ISBN: 9781314506501

Published by:
HardPress Publishing
8345 NW 66TH ST #2561
MIAMI FL 33166-2626

Email: info@hardpress.net
Web: http://www.hardpress.net

UNIV. OF
CALIFORNIA

1 Orthorhombic ρ - υ

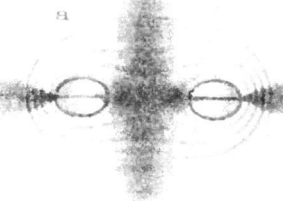
a

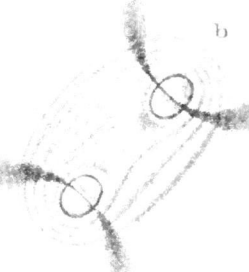
b

2 Monoclinic - Inclined Dispersion.

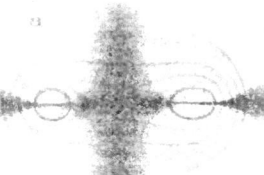
a

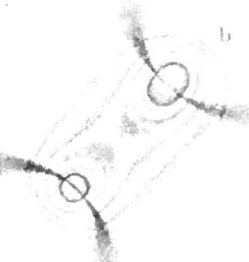
b

3 Monoclinic - Horizontal Dispersion.

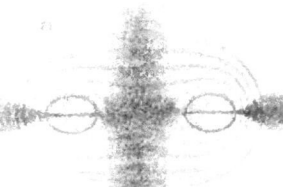
a

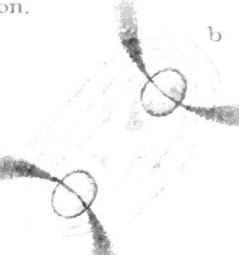
b

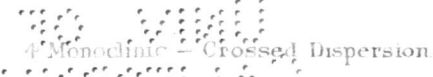

4 Monoclinic - Crossed Dispersion.

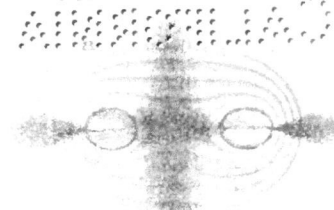
a

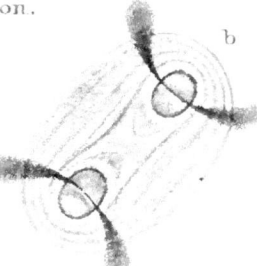
b

A TEXT-BOOK

OF

MINERALOGY.

WITH AN EXTENDED TREATISE ON

CRYSTALLOGRAPHY AND PHYSICAL MINERALOGY.

BY

EDWARD SALISBURY DANA,

CURATOR OF MINERALOGY, YALE COLLEGE.

ON THE PLAN AND WITH THE CO-OPERATION

OF

PROFESSOR JAMES D. DANA.

WITH UPWARDS OF EIGHT HUNDRED WOODCUTS AND ONE COLORED PLATE.

NEWLY REVISED AND ENLARGED.
(11TH EDITION.)

NEW YORK:
JOHN WILEY & SONS,
15 ASTOR PLACE.
1885.

COPYRIGHT BY
EDWARD S. DANA.
1877.

PREFACE.

The preparation of a "Text-Book of Mineralogy" was undertaken in 1868, by Prof. J. D. Dana, immediately after the publication of the fifth edition of the System of Mineralogy. The state of his health, however, early compelled him to relinquish the work, and he was not able subsequently to resume it. Finally, after the lapse of seven years, the editorship of the volume was placed in the hands of the writer, who has endeavored to carry out the original plan.

The work is intended to meet the requirements of class instruction. With this end in view the Descriptive part has been made subordinate to the more important subjects embraced under Physical Mineralogy.

The Crystallography is presented after the methods of Naumann; his system being most easily understood by the beginner, and most convenient for giving a general knowledge of the principles of the Science. For use in calculations, however, it is much less satisfactory than the method of Miller, and a concise exposition of Miller's System has accordingly been added in the Appendix. The chapter on the Physical Characters of Minerals has been expanded to a considerable length, but not more than was absolutely necessary in order to make clearly intelligible the methods of using the principles in the practical study of crystals. For a still fuller discussion of these subjects reference may be made to the works of Schrauf and of Groth, and for details in regard to the optical characters of mineral species to the Mineralogy of M. DesCloizeaux.

The Descriptive part of the volume is an abridgment of the System of Mineralogy, and to that work the student is referred for the history of each species and a complete list of its synonyms; for an enumeration of observed crystalline planes, and their angles; for all published analyses;

for a fuller description of localities and methods of occurrence, and also for an account of many species of uncertain character, not mentioned in the following pages. A considerable number of changes and additions, however, have been made in the preparation of the present work, made necessary by the progress in the Science, and among these are included many new species. The chemical formulas are those of modern Chemistry. The new edition of Rammelsberg's *Handbuch der Mineralchemie* has been often used in the preparation of the volume, and frequent references to him will be found in the text.

The work has throughout been under the supervision of Prof. Dana, and all the proofs have passed under his eye. Acknowledgments are also due to Prof. G. J. Brush and Prof. J. P. Cooke for friendly advice on many points.

PREFACE TO THE REVISED EDITION.

In this Revised Edition, the chief additions are contained in four supplementary chapters, covering about fifty pages. Of these, two are devoted to descriptions of new instruments and methods of research in Crystallography and Physical Mineralogy; and the others to brief descriptions of the minerals recently announced, and a concise statement of important new facts in regard to the characters or occurrence of old species. A number of new figures are introduced in illustration of these subjects. The work has been repaged; and a new index, much more complete than the former one, has been added.

New Haven, *January*, 1883.

TABLE OF CONTENTS.

INTRODUCTION.

PART I.

PHYSICAL MINERALOGY.

Section I. CRYSTALLOGRAPHY.

	PAGE
DESCRIPTIVE CRYSTALLOGRAPHY	1–83
General Characters of Crystals	1
Descriptions of some of the Simpler Forms of Crystals	3
Systems of Crystallization	8
Laws with reference to the Planes of Crystals	10
I. Isometric System	14
II. Tetragonal System	25
III. Hexagonal System	31
IV. Orthorhombic System	41
V. Monoclinic System	47
VI. Triclinic System	50
MATHEMATICAL CRYSTALLOGRAPHY	51
Methods of Calculation in General	53
Special Methods of Calculation in the different Systems	62
Measurement of the Angles of Crystals	83
COMPOUND OR TWIN CRYSTALS	88
IRREGULARITIES OF CRYSTALS	102
CRYSTALLINE AGGREGATES	111
PSEUDOMORPHOUS CRYSTALS	113

Section I. SUPPLEMENTARY CHAPTER.

Improved Instruments for the Measurement of the Angles of Crystals	115

Section II. PHYSICAL CHARACTERS OF MINERALS.

I. COHESION AND ELASTICITY	119
Cleavage and Fracture	119
Hardness	120
Tenacity	121
II. SPECIFIC GRAVITY	123
III. LIGHT	125
Fundamental Principles of Optics	125
Distinguishing Optical Characters of Crystals of the different Systems	135
Isometric Crystals	135
Uniaxial Crystals	136
Biaxial Crystals	144
Diaphaneity; Color	161
Lustre	167

TABLE OF CONTENTS.

	PAGE
IV. HEAT	168
V. ELECTRICITY—MAGNETISM	169
VI. TASTE AND ODOR	171

Section II. SUPPLEMENTARY CHAPTER.

I. COHESION AND ELASTICITY	173
II. SPECIFIC GRAVITY	173
III. LIGHT	177
Determination of Indices of Refraction	177
Polarization Instruments	178
Discussion of the Various Explanations offered for Observed "Optical Anomalies" of Crystals	185

PART II.

CHEMICAL MINERALOGY.

Chemical Constitution of Minerals	191
Dimorphism; Isomorphism	199
Chemical Examination of Minerals:	
In the Wet Way	202
In the Dry Way; Blowpipe Analysis	203

PART III.

DESCRIPTIVE MINERALOGY.

Classification of Mineral Species	215
Description of Mineral Species	221–419
Supplementary Chapter	420–440

APPENDIX A.	Miller's System of Crystallography	441
APPENDIX B.	On the Drawing of Figures of Crystals	463
APPENDIX C.	Catalogue of American Localities of Minerals	473
APPENDIX C.	Supplementary Chapter	503
GENERAL INDEX		

INTRODUCTION.

The Third Kingdom of Nature, the Inorganic, embraces all species not organized by living growth. Unlike a plant or animal, an inorganic species is a simple chemical compound, possessing unity of chemical and physical nature throughout, and alike in essential characters through all diversity of age or size.

The Science of Mineralogy treats of those inorganic species which occur ready formed in or about the earth. It is therefore but a fragment of the Science of Inorganic nature, and it owes its separate consideration simply to convenience.

The Inorganic Compounds are formed by the same forces, and on the same principles, whether produced in the laboratory of the chemist or in outdoor nature, and are strictly no more artificial in one case than in the other. Calcium carbonate of the chemical laboratory is in every character the same identical substance with calcium carbonate, or calcite, found in the rocks, and in each case is evolved by nature's operations. There is hence nothing whatever in the character of mineral species that entitles them to constitute a separate division in the natural classification of Inorganic species.

The objects of Mineralogy proper are three-fold : 1, to present the true idea of each species ; 2, to exhibit the means and methods of distinguishing species, which object is however partly accomplished in the former ; 3, to make known the modes of occurrence and associations of species, and their geographical distribution.

In presenting the science in this Text Book, the following order is adopted :

I. Physical Mineralogy, comprising that elementary discussion with regard to the structure and form, and the physical qualities essential to a right understanding of mineral species, and their distinctions.

II. Chemical and Determinative Mineralogy, presenting briefly the general characters of species considered as chemical compounds, also giving the special methods of distinguishing species, and tables constructed for this purpose. The latter subject is preceded by a few words on the use of the blow-pipe.

III. Descriptive Mineralogy, comprising the classification and descriptions of species and their varieties. The descriptions include the physical and chemical properties of the most common and important of the minerals, with some account also of their association and geographical distribution. The rarer species, and those of uncertain composition, are only very briefly noticed.

Besides the above, there is also the department of *Economic Mineralogy*, which is not here included. It treats of the uses of minerals, (1) as ores; (2) in jewelry; and (3) in the coarser arts.

The following subjects connected with minerals properly pertain to Geology: 1, *Lithological geology*, or *Lithology*, which treats of minerals as constituents of rocks. 2, *Chemical geology*, which considers in one of its subdivisions the origin of minerals, as determined, *in the light of chemistry*, by the associations of species, the alterations which species are liable to, or which they are known to have undergone, and the general nature, origin, and changes of the earth's rock formations. Under chemical geology, the department which considers especially the associations of species, and the order of succession in such associations, has received the special name of the *paragenesis* of minerals; while the origin of minerals or rocks through alteration, is called *metamorphism* or *pseudomorphism*, the latter term being restricted to those cases in which the crystalline form, and sometimes also the cleavage, of a mineral is retained after the change.

LITERATURE.

For a catalogue of mineralogical works, and of periodicals, and transactions of Scientific Societies in which mineralogical memoirs have been and are published, reference is made to the System of Mineralogy (1868), pp. xxxv–xlv., Appendix II. (1874), and Appendix III. (1882). The following works, however, deserve to be mentioned, as they will be found useful as books of reference.

In CRYSTALLOGRAPHY :
Naumann. Lehrbuch der reinen und angewandten Krystallographie. 2 vols., 8vo. Leipzig, 1829.
Naumann. Anfangsgründe der Krystallographie. 2d ed., 292 pp., 8vo. Leipzig, 1854.
Naumann. Elemente der theoretischen Krystallographie. 383 pp., 8vo. Leipzig, 1856.
Miller. A Treatise on Crystallography. Cambridge, 1839.
Grailich. Lehrbuch der Krystallographie von W. H. Miller. 328 pp., 8vo. Vienna, 1856.
Kopp. Einleitung in die Krystallographie. 348 pp., 8vo. Braunschweig, 1862.
Von Lang. Lehrbuch der Krystallographie. 358 pp., 8vo. Vienna, 1866.
Quenstedt. Grundriss der bestimmenden und rechnenden Krystallographie. Tübingen, 1873.
Rose-Sadebeck. Elemente der Krystallographie. 2d ed., vol. i., 181 pp., 8vo. Berlin, 1873. Vol. ii., Angewandte Krystallographie. 284 pp., 8vo. Berlin, 1876.
Schrauf. Lehrbuch der Physikalischen Mineralogie. Vol. i., Krystallographie. 251 pp., 8vo., 1866 ; vol. ii., Die angewandte Physik der Krystalle. 426 pp. Vienna, 1868.
Groth. Physikalische Krystallographie. 527 pp., 8vo. Leipzig, 1876.
Klein. Einleitung in die Krystallberechnung. 393 pp., 8vo. Stuttgart, 1876.
Mallard. Traité de Cristallographie géometrique et physique, vol. i. Paris, 1876.
Bauerman. Text-Book of Systematic Mineralogy. Vol. i., 367 pp, 12mo. London, 1881.
Liebisch. Geometrische Krystallographie. 464 pp., 8vo. Leipzig, 1881.
Tschermak. Lehrbuch der Mineralogie. Lief. I., II., pp. 1–368. Vienna, 1881–82.

In PHYSICAL MINERALOGY the works of *Schrauf* (1868) and *Groth* (1876), and *Tschermak*, titles as in the above list. Reference is also made to the works on Physics, mentioned on p. 160. In addition to these, on pp. 111, 122, 160, 167, 171, 190, a few memoirs of especial importance on the different subjects are enumerated.

In CHEMICAL MINERALOGY : *Rammelsberg,* Handbuch der Mineralchemie, 2d ed., Leipzig, 1875. In Determinative Mineralogy, *Brush,* New York, 1878.

In DESCRIPTIVE MINERALOGY : among recent works those of *Brooke* and *Miller* (2d ed. of Phillips' Min.), London, 1852 ; *Quenstedt,* 3d ed., Tübingen, 1877 ; *Schrauf,* Atlas der Krystallformen, Lief. I.–V., 1871–1878 ; *Groth* (Tabellarische Uebersicht der Mineralien, etc.), 2d ed., 1882 ; *v. Kokscharof,* Materialien zur Mineralogie Russlands, vol. i., 1865, vol. viii., 1881 ; *Des Cloizeaux,* vol. i., 1862, vol. ii., Paris, 1874 ; *Dana,* System of Mineralogy, 1868, App. I., 1872, App. II., 1874, App. III., 1882 ; *Blum,* 4th ed., 1874 ; *Naumann-Zirkel,* 11th ed., 1881.

The following publications are devoted particularly to Mineralogy :
Jahrbuch für Mineralogie ; G. Leonhard and H. B. Geinitz, Editors ; after 1879, E. W. Benecke, C. Klein, and H. Rosenbusch.
Mineralogische Mittheilungen ; commenced 1872, G. Tschermak, Editor ; since 1878, published as the Mineralogische und Petrographische Mittheilungen.
Mineralogical Magazine and Journal of the Mineralogical Society ; London, and Truro, Cornwall. Commenced 1875.
Zeitschrift für Krystallographie ; P. Groth. Editor ; Leipzig. Commenced 1876.
Bulletin de la Société Minéralogique de France. Commenced 1878.

ABBREVIATIONS.

For abbreviations of the names of Mineralogical works, of Journals, publications of Scientific Societies, etc., see System Min., 5th ed., pp. xxxv.-xlv., App. III., p. viii.
The following abbreviations are used in the Description of Species.

B.B.	Before the Blowpipe (p. 210).	Obs.	Observations on occurrence, etc.
Comp.	Composition.	O.F.	Oxidizing Flame (p. 204).
Diff.	Differences, or distinctive characters.	Pyr.	Pyrognostics.
G.	Specific Gravity.	Q. Ratio.	Quantivalent Ratio (p. 198).
Germ.	German.	R.F.	Reducing Flame (p. 204).
H.	Hardness.	Var.	Varieties.

An asterisk (*), appended to the name of a mineral species in the Descriptive part of this work, indicates that additional facts in regard to it are mentioned in the Supplementary Chapter, pp. 420 to 440.

PART I.

PHYSICAL MINERALOGY.

The grand departments of the science here considered are the following:
1. STRUCTURE.—Structure in Inorganic nature is a result of mathematical symmetry in the action of cohesive attraction. The forms produced are regular solids called *crystals;* whence morphology is, in the Inorganic kingdom, called CRYSTALLOLOGY. It is the science of structure in this kingdom of nature.

2. PHYSICAL PROPERTIES OF MINERALS, or those depending on relations to light, heat, electricity, magnetism; on differences as to density or specific gravity, hardness, taste, odor, etc.

Crystallology is naturally divided into, I. CRYSTALLOGRAPHY, which treats of the forms resulting from crystallization; II. CRYSTALLOGENY, which describes the methods of making crystals, and discusses the theories of their origin. Only the former of these two subjects is treated of in this work.

SECTION I.

CRYSTALLOGRAPHY.

Crystallography embraces the consideration of—(1) normally formed or regular crystals; (2) twin or compound crystals; (3) the irregularities of crystals; (4) crystalline aggregates; and (5) pseudomorphous crystals.

1. GENERAL CHARACTERS OF CRYSTALS.

(1) *External form.*—Crystals are bounded by plane surfaces, called simply planes or faces, symmetrically arranged in reference to one or more diametral lines called axes. In the annexed figure the planes 1 and the planes i are symmetrically arranged with reference to the vertical axis $c\ c$; and also the planes of each kind with reference to the three transverse axes.

(2) *Constancy of angle in the same species.*—The crystals of any species are essentially constant in the angle of inclination between like planes. The angle between 1 and i, in a given species, is always essentially the same, wherever the crystal is found, and whether a product of nature or of the laboratory.

CRYSTALLOGRAPHY.

(3) *Difference of angle of different species.*—The crystals of different species commonly differ in angles between corresponding planes. The angles of crystals are consequently a means of distinguishing species.

(4) *Diversity of planes.*—While in the crystals of a given species there is constancy of angle between like planes, the forms of the crystals may be exceedingly diverse. The accompanying figures are examples of a few of

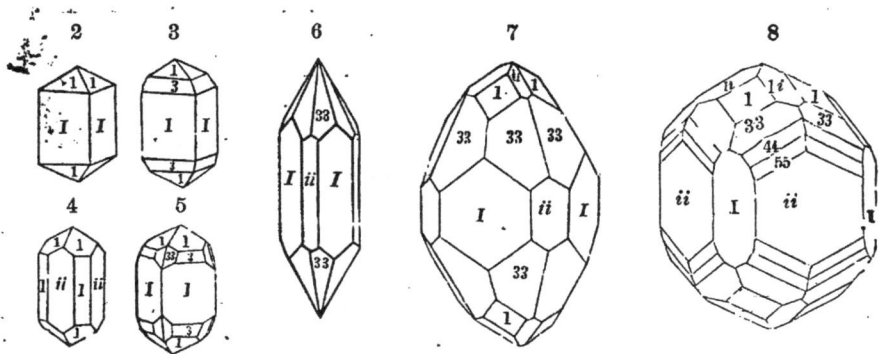

the forms of the species zircon. There is hardly any limit to the number of forms which may occur; yet for each the angles between like planes are essentially constant.

Crystals occur of all sizes, from the merest microscopic point to a yard or more in diameter. A single crystal of quartz, now at Milan, is three and a quarter feet long, and five and a half in circumference; and its weight is estimated at eight hundred and seventy pounds. A single cavity in a vein of quartz near the Tiefen Glacier, in Switzerland, discovered in 1867, has afforded smoky quartz crystals weighing in the aggregate about 20,000 pounds; a considerable number of the single crystals having a weight of 200 to 250 pounds, or even more. One of the gigantic beryls from Acworth, New Hampshire, measures four feet in length, and two and a half in circumference; and another, at Grafton, is over four feet long, and thirty-two inches in one of its diameters, and does not weigh less than two and a half tons. But the highest perfection of form and transparency are found only in crystals of small size.

In its original signification the term *crystal* was applied only to crystals of quartz (f. 1), which the ancient philosophers believed to be *water* congealed by intense cold. Hence the term, from κρύσταλλος, *ice.*

(5) *Symmetry in the position of planes.*—The planes on the crystals of any species, however numerous, are arranged in accordance with certain laws of symmetry and numerical ratio. If one of the simpler forms be taken as a primary or *fundamental form*, all other planes will be secondary planes, or modifications of the fundamental form. It should be observed, however, that the forms called primary and fundamental in crystallographic description, are in general merely so by assumption and for convenience of reference. (See also p. 12.)

Cleavage.—Besides external symmetry of form, crystallization produces also regularity of internal structure, and often of fracture. This regularity of fracture, or *tendency to break* or cleave along certain planes, is called *cleavage.* The surface afforded by cleavage is often smooth and brilliant. The directions of cleavage are those of least cohesive force in a crystal; it is not to be understood that the cleavage lamellæ are in any sense present before they are made to appear by fracture.

In regard to cleavage, two principles may be here stated:—(*a*) In any species, the direction in which cleavage takes place is always parallel to some plane which either actually occurs in the crystals or *may* exist there in accordance with the general laws which will be stated hereafter.

(*b*) Cleavage is uniform as to ease parallel to all like planes; that is, if it may be obtained parallel to one plane of a kind (as 1, f. 1), it may be obtained with equal facility parallel to each of the other planes 1; and will afford planes of like lustre. This is in accordance with the symmetry of crystallization. It will be evident from this that the angles between planes of like cleavage will be constant: thus, a mass of calcite under the blow of a hammer will separate into countless rhombohedrons, each of which affords on measurement the angles 74° 55′ and 105° 5′. In a shapeless mass of marble the minute grains have the same regularity of cleavage structure. See further, p. 119.

2. Descriptions of some of the simpler forms of Crystals.

PRELIMINARY DEFINITIONS. *Angles.*—In the descriptions of crystals three kinds of *angles* may come under consideration, *solid*, *plane*, and *interfacial*. The last are the inclinations between the faces or planes of crystals.

Axes.—The *crystallographic axes* are imaginary lines passing through the centre of a crystal. They are assumed as axes in order to describe, by reference to them, the relative positions of the different planes. One of the axes is called the *vertical*, and the others the *lateral*; the number of lateral axes is either *two* or *three*. The axes have essentially the same relative lengths in all the crystals of a species; but those of different species often differ widely

Diametral planes.—The planes in which any two axes lie are called the *axial* or *diametral planes* or sections; they are the *coördinate planes* of analytical geometry. They divide the space about the centre into *sectants;* into *eight* sectants, called *octants*, if there are but two lateral axes, as is generally the case; but into *twelve* sectants if there are three, as in hexagonal crystalline forms.

Diagonal planes are either diagonal to the *three* axes, as those through the centre connecting diagonally opposite solid angles of a cube, or diagonal to *two* axes, and passing through the third, as those connecting diagonally opposite edges of the cube.

Similar planes and *edges* are such as are similar in position, and of like angles with reference to the axes or axial planes. Moreover, in the case of similar edges, the two planes by whose intersection the edges are formed, meet at the same angle of inclination. For example, all the planes and edges of the tetrahedron (f. 9), regular octahedron (f. 11), cube (f. 14), rhombic dodecahedron (f. 19), are similar. In the rhombohedron (f. 16) there are two sets of similar edges, six being obtuse and six acute.

Solid angles are *similar* when alike in plane angles each for each, and when formed by the meeting of planes of the same kind.

A *combination-edge* is the edge formed by the meeting or intersection of two planes.

Truncations, bevelments.—In a crystal, an edge or angle is said to be *replaced* when the place of the edge or angle is occupied by one or more planes; and in the case of the *replacement* of an edge, the *replacing* planes make parallel intersections with the including planes, that is, with the direction of the replaced edge (f. 43).

A replacement of an edge or angle is a *truncation* when the replacing plane makes equal angles with the including planes. Thus, in f. 6, *i-i* truncates the edge between I and I.

An edge is said to be *bevelled* when it is replaced by two similar planes, that is, by planes having like inclinations to the adjoining planes. Thus, in f. 5, the edge between 3, 3, is bevelled by the two planes 3-3, 3-3, the right 3-3 and 3 having the same mutual inclination as the left 3-3 and 3. So, in f. 192, p. 43, the edge between I and I is *bevelled* by the planes i-$\bar{2}$, i-$\bar{2}$. Truncations and bevelments of edges take place only between similar planes. Thus I, I, and 3, 3, are similar planes in fig. 5. The edge 1|1 might be *truncated* or *bevelled*, for the same reason; but not the edge between 1 and I, since 1 and I are dissimilar planes.

A *zone* is a series of planes in which the *combination-edges* or mutual intersections are *parallel*. Thus, in fig. 3, the planes 1, 3, I make a vertical zone; so in f. 8, the planes between 1 and *i-i* make a zone, and this zone actually continues above and below, around the crystal; in f. 5, the planes 3, 3-3, 3-3, 3 are in one zone; and *i-i*, I, *i-i*, I, in another. On the true meaning of zones, see p. 53.

The above explanations are preliminary to the descriptions of the forms of all crystals.

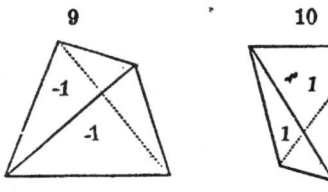

A. — FORMS CONTAINED UNDER FOUR EQUAL TRIANGULAR PLANES.—A. *Regular tetrahedron* (f. 9). Edges six; solid angles four. Faces equilateral triangles, and plane angles therefore 60°. Interfacial angles 70° 31' 44''. Named from τέτρακις, *four times*, and ἕδρα, *face*.

2. *Sphenoid* (f. 10). Faces isosceles triangles, not equilateral. Plane and interfacial angles varying; the latter of two kinds, (*a*) two terminal, (*b*) four lateral. Named from σφήν, *a wedge*.

B.—FORMS CONTAINED UNDER EIGHT TRIANGULAR PLANES.—The solids here included are called *octahedrons*, from ὀκτάκις, *eight times*, and ἕδρα, *face*. They have twelve edges; and six solid angles. One of the axes, when they differ in length, is made the vertical axis; and the others are the lateral axes. The solid angles at the extremities of the vertical axes are the vertical or terminal solid angles; the other four are the lateral. The four edges meeting in the apex of the terminal solid angle are the terminal edges; the others, the lateral or basal edges.

1. *Regular Octahedron* (f. 11). Faces equilateral triangles. Interfacial angles 109° 28' 16''; angle between the planes over the apex of a solid angle 70° 31' 44''; angle between edges over a solid angle 90°. The three axes are equal, and hence either may be made the vertical. Lines connecting the centres of opposite faces are called the *octahedral* or *trigonal inter-*

axes; and those connecting the centres of opposite edges the *dodecahedral* or *rhombic interaxes.*

2. *Square Octahedron* (f. 12, f. 12A). Faces equal isosceles triangles, not equilateral. The four terminal edges are equal and similar; and so also the four lateral.

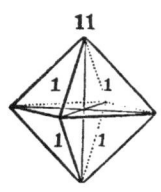
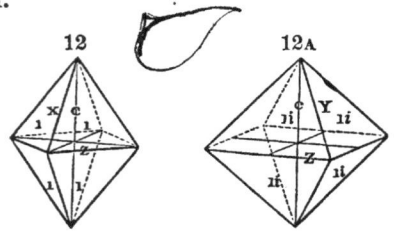
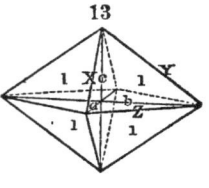

The lateral axes are *equal;* the vertical axis may be longer or shorter than the lateral.

3. The *rhombic octahedron* (f. 13) differs from the square octahedron in having a rhombic base, and consequently the three axes are unequal. The basal edges are equal and similar; but, owing to the unequal lengths of the lateral axes, the terminal edges are of two kinds, two being shorter and more obtuse than the other two.

C.—FORMS CONTAINED UNDER SIX EQUAL PLANES.—The forms here included have the planes parallelograms; the edges are twelve in number and equal; the solid angles eight.

1. *Cube* (f. 14). Faces equal squares, and plane angles therefore 90°. The twelve edges similar as well as equal; the eight solid angles similar and equal. Interfacial angles 90°. The three axes equal and intersecting at right angles.

Lines connecting the apices of the solid angles are the *octahedral* or *trigonal interaxes*, and those connecting the centres of opposite edges the *dodecahedral* or *rhombic interaxes*. If the cubic axis (=edge of the cube) =1, then the dodecahedral interaxes = $\sqrt{2}$ = 1.41421; and the octahedral interaxes = $\sqrt{3}$ = 1.73205. And if the dodecahedral axis = 1, then the octahedral = 1.224745.

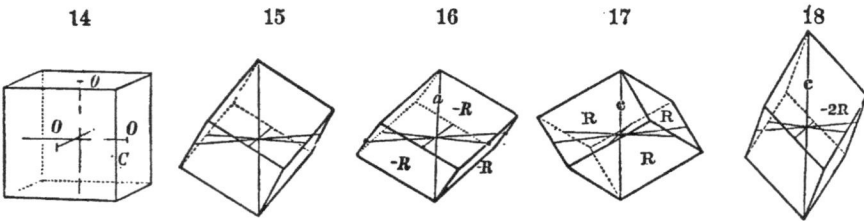

If a cube is placed with the apex of one angle vertically over that diagonally opposite, that is, with an octahedral interaxis vertical, the parts are all symmetrically arranged around this vertical axis. In this position (f. 15) the cube has three planes inclined toward one apex, and three toward the other; it has three *terminal* edges meeting at each apex; and six *lateral* edges situated symmetrically, but in a zigzag, around the vertical axis. If lines are drawn connecting the centres of the opposite lateral edges, and these are taken as the lateral axes, the lateral axes, three in number, will lie in a plane at right angles to the vertical, and will intersect at the centre at angles of 60°. The cube placed in this position would then have one vertical and three equal lateral axes; and as the lateral axes correspond to the dodecahedral interaxes of a cube, the ratio of a lateral axis to the vertical is 1 : 1.224745.

2. *Rhombohedron* (f. 16 to 18). Faces equal rhombs. The twelve edges of two kinds; six obtuse, and six acute. Solid angles of two kinds; two symmetrical, consisting each of three equal plane angles; the other six unsymmetrical, the plane angles enclosing them being of two kinds.

The rhombohedron resembles a cube that has been either shortened, or lengthened, in the direction of one of the octahedral axes, the former making an *obtuse* rhombohedron, the latter an *acute;* and it is in position when this axis is vertical, the parts being situated symmetrically about this axis, as in the second position of the cube above described. In an *obtuse* rhombohedron (f. 16, 17), the terminal solid angles are bounded by three obtuse plane angles, and the other six, which are the lateral, by two acute and one obtuse; the six terminal edges (three meeting at each apex) are obtuse, and the six lateral edges are acute. Conversely, in an acute rhombohedron (f. 18) the terminal angles are made up of acute plane angles, and the lateral of two obtuse and one acute; the six terminal edges are acute, and the six lateral obtuse. The axes are a vertical, and three lateral; the lateral axes connect the centres of opposite lateral edges and intersect at angles of 60°.

The cube in the second position (f. 15) corresponds to a rhombohedron of 90°, or is intermediate between the obtuse and the acute series.

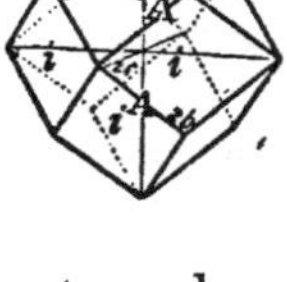

D.—FORMS CONTAINED UNDER TWELVE EQUAL PLANES. 1. *Rhombic Dodecahedron* (f. 19). Faces rhombs, with the plane angles 109° 28′ 16″, 70° 31′ 44″. Edges twenty-four, all similar; interfacial angle over each edge 120°. Solid angles of two kinds: (*a*) six acute tetrahedral, being formed of four acute plane angles; and (*b*) eight obtuse trihedral, being formed of three obtuse plane angles. Angle between planes over apex of tetrahedral solid angle, 90°; angle between edges over the same 109° 28′ 16″. The axes three, equal, rectangular, and therefore identical with those of the regular octahedron and cube. The dodecahedral interaxes connect the centres of opposite faces; and the octahedral the apices of the trihedral solid angles. Named from δώδεκα, *twelve*, and ἕδρα, *face*.

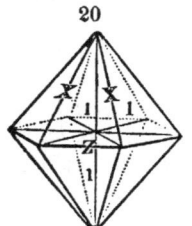

2. *Pyramidal dodecahedron, or Quartzoid.* (Called also Dihexagonal Pyramid, Isosceles Dodecahedron.) Faces isosceles triangles, and arranged in two pyramids placed base to base (f. 20). Edges of two kinds: twelve equal *terminal,* and six equal *basal;* axes, a vertical, differing in length in different species; and three lateral, equal, situated in a plane at right angles to the vertical, and intersecting one another at angles of 60°, as in the rhombohedron.

E.—PRISMS.—Prismatic forms consist of at least two sets of planes, the basal planes being unlike the lateral. The bases are always equal; and the lateral planes parallelograms. The vertical axis is unequal to the lateral. (*a*) *Three-sided prism.* A right (or erect) prism, having its bases equal equilateral triangles. (*b*) *Four-sided prisms.* Four-sided prisms are either right (erect), or oblique, the former having the vertical axis at *right angles* to the base or to the plane of the lateral axes, and the latter *oblique*.

1. *Square or Tetragonal Prism* (f. 21, 22). Base a square; lateral planes equal. Edges of two kinds: (*a*) eight basal, equal, each contained between the base and a lateral plane; (*b*) four lateral, contained between the equal lateral planes. Interfacial angles all 90°, plane angles 90°. Solid angles eight, of one kind. Axes: a vertical, differing in length in different species, and longer or shorter than the lateral; two lateral, equal, at right angles to one another and to the vertical, and connecting either the centres of opposite lateral planes (f. 21) or edges (f. 22). The cube is a square prism with the vertical axis equal to the lateral.

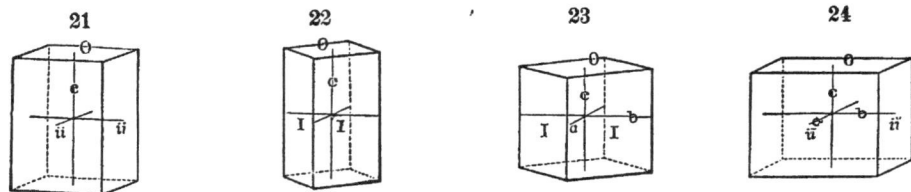

2. *Right Rhombic Prism* (f. 23). Base a rhomb; lateral planes equal parallelograms. Edges of three kinds: (*a*) eight basal, equal, and rectangular as in the preceding form; (*b*) two lateral, obtuse; and (*c*) two lateral, acute. Solid angles of two kinds: (*a*) obtuse at the extremities of the obtuse edge, and (*b*) acute at the extremities of the acute edge. Axes rectangular, unequal; a vertical; a longer lateral, the *macrodiagonal* axis (named from μάκρος, *large*), and a shorter lateral, the *brachydiagonal* axis (named from βραχύς, *short*).

3. *Right Rectangular Prism* (f. 24). Base a rectangle, and in consequence of its unequal sides, two opposite lateral planes of the prism are broader than the other two. Edges all rectangular, but of three kinds: (*a*) four longer basal; (*b*) four shorter basal; (*c*) four lateral. Axes connecting the centres of opposite faces, rectangular, unequal; a vertical, a macrodiagonal, and a brachydiagonal, being like those of the right rhombic prism. In the rectangular prism, either of the faces may be made the basal, and either axis, consequently, the vertical.

4. *Oblique Prisms*. Figs. 25 and 26 represent prisms oblique in the direction of one axis. As seen in them, the vertical axis *c* is oblique to the lateral axis *à*, called the *clinodiagonal* axis; but *b*, the *orthodiagonal* axis, is at right angles to both *c* and *à*. Similarly, the axial sections *cb*, *ba* are mutually oblique in their inclinations, while *ca*, *cb* and *ca*, *ba* are at right angles. The clinodiagonal section *ca* is called the section or plane of symmetry.

The form in f. 25 is sometimes called an *oblique rhombic* prism. The edges are of two kinds as to length, but of four kinds as to interfacial angles over them: (*a*) four basal obtuse; (*b*) four basal acute; (*c*) two lateral obtuse: (*d*) two lateral acute. The prism is in position when placed with the *clinodiagonal* section vertical.

Figs. 27 and 28 show the doubly oblique, or *oblique rhomboidal* prism, in which all the axes, and hence all the axial sections, are oblique to each other. All these cases will receive further attention in the description of actual crystalline forms.

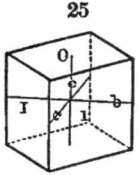 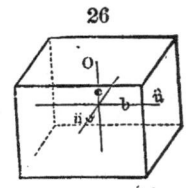 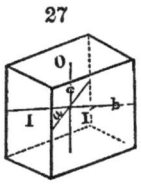 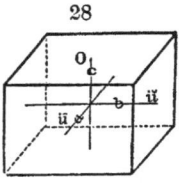

The prisms (in f. 21, 24, 26, 28) in which the planes are parallel to the three diametral sections, are sometimes called diametral prisms. This term also evidently includes the cube. The planes which form these diametral prisms are often called *pinacoids*. The terminal plane is the basal pinacoid, or simply base; also, in f. 24 the plane (lettered $i\text{-}\bar{i}$) parallel to the macrodiagonal section is called the *macropinacoid*, and the plane ($i\text{-}\bar{i}$) parallel to the brachydiagonal the *brachypinacoid*. In f. 26 the plane ($i\text{-}\bar{i}$) parallel to the orthodiagonal section is called the *orthopinacoid*, and the plane ($i\text{-}\bar{i}$) parallel to the clinodiagonal section the *clinopinacoid*. The word *pinacoid* is from the Greek πίναξ, a *board*.

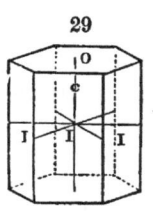 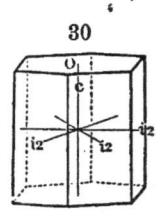

(c). SIX-SIDED PRISM.—*The Hexagonal prism*. Base an equilateral hexagon. Edges of two kinds: (a) twelve basal, equal and similar, (b) six lateral, equal and similar; interfacial angle over the former 90°, over the latter 120°. Solid angles, twelve, similar. Axes: a vertical, of different length in different species; three lateral equal, intersecting at angles of 60°, as in the rhombohedron, and the dihexagonal pyramid or quartzoid, connecting the centres either of the lateral edges (f. 29), or lateral faces (f. 30).

3. SYSTEMS OF CRYSTALLIZATION.

The systems of crystallization are based on the mathematical relations of the forms; the axes are lines assumed in order to exhibit these relations, they mark the degree of symmetry which belongs to each group of forms, and which is in fact the fundamental distinction between them. The number of axes, as has been stated, is either *three* or *four*—the number being four when there are three lateral axes, as occurs only in hexagonal forms.

Among the forms with three axes, all possible conditions of the axes exist both as to relative lengths and inclinations; that is, there are (as has been exemplified in the forms which have been described), (A) among *orthometric* kinds, or those with rectangular axial intersections; (a) the three axes equal; (b) two equal, and the other longer or shorter than the two; (c) the three unequal; and (B) among *clinometric* kinds, one or more of the intersections may be oblique (in all of these the three axes are unequal). The systems are then as follows:

A. Axes three; orthometric.

1. ISOMETRIC SYSTEM.—Axes equal. Examples, cube, regular octahedron, rhombic dodecahedron

2. TETRAGONAL SYSTEM.—Lateral axes equal; the vertical a varying axis Ex., square prism, square octahedron.
3. ORTHORHOMBIC SYSTEM.—Axes unequal. Ex., right rhombic prism, rectangular prism, rhombic octahedron.
B. Axes three; clinometric.
1. MONOCLINIC SYSTEM.—Axes unequal; one of the axial intersection oblique, the other two rectangular. Ex., the oblique prisms (f. 25, 26).
2. TRICLINIC SYSTEM.—Axes unequal; three of the axial intersections oblique. Ex., oblique rhomboidal prism (f. 27, 28).
C. Axes four.—HEXAGONAL SYSTEM.—Three lateral axes equal, intersecting at angles of 60°. The vertical axis of variable length. Example, hexagonal prisms (f. 29, 30).

The so-called Diclinic system (two oblique axes) is not known to occur, for the single substance, an artificial salt, supposed to crystallize in this system has been shown by von Zepharovich to be triclinic. Moreover, von Lang, Quenstedt, and others have shown mathematically that there can be only six distinct systems.

The six systems may also be arranged in the following groups:
1. *Isometric* (from ἴσος, *equal*, and μέτρον, *measure*), the axes being all equal; including: I. ISOMETRIC SYSTEM.
2. *Isodiametric*, the lateral axes or diameters being equal; including: II. TETRAGONAL SYSTEM; III. HEXAGONAL SYSTEM.
3. *Anisometric* (from ἄνισος, *unequal*, etc.), the axes being unequal; including: IV. ORTHORHOMBIC SYSTEM; V. MONOCLINIC SYSTEM; VI. TRICLINIC SYSTEM.
A further study of these different systems will show that in group 1 the crystals are formed or developed alike in all three axial directions; in group 2 the development is alike in the several lateral directions, but unlike vertically; and in group 3 the crystals are formed unlike in all three directions. These distinctions are of the highest importance in relation to the physical characters of minerals, especially their optical properties, and are often referred to beyond.

The numbers (in Roman numerals) here connected with the names of the system are often used in place of the names in the course of this Treatise.
The systems of crystallization have been variously named by different authors, as follows:
1. ISOMETRIC. *Tessular* of Mohs and Haidinger; *Isometric* of Hausmann; *Tesseral* of Naumann; *Regular* of Weiss and Rose; *Cubic* of Dufrenoy, Miller, Des Cloizeaux; *Monometric* of the earlier editions of Dana's System of Mineralogy.
2. TETRAGONAL. Pyramidal of Mohs; Viergliedriege, or *Zwei-und-einaxige*, of Weiss; *Tetragonal* of Naumann; *Monodimetric* of Hausmann; *Quadratic* of von Kobell; *Dimetric* of early editions of Dana's System.
3. HEXAGONAL. *Rhombohedral* of Mohs; Sechsgliedrige, or *Drei-und-einaxige* of Weiss; *Hexagonal* of Naumann; *Monotrimetric* of Hausmann.
4. ORTHORHOMBIC. *Prismatic*, or *Orthotype*, of Mohs; *Ein-und-einaxige* of Weiss; *Rhombic* and *Anisometric* of Naumann; *Trimetric* and *Orthorhombic* of Hausmann; *Trimetric* of earlier editions of Dana's System.
5. MONOCLINIC. *Hemiprismatic* and *Hemiorthotype* of Mohs; *Zwei-und-eingliederige* of Weiss; *Monoclinohedral* of Naumann; *Clinorhombic* of v. Kobell, Hausmann, Des Cloizeaux; *Augitic* of Haidinger; *Oblique* of Miller; *Monosymmetric* of Groth.
6. TRICLINIC. *Tetarto-prismatic* of Mohs; *Ein-und-eingliederige* of Weiss; *Triclinohedral* of Naumann; *Clinorhomboidal* of v. Kobell; *Anorthic* of Haidinger and Miller; *Anorthic*, or *Doubly Oblique*, of Des Cloizeaux; *Asymmetric*, of Groth.

4. Laws with reference to the planes of Crystals.

The laws with reference to the positions of the planes of crystals are two: first, *the law of simple mathematical ratio;* secondly, *the law of symmetry.*

1. The Law of simple Mathematical Ratio.

The crystallographic axes afford the means, after the methods of analytical geometry, of expressing with precision the relative positions of the planes of crystals, and so exhibiting the mathematical ratios pertaining to crystallization. These axes, as has been stated, are supposed to pass through the centre of the crystal, and every plane must intersect one, two, or three of them. The position of a plane is obviously determined by the position of the points in which it meets these axes.

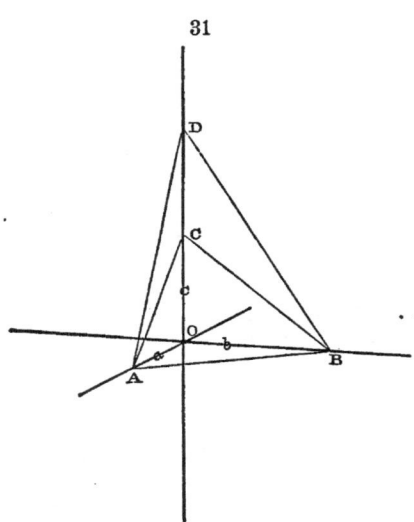

Thus the plane A B C, f. 31, meets the three axes at the points A, B, and C, and its position is determined by the distances O A, O B, O C, intercepted between these points and the centre O. Similarly the plane A B D meets the axes in the points A, B, and D, and its position is determined by the distances O A, O B, O D; and in the same manner with any other plane. On the crystals of a given species the occurring planes have exact numerical relations to each other, and it is to show these relations that certain lengths of the axes are assumed as units. Thus, in the case already given if O C, O B, O A, or more briefly c, b, a, are the lengths of the axes* (strictly speaking semi-axes) for a given species, then the position of the first plane is expressed by $1c : 1b : 1a$; that of the second by $2c : 1b : 1a$ (if OD=2OC), and still another plane might be $2c : 2b : 1a$, and so on. Consequently the general position of any plane may be expressed by $mc : nb : ra$,† or more simply $mc : nb : a$, as every plane is for simplicity supposed to meet *one* of the axes at the unit distance. In the first case mentioned above, $m = 1$ and $n = 1$; but in general m and n may vary in value from zero to infinity. The law of simple mathematical ratio, however, requires that m and n, which express the ratios in the lengths of the axes, should be invariably *rational numbers*, and in general they are either *whole numbers or simple fractions.*

This principle may be stated as follows:

The position of the planes in a given crystal is related in some simple ratio to the relative lengths of the axes.

---

* The vertical axis is throughout called c, see p. 53.
† It is more usual, and analytically more correct, to write this expression $ra : nb : mc$; but as the usual symbols take the form m-n, the order of the terms used here and elsewhere is more convenient.

This subject will become clear in the subsequent study of the different crystalline forms; in passing, however, reference may be made to f. 32 (zircon) as a single example. The planes lettered 1 and 3 have respectively the positions, $1c : 1b : 1a$, and $3c : 1b : 1a$, and in the second case the vertical axis has *exactly* three times the length of that of the former; any such multiples as 2.93 or 3.07 are crystallographically impossible. It is this principle which makes crystallography an exact mathematical science. Some apparent exceptions, such as occasionally occur, do not at all set aside this rule.

The expression $mc : nb : a$ is called the *symbol* of a plane, as it expresses its exact mathematical position, and the values of m and n are called its *parameters*. If a plane intersects two of the axes, but not the third, it is parallel to it, and mathematically it is said to cut it at infinity (∞); hence the general expression for a plane parallel to the vertical axis c (as in f. 33) will be $\infty c : nb : a$, or $\infty c : b : na$, according as a or b is taken as the unit; for a plane parallel to the lateral axis b (as in f. 34), it will be $mc : \infty b : a$; if parallel to the lateral axis a (as in f. 35), $mc : b : \infty a$.

If a plane is parallel to two axes, b and a, that is, intercepts these axes at

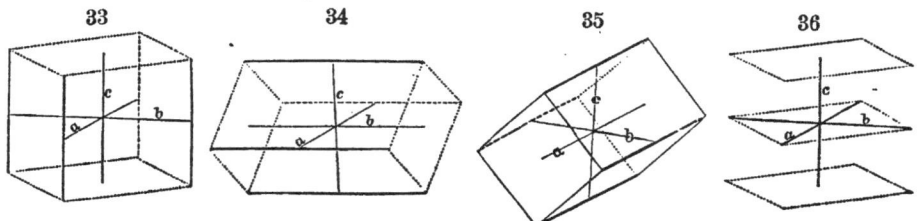

an infinite distance, its position is expressed by $c : \infty b : \infty a$, as is illustrated by f. 36; again, its position is expressed by $\infty c : b : \infty a$, if parallel to c and a; and by $\infty c : \infty b : a$, if parallel to c, b. These may also be written $0c : b : a$, etc.

The following important principle should be kept in mind. The *relative* not the *absolute* position of any plane has to be regarded, and hence all planes parallel to each other are crystallographically identical. A plane on the angle of the cube is the same, if the mutual inclinations remain unchanged, whether large or small, for, though the actual distances cut off on the axes may differ in each case, the *ratios* of these axes are identical. Again, in f. 37, the three planes, $4c : 4b : 2a$, and $2c : 2b : a$, and $c : b : \tfrac{1}{2}a$ are identical, for the ratios of the three axes are the same throughout, the planes being of course parallel. Similarly the symbol $1c : \tfrac{1}{3}b : \tfrac{1}{3}a$ may be written $3c : b : a$,

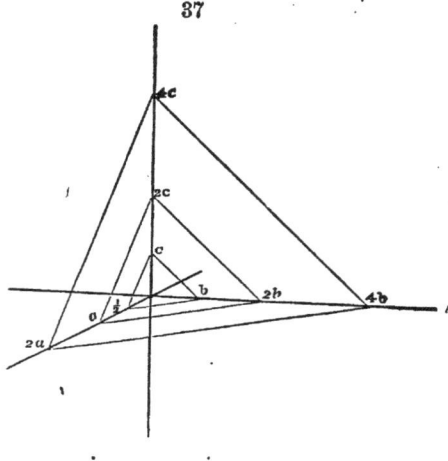

and $c : \infty b : \infty a$ is the same as $0c : b : a$. It will be seen that this principle makes it right to regard every plane as meeting one of the axes at the unit distance from the centre, which, as before stated, reduces the general expression of any plane $mc : nb : ra$ to the simpler form $mc : nb : a$, or $mc : b : na$.

The principle, which has just been stated, also makes it evident that when the axes are all equal, they are not necessarily considered in naming the position of any plane; when the lateral axes alone are equal, a certain length of the vertical axis must be assumed for each species; and when all the axes are unequal, certain lengths for two of the axes, expressed in terms of the third axis, must in every case be adopted.

Hence the *fundamental form* of any species may be regarded as that octahedron whose axes correspond in relative lengths with the axes c, b, a adopted for the species. The faces of this octahedron intersect the axes at distances from the centre equal to nc, nb, na (or $c : b : a$) respectively, and, since the ratio of the coefficients which expresses the position of these planes is $1 : 1 : 1$, this form is also called the unit octahedron. But the form is not necessarily fundamental; for it is frequently more or less arbitrarily assumed, and the structure or genesis of the crystals of a species may point to other forms, having very different axial relations, as will appear from facts stated beyond.

MODELS.—For clear illustration of the axes and axial ratios of planes it is well to have models of the axes made of rods of wood mortised and glued together at the crossing at centre. The rods may be half an inch in diameter and 10 or 12 inches long; for the Isometric system, three equal rods, say 12 inches long; for the Tetragonal system, two of 12 inches for the lateral axes and one of 8 or 14 inches for the vertical; for the Orthorhombic, one of 16 inches for axis b, one of 10 inches for axis c, and one of 14 inches for axis a. (Either axis may be made the vertical by way of change.)

For the Clinometric systems, make a second model like that for the Orthorhombic system, but with the rods but loosely mortised and tied together, so as to admit of a little movement at centre. Then, the model when in its more natural position will be that of the orthorhombic system, the intersections being all rectangular. But by pushing the front rod a down in the plane of ca, making it thus oblique to c while at right angles to b, the model will represent the monoclinic axes; if all the intersections of the rods are oblique, the model will represent the axes of the Triclinic system.

Now by taking a large piece of thick pasteboard, and placing it in different positions with reference to the three axes, the relations to the various planes may be readily illustrated.

Models of the various forms of crystals are also of the highest importance; and the best for general illustration are those made of plate glass, some of them having the positions of the axes within indicated by threads, and others consisting of one form inside of another to show their mutual relations. Such glass models (first made by Professor Dana, in 1835, and recommended in the first edition of his Mineralogy) are now manufactured of great perfection at Siegen, in Germany.

Pasteboard models, likewise useful aids to the study of crystallography, are easily made from the outlines of the faces of the various forms, which have been prepared by various authors.

Models cut in hard wood representing the actual forms of the various mineral species are very valuable, when accurately made. They not only show the relations of different planes, but may also be advantageously used to give the student practice in the mathematical calculations of the axes and parameters, the angles being measured by him as on an actual crystal. Such models have the advantage of being of convenient size, and symmetrically formed, which are conditions not often realized in the crystals furnished by nature.

2. LAW OF SYMMETRY.

The symmetry of crystals is based upon the law that either:

I. *All parts of a crystal similar in position with reference to the axes are similar in planes or modification,* or

II. *Each half of the similar parts of a crystal, alternate or symmetrical in position or relation to the other half, may be alone similar in its planes or modifications.*

The forms resulting according to the first method are termed *holohedral* forms, from ὅλος, *all,* ἕδρα, *face*; and those according to the second, *hemihedral,* from ἥμισυς, *half.*

According to the law of full or *holohedral* symmetry, each sectant in one of the rectangular systems (*a*) should have the same planes both as to number and kind ; and (*b*) whatever the kinds, in each sectant there should be as many of each kind as are geometrically possible. But in *hemihedrism,* either (*a*) planes of a kind occur only in half of the sectants; or else (*b*) half the full number occur in all the sectants.

In the isometric system, for example, if one solid angle of a cube has upon it a plane equally inclined to the diametral sections, so will each of the other angles (or sectants) (f. 39–42).

If one of the twelve edges of the cube has a plane equally inclined to the enclosing cubic faces (or diametral planes) the others will have the same (f. 43–46).

Again, one of the solid angles of a cube being replaced by six planes, as in f. 70, this law requires that the same six planes should appear on all the other solid angles.

But under the law of hemihedrism these planes may occur on half the solid angles of the cube, and not on the other half, as in f. 87, or half the full number of planes may occur on all the angles, as in f. 101. This subject is further elucidated in the discussion of the hemihedral forms belonging to each system of crystallization.

HEMIHEDRISM is of various kinds:

1. *Holomorphic,* in which the occuring planes pertain equally to both the upper and lower (or opposite) ranges of sectants, as in all ordinary hemihedral forms.

2. *Hemimorphic,* in which the planes pertain to either the upper or the lower range, and not to both, and hence the planes are only half enough of the kind to enclose a space, whence the term *hemimorphic,* from ἥμισυς, *half,* and μόρφη, *form.*

The holomorphic forms may be either:

A. *Hemiholohedral,* HALF the sectants having the FULL number of planes, or

B. *Holohemihedral,* ALL the sectants having HALF the whole number of planes.

Again, as to the relative positions of the sectants containing the planes, the forms may be:

a. Vertically-direct, in which the sectants of the upper and of the lower ranges are *alternate,* but the upper *not alternate* with reference to the lower, and, accordingly, each plane above is in the same vertical zone with a like plane below; as in forms described on pp. 34, 35.

b. *Vertically-alternate*, in which the sectants of the upper and lower ranges are *alternate*, and also the upper *are alternate* with reference to the lower, and, accordingly, each plane above is not in the same vertical zone with a like plane below; as in the tetrahedron (f. 9), rhombohedron (f. 16), and gyroidal forms (f. 182).

c. *Vertically-oblique*, in which the sectants of the upper and lower ranges are *adjacent*, but the upper are situated *diagonally* with reference to the lower, being on the opposite side of a transverse diametral or diagonal plane; as in hemihedrons of monoclinic habit under the orthorhombic system (p. 45).

Tetartohedrism.—Mathematically the rhombohedron is a *hemihedron* under the hexagonal system, consequently the forms that are hemihedral to the rhombohedron are *tetartohedrons*, or *quarter-forms*. See p. 39.

Tetartohedral forms, or those with one-fourth of the normal number of planes, have also been observed in the Isometric system. The term *merohedrism*, from μέρος, *part*, and ἕδρα, *face*, has been used in place of hemihedrism, to include both this and tetartohedrism.

I.—ISOMETRIC SYSTEM.

A. *Holohedral Forms.*

In the ISOMETRIC SYSTEM the axes are equal, so that either one may be the vertical axis, and each may be called a. It has already been shown that the general expression for any plane meeting the axes c, b, a is $mc : nb : a$; and in this system it will be $ma : na : a$, or, since the axes are equal, simply $m : n : 1$. Now it has been shown also that according as a plane intersects the several axes at different points, or is parallel to one or more of them, this fact is indicated by the values given for m and n in each case (p. 11). Hence expressions for all the forms geometrically possible in this system will be obtained if to m and n, in the general expression $ma : na : a$, successive values are given. These values may be in this system, 0, 1, a number greater than 1, or ∞. In this way are derived:—

1. $m : n : 1$ [m-n] when m and n have both different values greater than unity.
2. $m : m : 1$ [m-m] when $m > 1, n = m$.
3. $m : 1 : 1$ [m] when $m > 1, n = 1$.
4. $1 : 1 : 1$ [1] when m and $n = 1$.
5. $\infty : n : 1$ [i-n] when $m = \infty, n > 1$.
6. $\infty : 1 : 1$ [i] when $m = \infty, n = 1$.
7. $\infty : \infty : 1$ [H] when m and $n = \infty$.

In lettering the planes of the several forms only the essential part of the symbol is used: the cube is H (hexahedron); the octahedron $1 (= 1 : 1 : 1)$; the dodecahedron i ($\infty : 1 : 1$), (i stands for infinity); m is used for the planes $m : 1 : 1$; m-m for $m : m : 1$; i-n for $\infty : n : 1$.

ISOMETRIC SYSTEM.

m-n for $m : n : 1$. These symbols are the same as those of Naumann, except that he wrote ∞ instead of i for infinity, and introduced also the letter O (octahedron) as the sign of the system; $\infty O \infty$ of his system $= H$; $O = 1$; $\infty O = i$; $m O = m$; $m O m = m$-m, $\infty O n = i$-n, and $m O n = m$-n.

Each of these expressions, appearing at first sight possibly a little obscure, may be translated into simple language.

Cube.—The cube with the symbol $\infty : \infty : 1$, is composed of planes each one of which is parallel to two of the axes, and meets the third at its unit point (see f. 36). It is evident that there are *six* such planes, one at each extremity of the three axes, and the figure or crystal which is enclosed by these six planes has already been described (p. 5) as the *cube* (f. 38).

Octahedron.—The symbol $1 : 1 : 1$ comprises all those planes which meet the three axes at the same distance, that is, cut off the unit length of each. It is evident that there must be *eight* such planes, one in each octant, and they together form the regular *octahedron* (f. 42), which has already been described, p. 4.

Dodecahedron.—The symbol $\infty : 1 : 1$ includes those planes which intercept two of the axes at the same unit distance, and are parallel to the third. There can be twelve planes answering to these conditions, and they form together the *dodecahedron* (f. 45, see also p. 6).

These three forms, the cube, octahedron, and dodecahedron, are those most commonly occurring in this system, and it is important that their relation should be thoroughly understood. The transitions between these forms, as they modify one another, are exhibited in the following figures:

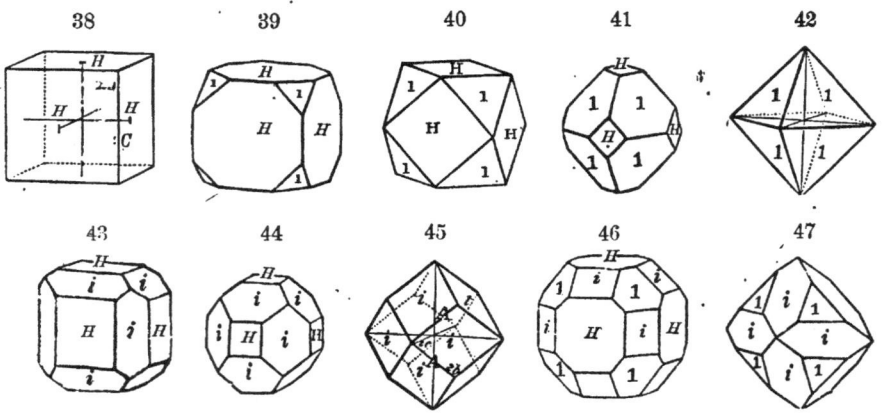

Figs. 38 and 42 represent the cube and octahedron, and 39, 40, 41, the intermediate forms. Slicing off from the eight angles of a cube piece after piece, such that the planes made are equally inclined to H, or the cubic faces, the cube is finally converted into the regular octahedron; and the last disappearing point of each face of the cube is the apex of each solid angle of the octahedron. The axes of the former, therefore, of necessity connect the apices of the solid angles of the latter.

The form in f. 40 is called a *cubo-octahedron.* $H \wedge 1 = 125° \, 15' \, 52''$.

If the twelve edges of the cube are truncated (for all will be truncated if one is) it affords the form in f. 43; then that of f. 44; then the dodecahedron, f. 45; the axes of the cube becoming, in the transition, the axes connecting the tetrahedral solid angles of the dodecahedron; $H \wedge i = 135°$. If the twelve edges of the octahedron (f. 42) are truncated, the form in f. 47 results; and by continuing the replacement, finally the dodecahedron again is formed (f. 45). $1 \wedge i = 144° \, 44' \, 8''$. The last point of the face of the octahedron, as it disappears, is the apex of the trihedral solid angle of the dodecahedron.

These forms are thus mutually derivable. The process may be reversed, the cube being derivable from the dodecahedron by the truncation of the tetrahedral solid angles of the latter (compare in succession f. 45, 44, 43, 38); and the octahedron by the truncation of the trihedral solid angles (compare f. 45, 47, 42). These remarks are important as showing the relations between these forms, though it is of course not intended to be understood that they are in any sense derived from each other in this manner in nature.

The *three axes* (or cubic axes) connect the centres of *opposite faces in the cube*; the apices of opposite solid angles in the octahedron; the apices of opposite tetrahedral solid angles in the dodecahedron.

The *eight trigonal* or *octahedral* interaxes connect the centres of *opposite faces in the octahedron*; the apices of opposite solid angles in the cube; the apices of opposite trihedral solid angles in the dodecahedron.

The *twelve rhombic* or *dodecahedral* interaxes connect the centres of *opposite faces in the dodecahedron*; the centres of opposite edges both in the cube and the octahedron.

In a vertical section, containing each of these kinds of axes, the octahedral interaxis intersects one of the three cubic axes at the angles 54° 44′ 8 and 125° 15′ 52″, and one of the dodecahedral interaxes, at the angles 35° 15′ 52″ and 144° 44′ 8″.

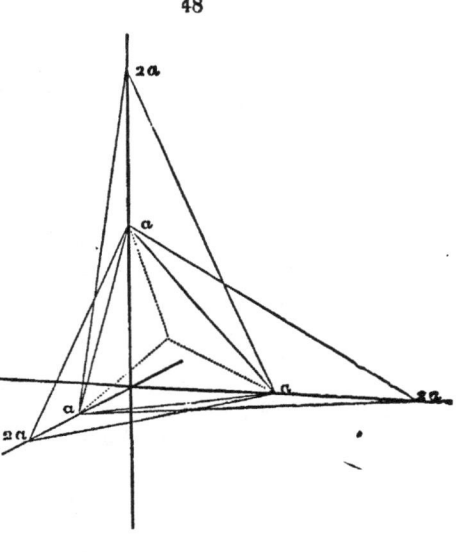

48

There remain four other holohedral forms belonging to the system as contained in the list on page 14.

Trisoctahedrons. — The symbol $m : 1 : 1$ is of that solid each of whose planes meets two of the axes at the unit distance, and the third axis at some distance which is a multiple of this unit length. It will be evident, as in f. 48, that there are three such planes in each of the eight sectants, and hence the total number of planes by which the solid is bounded is twenty-four. The resulting solid is called a *trigonal trisoctahedron*, and one, having $m = \frac{3}{2}$, is shown in f. 49.

It will be found a very valuable practice for the student to construct the figures of the successive crystalline forms in this way, laying off the proper lengths of the several axes and noting the points where the different planes intersect. Further remarks on the drawing o crystals will be found in the Appendix.

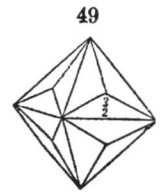

The symbol $m : m : 1$ belongs to all the planes which meet one axis at the unit distance, and the others at equal distances which are multiples of the former. As seen in the preceding case, there will be three such planes in each of the eight sectants, and the total number consequently will be twenty-four. The solid is seen in f. 50, and is called a *tetragonal trisoctahedron*, or a trapezohedron.

Both these forms are called trisoctahedrons, from τρὶς, *three times*, and octahedron, because in each a three-sided pyramid occupies the position of the planes of the regular octahedron. They are closely related to each other; starting with the form $m : 1 : 1$, if m is diminished till it equals unity, then the symbol becomes $1 : 1 : 1$, that is, it has passed into the octahedron. If m becomes less than unity, the symbol may be, for example, $\frac{1}{2} : 1 : 1$, which is identical, as has been explained (p. 11) with $1 : 2 : 2$ (2-2), and this is the symbol of the second trisoctahedron. This explains why, in the first list comprising all the possible forms, m was in no case made less than unity.

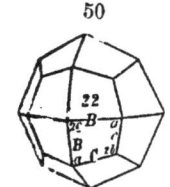

Trigonal-trisoctahedron.—In this form the solid angles are of two kinds: the trigonal or octahedral, and the octagonal or cubic. The edges are thirty-six in number, twenty-four of one kind, forming the octahedral or trihedral solid angles, and twelve edges meeting at the extremities of the cubic axes. Each of the twenty-four planes is an isosceles triangle.

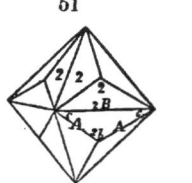 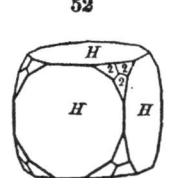 

In combination with the cube, the form 2 appears as a replacement of each of the solid angles by three planes equally inclined on the *edges;* this is seen in f. 52. With the octahedron, it appears as a bevelment of its twelve edges, as shown in f. 53. It also replaces the eight trigonal solid angles of a dodecahedron by three planes inclining on the faces. The more commonly occurring examples of this form are 2 (=2 : 1 : 1), also $\frac{3}{2}$ (=$\frac{3}{2}$: 1 : 1), and 3 (3 : 1 : 1).

The *Tetragonal-trisoctahedron* or trapezohedron, has three kinds of solid angles: six cubic, whose truncations are cubic faces (f. 56); eight octahedral, whose truncations are octahedral faces (f. 56); twelve dodecahedral, truncated by the dodecahedral planes (f. 60). It has forty-eight edges; twenty-four of one kind, those of the trihedral or octahedral solid angles, and the remaining twenty-four, also of one kind, meeting in the cubic solid angles. Each of the twenty-four faces is a quadrilateral.

In combination with the cube it is seen in f. 55, 56, appearing as a replacement of each of the solid angles by three planes equally inclined on the faces of the cube. Figs. 56, 57, 58, 59, 60, 62, also show it in combination with the octahedron and dodecahedron. The most commonly occurring of this series is 2-2 (=2 : 2 : 1), f. 54; as seen in f. 59, it truncates the twenty-four edges of the dodecahedron. On the other hand the form

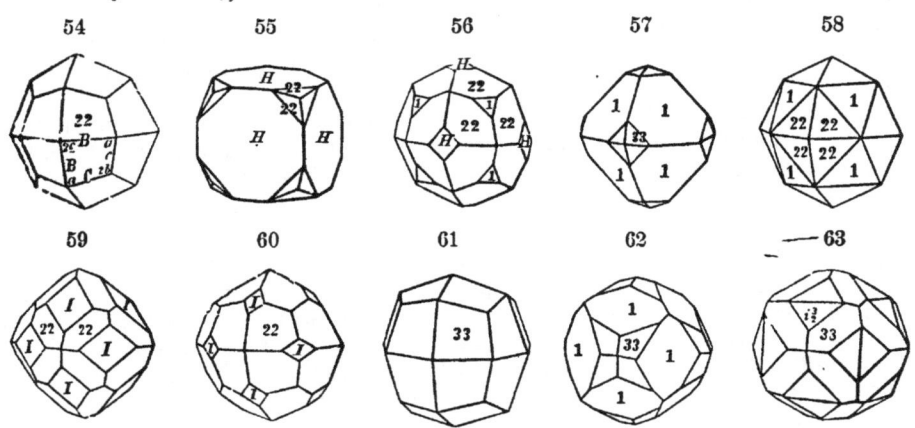

$\frac{3\text{-}3}{2}$ would replace the trihedral solid angles by planes inclined on the edges, while 3-3 replaces (f. 62), the tetrahedral solid angles of the dodecahedron, by planes also inclined on the edges.

Tetrahexahedron.—The symbol $\infty : n : 1$ (*i-n*) belongs to all the planes which are parallel to one axis, meet a second at the unit distance, and the third at some multiple of that. There are *twenty-four* planes which satisfy these conditions, and they form the *tetrahexahedron;* f. 64, 65, represent two varieties of tetrahexahedrons. It will be seen that the planes are so arranged that a square pyramid corresponds to each of the six faces of the cube; and hence the name from τετρακις, *four times,* ἕξ, *six,* and ἕδρα, *face,* it being a 4 × 6-faced solid. The tetrahexahedron has six tetrahedral solid angles and eight hexahedral or octahedral solid angles. There are twenty-four edges of one kind forming the former solid angles, and twelve edges occupying the position of the cubic edges. Each of the twenty-four faces is an isosceles triangle. In combination with the cube it produces a bevelment of its twelve edges, as represented in f. 64.

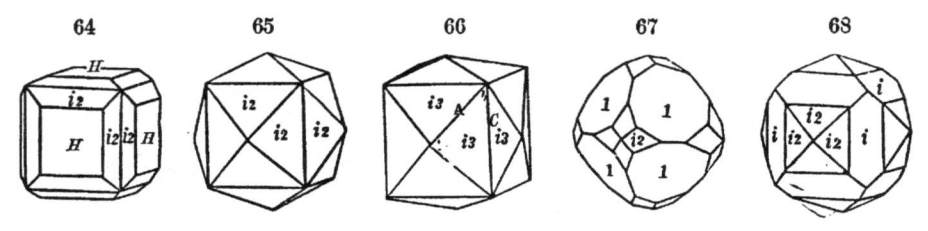

The tetrahexahedron, in f. 65, lettered *i*-2, has the symbol $\infty : 2 : 1$; and that of f. 66, lettered *i*-3, $\infty : 3 : 1$. Some of the other occurring kinds are those with the ratios, 2 : 3, 3 : 4, 4 : 5, etc., etc.

The relation of the tetrahexahedron to the octahedron is shown in f. 67. By comparing this figure with f. 42, it is seen that the planes *i*-2 replace

ISOMETRIC SYSTEM.

the solid angles of the octahedron by planes inclined on its edges. Its relation to the dodecahedron is presented in f. 68, which is a dodecahedron (planes i being the dodecahedral planes, see f. 45) with the tetrahedral solid angles replaced by four planes inclined each on an i.

The tetrahexahedron is called a *fluoroid*, by Haidinger, the form being common in fluorite. It is the *Tetrakishexahedron* (or Pyramidenwürfel) of Naumann.

In accordance with considerations already presented it is evident that n, in the symbol i-n, may always be written as a whole number, for the symbol $\infty : \frac{1}{2} : 1$ is identical with $\infty : 1 : 2$. Moreover it is seen that when n is ∞, the form passes into the cube ($\infty : \infty : 1$), and as n diminishes and becomes unity, it passes into the dodecahedron ($\infty : 1 : 1$).

Hexoctahedron.—The general form $m : n$ includes the largest number of similar planes geometrically possible in this system. This symbol requires six planes in each octant, as will be seen by a method of construction similar to that in f. 48, and consequently the whole solid has forty-eight planes. It is hence called a hexakisoctahedron (ἕξακις, *six times*, ὀκτω, *eight*, and ἕδρα, *face*, i.e., a 6 × 8-faced solid) or hexoctahedron. The form is shown in f. 69, where it will be seen that there are *three* different kinds of edges, and three kinds of solid angles; each of the forty-eight planes is a scalene triangle.

When modifying the cube it appears as six planes replacing each of the solid angles, f. 70. It replaces the eight angles of the octahedron, and the

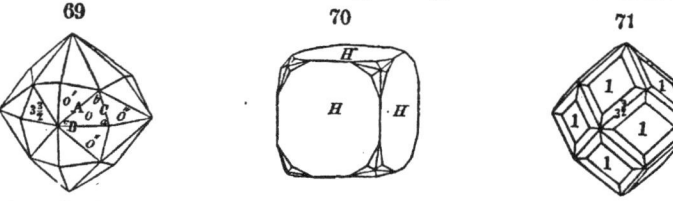

form 3-$\frac{3}{2}$ bevels the twenty-four edges of the dodecahedron (f. 71). Other hexoctahedrons, differing in their angles, may replace the *six* acute solid angles of the dodecahedron by *eight* planes, or the *eight* obtuse by *six* planes.

The hexoctahedron of f. 69, 70, 71 is that whose planes have the axial ratio $3 : \frac{3}{2} : 1$. Others have the ratio $4 : 2 : 1$, $2 : \frac{4}{3} : 1$ (=$6 : 4 : 3$), $5 : \frac{5}{3} : 1$ (=$15 : 5 : 3$), $7 : \frac{7}{3} : 1$ (=$21 : 7 : 3$), etc.

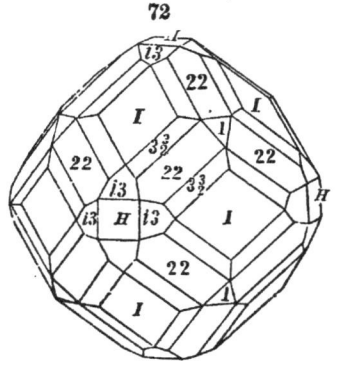

Amalgam.

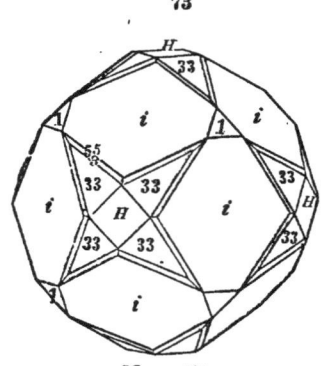

Magnetite.

The preceding figures show dodecahedrons variously modified. In f. 72, *I*, or *i*, are faces of the dodecahedron; *H* of the cube; 1 of the octahedron; *i*-3 of a tetrahexahedron (f. 66); 2-2 of the trapezohedron of f. 54 59; 3-$\frac{3}{2}$ of the hexoctahedron of f. 69, 70. In f. 73, *i*, *O*, and 1 are as in f. 72; 3-3 is the trapezohedron of f. 61, 62; and 5-$\frac{5}{2}$ (either side of 3-3) a hexoctahedron.

The hexoctahedron is called the *adamantoid* by Haidinger, in allusion to its being a common form of crystals of diamond. It is the *hexakisoctahedron* of Naumann.

B. *Hemihedral Forms.*

Of the kinds of hemihedral forms mentioned on page 13, the *hemiholohedral*, in which only half of the sectants are represented in the form, produces what are called *inclined hemihedrons;* and the *holohemihedral*, in which all the sectants are represented by half the full number of planes, *parallel hemihedrons.* In the former the sectants to which the occurring planes belong are diagonally opposite to those without the same planes; and hence no plane has another opposite and parallel to it; on the contrary, opposite planes are oblique to one another, and hence the name of *inclined* hemihedrons applied to them. They are also called *tetrahedral* forms, the tetrahedron being the simplest form of the number, and its habit characteristic of them all; while the latter are called *pyritohedral*, because observed in the species *pyrite.* The complete symbols of the inclined hemihedrons are written in the general form $\frac{1}{2}(m:n:1)$, of the parallel hemihedrons in the form $\frac{1}{2}[m:n:1]$; also written $\kappa(m:n:1)$ and $\pi(m:n:1)$ respectively.

a. Inclined or *Tetrahedral Hemihedrons.* 1. *Tetrahedron*, or *Hemi-octahedron.*—$\frac{1}{2}(1:1:1)$.

As has been shown, the form 1(1 : 1 : 1) embraces eight planes, and when holohedrally developed it produces the octahedron; in accordance, however, with the law of hemihedrism, *half* of the eight possible planes may

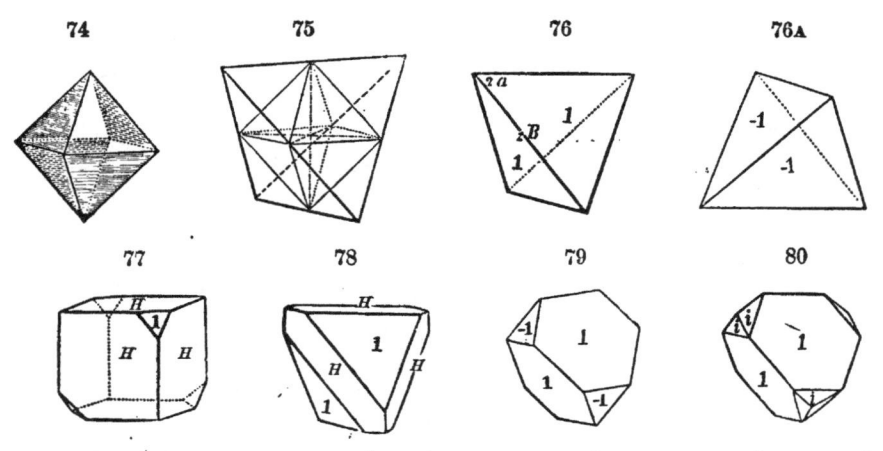

occur in alternate octants; thus in two opposite sectants above, and the two diagonally opposite below, as shown by the shaded planes in f. 74. If these four shaded planes are suppressed, while the other four of the octahedron are extended, the resulting form is the regular tetrahedron, f. 76. The relation of the octahedron and tetrahedron may be better understood from f. 75. If, as just remarked, the planes shaded in f. 74 are suppressed, while the others are extended, it will be seen in f. 75 that the two latter pairs intersect in edges parallel respectively to the basal edges of the octahedron, and the complete tetrahedron is the result. The axes, it is important to observe, connect the middle points of the opposite edges.

Further than this, since either set of four planes may go to form the solid, two tetrahedrons are evidently possible, and they may be distinguished by calling the first, f. 76, positive, and the second negative, f. 76A. These terms are of course only relative. The plus and the minus tetrahedrons may occur in combination, as in f. 79; and though there are here present the eight planes which in holohedral forms make the octahedron, and though they should happen to be equally developed so as to give the same shape, the crystal would still be pronounced tetrahedral, since the planes 1 and −1 are physically different. An example of this occurs in crystals of boracite, where the planes of one tetrahedron are polished while those of the other are without lustre.

The plane angles of the tetrahedron are 60°, and the interfacial angles 70° 31′ 44″.

The combinations of the cube and tetrahedron are shown in f. 77 and 78, and the dodecahedron and tetrahedron in f. 80. As the octahedron results geometrically from slicing off successively the solid angles of the cube, by planes of equal inclination on the cubic faces, so also the tetrahedron may be made mechanically by slicing off similarly *half* these solid angles.

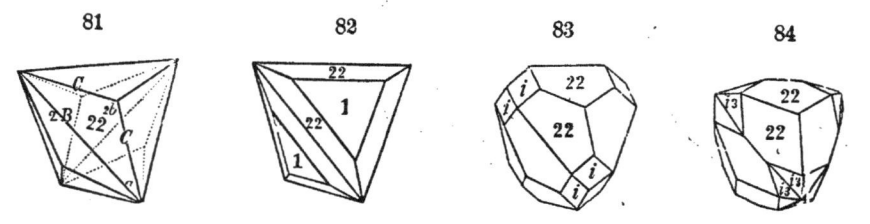

Hemi-trisoctahedrons, $\frac{1}{2}(m : m : 1)$ and $\frac{1}{2}(m : 1 : 1)$. In the same manner as with the tetrahedron, the form m-m, when hemihedral, may have half its twenty-four planes present, viz., those in the two opposite sectants above and the alternate sectants below. When these twelve planes are extended, the others being suppressed, they form the solid represented in f. 81; the symbol properly being $\frac{1}{2}(m$-$m)$, or here $\frac{1}{2}(2$-$2)$. The faces, as will be observed, are *trigonal*, and the solid is sometimes called a *cuproid*. There is the same distinction to be made here between the plus and the minus forms as with the tetrahedrons. Figs. 82, 83, 84 show combinations of $+\frac{1}{2}(m$-$m)$ with the plus tetrahedron, the dodecahedron, and the tetrahexahedron.

Similarly the form m, when hemihedral, according to the same principle results in the solid, f. 85. It is called the *deltohedron* by Haidinger; it has trapezoidal faces. In f. 86, $+\frac{1}{2}(\frac{5}{3})$ is shown in combination with $+\frac{1}{2}(2$-$2)$. Here also the distinction between the plus and minus forms is to be made in the same manner as that already explained.

22   CRYSTALLOGRAPHY.

Inclined or *tetrahedral Hemi-hexoctahedron* $\frac{1}{2}(m : n : 1)$. The form m-n when developed according to the law of inclined hemihedrism, that is, when of its forty-eight faces, half are present, viz., all in half the whole

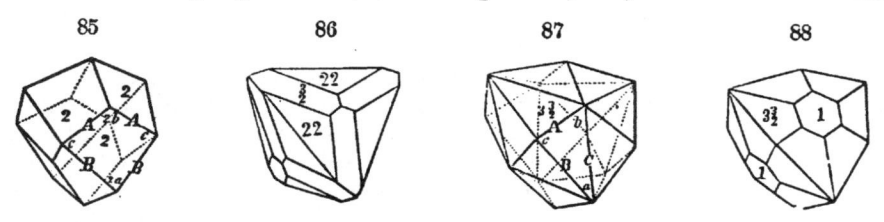

85   86   87   88

number of sectants, produces the solid seen in f. 87. There is here also a *plus* solid, and a *minus* solid, corresponding to the + and − tetrahedron. In f. 88 it is in combination with the plus tetrahedron.

If the same method of inclined hemihedrism be applied to the remaining solids of this system, the cube, dodecahedron, and tetrahexahedron, that is, if in each case the parts in two opposite sectants above, and the two diagonally opposite sectants below, be conceived to be extended, the other half being suppressed, it will be seen that the solid reproduces itself; the hemihedral form of the cube is the cube, and so of the others.

The following figures represent some other combinations of these forms.

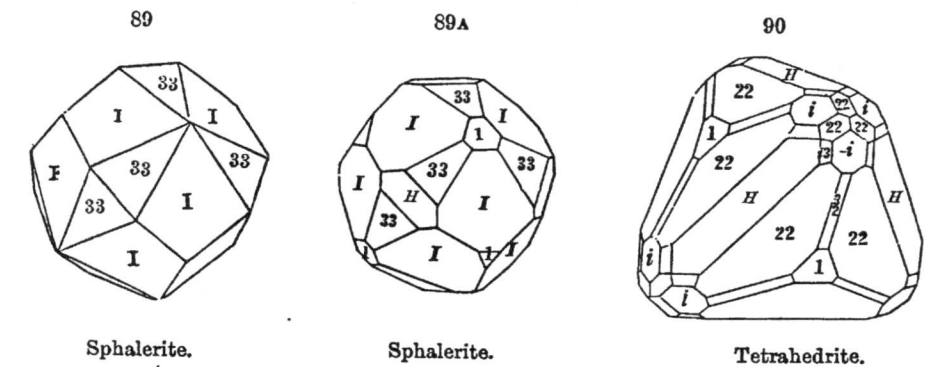

89   89A   90

Sphalerite.   Sphalerite.   Tetrahedrite.

In f. 89, the cuproid 3-3 is combined with the faces I of a dodecahedron. The form 3-3 resembles closely that of f. 81, but in its combination with the dodecahedron it does not truncate an edge of the dodecahedron, like 2-2 in f. 83. Fig. 89A contains the same planes combined with the *plus* tetrahedron, hexagonal planes 1, the minus tetrahedron, triangular planes 1, and the faces of the cube H. The presence of the plane H facilitates the comparison of the form with f. 55, 56, 57, p. 18, the plane 3-3 having the same position essentially with 2-2. Fig. 90 has as its most prominent planes those of f. 81, but the position given it is relatively to f. 81 that of the *minus* hemihedron; and there are also the small planes 2-2 about the angles, which are those of the minus hemihedron. H, are planes of the cube; 1, those of the tetrahedron; i, those of the dodecahedron; i-3 those of a tetrahexahedron (H, i, i-3 all holohedral); and $\frac{3}{2}$ the planes of a deltohedron similar to f. 85, and occurring with 2-2 in f. 86.

ISOMETRIC SYSTEM.

b. Parallel or *pyritohedral hemihedrons.*—According to the second law of hemihedrism, half the whole number of planes of any form may be present in all the sectants. In the resulting solids each plane has *another* parallel to it. This method of hemihedrism obviously produces *distinct forms* only in those cases where there is an even number of planes in each octant.

Pentagonal Dodecahedron, or *Hemi-tetrahexahedron*, $\frac{1}{2}(\infty : n : 1)$. If of the twenty-four planes of the form $i\text{-}n\,(\infty : n : 1)$, only half are present; viz., one of each pair in the manner indicated by shading in f. 91, these being extended while the others are suppressed, the solids in f. 92 and f. 93 result. The parallelism of each pair of opposite planes will be seen in these figures. These two possible forms, seen in the figures, are distinguished by calling one *plus* (arbitrarily), $+\frac{1}{2}[i\text{-}2]$, and the other minus, $-\frac{1}{2}[i\text{-}2]$. These solids are very common in the species pyrite, and are hence called *pyritohedrons*; they are also called pentagonal dodecahedrons, in allusion to their pentagonal faces. The regular dodecahedron of geometry belongs to this class, but is an impossible form in nature, since for it n must have an irrational value, viz., $\dfrac{1+\sqrt{5}}{2}$, see p. 10.

In combination with the cube the form $+\frac{1}{2}[i\text{-}2]$ is seen in f. 94 and f. 95, and in f. 96, 97, with the octahedron, and in f. 98, with the cube and octahedron.

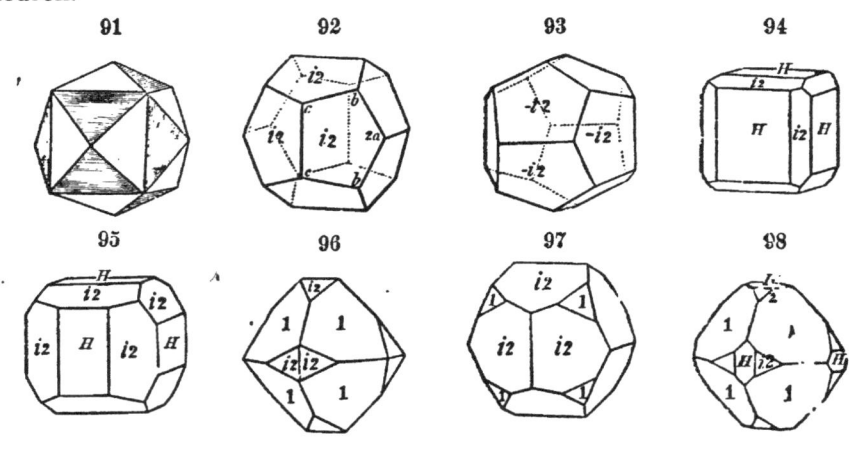

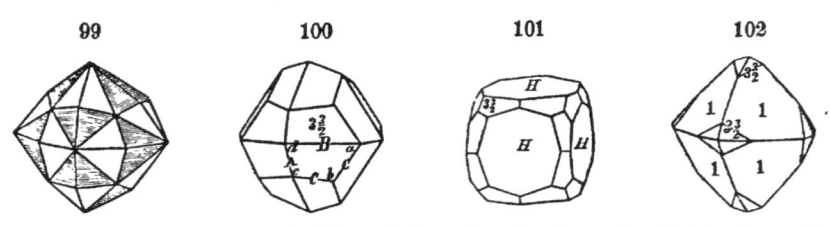

Parallel hemi-hexoctahedron, $\frac{1}{2}[m : n : 1]$. When of the forty-eight planes of the form $m\text{-}n$, only half are present, viz., the three *alternate* planes in each octant as indicated by the shading in f. 99, the solid in f. 100 results. This solid is called a *diploid* by Haidinger. It is also called a dyakis-dodecahedron. In f. 101 it is shown in combination with the cube and in f. 102 with the octahedron.

Figs. 103, 104, 105, of the species pyrite, represent various combinations of parallel hemihedrons with the cubic and other faces. In f. 103 there are planes of two hemi-tetrahexahedrons (pentagonal dodecahedrons) i-2, i-$\frac{3}{2}$; and of two diploids 4-2, 3-$\frac{3}{2}$, along with planes of the octahedron, 1, and of the trapezohedron 2-2. In f. 104 the dominant form is the dodecahedron, I; it has the faces of the cube, H; of the octahedron, 1; of the

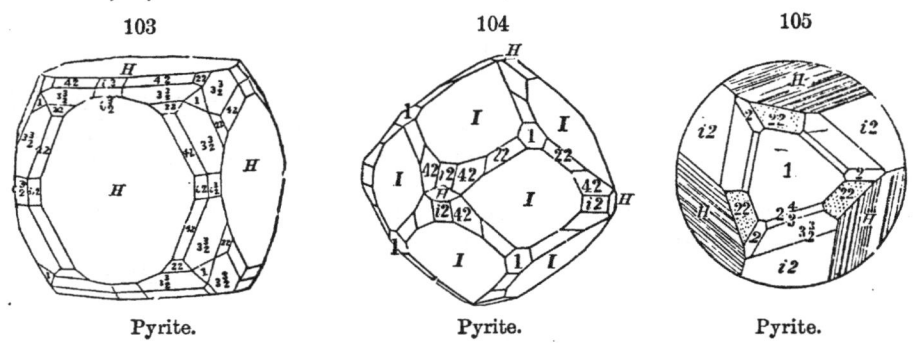

103   104   105

Pyrite.   Pyrite.   Pyrite.

trapezohedron, 2-2; and of the parallel hemihedrons, i-2 and 4-2. Fig. 105 represents a map of one angle of a cube, showing at centre the octahedral face 1, and around it the faces of the cube H, of the trapezohedron 2-2, the trigonal trisoctahedron 2, and the parallel hemihedrons, i-2, 2-$\frac{4}{3}$, 3-$\frac{3}{2}$. The axial ratio for 2-$\frac{4}{3}$ is 2 : $\frac{4}{3}$: 1 (or 6 : 4 : 2), and for 3-$\frac{3}{2}$, 3 : $\frac{3}{2}$: 1 (or 6 : 3 : 2).

Prominent distinctive characters.—The student, in order to facilitate his study of Isometric forms in nature, should be thoroughly familiar with the following points, from the study of models or natural crystals; (1) The *isometric* character of the symmetry, the planes being alike in grouping in the direction of the three axes. (2) The forms of the faces and solid angles of the octahedron, the dodecahedron, the trapezohedron 2-2, the pentagonal dodecahedron i-2. (3) The fact that the following are common angles in the system—135° (=H∧i); 109° 28' (angle of octahedron), 70° 32' (angle in octahedron and tetrahedron); 120° (angle of dodecahedron); 125° 16' (=H∧1); 144° 44' (=H∧2-2= 1∧i); 153° 26' (=H∧i-2); 161° 34' (=H ∧i-3). A list of the angles belonging to the various forms of this system is given on p. 67. (4) Cleavage may be *cubic, octahedral,* or *dodecahedral ;* and sometimes two of these kinds, and occasionally the three, occur in the same species, but always with great difference of facility between them. Galenite is an example of easy cubic cleavage; fluorite of easy octahedral; sphalerite (blende) of easy dodecahedral.

Planes of symmetry.—The seven kinds of solids described on pp. 15 to 19, include *all* the holohedral forms possible in this system, as is evident from their geometrical development. In them exists the highest degree of symmetry possible in any geometrical solids.

In the cube, as has already been stated, all planes, solid angles, and edges are equal and similar. The three diametral planes, passing each through two of the axes, are the chief planes of symmetry, every part of the crystal on one side of the plane having its equal and symmetrical part on the opposite side. Further than this, each of the six planes passing through the diagonal edges of the cube, and consequently parallel to the dodecahedral planes, are also planes of symmetry. There are hence in this system *nine* planes of symmetry.

II.—TETRAGONAL SYSTEM.

In the TETRAGONAL SYSTEM, there are three rectangular axes; but while the two lateral axes are equal, the remaining vertical axis is either longer or shorter than they are; there are consequently to be considered the lateral axes (a) and the vertical axis (c).

The general geometrical expression for the planes of crystals becomes for this system $mc : na : a$, and, if this be developed in the same way as the corresponding expression in the Isometric system, all the forms* geometrically possible are derived.

1. $mc : na : a$ $[m\text{-}n]$ when $m > 1, n > 1$.
2. $\begin{cases} c : a : a \\ mc : a : a \end{cases}$ $\begin{matrix}[1] \\ [m]\end{matrix}$ when $m = 1, n = 1$.
 when $m \gtrless 1, n = 1$.
3. $\begin{cases} c : \infty a : a \\ mc : \infty a : a \end{cases}$ $\begin{matrix}[1\text{-}i] \\ [m\text{-}i]\end{matrix}$ when $m = 1, n = \infty$.
 when $m \gtrless 1, n = \infty$.
4. $\infty c : na : a$ $[i\text{-}n]$ when $m = \infty, n > 1$.
5. $\infty c : a : a$ $[I]$ when $m = \infty, n = 1$.
6. $\infty c : \infty a : a$ $[i\text{-}i]$ when $m = \infty, n = \infty$.
7. $\begin{cases} (c : \infty a : \infty a) \\ \text{or } 0c : a : a. \end{cases}$ $[O]$ when $m = 0, n = 1$.

In lettering the planes the abridged symbols are used; here, as before, $i = \infty$, and the unit term is omitted as unnecessary, $mc : \infty a : a = m\text{-}i$, etc. These are the same as the symbols of Naumann, except that he wrote ∞, and added P as the sign of the systems which are not isometric; $0P = O$; $\infty P\infty = i\text{-}i$; $\infty P = I$; $\infty Pn = i\text{-}n$; $mP\infty = m\text{-}i$; $mP = m$; $P = 1$; and $mPn = m\text{-}n$.

A. *Holohedral Forms.*

Basal plane.—There are two similar planes corresponding to the symbol $c : \infty a : \infty a$ (or $0c : a : a$), parallel to both the lateral axes; each is called the basal plane. They do not inclose a space, and consequently they can occur only in combination with other planes.

Prisms.—The planes having the symbol $\infty c : \infty a : a$ are parallel to the vertical and one of the lateral axes. There are four such planes, one at each extremity of the two lateral axes, and, in combination with the plane O, they form the square prism, which has been called the *diametral* prism, seen in f. 106.

For the symbol $\infty c : a : a$, the planes are parallel to the vertical axis,

---

* The word *form* has been freely used in the preceding pages; from this point on, however, it needs to be more exactly defined. In a crystallographic sense it includes all the planes geometrically possible. never less than two, which have the same general symbol.

and meet the others at equal distances. There are, as in the preceding case, four such planes. They form, in combination with the plane O, that square prism which is seen in f. 107, and may be called the *unit* prism. Both the prisms i-i and I are alike in their degree of symmetry. Each has four similar vertical edges, and eight similar basal edges unlike the vertical. There are also in each case eight similar solid angles.

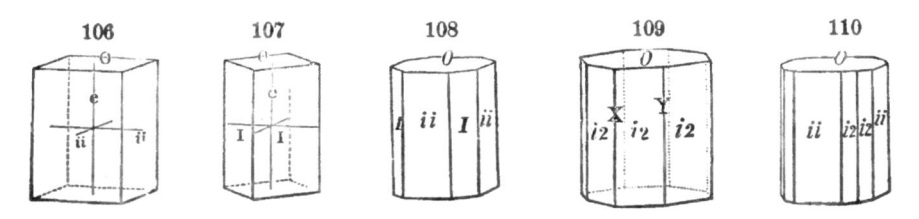

The form i-n ($\infty\, c : na : a$) is another prism, but in this each plane meets one of the lateral axes at the unit distance, and the other at some multiple of its unit distance. As is evident in the accompanying horizontal section (f. 113), this general symbol requires *eight* similar planes, two in each quadrant, and the complete form is shown in f. 109. The sixteen basal edges are all similar; the vertical edges are of two kinds, four axial X, and four diagonal Y (f. 109). The *regular* octagonal prism with eight similar vertical edges, each angle being 135°, is crystallographically impossible.

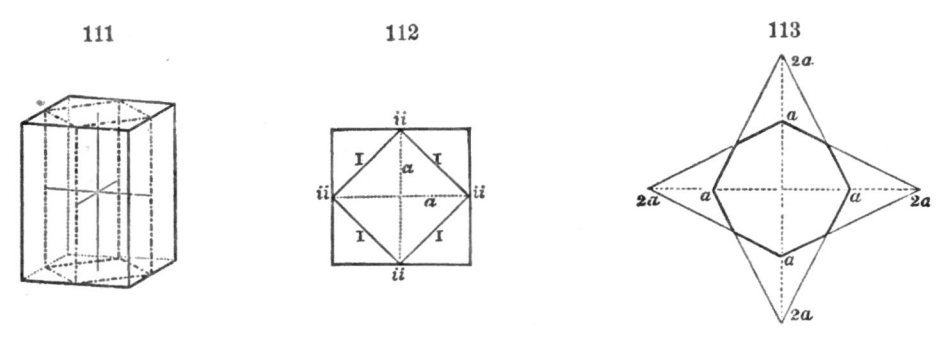

The planes I truncate the edges of the diametral prism i-i, as in f. 108. Similarly the planes i-i truncate the vertical edges of I. The prism i-n bevels the edges of i-i, as in f. 110, where i-$n = i$-2.

The relation of the two square prisms, i-i and I, may be further illustrated by the figs. 111 and 112. In f. 112 the sections of the two prisms are shown with the dotted lines for the axes, and in f. 111 there are the two forms complete, the one (I) within the other (i-i). The unit prism I is sometimes called the prism of the *first series*, and the prism i-i that of the *second series*.

Octahedrons or *Pyramids*.—The forms m-i and m both give rise to square octahedrons, corresponding to the two kinds of square prisms. In m-i the planes are parallel to one lateral axis and meet the vertical axis at variable distances, multiples (denoted by m) of the unit length. The total number of such planes, for a given value of m, is obviously eight, and the form is shown in f. 114 and 115. These planes replace the basal edges of the form shown in f. 106, and m varies in value from 0 to ∞. When $m=0$ the four planes above and below coincide with the two basal

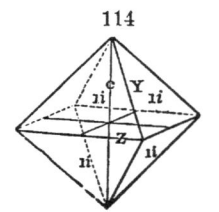

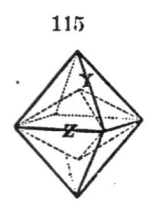

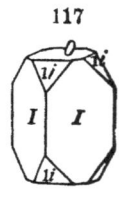

planes; as m increases, there arises a series, or zone, of planes, with mutually parallel intersections (f. 116); and when $m=\infty$, the octahedral planes $m\text{-}i$ coincide with the planes $i\text{-}i$. The value of m in a particular species depends upon the unit value assumed for the vertical axis c.

The same form replaces the vertical angles of the prism I, as in f. 117.

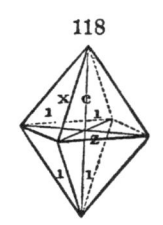

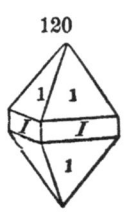

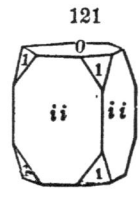

The octahedrons of the m series meet both of the lateral axes at equal distances and the vertical axis at variable distances. It is clear that the whole number of planes for this form, when the value of m is given, is also eight, one in each octant. When $m=1$ the solid in f. 118 is obtained, which is sometimes called the unit octahedron. As m decreases, the octahedrons become more and more obtuse, till $m=0$, when the eight planes coincide with the two basal planes. As m increases from unity, on the other hand, the octahedrons or pyramids become more and more acute, and when $m=\infty$ they coincide with the prism I; this series forms another zone of planes. These octahedrons replace the basal edges in the form f. 107, as seen in f. 119, and as the octahedron is more and more developed it passes to f. 120, and finally to f. 118.

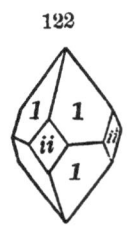

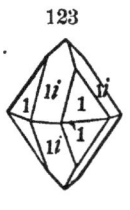

The same form replaces the solid angles of the form f. 106, as seen in f. 121, and this too gradually passes into f. 122 and f. 114.

28   CRYSTALLOGRAPHY.

The relation of the octahedrons 1 and 1-i (m and m-i) is the same as that of the prisms I and i-i (compare f. 112). Similarly, too, they are often called octahedrons (or pyramids) of the *first* (m) and *second* (m-i) series.

As will be seen in f. 123, 1-i truncates the pyramidal edges of the octahedron 1, and, conversely, the edges of the octahedron 2-i are truncated by the octahedron 1 (f. 124).

Octagonal pyramids.—The form m-n (mc : na : a) in this system has, as in the preceding system, the highest number of similar planes which are geometrically possible; in this case the number is obviously sixteen, two in each of the eight sectants, as in f. 125, where $m=1$, $n=2$. These sixteen similar planes together form the octagonal pyramid (strictly double pyramid) or zirconoid, f. 126. It has two kinds of terminal edges, the axial X and the diagonal Y; the basal edges are all similar. It is seen (m-$n=1$-2) in f. 127 in combination with the diametral prism, and in f. 128 with 1, where it bevels the vertical edges.

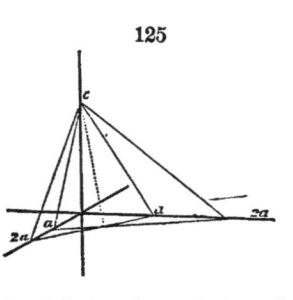

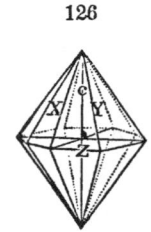

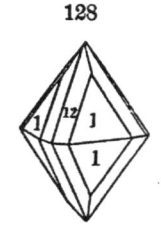

Other tetragonal forms are illustrated in figures 2 to 8, of zircon crystals, on p. 2; f. 8 is the most complex, and besides 3-3 shows also the related zirconoids 4-4 and 5-5.

Several series of forms occur in f. 129, of vesuvianite. In the unit series of planes there are the octahedrons (or pyramids) 1, 2, 3, and the prism I; in the diametral series 1-i, i-i; of octagonal prisms, i-2, i-3; of zirconoids 2-2, 3-3, 5-5, 4-2, ⅔-3, the whole number of planes being 154.

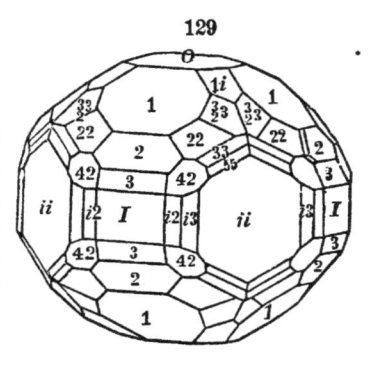

B. *Hemihedral Forms.*

Among hemihedral forms there are two divisions, as in the isometric system:

1. *Hemiholohedral*, having the full number of planes in half the sectants (*a*) *Vertically-alternate*, or *sphenoidal* forms.—The planes occur in two sectants situated in a diagonal line at one extremity, and two in the transverse diagonal at the other.

TETRAGONAL SYSTEM.

With octahedral planes $\frac{1}{2}(mc : a : a)$ the solid is a tetrahedron (f. 130, 131) called a *sphenoid*, having the same relation to the square prism of

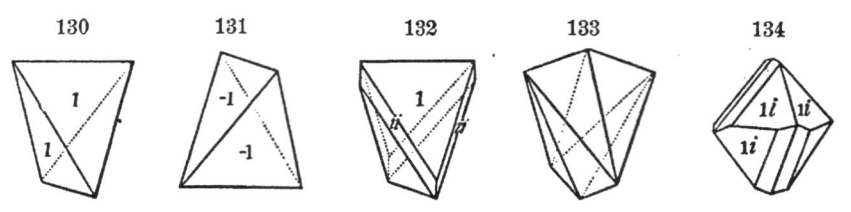

f. 106 that the regular tetrahedron has to the cube. Fig. 130 is the *positive* sphenoid or $+1$, and 131 the *negative*, or -1. The form $\frac{1}{2}(mc : \infty a : a)$ is similar. Fig. 132 represents the sphenoid in combination with the prism i-i.

If the planes of each sectant are the two of the octagonal pyramid $\frac{1}{2}(mc : na : a)$ (f. 126), the form is a *diploid* (f. 133). It is in combination with the octahedron 1-i in f. 134.

(*b*) *Vertically-direct*, or the planes occuring in two opposite sectants above, and in two on the same diagonal below. The result is a horizontal prism, or forms resembling those of the orthorhombic system. Characterizes crystals of edingtonite.

(*c*) *Vertically-oblique*. Planes occurring in two adjacent octants above, and in two diagonally opposite below, producing monoclinic forms, as in a hydrous ammonium sulphate.

2. *Holohemihedral*, all the sectants having half the full number of planes. As the largest number of planes of a kind is *two*, half the full number is in all cases *one*. Hemihedrism may occur in the forms m-n (f. 126, 127), or zirconoids, and in the forms i-n (f. 109), or the octagonal prism.

The following are the kinds:

(*a*) *Vertically-direct*. The occurring plane of the sectants, the *right* one in the upper series, and that in the same vertical zone below, as indicated by the shading in f. 135; or else the *left* one above, and that in the same vertical zone below, f. 136.

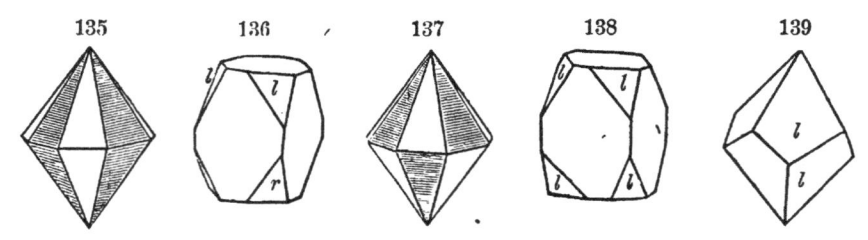

(*b*) *Vertically-alternate*. The occurring plane the *right* above, and that in the alternate zone below, as indicated in f. 137; or else the *left* above, and that in the alternate zone below, f. 138.

As the *right* of the two planes above is in the same vertical zone with the *left* of the two below (supposing the lower end made the upper), the two kinds of the first division will be the *rl m-n*; and the *lr m-n* (in f. 136 on the angles of the prism i-i); and the two of the second division the *rr m-n* and the *ll m-n* (in f. 138, on the angles of the prism i-i).

The completed form for the first methods has parallel faces, and is like the ordinary square octahedron in shape, because the upper and lower planes belong to the same vertical zone. But in the second it is *gyroidal;* the upper pyramid has its faces in the same vertical line with an edge of the lower, as represented in f. 139, the form *ll m-n*.

The first of these methods occurs in octagonal prisms, producing a square prism, either *r i-n*, or *l i-n*.

Fig. 140 represents a combination of the octahedron 1-*i* with the unit-octahedron 1, and two hemihedral forms, one of them *lr* 1-2, the other *rl* 3-3. The plane 1 shows the position of the octant; 3-3 is to the *right* of 1, and 1-2 to the *left*. In f. 141, which is a top view of a crystal of wernerite, there occurs *l* 3-3 large, along with *r* 3-3 small, indicating hemihedrism, and, judging from that of the allied species sarcolite, it is of the square octahedral kind, *rl* 3-3 and *lr* 3-3.

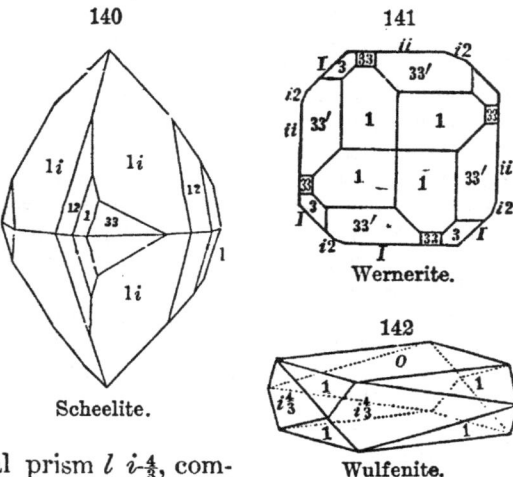

Scheelite.

Wernerite.

Wulfenite.

Fig. 142 contains the hemihedral prism l $i\text{-}\tfrac{4}{3}$, combined with the unit-octahedron 1, and the basal plane *O*.

Variable elements in this system.—In the tetragonal system two elements are variable, and in any given case must be decided before the relations of the forms can be definitely expressed.

(*a*) *The position of the lateral axes.*—These axes are equal, but there are two possible positions for them, for in a given square octahedron they may be either diagonal or diametral; in other words, given an octahedron, as in f. 115, 116, the prismatic planes may be made diametral (*i-i*), and the octahedron so belong to the *m-i* series, or the prismatic planes may be made diagonal, that is *I* ($\infty c : a : a$), when the corresponding octahedrons belong to the *m* series. The ratio of the lateral axes for the two cases is obviously $1 : \sqrt{2}$, or $1 : 1.4142 +$.

(*b*) *The length of the vertical axis.*—Among the several occurring octahedrons, one must be assumed as the unit, and the others referred to it. In f. 143, of zircon, the octahedron 1 is made the unit, and by measuring the basal angle it is found mathematically, as explained later, that the length of the vertical axis is 0.85 times that of the lateral axes. The octahedron 3 has then the symbol $3c : a : a$ as referred to this unit. If the latter octahedron had been taken as the fundamental form, the length of the vertical axis would have been 3×0.85 times that of the lateral axes, and the symbol of the first plane would have been $\tfrac{1}{3}c : a : a$. Which form is to be taken as the unit or fundamental, that is, what length of the vertical axis *c* is to be adopted, depends upon various considerations. In general that form is assumed as fundamental which is of most common occurrence or to which the cleavage is parallel; or which best shows the morphological relations of the given species to others related to it in chemical composition, or which gives the simplest symbols for the occurring forms of a species.

Prominent characteristics of ordinary tetragonal forms.—The prominent distinguishing characteristics of tetragonal forms are: (1) A symmetrical arrangement of the planes in *fours* or *eights*. (2) The frequent occurrence of a square prism diagonal to a square prism, the one making with the other an angle of 135°. (3) The occurrence of bevelling planes on the lateral edges of the square prism. (4) A resemblance of the octahedrons to the regular octahedron, in having a square base, but a dissimilarity in that the angles over the basal edges do not equal those over the terminal. (5) *Cleavage* may be either *basal, square-prismatic,* or *octahedral;* prismatic cleavage, when existing, is alike in two directions, parallel to the lateral faces of one of the square prisms, and is always dissimilar to the basal cleavage; the basal, or the lateral, is sometimes indistinct or wanting; the prismatic may occur parallel to the lateral planes of both square prisms, but when so, that of one will be always unlike in facility that of the other.

Planes of symmetry.—There are five planes of symmetry in the tetragonal system: one principal plane of symmetry normal to the vertical axis, and four others, intersecting in this axis; these four are in two pairs, the planes of each pair normal (90°) to each other, and diagonal (45°) to those of the other.

III.—HEXAGONAL SYSTEM.

The HEXAGONAL SYSTEM includes two grand divisions: 1. The HEXAGONAL proper, in which (1) symmetry is by *sixes*, and multiples of six; (2) hemihedral forms are of the kind called vertically-direct; and (3) cleavage and all physical characters have direct relations to the holohedral hexagonal form.

2. The RHOMBOHEDRAL, in which (1) symmetry is by *threes* and multiples of three, rhombohedral forms being *hemihedral* in mathematical relation to the hexagonal system, and of the kind called vertically-alternate; (2) cleavage, and many other physical characters, usually partake of the hemihedrism.

While the rhombohedron is mathematically a hemihedral form under the hexagonal system, and is properly so treated in a system of mathematical crystallography, it is not so genetically, or in its fundamental relations. Moreover, it has its own hemihedral forms, which, under the broad hexagonal system, are *tetartohedral*.

The *holohedral* forms, all of which belong to the Hexagonal division, are here first described; and then the *hemihedral* forms, which include, besides a few under the hexagonal division, the whole of the *Rhombohedral division*.

A. *Holohedral Forms*: HEXAGONAL DIVISION.

The general expression for planes of this system is $mc : na : a : pa$, where there are to be considered the vertical axis, c, and three equal lateral axes, a.

It is evident, however, that the position of any plane is determined by its intersections with two of the lateral axes, as its direction with the third follows directly from them. (Compare f. 146.) Consequently, in writing the symbol of any plane it is necessary to take into consideration only the vertical axis, and two of the lateral axes adjacent to each other.

The various holohedral forms possible in this system are derived after the analogy of those of the tetragonal system. The parameters for *all* the lateral axes are given below for sake of comparison. It is to be noted here that m may be either < 1, or > 1; n is always > 1 and < 2, while $p > 2$ and $< \infty$; further than this it is always true that $p = \dfrac{n}{n-1}$.

$mc : na : a : (pa)$ $[m\text{-}n]$ when $m \lessgtr 1$, $n > 1$ and < 2.
$mc : 2a : a : (2a)$ $[m\text{-}2]$ when $m \lessgtr 1$, $n = 2$.
$\{\ mc : a : a : (\infty a)$ $[m]$ when $m \gtrless 1$, $n = 1$.
$\{\ c : a : a : (\infty a)$ $[1]$ when $m = 1$, $n = 1$.
$\infty c : na : a : (pa)$ $[i\text{-}n]$ when $m = \infty$, $n > 1$ and < 2.
$\infty c : 2a : a : (2a)$ $[i\text{-}2]$ when $m = \infty$, $n = 2$.
$\infty c : a : a : (\infty a)$ $[I]$ when $m = \infty$, $n = 1$.
$0c : a : a : (a)$ $[O]$ when $m = 0$, $n = 1$.

The abridged symbols need no explanation beyond that which has been given on p. 25; $mPn = m\text{-}n$; $\infty Pn = i\text{-}n$, etc.

Basal planes.—The form $O = 0c : a : a$ includes the two basal planes above and below, parallel to the plane of the lateral axes.

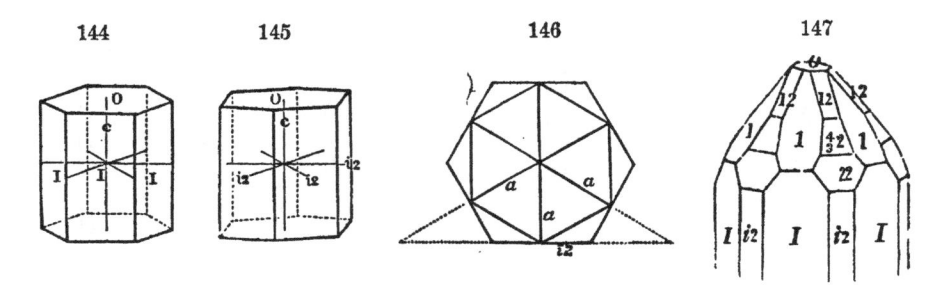

144   145   146   147

Prisms.—The form $I = \infty c : a : a$ comprises the six planes parallel to the vertical axis, and meeting the two adjoining lateral axes at equal distances. These six planes with the basal plane form the hexagonal unit prism, f. 144. The form $i\text{-}2 = \infty c : 2a : a$ includes the six planes which are parallel to the vertical axis but meet one of the lateral axes at the unit distance, and the other *two* at double that distance. These planes with the basal plane form the diametral prism, f. 145. The relations of the two prisms I and $i\text{-}2$ are shown in f. 146. In f. 147, it will be seen that the one prism truncates the vertical edges of the other. The faces of the $i\text{-}2$ make an angle of 150° with the faces of I. These two prisms have an intimate connection with each other, and together form a *regular* twelve-sided prism,—a prism which is crystallographically impossible except as the result of the combination of these two different forms.

HEXAGONAL SYSTEM.

The form i-2 is a special case of the general form i-n or $\infty c : na : a$. When n is some number less than 2, and greater than 1, there must be two planes answering the given conditions in each sectant, and twelve in all. Together they form the dihexagonal, or twelve-sided, prism. This prism bevels the edges of the prism I, and the vertical edges are of two kinds, axial and diagonal. The values of n must lie between 1 and 2; some of the occurring forms are i-$\frac{4}{3}$, i-$\frac{5}{4}$, etc.

Hexagonal pyramids, or Quartzoids.—The symbol $1 = c : a : a$ belongs to the twelve planes of the unit pyramid, f. 148, while the general form $m = mc : a : a$ includes all the pyramids in this series where the length of the vertical axis is some multiple of the assumed unit length. As in the tetragonal system, when m diminishes, the pyramids become more and more obtuse, and the form passes into the basal plane when m is zero; while as m increases, the pyramids become more and more acute, and finally coincide with the prism I. These pyramids consequently replace the basal edges between O and I, f. 149, and with them form a vertical *zone* of planes.

The pyramids of the m-2 series have the same relation to those of the m series, just described, that the prism i-2 has to the prism I. They replace the basal edges between i-2 and O (f. 145), and as the value of m varies, give rise to a series or *zone* of planes between these limits.

The pyramids of both the first (m) and the second (m-2) series are well shown in f. 150, of apatite. In the first series there are the pyramids $\frac{1}{2}$, 1, and 2; and in the second series the pyramids 1-2, 2-2, and 4-2. The cor-

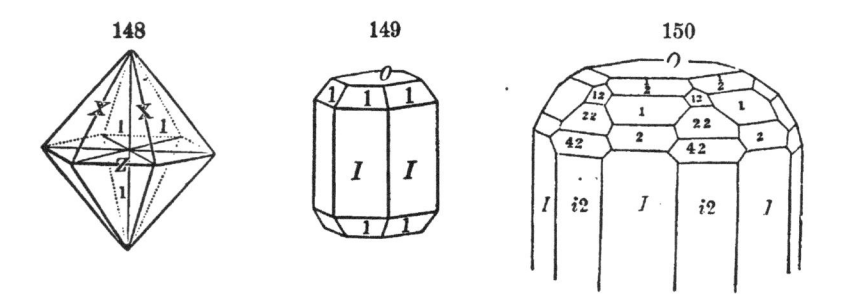

responding prisms I and i-2 are also shown, and the zones between each of them and the basal plane O are to be noticed. Attention may also be called to the fact, exemplified here, that the pyramid 2-2 truncates the vertical edges of the pyramid 2; also 1-2 truncates the vertical edges of 1; while the latter form (1) also truncates the vertical edges of $\frac{4}{3}$-2, as is seen in f. 147.

Dihexagonal pyramids, or Berylloids.—The general form $mc : na : a$ gives the largest number of similar planes possible in this system, which is here obviously twenty-four, that is, two in each of the twelve sectants. These pyramids correspond to the prisms of the i-n series, and form the dihexagonal pyramids, or berylloids, as in f. 151.

The berylloid has three kinds of edges: the axial edges X (f. 151, 152), connecting the apex with the extremity of one of the axes; the diagonal edges Y, and the basal edges Z

In the upper pyramid, one of these two planes for each sectant may be distinguished as the *right*, and the other the *left*, as lettered in f. 152; and the same, after inverting the crystal, for those of the other pyramid. It is to be observed that in a given position of the form, as that of f. 151, the *right*

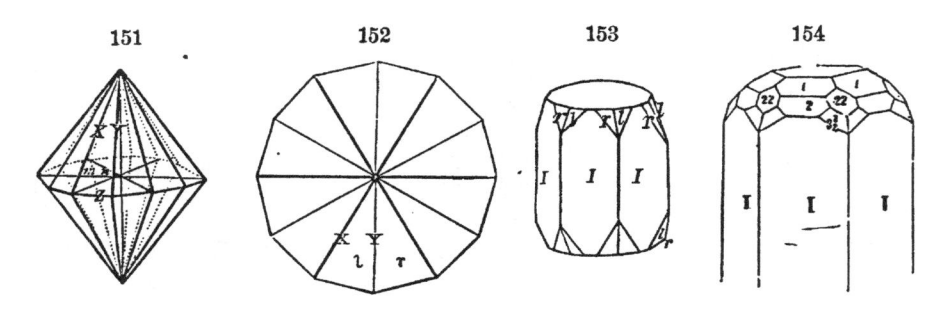

of the upper pyramid will be over the *left* of the lower pyramid, and the reverse. Fig. 153 represents the planes of such a form m-n combined with the unit prism I, and the planes are lettered l, r, in accordance with the above. In f. 154, of a crystal of beryl, the prism I is combined with the pyramids 1, 2, 2-2, and the berylloid 3-$\frac{3}{2}$.

B. *Hemihedral Forms.*

I. VERTICALLY DIRECT.—The planes of the upper range of sectants being in the same vertical zone severally with those below.

(*A*). *Hemiholohedral.*—Half the sectants having the full number of planes:

1. *Trigonal pyramids.*—The diametral pyramid m-2 is sometimes thus hemihedral, as in the annexed figure (f. 155) of a crystal of quartz, in which there are only three planes, 2-2, at each extremity, and each of those above is in the same zone with one below. The completed form would be an equilateral and symmetrical double three-sided pyramid.

2. *Trigonal prisms.*—The occurrence of three out of the six planes of the prism I, or i-2, produces a three-sided prism. The prism I is thus hemihedral in tourmaline (f. 156, a top view of a crystal), and the prism i-2 in quartz. Both these forms properly belong to the Rhombohedral division.

3. *Ditrigonal prisms.*—An hexagonal prism hemihedral to the dihexagonal prism occurs in quartz and tourmaline, the hexagonal prism sometimes having only the alternate vertical edges bevelled, as in f. 185, and f. 186, p. 40.

(*B*). *Holohemihedral.*—All the sectants having half the full number of planes:

1. *Hemi-dihexagonal pyramids.*—Each sectant has one out of the two planes of the dihexagonal pyramid (f. 151, 153); this is indicated by

the shading in f. 157. The occurring plane may be the right above and left below, or left above and right below, and the form accordingly

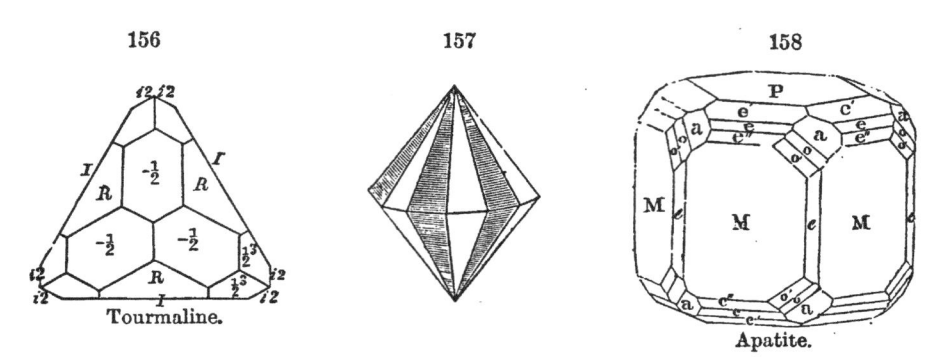

156
Tourmaline.

157

158
Apatite.

either *rl m-n*, or *lr m-n*. Examples of the first of these occur in f. 158, representing a crystal of apatite, the planes $o(3\text{-}\frac{3}{2})$, and $o'(4\text{-}\frac{4}{3})$ being of this kind. This method of hemihedrism occurs only in forms that are true hexagonal; it is often called *pyramidal hemihedrism*.

II. VERTICALLY ALTERNATE, the planes of the upper range of sectants being in zones alternate with those below.

(A) *Hemiholohedral forms*, or those in which half the sectants have the full number of planes as in the

RHOMBOHEDRAL DIVISION.

1. *Rhombohedrons, and their relation to Hexagonal forms.*—The rhombohedron is derivable from the hexagonal pyramid by a suppression of the alternate planes and the extension of the others. In f. 159, if the shaded planes in front and the opposite ones behind are suppressed, while the others are extended, a rhombohedron will be derived. This is further shown in f. 160, where the hexagonal pyramid is represented within the rhombohedron. Another similar rhombohedron, complementary to this, would result from the suppression of the other alternate half of the planes. One of these rhombohedrons is called *minus*, and the other *plus* (f. 161, 162). The form in f. 148 is made up, under the rhombohedral system, of $+R$ and $-R$ (or $+1$ and -1) combined, as in the annexed figure (f. 163), of a crystal of quartz.

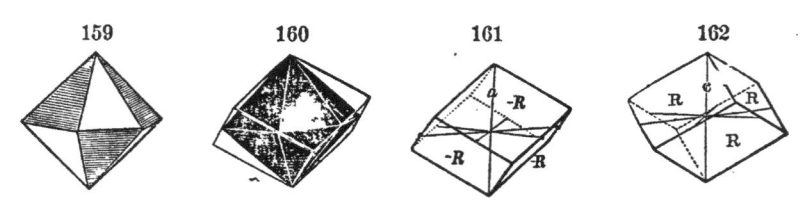

159 **160** **161** **162**

Fig. 164 shows the combination of the rhombohedron with the prism I; in f. 165 the former is more developed, and it finally passes into the com plete rhombohedron, f. 161. In f. 166 the rhombohedral planes occur on the alternate angles of the diagonal prism i-2.

The symbol of the unit rhombohedron as referred to the hexagonal system is $\frac{1}{2}(c : a : a)$, a second rhombohedron may be $\frac{1}{2}(2c : a : a)$ and so on; it is, however, more simple to write only $+R$ or $-R$, and $+2R$ or $-2R$, and so on; or, where there is no confusion with the symbols of hexagonal forms, as $+1, -1$, and $+m, -m$.

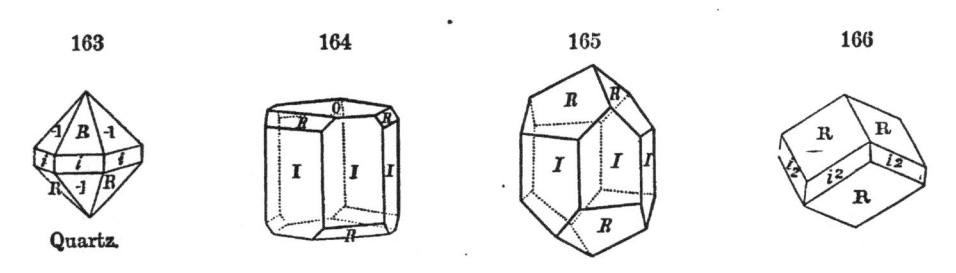

163   164   165   166

Quartz.

This hemihedrism resulting in the rhombohedron is analogous, in the alternate positions of the planes above and below, to that producing the tetrahedron in the isometric system. But owing to the fact that there are *three* lateral axes instead of *two*, the rhombohedron has its opposite faces parallel, unlike the tetrahedron.

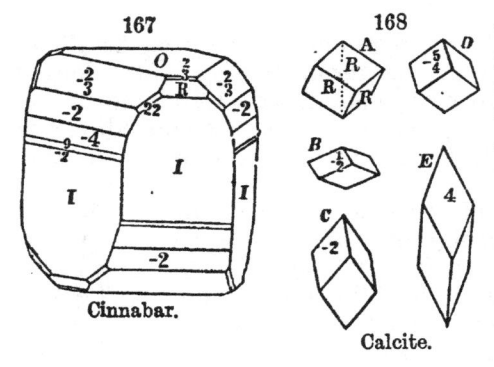

167   168

Cinnabar.   Calcite.

169

In f. 167 the planes R belong to the rhombohedron $+1$; $\frac{2}{3}$ to the rhombohedron $+\frac{2}{3}$, having the vertical axis $\frac{2}{3}c$; O is the basal plane, or mathematically the rhombohedron 0, the vertical axis being $0c$. I is the hexagonal prism $\infty : 1 : 1$, or more properly a rhombohedron with an infinite axis, ∞c. On the opposite side of I the planes are rhombohedral, but belong to the *minus* series; $-\frac{2}{3}$ has the vertical axis $\frac{2}{3}c$; $-4, 4c$; $-2, 2c$; $-\frac{2}{3}, \frac{2}{3}c$, this last being complementary to $+\frac{2}{3}$, and the same identical form, except that all the parts are reversed. Fig. 168, A–E represent different rhombohedrons of the species calcite: A, the rhombohedron 1; $B, -\frac{1}{2}$; $C, -2$; $D, -\frac{5}{4}$; $E, 4$; having respectively for the vertical axis, $1c, \frac{1}{2}c, 2c, \frac{5}{4}c, 4c$, with $c=0.8543$, the lateral axes being made equal to unity. In f. 169 the rhombohedron 2 (or $2R$) is combined with -1 (or $-R$), the latter truncating the terminal edges of the former.

In relation to the series of $+$ and $-$ rhombohedrons it is important to note that, since the position of $-\frac{1}{2}R$ is that of the vertical edge of $+R$, in combination with it, it truncates these edges. Similarly $+\frac{1}{4}R$ truncates the same edges of $-\frac{1}{2}R$, and so on.

HEXAGONAL SYSTEM. 37

Also $+R$ truncates the edges of $-2R$, and $-R$ the edges of $+2R$ (f. 169), $-2R$ truncates the edges of $+4R$, and so on.

2. *Scalenohedrons; forms hemihedral to the dihexagonal pyramid.*—As the rhombohedron is a hemihedral hexagonal pyramid or quartzoid, so a scalenohedron is a hemihedral dihexagonal pyramid or berylloid. The method of hemihedrism is similar by the suppression of the planes of the alternate sectants, as indicated by the shading in f. 170 (analogous to f. 159) and the extension of those of the other sectants. A scalenohedron is

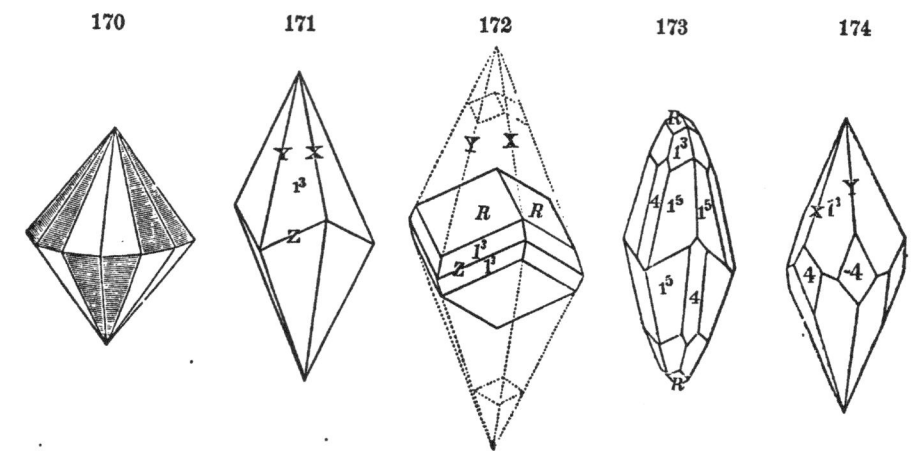

represented in f. 171, a hexagonal double pyramid with a zig-zag basal outline, and three kinds of edges; the shorter terminal edge X, the longer terminal edge Y, and the basal edge Z; the lateral axes terminate in the middle of the edges Z. There are *plus* and *minus* scalenohedrons, as there are *plus* and *minus* rhombohedrons, and they bear the same relation to each other.

The relations of the form to replacements of the rhombohedron are illustrated in the other figures. Fig. 172 represents a rhombohedron ($+1$ or R) with its basal edges bevelled; and this bevelment, continued to the obliteration of the planes R, produces the scalenohedron shown by the dotted lines. The scalenohedron in f. 171, 172 has the vertical axis equal to $3c$, or three times as long as that of R, the lateral axes of both being equal; and hence it is that the planes are lettered 1^3, the 1 referring to the rhombohedron and the index ^{3} being the multiple that gives the value of the vertical axis of the scalenohedron.

In f. 173 there are two scalenohedrons of the same series, viz., 1^5, 1^3, combined with the rhombohedrons R (or $+1$) and $+4$. Fig. 174 shows the scalenohedron -1^3 combined with the rhombohedron -4 (or $-4R$); and 175, the same with the rhombohedron 5 ($+5R$).

Other scalenohedrons replace the basal angles of a rhombohedron by two similar planes (f. 176); or bevel the terminal edges; or replace the terminal solid angles by six planes, two to each terminal edge, or to each

38   CRYSTALLOGRAPHY.

rhombohedral face; and they will be relatively + or −, according to their position in one or the other set of sectants, as has been explained. Fig. 177 represents the top view of a crystal of tourmaline. It contains the rhombo-

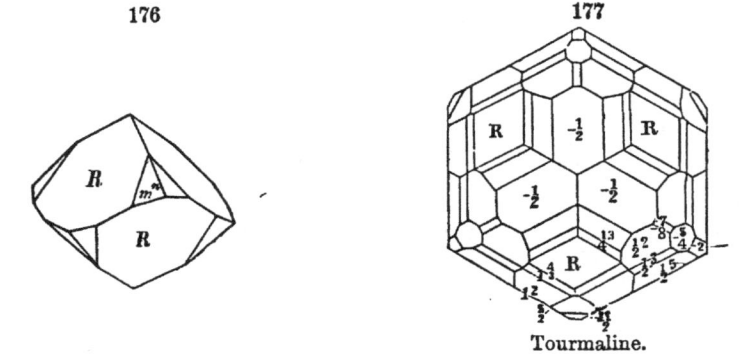

176

177

Tourmaline.

hedral planes, $R, \frac{5}{2}, 1\frac{1}{2}, -\frac{1}{2}, -\frac{7}{8}, -\frac{5}{4}, -2$, along with the scalenohedrons $-\frac{1}{2}^2$, $-\frac{1}{2}^3, -\frac{1}{2}^5, 1\frac{4}{3}, 1^2$, and also two others bevelling the terminal edges of the rhombohedron R.

The scalenohedrons $-\frac{1}{2}^2, -\frac{1}{2}^3, -\frac{1}{2}^5$, bevel the basal edges of the rhombohedron $-\frac{1}{2}$; and consequently the lengths of the axes are respectively 2, 3, 5 times that of the rhombohedron $\frac{1}{2}$, and hence, equal $1c$, $\frac{3}{2}c$, $\frac{5}{2}c$. Every scalenohedron corresponds to a bevelment of the basal edges of some rhombohedron—and that particular one whose lateral edges are parallel to those of the scalenohedron. The symbols for them accordingly are made up of the symbol of the rhombohedron and an index which expresses the relation of its vertical axis as to length to that of the rhombohedron, according to a method proposed by Naumann. (See p. 72.)

178

Corundum.

Hexagonal pyramids of the m-2 or diagonal series occur in many rhombohedral species; as f. 178 of corundum, which contains $\frac{4}{3}$-$2(r)$, 4-2, $\frac{28}{3}$-2 (for 9-2 on the figure read $\frac{28}{3}$-2, *Klein*), along with the rhombohedron 1, and the basal plane O; also f. 167; in which is the pyramid 2-2. Hemihedral forms of the same pyramids (of the kind described on p. 34) are met with in rhombohedral species, but only such as have also tetartohedral modifications. Hemihedral forms of the hexagonal and dihexagonal prisms (p. 34) are also characteristic of some rhombohedral species, and of those that have either tetartohedral or hemimorphic modifications.

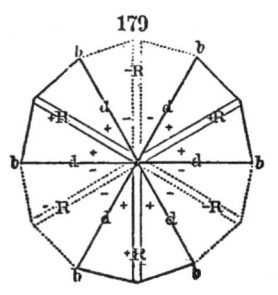

179

Fig. 179 illustrates the relative positions of the zones of the + and − rhombohedrons, and diagonal pyramids m-2 alternating with regions of + and − scalenohedrons in the scheme of the rhombohedral system. The figure is supposed to be a top view. It is similar to f. 152, p. 34, and like that contains the upper planes of the dihexagonal pyramid; but these are divided between a *plus* and a *minus* scalenohedron, those planes marked + being the former, and the others (−) the latter. The three lateral axes are lettered each bb. The position of the + mR zone of planes (or *plus* rhombohedrons) relative to the scalenohedrons is shown by the lettering +R; of the −mR zones (or *minus* rhombohedrons) by −R. The position of the vertical zone of m-2, or diametral pyramidal planes, is indicated by the letter d. The order of succession, beginning with one of the *plus* interaxial sectants (the one in the medial line below) and numbering it I, is as follows:

HEXAGONAL SYSTEM.

I.
- (1) Plus scalenohedrons, or planes of the general form $+m^n$.
- (2) Zone of plus rhombohedrons, $+mR$.
- (3) Plus scalenohedrons, or planes of the general form $+m^n$.
- (4) Zone of diagonal pyramids, m-2.

II.
- (5) Minus scalenohedrons, or planes of the general form $-m^n$.
- (6) Zone of minus rhombohedrons, $-mR$.
- (7) Minus scalenohedrons, $-m^n$.
- (8) Zone of diagonal pyramids, m-2.

III.
- (9) Plus scalenohedrons, $+m^n$.
- (10) Zone of plus rhombohedrons, $+mR$.
- (11) Plus scalenohedrons, $+m^n$.
- (12) Zone of diagonal pyramids.

And so on around, as the figure illustrates. In the *lower* pyramid the order of succession is the same; but the *plus* planes are directly below the *minus* of the above view of the upper pyramid.

The *plus* scalenohedrons have the pyramidal edge over the $+mR$ section, the more obtuse of the two (or edge Y); and the *minus* scalenohedrons have that edge the less obtuse (or edge X), and that over the $-mR$ section the more obtuse (or edge Y).

B. *Holohemihedral forms*, or those in which all the sectants have half the full number of planes (as shown by the shading in f. 180).

Gyroidal, or trapezohedral forms.—Of the planes, in f. 181 there would occur only those lettered r, r, above and below; or those lettered l, l, and, unlike f. 157, the planes above and below are not in the same zone. The

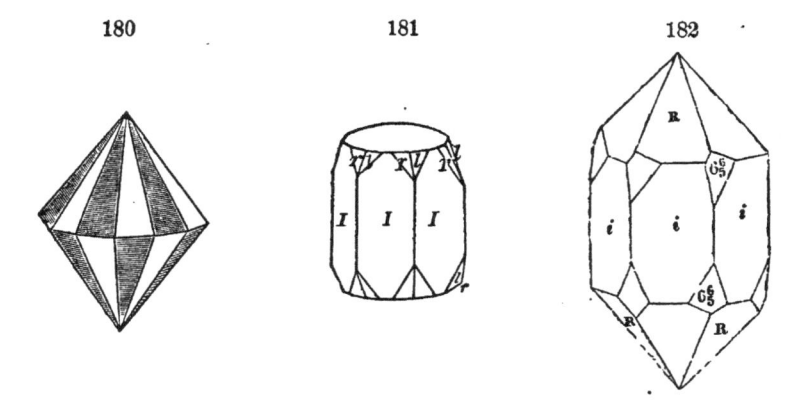

180   181   182

form is consequently *gyroidal*, the planes being inclined around the prism, both above and below, and in the same direction at the two extremities. It is also called *plagihedral*. The symbol for the planes is rr m-n, or ll m-n, according as the occurring planes of the two in the same sector are the *right* or the *left*. Fig. 182 is an example of ll 6-$\frac{6}{5}$ in the species quartz.

C. *Tetartohedral Forms.*

These forms are hemihedral to the Rhombohedron.

(A) *Holomorphic forms*, like the preceding hemihedral, the planes occurring equally in the upper and lower range of sectants.

1. *Rhombohedral tetartohedrism.*—Occurring planes the alternate of those mentioned on page 35, that is, the alternate planes r of one base, and l of the other. They are the r of three alternate sectants above, and

the l of three sectants below alternate with these. A form of this kind consists of six equal planes, equally spaced, and hence, equal in inclinations, and is therefore, in the completed state, a rhombohedron. It occurs in menaccanite or titanic iron, and in quartz (f. 183, planes 13-$\frac{4}{3}\frac{3}{2}$).

2. *Gyroidal or trapezohedral tetartohedrism.*—Occurring planes the alternate of those lettered r or l in f. 153, p. 34, that is, the alternate planes r, or alternate l, of both bases.

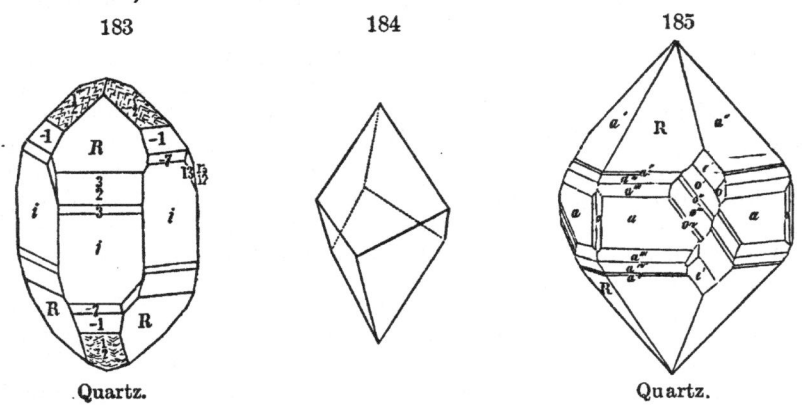

183   184   185

Quartz.   Quartz.

In f. 185, the planes o^{I}, o^{II}, o^{III}, o^{IV}, o^{V} (4-$\frac{4}{3}$, 5-$\frac{5}{4}$, 6-$\frac{6}{5}$, 8-$\frac{8}{7}$, 3-$\frac{3}{2}$, the first four *right*, the last *left*) are examples. The upper and lower of a kind adjoin the same diametral plane, but are on opposite sides of it, and therefore the three sectants containing planes below are alternate with the three above. The solid made of these six planes (f. 184) has trapezoidal faces, and is called a *trigonotype* by Naumann.

The tetartohedral planes on quartz and cinnabar have a remarkable connection with the circular polarization which is characteristic of them both, and which is further explained elsewhere (p. 142).

(B) *Hemimorphic forms;* the planes occurring either in the upper or the lower range of sectants and not in both.

There are two kinds of forms: (1) the *hemi-rhombohedron*, and (2) the *hemi-scalenohedron*. Fig. 186 illustrates each of these forms. The form R is properly hemihedral at the two extremities, its planes being very large at one, and quite small at the other. So with $-\frac{1}{2}$. Another rhombohedron, -2, occurs *only* at the upper extremity. Again, $\frac{1}{2}^{6}$ is a hemi-scalenohedron, the upper six planes being present, but not the lower.

186

The prism I in this figure is *hemihedral*, as explained on p. 34. It is not tetartohedral to the hexagonal system in the ordinary view. But since in a vertical zone $+mR$, ∞R, $-mR$, the ∞R may be regarded as the infinite term of either the $+mR$ series, or else the same of the $-mR$ series; and as this view accords with the tetartohedral character of the mR series in all such crystals, it might be ranked among tetartohedral forms.

From the same point of view, the ditrigonal prisms in tourmaline and quartz are tetartohedral, since they may be regarded as either plus or minus tetartohedral scalenohedrons, with an infinite vertical axis.

Variable elements.—In the hexagonal system the same elements are variable as in the tetragonal (see p. 30). In other words, the position of the vertical axis is fixed, but (1) a certain length must be assumed as the unit in a given species, and also (2) the position of the lateral axes must be fixed, for, as in f. 144, 145, either of the hexagonal prisms may be made I and the other i-2.

The *general characteristics* of this system which the student must be acquainted with are: (1) The planes constantly occur in threes or sixes, or their multiples; (2) The frequency of the angles 120° and 150° in the prismatic series; (3) The rhombohedral cleavage, common in species belonging to the rhombohedral division. It is also important to note that many forms *apparently* hexagonal really belong to the orthorhombic system, being produced by twinning parallel to the vertical prism; *e.g.*, the apparently hexagonal prisms of aragonite. The close relation of the two systems is spoken of elsewhere (p. 46).

The *planes of symmetry* for the holohedral forms are analogous to those in the tetragonal system; that is, one principal plane of symmetry normal to the vertical axis, and six others intersecting in this axis. These last belong to two sets, the planes of the one cutting each other at angles of 60°, and diagonal to those of the other.

IV.—ORTHORHOMBIC SYSTEM.

In the ORTHORHOMBIC SYSTEM the three axes are unequal $\acute{c}$, $\bar{b}$, $\breve{a}$; of these $\acute{c}$ is the vertical axis, $\bar{b}$ is made the longer of the two lateral axes, or the *macrodiagonal* axis, and $\breve{a}$ the shorter lateral, or *brachydiagonal*, axis.*

The different occurring forms, deduced as before from the general expression, are:

$$\begin{cases} mc : nb : a & [m\text{-}\bar{n}] \\ mc : b : na & [m\text{-}\breve{n}] \\ mc : b : a & [m] \\ c : b : a & [1] \\ mc : \infty b : a & [m\text{-}\bar{\imath}] \\ mc : b : \infty a & [m\text{-}\breve{\imath}] \end{cases} \qquad \begin{cases} \infty c : nb : a & [i\text{-}\bar{n}] \\ \infty c : b : na & [i\text{-}\breve{n}] \\ \infty c : b : a & [I] \\ \infty c : b : \infty a & [i\text{-}\bar{\imath}] \\ \infty c : \infty b : a & [i\text{-}\breve{\imath}] \\ 0c : b : a & [O] \end{cases}$$

The abridged symbols need very little explanation additional to that given on p. 25. As before, only the essential part of the symbol is given; m is written first, and refers in all cases to the vertical axis (c), and n refers to one of the lateral axes, whether the longer ($\bar{b}$) or the shorter ($\breve{a}$) is indicated by the sign placed over it, as $\bar{n}$ or $\breve{n}$. When $n=\infty$, this is indicated by the i hitherto used, and the sign is placed over it, $\bar{\imath}$, or $\breve{\imath}$, with the same signification. These correspond to the symbols used by Naumann, as follows: $O=0P$; $\breve{\imath}\text{-}\breve{\imath}=\infty\breve{P}\infty$; $i\text{-}\breve{\imath}=\infty\bar{P}\infty$; $\infty\bar{P}\breve{n}=i\text{-}\breve{n}$; $mP\breve{\imath}=m\text{-}\breve{\imath}$; $mP=m$; $m\text{-}\bar{n}=mP\bar{n}$, etc.

---

* For the relation of the axes thus lettered to those of Dana's System of Mineralogy and of other authors, see p. 53.

A. *Holohedral Forms.*

Pinacoids.—The final case mentioned in the above enumeration embraces, as before, the two basal planes, or basal pinacoids; the one preceding it includes the two planes parallel to the vertical and macrodiagonal axes (c and b), called the *macropinacoids*, and the next above includes the planes parallel to the vertical and brachydiagonal axes (c and a), called the *brachypinacoids*. These three sets of planes together form the solid in f. 188, which is called the diametral prism. In consequence of the inequality of the different pairs of planes there are only four similar edges in any set; thus four similar vertical edges; four macrodiagonal basal edges, two above and two below, between O and $i\text{-}\bar{\imath}$; and similarly four brachydiagonal basal edges between O and $i\text{-}\check{\imath}$; the eight solid angles are all similar.

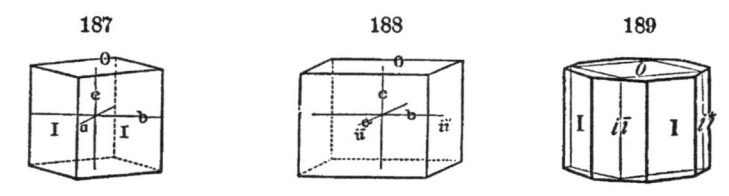

Prisms.—The form $\infty c : b : a$, or I, includes the four planes of the unit prism which, in combination with O, is seen in f. 187. In this case the eight basal edges are similar, being made in each case by a similar pair of planes O and I. Of the vertical edges there are two pairs, those at the extremity of the axis $\check{a}$, which are obtuse, and those at the extremity of $\bar{b}$, which are acute. Similarly, there are two sets of basal solid angles, four in each; for though each solid angle is formed by the meeting of the same three planes, the angles are different in the two cases. The form I replaces the four similar vertical edges of f. 188; the macropinacoids $i\text{-}\bar{\imath}$ truncate the obtuse vertical edges of the prism I, and the brachypinacoids $i\text{-}\check{\imath}$ truncate the acute vertical edges of I, as shown in f. 189.

There are two other series of prisms with symbols $\infty c : nb : a$ and $\infty c : b : na$. In the latter series the axis b is made the unit; the reason for this will be obvious when the relations of the two forms are explained.

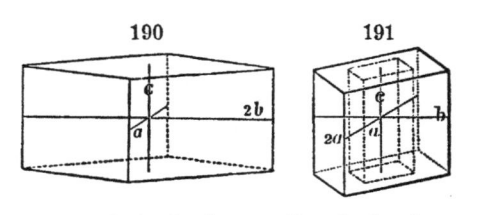

The prism I meets both axes a and b at their unit lengths, as in f. 187. If, now, the prismatic planes meet the longer lateral axis (b) at a greater distance, a prism is formed such as that in f. 190, whose symbol is $i\text{-}2$, or $\infty c : 2b : a$. This is a macrodiagonal prism; and others might have the symbols $i\text{-}3$ ($\infty c : 3b : a$), $i\text{-}4$ ($\infty c : 4b : a$), and so on, or in general $i\text{-}n$.

If n becomes less than unity, the case shown in f. 191 arises, where the inner prism has $n=\frac{1}{2}$, and the symbol is $i\text{-}\frac{1}{2}$ ($\infty c : \frac{1}{2}b : a$), still retaining $\check{a}$ as the unit axis. For convenience of reference, however, the principle before explained (p. 11) is made use of, and the plane is called $\infty c : b : 2a$, or $i\text{-}\check{2}$;

ORTHORHOMBIC SYSTEM.

these expressions and those before given being identical, except that in the latter case b is the unit axis. By this method the use of any fractions less than unity is avoided. The inner prism $i\text{-}\frac{1}{2}$, indicated by dotted lines in f. 191, then becomes the outer prism or $i\text{-}2$. The prisms of the general form $i\text{-}\check{n}$, are called brachydiagonal prisms.

The prisms $i\text{-}\bar{n}$ bevel the front and rear (obtuse) edges of the prism I, f. 192, and the prisms $i\text{-}\check{n}$ bevel the side (acute) edges as in f. 193. Further, the former, $i\text{-}\bar{n}$, replace the edges between $i\text{-}\bar{i}$ and I (f. 194), while the $i\text{-}\check{n}$ prisms replace the edges between $i\text{-}\check{i}$ and I (f. 194).

This series of planes (f. 194), from $i\text{-}\bar{i}$ to $i\text{-}\check{i}$, is another example of a zone; all the planes make parallel intersections with each other, being alike in that they are parallel to the vertical axis.

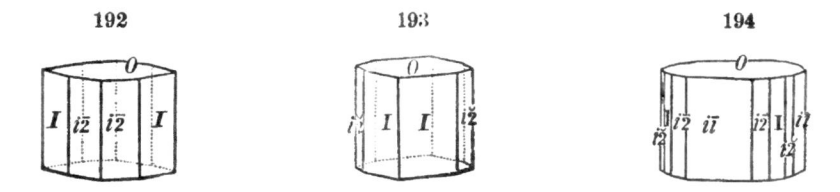

Domes.—The form $mc : \infty b : a$ includes the four planes which are parallel to the macrodiagonal axis, and meet the vertical axis at variable distances, multiples of the unit length (see f. 34, p. 11). An example of them in combination with $i\text{-}\check{i}$, the brachypinacoid, is shown in f. 195. These planes are called *macrodomes* (see also f. 196).

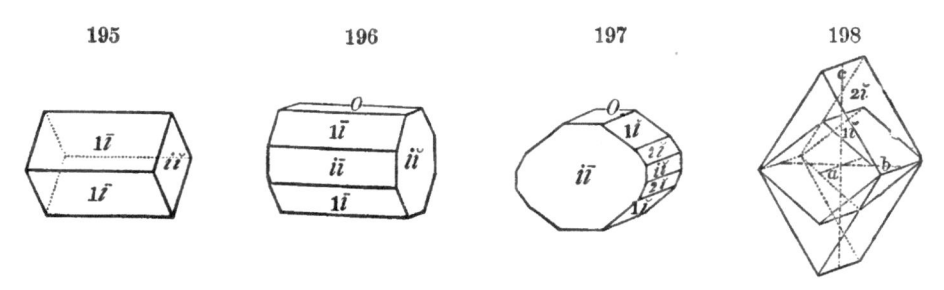

The form $mc : b : \infty a$ includes four analogous planes, which differ in this respect, that they are parallel to the brachydiagonal axis, and are hence called *brachydomes* (see f. 35, p. 11). In this case, the longer lateral axis is taken as the unit. Fig. 197 shows two such brachydomes, 1-$\check{i}$ and 2-$\check{i}$, in combination with other forms. (See also f. 198.) The word *dome*, used here and above, is derived from δομή, or domus, *a house*, the form resembling the roof of a house.

The combination of 1-$\bar{i}$ with 1-$\check{i}$ is shown in f. 199, forming a rectangular octahedron, and in f. 200 they are shown replacing the solid angles formed by I and O, as in f. 188. As either of the three directions may be made the vertical, it is evident that these domes differ from vertical prisms only in position.

The occurrence of these domes in combination with the other forms, O, $i\text{-}\breve{\imath}$, $i\text{-}\check{\imath}$, I, affords an illustration of the law of symmetry that all similar parts must be modified alike. Thus in f. 187, as has been shown, there are two sets of solid angles, four in each; one set is replaced by the four planes of the form $m\text{-}\bar{\imath}$, and if one is, all must be; and the other set (lateral) is replaced by the four planes of the form $m\text{-}\check{\imath}$, f. 200.

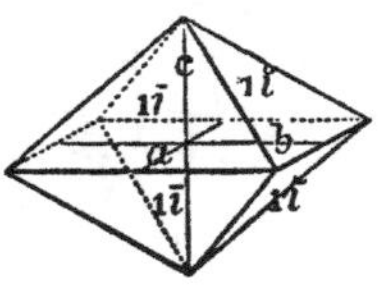

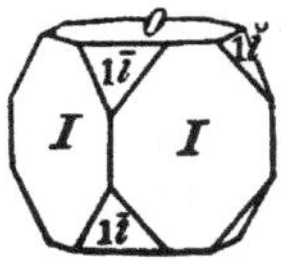

Octahedrons (or Pyramids).—The symbol $c : b : a$ (1) belongs to the unit octahedron (f. 201). It replaces the edges between the prism I and the basal plane O (f. 202). It also replaces the eight similar solid angles of the diametral prism, as in f. 203. This is a special case of the form $mc : b : a$, in which m may have values varying from 0 to ∞. Fig. 208, of sulphur, shows a zone of such planes, of the general symbol $mc : b : a$, with $m = \infty$ for I; also, $m=1$, $m=\frac{1}{2}$, $m=\frac{1}{3}$, $m=\frac{1}{4}$, and finally $m=0$, for the basal plane O.

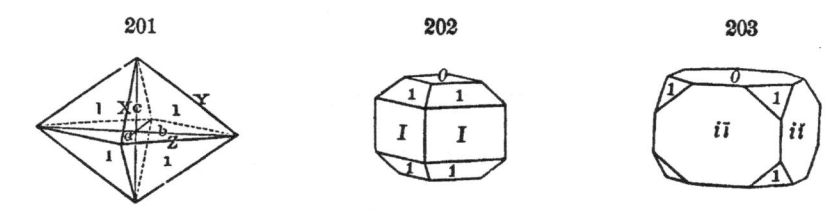

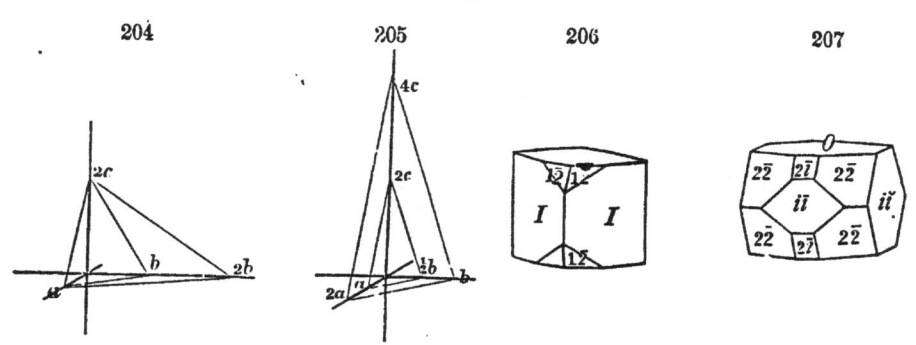

The general form in this system, consisting of eight similar planes, may be written either $mc : nb : a$ $(m\text{-}\bar{n})$ or $mc : b : na$ $(m\text{-}\check{n})$. The relation between the two is the same as that between the prisms $i\text{-}\bar{n}$ and $i\text{-}\check{n}$. Thus, in f. 204, one plane of the octahedron $2c : 2b : a$ (2-2) is given, and also one plane of another octahedron or pyramid, whose symbol is $2c : b : a$ (2). If n becomes less than unity, as $\frac{1}{2}$, the plane has the symbol $2c : \frac{1}{2}b : a$ $(2\text{-}\frac{1}{2})$. In order to avoid this use of fractions, the symbol is written $4c : b : 2a$, that is, 4-2. The plane is shown in f. 205, in its two positions corresponding to $2c : \frac{1}{2}b : a$, and $4c : b : 2a$, the two being crystallographically identical.

ORTHORHOMBIC SYSTEM.

Thus there are two series of pyramidal planes: a *macrodiagonal* $(m\text{-}\bar{n})$ where the shorter axis is taken as the unit, and a *brachydiagonal* $(m\text{-}\breve{n})$, where the unit is the longer lateral axis; and between the two lie the unit octahedron (1) and those of the m series, just as the prism I lies between the prisms $i\text{-}\bar{n}$ and $i\text{-}\breve{n}$. The macrodiagonal planes 1-2 and 2-2 are shown in f. 206 and f. 207. It is also seen in f. 207 that the planes 2-2, 2-$\bar{i}$, 2-2 all make parallel intersections with each other and with $i\text{-}\breve{i}$, being an example of a zone where the ratios of the vertical axes are the same. Further orthorhombic forms are displayed in f. 208, of sulphur, already referred to. The full symbol of the plane 1-3 is $c : b : 3a$.

208

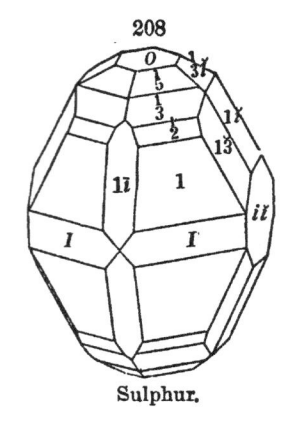

Sulphur.

B. *Hemihedral Forms.*

The hemihedral forms that have been observed are of two kinds: 1, The *vertically-oblique* (p. 14), producing *monoclinic* forms; and 2, the *hemimorphic*, in which the planes of the octahedrons or domes of one base have no corresponding planes at the opposite extremity. The former kind

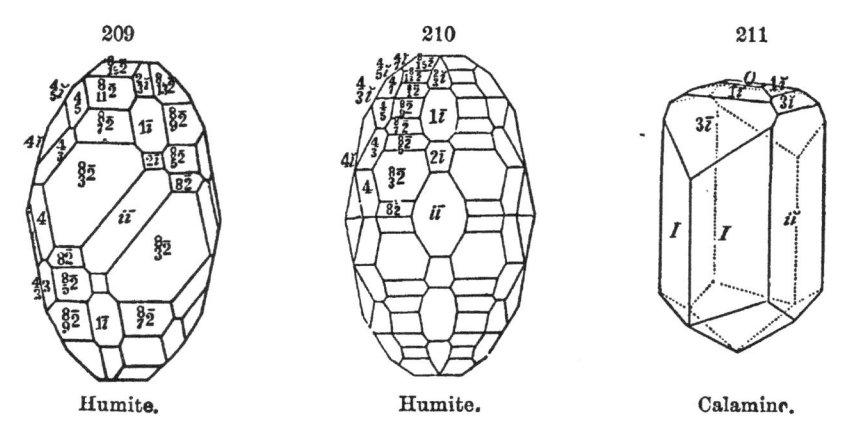

209

210

211

Humite.

Humite.

Calamine.

is illustrated in f. 209, of the species chondrodite (var. humite, type III). Fig. 210 represents the holohedral form of the same; the planes $\frac{2}{3}\text{-}\bar{i}$, 1-$\bar{i}$, 2-$\bar{i}$, are of macrodomes; $4\text{-}\breve{i}$, $\frac{4}{3}\text{-}\breve{i}$, $\frac{4}{3}\text{-}\breve{i}$, $4\text{-}\breve{i}$, of brachydomes; and the others of various octahedrons, mostly in two vertical zones, the unit zone $(mc : b : a)$, and the 1 : 2 zone $(ma : 2b : a)$. In f. 209 the alternate of the macrodomes and of the octahedral planes of the 1 : 2 zone are absent in the upper half of the form, and are present without those with which they alternate in the lower half. The crystal consequently resembles one under the monoclinic system.

Datolite was formerly cited as a hemihedral orthorhombic species, but it has been found to be really monoclinic. Furthermore, it has been recently shown by the author, by reference to the optical properties, that the chon drodite of the second and third types (see p. 327) is not orthorhombic but *monoclinic*, and this must be true also of humite.*

Hemimorphic forms characterize the species topaz and calamine. The latter (in f. 211) has only the planes of a hemioctahedron at one extremity, and planes of hemidomes at the other. For the pyro-electric properties of such forms, see p. 169.

Variable elements.—In the orthorhombic system the lengths of the three axes are variable, though their position is fixed, and after these are fixed the choice of one for the vertical axis must be arbitrarily made. In other words, given an orthorhombic crystal, the three rectangular *directions* are fixed, but *two* assumptions must be made which will mathematically determine the length of two of the axes in terms of the third. For instance, in a crystal, if certain occurring domes are adopted as the unit planes 1-$\bar{\imath}$ and 1-$\check{\imath}$, this will determine the relative lengths of the three axes, for which two measurements will be necessary; or, if an occurring octahedron is assumed as the unit octahedron (1,) this alone will obviously fix the axes; but here, also, two independent measurements are necessary in order to enable us to calculate their length, as is explained later, p. 74. Having determined upon the relative lengths of the axes, one of these must be made the vertical axis (c), and then, of the two remaining, the shorter will be the brachydiagonal (a), and the longer the macrodiagonal axis (b).

In deciding these arbitrary points, the following serve as guides: The habit of the crystals; the relations of the given species to those allied in composition; the cleavage, which is regarded as pointing to that form which is properly fundamental; and other considerations. How arbitrary the choice generally is is well shown by the fact that, in a considerable number of species belonging to this system, different lengths of axes, as also different positions for them, have been adopted by different authors. Where an optical examination can be made of an orthorhombic crystal, the results show what the true position of the axes is, in accordance with the principles proposed by Schrauf. This subject is alluded to again in its proper place (p. 151).

The *general characteristics* of the crystals of this system are not so marked as those of the preceding systems. The kind of symmetry should be well understood, though, as remarked on p. 50, crystals which are in appearance orthorhombic may be really monoclinic; the true test of the system is to be found in the three *rectangular* axial directions. A prismatic habit is very common, the prisms (except the diametral prism) *not* being square, also the prominence of some of the most commonly occurring macrodomes and brachydomes; a prismatic cleavage is common, and often a cleavage exists parallel to one of the pinacoids (*e.g.*, i-$\bar{\imath}$) and not to the other, which could not be true in the tetragonal system; similarly the planes i-$\bar{\imath}$, i-$\check{\imath}$ are sometimes physically different, *e.g.*, in regard to lustre.

As has already been remarked, forms apparently hexagonal are common among certain species belonging to this system; this is true in those cases

---

* Since the above paragraph was put into type, Des Cloizeaux has announced that an optical investigation by him has proved that humite crystals, of types II. and III., are really *monoclinic*, as suggested above. The figures are allowed to remain, however, since they illustrate the form which this method of hemihedrism *would* produce.

where the prism has an angle approximating to 120°. It is immediately evident, as is explained more thoroughly in the chapter on compound crystals, that if three individual crystals are united each by a prismatic face, when the prismatic angle is near 120°, they will form together a six-sided prism, approximating more or less closely to a regular hexagonal prism. Similarly, under the same circumstances, the corresponding pyramids will thus together form a more or less symmetrical hexagonal pyramid. This is illustrated by the accompanying figures of witherite, where the prismatic angle is 118° 30'. It need hardly be added that this is true in general, not only of the vertical prism, but also of a macrodome or brachydome, having an angle near 120°. The optical relations connected with this subject are alluded to elsewhere, p. 151.

Planes of Symmetry.—The three diametral planes are planes of symmetry in this system, and they are the only ones.

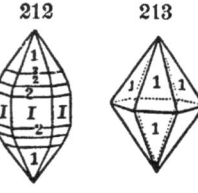

V. MONOCLINIC SYSTEM.

In the MONOCLINIC SYSTEM the three axes are unequal in length, and while two of them have rectangular intersections, the third is oblique. The position usually adopted for these axes is as shown in f. 214, where the vertical axis, $\acute{c}$, and lateral axis, b, make retangular intersections. The same is true of b and $\grave{a}$, while $\acute{c}$ and $\grave{a}$ are oblique to one another.

The following is an enumeration of the several distinct forms possible in this system, deduced, as before, from the general expression:

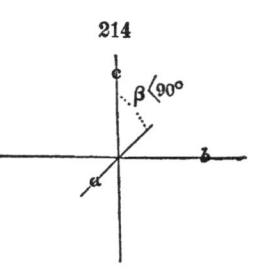

$$\begin{cases} -mc : nb : a \\ +mc : nb : a \\ -mc : b : na \\ +mc : b : na \\ -mc : b : a \\ -c : b : a \\ +mc : b : a \\ +c : b : a \\ mc : b : \infty a \end{cases} \quad \begin{array}{l} [-m\text{-}n] \\ [+m\text{-}n] \\ [-m\text{-}\grave{n}] \\ [+m\text{-}\grave{n}] \\ [-m] \\ [-1] \\ [+m] \\ [+1] \\ [m\text{-}\grave{\imath}] \end{array} \quad \begin{cases} -mc : \infty b : a \\ +mc : \infty b : a \\ \infty c : nb : a \\ \infty c : b : na \\ \infty c : b : a \\ \infty c : \infty b : a \\ \infty c : b : \infty a \\ 0c : b : a \end{cases} \quad \begin{array}{l} [-m\text{-}i] \\ [+m\text{-}i] \\ [i\text{-}n] \\ [i\text{-}\grave{n}] \\ [I] \\ [i\text{-}i] \\ [i\text{-}\grave{\imath}] \\ [O] \end{array}$$

The abridged symbols correspond to those in the orthorhombic system, explained on p. 42. The only point to be noted is that where n or i relates to the clinodiagonal axis, $\grave{a}$, this is indicated by an accent placed over it, as $m\text{-}\grave{\imath}$, $m\text{-}\grave{n}$; but in $m\text{-}i$, and $m\text{-}n$, etc., i and n refer to the orthodiagonal axis. Naumann wrote these $mP\bar{\infty}$, and $mP\bar{n}$, or else with the accent across the initial letter P. The minus signs are used in the same way as by Naumann (see p. 76).

Pinacoids.—As in the orthorhombic system, there are three pairs of pinacoidal planes: the base $O = 0c : b : a$; the *orthopinacoid*, parallel to the

48   CRYSTALLOGRAPHY.

ortho-axis (b) $\infty c : \infty b : a$, or $i\text{-}i$; and the *clinopinacoid*, parallel to the inclined axis (d), $\infty c : b : \infty a$, or $i\text{-}\grave{i}$.

In the solid (f. 216) or diametral prism formed of these three pairs of planes, the four vertical edges are similar, and this is also true of the four edges between O and $i\text{-}\grave{i}$. On the other hand, the four remaining edges are of two sets; that is, the edge in front above is similar to the edge behind and below, for the angles are equal and inclosed by similar planes; but these edges are not similar to the remaining two, since, though the planes are the same, the inclosed angles are unequal to the former. Further, there are two sets of solid angles, two in front and two diagonally opposite behind, being alike obtuse angles, and the other four alike and acute.

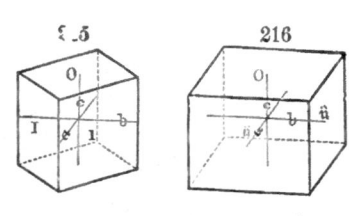

Prisms.—In consequence of the similarity of the vertical edges of the diametral prism, they must all be replaced if one is; this is done by the unit prism $I (\infty c : b : a)$, in f. 215, 217.

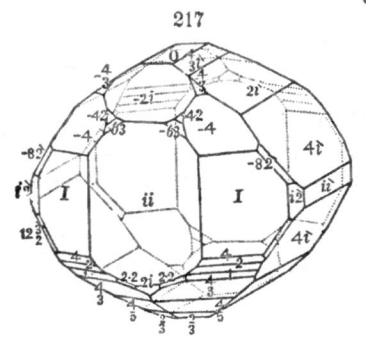

Of the other prisms, each obviously consisting of four planes, there are two series, the orthodiagonal, $i\text{-}n$, and clinodiagonal, $i\text{-}\grave{n}$, bearing the same relation to each other as the macro- and brachy-diagonal prisms in the orthorhombic system, in fact, the same explanation may be made use of here. Fig. 217, of a crystal of datolite from Toggiana, shows the pinacoid planes, as also the unit prism, I, and the clinodiagonal prism, $i\text{-}2$.

Clinodomes.—The form $m\text{-}\grave{i}$ ($mc : b : \infty a$) includes the four planes parallel to the clinodiagonal axis, and meeting the others at variable distances. They are analogous to the brachydomes of the orthorhombic system. There are four of these planes, because the two axes, c and b, make rectangular intersections. This is also seen in f. 218, since, as has been remarked, the four clinodiagonal edges in f. 216 are similar, and hence are simultaneously replaced by these clinodomes.

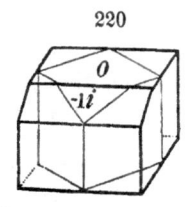

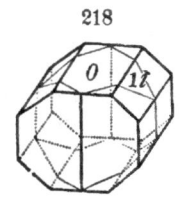

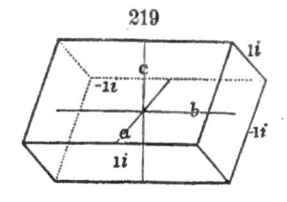

Orthodomes.—Of the general form, $mc : \infty b : a$, there are two sets of planes, two in each (*hemi-orthodomes*), both of which are alike in that they are parallel to the orthodiagonal (b) axis (see f. 219). They are unlike, however, in that two are opposite an obtuse angle, and two opposite the acute angle. Consequently these two pairs of planes are distinct, and must occur independently of each other. To distinguish between them, those belonging to the obtuse sectants receive the minus sign ($-m$-i), and those belonging to the acute sectants the plus sign ($+m$-i), f. 219. This same point is illustrated by f. 220, where, as has been remarked, the obtuse edges, above in

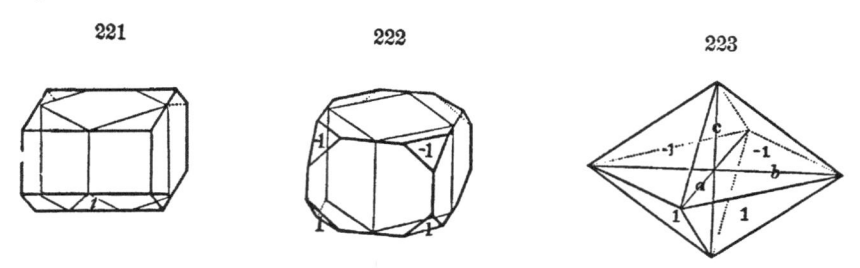

221 222 223

front, and below behind, are similar, and are hence replaced by planes of the $-m$-i series, while the remaining two (f. 221), are also similar, and are replaced by $+m$-i planes.

Hemi-octahedrons.—The same distinction of plus and minus belongs to all the pyramidal planes, and the signs are used in the same way. For each form there are only four similar planes.

The m series is that of the unit octahedrons,—properly hemi-octahedrons, or hemi-pyramids $+m$ and $-m$. The form made up of $+1$ and -1 is seen in f. 223, and in f. 222 the same planes are in combination with the three pinacoids.

The general form, $+m$-n, $-m$-n, and $+m$-$ň$, $-m$-$ň$, give each four similar planes. They bear exactly the same relation to each other as the m-$ň$ and m-$ň$ of the orthorhombic system, so that no additional explanation is needed here in regard to them.

The figure (f. 217) of datolite may be referred to for illustrations of the different forms which have been named. There are here three different clinodomes $\frac{4}{3}$-i, 2-i, and 4-i, each comprising four planes; a minus hemi-orthodome (opposite the obtuse angle), -2-i, and also a plus orthodome, $+2$-i (these two planes are quite distinct, though numerically the symbols are the same); moreover, of hemi-octahedrons of the unit series, there are -4, $-\frac{4}{3}$, and $+4$, $+2$, $+\frac{4}{3}$, $+1$, $+\frac{4}{5}$, $+\frac{2}{3}$; also of orthodiagonal pyramids, -4-2, -6-3, also $+2$-2, and of clinodiagonal planes, -8-$\frac{3}{2}$, and $+12$-$\frac{3}{2}$. A careful study of a few such figures, especially with the help of models, will give the student a clear idea of the symmetry of this system. It will be noticed that all the planes above in front are repeated below behind, and those below in front appear again above behind. More important than this, it will be seen that the clinodiagonal diametral plane divides the crystal into two symmetrical halves, right and left; in other words, as remarked later, it is a plane of symmetry.

Hemihedral forms occur of a *hemimorphic* character, in which the planes about the opposite extremities of the vertical axis are unlike; thus, the planes of one or more hemi-pyramids may occur at one extremity, without those corresponding at the other, as in tartaric acid, ammonium tartrate, etc.

With many monoclinic crystals the obliquity is obvious at sight; but with many others it is slight, and can be determined only by exact measurements.

In datolite it is only six minutes. The character of the symmetry exhibits further the obliquity. But, as seen above, both + and − planes of the same value do occur together, and though they are really distinct yet they may give a monoclinic crystal the aspect of an *orthorhombic* crystal. On the other hand, true orthorhombic crystals may be hemihedral, and thus may be *monoclinic* in the character of the symmetry (p. 45).

Variable elements.—In the monoclinic system, the only element which is fixed is the position of the orthodiagonal axis (b) at right angles to the plane in which the other axes must lie. The lengths of these axes must obviously be assumed in the same way as in the preceding system; but, further than this, their position in the given plane, and the angle they make with each other, are both arbitrary; in other words, any plane in the zone at right angles to the clinopinacoid may be taken as the base (O) and any other as the orthopinacoid ($i\text{-}i$). The existence of a prismatic cleavage, or one parallel to a plane in the orthodiagonal zone often points to the planes which are really to be considered fundamental. In many cases it is considered desirable to assume an angle near 90° as the angle of obliquity, so as to show the degree of divergence from the rectangular type. It need hardly be added that authorities differ widely both as to the position and lengths given to the axes of the same species.

Plane of symmetry.—Monoclinic crystals have but one plane of symmetry, the diametral plane in which the vertical and clinodiagonal axes lie, that is, the plane parallel to the clinopinacoids. The maximum number of similar planes for any form is four, and it will be noticed that there is no single form which alone can enclose a space, or form a geometrical solid.

VI.—TRICLINIC SYSTEM.

In the TRICLINIC SYSTEM the three axes are unequal, and their intersections are mutually oblique. In consequence of this fact, there is *no* plane of symmetry. Only diagonally opposite octants are similar; there can consequently be only two planes of any one kind. There are no truncations or bevelments, and no interfacial angles of 90°, 135°, or 120°. The prisms are all *hemiprisms*, and the octahedrons *tetarto-octahedrons*.

The lateral axes are called the *macrodiagonal* ($\bar{b}$), and the *brachydiagonal* ($\breve{a}$). In f. 225 the diametral prism (made up of three pairs of different

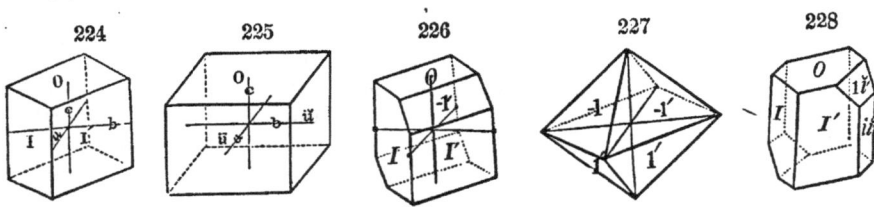

planes) is represented, and in f. 224 the unit prism. To the latter is added (in f. 226) one plane −1 on two diagonally opposite edges, which are two out of the eight of the unit octahedron (f. 227). This octahedron, as will be seen, is made up of *four* sets of different planes. The different kinds of planes are distinguished by the long or short mark over the n (*ñ* or *ñ̆*) and also by giving those which occur in the right-hand octants, in front, an accent; those above (in the obtuse octants) are minus, and the others plus. The form *m-ñ̆* consequently may be $-m\text{-}ñ̆'$, or $-m\text{-}ñ̆$, $+m\text{-}ñ̆'$, or $+m\text{-}ñ̆$; and similarly with *m-ñ*. In f. 228 the unit prism is combined with a hemidome and a vertical plane parallel to the brachydiagonal section.

The forms, although oblique in every direction, may still be closely similar to monoclinic forms of related species.

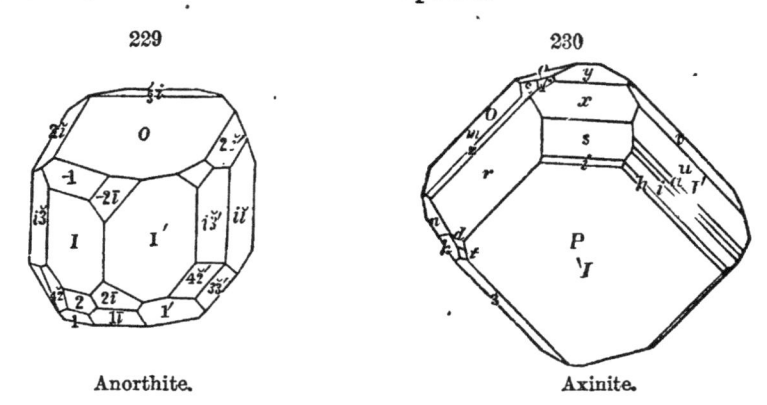

229

230

Anorthite.   Axinite.

The annexed figures are of triclinic species. In f. 229, of anorthite, of the feldspar group, the form is very similar to those of the monoclinic feldspar, orthoclase; in orthoclase, *O* on the brachydiagonal (clinodiagonal) section is 90°, whence it is monoclinic, while in anorthite this angle is 85° 50′, or 4° 10′ from 90°, and this is the principal source of the diversity of angle and form.

Fig. 230 represents one of the crystalline forms of axinite, nearly all of which fail of any special monoclinic habit.

MATHEMATICAL CRYSTALLOGRAPHY.

Introductory remarks on the proper symbol of each plane of a general crystalline form.—Hitherto the symbol *mc* : *nb* : *a* has been employed to express the general position of all the planes comprising any crystalline form, and it has been shown that there are in some cases forty-eight similar planes answering to the general symbol, and in other cases only two. In order, however, to express the exact position of each individual plane belonging to such a form, it becomes necessary to resort to the methods of analytical geometry. As shown in f. 231, the portions of the axes, when the centre is the starting point, which lie *above*, to the *right*, and in *front* of the centre, are called *plus* (+); the corresponding portions of the axes measured from the centre *below*, to the *left*, and *behind*, are called, for the sake of distinction, *minus* (−). The planes of the first quadrant (see also f. 232) are all positive (+); the planes of the second positive (+) with reference to the axes c and a, but negative (−) with reference to b; in the

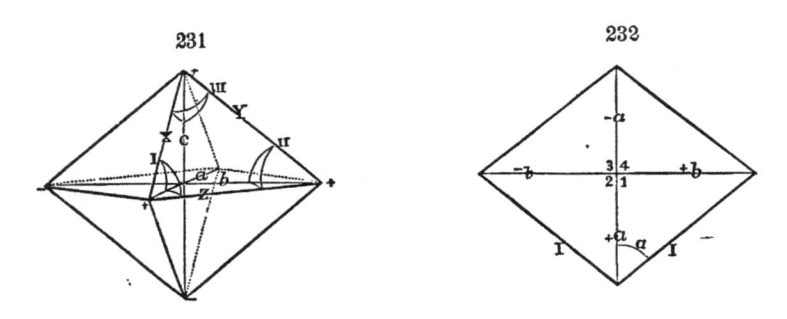

231

232

third, both lateral axes are negative (−); in the fourth quadrant the planes are positive in regard to c and b, but negative with respect to a. The lower quadrants are respectively similar, except that the vertical axis is always negative. The symbols for each plane of the orthorhombic octahedron (f. 231), taken in the same order, will be as follows:

Above, $+c : +b : +a$; $+c : -b : +a$; $+c : -b : -a$; $+c : +b : -a$.
Below, $-c : +b : +a$; $-c : -b : +a$; $-c : -b : -a$; $-c : +b : -a$.

The hexoctahedron ($ma : na : a$) may be taken as another example. The general symbol of the form of f. 247, p. 64, is $3\text{-}\tfrac{3}{2}$ ($3a : \tfrac{3}{2}a : a$), but the symbol of each plane is distinct. The same principle applies here as in the other case. Several of the planes in f. 247 are numbered to allow of convenient reference to them as examples, the appropriate symbols are written below; the order in the symbols is the same as that uniformly used in the work: 1st, the vertical axis (c); 2d, the lateral axis extending right and left (b); and 3d, the lateral axis, in front and behind (a).

	c	b	a			c	b	a
1 =	$3a$:	$\tfrac{3}{2}a$:	a		6 =	$3a$:	a :	$\tfrac{3}{2}a$
2 =	$\tfrac{3}{2}a$:	$3a$:	a		7 =	$-3a$:	$\tfrac{3}{2}a$:	a
3 =	a :	$3a$:	$\tfrac{3}{2}a$		8 =	$-3a$:	a :	$\tfrac{3}{2}a$
4 =	a :	$\tfrac{3}{2}a$:	$3a$		9 =	$\tfrac{3}{2}a$:	$-3a$:	a
5 =	$\tfrac{3}{2}a$:	a :	$3a$		10 =	$-3a$:	$-\tfrac{3}{2}a$:	a, and so on.

It will be evident from these examples that to express the position of an individual plane the numbers expressing its relations to the three axes must all be regarded, each with its appropriate sign; in other words, the values of m, n, r, in the general form, $mc : nb : ra$, must all be given, one of them being unity; m always refers to the vertical axis, c; n to the lateral axis, b; r to the lateral axis, a; as has already been remarked, a is usually made the unit axis. In the example last given the axes, being all equal, are all called a.

MATHEMATICAL CRYSTALLOGRAPHY.

Reference must be made here to the method of lettering the axes adopted in this work. The usage of the majority of authors is followed, and the subject is illustrated in the following table.

	Isometric.	Tetrag. (Hexag.)		Orthorhombic.	Triclinic.		Monoclinic.		
		vert.	lat.	vert.	macrodiag.	brachydiag.	vert.	orthodiag	clinodiag
Common usage. This work (Weiss, Rose.)	a	$\acute{c}$	a	$\acute{c}$	$\bar{b}$	$\acute{a}$	$\acute{c}$	b	$\acute{d}$
Miller's School,		c		c	a	b	c	b	a
Mohs, Naumann,	a	a		a	b	c	a	c	b
Dana (System 1868)	a	a		a	c	b			

It is certainly very desirable to indicate to which axis each letter refers by the mark placed above it; in doing which, we follow Klein's *Einleitung in die Krystallberechnung.*

DETERMINATION OF PLANES BY ZONES.

The subject of zones has been briefly explained on page 4 and various examples have been pointed out. The principle is one of the highest importance, both practically, since it gives the means of determining the symbols of many planes without calculation, and also theoretically. The *law of zones*, which states simply that the planes of a crystal lie in zones, is one of the most important of the science, and second only to that of the rationality of the indices. The planes of a crystal thus may be said to be connected together by these zones, a single plane often lying in a large number of zones.

Parallelism in the combination edges, or mutual intersections of planes, is based upon some common geometrical ratio, and this common ratio belongs to the symbols of all the planes of the zone.

All planes which lie in the same zone will give exactly parallel reflections with the reflective goniometer, as explained on p. 87. This is the only decisive test, and when possible should be made use of, since combination-edges often appear parallel when the planes forming them are not really in the same zone. Furthermore, inasmuch as parallel intersections are observed between planes of a zone only when they actually intersect, the goniometer may often serve to detect the existence of zones not otherwise manifest.

233

Acanthite.

In f. 194, p. 43, the planes $i\text{-}\bar{\imath}$, $i\text{-}2$, I, $i\text{-}2$, $i\text{-}\bar{\imath}$, all lie in a vertical zone, and they are all obviously alike in this, that they are parallel to the vertical axis; in other words, the common value $\acute{c} = \infty$ belongs to them all. Again, in the zone O, 1-$\breve{\imath}$, 2-$\breve{\imath}$, $i\text{-}\breve{\imath}$, etc. (f. 197, p. 43), the planes are alike in that they are all parallel to the brachydiagonal axis; in other words, $\acute{a} = \infty$ is true of all of them. Still again, the pyramidal planes $\frac{1}{2}$, 1, 2 (f. 150, p. 33), are also in a zone between O and I, and here the ratio 1 : 1 for the lateral axes applies to all; also, 1-2, 2-2, 4-2, are in a zone from O to $i\text{-}2$, and for them the lateral axes have the ratio 1 : 2. In the case of an oblique zone, as $i\text{-}\breve{\imath}$, 3-$\breve{\jmath}$, 2-$\breve{\imath}$, 1, etc. (f. 233), this fact is less evident on inspection, but is equally true, as will be seen later. The common ratio in this case is $m = r$.

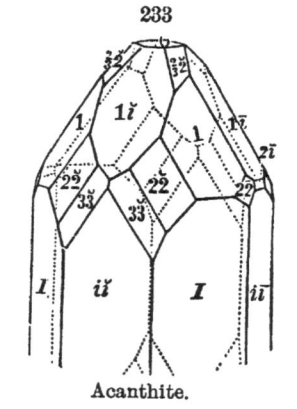

Since all the planes of a zone have a common ratio, which has been shown to be true in several examples but also admits of rigid proof, it is evident that a plane which lies in *two* zones has its position determined by that fact, since it must answer to two known conditions. In other words, the algebraic equation of a zone is known when the parameters of two of its planes are given, for they are sufficient to determine the common ratio, and by combining them the zone equation is obtained; and further, when the equations of two zones are given, combining them will give the equation, that is, the parameters, of the plane common to both.

The general equation, derived from Analytical Geometry, for any plane $mc : nb : ra$, making parallel intersections with the planes $m'c : n'b : r'a$ and $m''c : n''b : r''a$ is,

$$\frac{M}{m} + \frac{N}{n} + \frac{R}{r} = 0; \text{ in which,}$$

$M = m'm''(n'r'' - n''r'); \quad N = n'n''(r'm'' - r''m'); \quad R = r'r''(m'n'' - m''n').$

By substituting the values of the parameters of two given planes for m', n', r', and m'', n'', r'' in the zone equation, a derived equation is obtained which expresses the relations between m, n, r of all the planes of the zone. The form of the general zone equation is so symmetrical that the calculations are in any case quickly and easily made by a method analogous to that used in Miller's system (as suggested by Prof. J. P. Cooke). If we write the parameters in parallel lines, repeating the first two terms, we have

$$\begin{matrix} m' , n' \\ m'' , n'' \end{matrix} \times \begin{matrix} r' \\ r'' \end{matrix} \times \begin{matrix} m' \\ m'' \end{matrix} \times \begin{matrix} n' \\ n'' \end{matrix}$$

and it will be seen that the coefficients M, N, R are found by multiplying together the parameters in the manner which the scheme indicates.

$M = m'm''(n'r'' - r'n''). \quad N = n'n''(r'm'' - m'r''). \quad R = r'r''(m'n'' - n'm'').$

Take, for example, the zone of planes between $i\text{-}i$ and 1 (f. 233). For $i\text{-}i$, $m' = i$, $n' = 1$, $r' = i$; for 1, $m'' = 1$, $n'' = 1$, $r'' = 1$ ($i = \infty$); hence the scheme becomes

$$\begin{matrix} i , 1 \\ 1 , 1 \end{matrix} \times \begin{matrix} i \\ 1 \end{matrix} \times \begin{matrix} i \\ 1 \end{matrix} \times \begin{matrix} 1 \\ 1 \end{matrix}$$

and for the several values of the coefficients

$$M = i(1 - i) = -i^2. \quad N = 1(i - i) = 0. \quad R = i(i - 1) = i^2.$$

This reduces the zone equation to $m = r$ (after dividing by $i^2 = \infty^2$), and to this all the planes of the zone conform. So also for the zone of 1-i, I, 3-$\frac{3}{2}$, 1-i, etc., in f. 234. The parameters of the plane I and 1-i arranged as above give

$$\begin{matrix} i & 1 & 1 & i & 1 \\ 1 & i & 1 & 1 & i \end{matrix}$$

and the values of M, N, R are $-i^2$, $-i^2$ and $+i^2$ respectively. Hence the zone equation becomes

$$-\frac{1}{m} - \frac{1}{n} + \frac{1}{r} = 0;$$

MATHEMATICAL CRYSTALLOGRAPHY. 55

and if $r = 1$, the general formula $n = \dfrac{m}{m-1}$ is derived. Between $i:1:1$ (I) and $1:i:1$ (1-i) the values of n are positive, as with the series of planes $i:1$-$i:1$-i; $6c:\tfrac{6}{5}b:a$; $5:\tfrac{5}{4}:1$; $4:\tfrac{4}{3}:1$; $3:\tfrac{3}{2}:1$; $2:2:1$; $\tfrac{3}{2}:3:1$, etc., $1:i:1$. Between $1:i:1$ and $\tfrac{1}{2}$ the values of n are negative, that is, are measured on the back half of the axis b; as, for example, $\tfrac{4}{5}:-4:1$; $\tfrac{3}{4}:-3:1$; $\tfrac{2}{3}:-2:1$; $\tfrac{1}{2}:-1:1$. As the zone continues on from $\tfrac{1}{2}:-1:1$ to $1:-1:\pm i$ (1-i), and $i:-1:-1$ (I), the unit axis is changed, making $n=-1$. The zone equation then becomes $r = \dfrac{-m}{m-1}$, the values of r being positive between $\tfrac{1}{2}:-1:1$ and $1:-1:\pm i$, and negative between $1:-1:\pm i$ and $i:-1:-1$. The successive planes are $\tfrac{2}{8}:-1:2$; $\tfrac{3}{4}:-1:3$; $\tfrac{4}{5}:-1:4$; $1:-1:\pm i$; $\tfrac{4}{3}:-1:-4$; $\tfrac{3}{2}:-1:-3$; $2:-1:-2$, etc. Both figures 233 and 234 are illustrations of this zone.

If the student will select a variety of examples of zones from the figures in the descriptive part of this work, and will apply the zone equation as given above to them, paying special attention to the *signs* of the parameters of each plane, he will soon find that the apparent difficulties of the subject disappear.

EXHIBITION OF THE ZONE-RELATIONS OF DIFFERENT PLANES BY MEANS OF METHODS OF PROJECTION.

The relations of the different planes of a crystal are to some extent exhibited graphically in such figures as have been already given. Other methods, however, are used which have special advantages. The two most important are briefly mentioned here.

1. *Quenstedt's method of projection.*—In this method the planes of a crystal are projected upon a horizontal plane, usually that of the base (O). Every plane is regarded as passing through the unit-length of the axis which is taken as the vertical; these planes consequently appear as straight lines intersecting each other on the plane of projection.

The following are examples. In f. 235, of galenite, there are present the planes of the cube, octahedron, dodecahedron, and tetragonal trisoctahedron $\tfrac{3}{2}$-$\tfrac{3}{2}$. In the projection (f. 236) the plane of the paper is taken as that of the cubic plane, the two equal lateral axes (a) are shown in the dotted lines, and the vertical axis is perpendicular to the plane of the paper at their point of intersection. Any arbitrary length of the lateral axes, as ca, is taken as the unit. One of the cubic planes coincides with the plane of the paper, and the others, since they are supposed to pass through the unit point of the vertical axis, coincide with the projections of the lateral axes, and are marked II, II.

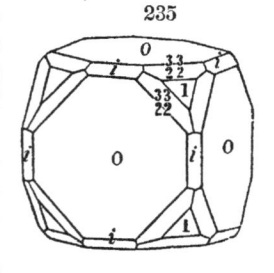

The octahedral planes (1) appear as lines connecting the unit lengths of the equal lateral axes; of the dodecahedral planes, four pass each through the extremity of one lateral axis, and parallel to the other, and four others are diagonal lines passing through the centre; they are marked i in the figure. The other planes, $\frac{3}{2}$-$\frac{3}{2}$, when passing through the unit point of the vertical axis, are represented by the symbols $1 : \frac{2}{3} : 1$, and $1 : 1 : \frac{2}{3}$, and $1 : \frac{3}{2} : \frac{3}{2}$, in the first quadrant, and similarly in the other three.

236

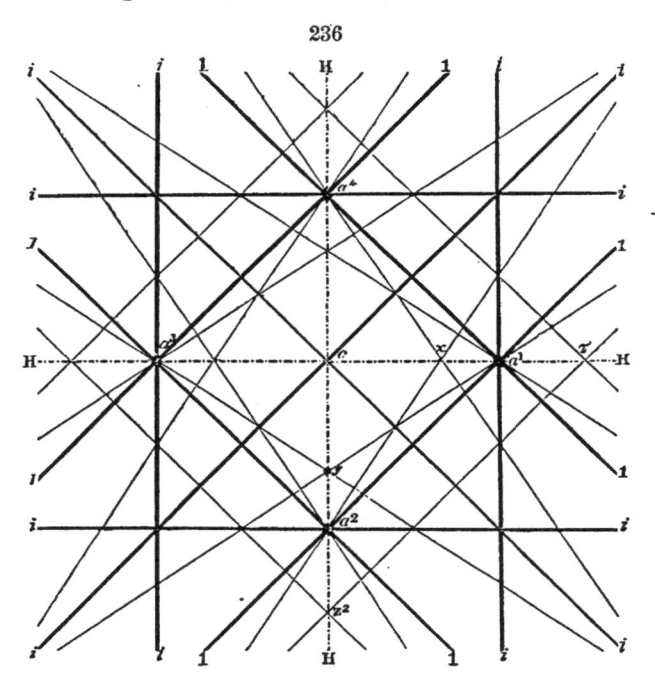

The projection of the first of these planes is the line joining the points x ($cx = \frac{2}{3}$ of ca^1) and a^2; that of the second plane is the line joining the points a^1 and y ($cy = \frac{2}{3}$ of ca^2); that of the third plane is the line joining the points z^1 and z^2 ($cz^1 = cz = \frac{2}{3}$ of ca). The same method is followed in the other quadrants, the twelve lines, lightly drawn, in the figure are the projections of the twelve corresponding planes of the form $\frac{3}{2}$-$\frac{3}{2}$.

237

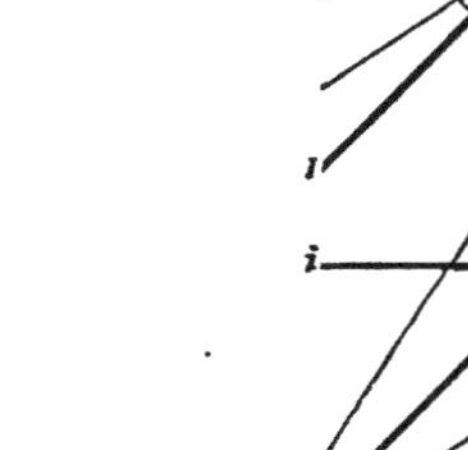

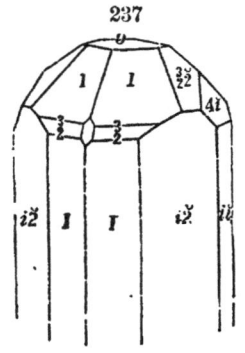

Fig. 237, 238, give another example (topaz) from the orthorhombic system. The dotted lines, as before (f. 238), show the lateral axes on which the relative unit lengths of $\bar{b}$ and $\check{a}$ belonging to this species have been marked off ($\bar{b} = 1.892$, $\check{a} = 1$). The four lines passing through these unit points, a and b, are the projections of the unit octahedron 1. The unit-prism, I, is projected in lines parallel to these, and passing through the centre. The prism i-2 also passes through the centre, but the direction is that of a line joining the unit length of the axis $\bar{b}$ with two times that of $\check{a}$. The symbol of the octahedron $\frac{3}{2}$ ($= \frac{3}{2}c : b : a$), becomes, on supposing the plane to pass through the unit point of the vertical axis $c : \frac{2}{3}b : \frac{2}{3}a$, and it is consequently projected in the lines joining the points t ($ct = \frac{2}{3}$ of cb), and s ($cs = \frac{2}{3}$ of ca). The symbol of the plane $\frac{3}{2}$ $\check{2}$ ($= \frac{3}{2}c : b : 2a$) becomes, on the same condition, $c : \frac{2}{3}b : \frac{4}{3}a$, and its projection lines consequently connect the points t ($ct = \frac{2}{3}$ of cb) and u ($cu = \frac{4}{3}$ of ca). The same method is followed in the other systems; in the hexagonal there are on the plane of projection three equal lateral axes cutting each other at angles of 60°.

238

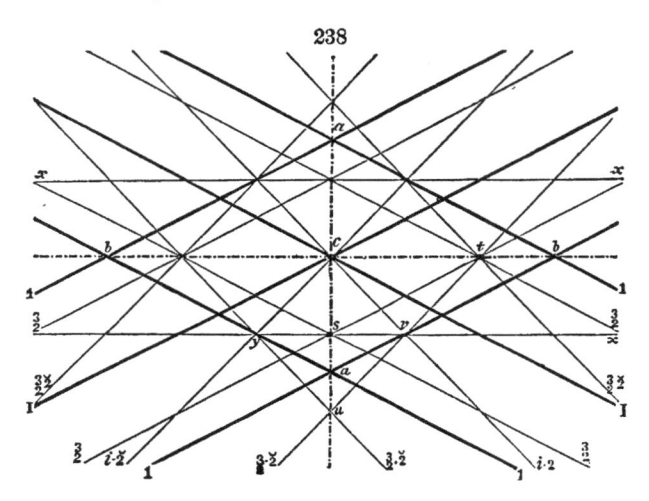

It will be seen from these examples that planes in a zone all pass through the same point of intersection; as in f. 234, O, $\frac{3}{2}$-$\frac{3}{2}$, 1, i (a^2), and, f. 237, I, i-$\check{2}$, i-$\check{i}$ (c); this is also true mathematically of the planes O, 1, $\frac{3}{2}$, I, whose projections are parallel. This principle, which follows immediately from the fact stated above that planes in a zone have a common ratio for two of the axes, is very important. If a given plane lie in two zones its projection must necessarily pass through the two points of intersections which belong to each of these respectively, and consequently its position is determined. The plane on f. 237 which has no written symbol for instance, lying in the zone with $\frac{3}{2}$ and $\frac{3}{2}$, and the zone with 1 and $\frac{3}{2}$-$\check{2}$, must, when projected, pass through the intersection point (f. 238) s of the former zone, and also through v that of the second zone. The plane itself, then, is one which meets the vertical axis at its unit length, the axis b obviously at an infinite distance, and the axis a at a distance $\frac{2}{3}$ of its unit length; hence, the symbol is $c : \infty b : \frac{2}{3}a$, or $\frac{3}{2}c : \infty b : a$ ($\frac{3}{2}$-$\check{i}$) in the form it is usually written. In many cases the ratios of the lateral axes are obvious at sight, as here; in every case, however, the position of the zonal point, and of the two points of intersection on the axes, admits of exact determination by a series of simple equations.

These equations it is unnecessary to add here; reference for them may be made to Quenstedt's Crystallography, or that of Klein, mentioned on p. 59. This method is of so general use and of so easy application that every student should be familiar with it. Its advantages are that it leads to a clearer comprehension of the relations of the different forms, showing immediately *all* the zones in which they lie, and in many cases—without the use of equations—suffices to determine the symbols of an unknown plane, and that more simply than by the use of the zonal equation. The general principles contained in the method have been made by its proposer (Quenstedt) the basis of an ingenious and philosophical system of Crystallography (Grundriss der bestimmenden und rechnenden Krystallographie von Fr. Aug. Quenstedt, Tübingen, 1873).

2. *Spherical projection of Neumann and Miller.*—In this subject, as viewed by Miller, a crystal is situated within a sphere so that the centres of the two coincide. If now perpendiculars, or normals, be drawn from this centre to each plane, and be produced, they will meet the surface of the sphere, and these normal points will determine the position of each plane. If, then, this sphere is regarded as projected upon a horizontal plane it will appear as a circle, and the various normal points will occupy each its proper position on or within this circle. This will be made more clear by an example. If the crystal (f. 237) be supposed to occupy the centre of a sphere, and if the terminal plane coincide with the plane of the paper, a normal to the plane O will meet the sphere of projection at the central point (f. 239); the planes $i\text{-}\bar{\imath}$ at the points indicated, and so of the other planes 1, $\frac{3}{2}$, $i\text{-}\bar{2}$, etc.

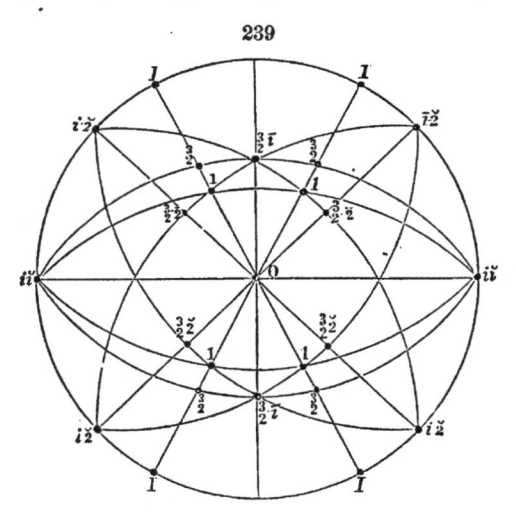

239

Two principles here are of fundamental importance: 1st, all planes of a zone have their normals in the same great circle, as $i\text{-}\bar{\imath}$, $\frac{3}{2}$, $\frac{3}{2}\text{-}\bar{\imath}$, etc.; and 2d, the angles between these normal points are the supplements of the angles between the actual planes. These having been stated, it will be clear at once that the calculation of the angles between different planes, *i.e.*, their normals, becomes merely a matter of solving a series of spherical triangles in which some parts are given and others obtained by calculation. Upon this basis a system of crystallography was constructed by Miller in 1839, which, as further developed by Grailich, Schrauf, von Lang and Maskelyne, has every advantage over that of Naumann in the matter of facility of calculation as in some other even more important respects.

The method of construction of the circle of projection, for a given crystal, is in most cases very simple. The position of the crystal is commonly so taken that the prismatic zone is represented by the circumference of the circle, and the position of the normal-points of all prismatic planes lie upon it. The normal-points of the pinacoid planes are at 90° from one another (the macropinacoid is not present on the crystal, f 237). The two corresponding diameters, at right angles to each other, which are properly the projections of two great circles, intersect at the centre the normal-point of the basal plane, O; these diameters represent respectively the macrodome ($m\text{-}\bar{\imath}$) and brachydome ($m\text{-}\bar{\imath}$) zones of planes. The several positions of the normal-points of the prismatic planes are determined by laying off the supplement angles of each with a protractor; that of $i\text{-}\bar{2}$ is 43° 25′, and of I, 62° 8½′, from the normal-point of $i\text{-}\check{\imath}$. The lines drawn between $i\text{-}\check{2}$, O, and $i\text{-}\check{2}$ (behind), and I, O, I (behind) represent the zones of the $m\text{-}\check{2}$ and m pyramids respectively. The position of the normal-points of a dome or pyramid upon its respective zonal line (great circle) is formed by laying off from the centre a distance equal to the tangent of half the supplement angle of the given plane on O, taking the radius as unity. For example, $O \wedge \frac{1}{2}\text{-}\check{\imath} = 126°\,27'$, hence the position of the required normal-point will be about $\frac{1}{2}$ (.5046) of the radius measured from O.

It is in general necessary to determine in this way the normal-points of but very few of the planes, since those of the others are given by the zonal connection between the planes. Thus in this case, having determined in the way explained the positions of the points $i\text{-}\check{\imath}$, $i\text{-}\check{2}$, I, and $\frac{3}{2}\text{-}\check{\imath}$, no further calculation is needed; the point of intersection of the great circle joining $i\text{-}\check{\imath}$, $\frac{3}{2}\text{-}\check{\imath}$, and $i\text{-}\check{\imath}$, and that joining I, O, I, is the normal-point of $\frac{3}{2}$; also the point of intersection of the great circle $i\text{-}\check{2}$, $\frac{3}{4}\text{-}\check{\imath}$, $i\text{-}\check{2}$ with I, O, I, is the normal-point of 1, and with $i\text{-}\check{2}$, O, $i\text{-}\check{2}$ that of $\frac{3}{2}\text{-}\check{2}$.

The method explained is the same for all the orthometric systems; for the clinometric systems the same principle is made use of, though the application is not quite so simple, since the basal plane does not fall at the centre of the circle.

In the system of Miller the general form of the symbol is hkl, in which h, k, and l are always whole numbers, and, the reciprocals of Naumann's symbols. To translate the latter into the former it is only necessary to take the reciprocals and reduce the result to three whole numbers and write them in the proper order. In general, for $m\text{-}n$ $(mc : nb : a)$, $h : k : l = mn : m : n$, the latter expression being written in its simplest form, and, if necessary; fractional forms must be reduced to whole numbers by multiplication. Conversely, from hkl is obtained $m = \dfrac{h}{l}$, $n = \dfrac{h}{k}$, and hence, $\dfrac{h}{l} - \dfrac{h}{k} = m\cdot n$. This applies to all the systems except the hexagonal, where a special process is required. See Appendix (p. 441).

METHODS OF CALCULATION.

In mathematical crystallography there are three problems requiring solution: 1st, The determination of the elements of the crystallization of a species, that is, the lengths and mutual inclination of the axes; 2d, The determination of the mutual interfacial angles of like or unlike known planes; and 3d, The determination of the symbols, that is, values of the parameters m and n for unknown planes.

This whole subject has been exhaustively discussed by Naumann in his several works on crystallography. (For titles, see p. iv.) The long series of formulas deduced by him cover almost every case which can arise. In the present place the matter is treated briefly, since for all ordinary problems in crystallography the amount of mathematics required is very small. This is especially true in view of the fact that a large part of unknown planes can be determined by the zonal equation already given. When complicated problems do arise, the methods of spherical trigonometry (based on the spherical projection of Miller) offer, in the opinion of most crystallographers, the simplest and shortest mode of solution. It is believed that the student who has mastered the elements of the subject, after the method of Naumann here followed, will, if he desire to go further, find it to his advantage to turn to the system of Miller, referred to on p. 58 (See also Appendix.) The formulas given under the different systems in the following pages are mostly those of Naumann, and it has been deemed desirable to explain at length, in most cases, the methods by which these formulas are deduced. If the student will follow these explanations through, he will find himself in a position to solve more difficult problems involving similar methods. Spherical triangles are employed in most cases, as early used by Hausmann (1813), by Naumann (1829), and others; and carefully explained by Von Kobell in 1867 (Zur Berechnung der Krystallformen). The same methods have been elaborated by Klein (Einleitung in die Krystallberechnung, Stuttgart, 1875).

THE RATIO OF THE TANGENTS IN RECTANGULAR ZONES.

Tangent principle.—In any rectangular zone of planes, that is, a zone lying between two planes at right angles to each other, one of them being a diametral plane, the tangents of the supplement angles made with this diametral plane are proportional to the lengths of the axis corresponding to it.

Examples of rectangular zones are afforded by the zones between i-i and i-i, also I and O, f. 130, and I and O, in f. 208; still again between I and O, in f. 167; I and O, also i-2 and O, in f. 150. In f. 217, the zone between i-i and i-i, and O and i-i, as also the zones between i-i and any one of the orthodomes, are rectangular zones, but not the zones between the basal and vertical planes (except i-i), nor those between i-i and a clinodome.

The truth of the above law is evident from the accompanying figures. If the angles between the planes e^1, e^2, e^3 (f. 240) and the basal plane O are given, their supplements are the angles with the basal diametral section a^1, a^2, a^3, respectively (f. 241). The tangents of these angles are the respective lengths of the vertical axis, corresponding to each plane, as seen in the successive triangles. In each case we have $b \tan a = c$, and hence, $\tan a^1 : \tan a^2 : \tan a^3 = c^1 : c^2 : c^3$.

By the law stated on p. 10, the ratio of the axes must have some simple numerical value. In other words, if c^1 be taken as the unit, c^2 and c^3 must bear some simple ratio to it (denoted generally by m). In general, if a^1, a^2, a^3 are the supplement angles of three planes of a vertical zone upon a basal plane, then,

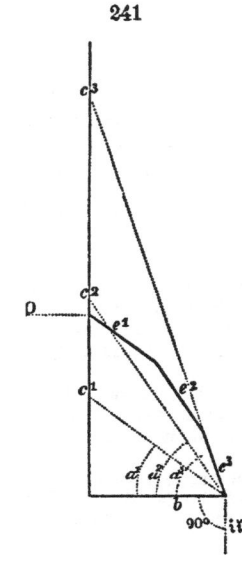

$$\tan a^1 : \tan a^2 : \tan a^3 = m^1 c : m^2 c : m^3 c = m^1 : m^2 : m^3.$$

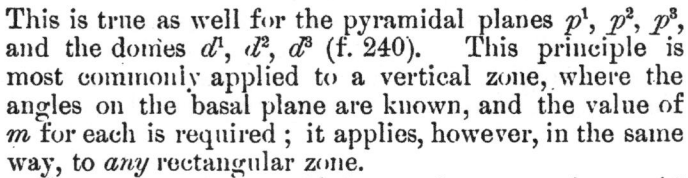

This is true as well for the pyramidal planes p^1, p^2, p^3, and the domes d^1, d^2, d^3 (f. 240). This principle is most commonly applied to a vertical zone, where the angles on the basal plane are known, and the value of m for each is required; it applies, however, in the same way, to *any* rectangular zone.

For a prismatic zone, if the supplement angles on i-i are given $= \gamma^1, \gamma^2$, etc., then,

$$\tan \gamma^1 : \tan \gamma^2 : \tan \gamma^3 = b^1 : b^2 : b^3 = n^1 : n^2 : n^3.$$

These relations may perhaps be made more clear by a little further explanation. Suppose a plane to pass through the vertical axis at right angles to the given zone O, e^1, e^2, e^3, and intersecting it in the dotted line (see also f. 241). A similar section may be made with the planes d^1, d^1, d^3, or with p^1, p^2, p^3. From the section (f. 241), the relation of the vertical axes to the tangents of the basal angles is at once obvious. It will be seen here that a^1, a^2, etc., are not only the supplements of the interfacial angles measured on O, but are also equal to the angles measured on i-i diminished by 90°, and this is true in general. It will be also seen that the angles a^1, a^2, etc., may be obtained from the angles of the planes measured on each other. Thus, given $e^1 \wedge O = 180° - a^1$, and given $e^1 \wedge e^2$, obviously a^2 (supplement of $e^2 \wedge O) = a^1 + (180° - e^1 \wedge e^2)$.

USE OF SPHERICAL TRIGONOMETRY.

The use of a spherical triangle often simplifies very much the operation of calculating the various angles and axial ratios. The following example will exemplify the principle involved. Fig. 242 represents a square octahedron of zircon. If we take the front solid angle of the octahedron as a centre, and from it imagine three arcs to be described with any radius—one on the octahedral plane BA, another on the basal section CA, and a third on the diametral section CB, it is evident that a spherical triangle will be formed. In other words, the point a is imagined to be the centre of a sphere and the triangle ABC is that portion of its surface included between the three planes in question.

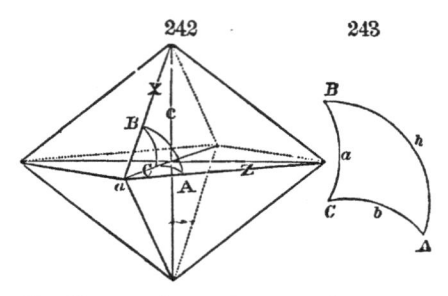

In this triangle (f. 243) the successive parts are as follows:

$C =$ the angle between the basal and vertical diametral sections; here 90°.
$a =$ the inclination of the vertical edge on the lateral axis.
$B =$ the semi-vertical angle of the octahedron ($= \frac{1}{2}X$).
h (the hypothenuse) $=$ the plane angle of the octahedral face.
$A =$ the semi-basal angle ($= \frac{1}{2}Z$).
$b =$ the inclination of the basal edge on the lateral axis.

In the case given, $b = 45°$, since in this, the tetragonal system, the lateral axes are equal and the basal edge makes an angle of 45° with each. Now if either A or B (that is, X or Z) is given by measurement, two parts in the triangle will be known and the others can be readily calculated as they may be required. Other examples will be found in the pages which follow.

In the majority of cases the spherical triangles obtained in the manner described are right-angled, and the problems resolve themselves into the solution of right-angled spherical triangles. In performing these operations practically, the student may be assisted by the following graphic method (used by Prof. Cooke, of Harvard University). It is based upon Napier's rules, which are familiar to every student:

In a right-angled spherical triangle the sine of any part is equal to the product of the cosines of the opposite parts, or the product of the tangents of the adjacent parts. Here it is to be remembered that for the two angles and hypothenuse the complements are to be taken.

The problems are represented graphically as follows: In the case given, suppose that the basal angle (Z) on the given octahedron has been measured and found to be 84° 19' 46", that is, the angle $A = \frac{1}{2}Z = 42° 9' 53"$, and hence $90° - A = 47° 50' 7"$. Then the parts of the triangle may be written, commencing with C,

$$\begin{array}{ccc} & 90° (C) & a \\ b\ (45°) & & (90° - B) \\ & (90° - A) & (90° - h) \end{array}$$

If B is required, we have (for zircon) $\sin (90° - B) = \cos 45° \times \cos 47° 50' 7"$;
whence $B = 61° 39' 47"$,
and the vertical angle (X) is 123° 19' 34".
Also, $\sin 45° = \tan a \times \tan 47° 50' 7"$,
$\tan a = 0.640373 = \dot{c}$, the vertical axis.

For convenience, some of the more important formulas for the solution of spherical triangles are here added.

In spherical right triangles $C = 90°$.

$$\operatorname{Sin} A = \frac{\sin a}{\sin h} \qquad \sin B = \frac{\sin b}{\sin h}$$

$$\operatorname{Cos} A = \frac{\tan b}{\tan h} \qquad \cos B = \frac{\tan a}{\tan h}$$

$$\operatorname{Tan} A = \frac{\tan a}{\sin b} \qquad \tan B = \frac{\tan b}{\sin a}$$

$$\operatorname{Sin} A = \frac{\cos B}{\cos b} \qquad \sin B = \frac{\cos A}{\cos a}$$

$$\cos h = \cos a \cos b$$
$$\cos h = \cot A \cot B$$

In oblique-angled spherical triangles:

(1) $\operatorname{Sin} A : \sin B = \sin a : \sin b$;
(2) $\operatorname{Cos} a = \cos b \cos c + \sin b \sin c \cos A$;
(3) $\operatorname{Cot} b \sin c = \cos c \cos A + \sin A \cot B$;
(4) $\operatorname{Cos} A = - \cos B \cos C + \sin B \sin C \cos a$.

In calculation it is often more convenient to use, instead of the latter formulas, those especially arranged for logarithms, which will be found in any of the many books devoted to mathematical formulas.

Cosine formula.—General equation for the inclination of two planes in the orthometric systems.

Representing the parameters of any plane by $c : b : a$, and also of any other plane by $c' : b' : a'$, and placing W for the supplement of their mutual inclination,

$$\operatorname{Cos} W = - \frac{aa'bb' + cc'aa' + bb'cc'}{\sqrt{(a^2b^2 + c^2a^2 + b^2c^2)} \sqrt{(a'^2b'^2 + c'^2a'^2 + b'^2c'^2)}}$$

In using this equation, the actual values of the parameters are to be substituted for the letters. For the planes *m-n*, *m'-n'*, in the same octant, in which the parameters would be $mc : nb : a$, and $m'c : n'b : a$,

mc, nb, a are substituted severally for c, b, a.
$m'c, n'b, a$ "   "   " c', b', a'.

I. ISOMETRIC SYSTEM.

The equality of the axes in the Isometric system makes it unnecessary to consider them in the calculations. The most commonly occurring problems are the determination of the symbols in the various forms, *i-n*, *m*, *m-m*, *m-n* (f. 51, 54, 65, 69). These cases will be considered in succession. In all but the last, but a single measurement is necessary.

1. Form *i-n, tetrahexahedron.*—The edges are of two kinds (p. 18), as A and C in f. 244; a measurement of either is sufficient to determine the value of n. (*a*) Given the angle of the edge A. Suppose a plane to

MATHEMATICAL CRYSTALLOGRAPHY.

pass through the edge A and the adjoining axis, ac, also a second plane through the two lateral axes, and imagine a spherical triangle constructed, as explained on p. 61. This triangle (see f. 244A) is right angled at C, and the other angles are $\frac{1}{2}A$, (half the measured angle of the crystal) and 45°, respectively. Hence, if ν is the inclination of the plane on the lateral axis, ac,

$$\cos \nu = \cos \tfrac{1}{2}A \sqrt{2},$$
$$\text{and } \tan \nu = na = n.$$

(b) Suppose the angle of the edge C to be given. In the plane triangle (abc) of the section in f. 244, $\frac{1}{2}C + 45° + \nu = 180°$, or $\nu = 135° - \frac{1}{2}C$, and, as before, $\tan \nu = n$. If the angle of two opposite planes, meeting at the extremity of an axis, were given, half this angle would be the angle ν. For a series of tetrahexahedrons the tangent law may be applied, since they form a zone between two cubic planes; the dodecahedron falls in this zone, being a special case of the tetrahexahedron where $n = 1$. The angle between a plane i-n and the adjoining cubic face (H) is equal to $\nu + 90°$, hence, $\cot H = n$.

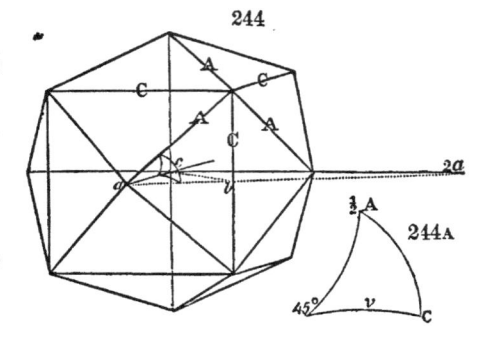

2. Form m, *trigonal trisoctahedron.*—The edges are of two kinds, A and B. (a) If the angle over B is given, suppose a diagonal plane to pass through the vertical axis and the edge A, meeting the planes, as indicated in the figure. A right-angled plane triangle is formed, of which the basal angle is equal to $\frac{1}{2}B$, and the base is the diagonal line x. Then $x \tan \frac{1}{2}B =$ the vertical side of the triangle (ma), but $x = \sqrt{\tfrac{1}{2}}$ when $a = 1$, whence $\tan \frac{1}{2}B\sqrt{\tfrac{1}{2}} = ma$ or m. (b) If the given angle is that of the edge A, place a spherical triangle (ma), as indicated in the figure. In this triangle $C = 90°$ (for the diagonal plane is perpendicular to the plane m), and the other angles are respectively $\frac{1}{2}A$ (half the measured angle) and 60°; hence, the side opposite $\frac{1}{2}A$ ($=$ the angle ρ) is obtained. Further, the angle of the two dotted diagonals (the octahedral and dodecahedral axes) is 35° 16′ (p. 16), whence, $\frac{1}{2}B = 144° 44' - \rho$, and, as before, $\tan \frac{1}{2}B\sqrt{\tfrac{1}{2}} = m$. See further the following case. The general equations are thus:

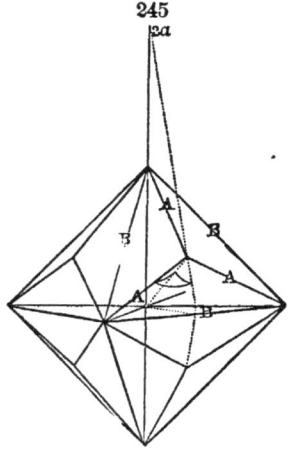

(a) $\qquad\qquad \tan \tfrac{1}{2}B \sqrt{\tfrac{1}{2}} = m.$
(b) $\qquad \cos \rho = 2 \cos \tfrac{1}{2}A\sqrt{\tfrac{1}{3}}; \quad \tfrac{1}{2}B = 144° 44' - \rho.$

3. Form m-m, *tetragonal trisoctahedron.*—Suppose (a) that the angle of the edge B is given. In the spherical triangle 1, in f. 246, $C = 90°$, and

each of the other angles equals $\frac{1}{2}B$. Hence, one of the equal sides (= angle ν) is obtained, and $\tan \nu = m$. (*b*) If the angle C is given, the triangle 2, in f. 246, is employed; here one angle is $= 90°$, a second $= 60°$, and the third $= \frac{1}{2}C$, half the measured angle of the edge C. The side of the triangle $=$ the angle ρ is calculated, and, as in the preceding case, $\zeta = 144° \, 44' - \rho$, then $m + 1 = \tan \zeta \sqrt{2}$.

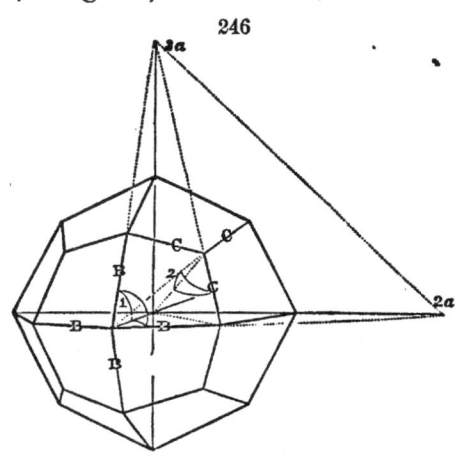

The planes *m-m*, 1, *m*, form a zone between the cubic and dodecahedral planes as f. 461, p. 244, to which the tangent law may be often conveniently applied. The form *m* passes into the octahedron 1 when $m = 1$, and when *m* is less than unity it becomes *m-m*, as explained on p. 17.

Since these planes form a rectangular zone the tangent of the supplement angles between them and a cubic plane are proportional to the values of *m* for the given forms; only by applying this principle for *m-m*, the index $\frac{1}{m}$ ($= \frac{1}{m} : 1 : 1$) will be obtained, which is equivalent to *m-m* ($= 1 : m : m$).

The general equations for the form *m-m* are:

(*a*) $\qquad \cos \nu = \cot \frac{1}{2}B; \; \tan \nu = m.$

(*b*) $\quad \cos \rho = \cot \frac{1}{2}C \sqrt{\frac{1}{3}}; \; \zeta = 144° \, 44' - \rho; \; \tan \zeta \sqrt{2} = m + 1.$

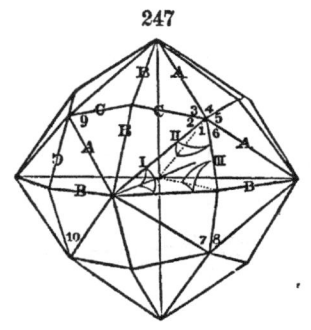

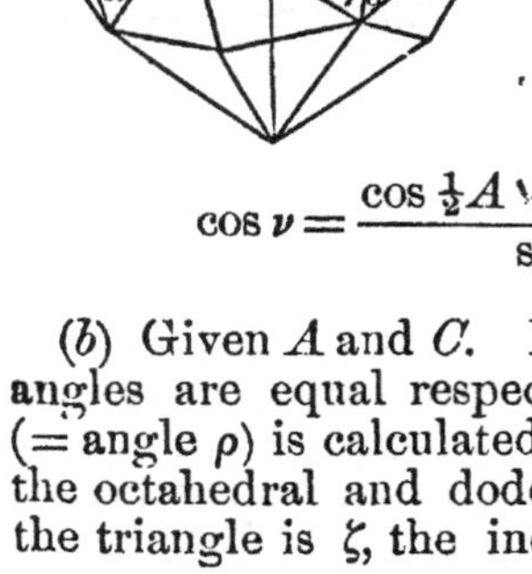

4. **Form *m-n*, hexoctahedron.**—The edges of the hexoctahedron are of three kinds, A, B, C (f. 247), and two measurements are, in general, needed in order to deduce the values of *m* and *n*.

(*a*) Given A and B. In the oblique-angled spherical triangle I (f. 247), the three angles are $\frac{1}{2}A$, $\frac{1}{2}B$, and 45°. In this triangle, the side opposite $\frac{1}{2}A$ ($=$ angle ν) is calculated, and from it are obtained the values of *m* and *n*, as follows:

$$\cos \nu = \frac{\cos \frac{1}{2}A \sqrt{2} + \cos \frac{1}{2}B}{\sin \frac{1}{2}B}; \; \tan \frac{1}{2}B \sin \nu = m; \; \tan \nu = n.$$

(*b*) Given A and C. In the oblique-angled triangle II (f. 247), the three angles are equal respectively to $\frac{1}{2}A$, $\frac{1}{2}C$, and 60°. The side opposite $\frac{1}{2}A$ ($=$ angle ρ) is calculated. But the angle between the diagonals, that is, the octahedral and dodecahedral axes, is 35° 16', and the third angle of the triangle is ζ, the inclination of the edge C on the dodecahedral axis;

hence, $\zeta = 144° 44' - \rho$. Again, in the right-angled triangle III (f. 247), one angle $= \frac{1}{2}C$, and the adjacent side $= \zeta$, whence the other side, δ (the inclination of the edge B on the dodecahedral axis), is obtained; $\nu = 135° - \delta$, and from this, as above, and from the angle ρ, are deduced the values of n and n. The formulas are:

$$\cos \rho = \frac{2 \cos \frac{1}{2}A + \cos \frac{1}{2}C}{\sin \frac{1}{2}C \sqrt{3}}; \quad \zeta = 144° 44' - \rho; \quad \tan \delta = \sin \zeta \tan \frac{1}{2}C$$

$$\nu = 135° - \delta; \quad \tan \nu = n; \quad \frac{n\sqrt{2}}{n+1} \tan \zeta = m.$$

(c) Given B and C. In the right-angled triangle, III (f. 247), the two angles are given, equal respectively to $\frac{1}{2}B$ and $\frac{1}{2}C$. From the triangle is deduced the side opposite $\frac{1}{2}C$ (= angle δ defined before), and from it is obtained ν, and from ν and $\frac{1}{2}B$, the values of m and n, as in the first case. The formulas are:

$$\cos \delta = \frac{\cos \frac{1}{2}C}{\sin \frac{1}{2}B}; \quad \nu = 135° - \delta; \quad \tan \nu = n; \quad \tan \frac{1}{2}B \sin \nu = m.$$

If, instead of m-n, the form is m-$\frac{m}{m-1}$, only one measurement is needed, and the process is simplified.

When the angles of any plane m-n on two cubic planes are given, their supplements will be the angles of the plane upon the corresponding diametral sections, and from them the values of m-n may be readily calculated. Thus (in f. 248), the angles of a given plane on a cubic plane at a^2 will be the supplement of its angle upon the section a^1a^2, that is, the angle B in the spherical triangle; similarly, the angle of a cubic plane at a^3 will be the supplement of its angle on the section a^1a^2, the angle A in the spherical triangle. In this same triangle $C = 90°$. Hence, the sides opposite A and B, that is, the inclinations of the two edges on the adjacent axis, may be calculated, and this axis being equal to unity, their *tangents* will give the corresponding lengths of the other axes. These lengths may not be the values of m and n in the form in which the symbol is generally written, where the unit axis is always the shortest, but the latter are immediately deducible. For example, if the angles here mentioned for the plane numbered 4 (in f. 247) had been measured, the values of the axes obtained by calculation, when the front axis is the unit, would be $\frac{1}{3}$ and $\frac{1}{2}$ respectively, and the symbol, hence, $\frac{1}{3} : \frac{1}{2} : 1$, which is equivalent to $1 : \frac{3}{2} : 3$, or m-$n = 3$-$\frac{3}{2}$ for the general form.

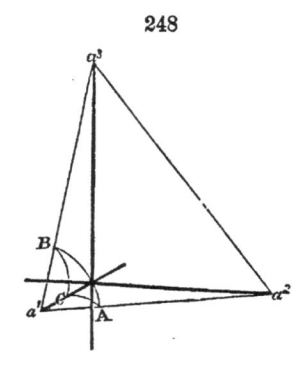

Hemihedral forms.—For each hemihedral form the formulas are identical with those already given for the corresponding holohedral, so far as the edges of the two are the same. For example, in comparing f. 69 and f. 87 it is seen that the edges A and C are the same in both, while B of the holohedral form differs from B' of the hemihedral. The formulas required to cover these additional cases are given below, they are obtained in a manner similar to those in the preceding pages.

Form $\frac{1}{2}(m)$, f. 85. Given B'.

$$\cos \epsilon = 2 \cos \tfrac{1}{2} B' \sqrt{\tfrac{1}{3}}; \quad \zeta = 35° \ 16' + \epsilon; \quad \tan \zeta \sqrt{\tfrac{1}{2}} = m.$$

Form $\frac{1}{2}(m\text{-}m)$, f. 81. Given B'.

$$\tan \tfrac{1}{2} B' \sqrt{2} = m.$$

Form $\frac{1}{2}(m\text{-}n)$, f. 87. (a) Given A' and B'.

$$\cos a = \frac{\cos \tfrac{1}{2} B'}{\sin \tfrac{1}{2} A'}; \quad \cos \beta = \frac{\cos \tfrac{1}{2} A'}{\sin \tfrac{1}{2} B'}; \quad m = \frac{\sqrt{2}}{\cot a - \cot \beta}; \quad n = \frac{\sqrt{2}}{\cot a + \cot \beta}.$$

(b) Given B' and C'.

$$\cos \epsilon = \frac{2 \cos \tfrac{1}{2} B' + \cos \tfrac{1}{2} C'}{\sin \tfrac{1}{2} C' \sqrt{3}}; \quad \zeta = 35° \ 16' + \epsilon; \quad \cot \delta = \tan \tfrac{1}{2} C' \sin \zeta.$$

$$\tan (\delta + 45°) = n; \quad \frac{n \sqrt{2}}{n+1} \tan \zeta = m.$$

Form $\frac{1}{2}[i\text{-}n]$, f. 92. Given A''.

$$\tan \tfrac{1}{2} A'' = n.$$

Form $[m\text{-}n]$, f. 100. (a) Given A'' and B''.

$$\frac{\cos \tfrac{1}{2} A''}{\sin \tfrac{1}{2} B''} = \cos \nu; \quad \tan \nu = n; \quad \frac{n \cos \tfrac{1}{2} A''}{\cos \tfrac{1}{2} B''} = m.$$

(b) Given A'' and C''

$$2 \cos \tfrac{1}{2} C'' \sqrt{\tfrac{1}{3}} = \sin O; \quad \cos \theta = \frac{\cos O \sqrt{3} - \cos \tfrac{1}{2} A''}{\sin \tfrac{1}{2} A'' \cdot \sqrt{2}}.$$

$$\tan (45° + \theta) = m; \quad \sin (45° + \theta) \tan \tfrac{1}{2} A'' = n.$$

(c) Given B'' and C''.

$$2 \cos \tfrac{1}{2} C'' \sqrt{\tfrac{1}{3}} = \sin O; \quad \cos \delta = \frac{\cos O \sqrt{3} - \cos \tfrac{1}{2} B''}{\sin \tfrac{1}{2} B'' \sqrt{2}}.$$

$$\tan (45° + \delta) = n; \quad \sin (45° + \delta) \tan \tfrac{1}{2} B'' = m.$$

The various combinations of holohedral and hemihedral forms which may occur are unlimited, and it would be unwise to attempt here to show the methods of working them out. It is only necessary to remark that the solution can generally be readily obtained by the use of one or two spherical triangles in the way shown in the preceding cases.

The calculation of the interfacial angles between two known forms can often be performed by the formulas already given, or by similar methods. For the more general cases, reference must be made to the cosine formula, p. 62.

Interfacial Angles.—I. Holohedral Forms.

The following are some of the angles among the more common of Isometric holohedral forms; adjacent planes are to be understood, unless it is stated otherwise. The angles A, B, C, above, are those over the edges so lettered in the figures referred to (see pp. 15–19), or over the corresponding edges in related forms:

$H \wedge H = 90°$, f. 38
$H \wedge 1 = 125\ 16'$, f. 40, 41
$H \wedge i = 135$, f. 43, 45.
$H \wedge i\text{-}\frac{3}{2} = 146\ 19$
$H \wedge i\text{-}2 = 153\ 26$, f. 64
$H \wedge i\text{-}3 = 161\ 34$
$H \wedge \frac{1}{2}\text{-}\frac{1}{2} = 133\ 19$
$H \wedge \frac{3}{2}\text{-}\frac{3}{2} = 136\ 45$
$H \wedge 2\text{-}2 = 144\ 44$, f. 55
$H \wedge 3\text{-}3 = 154\ 46$
$H \wedge \frac{3}{2}$, ov. 1, $= 115\ 14$
$H \wedge 2,\ " \ = 109\ 28$, f. 52
$H \wedge 3,\ " \ = 103\ 16$
$H \wedge 3\text{-}\frac{3}{2} = 143\ 18$, f. 70
$H \wedge 4\text{-}2 = 150\ 48$
$H \wedge 5\text{-}\frac{5}{3} = 147\ 41$
$1 \wedge 1 = 109\ 28$, f. 42
$1 \wedge 1,\ \text{top,} = 70\ 32$
$1 \wedge i = 144\ 44$, f. 47
$1 \wedge i\text{-}\frac{3}{2} = 143\ 11$
$1 \wedge i\text{-}2 = 140\ 16$, f. 67
$1 \wedge i\text{-}3 = 136\ 54$
$1 \wedge \frac{3}{2}\text{-}\frac{3}{2} = 168\ 41$

$1 \wedge 2\text{-}2 = 160°\ 32'$, f. 58
$1 \wedge 3\text{-}3 = 150\ 30$, f. 57
$1 \wedge \frac{3}{2} = 169\ 49$
$1 \wedge 2 = 164\ 12$, f. 53
$1 \wedge 3 = 158$
$1 \wedge 3\text{-}\frac{3}{2} = 157\ 45$
$1 \wedge 4\text{-}2 = 151\ 52$
$1 \wedge 5\text{-}\frac{5}{3} = 151\ 25$
$i \wedge i = 120$ f. 45
$i \wedge i,$ ov. top, $= 90$
$i \wedge i\text{-}\frac{3}{2} = 167\ 42$
$i \wedge i\text{-}2 = 161\ 34$, f. 68
$i \wedge i\text{-}3 = 153\ 26$
$i \wedge 2\text{-}2 = 150$
$i \wedge 3\text{-}\frac{3}{2} = 160\ 54$
$i \wedge 3\text{-}3 = 148\ 31$
$i \wedge 4\text{-}\frac{4}{3} = 166\ 6$
$i \wedge 5\text{-}\frac{5}{3} = 162\ 58\frac{1}{2}$
$2\text{-}2 \wedge 2\text{-}2, B, = 131\ 49$, f. 54
$2\text{-}2 \wedge 2\text{-}2, C, = 146\ 27$
$2\text{-}2 \wedge 2\text{-}2,$ ov. top. $= 109\ 28$
$3\text{-}3 \wedge 3\text{-}3, B, = 144\ 54$, f. 61
$3\text{-}3 \wedge 3\text{-}3, C, = 129\ 31$

$i\text{-}\frac{3}{2} \wedge i\text{-}\frac{3}{2}, A, = 133°\ 49'$
$i\text{-}\frac{3}{2} \wedge i\text{-}\frac{3}{2}, C, = 157\ 23$
$i\text{-}2 \wedge i\text{-}2, A, = 143\ 8$, f. 65
$i\text{-}2 \wedge i\text{-}2, C, = 143\ 8$
$i\text{-}2 \wedge i\text{-}2,$ ov. top, $= 126\ 52$
$i\text{-}2 \wedge i\text{-}3 = 171\ 52$
$i\text{-}2 \wedge 2\text{-}2 = 155\ 54$
$i\text{-}3 \wedge i\text{-}3, A, = 154\ 9$, f. 66
$i\text{-}3 \wedge i\text{-}3, C, = 126\ 52$
$2 \wedge 2, A, = 152\ 44$, f. 51
$2 \wedge 2, B, = 141\ 3\frac{1}{4}$
$3 \wedge 3, A, = 142\ 8$
$3 \wedge 3, B, = 153\ 28\frac{1}{4}$
$3\text{-}\frac{3}{2}, A, = 158\ 13$, f. 69
$3\text{-}\frac{3}{2}, B, = 149$
$3\text{-}\frac{3}{2}, C, = 158\ 13$
$4\text{-}2, A, = 162\ 15$
$4\text{-}2, B, = 154\ 47\frac{1}{4}$
$4\text{-}2, C, = 144\ 3$
$5\text{-}\frac{5}{3}, A, = 152\ 20$
$5\text{-}\frac{5}{3}, B, = 160\ 32$
$5\text{-}\frac{5}{3}, C, = 152\ 20$

II. Hemihedral Forms.

The following are the angles for the corresponding hemihedral forms:

$1 \wedge 1 = 70°\ 32'$, f. 76, 76A
$\frac{3}{2} \wedge \frac{3}{2}, A, = 162\ 39\frac{1}{2}$
$\frac{3}{2} \wedge \frac{3}{2}, B, = 82\ 10$
$2 \wedge 2, A, = 152\ 44$, f. 85
$2 \wedge 2, B, = 90$
$3 \wedge 3, A, = 142\ 8$
$3 \wedge 3, B, = 99\ 5$
$\frac{3}{2}\text{-}\frac{3}{2} \wedge \frac{3}{2}\text{-}\frac{3}{2}, B, = 93\ 22$
$\frac{3}{2}\text{-}\frac{3}{2} \wedge \frac{3}{2}\text{-}\frac{3}{2}, C, = 160\ 15$
$2\text{-}2 \wedge 2\text{-}2, B, = 109\ 28$, f. 81
$2\text{-}2 \wedge 2\text{-}2, C, = 146\ 26\frac{1}{4}$
$3\text{-}3 \wedge 3\text{-}3, B, = 124\ 7$

$3\text{-}3 \wedge 3\text{-}3, C, = 134°\ 2'$
$3\text{-}\frac{3}{2} \wedge 3\text{-}\frac{3}{2}, A, = 158\ 13$, f. 87
$3\text{-}\frac{3}{2} \wedge 3\text{-}\frac{3}{2}, B, = 110\ 55\frac{1}{2}$
$3\text{-}\frac{3}{2} \wedge 3\text{-}\frac{3}{2}, C, = 158\ 13$
$4\text{-}2 \wedge 4\text{-}2, A, = 162\ 15$
$4\text{-}2 \wedge 4\text{-}2, B, = 124\ 51$
$4\text{-}2 \wedge 4\text{-}2, C, = 144\ 3$
$i\text{-}\frac{3}{2} \wedge i\text{-}\frac{3}{2}, A, = 112\ 37$
$i\text{-}\frac{3}{2} \wedge i\text{-}\frac{3}{2}, C, = 117\ 29$
$i\text{-}2 \wedge i\text{-}2, A, = 126\ 52$, f. 92, 93
$i\text{-}2 \wedge i\text{-}2, C, = 113\ 35$
$i\text{-}3 \wedge i\text{-}3, A, = 143\ 8$

$i\text{-}3 \wedge i\text{-}3, C, = 107°\ 27\frac{1}{4}'$
$4\text{-}2 \wedge 4\text{-}2, A, = 128\ 15$
$4\text{-}2 \wedge 4\text{-}2, B, = 154\ 47\frac{1}{4}$
$4\text{-}2 \wedge 4\text{-}2, C, = 131\ 49$
$3\text{-}\frac{3}{2} \wedge 3\text{-}\frac{3}{2}, A, = 115\ 23$, f. 100
$3\text{-}\frac{3}{2} \wedge 3\text{-}\frac{3}{2}, B, = 149$
$3\text{-}\frac{3}{2} \wedge 3\text{-}\frac{3}{2}, C, = 141\ 47$
$5\text{-}\frac{5}{3} \wedge 5\text{-}\frac{5}{3}, A, = 119\ 3\frac{1}{4}$
$5\text{-}\frac{5}{3} \wedge 5\text{-}\frac{5}{3}, B, = 160\ 32$
$5\text{-}\frac{5}{3} \wedge 5\text{-}\frac{5}{3}, C, = 131\ 5$

In the forms $i\text{-}\frac{3}{2}$, $i\text{-}2$ (f. 92), $i\text{-}3$, $i\text{-}4$, A is the angle at the longer edge, and C that at either of the others.

II.—TETRAGONAL SYSTEM.

In the Tetragonal system, as has been fully explained (p. 30), the length of the vertical axis is variable, and must be determined for each species. If the length of c is known, then it may be required to determine the symbols of certain planes by means of measured angles. These two problems are in a measure complementary to each other, and the same methods will give a solution to either case. (For figures of the forms see pages 27 and 28.) The calculation of the interfacial angles can be performed by similar methods or by the cosine formula.

1. Form m.—The edges are of two kinds, pyramidal X, and basal Z. If either angle is known, the angle a, which is the inclination of the edge X on the lateral axis, may be calculated by the spherical triangle, as in f. 242, 243. (Compare the explanation of this case, p. 62.) Obviously in the plane right-angled triangle formed by the two axes and the edge X, $\tan a = mc$ (since $a = 1$). If c is known, then m is determined; and, conversely, a value being assumed for m, in the special case, c is given by the calculation. The general formulas are:

$$\cot \tfrac{1}{2}X = \sin a, \text{ or } \tan \tfrac{1}{2}Z \sqrt{\tfrac{1}{2}} = \tan a; \text{ then } \tan a = mc.$$

2. Form m-i.—(a) Given the angle Z, mc is found immediately; the solution is obvious, for in the section indicated by the dotted line (f. 249), $\tfrac{1}{2}Z = a$, and the tangent of this angle is equal to the vertical axis. (b) Given the angle Y. A spherical triangle placed as in f. 249, has one angle $= \tfrac{1}{2}Y$, a second $= 45°$, and the third $= 90°$, whence the side opposite $\tfrac{1}{2}Y$ is calculated, which is the complement of a.

The general formulas, which may serve to deduce the value of m, when c is given, or the converse, are:

$$\cos \tfrac{1}{2}Y \sqrt{2} = \sin a, \text{ or } \tan \tfrac{1}{2}Z = \tan a, \text{ and } \tan a = mc.$$

If a series of square octahedrons m, or m-i, occur in a vertical zone, their symbols may be calculated in both cases alike by the law of the tangents, the angles of the planes on O, or on I, or i-i, respectively, being given. (See p. 60.)

3. Form i-n.—For the angle of the edge X (f. 109, p. 26), at the extremity of a lateral axis, $\tan \tfrac{1}{2}X = n$. From the angle of the other edge Y, we have $\tfrac{1}{2}X = 135° - \tfrac{1}{2}Y$; and hence, $\tan (135° - \tfrac{1}{2}Y) = n$.

4. Form m-n.—The edges are of three kinds, X, Y, Z (f. 250), and two angles must be given in the general case to determine m and n.

(a) Given X and Z. A spherical triangle having its vertices on the edges X and Z, and the lateral axis, as 1, f. 250, will have two of its angles equal to $\tfrac{1}{2}X$, $\tfrac{1}{2}Z$, respectively, and the third equal to $90°$. The solution of this triangle gives the sides, viz., a and v, the inclinations of the edges X and

Z, respectively, on the lateral axis. The tangents of these angles give the values of m and n. The formulas are as follows:

$$\frac{\cos \tfrac{1}{2}Z}{\sin \tfrac{1}{2}X} = \cos a, \ \tan a = mc; \ \frac{\cos \tfrac{1}{2}X}{\sin \tfrac{1}{2}Z} = \cos \nu, \ \tan \nu = n.$$

(*b*) Given Y and Z. In a second triangle placed as indicated (2, f. 250), two of the angles are $\tfrac{1}{2}Y$ and $\tfrac{1}{2}Z$ respectively, and the third is 90°. The solution of this second triangle gives δ, the inclination of the edge Z on the diagonal axis, from which, in the plane triangle we have $\nu = 135° - δ$, and from ν is obtained n. Still again from the triangle 1 (f. 250), and its solution used in the preceding case, having given Z and ν, a is obtained, and from it m; as by the following formulas:

$$\frac{\cos \tfrac{1}{2}Y}{\sin \tfrac{1}{2}Z} = \cos δ, \ \nu = 135° - δ, \ \tan \nu = n;$$

$$\tan \tfrac{1}{2}Z \sin \nu = \tan a = mc.$$

(*c*) Given X and Y. A third triangle, numbered 3 in the figure, has two of the angles equal to $\tfrac{1}{2}X$ and $\tfrac{1}{2}Y$ respectively, and the third is 45°. Solving this oblique-angled triangle, the angle of the inclination of the edge Y on the vertical axis is obtained, and its complement is the angle ε, the inclination of the edge Y on the diagonal axis; from ε and $\tfrac{1}{2}Y$ are obtained, by triangle 2, δ, and thence, as above, n; and finally, from X and ν, is obtained a, and from that the value of m. The simplified formulas are as follows:

$$\frac{\cos \tfrac{1}{2}Y \sqrt{2}}{\cos \tfrac{1}{2}X} = n - 1; \ \sin a = n \cot \tfrac{1}{2}X, \ \tan a = mc.$$

Pyramids of the general symbol 1-n, m-m, etc., are especial cases of the preceding, the processes being for them, however, somewhat simplified. A single measurement is sufficient.

III. HEXAGONAL SYSTEM.

In the Hexagonal system there are three equal lateral axes (a) intersecting at angles of 60°, and a fourth vertical axis (c) at right angles to the plane of the others. Taking $a = 1$, there remains but one unknown quantity in the elements of a crystal, that is the length of c, and a single measurement is sufficient to determine this. The relations of the three lateral axes have been explained on p. 32.

The hexagonal system is closely allied to the tetragonal, and optically they are identical, as is shown beyond.

Schrauf refers all hexagonal forms to two lateral axes crossing at right angles and a vertical axis, in order to show this relation. According to him, in this system, the axes are $\dot{c} : a\sqrt{3} : a$; in the tetragonal they are $\dot{c} : a : a$. Miller's school, on the contrary, employ three equal axes, making equal angles with each other, and each normal to a face of the fundamental rhombohedron. In each of these methods a holohedral form, for instance a hexagonal pyramid, is considered as made up of two sets of forms, having different indices.

A.—*Holohedral Forms.*

1. Form m: hexagonal pyramid, first series.—Suppose a spherical triangle, inscribed in f. 148, p. 33, having its vertices upon the edges X and Z, and the corresponding lateral axis respectively, similar to the triangle of f. 242. This will be a right-angled triangle.

(*a*) When the angle of the edge X is given, then ξ, the inclination of the edge X upon the adjoining lateral axis, is calculated:

$\sin \xi = \cot \tfrac{1}{2} X \sqrt{3}$, and $\tan \xi = mc$, or $= \dot{c}$, the vertical axis, when $m = 1$.

(*b*) Given the angle Z.

$$\tan \tfrac{1}{2} Z \sqrt{\tfrac{3}{4}} = mc, \text{ or } = \dot{c} \text{ when } m = 1.$$

2. Form m-2: hexagonal pyramid, second series.—These pyramids bear the same relation to those of the m series as the m-i octahedrons to m octahedrons of the tetragonal system. (Compare f. 112, 146.) The methods of calculation are similar (f. 249.) The edges are of two kinds, vertical Y and basal Z.

(*a*) Given the angle Y.

$2 \cos \tfrac{1}{2} Y = \sin \tfrac{1}{2} Z$, and $\tan \tfrac{1}{2} Z = mc$, or $\dot{c}$ when $m = 1$.

(*b*) Given the angle Z. Then simply

$$\tan \tfrac{1}{2} Z = mc.$$

3. Form i-n: dihexagonal prism.—The vertical edges are of two kinds, axial X, and diagonal Y; the solution in either case is by means of a plane triangle, in a cross-section analogous to that of f. 146.

(*a*) Given X.

$$\tan \tfrac{1}{2} X \sqrt{\tfrac{1}{3}} = \frac{n}{2-n}.$$

(*b*) Given Y.

$$\tan \tfrac{1}{2} Y \sqrt{3} = \frac{n+1}{n-1}.$$

4. Form *m-n*: dihexagonal pyramid.—The edges (f. 251) are of three kinds, X and Y terminal, and Z basal; measurements of two of these are required to give the values of m and n; this is analogous to the calculation for the form *m-n* in the preceding system.

251

(*a*) Given X and Z. In a spherical triangle having its vertices on the edges X and Z, and the adjoining lateral axis respectively, two angles are given. If $\nu =$ the inclination of the edge Z upon the lateral axis (the side of the spherical triangle opposite the angle $\frac{1}{2}X$), then

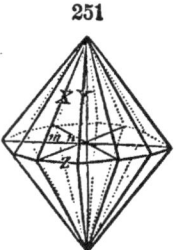

$$\cos \nu = \frac{\cos \frac{1}{2}X}{\sin \frac{1}{2}Z}, \; n - \tfrac{1}{2} = \tan(\nu - 30°)\sqrt{\tfrac{3}{4}}; \; \tan \tfrac{1}{2}Z \sin \nu = mc.$$

(*b*) Given Y and Z. The right-angled spherical triangle has its vertices on the edges Y and Z and the diagonal axis. If $\delta =$ the inclination of the edge Z upon this diagonal lateral axis, then:

$$\cos \delta = \frac{\cos \frac{1}{2}Y}{\sin \frac{1}{2}Z}; \; \text{but } n - \tfrac{1}{2} = \tan(120°-\delta)\sqrt{\tfrac{3}{4}},$$

also

$(150° - \delta) = \nu$; and, as before, $\tan \frac{1}{2}Z \sin \nu = mc$.

(*c*) Given X and Y. In the oblique-angled spherical triangle, with its vertices upon the edges X and Y and the vertical axis, the three angles are known, viz., $\frac{1}{2}X$, $\frac{1}{2}Y$, and 30°, hence:

$$\frac{2-n}{n-1} = \frac{\cos \frac{1}{2}X \sqrt{3}}{\cos \frac{1}{2}Y}$$

Further, if $\xi =$ the angle of inclination of the edge X upon a lateral axis, that is, the complement of the same edge upon the vertical axis (the side of the spherical triangle opposite the angle $\frac{1}{2}Y$),

$$\sin \xi = n \frac{\sqrt{3}}{2-n} \cot \tfrac{1}{2}X, \text{ and } \tan \xi = mc.$$

If the pyramid *m-n* takes the form $m\text{-}\dfrac{m}{m-1}$, as determined by its zonal relations, the calculations are simplified, since one unknown quantity only, m, has to be determined, and one measurement is sufficient.

B.—*Rhombohedral Division.*

The relation of the rhombohedrons and scalenohedrons to the true hexagonal forms has been made clear in another place. The rhombohedron is the hemihedral form of the hexagonal pyramid m, and its symbol is written $\frac{m}{2}$, or usually mR. The scalenohedron is the corresponding hemihedral form of the twelve-sided pyramid, and its symbol is written $\frac{1}{2}(m\text{-}n)$ or $m'R^{n'}$. The latter symbol, proposed by Naumann, has reference to the rhombohedron whose lateral edge corresponds to the edge Z of the given scalenohedron.

The formulas given by Naumann for reducing the symbol $\frac{1}{2}(m\text{-}n)$ to the form $m'R^{n'}$ are as follows:

$$m' = \frac{m(2-n)}{n}, \text{ and } n' = \frac{n}{2-n},$$

For the converse, to reduce $m'R^{n'}$ to the form $\frac{1}{2}(m\text{-}n)$,

$$m = m'n' \text{ and } n = \frac{2n'}{n'+1}$$

1. *Rhombohedrons, mR.*—The methods of calculation are simple, and will be understood from f. 252. The edges are of two kinds, X and Z, and their relation is such that the corresponding angles are the supplements of each other.

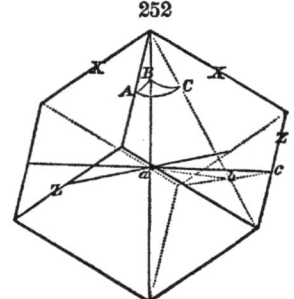

Given the angle of the edge X. A spherical triangle is placed, as indicated by ABC, in f. 252, with its vertices respectively on the edge X, the vertical axis, and the diagonal of the rhombohedral face. In this triangle $A = \frac{1}{2}X$, $B = 60°$, and $C = 90°$, but $\cos a = \dfrac{\cos A}{\sin B} = \dfrac{\cos \frac{1}{2}X}{\sin 60°}$; here a is the inclination of the diagonal line upon the vertical axis, that is, the complement of a, its inclination upon the basal section. Now in the plane triangle abc, where $ac =$ the lateral axis $= 1$, $ab = \sqrt{\frac{3}{4}}$, hence, $\tan a \sqrt{\frac{3}{4}} = mc$, or $= c$, the vertical axis of the rhombohedron, when $m = 1$.

The general formulas are then:

$$\sin a = \frac{\cos \frac{1}{2}X}{\sin 60°}, \text{ and } \tan a \sqrt{\frac{3}{4}} = mc.$$

Obviously, when the angle of R (or mR) upon the basal plane O can be measured, the supplement of this is the angle a. Similarly the angle $R \wedge 1 - 90° = a$.

In a series of rhombohedrons in a vertical zone, the tangent law can be advantageously applied. Attention must also be called to the zonal relations of certain $+$ and $-$ rhombohedrons, remarked on p. 36; these relations may be conveniently shown by means of Quenstedt's method of projection.

2. *Scalenohedrons, mR^n.*—As seen in f. 171, p. 37, the edges are of three kinds, X, Y, Z, and two angles, must in general be measured to allow of

the determination of m and n. The methods of calculation are not altogether simple. The following equations are from Naumann.

(*a*) Given X and Y.

n is found from $\dfrac{n+1}{n-1} = \dfrac{\cos \frac{1}{2}X}{\cos \frac{1}{2}Y}$; further, $\sin \frac{1}{2}Z = \dfrac{2n}{n+1} \cos \frac{1}{2}X$

also,

$$\cos \xi' = \dfrac{\tan \frac{1}{2}Z}{n\sqrt{3}}, \text{ and } \cot \xi' \sqrt{3} = mc.$$

(*b*) Given X and Z.

$$\dfrac{2n}{n+1} = \dfrac{\sin \frac{1}{2}Z}{\cos \frac{1}{2}X}\ ;\ \cos \xi' = \dfrac{\tan \frac{1}{2}Z}{n\sqrt{3}}\ ;\ \cot \xi' \sqrt{3} = mc.$$

(*c*) Given Y and Z.

$$\dfrac{2n}{n-1} = \dfrac{\sin \frac{1}{2}Z}{\cos \frac{1}{2}Y}\ ;\quad \cos \xi' = \dfrac{\tan \frac{1}{2}Z}{n\sqrt{3}}, \text{ and } \cot \xi' \sqrt{3} = mc.$$

If m, that is the inscribed rhombohedron, is known, one measurement will give the value of n. Z' = basal edge of the inscribed rhombohedron (care must be taken to note whether ϕ is obtuse or acute).

(*d*) Given X. $\quad \sin \phi = 2 \cos \frac{1}{2}X \cos \frac{1}{2}Z'.$

$\quad\quad\quad\quad\quad\quad \tan (\phi - \frac{1}{2}Z') \cot \frac{1}{2}Z' = n.$

(*e*) Given Y. $\quad \sin \phi = 2 \cos \frac{1}{2}Y \cos \frac{1}{2}Z'.$

$\quad\quad\quad\quad\quad\quad \tan (\phi + \frac{1}{2}Z') \cot \frac{1}{2}Z' = n.$

(*f*) Given Z. $\quad \tan \frac{1}{2}Z, \cot \frac{1}{2}Z' = n.$

If n is known. From X, we have $\sin \frac{1}{2}Z = \dfrac{2n}{n+1} \cos \frac{1}{2}X$; then, as under (*a*). From Y, $\sin \frac{1}{2}Z = \dfrac{2n}{n-1} \cos \frac{1}{2}Y$, and then as above. From Z, $\cos \xi'$ is obtained as under (*a*), and then mc.

IV. Orthorhombic System.

Of the three rectangular axes in the Orthorhombic system, one is always taken equal to unity, in this work the shortest ($\check{a}$). This leaves two unknown quantities to be determined for each species, namely, the lengths of the axes $\dot{c}$ and $\bar{b}$, expressed in terms of the unit axis $\breve{a}$, and for this end two independent measurements are required. The simpler cases are considered here.

Calculation of the Lengths of the Axes.

Let $a =$ the inclination of the edge Z to the axis $\breve{a}$ (f. 253).
$\beta =$ the inclination of the edge X to the axis $\breve{a}$.
$\gamma =$ the inclination of the edge Y to the axis $\bar{b}$.

From the plane triangle formed by each edge and the axes adjacent (f. 253, 254) the following relations are deduced, when $\breve{a} = 1$:

(1) Given a and β, $\tan \beta = \dot{c}$ and $\tan a = \bar{b}$.
(2) Given a and γ, $\tan a = \bar{b}$, and $\bar{b} \tan \gamma = \dot{c}$.
(3) Given β and γ, $\tan \beta = \dot{c}$, and $\dot{c} \cot \gamma = \bar{b}$.

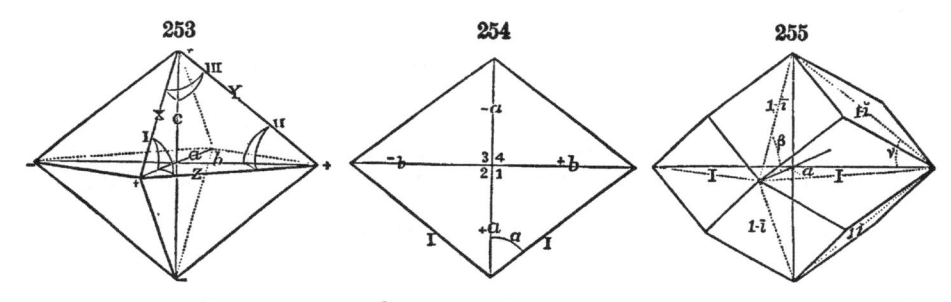

The angles a, β, γ are often given direct by measurement; for, obviously (f. 254, 255),
$a =$ the semi-prismatic angle $I \wedge I$ (over $i\text{-}\bar{i}$).
$\beta =$ the semi-basal angle of $1\text{-}\bar{i} \wedge 1\text{-}\bar{i}$.
$\gamma =$ the semi-basal angle of $1\text{-}\check{i} \wedge 1\text{-}\check{i}$.
Also $I \wedge i\text{-}\bar{i} = a + 90°$; $1\text{-}\bar{i} \wedge i\text{-}\bar{i} = \beta + 90°$; $1\check{i} \wedge O = 180° - \beta$, etc.
From the octahedron (f. 253), the angles a, β, γ are calculated immediately by the following formulas, and from them the length of the axes as above.

(*a*) Given X and Z (spherical triangle I, f. 253),

$$\cos a = \frac{\cos \tfrac{1}{2} X}{\sin \tfrac{1}{2} Z}; \quad \cos \beta = \frac{\cos \tfrac{1}{2} Z}{\sin \tfrac{1}{2} X}.$$

(*b*) Given Y and Z (spherical triangle II, f. 253),

$$\sin a = \frac{\cos \tfrac{1}{2} Y}{\sin \tfrac{1}{2} Z}; \quad \cos \gamma = \frac{\cos \tfrac{1}{2} Z}{\sin \tfrac{1}{2} Y}.$$

(*c*) Given X and Y (spherical triangle III, f. 253),

$$\sin \beta = \frac{\cos \tfrac{1}{2} Y}{\sin \tfrac{1}{2} X}; \quad \sin \gamma = \frac{\cos \tfrac{1}{2} X}{\sin \tfrac{1}{2} Y}.$$

If any one of the angles a, β, or γ is given, as from the measurement of a prism or dome, and also any one of the angles of the octahedral edges X, Y, or Z, a second of the former angles may be calculated, and from the two the axes are obtained as before. The formulas, derived from the same spherical triangles, are as follows:

(1) Given X and a, $\sin \beta = \cot \tfrac{1}{2} X \tan a$.
    X and β, $\tan a = \tan \tfrac{1}{2} X \sin \beta$.
    X and γ, $\cos \beta = \cot \tfrac{1}{2} X \cot \gamma$.
(2) Given Y and a, $\sin \gamma = \cot \tfrac{1}{2} Y \cot a$.
    Y and β, $\cos \gamma = \cot \tfrac{1}{2} Y \cot \beta$.
    Y and γ, $\cot a = \tan \tfrac{1}{2} Y \sin \gamma$.
(3)* Given Z and a, $\tan \gamma = \tan \tfrac{1}{2} Z \cos a$.
    Z and β, $\cos a = \cot \tfrac{1}{2} Z \tan \gamma$.
    Z and γ, $\sin a = \cot \tfrac{1}{2} Z \tan \beta$.

Calculation of the values of m and n.

The above formulas cover all the ordinary cases, the only change that is required in them is to write for c, b, a, in equations (1), (2), (3), above, c', b', a', the lengths of the axes for the given form, noting that $c' = mc$, and so on.

1. *Prisms, $i\text{-}\bar{n}$ or $i\text{-}\check{n}$.*—As remarked, the semi-prismatic angle (over $i\text{-}\bar{\imath}$) is the angle a (f. 254), and $\tan a = nb$. If the calculated value of n is greater than unity, the form is written $\infty c : nb : a \, (i\text{-}\bar{n})$; if less than unity, the form is written $\infty c : b : na \, (i\text{-}\check{n})$, b being the unit axis. Thus $i\text{-}\tfrac{1}{2}$ ($\infty c : \tfrac{1}{2} b : a$) becomes $i\,2\,(\infty c : b : 2a)$.

2. *Domes, $m\text{-}\bar{\imath}$ and $m\text{-}\check{\imath}$.*—No further explanation is needed (f. 255); here $\tan \beta = mc$, or $b \tan \gamma = mc$.

3. *Octahedrons, m.*—Here the angle a is always known (it being the same as for the unit-octahedron where $\tan a = b$), and hence a single measured angle, X, Y, or Z will give the values of either β or γ for the given form, and $\tan \beta = mc$, $b \tan \gamma = mc$.

4. *Forms $m\text{-}\bar{n}$ or $m\text{-}\check{n}$.*—The measurement of the angles X, Y, Z will give the values of a, β, and γ belonging to the given form, and $\tan \beta = mc$, $\tan a = nb$, etc.

Here, as in the prisms, if n is less than unity, when the axis $\check{a}$ is the unit, the symbol is transposed, and the axis $\bar{b}$ made the unit, thus $2c : \tfrac{1}{2} b : a \,(2\,\tfrac{1}{2})$ becomes $4c : b : 2a \,(4\text{-}2)$.

If the angle between the form $m\text{-}\bar{n}$ (or $m\text{-}\check{n}$) and either of the pinacoids can be measured, the method of calculation is essentially the same (Compare f. 248); for

$m\text{-}n \wedge O$ (base) = supplement of the angle $\tfrac{1}{2} Z$;
$m\text{-}n \wedge i\text{-}\bar{\imath}$ (macropinacoid) = supplement of the angle $\tfrac{1}{2} Y$; and
$m\text{-}n \wedge i\text{-}\check{\imath}$ (brachypinacoid) = supplement of the angle $\tfrac{1}{2} X$.

The method of calculation of planes in a rectangular zone by means of the tangents of their supplement basal angles finds a wide application in this system. It applies not only to the main zones O to $i\text{-}\bar{\imath}$ (macrodomes),

O to $i\text{-}\check{\imath}$ (brachydomes), $\check{\imath}\text{-}\check{\imath}$ to $i\text{-}\check{\imath}$ (vertical prisms), and I to O (unit octahedrons), but also to any zone of octahedrons $m\text{-}\bar{n}$ (or $m\text{-}\check{n}$) between O and $i\,\bar{n}$ (or $i\text{-}\check{n}$), and any transverse zone from $i\text{-}\check{\imath}$ to $m\text{-}\check{\imath}$, and $i\text{-}\check{\imath}$ to $m\text{-}\check{\imath}$.

V. Monoclinic System.

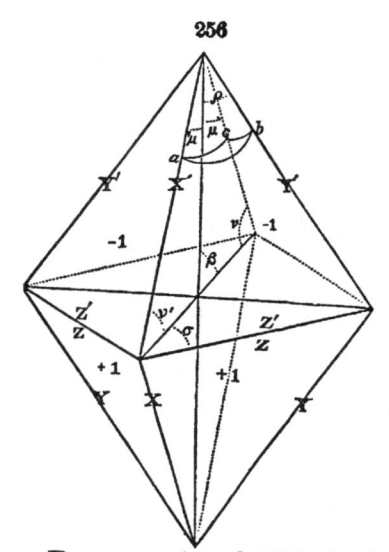

256

In the Monoclinic system the number of unknown quantities is three, viz., the lengths of the axes $\dot{c}$ and b, expressed in terms of the unit clinodiagonal axis $\dot{a}$, and the oblique angle β (also called C), between the basal and vertical diametral sections, that is, between the axes $\dot{c}$ and $\dot{a}$. Three independent measurements are needed to determine these crystallographic elements.

The angle β is obtuse in the upper front quadrants, and acute in the lower front quadrants; the planes in the first mentioned quadrants are distinguished from those below by the minus sign. The unit octahedron is made up of two hemi-octahedrons (-1 and $+1$), as shown in f. 256.

Calculation of the Lengths of the Axes, and the Angles of obliquity.

Represent (see f. 256) the inclination of the

Edge X on the axis $\dot{c}$ by μ. X on $\dot{a}$ by ν. Y on $\dot{c}$ by ρ.
X' " " $\dot{c}$ " μ'. X' on $\dot{a}$ by ν'. Z on $\dot{a}$ by σ.

For the relation of the axes in terms of these angles we have:

(1) In the oblique-angled plane triangle, in the clinodiagonal section

$$a : c = \sin \mu : \sin \nu, \text{ or, } c = \frac{\sin \nu}{\sin \mu} \text{ when } a = 1.$$

$$\tan \mu = \frac{a \sin \beta}{c - a \cos \beta}. \qquad \tan \mu' = \frac{a \sin \beta}{c + a \cos \beta}.$$

$$\tan \nu = \frac{c \sin \beta}{a - c \cos \beta}. \qquad \tan \nu' = \frac{c \sin \beta}{a + c \cos \beta}.$$

$$\tan \beta = \frac{2 \sin \mu \sin \mu'}{\sin (\mu - \mu')}. \qquad \tan \beta = \frac{2 \sin \nu \sin \nu'}{\sin (\nu - \nu')}.$$

Further, $\quad \mu + \nu + \beta = 180° \qquad \mu' + \nu' = \beta.$

(2) In the right-angled triangle of the orthodiagonal section, $b \cot \rho = \dot{c}$.

(3) In the basal section, $\dot{a} \tan \sigma = b$.

The above formulas serve to determine the lengths of the axes, and the angle of obliquity, or, if these are known, to determine the values of m and n by substituting mc for c, etc.

The angles μ, ν, ρ, σ, etc., must, in general, be determined by calculation from measured angles.

Let the inclination of a plane in the positive quadrant on the clinodiagonal section be denoted by X; that on the orthodiagonal section by Y; that on the basal section by Z. Let also the corresponding inclinations of a plane in the negative quadrants be indicated by X', Y', Z', respectively (see f. 256).

It is to be noted, when the pinacoids are present, that

$$+1 \wedge O = 180° - Z; \quad +1 \wedge i\text{-}i = 180° - Y; \quad +1 \wedge i\text{-}\check{\imath} = 180° - X;$$
$$-1 \wedge O = 180° - Z'; \quad -1 \wedge i\text{-}i = 180° - Y'; \quad -1 \wedge i\text{-}\check{\imath} = 180° - X'.$$

The same is true for the corresponding angles of the general form $\pm m\text{-}n$, or $m\text{-}\check{n}$.

Also, when ± 1 (f. 256) alone are present (or $m\text{-}n$) note that

$$+1 \wedge +1 = 2X; \quad -1 \wedge -1 = 2X'; \quad +1 \wedge -1 \text{ (orthodiag.)} = Y + Y';$$
$$\text{(basal)} = Z + Z'.$$

Any three of these angles will serve to give for the unit form (± 1) the length and obliquity of the axes, or, when these are known, two of these angles are sufficient to deduce the values of m and n for any unknown form.

In the first case, as one of the three measured angles must be either $Y + Y'$ or $Z + Z'$, the formulas given above do not immediately apply.

For example, if X, X' and $Y + Y'$ are given. Placing a spherical triangle, abc, in f. 256, with its vertices on the edges X, X', and Y, in this the three angles will equal X, X' and $Y + Y'$ respectively; here the side, ac, opposite the angle ($Y + Y'$) is calculated, which gives the value of $\mu + \mu'$, also the side, bc, opposite X'; then, again, in the right-angled spherical triangle, where bc and X are known, μ is obtained, thus μ' is known and also β. The lengths of the axes follow from the formulas given above.

The following are some of the cases which may occur:

(a) Given O, and $i\text{-}i$. $O \wedge i\text{-}i$ (front) $= 180° - \beta$, behind $= \beta$.

(b) Given $O, -1\text{-}i,$ and $+1\text{-}i$. $O \wedge -1\text{-}i = 180° - \nu'$; $O \wedge +1\text{-}i = 180° - \nu$. By the formula given above, $\tan \beta = \dfrac{2 \sin \nu \sin \nu'}{\sin (\nu - \nu')}$, also, $\mu = 180° - (\beta + \nu)$. Thus β, μ, and ν are known, and from them the relation of the axes $\dot{a}$ and $\dot{c}$ is deduced.

(c) Given $i\text{-}i, -1\text{-}i$ and $+1\text{-}i$. $i\text{-}i \wedge -1\text{-}i = 180° - \mu', i\text{-}i \wedge +1\text{-}i = 180° - \mu$. As before, $\tan \beta = \dfrac{2 \sin \mu \sin \mu'}{\sin (\mu - \mu')}$, and $\nu = 180° - (\beta + \mu)$.

(d) Given the prism I and O (f. 257). In the spherical triangle ABC, $C = 90°$ (inclination of base on clinodiagonal section), $B = O \wedge I$, $A = \frac{1}{2}(I \wedge I)$. Hence, the sides CA and CB are calculated; $CA = \beta$ (or, as in this case, $180° - \beta$); $CB = \sigma$, which gives the ratio of the lateral axes, $\dot{a}$ and b.

257

(e) Given $i\text{-}i$, $1\text{-}i$ and O. $O \wedge i\text{-}i$ (behind) $= \beta$, and $\sin \beta \tan [(O \wedge 1\text{-}i) - 90°] = \tan \rho$.

(f) Given $+1$ and -1, form as in f. 256. The angles between the planes $+1$ and -1 and the diametral sections are indicated by the letters X, Y, etc., as before explained (p. 77). The relations between these angles and the angles μ, ν, ρ, etc., are given in the following formulas, deduced by means of spherical triangles:

$$\cos \mu = \frac{\cos Y}{\sin X}, \quad \cos \mu' = \frac{\cos Y'}{\sin X'}, \quad \cos \rho = \frac{\cos X}{\sin Y} = \frac{\cos X'}{\sin Y'}.$$

$$\cos \nu = \frac{\cos Z}{\sin X}, \quad \cos \nu' = \frac{\cos Z'}{\sin X'}, \quad \cos \sigma = \frac{\cos X}{\sin Z} = \frac{\cos X'}{\sin Z'};$$

also,

$$\tan X = \frac{\tan \sigma}{\sin \nu} = \frac{\tan \rho}{\sin \mu}, \quad \tan X' = \frac{\tan \sigma}{\sin \nu'} = \frac{\tan \rho}{\sin \mu'}.$$

$$\tan Y = \frac{\tan \mu}{\sin \rho}, \quad \tan Y' = \frac{\tan \mu'}{\sin \rho}, \quad \tan Z = \frac{\tan \nu}{\sin \sigma}, \quad \tan Z' = \frac{\tan \nu'}{\sin \sigma}.$$

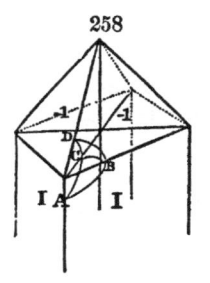

258

(g) Given the prism I and -1 (or $+1$). The angles $I \wedge I$, $-1 \wedge I$, $-1 \wedge -1$ are measured. In the spherical triangle ABD (f. 258), the angle $A = \frac{1}{2}(I \wedge I)$, $B = -1 \wedge I$, $D = \frac{1}{2}(-1 \wedge -1) = X'$, from which the sides $AD = \nu' + (180° - \beta)$ and AB are calculated. Then in the second triangle, ABC, $C = 90°$, AB is known, also A; hence, $CB = \sigma$ and $CA = 180° - \beta$ are calculated. Thus ν' and μ' and β become known, and the relation of $\dot{a}$ to $\dot{c}$; also from σ follows the ratio of $\dot{a}$ to b.

Calculation of the values of m and n.

In general, it may be said that the methods of calculation are the same as those already given. In each case the values of μ, ν, ρ, σ are to be obtained, and those introduced into the axial equations (1, 2, 3) given above give the values of mc, nb, etc., from which m and n are derived. When in the general form m-n ($mc : nb : a$) n is found to be less than unity, then b is made the unit axis and the form is written m-$\dot{n}$ ($mc : b : na$), thus $2c : \frac{1}{2}b : a$ becomes $4c : b : 2a$ (4-2), the same is true for i-n and i-$\dot{n}$.

1. Hemi-octahedrons, $\pm$ m-n.— Two measurements are needed, giving

two of the angles X, Y, Z, etc., from which are derived μ (or ν), ρ (or σ), and from the proper formulas m and n.

The following hemi-octahedrons require one measurement only: $\pm m$, $\pm m\text{-}m$, $\pm m\text{-}\check{m}$, $\pm 1\text{-}n$, $\pm 1\text{-}\check{n}$. Further, it is to be noted in regard to them that the forms $\pm m$ have the same ratio of the lateral axes as ± 1, that is, the same value of σ.

Forms $\pm 1\text{-}n$, and $\pm m\text{-}m$, have the same ratio of the axes $\acute{c}$ and $\acute{a}$ as the unit form ± 1, that is, the same values of μ, ν (μ', ν').

Forms $\pm m\text{-}m$, $\pm 1\text{-}\check{n}$, have the same ratio of the axes $\acute{c}$ and b with ± 1, that is, the same value of ρ.

2. Form $i\text{-}n$ (or $i\text{-}\check{n}$).—If, as before, X, Y represent the inclinations of the given prism on the clinodiagonal and orthodiagonal sections respectively, it is to be noted that:

$$X + Y = 90°.$$

Similarly to f. 257, we obtain, in general, for any form, $i\text{-}n$,

$$n = \frac{\sin \beta \ \tan X}{b}; \text{ and for } i\text{-}\check{n},\ n = \frac{b \cot X}{\sin \beta}.$$

Since $i\text{-}i \wedge i\text{-}\check{i} = 90°$, the tangent law can be applied in this zone advantageously. If X^1, Y^1 are the corresponding angles for the unit prism I, then for $i\text{-}n$,

$$n = \frac{\tan X}{\tan X^1} = \frac{\tan Y^1}{\tan Y}, \quad \text{and for } i\text{-}\check{n},\ n = \frac{\tan X^1}{\tan X} = \frac{\tan Y}{\tan Y^1}.$$

3. Forms $\pm m\text{-}i$, hemi-orthodomes.—For each form the corresponding values of μ, ν (μ', ν') are to be obtained by measurement or else calculated, and from them the value of mc obtained from the formulas (1), $mc = \dfrac{\sin \nu}{\sin \mu}$, etc.

4. Forms $m\text{-}\check{i}$, clinodomes.—Similarly as with the prisms, when X and Z denote the angles with the clinodiagonal and basal sections,

$$X + Z = 90°.$$

For any form $m\text{-}\check{i}$,

$$m = \frac{b \cot X}{c \sin \beta},$$

Or by the tangent law, X^1 being the corresponding angle for $1\text{-}\check{i}$,

$$m = \frac{\tan X^1}{\tan X}.$$

TRICLINIC SYSTEM.

The triclinic system is characterized by its entire want of symmetry. The inclinations of all the diametral planes, and hence, the inclination of the axes, are oblique to one another. There are, then, five unknown quantities to be determined in each case, viz., the three angles of obliquity of the axes, and the lengths of the axes $\bar{b}$ and $\dot{c}$, $\breve{a}$ being made = 1.

The axes are lettered as in the orthorhombic system: $\dot{c}$ = the vertical axis, $\bar{b}$ = the macrodiagonal axis, and $\breve{a}$ = the brachydiagonal axis.

Let (f. 259) a = angle between the axes $\dot{c}$ and $\bar{b}$;
β = angle between the axes $\dot{c}$ and $\breve{a}$;
γ = angle between the axes $\bar{b}$ and $\breve{a}$.

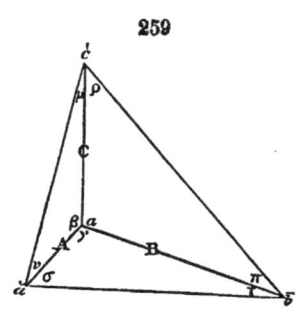

Also, let A = angle of inclination of the diametral planes meeting in the axis $\breve{a}$; B = angle of inclination for those intersecting in the axis $\bar{b}$, and C = the angle of those meeting in $\dot{c}$.

The macrodiagonal (m-$\bar{n}$) and brachydiagonal (m-$\breve{n}$) planes are indicated as in the orthorhombic system, also the planes opposite the acute angle (β) are called +, and those opposite the corresponding obtuse angle —; furthermore, the planes in front, to the right (and behind, to the left) are distinguished by an accent, as m-n'.

In the fundamental octahedron formed by four sets of planes, these are, taken in the usual order (f. 227), — 1', — 1, + 1', + 1, and below, + 1', + 1, — 1', — 1.

In the determination of any individual crystal belonging to this system, the axial directions as well as unit values have to be assumed arbitrarily; in many cases (*e.g.*, axinite) the custom of different authors has varied much. Two points are to be considered in making the choice: 1, the correspondence in form with related species, even if these be not triclinic, as, for example, in the feldspar family; and 2, the ease of calculation, which is much facilitated if, of the planes chosen as fundamental, the pinacoids are all, or at least in part, present.

In general, the methods of calculation are not simple. Some of the most important relations are given here (from Naumann). In actual practice, problems which arise may be solved by some of the following formulas, or by means of a series of appropriate spherical triangles, used as in the preceding pages, and by which, from the measured angles, the required elements of the forms may be obtained.

In addition to the angles already defined, let, as follows (f. 259),

X = inclination of a plane on the brachydiagonal section;
Y = " " " " macrodiagonal "
Z = " " " " basal "

Let the inclination of the edge,

X on $\dot{c} = \mu$, Y on $\dot{c} = \rho$, Z on $\breve{a} = \sigma$,
X on $\breve{a} = \nu$, Y on $\bar{b} = \pi$, Z on $\bar{b} = \tau$,

MATHEMATICAL CRYSTALLOGRAPHY.

When the three pinacoids are present, the angles A, B, C are given by measurement. These angles are connected with the axial angles by the following equations:

$$\cos a = \frac{\cos A + \cos B \cos C}{\sin B \sin C}; \quad \cos \beta = \frac{\cos B + \cos C \cos A}{\sin C \sin A};$$

$$\cos \gamma = \frac{\cos C + \cos A \cos B}{\sin A \sin B};$$

also,

$$\sin a : \sin \beta : \sin \gamma = \sin A : \sin B : \sin C.$$

The relations between the angles a, β, γ, and the angles μ, ν, etc., are as follows:

$$\tan a = \frac{2 \sin \rho \sin \rho'}{\sin (\rho - \rho')} = \frac{2 \sin \pi \sin \pi'}{\sin (\pi - \pi')}.$$

$$\tan \beta = \frac{2 \sin \mu \sin \mu'}{\sin (\mu - \mu')} = \frac{2 \sin \nu \sin \nu'}{\sin (\nu - \nu')}.$$

$$\tan \gamma = \frac{2 \sin \tau \sin \tau'}{\sin (\tau - \tau')} = \frac{2 \sin \sigma \sin \sigma'}{\sin (\sigma - \sigma')}.$$

Also,

$$a + \pi + \rho = \beta + \mu + \nu = \gamma + \sigma + \tau = 180°.$$

The relations between X, Y, Z, and A, B, C, and μ, ν, etc., are given by the following formulas, in which the sum and difference of X and Y, etc., are calculated, and from them the angles X, Y, etc., themselves are obtained:

$$\tan \tfrac{1}{2}(X+Y) = \cot \tfrac{1}{2}C \cdot \frac{\cos \tfrac{1}{2}(\rho - \mu)}{\cos \tfrac{1}{2}(\rho + \mu)}.$$

$$\tan \tfrac{1}{2}(X-Y) = \cot \tfrac{1}{2}C \cdot \frac{\sin \tfrac{1}{2}(\rho - \mu)}{\sin \tfrac{1}{2}(\rho + \mu)}.$$

$$\tan \tfrac{1}{2}(X+Z) = \cot \tfrac{1}{2}A \cdot \frac{\cos \tfrac{1}{2}(\sigma - \nu)}{\cos \tfrac{1}{2}(\sigma + \nu)}.$$

$$\tan \tfrac{1}{2}(X-Z) = \cot \tfrac{1}{2}A \cdot \frac{\sin \tfrac{1}{2}(\sigma - \nu)}{\sin \tfrac{1}{2}(\sigma + \nu)}.$$

$$\tan \tfrac{1}{2}(Y+Z) = \cot \tfrac{1}{2}B \cdot \frac{\cos \tfrac{1}{2}(\tau - \pi)}{\cos \tfrac{1}{2}(\tau + \pi)}.$$

$$\tan \tfrac{1}{2}(Y-Z) = \cot \tfrac{1}{2}B \cdot \frac{\sin \tfrac{1}{2}(\tau - \pi)}{\sin \tfrac{1}{2}(\tau + \pi)}.$$

CRYSTALLOGRAPHY.

$$\cos \mu = \frac{\cos Y + \cos X \cos C}{\sin X \sin C}, \quad \cos \nu = \frac{\cos Z + \cos X \cos A}{\sin X \sin A}.$$

$$\cos \rho = \frac{\cos X + \cos Y \cos C}{\sin Y \sin C}, \quad \cos \pi = \frac{\cos Z + \cos Y \cos B}{\sin Y \sin B}.$$

$$\cos \sigma = \frac{\cos X + \cos Z \cos A}{\sin Z \sin A}, \quad \cos \tau = \frac{\cos Y + \cos Z \cos B}{\sin Z \sin B}.$$

Further,
$$\sin X : \sin Y = \sin \rho : \sin \mu.$$
$$\sin Y : \sin Z = \sin \tau : \sin \pi.$$
$$\sin Z : \sin X = \sin \nu : \sin \sigma.$$

The following equations give the relations of the angles μ, ν, ρ, etc. to the axes and axial angles:

$$\tan \mu = \frac{a \sin \beta}{c - a \cos \beta}; \quad \tan \nu = \frac{c \sin \beta}{a - c \cos \beta}.$$

$$\tan \rho = \frac{b \sin \alpha}{c - b \cos \alpha}; \quad \tan \pi = \frac{c \sin \alpha}{b - c \cos \alpha}.$$

$$\tan \tau = \frac{a \sin \gamma}{b - a \cos \gamma}; \quad \tan \sigma = \frac{b \sin \gamma}{a - b \cos \gamma}.$$

Also,
$$\sin \tau : \sin \sigma = \breve{a} : \bar{b},$$
$$\sin \rho : \sin \pi = \bar{b} : \breve{c},$$
$$\sin \nu : \sin \mu = \breve{c} : \breve{a}.$$

For any form m-n,

$$m\text{-}n \wedge \bar{i}\text{-}\bar{i} = 180° - Y; \quad m\text{-}n \wedge \breve{i}\text{-}\breve{i} = 180° - X; \quad m\text{-}n \wedge O = 180° - Z.$$

For a vertical hemiprism, $X + Y + C = 180°$,

$$\breve{a} : \bar{b} = \sin Y \cdot \sin \alpha : \sin X : \sin \beta.$$

For a macrodiagonal hemidome, $Y + Z + B = 180°$,

$$\breve{a} : \breve{c} = \sin Y \cdot \sin \alpha : \sin Z \cdot \sin \gamma.$$

For a brachydiagonal hemidome, $X + Z + A = 180°$,

$$\bar{b} : \breve{c} = \sin X \sin \beta : \sin Z \sin \gamma.$$

By writing mc for c, nb for b, etc., these formulas will answer also for the determination of m and n. It is supposed in the above that the measured edge is parallel to the axis of the given hemiprism, etc.; when this is not the case the relations are a little less simple.

MATHEMATICAL CRYSTALLOGRAPHY. 83

Measurement of the Angles of Crystals.*

The angles of crystals are measured by means of instruments which are called *goniometers*.

The simplest form of these instruments is the hand-goniometer, represented in f. 260. It consists of an arc, graduated to half degrees, or finer,

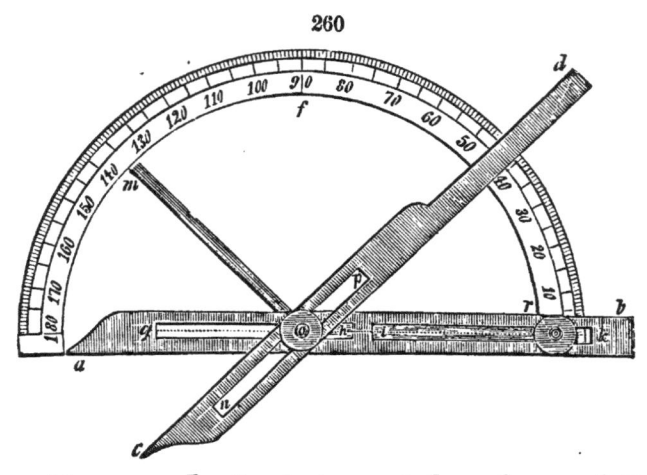

260

and two movable arms. In the instrument figured, one of the arms, ao, has the motion forward and backward by means of slits gh, ik; the other arm, cd, has also a similar slit, and in addition it turns around the centre of the arc as an axis. The planes whose inclination is to be measured are applied between the arms ao, co, and the latter adjusted so that they and the surfaces of the planes are in close contact. This adjustment must be made with care, and when the instrument is held up to the light none must pass through between the arm and the plane. The number of degrees read off on the arc between k and the left edge of d (this edge being in the line of the centre, o, of the arc) is the angle required. The motion to and fro by means of the slits is for the sake of convenience in measuring small or imbedded crystals. In a much better form of the instrument the arms are wholly separated from the arc; and the arc is a delicately graduated circle to which the arms are adjusted after the measurement.

The hand-goniometer is useful in the case of large crystals, and those whose faces are not well polished; the measurements with it, however, are seldom within a quarter of a degree of accuracy. In the finest specimens of crystals, where the planes are smooth and lustrous, results far more accurate may be obtained by means of a different instrument, called the reflecting goniometer.

Reflecting Goniometer.—This instrument was devised by Wollaston, in 1809, but it has been much improved in its various parts since his time, especially by Mitscherlich. The principle on which it is constructed may be understood by reference to the following figure (f. 261), which represents a crystal, whose angle, abc. is required.

The eye at P, looking at the face of the crystal, bc, observes a reflected image of *m*, in the direction of *Pn*. The crystal may now be so changed in its position, that the same image is seen reflected by the next face and in the same direction, *Pn*. To effect this, the crystal must be turned around, until *abd* has the present direction of *bc*. The angle *dbc*, measures, therefore, the number of degrees through which the crystal must be turned. But *dbc*, subtracted from 180°, equals the required angle of the crystal, *abc*. The crystal is, therefore, passed in its revolution through an angle which is the supplement of the required angle. This angle evidently may be measured by attaching the crystal to a graduated circle, which should turn with the crystal.

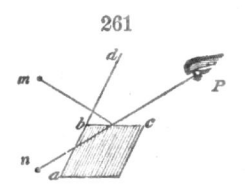

The accompanying cut (f. 262) represents a reflecting goniometer made by Oertling, in Berlin. It will suffice to make clear the general character of the instrument, as well as to exhibit some of the refinements added for the sake of greater exactness.

The circle, C, is graduated, in this case, to twenty minutes, and by means of the vernier at v the readings may be made to minutes and half minutes. The crystal is attached by means of wax to the little plate at k; this may be removed for convenience, but in its final position it is, as here, at the extremity of the axis of the instrument. This axis is moved by means of the wheel, n; the graduated circle is moved by the wheel, m. These motions are so arranged that the motion of n is independent, its axis being within the other, while on the other hand the revolution of m moves both the circle and the axis to which the crystal is attached. This arrangement is essential for convenience in the use of the instrument, as will be seen in the course of the following explanation.

The screws, c, d, are for the adjustment of the crystal, and the slides, a, b, serve to centre it.

The method of procedure is briefly as follows: The crystal is attached by means of suitable wax at k, and adjusted so that the direction of the combination-edge of the two planes to be measured coincides with the axis of the instrument; the wheel, n, is turned until an object (*e.g.*, a window-bar) reflected in one plane is seen to coincide with another object not reflected (*e.g.*, a chalk line on the floor), the position of the graduated circle is observed, and then both crystal and circle revolved together by means of the wheel, m, till the same reflected object now seen in the *second* plane again coincides with the fixed object (that is, the chalk line); the angle through which the circle has been moved, as read off by means of the vernier, is the supplement angle between the two planes.

In order to secure accuracy, several conditions must be fulfilled, of which the following are the most important:

1. The position of the eye of the observer must remain perfectly stationary.

2. The object reflected and that with which it is brought in coincidence, should be at an equal distance from the instrument, and this distance should not be too small.

3. The crystal must be accurately *adjusted;* this is so when the line seen reflected in the case of each plane and that seen directly with which it is in coincidence are horizontal and parallel. It can be true only when the intersection edge of the two planes measured is exactly in the *direction* of the axis of the instrument, and perpendicular to the plane of the circle.

4. The crystal must be *centered* as nearly as possible, or, in other words, the same intersection-edge must *coincide* with a line drawn through the revolving axis. This condition will be seen to be distinct from the preceding, which required only that the two *directions* should be the same. The error arising when this condition is not satisfied diminishes as the object reflected is removed farther from the instrument, and becomes zero if the object is at an infinite distance.

The first and second conditions are both satisfactorily fulfilled by the use of a telescope, as t, f. 262, with slight magnifying power. This is arranged for parallel light, and provided with spider lines in its focus. It admits also of some adjustments, as seen in the figure, but when used it must be directed exactly toward the axis of the goniometer. This telescope has also a little magnifying glass (g, f. 262) attached to it, which allows of the crystal itself being seen when mounted at k. This latter is used for the first adjustments of both planes, and then slipped aside, when some distant object which has been selected must be seen in the field of the telescope as reflected, first by the one plane and then by the other as the wheel n is revolved. When the final adjustments have been made so that in each case the object coincides with the centre of the spider-cross of the telescope, and when further the edge to be measured has been centered, the crystal is ready for measurement.

This telescope, obviously, can be used only when the plane is smooth and large enough to give distinct and brilliant reflections. In many cases sufficient accuracy is obtained without it by the use of a window-bar and a white chalk line on the floor below for the two objects; the instrument in this case is placed at the opposite end of the room, with its axis parallel to the window; the eye is brought very close to the crystal and held motionless during the measurement.

The best instruments are provided with two telescopes. The second stands opposite the telescope, t (see figure), the centres of both telescopes being in the same plane perpendicular to the axis of the instrument. This second telescope has also a hair cross in the focus, and this, when illuminated by a brilliant gas burner (the rest of the instrument being protected from the light by a screen) will be reflected in the successive faces of the crystal. The reflected cross is brought in coincidence with the cross in the first telescope, first for one and then for the other plane. As the lines are delicate, and as exact coincidence can take place only after perfect adjustment, it is evident that a high degree of accuracy is possible.

Still more than before, however, are well-polished crystals required, so that in the majority of cases the use of the ordinary double telescopes is impossible. Very often, however, the second telescope may be advantageously replaced by another having an adjustable slit in its focus, as proposed by Websky, allowing of being made as narrow as is convenient; or, as suggested by Schrauf, the spider-lines of the second telescope may be replaced by a piece of tin-foil, in which two fine cross lines have been cut; these are illuminated by a gas-burner. By these methods the reflected object is a bright line or cross, instead of the dark spider-lines, and it is visible in the first telescope even when the planes are extremely minute, or, on the other hand, somewhat rough and uneven; the image is naturally not perfectly distinct, but sufficiently so to admit of good measurements (*e.g.*, within two or three minutes).

The third and fourth conditions are the most difficult to fulfil absolutely. In the cheaper instruments the contrivance to accomplish the end often consists of a jointed arm so placed as to have two independent motions at right angles to each other. In the best instruments the greatest care and attention is paid to this point, and a great variety of ingenious contrivances have been devised to overcome the various practical difficulties arising.

The cut (f. 262) shows one of these in its simpler form. The crystal is approximately adjusted by the hand, and then the operation completed by means of the screws c and d. These give two motions at right angles to each other, and the arrangement is such that the motions are made on the surface of a spherical segment of which the crystal itself occupies the centre, so that it is not thrown entirely out of the axis of the instrument by the motions of the screws. The adjustment having been accurately made, the edge is *centered* by means of two sliding carriages, a, b, moving at right angles to each other; here they are moved by hand, but in better instruments by fine screws. The edge must be first centered as carefully as practicable, then the complete adjustments made, and finally again centered, as before, to remove the excentricity caused by the movement of the adjustment screws. The successful use of the most elaborate instruments is only to be attained after much patient practice.

Theoretical discussions of the various errors arising in measurements and the weight to be attached to them have been given by Kuppfer (Preisschrift über genaue Messung der Winkel an Krystallen, 1825), also by Naumann, Grailich, Schrauf, and others (see literature, p. iv).

It has been stated that when the two planes have been adjusted in the goniometer so that their combination-edge is parallel to the axis of the instrument, the reflections given by them will be parallel. It is evident from this that any other planes on the crystal which are in the same zone with the two mentioned planes will also give, as the circle is revolved, reflections parallel to these. This means gives the test referred to on p. 53, leading on the one hand to the discovery of zones not indicated by parallel intersections, and on the other hand showing, in regard to supposed zones, whether they are so in fact or not.

The degree of accuracy and constancy in the angles of crystals as they are given by nature is an important subject. Crystallography as a science is based upon the assumption that the forms made by nature are perfectly accurate, and whenever exact measurements are possible, supposing the crystals to have been free from disturbing influences, it has been found that this assumption is warranted by the facts; in other words, the more accurate the measurements the more closely do the angles obtained agree with those required by theory. An example may illustrate this:—On a crystal of sphalerite (zinc-blende), from the Binnenthal, exact measurements were made by Kokscharow to test the point in question. He found for the angle of the tetrahedron 70° 31' 48", required 70° 31' 44"; for the octahedral angle 109° 27' 42", required 109° 28' 16"; and for the angle between the tetrahedron and cube 125° 15' 52", required 125° 15' 52". The crystallographic works of the same author, as well as those of many other workers in the same field, contain many illustrations on the same subject. At the same time variations in angle do occasionally occur, from a change in chemical composition, and from various disturbing causes, such as heat and pressure (see further, p. 107). Further than this, it is universally true that exact measurements are in comparatively few cases possible. Many crystals are large and rough, and admit of only approximate results with the hand goniometer; others have faces which are more or less polished, but which give uncertain reflections. This is due in some cases to striations, in others to the fact that the surfaces are curved or more or less covered with markings or etchings, like those common on the pyramidal planes of quartz. In all such cases there is a greater or less discrepancy between the measured and calculated angles.

The important point to be noted always is the degree of accuracy attainable, or, in other words, the probable error. The true result to be accepted is always to be obtained by the discussion of all the measurements in accordance with the methods of least squares. This method involves considerable labor, and in most cases it is sufficient to take the arithmetical mean, noting what degree of weight is to be attached to each measurement. It is to be noted that where measurements vary largely the probable error in the mean accepted will be considerable; moreover an approximate measurement may not be the more accurate because it *happens* to agree closely with the theoretical angle.

For the determination of the symbols of planes, measurement accurate within 30', or even 1°, are generally sufficient.

When planes are rough and destitute of lustre the angles can best be obtained with the reflecting goniometer, the reflections of the light from an object like a candle-flame, being taken in place of more distinct images.

For imbedded crystals, and often in other cases, measurements may be very advantageously made from impressions in some material, like sealing-wax. Angles thus obtained ought to be accurate within one degree, and suffice for many purposes. It is sometimes of advantage to attach to the planes to be measured, when quite rough, fragments of thin glass, from which reflections can be obtained; this must, however, be done with care, to avoid considerable error.

COMPOUND, OR TWIN CRYSTALS.

TWIN CRYSTALS are those in which one or more parts regularly arrranged are in reverse position with reference to the other part or parts. They often appear externally to consist of two or more crystals symmetrically united, and sometimes have the form of a cross or star. They also exhibit the composition in the reversed arrangement of part of the planes, in the striæ of the surface, and in re-entering angles; in other cases the compound structure is detected only by polarized light. The following figures are examples of the simpler kinds. Fig. 263 is a twinned octahedron with

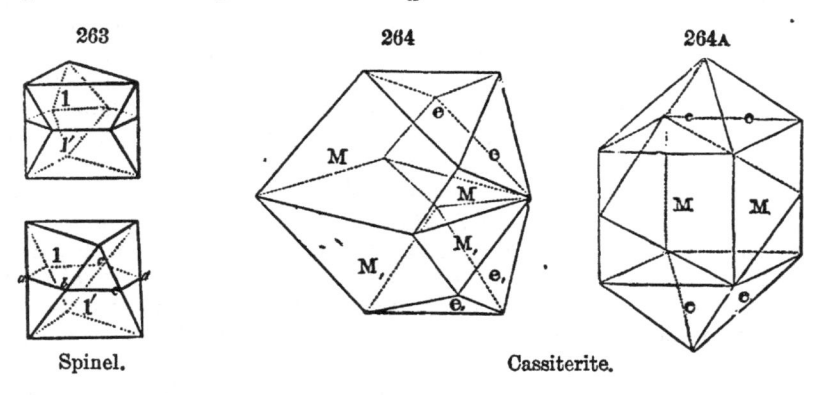

263   264   264A

Spinel.   Cassiterite.

re-entering angles. Fig. 263A represents the regular octahedron divided into two halves by a plane parallel to an octahedral face; the revolving of the upper half around 180° produces the twinned form. Fig. 264 consists of a square prism, with pyramidal terminations, twinned parallel to a diagonal plane between opposite solid angles, as illustrated in f. 264A, a representation of the simple form. A revolution of one of the two halves of f. 264A 180° about an axis at right angles to the diagonal plane outlined in the figure, would produce the form in fig. 264.

Crystals which occupy parallel positions with reference to each other, that is, those whose similar axes and planes are parallel, are not properly called twins; the term is applied only where the crystals are united in their reversed position in accordance with some deducible mathematical law. In conceiving of them we imagine first the two individuals or portions of the same individual to be in a parallel position, and then a revolution of 180° to take place about a certain line, as axis, which will bring them into the twinning position.

An exception to the principle in regard to parallel axes is afforded in the case of hemihedral crystals, in some of which a revolution of 180° has the effect of producing an apparently holohedral form, the axes of the parts revolved remaining parallel.

In some cases (e.g., hexagonal forms), a revolution of 60° would produce the twinned form, but in treating of the subject it is better to make the uniform assumption of a revolution of 180°, which will answer in all cases.

It is not to be supposed that twins have actually been formed by such a revolution of the parts of crystals, for the twin is the result of regular molecular growth or enlargement, like that of the simple crystal. This reference to a *revolution*, and an *axis of revolution*, is only a convenient means of describing the forms. But while this is true, it is important to observe that the *laws* deduced to explain the twinning of a crystal have, from a molecular standpoint, a real existence. The measurements of Schrauf on twins of cerussite (Tsch. Min. Mitth., 1873, 209) show the complete correspondence between the actual angles and those required in accordance with the law of twinning.

Twinning axis.—The line or axis about which the revolution of 180° is supposed to take place is called the twinning-axis (Zwillingsaxe, *Germ.*), or axis of revolution.

The following law has been deduced in regard to this axis, upon which the theory of the whole subject depends:

The twinning axis is always a possible crystallographic line, usually either an axis or a normal to some possible *crystalline plane*.

Twinning-plane.—The plane normal to the axis of revolution is called the twinning-plane (Zwillingsfläche, *Germ.*). The axis and plane of twinning bear the same relation to both individuals in their reversed position; consequently (except in some of hemihedral and triclinic forms) the twinned crystals are symmetrical with reference to the twinning-plane.

Composition-plane.—The plane by which the reversed crystals are united is the *composition-plane* or *-face* (Zusammensetzungsfläche, *Germ.*). This and the twinning-plane very commonly coincide; this is true of the simple examples given above (f. 263, 264) where the plane about which the revolution is conceived as having taken place (normal to the twinning axis), and the plane by which the semi-individuals are united, are identical. When not coinciding the two planes are generally at right angles to each other, that is, the composition face is parallel to the axis of revolution. Examples of this are given beyond (p. 99). Still again, where the crystals are not regularly developed, and where they interpenetrate, and, as it were, exercise a disturbing influence upon each other, the contact surface may be interrupted, or may be exceedingly irregular. In such cases the axis and plane of twinning have, as always, a definite position, but the composition-face has lost its significance.

Thus in quartz the interpenetrating parts have often no rectilinear boundary, but mingle in the most irregular manner throughout the mass, and showing this composite irregularity by abrupt variations of the planes at the surface. Fig. 265 exhibits by its shaded part the parts of the plane − 1 that appear over the surface of the plane R, owing to the interior composition. This internal structure of quartz, found in almost all quartz crystals, even the common kinds, is well brought out by means of polarized light; also, by etching with hydrofluoric acid, the plane − 1 and R becoming etched unequally on the same amount of exposure to the acid.

The twinning-plane is, with rare exceptions, a possible occurring plane on the given species, and usually one of the more frequent or fundamental planes. The exceptions occur only in the triclinic and monoclinic systems, where the twinning axis is sometimes one of the oblique crystallographic axes, and then the plane of twinning normal to it is obviously not necessarily a crystallographic plane, this is conspicuous in albite. In these cases the composition-face is often of more significance than the twinning-plane, the former being distinct and parallel to the axis, in accordance with the principle stated above.

With reference to the composition-face, the twinning may be described as taking place (1) by a revolution on an axis at right angles to the composition-face, (2) on an axis parallel to it and vertical, (3) by an axis parallel to it and horizontal; whether the revolution takes place with the right or left half of the crystal, the twin is right- or left-handed.

One further principle is of theoretical importance in the mathematical explanation of the forms. The twinning axis may, in many cases, be exchanged for another line at right angles with it, a revolution about which will also satisfy the conditions of producing the required form. An example of this is furnished by f. 318, of orthoclase; the composition-face is parallel to $i\text{-}i$, the axis of revolution also parallel to this plane, and (a) normal to $i\text{-}i$, which is then consequently the twinning-plane, though the axis does not coincide with the crystallographic axis, or (b) it may coincide with the vertical axis, and then the twinning-plane normal to it is not a crystallographic plane. In other simpler cases also, the same principle holds good, generally in consequence of the possible mutual interchange of the planes of twinning and composition. In most cases the true twinning-plane is evident, since it is parallel to some plane on the crystal of simple mathematical ratio.

An interesting example of the above principle is furnished by the species staurolite. Fig. 307, p. 98, shows a prismatic twin observed by the author among crystals from Fannin Co., Ga. The measured angle for $i\text{-}i \wedge i\text{-}i'$ was 70° 30'; the twinning-axis deduced from this may be the normal to the plane $i\text{-}\frac{3}{2}$, which would then be the twinning-plane. Instead of this axis, its complementary axis at right angles to it may be taken, which will equally well produce the observed form. Now in this species it happens that the planes $i\text{-}3$ and $i\text{-}\frac{3}{2}$ (over $i\text{-}i$) are almost exactly at right angles (90° 8') with each other, and hence, according to this latter supposition, $i\text{-}3$ becomes the twinning-plane, and the axis of revolution is normal to it. Hence, either $i\text{-}\frac{3}{2}$ or $i\text{-}3$ may be the twinning-plane, either supposition agrees closely with the measured angle, which could not be obtained with great accuracy. The former method of twinning ($i\text{-}\frac{3}{2}$) conforms to the other twins observed on the species, and hence it may be accepted. What is true in this case, however, is not always true, for it will seldom happen that of the two complementary axes each is so nearly normal to a plane of the crystal. In most cases one of the two axes conforms to the law in being a normal to a possible plane, and the other does not, and hence there is no doubt as to which is the true twinning axis.

Contact-twins and Penetration-twins.—In contact-twins, when normally formed, the two halves are simply connate, being united to each other by the composition-face; this is illustrated by f. 263, 264. In actually occurring crystals the two parts are seldom symmetrical, as demanded by theory, but one may preponderate to a greater or less extent over the other; in some cases only a small portion of the second individual in the reversed position may exist. Very great irregularities are observed in nature in this respect. Moreover, the re-entering angles are often obliterated by the abnormal developments of one or other of the parts, and often only an indistinct line on some of the faces marks the division between the two individuals.

Penetration-twins are those in which two or more complete crystals interpenetrate, as it were crossing through each other. Normally, the crystals have a common centre, which is the centre of the axial system for both; practically, however, as in contact-twins, great irregularities occur.

Examples of these twins are given in the annexed figures, f. 266, of fluorite, and f. 267, of hematite. Other examples occur in the pages following, as, for instance, of the species staurolite, f. 309 to 312, the crystals of which sometimes occur in nature with almost the perfect symmetry demanded by theory. It is obvious that the distinction between contact and penetration-twins is not a very important one, and the line cannot always be clearly drawn between them.

266. Fluorite.

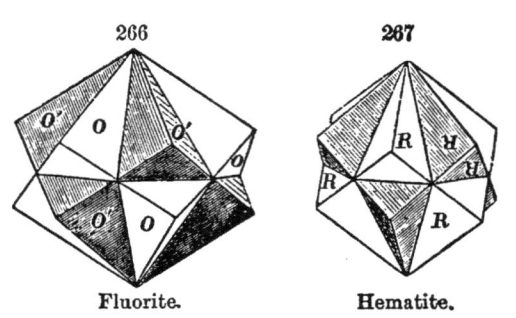

267. Hematite.

Paragenic and Metagenic twins.—The distinction of paragenic and metagenic twins belongs rather to crystallogeny than crystallography. Yet the forms are often so obviously distinct that a brief notice of the distinction is important.

In ordinary twins, the compound structure had its beginning in a nucleal compound molecule, or was compound in its very origin; and whatever inequalities in the result, these are only irregularities in the development from such a nucleus. But in others, the crystal was at first simple; and afterwards, through some change in itself or in the condition of the material supplied for its increase, received new layers, or a continuation, in a reversed position. This mode of twinning is *metagenic*, or a result subsequent to the origin of the crystal; while the ordinary mode is *paragenic*. One form of it is illustrated in f. 268. The middle portion had attained a length of half an inch or more, and then became geniculated simultaneously at either extremity. These geniculations are often repeated in rutile, and the ends of the crystal are thus bent into one another, and occasionally produce nearly regular prismatic forms.

This metagenic twinning is sometimes presented by the successive layers of deposition in a crystal, as in some quartz crystals, especially amethyst, the inseparable layers, exceedingly thin, being of opposite kinds. So calcite crystals are sometimes made up of twinned layers, which are due to an oscillatory process of twinning attending the progress of the crystal. In a similar manner, crystals of the triclinic feldspars, albite, etc., are often made up of thin plates parallel to $i\text{-}\breve{\imath}$, by oscillatory composition, and the face O, accordingly, is finely striated parallel to the edge $O \wedge i\text{-}\breve{\imath}$.

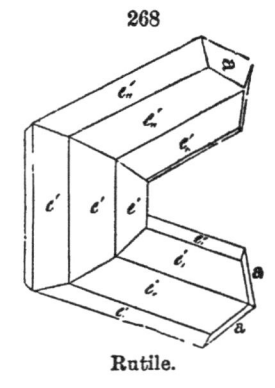

268. Rutile.

92   CRYSTALLOGRAPHY.

Repeated twinning.—In the preceding paragraph one case of repeated twinning has been mentioned, that of the feldspars; it is a case of *parallel* repetition or parallel grouping of the successive crystals. Another kind is that which is illustrated by f. 295, 297, 311, where the successively reversed individuals are not parallel. In this case the axes may, however, lie in a zone, as the prismatic twins of aragonite, or they may be inclined to each other, as in f. 311, of staurolite. In all such cases where the repetition of the twinning tends to produce circular forms, as f. 281, of rutile, the number of individuals is equal to the number of times the angle between the two axial systems is contained in 360°. For example, five-fold twins occur in the tetrahedrons of gold and sphalerite, since 5 × 70° 32′ (the tetrahedral angle) = 360° (approx.). A compound crystal, when there are three individuals, is called a *Trilling* (Drilling, *Germ.*), where there are four individuals, a *Fourling* (Vierling, *Germ.*), etc. (See also on p. 186.)

Compound crystals in which twinning exists in accordance with two laws at once are of rare occurrence; an excellent example is afforded by staurolite, f. 312. They have also been observed on albite (f. 333), orthoclase, chalcocite, and in other less distinct cases.

*Examples of different methods of Twinning.**

ISOMETRIC SYSTEM.—With few exceptions the twins of this system are of one kind, the twinning axis an octahedral axis, and the twinning plane consequently an *octahedral plane*; in most cases also the latter coincides

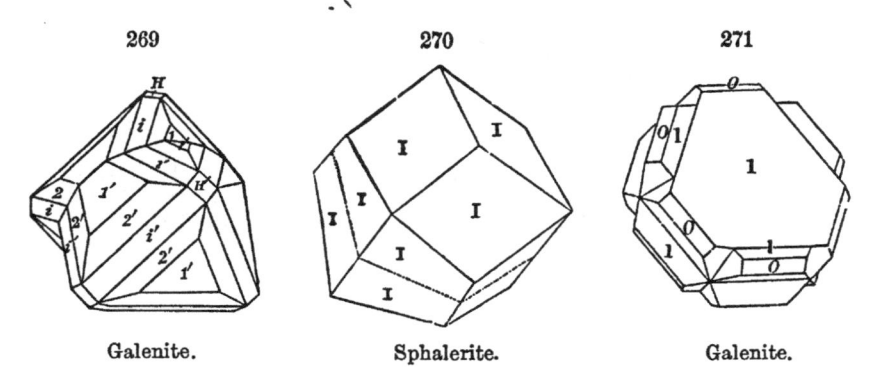

269   270   271

Galenite.   Sphalerite.   Galenite.

with the composition-face. Fig. 263 shows this kind as applied to the simple octahedron, it is especially common with the spinel group of minerals; similarly, f. 269, a more complex form, and also, f. 270, a dodecahedron twinned; all these are contact twins. Fig. 271 is a penetration twin following the same law; the twinning being repeated, and the form flattened parallel to an octahedral face. Fig. 266, p. 91, shows a twin of

---

* A complete enumeration of the different methods of twinning observed under the different systems, with detailed descriptions and many figures, will be found in Vol. II. of Rose-Sadebeck's Crystallography (Angewandte Krystallographie, 284 pp., 8vo, Berlin, 1876).

fluorite, two interpenetrating cubes; f. 272 exhibits a dodecahedral twin of sodalite occurring in nature of almost ideal symmetry, and f. 273 is a tetrahedral twin of the species tetrahedrite; the same law is true for all.

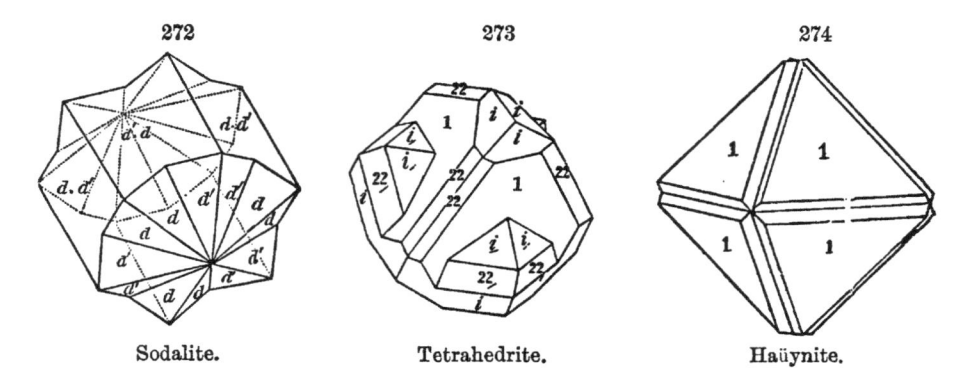

272
Sodalite.

273
Tetrahedrite.

274
Haüynite.

Figs. 274, 275, 276, are twins whose axes are parallel; these forms are possible only with hemihedral crystals. The twinning axis is here a *dodecahedral axis* and the twinning plane a *dodecahedral plane*. The same

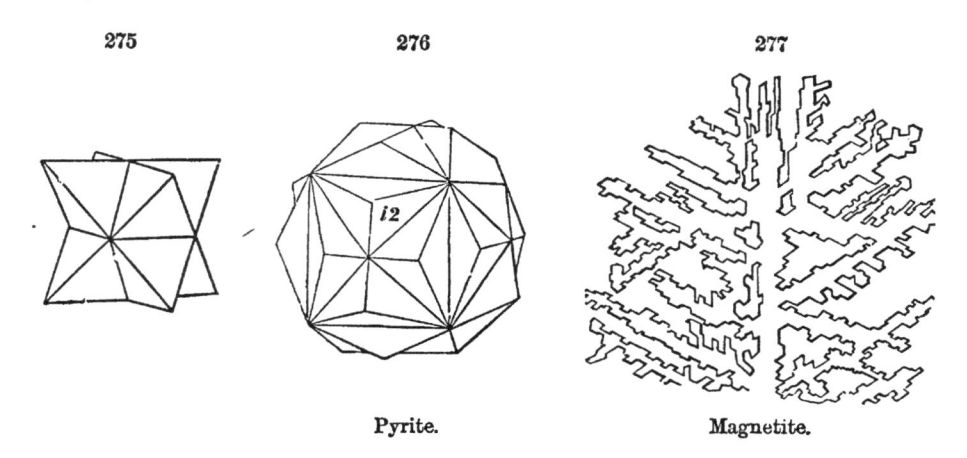

275

276
Pyrite.

277
Magnetite.

method of composition is often seen in dendritic crystallizations of native gold and copper, in which the angle of divergence of the branches is 60° and 120°, the interfacial angles of a dodecahedron. The brownish-black mineral in the mica from Pennsbury, Pa., is magnetite in this form (f. 277), as first observed by G. J. Brush.

TETRAGONAL SYSTEM.—The most common method is that where the twinning-plane is parallel to 1-i. It is especially characteristic of rutile and cassiterite. This is illustrated in f. 264 and similarly in f. 278. Fig. 268 shows a similar twin of rutile, and in f. 281 to 283 the twinning according to this law is repeated. In f. 281 the vertical axes of the successive six individuals lie in a plane, and an enclosed circle is the result; in f. 282 the successive vertical axes form a zig-zag line; there are here four individuals, add four more behind, the last (VIII) uniting with the first (I), and let it be developed vertically, and the complex form produced results in the scalenohedron twin of f. 283. In chalcopyrite, the octahedron 1, which is

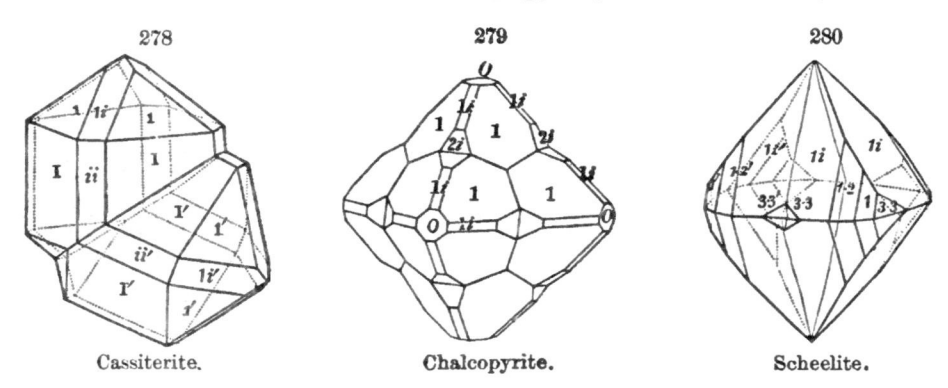

278
Cassiterite.

279
Chalcopyrite.

280
Scheelite.

very near a regular octahedron in angle, may be the twinning-plane, and forms are thus produced very similar to f. 263. With hemihedral forms twinning may take place as shown in f. 280, where the axis of revolution

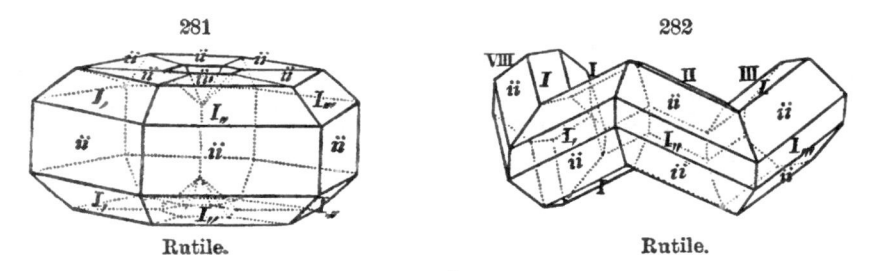

281
Rutile.

282
Rutile.

is a diagonal axis, and the plane of twinning the prism I. It is not always indicated by a re-entering angle, but is sometimes only shown by the oblique striations in two directions meeting in the line of contact.

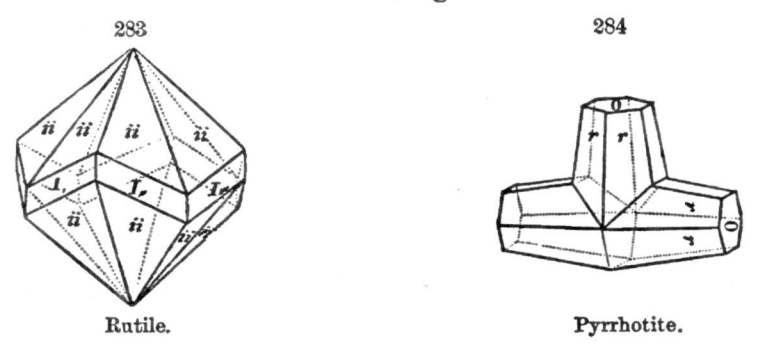

283
Rutile.

284
Pyrrhotite.

Another mode of twinning is that occurring in leucite, observed by vom Rath, who showed the species to be tetragonal. The twinning-plane is here $2 \cdot i$. (Jahrb. Min., 1873, 113.)

TWIN CRYSTALS.

HEXAGONAL SYSTEM.—In the holohedral division of this system twins are rare. An example is furnished by pyrrhotite, f. 284, where the twinning-plane is the pyramid 1, the vertical axes of the individual crystals being nearly at right angles to each other ($O \wedge 1 = 135° 8'$). Another example is tridymite * (see p. 288), where the twinning-plane is either the pyramid $\frac{1}{4}$ or $\frac{3}{4}$.

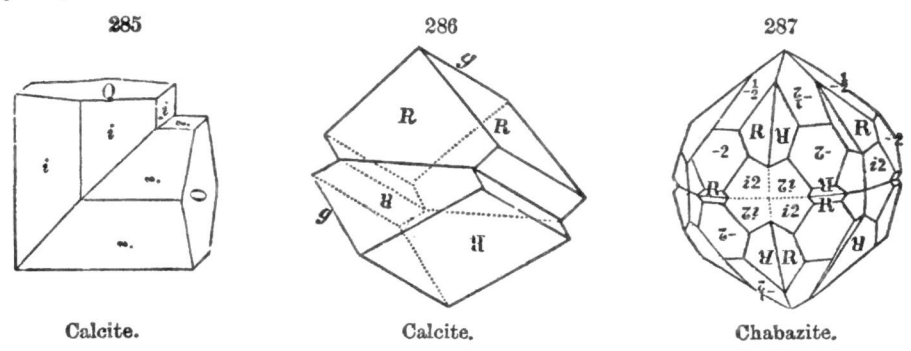

285   **286**   **287**

Calcite.   Calcite.   Chabazite.

In the species of the rhombohedral division twins are numerous; the ordinary methods are the following: the twinning-plane the rhombohedron R, f. 285; the rhombohedron $-2R$, f. 288; the rhombohedron $-\frac{1}{2}R$, f. 286. The last mentioned method is common in masses of calcite, where by its frequent repetition it gives rise to thin lamellæ; these are observed often in crystalline limestones. (See p. 173.)

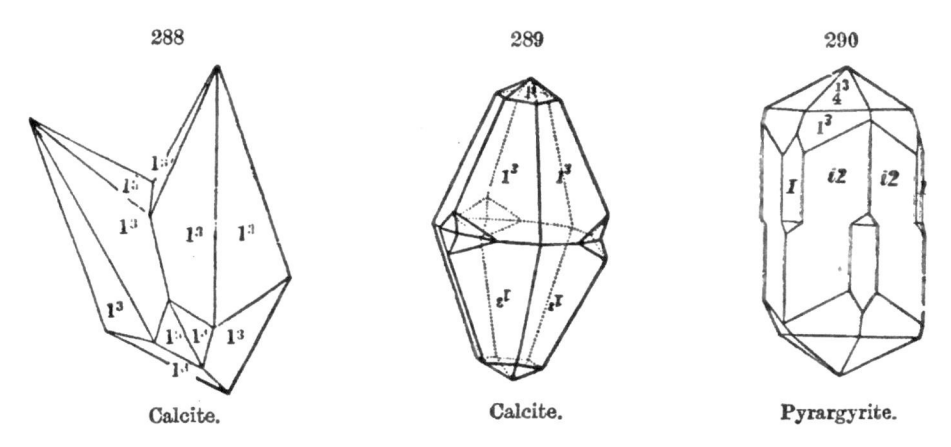

288   **289**   **290**

Calcite.   Calcite.   Pyrargyrite.

The twinning-plane may also be the basal plane, the axis of revolution consequently the vertical axis. This is illustrated in f. 287, a complex penetration twin of chabazite, also f. 267 (hematite), and in f. 289, 290. It is also common with quartz, the two crystals sometimes distinct, and joined by a prismatic plane, sometimes interpenetrating each other very irregularly, as shown in f. 265.

---

* G. vom Rath, Pogg. Ann., cxxxv. 437; clii. 1.

ORTHORHOMBIC SYSTEM.—In the orthorhombic system twins are exceedingly common, and the variety of methods is very great. These may, however, be brought into two groups, according as the twinning-plane is (1) a prismatic plane, vertical or horizontal, or (2) an octahedral plane. The twinning is very often repeated, and always in accordance with the law already stated, that the number of individuals is determined by the number of times that the angle of the two axial systems is contained in 360°.

(*a*) Twinning parallel to a prism whose angle is approximately 120°.

1. *Prism vertical.*—The principal examples are aragonite, $I \wedge I = 116°$ 10'; cerussite, $I \wedge I = 117° 13'$; witherite, $I \wedge I = 118° 30'$; bromlite, $I \wedge I = 118° 50'$; chalcocite, $I \wedge I = 119° 35'$; stephanite, $I \wedge I = 115° 39'$; dyscrasite, $I \wedge I = 119° 59'$. Figs. 291, 292, represent twins of aragonite in accordance with this law. Figs. 293, 294, show cross-sections of the two prisms of the preceding figures, in the latter the form is hexagonal, though not regularly so. Fig. 295 is a cruciform twin of the same species.

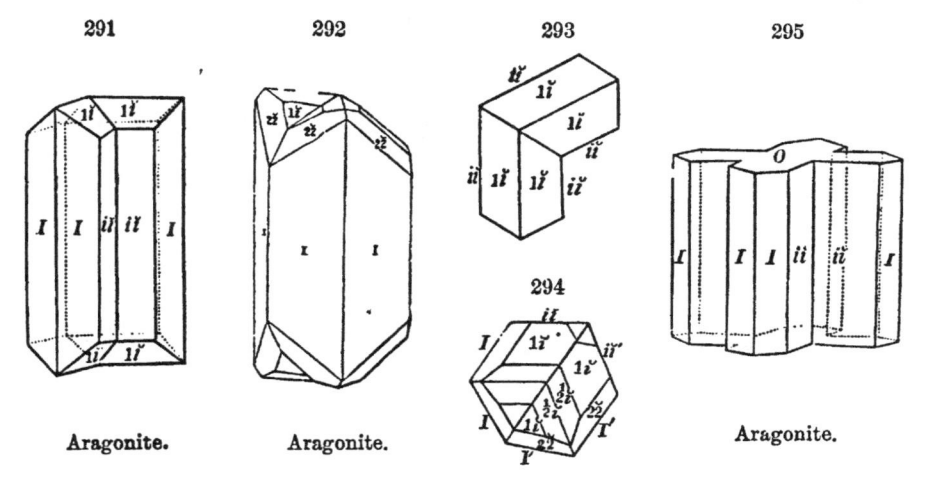

291   292   293   295

Aragonite.   Aragonite.   294   Aragonite.

2. *Prism horizontal*; that is, a macrodome.—Examples: arsenopyrite, $1\text{-}\bar{\imath} \wedge 1\text{-}\bar{\imath} = 120° 46'$; leadhillite, $1\text{-}\bar{\imath} \wedge 1\text{-}\bar{\imath} = 119° 20'$; humite, type I.

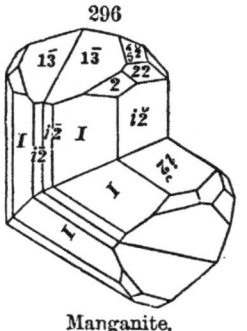

296

3. *Prism horizontal*; that is, a brachydome.—Examples: manganite, $1\text{-}\breve{\imath} \wedge 1\text{-}\breve{\imath} = 122° 50'$ (f. 296); chrysoberyl, $3\,\breve{\imath} \wedge 3\text{-}\breve{\imath}$ (f. 300) $= 120° 13'$; columbite, $2\text{-}\breve{\imath} \wedge 2\text{-}\breve{\imath} = 117° 20'$.

In all these cases there is a strong tendency toward repetition of the twinning, by which forms often stellate, sometimes apparently hexagonal, result. These forms are illustrated in the following figures: f. 297 is of witherite; f. 298 a crystal of leadhillite, in its twinned form of very rhombohedral aspect. Figs. 299 and 300 are both chrysoberyl, where $3\text{-}\breve{\imath}$ is the twinning-plane; six-rayed twins are very common in this species.

Manganite.

The genesis of these forms is further illustrated by the following cross-

TWIN CRYSTALS.

sections. Fig. 301 shows a cross-section of a cerussite twin, and f. 302 one of the crystal of leadhillite figured above (f. 298).

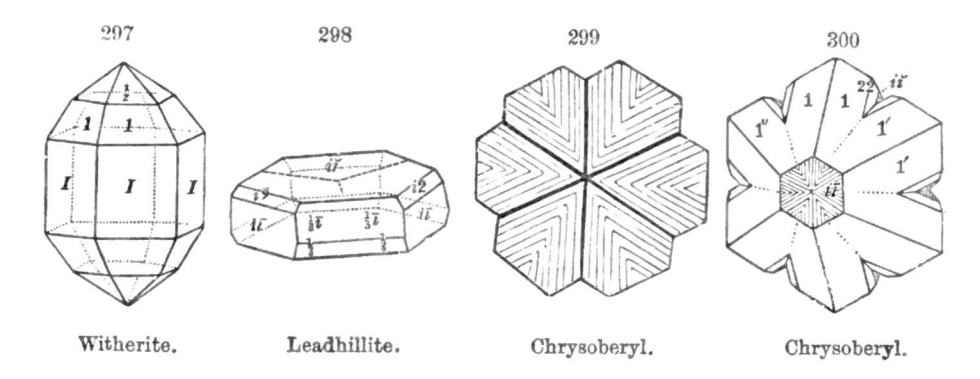

297 — Witherite. 298 — Leadhillite. 299 — Chrysoberyl. 300 — Chrysoberyl.

In f. 303, three rhombic prisms, I, of aragonite, are combined about their acute angles, the dotted lines showing the outlines of the prisms, and the cross lining the direction of the brachydiagonal; and in f. 304, four are similarly united. In f. 305, three similar prisms, I, are combined about the

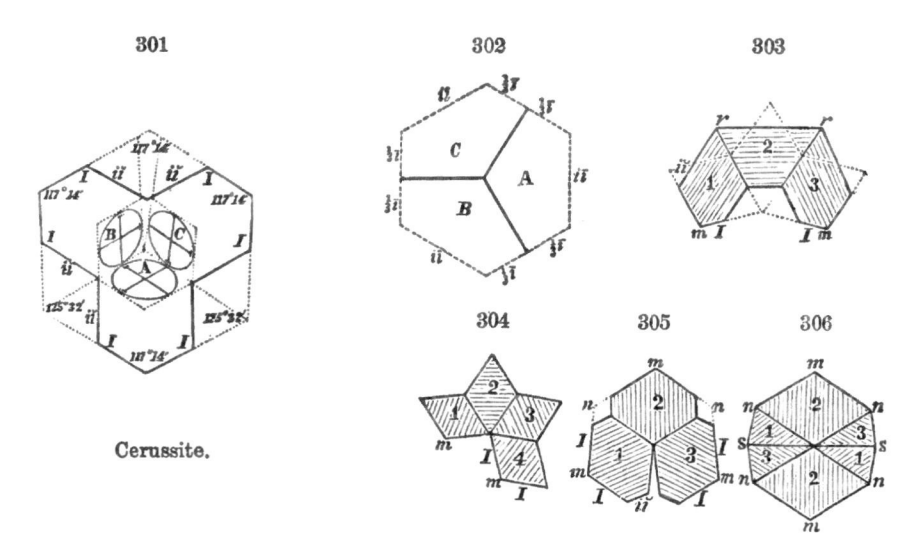

301 — Cerussite. 302. 303. 304. 305. 306.

obtuse angle. This twin combination may take the form of a hexagonal prism, with or without re-entering angles; of a three-rayed twin, like f. 301, and if a penetration-twin, of a composite prism, like f. 306 (the numbering of the parts showing the relation), or a six-rayed twin. In all these cases the stellate form depends on the extension of the individuals beyond the normal limits.

(*b*) Prismatic angle approximately that of the regular octahedron, 109° 28′. An example is furnished by the species staurolite (f. 307), where th twinning-plane is $i\text{-}\breve{\tfrac{3}{2}}$, and the corresponding prismatic angle is 109° 14' (over $i\text{-}\breve{\imath}$, or 70° 46' over $i\text{-}\bar{\imath}$). Another example is furnished by marcasite, whose prismatic angle is 106° 5'. The twins are generally compound, the repetition with the twinning-plane sometimes parallel, sometimes oblique, see p. 247. In f. 308 the compound crystal consists of five individuals, since five times 73° 55' is approximately equal to 360°.

Staurolite. Marcasite.

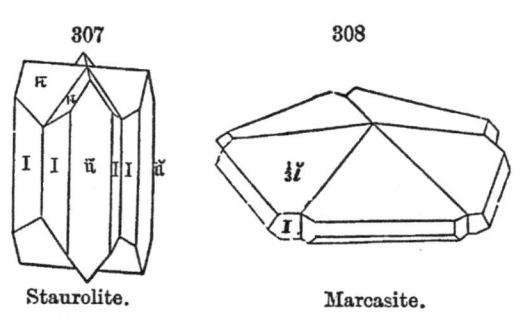

(c) Prismatic angle approximately 90°. Examples are furnished by bournonite, $I \wedge I = 91°\ 12'$, see p. 254, and staurolite. In the latter case the twinning-plane is a brachydome, $\tfrac{3}{2}\text{-}\breve{\imath}$, and the angle is 91° 18'; the form is shown in f. 309, it being that of a nearly rectangular cross. See also phillipsite, p. 345.

2. The twinning-plane may be also an octahedral plane. An excellent example is furnished by staurolite, where the twinning-plane is $\tfrac{3}{2}\text{-}\breve{\tfrac{3}{2}}$ (f. 310). The crystals cross at angles of nearly 120° and 60°, hence the form in f. 311, consisting of three individuals (trilling) forming a six-rayed star. In f. 312 both this method of twinning and that mentioned above are com-

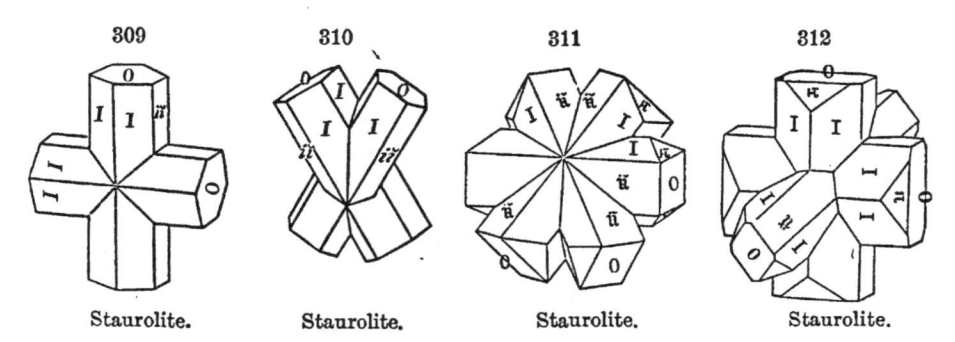

Staurolite. Staurolite. Staurolite. Staurolite.

bined. There are thus for the species staurolite three methods of twinning, parallel to $i\text{-}\breve{\tfrac{3}{2}}$, to $\tfrac{3}{2}\text{-}\breve{\imath}$, and to $\tfrac{3}{2}\text{-}\breve{\tfrac{3}{2}}$. If the occurring prism is made $i\text{-}\breve{\tfrac{3}{2}}$, then the three twinning-planes become I, 1-$\breve{\imath}$, 1, or fundamental planes, as is usually true.

MONOCLINIC SYSTEM.—The following examples comprise the more commonly occurring methods of twinning in this system.

(a) The twinning-plane is the orthopinacoid ($i\text{-}\bar{\imath}$). This is true in the case of the common twins of orthoclase (f. 318), called the *Carlsbad twins*. The axis of revolution is normal to $i\text{-}\bar{\imath}$ (see also p. 90), while the two crystals are united by the clinopinacoid, which is consequently the composition-face. These twins may be either right- or left-handed (f. 318 or f. 319), according as the right or left half of the simple form (f. 317) has been revolved.

Fig. 313, of pyroxene, is another familiar example; so also f. 314, of which f. 315 is the simple form. Fig. 320 is a twin of scolecite, where the twin structure is shown by the striations on the clinopinacoid.

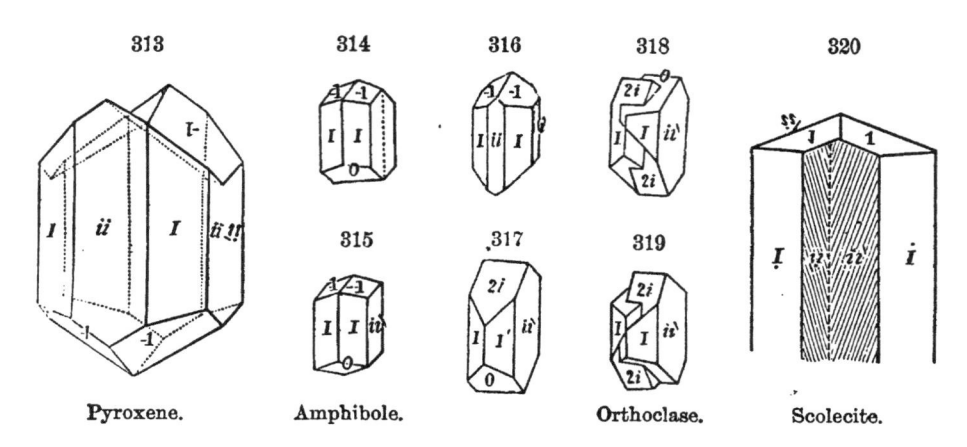

Pyroxene. Amphibole. Orthoclase. Scolecite.

A form of penetration-twin, with $i\cdot i$ the twinning-plane, is shown in f. 321 (from von Lang). The mode of combination and cross-penetration of the two crystals 1, 2, is illustrated in f. 322; it is a medial section of f. 321 from front to back.

(b) The twinning-plane may also be the basal plane. This is common with orthoclase (f. 324); also with gypsum (f. 323). It has also been observed by the author in chondrodite, type II and III, from Brewster, N. Y., see p. 305.

(c) Figs. 325, 326, 327 show another method of twinning of orthoclase parallel to the clinodome, $2\text{-}i$. These twins are peculiar in that they form nearly rectangular prisms, since $O \wedge 2\text{-}i = 135° \ 3\frac{1}{2}'$. They are common among the orthoclase crystals from Baveno, and hence are called *Baveno twins*. This method of twinning is also common with the amazon-stone of Pike's Peak.

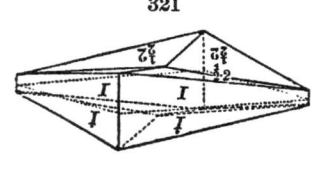

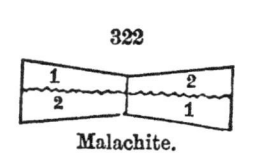

Malachite.

The union of four crystals of this kind produces the form represented in f. 325; and the same, by penetration, develops the penetration-twin of f. 327 (from v. Rath), which apparently consists of four pairs of twins, but may be regarded as made by the cross-penetration of the crystals of two pairs, or of the four of f. 325.

Forms like f. 325 may have one of the four parts undeveloped and so consist of three united crystals, and also the other parts, as in such compound twins generally, may be very unequal.

Twins corresponding to those of the orthorhombic system, where the twinning-plane is a prism whose angle is nearly 120°, have been observed by vom Rath in humite, types II and III.

TRICLINIC SYSTEM.—In the twins of the triclinic system, the three axes

100   CRYSTALLOGRAPHY.

may be axes of revolution, in which case the twinning-planes are not occurring crystallographic planes; or, the pinacoid planes may be the planes of twinning and the normals to them the axes of revolution. Some of the cases are illustrated in the following figures of albite. In f. 329 the brachy pinacoid (i-$\check{\imath}$) is the twinning-plane; f. 328 is the same, but it is a penetration-twin; this is the most common method of twinning with this species.

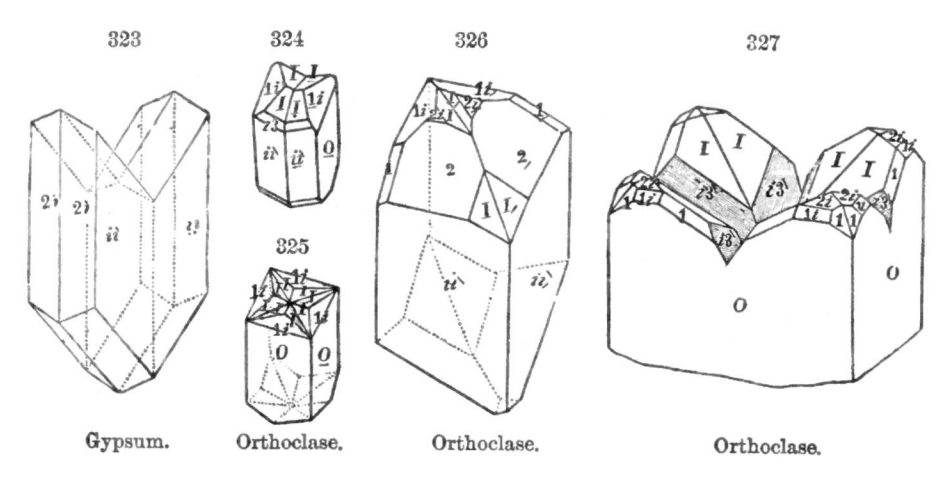

323   324   326   327
           325

Gypsum.   Orthoclase.   Orthoclase.   Orthoclase.

In f. 332 the vertical axis is the twinning-axis. Fig. 333 (from G. Rose) is a double twin, the two halves of which are like f. 328, but they are twinned together like f. 332. It happens in albite that the plane angles

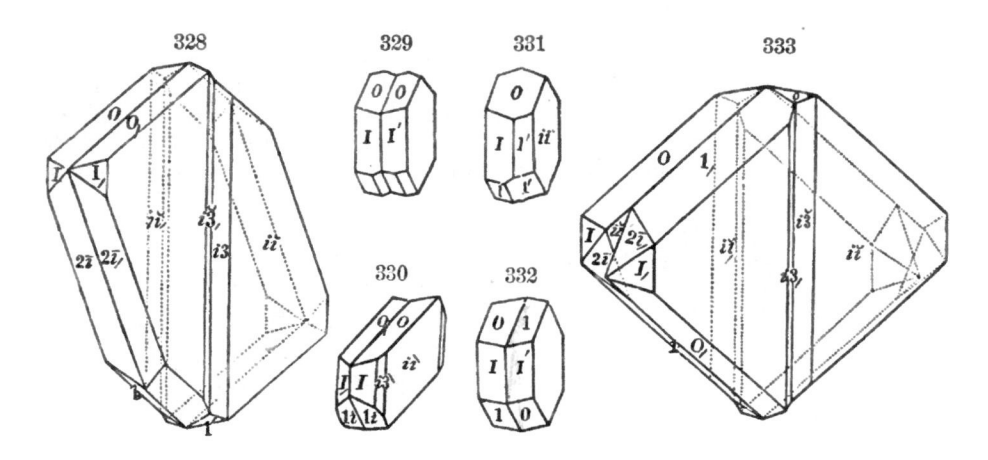

328   329   331   333
     330   332

on i-$\check{\imath}$, made by the edges $I \wedge O$ and $I \wedge 1$ differ but 37' (the former being 116° 26', the latter 115° 55'), and hence it is that in the twin O and 1 fall nearly into one plane.

TWIN CRYSTALS.   101

Composition parallel to O, where the revolution is on a horizontal axis normal to the shorter diagonal of O, is exemplified in f. 334 (from G. Rose). Both right- and left-handed twins of this kind occur; also double twins in which this method is *combined* with twinning (like that in f. 329, 330), parallel to $i\text{-}\check{\imath}$.

A thorough discussion of the method of twinning in the triclinic system has been given by Schrauf in his monograph of the species brochantite (Ber. Ak., Wien, lxvii., 275, 1873).

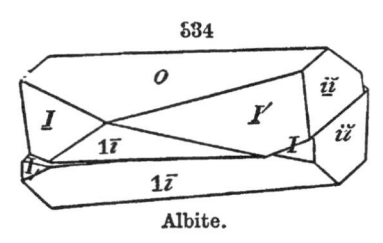

334

Albite.

REGULAR GROUPING OF CRYSTALS.

Connected with the subject of twin crystals is that of the parallel position of associated crystals of the same species, or of different species. Crystals of the same species occurring together are very commonly in parallel position. In this way large crystals are sometimes built up of smaller individuals grouped together with corresponding planes parallel. This parallel grouping is often seen in crystals as they lie on the supporting rock. On glancing the eye over a surface covered with crystals, a reflection from one face will often be accompanied with reflections from the corresponding face in each of the other crystals, showing that the crystals are throughout similar in their positions.

Crystals of different species often show the same tendency to parallelism in mutual position. This is true most frequently of species which, from similarity of form and composition, are said to be isomorphous (see p. 199). Crystals of albite, implanted on a surface of orthoclase, are sometimes an example of this; crystals of hornblende and pyroxene, and of various kinds of mica are also at times observed associated in parallel position.

The same relation of position also occasionally occurs where there is no connection in composition, as the crystals of rutile on tabular crystals of hematite, the vertical axes of the former coinciding with the lateral axes of the latter. Breithaupt has figured crystals of calcite, whose rhombo-

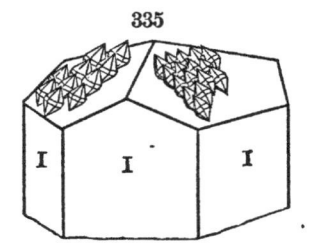

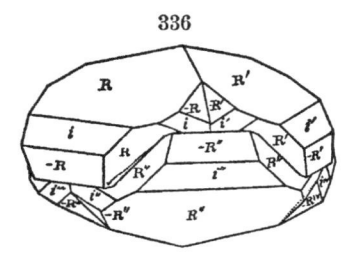

335

336

hedral faces ($-\frac{1}{2}R$) had a series of quartz crystals upon them, all in parallel position (f. 335); and Frenzel and vom Rath have described the same association where three such quartz crystals, one on each rhombohedral face, entirely enveloped the calcite, and uniting with re-entering angles formed pseudo-twins (rather trillings) of quartz after calcite. The author has described a similar occurrence from "Specimen Mountain," in the Yellowstone Park; the form is shown in f. 336. (Am. J. Sci., III., xii., 1876.)

IRREGULARITIES OF CRYSTALS.

The laws of crystallization, when unmodified by extrinsic causes, should produce forms of exact symmetry; the angles being not only equal, but also the homologous faces of crystals and the dimensions in the directions of like axes. This symmetry is, however, so uncommon, that it can hardly be considered other than an ideal perfection. Crystals are very generally distorted, and often the fundamental forms are so completely disguised, that an intimate familiarity with the possible irregularities is required in order to unravel their complexities. Even the angles may occasionally vary rather widely.

The irregularities of crystals may be treated of under several heads: 1, *Imperfections of surface;* 2, *Variations of form and dimensions;* 3, *Variations of angles;* 4, *Internal imperfections and impurities.*

I. IMPERFECTIONS IN THE SURFACES OF CRYSTALS.

1. *Striations or angular elevations arising from oscillatory combinations.*—The parallel lines or furrows on the surfaces of crystals are called *striæ*, and such surfaces are said to be *striated*.

Each little ridge on a striated surface is enclosed by two narrow planes more or less regular. These planes often correspond in position to different planes of the crystal, and we may suppose these ridges to have been formed by a continued oscillation in the operation of the causes that give rise, when acting uninterruptedly, to enlarged planes. By this means, the surfaces of a crystal are marked in parallel lines, with a succession of narrow planes meeting at an angle and constituting the ridges referred to.

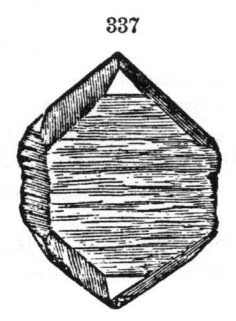

337

Magnetite.

This combination of different planes in the formation of a surface has been termed *oscillatory combination*. The horizontal striæ on prismatic crystals of quartz are examples of this combination, in which the oscillation has taken place between the prismatic and pyramidal planes. As the crystals lengthened, there was apparently a continual effort to assume the terminal pyramidal planes, which effort was interruptedly overcome by a strong tendency to an increase in the length of the prism. In this manner, crystals of quartz are often tapered to a point, without the usual pyramidal terminations.

Other examples are the striation on the cubic faces of pyrite parallel with the intersections of the cube with the planes of the pyritohedron; also the striations on magnetite (f. 337) due to the oscillation between the octahedron and dodecahedron.

Prisms of tourmaline are very commonly bounded vertically by three convex surfaces, owing to an oscillatory combination of the planes I and i-2.

Faces of crystals are often marked with angular elevations more or less distinct, due sometimes also to oscillatory combination. Octahedrons of fluorite are common which have for each face a surface of minute cubes, proceeding from an oscillation between the cube and octahedron. This is a common cause of *drusy* surfaces with the crystals of many minerals.

2. *Striations from oscillatory composition.*—The striations of the plane O of albite and other triclinic feldspars, and of the rhombohedral surfaces some calcite, have been attributed, on p. 91, to oscillatory twinning.

3. *Markings from erosion and other causes.*—It is not uncommon that the faces of crystals are uneven, or have the crystalline structure developed as a consequence of etching by some chemical agent. Cubes of galenite are often thus uneven, and crystals of lead sulphate or lead carbonate are sometimes present as evidence with regard to the cause. Crystals of numerous other species, even of corundum, spinel, quartz, etc., sometimes show the same result of partial change over the surface—often the incipient stage in a process tending to a final removal of the whole crystal. Interesting investigations have been made by various authors on the action of solvents on different minerals, the actual structure of the crystals being developed in this way. These are referred to again in another place (p. 122).

The markings on the surfaces of crystals are not, however, always to be ascribed to etching. In most cases etchings, as well as the minute angular elevations upon the planes, are a part of the original molecular growth of the crystal, and often serve to show the successive stages in its history. They are the imperfections arising from an interrupted or disturbed development of the form, the perfectly smooth and even crystalline faces being the result of completed action free from disturbing causes. Examples of the marking referred to occur on the crystals of most minerals, and conspicuously so on the pyramidal planes of quartz.

The development of this subject belongs rather to *crystallogeny*; reference may, however, be made here to the memoirs of Scharff, bearing on this subject, especially one entitled "Ueber den Quarz, II., die Uebergangsflächen," Frankfort, 1874; also to the Crystallography of Sadebeck (for title see Introduction).

It follows from the symmetry of crystallization that like planes should be physically alike, that is in regard to their surface character; it thus often happens that on all the crystals of a species from a given locality, or perhaps from all localities, the same planes are etched or roughened alike. For example, on crystals of datolite from Bergen Hill, the plane -2-i is almost uniformly destitute of lustre; there is much uniformity on the crystals of quartz in this respect.

4. *Curved surfaces* may result from (*a*) oscillatory combination; or (*b*) some independent molecular condition producing curvatures in the laminæ of the crystal; or (*c*) from a mechanical cause.

Curved surfaces of the first kind have been already mentioned, p. 102. A singular curvature of this nature is seen in f. 339, of calcite; and another in the same mineral in the lower part of f. 338, in which traces of a scalenohedral form are apparent which was in oscillatory combination with the prismatic form.

104 CRYSTALLOGRAPHY.

Curvatures of the *second* kind sometimes have all the faces convex. This is the case in crystals of diamond (f. 340), some of which are almost spheres. The mode of curvature, in which all the faces are equally convex, is less common than that in which a convex surface is opposite and parallel to a corresponding concave surface. Rhombohedrons of siderite (see p. 403) are usually thus curved. The feathery curves of frost on windows and the flagging stones of pavements in winter are other examples of curves of the second kind. The alabaster rosettes from the Mammoth Cave, Ky., are similar.

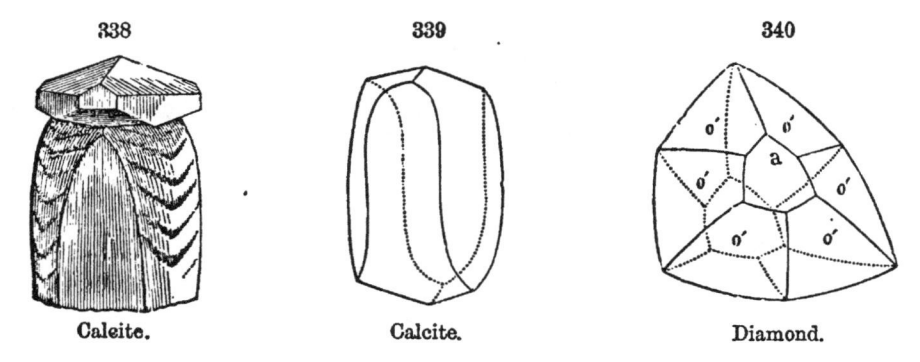

338　　　　　　　339　　　　　　　340

Calcite.　　　　Calcite.　　　　Diamond.

A *third* kind of curvature is of *mechanical origin*. In many species crystals appear as if they had been broken transversely into many pieces, a slight displacement of which has given a curved form to the prism. This is common in tourmaline and beryl. The beryls of Monroe, Conn., often present these interrupted curvatures, as represented in f. 341.

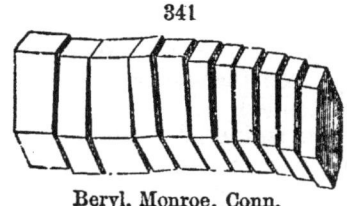

341

Beryl, Monroe, Conn.

Crystals not unfrequently occur with a deep pyramidal depression occupying the place of each plane, as is often observed in common salt, alum, and sulphur. This is due in part to their rapid growth.

II. Variations in the Forms and Dimensions of Crystals.

The simplest modification of form in crystals consists in a simple variation in length or breadth, without a disparity in similar secondary planes. The distortion, however, extends very generally to the secondary planes, especially when the elongation of a crystal takes place in the direction of a diagonal, instead of the crystallographic axes. In many instances, one or more planes are *obliterated* by the enlargement of others, proving a source of much perplexity to the student. The interfacial angles remain constant, unaffected by these variations in form. These changes in form often give rise to what is called by Sadebeck *pseudo-symmetry ;* the distorted forms of one system appearing similar to the normal forms of another. (Compare the descriptions of the following figures.) As most of the difficulties in the

---

* See p. 188 for another use of this word.

study of crystals arises from these distortions, this subject is one of great importance.

Figs. 342 to 353 represent examples from the isometric system.

A *cube* lengthened or shortened along one axis becomes a right square prism, and if varied in the direction of two axes is changed to a rectangular prism Cubes of pyrite, galenite, fluorite, etc., are generally thus distorted. It is very unusual to find a cubic crystal that is a true symmetrical cube. In some species the cube or octahedron (or other isometric form) is lengthened into a capillary crystal or needle, as happens in cuprite and pyrite.

An octahedron *flattened* parallel to a face, or in the direction of a trigonal interaxis, is reduced to a tabular crystal (f. 342). If *lengthened* in the same direction, it takes the form in f. 343; or if still farther lengthened to the obliteration of A', it becomes an acute rhombohedron (same figure).

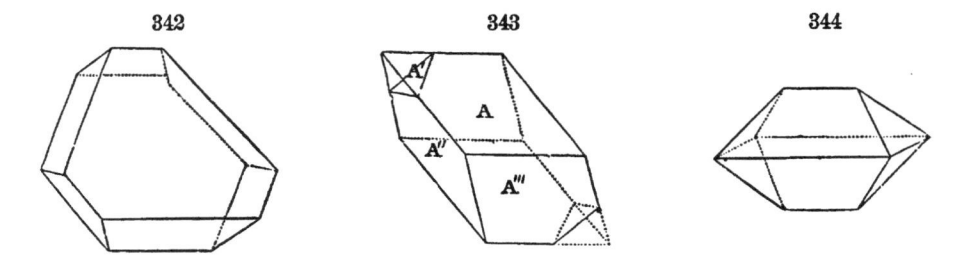

When an octahedron is extended in the direction of a line between two opposite edges, or that of a rhombic interaxis, it has the general form of a rectangular octahedron; and still farther extended, as in f. 344, it is changed to a rhombic prism with dihedral summits (spinel, fluorite, magnetite). The figure represents this prism lying on its acute edge.

The *dodecahedron* lengthened in the direction of a diagonal between the

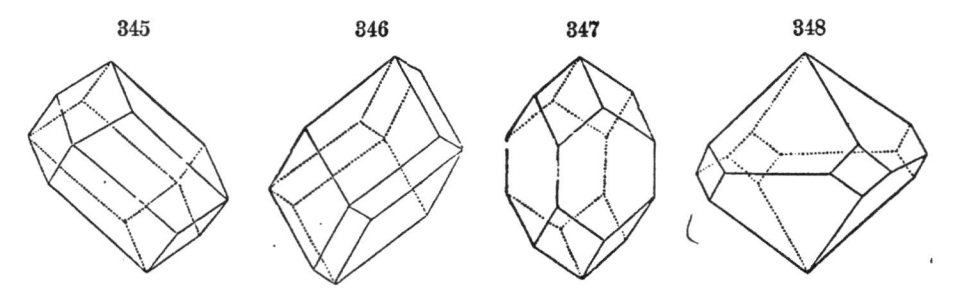

obtuse solid angles, that is, that of a trigonal interaxis, becomes a six-sided prism with three-sided summits, as in f. 345; and shortened in the same direction is a *short* prism of the same kind (f. 346). Both resemble rhombohedral forms and are common in garnet and zinc blende. When lengthened in the direction of one of the cubic axes, it becomes a square prism with pyramidal summits (f. 347), and shortened along the same axis it is reduced to a square octahedron, with truncated basal angles (f. 348).

The trapezohedron is still more disguised by its distortions. When elongated in the line of a trigonal interaxis, it assumes the form in f. 349; and still farther lengthened, to the obliteration of some of the planes, becomes a scalene dodecahedron (f. 350). This has been observed in fluor spar. Only twelve planes are here present out of the twenty-four. Threads of native gold from Oregon, are strings of crystals presenting the form of this very acute rhombohedron, with the other planes of the trapezohedron 2-2 (the scalenohedral and the terminal obtuse rhombohedral) quite small at the extremities.

If the elongation of the trapezohedron takes place along a cubic axis, it becomes a double eight-sided pyramid with four-sided summits (f. 351); or if these summit planes are obliterated by a farther extension, it becomes a complete eight-sided double pyramid (f. 352).

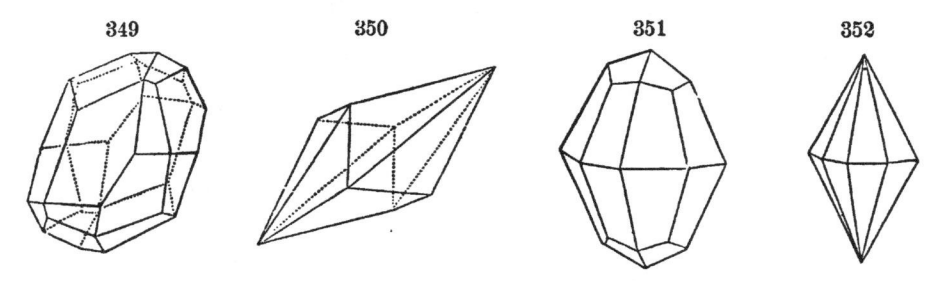

A scaleno-dodecahedron of calcite is shown distorted in f. 353, which appears, however, to be an eight-sided prism, bounded laterally by the planes R, 1^3, 1^3, and R, and their opposites, and terminated by the remaining planes. The following figures of quartz (f. 354, 355) represent distorted forms of this mineral, in which some of the pyramidal faces by enlargement displace the prismatic faces, and nearly obliterate some of the other pyramidal faces; see also f. 336.

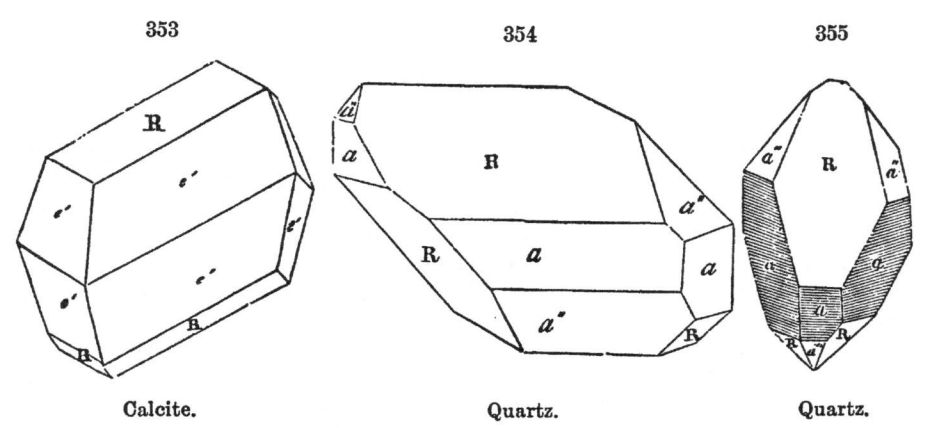

Calcite.　　　　Quartz.　　　　Quartz.

Fig. 356 is a distorted crystal of apatite; the same is shown in f. 357 with the normal symmetry. The planes between O and the right I are enlarged, while the corresponding planes below are in part obliterated.

By observing that similar planes are lettered alike, the correspondence of the two figures will be understood.

In deciphering the distorted crystalline forms it must be remembered that while the appearance of the crystals may be entirely altered, the angles remain the same; moreover, like planes are physically alike, that is, alike in degree of lustre, in striations, and so on.

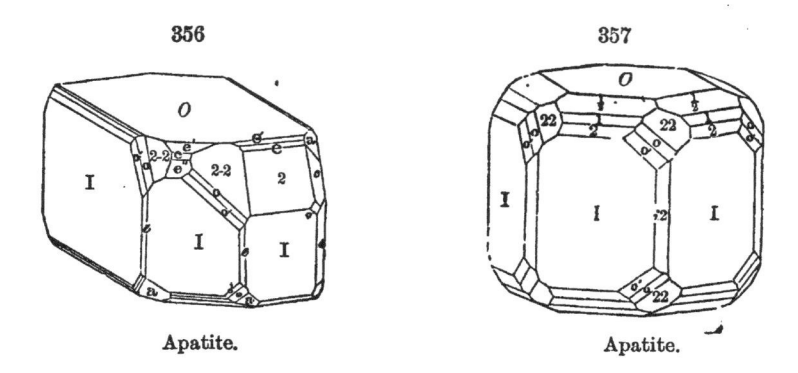

356

357

Apatite.

Apatite.

In addition to the variations in form which have just been described, still greater irregularities are due to the fact that, in almost all cases, crystals in nature are attached either to other crystals or to some rock surface, and in consequence of this are only partially developed. Thus quartz crystals are generally attached by an extremity of the prism, and hence have only one set of pyramidal planes; perfectly formed crystals, as those from Herkimer Co., N. Y., having the double pyramid complete, are rare. The same statement may be made for nearly all species.

III. Variations in the Angles of Crystals.

The greater part of the distortions described occasion no change in the interfacial angles of crystals. But those imperfections that produce convex, curved, or striated faces, necessarily cause such variations. Furthermore, circumstances of heat or pressure under which the crystals were formed may sometimes cause not only distortion in form, but also some variation in angle. The presence of impurities at the time of crystallization may also have a like effect.

Still more important is the change in the angles of completed crystals which is caused by subsequent pressure on the matrix in which they were formed, as, for example, the change which may take place during the more or less complete metamorphism of the enclosing rock.

The change of composition resulting in pseudomorphous crystals (see p. 113) is generally accompanied by an irregular change of angle, so that the pseudomorphs of a species vary much in angle.

In general it is safe to affirm that, with the exception of the irregularities arising from imperfections in the process of crystallization, or from changes produced subsequently, variations in the angles are rare, and the constancy of angle alluded to on p. 87 is the universal law.*

In cases where a greater or less variation in angle has been observed in the crystals of the same species from different localities, the cause for this can usually be found in a difference of chemical composition. In the case of isomorphous compounds it is well known that an exchange of corresponding chemically equivalent elements may take place without a change of form, though usually accompanied with a slight variation in the fundamental angles.

The effect of heat upon the form of crystals is alluded to upon p. 168.

IV. Internal Imperfections and Impurities.

The transparency of crystals is often destroyed by disturbed crystallization, or by impurities taken up from the solution during the process of crystallization. These impurities may be simply coloring ingredients, or they may be inclosed particles, fluid or solid, visible to the eye or under the microscope. The coloring ingredients may vary in the course of formation of the crystals, and thus layers of different colors result; the tourmaline crystals of Chesterfield, Mass., have a red centre and blue exterior; others from Elba are sometimes light-green below and black at the extremity; many other examples might be given.

The subject of the fluid and solid inclosures in crystals is one to which much attention has been directed of late years. Attention was early called to its importance by Brewster, who described the presence of fluids in quartz, topaz, beryl, chrysolite, and other minerals. In later years the matter has been more thoroughly studied by Sorby, Zirkel, Vogelsang, Fischer, Rosenbusch, and many others. (See Literature, p. 111.)

Many crystals contain empty cavities; in others the cavities are filled sometimes with water, or with the salt solution in which the crystal was formed, and not infrequently, especially in the case of quartz, with liquid carbonic acid, as first proved by Vogelsang, and recently followed out by Hartley. These liquid inclosures are marked as such, in many cases, by the presence in the cavity of a movable bubble.

The solid inclosures are almost infinite in their variety. Sometimes they are large and distinct, and can be referred to known mineral species, as the scales of hematite to which the peculiar character of aventurine feldspar is due. Magnetite is a very common impurity for many minerals, appearing, for example, in the Pennsbury mica; quartz is also often mechanically mixed, as in staurolite and gmelinite. On the other hand, quartz crystals very commonly inclose foreign material, such as chlorite, tourmaline, rutile, hematite, asbestos, and many other minerals.

---

* Reference must be made here to the discussion by Scacchi of the principle of "Polysymmetry." (Atti Accad. Napoli, i., 1864.) See also *Hirschwald*, Zur Kritik des Leucitsystems, Tsch. Min. Mitth., 1875, 227. See further the discussion on pp. 185 et seq.

IRREGULARITIES OF CRYSTALS.

The inclosures may also consist of a heterogeneous mass of material; as the granitic matter seen in orthoclase crystals in a porphyritic granite; or the feldspar, quartz, etc., sometimes inclosed in large coarse crystals of beryl, occurring in granite veins.

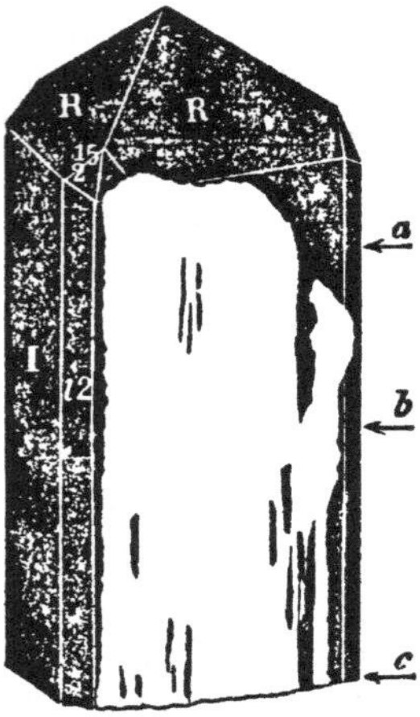

An interesting example of the inclosure of one mineral by another is afforded by the annexed figures of tourmaline, enveloping orthoclase (E. H. Williams, Am. J. Sci., III., xi., 273, 1876). Fig. 358 shows the crystal of tourmaline; and cross-sections of it at the points indicated (a, b, c) are given by f. 359, 360, 361. The latter show that the feldspar increases in amount in the lower part of the crystal, the tourmaline being merely a thin shell. Similar specimens from the same locality (Port Henry, Essex Co., N. Y.) show that there is no necessary connection between the position of the tourmaline and that of the feldspar.

Similar occurrences are those of trapezohedrons of garnet, where the latter is a mere shell, enclosing calcite, or sometimes epidote. Analogous cases have been explained by some authors as being due to partial pseudomorphism, the alteration progressing from the centre outward.

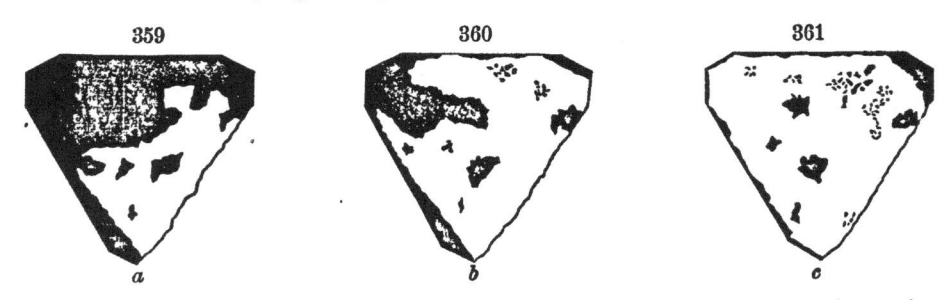

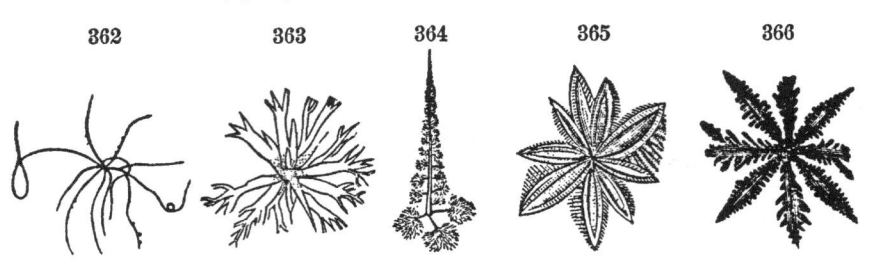

The microscopic crystals observed as inclosures may sometimes be referred to known species, but more generally their true nature is doubtful. The term *microlites*, proposed by Vogelsang, is often used to designate the minute inclosed crystals; they are generally of needle-like form, sometimes quite irregular, and often very remarkable in their arrangement and groupings; some of them are exhibited in f. 367 and f. 368, as explained below. Trichite and belonite are names introduced by Zirkel; the former name is derived from θρίξ, *hair*, the forms, like that in f. 362, are common in obsidian. Where the minute individuals belong to known species they are called, for example, feldspar microlites, etc.

Crystallites is an analogous term which is intended by Vogelsang to cover those minute forms which have not the regular exterior form of crystals, but may be considered as intermediate between amorphous matter and true crystals. Some of the forms, figured by Vogelsang, are shown in f. 363 to 366; they are often observed in glassy volcanic rocks, and also in furnace slags. A series of names have been given to varieties of crystallites, such as globulites, margarites, etc.*

The microscopic inclosures may also be of an irregular glassy nature; a kind that exists in crystals which have formed from a melted mass, as lavas or the slag of iron furnaces.

In general, it may be said that while the solid inclosures occur sometimes quite irregularly in the crystals, they are more generally arranged with some evident reference to the symmetry of the form, or planes of the crystals. Examples of this are shown in the following figures: f. 367 ex

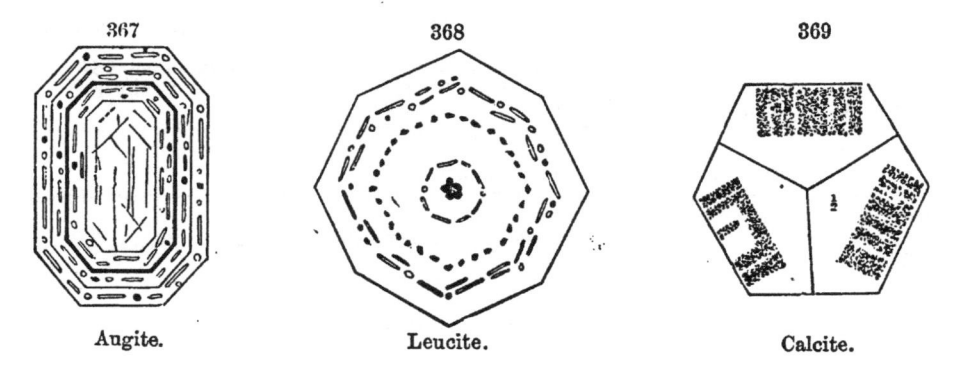

367   368   369
Augite.   Leucite.   Calcite.

hibits a crystal of augite, inclosing magnetite, feldspar and nephelite microlites, etc., and f. 368 shows a crystal of leucite, a species whose crystals very commonly inclose foreign matter. Fig. 369 shows a section of a crystal of calcite, containing pyrite.

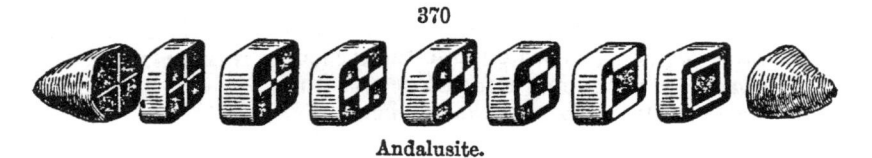

370
Andalusite.

Another striking example is afforded by andalusite, in which the inclosed impurities are of considerable extent and remarkably arranged. Fig. 370 shows the successive parts of a single crystal, as dissected by B. Horsford

---

* Die Krystalliten von Hermann Vogelsang. Bonn, 1875.

of Springfield, Mass.; 371, one of the four white portions; and 372, the central black portion.

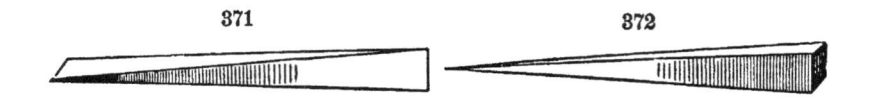

Literature.

Some of the most important works on the subject are referred to here, but for a complete list of the literature up to 1873, reference may be made to Rosenbusch (see below).

Blum, Leonhard, Seyfert, and *Söchting*, die Einschlüsse von Mineralien in krystallisirten Mineralien. (Preisschrift.) Haarlem, 1854.

Brewster. Many papers published mostly in the Philosophical Magazine, and the Edinburgh Phil. Journal, from 1822-1856.

Fischer. Kritische-microscopische mineralogische Studien. Freiburg in Br., 64 pp., 1869; 1te Fortsetzung, 64 pp., 1871; 2te Forts., 96 pp., 1873.

Kosmann. Ueber das Schillern und den Dichroismus des Hypersthens. Jahrb. Min., 1869, 368 (ibid. p. 532, 1871, p. 501).

Rosenbusch. Microscopische Physiographie der petrographisch wichtigen Mineralien. 395 pp., Leipzig, 1873

Schrauf. Studien an der Mineralspecies Labradorit. Ber. Ak. Wien, lx., Dec., 1869.

Sorby. On the microscopical structure of crystals, indicating the origin of minerals and rocks. Q. J. Geol. Soc., xiv., 453, 1858, (and many other papers).

Sorby and *Butler.* On the structure of rubies, sapphires, diamonds, and some other minerals. Proc. Roy. Soc., No. 109, 1869.

Vogelsang. Die Krystalliten. 175 pp., Bonn, 1875.

Vogelsang and *Geissler.* Ueber die Natur der Flüssigkeitseinschlüsse in gewissen Mineralien. Pogg. Ann., cxxxvii., 56, 1869 (ibid. p. 257).

Zirkel. Die microscopische Beschaffenheit der Mineralien und Gesteine. 502 pp., Leipzig, 1873.

CRYSTALLINE AGGREGATES.

The greater part of the specimens or masses of minerals that occur, may be described as aggregations of imperfect crystals. Even those whose structure appears the most purely impalpable, and the most destitute internally of anything like crystallization, are probably composed of crystalline grains. Under the above head, consequently, are included all the remaining varieties of structure in the mineral kingdom.

The individuals composing imperfectly crystallized individuals, may be:
1. *Columns, or fibres*, in which case the structure is *columnar*.
2. *Thin laminæ*, producing a *lamellar* structure.
3. *Grains*, constituting a *granular* structure.

1. *Columnar Structure.*

A mineral possesses a columnar structure when it is made up of slender columns or fibres. There are the following varieties of the columnar structure:

Fibrous : when the columns or fibres are parallel. Ex. gypsum, asbestus Fibrous minerals have often a silky lustre.

Reticulated : when the fibres or columns cross in various directions, and produce an appearance having some resemblance to a net.

Stellated or *stellular :* when they radiate from a centre in all directions, and produce star-like forms. Ex. stilbite, wavellite.

Radiated, divergent : when the crystals radiate from a centre, without producing stellar forms. Ex. quartz, stibnite.

2. *Lamellar Structure.*

The structure of a mineral is lamellar when it consists of plates or leaves. The laminæ may be curved or straight, and thus give rise to the *curved* lamellar, and *straight* lamellar structure. Ex. wollastonite (tabular spar), some varieties of gypsum, talc, etc. When the laminæ are thin and easily separable, the structure is said to be foliaceous. Mica is a striking example, and the term *micaceous* is often used to describe this kind of structure.

3. *Granular Structure.*

The particles in a granular structure differ much in size. When coarse, the mineral is described as *coarsely granular ;* when fine, *finely granular ;* and if not distinguishable by the naked eye, the structure is termed *impalpable*. Examples of the first may be observed in granular crystalline limestone, sometimes called saccharoidal; of the second, in some varieties of hematite ; of the last, in chalcedony, opal, and other species.

The above terms are indefinite, but from necessity, as there is every degree of fineness of structure in the mineral species, from perfectly impalpable, through all possible shades, to the coarsest granular. The term *phanero-crystalline* has been used for varieties in which the grains are distinct, and *crypto-crystalline*, for those in which they are not discernible.

Granular minerals, when easily crumbled in the fingers, are said to be *friable*.

4. *Imitative Shapes.*

Reniform : kidney shape. The structure may be radiating or concentric.

Botryoidal : consisting of a group of rounded prominences. The name is derived from the Greek βοτρυς, *a bunch of grapes*. Ex. limonite, chalcedony.

Mammillary : resembling the botryoidal, but composed of larger prominences.

Globular : spherical or nearly so ; the globules may consist of radiating fibres or concentric coats. When attached, as they usually are, to the surface of a rock, they are described as *implanted globules*.

Nodular : in tuberose forms, or having irregular protuberances over the surface.

Amygdaloidal : almond-shaped, applied usually to a greenstone containing almond-shaped or sub-globular nodules.

Coralloidal: like coral, or consisting of interlaced flexuous branchings of a white color, as in some aragonite.

Dendritic: branching tree-like.

Mossy: like moss in form or appearance.

Filiform or *Capillary:* very slender and long, like a thread or hair; consists ordinarily of a succession of minute crystals.

Acicular: slender and rigid like a needle.

Reticulated: net-like.

Drusy: closely covered with minute implanted crystals.

Stalactitic: when the mineral occurs in pendant columns, cylinders, or elongated cones.

Stalactites are produced by the percolation of water, holding mineral matter in solution, through the rocky roofs of caverns. The evaporation of the water produces a deposit of the mineral matter, and gradually forms a long pendant cylinder or cone. The internal structure may be imperfectly crystalline and granular, or may consist of fibres radiating from the central column, or there may be a broad cross-cleavage.

Common stalactites consist of calcium carbonate. Chalcedony, gibbsite, brown iron ore, and many other species, also present stalactitic forms.

The term *amorphous* is used when a mineral has not only no crystalline form or imitative shape, but also does not polarize the light even in its minute particles, and thus appears to be destitute wholly of a crystalline structure internally, as most opal. Such a structure is also called *colloid* or jelly-like, from the Greek for glue. Whether there is a total absence of crystalline structure in the molecules is a debated point. The word is from a, *privative*, and μόρφη, shape.

PSEUDOMORPHOUS CRYSTALS.

Every true mineral species has, when crystallized, a form peculiar to itself; occasionally, however, crystals are found that have the form, both as to angles and general habit, of a certain species, and yet differ from it entirely in chemical composition. Moreover it is often seen that, though in outward form complete crystals, in internal structure they are granular, or waxy, and have no regular cleavage.

Such crystals are called *pseudomorphs*, and their existence is explained by the assumption, often admitting of direct proof, that the original mineral has been changed into the new compound, or has disappeared through some agency, and its place been taken by another chemical compound to which the form does not belong.

Pseudomorphs have been classed under several heads.

1. Pseudomorphs by *substitution*.
2. Pseudomorphs by simple *deposition*, (*a*) *incrustation* or (*b*) *infiltration*.
3. Pseudomorphs by *alteration*; and these may be altered
    (*a*) without a change of composition, by paramorphism;
    (*b*) by the loss of an ingredient;
    (*c*) by the assumption of a foreign substance;
    (*d*) by a partial exchange of constituents.

1. The first class of pseudomorphs, by *substitution*, embrace those cases where there has been a gradual removal of the original material and a corresponding and simultaneous replacement of it by another, without, however, any chemical reaction between the two. A common example of this is a piece of fossilized wood, where the original fibre has been replaced entirely by silica. The first step in the process was the filling of all the pores and cavities by the silica in solution, and then as the woody fibre by gradual decomposition disappeared, the silica further took its place. Other examples are quartz after fluorite, calcite, and many other species, cassiterite after orthoclase, etc.

2. Pseudomorphs by *incrustation*, form a less important class. Such are the crusts of quartz formed over fluorite. In most cases the removal of the original mineral has gone on simultaneously with the deposit of the second, so that the resulting pseudomorph is properly one of substitution. In pseudomorphs by *infiltration*, a cavity made by the removal of a crystal has been filled by another mineral.

3. The third class of pseudomorphs, by *alteration*, include a considerable proportion of the observed cases, of which the number is very large. Conclusive evidence of the change which has gone on is often furnished by a kernel of the original mineral in the centre of the altered crystal; *e.g.*, a kernel of cuprite in a pseudomorphous octahedron of malachite; also of chrysolite in a pseudomorphous crystal of serpentine; of corundum in fibrolite, or spinel (Genth).

(*a*) An example of paramorphism is furnished by the change of aragonite to calcite at a certain temperature; also the *paramorphs* of rutile after arkansite from Magnet Cove.

(*b*) An example of the pseudomorphs in which alteration is accompanied by a loss of ingredients is furnished by crystals of limonite in the form of siderite, the carbonic acid having been removed; so also calcite after gay-lussite; native copper after cuprite.

(*c*) In the change of cuprite to malachite, *e.g.*, the familiar crystals from Chessy, France, an instance is afforded of the assumption of an ingredient, viz., carbonic acid. Pseudomorphs of gypsum after anhydrite occur, where there has been an assumption of water.

(*d*) A partial exchange of constituents, in other words, a loss of one and gain of another, takes place in the change of feldspar to kaolin, in which the potash silicate disappears and water is taken up; pseudomorphs of chlorite after garnet, pyromorphite after galenite, are other examples.

The chemical processes involved in such changes open a wide field for investigation, in which Bischof, Delesse and others have done much.

SECTION I.—SUPPLEMENTARY CHAPTER.

IMPROVEMENTS IN THE INSTRUMENTS FOR THE MEASUREMENT OF THE ANGLES OF CRYSTALS (see pp. 83–87).

Reflecting Goniometer.—A form of reflecting goniometer, well adapted for accurate measurements, and at the same time thoroughly practical, is shown in f. 372A. It is made on the Babinet type, with a horizontal graduated circle; the instruments of the Mitscherlich type, alluded to on p. 86, having a vertical circle. The horizontal circle has many advantages, especially when it is desired to measure the angles of large crystals or those which are

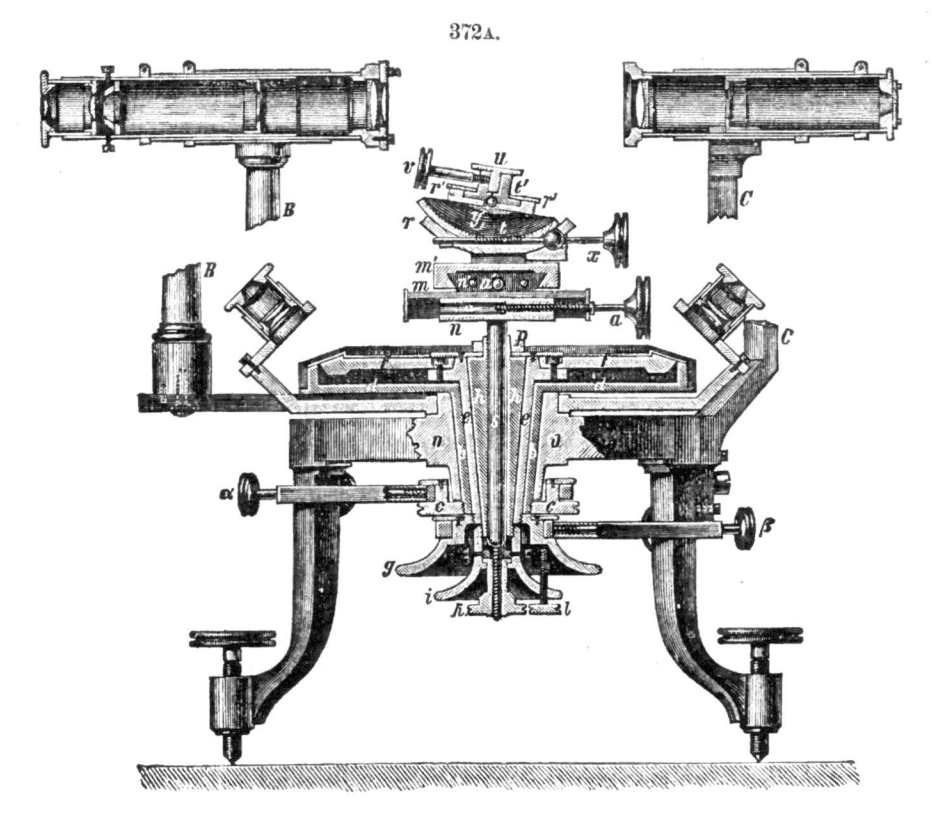

372A.

attached to a large piece of rock. This particular form of instrument here figured is made by R. Fuess,* in Berlin (Alte Jacobstrasse 108), and has

---

* The author is indebted to R. Fuess for the electrotypes from which this and the following figures (372A, B, C, D, also, f. 412C, D, E, F, H, K, L) have been printed.

many improvements suggested by WEBSKY (Zeitschr. Kryst., iv., 545, 1880. See also Liebisch, Bericht über die wissenschaftlichen Instrumente auf der Berliner Gewerbeausstellung im Jahre 1879, pp. 330–332).

The instrument stands on a tripod with leveling screws. The central axis, o, has within it a hollow axis, b, with which turns the plate, d, carrying the verniers and also the observing telescope, the upright support of which is shown at B. Within b is a second hollow axis, e, which carries the graduated circle, f, above, and which is turned by the screw-head, g; the tangent screw, α, serves as a fine adjustment for the observing telescope, B, the screw, c, being for this purpose raised so as to bind b and e together. The tangent screw, β, is a fine adjustment for the graduated circle. Again, within e is the third axis, h, turned by the screw-head, i, and within h is the central rod, s, which carries the support for the crystal, with the adjusting and centering contrivances mentioned below. The rod, s, can be raised or lowered by the screw, h, so as to bring the crystal to the proper height, that is up to the axis of the telescope; when this has been accomplished, the clamp at p, turned by a set-key, binds s to the axis, h. The movement of h can take place independently of g, but after the crystal is ready for measurement these two axes are bound together by the set-screw, l. The signal telescope is supported at C, firmly attached to one of the legs of the tripod. The crystal is mounted on the plate, u, with wax, the plate is clamped by the screw, v. The centering apparatus consists of two slides at right angles to each other (one of these is shown in the figure) and the screw, a, which works it; the end of the other corresponding screw is seen at a'. The adjusting arrangement consists of two cylindrical sections, one of them, r, shown in the figure, the other is at r'; the cylinders have a common centre.

The circle is graduated to degrees and quarter degrees, and the vernier gives the readings to 30'', but by estimate they can be obtained to 10''. The signals provided are four in number, each in its own tube, to be inserted behind the collimator lens; these are: (1) the ordinary telescope with the hair cross, to be used in the case of the most perfect planes; (2) the commonly used signal,* proposed by Websky, consisting of two small opaque circles, whose distance apart can be adjusted by a screw between them; the light passing between these circles enters the tube in a form resembling a double concave lens; also (3) an adjustable slit; and, finally, (4) a tube with a single round opening, very small. There are four observing telescopes of different angular breadth of field and magnifying power, and hence suitable for planes varying in size and in degree of polish. A Nicol prism is also added.

The methods to be employed, both in making the preliminary adjustments required by every instrument before it can be used, and in the actual measurement of the angles of crystals, have been described by Websky (l. c.) with a fullness and clearness which leaves nothing to be desired, and reference must be here made to this memoir.

Microscope-Goniometer of Hirschwald.—For the measurement of the angles of crystals whose planes are destitute of polish, HIRSCHWALD has devised a "microscope-goniometer" (Jahrb. Min., 1879, 301, 539; 1880, i., 156.— See also Liebisch, l. c., pp. 336, 377); the actual construction has been made by Fuess. The instrument consists of a Wollaston goniometer with a centering telescope and a vertical microscope. The principle upon which the use of the instrument is based is this: that a plane seen through a microscope

---

* See Websky, Z. Kryst., iii., 241.

will be in focus over its entire extent only when the plane is exactly at right angles to the axis of the microscope. The microscope stands vertically above the crystal, and is supported on a double slide, which allows of its being moved parallel and perpendicular to the axis of the goniometer, so that it is possible to see successively every portion of a crystal face fastened to the goniometer, and at the proper focal distance. The slide perpendicular to the axis of the goniometer carries a vernier, so that the position of the microscope can be measured on the fixed scale to a half millimeter. The micrometer screw of the microscope is arranged so that the raising or lowering of the microscope can be measured to 0·004 mm. The spider line in the eye-piece, parallel to the axis of rotation of the goniometer, is so adjusted that when the slide just mentioned stands at the zero of its scale, it lies exactly in the vertical plane through the axis. The horizontal centering telescope is placed opposite the crystal support, and moves on a slide parallel to the axis of the graduated circle. Its spider lines are so adjusted that their centre exactly coincides with this axis. The apparatus for centering and adjusting the crystal consists of a vertical disk allowing of motion in any direction perpendicular to the axis of rotation, and a spherical segment moved by four arms (Petzval support). In use the edge of the two planes to be measured is brought by means of the spider line of the microscope parallel to the axis of rotation of the goniometer, and there centered, by means of the telescope, so that as the crystal is turned this edge remains in the centre of the spider line of the centering telescope; then the two planes which form this edge are, by successive adjustments by help of the microscope, brought each successively into an exactly horizontal position as the circle is revolved. The angle (normal angle) between the two planes is obtained in the usual manner. Hirschwald calculates that, with a sufficiently delicate arrangement of lenses, for planes whose width is 5 mm., the theoretical error of measurement is 2′ 40″; for those with a width of 10 mm., the error is only 1′. The improved support for the crystal is so arranged that when the edge is exactly adjusted and one of the two planes carefully placed with the microscope, the second plane must be for its whole extent in the proper position as soon as this is true for a single point of the plane.

Contact-lever Goniometer of Fuess.— Another form of goniometer has been invented by FUESS (see Liebisch, l. c., pp. 337–339) which aims to accomplish the same end as that of Hirschwald — the exact measurement of the angle between two unpolished surfaces — but in this case the adjustment is accomplished by mechanical means. The essential arrangement is shown in f. 372B, 372C. It consists of a Wollaston goniometer, G, supported upon a perfectly even unpolished glass plate, *A*. The contact-lever is carried by *B*, which rests on the glass plate by two pegs, *o*, and by the screw, *n*, with a graduated head turning in connection with the index, *y*. Two arms, *FF*, go down from *B*, carrying the nut in which the screw, *r*, turns; this screw moves *B* in a direction at right angles to the axis of the goniometer. The arm, *D*, contains the nut for the adjusting screw, *m* (similar to *n*), which belongs immediately to the lever system. On the arm *C* is attached the knife edge, *l*, which meets the edge, *c*, fastened to the arm, *i*; this arm, *i*, turns about *a*, and is supported by the screw, *m*. The adjustable ball, *b*, supported on *t*, is to be placed so that the ivory index rests with the least possible pressure on the crystal-face at *K* (see also f. 372c). The contact-lever, *E*, whose longer arm marks on the scale, *S*, lies between *l* and *c*; its head, *d*, is so to be adjusted that the lever resting on the lower edge, *c*, has a slight excess of weight on the side of the goniometer, so that it touches both edges. A perceptible play of the long arm corresponds to a raising or lowering of the ivory index of 0·0005 mm. If the plane has a width of 1 mm., the degree of accuracy attainable is theoretically 2'.

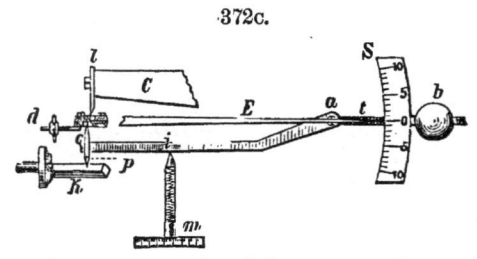

In the preliminary centering and adjusting the work is facilitated by the arrangement shown in f. 372D. It consists of a plate, *p*, which rests on *A* by the three set-screws, *s*. Two arms, with set-screws, *t*, resting on the side of the supporting plate, make possible, similar to *r*, a movement parallel to this side. An index finger, *l*, is supported above the plate, *p*. The screws, *s* and *t*, are now set so that the sharp edge of *l* is exactly in the prolongation of the axis of rotation of the goniometer, which is necessarily parallel to the upper and side surfaces of the supporting plate. By the help of this arrangement, the approximate centering and adjusting of the crystal-edge can be readily accomplished, and also the parallelism between the crystal-face and the supporting plate be proved.

Measurement of the Angles of microscopic Crystals.—BERTRAND (C. R., lxxxv., 1175, 1877; Bull. Soc. Min., i., 22, 96, 1878) has described a method for obtaining the interfacial angles of microscopic crystals, which may be briefly alluded to here. It is based on the geometrical principle that if the plane angles are known which the projections of a plane make with three perpendicular co-ordinate axes, the angular inclination of the plane to the three axes can be calculated. The crystal to be measured is fastened on a small cube of glass held in a pincer arrangement, on a secondary microscope stage; this stage is, like the principal stage below it, movable about a vertical axis, and besides has by means of screws a motion in two perpendicular directions in a horizontal plane. The method of obtaining the desired angles is very ingenious, but too complex to allow of explanation here; reference must be made to the original paper. With crystals of from 1-20 to 1-30 mm., Bertrand obtained results accurate within 6', and he states that the method can be extended to crystals which have a magnitude of only 1-100 mm.

SECTION II.

PHYSICAL CHARACTERS OF MINERALS.

The physical characters of minerals are those which relate: I., to Cohesion and Elasticity, that is: *cleavage* and *fracture, hardness*, and *tenacity;* II., to the Mass and Volume, the *specific gravity;* III., to Light, the *optical properties* of crystals; also *color, lustre*, etc.; IV., to Heat; V., to Electricity and Magnetism; VI., to the action on the Senses, as *taste, feel,* etc.

I. COHESION AND ELASTICITY.*

By *cohesion* is understood the attraction existing between the molecules of a body, in consequence of which they offer resistance to a force tending to separate them, as in breaking or scratching. This principle leads to some of the most universally important physical characters of minerals,—*cleavage, fracture,* and *hardness.*

Elasticity, on the other hand, is the force which tends to bring the molecules of a body back into their original position, from which they have been disturbed. Upon elasticity depends, for the most part, the degree of *tenacity* possessed by different minerals.

A. Cleavage and Fracture.

1. *Cleavage.* — Most crystallized minerals have certain directions in which their cohesive power is weakest, and in which they consequently yield most readily to an exterior force. This tendency to break in the direction of certain planes is called *cleavage*, and being most intimately connected with the crystalline form it has already been necessary to define it, and to mention some of its most important features (p. 2). Cleavage differs (*a*) according to the ease with which it is obtained, and (*b*) according to its direction, crystallographically determined.

(*a*) Cleavage is called *perfect* or *eminent* when it is obtained with great ease, affording smooth, lustrous surfaces, as in mica, topaz, calcite. Inferior degrees of cleavage are spoken of as *distinct, indistinct* or *imperfect, interrupted*, in *traces, difficult*. These terms are sufficiently intelligible without further explanation. It may be noticed that the cleavage of a species is sometimes better developed in some of its varieties than in others.

(*b*) Cleavage is also named according to the direction, crystallographically defined, which it takes in a species. When parallel to the basal section (O) it is called *basal*, as in topaz; parallel to the prism, as in amphibole, it is called *prismatic;* also *macrodiagonal, orthodiagonal*, etc., when parallel to the several diametral sections; parallel to the faces of the cube, octa-

---

* See further on p. 173.

hedron, dodecahedron, or rhombohedron, it is called *cubic*, as galenite; *octahedral*, as fluorite; *dodecahedral*, as sphalerite; *rhombohedral*, as calcite.

Intimately connected with the cleavage of crystallized minerals are the divisional planes investigated by Reusch (see Literature, p. 122). He has found that by pressure, or by a sudden blow, divisional planes are in many cases produced which are analogous to the cleavage planes. The first he calls *Gleitflächen*, or planes in which a sliding of the molecules upon each other takes place. Thus, for example, if two opposite dodecahedral edges of a cubic cleavage mass of rock-salt are regularly filed away, and the mass then subjected to pressure in this direction, a *Gleitfläche* is obtained parallel to the dodecahedral face.

The figures, on the other hand, obtained by a blow on a rounded steel point, placed perpendicular to the natural or cleavage face of a crystal, are called by him *fracture-figures* (Schlagfiguren). The divisional-planes in this case appear as cracks diverging from the point where the blow has been made. For instance, on a cubic face of rock-salt two planes, forming a rectangular cross, are obtained; on biaxial mica, a six-rayed (sometimes three-rayed) star results from the blow, one ray of which is always parallel to the brachydiagonal axis of the prism.

2. *Fracture.*—The term fracture is used to define the form or kind of surface obtained by breaking in a direction other than that of the cleavage in crystallized minerals, and in any direction in massive minerals. When the cleavage is highly perfect in several directions, as the cubic cleavage of galenite, fracture is often not readily obtainable.

Fracture is defined as:

(*a*) *Conchoidal;* when a mineral breaks with curved concavities, more or less deep. It is so called from the resemblance of the concavity to the valve of a shell, from concha, *a shell;* flint.

(*b*) *Even;* when the surface of fracture, though rough, with numerous small elevations and depressions, still approximates to a plane surface.

(*c*) *Uneven;* when the surface is rough and entirely irregular.

(*d*) *Hackley;* when the elevations are sharp or jagged; broken iron.

Other terms also employed are *earthy, splintery*, etc.

B. Hardness.

By the hardness of a mineral is understood the resistance which it offers to abrasion. The degree of hardness is determined by observing the ease or difficulty with which one mineral is scratched by another, or by a file or knife.

In minerals there are all grades of hardness, from that of a substance impressible by the finger-nail to that of the diamond. To give precision to the use of this character, a *scale of hardness* was introduced by Mohs. It is as follows:

1. *Talc;* common laminated light-green variety.
2. *Gypsum;* a crystallized variety.
3. *Calcite;* transparent variety.
4. *Fluorite;* crystalline variety.
5. *Apatite;* transparent variety.
(5.5. *Scapolite;* crystalline variety.)
6. *Feldspar* (orthoclase); white cleavable variety.
7. *Quartz;* transparent.

8. *Topaz;* transparent.
9. *Sapphire;* cleavable varieties.
10. *Diamond.*

If the mineral under trial is scratched by the file or knife as easily as apatite, its hardness is called 5; if a little more easily than apatite and not so readily as fluorite, its hardness is called 4.5, etc. For minerals as hard or harder than quartz, the file will not answer, and the relative hardness is determined by finding by experiment whether the given mineral will scratch, or can be scratched by, the successive minerals in the scale.

It need hardly be added that great accuracy is not attainable by the above methods, though, indeed, for all mineralogical purposes exactness is quite unnecessary.

The interval between 2 and 3, and 5 and 6, in the scale of Mohs, being a little greater than between the other numbers, Breithaupt proposed a scale of *twelve* minerals; but the scale of Mohs is now universally accepted.

Accurate determinations of the hardness of minerals have been made by *Frankenheim, Franz, Grailich* and *Pekarek,* and others (see Literature, p. 122), with an instrument called a *sclerometer.* The mineral is placed on a movable carriage with the surface to be experimented upon horizontal; this is brought in contact with a steel point (or diamond-point), fixed on a support above; the weight is then determined which is just sufficient to move the carriage and produce a scratch on the surface of the mineral.

By means of such an instrument the hardness of the different faces of a given crystal has been determined in a variety of cases. It has been found that different planes of a crystal differ in hardness, and the same plane differs as it is scratched in different directions. In general, the hardest plane is that which is intersected by the plane of most complete cleavage. And of a single plane, which is intersected by cleavage planes, the direction perpendicular to the cleavage direction is the softer, those parallel to it the harder.

This subject has been recently investigated by Exner (p. 122), who has given the form of the *curves of hardness* for the different planes of many crystals. These curves are obtained as follows: the least weight required to scratch a crystalline surface in different directions, for each 10° or 15°, from 0° to 180°, is determined with the sclerometer; these directions are laid off as radii from a centre, and the length of each is made proportional to the weight fixed by experiment, that is, to the hardness thus determined; the line connecting the extremities of these radii is the curve of hardness for the given plane.

C. Tenacity.

Solid minerals may be either brittle, sectile, malleable, flexible, or elastic.

(*a*) *Brittle;* when parts of a mineral separate in powder or grains on attempting to cut it; calcite.

(*b*) *Sectile;* when pieces may be cut off with a knife without falling to powder, but still the mineral pulverizes under a hammer. This character is intermediate between brittle and malleable; gypsum.

(*c*) *Malleable;* when slices may be cut off, and these slices flattened out under a hammer; native gold, native silver.

(*d*) *Flexible;* when the mineral will bend, and remain bent after the bending force is removed; talc.

(*e*) *Elastic;* when after being bent, it will spring back to its original position; mica.

The *elasticity* of crystallized minerals is a subject of theoretical rather than practical importance. The subject has been acoustically investigated by Savart with very interesting results. Reference may also be made to the investigations of Neumann, and later those of Voigt and Groth. The most important principle established by these researches is, as stated by Groth, that in crystals the elasticity (coefficient of elasticity) differs in different directions, but is the same in all directions which are crystallographically identical; hence he gives as the definition of a crystal, a solid in which the elasticity is a function of the direction.

Intimately connected with the general subjects here considered, of cohesion in relation to minerals, are the figures produced by etching on crystalline faces (Aetzfiguren, *Germ.*), investigated by Leydolt, and later by Baumhauer, Exner, and others. This method of investigation is of high importance as revealing the molecular structure of the crystal; reference, however, must be made to the original memoirs, whose titles are given below, for the full discussion of the subject.

The etching is performed mostly by solvents, as water in some cases, more generally the ordinary mineral acids, or caustic alkalies, also by steam and hydrofluoric acid; the latter is especially powerful in its action. The figures produced are in the majority of cases angular depressions, such as low triangular, or quadrilateral pyramids, whose outlines run parallel to some of the crystalline edges. In some cases the planes produced can be referred to occurring crystallographic planes. They appear alike on similar planes of crystals, and hence serve to distinguish different forms, perhaps in appearance identical, as the two sets of planes in the ordinary double pyramid of quartz; so, too, they reveal the compound twinning structure common on some crystals, as quartz (p. 89) and aragonite.

Analogous to the etching-figures are the figures produced on the faces of some crystals by the loss of water (Verwitterungsfiguren, *Germ.*) This subject has been investigated by Pape (see below).

LITERATURE.

Cohesion; Hardness.

Frankenheim. De Crystallorum Cohæsione, 1829; also in Baumgartner's Zeitschrift für Physik, ix., 94, 194. 1831.
Frankenheim. Ueber die Anordnung der Molecule in Krystallen; Pogg. xcvii., 337. 1856.
Sohncke. Ueber die Cohäsion des Steinsalzes in krystallographisch verschiedenen Richtungen; Pogg. cxxxvii., 177. 1869.
Franz. Ueber die Härte der Mineralien und ein neues Verfahren dieselbe zu messen; Pogg. lxxx., 37. 1850.
Grailich und Pekárek. Ber. Ak. Wien, xiii., 410. 1854.
Exner. Ueber die Härte der Krystallflächen; 166 pp. Wien, 1873.

Elasticity.

Savart. Pogg. Ann., xvi., 206.
Neumann. Pogg. Ann., xxxi., 177.
Voigt. Pogg. Ann. Erg. Bd., vii, i, 177, 1875.
Groth. Pogg. Ann., clvii., 115, 787. 1876.

Bauer. Untersuchung über den Glimmer und verwandte Minerale; Pogg. cxxxviii., 337, 1869.
Reusch. Ueber die Körnerprobe am Steinsalz u. Kalkspath. Pogg. cxxxii., 441, 1867;— am zwei-axigen Glimmer, Pogg. Ann. cxxxvi, 430, 632;—am krystallirten Gyps, ibid., p. 135.

Baumhauer. Ueber Aetzfiguren und die Erscheinungen des Asterismus an Krystallen; Pogg. Ann. cxxxviii., 163; cxxxix., 349; cxl., 271; cxlv., 459; cliii., 621; Ber. Ak. München, 1875, 169.
Daniell. Quarterly Journal of Science, i., 24. 1816.
Exner. An Lösungsfiguren in Krystallen; Ber. Ak. Wien, lxix., 6. 1874.
Hirschwald. Aetzfiguren an Quarz-Krystallen; Pogg. cxxxvii., 548. 1869.
Knop. Jahrb. Min., 1872, 785.
Leydolt. Ueber Aetzungen; Ber. Ak. Wien, xv., 58; xix., 10.
Pape. Ueber das Verwitterungs-Ellipsoid wasserhaltiger Krystalle; Pogg. cxxiv., 329: cxxv., 513. 1865.

II. SPECIFIC GRAVITY.*

The specific gravity of a mineral is its weight compared with that of another substance of equal volume, whose gravity is taken at unity. In the case of solids or liquids, this comparison is usually made with water. If a cubic inch of any mineral weighs twice as much as a cubic inch of water (water being the unit), its specific gravity is 2, if three times as much, its specific gravity is 3, etc.

The direct comparison by weight of a certain volume of water with an equal volume of a given solid is not often practicable. By making use, however, of a familiar principle in hydrostatics, viz., that the weight lost by a solid immersed in water is equal to the weight of an equal volume of water, that is of the volume of water it displaces,—the determination of the specific gravity becomes a very simple process.

The weight of the solid out of water (w) is determined by weighing in the usual manner; then the weight in water is found (w'), when the loss by immersion or the difference of the two weights ($w - w'$) is the weight of a volume of water equal to that of the solid; finally the quotient of the first weight (w) by that of the equal volume of water as determined ($w - w'$) is the specific gravity (G).

Hence, $$G = \frac{w}{w - w'}.$$

For example, the weight of a fragment of quartz is found to be 4.534 grains. Its weight in water = 2.817 grains, and therefore the loss of weight, or the weight of an equal volume of water = 1.717. Consequently the specific gravity is equal to $\frac{4.534}{1.717}$, or 2.641.

The ordinary method for obtaining the specific gravity of firm, solid minerals is first to weigh the specimen accurately on a good chemical balance, then suspend it from one pan of the balance by a horse-hair, silk thread, or better still by a fine platinum wire, in a glass of water conveniently placed beneath. The platinum wire may be wound around the specimen, or where the latter is small it may be made at one end into a little spiral support. While thus suspended, the weight is again taken with the same care as before.

The water employed for this purpose should be distilled, to free it from all foreign substances. Since the density of water varies with its temperature, a particular temperature has to be selected for these experiments, in

* See further on p. 173.

order to obtain uniform results: 60° F. is the most convenient, and has been generally adopted. But the temperature of the maximum density of water, 39.2° F. (4° C.), has been recommended as preferable. For minerals soluble in water some other liquid, as alcohol, benzene, etc., must be employed, whose specific gravity (g) is accurately known; from the comparison with it, the specific gravity (G) of the mineral as referred to water is determined, as by the formula:

$$G = \frac{w}{w - w'} g.$$

A very convenient form of balance is the spiral balance of Jolly, where the weight is measured by the torsion of a spiral brass wire. The readings, which give the weight of the mineral in and out of water, are obtained by observing the coincidence of the index with its image reflected in the mirror on which the graduation is made.

A form of balance in which weights are also dispensed with, the specific gravity being read off from a scale without calculation, has recently been described by Parish (Am. J. Sci., III., x., 352). Where great accuracy is not required, it can be very conveniently used.

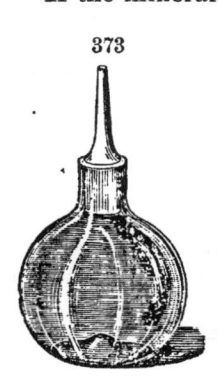

If the mineral is not solid, but pulverulent or porous, it is best to reduce it to a powder and weigh it in a little glass bottle (f. 373) called a pygnometer. This bottle has a stopper which fits tightly and ends in a tube with a very fine opening. The bottle is filled with distilled water, the stopper inserted, and the overflowing water carefully removed with a soft cloth. It is now weighed, and also the mineral whose density is to be determined. The stopper is then removed and the mineral in powder or in small fragments inserted, with care, so as not to introduce air-bubbles. The water which overflows on replacing the stopper is the amount of water displaced by the mineral. The weight of the pygnometer with the enclosed mineral is determined, and the weight of the water lost is obviously the difference between this last weight and that of the bottle and mineral together, as first determined. The specific gravity of the mineral is equal to its weight alone divided by the weight of the equal volume of water thus determined.

Where this method is followed with sufficient care, especially avoiding any change of temperature in the water, the results are quite accurate. Other methods of determining the specific gravity will be found described in the literature notices which follow.

It has been shown by Rose that chemical precipitates have uniformly a higher density than belongs to the same substance in a less finely divided state. This increase of density also characterizes, though to a less extent, a mineral in a fine state of *mechanical* subdivision. This is explained by the condensation of the water on the surface of the powder.

It may also be mentioned that the density of many substances is altered by fusion. The same mineral in different states of molecular aggregation may differ somewhat in density. Furthermore, minerals having the same chemical composition have sometimes different densities corresponding to the different crystalline forms in which they appear (see p. 199).

For all minerals in a state of average purity the specific gravity is one of the most important and constant characteristics, as urged especially by Breithaupt. Every chemical analysis of a mineral should be accompanied by a careful determination of its density.

Practical suggestions.—The fragment taken should not be too large, say from two to five grams for ordinary cases, varying somewhat with the density of the mineral. The substance must be free from impurities, internal and external, and not porous. Care must be taken to exclude air-bubbles, and it will often be found well to moisten the surface of the specimen before inserting it in the water, and sometimes boiling is necessary to free it from air. If it absorbs water this latter process must be allowed to go on till the substance is fully saturated. No accurate determinations can be made unless the changes of temperature are rigorously excluded and the actual temperature noted.

In a mechanical mixture of two constituents in known proportions, when the specific gravity of the whole and of one are known, that of the other can be readily obtained. This method is often important in the study of rocks.

LITERATURE.—SPECIFIC GRAVITY.

Beudant. Pogg. Ann., xiv., 474. 1828.
Jenzsch. Ueber die Bestimmung der specifischen Gewichte; Pogg. xcix., 151. 1856.
Jolly. Ber. Ak. München, 1864, 162.
Gadolin. Eine einfache Methode zur Bestimmung des specifischen Gewichtes der Mineralien; Pogg., cvi., 213. 1859.
G. Rose. Ueber die Fehler, welche in der Bestimmung des specifischen Gewichtes der Körper entstehen, wenn man dieselben im Zustande der feinsten Vertheilung wägt; Pogg. lxxiii., lxxv., 403. 1848.
Scheerer. Ueber die Bestimmung des specifischen Gewichtes von Mineralien; Pogg. Ann., lxvii., 120, 1846. Journ. pr. Ch., xxiv., 139.
Schiff. Ann. Ch. Pharm., cviii., 29. 1858.
Schröder. Neue Beiträge zur Volumentheorie; Pogg. cvi., 226. 1859.
———; Die Volumconstitution einiger Mineralien; Jahrb. Min., 1873, 561, 932; 1874, 399, etc.
Tschermak. Ber. Ak. Wien, 292, 1863.
Websky. Die Mineralien nach den für das specifische Gewicht derselben angenommenen und gefundenen Werthen; 170 pp. Breslau, 1868.

III. LIGHT.*

Before considering the distinguishing optical properties of crystals of the different systems, it is desirable to review briefly some of the more important principles of optics upon which the phenomena in question depend.

Nature of light.—In accordance with the undulatory theory of Huyghens, as further developed by Young and Fresnel, light is conceived to consist in the vibrations, transverse to the direction of propagation, of the particles of imponderable, elastic *ether*, which it is assumed pervades all space as well as all material bodies. These vibrations are propagated with great velocity in straight lines and in all directions from the luminous point, and the sensation which they produce on the nerves of the eye is called *light*.

The nature of the vibrations will be understood from f. 374. If AB represents the direction of propagation of the light-ray, each particle of ether vibrates at right angles to this as a line of equilibrium. The vibration of the first particle induces a similar movement in the adjacent particle; this is communicated to the next, and so on. The particles vibrate successively from the line AB to a distance corresponding to bb', called the *amplitude* of the vibration, then return to b and pass on to b'', and so

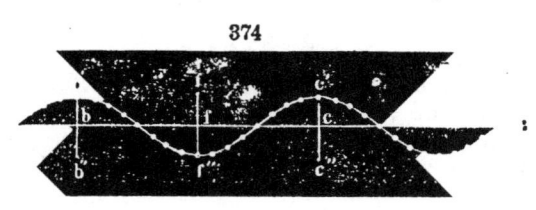

374

on. Thus at a given instant there are particles occupying all positions, from that of the extreme distance b', or c', from the line of equilibrium to that on this line. In this way the wave of vibration moves forward, while the motion of the particles is only transverse. In the figure the vibrations are represented in one plane only, but in ordinary light they take place in all directions about the line AB. The distance between any two particles, which are in like positions, of like *phase*, as b' and c', is called the *wave-length;* and the time required for this completed movement is called the *time* of vibration. The intensity of the light varies with the amplitude of the vibrations, and the color depends upon the length of the waves; the wave-lengths of the violet rays are shorter than those of the red rays.

Two waves of like phase, propagated in the same direction and of equal intensity, on meeting unite to form a wave of double intensity (double amplitude). If the waves differ in phase by half a wave-length, or an odd multiple of this, they *interfere* and extinguish each other. For other relations of phase they are also said to interfere, forming a new resultant wave, differing in phase and amplitude from each of the component waves; if they are waves of white light, their interference is indicated by the appearance of the successive colors of the spectrum. The propagation of the vibration-waves of light is sometimes compared to the effect produced when a pebble is thrown in a sheet of quiet water—a series of concentric circular waves are sent out from the point of agitation. These waves consist in the transverse vibration of the particles of water, the waves move forward, but the water simply vibrates to and fro vertically.

The waves of light are propagated forward, in an analogous manner, in all directions from the luminous point, and the surface which contains all the particles which commence their vibrations simultaneously is called the *wave-surface* (Wellenfläche, *Germ.*).

If the propagation of light goes on with the same velocity in all directions in a homogeneous medium, the wave-surface is obviously that of a sphere and the medium is said to be *isotrope*. If it takes place with different velocities in different directions in a body, the wave-surface is sometimes an ellipsoid, but never spherical, as is shown later; such a body is called *anisotrope*.

All the phenomena of optics are explained upon the supposition of *waves of light*, whose change of direction accompanies refraction, whose interference produces the colored bands of the diffraction spectra, etc. For the full discussion of the subject reference must be made to works on optics.

Refraction.—A ray of light passing through a homogeneous medium is always propagated in a straight line without deviation. When, however, the light-ray passes from one medium to another, which is of different density, it suffers a change of direction, which is called refraction. For instance, in f. 375, if *ca* is a ray of light passing from air into water, its path will be changed after passing the surface at *a*, and it will continue in the direction *ab*. Conversely, if a ray of light, *ba*, pass from the denser medium, water, into the rarer medium, air, at *a*, it will take the direction *ac*.

If now *mao* is a perpendicular to the surface at *a*, it will be seen that the angle *cam*, called the *angle of incidence* (i) of the ray *ca* is greater than the angle *bao*, called the angle of *refraction* (r), and what is observed in this case is found to be universally true, and the law is expressed as follows:

A ray of light in passing from a rarer to a denser medium is refracted TOWARDS *the perpendicular; if from a denser to a rarer medium it is refracted* AWAY FROM *the perpendicular.*

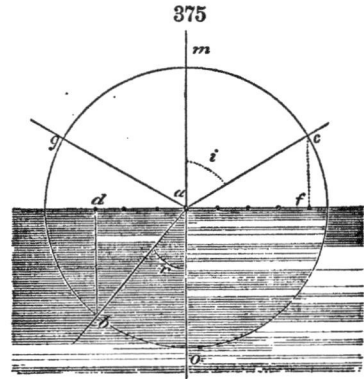

A further relation has also been established by experiment: however great or small the angle of incidence, *cam* (i), may be, there is always a constant relation between it and the angle of refraction, *gam* (r), for two given substances, as here for air and water. This is seen in the figure where *af* and *da* are the sines of the two angles, and their ratio ($= \frac{4}{3}$ nearly) is the same as that of the sine of any other angle of incidence to the sine of its angle of refraction. This principle is expressed as follows:

The sine of the angle of incidence bears a constant ratio to the sine of the angle of refraction.

This constant ratio between these two angles is called the *index of refraction*, or simply n. In the example given for air and water $\frac{\sin i}{\sin r} = 1.335$, and consequently the value of the index of refraction, or n, is 1.335.

The following table includes the values of n for a variety of substances. For all crystallized minerals, except those of the isometric system, the index of refraction has more than one value, as is explained in the pages which follow.

Ice	1.308	Calcite	1.654
Water	1.335	Aragonite	1.693
Fluorite	1.436	Boracite	1.701
Alum	1.457	Garnet	1.815
Chalcedony	1.553	Zircon	1.961
Rock-salt	1.557	Blende	2.260
Quartz	1.548	Diamond	2.419

In the principle which has been stated, $\frac{\sin i}{\sin r} = n$, two points are to be noted. First, if the angle $i = 0°$, then $\sin i = 0$, and obviously also $r = 0$, in other words, when the ray of light coincides with the perpendicular no refraction takes place, the ray proceeding onward into the second medium without deviation.

Again, if the angle $i = 90°$, then $\sin i = 1$, and the equation above becomes $\dfrac{1}{\sin r} = n$, or $\sin r = \dfrac{1}{n}$. As n has a fixed value for every substance, it is obvious that there will also be a corresponding value of the angle r for the case mentioned. From the above table it is seen that for water $\sin r = \dfrac{1}{1.335}$, and $r = 48° 35'$; for diamond, $\sin r = \dfrac{1}{2.42}$, and $r = 24° 25'$.

In the example employed above, if the angle bao $(r) = 48° 35'$, the line ac will coincide with af, supposing the light to go from b to a. If r is greater than $48° 35'$, the ray no longer passes from the water into the air, but suffers *total reflection* at the surface a. This value of r is said to be the limiting value for the given substance. The smaller it is the greater the amount of light reflected, and the greater the apparent *brilliancy* of the substance in question. This is the explanation of the brilliancy of the diamond.

Determination of the index of refraction.*—By means of a prism, as MNP in f. 376, it is possible to determine the value of n, or index of refraction of a given substance. The full explanation of this subject belongs to works on optics, but a word is devoted to it here. If the material is solid, a prism must be cut and polished, with its edge in the proper direction, and having not too small an angle. If the refractive index of a liquid is required, it is placed within a hollow prism, with sides of plates of glass having both surfaces parallel.

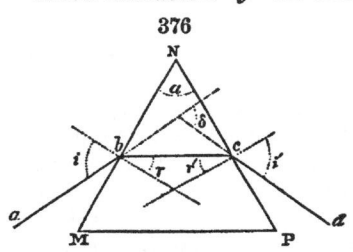

The angle of the prism, MNP (a), is, in each case, measured in the same manner as the angle between two planes of a crystal, and then the *minimum* amount of deviation (δ) of a *monochromatic* ray of light passing from a slit through the prism is also determined. The amount of deviation of a ray in passing through the prism varies with its position, but when the prism is so placed that the ray makes equal angles with the sides of the prism ($i = i'$, f. 376), both when entering and emerging, this deviation has a *fixed minimum* value.

If $\delta =$ the minimum deviation of the ray, and
$a =$ the angle of the prism, then $n = \dfrac{\sin \frac{1}{2}(a + \delta)}{\sin \frac{1}{2}a}$.

In determining the value of n for different colors, it is desirable to employ rays of known position in the spectrum.

Double refraction.—Hitherto the existence of only one refracted ray has been assumed when light passes from one medium to another. But it is a well-known fact that there are sometimes *two* refracted rays. The most familiar example of this is furnished by the mineral calcite, also called on account of this property "doubly-refracting spar."

If $mnop$ (f. 377) be a cleavage piece of calcite, and a ray of light meets

---

* See further on p. 177.

it at *b*, it will, in passing through, be divided into two rays, *bc*, *bd*. Similarly a line seen through a piece of calcite ordinarily appears double.

377

It will be seen, however, that the same property is enjoyed by the great majority of crystallized minerals, though in a less striking degree.

Reflection.—When a ray of light passes from one medium to another, for example, from air to a denser substance, as has been illustrated, the light will be partially transmitted and refracted by the latter, in the manner illustrated, but a portion of it (the ray *ag*, in f. 375), is always reflected back into the air. The direction of the reflected ray is known in accordance with the following law:

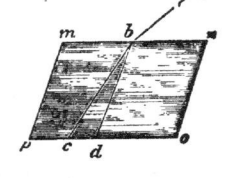

The angles of incidence and reflection are equal.—In f. 375 the angle *cam* is equal to the angle *mag*.

The relative amount of light reflected and transmitted depends upon the angle of incidence, and also upon the transparency of the second medium. If the surface of the latter is not perfectly polished, diffuse reflection will take place, and there will be no distinct reflected ray.

Still another important principle, in relation to the same subject, remains to be enunciated: *The rays of incidence, reflection, and refraction all lie in the same plane.*

Dispersion.—Thus far the change in direction which a ray of light suffers on refraction has alone been considered. It is also true that the amount of refraction differs for the different colors of which ordinary white light is composed, being greater for blue than for red. In consequence of this fact, if a ray of ordinary light pass through a prism, as in f. 376, it will not only be refracted, but it will also be separated into its component colors, thus forming the *spectrum*.

This variation for the different colors depends directly upon their wave-lengths; the red rays have longer waves, and vibrate more slowly, and hence suffer less refraction than the violet rays, for which the wave-lengths are shorter and the velocity greater.

Interference of light; diffraction.—When a ray of monochromatic light is made to pass through a narrow slit, or by the edge of an opaque body, it is *diffracted*, and there arise, as may be observed upon an appropriately placed screen, a series of dark and light bands, growing fainter on the outer limits. Their presence, as has been intimated, is explained in accordance with the undulatory theory of light, as due to the *interference*, or mutual reaction of the adjoining waves of light. If ordinary light is employed, the phenomena are the same and for the same causes, except that the bands are successive spectra. Diffraction gratings, consisting of a series of extremely fine lines very closely ruled upon glass, are employed for the same purpose as the prism to produce the colored spectrum. The familiar phenomena of the colors of thin plates and of Newton's rings depend upon the same principle of the interference of the light waves. This subject is one of the highest importance in its connection with the optical properties of crystals, since the phenomena observed when they are viewed, under certain circumstances, in polarized light are explained in an analogous manner. (Compare the colored plate, frontispiece.)

Polarization by reflection.—By *polarization* is understood, in general, that change in the character of reflected or transmitted light which diminishes its power of being further reflected or transmitted. In accordance with the undulatory theory of light a ray of polarized light is one whose vibrations take place in a single plane only.

Suppose (f. 378) *mn* and *op* to be two parallel mirrors, say simple polished pieces of black glass; a ray of light, AB, will be reflected from *mn* in the direction BC, and meeting *op*, will be again reflected to D. When, as here, the two mirrors are in a parallel position, the plane of reflection is clearly the same for both, the angles of incidence are equal, and the rays AB and CD are parallel. The ray CD is *polarized*, although this does not show itself to the eye direct.

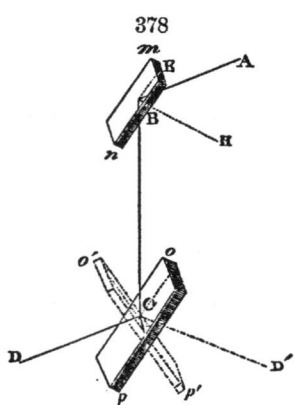

Now let the mirror, *op*, be revolved about BC as an axis, and let its position otherwise be unchanged, so that the angles of incidence still remain equal, it will be found that the reflected ray, CD, loses more and more of its brilliancy as the revolution continues, and when the mirror, *op*. occupies a position at right angles to its former position, the amount of light reflected will be a minimum, the planes of reflection being in the two cases perpendicular to one another.

If the revolution of the mirror be continued with the same conditions as before, and in the same direction, the reflected ray will become brighter and brighter till the mirror has the position indicated by the dotted line, $o'p'$, when the planes of reflection again coincide, and the reflected ray, CD', is equal in brilliancy to that previously obtained for the position CD.

The same diminution to a minimum will be seen if the revolution is continued 90° farther, and the reflected ray again becomes as brilliant as before when the mirror resumes its first position *op*.

In the above description it was asserted that, when the planes of incidence of the mirrors were at right angles to each other, the amount of light reflected would be less than in any other position, that is a minimum. For one single position of the mirrors, however, as they thus stand perpendicular to each other, that is for one single value of the angle of incidence, the light will be practically extinguished, and no reflected ray will appear from the second mirror.

The angle of incidence, ABH, for this case is called the *angle of polarization*, and its value varies for different substances. It was shown further by Brewster that:

The angle of polarization is that angle whose tangent is the index of refraction of the reflecting substance, i.e., $\tan i = n$.

Exactly the same phases of change would have been observed if the upper mirror had been revolved in a similar manner. The first mirror is often called the *polarizer*, the second the *analyzer*.

This change which the light suffers in this case, in consequence of reflection, is called *polarization*.

In order to give a partial explanation of this phenomenon and to make the same subject intelligible as applied to other cases in which polarization occurs, reference must be made to the commonly received theory of the nature of light already defined.

The phenomena of light are explained, as has been stated, on the assumption that it consists of the vibrations of the ether, the vibrations being transverse, that is in a plane perpendicular, to the direction in which the light is propagated. These vibrations in ordinary light take place in all directions in this plane at sensibly the same time; strictly speaking, the vibrations are considered as being always transverse, but their directions are constantly and instantaneously changing in azimuth. Such a ray of light is alike on all sides or all around the line of propagation, AB, f. 374. A ray of completely polarized light, on the other hand, has vibrations in *one* direction only, that is in a single plane.

These principles may be applied to the case of reflection already described. The ray of ordinary light, AB, has its vibrations sensibly simultaneous in all directions in the plane at right angles to its line of propagation, while the light reflected from each mirror has only those vibrations which are in *one* direction, at right angles to the plane of reflection—supposing that the mirrors are so placed that the angle of incidence (ABH) is also the angle of polarization.

If the mirror occupy the position represented in f. 378, the ray of light, BC, after being reflected by the first mirror, mn, contains that part of the vibrations whose direction is normal to its plane of reflection called the *plane of polarization*. This is also true of the second mirror, and when they are parallel and their planes of reflection coincide, the ray of light is reflected a second time without additional change.

If, however, the second mirror is revolved in the way described (p. 130), less and less of the light will be reflected by it, since a successively smaller part of the vibrations of the ray BC take place in a direction normal to *its* plane of reflection. And when the mirrors are at right angles to each other, after a revolution of *op* 90° about the line BC as an axis, no part of the vibrations of the ray BC are in the plane at right angles to the reflection-plane of the second mirror, and hence the light is extinguished.

By reference to f. 375 this subject may be explained a little more broadly. It was seen that of the ray *ca*, meeting the surface of the water at *a*, part is reflected and part transmitted in accordance with the laws of reflection and refraction. It has been shown further that the reflected ray is polarized, that is, it is changed so that the vibrations of the light take place in one direction, at right angles to the plane of incidence. It is also true that the *refracted ray is polarized*, it containing only those vibrations which were lost in the reflected ray, that is, those which *coincide* with the plane of incidence and reflection.

It was stated that the vibrations of the polarized reflected ray take place *at right angles* to the plane of polarization. This is the assumption which is commonly made; but all the phenomena of polarization can be equally well explained upon the other supposition that they *coincide* with this plane.

The separation of the ray of ordinary light into two rays, one reflected the other refracted, vibrating at right angles to each other, takes place most completely when the reflected and refracted rays are 90° from one another, as proved by Brewster. From this fact follows the law already stated, that the tangent of the angle of polarization is equal to the index of refraction. The angle of polarization for glass is about 54° 35'.

This separation is in no case absolutely complete, but varies with different substances. In the case of opaque substances the vibrations belonging to the refracted ray are more or less completely absorbed (compare remarks on *color*, p. 168). Metallic surfaces polarize the light very slightly.

Polarization by means of thin plates of glass.—It has been explained that the light which has been transmitted and refracted is always at least in part polarized. It will be readily understood from this fact that when a number of glass plates are placed together, the light which passes through them all will be more and more completely polarized as their number is increased. This is a second convenient method of obtaining polarized light.

Polarization by means of tourmaline plates.—The phenomena of polarized light may also be shown by means of tourmaline plates. If from a crystal of tourmaline, which is suitably transparent, two sections be obtained, each cut parallel to the vertical axis, it will be found that these, when placed together with the direction of their axes coinciding, allow the light to pass through. If, however, one section is revolved upon the other, less and less of the light is transmitted, until, when their axes are at right angles (90°) to each other, the light is (for the most part) extinguished. As the revolution is continued, more and more light is obtained through the sections, and after a revolution of 180°, the axes being again parallel, the appearance is as at first. A further revolution (270°) brings the axes again at right angles to each other, when the light is a second time extinguished, and so on around.

The explanation of these phenomena, so far as it can be given here, is analogous to that employed for the case of polarization by reflection. Each plate so affects the ray of light that after having passed through it there exist vibrations in one direction only, and that parallel to the vertical axis, the other vibrations being absorbed. If now the two plates are placed in the same position, *abdc*, and *efgh* (f. 379), the light passes through both in succession. If, however, the one is turned upon the other, only that portion of the light can pass through which vibrates still in the direction *ac*. This portion is determined by the resolution of the existing vibrations in accordance with the principle of the parallelogram of forces. Consequently, when the sections stand at right angles to each other (f. 380) the amount of transmitted light is nothing (not strictly true), that is, the light is extinguished.

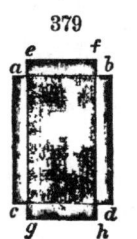

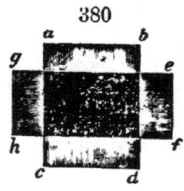

The tourmaline plates, which have been described, are mounted in pieces of cork and held in a kind of wire pincers (f. 381). The object to be examined is placed between them and supported there by the spring in the wire. In use they are held close to the eye, and in this position the object is viewed in *converging* polarized light.

Polarization by means of Nicol prisms.—The most convenient method of obtaining polarized light is by means of a *Nicol prism* of calcite. A

POLARIZATION OF LIGHT. 133

cleavage rhombohedron of calcite (the variety *Iceland spar* is universally used in consequence of its transparency) is obtained, having four large and two small rhombohedral faces opposite each other. In place of the latter

381

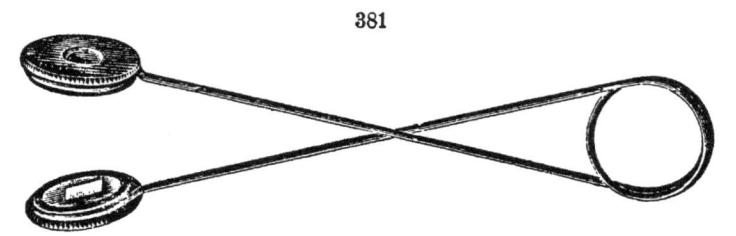

planes two new surfaces are cut, making angles of 68° (instead of 71°) with the obtuse vertical edges; these then form the terminal faces of the prism. In addition to this, the prism is cut through in the direction HH (f. 382), the parts then polished and cemented together again with Canada balsam. A ray of light, ab, entering the prism is divided into two rays polarized at right angles to each other. One of these, bc, on meeting the layer of balsam (whose refractive index is greater than that of calcite) suffers total reflection (p. 128), and is deflected against the blackened sides of the prism and extinguished. The other passes through and emerges at e, a completely polarized ray of light, that is. a ray with vibrations in one direction only, and that the direction of the shorter diagonal of the prism (f. 383).

382

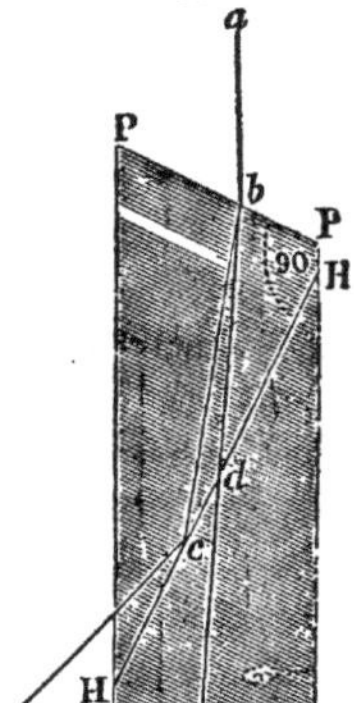

It is evident that two Nicol prisms can be used together in the same way as the two tourmaline plates, or the two mirrors; one is called the *polarizer*, and the other the *analyzer*. The plane of polarization of the Nicol prisms has the direction PP (f. 383) at right angles to which the vibrations of the light take place. A ray of light passing through one Nicol will be extinguished by a second when its plane of polarization is at right angles to that of the first prism; in this case the Nicols are said to be *crossed*. The Nicol prisms have the great advantage over the tourmaline plates, that the light they transmit is uncolored and more completely polarized.

Either a tourmaline plate or a Nicol prism may also be used in connection with a reflecting mirror. The light reflected by such a mirror vibrates in a plane at right angles to the plane of incidence (plane of polarization); that transmitted by the Nicol prism vibrates in the direction of the shorter diagonal (f. 383). Hence, when the plane of this diagonal is at right angles to the plane of polarization of the mirror, the reflected ray will pass through the prism; but when the two planes mentioned coincide, the planes of vibration are at right angles and the reflected ray is extinguished by the prism.

383

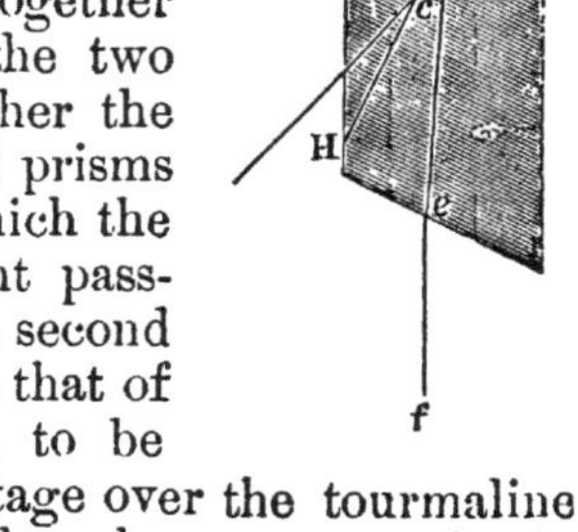

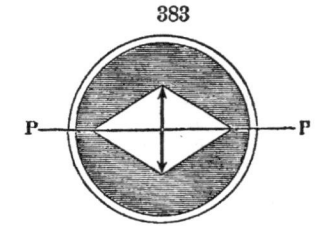

PHYSICAL CHARACTERS OF MINERALS.

Polariscopes.*—The Nicol prisms, when ready for use, are mounted in an upright instrument, called a *polariscope*. Sometimes *parallel*, and sometimes *converging*, light is required in the investigations for which the instrument is used. Fig. 384 shows the polarization-microscope of Nörrenberg as altered and improved by Groth (see Literature, p. 160). The Nicol prisms are at d and r, and are so mounted as to admit of a motion of revolution independent of the other parts of the instrument. The lense e causes the light from the ordinary mirror, a, to pass as a cone through the prism d, and the lenses at h converge the light upon the plate to be examined placed at i. The other lenses (o) above act as a weak microscope, having a field of vision of 130°. The stage (l and k), carrying the object, admits of a horizontal revolution. The distance between the two halves of the instrument is adjusted by the screws m and n.

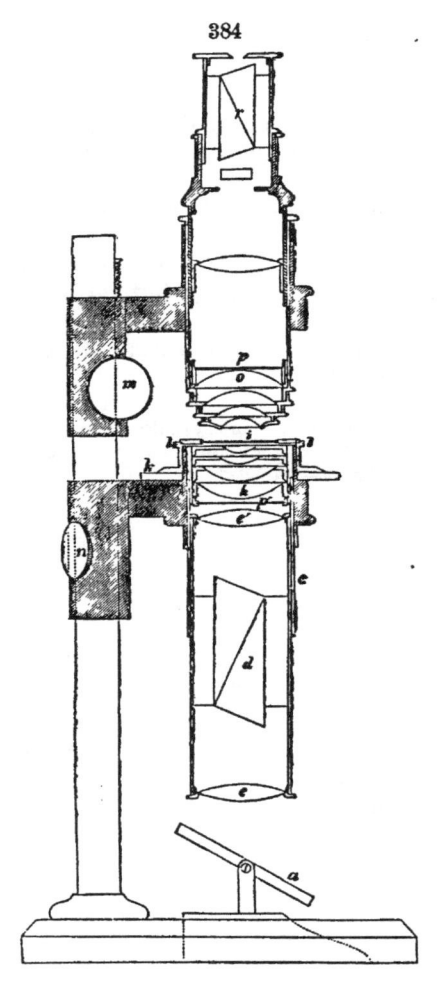

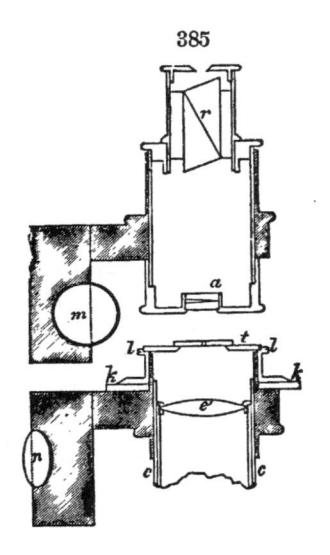

When *parallel* light is required, a similar instrument is employed, which has, however, a different arrangement of the lenses, as shown in f. 385. The objects for which these instruments, as well as the tourmaline plates, are employed, will be found described in the following pages.

The Nicol prisms are often used as an appendage to the ordinary compound microscope, and in this form are important as enabling us to examine very minute crystals in polarized light.†

---

* See further on pp. 178, 179.   † See pp. 182 et seq.

DISTINGUISHING OPTICAL CHARACTERS OF THE CRYSTALS OF THE DIFFERENT SYSTEMS.

It has already been remarked that all crystallized minerals group themselves into three grand classes, which are distinguished by their physical properties, as well as their geometrical form:

A. Isometric, in which the crystals are developed alike in all the several axial directions.

B. Isodiametric, including the tetragonal and hexagonal systems, whose crystals are alike in the directions of the several lateral axes, but vertically the development is unlike that laterally.

C. Anisometric, embracing the three remaining systems, where the crystals are developed in the three axial directions dissimilarly.

Between these classes there are many cases of gradual transition in crystalline form, and, similarly and necessarily, in optical character. The line between uniaxial and biaxial crystals, for instance, cannot be considered a very sharply defined one.*

A. ISOMETRIC CRYSTALS.

General Optical Character.

All *isometric* crystals are alike in this respect that they simply refract, but do not *doubly refract* the light they transmit. They are optically *isotrope.* This follows directly from the symmetry of the crystallization. In the language of Fresnel, the elasticity of the light-ether is throughout them the same, and the light is propagated in every direction with the same velocity. There is, consequently, but one value of the index of refraction. The wave-surface is spherical. This class also includes all transparent amorphous substances, like glass.

Optical Investigation of Isometric Crystals.

In consequence of their isotropic character, isometric crystals exhibit no special phenomena in polarized light. Sections of isometric crystals may be always recognized as such by the fact that they behave as an amorphous substance in polarized light; in other words, when the Nicol prisms are crossed they appear dark, and a revolution of the section in any plane produces no change in appearance. Similarly they appear light when placed between parallel Nicols. Some anomalies are mentioned on p. 158.

Isometric crystals have but a single index of refraction, and that may be determined in the way described by means of a prism cut with its edge in any direction whatever.

Crystals of the second and third classes are optically *anisotrope.*

B. Uniaxial Crystals.

General Optical Character.

In the *isodiametric* crystals, those of the tetragonal and hexagonal systems, there is crystallographically one axial direction, that of the vertical axis, which is distinguished from the other lateral directions which are among themselves alike. So also the optical investigations of these crystals show that with reference to the action of light there exists a similar kind of symmetry. Light is propagated in the direction of the vertical axis with a velocity different from that with which it passes in any other direction, but for all directions at right angles to the vertical axis, or all directions making the same angle with it, the velocity of propagation is the same. In other words, the elasticity of the ether in the direction of the vertical axis is either greater or less than that in directions normal to it (analogous to the crystallographical relation $c \gtreqless a$), while in the latter directions it is everywhere alike.

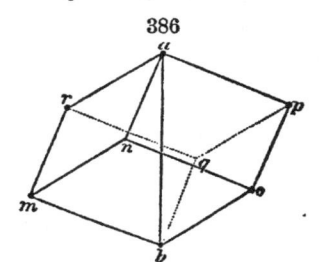

Optic axis.—Let a ray of light pass through the crystal in the direction of the vertical axis, ab, in f. 386, its vibrations must take place in the plane at right angles to this axis; but in all directions in this plane the elasticity of the ether is the same, hence for such a ray the crystal must act as an isotrope medium; and the ray is consequently not doubly refracted and not polarized. This direction is called the OPTIC AXIS.*

Double refraction.—If, on the other hand, the ray of light passes through the crystal in any other direction, it is divided into two rays, or doubly refracted (see f. 377), and this in consequence of the difference in the elasticity of the ether in the plane in which the vibrations take place. Of these two rays, one follows the law of ordinary refraction, and this is called the *ordinary* ray; the other does not conform to this law, and is called the *extraordinary* ray. Both these rays are polarized, and in planes at right angles to each other; the vibrations of the extraordinary ray take place in the plane passing through the incident ray and vertical axis, called the *principal section*, those of the ordinary ray are in a plane at right angles to this.

Wave-surface of the ordinary ray.—The meaning of the statement that the ordinary ray follows the law of the simple refraction is this:—the index of refraction (ω) of the ordinary ray has invariably the same value, whatever be the direction in which the light passes through the crystal; the amount of deviation from the perpendicular is always in accordance with the law $\dfrac{\sin i}{\sin r} = n\ (\omega)$. In other words, the ordinary ray is propagated in all directions in the medium with the same velocity; and hence the wave-

---

* It will be understood that the *optic axis* is always a *direction*, not a fixed line in the crystals.

OPTICAL CHARACTERS OF UNIAXIAL CRYSTALS. 137

surface is that of a sphere. Moreover, the ordinary ray always remains in the plane of incidence.

Wave-surface of the extraordinary ray.—For the extraordinary ray the law of simple refraction does not hold good. If experiments be made upon any uniaxial crystal, it will be found that the two rays are most separated when (1) the light falls PERPENDICULAR to the vertical axis. As its inclination toward the axis is diminished, the extraordinary ray approaches the ordinary ray, and coincides with it when (2) the light passes through PARALLEL to the vertical axis. The index of refraction of the extraordinary ray varies in value, being most unlike ω for the first case supposed when the vibrations of the extraordinary ray are parallel to the axis (when it is called ϵ), and is equal to ω for the second case supposed. The velocity of this ray is then variable in a corresponding manner. The wave-surface of the extraordinary ray is an ellipsoid of rotation. Moreover it ordinarily does not remain in the plane of incidence.

Two cases are now possible: the index (ω) of the ordinary ray may be (1) *greater* than that of the extraordinary ray (ϵ), in which case the velocity of the light in the direction of the vertical axis is *less* than that in any other direction; or (2) ω may be *less* than ϵ, and in this case the velocity of propagation for the light has its maximum parallel to the vertical axis. The former are called *negative*, the latter *positive* crystals. The fact alluded to here should be noted that the value of the refractive index is inversely proportional to the velocity of the light, or elasticity of the ether, in the given direction.

Negative crystals; Wave-surface.—For calcite $\omega = 1.654$, $\epsilon = 1.483$, it is hence one of the class of negative crystals. The former value (ω) belongs to the ray vibrating at right angles to the vertical axis, and the latter value (ϵ) to the ray with vibrations parallel to the axis. As has been stated, the refractive index for the extraordinary ray increases from 1.483 to 1.654, as the ray becomes more and more nearly parallel to the vertical axis. Fig. 387 illustrates graphically the relation between the two indices of refraction, and the corresponding velocities of the rays; *ab* represents the direction of the vertical axis, that is, the *optic axis*. Also *ma*, *mb* represent the velocity of the light parallel to this axis, corresponding to the *greater* index of refraction (1.654). The circle described with this radius will represent the constant velocity of the ordinary ray in any direction whatever. Let further *md*, *mc* represent the velocity of the extraordinary ray passing at right angles to the axis, hence corresponding to the *smaller* index of refraction (1.483). The ellipse, whose major and minor axes are *cd* and *ab*, will express the law in accordance with which the velocity of the extraordinary ray varies, viz., greatest in the direction *md*, least in the direction *ab* in which it coincides with the ordinary ray. For any intermediate direction, *hgm*, the velocity will be expressed by the length of the line, *hm*.

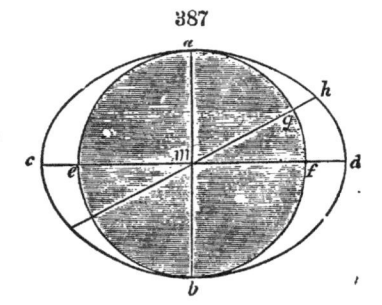

Now let this figure be revolved about the axis *ab*; there will be generated a circle within an oblate ellipsoid of rotation (f. 388). The surface of the sphere is the *wave-surface* of the ordinary ray, and that of the ellipsoid of the extraordinary ray; the line of their intersection is the optic axis.

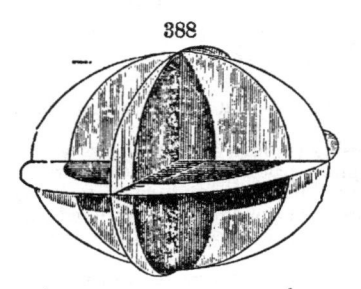

In f. 377, p. 147, the ray of light is shown divided into two by the piece of calcite; of these, *bd*, which is the more refracted, is the ordinary ray, and *bc*, which is less refracted, is the extraordinary ray.

Positive crystals; Wave-surface. —For quartz $\omega = 1.548$, $\epsilon = 1.558$. The index of refraction for the ordinary ray (ω) is *less* than that of the extraordinary ray (ϵ); quartz hence belongs to the class of positive crystals. The value of ϵ (1·558) for the extraordinary ray corresponds to the direction of the ray at right angles to the vertical axis, when its vibrations are parallel to this axis. As the direction of the ray changes and becomes more and more nearly parallel to the axis, the value of its index of refraction decreases, and when it is parallel to the latter, it has the value 1·548. The extraordinary ray then coincides with the ordinary, and there is no double refraction; this is, as before, the line of the *optic axis*. The law for both rays can be represented graphically in the same way as for negative crystals. In f. 389, *amb* is the direction of the optic axis; let *ma*, *mb* represent the velocity of the ordinary ray, which corresponds to the *least* refractive index (1·548), the circle *afbe* will express the law for this ray, viz., the velocity the same in every direction. Moreover, let *md*, *mc* represent the velocity of the extraordinary ray, at right angles to the axis, which corresponds to the maximum refractive index (1·558); the ellipse, *adbc*, will express the law for velocity of the extraordinary ray, viz., least in the direction *md*, and greatest in the direction *ab*, when it is equal to that of the ordinary ray, and varying uniformly between these limits. If the figure be revolved as before, there will be generated a sphere, whose surface is the wave-surface of the ordinary ray, and *within* it a prolate ellipsoid whose surface represents the wave-surface of the extraordinary ray.

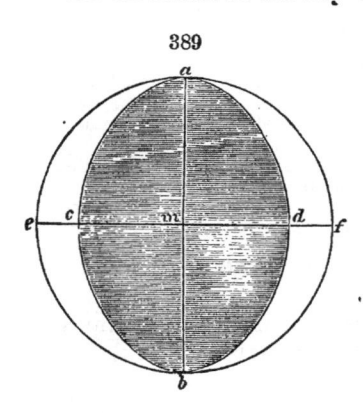

The following list includes examples of both classes of uniaxial crystals:

Negative crystals (−),	*Positive crystals* (+),
Calcite,	Quartz,
Tourmaline,	Zircon,
Corundum,	Hematite,
Beryl,	Apophyllite,
Apatite.	Cassiterite.

It may be remarked that in some species both + and − varieties have been observed. Certain crystals of apophyllite are positive for one end of the spectrum and negative for the other, and consequently for some color between the two extremes it has no double refraction.

These principles make the explanation of the use of tourmaline plates and calcite prisms as polarizing instruments (p. 150) more intelligible.

The two rays into which the single ray is divided on passing through a uniaxial crystal are, as has been said, both polarized, the ordinary ray in a plane passing through the vertical axis and the extraordinary ray perpendicular to this. In a tourmaline plate of the proper thickness, cut parallel to the axis c, the ordinary ray is absorbed (for the most part) and the extraordinary ray alone passes through, having its vibrations in the direction of the vertical axis.

In the calcite prism, of the two refracted and polarized rays, the ordinary ray is disposed of artificially in the manner mentioned (p. 151), and the extraordinary ray alone passes through, vibrating as already remarked, in the direction of the axis c, or, in other words, of the shorter diagonal of the Nicol prism.

The relation of these phenomena to the molecular structure of the crystal is well shown by the effect of pressure upon a parallelopiped of glass. Glass, normally, exhibits no colored phenomena in polarized light, since the elasticity of the ether is the same in all directions, and there is hence no double refraction. But if the block be placed under pressure, exerted on two opposite faces, the conditions are obviously changed, the density is the same in the both lateral directions but differs from that in the direction of the axis of pressure. The symmetry in molecular structure becomes that of a uniaxial crystal, and, as would be expected, on placing the block in the polariscope, a black cross with its colored rings is observed, exactly as with calcite. Similarly when glass has been suddenly and unevenly cooled its molecular structure is not homogeneous, and it will be found to polarize light, although the phenomena, for obvious reasons, will not have the regularity of the case described.

It may be added here that recent investigations by Mr. John Kerr have shown that electricity calls out birefringent phenomena in a block of glass. (Phil. Mag., l., 337.)

Optical Investigation of Uniaxial Crystals.

Sections normal or parallel to the axis in polarized light.—Suppose a section to be cut perpendicular to the vertical axis (axial section), it has already been shown that a ray of light passing through the crystal in this direction suffers no change, consequently, such a section examined in *parallel* polarized light, in the instrument (f. 385), appears as a section of an isometric crystal.

If the same section be placed in the other instrument (f. 384, p. 152), arranged for viewing the object in *converging* light, or in the tourmaline tongs, a beautiful phenomenon is observed; a symmetrical black cross—when the Nicols or tourmaline plates are crossed—with a series of concentric rings, dark and light, in monochromatic light, but in white light, showing the prismatic colors in succession in each ring. This is shown without the colors in f. 390, the arrangement of the colors in the elliptical rings of the colored plate (frontispiece) is similar.

This cross becomes white when the Nicols or tourmalines are in a parallel position, and each band of color in white light changes to its complementary tint (f. 391). These interference figures are seen* in this form only in a plate cut perpendicular to the vertical axis, and marks the *uniaxial* character of the crystal.

The explanation of this phenomenon can be only hinted at in this place

---

* Uniaxial crystals which produce circular polarization exhibit interference figures which differ somewhat from those described. Some anomalies are mentioned on p. 158. See also pp. 185 et seq.

All the rays of light, whose vibrations coincide with the vibration-planes of either of the crossed Nicols, must necessarily be extinguished. This gives rise to the black cross in the centre, with its arms in the direction of the planes mentioned. All other rays passing through the given plate obliquely will be doubly refracted, and after passing through the second Nicol, thus being referred to the same plane of polarization, they will

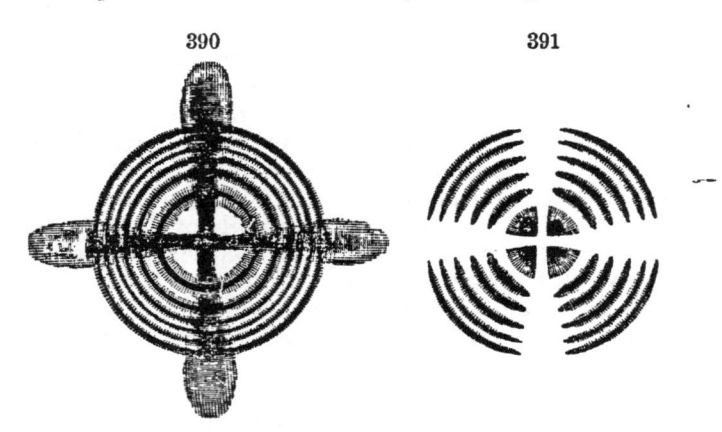

390 391

interfere, and will give rise to a series of concentric rings, light and dark in homogeneous light, but in ordinary light showing the successive colors of the spectrum. In regard to the interference of polarized rays, the fact must be stated that that can take place only when they vibrate in the same plane; two rays vibrating at right angles to each other cannot interfere. These interference phenomena are similar to the successive spectra obtained by diffraction gratings alluded to on p. 129. It is evident that, in order to observe the phenomena most advantageously, the plate must have a suitable thickness, which, however, varies with the refractive index of the substance. The thicker the plate the smaller the rings and the more they are crowded together; when the thickness is considerable, only the black brushes are seen.

Section parallel (or sharply inclined) to the axis.—If a section of a uniaxial crystal, cut parallel or inclined to the vertical axis, be examined in *parallel* polarized light, it will, when its axis coincides with the direction of vibration of one of the Nicol prisms, appear dark when the prisms are crossed. If, however, it be revolved horizontally on the stage of the polariscope (l, l, f. 384) it will appear alternately dark and light at intervals of 45°, dark under the conditions mentioned above, otherwise more or less light, the maximum of light being obtained when the axis of the section makes an angle of 45° with the plane of the Nicol. Between parallel Nicols the phenomena are the same except that the light and darkness are reversed. When the plate is not too thick the polarized ray, after passing the upper Nicol, will interfere, and in white light, the plate will show bright colors, which change as one of the Nicols or the plate is revolved.

Examined in converging light, similar sections, when very thin, show in white light a series of parallel colored bands.

Determination of the indices of refraction ω and ϵ.—One prism will

OPTICAL CHARACTERS OF UNIAXIAL CRYSTALS.

suffice for the determination of both indices of refraction, and its edge may be either parallel or perpendicular to the vertical axis.

(a) If *parallel* to the vertical axis, the angle of minimum deviation for each ray in succession must be measured. The extraordinary ray vibrates parallel to, and the ordinary ray at right angles to, the direction of the edge of the prism. For convenience it is better to isolate each of the rays in succession, which is done with a single Nicol prism. If this is held before the observing telescope with its shorter diagonal parallel to the refracting edge of the prism, the ordinary ray will be extinguished and the image of the slit observed will be that due to the extraordinary ray. If held with its plane of vibration at right angles to the prismatic edge, the extraordinary ray will be extinguished and the other alone observed. From the single observed angle, for the given color, the index of refraction can be calculated, ω or ϵ, by the formula given on p. 128, the angle of the prism being known.

(b) If the refracting edge of the prism is perpendicular to the vertical axis of the crystal, the same procedure is necessary, only in this case the ordinary ray will vibrate parallel to the prismatic edge, and the extraordinary ray at right angles to it. The two rays are distinguished, as before, by a Nicol prism.

Determination of the positive or negative character of the double refraction.—The most obvious way of determining the character of the double refraction ($\omega > \epsilon$ or $\omega > \epsilon$) is to measure the indices of refraction in accordance with the principles explained in the preceding paragraphs. It is not always possible, however, to obtain a prism suitable for this purpose, and in any case it is convenient to have a more simple method of accomplishing the result.

To do this, use may be made of a very simple principle:—the + or − character of a given crystal is determined by observing the effect produced when an axial section from it is combined in the polariscope with that of a crystal of known character.

For instance, calcite is negative, and if it be placed in conjunction with the section of a positive crystal, the whole effect observed is the same as that which would be produced if the original plate were diminished in thickness, while, if combined with a negative crystal, it is as if the plate were made thicker. It has already been remarked that, as the axial plate of a crystal increases in thickness, the number of rings visible in the field of the polariscope increases, and they become more crowded together; but, if the section is made thinner, the successive rings widen out and become less numerous. One or the other of these effects is produced by the use of the intervening section.

In the case of uniaxial crystals, however, the method which is practically most simple is that suggested by Dove—the use of an axial plate of mica of a certain thickness. The section required is a cleavage piece of such a thickness that the two rays in passing through suffer a difference of phase which is equal to a quarter wave-length, or an odd multiple of this.

Suppose that the section of the crystal to be examined, cut perpendicular to the axis, is brought between the crossed Nicols in the polariscope; the black cross and the concentric colored rings are of course visible. Let now, while the given section occupies this position, the mica plate be placed upon it, with the plane of its optic axes (determined beforehand, and the direction marked by a line for convenience) making an angle of 45° with the vibration-planes of the Nicols; the black cross disappears and there remain only two diagonally situated dark spots in the place of it. Moreover, the colored curves in the two quadrants with these spots are pushed farther away from the centre than the others. The effect produced is represented in f. 392 and f. 393. If the line joining these two dark spots stands at right angles to the axial plane of the mica, the crystal is positive (f. 392), if this line coincides with the axial plane, the crystal is negative (f. 393). The explanation of this effect is not so simple as to allow of being introduced here; the effect of the mica is to produce circular polarization of the light which it transmits.

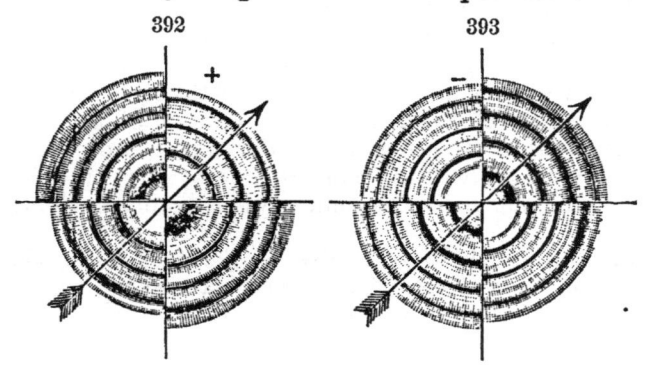

With both uniaxial and biaxial crystals the student will find it of great assistance always to have at his side a good section of a positive and a negative crystal. By comparing the phenomena observed in the section under examination with those shown by crystals of known character, he will often be saved much perplexity.

For the investigation of the *absorption phenomena* of uniaxial crystals see p. 165.

CIRCULAR POLARIZATION.

In what has been said of polarized light, in the preceding pages, it has been assumed that a polarized ray was one whose vibrations took place in a single plane, so that the plane of polarization at right angles to this was a fixed plane. Such a ray is said to be linearly polarized. There are some uniaxial crystals, however, which have the power to *rotate* the plane of polarization; the ray is said to be *circularly* polarized. They manifest this in the phenomena observed when an axial section is examined in the polariscope.

An axial section of a uniaxial crystal normally exhibits, in converging polarized light, a black cross with a series of concentric colored circles, f. 390, p. 140. If, however, a section of quartz be cut perpendicular to the axis and viewed between the crossed Nicols, the phenomena observed are different from these:—the central portion of the black cross has disappeared, and instead, the space within the inner ring is brilliantly colored. Furthermore, when the analyzing Nicol is revolved, this color changes from blue to yellow to red, and it is found that in some cases this change is produced by revolving the Nicol to the *right*, and in other cases to the *left*. To distinguish between these the first are called right-handed rotating crystals, and the others left-handed. The relations here involved will be better understood if the quartz section is viewed in parallel monochromatic light. Under these circumstances a similar plate of calcite appears dark when the Nicols are crossed, but with quartz the maximum darkness is only obtained when the analyzer has been revolved beyond its first position a certain angle; this angle increasing with the thickness of the section, and also varying with the color of the light employed.

For a section 1 mm. thick in red light, a rotation of the analyzer of 19° is required to produce the maximum darkness. For yellow light the rotation is 24° with a plate of the same thickness; with blue, 32°, and so on. The rotation of the analyzer with some crystals is to the right, with others to the left.

The explanation of these facts lies in the fact stated above, that the quartz rotates the plane of vibration of the polarized light, and the angle of rotation is different for rays of different wave-lengths. Furthermore, this rotation of the plane of vibration results from the fact that in quartz, even in the direction of its axis, double refraction takes place. The oscillations of the particles of ether take place not in straight lines but in circles, and they move in opposite directions for the two rays, ordinary and extraordinary.

An axial section of a quartz crystal can never appear dark between crossed Nicols in ordinary light, since there is no point at which all the colors are extinguished; on the contrary, it appears highly colored. The color depends upon the thickness of the section, and is the same as that observed in the centres of the rings in converging polarized light. If sections of a right-handed and left-handed crystal are placed together in the polariscope, the centre of the interference figure is occupied with a four-rayed spiral curve, called from the discoverer Airy's spiral. Twins of quartz crystals are not uncommon, consisting of the combination of right- and left-handed individual, which sometimes show the spirals of Airy.

It is a remarkable fact, discovered by Herschel, that the right- or left-handed optical character of quartz is often indicated by the position of the trapezohedral planes on the crystals. When a given trapezohedral plane appears as a modification of the prism, to the right above and left below, the crystal is optically *right-handed ;* if to the left above and right below, the crystal is *left-handed.* In f. 394 the plane is, as last remarked, left above and right below, and the crystal is hence left-handed. Cinnabar has been shown by Des Cloizeaux to possess the same property as quartz; and this is true also of some artificial salts, also solutions of sugar, etc.

In twins of quartz, the component parts may be both right-handed or both left-handed (as in those of Dauphiny and the Swiss Alps); or one may be of one kind and the other of the other. Moreover, successive layers of deposition (made as the crystal went on enlarging, and often exceedingly thin) are sometimes alternately right- and left-handed, showing a constant oscillation of polarity in the course of its formation ; and, when this is the case, and the layers are *regular*, cross-sections, examined by polarized light, exhibit a division, more or less perfect, into sectors of 120°, parallel to the plane *R*, or into sectors of 60°. If the layers are of unequal thickness

144   PHYSICAL CHARACTERS OF MINERALS.

there are broad areas of colors without sectors. In f. 395 (by Des Cloizeaux, from a crystal from the Dept. of the Aude), half of each sector of 60° is

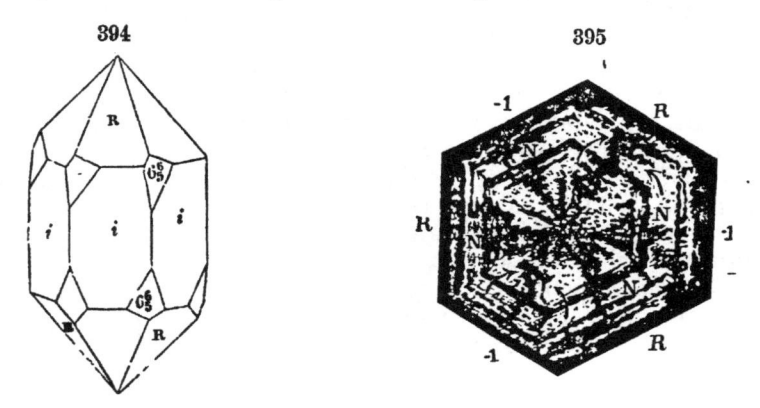

right-handed, and the other half left (as shown by the arrows), and the dark radii are neutral bands produced by the overlapping of layers of the two kinds. These overlapping portions often exhibit the phenomenon of Airy's spiral.

C. BIAXIAL CRYSTALS.

General Optical Character.

As in the crystalline systems, thus far considered, so also in the *anisometric* systems, the orthorhombic, monoclinic, and triclinic, there is a strict correspondence between the molecular structure, as exhibited in the geometrical form of the crystals, and their optical properties. In the crystals of these systems there is no longer one axis around about which the elasticity of the light-ether, that is, the velocity of the light, is everywhere alike. On the contrary, the relations are much less simple, and less easy to comprehend. There are two directions in which the light passes through the crystal without double refraction—these are called the *optic axes*, and hence the crystals are *biaxial*—but in every other direction a ray of light is separated into two rays, polarized at right angles to each other. Neither of these conforms to the law of simple refraction. The subject was first developed theoretically by Fresnel, and his conclusions have since been fully verified by experiment.

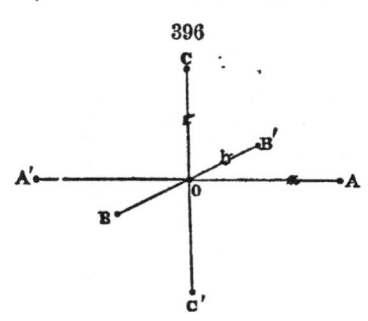

Axes of elasticity.—In regard to the elasticity of the ether in a biaxial crystal there are (1) a maximum value, (2) a minimum value, and (3) a mean value, and these values in the crystal are found in directions at right angles to each other. In f. 396, CC' represents the axis (c) of least elasticity, AA' of greatest elasticity (a), and BB' of mean elasticity (b). A ray passing in the direc-

OPTICAL CHARACTERS OF BIAXIAL CRYSTALS. 145

tion CC' vibrates in a plane at right angles, that is, parallel to BB' and AA'. Similarly for the ray BB' the vibrations are parallel to AA' and CC', and for the ray AA' parallel to BB' and CC'. Between these extreme values of the axes of elasticity, the elasticity varies according to a regular law, as will be seen in the following discussion. The form of the wave-surface for a biaxial crystal may be determined by fixing its form for the planes of the axes $\mathfrak{a}$, $\mathfrak{b}$, and $\mathfrak{c}$.

Wave-surface.—First consider the case of rays in the plane of the axes BB' and CC' (f. 397). A ray passing in the direction BB' is separated into two sets of vibrations, one parallel to AA', corresponding to the greatest elasticity, moving more rapidly than the other set, parallel to CC', which correspond to the least elasticity. The velocities of the two sets of vibrations are made proportional to the lengths of the lines mn, and mo respectively, in f. 397. Again, for a ray in the same plane, parallel to CC', the vibrations are (1) parallel to AA', and propagated faster (greatest elasticity) than the other set; (2) parallel to BB' (mean elasticity). Again, in f. 397, on the line CC'', mn'', and mq'' are made proportional to these two velocities; here $mn = mn''$, and for a ray in the same plane in any other direction, there will be one set of vibrations parallel to AA', with the same velocity as before, and another set at right angles with a velocity between mo and mq'', determined by the ellipse whose semi-axes are proportional to the mean and least axes of elasticity.

Fig. 397 then represents the section of the wave-surface through the axes CC' and BB'. The circle nn'' shows the constant velocity for all vibrations parallel to AA', and the ellipse the variable values of the velocity for the other set of vibrations at right angles to the first.

Again, for a ray in the plane AA', BB', the method of the construction is similar. The vibrations will in every case take place in the plane at right angles to the direction of the ray, which plane must always pass through the axis CC' of least elasticity. Hence for every direction of the ray in the plane mentioned, one set of vibrations will always be parallel to CC', and hence be propagated with a constant velocity

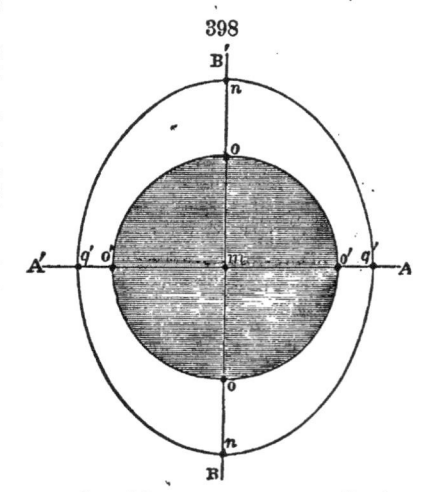

$= mo'$, f. 398), and hence this is expressed by the circle oo'. The other set of vibrations will be at right angles to CC', and the velocity with which they are propagated will vary according as they are parallel to AA' ($= mn$, f. 398), or parallel to BB' ($= mq'$), or some intermediate value for an intermediate position. The section of the wave-surface is consequently a circle within an ellipse.

Finally, let the ray pass in some direction in the plane CC', AA', of least and greatest elasticity, the section of the wave-surface is also a circle and ellipse. Suppose the ray passes in the direction parallel to AA', the vibrations will be (1) parallel to CC', and (2) parallel to BB', those (1) parallel to CC' (least axis of elasticity) are propagated more slowly than those (2) parallel to BB' (axis of mean elasticity). In f. 399, on the line AA', lay off mo' and mq' proportional to these two values.

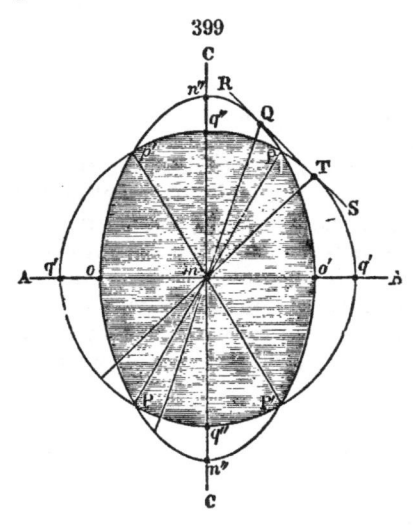

Again, for a ray parallel to CC' the vibrations will take place (1) parallel to AA', and (2) parallel to BB', the former will be propagated with greater velocity than those latter. These two values of the velocity in the direction CC' are represented by mn'' and mq'' ($= mq'$). For any intermediate position of the ray in the same plane there will always be one set of vibrations parallel to BB' ($mq' = mq''$, f. 399, hence the circle). The other set at right angles to these will be propagated with a velocity varying according to the direction, from that corresponding to the least axis of elasticity (represented by mo', f. 399), to that of the greatest axis of elasticity (mn'').

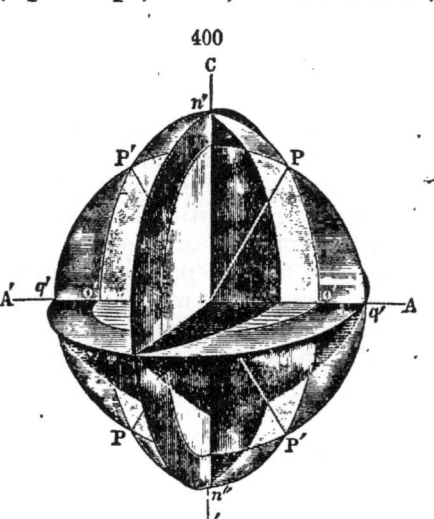

Optic axes.—It is seen that the circle, representing the uniform velocity of vibrations parallel to b, and the ellipse representing the varying value of the velocity for the vibrations at right angles to these, intersect one another at P, P', f. 399. The obvious meaning of this fact is that, for the directions mP, and mP', making equal angles with the axis CC', the velocity is the same for both sets of vibrations; these are not separated from each other, the ray is *not doubly refracted*, and *not polarized*.

These two directions are called the OPTIC AXES. All anisometric crystals have, as has been stated, two optic axes, and are hence called *biaxial*.

The complete wave-surface of a biaxial crystal is constructed from the three sections given in f. 397, 398, 399. It is shown graphically in f. 400, where the lines PP, and $P'P'$ are the two optic axes.

Bisectrices, or Mean-lines.—As shown in f. 399, the optic axes always lie in the plane of greatest (𝔞) and least (𝔠) elasticity, and the value of the optic axial angle is known when the axes of elasticity are given as stated below. The axis of elasticity which, as the line CC', f. 399, bisects the acute angle is called the *acute bisectrix*, or *first mean-line* (erste Mittellinie, *Germ.*), and that bisecting the obtuse angle, the *obtuse bisectrix*, or *second mean-line* (zweite Mittellinie, *Germ.*).

Positive and negative crystals.—When the acute bisectrix is the axis of least elasticity (𝔠), it is said to be *positive*, and when it is the axis of greatest (𝔞) elasticity, it is said to be *negative*. Barite is positive, mica negative.

Indices of refraction.—It has been seen that in uniaxial crystals there are two extreme values for the velocity with which light is propagated, and corresponding to them, and inversely proportional to them, *two* indices of refraction. Similarly for biaxial crystals, where there are three axes of elasticity, there are three indices of refraction—a maximum index a, a minimum γ, and a mean value β; a is the index for the rays propagated at right angles to 𝔞, but vibrating parallel to 𝔞; β is the index for rays propagated perpendicularly to 𝔟, by vibrations parallel to 𝔟; γ is the index for rays propagated perpendicularly to 𝔠, but vibrating parallel to 𝔠. $a = \frac{1}{𝔞}, \beta = \frac{1}{𝔟}, \gamma = \frac{1}{𝔠}.$

If a, β, and γ are known, the value of the optic axial angle $(2V)$ can be calculated from them by the following formula:

$$\cos V = \sqrt{\frac{\frac{1}{\beta^2} - \frac{1}{\gamma^2}}{\frac{1}{a^2} - \frac{1}{\gamma^2}}}$$

Dispersion of the optic axes.—It is obvious that the three indices of refraction may have different values for the different colors, and as the angle of the optic axes, as explained in the last paragraph, is determined by these three values, the axial angle will also vary in a corresponding manner.

This variation in the value of the axial angle for rays of different wave lengths is called the dispersion of the axes, and the two possible cases are distinguished by writing $\rho > \upsilon$ when the angle for the red rays (ρ) is greater than for the blue (violet, υ), and $\rho < \upsilon$ when the reverse is true.

In the properties thus far mentioned, the three systems are alike; in details, however, they differ widely.

Practical Investigation of Biaxial Crystals.

Interference figures.—A section cut perpendicular to either axis will show, in converging polarized light, a system of concentric rays analogous to those of uniaxial crystals, f. 390, but more or less elliptical. There is, moreover, no black cross, but a single black line, which changes its position as the Nicols are revolved.

If a section of a biaxial crystal, cut perpendicularly to the first, that is acute, bisectrix, is viewed in the polariscope, a different phenomenon is observed.

There are seen in this case, supposing the plane of the axes to make an angle of 45° with the planes of polarization of the crossed Nicols, two black hyperbolas, marking the position of the axes, a series of elliptical curves surrounding the two centres and finally uniting, forming a series of lemniscates. If monochromatic light is employed, the rings are alternately light and dark; if white light, each ring shows the successive colors of the spectrum. If one of the Nicol prisms be revolved, the dark hyperbolic brushes gradually become white, and the colors of the rings take the complementary tints after a revolution of 90°. Since the black hyperbolic brushes mark the position of the optic axes, the smaller the axial angle the nearer together are the hyperbolas, and when the angle is very small, the axial figure

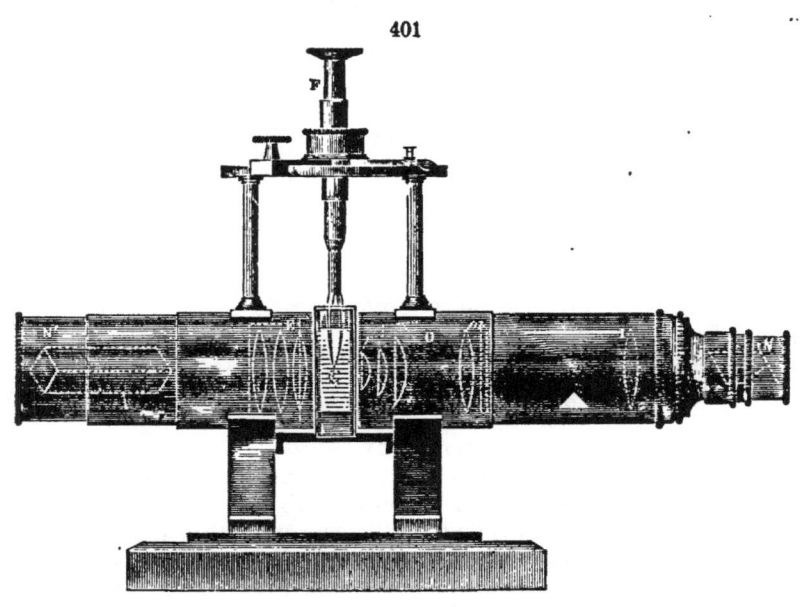

401

observed closely resembles the simple cross of a uniaxial crystal. On the other hand, when the axial angle is large the hyperbolas are far apart, and may even be so far apart as to be invisible in the field of the polariscope.

When the plane of the axes coincides with the plane of vibration for either Nicol, these being crossed, an unsymmetrical black cross is observed, and also a series of elliptical curves. Both these figures are well exhibited on the frontispiece; the one gradually changes into the other as the crystal-section is revolved in the horizontal plane, the Nicols remaining stationary.

A section of a biaxial crystal cut perpendicular to the obtuse bisectrix will exhibit the same figures under the same conditions in polarized light, when the angle is not too large. This is, however, generally the case, and in consequence the axes suffer *total reflection* on the inner surface of the section, and no axial figures are visible. This is sometimes the case also with a section cut normal to the acute bisectrix, when the angle is large. A micrometer scale in the polariscope, f. 384, allows of an approximate measurement of the axial angle; the value of each division of the scale being known.

Measurement of the axial angle.*—The determination of the angle made by the optic axes is of the highest importance, and the method of procedure offers no great difficulties. Fig. 401 shows the instrument recommended for this purpose by DesCloizeaux; its general features will be understood without detailed description; some improvements have been introduced by Groth, which make the instrument more accurate and convenient of use. The section of the crystal, cut at right angles to the bisectrix, is held in the pincers at c, with the plane of the axes *horizontal*, making an angle of 45° with the plane of vibration of the Nicols (NN). There is a cross-wire in the focus of the eye-piece, and as the pincers holding the section are turned by the screw F, one of the axes, that is one black hyperbola, is brought in coincidence with the vertical cross-wire, and then, by a further revolution of F, the second. The angle which the section has been turned from one axis to the second, as read off at the vernier H on the graduated circle above, is the *apparent* angle for the axes of the given crystal as seen in the air (aca, f. 402). It is only the *apparent* angle, for, owing to the refraction suffered on passing from the section of the crystal to the air, the true axial angle is more or less increased, according to the refractive index of the given crystal.

This being understood, the fact already stated is readily intelligible, that when the axial angle exceeds a certain limit, the axes will suffer total reflection (p. 128), and they will be no longer visible at all. When this is the case, oil† or some other medium with high refractive power is made use of, into which the axes pass when no longer visible in the air. In the instrument described a small receptacle holding the oil is brought between the tubes, as seen in the figure, and the pincers holding the section are immersed in this, and the angle measured as before.

In the majority of cases it is only the acute axial angle that it is practicable to measure; but sometimes, especially when oil is made use of, the obtuse angle can also be determined from a second section normal to the obtuse bisectrix.

If E = the apparent semi-axial angle in air (f. 402).
H_a = the apparent semi-acute angle in oil.
H_o = "   "   "   " obtuse "   "   "
V_a = the real (or interior) semi-acute angle (f. 402).
V_o = "   "   "   "   " semi-obtuse " (f. 402).
n = index of refraction for the oil.
β = the mean refractive index for the given crystallized substance.

---

* See further on p. 180.
† Almond oil, which has been decolorized by exposure to the light, is commonly employed.

$$\sin E = n \sin H_a; \quad \sin V_a = \frac{n}{\beta} \sin H_a; \quad \sin V_o = \frac{n}{\beta} \sin H_o.$$

These formulas give the true interior angle from the measured apparent angle when the mean refractive index (β) is known.

If, however, it is possible to measure both the acute and obtuse apparent angles, the true angle, and also the value of β, can be determined from them. For $\sin V_o = \cos V_a$, hence:

$$\tan V_a = \frac{\sin H_a}{\sin H_o}; \quad \beta = n \frac{\sin H_a}{\sin V_a} = n \frac{\sin H_o}{\cos V_a} = \frac{\sin E}{\sin V_a}.$$

In measuring this angle, if white light is employed, the colors being separated, the position of the hyperbolas is a little uncertain; hence it is always important to measure the angle for monochromatic light, red and yellow and blue particularly. This is especially essential where the dispersion of the axes is considerable.

Determination of the indices of refraction.*—The values of the three indices of refraction, a, β, γ, for biaxial crystals, may be determined from three prisms cut with their refracting edges parallel respectively to the three axes of elasticity a, b, and c. In each case, after the angle of the prism has been measured, the angle of minimum deviation must be measured for that one of the two refracted rays whose vibrations are parallel to the edge of the prism; the formula of p. 128 is then employed.

It is possible, however, to obtain the values of a, β, and γ with *two* prisms; in this case one of the prisms must be so made that its vertical edge is parallel to one axis of elasticity, while the line bisecting its refracting angle at this edge is parallel to a second. In the case of such a prism the minimum deviation of the ray is obtained for both rays, that having its vibrations parallel to the prism-edge, and that vibrating at right angles to this, that is parallel to the bisector of the prismatic angle.

Of the three indices of refraction, β is one which it is most important to determine, since by means of it, in accordance with the above formulas, the true value of the axial angle can be calculated from its apparent value in air. The prism to give the value of β should obviously have its refracting edge parallel to the mean axis of elasticity b, that is at right angles to the plane of the optic axes.

Determination of the positive or negative character of biaxial crystals.—The question of the positive or negative character of a biaxial crystal is determined from the values of the indices of refraction, where these can be obtained. If c, the axis of least elasticity, is the acute bisectrix, the crystal is optically *positive*; if a, the axis of greatest elasticity, is the acute bisectrix, the crystal is optically *negative*; in the former case the value of b is nearer that of c than of a, in the second case the reverse of this is true.

There is, however, a more simple method of solving the problem, as was remarked also in regard to uniaxial crystals. The methods are similar.

The quarter-undulation mica plate may be employed just as with uniaxial crystals, but its use is not very satisfactory excepting when the axial divergence is quite small. In this case it can be employed to advantage, the

---

* See further on pp. 177 et seq.

plane of the axes of the crystal investigated being made to coincide with the vibration-plane of one of the Nicols. The more general method is the employment of a wedge-shaped piece of quartz; this is so cut that one surface coincides with the direction of the vertical axis, and the other makes an angle of 4° to 6° with it. By this means a section of varying thickness is obtained. The section to be examined normal to the acute bisectrix is brought between the crossed Nicols of the polariscope (f. 384), and with its axial plane making an angle of 45° with the polarization-plane of the Nicol prisms; that is, so that the black hyperbolas are visible. The quartz wedge is now introduced slowly between the section examined and the analyzer; in the instrument figured a slit above gives an opportunity to insert it. The quartz section is introduced first, in a direction at right angles to the axial plane, that is, to the line joining the hyperbolas, of the plate investigated; and second, parallel to the axial plane, that is, in the direction of the line joining the hyperbolas. In one direction or the other it will be seen, when the proper thickness of the quartz wedge is reached, that the central rings appear to increase in diameter, at the same time advancing from the centre to the extremities.

The effect, in other words, is that which would have been produced by the *thinning* of the given section. If the phenomenon is observed in the first case when the axis of the quartz is parallel to the axial plane, that is to the obtuse bisectrix, it shows that this bisectrix must have an opposite sign to the quartz, that is, the obtuse bisectrix is negative, and the acute bisectrix *positive*. If the mentioned change in the interference figures takes place when the axis of the quartz is at right angles to the axial plane, then obviously the opposite must be true and the acute bisectrix is *negative*.

The same effect may be obtained by bringing an ordinary quartz section of greater or less thickness, cut normal to the axis, between the analyzer and the crystal examined, and then inclining it, first in the direction of the axial plane, and again at right angles to it. The method of investigation with the quartz wedge can be applied even in those cases where the axial angle is too large to appear in the air.

For the investigation of the *absorption phenomena* of biaxial crystals, see p. 165.

Distinguishing Optical Characters of Orthorhombic Crystals.

In the *Orthorhombic System*, in accordance with the symmetry of the crystallization, the three axes of elasticity *coincide* with the three crystallographic axes. Further than this, there is no immediate relation between the two sets of axes in respect to magnitude, for the reason that, as has been stated, the choice of the crystallographic axes is arbitrary, and has been made, in most cases, without reference to the optical character.

Schrauf has proposed that the crystallographic vertical axis ($\dot{c}$) should be always made to coincide with the acute bisectrix, which would be very desirable, especially, as urged by him, in showing the true relations between the orthorhombic and hexagonal systems. Of course, this suggestion can be carried out only in those species in which the optical character is known.

Schrauf (Phys. Min., p. 302, 303) has shown there is a close analogy between certain orthorhombic crystals whose prismatic angle is near 120° (compare remarks on twins, p 96), and the crystals of the hexagonal system. With these the acute bisectrix is uniformly parallel to the prismatic edge, and normal to the six-sided basal plane, analogous to the one optic axis of true hexagonal forms. Moreover, he shows that the nearer the prismatic angle approaches 120°, the less the difference between the three axes of elasticity, and the nearer the approach to the uniaxial character.

By the combination of thin plates of a biaxial mica optical phenomena may, under some conditions, be observed in polarized light which are similar to those shown by uniaxial crystals. Similarly twins of chrysoberyl (p. 97) have been described which in spots gave the axial image of uniaxial crystals. This subject has been investigated by Reusch (Pogg. cxxxvi., 626, 637, 1869), and later by Cooke (Am. Acad. Sci., Boston, p, 35, 1874).

Practical Optical Investigation of Orthorhombic Crystals.

Determination of the plane of the optic axes.—The *position* of the three axes of elasticity in an orthorhombic crystal is always known, since they must coincide with the crystallographic axes; but the plane of the *optic axes*, that is, of the axes of greatest (a) and least (c) elasticity, must in each case be determined. This plane will be parallel to one of the three diametral or pinacoid planes. In order to determine in which the axes lie, it is necessary to cut sections parallel to these three directions; one of these three sections will in all ordinary cases show, in converging polarized light, the interference figures peculiar to biaxial crystals. It is evident, too, that two of the three sections named determine the character of the third, so that the plane of the optic axes and the position of the acute bisectrix can be in practice generally told from them.

Measurement of the axial angle, $\rho \lessgtr v$.—From the section showing the axial figures, that is, normal to the acute bisectrix, the axial angle can be measured in the manner which has been described (p. 149). If it is practicable to determine also the obtuse axial angle, from a second section normal to the obtuse bisectrix, it will be possible to calculate the true axial angle from these data, and also the mean index of refraction (β).

There is further to be determined the dispersion of the axes. Whether the axial angle for red rays is greater or less than for blue ($\rho > v$, or $\rho < v$) can be seen immediately from the figure of the axes, as in f. 1a, 1b, in the colored plate, (frontispiece). It is obviously true in this case, from f. 1a, as also f. 1b, that the angle for the blue rays is greater than that for the red ($\rho < v$), and so in general. This same point is also accurately determined, of course, by the measured angle for the two monochromatic colors.

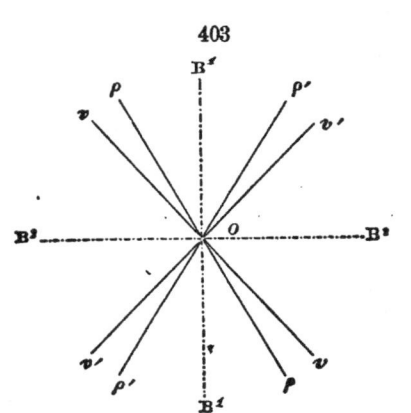

In all cases the same line will be the bisectrix of the axial angle for both blue and red rays, so that the position of the respective axes is symmetrical with reference to the bisectrix. In f. 403, the dispersion of the axes is illustrated, where $\rho < v$; it is shown also that the lines, $B^1 B^1$ and $B^2 B^2$, bisect the angles of both red ($\rho O \rho'$) and blue ($v O v'$) rays. It also needs no further explanation that for a certain relation of the refractive indices of the different colors, the acute bisectrix of the axial angle for red rays may be the obtuse bisectrix for the angle for blue rays.

Indices of refraction, etc.—The determination of the indices of refraction and the character (+ or −) of the acute bisectrix is made for orthorhombic crystals in the same way as for all biaxial crystals (p. 150). It is merely to be mentioned that, since the axes of elasticity always coincide with the crystallographic axes, it will happen not infrequently that crystals without artificial preparation will furnish, in their prismatic or dome series, prisms whose edges are parallel to the axes of elasticity, and consequently at once suitable for the determination of the indices of refraction.

DISTINGUISHING OPTICAL CHARACTERS OF MONOCLINIC CRYSTALS.

Position of the axes of elasticity.—In crystals belonging to the *monoclinic system* one of the axes of elasticity always coincides with the orthodiagonal axis b, and the other two lie in the plane of symmetry at right angles to this axis. Here obviously three cases are possible, according to which two of the axes, a, b, or c, lie in the plane of symmetry.

Corresponding to these three positions of the axes of elasticity, there may occur three kinds of dispersion of these axes, or *dispersion of the bisectrices*. This dispersion arises from the fact that, while the position of one axis of elasticity is always fixed, the position of the other two is indeterminate and for the same crystal may be different for the different colors, so that the bisectrices of the different colors may not coincide.

Dispersion of the bisectrices.—1. The bisectrices, that is, the axes of greatest and least elasticity, lie in the plane of symmetry, while the orthodiagonal axis b coincides with **b**. The optic axes here suffer a dispersion in this plane of symmetry, and, as already stated, they do not lie symmetrically with reference to the acute bisectrix. This is illustrated in f. 404, where MM is the bisectrix for the angle, vOv', and BB for the angle $\rho O \rho'$. This kind of dispersion is called by DesCloizeaux *inclined* (dispersion inclinée).

2. The second case is that where the plane of the optic axes is perpendicular to the plane of symmetry, and the acute bisectrix stands at right angles to the orthodiagonal axis b. In other words, the acute bisectrix and the axis of mean elasticity both lie in the plane of symmetry. In this case also dispersion of the axes may take place, and in this way—the plane of the optic axes for all the colors lies parallel to the orthodiagonal, but these planes may have different inclinations to the vertical axis. This is called *horizontal* dispersion by DesCloizeaux.

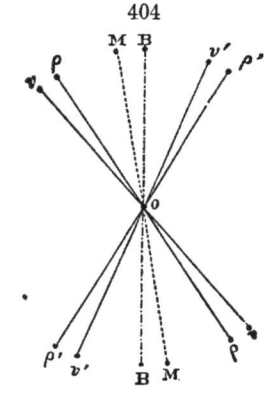

3. Still again, in the third place, the plane of the optic axes lies perpendicular to the plane of symmetry; but in this case the acute bisectrix is parallel to the crystallographic axis b, so that the obtuse bisectrix and axis of mean elasticity lie in the plane of symmetry. The dispersion which

results in this case is called by DesCloizeaux *crossed* (dispersion tournante or croisée).

Dispersion as shown in the interference figures.—If an axial section of a monoclinic crystal be examined in converging polarized light, the kind of dispersion which characterizes it will be indicated by the nature of the interference figures observed; the three cases are illustrated by the figures upon the frontispiece, taken from DesCloizeaux. (frontispiece).

Figs. 1*a*, 1*b* represent the interference figures for an orthorhombic crystal (nitre), characterized by the symmetry in the size of the rings, and the distribution of the colors. Figs. 2*a*, 2*b* (diopside), 3*a*, 3*b* (orthoclase), 4*a*, 4*b* (borax), are examples of the corresponding figures for monoclinic crystals, characterized as such more or less distinctly by the want of symmetry in the size of the rings about the two axes, and the irregularity in the arrangement of the colors.

(1) *Inclined dispersion.*—Where the axes are not symmetrically situated with reference to the acute bisectrix. The relation of the two axial figures is illustrated by f. 405. In f. 2*a*, 2*b* this kind of dispersion is indicated by

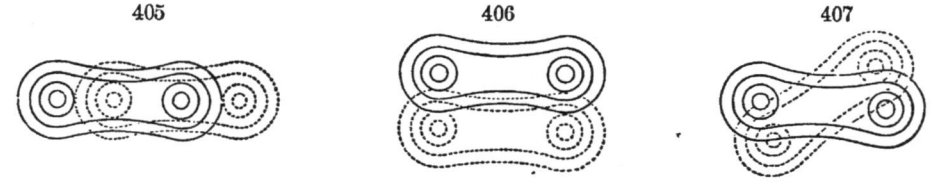

the position of the red and blue at the centres of the rings, and on the borders of the hyperbolas, compare f. 1*a*, 1*b* of the normal figure, where there is no dispersion of the bisectrices.

(2) *Horizontal dispersion*, where the planes of the optic axes for the different colors make different angles with the axis.—This is illustrated by f. 406. The effect upon the interference figures is seen in f. 3*a*, 3*b* of the plate, by comparing the colors within the rings (f. 3*a*), and on the borders of the hyperbolas (f. 3*b*), with f. 1*a*, 1*b*.

(3) *Crossed dispersion*, where the acute bisectrix coincides with the crystallographic axis *b*.—This is illustrated in f. 407, and the interference figures belonging to this kind of dispersion are seen in f. 4*a*, 4*b* of the plate, compared as before with 1*a*, 1*b*, and with the other figures.

Practical Optical Investigation of Monoclinic Crystals.

Determination of the position of the axes of elasticity, that is, the directions of vibration. Stauroscope.—The position of one axis of elasticity is alone known, since, as has been stated, it coincides with the crystallographic axis *b*. In order to determine the position of the other axes in the plane of symmetry, where they necessarily lie, use is made of an instrument, first proposed by von Kobell, called the STAUROSCOPE. The principle of this instrument is very simple. Suppose that the two Nicols in the polariscope (f. 385) have their planes of polarization crossed, causing the maximum extinction of light. Now, if a section of any biaxial crystal is brought between them, obviously, if the position of its two rectangular axes of elasticity, which are its two directions of vibration, coincide with those of the two Nicols, it will produce no change in appearance: the field of the polariscope, which was dark before, remains dark. But suppose, on the other hand, that it is placed in any other position in the plane, so that its two rectangular directions of vibration do *not* coincide with those of the Nicols, the field is no longer dark, but more or less light. The reason for this is, that the light from the lower Nicol meeting the crystal plate is separated, according to the law of the parallelogram of forces, into two sets of vibrations, which are again resolved by the analyzing Nicol, and only one set extinguished by it. If, however, the plate be gradually changed in position, that is, revolved horizontally, until its vibration-directions (axes of elasticity) coincide with those of the Nicols, then, as at first, the light is extinguished. If the angle is measured which it is necessary to revolve the section to accomplish the result just remarked, that will be the angle between the direction of one of the axes of elasticity of the plate in its original position and the vibration-plane of the Nicol.

In figure 408, let the two larger rectangular arrows represent the vibration-directions for the two Nicols, and between the two prisms suppose a section of a monoclinic crystal, $abcd$, to be placed so that one edge of a known crystallographic plane (*eg.*, $i\text{-}i$) coincides with one of these lines. The field of the microscope, dark before, since the prisms were crossed, is no longer so, and becomes dark again, as explained, only when the crystal is revolved so that its vibration-directions (the smaller dotted arrows) coincide with those of the Nicols, which is indicated by the maximum extinction of the light. The crystal has then the position $a'b'c'd'$. The angle (f. 408), which it has been necessary to revolve the plate to obtain the effect described, is the angle which one of the axes of elasticity in the given plate makes with the given crystallographic edge $i\text{-}i$.

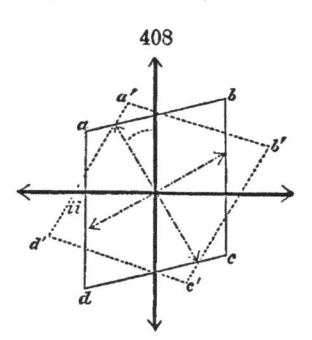

The preceding explanations cover everything that is essential in the Stauroscope; but a variety of improvements have been introduced, which practically make the measurements by means of the instrument much more easy and accurate.

It will be seen that the most important feature is the point where the maximum extinction of the light occurs; this, however, is not easy for the eye to decide upon, and if the trial is made, it will be found that the change produced by a revolution of several degrees is hardly perceptible. To overcome this difficulty, von Kobell proposed to introduce a section of calcite just below the analyzer, because its interference figure gives a better opportunity to judge of a change in the intensity of the light. A still better plan is to introduce a composition plate of calcite, as proposed by Brezina, giving a peculiar interference figure, a very slight change in which destroys its symmetry, and it takes its normal form only when the planes of polarization of the two Nicols are *exactly* at right angles. Supposing this to be the case, when the crystal has been introduced the interference figure is disturbed, it returns to its normal appearance only when the crystal has been revolved to the point where the vibration-directions of the Nicols and crystal section exactly coincide.*

It will be observed again, that it is essential that the direction of the known edge of the crystal should be exactly parallel to the vibration-direction of one of the Nicols. This condition, in the case of small crystals especially, is hard to fulfil, and to accomplish it most satisfactorily Groth has proposed to use the plate shown in f. 409.

The plate of glass, v, held in its present position by the spring, has one edge polished, which adjoins u, and the direction of this is made to coincide exactly with the line joining the opposite zero points of the graduation. The crystal section is attached to this plate over the hole seen in v, and with a plane of known crystallographic position, either O, $i\text{-}\bar{\imath}$ or a plane in that zone or a corresponding edge, coinciding with the direction of the polished edge of the plate. Whether this coincidence is exact can be tested by the reflective goniometer. In order to eliminate any small error, Groth proposes to measure the divergence from the exact coincidence, and then to make a corresponding correction, for which he furnishes a series of tables.

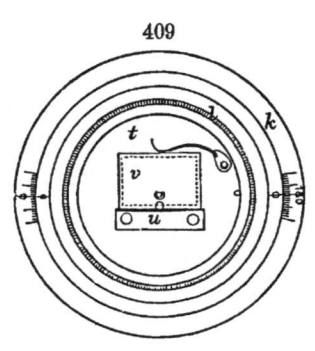

After the adjustment of the crystal section on the plate, the latter is inserted in its place, the whole plate, l, k, occupying the position indicated in f. 385, and the Nicols so adjusted that the plane of vibration of one coincides with the line 0° to 180°. The angle of revolution of the plate, l, is obtained from the graduated scale on k.

It is not always easy to make the adjustment of the Nicols alluded to, but the error arising when the vibration-plane of the Nicol does not coincide with the line 0° to 180° is easily eliminated. This is accomplished by removing the plate v, and, without disturbing the crystal section, restoring it to its place in an inverted position. The measured angle, if before too great, will now be as much too small, and the arithmetical mean of the two measurements will be the true angle.

Reference further may be made to Groth, Pogg. Ann., cxliv., 34, 1871.

Determination of the plane of the optic axes.—The investigation of a section of a monoclinic crystal parallel to the plane of symmetry determines the position of the two remaining axes of elasticity, but it does not fix the relative position of the greatest and least axes of elasticity, that is, the plane of the optic axes. To solve the latter point, sections normal to each of the three axes must be examined in converging polarized light, and one of them will show the characteristic interference figures. The section parallel to the plane of symmetry is first to be examined, and if it does not show the axes even in oil, one or both of the other sections spoken of must be employed.

Axial angle, dispersion, etc.—The method of measuring the axial angle has been already explained, and if this is determined for the different colors it will determine the dispersion of the axes $\rho \lessgtr v$.

The dispersion of the axes of elasticity has been shown to be always indicated by the character of interference figures; its amount, where con-

---

* See p. 180 for a description of the Calderon plate.

siderable, may be determined by making the stauroscopic measurements for different colors.

The remaining points to be investigated, the indices of refraction, and the + or − character of the crystal, need no further explanation beyond that which has been given, pp. 150, 151.

DISTINGUISHING OPTICAL CHARACTERS OF TRICLINIC CRYSTALS.

The crystals of the triclinic system are characterized by their entire want of crystallographic symmetry, the position and inclination of the axes being entirely arbitrary, and it follows from this that there is no necessary connection between them and the rectangular axes of elasticity. More than one of the three kinds of dispersion mentioned on p. 154 may occur in a single crystal, and the interference figures will indicate the existence of both.

The *practical investigation* of triclinic crystals optically involves great difficulty; in general a series of successive trials are required to determine the position of the axes of elasticity. When these are found, the axial sections can be prepared and the axial angle determined, and the other points settled as with other biaxial crystals.

EFFECT OF HEAT UPON THE OPTICAL CHARACTERS OF CRYSTALS.

In addition to the ordinary investigation of crystal-sections in the polariscope, it is often important to determine the influence of heat upon the optical character of crystals. The axial angle may be measured at any required temperature by the use of a metal air-bath. This is placed at C, (f. 401), and extends beyond the instrument on either side, so as to allow of its being heated with gas burners; a thermometer inserted in the bath makes it possible to regulate the temperature as may be desired. This bath has two openings, closed with glass plates, corresponding to the two tubes carrying the lenses, and the crystal-section, held as usual in the pincers, is seen through these glass windows.

The conclusions of DesCloizeaux (see Literature) as to the influence of heat upon the optical characters of crystals are as follows:

(1) *Uniaxial* crystals appear to be uninfluenced by a heating of from 10° to 190° C. (2) *Biaxial* crystals of the *orthorhombic* system suffer a greater or less change in axial angle. (3) *Biaxial* crystals of the *monoclinic* system suffer a change in axial angle, and in addition also in the plane of the axes when it is not the plane of symmetry. *Triclinic* crystals also show a little change in the position of the axes.

A striking example of the change in axial divergence is furnished by gypsum. At ordinary temperatures the axes lie in the plane of symmetry (i-i); at 80° C. they unite in a line making an angle of 37° 28' with a normal to O; and with an increased temperature they again separate in a plane perpendicular to i-i. DesCloizeaux found that the feldspars, when heated up to a certain point, suffer a change in the position of the axes, and if the heat becomes greater and is long continued, they do not return again to their original position, but remain altered. Weiss* has made use of this principle

---

* Zur Kenntniss der Feldspathbildung; Haarlem Soc. Verhandl., **xxv.**, 1866.

to determine at what temperature certain feldspathic rocks were formed This constant change of axial angle upon heating is true also of brookite, zoisite, and other minerals. The investigations of Pfaff show that the optical properties of some uniaxial crystals also are affected by heating, though to no great extent. Pogg., cxxiii., 179, cxxiv., 448, etc.

ANOMALIES EXHIBITED BY SOME CRYSTALS IN THEIR OPTICAL PHENOMENA.*

There are a considerable number of crystals of the three classes, which, from a variety of causes, exhibit irregularities in their optical characters; some of the more important cases are mentioned here.

Isometric crystals.—Boracite, and also senarmontite, sometimes exhibit interference figures resembling closely those of biaxial crystals. In the case of boracite this is explained by DesCloizeaux as due to the presence of enclosed crystals of parasite formed by alteration. Perofskite is also strongly doubly refracting, and in polarized light appears to be biaxial, although, as shown by Kokscharow, it is isometric in crystallographic relations. The irregularities are supposed by him to be caused by the want of homogeneity in the internal structure of the crystals.

The properties of double refraction possessed by some substances, crystallized and non-crystallized, which are normally isotrope, are explained by Biot to be due to lamellar polarization. This is analogous to the production of polarized light by means of a series of thin plates (see p. 132). Alum crystals have often the lamellar structure, which causes these phenomena.

Analcite and leucite have been included in the list of isometric crystals, which exhibit anomalous optical characters; but the most accurate crystallographic determination has referred both species to the tetragonal system. Tension or compression at the time of crystallization may cause isotropic crystals to polarize light; Schrauf has described a *uniaxial* diamond, and it was long since shown by Brewster that some diamonds give evidence in polarized light of compression about interior cavities.

Uniaxial crystals.—A want of homogeneity in the crystals, as shown by DesCloizeaux, may cause uniaxial crystals to exhibit in polarized light a variety of abnormal phenomena. In some cases the axial figures resemble those of biaxial crystals, the cross in the middle of the field (f. 390) not being closed, but separated into two hyperbolas, lying near each other. Beryl, zircon, vesuvianite, and apatite are examples. That such crystals are nevertheless *uniaxial* is proved by the fact that the opening of the cross is independent of the position of the Nicols, and is not altered if the section is turned in a horizontal plane. If this is not true, or if, when the section is heated (p. 157) the distance between the hyberbolas is altered, it is a proof that the irregularity is not due to lamellar polarization, but that the two indices of refraction are not exactly equal, and consequently that the crystal is not *strictly* uniaxial. In such cases a revision of the crystallographical elements is desirable.

The axial figure shown by a section of apophyllite is peculiar, exhibiting

---

* For a discussion of this subject in the light of recent (1882) investigations, see pp. 185 et seq.

a series of rings alternately dark violet, and yellow. The explanation is found in the fact previously stated, that it is positive for red rays, negative for blue, and does not doubly refract yellow light.

Among *biaxial crystals* irregularities in the optical phenomena are often observed. They are due in part to want of homogeneity, in part to twin structure, and also to other causes. In brookite the planes of the axes for red and blue rays are at right angles to each other, and hence the axial figures vary much from those normally observed; in titanite the axial angle for the two colors is widely different, and this also gives rise to an axial figure of abnormal appearance.

Irregular structure, due to twinning, is a frequent cause of peculiar optical phenomena; crystals, in external form apparently simple, often show themselves to be made up of irregular banded layers in twinned position, when examined in polarized light; this is true of many minerals.

In some crystals, as occasionally in the epidote from the Untersulzbachthal in the Tyrol, the biaxial figures may be observed immediately, without the use of the polariscope. This is due to the complex twinned structure of the crystal, a thin lamella in reverse position being enclosed in the interior, so that the parts of the crystal on either side act as polarizer and analyzer.

Practical Suggestions in regard to the Preparation and use of Crystal Sections made for Optical Examination.

The most important task is the preparation of a plate for examination in the Stauroscope, or for the observation of the axial interference-figures. In this we are often assisted by the cleavage, which sometimes makes it possible to obtain the required section without the labor of cutting it. This is conspicuously the case with mica; also with topaz and anhydrite, and other minerals. Sometimes the natural surfaces need to be made smooth and polished. Furthermore natural crystals sometimes occur in a tabular form, thin and transparent enough to answer the purpose; this is true of the crystals of wulfenite from Utah. In most cases, however, the section must be actually cut. The means required in such cases vary with the hardness of the mineral under examination. For the hardest minerals diamond powder is made use of in grinding; it is employed after the manner of the lapidary. (It may be mentioned here that the investigator will generally find it for his interests, both as regards time, money, and accuracy of results, to employ a lapidary to do this work for him.) The diamond powder is applied to a thin wheel of soft iron or copper, rotating on a lathe.

For minerals which are not so extremely hard, good emery may be used instead of diamond powder. It is merely necessary to apply the emery and water to the edge of the wheel as it revolves, the mineral being held firmly against. A neater and more advantageous method, where the amount of material is small, is the use of a fine saw, or better wire, mounted in a frame, and used with either diamond powder or emery moistened with water or oil. The crystal may be mounted in wax or otherwise, if very small; sometimes a holder made of cork is convenient.

The direction in which the slice is to be cut is of the highest importance, and can often be indicated at first by a scratch across a plane of a crystal. In many cases it is more simple to grind on a surface in the proper direction, and this can be easily accomplished by holding the crystal against a fine-grained emery wheel rotating on a lathe. It can be held either in the fingers, or cemented to a small piece of glass, for instance with Canada balsam.

Another way, more simple as demanding no instruments, is to make use of a flat piece of plate glass, not too small, on which the crystal is ground with moistened emery, being carefully moved about with the hand. In some cases a file, or even a knife, may be used, where the mineral in hand is soft.

Whatever method of grinding is adopted, it is necessary to exercise great care to bring the artificial surface into exactly the proper direction. This can be determined only as its inclinations to existing crystalline planes, or cleavage surfaces, are measured, and practically it is necessary often to stop the work and test what has been done. The parallel intersections will often show the degree of correctness in the work. For purposes of measurement it is necessary to polish the artificial plane, or instead, a small piece of thin glass may be cemented on where the crystal is too small for the use of the hand-goniometer. It is of course necessary to know, before starting, the angle which the new plane will make with the natural planes which are already present. When one plane in the required direction has been obtained, it is a comparatively simple process to obtain a second parallel to it, though care must be exercised to attain accuracy.

The required section having been cut, it remains only to polish the surfaces. The means required differ so widely, according to the hardness of the mineral, that no fixed rule can be given. The most commonly used polishing powder is the English red, or colcothar, which may be used on the plate of glass, or leather surface, or on a revolving wheel covered with a soft cloth. In other cases oxide of tin or fine chalk is used; and again the simple plate of ground glass will answer the purpose without the use of any other means. As a rule, the hardest minerals take the polish most readily. Sometimes the only method practicable is to use small fragments of thin glass, adhering with balsam, by which transparency is obtained without polish, though errors are easily introduced by this means when sufficient care is not exercised.

The preparation of prisms for the measurement of the indices of refraction is practically much more difficult than that of a simple section, but in general the methods are the same.

It is often advisable to examine a mineral microscopically when a slice in a particular direction is not needed. In such cases use can be made of the methods employed in making rock slices. A revolving wheel of soft iron, vertical or horizontal, is employed, on the lateral surface of which the substance is ground with the use of emery moistened with water. A thin slice, or thin fragment broken off, is taken to commence with. First one surface is ground smooth and polished. The piece is then cemented to a little plate of thick glass with balsam, and the other side ground down parallel to the first, the grinding being continued until the required degree of transparency is obtained. Obviously when the section becomes thin and fragile, the coarse emery must be replaced with fine, and a considerable degree of care exercised. The section obtained is generally removed to another slip of glass and mounted with balsam under a thin glass cover.

The microscopic investigation of minerals, by means of thin slices, is of the highest importance, aside from optical investigations. Every chemical analysis should be preceded by such an examination to test the purity of the material in hand. Where a transparent section cannot be obtained, a single polished surface, examined by reflected light, will often suffice to decide the same point.

The valuable investigations of Vogelsang, Fischer, Rosenbusch, and others, referred to on pp. 108 to 111, show how many minerals, which at first glance seem perfectly pure, are found to enclose impurities considerable in variety and amount.

LITERATURE.—OPTICAL CHARACTERS OF CRYSTALS.

Brewster. Treatise on Optics, and many minor papers in Ed. Phil. Mag., etc.
Beer. Einleitung in die höhere Optik; Braunschweig, 1853.
Dove. Darstellung der Farbenlehre und optische Studien; Berlin, 1853.
Grailich. Krystallographisch-optische Untersuchungen; Wien, 1858.
Grailich u. von Lang. Untersuchungen über das physikalische Verhalten krystallisirter Körper; Ber. Ak. Wien, xxvii. 3; xxxii., xxxiii., and other papers.
Des Cloizeaux. Mémoire sur les propriétés biréfringentes en Mineralogie, Ann. d. Mines; V., xi., 1857; xiv., 1858.
——— Mémoire sur l'emploi du microscope polarisant, etc.; Paris, 1864.
——— Nouvelles Recherches sur les propriétés optiques des Cristaux, etc., et sur les variations que ces propriétés éprouvent sous l'influence de la chaleur; C. R., lxii., 987, 1866.
Schrauf. Lehrbuch der physikalischen Mineralogie; vol. ii., Wien, 1868.
Müller-Pouillet. Lehrbuch der Physik; vol. i., Braunschweig, 1875.
Wüllner. Lehrbuch der Experimental-Physik; vol. ii. Die Lehre vom Licht; Leipzig, 1871.
Rosenbusch. Microscopische Physiographie der petrographisch wichtigen Mineralien, pp. 55-107; Stuttgart, 1873.
Groth. Physikalische Krystallographie; Leipzig, 1876.

Von Kobell. Ueber ein neues Polariskop—Stauroskop; Pogg., xcv., 320, 1855.
Brezina. Eine neue Modification des Stauroskops, etc.; Pogg., cxxviii., 448, 1866; cxxx., 141, 1867.
Groth. Ueber Apparate und Beobachtungsmethoden für krystallographisch-optische Untersuchungen; Pogg., cxliv., 34, 1871.

DIAPHANEITY; COLOR; LUSTRE.

There are certain characteristics belonging to all minerals alike, crystallized and non-crystallized, in their relation to light. These are:
1. DIAPHANEITY; depending on the power of transmitting light.
2. COLOR; depending on the kind of light reflected or transmitted.
3. LUSTRE; depending on the power and manner of reflecting light.

1. DIAPHANEITY.

The amount of light transmitted by a solid varies in intensity, or, in other words, of the light received more or less may be *absorbed*. The amount of absorption is a minimum in a perfectly transparent solid, as ice, while it is greatest in one which is opaque, as iron. The following terms are adopted to express the different degrees in the power of transmitting light:

Transparent: when the outline of an object seen through the mineral is perfectly distinct.

Subtransparent, or *semi-transparent:* when objects are seen, but the outlines are not distinct.

Translucent: when light is transmitted, but objects are not seen.

Subtranslucent: when merely the edges transmit light or are translucent.

When no light is transmitted, the mineral is said to be *opaque*. This is properly only a *relative* term, since no substance fails to transmit some light, if made sufficiently thin. Magnetite is translucent in the Pennsbury mica. The recent researches of Prof. A. W. Wright have shown that by means of the electrical current the metals may be volatilized and deposited again on the sides of the surrounding glass tube. The layers thus formed are perfectly continuous, but so thin as to be transparent. By transmitted light the layer of gold thus obtained appears green, and that of silver a beautiful blue.

The property of diaphaneity occurs in the mineral kingdom, in every degree from nearly perfect opacity to a perfect transparency, and many minerals present, in their numerous varieties, nearly all the different shades.

The absorption of light in its relation to the axes of elasticity is spoken of on p. 165.

2. COLOR.

Cause of color.—The color of a substance depends upon its power of absorbing certain portions of the light, that is, certain rays of the spectrum; a yellow mineral, for instance, absorbs all the rays of the spectrum with the exception of the yellow. In general the color which the eye perceives is the result of the mixture of those rays which are not absorbed. All minerals may be divided into two classes: (1) those whose color is essential and belongs to the finest particles mechanically made; (2) those whose color is non-essential and in the fine powder is different from what it is in the mass.

Streak.—It is obvious from these distinctions that the color of the powder, or the *streak*, as it is called, is often a very important quality in distinguishing minerals. The *streak* is obtained by scratching the surface of the mineral with a knife or file, or still better, if not too hard, by rubbing it on an unpolished porcelain surface.

To the first class, mentioned above, belong the metals, and many metallic minerals; for instance, the *streak* of the black manganese oxides is black; that of hematite, which is red by transmitted light, is red, and so on. To the second class belong the silicates, and in fact the large part of all minerals. With them the color is often quite unessential, being generally due to small admixtures of some metallic oxide, to some carbon compound, or some foreign substance in a finely divided state. Most of these have a white or light-colored streak. For example, the streak of *black, green, red,* and *blue* tourmaline varies little from *white.*

VARIETIES OF COLOR.

The following eight colors have been selected as fundamental, to facilitate the employment of this character in the description of minerals: *white, gray, black, blue, green, yellow, red,* and *brown.*

a. Metallic Colors.

1. *Copper-red:* native copper.—2. *Bronze-yellow:* pyrrhotite.—3. *Brass-yellow:* chalcopyrite.—4. *Gold-yellow.*—5. *Silver-white:* native silver, less distinct in arsenopyrite.—6. *Tin-white:* mercury, cobaltite.—7. *Lead-gray:* galenite, molybdenite.—8. *Steel-gray:* nearly the color of fine-grained steel on a recent fracture; native platinum, and palladium.

b. Non-metallic Colors.

A. WHITE. 1. *Snow-white:* Carrara marble.—2. *Reddish-white:* some varieties of calcite and quartz.—3. *Yellowish-white:* some varieties of calcite and quartz.—4. *Grayish-white:* some varieties of calcite and quartz.—5. *Greenish-white:* talc.—6. *Milk-white:* white, slightly bluish; some chalcedony.

B. GRAY. 1. *Bluish-gray:* gray, inclining to a dirty blue color.—2. *Pearl-gray:* gray, mixed with red and blue; cerargyrite.—3. *Smoke-gray:* gray, with some brown; flint.—4. *Greenish-gray:* gray, with some green; cat's eye, some varieties of talc.—5. *Yellowish-gray:* some varieties of compact limestone.—6. *Ash-gray:* the purest gray color; zoisite.

C. BLACK. 1. *Grayish-black:* black, mixed with gray (without any green, brown, or blue tints); basalt, Lydian stone.—2. *Velvet-black:* pure black; obsidian, black tourmaline.—3. *Greenish-black:* augite.—4 *Brownish-black:* brown coal, lignite.—5. *Bluish-black:* black cobalt.

D. BLUE. 1. *Blackish-blue:* dark varieties of azurite.—2. *Azure-blue:* a clear shade of bright blue; pale varieties of azurite, bright varieties of azulite.—3. *Violet-blue:* blue, mixed with red; amethyst, fluorite.—4 Lavender-blue: blue with some red and much gray.—5. *Prussian-blue,* or Berlin blue: pure blue; sapphire, cyanite.—6. *Smalt-blue:* some varieties of gypsum.—7. *Indigo-blue:* blue with black and green; blue tourmaline.—8. *Sky-blue:* pale blue with a little green; it is called mountain blue by painters.

E. GREEN. 1. *Verdigris-green:* green inclining to blue; some feldspar (amazon-stone).—*Celandine-green:* green with blue and gray; some varieties of talc and beryl. It is the color of the leaves of the celandine (Chelidonium majus).—3. *Mountain-green:* green with much blue; beryl.—4. *Leek-green:* green with some brown; the color of leaves of garlic; distinctly seen in prase, a variety of quartz.—5. *Emerald-green:* pure deep green; emerald.—6. *Apple-green:* light green with some yellow; chrysoprase.—7. *Grass-green:* bright green with more yellow; green diallage.— 8. *Pistachio-green:* yellowish green with some brown; epidote.—9. *Asparagus-green:* pale green with much yellow; asparagus stone (apatite).— 10. *Blackish-green:* serpentine.—11. *Olive-green:* dark green with much brown and yellow; chrysolite.—12. *Oil-green:* the color of olive oil; beryl, pitchstone.—13. *Siskin-green:* light green, much inclining to yellow; uranite.

F. YELLOW. 1. *Sulphur-yellow:* sulphur.—2. *Straw-yellow:* pale yellow; topaz.—3. *Wax-yellow:* grayish yellow with some brown; blende, opal.—4. *Honey-yellow:* yellow with some red and brown; calcite.—5. *Lemon-yellow:* sulphur, orpiment.—6. *Ochre-yellow:* yellow with brown; yellow ochre.—7. *Wine-yellow:* topaz and fluorite.—8. *Cream-yellow:* some varieties of lithomarge.—9. *Orange-yellow:* orpiment.

G. RED. 1. *Aurora-red:* red with much yellow; some realgar.—2. *Hyacinth-red:* red with yellow and some brown; hyacinth garnet.—3. *Brick-red:* polyhalite, some jasper.—4. *Scarlet-red:* bright red with a tinge of yellow; cinnabar.—5. *Blood-red:* dark red with some yellow; pyrope.—6. *Flesh-red:* feldspar.—7. *Carmine-red:* pure red; ruby sapphire.—8. *Rose-red:* rose quartz.—9. *Crimson-red:* ruby.—10. *Peach-blossom-red:* red with white and gray; lepidolite.—11. *Columbine-red:* deep red with some blue; garnet.—12. *Cherry-red:* dark red with some blue and brown: spinel, some jasper.—13. *Brownish-red:* jasper, limonite.

H. BROWN. 1. *Reddish-brown:* garnet, zircon.—2. *Clove-brown:* brown with red and some blue; axinite.—3. *Hair-brown:* wood opal.—4. *Broccoli-brown:* brown, with blue, red, and gray; zircon.—5. *Chestnut-brown:* pure brown.—6. *Yellowish-brown:* jasper.—7. *Pinchbeck-brown:* yellowish-brown, with a metallic or metallic-pearly lustre; several varieties of talc, bronzite.—8. *Wood-brown:* color of old wood nearly rotten; some specimens of asbestus.—9. *Liver-brown:* brown, with some gray and green; jasper.—10. *Blackish-brown:* bituminous coal, brown coal.

c. *Peculiarities in the Arrangement of Colors.*

Play of Colors.—An appearance of several prismatic colors in rapid succession on turning the mineral. This property belongs in perfection to the diamond; it is also observed in precious opal, and is most brilliant by candle-light.

Change of Colors.—Each particular color appears to pervade a larger space than in the play of colors, and the succession produced by turning the mineral is less rapid; Ex. labradorite.

Opalescence.—A milky or pearly reflection from the interior of a specimen. Observed in some opal, and in cat's eye.

Iridescence.—Presenting prismatic colors in the interior of a crystal. The phenomena of the play of colors, iridescence, etc., are sometimes to be explained by the presence of minute foreign crystals, in parallel positions; more generally, however, they are caused by the presence of fine cleavage lamellæ, in the light reflected from which interference takes place, analogous to the well-known Newton's rings.

Tarnish.—A metallic surface is tarnished, when its color differs from that obtained by fracture; Ex. bornite. A surface possesses the *steel tarnish*, when it presents the superficial blue color of tempered steel; Ex. columbite. The tarnish is *irised*, when it exhibits fixed prismatic colors; Ex. hematite of Elba. These tarnish and iris colors of minerals are owing to a thin surface film, proceeding from different sources, either from a change in the surface of the mineral, or foreign incrustation; hydrated iron oxide, usually formed from pyrite, is one of the most common sources of it, and produces the colors on anthracite and hematite.

Asterism.—This name is given to the peculiar star-like rays of light observed in certain directions in some minerals by reflected or transmitted light. This is seen in the form of a six-rayed star in sapphire, and is also well shown in mica from South Burgess, Canada. In the former case it has been attributed by Volger to a repeated lamellar twinning; in the other case, by Rose, to the presence of minute inclosed crystals, which are a uniaxial mica, according to DesCloizeaux. Crystalline planes, which have been artificially etched, also sometimes exhibit asterism. In general the phenomenon is explained by Schrauf as caused by the interference of the light, due to fine striations or some other cause.

(Upon the above subjects, see Literature, p. 167.)

PHOSPHORESCENCE.

Phosphorescence,[*] or the emission of light by minerals, may be produced in different ways: by *friction*, by *heat*, or by *exposure to light*.

By friction.—Light is readily evolved from quartz or white sugar by the friction of one piece against another, and merely the rapid motion of a feather will elicit it from some specimens of sphalerite. Friction, however, evolves light from a few only of the mineral species.

By heat.—Fluorite is highly phosphorescent at the temperature of 300° F. Different varieties give off light of different colors; the *chlorophane* variety, an emerald-green light; others purple, blue, and reddish tints. This phosphorescence may be observed in a dark place, by subjecting the pulverized mineral to a heat below redness. Some varieties of white limestone or marble emit a yellow light.

---

[*] This subject has been investigated by *Becquerel*, Ann. Ch. Phys., III., lv., 5–119, 1859; *Faster*, Mitth. nat. Ges. Bern, 1867, 62; and *Hahn*, Zeitsch. Ges. nat. Wiss. Berlin, II., ix., 1,131, 1874.

By the application of heat, minerals lose their phosphorescent properties. But on passing electricity through the calcined mineral, a more or less vivid light is produced at the time of the discharge, and subsequently the specimen when heated will often emit light as before. The light is usually of the same color as previous to calcination, but occasionally is quite different. It is in general less intense than that of the unaltered mineral, but is much increased by a repetition of the electric discharges, and in some varieties of fluorite it may be nearly or quite restored to its former brilliancy. It has also been found that some varieties of fluorite and some specimens of diamond, calcite, and apatite, which are not naturally phosphorescent, may be rendered so by means of electricity. Electricity will also increase the natural intensity of the phosphorescent light.

Light of the sun.—The only substance in which an exposure to the light of the sun produces very apparent phosphorescence is the diamond, and some specimens seem to be destitute of this power. This property is most striking after exposure to the blue rays of the spectrum, while in the red rays it is rapidly lost.

PLEOCHROISM.

Dichroism, Trichroism.—In addition to the general phenomena of color, which belong to all minerals alike, some of those which are crystallized show *different* colors under certain circumstances. This is due to the fact that in them the absorption of parts of the spectrum takes place unequally in different directions, and hence their color by transmitted light depends upon the direction in which they are viewed. This phenomenon is called in general *pleochroism.*

In uniaxial crystals it has been seen that, in consequence of their crystallographic symmetry, there are two distinct values for the velocity of light transmitted by them, according as the vibrations take place, *parallel* or at *right angles* to the vertical axis. Similarly the crystal may exert different degrees of absorption upon the rays vibrating in these two directions. For example, a transparent crystal of zircon looked through in the direction of the vertical axis appears of a pinkish-brown color, while in a lateral direction the color is asparagus-green. This is because the rays (extraordinary) vibrating *parallel* to the axis are absorbed with the exception of those which together give the green color, and those vibrating *laterally* (ordinary) are absorbed except those which together appear pinkish-brown.

Again, all crystals of tourmaline in the direction of the vertical axis are opaque, since the ordinary ray, vibrating normal to the axis $\dot{c}$, is absorbed, while light-colored varieties, looked through laterally, are transparent, for the extraordinary ray, vibrating parallel to $\dot{c}$, is not absorbed; the color differs in different varieties. Thus, all uniaxial crystals may be *dichroic*, or have two distinct axial colors.

Similarly all biaxial crystals may be *trichroic*. For the rays vibrating in the directions of the three axes of elasticity may be differently absorbed. For diaspore the three axial colors are azure-blue, wine-yellow, and violet-blue. It will be understood that, while these three different colors are possible, they may not exist; or only two may be prominent, so that a biaxial mineral may be called dichroic.

In order to investigate the absorption-properties of any uniaxial or biaxial crystal, it is evident that sections must be obtained which are parallel to the several axes of elasticity. Suppose that f. 410 represents a rectangular solid with its sides parallel to the three axes of elasticity of a biaxial crystal. In an orthorhombic crystal the faces are those of the three diametral planes or pinacoids; in a monoclinic crystal one side coincides with the clinopinacoid, the others are to be determined for each species. The light transmitted by this solid is examined by means of a single Nicol prism. Suppose, first, that the light transmitted by the parallelopiped (f. 410) in the direction of the vertical axis is to be examined. When the shorter diagonal of the Nicol coincides with the direction of the axis b, the color observed belongs to that ray vibrating parallel to this direction; when it coincides with the axis a, the color for the ray with vibrations parallel to a is observed. In the same way the Nicol separates the different colored rays vibrating parallel to c and a respectively, when the light passes through in the direction of b.

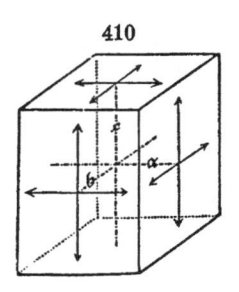

So also finally when the section is looked through in the direction of the axis a, the colors for the rays vibrating parallel to b and c, respectively, are obtained. It is evident that the examination in two of the directions named will give the three possible colors.

For epidote, according to Klein, the colors for the three axial directions are:

1. Vibrations parallel to b, brown (absorbed).
   "   "   a, yellow.
2. Vibrations parallel to c, green.
   "   "   a, yellow.
3. Vibrations parallel to c, green,
   "   "   b, brown (absorbed).

The colors observed by the eye alone are the resultants of the double set of vibrations, in which the stronger color predominates; thus, in the above example, the plane, normal to c is brown, to b, yellowish-green, to a, green. In any other direction in the crystal, the apparent color is the result of a mixture of those corresponding to the three directions of vibrations in different proportions. Dichroite is a striking example of the phenomenon of pleochroism.

An instrument called a *dichroscope* has been contrived by Haidinger for examining this property of crystals. An oblong rhombohedron of Iceland spar has a glass prism of 18° cemented to each extremity. It is placed

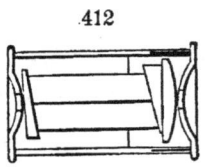

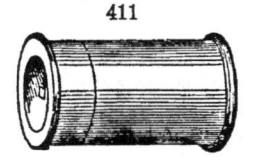

in a metallic cylindrical case, as in the figure, having a convex lens at one end, and a square hole at the other. On looking through it, the square hole appears double; one image belongs to the ordinary and the other to the extraordinary ray. When a pleochroic crystal is examined with it, by transmitted light, on revolving it, the two squares, at intervals of 90° in the revolution, have different colors, corresponding to the direction of the vibrations of the ordinary and extraordinary ray in calcite. Since the two images are situated side by side, a very slight difference of color is perceptible.

LITERATURE.—PLEOCHROISM, ASTERISM, ETC.

Haidinger. Ueber den Pleochroismus der Krystalle ; Pogg. lxv., 1, 1845.
——— Ueber das Schillern der Krystallflächen ; Pogg. lxx., 574, 1847 ; lxxi., 321 ; lxxvi., 99, 1849.
Reusch. Ueber das Schillern gewisser Krystalle ; Pogg. cxvi., 392, 1862 ; cxviii., 256, 1863 ; cxx., 95, 1863.
v. Kobell. Ueber Asterismus ; Ber. Ak. München, 1863, 65.
Haushofer. Der Asterismus des Calcites ; Ber. Ak. München, 1869.
Vogelsang. Sur le Labradorite coloré ; Arch. Neerland., iii., 32, 1868.
Schrauf. Labradorit ; Ber. Ak., Wien, lx., 1869.
Kosmann. Ueber das Schillern und den Dichroismus des Hypersthens ; Jahrb. Min., 1869, 368, 532 ; 1871, 501.
Rose. Ueber den Asterismus der Krystallen ; Ber. Ak. Berlin, 1862, 614 ; 1869, 344.

3. LUSTRE.

The lustre of minerals varies with the nature of their surfaces. A variation in the quantity of light reflected, produces different degrees of intensity of lustre ; a variation in the nature of the reflecting surface produces different kinds of lustre.

A. The *kinds of lustre* recognized are as follows :

1. *Metallic :* the lustre of metals. Imperfect metallic lustre is expressed by the term *sub-metallic.*

2. *Adamantine :* the lustre of the diamond. When also sub-metallic, it is termed *metallic-adamantine.* Ex. cerussite, pyrargyrite.

3. *Vitreous :* the lustre of broken glass. An imperfectly vitreous lustre is termed *sub-vitreous.* The vitreous and sub-vitreous lustres are the most common in the mineral kingdom. Quartz possesses the former in an eminent degree ; calcite, often the latter.

4. *Resinous :* lustre of the yellow resins. Ex. opal, and some yellow varieties of sphalerite.

5. *Pearly :* like pearl. Ex. talc, brucite, stilbite, etc. When united with sub-metallic, as in hypersthenite, the term *metallic-pearly* is used.

6. *Silky :* like silk ; it is the result of a fibrous structure. Ex. fibrous calcite, fibrous gypsum.

B. The *degrees of intensity* are denominated as follows :

1. *Splendent :* reflecting with brilliancy and giving well-defined images. Ex. hematite, cassiterite.

2. *Shining :* producing an image by reflection, but not one well defined. Ex. celestite.

3. *Glistening :* affording a general reflection from the surface, but no image. Ex. talc, chalcopyrite.

4. *Glimmering :* affording imperfect reflection, and apparently from points over the surface. Ex. flint, chalcedony.

A mineral is said to be *dull* when there is a total absence of lustre. Ex. chalk, the ochres, kaolin

The true difference between metallic and vitreous lustre is due to the effect which the different surfaces have upon the reflected light; in general, the lustre is produced by the union of two simultaneous impressions made upon the eye. If the light reflected from a metallic surface be examined by a Nicol prism (or the dichroscope of Haidinger), it will be found that both rays, that vibrating in the plane of incidence and that whose vibrations are normal to it, are alike, each having the color of the material, only differing a little in brilliancy; on the contrary, of the light reflected by a vitreous substance, those rays whose vibrations are at right angles to the plane of incidence are more or less polarized, and are colorless, while those whose vibrations are in this plane, having penetrated somewhat into the medium and suffered some absorption, show the color of the substance itself. A plate of red glass thus examined will show a colorless and a red image. Adamantine lustre occupies a position between the others.

The different degrees and kinds of lustre are often exhibited differently by unlike faces of the same crystal, but always similarly by like faces. The lateral faces of a right square prism may thus differ from a terminal, and in the right rectangular prism the lateral faces also may differ from one another. For example, the basal plane of apophyllite has a pearly lustre wanting in the prismatic planes. The surface of a cleavage plane in foliated minerals, very commonly differs in lustre from the sides, and in some cases the latter are vitreous, while the former is pearly. As shown by Haidinger, only the vitreous, adamantine, and metallic lustres belong to faces perfectly smooth and pure. In the first, the index of refraction of the mineral is 1·3—1·8; in the second, 1·9—2·5; in the third, about 2·5. The pearly lustre is a result of reflection from numberless lamellæ or lines within a translucent mineral, as long since observed by Breithaupt.

IV. HEAT.

The expansion of crystallized minerals by heat depends, as directly as their optical properties, on the symmetry of their molecular structure as shown in their crystalline form. The same three classes as before are distinguished:

A. Isometric crystals, where the expansion is in all directions alike.

B. Isodiametric crystals, of the tetragonal and hexagonal systems. Expansion vertically unlike that laterally, but in all lateral directions alike.

C. Anisometric, of the orthorhombic, monoclinic, and triclinic systems. Expansion unlike in the three axial directions. The expansion by heat in the case of crystals may serve to alter the angles of the form, but it has been shown that the zone relations and the crystalline system remain constant.

Mitscherlich found that in calcite there was a diminution of 8' 37" in the angle of the rhombohedron, on passing from 32° to 212° F., the form thus approaching that of a cube, as the temperature increased. Dolomite, in the same range of temperature, diminishes 4' 46"; and in aragonite, between 63° and 212° F., the angle of the prism diminishes 2' 46", and 1-i : 1-i increases 5' 30"; in gypsum, I : i-i is increased 5' 24", I : 1, 4' 12", and 1-i : i-i is diminished 7' 24". In some rhombohedrons, as of calcite, the vertical axis is lengthened (and the lateral shortened), while in others, like quartz, the reverse is true. The variation is such either way that the double refraction is diminished with the increase of heat; for calcite possesses negative double refraction, and quartz, positive.

The conductive power of a crystal depends, as does expansion, on the symmetry of its crystalline form; this is also true of its power of transmitting or absorbing heat. It follows, moreover, from the analogous nature of heat and light, that heat rays are polarized by reflection, and by transmission in anisotrope media, in the same way as the rays of light. These subjects, considered solely in their relation to Mineralogy, are of minor importance; they belong to works on Physics, and reference may be made to those whose titles are given in the Introduction, as also to the works of Schrauf and Groth.

The change in the optical properties of crystals produced by heat has already been noticed (p. 151).

V. ELECTRICITY—MAGNETISM.

The electric and magnetic characters of crystals, as their relations to heat, bear but slightly upon the science of mineralogy, although of high interest to the student of physics.

Frictional electricity.—The development of electricity *by friction* is a familiar fact. All minerals become electric by friction, although the degree to which this is manifested depends upon their conducting or non-conducting power. There is no line of distinction among minerals, dividing them into *positively* electric and *negatively* electric; for both kinds of electricity may be presented by different varieties of the same species, and by the same variety in different states. The gems are positively electric only when polished; the diamond alone among them exhibits positive electricity whether polished or not. The time of retaining electric excitement is widely different in different species, and topaz is remarkable for continuing excited many hours.

Pressure also develops electricity in many minerals; calcite and topaz are examples.

Pyro-electricity.—A decided change of temperature, through heat or cold, develops electricity in a large number of minerals, which are hence called *pyro-electric*. This property is most decided, and was first observed in a series of minerals which are hemimorphic or hemihedral in their development. The electricity in these minerals is of opposite character in the parts dissimilarly modified. Thus in tourmaline and calamine, the crystals of which are often differently modified at the two extremities, positive and negative electricity are developed at these extremities or *poles* respectively. When the extremity becomes positive on heating it has been called the *analogue* pole, and when it becomes negative, it has been called the *antilogue*. The names were given by Rose and Riess, who investigated these phenomena. For a change of temperature in the opposite direction, that is, cooling, the reverse electrical effect is observed.

Boracite, on whose crystals the + and − tetrahedrons often occur, shows by heating the positive electricity for the faces of one tetrahedron and the negative for those of the other.

Further investigations by Hankel and others (see Literature) have extended the subject and shown that the phenomena of pyro-electricity belong to the crystals of a large number of species. Moreover, it is not, as once supposed, essentially connected with hemihedral development. The number of poles, too, may be more than two, that is, the points at which posi tive and negative electricity is developed. Thus for prehnite there is a large series of such poles, distributed over the surface of a crystal. The investigations of Hankel have shown in general, that in crystals not hemihedrally developed, the same electricity is developed at both extremities of the same axis, and the distinction between positive and negative electricity is only shown by reference to the different crystallographic axes; on symmetrically formed crystals of the isodiametric class the electricity is the same in all lateral directions, that is, on all prismatic planes, while different at the extremities of the vertical axis.

Thermo-electricity.—When two different metals are brought into contact, a stream of electricity passes from one to the other. If one is heated the effect is more decided and is sufficient to deflect more or less vigorously the needle of a galvanometer. According to the direction of the current produced by the different metallic substances, they are arranged in a thermo-electrical series; the extremes are occupied by antimony (+) and bismuth (—), the electrical stream passing from bismuth to antimony.

This subject is so far important for mineralogy, as it was shown by Bunsen that the natural metallic sulphides stand further off in the series than antimony and bismuth, and consequently by them a stronger stream is produced. The thermo-electrical relations of a large number of minerals was determined by Flight (Ann. Ch. Pharm., cxxxvi.).

It was early observed that some minerals have varieties which are both + and —. This fact was made use of by Rose to show a relation between the plus and minus hemihedral varieties of pyrite and cobaltite. The later investigations of Schrauf and Dana have shown, however, that the same peculiarity belongs also to glaucodot, tetradymite, skutterudite, danaite, and other minerals, and it is demonstrated by them that it cannot be dependent upon crystalline form, but, on the contrary, upon chemical composition.

MAGNETISM.—The magnetic properties of crystals are theoretically of interest, since they, too, like the optical and thermic, are directly dependent upon the form; hence, with relation to magnetism they group themselves into the same three classes before referred to.

All substances are divided into two classes, the *paramagnetic* and *diamagnetic*, according as they are attracted or repelled by the poles of a magnet. For purposes of experiment the substance in question, in the form of a rod, is suspended between the poles of the magnet, being movable on a horizontal axis. If of the first class, it will take a position *parallel*, and if of the second class, *transverse*, to the magnetic axis.

By the use of a sphere it is possible to determine the relative amount of magnetic induction in different directions of the same substance. Experiment has shown that in *isometric* crystals the magnetism is alike in all directions; in those optically uniaxial, that there is a direction of maximum and, normal to it, one of minimum magnetism; in biaxial crystals, that there are three unequal axes of magnetism, the position of which may be determined.

A few minerals have the power of exerting a sensible influence upon the magnetic needle, and are hence said to be magnetic. This is true of magnetite and pyrrhotite (magnetic pyrites) in particular, also of franklinite, almandite, and other minerals, containing considerable iron protoxide (FeO). When such minerals in one part attract and in another repel the poles of the magnet, they are said to possess *polarity*. This is true of the variety of magnetite called in popular language loadstone.

LITERATURE.—ELECTRICITY.*

Hankel. Ueber die Thermo-Electricität der Krystalle; Pogg., xlix., 493; l., 237, 1840; lxi., 281.
Rose u. Ries. Ueber die Pyro-Electricität der Mineralien; Ber. Ak. Berlin, 1843.
——— Ueber den Zusammenhang zwischen der Form und der elektrischen Polarität der Krystalle; Ber. Ak. Berlin, 1836.
v. Kobell. Ueber Mineral-Electricität; Pogg., cxviii., 594, 1863.
Bunsen. Thermo-Ketten von grosser Wirksamkeit; Pogg., cxxiii., 505, 1864.
Friedel. Sur les propriétés pyro-électrique des Cristaux bons conducteurs de l'electricité; Ann. Ch. Phys., IV., xvii., 79, 1869.
Rose. Ueber den Zusammenhang zwischen hemiëdrischer Krystallform und thermo-elektrischem Verhalten beim Eisenkies und Kobaltglanz; Pogg., cxlii., 1, 1871.
Schrauf u. E. S. Dana. Ueber die thermo-elektrischen Eigenschaften von Mineralvarietäten; Ber. Ak. Wien, lxix., 1874 (Am. J. Sci., III., viii., 255).
Hankel. Ueber die thermo-elektrischen Eigenschaften des Boracites; Sächs. Ges. Wiss., vi., 151, 1865; ibid., viii., 323, 1866; Topaz, ix., 1870, 359; 10 Abhandlung, 1872, 24; calcite, beryl, etc., 1876.
On MAGNETISM reference may be made to Faraday (Experimental Researches); Tyndall, Phil. Mag.; Knoblauch and Tyndall, Pogg., lxxxi., 481, 498; lxxxiii., 384; Pflücker, Pogg., lxxii., 315; lxxvi., 576; lxxvii., 417; lxxxvi., 1; Grailich u. von Lang, Ber. Ak., Wien, xxxii., 43; xxxiii., 439, etc., etc.

VI. TASTE AND ODOR.

In their action upon the senses a few minerals possess *taste*, and others under some circumstances give off *odor*.

TASTE belongs only to soluble minerals. The different kinds of taste adopted for reference are as follows:
1. *Astringent ;* the taste of vitriol.
2. *Sweetish astringent ;* taste of alum.
3. *Saline ;* taste of common salt.
4. *Alkaline ;* taste of soda.
5. *Cooling ;* taste of saltpeter.
6. *Bitter ;* taste of epsom salts.
7. *Sour :* taste of sulphuric acid.

ODOR.—Excepting a few gaseous and soluble species, minerals in the dry unchanged state do not give off odor. By friction, moistening with the breath, and the elimination of some volatile ingredient by heat or acids, odors are sometimes obtained which are thus designated:
1. *Alliaceous ;* the odor of garlic. Friction of arsenical iron elicits this odor; it may also be obtained from arsenical compounds, by means of heat.
2. *Horse-radish odor ;* the odor of decaying horse-radish. This odor is strongly perceived when the ores of selenium are heated.
3. *Sulphureous ;* friction elicits this odor from pyrite and heat from many sulphides.
4. *Bituminous ;* the odor of bitumen.
5. *Fetid ;* the odor of sulphuretted hydrogen or rotten eggs. It is elicited by friction from some varieties of quartz and limestone.
6. *Argillaceous ;* the odor of moistened clay. It is obtained from ser-

---
* See also on p. 190.

pentine and some allied minerals, after moistening them with the breath; others, as pyrargillite, afford it when heated.

The FEEL is a character which is occasionally of some importance; it is said to be *smooth* (sepiolite), *greasy* (talc), *harsh*, or *meagre*, etc. Some minerals, in consequence of their hygroscopic character, *adhere to the tongue*, when brought in contact with it.

SECTION II.—SUPPLEMENTARY CHAPTER.

I. COHESION AND ELASTICITY (pp. 119 to 122).

The etching-figures (*Aetzfiguren*) produced by the action of appropriate solvents upon the surfaces of crystals have been further investigated in the case of a considerable number of minerals, and the results have in some cases served to throw light upon the question as to which crystalline system a given species belongs. See the investigations of BAUMHAUER of the etching-figures of lepidolite, tourmaline, topaz, calamine, Jahrb. Min., 1876, i. ; pyromorphite, mimetite, vanadinite, ib., 1876, 411 ; of adularia, albite, fluorite, ib., 1876, 602 ; of leucite, Z. Kryst., i., 257, 1877 ; quartz, ib., ii., 117, 1878 ; mica (zinnwaldite), ib., iii., 113, 1878; boracite, ib., iii., 337, 1879 ; perofskite, ib., iv., 187, 1879 ; nephelite, ib., vi., 209, 1882. (For earlier papers giving results of etching experiments on muscovite, garnet, linnæite, biotite, epidote, apatite, gypsum, in Ber. Ak. München, 1874, 245 ; 1876, 99.) On the etching-figures of alum, see FR. KLOCKE, Z. Kryst., ii., 126, 1878 ; of the different micas, F. J. WIIK, Oefv. Finsk. Vet. Soc., xxii., 1880.

On the artificial twins (twinning-plane $-\frac{1}{2}R$) of calcite produced by simple pressure with a knife-blade on the obtuse edge of a cleavage fragment, see BAUMHAUER, Zeitschr. Kryst., iii., 588, 1879 ; BREZINA, ib., iv., 518, 1880. The fragment should have a prismatic form, say 6–8 mm. in length and 3–6 mm. in breadth, and be placed with the obtuse edge on a firm horizontal support. The blade of an ordinary table-knife is then applied to the other obtuse edge, as at a (f. 412A), and pressed gradually and firmly down. The result is that the portion of the crystal lying between a and b is reversed in position, as if twinned parallel to the horizontal plane $-\frac{1}{2}R$. The twinning surface, gce, is perfectly smooth, and the re-entrant angle corresponds very exactly with that required by theory (Brezina). Earlier observations by Pfaff and Reusch have shown that twin lamellæ ($-\frac{1}{2}R$) may be produced in a cleavage mass of calcite of prismatic form, by simple pressure exerted perpendicular to a straight terminal plane. Such twinning lamellæ are often observed in thin sections of a crystalline limestone when examined in polarized light under the microscope.

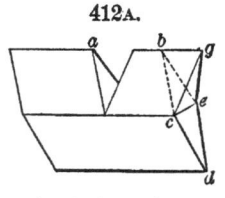

On the application of the fracture-figures (Schlagfiguren) in the optical examination of the mica species see Bauer, ZS. G. Ges., xxvi., 137, 1874 (for earlier papers see p. 122) ; Tschermak, Z. Kryst., ii., 14, 1877. On the occurrence of *Gleitflächen* on galena see Bauer, Jahrb. Min., 1882, i., 183.

II. SPECIFIC GRAVITY (pp. 123, 124).

Use of a Solution of high Specific Gravity.—A solution of *mercuric iodide* in *potassium iodide* (Hg_2I in KI) affords a means of readily obtaining the specific gravity of any mineral not acted upon by it chemically, and for which $G. < 3.1$; and also of separating from each other minerals of different densities, when intimately mixed in the form of small fragments. The solution is called the Sonstadt solution, having been first proposed by E. SONSTADT in 1873 (Chem. News, xxix., 127); its application for the above objects was proposed by CHURCH in 1877 (Min. Mag., i., 237); and the method elaborated by THOULET in 1878 (C. R., Feb. 18, 1878; Bull. Soc. Min., ii., 17, 189, 1879), and later by GOLDSCHMIDT (J. Min., Beil.-Bd., i., 179, 1881).

The solution is prepared (Goldschmidt) as follows: The KI and Hg_2I are taken in the ratio of 1:1.239, and introduced into a volume of water slightly greater than is required to dissolve them (say 80 cc. to 500 gr. of the salts); the solution is then filtered in the usual way and afterward evaporated down in a porcelain vessel, over a water-bath, until a crystalline scum begins to form, or when a fragment of tourmaline ($G. = 3.1$) floats; on cooling, the solution has its maximum density. If the mercuric iodide is not quite pure a small quantity in excess of that required by the above ratio must be taken. The highest specific gravity for the solution obtained by Goldschmidt was 3.196, a solution in which fluorite floats. This maximum is not quite constant, varying with the moisture of the atmosphere and with the temperature.

The method of using the solution for obtaining the specific gravity of small fragments of any mineral is, according to Goldschmidt, as follows: The fragments are introduced into a tall beaker, say 40 cc. capacity, with a portion of the concentrated solution; then water is added drop by drop (or a dilute solution of the same for high densities) from a burette, until the fragments, after being agitated, are just suspended, and remain so without either rising or falling. This process requires care and precision, since the principal error to which the method is liable is involved here. The solution is now introduced into a little glass flask, graduated say to hold just 25 cc., and this amount having been exactly measured off, the weight is taken; then the solution is poured back into the original beaker and the fact noted whether the fragments still remain suspended; then introduced again into the flask and weighed, and so a third time. The average result of the three weighings, diminished by the known weight of the flask and divided by 25, gives the specific gravity. The exact measurement of the 25 cc. is a matter of importance, and is most easily accomplished by adding at first a little more than enough and then removing the excess by a capillary tube or a piece of filter paper; the reading is best taken from the lower edge of the meniscus. It is not necessary to clean and dry the flask each time. The weighing need not be very accurate, as an error of 25 mgr. only involves a change of a unit in the third decimal place (·001). The describer readily obtained results accurate to three decimals. The advantages of the method are that it is readily applicable in the case of small fragments (dust is to be avoided), it is easily used, and any want of homogeneity in the mineral makes itself at once apparent.

This solution is also most useful in affording a means of separating mechanically different minerals when intimately mixed together; as, for example, in a fine-grained rock. For this purpose the rock must first be pulverized in a steel mortar, then put through a sieve, or better, through several, so as to obtain a series of sets of fragments of different size; the dust is rejected. The fragments should be examined under the microscope, to see that they are homogeneous; the largest fragments satisfying this condition will give the best results.

According to Thoulet the best method of procedure is to first determine the density of the fragments approximately by inserting typical ones in a series of samples of the solution of gradually increasing density. This point determined, some 60 cc. of the concentrated solution are introduced into the tube, A, and 1 or 2 grams of the weighed fragments added. Then the tightly-fitting rubber cork with the tube, F', is inserted ; the tube, F, is connected by a rubber tube with an air pump, and the air bubbles are in this way removed from the powder. The heavy parts of the mixture fall to the bottom, and are removed by opening the stop-cock at C, and are washed out by use of the tube, B ; the other fragments float. Now a quantity of distilled water is added in order so to dilute the solution as to cause the next heavier portions to sink, as determined by the equation

$$v_1 = \frac{v(D - \Delta)}{\Delta - 1}$$

where $v =$ volume of the solution, D its specific gravity, v_1 the volume of the water, and Δ the density desired. The cock at D is shut and that at C opened and air blown through the side tube, so as to mix the solution thoroughly ; then the original operation is repeated, and so on.

GOLDSCHMIDT recommends the following method of procedure. The separation is conducted in a small slender beaker of about 40–50 cc. capacity. Instead of the series of standard solutions (the density of which is liable to alter) a series of minerals of known specific gravity are used as *indicators ;* by means of them it is easy to determine the limits as to density which are required to make the separation desired, the constituent minerals having been determined by the microscope. For example, suppose it to be desired to separate augite, hornblende, oligoclase, and orthoclase ; labradorite and albite are taken as indicators. Augite falls at once in the concentrated solution ; if diluted till the labradorite sinks, all the hornblende goes down ; before or with the albite the oligoclase sinks, and the orthoclase is left suspended. By the use of the 25 cc. flask, the exact specific gravity in each case can be obtained if desired. The operation of separation goes on as follows : The rock powder and the indicators are inserted with say 30 cc. of the concentrated solution into the beaker spoken of, then the whole is stirred vigorously and allowed to settle, and the lighter part decanted off. The heavier part which has settled is removed with a jet from a wash bottle, without disturbing the lighter fragments adhering to the upper part of the beaker. The latter are subsequently removed, washed, dried, again washed in the solution, and added to the rest for the further separation. If the separations accomplished in this way are not complete, they may be repeated most conveniently with the Thoulet apparatus. Under favorable conditions, and if the manipulation is skilful, the separation can be accomplished with considerable exactness. For the best results the process must be repeated several times.

THOULET recommends also (l. c.) this method of determining the specific gravity of small fragments of minerals. A float of wax (inclosing any suitable solid body) is made with a specific gravity of from 1 to 2. The fragments of the mineral are lightly pressed into the wax float, and this introduced into the Sonstadt solution, of such strength that the float remains in equilibrium at any level. If P, V, D are respectively the weight, volume, and density of the float alone $\left(V = \dfrac{P}{D}\right)$ and p, v, d the same values for the fragments alone $\left(v = \dfrac{p}{d}\right)$ and finally $\triangle$ the density of the liquid in which the loaded float is in equilibrium; then

$$\triangle = \frac{P + p}{V + \dfrac{p}{d}} \quad \text{or} \quad d = \frac{p \triangle}{P + p - \triangle V}$$

BREON has proposed (Bull. Soc. Min., iii., 46, 1880) the following method for separating different minerals intimately mixed, which is applicable in cases where their density is greater than that of the Sonstadt solution. Lead chloride and zinc chloride, in appropriate proportions, are fused together (at 400° C.) and by this means a transparent or translucent solution is obtained of high specific gravity. Briefly, the method of procedure is as follows: A conical tube of glass is taken, of about 12 to 15 cc. capacity; this will allow of the treatment of 4 or 5 grams of the mixed minerals. The chlorides of lead and zinc, in approximately the proper proportions, are placed in the glass tube and this, surrounded by sand, inserted in a platinum crucible. On the application of heat the zinc chloride fuses first, but finally a homogeneous mixture of the two liquids is obtained. Now, little by little, the mineral fragments are introduced and the liquid stirred; then on allowing it to stand for a moment the heavier particles sink to the bottom and the lighter ones float. The tube is now removed from its sand bath and cooled rapidly. When solidified but still hot the glass may be plunged into cold water, in which case it will be broken and the fragments can be removed, so that the fused mass within can be obtained free. Subsequently the fragments in the upper and lower parts of the mass can be separated by solution in water to which a little acetic acid has been added. The author has operated on minerals varying from wolframite (G. = 7·5) to beryl (G. = 2·7), and in some samples of sand has separated as many as 12 constituent minerals.

D. KLEIN (Bull. Soc. Min., iv., 149, 1881) has proposed to use one of the boro-tungstate salts in the place of the Sonstadt solution for the separation of minerals whose specific gravity is as high as 3·6. The most suitable salt for this purpose is the cadmium compound, $H_4Cd_2B_2W_9O_{34} + 16$ aq. It dissolves at 22° C. in about $\tfrac{1}{10}$ its weight of water, and crystallizes out both on evaporation and cooling. At 75° C. it melts (best over a water-bath) in its water of crystallization to a yellow liquid, on the surface of which a spinel crystal (G. = 3·55) floats. By the application of the Thoulet apparatus (see above), so arranged as to allow of the application of heat, solutions of any specific gravity, hot or cold, from 1 to 3·6, can be obtained. A number of common minerals (e. g. chrysolite, epidote, vesuvianite, some varieties of amphibole and mica) can be separated by the use of this liquid, while the Sonstadt solution is inapplicable. The fragments under examination must be free from the carbonates of calcium or magnesium, which decompose the boro-tungstate of cadmium.

III. LIGHT (pp. 125–168).

Measurement of Indices of Refraction.

For the determination of the indices of refraction of crystallized minerals, various improvements have been made in former methods and some new methods devised.

Use of the Horizontal Goniometer.—The ordinary method for determining the index of refraction, requiring the observation of the angle of minimum deviation (δ) of a light-ray on passing through a prism of the given material, having a known angle (α), and with its edge cut in the proper direction, has already been mentioned (p. 128). The two measurements required in this case can be readily made with the horizontal goniometer of Fuess, described on p. 115. In this instrument the collimator is stationary, being fastened to a leg of the tripod support, but the observing telescope with the verniers moves freely. In the use for this object the graduated circle is to be clamped, and the screw attachments connected with the axis carrying the support, and the vernier circle and observing telescope are to be loosened. The method of observation requires no further explanation (see also pp. 141, 150).

Total Reflectrometer.—F. Kohlrausch has shown (Wied. Ann., iv., 1, 1878) that the principle of total reflection (p. 128) may be made use of to determine the index of refraction in cases where other methods are inapplicable. No prism is required, but only a small fragment having a single polished surface; this may be cut in any direction for an isotrope medium; it should be parallel to the vertical axis in a uniaxial crystal, and perpendicular to the acute bisectrix with a biaxial crystal. The arrangements required are, in their simplest form, a wide-mouthed bottle filled with carbon disulphide (refractive index 1·6); the top of this is formed by a fixed graduated circle, and a vertical rod, with a vernier attached, passes through the plate and carries the crystal section on its extremity, immersed in the liquid. The angle through which the crystal surface lying in the axis is turned is thus measured in the same way as in f. 412H, by the vernier on the stationary graduated circle. The front of the bottle is made of a piece of plate glass, and through this passes the horizontal observing telescope, arranged for parallel light. The rest of the surface of the bottle is covered with tissue-paper, through which the diffuse illumination from say a sodium flame has access; the rear of the bottle is suitably darkened. When now the observer looks through the telescope, at the same time turning the axis carrying the crystal section, he will finally see, if the source of illumination is in a proper oblique direction, a sharp line marking the limit of the total reflection. The angle is then measured off on the graduated circle, when this line coincides with one of the spider lines of the telescope. Now the crystal is turned in the opposite direction, and the angle again read off. Half the observed angle (2α) is the angle of total reflection; if n is the refractive index of the carbon disulphide, then the required refractive index is equal to

$$n \sin \alpha.$$

Under favorable conditions the results are accurate to four decimal places. This method is limited, of course, to substances whose refractive index is less than that of the liquid medium with which the bottle is filled. With a section of a uniaxial crystal, whose surface is most conveniently parallel to the vertical axis, the method is essentially the same. The section is so placed that in it the direction normal to the optic axis is horizontal. The light will be here separated into two rays, having separate limiting surfaces, and with a Nicol prism it is easy to determine which of them corresponds to the vibrations parallel and perpendicular, respectively, to the optic axis. For biaxial crystals the surface should be normal to the acute bisectrix. This will give by actual observation the values of α and γ, and if $2E$, the apparent axial angle in air, is known, then β, the mean index can be calculated (see p. 150). Instead of carbon disulphide the Sonstadt solution, with $n = 1\cdot 73$, can be employed. The total reflectrometer of Kohlrausch has been adapted in practical form to the horizontal goniometer (f. 372A) of Fuess (see Liebisch, Ber. Ges. Nat. Fr. Berlin, Dec. 16, 1879). Klein has suggested some improvements (J. Min., 1879, 880), and Bauer (J. Min., 1882, i., 132) has shown how the method can be simply applied to the instrument for the measurement of the optic axial angle (f. 412H), and without its modification in any important respect.

QUINCKE (abstract in Z. Kryst., iv., 540) has described another method for obtaining the refractive index of a substance on the principle of total reflection. In a word, it consists in observing on a spectrometer the limiting angle of total reflection for a plane section of the substance to be investigated, brought with oil of cassia between two flint glass prisms.

SORBY (Proc. Roy. Soc., xxvi., 384; Min. Mag., i., 97, 194; ii., 1, 103) has developed the method of obtaining the refractive index of a transparent medium, first described by Duke de Chaulnes (1767), and has shown that under suitable conditions it allows of determinations being made with considerable accuracy. This method consists in observing the distance (d) which the focal distance of the objective is changed when a plane-plane plate of known thickness (t) is introduced perpendicular to the axis of the microscope between the objective and the focal point—here

$$\mu = \frac{t}{t-d}$$

Sorby makes use of a glass micrometer, upon which two systems of lines perpendicular to each other are ruled. The micrometer screw at g, in the Rosenbusch microscope (f. 412K, p. 181), makes it possible to measure the distance through which the tube is to be raised and lowered down to $\cdot 001$ mm.; consequently both t and d can be obtained with a high degree of accuracy.

BAUER has shown that the indices of refraction may be obtained with considerable accuracy from measurements, in the plane of the axes, of the distances between the black rings in the interference figures as seen in homogeneous light. The relation between these distances and the optical axes of elasticity was established by Neumann (Pogg. Ann., xxxiii., 257, 1834). Bauer has made use of this method in the case of muscovite (Ber. Ak. Berlin, 1877, 704). He has also developed the same method as applied to uniaxial crystals and employed it in the case of brucite (ib., 1881, 958).

Polarization Instruments.

Polariscope.—The earlier forms of polariscope for converging and for par-

POLARIZATION INSTRUMENTS—POLARISCOPE. 179

allel light, as arranged by Groth and constructed by Fuess, are shown in figs. 384, 385, p. 134. The more recently constructed instruments (see Liebisch, l. c., p. 342 et seq.), with some important improvements, are shown in f. 412c and f. 412d. The lower tube, f, containing the analyzer, has about it a collar, f' (see details, figure 412f), with a triangular projection on the upper edge; this fits into one of two corresponding triangular depressions (0° and 45°) in the surrounding tube, g. This serves to fix the position of the tube, that is, of the vibration-plane of the enclosed Nicol, with reference to the fixed arm, B, to which the verniers are attached, so that the principal section of the Nicol either coincides with, or makes an angle of 45° with the 0° line of the verniers. The circle, i, is graduated to 1°, and with the vernier gives readings to 2′; the section to be examined is supported at k. A similar collar, u, surrounds the upper tube, v, by which the position of the micrometer (at r) (this micrometer consists of two lines at right angles, one of which is graduated) can also be fixed relatively to the vernier so that the graduated line of the micrometer is perpendicular to the plane through the axis of the instrument and the zero of the vernier. The tube above carrying the Nicol has at s a graduated circle which shows the relative directions of the vibration-planes of the two Nicols. The lenses at n and o are arranged so that they may be used all together, when strongly converging light is needed, or the small lenses may be removed, so that three combinations are possible. A small screw at a makes it possible to adjust the position of the glass micrometer so that it shall always be in the focus of the lenses at o, a point which varies according to the combination of lenses employed.

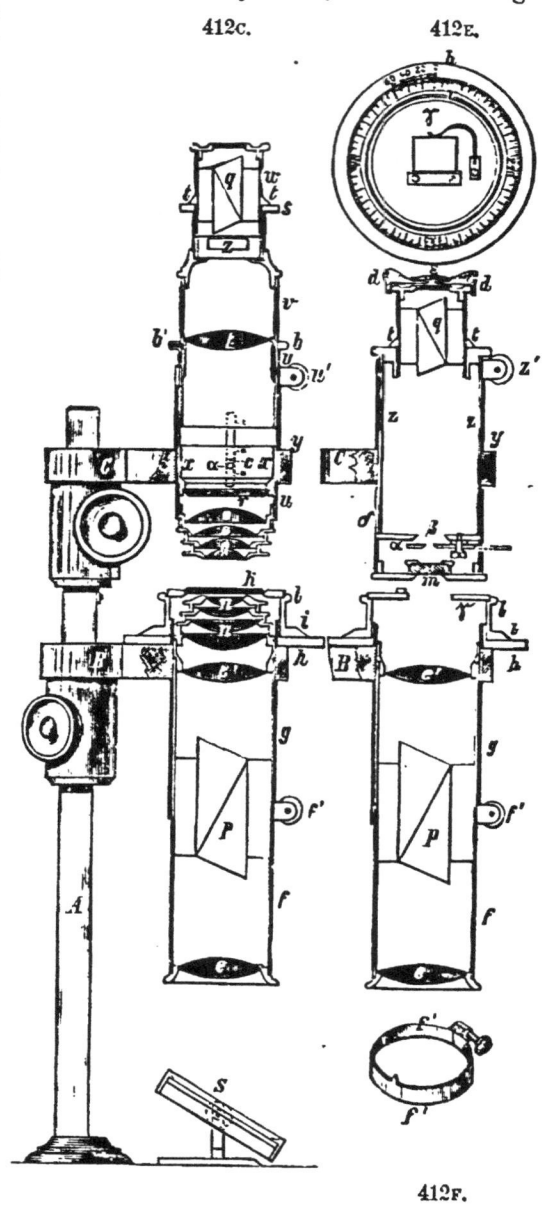

Stauroscope—Calderon's Plate.—The stauroscope is essentially the same instrument as that mentioned in f. 385. Instead, however, of employing the Brezina interference-plate of calcite, a double plate is used, as suggested by Calderon (Z. Kryst., ii., 68). This plate is, in fact, an artificial twin, and is made as follows: A calcite rhombohedron is cut through along the shorter diagonal; from each half a wedge-shaped portion is cut away and the two surfaces thus produced, after being polished, are cemented together. A plane-plane plate is then cut from this (compare figure) by grinding away the angles as indicated; this plate is divided into two halves by the line of separation of the artificial twin. Such a plate is very sensitive, and allows of very exact observations. It is placed at m (f. 412D), and when the arrangements are completed the dividing line of the calcite exactly coincides with a vibration-plane of one of the two Nicols. A diaphragm is placed above with holes of varying size according to the minuteness of the crystal to be examined. The stauroscopic determinations made by Calderon showed an error of only 3' to 7'.

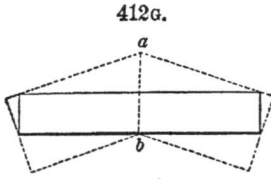

Axial-angle Instrument (see p. 148).—The instrument for the measurement of the angle of the optic axes is in principle essentially that of Des Cloizeaux, but in the details of the construction various improvements have been introduced (see f. 412H). The same arrangement of adjustable collars at u' and f' is employed as in the other instruments, to fix the position of the principal sections of the Nicols relatively to the plane passing through the axis of the observing telescope and the axis of rotation. Instead of the straight rod in f. 401, in the pincers at the extremity of which the crystal section is

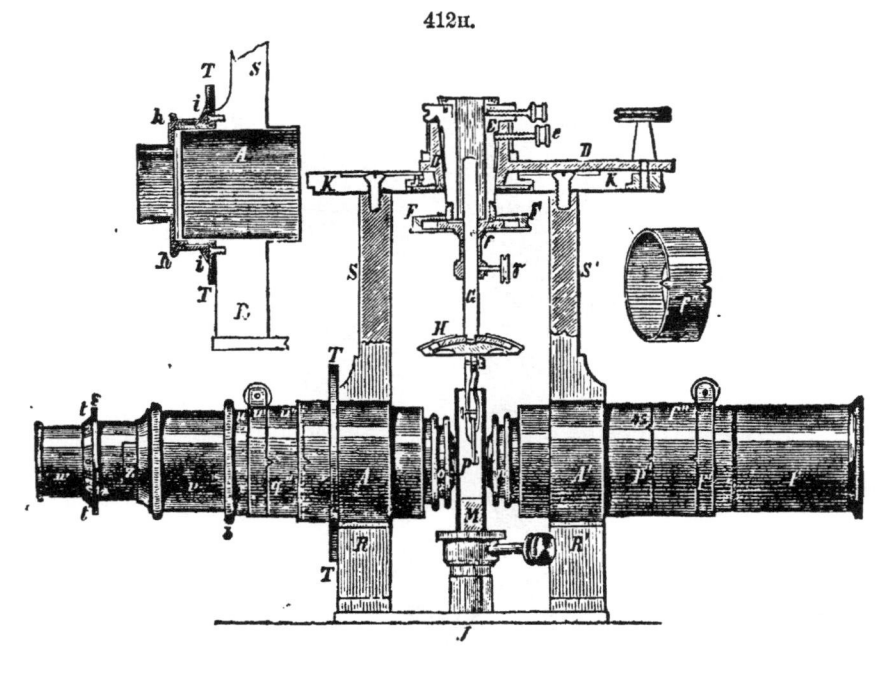

POLARIZATION MICROSCOPE.

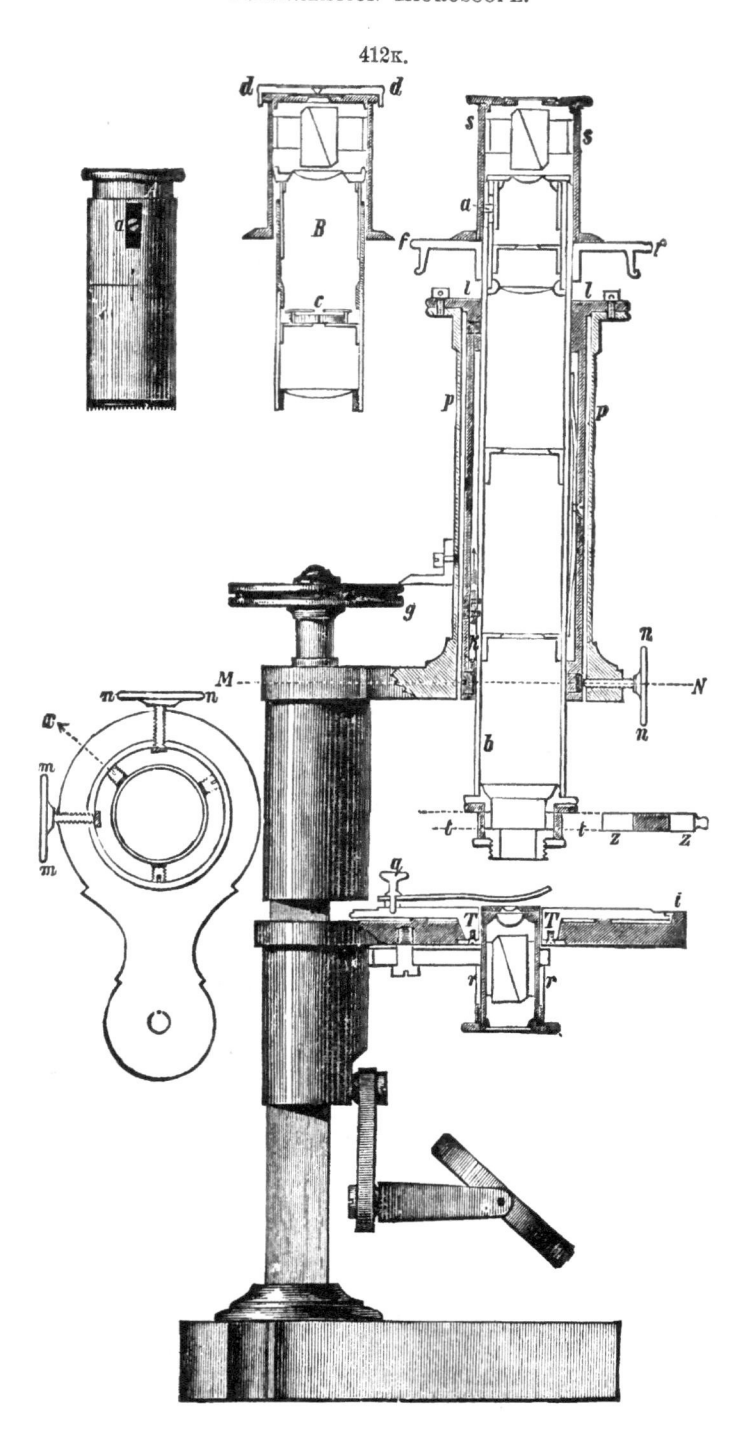

412K.

held, there is here an arrangement consisting of two concentric tubes, turning independently, but so as to be clamped at e. The adjustable disk having a horizontal motion at F, and the spherical segment at H (Petzval support) allow of the section being both centered and adjusted.

Polariscope of Adams-Schneider.—A polariscope of peculiar construction, giving a very large field of view, and at the same time allowing of the measurement of the axial angle, was proposed in 1875 by ADAMS (Phil. Mag., IV., 1., p. 13, 1875; V., viii., 275). The same instrument has been further developed by SCHNEIDER (Carl. Rep., xv., 744), and is also described by BECKE (Min. Petr. Mitth., ii., 430, 1879). The peculiarity of the instrument consists in this, that the middle plano-convex lenses which ordinarily are fixed to the upper and lower lens systems, respectively (see o, o, o, and n, n, n, in f. 412c), are here separated from the others in a common support, and together form a sphere. The course of the light-rays will be always the same, however the sphere is rotated about its fixed centre. Between the semi-spherical lenses a space is left, and here is introduced the section to be examined, which, turning with the surrounding lenses, can obviously be made to take any desired position with reference to the axis of the instrument. An appropriate arrangement makes it possible to measure the angle through which the section must be rotated to bring first one and then the second optic axis in coincidence with the axis of the instrument. The advantages of the instrument consist in the fact that the field of view is very large, and at the same time it allows of placing the section in any desired position relatively to the axis. Moreover, the angle measured is the apparent angle for the glass of which the lenses are made, so that the axes are visible in cases where this would not be the case, because of total reflection, either in air or in oil.

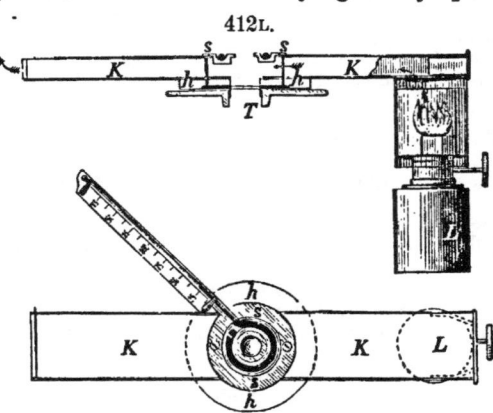

Polarization-Microscope.—The investigation of the form and optical properties of minerals when in microscopic form, as they occur, for example, in rocks of fine crystalline structure, has been much facilitated by the use of instruments specially adapted for this purpose. The most serviceable polarizing microscope, for general use, is that described by Rosenbusch (Jahrb. Min., 1876, 504), and made by R. Fuess, of Berlin. A sectional view is given in f. 412K. The essential arrangements are as follows: The coarse adjustment of the tube carrying the eye-piece and objective is accomplished by the hand, the tube sliding freely in the support, p. The fine adjustment is made by the screw, g; the screw-head is graduated and turns about a fixed index attached to p, by this means the distance through which the tube is raised or lowered can be measured to 0·001 mm.; this is important in determining the indices of refraction by the De Chaulnes-Sorby method (see p. 178). The polarizing prism (Razumovsky) is placed below the stage at r, in a support, with a graduated circle, so that the position of its vibration-plane can be fixed. The analyzing prism is placed above the eye-piece in a support, s, which may be removed at pleasure; the edge of this is graduated and a fixed mark on the plate, f, makes it possible to set the vibration-plane in any desired position. When both prisms are set at the zero mark, their vibration-planes are crossed ($\perp$); when either is turned 90°, the planes are parallel ($\parallel$). The stage is made to rotate about the vertical axis, but otherwise is fixed; its edge is graduated, so that the angle through which it is turned can be measured to $\frac{1}{2}°$. Three adjustment screws, of which one is shown at n, n, make it possible to bring the axis of the object glass in coincidence with axis of rotation of the stage (see further the detailed drawing at the side).

This instrument is especially applicable to the study of the form and optical properties of minerals as they are found in thin sections of rocks (on the method of preparing see p. 159), although it can also be used with small independent crystals and crystalline sections or fragments. The more important points to which the attention is to be directed, more particularly in the case of minerals in sections of rocks, are: (1) crystalline form, as shown in the outline; (2) direction of cleavage lines; (3) index of refraction; (4) light absorption in different directions, i. e., dichroism or pleochroism; (5) the isotrope or anisotrope character, and if the latter, the direction of the planes of light-vibration—this will generally decide the question as to the crystalline system; (6) position of the axial plane and nature of the axial interference figures when they can be observed, and the positive or negative character of the double refraction; (7) inclosures, solid, liquid or gaseous.

In regard to these several points a few general remarks may be made.*

(1) *Crystalline Form.*—In most rocks well defined crystals are rather the exception than the rule. It will be consequently only in occasional sections (e. g. more commonly in volcanic rocks) that a clear crystalline outline is observed. The form of this outline will depend upon the direction in which the section is cut, and will vary as it varies; this fact will explain why in a given rock section so many widely different forms of a given mineral are observed; this irregularity is increased by the fact that the crystals may be more or less distorted. For the recognition of the form, consequently, considerable familiarity with the various outlines likely to occur in the case of a given species is very desirable.

The angles between any two crystalline directions is obtained by first bringing one of them in coincidence with a spider line in the eye-piece, the adjustment at N having been previously made, and then noting the angle through which the crystal, i. e., the stage, must be rotated to bring the other direction in coincidence with the same spider line.

(2) *Cleavage.*—The process of grinding involved in the making of a thin section tends to develop the cleavage lines. Here are to be noted, (1) the direction of cleavage (measured as above), depending on the direction in which the section is cut; and (2) the character of the cleavage. For example, a basal section of a crystal of amphibole shows the cleavage lines parallel to the prism ($124\frac{1}{2}°$); a vertical section shows one set of vertical and parallel

---

* For the full development of this subject, see the works of ROSENBUSCH and ZIRKEL (titles on p. 111.); also the following:

BORICKY, E. Elemente einer neuen chemisch-mikroskopischen Mineral- und Gesteinsanalyse, 72 pp. 4to, Prag, 1877.

COHEN, E. Sammlung von Mikrophotographieen zur Veranschaulichung der mikroskopishen Structur von Mineralien und Gesteinen, aufgenommen von J. Grimm in Offenburg, 1, 2, 3, 4, 5 Lfg., Stuttgart, 1881-82.

DOELTER. Die Bestimmung der petrographisch wichtigeren Mineralien durch das Mikroskop; Eine Anleitung zur mikroskop. Gesteins-Analyse, 33 pp. 8vo, Vienna, 1876.

FOUQUÉ, F. and MICHEL-LÉVY, A. Minéralogie micrographique, roches éruptives Françaises, 509 pp. 4to, Paris, 1879.

RUTLEY, F. The Study of Rocks, 319 pp. 12mo, London, 1879.

THOULET. Contributions à l'étude des propriétés physiques et chemiques des minéraux microscopiques, 77 pp. 8vo, Paris.

HAWES, G. W. The Mineralogy and Lithology of New Hampshire (Geology of New Hampshire, vol. iii.), 262 pp. 4to, with 12 plates. Pages 8–18 of this work give an excellent summary of microscopic methods of investigation, as applied to rocks and minerals.

cleavage lines. On the other hand, a basal section of a crystal of pyroxene shows the prismatic cleavage, here less perfect than in the amphibole, and at an angle of 87° and 93°; a vertical section again shows only one set. Also a basal section of mica shows no cleavage lines, but a vertical section shows a series of very fine parallel lines corresponding to the highly perfect basal cleavage.

(3) The *index of refraction* is obtained by the method of the Duke de Chaulnes, as developed by Sorby (see p. 178).

(4) *Pleochroism.*—To examine the pleochroism of a mineral section, the lower prism is inserted and set at 0°, so that its vibration-plane coincides with the direction 0° to 180° on the stage. If now the section be placed on the stage and the latter rotated, the absorption of the light vibrating in the same plane with the prism can be observed. For example, a vertical section of biotite is dark when the direction of the cleavage lines is ∥ with the above named line (0° to 180° of stage), for the light which it transmits has vibrations in this plane only, and these are strongly absorbed; on the contrary, when the stage is rotated 90° the section becomes light, because the light vibrating ∥ to this direction, is but slightly absorbed; on the other hand, a basal section shows no difference of light absorption.

(5) *Isotrope or Anisotrope*, etc.—Supposing the prisms in position and placed with their vibration-planes perpendicular, a section of an *amorphous* substance, as glass, will remain dark in all positions as it is rotated upon the stage, for it has sensibly the same light-elasticity in all directions, since no one direction has any advantage over another.

A section of an *isometric* mineral will also remain dark as it is revolved between the crossed prisms. A section of a *tetragonal* or *hexagonal* crystal parallel to the base will also remain unchanged between crossed prisms; a vertical section, or one inclined to the base, will be dark only when the directions of the spider lines coincide with the vertical and transverse directions; in other words, the extinction directions are ∥ and ⊥ to the prism. A section of an orthorhombic crystal will have its directions of extinction coincident with the crystallographic axes. A section of a monoclinic crystal cut parallel to any direction in the orthodiagonal zone will have its extinction directions parallel to the clinodiagonal axis and perpendicular; that is, if prismatic in habit, ∥ and ⊥ to the prism, hence in this position it cannot be distinguished from an orthorhombic crystal. On the other hand, in the case of a section cut in any other plane, the position of the extinction directions will depend upon the individual crystal. For the exact determination of these directions with reference to any crystallographic lines present, the method of the stauroscope must be employed. For minute sections a quartz plate (⊥ vertical axis) is sometimes inserted (ZZ at tt in f. 412K); this gives for a proper position of the upper prism a field of uniform delicate color (say violet). A section of an anisotrope mineral placed on the stage will have the same color only when its extinction directions are ∥ and ⊥ to the vibration plane of the lower prism (rr, in f. 412K). A special eye-piece (see f. 412K) provided with a Calderon plate is also sometimes employed.

(6) If the eye-piece is removed, and at the same time suitable lenses added, two at T (f. 412K) and one above, strongly converging light is obtained. In many cases when the section is cut in the proper direction, the axial interference figures can be seen as distinctly as in the ordinary polariscope. A ¼-undulation mica plate makes it possible in such cases to determine the + or − character of the double refraction. On the use of microscope for the observation of the optic axes, see v. Lasaulx, J. Min., 1878, 377, and Z. Kryst., ii., 256; Bertrand, Bull. Soc. Min., 1878, 27; Klein, Nachr. Ges. Wiss. Göttingen, 1878, 461; Laspeyres, Z. Kryst., iv., 460.

(7) For a description of the various inclosures often observed in sections of minerals, and the method of studying them, reference must be made to the works referred to above.

When it is desired to observe the effect of increased temperature on the mineral sections or their enclosures (e.g. liquid CO_2) the air bath (f. 412L) heated by the lamp, L, and provided with a delicate thermometer, is employed. This fits into the stage at T, and the section is placed above at ss.

Microscope of Bertrand.—Bertrand (Bull. Soc. Min., iv., 97–100, 1880) has devised a form of microscope especially adapted for mineralogical work, and allowing of the determination of the form and optical properties of minerals in crystals or sections so small that they cannot be employed in the ordinary polariscopes. The tube carrying the eye-piece and objective has the ordinary coarse and fine adjustments; the former is accomplished by a rack and pinion movement, and is measured by a scale and vernier; the latter is made by a screw with a graduated head situated similarly to that in the Rosenbusch microscope. An opening in the tube above the objective allows of the introduction of a little slide carrying a small lens, whose vertical position can be adjusted by an appropriate rack and pinion turned by a screw head; this auxiliary lens may either magnify the interference figures of the crystal section or else the section itself, when the position of the former is properly adjusted. The objective can be centered by horizontal screws, and immediately above it a quartz wedge, or quarter-undulation plate of mica, can be introduced for the determination of the character of the double refraction. The stage has two movements in directions at right angles to each other, for each of which a special scale with a vernier is supplied; also, the stage rotates in a horizontal plane, and is supplied with a graduation to allow of the measurement of the angle of rotation. The lower polarizing prism is supplied with several lenses for producing strongly converging light, and by a screw can be moved in a vertical direction. In addition, a small goniometer with oil bath is provided, which can be placed upon the stage, and which allows of the measurement of the optic axial angle of the section under examination. The special advantages of this instrument, as shown by the observations of the inventor with it, as also those of Des Cloizeaux, are that it allows of all the necessary optical determinations even in crystals or crystal sections which are extremely minute.

On the Cause of the so-called Optical Anomalies of Crystals.

[The following paragraphs contain a brief statement of the results of some of the more important of recent investigations bearing upon the subject of the "Optical Anomalies" of crystals. It will be seen that the main point at issue is as to the true explanation of the phenomena of double-refraction, observed in many crystallized minerals of apparent isometric form (as garnet, fluorite, boracite, analcite, etc.), and analogous variations from the theoretical optical character in crystals apparently tetragonal, hexagonal, etc. (as vesuvianite, zircon, corundum, beryl, etc.). Are these "optical anomalies" a proof that the apparent symmetry of the observed form is only *pseudo-symmetry*, being due to the complex twinning of parts of lower grade of symmetry than that which the crystal as a whole simulates? In other words, do the optical properties actually belong to the inherent molecular structure of the parts of the crystal ? Or, does the geometrical form of the whole really represent the true symmetry of the crystal, and are these phenomena (of double-refraction in isometric crystals, for example) due to secondary causes, such as internal tension produced during the growth of the crystal, and so on ?
In regard to this subject, it may be remarked that it is beyond question, on the one hand, that *pseudo-symmetry* is to some extent a law of nature, for the crystals of many minerals of unquestioned orthorhombic character simulate hexagonal forms (e. g., aragonite) ; on the other hand, it is equally certain that the phenomena of double-refraction may be produced in colloid or crystalline isotrope media by a state of tension, and similarly that uniaxial crystals may be made biaxial by pressure, and so on. Which of these two explanations is to be applied in the large number of cases now under discussion cannot be regarded as settled, although the writer inclines to the opinion that the second explanation, more fully detailed later, will be found to hold true in the case of the majority. This does not seem, however, to be the place nor the time for a full review of the testimony which has been accumulated on both sides of the question.]

There are a considerable number of minerals, the crystals of which exhibit optical phenomena which are not in accordance with the apparent symmetry of the crystalline form. Cases of this kind were observed by Brewster (1815 and later), and investigated by him with a remarkable acuteness considering the imperfect instruments then available. For example, alum, analcite, boracite, diamond, fluorite, halite were shown by Brewster to exert an effect on polarized light not in accordance with their apparent isometric form. With the improved methods and means of investigation at the disposal of mineralogists in recent times, the list of minerals whose crystals exhibit "optical anomalies" has been very largely increased.

In explanation of these anomalies, various hypotheses have been advanced. BREWSTER explained them in the case of diamond as due to local tension connected with solid or gaseous inclosures. In 1841 BIOT published his memoir on *lamellar polarization* (C. R. xii., 967 ; xiii., 155, 391, 839), and explained the optical characters of the minerals named above, as also the tetragonal apophyllite, as due to that cause. The idea advanced by him was that the crystal was made up of thin lamellæ, which exerted on transmitted light an effect analogous to that of a bundle of parallel glass plates. VOLGER (1854–5) attempted to show that in the case of boracite the anomalous optical properties were due to the presence of a doubly-refracting anisotrope mineral, parisite, derived from alteration ; much later (1868) this view was accepted by Des Cloizeaux. MARBACH (Pogg. Ann., xciv., 412, 1855) discussed the question more broadly, and concluded that the phenomena observed were due to the presence in the normal substance of abnormal anisotrope portions, which last owed their existence to a tension produced at the time the crystal was formed. It was further shown by VON REUSCH (ib. cxxxii., 618, 1867) that the hypothesis of Biot was not sufficient to explain the observed facts in the case of alum. He also took up the view of Marbach, and following out much the same idea as that of Marbach, reached the conclusion that the anisotrope characters of isometric crystals were due to the condition of internal tension existing within the crystal. As bearing upon the question he proved by experiment that by suitable pressure, in the case for example of alum crystals, the double-refraction could be removed. The influence of pressure in causing double refraction was early investigated by F. E. NEUMANN (Pogg. Ann., liv., 449, 1841), and by PFAFF (ib., cvii., 333 ; cviii., 578, 1859). The subject has also been discussed by HIRSCHWALD (Min. Mitth., 1875, 227).

More recently the idea of internal molecular tension as a cause of anomalous optical characters has been developed by Klocke, Jannettaz, Klein, Ben Saude and others, as more particularly described later.

In 1876 MALLARD published his most important memoir (Ann. Min., VII., x., 60–196) upon this subject, in which he not only gave a very large number of new facts of a similar nature, but also advanced a new explanation which has been warmly accepted by some mineralogists. He regards all the indications of double-refraction observed in apparent isometric crystals, and analogous variations from the normal character in crystals of other systems, as proof that the form is only apparently isometric, tetragonal, and so on (*pseudo-isometric, pseudo-tetragonal*, etc.), the union of several individual crystals giving rise to an external form of a higher grade of symmetry than that which they themselves possess. On his view, an apparent isometric cube may, in fact, be a combination of six uniaxial crystals (counting two parallel as one, in fact only three independent), each having the form of a square pyramid, united so that their bases form the sides of the cube, and their vertices are combined at the centre. Again, an apparent regular octahedron may be made up of eight uniaxial triangular pyramids, similarly placed ; a dodecahedron of twelve rhombic pyramids (boracite), or perhaps of forty-eight triclinic triangular pyramids, the bases of four combining to form a rhombic face. In most of these cases the optic axis coincides with the axis of the pyramid.

Mallard thus includes among *pseudo-isometric* species : alum, analcite, boracite, fluorite, garnet, senarmontite ; among *pseudo-tetragonal* species : apophyllite, mellite, octahedrite, rutile, vesuvianite, zircon ; among *pseudo-*

hexagonal species: apatite, beryl, corundum, penninite, ripidolite, tourmaline; *pseudo-orthorhombic* species: harmotome, topaz; *pseudo-monoclinic:* orthoclase.

Many observations similar to those of Mallard have been made by BERTRAND (in Bull. Soc. Min., 1878-1882), who applies the same method of explanation to them. For explanation, Bertrand has described crystals of garnet which were biaxial, with an angle of about 90°; a hexoctahedron being made up, in his view, of forty-eight triangular pyramids, four to each pseudo-rhombic pyramid. Each pyramid is biaxial, with the acute negative bisectrix nearly normal to the base, and the axial plane coincides with the direction of the longer diameter of the rhombic face. Further, apparent tetrahedral crystals of romeite are regarded as formed of four rhombohedrons of 120°, placed with their vertices at a common point. Also in the case of romeite the octahedrons are, in his view, formed by the grouping of eight rhombohedral crystals of 90° about a central point. The above will serve as illustrations. Bertrand has extended his observations over a considerable number of species, and the explanation given by Mallard of the optical phenomena just described is strongly supported by him, as against the Marbach-Reusch theory of molecular tension, more minutely described below. Bertrand urges (Bull. Soc. Min., v., 3, 1882) that a true doubly-refracting crystal, whether simple or a complex twin, can always be distinguished from a crystal normally isotrope, but modified through internal tension or any other cause. The difference, he states, is to be seen in parallel polarized light, where the former will show a distinctness and uniformity of character which does not belong to the latter; still more clearly in converging light, where the truly doubly-refracting crystal shows throughout the same characters, each fragment into which the section may be broken giving the identical uniaxial or biaxial figures with the whole; on the other hand, this cannot be true of the different parts of a crystal made doubly-refracting through some cause, as contraction, and so on. As illustrations of these facts, he appeals to boracite, garnet, pharmacosiderite, etc., stating that, as the result of his observations, they fall into the former class. He speaks further of octahedrons of boracite formed of twelve biaxial crystals, and of romeite formed of eight uniaxial crystals, as showing that the internal structure is independent of the external form; as bearing further upon this point, it is stated that the imperfect crystals of the garnet rock of Jordansmühl show the same twinning of biaxial individuals as do isolated crystals of garnet, whose external form is complete. But reference must be made to the observations alluded to beyond, which do not entirely support the conclusions of Bertrand.

This subject has been discussed by GRATTAROLA, who includes calcite, quartz, nephelite, barite, etc., in the list of species which have an apparent symmetry higher than that which really belongs to them; his conclusions, however, are not based upon observations (Dell' unità cristallonomica in Mineralogia, Florence, 1877).

In many other cases, besides those mentioned above, observers have, on the basis of variation in angles, or of optical characters, reached the conclusion that the species in question really belongs to a system of lower symmetry than that to which it has been ordinarily referred. For example, see Des Cloizeaux on microcline and milarite; Rumpf on apophyllite (Min. Petr. Mitth., ii., 369); Becke on chabazite (ib., ii., 391), and hessite (ib., iii., 301); Schrauf on brookite (Ber. Ak. Wien, lxxiv., 535 and Z. Kryst., i., 274) and other species; Brezina on autunite (Z. Kryst., iii., 273); Tschermak on the micas (Z. Kryst., ii., 14) and corundum (Min. Petr. Mitth., ii., 362); and many other cases. These last named observations, however, do not generally admit of being explained on the hypothesis of Mallard. In many of them the conclusions reached are beyond doubt correct, in others the question must be regarded as still undecided.

TSCHERMAK proposes the term *mimetic* for those forms ("mimetische Formen"), which imitate a higher grade of symmetry by the grouping (twinning) of individuals of a lower grade of symmetry, as for example, aragonite; also, chabazite, which, according to Becke, is apparently rhombohedral, but, in fact, formed by a complex twinning of triclinic individuals (this conclusion, however, is not universally accepted). He also uses the term *pseudo-symmetry* to describe the phenomena in general (ZS. G. Ges., xxxi., 657, 1879, and Lehrb. Min., p. 89 et seq., 1881).

The explanation of the optical phenomena referred to above, which was presented by Marbach and later developed by Reusch, has been recently still further elaborated by Klocke (J. Min., 1880, i., 53, 158), Klein, Jannettaz, Ben Saude. KLOCKE'S first observations were made upon artificial crystals of alum. He found that each crystal (contrary to earlier statements) showed doubly refracting properties as strongly normal to an octahedral plane as in other directions. A section parallel to this plane was divided into six sectors by radial lines passing from the angles to the centre; the directions of extinction in each sector being || (parallel) and ⊥ (perpendicular) to its outer edge, these directions consequently coinciding for each pair of opposite sectors. These sectors behaved as if made up of bands in a state of tension parallel to their longer direction; a similar result was obtained by subjecting a six-sided octahedral and *isotrope* alum section to pressure perpendicular to two of its edges. He found further that all the sections of the same crystal, independent of the crystallographic orientation, were alike as regards the direction of the tension, and that all crystals made at the same time, that is, under the same conditions, yielded identical results; but this was not true of crystals made at different times. Further it was found that the distortion peculiar to the crystal exerted an essential effect upon the number and arrangement of the optical sectors, and that the position which the crystal occupied in the vessel during its formation was also an important factor.

Later the same author (J. Min., 1881, ii., 249) has extended his observations to some of the species exhibiting *pseudo-symmetry*. He shows, among other results, that pressure exerted normal to the vertical axis of a section of a tetragonal or hexagonal crystal which has been cut ⊥ c (vert.), changes the uniaxial interference figure into a biaxial, and with substances optically positive, the plane of the optic axes is parallel, and with negative substances normal, to the direction of pressure. This was observed on sections of vesuvianite and apophyllite which exhibited uniaxial portions. Many sections are divided into four optical fields (biaxial) with the axial plane perpendicular to the edge. The behavior of each field in a section of apophyllite consequently is (optically +, see above) as if in a state of tension *parallel* to the adjacent combination-edge with the prism; but with vesuvianite (optically −) the direction of tension is perpendicular. This explanation is supported by the fact that pressure exerted in the proper direction serves, in accordance with the above principles, respectively to increase or diminish the axial angle. The author also succeeded in obtaining axial interference figures visible in converging polarized light in gelatine sections when under pressure; the same phenomenon in parallel light had been earlier observed.

On the observations of JANNETTAZ, showing the effect of internal tension in causing double-refraction, see Bull. Soc. Min., ii., 124; ii., 191; iii, 20.

The results of the observations of KLEIN (J. Min., 1880, ii., 209; 1881, i., 239) on boracite have an important bearing upon this subject. As stated above, it is included by Mallard among the pseudo-isometric species. Basing his results more especially upon the examination of crystals of dodecahedral habit, Mallard concluded that the apparent simple form is made up of twelve rhombic pyramids whose basal planes form the twelve faces of the dodecahedron. Baumhauer, on the basis of results of etching experiments, more particularly on crystals of octahedral habit, concluded that the species was orthorhombic, the apparent simple form being made up of six individuals whose bases would coincide with the cubic planes (p. 187). The observations of Klein show that the structure of the crystals of different habits vary—some agreeing with the scheme of Mallard—some with that of Baumhauer; he shows, however, very conclusively (as it seems to the writer) that this apparently complicated structure is probably due to internal tension produced during the growth of the crystals. Crystallographically there is no variation in angle from the requirements of the isometric system to be observed. In regard to the optical characters, he shows that the interior optical structure does not correspond to the exterior planes; that the etching figures do not correspond to the optical limits; that a change of temperature alters the relative position of the optical fields without influencing the form of the etching figures; that the differently orientired optical portions lose their sharp limits, they change their position relatively, some disappearing in part or whole, and others appearing.* Klein has also made a series of optical studies on garnet (Nachr. Ges. Wiss. Göttingen, June 28, 1882), and after a review of the whole subject decides in favor of the true isometric character of the species; the double-refraction phenomena observed being due to secondary causes.

BEN SAUDE (J. Min., 1882, i., 41) has investigated analcite, and arrived at the conclusion that with it also the abnormal optical characters are to be explained by internal molecular tension. He shows that the crystals are formed of different optical parts, in combinations of 30 with the cube and trapezohedron together, and 24 for the trapezohedron alone, the form of which changes as the outer surfaces of the crystals change. The structure can be explained in this way, as made up of pyramids going from each plane to the middle of the crystal having the plane as its base, with as many sides as there are edges to the plane; as the outer form changes the optical structure changes correspondingly; every edge corresponds to an optical boundary, and every plane to an optical field. All these double-refraction phenomena are explained as due to secondary causes. Moreover, the author has proved that gelatine cast into the form of the natural crystals has on solidifying an analo-

---

* A memoir by Mallard (Bull. Soc. Min., v., 144, 1882) upon the effect of heat upon boracite crystals was received just as these pages were going to press. Mallard details the results of numerous experiments, and concludes that the effect of heat does not modify the form of the ellipsoid of elasticity, nor the position of the six different orientations which it can have; it only modifies the choice made by each of the crystal sections between the six orientations. From this it is concluded that this ellipsoid is in fact characteristic of the crystalline *réseau* of the species, and that the apparent isometric symmetry is due to the method of grouping alluded to. Analogous results were obtained with crystals of potassium sulphate (orthorhombic, pseudo-hexagonal like aragonite), and the conclusion is drawn from this that a perfect analogy exists between the so-called pseudo-isometric crystals and the pseudo-hexagonal.

gous optical structure, showing the same sections, the same directions of light-extinction, and under favoring conditions the same position of the optic axes. Ben Saude has also examined perofskite (Gekrönte Preisschrift der Universität Göttingen, 1882) from the same standpoint, with reference to the etching-figures and optical phenomena. He concludes that it is to be referred to the isometric system, and that the double refraction is to be explained as caused by changes in the original position of equilibrium produced in the growth of the crystals. This conclusion, however, is at variance with the results of the observations of others.

References to some important Recent Papers upon the Subjects of Heat and Electricity.

A. Arzruni. Ueber den Einfluss der Temperatur auf die Brechungsexponenten der natürlichen Sulfate des Baryum, Strontium und Blei, Zeitsch. Kryst., i., 165, 1877.
J. Beckenkamp. Ueber die Ausdehnung monosymmetrischer und asymmetrischer Krystalle durch die Wärme, Z. Kryst., v., 436, 1881.
H. Dufet. Influence de la température sur la double réfraction du gypse, Bull. Soc. Min., iv., 113, 1881 ; Influence de la température sur les indices principaux du gypse, ib., iv., 191.
L. Fletcher. Ueber die Ausdehnung der Kristalle durch die Warme, Zeitschr. Kryst., iv., 336.
Jannettaz. Mémoire sur la propagation de la chaleur dans les corps cristallisés, Bull. Soc. Géol., IV., xxix., 5 ; Note sur la conductibilité des corps cristallisés pour la chaleur, etc., ib., III., i., 117 ; Sur les propriétés thermiques des cristaux, ib., p. 252; see also ib., ii., p. 264; iii., 499; iv., 1, 553 ; ix. ; Sur un appareil à conductibilité thermique, Bull. Soc. Min., i., 119.
Joubert. Sur le pouvoir rotatoire du Quartz et sa variation avec la température, C. R., lxxxvii., 497, 1878.
V. von Lang. Ueber die Abhängigkeit der circularpolarization des Quarzes von der Temperatur, Ber. Ak. Wien., lxxi., 707, 1875. Grösse und Lage der optischen Elasticitätsaxen beim Gypse, Ber. Ak. Wien., lxxvi., 793, 1877.
O. J. Lodge. On a method of measuring the absolute thermal conductivity of crystals and other rare substances, Phil. Mag., V., v., 110, 1878.
C. Pape. Die Wärmeleitung im Kupfervitriol, Wied. Ann., i., 126, 1877.
W. C. Röntgen. Ueber eine Variation der Senarmont'schen Methode zur Bestimmung der Isothermenflächen in Krystallen, Pogg. Ann., cli., 603, 1874. Ueber eine Methode zur Erzeugung von Isothermen auf Krystallen, Zeitschr. Kryst., iii., 17, 1878.
L. Sohncke. Ueber den Einfluss der Temperatur auf das optische Drehvermögen des Quarzes und des Chlorsauren Natrons, Weid. Ann., iii., 516, 1878.
S. P. Thompson and O. J. Lodge. On unilateral conductivity in tourmaline crystals, Phil. Mag., V., viii., 18, 1879.

Jacques et Pierre Curie. Développement par compression de l'électricité polaire dans les cristaux hemièdres à faces inclinées, C. R., xci., 294, 383, 1880; Lois du dégagement de l'électricité par pression dans la tourmaline, ib., xcii., 186, 1881; Sur les phénomènes électriques de la tourmaline et des cristaux hemièdres à faces inclinées, ib., xcii., 350; Les cristaux hemièdres à faces inclinées comme sources constantes d'électricité, ib., xciii., 204.
C. Friedel. Sur la pyroélectricité dans la topaze, la blende et le quartz.
W. G. Hankel. Elektrische Untersuchungen (I. Thermoelektricität, II. Aktinolektricität, III. Piezoelectricität), Abhandl. K. Sächs Ges. Wiss., xii., 459, 1881. Ueber eine directe Umwandlung der Schwingungen der strahlenden Wärme in Electricität, Ber. Sächs Ges. Wiss., April 23, 1880, or Wied. Ann., x., 618. On the thermo-electrical properties of various minerals see earlier papers (p. 171), and also (gypsum, diopside, orthoclase, albite, pericline), Wied. Ann., i., 276.

PART II.

CHEMICAL MINERALOGY.

Minerals are either the uncombined elements in a native state, or compounds of these elements formed in accordance with chemical laws. It is the object of Chemical Mineralogy to determine the chemical composition of each species; to show the chemical relations of different species to each other where such exist; and also to explain the methods of distinguishing different minerals by chemical means. It thus embraces the most important part of Determinative Mineralogy.

CHEMICAL CONSTITUTION OF MINERALS.

In order to understand the chemical constitution of minerals, some knowledge of the fundamental principles of Chemical Philosophy is required; and these are here briefly recapitulated.

Chemical elements.—Chemistry recognizes sixty-four substances which cannot be decomposed, or divided into others, by any processes at present known; these substances are called the chemical *elements*. Of these oxygen, hydrogen, and nitrogen are fixed gases; chlorine and fluorine are generally gases, but may be condensed to the liquid state; bromine is a volatile liquid; and the rest, under ordinary conditions, quicksilver excepted, are solids. Of these last carbon, phosphorus, arsenic, sulphur, boron, (tellurium), selenium, iodine, silicon, generally rank as non-metallic elements, and the others as metallic.*

Molecules; Atoms.—By a *molecule* is understood the smallest portion of a substance which possesses all the properties of the matter itself; it is the smallest division into which the substance can be divided without loss or change of character. The molecule of water is the smallest conceivable particle which can exist alone, and which has all the properties of water. An *atom* is the smallest mass of each element which enters into combination with others to form the molecule. Thus two *chemical* units, or atoms, of hydrogen unite with one atom of oxygen to form the *physical* unit, or molecule, of water.

Atomic weights.—The relative weights of the chemical units, or atoms, of the different elements are their atomic weights. For the sake of uni-

---

* Recent investigations have added a considerable number of supposed new elements to the list on the following page.

formity the atom of hydrogen, the lightest of all the elements, has been adopted as the standard or unit. The absolute weight of the atoms cannot be determined; but their relative weight can in many cases be fixed beyond question. When the elements are gases, or form gaseous compounds, the atomic weights are determined directly. Thus in hydrochloric acid gas there are equal volumes of hydrogen and chlorine, or, chemically expressed, one atom of hydrogen combines with one atom of chlorine; by analysis it is found that in 100 parts there are 2·74 by weight of hydrogen, and 97·26 of chlorine; hence if hydrogen be taken as the unit, the atomic weight of chlorine is 35·5, since 2·94 : 97·26 = 1 : 35·5.

Where the elements, or their compounds, are not gases, the atomic weights are determined more or less indirectly, and are sometimes not entirely free from doubt. The analysis of rock-salt gives us, in 100 parts, 60·68 parts of chlorine, and 39·32 parts of sodium; now if, as is believed, the number of units of each element involved is the same, or in other words, if the molecule consists of one atom each of chlorine and sodium, then the atomic weights will be as 60·68 : 39·32; or 35·5 : 23, since that of chlorine = 35·5. Hence the atomic weight of sodium is 23, when referred, like chlorine, to that of hydrogen as the unit. There is an assumption in such cases as to the number of units of each element involved which may introduce doubt, so that other methods are applied which need not be here detailed.

The following table gives the atomic weights of the elements. The symbols used to represent an atom of each element are shown in the table; in most cases they are the initial letter or letters of the Latin name. When more than one atom is involved in the formation of a compound, it is indicated by a small index number placed below, to the right: as Sb_2O_3, which signifies 2 of antimony to 3 of oxygen. The quantity by weight of any element entering into a compound is always expressed either by the atomic weight or some multiple of it; hence the atomic weights are strictly the *combining weights* of the different elements.

Atomic Weights.

Aluminum	Al	27·3	Cobalt	Co		59
Antimony	Sb	122	Columbium (Niobium)	Cb	(Nb)	94
Arsenic	As	75	Copper	Cu		63·4
Barium	Ba	137	Didymium*	D		96·5
Bismuth	Bi	208	Erbium	E		112·6
Boron	B	11	Fluorine	F		19
Bromine	Br	80	Gallium	Ga		69·8
Cadmium	Cd	112	Glucinum (Beryllium)	G	(Be)	9
Cæsium	Cs	133	Gold	Au		196
Calcium	Ca	40	Hydrogen	H		1
Carbon	C	12	Indium	In		113·4
Cerium*	Ce	92	Iodine	I		127
Chlorine	Cl	35·5	Iridium	Ir		198
Chromium	Cr	52	Iron	Fe		56

* By the determination of the specific heats of cerium, didymium, and lanthanum, Dr. Hillebrand has shown recently that the oxides of the three metals are *sesquioxides* (Ce_2O_3, Di_2O_3, La_2O_3), and corresponding to them the atomic weights should be Ce = 138, Di = 144·8, La = 139. (Pogg. Ann., clviii., 71, 1876.)

Lanthanum	La	92·5	Selenium	Se		79
Lead	Pb	207	Silver	Ag		108
Lithium	Li	7	Silicon	Si		28
Magnesium	Mg	24	Sodium	Na		23
Manganese	Mn	55	Strontium	Sr		88
Mercury	Hg	200	Sulphur	S		32
Molybdenum	Mo	96	Tantalum	Ta		182
Nickel	Ni	59	Tellurium	Te		128
Nitrogen	N	14	Thallium	Tl		204
Osmium	Os	200	Thorium	Th		231
Oxygen	O	16	Tin	Sn		118
Palladium	Pd	106	Titanium	Ti		50
Phosphorus	P	31	Tungsten	W		184
Platinum	Pt	198	Uranium	U		240
Potassium	K	39	Vanadium	V		51·4
Rhodium	Ro	104	Yttrium	Y		61·7
Rubidium	Rb	85·4	Zinc	Zn		65
Ruthenium	Ru	104	Zirconium	Zr		90

Atomicity; Quantivalence.—The combining power of each element is measured by the number of hydrogen atoms with which it combines in forming a chemical compound. In hydrochloric acid (HCl), one atom of hydrogen combines with one of chlorine; in water (H_2O), two atoms of hydrogen combine with one of oxygen; in ammonia (H_3N), three atoms of hydrogen combine with one of nitrogen; and in marsh gas (H_4C), four atoms of hydrogen are required to enter into combination with one carbon atom.

By the examination of compounds of all the elements we are able to fix the combining power, or *quantivalence*, of each, expressed in hydrogen units. All those elements which combine with *one* atom of hydrogen, or an element which (like chlorine) has the same quantivalence, are called *monads*; those which require two of hydrogen, or two other monad atoms, in forming the compound, are called *dyads*; those uniting with three atoms of hydrogen are called *triads*; and similarly *tetrads, pentads, hexads,* and *heptads.*

The adjective terms *univalent, bivalent, trivalent, quadrivalent,* etc., are also employed with similar meaning. Atoms having the same degree of quantivalence are said to be *equivalent;* this is true of Na and K, both monads, and they may replace each other in similar compounds; but it requires two sodium atoms to be equivalent to one calcium atom, since the latter is a dyad.

The degree of quantivalence may vary for many of the elements in different compounds; for example, in FeO or FeS, iron (Fe) is bivalent, since it satisfies or is combined with simply a dyad; in FeS_2, it is quadrivalent, since it is united to two atoms of a dyad; and, similarly, in $[Fe_2]O_3$ it is sexivalent (for the double atom).

Perissads; Artiads.—Those elements whose atoms have an odd quantivalence (I, III, V, or VII), are called *perissads;* those whose quantivalence is even (II, IV, VI) are called *artiads.* These terms, perissad and artiad, are derived from περισσός and ἄρτιος, the words for odd and even in ancient arithmetic. The following table gives the division of the elements into these two classes, and shows, also, the quantivalence of each element:

CHEMICAL MINERALOGY.

PERISSADS.		ARTIADS.	
Monads:—		*Dyads:*—	*Tetrads:*—
Hydrogen.		Oxygen.	Carbon, II, IV.
		Sulphur, II, IV, VI.	Silicon.
Fluorine.		Selenium, II, IV, VI.	Titanium, II, IV.
Chlorine,	I, III, V, VII.	Tellurium, II, IV, VI.	Tin, II, IV.
Bromine,	I, III, V, VII.		
Iodine,	I, III, V, VII.	Calcium, II, IV.	Thorium,
		Strontium, II, IV.	Zirconium.
Lithium.		Barium, II, IV.	
Sodium,	I, III.		Platinum, II, IV.
Potassium,	I, III, V.	Magnesium.	Palladium, II, IV.
Rubidium.		Zinc.	
Cæsium.		Cadmium.	Lead, II, IV.
			Indium.
Silver,	I, III.	Glucinum.	
Thallium,	I, III.	Yttrium.	*Hexads:*—
		Cerium.	Molybdenum, II, IV, VI.
Triads:—		Lanthanum.	Tungsten, IV, VI.
Nitrogen,	I, III, V.	Didymium.	
Phosphorus,	I, III, V.	Erbium.	Ruthenium, II, IV, VI.
Arsenic,	I, III, V.	Mercury [Hg$_2$]^{II}, II.	Rhodium, II, IV, VI.
Antimony,	III, V.	Copper [Cu$_2$]^{II}, II.	Iridium, II, IV, VI.
Bismuth,	III, V.		Osmium, II, IV, VI.
Boron.			Aluminum, IV, [Al$_2$]^{VI}.
			Chromium, II, IV, VI.
Gold,	I, III.		
			Manganese, II, IV, VI.
Pentads:—			Iron, II, IV, VI.
Columbium.			Cobalt, II, IV.
Tantalum.			Nickel, II, IV.
			Uranium, II, IV.
Vanadium,	III, V.		

The general divisions of chemical compounds now accepted are as follows.

1. *Binaries*, where the atoms are directly united. Examples are given by the compounds of a positive (basic) element with oxygen (Na_2O, CaO, CO_2), called *oxides;* those with sulphur, chlorine, bromine, iodine, etc., called *sulphides, chlorides,* etc. Binary compounds of a negative element with hydrogen (as HCl, HBr) form acids.

2. *Ternaries*, where the atoms are united by means of a third atom, as oxygen, sulphur, etc., as $CaSO_4$, Mg_2SiO_4, etc.

Among minerals there are three classes of compounds: (1) The Native Elements; (2) Binary compounds, including the *sulphides, oxides, chlorides, iodides, fluorides;* (3) Ternary compounds, including *sulph-arsenites,* etc., *hydrates* (hydrated oxides), *silicates,* mostly salts of the acids H_4SiO_4 and H_2SiO_3, tantalates, columbates, phosphates, arsenates, sulphates, chromates, carbonates, etc. The full enumeration of these compounds, with their general chemical formulas, are given in the synopsis which precedes the Descriptive Mineralogy.

The position of water in the composition of minerals.—Many minerals lose water, especially upon the application of heat. With some of these it is given off upon mere exposure to dry air at ordinary temperature, and such crystals are said to *effloresce;* others lose water when they are placed in a desiccator over sulphuric acid, or when they are subjected to a slightly elevated temperature; with others, again, a greater heat is required; and with a few silicates water is yielded only upon long continued heating at a very high temperature. It is evidently possible that either, (1) the mineral contains water as such, or (2) the water is formed by the process of decomposition caused by the application of heat. In the cases first mentioned, where water is readily given off, it is believed that the water actually exists as such in the compound. It is found that many salts take up water when they crystallize, and in some cases the amount of water depends upon the temperature at which the salt is formed; this water is called *water of crystallization*. For example: manganous sulphate has three definite amounts of this water of crystallization, according to the temperature at which it has been formed. When crystallized below 7°, its composition is $MnSO_4 + 7H_2O$; between 7° and 20°, $MnSO_4 + 5H_2O$; and between 20° and 30°, $MnSO_4 + 4H_2O$.

In those cases where a very high temperature is required to make a loss of water, it is quite certain the water has no place as such in the original constitution, but, on the contrary, that the mineral contains basic hydrogen, replacing the other basic elements. In some cases, where part of the water is yielded at a low and the rest at a very high temperature, this shows that a difference exists in regard to the part which the water plays in the two cases; for example, crystallized sodium phosphate yields readily 24 equivalents of water, while the remaining 1 molecule is given off only at a temperature between 300° and 400°; from this it is concluded that in the latter case the elements forming the water exist actually in the salt, and that its composition is:

$$H_2Na_4P_2O_8 + 24aq.$$

The part played by the water in the silicates is in most cases still undecided, though in many species the hydrogen is undoubtedly basic. The latter is doubtless true of many of the so-called hydrous silicates. The views commonly held in regard to them will be gathered from the descriptive part of this work.

Chemical formulas for minerals.—A chemical formula expresses the relative amounts of the different elements present in the compound, in terms of their atomic weights—or, in other words, more strictly the number of atoms of each element in a given molecule with or without the expression of their probable grouping.

Empirical formulas simply state in the briefest form the result of the analysis, giving the number of atoms of each element present without any theoretical considerations. For example, the empirical formula of epidote is $Si_6Al_3Ca_4H_2O_{26}$.

The object of the *rational* formulas is to express not only the number of atoms of each element present, but also their probable method of grouping, and relation to each other, in the molecule. These are called *typical formulas* when the attempt is made to arrange the atoms in accordance with the type of water, or some other type.

In the rational formulas of the old chemistry the oxygen (or sulphur) was apportioned to the several elements, according to their combining power, and the basic and acid oxides, or sulphides, thus obtained were written consecutively. For example, the formula of wollastonite (calcium silicate), according to the old dualistic method, was written CaO, SiO_2, and of anhydrite (calcium sulphate), CaO, SO_3. The principles of the new chemistry have set aside these rational formulas; but as others consistent with the new principles now adopted have not in all cases been accepted, it is customary to give the formulas of minerals empirically. For those above the empirical formulas are $CaSiO_3$ and $CaSO_4$.

Relation between the old and new systems.—The points of difference between the old and new chemistry have already been hinted at. The principal changes which have been introduced by the latter are: (1) The doubling of all the atomic weights, except those of the monad elements, and also of bismuth, arsenic, antimony, nitrogen, phosphorus, and boron, whose oxides are now written Bi_2O_3, instead of BiO_3, etc. Corresponding to this change, binary compounds involving the monad elements are written: H_2O instead of HO, Na_2O for NaO, Na_2S, etc., also $CaCl_2$ instead $CaCl$, SiF_4 instead of SiF_2, and so on. (2) The method of viewing the composition of ternary compounds—these being now regarded *not* as compounds of an oxide and a so-called acid, but as compounds for the most part of the several elements concerned, and hence a metal in a compound is believed to be replaced by another metal, not one oxide by another. Hence we say calcium carbonate, or carbonate of calcium instead of carbonate of lime, and write the formula $CaCO_3$, not CaO, CO_2; and so in the other cases.

Replacing power of the different elements.—It has been mentioned that the replacing power of the elements is in proportion to their combining power, that is, to their quantivalence. For example, one atom of Mg or of Ba may replace one atom of Ca, all being dyads; but two atoms of Na (monad) are required to replace one of Ca; similarly three dyad atoms are equivalent, or may replace, one hexad atom, thus, $3Ca = [Al_2]$.

The relation of the different oxides may be understood from the following scheme, in which the above principle is made use of. The line A below contains the different kinds of oxides. B the same divided each by its number of atoms of oxygen (that is, severally, for the successive terms, by 1, 3, 2, 5, 3, 7, 4), by which division they are reduced to the protoxide form. C the basic elements alone:

A	RO	R^2O^3	RO^2	R^2O^5	RO^3	R^2O^7	RO^4
B	RO	$R^{\frac{2}{3}}O$	$R^{\frac{1}{2}}O$	$R^{\frac{2}{5}}O$	$R^{\frac{1}{3}}O$	$R^{\frac{2}{7}}O$	$R^{\frac{1}{4}}O$
C	R	$R^{\frac{2}{3}}$	$R^{\frac{1}{2}}$	$R^{\frac{2}{5}}$	$R^{\frac{1}{3}}$	$R^{\frac{2}{7}}$	$R^{\frac{1}{4}}$

According to the above law the R, $R^{\frac{2}{3}}$, $R^{\frac{1}{2}}$, etc., in the last line, are mutually replaceable, 1 for 1, though varying in atomic weight from 1 to $\frac{1}{4}$. They represent different states in which elements may exist, and have, to a certain extent, independent element-like relations. In some cases, as in iron, four of these states are represented in a single element, the compounds (1) FeO, FeS, (2) Fe^2O^3, (3) FeS^2, (4) FeO^3, containing this metal in four states Fe, $Fe^{\frac{2}{3}}$, $Fe^{\frac{1}{2}}$, $Fe^{\frac{1}{3}}$.

The use of the fractions can be avoided by multiplying, instead of dividing, thus, $Fe^{\frac{2}{3}}$ of Fe^2O^3 replaces Fe of FeO, we might have said, 2Fe of Fe^2O^3 replaces 3Fe of FeO (Fe^2O^3, Fe^3O^3), and so for the others.

These different states of the elements are best designated in the symbols by the Greek letters a, β, etc., thus avoiding all confusion. The above lines A, B, C then become

A	aRO	3βRO	2γRO	5δRO	3ϵRO	7ζRO	4ηRO
B	aRO	βRO	γRO	δRO	ϵRO	ζRO	ηRO
C	aR	βR	γR	δR	ϵR	ζR	ηR

By means of this system all the different oxides may be reduced to the common protoxide form, and thus the true relations of the silicates may be clearly expressed. This is exhibited in the formulas for the silicates given in Dana's System of Mineralogy (1868).

Calculation of a formula from an analysis.—The result of an analysis gives the proportions, in a hundred parts of the mineral, of either the elements themselves, or of their oxides or other compounds obtained in the chemical analysis. In order to obtain the atomic proportions of the elements: *Divide the percentages of the elements by the respective* ATOMIC WEIGHTS; or, for those of the oxides: *Divide the percentage amounts of each by their* MOLECULAR WEIGHTS; then, *find the simplest ratio in whole numbers for the numbers thus obtained.*

Examples.—An analysis of bournonite from Meiseberg gave Rammelsberg: Lead (Pb) 42·88, copper (Cu) 13·06, antimony (Sb) 24·34, and sulphur (S) 19·76 = 100·04. Dividing each amount by its atomic weight we obtain:

$$\frac{42\cdot 88}{207} = \cdot 207; \quad \frac{13\cdot 06}{63\cdot 4} = \cdot 206; \quad \frac{24\cdot 34}{122} = \cdot 217; \quad \frac{19\cdot 76}{32} = \cdot 6175.$$

The atomic ratio is hence:—Pb : Cu : Sb : S = ·207 : ·206 : ·217 : ·6175; that is, 1·005 : 1 : 1·053 : 2·998, or in whole numbers, 1 : 1 : 1 : 3. The empirical formula is consequently $CuPbSbS_3$.

An analysis of epidote from Untersulzbach gave Ludwig:

SiO_2	AlO_3	FeO_3	FeO	CaO	H_2O
37·83	22·63	15·02	0·93	23·27	2·05 = 101·73.

From the results of the analysis given in this form, the percentage amount of each element may be calculated in the usual way; we obtain: Si 17·65, Al 12·06, Fe 10·51, FeO 0·72, Ca 16·62, H 0.23, O 43·64. The number of atoms of each element may be calculated from the last given percentages by dividing each by the atomic weight, that is $\frac{17\cdot 65}{28} = \cdot 630$ for Si, $\frac{12\cdot 06}{55} = 0\cdot 22$ for Al ($= Al_2$), etc. Or, the percentage amounts of each oxide may be divided by its molecular weight, and the result will be the same; for SiO_2, the molecular weight is 60 ($28 + 2\times 16$), hence, $\frac{37\cdot 83}{60} = \cdot 630$ as before; also for Al, 103 ($= 2\times 27\cdot 5 + 3\times 16$), and $\frac{22\cdot 63}{103} = 0\cdot 22$, etc. The atomic proportions thus obtained are:

Si	Al	Fe	Fe	Ca	H	O
0·630	0·220	0·094	0·013	0·415	0·230	2·727, or simply
	·314		0·428			
6	2·99		4·07		2·2	25·79, or again,
6	3		4		2	26.

The empirical formula is consequently $Si_6Al_3Ca_4H_2O_{26}$. As in the above case, it is necessary, when very small quantities only of certain elements are present, to neglect them in the final formula, reckoning them in with the elements which they replace, that is, with those of the same quantivalence. The degree of correspondence between the analysis and the formula deduced, if the latter is correctly assumed, depends entirely upon the accuracy of the former.

Quantivalent Ratio.—In the chemical constitution of most minerals there exists a strong distinction between the basic and acidic elements, and this relation, in the case of substances of complex character, is often fixed when otherwise the composition is exceedingly varied. In the dualistic formulas of the old chemistry this relation was expressed in the "*oxygen-ratio*," which gave the ratio between the number of oxygen atoms belonging respectively to the bases, protoxide and sesquioxide, and to the acid. The expression, "oxygen-ratio," is not in harmony with the present method of viewing chemical compounds, and the term has consequently been, to some extent, abandoned; the same relation, however, between the different classes of elements still exists, but the ratio must be regarded as that existing between the total quantivalences of each group of elements, and hence may be called the QUANTIVALENT RATIO.*

The old formula for all the members of the garnet family is $3\dot{R}, \ddot{R}, 3\ddot{S}i = 3RO, RO_3, 3SiO_2$, and the *oxygen ratio* for $\dot{R} : \ddot{R} : \ddot{S}i = 1 : 1 : 2$, or for bases to silica, $1 : 1$. Here $\dot{R}$ may be either $\dot{C}a, \dot{M}g, \dot{F}e, \dot{M}n$, or $\dot{C}r$, and $\ddot{R}$ either $\ddot{A}l, \ddot{F}e, \ddot{C}r$. This formula, however, written according to the new system (the quantivalence being expressed by Roman numerals over the symbols), is:

$$\overset{II}{R_3}\overset{VI}{R}\overset{IV}{Si_3}\overset{II}{O_{12}}; \text{ or } \overset{II}{R_3}\overset{VI}{R}\|O_{12}\|\overset{IV}{Si_3},$$

to indicate that the oxygen is regarded as all linking oxygen. The ratio of the total quantivalences for each class of elements, dyads and hexads (basic), and the tetrad silicon (acidic), is:—$3 \times II : VI : 3 \times IV$, or, Q. ratio for $R : \ddot{R} : Si\dagger = 6 : 6 : 12$, that is, $1 : 1 : 2$.

The same ratio for $(\dot{R}+\ddot{R}) : Si = 1 : 1$, both of which are identical with the previously given oxygen ratio.

---

* This relation was brought out by Prof. Dana in 1867 (Am. J. Sci., xliv., 89, 252, 398), and it forms the basis of all the formulas, according to the new system, in Dana's System of Mineralogy, 1868. Prof. Cooke has discussed the same subject (Am. J. Sci., II., xlvii., 386, 1869), he calls the ratio, the Atomic Ratio; the latter term, however, is generally used in a different sense, hence the expression Quantivalent Ratio employed here.

† Throughout this work the letter R, unless otherwise indicated, represents a *bivalent* metal, and $\ddot{R}$ either Fe, Al, Cr, Mn, where the quantivalence of the double atom is *six*. In a few cases, to indicate further relations, the sign of the quantivalence is sometimes employed

Thus the *oxygen* ratio of the old system becomes the *quantivalent* ratio of the new, "a term, too, which has a wider meaning and bearing than that which it replaces." This principle of the ratio between the total quantivalences is an important one, and fundamental in the character of chemical compounds. This is well shown in the example here given, where, for a family of minerals of so varied composition as the garnets, it remains constant in all varieties. Its importance is even more marked in the many silicates where $\dot{R}$ replaces $3R$ (as in spodumene in the pyroxene family).

The quantivalent ratio is obtained by multiplying the quantivalence of each class of elements present by their number of atoms; or by dividing the percentage amount of each element by the atomic weight and multiply by its quantivalence. When the basic or acid oxides are given, divide the percentage amount of each by the molecular weight, and multiply as before by the number expressing the quantivalence, and the result is the total quantivalence for the given element.

Dimorphism. Isomorphism.

A chemical compound, which crystallizes in two forms genetically distinct, is said to be *dimorphous*; if in three, *trimorphous*, or in general *pleomorphous*. The phenomenon is called DIMORPHISM, or PLEOMORPHISM.

On the other hand, chemical compounds, which are of dissimilar though analogous composition, are said to be *isomorphous* when their crystalline forms are identical, or at least very closely related (sometimes called homœomorphous). This phenomenon is called ISOMORPHISM.

An example of *pleomorphism* is given by the compound calcium carbonate ($CaCO_3$), which is *trimorphous*: appearing as calcite, as aragonite, and as baryto-calcite. As *calcite*, it crystallizes in the rhombohedral system, and, unlike as its many crystalline forms are, they may be all referred to the same fundamental rhombohedron, and, what is more, they have all the same cleavage and the same specific gravity (2·7), and, of course, the same optical characters. As *aragonite*, calcium carbonate appears in orthorhombic crystals, whose optical characters are entirely different from those of calcite, as will be understood from the explanations made in the preceding chapter. Moreover, the specific gravity of aragonite (2·9) is higher than that of calcite (2·7). Again, as *baryto-calcite*, calcium carbonate crystallizes in a monoclinic form.

The explanation of the phenomenon of pleomorphism in this case—and an analogous explanation must answer for all such cases—is to be found, not as was once proposed in a slight variation of chemical composition, but in the different conditions in which the same compound has been formed. Thus Rose has shown that the calcium carbonate precipitated from a solution by the alkaline carbonates in the cold has the form of calcite, whereas, if the precipitation takes place at a temperature of 100° C., it takes the form of aragonite. Moreover, he found that aragonite on heating fell to powder, and though no loss of weight took place, the specific gravity (2·9) became that of calcite (2·7).

Many other examples of pleomorphism may be given: Silica (SiO_2) is trimorphous; appearing as *quartz*, rhombohedral, $G = 2\cdot66$; as *tridymite*, hexagonal, $G = 2.3$; and as *asmanite*, orthorhombic, $G = 2.24$. Titanic oxide (TiO_2) is also trimorphous, the species being called *rutile*, tetragonal ($\dot{c} = .6442$), $G = 4.25$; *octahedrite* ($\dot{c} = 1.778$), $G = 3.9$; and *brookite*, orthorhombic or monoclinic, $G = 4.15$. Carbon appears in two forms, in diamond and graphite. Other familiar examples are pyrite and marcasite (FeS_2); acanthite and argentite (Ag_2S); sphalerite and würtzite (ZnS); sulphur natural, orthorhombic, if artificial and crystallizing from a molten condition, monoclinic. The relation in form of the species mentioned, and also of those of other dimorphous groups, will be found in Part III., Descriptive Mineralogy.

Isomorphism is well illustrated by the group of rhombohedral carbonates, with the general formula RCO_3. Here R may be Ca, Mg, Fe, Mn, or Zn; or further, in the same species, the R may be represented by both Ca and Mg in varying proportions, as remarked on the following page, or both Ca and Fe, etc. The group is as follows:

Calcite.	Dolomite.	Magnesite.	Rhodochrosite.	Siderite.	Smithsonite.
$CaCO_3$	$\left.\begin{array}{c}Ca\\Mg\end{array}\right\} 2CO_3$	$MgCO_3$	$MnCO_3$	$FeCO_3$	$ZnCO_3$
105° 5'	106° 15'	107° 29'	106° 51'	107° 0'	107° 40'.

Ankerite (parankerite), breunerite, mesitite, and pistomesite belong to the same group. All the above species have an analogous composition, and all crystallize in the rhombohedral system, the angle of the fundamental form varying somewhat in the different cases.

Mitscherlich, who, by a series of experimental researches, established the principle of isomorphism, expressed it as follows: *Substances, which are analogous chemical compounds, have the same crystalline form, or are* ISOMORPHOUS.

Some of the more important isomorphous groups are mentioned below, for the description of the different species reference must be made to Part III.

Isometric system.—(1) The SPINEL group, having the general formula $\dot{R}\ddot{R}O_4$, including spinel $Mg\ddot{A}lO_4$, magnetite $Fe\ddot{F}eO_4$, chromite $Fe\ddot{C}rO_4$. also franklinite, gahnite, etc. (2) The ALUM group, for example, potash-alum $K_2\ddot{A}lS_4O_{16} + 24aq$, etc. (3) The GARNET group, having the general formula $\dot{R}_3\ddot{R}Si_3O_{12}$.

Tetragonal system.—RUTILE group, RO_2; including rutile TiO_2, and cassiterite SnO_2. The SCHEELITE group; including scheelite $CaWO_4$, stolzite $PbWO_4$, wulfenite $PbMO_4$.

Hexagonal system.—APATITE group; apatite $3Ca_3P_2O_8 + Ca(Cl, F)_2$, pyromorphite $3Pb_3P_2O_8 + PbCl_2$, mimetite $3Pb_3As_2O_8 + PbCl_2$, and vanadinite $3Pb_3V_2O_8 + PbCl_2$. CORUNDUM group, $\ddot{R}O_3$; corundum $\ddot{A}lO_3$, hematite $\ddot{F}eO_3$, menaccanite.

Rhombohedral system.—CALCITE group, RCO_3, already mentioned.

Orthorhombic system.—ARAGONITE group, RCO_3; aragonite $CaCO_3$, witherite $BaCO_3$, strontianite $SrCO_3$, cerussite $PbCO_3$. BARITE group, RSO_4; barite $BaSO_4$, celestite $SrSO_4$, anhydrite $CaSO_4$, anglesite $PbSO_4$. CHRYSOLITE group, general formula, R_2SiO_4.

Monoclinic system.—COPPERAS group; melanterite $FeSO_4+7aq$; bieberite $CoSO_4+7aq$, etc. Pyroxene group, $RSiO_3$, etc.
Monoclinic and Triclinic. Feldspar group.

The above enumeration includes only the more prominent among the isomorphous groups. In many other cases a close relationship exists among species, both in form and composition, as brought out in Dana's System of Mineralogy (1854), and as also to some extent exhibited in the grouping of the species in the descriptive part of this work.

(1) It will be observed in the above that a replacement of an element in a compound by one or more other elements, chemically equivalent, may take place without any essential change of the crystalline form. Besides this a part of one element may be similarly replaced. This is illustrated in the case of the rhombohedral carbonates: calcite has the composition $CaCO_3$, and magnesite $MgCO_3$; but in dolomite the place of the basic element is taken by Ca and Mg in equal proportions, so that the formula may be written $(\frac{1}{2}Ca+\frac{1}{2}Mg)CO_3$, or more properly $CaMgC_2O_6$. But besides this compound there are others where the ratio of Ca to Mg is 3 : 2, also 2 : 1, and 3 : 1, etc. Further than this the Ca or Mg may be in part replaced by Mn, Fe, or Zn.

The mineral ankerite is one in which Ca, Mg, Fe (Mn), all enter, and in different proportions. Boricky has shown that the composition of the ankerite group of compounds is expressed by the formula:—$CaCO_3+FeCO_3+x(CaMgC_2O_6)$, where x may be $\frac{1}{2}$, 1, $\frac{4}{3}$, $\frac{3}{2}$, $\frac{5}{3}$, 2, 3, 4, 5, 10. This and all similar cases are examples of *isomorphous replacement*.

It is not essential that the replacing elements in an isomorphous series should have the same quantivalence, although this is generally true. For example, spodumene is isomorphous with the pyroxene group, though in it the bivalent element is replaced by a sexivalent ($3\overset{\text{II}}{R} = \overset{\text{VI}}{R}$). So, too, menaccanite was included in the corundum group, since here $\overset{\text{II}}{R}\overset{\text{IV}}{R}O_3$ is isomorphous with RO_3. This relation of the elements, which are not equivalent, is brought out by the method of viewing the oxides presented on p. 174.

(2). Minerals which crystallize in different systems may yet be isomorphous, when the difference between their geometrical form is slight; this is conspicuously true of the members of the feldspar family.

(3). Minerals may be closely related in form, although there is no analogy whatever between their chemical composition; many such cases have been noted, *e.g.*, axinite and glauberite, azurite and epidote.

Two substances may be both homœomorphous and correspondingly dimorphous; and they are then described as *isodimorphous*. Titanic oxide (TiO_2), and stannic oxide (SnO_2), are both dimorphous, and they are also homœomorphous severally in each of the two forms. This is an example of *isodimorphism*.

There are also cases of *isotrimorphism*. Thus there are the following related groups; the angle of the rhombohedral forms here given is $R : R$; of the orthorhombic and monoclinic $I : I$ (for baryto-calcite 2-2 on 2-2):

	Rhombohedral.	*Orthorhombic.*	*Monoclinic.*
RCO_3	Calcite, 105° 5′.	Aragonite, 116° 10′.	Barytocalcite, 95° 8′.
RSO_4	Dreelite, 93°–94°.	Anglesite, 103° 38′.	Glauberite, 83°–83° 20′.
RSO_4+nRCO_3	Susannite, 94°.	Leadhillite, 103° 16′.	Lanarkite, 84°.

Calcite, aragonite, and barytocalcite form an undoubted case of *trimorphism*, as has already been shown. Dreelite, anglesite, and glauberite constitute another like series, and moreover it is closely parallel in angle with the former. In the third line we have the sulphato-carbonate susannite near dreelite in angle, leadhillite (identical with susannite in composition) near anglesite, and lanarkite, another sulphato-carbonate, near glauberite, forming thus a third parallel line. The sulphuric acid in these sulphato-carbonates dominates over the carbonic acid, and gives the form of the sulphates enumerated in the second line of the table.

Chemical Examination of Minerals.

The chemical characters of minerals are ascertained (*a*) by the action of acids and other reagents; (*b*) by means of the blowpipe assisted by a few chemical reagents; (*c*) by chemical analysis. The last method is the only one by which the exact chemical composition of a mineral can be determined. It belongs, however, wholly to chemistry, and it is unnecessary to touch upon it here except to call attention to the remarks already made (p. 160) upon the essential importance of the use of pure material for analysis.

The various tests and reactions of the wet and dry methods are important, since they often make it possible to determine a mineral with very little labor, and this with the use of the minimum amount of material.

a. Examination in the Wet Way.

The most common chemical reagents are the three mineral acids, hydrochloric, nitric, and sulphuric. In testing the powdered mineral with these acids, the important points to be noted are: (1) the degree of solubility, and (2) the phenomena attending entire or partial solution; that is, whether a gas is evolved, producing *effervescence*, or a solution is obtained without effervescence, or an insoluble constituent is separated out.

Solubility.—In testing the degree of solubility hydrochloric acid is most commonly used, though in the case of sulphides, and compounds of lead and silver, nitric acid is required. Less often sulphuric acid, and aqua regia (nitro-hydrochloric acid), are resorted to.

Many minerals are completely *soluble without effervescence:* among these are some of the oxides, hematite, limonite, göthite, etc., some sulphates, many phosphates and arseniates, etc.

Solubility with effervescence takes place when the mineral loses a gaseous ingredient, or when one is generated by the mutual decomposition of acid and mineral. Most conspicuous here are the *carbonates*, all of which dissolve with effervescence, giving off carbonic acid (properly carbon dioxide, CO_2), though some of them only when pulverized, or again, on the addition of heat. In applying this test dilute hydrochloric acid is employed. Sulphuretted hydrogen (H_2S) is evolved by some sulphides, when dissolved in hydrochloric acid: this is true of sphalerite, stibnite, greenockite, etc. Chlorine is evolved by oxides of manganese and also chromic and vanadic acid salts, when dissolved in hydrochloric acid. Nitric peroxide is given off by many metallic minerals, and also some of the lower oxides (cuprite, etc.), when treated with nitric acid.

The *separation of an insoluble ingredient* takes place: With many silicates, the silica separating sometimes as a fine powder, and again as a jelly; in the latter case the mineral is said to *gelatinize* (sodalite, analcite). In order to test this point the finely pulverized silicate is digested with strong hydrochloric acid, and the solution afterward slowly evaporated nearly to dryness. With a considerable number of silicates the gelatinization takes place only after ignition; while others, which ordinarily gelatinize, are rendered insoluble by ignition.

With many sulphides a separation of sulphur takes place when they are treated with nitric acid. Compounds of titanic and tungstic acids are decomposed by hydrochloric acid with the separation of the oxides named. The same is true of salts of molybdic and vanadic acids, only that here the oxides are soluble in an excess of the acid.

Compounds containing silver, lead, and mercury give with hydrochloric acid insoluble residues of the chlorides. These compounds are, however, soluble in nitric acid.

When compounds containing tin are treated with nitric acid, the stannic oxide separates as a white powder. A corresponding reaction takes place under similar circumstances with minerals containing arsenic and antimony.

Insoluble minerals.—A large number of minerals are not sensibly attacked by any of the acids. Among these may be named the following oxides: corundum, spinel, chromite, diaspore, rutile, cassiterite, quartz; also cerargyrite; many silicates, titanates, tantalates, and columbates; also the sulphates (barite, celestite, anglesite); many phosphates (xenotime, lazulite, childrenite, amblygonite), and the borate, boracite.

b. *Examination of Minerals by means of the Blowpipe.*

Blowpipe.—The simplest form of the blowpipe is a tapering tube of brass (f. 413, 1), with a minute aperture at the extremity. A chamber is advantageously added (f. 413, 2) at o, to receive the condensed moisture, and an ivory mouth-piece is often very convenient. In the better forms of the instrument (see f. 413, 3), the tip is made of solid platinum (f), which admits of being readily cleaned when necessary. Operations with the blowpipe often require an unintermitted heat for a considerable length of time, and always longer than a single breath of the operator. It is therefore requisite that breathing and blowing should go on together. This may be difficult at first, but the necessary skill or tact is soon acquired.

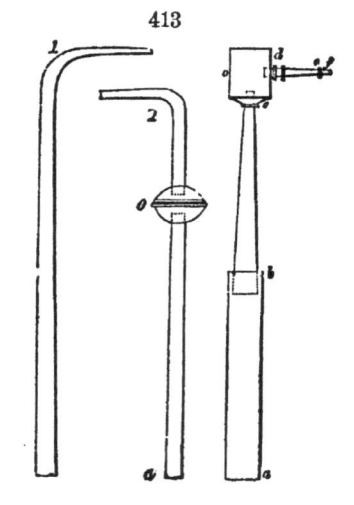

Blowpipe-flame.—The best and most convenient source of heat for blowpipe purposes is ordinary illuminating gas. The burner is a simple tube, flattened at the top, and cut off a little obliquely; it thus furnishes a flame of convenient shape. A similar jet may also be used in conjunction with the ordinary Bunsen burner, it being so made as to slip down within the outer tube, and cut off the supply of air, thus giving a luminous flame. The gas flame required need not be more than an inch and a half in height. In place of the gas, a lamp fed with olive oil will answer, or even a good candle.

The jet of the blowpipe is brought close to the gas flame on the higher side of the obliquely terminated burner. The arm of the blowpipe is inclined a little downward, and the blast of air produces an oblique conical flame of intense heat. This blowpipe flame consists of two cones: an inner of a blue color, and an outer cone which is yellow. The heat is most intense just beyond the extremity of the blue flame, and the mineral is held at this point when its *fusibility* is to be tested.

The inner flame is called the REDUCING FLAME (R.F.); it is characterized by the excess of the carbon or hydrocarbons of the gas, which at the high temperature present tend to combine with the oxygen of the mineral brought into it, or in other words, *to reduce* it. The best reducing flame is produced when the blowpipe is held a little distance from the gas flame; it should retain the yellow color of the latter.

The outer cone is called the OXIDIZING FLAME (O.F.); it is characterized by the excess of the oxygen of the air over the carbon of the gas to be combined with it, and has hence an *oxidizing* effect upon the assay. This flame is best produced when the jet of the blowpipe is inserted a very little in the gas flame; it should be entirely non-luminous.

Supports.—Of other apparatus required, the most essential articles are those which serve to support the mineral in the flame; these supports are: (1) charcoal, (2) platinum forceps, (3) platinum wire, and (4) glass tubes.

(1) *Charcoal* is especially useful as a support in the case of the examination of metallic minerals, where a reduction is desired. It must not crack when heated, and should not yield any considerable amount of ash on combustion; that made from soft wood (pine or willow) is the best. Pieces of convenient size for holding in the hand are employed; they should have a smooth surface, and a small cavity should be in it made for the mineral.

(2) A convenient kind of *platinum forceps* is represented in f. 414; it is made of steel with platinum points. These open by means of the pins

414

pp; other forms open by the spring of the wire in the handle. Care must be taken not to heat any substance (*e.g.*, metallic) in the forceps, which when fused might injure the platinum.

(3) *Platinum wire* is employed with the use of fluxes, as described in another place.

(4) The *glass tubes* required are of two kinds: *closed* tubes, having only one open end, about four inches long; and *open* tubes, having both ends open, four to six inches in length. Both kinds can be easily made by the student from ordinary tubing (best of rather hard glass), having a bore of $\frac{1}{4}$ to $\frac{1}{8}$ of an inch.

In the way of additional apparatus, the following articles are useful; they need no special description: hammer, small anvil, three-cornered file, magnet, pliers, pocket-lens, and a small mortar, as also a few of the test-tubes, etc., used in the laboratory.

Chemical reagents.—The commonest reagents employed are the *fluxes*, viz., soda (sodium carbonate); salt of phosphorus (sodium-ammonium phosphate); and borax (sodium biborate). The method of using them is spoken of on p. 208.

Nitrate of cobalt in solution is also employed. It is conveniently kept in a small bulb from which a drop or two may be obtained as it is needed. This is used principally as a test for aluminum or magnesium with infusible minerals, as remarked beyond. The fragment of the mineral held in the forceps is first ignited in the blowpipe flame, a drop of the cobalt solution is placed on it, and then it is heated again; the presence of either constituent named is manifested by the color assumed by the ignited mineral. It is also used as a test for zinc. Potassium bisulphate and calcium fluoride (fluorite) in powder, metallic magnesium (foil or wire), and tin foil, are other reagents, the use of which is explained later. Test-papers are also needed, viz., blue litmus paper, and turmeric paper.

The wet reagents required are: the ordinary acids, and most important of these hydrochloric acid, generally diluted one-half for use, and also barium chloride, silver nitrate, ammonium molybdate.

The blowpipe investigation of minerals includes their examination, (1) in the platinum-pointed forceps, (2) in the closed tube, (3) in the open tube, (4) on charcoal, and (5) with the fluxes.

(1) *Examination in the forceps.*—The most important use of the platinum-pointed forceps is to hold the fragment of the mineral while its fusibility is tested.

The following practical points must be regarded: (1) Metallic minerals, which when fused may injure the platinum, should be examined on charcoal; (2) the fragment taken should be thin, and as small as can conveniently be held; (3) when decrepitation takes place, the heat must be applied slowly, or, if this does not prevent it, the mineral may be powdered and a paste made with water, thick enough to be held in the forceps or on the platinum wire; or the paste may, with the same end in view, be heated on charcoal; (4) the fragment whose fusibility is to be tested must be held in the hottest part of the flame, just beyond the extremity of the blue cone.

In connection with the trial of fusibility, the following phenomena may be observed: (*a*) a coloration of the flame; (*b*) a swelling up (stilbite), or an exfoliation of the mineral (vermiculite); or (*c*) a glowing without fusion (calcite); and (*d*) an intumescence, or a spirting out of the mass as it fuses (scapolite). The color of the mineral after ignition is to be noted; and the nature of the fused mass is also to be observed, whether a clear or blebby glass is obtained, or a black slag, or whether magnetic or not, etc.

The ignited fragment, if nearly or quite infusible, may be moistened with the cobalt solution and again ignited (see above); also, if not too fusible, it may, after treatment in the forceps, be placed upon a strip of moistened turmeric paper, in which case an alkaline reaction shows the presence of the alkaline earths.

Fusibility.—All grades of fusibility exist among minerals, from those which fuse in large fragments in the flame of the candle (stibnite, see below), to those which fuse only on the thinnest edges in the hottest blowpipe flame (bronzite); and still again there are a considerable number which are entirely infusible (*e.g.*, corundum).

The following scale of fusibility, proposed by von Kobell, is made use of: 1, stibnite; 2, natrolite; 3, almandine garnet; 4, actinolite; 5, orthoclase; 6, bronzite.

A little practice with these minerals will show the student what degree of fusibility is expressed by each number, and render him quite independent of the table; he will thus be able also to judge of his power to produce a hot flame by the blowpipe, which requires practice.

Flame coloration.—When coloration is produced it is seen on the exterior portion of the flame, and is best observed when shielded from the direct light.

The presence of soda, even in small quantities, produces a yellow flame, which (except in the spectroscope) more or less completely masks the coloration of the flame due to other substances; phosphates and borates give the green flame in general best when they have been pulverized and moistened with sulphuric acid; moistening with hydrochloric acid makes the coloration in many cases (barium, strontium) more distinct.

The colors which may be produced, and the substances to whose presence they are due, are as follows: (1) yellow, *sodium;* (2) violet, *potassium;* (3) purple-red, *lithium;* red, *strontium;* yellowish-red, *calcium* (lime); (4) yellowish-green, *barium, molybdenum;* emerald-green, *copper;* bluish-green, *phosphorus* (phosphates); yellowish-green, *boron* (borates); (5) blue, azure-blue, *copper chloride;* light-blue, *arsenic;* greenish-blue, *antimony.*

(2) *Heating in the closed tube.*—The closed tube is employed to show the effect of heating the mineral out of contact with the air. A small fragment is taken, or sometimes the powdered mineral is inserted, though in this case with care not to soil the sides of the tube. The phenomena which may be observed are as follows: *decrepitation,* as shown by fluorite, calcite, etc.; *glowing,* as exhibited by gadolinite; *phosphorescence,* of which fluorite is an example; *change of color* (limonite), and here the color of the mineral should be noted both when hot, and again after cooling; *fusion;* giving off *oxygen,* as mercuric oxide; yielding *water* at a low or high temperature, which is true of all hydrous minerals; yielding *acid* or *alkaline vapors,* which should be tested by inserting a strip of moistened litmus or turmeric paper in the tube; yielding a *sublimate,* which condenses in the cold part of the tube.

Of the *sublimates* which form in the tube, the following are those with which it is most important to be familiar: Sublimate yellow, *sulphur;* dark brown-red when hot, and red or reddish-yellow when cold, *arsenic sulphide;* brilliant black, *arsenic* (also giving off a garlic odor); black when hot, brown-red when cold, formed near the mineral by strong heating, *antimony oxysulphide;* dark-red, *selenium* (also giving the odor of decaying horseradish); sublimate consisting of small drops with metallic lustre, *tellurium;* sublimate gray, made up of minute metallic globules, *mercury;* sublimate black, lustreless, red when rubbed, *mercury sulphide.*

(3) *Heating in the open tube.*—The small fragment is placed in the tube about an inch from the lower end, the tube being inclined sufficiently to prevent the mineral from slipping out. The current of air, passing through

the tube during the heating process, has an oxidizing effect. The special phenomena to be observed are the formation of a *sublimate* and the *odor* of the escaping gases. The acid or alkaline character of the vapors are tested in the same way as with the closed tube. Fluorides, when heated in the open tube with previously fused salt of phosphorus, yield hydrofluoric acid, which gives an acid reaction with test-paper, has a peculiar pungent odor, and corrodes the glass.

The *sublimates* which may be formed, as far as they differ from those already mentioned, as obtained in the closed tube, are as follows: Sublimate, white and crystalline, volatile, *arsenous oxide;* white, near the mineral crystalline, fusible to minute drops, yellowish when hot, nearly colorless when cold, *molybdic oxide;* sublimate white, yielding dense white fumes, at first mostly volatile, forming on the upper side of the tube, and afterward generally non-volatile on the under side of the tube, *antimonous* and *antimonic oxides;* sublimate dark brown when hot, lemon-yellow when cold, fusible, *bismuth oxide;* sublimate gray, fusible to colorless drops, *tellurous oxide;* sublimate steel-gray, the upper edge appearing red, *selenium;* sublimate bright metallic, *mercury.*

The *odors* which may be perceived are the same as those mentioned in the following article.

(4) *Heating alone on charcoal.*—The substance to be examined is placed in a shallow cavity; it may simply be a small fragment, or, where the mineral decrepitates, it may be powdered, mixed with water, and thus the material employed as a paste. The points to be noticed are:

(*a*) The *odor* given off after short heating. In this way the presence of sulphur, arsenic (garlic odor), and selenium (odor of decayed horseradish), may be recognized.

(*b*) *Fusion.*—In the case of the salts of the alkalies the fused mass is absorbed into the charcoal; this is also true, after long heating, of the carbonates and sulphates of barium and strontium.

(*c*) The *infusible residue.*—This may (1) glow brightly in the O.F., indicating the presence of calcium, strontium, magnesium, zirconium, zinc, or tin. (2) It may give an alkaline reaction after ignition: alkaline earths. (3) It may be magnetic, showing the presence of iron.

(*d*) The *sublimate.*—By this means the presence of many of the metals may be determined. The color of the sublimate, both near the assay (N), and at a distance (D); as also when hot and when cold is to be noted.

The most important of the sublimates, with the metals to which they are due, are contained in the following list: Sublimate, steel-gray (N), and dark gray (D), in R.F. volatile with a blue flame, *selenium* (also giving a peculiar odor); white (N) and red or deep yellow (D), in R.F. volatile with green flame, *tellurium;* white (N) and grayish (D), *arsenic* (giving also a peculiar alliaceous odor); white (N) and bluish (D), *antimony* (also giving off dense white fumes). Reddish-brown, *silver;* dark orange-yellow when hot, and lemon-yellow when cold (N), also bluish-white (D), *bismuth;* dark lemon-yellow when hot, sulphur-yellow when cold, *lead;* red-brown (N) and orange-yellow (D), *cadmium;* yellow when hot, white on cooling, *zinc* (the sublimate becomes green if moistened with cobalt solution and again ignited); faint yellow when hot, white on cooling, *tin* (the sublimate becomes bluish-green when ignited after being moistened with the cobalt solution, in the R.F. it is reduced to metallic tin); yellow, sometimes crystalline when hot, white when cold (N), bluish (D), *molybdenum* (in O.F. the sublimate volatilizes, leaving a permanent stain of the oxide, in R.F. gives an azure blue color when touched for a moment with the flame).

(5) *Treatment with the fluxes.*—The three fluxes have been mentioned on p. 205. They are used either on charcoal or with the platinum wire. If the latter is employed it must have a small loop at the end; this is heated to redness and dipped into the powdered flux, and the adhering particles fused to a bead; this operation is repeated until the loop is filled. Sometimes in the use of soda the wire may at first be moistened a little to cause it to adhere. When the bead is ready it is, while hot, brought in contact with the powdered mineral, some of which will adhere to it, and then the heating process may be continued. Very little of the mineral is in general required, and the experiment should be commenced with a minute quantity and more added if necessary. The bead must be heated successively in the reducing and oxidizing flames, and in each case the color noted when hot and when cold. The phenomena connected with fusion, if it takes place, must also be observed.

Minerals containing sulphur or arsenic, or both, must be first roasted, that is, heated on charcoal, first in the oxidizing and then in the reducing flame, till these substances have been volatilized. If too much of the mineral has been added and the bead is hence too opaque to show the color, it may, while hot, be flattened out with the hammer, or drawn out into a wire, or part of it may be removed and the remainder diluted with more of the flux.

BORAX.—The following list enumerates the different colored beads obtained with borax, and also the metals to the presence of whose oxides the colors are due:

Colorless; silica, aluminum, the alkaline earths, etc. (both O.F. and R.F.); also silver, zinc, cadmium, lead, bismuth, and nickel, O.F., and also R.F., after long heating, but when first heated, gray or turbid; R.F., manganese.

Yellow; in O.F., titanium, tungsten, and molybdenum, also zinc and cadmium, when strongly saturated and *hot;* vanadium (greenish when hot); iron, uranium, and chromium, when feebly saturated.

Red to brown; in O.F., iron, hot (on cooling, yellow); O.F., chromium, hot (yellowish-green when cold); O.F., uranium, hot (yellow when cold); nickel, manganese, cold (violet when hot).

Red; R.F., copper, if highly saturated, cold (colorless when hot).

Violet; O.F., nickel, hot (red-brown to brown on cooling); O.F., manganese.

Blue; O.F. and R.F., cobalt, both hot and cold; O.F., copper, cold (when hot, green).

Green; O.F., copper, hot (blue or greenish-blue on cooling), R.F., bottle-green; O.F., chromium, cold (yellow to red when hot), R.F., emerald-green; O.F., vanadium, cold (yellow when hot), R.F., chrome-green, cold (brownish when hot); R.F., uranium, yellowish-green (when highly saturated).

SALT OF PHOSPHORUS.—This flux gives for the most part reactions similar to those obtained with borax. The only cases enumerated here are those which are distinct, and hence those where the flux is a good test.

With *silicates* this flux forms a glass in which the bases of the silicate are dissolved, but the silica itself is left insoluble. It appears as a skeleton readily seen floating about in the melted bead.

The colors of the beads and the metals to whose oxides these are due, are:

Blue; R.F., tungsten, cold (brownish when hot); R.F., columbium, cold and when highly saturated (dirty-blue when hot). Both these give colorless beads in the O.F.

Green; R.F., uranium, cold (yellowish-green when hot); O.F., molybdenum, pale on cooling, also R.F., dirty-green when hot, green when cold.

Violet; R.F., columbium (see above); R.F., titanium cold (yellow when hot).

SODA is especially valuable as a flux in the case of the reduction of the metallic oxides; this is usually performed on charcoal. The finely pulverized mineral is intimately mixed with soda, and a drop of water added to form a paste. This is placed in a cavity in the charcoal, and subjected to a strong reducing flame. More soda is added as that present sinks into the coal, and, after the process has been continued some time, the remainder of the flux, the assay, and the surrounding coal are cut out with a knife, and the whole ground up in a mortar, with the addition of a little water. The charcoal is carefully washed away and the metallic globules, flattened out by the process, remain behind. Some metallic oxides are very readily reduced, as lead, while others, as copper and tin, require considerable skill and care.

The metals obtained may be: iron, nickel, or cobalt, recognized by their being attracted by the magnet; or copper, marked by its red color; bismuth and antimony, which are brittle; gold or silver; antimony, tellurium, bismuth, lead, zinc, cadmium, which volatilize more or less completely and may be recognized by their sublimates (see p. 207); arsenic and mercury are also reduced, but must be heated with soda in the closed tube in order to collect the sublimates. The metals obtained may be also tested with borax on the platinum wire.

By means of soda on charcoal the presence of sulphur in the sulphates may be shown, though they do not yield it upon simple heating. When soda is fused on charcoal with a compound of sulphur (sulphide or sulphate), sodium sulphide is formed, and if much sulphur is present the mass will have the *hepar* (liver-brown) color. In any case the presence of the sulphur is shown by placing the fused mass on a clean surface of silver, and adding a drop of water; a black or yellow stain of silver sulphide will be formed. Illuminating gas often contains sulphur, and hence, when it is used, the soda should be first tried alone on charcoal, and if a sulphur reaction is obtained (due to the gas), a candle or lamp must be employed in the place of the gas.

It is also useful in the case of many minerals to test their fusibility or infusibility with soda, generally on the platinum wire. Silica forms if not in excess a clear glass with soda, so also titanic acid. Salts of barium and strontium are fusible with soda, but the mass is absorbed by the coal. Many silicates, though alone difficultly fusible, dissolve in a little soda to a clear glass, but with more soda they form an infusible mass. Manganese, when present even in minute quantities, gives a bluish-green color to the soda bead.

CHARACTERISTIC REACTIONS OF THE MOST IMPORTANT ELEMENTS AND OF SOME OF THEIR COMPOUNDS.

The following list contains the most characteristic reactions, both before the blowpipe (B.B.) and in some cases in the wet way, of the different elements and their oxides. It is desirable for every student to be familiar with them. Many of them have already been briefly mentioned in the preceding pages. It is to be remembered that while the reaction of a single substance may be perfectly distinct if alone, the presence of other substances may more or less entirely obscure these reactions; it is consequently obvious that in the actual examination of minerals precautions have to be taken, and special methods have to be devised, to overcome the difficulty arising from this cause. These will be gathered from the pyrognostic characters given (by Prof. Brush) in connection with the description of each species in the Third Part of this work.

For many substances the most satisfactory and delicate tests are those which have been given by Bunsen in his important paper on Flame-reactions (Flammenreactionen, Ann. Ch. Pharm., cxxxviii., 257, or Phil. Mag., IV., xxxii., 81). The methods, however, require for the most part much detailed explanation, and in this place it is only possible to make this general reference to the subject.

Alumina. B.B.; the presence of alumina in most infusible minerals, containing a considerable amount, may be detected by the blue color which they assume when, after being heated, they are moistened with cobalt solution and again ignited. Very hard minerals (*e.g.*, corundum) must be first finely pulverized.

Antimony. B.B.; antimonial minerals on charcoal give dense white inodorous fumes. Antimony sulphide gives in a strong heat in the closed tube a sublimate, black when hot, brown-red when cold. See also p. 207.

In nitric acid compounds containing antimony deposit white antimonic oxide (Sb_2O_5).

Arsenic. B.B.; arsenical minerals give off fumes, usually easily recognized by their peculiar garlic odor. In the open tube they give a white, volatile, crystalline sublimate of arsenious oxide. In the closed tube arsenic sulphide gives a sublimate dark brown-red when hot, and red or reddish-yellow when cold. The presence of arsenic in minerals is often proved by testing them in the closed tube with sodium carbonate and potassium cyanide. Strong heating produces a sublimate of metallic arsenic, proper precautions being observed.

Baryta. B.B.; a yellowish-green coloration of the flame is given by all baryta salts, except the silicates.

In solution the presence of barium is proved by the heavy white precipitate formed upon the addition of dilute sulphuric acid.

Bismuth. B.B.; on charcoal alone, or with soda, bismuth gives a very characteristic orange-yellow sublimate (p. 207). Also when treated with equal parts of potassium iodide and sulphur, and fused on charcoal, a beautiful red sublimate of bismuth iodide is obtained.

Boracic acid. Borates. B.B.; many compounds tinge the flame intense yellowish-green, especially if moistened with sulphuric acid. For silicates the best method is to mix the powdered mineral with one part powdered fluorite and two parts potassium bisulphate. The mixture is moistened and placed on platinum wire. At the moment of fusion the green color appears, but lasts but a moment (ex. tourmaline).

Heated in a dish with sulphuric acid, and alcohol being added and ignited, the flames of the latter will be distinctly tinged green.

Cadmium. B.B.; on charcoal cadmium gives a characteristic sublimate of the reddish-brown oxide (p. 207)

Carbonates. Effervesce with dilute hydrochloric acid; many require to be pulverized, and some need the addition of heat.

Chlorides. B.B.; if a small portion of a chloride is added to the bead of salt of phosphorus, saturated with copper oxide, the bead is instantly surrounded with an intense purplish flame.

In solution they give with silver nitrate a white curdy precipitate, which darkens in color on exposure to the light; it is insoluble in nitric acid, but entirely so in ammonia.

Chromium. B.B.; chromium gives with borax and salt of phosphorus an emerald-green bead (p. 208).

Cobalt. B.B.; a beautiful blue bead is obtained with borax in both flames from minerals containing cobalt. Where sulphur or arsenic is present it should first be roasted off on charcoal.

Copper. B.B.; on charcoal the metallic copper can be reduced from most of its compounds. With borax it gives a green bead in the oxidizing flame, and in the reducing an opaque red bead (p. 208).

Most metallic compounds are soluble in nitric acid. Ammonia produces a green precipitate in the solution, which is dissolved when an excess is added, the solution taking an intense blue color.

Fluorine. B.B.; heated in the closed tube fluorides give off fumes of hydrofluoric acid, which react acid with test-paper and etch the glass. Sometimes potassium bisulphate must be added (see also p. 207).

Heated gently in a platinum crucible with sulphuric acid, most compounds give off hydrofluoric acid, which corrodes a glass plate placed over it.

Iron. B.B.; with borax iron gives a bead (O.F.) which is yellow while hot, but is colorless on cooling; R.F., becomes bottle-green (see p. 208). On charcoal with soda gives a magnetic powder. Minerals which contain even a small amount of iron yield a magnetic mass when heated in the reducing flame.

Lead. B.B.; with soda on charcoal a malleable globule of metallic lead is obtained from lead compounds; the coating has a yellow color near the assay and farther off a white color (carbonate); on being touched with the reducing flame both of these disappear, tinging the flame azure blue.

In solutions dilute sulphuric acid gives a white precipitate of lead sulphate; when delicacy is required an excess of the acid is added, the solution evaporated to dryness, and water added, the lead sulphate, if present, will then be left as a residue.

Lime. B.B.; it imparts a yellowish-red color to the flame. In the presence of other alkaline earths the spectroscope gives a sure means of detecting even when in small quantities. Many lime salts give an alkaline reaction with test-paper after ignition.

In solutions containing lime salts, even when dilute, ammonium oxalate throws down a white precipitate of calcium oxalate.

Lithia. B.B.; lithia gives an intense red to the outer flame; in very small quantities it is evident in the spectroscope.

Magnesia. B.B.; moistened, after heating, with cobalt nitrate and again ignited, a pink color is obtained from infusible minerals.

Manganese. B.B.; with borax manganese gives a bead violet-red (O.F.), and colorless (R.F.). With soda (O.F.) it gives a bluish-green bead; this reaction is very delicate and may be relied upon, even in presence of almost any other metal.

Mercury. B.B.; in the closed tube a sublimate of metallic mercury is yielded when the mineral is heated with soda. Mercuric sulphide gives a black lustreless sublimate in the tube, red when rubbed (p. 207).

Molybdenum. B.B.; on charcoal molybdenum gives a copper-red stain (O.F.) which becomes azure-blue when for a moment touched with the R.F. (p. 208).

Nickel. B.B.; with borax nickel oxide gives a bead which (O.F.) is violet when hot and red-brown on cooling; (R.F.) the glass becomes gray and turbid from the separation of metallic nickel, and on long blowing colorless.

Nitrates. Detonate when heated on charcoal. Heated in a tube with sulphuric acid give off red fumes of nitric peroxide.

Phosphates. B.B.; most phosphates impart a green color to the flame, especially after having been moistened with sulphuric acid, though this test may be rendered unsatisfactory by the presence of other coloring agents. If they are used in the closed tube with a fragment of metallic magnesium or sodium, and afterward moistened with water, phosphuretted hydrogen is given off, recognizable by its disagreeable odor.

A few drops of a neutral or acid solution, containing phosphoric acid, produces in a solution of ammonium molybdate with nitric acid a pulverulent yellow precipitate.

Potash. B.B.; potash imparts a violet color to the flame when alone. It is best detected in small quantities, or when soda or lithia is present, by the aid of the spectroscope.

Selenium. B.B.; on charcoal selenium fuses easily, giving off brown fumes with a peculiar disagreeable organic odor (see also p. 207).

Silica. B.B.; a small fragment of a silicate in the salt of phosphorus bead leaves a skeleton of silica, the bases being dissolved.

If a silicate in a fine powder is fused with sodium carbonate and the mass then dissolved in hydrochloric acid and evaporated to dryness, the silica is made insoluble, and when strong hydrochloric acid is added and then water, the bases are dissolved and the silica left behind.

Many silicates, especially those which are hydrous, are decomposed by strong hydrochloric acid, the silica separating as a powder or as a jelly (see p. 203).

Silver. B.B.; on charcoal in O.F. silver gives a brown coating (p. 207). A globule of metallic silver may generally be obtained by heating on charcoal in O.F., especially if soda is added. Under some circumstances it is desirable to have recourse to cupellation.

From a solution containing any salt of silver, the insoluble chloride is thrown down when hydrochloric acid is added. This precipitate is insoluble

In acid or water, but entirely so in ammonia. It changes color on exposure to the light.

Soda. B.B.; gives a strong yellow flame.

Sulphur, sulphides, sulphates. B.B.; in the closed tube some sulphides give off sulphur, others sulphurous oxide which reddens a strip of moistened litmus paper. In small quantities, or in sulphates, it is best detected by fusion on charcoal with soda. The fused mass, when sodium sulphide has thus been formed, is placed on a clean silver coin and moistened; a distinct black stain on the silver is thus obtained (the precaution mentioned on p. 209 must be exercised).

A solution in hydrochloric acid gives with barium chloride a white insoluble precipitate of barium sulphate.

Tellurium. B.B.; tellurides heated in the open tube give a white or grayish sublimate, fusible to colorless drops (p. 207). On charcoal they give a white coating and color the R.F. green.

Tin. B.B; minerals containing tin, when heated on charcoal with soda or potassium cyanide, yield metallic tin in minute globules (see also p. 209).

Titanium. B.B.; titanium gives a violet color to the salt of phosphorus bead. Fused with sodium carbonate and dissolved with hydrochloric acid, and heated with a piece of metallic tin or zinc, the liquid takes a violet color, especially after partial evaporation.

Tungsten. B.B.; tungsten oxide gives a blue color to the salt of phosphorus bead (R.F.). Fused and treated as titanic acid (see above) with the addition of zinc instead of tin, gives a fine blue color.

Uranium. B.B.; salt of phosphorus bead, in O.F., a greenish-yellow bead when cool. In R.F. a fine green on cooling (p. 209).

Vanadium. B.B.; the characteristic reactions of vanadium with the fluxes are given on p. 208.

Zinc. B.B.; on charcoal compounds of zinc give a coating which is yellow while hot and white on cooling, and moistened by the cobalt solution and again heated becomes a fine green (p. 207).

Zirconia. A dilute hydrochloric acid solution, containing zirconia, imparts an orange-yellow color to turmeric paper, moistened by the solution.

Students who desire to become thoroughly acquainted with the use of the blowpipe should provide themselves with a thorough and systematic book devoted to the subject. The most complete American book is that by Prof. Brush (Manual of Determinative Mineralogy, with an introduction on blowpipe analysis, New York, 1875). Other standard works are those of Berzelius (The use of the Blowpipe in Chemistry and Mineralogy, translated into English by Prof. J. D. Whitney, 1845), and Plattner (Manual of Qualitative and Quantitative Analysis with the Blowpipe, translated by Prof. H. B. Cornwall, 1872). The work of Prof. Brush has been freely used in the preparation of the preceding notes upon blowpipe methods and reactions.

Determinative Mineralogy.

Determinative Mineralogy may be properly considered under the general head of Chemical Mineralogy, since the determination of minerals depends mostly upon chemical tests. But crystallographic and all physical characters have also to be used.

There is but one satisfactory way in which the identity of an unknown mineral may in all cases be fixed beyond question, and that is by the use of a complete set of determinative tables. By means of such tables the mineral in hand is referred successively from a general group into a more special one, until at last all other species have been eliminated, and the identity of the one given is beyond doubt.

A careful preliminary examination of the unknown mineral should, however, always be made before final recourse is had to the tables. This examination will often suffice to show what the mineral in hand is, and in any case it should not be omitted, since it is only in this way that a practical familiarity with the appearance and characters of minerals can be gained.

The student will naturally take note first of those characters which are at once obvious to the senses, that is: the *color, lustre, feel, general struc ture, fracture, cleavage*, and also *crystalline form*, if distinct; also, if the specimen is not too small, the apparent weight will suggest something as to the *specific gravity*. The above characters are of very unequal importance. Structure, if crystals are not present, and fracture are generally unessential except in distinguishing varieties; color and lustre are essential with metallic, but generally very unimportant with unmetallic minerals. *Streak* is of importance only with colored minerals and those of metallic lustre (p. 162). Crystalline form and cleavage are of the highest importance, but usually require careful study.

The first trial should be the determination of the *hardness* (for which end the pocket-knife is often sufficient in experienced hands). The second trial should be the determination of the *specific gravity*. Treatment of the powdered mineral with acids may come next; by this means (see p. 202) the presence of carbonic acid is detected, and also other results obtained (p. 203). Then should follow blowpipe trials, to ascertain the *fusibility*, the *color* given to the flame, if any, the character of the *sublimate* given off and the reactions with the *fluxes* and other points as explained in the preceding pages.

How much the observer learns in the above way, in regard to the nature of his mineral, depends upon his knowledge of the characters of minerals in general, and upon his familiarity with the chemical behavior of the various elementary substances (pp. 210 to 213) with reagents, and before the blowpipe. If the results of such a preliminary examination are sufficiently definite to suggest that the mineral in hand is one of a small number of species, reference may be made to their full description in Part III. of this work for the final decision.

A number of minor tables, embracing under appropriate heads minerals which have some striking physical characters, are added in the Appendix. They will in many cases aid the observer in reaching a conclusion. In addition to these tables, an extended table is also given for the systematic determination of the more important minerals, those described in full in the following pages.

PART III.*

DESCRIPTIVE MINERALOGY.

The following is the system of classification employed in the arrangement of the species in this work. It is identical with that adopted in Dana's System of Mineralogy, 1868, to which treatise reference may be made for the discussion of the principles upon which it is based. In general only the more prominent species are enumerated under the successive heads.

The native elements are grouped as follows:

SERIES I.—The more basic, or electro-positive elements.
    1. GOLD GROUP.—Gold, silver (also hydrogen, potassium, sodium, etc.).
    2. IRON GROUP.—Platinum, palladium, mercury, copper, iron, zinc, lead (also cobalt, nickel, chromium, manganese, calcium, magnesium, etc.).
    3. TIN GROUP.—Tin (also titanium, zirconium, etc.).

SERIES II.—Elements generally electro-negative.
    1. ARSENIC GROUP.—Arsenic, antimony, bismuth, phosphorus, vanadium, etc.
    2. SULPHUR GROUP.—Sulphur, tellurium, selenium.
    3. CARBON-SILICON GROUP.—Carbon, silicon.

SERIES III.—Elements always negative.
    1. Chlorine, bromine, iodine.
    2. Fluorine.
    3. Oxygen.

CLASSIFICATION OF MINERAL SPECIES.

I. NATIVE ELEMENTS.

Gold; silver.—Platinum; palladium; iridosmine, $IrOs$, etc.; mercury; amalgam, $AgHg$, etc.; copper; iron.—Arsenic; antimony; bismuth.—Tellurium; sulphur.—Diamond; graphite.

II. SULPHIDES, TELLURIDES, SELENIDES, ARSENIDES, ANTIMONIDES, BISMUTHIDES.

1. BINARY COMPOUNDS.—SULPHIDES AND TELLURIDES OF METALS OF THE SULPHUR AND ARSENIC GROUPS.
   (a) *Realgar group.* Composition RS. Monoclinic. Realgar.
   (b) *Orpiment group.* Composition R_2S_3. Orthorhombic. Orpiment; stibnite; bismuthinite.
   (c) *Tetradymite group.* Tetradymite $Bi_2(Te,S)_3$.
   (d) *Molybdenite group.* Composition RS_2. Molybdenite.

2. BINARY COMPOUNDS.—SULPHIDES, TELLURIDES, ETC., OF METALS OF THE GOLD, IRON, AND TIN GROUPS.

   A. BASIC DIVISION.—Dyscrasite; domeykite.

   B. PROTO DIVISION.—Composition RS (or $\overset{\text{\tiny I}}{R}_2S$), RSe, RTe.

   (a) *Galenite group.* Isometric; holohedral.—Argentite; galenite; clausthalite; bornite; alabandite.
   (b) *Blende group.* Isometric; tetrahedral.—Sphalerite.
   (c) *Chalcocite group.* Orthorhombic.—Chalcocite; acanthite; hessite; stromeyerite.
   (d) *Pyrrhotite group.* Hexagonal.—Cinnabar; millerite; pyrrhotite (Fe_7S_8); greenockite; niccolite.

   C. DEUTO OR PYRITE DIVISION.—Composition RS_2, etc.

   (a) *Pyrite group.* Isometric.—Pyrite; linnæite; smaltite; cobaltite; gersdorffite.—Chalcopyrite.
   (b) *Marcasite group.* Orthorhombic.—Marcasite; arsenopyrite; sylvanite.
   (c) Nagyagite. (d) Covellite.

3. TERNARY COMPOUNDS.—SULPHARSENITES, SULPHANTIMONITES, SULPHOBISMUTHITES.
   (a) GROUP I. Atomic ratio, $R : As(Sb) : S = 1 : 2 : 4$. Formula $R(As,Sb)_2S_4 = RS + (As,Sb)_2S_3$. Miargyrite; sartorite; zinkenite.
   (b) SUB GROUP. At. Ratio, $R : As(Sb) : S = 3 : 4 : 9$. Formula $R_3(As,Sb,Bi)_4S_9 = 3RS + 2(As,Sb,Bi)_2S_3$. Jordanite; schirmerite, etc.
   (c) GROUP II. At. Ratio, $R : (As, Sb) : S = 2 : 2 : 5$. Formula $R_2(Sb,As)_2S_5 = 2RS + (Sb,As)_2S_3$. Jamesonite; dufrenoysite.
   (d) GROUP III. At. Ratio, $R : (As,Sb) : S = 3 : 2 : 6$. Formula $R_3(As,Sb)_2S_6 = 3RS + (As,Sb)_2S_3$. **Pyrargyrite**, proustite; bournonite; boulangerite.

(e) GROUP IV. At. Ratio, $R : (As,Sb,Bi) : S = 4 : 2 : 7$. Formula $R_4(As,Sb,Bi)_2S_7 = 4RS + (As,Sb,Bi)_2S_3$. Tetrahedrite; tennantite.
(f) GROUP V. At. Ratio, $R : (As,Sb) : S = 5 : 2 : 8$. Formula $R_5(As,Sb)_2S_8 = 5RS + (As,Sb)_2S_3$. Stephanite; geocronite Polybasite.—Enargite.

III. CHLORIDES, BROMIDES, IODIDES.

1. ANHYDROUS CHLORIDES.—Composition mostly $R(Cl, Br, I)$; also $R_2(Cl,Br,I)$ (calomel), and RCl_6 (molysite).
Halite; sylvite; cerargyrite; embolite; bromyrite.
2. HYDROUS CHLORIDES.—Carnallite. Tachhydrite.
3. OXYCHLORIDES.—Atacamite; matlockite.

IV. FLUORIDES.

1. ANHYDROUS FLUORIDES. Fluorite; sellaite.—Cryolite.
2. HYDROUS FLUORIDES.—Pachnolite; ralstonite.

V. OXYGEN COMPOUNDS.

I. OXIDES.

1. OXIDES OF METALS OF THE GOLD, IRON, AND TIN GROUPS.

A. ANHYDROUS OXIDES.—(a) PROTOXIDES.—Binary compounds of oxygen with a univalent or bivalent element. Formula RO or ($\overset{I}{R}_2O$). Cuprite; zincite; tenorite.
(b) SESQUIOXIDES.—Binary compounds of oxygen with a sexivalent element. Formula RO_3. Corundum; hematite. This group also includes menaccanite and perofskite.
(c) COMPOUNDS OF PROTOXIDES AND SESQUIOXIDES.—Ternary compounds of oxygen with a bivalent and a sexivalent element. Formula $RRO_4 = RO + RO_3$.
Spinel Group. Isometric.—Spinel; gahnite; magnetite; franklinite; chromite. Orthorhombic.—Chrysoberyl.
(d) DEUTOXIDES.—Binary compounds of oxygen with a quadrivalent element. Formula RO_2.
TETRAGONAL.—*Rutile Group.*—Cassiterite; rutile; octahedrite; hausmannite; braunnite. Orthorhombic.—Brookite; pyrolusite.

B. HYDROUS OXIDES.—Turgite.—Diaspore; göthite; manganite.—Limonite.—Brucite; gibbsite.—Psilomelane.

2. OXIDES OF METALS OF THE ARSENIC AND SULPHUR GROUPS.
Isometric.—Arsenolite; senarmontite. Orthorhombic. — Claudetite; valentinite; bismite, etc.

3. OXIDES OF THE CARBON-SILICON GROUP.—Quartz; tridymite; asmanite; opal.

II. TERNARY OXYGEN COMPOUNDS.

1. SILICATES.—A. ANHYDROUS SILICATES.

(a) BISILICATES.—Salts of meta-silicic acid, H_2SiO_3. Quantivalent ratio for basic elements and silicon, 1 : 2. General formula $RSiO_3$. This may be written: $R \parallel O_2 \parallel SiO$, to indicate that part only of the oxygen is regarded as linking oxygen, or, taking into account the quantivalence of the various basic elements that may be present, $R_2, aR, \beta R \parallel O_2 \parallel SiO$.

(a) *Amphibole group.* Pyroxene section ($I \wedge I = 86°$–$88°$). Orthorhombic.—Enstatite; hypersthene. Monoclinic.—Wollastonite; pyroxene; acmite; ægirite. Triclinic.—Rhodonite; babingtonite.—Spodumene; petalite.

(b) *Amphibole section* ($I \wedge I = 123°$–$125°$). Orthorhombic.—Anthophyllite, kupfferite. *Monoclinic*, amphibole; arfvedsonite.

Beryl. Eudialyte. Pollucite.

(β) UNISILICATES.—Salts of the normal silicic acid, H_4SiO_4. Quantivalent ratio for basic elements and silicon, 1 : 1. General formula R_2SiO_4. This may be written: $R_2 \parallel O_4 \parallel Si$, to show that all the oxygen is regarded as linking oxygen, or, $R_2, aR, \beta R \parallel O_4 \parallel Si$. The latter formula shows that, though elements of different quantivalence may be present, the same unisilicate type still exists. The excess of silica sometimes present in both bisilicates and unisilicates, as well as other deviations from the ordinary types, are remarked upon in the pages which follow.

(a) *Chrysolite group.* Orthorhombic, $I \wedge I = 91°$–$95°$; $O \wedge 1\text{-}\bar{\imath} = 124°$–$129°$.—Chrysolite, forsterite, tephroite, monticellite, etc.

(b) *Willemite group.* Hexagonal, $R \wedge R = 116°$–$117°$.—Willemite, dioptase, phenacite.

(c) Isometric. Helvite. Danalite, $R_2SiO_4 + RS$.

(d) *Garnet group.* Isometric.—Q. ratio for $R : R : Si = 1 : 1 : 2$. General formula $R_3 R Si_3 O_{12}$.

(e) *Vesuvianite group.* Tetragonal.—Zircon, vesuvianite.

(f) *Epidote group.* Anisometric.—Epidote; allanite; zoisite; gadolinite; ilvaite.

(g) Triclinic. Axinite. Danburite.—(h) Iolite.

(k) *Mica group.* $I \wedge I = 120°$. Cleavage basal perfect; optic axis or acute bisectrix normal to the cleavage-plane.—Phlogopite; biotite; lepidomelane; muscovite; lepidolite.

(l) *Scapolite group.* Tetragonal.—Sarcolite; meionite; wernerite; ekebergite.

(m) Hexagonal. Nephelite. Isometric.—Sodalite; haüynite; nosite; leucite.

Feldspar group. Monoclinic or triclinic. $I \wedge I$ near $120°$; Q. ratio for $R : \ddot{R} = 1 : 3$. Anorthite; labradorite; andesite; hyalophane; oligoclase; albite; orthoclase (microcline).

(γ) SUBSILICATES.—(*a*) Q. ratio for bases to silicon, $4 : 3$. Chondrodite Tourmaline.
(*b*) Q. ratio for bases to silicon, $3 : 2$. Gehlenite.—Andalusite; fibrolite; cyanite ($\text{\AA}lSiO_6$).—Topaz; euclase; datolite.—Guarinite; titanite; keilhauite; tscheffkinite.
(*c*) Q. ratio for bases to silicon, $2 : 1$. Staurolite.

B. HYDROUS SILICATES—GENERAL SECTION.

BISILICATES.—Pectolite; laumontite; okenite.—Chrysocolla; alipite, etc.
UNISILICATES.—Calamine; prehnite.—Thorite. Pyrosmalite.—Apophyllite.
SUBSILICATES.—Allophane.

ZEOLITE SECTION.

Thomsonite; natrolite; scolecite; mesolite.—Levynite.—Analcite.—Chabazite; gmelinite; herschelite.—Phillipsite.—Harmotome.—Stilbite; heulandite.

MARGAROPHYLLITE SECTION.

BISILICATES.—Talc. Pyrophyllite.—Sepiolite; glauconite.
UNISILICATES.—*Serpentine group.* Serpentine; deweylite; genthite.
Kaolinite group. Kaolinite; pholerite; halloysite.
Pinite group. Pinite, etc.; palagonite.
Hydro-mica group. Fahlunite; margarodite; damourite; paragonite; cookeite.—Hisingerite.
Chlorite group. Vermiculites, Q. ratio of bases to silicon, $1 : 1$. Pyrosclerite; jefferisite, etc.—Penninite.—Ripidolite; prochlorite.—Chloritoid; margarite. Seybertite.

2. TANTALATES, COLUMBATES.

Pyrochlore.—Tantalite; columbite; yttrotantalite; samarskite; euxenite; æschynite, etc.

3. PHOSPHATES, ARSENATES, VANADATES.

ANHYDROUS.—Xenotime $Y_3P_2O_8$; pucherite.—Descloizite.
Hexagonal.—Formula $3R_3(P,As,V)_2O_8 + R(Cl,F)_2$. Apatite; pyromorphite; mimetite; vanadinite.
Wagnerite; monazite.—Triphylite; triplite.—Amblygonite (hebronite)

220   DESCRIPTIVE MINERALOGY.

Hydrous.—Pharmacolite; brushite.—Vivianite; erythrite.—Libethinite; olivenite.—Liroconite; pseudomalachite.—Clinoclasite.—Lazulite; scorodite; wavellite; pharmacosiderite.—Childrenite.—Turquois; cacoxenite.—Torbernite; autunite.
Hydrous antimonate.—Bindheimite.

4. BORATES.

Sassolite; sussexite; ludwigite.—Boracite; ulexite; priceite.—Warwickite.

5. TUNGSTATES, general formula RWO_4; MOLYBDATES, $RMoO_4$; CHROMATES, $RCrO_4$.

Wolframite; scheelite; stolzite.—Wulfenite.—Crocoite; phœnicochroite.

6. SULPHATES.

Anhydrous.—General formula RSO_4. Orthorhombic $I \wedge I = 100°-105°$.—Barite; celestite; anhydrite; anglesite; zinkosite; leadhillite.
Caledonite.—Dreelite; susannite; connellite.—Glauberite; lanarkite.
Hydrous sulphates.—Mirabilite.—Gypsum.—Polyhalite.—Epsomite.
Copperas group. Chalcanthite, $CuSO_4 + 5aq$, also the other vitriols, $RSO_4 + 7aq$.
Copiapite.—Aluminite.—Linarite; brochantite, etc.
Tellurates.—Montanite, $Bi_2TeO_6 + 2aq$.

7. CARBONATES.

Anhydrous.—*Calcite group.* Rhombohedral. General formula, RCO_3.—Calcite; dolomite; magnesite; siderite; rhodochrosite; smithsonite.
Aragonite group. Orthorhombic.—Aragonite; witherite; strontianite; cerussite; baryto-calcite.—Phosgenite.
Hydrous carbonates.—Gaylussite,—Hydromagnesite.—Hydrozincite; malachite; azurite.—Bismutite, etc.

VI. HYDROCARBON COMPOUNDS.

I. NATIVE ELEMENTS.

GOLD.

Isometric. The octahedron and dodecahedron the most common forms. Crystals sometimes acicular through elongation of octahedral or other forms; also passing into filiform, reticulated, and arborescent shapes; and occasionally spongiform from an aggregation of filaments; edges of crystals often salient (f. 415). Cleavage none. Twins: twinning-plane octahedral. Also massive and in thin laminæ. Often in flattened grains or scales, and rolled masses in sand or gravel.

H.=2·5–3. G.=15·6–19·5; 19·30–19·34, when quite pure, G. Rose. Lustre metallic. Color and streak various shades of gold-yellow, sometimes inclining to silver-white. Very ductile and malleable.

Composition, Varieties.—Gold, but containing silver in different proportions, and sometimes also traces of copper, iron, bismuth (*maldonite*), palladium, rhodium. Var. 1. *Ordinary*. Containing 0·16 to 16 p. c. of silver. Color varying, accordingly, from deep gold-yellow to pale yellow; G.=19–15·5. 2. *Argentiferous; Electrum*. Color pale yellow to yellowish-white; G.=15·5–12·5. Ratio for the gold and silver of 1 : 1 corresponds to 35·5 p. c. of silver, 2 : 1, to 21·6 p. c.

The average proportion of gold in the native gold of California, as derived from assays of several hundred millions of dollars' worth, is 880 thousandths; while the range is mostly between 870 and 890 (Prof. J. C. Booth, of U. S. Mint). The range in the metal of Australia is mostly between 900 and 960, with an average of 925. The gold of the Chaudière, Canada, contains usually 10 to 15 p. c. of silver; while that of Nova Scotia is very nearly pure. The Chilian gold afforded Domeyko 84 to 96 per cent. of gold and 15 to 3 per cent. of silver. (Ann. d. Mines, IV. vi.)

Pyrognostic and other Chemical Characters.—B.B. fuses easily. Not acted on by fluxes. Insoluble in any single acid; soluble in nitro-hydrochloric acid (aqua-regia).

D.ff.—Readily recognized by its malleability and specific gravity. Distinguished by its insolubility in nitric acid from pyrite and chalcopyrite.

Observations.—Native gold is found, when *in situ*, with comparatively small exceptions, in the quartz veins that intersect metamorphic rocks, and to some extent in the wall rock of these veins. The metamorphic rocks thus intersected are mostly chloritic, talcose, and argillaceous schist of dull green, dark gray, and other colors; also, much less commonly, mica and hornblendic schist, gneiss, diorite, porphyry; and still more rarely, granite. A laminated quartzyte, called itacolumyte, is common in many gold regions, as those of Brazil and North Carolina, and sometimes specular schists, or slaty rocks containing much foliated specular iron (hematite), or magnetite in grains.

The gold occurs in the quartz in strings, scales, plates, and in masses which are sometimes an agglomeration of crystals; and the scales are often invisible to the naked eye, massive quartz that apparently contains no gold frequently yielding a considerable percentage to the assayer. It is always very irregularly distributed, and never in continuous pure bands of metal, like many metallic ores. It occurs both disseminated through the mass of the quartz, and in its cavities. The associated minerals are: pyrite, which far exceeds in quantity all others, and is generally *auriferous;* next, chalcopyrite, galenite, sphalerite, arsenopyrite, each frequently auriferous; often tetradymite and other tellurium ores, native bismuth, stibnite, magnetite, hematite; sometimes barite, apatite, fluorite, siderite, chrysocolla.

The gold of the world has been mostly gathered, not directly from the quartz veins, but from the gravel or sands of rivers or valleys in auriferous regions, or the slopes of mountains or hills, whose rocks contain in some part, and generally not far distant, auriferous veins, such mines are often called *alluvial washings;* in California *placer-diggings*. Most of the gold of the Urals, Brazil, Australia, and all other gold regions, has come from such alluvial washings. The alluvial gold is usually in flattened scales of different degrees of fineness, the size depending partly on the original condition in the quartz veins, and partly on the distance to which it has been transported. Transportation by running water is an assorting process; the coarser particles or largest pieces requiring rapid currents to transport them, and dropping first, and the finer being carried far away—sometimes scores of miles. A cavity in the rocky slopes or bottom of a valley, or a place where the waters may have eddied, generally proves in such a region to be a *pocket* full of gold.

In the auriferous sands, crystals of zircon are very common; also garnet and cyanite in grains; often also monazite, diamonds, topaz, magnetite, corundum, iridosmine, platinum. The zircons are sometimes mistaken for diamonds.

Gold exists more or less abundantly over all the continents in most of the regions of crystalline rocks, especially those of the semi-crystalline schists; and also in some of the large islands of the world where such rocks exist. In Europe, it is most abundant in Hungary and in Transylvania; it occurs also in the sands of the Rhine, the Reuss, the Aar, the Rhone, and the Danube; on the southern slope of the Pennine Alps, from the Simplon and Monte Rosa to the valley of Aosta; in Piedmont; in Spain, formerly worked in Asturias; in many of the streams of Cornwall; near Dolgelly and other parts of North Wales; in Scotland; in the county of Wicklow, Ireland; in Sweden, at Edelfors.

In Asia, gold occurs along the eastern flanks of the Urals for 500 miles, and is especially abundant at the Beresov mines near Katharinenburg (lat. 56° 40′ N.); also obtained at Petropavlovski (60° N.); Nischne'Tagilsk (59° N.); Miask, near Slatoust and Mt. Ilmen (55° N., where the largest Russian nugget was found), etc. Asiatic mines occur also in the Cailas Mountains, in Little Thibet, Ceylon, and Malacca, China, Corea, Japan, Formosa, Sumatra, Java, Borneo, the Philippines, and other East India Islands.

In Africa, gold occurs at Kordofan, between Darfour and Abyssinia; also, south of the Sahara in Western Africa, from the Senegal to Cape Palmas; in the interior, on the Somat, a day's journey from Cassen; along the coast opposite Madagascar, between 22° and 35° S., supposed by some to have been the *Ophir* of the time of Solomon.

In South America, gold is found in Brazil; in New Granada; Chili; in Bolivia; sparingly in Peru. Also in Central America, in Honduras, San Salvador, Guatemala, Costa Rica, and near Panama; most abundant in Honduras.

In North America, there are numberless mines along the mountains of Western America, and others along the eastern range of the Appalachians from Alabama and Georgia to Labrador, besides some indications of gold in portions of the intermediate Archean region about Lake Superior. They occur at many points along the higher regions of the Rocky Mountains, in Mexico, and in New Mexico, in Arizona, in the San Francisco, Wauba, Yuma, and other districts; in Colorado, abundant, but the gold largely in auriferous pyrite; in Utah, and Idaho, and Montana. Also along ranges between the summit and the Sierra Nevada, in the Humboldt region and elsewhere. Also in the Sierra Nevada, mostly on its western slope (the mines of the eastern being principally silver mines). The auriferous belt may be said to begin in the Californian peninsula. Near the Tejon pass it enters California, and beyond for 180 miles it is sparingly auriferous, the slate rocks being of small breadth; but beyond this, northward, the slates increase in extent, and the mines in number and productiveness, and they continue thus for 200 miles or more. Gold occurs also in the Coast ranges in many localities, but mostly in too small quantities to be profitably worked. The regions to the north in Oregon and Washington Territory, and the British Possessions farther north, as also our possessions in Alaska, are at many points auriferous, and productively so, though to a less extent than California.

In eastern North America, the mines of the Southern United States produced before the California discoveries, in 1849, about a million of dollars a year. They are mostly confined to the States of Virginia, North and South Carolina, and Georgia, or along a line from the Rappahannock to the Coosa in Alabama. But the region may be said to extend north to Canada; for gold has been found at Albion and Madrid in Maine; Canaan and Lisbon, N. H.; Bridgewater, Vermont; Dedham, Mass. Traces occur also in Franconia township, Montgomery Co., Pennsylvania. In Canada, gold occurs to the south of the St. Lawrence, in the soil on the Chaudière, and over a considerable region beyond. In Nova Scotia, mines are worked near Halifax and elsewhere.

In Australia, which is fully equal to California in productiveness, and much superior in the purity of the metal, the principal gold mines occur along the streams in the mountains of N. S. Wales (S. E. Australia), and along the continuation of the same range in Victoria (S. Australia).

SILVER.

Isometric. Cleavage none. Twins: twinning-plane octahedral. Commonly coarse or fine filiform, reticulated, arborescent; in the latter, the branches pass off either (1) at right angles, and are crystals (usually octahedrons) elongated in the direction of a cubic axis, or else a succession of partly overlapping crystals; or (2) at angles of 60°, they being elongated in the direction of a dodecahedral axis. Crystals generally obliquely prolonged or shortened, and thus greatly distorted. Also massive, and in plates or superficial coatings.

H.=2·5–3. G.=10·1–11·1, when pure 10·5. Lustre metallic. Color and streak silver-white; subject to tarnish, by which the color becomes grayish-black. Ductile.

Comp., Var.—Silver, with some copper, gold, and sometimes platinum, antimony, bismuth, mercury.

Ordinary. (*a*) crystallized; (*b*) filiform, arborescent; (*c*) massive. *Auriferous.* Contains 10 to 30 p. c. of gold; color white to pale brass-yellow. There is a gradual passage to argentiferous gold. *Cupriferous.* Contains sometimes 10 p. c. of copper.

Pyr., etc.—B.B. on charcoal fuses easily to a silver-white globule, which in O.F. gives a faint dark-red coating of the oxide; crystallizes on cooling. Soluble in nitric acid, and deposited again by a plate of copper.

Obs.—Native silver occurs in masses, or in arborescent and filiform shapes, in veins traversing gneiss, schist, porphyry, and other rocks. Also occurs disseminated, but usually invisibly, in native copper, galenite, chalcocite, etc.

The mines of Kongsberg, in Norway, have afforded magnificent specimens of native silver. The principal Saxon localities are at Freiberg, Schneeberg, and Johanngeorgenstadt; the Bohemian, at Przibram, and Joachimsthal. It also occurs in small quantities with other ores, at Andreasberg, in the Harz; in Suabia; Hungary; at Allemont in Dauphiny; in the Ural near Beresof; in the Altai, at Zméoff; and in some of the Cornish mines.

Mexico and Peru have been the most productive countries in silver. In Mexico it has been obtained mostly from its ores, while in Peru it occurs principally native. In Durango, Sinaloa, and Sonora, in Northern Mexico, are noted mines affording native silver.

In the United States it is disseminated through much of the copper of Michigan, occasionally in spots of some size, and sometimes in cubes, skeleton octahedrons, etc., at various mines. In Idaho, at the "Poor Man's lode," large masses of native silver have been obtained. In Nevada, in the Comstock lode, it is rare, and mostly in filaments; at the Ophir mine rare, and disseminated or filamentous; in California, sparingly, in Silver Mountain district, Alpine Co.; in the Maris vein, in Los Angeles Co.; in the township of Ascot, Canada.

PLATINUM.

Isometric. Rarely in cubes or octahedrons. Usually in grains; occasionally in irregular lumps, rarely of large size. Cleavage none.

H.=4–4·5. G.=16–19; 17·108, small grains, 17·608, a mass, Breith. Lustre metallic. Color and streak whitish steel-gray; shining. Opaque. Ductile. Fracture hackly. Occasionally magneti-polar.

Comp.—Platinum combined with iron, iridium, osmium, and other metals. The amount of iron varies from 4–20 p. c.

Pyr., etc.—Infusible. Not affected by borax or salt of phosphorus, except in the state of fine dust, when reactions for iron and copper may be obtained. Soluble only in heated nitro-hydrochloric acid.

Diff.—Distinguished by its malleability, high specific gravity, infusibility, and entire insolubility in the ordinary acids.

Obs.—Platinum was first found in pebbles and small grains in the alluvial deposits of the river Pinto, in the district of Choco, near Popayan, in South America, where it received its name *platina*, from *plata*, *silver*. In the province of Antioquia, in Brazil, it has been found in auriferous regions in syenite (Boussingault).

In Russia, it occurs at Nischne Tagilsk, and Goroblagodat, in the Ural, in alluvial material. Formerly used as coins by the Russians. Russia affords annually about 800 cwt. of platinum, which is nearly ten times the amount from Brazil, Columbia, St. Domingo, and Borneo. Platinum is also found on Borneo; in the sands of the Rhine; at St. Aray, val du Drac; county of Wicklow, Ireland; on the river Jocky, St. Domingo; in California, but not abundant: in traces with gold in Rutherford Co., North Carolina; at St. Francois Beauce, etc., Canada East.

PLATINIRIDIUM.—Platinum and iridium in different proportions. Urals; Brazil.

PALLADIUM.

Isometric. In minute octahedrons, Haid. Mostly in grains, sometimes composed of diverging fibres.

H.$=4\cdot5$–5. G.$=11\cdot3$–$11\cdot8$, Wollaston. Lustre metallic. Color whitish steel-gray. Opaque. Ductile and malleable.

Comp.—Palladium, alloyed with a little platinum and iridium, but not yet analyzed.
Obs.—Palladium occurs with platinum, in Brazil, where quite large masses of the metal are sometimes met with; also reported from St. Domingo, and the Ural.
Palladium has been employed for balances; also for the divided scales of delicate apparatus, for which it is adapted, because of its not blackening from sulphur gases, while at the same time it is nearly as white as silver.

IRIDOSMINE. Osmiridium.

Hexagonal. Rarely in hexagonal prisms with replaced basal edges. Commonly in irregular flattened grains.

H.$=6$–7. G.$=19\cdot3$–$21\cdot12$. Lustre metallic. Color tin-white, and light steel-gray. Opaque. Malleable with difficulty.

Comp., Var.—Iridium and osmium in different proportions. Two varieties depending on these proportions have been named as species, but they are isomorphous, as are the metals (G. Rose). Some rhodium, platinum, ruthenium, and other metals are usually present.
Var. 1. *Newjanskite*, Haid.; H.$=7$; G.$=18\cdot8$–$19\cdot5$. In flat scales; color tin-white. Over 40 p. c. of Iridium. Probably IrOs.
2. *Sisserskite*, Haid. In flat scales, often six-sided, color grayish-white, steel-gray. G.$=20$–$21\cdot2$. Not over 30 p. c of iridium. One kind from Nischne Tagilsk afforded Berzelius IrOs$_4$=Iridium $19\cdot9$, osmium $80\cdot1=100$; G.$=21\cdot118$. Another corresponded to the formula IrOs$_3$.
Pyr., etc.—At a high temperature the sisserskite gives out osmium, but undergoes no further change. The newjanskite is not decomposed and does not give an osmium odor until fused with nitre.
Diff.—Distinguished from platinum by its superior hardness.
Obs.—Occurs with platinum in the province of Choco in South America; in the Ural mountains; in Australia. It is rather abundant in the auriferous beach-sands of northern California, occurring in small bright lead-colored scales, sometimes six-sided. Also traces in the gold-washings on the rivers du Loup and des Plantes, Canada.

MERCURY. Quicksilver. Gediegen Quecksilber, *Germ.*

Isometric. Occurs in small fluid globules scattered through its gangue. G.$=13.568$. Lustre metallic. Color tin-white. Opaque.

NATIVE ELEMENTS. 225

Comp.—Pure mercury (Hg); with sometimes a little silver.
Pyr., etc.—B.B., entirely volatile. Dissolves readily in nitric acid.
Obs.—Mercury in the metallic state is a rare mineral; the quicksilver of commerce is obtained mostly from cinnabar, one of its ores. The rocks affording the metal and its ores are mostly clay shales or schists of different geological ages.
Its most important mines are those of Idria in Carniola, and Almaden in Spain. It is found in small quantities in Carinthia, Hungary, Peru, and other countries; in California, especially in the Pioneer mine, in the Napa Valley.

AMALGAM.

Isometric. The dodecahedron a common form, also the cube and octahedron in combination (see f. 40, 41, etc., p. 15). Cleavage: dodecahedral in traces. Also massive.
H.=3–3.5. G.=13.75–14. Color and streak silver-white. Opaque. Fracture conchoidal, uneven. Brittle, and giving a grating noise when cut with a knife.

Comp.—Both Ag Hg (=Silver 35·1, mercury, 64·9), and Ag_2Hg_3 (=Silver 26·5, and mercury, 73·5), are here included.
Pyr., etc.—B.B., on charcoal the mercury volatilizes and a globule of silver is left. In the closed tube the mercury sublimes and condenses on the cold part of the tube in minute globules. Dissolves in nitric acid.
Obs.—From the Palatinate at Moschellandsberg. Also reported from Rosenau in Hungary, Sala in Sweden, Allemont in Dauphiné, Almaden in Spain.
ARQUERITE.—Composition $Ag_{12}Hg$=silver 86·6, mercury, 13·4=100. Chili. KONGSBERGITE, $Ag_{18}Hg$ (?) Kongsberg, Norway.

COPPER.

Isometric. Cleavage none. Twins: twinning-plane octahedral, very common. Often filiform and arborescent; the latter with the branches passing off usually at 60°, the supplement of the dodecahedral angle. Also massive.
H.=2·5–3. G.=8·838, Whitney. Lustre metallic. Color copper-red. Streak metallic shining. Ductile and malleable. Fracture hackly.

Comp.—Pure copper, but often containing some silver, bismuth, etc.
Pyr., etc.—B.B., fuses readily; on cooling, becomes covered with a coating of black oxide. Dissolves readily in nitric acid, giving off red nitrous fumes, and producing a deep azure-blue solution upon the addition of ammonia.
Obs.—Copper occurs in beds and veins accompanying its various ores, and is most abundant in the vicinity of dikes of igneous rocks. It is sometimes found in loose masses imbedded in the soil.
Found at Turinsk, in the Urals, in fine crystals. Common in Cornwall. In Brazil, Chili, Bolivia, and Peru. At Walleroo, Australia.
This metal has been found native throughout the red sandstone (Triassico-Jurassic) region of the eastern United States, in Massachusetts, Connecticut, and more abundantly in New Jersey, where it has been met with sometimes in fine crystalline masses. No known locality exceeds in the abundance of native copper the Lake Superior copper region, near Keweenaw Point, where it exists in veins that intersect the trap and sandstone, and where masses of immense size have been obtained. It is associated with prehnite, datolite, analcite, laumontite, pectolite, epidote, chlorite, wollastonite, and sometimes coats amygdules of calcite, etc., in amygdaloid. Native copper occurs sparingly in California. Also on the Gila river in Arizona; in large drift masses in Alaska.

IRON.*

Isometric. Cleavage octahedral.
$H.=4·5$. $G.=7·3–7·8$. Lustre metallic. Color iron-gray. Streak shining. Fracture hackly. Malleable. Acts strongly on the magnet.

Obs.—The occurrence of masses of native iron of terrestrial origin has been several times reported, but it is not yet placed beyond doubt. The presence of metallic iron in grains in basaltic rocks has been proved by several observers. It has also been noticed in other related rocks. The so-called meteoric iron of Ovifak, Greenland, found imbedded in basalt, is considered by some authors to be terrestrial.

Meteoric iron usually contains 1 to 20 per cent. of nickel, besides a small percentage of other metals, as cobalt, manganese, tin, copper, chromium; also phosphorus common as a phosphuret (schreibersite), sulphur in sulphurets, carbon in some instances, chlorine. Among large iron meteorites, the Gibbs meteorite, in the Yale College cabinet, weighs 1,635 lbs.; it was brought from Red River. The Tucson meteorite, now in the Smithsonian Institution, weighs 1,400 lbs.; it was originally from Sonora. It is ring-shaped, and is 49 inches in its greatest diameter. Still more remarkable masses exist in northern Mexico; also in South America; one was discovered by Don Rubin de Celis in the district of Chaco-Gualamba, whose weight was estimated at 32,000 lbs. The Siberian meteorite, discovered by Pallas, weighed originally 1,600 lbs. and contained imbedded crystals of chrysolite. Smaller masses are quite common.

ZINC.--Native zinc has been reported to occur in Australia; and more recently Mr. W. D. Marks reports its discovery in Tennessee, under circumstances not altogether free from doubt.

LEAD.—Native lead occurs very sparingly. It has been found in the Urals, in Spain, Ireland, etc. Dr. Genth speaks of its discovery in the bed rock of the gold placers at Camp Creek, Montana.

TIN is probably only an artificial product.

ARSENIC.

Rhombohedral. $R \wedge R = 85° \ 41'$, $O \wedge R = 122° \ 9'$, $c = 1·3779$, Miller. Cleavage: basal, imperfect. Often granular massive; sometimes reticulated, reniform, and stalactitic. Structure rarely columnar.

$H.=3·5$. $G.=5·93$. Lustre nearly metallic. Color and streak tin-white, tarnishing soon to dark-gray. Fracture uneven and fine granular.

Comp.—Arsenic, often with some antimony, and traces of iron, silver, gold, or bismuth.
Pyr.—B.B., on charcoal volatilizes without fusing, coats the coal with white arsenous oxide, and affords the odor of garlic; the coating treated in R.F. volatilizes, tinging the flame blue.
Obs.—Native arsenic commonly occurs in veins in crystalline rocks and the older schists, and is often accompanied by ores of antimony, red silver ore, realgar, sphalerite, and other metallic minerals.

The silver mines of Saxony afford this metal in considerable quantities; also Bohemia, the Harz, Transylvania, Hungary, Norway, Siberia; occurs at Chanarcillo, and elsewhere in Chili; and at the mines of San Augustin, Mexico. In the United States it has been observed at Haverhill and Jackson, N. H., at Greenwood, Me.

ANTIMONY.

Rhombohedral. $R \wedge R = 87° \ 35'$, Rose; $O \wedge R = 123° \ 32'$; $c = 1·3068$. $2 \wedge 2 = 89° \ 25'$. Cleavage: basal, highly perfect; $-\frac{1}{2}$ distinct. Generally massive, lamellar; sometimes botryoidal or reniform with a granular texture.

---

* The asterisk in this and similar cases indicates that the species is mentioned again in the Supplementary Chapter, pp. 420 to 440.

NATIVE ELEMENTS.

H.$=3-3·5$. G.$=6·646-6·72$. Lustre metallic. Color and streak tin-white. Very brittle.

Comp.—Antimony, containing sometimes silver, iron, or arsenic.

Pyr.—B.B., on charcoal fuses, gives a white coating in both O. and R.F.; if the blowing be intermitted, the globule continues to glow, giving off white fumes, until it is finally crusted over with prismatic crystals of antimonous oxide. The white coating tinges the R.F. bluish-green. Crystallizes readily from fusion.

Occurs near Sahl in Sweden; at Andreasberg in the Harz; at Przibram; at Allemont in Dauphiny; in Mexico; Chili; Borneo; at South Ham, Canada; at Warren, N. J., rare; at Prince William antimony mine, N. Brunswick, rare.

ALLEMONTITE.—Arsenical antimony, $SbAs_3$. Color tin-white or reddish-gray. Occurs at Allemont; in Bohemia; the Harz.

BISMUTH. Gediegen Wismuth, *Germ.*

Hexagonal. $R \wedge R = 87° 40'$, G. Rose; $O \wedge R = 123° 36'$; $c = 1·3035$. Cleavage: basal, perfect; 2, —2, less so. Also in reticulated and arborescent shapes; foliated and granular.

H.$=2-2·5$. G.$=9·727$. Lustre metallic. Streak and color silver-white, with a reddish hue; subject to tarnish. Opaque. Fracture not observable. Sectile. Brittle when cold, but when heated somewhat malleable.

Comp., Var.—Pure bismuth, with occasional traces of arsenic, sulphur, tellurium.

Pyr., etc.—B.B., on charcoal fuses and entirely volatilizes, giving a coating orange-yellow while hot, and lemon-yellow on cooling. Dissolves in nitric acid; subsequent dilution causes a white precipitate. Crystallizes readily from fusion.

Diff.—Distinguished by its reddish color, and high specific gravity, from the other brittle metals.

Obs.—Bismuth occurs in veins in gneiss and other crystalline rocks and clay slate, accompanying various ores of silver, cobalt, lead, and zinc. Abundant at the silver and cobalt mines of Saxony and Bohemia; also found in Norway, and at Fahlun in Sweden. At Wheal Sparnon, and elsewhere in Cornwall, and at Carrack Fell in Cumberland; at the Atlas mine, Devonshire; at Meymac, Corrèze; at San Antonio, Chili; Mt. Illampa (Sorata), in Bolivia; in Victoria.

At Lane's mine in Monroe, and near Seymour, Conn., in quartz; occurs also at Brewer's mine, Chesterfield district, South Carolina; in Colorado.

TELLURIUM.*

Hexagonal, $R \wedge R = 86° 57'$, G. Rose; $O \wedge R = 123° 4'$, $c = 1·3302$. In six-sided prisms, with basal edges replaced. Cleavage: lateral perfect, basal imperfect. Commonly massive and granular.

H.$=2-2·5$. G.$=6·1-6·3$. Lustre metallic. Color and streak tin-white. Brittle.

Comp.—According to Klaproth, Tellurium 92·55, iron 7·20, and gold 0·25.

Pyr.—In the open tube fuses, giving a white sublimate of tellurous oxide, which B.B. fuses to colorless transparent drops. On charcoal fuses, volatilizes almost entirely, tinges the flame green, and gives a white coating of tellurous oxide.

Obs.—Native tellurium occurs in Transylvania (whence the name *Sylvanite*); also at the Red Cloud mine, near Gold Hill, Boulder Co., Colorado.

NATIVE SULPHUR.

Orthorhombic. $I \wedge I = 101° \ 46'$, $O \wedge 1\text{-}\bar{\imath} = 113° \ 6'$; $\check{c} : \bar{b} : \check{a} = 2{\cdot}344 : 1{\cdot}23 : 1$. $O \wedge 1\text{-}\check{\imath} = 117° \ 41'$; $O \wedge 1 = 108° \ 19'$.

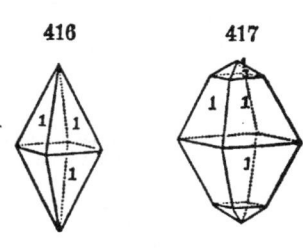

Cleavage: I, and 1, imperfect. Twins, composition-face, I, sometimes producing cruciform crystals. Also massive, sometimes consisting of concentric coats.

H.=1·5–2·5. G.=2·072, of crystals from Spain. Lustre resinous. Streak sulphur-yellow, sometimes reddish or greenish. Transparent—subtranslucent. Fracture conchoidal, more or less perfect. Sectile.

Comp.—Pure sulphur; but often contaminated with clay or bitumen.

Pyr., etc.—Burns at a low temperature with a bluish flame, with the strong odor of sulphurous oxide. Becomes resinously electrified by friction. Insoluble in water, and not acted on by the acids.

Obs.—Sulphur is dimorphous, the crystals being monoclinic when formed at a moderately high temperature (125° C., according to Frankenheim).

The great repositories of sulphur are either beds of gypsum and the associate rocks, or the regions of active and extinct volcanoes. In the valley of Noto and Mazarro, in Sicily; at Conil, near Cadiz, in Spain; Bex, in Switzerland; Cracow, in Poland, it occurs in the former situation; also Bologna, Italy. Sicily and the neighboring volcanic isles; the Solfatara, near Naples; the volcanoes of the Pacific ocean, etc., are localities of the latter kind. Abundant in the Chilian Andes.

Sulphur is found near the sulphur springs of New York, Virginia, etc., sparingly; in many coal deposits and elsewhere, where pyrite is undergoing decomposition; at the hot springs and geysers of the Yellowstone park; in California, at the geysers of Napa valley, Sonoma Co.; in Santa Barbara in good crystals; near Clear lake, Lake Co.; in Nevada, in Humboldt Co., in large beds; Nye and Esmeralda Cos., etc.

The sulphur mines of Sicily, the crater of Vulcano, the Solfatara near Naples, and the beds of California, afford large quantities of sulphur for commerce.

DIAMOND.*

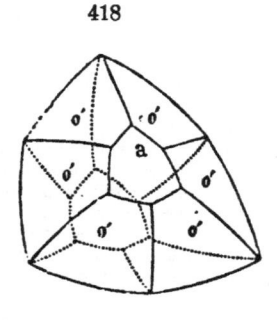

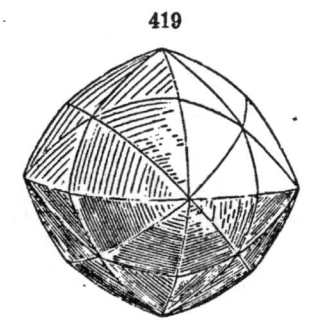

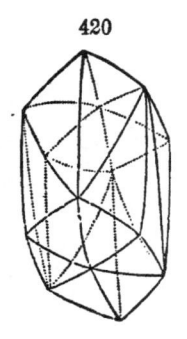

Isometric. Often tetrahedral in planes, 1, 2, and 3-$\frac{2}{3}$. Usually with curved faces, as in f. 419 (3-$\frac{2}{3}$); f. 420 is a distorted form. Cleavage: octahedral, highly perfect. Twins: twinning-plane, octahedral; f. 418, is an elliptic twin of f. 419, the middle portion between two opposite sets of six planes being wanting. Rarely massive.

H.=10. G.=3.5295, Thompson. Lustre brilliant adamantine. Color white or colorless: occasionally tinged yellow, red, orange, green, blue, brown, sometimes black. Transparent; translucent when dark colored. Fracture conchoidal. Index of refraction 2·4. Exhibits vitreous electricity when rubbed.

Comp.—Pure carbon, isometric in crystallization.

Var.—1. *Ordinary*, or crystallized. The crystals often contain numerous microscopic cavities, as detected by Brewster; and around these cavities the diamond shows evidence, by polarized light, of compression, as if from pressure in the included gas when the diamond was crystallized. The coarse varieties, which are unfit, in consequence of imperfections, for use in jewelry, are called *bort*; they are sold to the trade for cutting purposes.

2. *Massive.* In black pebbles or masses, called *carbonado*, occasionally 1,000 carats in weight. H =10; G.=3·012-3·416. Consists of pure carbon, excepting 0·27 to 2·07 p. c. (Brazil).

3. *Anthracitic.* Like anthracite, but hard enough to scratch even the diamond. In globules or mammillary masses, consisting partly of concentric layers; fragile; G.=1·66; composition, Carbon 97, hydrogen 0·5, oxygen 1·5. Cut in facets and polished, it refracts and disperses light, with the white lustre peculiar to the diamond. Locality unknown, but supposed to come from Brazil.

Pyr., etc.—Burns, and is wholly consumed at a high temperature, producing carbonic dioxide. It is not acted on by acids or alkalies.

Diff.—Distinguished by its extreme hardness, brilliancy of reflection, and adamantine lustre.

Obs.—The diamond often occurs in regions that afford a laminated granular quartz rock, called *itacolumyte*, which pertains to the talcose series, and which in thin slabs is more or less flexible. This rock is found at the mines of Brazil and the Urals; and also in Georgia and North Carolina, where a few diamonds have been found. It has also been detected in a species of conglomerate, composed of rounded siliceous pebbles, quartz, chalcedony, etc., cemented by a kind of ferruginous clay. Diamonds are usually, however, washed out from the soil. The Ural diamonds occur in the detritus along the Adolfskoi rivulet, where worked for gold, and also at other places. In India the diamond is met with at Purteal, between Hyderabad and Masulipatam, where the famous Kohinoor was found. The locality on Borneo is at Pontiana, on the west side of the Ratoos mountain. Also found in Australia.

The diamond region of South Africa, discovered in 1867, is the most productive at the present time. The diamonds occur in the gravel of the Vaal river, from Potchefström, capital of the Transvaal Republic, down its whole course to its junction with the Orange river, and thence along the latter stream for a distance of 60 miles. In addition to this the diamonds are found also in the Orange River Republic, in isolated fields or *Pans*, of which Du Toit's Pan is the most famous. The number of diamonds which have been found at the Cape is very large, and some of them are of considerable size. It has been estimated that the value of those obtained from March, 1867, to November, 1875, exceeded sixty millions of dollars. As a consequence of this production the market value of the stones has been much diminished.

In the United States a few crystals have been met with in Rutherford Co., N. C., and Hall Co., Ga.; they occur also at Portis mine, Franklin Co., N. C. (Genth); one handsome one, over ⅛ in. in diameter, in the village of Manchester, opposite Richmond, Va. In California, at Cherokee ravine, in Butte Co.; also in N. San Juan, Nevada Co., and elsewhere in the gold washings. Reported from Idaho, and with platinum of Oregon.

The largest diamond of which we have any knowledge is mentioned by Tavernier as in possession of the Great Mogul. It weighed originally 900 carats, or 2769·3 grains, but was reduced by cutting to 861 grains. It has the form and size of half a hen's egg. It was found in 1550, in the mine of Colone. The Pitt or Regent diamond weighs but 136·25 carats, or 419¼ grains; but is of unblemished transparency and color. It is cut in the form of a brilliant, and its value is estimated at £125,000. The Kohinoor measured, on its arrival in England, about 1⅜ inches in its greatest diameter, over ⅜ of an inch in thickness, and weighed 186$\frac{7}{16}$ carats, and was cut with many facets. It has since been recut, and reduced to a diameter of 1$\frac{7}{16}$ by 1⅜ nearly, and thus diminished over one-third in weight. It is supposed by Mr. Tennant to have been originally a dodecahedron, and he suggests that the great Russian diamond and another large slab weighing 130 carats were actually cut from the original dodecahedron. Tavernier gives the original weight at 787½ carats. The Rajah of Mattan has in his possession a diamond from Borneo, weighing 367 carats. The mines of Brazil were not known to afford diamonds till the commencement of the eighteenth century.

GRAPHITE. Plumbago.

Hexagonal. In flat six-sided tables. The basal planes (O) are often striated parallel to the alternate edges. Cleavage: basal, perfect. Commonly in imbedded, foliated, or granular masses. Rarely in globular concretions, radiated in structure.

H.=1–2. G.=2·09–2·229. Lustre metallic. Streak black and shining. Color iron-black—dark steel-gray. Opaque. Sectile; soils paper. Thin laminæ flexible. Feel greasy.

Var.—(a) Foliated; (b) columnar, and sometimes radiated; (c) scaly, massive, and slaty; (d) granular massive; (e) earthy, amorphous, without metallic lustre except in the streak; (f) in radiated concretions.

Comp.—Pure carbon, with often a little iron sesquioxide mechanically mixed.

Pyr., etc.—At a high temperature it burns without flame or smoke, leaving usually some red oxide of iron. B.B. infusible; fused with nitre in a platinum spoon, deflagrates, converting the reagent into potassium carbonate, which effervesces with acids. Unaltered by acids.

Diff.—See molybdenite, p. 233.

Obs.—Graphite occurs in beds and imbedded masses, laminæ, or scales, in granite, gneiss, mica schists, crystalline limestone. It is in some places a result of the alteration by heat of the coal of the coal formation. Sometimes met with in greenstone. It is a common furnace product.

Occurs at Borrowdale in Cumberland; in Glenstrathfarrar in Invernesshire; at Arendal in Norway; in the Urals, Siberia, Finland; in various parts of Austria; Prussia; France. Large quantities are brought from the East Indies.

In the United States, the mines of Sturbridge, Mass., of Ticonderoga and Fishkill, N. Y., of Brandon, Vt., and of Wake, N. C., are worked; and that of Ashford, Conn., formerly afforded a large amount of graphite. It occurs sparingly at many other localities.

The name *black lead*, applied to this species, is inappropriate, as it contains no lead. The name graphite, of Werner, is derived from γράφω, *to write*.

Nordenskiöld makes the graphite of Ersby and Storgard *monoclinic*.

II. SULPHIDES, TELLURIDES, SELENIDES, ARSENIDES, BISMUTHIDES.

1. BINARY COMPOUNDS.—Sulphides and Tellurides of the Metals of the Sulphur and Arsenic Groups.

REALGAR.*

Monoclinic. $C = 66° 5'$, $I \wedge I = 74° 26'$, Marignac, Scacchi, $O \wedge 1\text{-}\check{\imath} = 138° 21'$; $\check{c} : \check{b} : \check{a} = 0{\cdot}6755 : 0{\cdot}6943 : 1$. Habit prismatic. Cleavage: $i\text{-}\check{\imath}$, O rather perfect; I, $i\text{-}\check{\imath}$ in traces. Also granular, coarse or fine; compact.

H.=1·5–2. G.=3·4–3·6. Lustre resinous. Color aurora-red or orange-yellow. Streak varying from orange-red to aurora-red. Transparent—translucent. Fracture conchoidal, uneven.

Comp.—AsS = Sulphur 29.9, arsenic 70·1=100.
Pyr., etc.—In the closed tube melts, volatilizes, and gives a transparent red sublimate; in the open tube, sulphurous fumes, and a white crystalline sublimate of arsenous oxide. B.B. on charcoal burns with a blue flame, emitting arsenical and sulphurous odors. Soluble in caustic alkalies.
Obs.—Occurs with ores of silver and lead, in Upper Hungary; in Transylvania; at Joachimsthal; Schneeberg; Andreasberg; in the Binnenthal, Switzerland, in dolomite; at Wiesloch in Baden; near Julamerk in Koordistan; in Vesuvian lavas, in minute crystals.

ORPIMENT.*

Orthorhombic. $I \wedge I = 100° 40'$, $O \wedge 1\text{-}\check{\imath} = 126° 30'$, Mohs. $\check{c} : \bar{b} : \check{a} = 1{\cdot}3511 : 1{\cdot}2059 : 1$. Cleavage: $i\text{-}\check{\imath}$ highly perfect, $i\text{-}\check{\imath}$ in traces. $i\text{-}\check{\imath}$ longitudinally striated. Also, massive, foliated, or columnar; sometimes reniform.

H.=1·5–2. G.=3·48, Haidinger. Lustre pearly upon the faces of perfect cleavage; elsewhere resinous. Color several shades of lemon-yellow. Streak yellow, commonly a little paler than the color. Subtransparent—subtranslucent. Sub-sectile. Thin laminæ obtained by cleavage flexible but not elastic.

Comp.—As_2S_3 = Sulphur 39, arsenic 61=100.
Pyr., etc.—In the closed tube, fuses, volatilizes, and gives a dark yellow sublimate; other reactions the same as under realgar. Dissolves in nitro-hydrochloric acid and caustic alkalies.
Obs—Orpiment in small crystals is imbedded in clay at Tajowa, in Upper Hungary. It is usually in foliated and fibrous masses, and in this form is found at Kapnik, at Moldawa, and at Felsöbanya; at Hall in the Tyrol it is found in gypsum; at St. Gothard in dolomite; at

the Solfatara near Naples. Near Julamerk in Koordistan. Occurs also at Acobambillo, Peru. Small traces are met with in Edenville, Orange Co., N. Y.

The name orpiment is a corruption of its Latin name auripigmentum, "*golden paint*," which was given in allusion to the color, and also because the substance was supposed to contain gold.

DIMORPHITE of Scacchi may be, according to Kenngott, a variety of orpiment.

STIBNITE. Antimonite. Gray Antimony. Antimony Glance. Antimonglanz, *Germ.*

Orthorhombic. $I \wedge I = 90° 54'$, $O \wedge 1\text{-}\bar{\imath} = 134° 16'$, Krenner; $\breve{c} : \bar{b} : \breve{a} = 1·0259 : 1·0158 : 1$. $O \wedge 1 = 124° 45'$; $O \wedge 1\text{-}\breve{\imath} = 134° 42\tfrac{1}{2}'$.

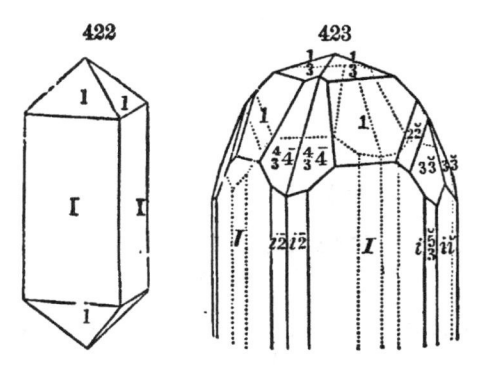

Lateral planes deeply striated longitudinally. Cleavage: $i\text{-}\bar{\imath}$ highly perfect. Often columnar, coarse or fine; also granular to impalpable.

H.=2. G.=4·516, Haüy. Lustre metallic. Color and streak lead-gray, inclining to steel-gray: subject to blackish tarnish, sometimes iridescent. Fracture small sub-conchoidal. Sectile. Thin laminæ a little flexible.

Comp.—Sb_2S_3=Sulphur 28·2, antimony 71·8=100.

Pyr., etc.—In the open tube sulphurous and antimonous fumes, the latter condensing as a white sublimate which B.B. is non-volatile. On charcoal fuses, spreads out, gives sulphurous and antimonous fumes, coats the coal white; this coating treated in R.F. tinges the flame greenish-blue. Fus.=1. When pure perfectly soluble in hydrochloric acid.

Diff.—Distinguished by its perfect cleavage; also by its extreme fusibility and other blowpipe characters.

Obs.—Occurs with spathic iron in beds, but generally in veins. Often associated with blende, barite, and quartz.

Met with in veins at Wolfsberg, in the Harz; at Bräunsdorf, near Freiberg; at Przibram; in Hungary; at Pereta, in Tuscany; in the Urals; in Dumfriesshire; in Cornwall. Also found in different Mexican mines. Also abundant in Borneo.

In the United States, it occurs sparingly at Carmel, Me.; at Cornish and Lyme, N. H.; at "Soldier's Delight," Md.; in the Humboldt mining region in Nevada; also in the mines of Aurora, Esmeralda Co., Nevada. Also found in New Brunswick, 20 m. from Fredericton, S. W. side of St. John R.

This ore affords much of the antimony of commerce. The crude antimony of the shops is obtained by simple fusion, which separates the accompanying rock. From this product most of the pharmaceutical preparations of antimony are made, and the pure metal extracted.

LIVINGSTONITE (*Barcena*).—Resembles stibnite in physical characters, but has a *red* streak, and contains, besides sulphur and antimony, 14 p. c. mercury. Huitzuco, State of Guerrero, Mexico. See p. 430.

BISMUTHINITE. Bismuth Glance. Wismuthglanz, *Germ.*

Orthorhombic. $I \wedge I = 91° 30'$, Haidinger. Cleavage: brachydiagonal perfect; macrodiagonal less so; basal perfect. In acicular crystals. Also massive, with a foliated or fibrous structure.

H.=2. G.=6·4–6·459; 7·2; 7·16, Bolivia, Forbes. Lustre metallic. Streak and color lead-gray, inclining to tin-white, with a yellowish or iridescent tarnish. Opaque.

Comp.—Bi$_2$S$_3$=Sulphur 18·75, bismuth 81·25=100; isomorphous with stibnite.

Pyr., etc.—In the open tube sulphurous fumes, and a white sublimate which B.B. fuses into drops, brown while hot and opaque yellow on cooling. On charcoal at first gives sulphurous fumes, then fuses with spirting, and coats the coal with yellow bismuth oxide. Fus.=1. Dissolves readily in hot nitric acid, and a white precipitate falls on diluting with water.

Obs.—Found at Brandy Gill, Carrock Fells, in Cumberland; near Redruth; at Botallack near Land's End; at Herland Mine, Gwennap; with childrenite, near Callington; in Saxony; at Riddarhyttan, Sweden; near Sorata, Bolivia. Occurs in Rowan Co., N. C., at the Barnhardt vein; at Haddam, Ct.; Beaver Co., Utah.

GUANAJUATITE; *Frenzelite. Fernandez*, 1873; *Castillo*, 1873; *Frenzel*, 1874.—A bismuth selenide, Bi$_2$Se$_3$; sometimes with part of the selenium replaced by sulphur, that is, Bi$_2$(Se,S)$_3$, with Se : S = 3 : 2, which requires Selenium 23·8, sulphur 6·5, bismuth 69·7=100. Isomorphous with stibnite and bismuthinite (*Schrauf*). Guanajuato, Mexico. SILAONITE from Guanajuato is Bi$_2$Se (Fernandez). See p. 428.

TETRADYMITE. Tellurwismuth, *Germ.*

Hexagonal. $O \wedge R = 118° 38'$, $R \wedge R = 81° 2'$; $c = 1·5865$. Crystals often tabular. Cleavage: basal, very perfect. Also massive, foliated, or granular.

H.=1·5-2. G.=7·2-7·9. Lustre metallic, splendent. Color pale steel-gray. Not very sectile. Laminæ flexible. Soils paper.

Comp., Var.—Consists of bismuth and tellurium, with sometimes sulphur and selenium. If sulphur, when present, replaces part of the tellurium, the analyses for the most part afford the general formula Bi$_2$(Te, S)$_3$. Var. 1.—*Free from sulphur*. Bi$_2$Te$_3$=Tellurium 48·1, bismuth 51·9; G.=7·868, from Dahlonega, Jackson; 7·642, id., Balch. 2. *Sulphurous*. Containing 4 or 5 p. c. sulphur. G.=7·500, crystals from Schubkau, Wehrle.

Pyr.—In the open tube a white sublimate of tellurous oxide, which B.B. fuses to colorless drops. On charcoal fuses, gives white fumes, and entirely volatilizes; tinges the R.F. bluish-green; coats the coal at first white (tellurous oxide), and finally orange-yellow (bismuth oxide); some varieties give sulphurous and selenous odors.

Diff.—Distinguished by its easy fusibility; tendency to foliation, and high specific gravity.

Obs.—Occurs at Schubkau, near Schemnitz; at Retzbanya; Orawicza; at Tellemark in Norway; at Bastnaes mine, near Riddarhyttan, Sweden.

In the United States, associated with gold ores, in Virginia; in North Carolina, Davidson Co., etc. Also occurs in Georgia, 4 m. E. of Dahlonega, and elsewhere; Highland, Montana T.; Red Cloud mine, Colorado, rare; Montgomery mine, Arizona.

JOSEITE.—A bismuth telluride, in which half the tellurium is replaced by sulphur and selenium; Brazil.

WEHRLITE.—Composition probably Bi(Te, S). G.=8·44. Deutsch Pilsen, Hungary.

MOLYBDENITE.* Molybdänglanz, *Germ.*

In short or tabular hexagonal prisms. Cleavage: eminent, parallel to base of hexagonal prisms. Commonly foliated, massive, or in scales: also fine granular.

H.=1-1·5, being easily impressed by the nail. G.=4·44-4·8. Lustre metallic. Color pure lead-gray. Streak similar to color, slightly inclined to green. Opaque. Laminæ very flexible, not elastic. Sectile, and almost malleable. Bluish-gray trace on paper.

Comp.—MoS_2 = Sulphur 41·0, molybdenum 59·0 = 100.

Pyr., etc.—In the open tube sulphurous fumes. B.B. in the forceps infusible, imparts a yellowish-green color to the flame; on charcoal the pulverized mineral gives in O.F. a strong odor of sulphur, and coats the coal with crystals of molybdic oxide, which appear yellow while hot, and white on cooling; near the assay the coating is copper-red, and if the white coating be touched with an intermittent R.F., it assumes a beautiful azure-blue color. Decomposed by nitric acid, leaving a white or grayish residue (molybdic oxide).

Diff.—Distinguished from graphite by its color and streak, and also by its behavior (yielding sulphur, etc.) before the blowpipe.

Obs.—Molybdenite generally occurs imbedded in, or disseminated through, granite, gneiss, zircon-syenite, granular limestone, and other crystalline rocks. Found in Sweden; Norway; Russia. Also in Saxony; in Bohemia; Rathausberg in Austria; near Miask, Urals; Chessy in France; Peru; Brazil; Calbeck Fells, and elsewhere in Cumberland; several of the Cornish mines; in Scotland at East Tulloch, etc.

In *Maine*, at Blue Hill Bay and Camdage farm. In *Conn.*, at Haddam. In *Vermont*, at Newport. In *N. Hampshire*, at Westmoreland; at Llandaff; at Franconia. In *Mass.*, at Shutesbury; at Brimfield. In *N. York*, near Warwick. In *Penn.*, in Chester, on Chester Creek; near Concord, Cabarrus Co., N. C. In *California*, at Excelsior gold mine, in Excelsior district. In *Canada*, at several places.

2. BINARY COMPOUNDS.—Sulphides, Tellurides, etc., of Metals of the Gold, Iron, and Tin Groups.

A. BASIC DIVISION.

DYSCRASITE. Antimonial Silver. Antimon-Silber, *Germ.*

Orthorhombic. $I \wedge I = 119°\ 59'$; $O \wedge 1\text{-}\check{\imath}\ 130°\ 41'$; $\check{c} : \bar{b} : \check{a} = 1·1633 : 1·7315 : 1$; $O \wedge 1 = 126°\ 40'$; $O \wedge 1\text{-}\check{\imath} = 146°\ 6'$. Cleavage: basal distinct: 1-$\check{\imath}$ also distinct; I imperfect. Twins: stellate forms and hexagonal prisms. Prismatic planes striated vertically. Also massive, granular; particles of various sizes, weakly coherent.

H. = 3·5–4. G. = 9·44–9·82. Lustre metallic. Color and streak silverwhite, inclining to tin-white; sometimes tarnished yellow or blackish. Opaque. Fracture uneven.

Comp.—Ag_4Sb = Antimony 22, silver 78 = 100. Also Ag_6Sb = Antimony 15·66, silver 84·34, and other proportions.

Pyr., etc.—B.B. on charcoal fuses to a globule, coating the coal with white antimonous oxide, and finally giving a globule of almost pure silver. Soluble in nitric acid, leaving antimonous oxide.

Obs.—Occurs near Wolfach in Baden, Wittichen in Suabia, and at Andreasberg; also at Allemont in Dauphiné, Casalla in Spain, and in Bolivia, S. A.

DOMEYKITE. Arsenikkupfer, *Germ.*

Reniform and botryoidal; also massive and disseminated.

H. = 3–3·5. G. = 7–7·50, Portage Lake, Genth. Lustre metallic but dull on exposure. Color tin-white to steel-gray, with a yellowish to pinchbeck-brown, and, afterward, an iridescent tarnish. Fracture uneven.

Comp.—Cu₃As=Arsenic 28·3, copper 71·7=100.
Pyr., etc.—In the open tube fuses and gives a white crystalline sublimate of arsenous oxide. B.B. on charcoal arsenical fumes and a malleable metallic globule, which, on treatment with soda, gives a globule of pure copper. Not dissolved in hydrochloric acid, but soluble in nitric acid.
Obs.—From the mines of Chili. In N. America, found on the Sheldon location, Portage Lake; and at Michipicoten Island, in L. Superior.
ALGODONITE.—Composition, Cu₆As=Arsenic 16·5, copper 83·5. Chili; also Lake Superior.
WHITNEYITE.—Cu₉As=Arsenic 11·6, copper 88·4=100. Houghton, Mich., also California, Arizona.

B. PROTO DIVISION.

(a) *Galenite Group.* Isometric; holohedral.

ARGENTITE. Silver Glance. Vitreous Silver. Silberglanz, *Germ.*

Isometric. Cleavage: dodecahedral in traces. Also reticulated, arborescent, and filiform; also amorphous.

H.=2–2·5. G.=7·196–7·365. Lustre metallic. Streak and color blackish lead-gray; streak shining. Opaque. Fracture small sub-conchoidal, uneven. Malleable.

Comp.—Ag₂S=Sulphur 12·9, silver 87·1=100.
Pyr., etc.—In the open tube gives off sulphurous oxide. B.B. on charcoal fuses with intumescence in O.F., emitting sulphurous fumes, and yielding a globule of silver.
Diff.—Distinguished from other silver ores by its malleability.
Obs.—Found in the Erzgebirge; in Hungary; in Norway, near Kongsberg; in the Altai; in the Urals at the Blagodat mine; in Cornwall; in Bolivia; Peru; Chili; Mexico, etc. Occurs in Nevada, at the Comstock lode, and elsewhere.
OLDHAMITE from the Busti meteorite is essentially CaS.
NAUMANNITE.—A silver selenide, containing also some lead. Color iron-black. From the Harz.
EUCAIRITE.—A silver-copper selenide, (Cu, Ag)₂Se. Color silver-white to gray. Sweden; Chili.

CROOKESITE.

Massive, compact; no trace of crystallization.
H.=2·5–3. G.=6·90. Lustre metallic. Color lead-gray. Brittle.

Comp.—(Cu₂,Tl,Ag) Se=Selenium 33·28, copper 45·76, thallium 17·25, silver 3·71=100.
Pyr., etc.—B.B. fuses very easily to a greenish-black shining enamel, coloring the flame strongly green. Insoluble in hydrochloric acid; completely soluble in nitric acid.
Obs.—From the mine of Skrikerum in Norway. Formerly regarded as selenide of copper or berzelianite.

GALENITE. Galena. Bleiglanz, *Germ.*

Isometric; habit cubic (see f. 38, 39, etc., p. 15). Cleavage, cubic, perfect; octahedral in traces. Twins: twinning-plane, the octahedral plane, f. 425 (f. 263, p. 88); the same kind of composition repeated, f. 426, and flattened parallel to 1. Also reticulated, tabular; coarse or fine granular; sometimes impalpable; occasionally fibrous.

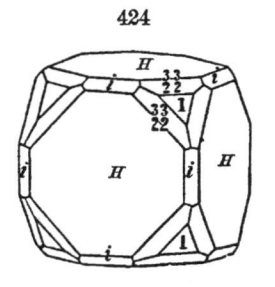

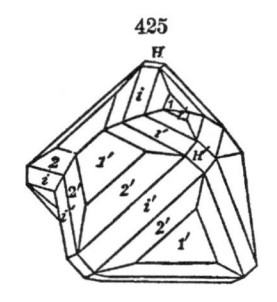

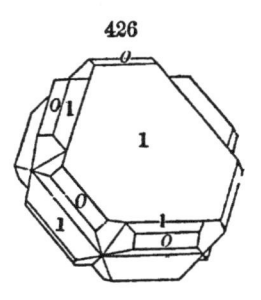

$H.=2\cdot5-2\cdot75.$ $G.=7\cdot25-7\cdot7.$ Lustre metallic. Color and streak pure lead-gray. Surface of crystals occasionally tarnished. Fracture flat subchonchoidal, or even. Frangible.

Comp., Var.—PbS=Sulphur 13·4, lead 86·6=100. Contains silver, and occasionally selenium, zinc, cadmium, antimony, copper, as sulphides; besides, also, sometimes native silver and gold; all galenite is more or less argentiferous, and no external characters serve to distinguish the relative amount of silver present.
Pyr.—In the open tube gives sulphurous fumes. B.B. on charcoal fuses, emits sulphurous fumes, coats the coal yellow, and yields a globule of metallic lead. Soluble in nitric acid.
Diff.—Distinguished in all but the finely granular varieties by its perfect cubic cleavage.
Obs.—Occurs in beds and veins, both in crystalline and uncrystalline rocks. It is often associated with pyrite, marcasite, blende, chalcopyrite, arsenopyrite, etc., in a gaugue of quartz, calcite, barite, or fluorite, etc.; also with cerussite, anglesite, and other salts of lead, which are frequent results of its alteration. It is also common with gold, and in veins of silver ores. Some prominent localities are:—Freiberg in Saxony, the Harz, Przibram and Joachimsthal, Styria; and also Bleiberg, and the neighboring localities of Carinthia, Sala in Sweden, Leadhills and the killas of Cornwall, in veins; Derbyshire, Cumberland, and the northern districts of England; in Nertschinsk, East Siberia; in Algeria; near Cape of Good Hope; in Australia; Chili; Bolivia, etc.
Extensive deposits of this ore in the United States exist in Missouri, Illinois, Iowa, and Wisconsin. Other important localities are:—in *New York*, Rossie, St. Lawrence Co.; Wurtzboro, Sullivan Co.; at Ancram, Columbia Co.; in Ulster Co. In *Maine*, at Lubec. In *New Hampshire*, at Eaton and other places. In *Vermont*, at Thetford. In *Connecticut*, at Middletown. In *Massachusetts*, at Newburyport, at Southampton, etc. In *Pennsylvania*, at Phenixville and elsewhere. In *Virginia*, at Austin's mines in Wythe Co., Walton's gold mine in Louisa Co., etc. In *Tennessee*, at Brown's Creek, and at Haysboro, near Nashville. In *Michigan*, in the region of Chocolate river, and Lake Superior copper districts, on the N. shore of L. Superior, in Neebing on Thunder Bay, and around Black Bay. In *California*, at many of the gold mines. In *Nevada*, abundant on Walker's river, and at Steamboat Springs, Galena district. In *Arizona*, in the Castle Dome, Eureka, and other districts. In *Colorado*, at Pike's Peak, etc.

CLAUSTHALITE. Selenblei, *Germ.*

Isometric. Occurs commonly in fine granular masses; some specimens foliated. Cleavage cubic.

$H.=2\cdot5-3.$ $G.=7\cdot6-8\cdot8.$ Lustre metallic. Color lead-gray, somewhat bluish. Streak darker. Opaque. Fracture granular and shining.

Comp., Var.—PbSe=Selenium 27·6, lead 72·4=100. Besides the pure selenide of lead, there are others, often arranged as distinct species, which contain cobalt, copper, or mercury in place of part of the lead, and sometimes a little silver or iron.

Pyr.—Decrepitates in the closed tube. In the open tube gives selenous fumes and a red sublimate. B.B. on charcoal a strong selenous odor; partially fuses. Coats the coal near the assay at first gray, with a reddish border (selenium), and later yellow (lead oxide); when pure entirely volatile; with soda gives a globule of metallic lead.

Obs.—Much resembles a granular galenite; but the faint tinge of blue and the B.B selenium fumes serve to distinguish it.

Found at Clausthal, Tilkerode, Zorge, Lehrbach, etc., in the Harz; at Reinsberg in Saxony; at the Rio Tinto mines, Spain; Cacheuta mine, Mendoza, S. A.

ZORGITE and LEHRBACHITE occur with clausthalite in the Harz. Zorgite is a lead-copper selenide. Lehrbachite is a lead-mercury selenide.

BERZELIANITE.—Cu_2Se=Selenium 38·4, copper 61·6=100. Color silver-white. From Sweden, also the Harz.

ALTAITE.—Composition PbTe=Tellurium 38·3, lead 61·17. Isometric. Color tin-white. From Savodinski in the Altai; Stanislaus mine, Cal.; Red Cloud mine, Colorado; Province of Coquimbo, Chili.

TIEMANNITE (Selenquecksilber, *Germ.*).—A mercury selenide, probably HgSe. Massive. Found in the Harz; also California.

BORNITE. Erubescite. Purple Copper Ore. Buntkupfererz, *Germ.*

Isometric. Cleavage: octahedral in traces. Massive, structure granular or compact.

H.=3. G.=4·4–5·5. Lustre metallic. Color between copper-red and pinchbeck-brown; speedily tarnishes. Streak pale grayish-black, slightly shining. Fracture small conchoidal, uneven. Brittle.

Comp.—For crystallized varieties $FeCu_2S_3$, or sulphur 28·06, iron 16·36, copper 55·58=100. Other varieties are: $Fe_2Cu_3S_4$, $FeCu_5S_3$, and so on. The ratio of R (Cu or Fe) to S has the values 5 : 4, 4 : 3, 3 : 2, 7 : 3 (Rammelsberg). Analysis, Collier, from Bristol, Ct. Sulphur 25·83, copper 61·79, iron 11·77, silver tr. =99·39 (R : S=3 : 2).

Pyr., etc.—In the closed tube gives a faint sublimate of sulphur. In the open tube yields sulphurous oxide, but gives no sublimate. B.B. on charcoal fuses in R. F. to a brittle magnetic globule. The roasted mineral gives with the fluxes the reactions of iron and copper, and with soda a metallic globule. Soluble in nitric acid with separation of sulphur.

Diff.—Distinguished by its copper-red color on the fresh fracture.

Obs.—Found in the mines of Cornwall; at Ross Island in Killarney, Ireland; at Mount Catini, Tuscany; in the Mansfeld district, Germany; and in Norway, Siberia, Silesia, and Hungary. It is the principal copper ore at some Chilian mines; also common in Peru, Bolivia, and Mexico. At Bristol, Conn., it has been found abundantly in good crystals. Found massive at Mahoopeny, Penn., and in other parts of the same State; also at Chesterfield, Mass.; also in New Jersey. A common ore in Canada, at the Acton and other mines.

ALABANDITE (Manganglanz, *Germ.*).—MnS=Sulphur 36·7, manganese 63.3=100. Isometric. Cleavage cubic. Color black. Streak green. From Transylvania, etc.

GRÜNAUITE.—A sulphide containing nickel, bismuth, iron, cobalt, copper. From Grünau.

(b) Blende Group. Isometric; tetrahedral.

SPHALERITE or **ZINC BLENDE.** Black-Jack, *Engl. Miners.*

Isometric: tetrahedral. Cleavage: dodecahedral, highly perfect. Twins: twinning-plane 1, as in f. 429. Also botryoidal, and other imitative shapes; sometimes fibrous and radiated; also massive, compact.

H.=3·5–4. G.=3·9–4·2. 4·063, white, New Jersey. Lustre resinous to adamantine. Color brown, yellow, black, red, green; white or yellow when pure. Streak white—reddish-brown. Transparent—translucent. Fracture conchoidal. Brittle.

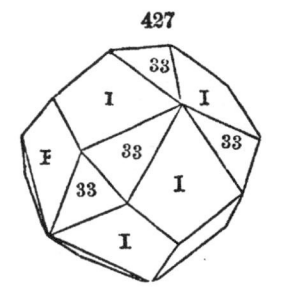

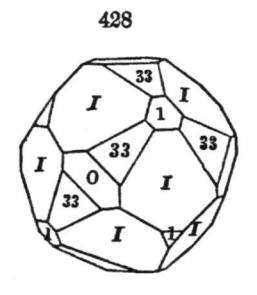

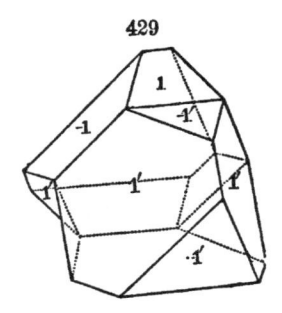

Comp., Var.—ZnS=Sulphur 33, zinc 67=100. But often having part of the zinc replaced by iron, and sometimes by cadmium; also containing in minute quantities, thallium, indium, and gallium. Var. 1. *Ordinary.* Containing little or no iron; colors white to yellowish-brown, sometimes black; G.=3.9–4.1. 2. *Ferriferous; Marmatite.* Containing 10 p. c. or more of iron; dark-brown to black; G.=3.9–4.2. The proportion of iron sulphide to zinc sulphide varies from 1 : 5 to 1 : 2. 3. *Cadmiferous; Przibramite.* The amount of cadmium present in any blende thus far analyzed is less than 5 per cent. Each of the above varieties may occur (*a*) in crystals; (*b*) firm, fibrous, or columnar, at times radiated or plumose; (*c*) cleavable, massive, or foliated; (*d*) granular, or compact massive.

Pyr., etc.—In the open tube sulphurous fumes, and generally changes color. B.B. on charcoal, in R.F., some varieties give at first a reddish-brown coating of cadmium oxide, and later a coating of zinc oxide, which is yellow while hot and white after cooling. With cobalt solution the zinc coating gives a green color when heated in O.F. Most varieties, after roasting, give with borax a reaction for iron. With soda on charcoal in R.F. a strong green zinc flame. Difficultly fusible.

Dissolves in hydrochloric acid, during which sulphuretted hydrogen is disengaged. Some specimens phosphoresce when struck with a steel or by friction.

Diff.—Generally to be distinguished by its perfect cleavage, giving angles of 60° and 120°; by its resinous lustre, and also by its infusibility.

Obs.—Occurs in both crystalline and sedimentary rocks, and is usually associated with galenite; also with barite, chalcopyrite, fluorite, siderite, and frequently in silver mines.

Derbyshire. Cumberland, and Cornwall, afford different varieties; also Transylvania; Hungary; the Harz; Sahla in Sweden; Ratieborzitz in Bohemia; many Saxon localities. Splendid crystals in dolomite are found in the Binnenthal.

Abounds with the lead ore of Missouri, Wisconsin, Iowa, and Illinois. In *N. York*, Sullivan Co., near Wurtzboro'; in St. Lawrence Co., at Cooper's falls, at Mineral Point; at the Ancram lead mine in Columbia Co.; in limestone at Lockport and other places. In *Mass.*, at Sterling; at the Southampton lead mines; at Hatfield. In *N. Hamp.*, at the Eaton lead mine; at Warren, a large vein of black blende. In *Maine*, at the Lubec lead mines, etc. In *Conn.*, at Roxbury, and at Lane's mine, Monroe. In *N. Jersey*, a *white* variety at Franklin. In *Penn.*, at the Wheatley and Perkiomen lead mines; near Friedensville, Lehigh Co. In *Virginia*, at Austin's lead mines, Wythe Co. In *Michigan*, at Prince vein, Lake Superior. In *Illinois*, near Rosiclare; near Galena, in stalactites, covered with pyrite, and galenite In *Wisconsin*, at Mineral Point. In *Tennessee*, at Haysboro', near Nashville.

Named *blende* because, while often resembling galena, it yielded no lead, the word in German meaning *blind* or *deceiving. Sphalerite* is from σφαλερός, *treacherous.*

(*c*) *Chalcocite Group.* Orthorhombic.

HESSITE.* Tellursilber, *Germ.*

Orthorhombic, and resembling chalcocite. Cleavage indistinct Massive; compact or fine grained; rarely coarse-granular.

SULPHIDES, TELLURIDES, SELENIDES, ETC.   239

H.$=2$-$3\cdot 5$.   G.$=8\cdot 3$-$8\cdot 6$.   Lustre metallic.   Color between lead-gray and steel-gray.   Sectile.   Fracture even.

Comp.—$Ag_2Te=$Tellurium 37·2, silver 62·8=100.   Silver sometimes replaced in part by gold.
Pyr.—In the open tube a faint white sublimate of tellurous oxide, which B.B. fuses to colorless globules.   On charcoal fuses to a black globule; this treated in R.F. presents on cooling white dendritic points of silver on its surface; with soda gives a globule of silver.
Obs.—Occurs in the Altai, in Siberia, in a talcose rock; at Nagyag in Transylvania, and at Retzbanya in Hungary; Stanislaus mine, Calaveras Co., Cal.; Red Cloud mine, Colorado; Province of Coquimbo, Chili.
PETZITE.—Differs from hessite in that gold replaces much of the silver.   H.$=2\cdot 5$.   G.$=8\cdot 72$-$8\cdot 83$, Petz; 9–9·4, Küstel.   Color between steel-gray and iron-black, sometimes with pavonine tarnish.   Streak iron-black.   Brittle.   Analysis by Genth, from Golden Rule mine, tellurium 32·68, silver 41·86, gold 25·60 = 100·14.   Occurs at Nagyag, Stanislaus mine, California, and several localities in Colorado.
TAPALPITE (Tellurwismuthsilber).—Composition (Ramm.), $Ag_2Bi_2Te_2S(Ag_2S + 2BiTe)$. Granular.   Color gray.   Sierra de Tapalpa, Mexico.

ACANTHITE.

Orthorhombic. $I \wedge I = 110° 54'$; $O \wedge 1\text{-}\bar{i} = 124° 42'$, Dauber; $\check{c} : \bar{b} : \check{a} = 1\cdot 4442 : 1\cdot 4523 : 1$. $O \wedge 1\text{-}\check{i} = 135° 10'$; $O \wedge 1 = 119° 42'$.   Twins: parallel to 1-$\check{i}$.   Crystals usually slender-pointed prisms.   Cleavage indistinct.

H.$=2\cdot 5$ or under.   G.$=7\cdot 16$-$7\cdot 33$.   Lustre metallic.   Color iron-black or like argentite.   Fracture uneven, giving a shining surface.   Sectile.

Comp.—Ag_2S, or like argentite.   Sulphur 12·9, silver 87·1=100.
Pyr.—Same as for argentite, p. 235.
Obs.—Found at Joachimsthal; also near Freiberg in Saxony.

CHALCOCITE.   Chalcosine.   Vitreous Copper.   Copper Glance.   Kupferglanz, *Germ.*

Orthorhombic. $I \wedge I = 119° 35'$, $O \wedge 1\text{-}\bar{i} = 120° 57'$; $\check{c} : \bar{b} : \check{a} = 1\cdot 6676 : 1\cdot 7176 : 1$; $O \wedge 1 = 117° 24'$; $O \wedge 1\text{-}\check{i} = 135° 52'$.   Cleavage: I, indistinct. Twins: twinning-plane, I, producing hexagonal, or stellate forms (left half

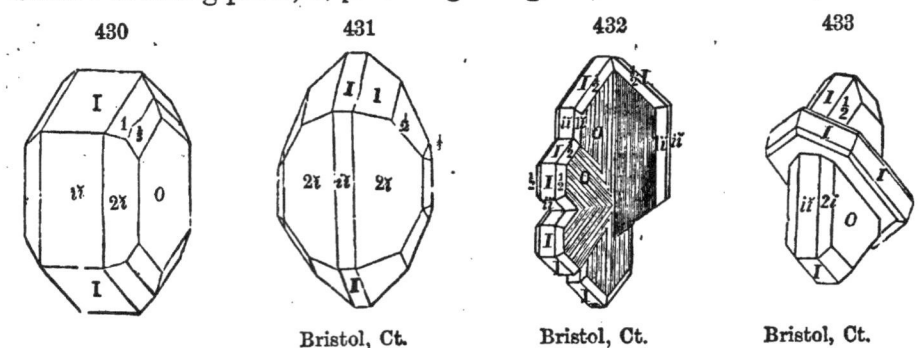

430   431   432   433

Bristol, Ct.   Bristol, Ct.   Bristol, Ct.

of f. 432); also $\frac{1}{2}$-$\check{i}$, a cruciform twin (f. 432), crossing at angles of 111° and 69°; f. 433, a cruciform twin, having O and I of one crystal parallel respectively to i-$\check{i}$ and O of the other.   Also massive, structure granular, or compact and impalpable

H.=2·5–3. G.=5·5–5·8. Lustre metallic. Color and streak blackish lead-gray: often tarnished blue or green; streak sometimes shining. Fracture conchoidal.

Comp.—Cu_2S=Sulphur 20·2, copper 79·8=100.
Pyr., etc.—Yields nothing volatile in the closed tube. In the open tube gives off sulphurous fumes. B.B. on charcoal melts to a globule, which boils with spirting; with soda is reduced to metallic copper. Soluble in nitric acid.
Obs.—Cornwall affords splendid crystals. The compact and massive varieties occur in Siberia, Hesse, Saxony, the Banat, etc.; Mt. Catini mines in Tuscany; Mexico, Peru. Bolivia, Chili.
In the United States, it has been found at Bristol, Conn., in large and brilliant crystals. In Virginia, in the United States copper mine district, Orange Co. Between Newmarket and Taneytown, Maryland. In Arizona, near La Paz; in N. W. Sonora. In Nevada, in Washoe, Humboldt, Churchill, and Nye Cos.
HARRISITE of Shepard, from Canton mine, Georgia, is chalcocite with the cleavage of galenite (pseudomorphous, *Genth*).

STROMEYERITE. Silberkupferglanz, *Germ.*

Orthorhombic: isomorphous with chalcocite. $I \wedge I = 119°\ 35'$. Also massive, compact.
H.=2·5–3. G.=6·2–6·3. Lustre metallic. Color dark steel-gray. Streak shining. Fracture subconchoidal.

Comp.—$AgCuS$=Ag_2S+Cu_2S=Sulphur 15·7, silver 53·1, copper 31·2=100.
Pyr., etc.—Fuses, but gives no sublimate in the closed tube. In the open tube sulphurous fumes. B.B. on charcoal in O.F. fuses to a semi-malleable globule, which, treated with the fluxes, reacts strongly for copper, and cupelled with lead gives a silver globule. Soluble in nitric acid.
Obs.—Found at Schlangenberg, in Siberia; at Rudelstadt, Silesia; also in Chili; at Combavalla in Peru; at Heintzelman mine in Arizona.
STERNBERGITE.*—An iron-silver sulphide, $AgFe_2S_3$. Johanngeorgenstadt and Joachimsthal.

(d) *Pyrrhotite Group.* Hexagonal.

CINNABAR. Zinnober, *Germ.*

Rhombohedral. $R \wedge R = 92°\ 36'$, $R \wedge O = 127°\ 6'$; $c = 1·1448$. According to DesCloizeaux, tetartohedral, like quartz. Also granular, massive; sometimes forming superficial coatings.

434

Cleavage: I, very perfect. Twins: twinning-plane O.
H=2–2·5. G=8·998, a cleavable variety from Neumarktel. Lustre adamantine, inclining to metallic when dark-colored, and to dull in friable varieties. Color cochineal-red, often inclining to brownish-red and lead-gray. Streak scarlet, subtransparent, opaque. Fracture subconchoidal, uneven. Sectile. Polarization circular.

Comp.—HgS (or Hg_3S_3)=Sulphur 13·8, mercury 86·2=100. Sometimes impure from clay iron sesquioxide, bitumen.

Pyr.—In the closed tube a black sublimate. Carefully heated in the open tube gives sulphurous fumes and metallic mercury, condensing in minute globules on the cold walls of the tube. B. B. on charcoal wholly volatile if pure.

Obs.—Cinnabar occurs in beds in slate rocks and shales, and rarely in granite or porphyry. It has been observed in veins, with ores of iron. The most important European beds of this ore are at Almaden in Spain, and at Idria in Carniola. It occurs at Reichenau and Windisch Kappel in Carinthia; in Transylvania; at Ripa in Tuscany; at Schemnitz in Hungary; in the Urals and Altai; in China abundantly, and in Japan; San Onofre and elsewhere in Mexico; in Southern Peru; forming extensive mines in California, in the coast ranges the principal mines are at New Almaden and the vicinity, in Santa Clara Co. Also in Idaho, in limestone, abundant.

This ore is the source of the mercury of commerce, from which it is obtained by sublimation. When pure it is identical with the manufactured *vermilion* of commerce.

METACINNABARITE (*Moore*).—A black mercury sulphide (HgS). Rarely crystallized. H.=3. G.=7·75. Lustre metallic. Redington mine, Lake Co., Cal.

GUADALCAZARITE.—Essentially HgS, with part ($\frac{1}{13}$) of the sulphur replaced by selenium, and part of the mercury replaced by zinc (Hg : Zn=6 : 1, Petersen; =12 : 1, Ramm.). Massive. Color deep black. Guadalcazar, Mexico. LEVIGLIANITE is a ferruginous variety from Levigliani, Italy.

MILLERITE.* Capillary Pyrites. Haarkies; Nickelkies, *Germ.*

Rhombohedral. $R \wedge R = 144° 8'$, Miller. $c = 0.32955$. $O \wedge R = 159° 10'$. Cleavage: rhombohedral, perfect. Usual in capillary crystals. Also in columnar tufted coatings, partly semi-globular and radiated.

H.=3–3·5. G.=4·6–5·65. Lustre metallic. Color brass-yellow, inclining to bronze-yellow, with often a gray iridescent tarnish. Streak bright. Brittle.

Comp.—NiS=Sulphur 35·6, nickel 64·4=100.

Pyr., etc.—In the open tube sulphurous fumes. B.B. on charcoal fuses to a globule. When roasted, gives with borax and salt of phosphorus a violet bead in O.F., becoming gray in R.F. from reduced metallic nickel. On charcoal in R.F. the roasted mineral gives a coherent metallic mass, attractable by the magnet. Soluble in nitric acid.

Obs.—Found at Joachimsthal; Przibram; Riechelsdorf; Andreasberg; several localities in Saxony; Cornwall.

Occurs at the Sterling mine, Antwerp, N. Y.; in Lancaster Co., Pa., at the Gap mine; with dolomite, and penetrating calcite crystals, in cavities in limestone, at St. Louis, Mo.

BEYRICHITE (*Liebe*).—Formula Ni_5S_7=Sulphur 43·6, nickel 56·4=100. Color lead-gray. Occurs in radiated groups with millerite in the Westerwald.

PYRRHOTITE. Magnetic Pyrites. Magnetkies, *Germ.*

Hexagonal. $O \wedge 1 = 135° 8'$; $c = 0.862$. Twins: twinning-plane 1 (f. 435). Cleavage: O, perfect; I, less so. Commonly massive and amorphous; structure granular.

H.=3·5–4·5. G.=4·4–4·68. Lustre metallic. Color between bronze-yellow and copper-red, and subject to speedy tarnish. Streak dark grayish-black. Brittle. Magnetic, being attractable in fine powder by a magnet, even when not affecting an ordinary needle.

435

Comp.—(1) Mostly Fe_7S_8=Sulphur 39·5, iron 60·5=100; but varying to Fe_8S_9, Fe_9S_{10} and $Fe_{10}S_{11}$. Some varieties contain 3–6 p. c. nickel. *Horbachite* contains (Wagner) 12 p. c. Ni.

Pyr., etc.—Unchanged in the closed tube. In the open tube gives sulphurous oxide. On charcoal in R. F. fuses to a black magnetic mass; in O.F. is converted into iron sesquioxide, which with fluxes gives only an iron reaction when pure, but many varieties yield small amounts of nickel and cobalt. Decomposed by muriatic acid, with evolution of sulphuretted hydrogen.

Diff.—Distinguished by its magnetic character, and by its bronze color on the fresh fracture.

Obs.—Occurs in Norway; in Sweden; at Andreasberg; Bodenmais in Bavaria; N. Tagilsk; in Spain; the lavas of Vesuvius; Cornwall.

In N. America, in Vermont, at Stafford, Corinth, and Shrewsbury; in many parts of Massachusetts; in Connecticut, in Trumbull, in Monroe; in N. York, near Natural Bridge in Diana, Lewis Co.; at O'Neil mine and elsewhere in Orange Co. In N. Jersey, Morris Co., at Hurdstown. In Pennsylvania, at the Gap mine, Lancaster Co., niccoliferous. In Tennessee, at Ducktown mines. In Canada, at St. Jerome; Elizabethtown, Ontario (f. 435), etc.

The niccoliferous pyrrhotite is the ore that affords the most of the nickel of commerce.

TROILITE.—According to the latest investigations of J. Lawrence Smith, composition FeS, iron proto-sulphide; that is, iron 63·6, sulphur 36·4=100. Occurs only in iron meteorites. DAUBRÉELITE (Smith).—Composition Cr_2S_3. Observed in the meteoric iron of Northern Mexico; occurring on the borders of troilite nodules. Similar to *shepardite*, Haidinger (=*schreibersite*, Shepard), described by Shepard (1846) as occurring in the Bishopville, S. C., meteoric iron.

SCHREIBERSITE also solely a meteoric mineral. Contains iron, nickel, and phosphorus.

WURTZITE (Spiauterite).—ZnS, like sphalerite, but hexagonal in crystallization. Bolivia.

GREENOCKITE.

Hexagonal; hemimorphic. $O \wedge 1 = 136° 24'$; $\breve{c} = 0·8247$. Cleavage: I, distinct; O, imperfect.

H.=3–3·5. G.=4·8–4·999. Lustre adamantine. Color honey-yellow; citron-yellow; orange-yellow—veined parallel with the axis; bronze-yellow. Streak-powder between orange-yellow and brick-red. Nearly transparent. Strong double refraction. Not thermoelectric, Breithaupt.

Comp.—CdS (or Cd_3S_3)=Sulphur 22·2, cadium 77·8.

Pyr., etc.—In the closed tube assumes a carmine-red color while hot, fading to the original yellow on cooling. In the open tube gives sulphurous oxide. B.B. on charcoal, either alone or with soda, gives in R.F. a reddish-brown coating. Soluble in hydrochloric acid, evolving sulphuretted hydrogen.

Obs.—Occurs at Bishoptown, in Renfrewshire, Scotland; also at Przibram in Bohemia; on sphalerite at the Ueberoth zinc mine, near Friedensville, Lehigh Co., Pa., and at Granby, Mo.

NICCOLITE. Copper Nickel. Kupfernickel, Rothnickelkies, *Germ.*

Hexagonal. $O \wedge 1 = 13°6 35'$; $\breve{c} : 0·81944$. Usually massive, structure nearly impalpable; also reniform with a columnar structure; also reticulated and arborescent.

H.=5–5·5. G.=7·33–7·671. Lustre metallic. Color pale copper-red, with a gray to blackish tarnish. Streak pale brownish-black. Opaque. Fracture uneven. Brittle.

Comp.—NiAs (or Ni_3As_3)=Arsenic 56·4, nickel 43·6=100; sometimes part of the arsenic replaced by antimony.

Pyr., etc.—In the closed tube a faint white crystalline sublimate of arsenous oxide. In the open tube arsenous oxide, with a trace of sulphurous oxide, the assay becoming yellowish-green. On charcoal gives arsenical fumes and fuses to a globule, which, treated with borax glass, affords, by successive oxidation, reactions for iron, cobalt, and nickel. Soluble in nitro-hydrochloric acid.

Diff.—Distinguished by its color from other similar sulphides, as also by its pyrognostics.

Obs.—Occurs at several Saxon mines, also in Thuringia, Hesse, and Styria, and at Allemont in Dauphiny; occasionally in Cornwall; Chili; abundant at Mina de la Rioja, in the Argentine Provinces. Found at Chatham, Conn., in gneiss, associated with smaltite.

BREITHAUPTITE.—Composition NiSb=Antimony 67·8, nickel 32·2=100. Color light copper-red. Andreasberg.

ARITE.—An antimoniferous niccolite, containing 28 p. c. Sb. Basses-Pyrenées; Wolfach, Baden.

C. DEUTO OR PYRITE DIVISION.

(a) *Pyrite Group.*

PYRITE.* Iron Pyrites. Schwefelkies, Eisenkies, *Germ.*

Isometric; pyritohedral. The cube the most common form; the pyritohedron, f. 92, p. 23, and related forms, f. 94, 95, 96, also very common. See also f. 103, 104, 105, p. 24. Cubic faces often striated, with striations of adjoining faces at right angles, and due to oscillatory combination of the cube and pyritohedron, the striæ having the direction of the edges between O and i-2. Crystals sometimes acicular through elongation of cubic and other forms. Cleavage: cubic and octahedral, more or less distinct. Twins: twining-plane I, f. 276, p. 93. Also reniform, globular, stalactitic, with a crystalline surface; sometimes radiated subfibrous. Massive.

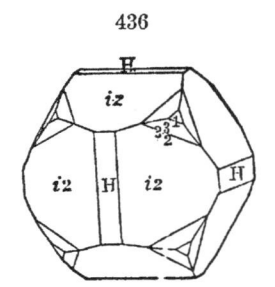

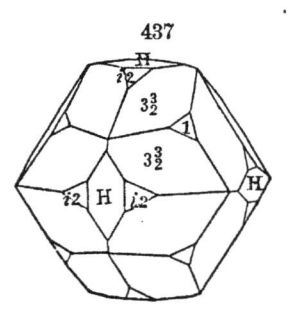

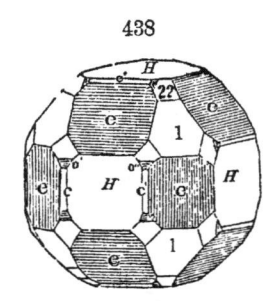

436   437   438

Rossie.

H.=6–6·5. G.=4·83–5·2. Lustre metallic, splendent to glistening. Color a pale brass-yellow, nearly uniform. Streak greenish or brownish-black. Opaque. Fracture conchoidal, uneven. Brittle. Strikes fire with steel.

Comp., Var.—FeS_2=Sulphur 53·3, iron 46·7=100. Nickel, cobalt, and thallium, and also copper, sometimes replace a little of the iron, or else occur as mixtures; and gold is sometimes present, distributed invisibly through it.

Pyr., etc.—In the closed tube a sublimate of sulphur and a magnetic residue. B.B. on charcoal gives off sulphur, burning with a blue flame, leaving a residue which reacts like pyrrhotite. Insoluble in hydrochloric acid, but decomposed by nitric acid.

Diff.—Distinguished from chalcopyrite by its greater hardness, since it cannot be cut with a knife; as also by its pale color; from marcasite by its specific gravity and color. Not malleable like gold

Obs.—Pyrite occurs abundantly in rocks of all ages, from the oldest crystalline rocks to the most recent alluvial deposits. It usually occurs in small cubes, also in irregular spheroidal nodules and in veins, in clay slate, argillaceous sandstones, the coal formation, etc. The Cornwall mines, Alston-Moor, Derbyshire, Fahlun in Sweden, Kongsberg in Norway, Elba, Traversella in Piedmont, Peru, are well-known localities.

Occurs in New England at many places: as the Vernon slate quarries; Roxbury, Conn., etc. In *N. York*, at Rossie, at Schoharie; in Orange Co., at Warwick and Deerpark, and many other places. In *Pennsylvania*, at Little Britain, Lancaster Co.; at Chester, Delaware Co.; in Carbon, York, and Chester Cos.; at Cornwall, Lebanon Co., etc. In *Wisconsin*, near Mineral Point. In *N. Car.*, near Greensboro', Guilford Co. Auriferous pyrite is common at the mines of Colorado, and many of those of California, as well as in Virginia and the States south.

This species affords a considerable part of the iron sulphate and sulphuric acid of commerce and also much of the sulphur and alum. The auriferous variety is worked for gold in many gold regions.

The name *pyrite* is derived from πῦρ, fire, and alludes to the sparks from friction.

HAUERITE.—Composition MnS_2=Sulphur 53·7, manganese 46·3=100. Isometric. Color reddish-brown. Kalinka, Hungary.

CHALCOPYRITE.* Copper Pyrites. Kupferkies, *Germ.*

Tetragonal; tetrahedral. $O \wedge 1\text{-}i = 135° 25'$; $\dot{c} = 0.98556$; $O \wedge 1 = 125° 40'$; $1 \wedge 1$, pyr., $= 109° 53'$; $1 \wedge 1$ (f. 440) $= 71° 20'$ and $70° 7'$. Cleavage: $2\text{-}i$ sometimes distinct; O, indistinct. Twins: twinning-plane $1\text{-}i$; the plane 1 (see p. 94). Often massive.

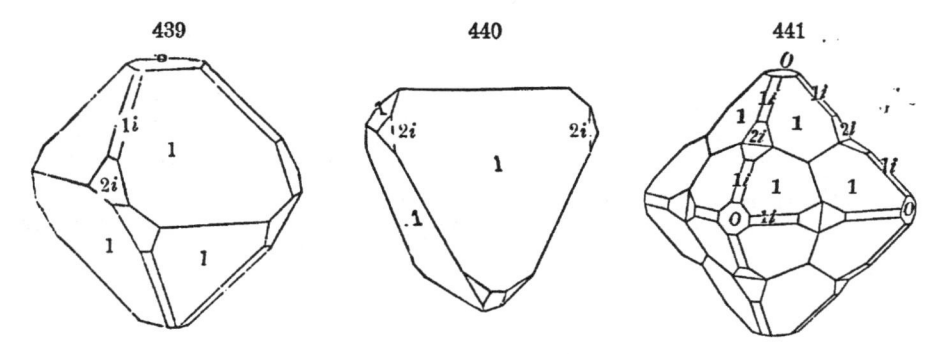

439   440   441

H.=3·5–4. G.=4·1–4·3. Lustre metallic. Color brass-yellow; subject to tarnish, and often iridescent. Streak greenish-black—a little shining. Opaque. Fracture conchoidal, uneven.

Comp.—$CuFeS_2$=Sulphur 34·9, copper 34·6, iron 30·5=100. Some analyses give other proportions; but probably from mixture with pyrite. There are indefinite mixtures of the two, and with the increase of the latter the color becomes paler.

This species, although tetragonal, is very closely isomorphous with pyrite, the variation from the cubic form being slight, the vertical axis being 0·98556 instead of 1.

Traces of selenium have been noticed by Kersten in an ore from Reinsberg near Freiberg. Thallium is also present in some kinds, and more frequently in this ore than in pyrite.

Pyr., etc.—In the closed tube decrepitates, and gives a sulphur sublimate; in the open tube sulphurous oxide. B.B. on charcoal gives sulphur fumes and fuses to a magnetic globule. The roasted ore reacts for copper and iron with the fluxes; with soda on charcoal gives a globule of metallic iron with copper. Dissolves in nitric acid, excepting the sulphur, and forms a green solution; ammonia in excess changes the green color to a deep blue.

Diff.—Distinguished from pyrite by its inferior hardness, it can be easily scratched with the knife; and by its deeper color. Not malleable like gold, from which it differs also in being decomposed by nitric acid.

SULPHIDES, TELLURIDES, SELENIDES, ETC.   245

Obs.—Chalcopyrite is the principal ore of copper at the Cornwall mines. Occurs at Freiberg; in the Bannat; Hungary; and Thuringia; in Scotland; in Tuscany; in South Australia; in fine crystals at Cerro Blanco, Chili.
A common mineral in America, some localities are: Stafford, Vt.; Rossie, Ellenville, N. Y.; Phenixville, etc., Penn. The mines in North Carolina and eastern Tennessee afford large quantities. Occurs in *Cal.*, in different mines along a belt between Mariposa Co. and Del Norte Co., on west side of, and parallel to, the chief gold belt; occurring massive in Calaveras Co.; in Mariposa Co., etc. In *Canada*, in Perth and near Sherbrooke; extensively mined at Bruce mines, on Lake Huron.
Named from χαλκός, *brass*, and *pyrites*, by Henckel, who observes in his Pyritology (1725) that chalcopyrite is a good distinctive name for the ore.

CUBANITE is $CuFe_2S_4$, or $CuFe_2S_3$ (Scheidhauer).—Occurs massive at Barracanao, Cuba; Tunaberg, Sweden.

BARNHARDTITE, from North Carolina.—Composition uncertain, perhaps $Cu_4Fe_2S_5$. It may be partly altered from chalcopyrite.

STANNITE (Zinnkies, *Germ.*).—A sulphide containing 26 p. c. tin; also copper, iron, and zinc. Massive. Color steel-gray. Chiefly from Cornwall, also Zinnwald.

LINNÆITE. Kobaltnickelkies, *Germ.*

Isometric. Cleavage: cubic, imperfect. Twins: twinning-plane octahedral. Also massive, granular to compact.

H.=5·5. G.=4·8–5. Lustre metallic. Color pale steel-gray, tarnishing copper-red. Streak blackish-gray. Fracture uneven or subconchoidal.

Comp.—Co_3S_4 (or $2CoS + CoS_2$) = Sulphur 42·0, cobalt 58·0 = 100; but having the cobalt replaced partly by nickel or copper, the proportions varying very much. The Müsen ore (*siegenite*) contains 30–40 p. c. of nickel.

Pyr., etc.—The variety from Müsen gives, in the closed tube, a sulphur sublimate; in the open tube, sulphurous fumes, with a faint sublimate of arsenous oxide. B.B. on charcoal gives arsenical and sulphurous odors, and fuses to a magnetic globule. The roasted mineral gives with the fluxes reactions for nickel, cobalt, and iron. Soluble in nitric acid, with separation of sulphur.

Diff.—Distinguished by its color, and isometric crystallization.

Obs.—In gneiss, at Bastnaes, Sweden; at Müsen, near Siegen, in Prussia; at Siegen (*siegenite*), in octahedrons; at Mine la Motte, in Missouri, mostly massive, also crystalline; and at Mineral Hill, in Maryland.

SMALTITE.* Speiskobalt, *Germ.*

Isometric. Cleavage: octahedral, distinct; cubic, in traces. Also massive and in reticulated and other imitative shapes.

H.=5·5–6. G.=6·4 to 7·2. Lustre metallic. Color tin-white, inclining, when massive, to steel-gray, sometimes iridescent, or grayish from tarnish. Streak grayish-black. Fracture granular and uneven. Brittle.

Comp., Var.—For typical kind $(Co,Fe,Ni)As_2 =$ (if Co, Fe, and Ni be present in equal parts) Arsenic 72·1, cobalt 9·4, nickel 9·5, iron 9·0 = 100. It is probable that nickel is never wholly absent, although not detected in some of the earlier analyses; and in some kinds it is the principal metal. The proportions of cobalt, nickel, and iron vary much.
The following analyses will serve as examples of the different varieties:

	As	Co	Ni	Fe	Cu	
1. Schneeberg	70·37	13·95	1·79	11·71	1·39	S 0·66, Bi 0·01 = 99·88 Hofmann.
2. Allemont (*chloanthite*)	71·11	——	18·71	6·82	——	S 2·29 = 98·93 Rammelsberg.
3. Riechelsdorf	60·42	10·80	25·87	0·80	——	S 2·11 = 100. "
4. Schneeberg	74·80	3·79	12·86	7·33	——	S 0·85 = 99·63 Karstedt.

Pyr., etc.—In the close tube gives a sublimate of metallic arsenic; in the open tube a white sublimate of arsenous oxide, and sometimes traces of sulphurous oxide. B.B. on charcoal gives an arsenical odor, and fuses to a globule, which, treated with successive portions of borax-glass, affords reactions for iron, cobalt, and nickel.

Obs.—Usually occurs in veins, accompanying ores of cobalt or nickel, and ores of silver and copper; also, in some instances, with niccolite and arsenopyrite; often having a coating of annabergite.

Occurs at Schneeberg, etc., in Saxony; at Joachimsthal; also at Wheal Sparnon in Cornwall; at Riechelsdorf in Hesse; at Tunaberg in Sweden; Allemont in Dauphiné. Also in crystals at Mine La Motte, Missouri. At Chatham, Conn., the chloanthite (*chathamite*) occurs in mica slate, associated generally with arsenopyrite and sometimes with niccolite.

SPATHIOPYRITE is closely allied to smaltite, with which it occurs at Bieber in Hessen.

SKUTTERUDITE (Tesseralkies, *Germ.*).—$CoAs_3$=Arsenic 79·2, cobalt 20·8=100. Isometric. Skutterud, Norway.

COBALTITE. Glance Cobalt. Kobaltglanz, *Germ.*

Isometric; pyritohedral. Commonly in pyritohedrons (f. 92, 95, etc., p. 23). Cleavage: cubic, perfect. Planes O striated. Also massive, granular or compact.

H.=5·5. G.=6–6·3. Lustre metallic. Color silver-white, inclined to red; also steel-gray, with a violet tinge, or grayish-black when containing much iron. Streak grayish-black. Fracture uneven and lamellar. Brittle.

Comp., Var.—CoAsS (or $CoS_2 + CoAs_2$)=Sulphur 19·3, arsenic 45·2, cobalt 35·5=100. The cobalt is sometimes largely replaced by iron, and sparingly by copper.

Pyr., etc.—Unaltered in the closed tube. In the open tube, gives sulphurous fumes and a crystalline sublimate of arsenous oxide. B.B. on charcoal gives off sulphur and arsenic, and fuses to a magnetic globule; with borax a cobalt-blue color. Soluble in warm nitric acid, separating arsenous oxide and sulphur.

Diff.—Distinguished by its reddish-white color; also by its pyritohedral form.

Obs.—Occurs at Tunaberg, Hokansbö, in Sweden; also at Skutterud in Norway. Other localities are at Querbach in Silesia, Siegen in Westphalia, and Botallack mine, in Cornwall. The most productive mines are those of Vena in Sweden.

This species and smaltite afford the greater part of the smalt of commerce. It is also employed in porcelain painting.

GERSDORFFITE. Nickelarsenikkies, Arseniknickelglanz, *Germ.*

Isometric; pyritohedral. Cleavage: cubic, rather perfect. Also lamellar and granular massive.

H.=5·5. G.=5.6–6·9. Lustre metallic. Color silver-white—steel-gray, often tarnished gray or grayish-black. Streak grayish-black. Fracture uneven.

Comp., Var.—Normal, NiAsS (or $NiS_2 + NiAs_2$)=Arsenic 45·5, sulphur 19·4, nickel 35·1=100. The composition varies in atomic proportions rather widely.

Pyr., etc.—In the closed tube decrepitates, and gives a yellowish-brown sublimate of arsenic sulphide. In the open tube yields sulphurous fumes, and a white sublimate of arsenous oxide. B.B. on charcoal gives sulphurous and garlic odors and fuses to a globule, which, with borax-glass, gives at first an iron reaction, and, by treatment with fresh portions of the flux, cobalt and nickel are successively oxidized.

Decomposed by nitric acid, forming a green solution, with separation of sulphur and arsenous oxide.

Obs.—Occurs at Loos in Sweden; in the Harz; at Schladming in Styria; Kamsdorf in Lower Thuringia; Haueisen, Voigtland; near Ems. Also found as an incrustation at Phenixville, Pa.

ULLMANNITE.—NiSbS (NiS$_2$+NiSb$_2$)=Antimony 57·2, sulphur 15·1, nickel 27·7=100. Generally contains also some arsenic. Color steel-gray. Siegen, Harzgerode, etc.

CORYNITE.—Ni(As,Sb)S, but the arsenic (38 p. c.) in excess of the antimony. Olsa, Corinthia. WOLFACHITE (Petersen), from Wolfach, Baden, is similar in composition, but is orthorhombic in form.

LAURITE.—An osmium-ruthenium sulphide. Analysis (Wöhler) Sulphur 31·79 [Osmium 3·03], Ruthenium 65.18=100. Occurs in minute octahedrons from the platinum-washings of Borneo; as also those in Oregon.

(b) Marcasite Group. Orthorhombic.

MARCASITE. White Iron Pyrites. Strahlkies, etc., *Germ.*

Orthorhombic. $I \wedge I = 106° 5'$, $O \wedge 1\text{-}\check{\imath} = 122° 26'$, Miller; $\check{c} : \bar{b} : \check{a} =$ 1·5737 : 1·3287 : 1. $O \wedge 1 = 116° 55'$; $O \wedge 1\text{-}\check{\imath} = 130° 10'$. Cleavage: I rather perfect; 1-$\check{\imath}$ in traces. Twins: twinning-plane I, sometimes consisting of five individuals (see f. 308, p. 98); also 1-$\check{\imath}$. Also globular, reniform, and other imitative shapes—structure straight columnar; often massive, columnar, or granular.

442

H.=6-6·5. G.=4·678-4·847. Lustre metallic. Color pale bronze-yellow, sometimes inclined to green or gray. Streak grayish- or brownish-black. Fracture uneven. Brittle.

Comp., Var.—FeS$_2$, like pyrite=Sulphur 53·3, iron 46·7=100.

The varieties that have been recognized depend mainly on state of crystallization; as the *Radiated* (*Strahlkies*): Radiated; also the simple crystals. *Cockscomb* (*Kammkies*): Aggregations of flattened crystals into crest-like forms. *Spear* (*Speerkies*): Twin crystals, with reëntering angles a little like the head of a spear in form. *Capillary* (*Haarkies*): In capillary crystallizations, etc.

Pyr.—Like pyrite. Very liable to decomposition; more so than pyrite.

Diff.—Distinguished from pyrite by its paler color, especially marked on a fresh surface; by its tendency to tarnish; by its inferior specific gravity.

Obs.—Occurs near Carlsbad in Bohemia; at Joachimsthal, and in several parts of Saxony; in Derbyshire; near Alston Moor in Cumberland; near Tavistock in Devonshire, and in Cornwall.

At Warwick, N. Y. Massive fibrous varieties abound throughout the mica slate of New England, particularly at Cummington, Mass. Occurs at Lane's mine, in Monroe, Conn.; in Trumbull; at East Haddam; at Haverhill, N. H.; Galena, Ill., in stalactites. In Canada in Neebing.

Marcasite is employed in the manufacture of sulphur, sulphuric acid, and iron sulphate, though less frequently than pyrite.

ARSENOPYRITE, or MISPICKEL. Arsenical Pyrites. Arsenikkies, *Germ.*

Orthorhombic. $I \wedge I = 111° 53'$, $O \wedge 1\text{-}\check{\imath} = 119° 37'$; $\check{c} : \bar{b} : \check{a} = 1·7588 :$ 1·4793 : 1. $O \wedge 1 = 115° 12'$, $O \wedge 1\text{-}\check{\imath} = 130° 4'$. Cleavage: I rather distinct; O, faint traces. Twins: twinning-plane I, and 1-$\check{\imath}$. Also columnar, straight and divergent; granular, or compact.

H.=5·5-6. G.=6·0-6·4; 6·269, Franconia, Kenngott. Lustre metallic.

Color silver-white, inclining to steel-gray. Streak dark grayish-black. Fracture uneven. Brittle.

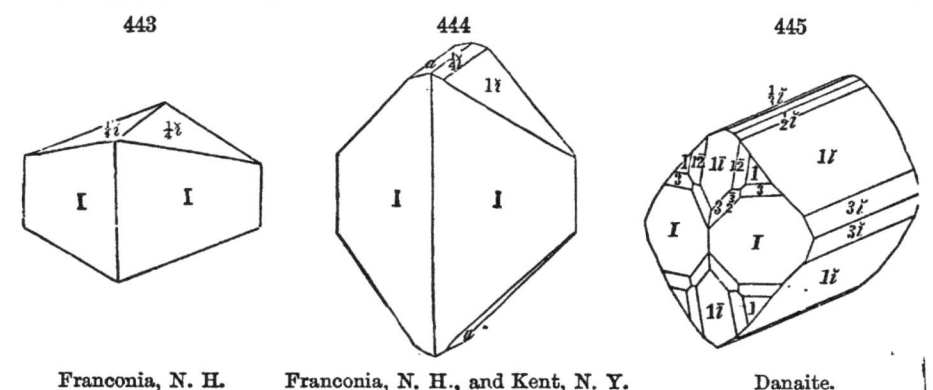

Franconia, N. H.   Franconia, N. H., and Kent, N. Y.   Danaite.

Comp., Var.—FeAsS=FeS$_2$+FeAs$_2$=Arsenic 46·0, sulphur 19·6, iron 34·4=100. Part of the iron sometimes replaced by cobalt; a little nickel, bismuth, or silver are also occasionally present. The cobaltic variety, called *danaite* (after J. Freeman Dana), contains 4-10 p. c. of cobalt.

Pyr., etc.—In the closed tube at first gives a red sublimate of arsenic sulphide, then a black lustrous sublimate of metallic arsenic. In the open tube gives sulphurous fumes and a white sublimate of arsenous oxide. B.B. on charcoal gives the odor of arsenic. The varieties containing cobalt give a blue color with borax-glass when fused in O.F. with successive portions of flux until all the iron is oxidized. Gives fire with steel, emitting an alliaceous odor. Decomposed by nitric acid with separation of arsenous oxide and sulphur.

Diff.—Distinguished by its form from smaltite. Leucopyrite (löllingite) do not give decided sulphur reactions.

Obs.—Found principally in crystalline rocks, and its usual mineral associates are ores of silver, lead, and tin; pyrite, chalcopyrite, and spalerite. Occurs also in serpentine.

Abundant at Freiberg; at Reichenstein in Silesia; at Schladming; Andreasberg; Joachimsthal; at Tunaberg in Sweden; at Skutterud in Norway; in Cornwall; in Devonshire at the Tamar mines.

In *New Hampshire*, in gneiss, at Franconia (*danaite*); also at Jackson and at Haverhill. In *Maine*, at Blue Hill, Corinna, etc. In *Vermont*, at Brookfield, Waterbury, and Stockbridge. In *Mass.*, at Worcester and Sterling. In *Conn.*, at Monroe, at Mine Hill, Roxbury. In *New Jersey*, at Franklin. In *N. York*, massive, in Lewis, Essex Co., near Edenville, and elsewhere in Orange Co.; in Carmel; in Kent, Putnam Co. In *California*, Nevada Co., Grass valley. In S. America, in Bolivia; also, *niccoliferous* var., between La Pas and Yungas in Bolivia (anal. by Kræber).

LÖLLINGITE is FeAs$_2$ (=Arsenic 72·8, iron 27·2), and LEUCOPYRITE is Fe$_2$As$_3$ (=Arsenic 66·8, iron 33·2). They are both like arsenopyrite in form. Found, the former at Lölling; Schladming; Sätersberg, near Fossum, Norway; the latter at Reichenstein; Geyer (geyerite) near Hüttenberg, Carinthia.

GLAUCODOT (Co,Fe)S$_2$+(Co,Fe)As$_2$, with Co : Fe=2 : 1=Sulphur 19·4, arsenic 45·5, cobalt 23·8, iron 11·3=100. Form like arsenopyrite. Huasco, Chili; Hakansbö, Sweden.

ALLOCLASITE R$_4$(As,Bi)$_7$S$_6$, with R=Bi,Co,Ni,Fe,Zn. Orawicza, Hungary.

SYLVANITE. Graphic Tellurium. Schrifterz, Schrift-Tellur, *Germ.*

Monoclinic. $C = 55° 21\frac{1}{2}'$, $I \wedge I = 94° 26'$, $O \wedge 1\text{-}\check{\imath} = 121° 21'$; $\dot{c} : b : \dot{a} = 1·7732 : 0·889 : 1$, Kokscharof. Cleavage: $i\text{-}\check{\imath}$ distinct. Also massive; imperfectly columnar to granular.

H.=1·5-2. G.=7·99-8·33. Lustre metallic. Streak and color pure steel-gray to silver-white, and sometimes nearly brass-yellow. Fracture uneven.

Comp., Var.—(Ag,Au)Te$_2$=(if Ag : Au=1 : 1) Tellurium 55·8, gold 28·5, silver 15·7=100. Antimony sometimes replaces part of the tellurium, and lead part of the other metals.

Pyr., etc.—In the open tube gives a white sublimate which near the assay is gray; when treated with the blowpipe flame the sublimate fuses to clear transparent drops. B.B. on charcoal fuses to a dark gray globule, covering the coal with a white coating, which treated in R.F. disappears, giving a bluish-green color to the flame; after long blowing a yellow malleable metallic globule is obtained. Most varieties give a faint coating of the oxides of lead and antimony on charcoal.

Obs.—Occurs at Offenbanya and Nagyag in Transylvania. In California, Calaveras Co., at the Melones and Stanislaus mines; Red Cloud mine, Colorado.

Named from Transylvania, the country in which it occurs, and in allusion to *sylvanium*, one of the names at first proposed for the metal tellurium. Called *graphic* because of a resemblance in the arrangement of the crystals to writing characters.

Schrauf has stated that, according to his measurements, sylvanite is *orthorhombic*.

CALAVERITE (*Genth.*) has the composition $AuTe_4$ = Tellurium 55·5, gold 44·5 = 100. Massive. Color bronze-yellow. Stanislaus mine, Cal.; Red Cloud mine, Colorado.

NAGYAGITE.* Blättererz, Blättertellur, *Germ.*

Tetragonal. $O \wedge 1\text{-}i = 127° 37'$; $\check{c} = 1·298$. $O \wedge 1 = 118° 37'$. Cleavage: basal. Also granularly massive, particles of various sizes; generally foliated. $H. = 1\text{-}1·5$. $G. = 6·85\text{-}7·2$. Lustre metallic, splendent. Streak and color blackish lead-gray. Opaque. Sectile. Flexible in thin laminæ.

446

Comp.—Uncertain, perhaps $R(S,Te)_2$, with $R = Pb, Au$ (Ramm.). Analysis, Schönlein, Te 30·52, S 8·07, Pb 50·78, Au 9·11, Ag 0·53, Cu 0·99 = 100.

Pyr., etc.—In the open tube gives, near the assay, a grayish sublimate of antimonate and tellurate, with perhaps some sulphate of lead; farther up the tube the sublimate consists of antimonous oxide, which volatilizes when treated with the flame, and tellurous oxide, which at a high temperature fuses into colorless drops. B.B. on charcoal forms two coatings: one white and volatile, consisting of a mixture of antimonite, tellurite, and sulphate of lead; and the other yellow, less volatile, of oxide of lead quite near the assay. If the mineral is treated for some time in O.F. a malleable globule of gold remains; this cupelled with a little assay lead assumes a pure gold color. Decomposed by nitro-hydrochloric acid.

Obs.—At Nagyag and Offenbanya in Transylvania, in foliated masses and crystalline plates.

COVELLITE (Kupferindig, *Germ.*).—Composition CuS = Sulphur 33·5, copper 66·5 = 100. Hexagonal. Commonly massive. Color indigo-blue. Mansfeld, etc.; Vesuvius, on lava; Chili.

MELONITE (*Genth.*).—A nickel telluride, formula probably Ni_2Te_3 = tellurium 76·5, nickel 23·5 = 100. Hexagonal. Cleavage basal eminent. Color reddish-white. Streak dark-gray. Occurs mixed with other tellurium minerals at the Stanislaus mine, Cal.

---

3. TERNARY COMPOUNDS. SULPHARSENITES, SULPHANTIMONITES, SULPHOBISMUTHITES.*

(*a*) GROUP I. Formula $R(As,Sb)_2S_4 = RS + (As,Sb)_2S_3$.

MIARGYRITE.

Monoclinic. $C = 48° 14'$; $I \wedge I = 106° 31'$, $O \wedge 1\text{-}\bar{i} = 136° 8'$; $\check{c} : \bar{b} : \bar{a} = 1·2883 : 0·9991 : 1$, Naumann. Crystals thick tabular, or stout, or short prismatic, pyramidal. Lateral planes deeply striated.. Cleavage: $\frac{1}{2}\text{-}i$, $1\text{-}i$ imperfect.

---

* The species of this group contain as bases chiefly copper, lead, and silver. They can be most readily distinguished by their behavior before the blowpipe. Attention may be called to the group of lead sulphantimonites, *zinkenite, plagionite,* (*jamesonite*) *boulangerite, meneghinite, geocronite,* for which the pyrognostics are nearly similar, and which are most surely distinguished by their specific gravity.

H.$=2$-$2\cdot 5$. G.$=5\cdot 2$-$5\cdot 4$. Lustre submetallic-adamantine. Color iron black. Streak dark cherry-red. Opaque, except in thin splinters, which, by transmitted light, are deep blood-red. Fracture subconchoidal.

Comp.—$AgSbS_2$ (or $Ag_2S + Sb_2S_3$) = Sulphur 21·8, antimony 41·5, silver 36·7 = 100.

Pyr., etc.—In the closed tube decrepitates, fuses easily, and gives a sublimate of antimony sulphide; in the open tube sulphurous and antimonous fumes, the latter as a white sublimate. B.B. on charcoal fuses quietly, with emission of sulphur and antimony fumes, to a gray bead, which after continued treatment in O.F. leaves a bright globule of silver. If the silver globule be treated with phosphorus salt in O.F., the green glass thus obtained shows traces of copper when fused with tin in R.F.

Decomposed by nitric acid, with separation of sulphur and antimonous oxide.

Obs.—At Braünsdorf, near Freiberg in Saxony; Felsobanya (*kenngottite*); Przibram in Bohemia; Clausthal (*hypargyrite*); Guadalajara in Spain; at Parenos, and the mine Sta. M. de Catorce, near Potosi; also at Molinares, Mexico.

SARTORITE. SCLEROCLASE.

Orthorhombic. $I \wedge I = 123°\ 21'$, $O \wedge 1\text{-}\bar{i} = 131°\ 3'$; $\dot{c} : \bar{b} : \breve{a} = 1\cdot 1483 : 1\cdot 8553 : 1$. Crystals slender. Cleavage: O quite distinct.

447

H.$=3$. G.$=5\cdot 393$. Lustre metallic. Color dark lead-gray. Streak reddish-brown. Opaque. Brittle.

Comp.—$PbAs_2S_4 (PbS + As_2S_3) =$ Sulphur 26·4, arsenic 30·9, lead 42·7 = 100.

Pyr., etc.—Nearly the same as for dufrenoysite (q. v.), but differing in strong decrepitation.

Obs.—From the Binnen valley with dufrenoysite and binnite. As the name Scleroclase is inapplicable, and the mineral was first announced by Sartorius v. Waltershausen, the species may be appropriately called *Sartorite*. It is the *binnite* of Heusser.

ZINKENITE.

Orthorhombic. $I \wedge I = 120°\ 39'$, Rose. Usual in twins, as hexagonal prisms, with a low hexagonal pyramid at summit. Lateral faces longitudinally striated. Sometimes columnar, fibrous, or massive. Cleavage not distinct.

H.$=3$-$3\cdot 5$. G.$=5\cdot 30$-$5\cdot 35$. Lustre metallic. Color and streak steel-gray. Opaque. Fracture slightly uneven.

Comp.—$PbSb_2S_4$ (or $PbS + Sb_2S_3$) = Sulphur 22·1, antimony 42·2, lead 35·7 = 100.

Pyr., etc.—Decrepitates and fuses very easily; in the closed tube gives a faint sublimate of sulphur and antimonous sulphide; in the open tube sulphurous fumes and a white sublimate of oxide of antimony. B.B. on charcoal is almost entirely volatilized, giving a coating which on the outer edge is white, and near the assay dark-yellow; with soda in R.F. yields globules of lead.

Soluble in hot hydrochloric acid with evolution of sulphuretted hydrogen and separation of lead chloride on cooling.

Resembles stibnite and bournonite, but may be distinguished by its superior hardness and specific gravity.

Obs.—Occurs at Wolfsberg in the Harz.

CHALCOSTIBITE (Kupferantimonglanz, *Germ.*).—Composition $CuSbS_2$ (or $Cu_2S + Sb_2S_3$) = Sulphur 25·7, antimony 48·9, copper 25·4. Color lead-gray to iron-gray. Wolfsberg in the Harz.

EMPLECTITE (Kupferwismuthglanz, *Germ.*).—Composition $CuBiS_2$ (or $Cu_2S + Bi_2S_3$) = Sulphur 19·1, bismuth 62·0, copper 18·9 = 100. Color grayish to tin-white. Schwarzenberg, Saxony; Copiapo, Chili.

SULPHARSENITES, SULPHANTIMONITES, ETC.   251

BERTHIERITE.—Composition approximately $FeSb_2S_4$ (or $FeS+Sb_2S_3$)=Sulphur 30·0, antimony 57·0, iron 13·0=100. Color dark steel-gray. Auvergne; Bräunsdorf, Saxony; Cornwall, etc.; San Antonio, Cal.

(b) SUB-GROUP. Formula $R_3(As,Sb,Bi)_4S_9 = 3RS + 2(As,Sb,Bi)_2S_3$.

PLAGIONITE.—Composition (Rose) $Pb_4Sb_6S_{13}$ (or $4PbS+3Sb_2S_3$)=Sulphur 21·1, antimony 37·0, lead 41·9. Monoclinic. G.=5·4. Found at Wolfsberg in the Harz.
JORDANITE (v. Rath).—Composition $Pb_3As_4S_9$ (or $3PbS+2As_2S_3$)=Sulphur 23·8, arsenic 24·8, lead 51·4. Orthorhombic. Resembles sartorite, but distinguished by its black streak, its six-sided twins, and by not decrepitating B.B. Binnenthal, Switzerland.
BINNITE.—Composition probably $Cu_6As_4S_9$ (or $3Cu_2S+2As_2S_3$)=Sulphur 29·7, arsenic 31·0, copper 39·3=100. Isometric. Streak cherry-red. Binnenthal in dolomite (*dufrenoysite* of v. Waltershausen).
KLAPROTHOLITE (*Petersen*).—Composition $Cu_6Bi_4Sb_9$ (or $3Cu_2S+2Bi_2S_3$). Orthorhombic. Cleavage *i-i* distinct. Color steel-gray. G.=4·6. Wittichen, Baden.
SCHIRMERITE (*Genth*).—Composition $R_3Bi_4S_9$ (or $3RS+2Bi_2S_3$), with $R=Ag_2 : Pb=2 : 1$. This requires sulphur 16·4, bismuth 47·3, silver 24·5, lead 11·8=100. Massive, disseminated in quartz. Color lead-gray. Red Cloud mine, Colorado.

(c) GROUP II. Formula $R_2(Sb,As)_2S_5 = 2RS + (Sb,As)_2S_3$.

JAMESONITE. Federerz, *Germ.*

Orthorhombic. $I \wedge I = 101° 20'$ and $78° 40'$. Cleavage basal, highly perfect; I and $i\text{-}i$ less perfect. Usually in acicular crystals. Also fibrous massive, parallel or divergent; also in capillary forms; also amorphous massive.
H.=2–3. G.=5·5–5·8. Color steel-gray to dark lead-gray. Streak gray.

Comp.—$Pb_2Sb_2S_5$ (or $2PbS+Sb_2S_3$); more strictly $2PbS=2$ (or Pb,Fe)S. If Fe : Pb=1 : 4, Sulphur 21·1, antimony 32·2, lead 43·7, iron 3·0=100. Small quantities of zinc, bismuth, silver, and copper are also sometimes present.
Pyr.—Same as for zinkenite.
Diff.—Distinguished from other related species by its perfect basal cleavage.
Obs.—*Jamesonite* occurs principally in Cornwall, in Siberia, Hungary, at Valentia, d'Alcantara in Spain, and Brazil.
The *feather ore* occurs at Wölfsberg in the Eastern Harz; also at Andreasberg and Clausthal; at Freiberg and Schemnitz; at Pfaffenberg and Meiseberg; in Tuscany, near Bottino; at Chonta in Peru.

DUFRENOYSITE.

Orthorhombic. $I \wedge I = 93° 39'$, $O \wedge 1\text{-}i = 121° 30'$, $\dot{c} : \bar{b} : \check{a} = 1·6318 : 1·0658 : 1$. Usual in thick rectangular tables. Cleavage: O perfect. Also massive.
H.=3. G.=5·549–5·569. Lustre metallic. Color blackish lead-gray. Streak reddish-brown. Opaque. Brittle.

448

Comp.—$Pb_2As_2S_5$ (or $2PbS+2As_2S_3$)=Sulphur 22·10, arsenic 20·72, lead 57·18=100.
Pyr., etc.—Easily fuses and gives a sublimate of sulphur and arsenous sulphide; in the open tube a smell of sulphur only, with a sublimate of sulphur in upper part of tube, and

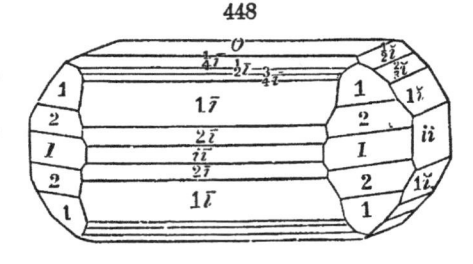

of arsenous oxide below. On charcoal decrepitates, melts, yields fumes of arsenic and a globule of lead, which on cupellation yields silver.

Obs.—From the Binnenthal in the Alps, in crystalline dolomite, along with sartorite, jordanite, binnite, etc.

Damour, who first studied the arsenio-sulphides of the Binnenthal, analyzed the massive ore and named it *dufrenoysite*. He inferred that the crystallization was isometric from some associated crystals, and so published it. This led von Waltershausen and Heusser to call the isometric mineral dufrenoysite, and the latter to name the orthorhombic species *binnite*. Von Waltershausen, after studying the prismatic mineral, made out of the species *arsenomelan* and *scleroclase*, yet partly on hypothetical grounds. Recently it has been found that three orthorhombic minerals exist at the locality, as announced by vom Rath, who identifies one, by specific gravity and composition, with Damour's *dufrenoysite;* another he makes *scleroclase* of von Waltershausen (sartorite, p. 250); and the other he names *jordanite* (p. 251). The isometric mineral was called *binnite* by DesCloizeaux.

FREIESLEBENITE. Schilfglaserz, *Germ.*

Monoclinic. $C = 87° 46', I \wedge I = 119° 12', O \wedge 1\text{-}i = 137° 10'$ (B. & M.); $\dot{c} : \bar{b} : \dot{a} = 1.5802 : 1.7032 : 1.$ $O \wedge 1\text{-}i = 123° 55'.$

449

Prisms longitudinally striated. Cleavage: I perfect. H.=2–2.5. G.=6–6.4. Lustre metallic. Color and streak light steel-gray, inclining to silver-white, also blackish lead-gray. Yields easily to the knife, and is rather brittle. Fracture subconchoidal—uneven.

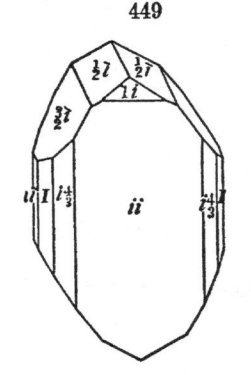

Comp.—$Pb_2Ag_2Sb_2S_6$. Ramm. (or $7RS+3Sb_2S_3$, with $7RS=4PbS+3Ag_2S$)=Sulphur 18.8, antimony 26.9, lead 30.5, silver 23.8=100.

Pyr.—In the open tube gives sulphurous and antimonial fumes, the latter condensing as a white sublimate. B.B. on charcoal fuses easily, giving a coating on the outer edge white, from antimonous oxide, and near the assay yellow, from oxide of lead; continued blowing leaves a globule of silver.

Obs.—Occurs at Freiberg in Saxony and Kapnik in Transylvania; at Ratieborzitz; at Przibram; at Felsöbanya; at Hiendelencina in Spain. According to v. Zepharovich, the mineral from Przibram and Bräunsdorf, and part of that from Freiberg, while identical in composition with freieslebenite, has an *orthorhombic* form. It is called by him DIAPHORITE.

BRONGNIARDITE.—Composition $Ag_2PbSb_2S_5$ (or $PbS+Ag_2S+Sb_2S_3$)=Sulphur 19.4, antimony 29.5, silver 26.1, lead 25.0=100. Isometric; in octahedrons, also massive. Color grayish-black. Mexico.

COSALITE (*Genth*).—Composition $Pb_2Bi_2S_5$ (or $2PbS+Bi_2S_3$)=Sulphur 16.1, bismuth 42.2, lead 41.7=100. Color lead-gray. Soft and brittle. Cosala, Sinaloa, Mexico. Identical (Frenzel) with Hermann's *retzbanyite*.

PYROSTILPNITE (Feuerblende, *Germ.*).—In delicate crystals; color hyacinth-red. Contains 62.3 p. c. silver, also sulphur and antimony. Freiberg; Andreasberg; Przibram.

RITTINGERITE.—In minute tabular crystals. Color black. Streak orange-yellow. Contains sulphur, antimony, and silver. Joachimsthal.

(*d*) GROUP III. Formula $R_3(As,Sb)_2S_6 = 3RS + (As,Sb)_2S_3$.

PYRARGYRITE. Ruby Silver. Dark Red Silver Ore. Dunkles Rothgültigerz, *Germ.*

Rhombohedral. Opposite extremities of crystals often unlike. $R \wedge R = 108° 42'$ (B. & M.); $O \wedge R = 137° 42'$; $\dot{c} = 0.788$. $O \wedge 1^3 = 112° 33'$, $O \wedge 1^7 = 100° 14'$, $R \wedge \tfrac{1}{2} = 144° 21'$. Cleavage: R rather imperfect.

Twins: composition-face $-\frac{1}{2}$; O or basal plane, as in f. 290, p. 95; also R and I. Also massive, structure granular, sometimes impalpable.

$H.=2-2\cdot5$. $G.=5\cdot7-5\cdot9$. Lustre metallic-adamantine. Color black, sometimes approaching cochineal-red. Streak cochineal-red. Translucent—opaque. Fracture conchoidal.

Comp. — Ag_3SbS_3 (or $3Ag_2S+Sb_2S_3$)=Sulphur 17·7, antimony 22·5, silver 59·8=100.

Pyr., etc.—In the closed tube fuses and gives a reddish sublimate of antimonous sulphide; in the open tube sulphurous fumes and a white sublimate of antimonous oxide. B.B. on charcoal fuses with spirting to a globule, gives off antimonous sulphide, coats the coal white, and the assay is converted into silver sulphide, which, treated in O.F., or with soda in R.F., gives a globule of fine silver. In case arsenic is present it may be detected by fusing the pulverized mineral with soda on charcoal in R.F.

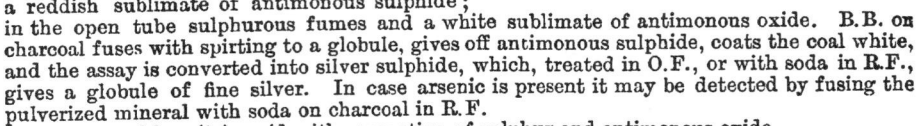

Decomposed by nitric acid with separation of sulphur and antimonous oxide.

Obs.—Occurs principally with calcite, native arsenic and galenite, at Andreasberg; also in Saxony, Hungary, Norway, at Gaudalcanal in Spain, and in Cornwall. In Mexico abundant. In Chili; in Nevada, at Washoe in Daney Mine; abundant about Austin, Reese river; at Poor Man lode, Idaho.

PROUSTITE. Light Red Silver Ore. Lichtes Rothgültigerz, *Germ.*

Rhombohedral. $R \wedge R = 107°\ 48'$, $O \wedge R = 137°\ 9'$; $\check{c} = 0\cdot78506$. Also granular massive.

$H.=2-2\cdot5$. $G.=5\cdot422-5\cdot56$. Lustre adamantine. Color cochineal-red. Streak cochineal-red, sometimes inclined to aurora-red. Subtransparent—subtranslucent. Fracture conchoidal—uneven.

Comp.—Ag_3AsS_3 (or $3Ag_2S+As_2S_3$)=Sulphur 19·4, arsenic 15·1, silver 65·5=100.

Pyr., etc.—In the closed tube fuses easily, and gives a faint sublimate of arsenous sulphide; in the open tube sulphurous fumes and a white crystalline sublimate of arsenous oxide. B.B. on charcoal fuses and emits odors of sulphur and arsenic; by prolonged heating in O.F., or with soda in R.F., gives a globule of pure silver. Some varieties contain antimony.

Decomposed by nitric acid, with separation of sulphur and arsenous oxide.

Obs.—Occurs at Freiberg and elsewhere in Saxony; at Joachimsthal; Wolfach in Baden; Chalanches in Dauphiné; Guadalcanal in Spain; in Mexico: Peru; Chili, at Chanarcillo, in magnificent crystals. In Nevada, in the Daney mine, and in Comstock lode, but rare; in veins about Austin, Lander Co.; in microscopic crystals in Cabarrus Co., N. C., at the McMakin mine; in Idaho, at the Poor Man lode.

BOURNONITE. Rädelerz, *Germ.*(=Wheel Ore).

Orthorhombic. $I \wedge I = 93°\ 40'$, $O \wedge 1\text{-}\bar{i} = 136°\ 17'$ (Miller); $\check{c}\ \bar{b}: \check{a} = 0\cdot95618 : 1\cdot0662 : 1$. $O \wedge 1\text{-}\bar{\imath} = 133°\ 26'$, $O \wedge 1 = 127°\ 20'$, $O \wedge 1\text{-}\check{\imath} = 138°\ 6'$. Cleavage: $i\text{-}\bar{\imath}$ imperfect; $i\text{-}\check{\imath}$ and O less distinct. Twins: twinning-plane face I; crystals often cruciform (f. 453), crossing at angles of $93°\ 40'$ and $86°\ 20'$; hence, also, cog-wheel shaped. Also massive; granular, compact.

H.=2·5–3. G.=5·7–5·9. Lustre metallic. Color and streak steel-gray, inclining to blackish lead-gray or iron-black. Opaque. Fracture conchoidal or uneven. Brittle.

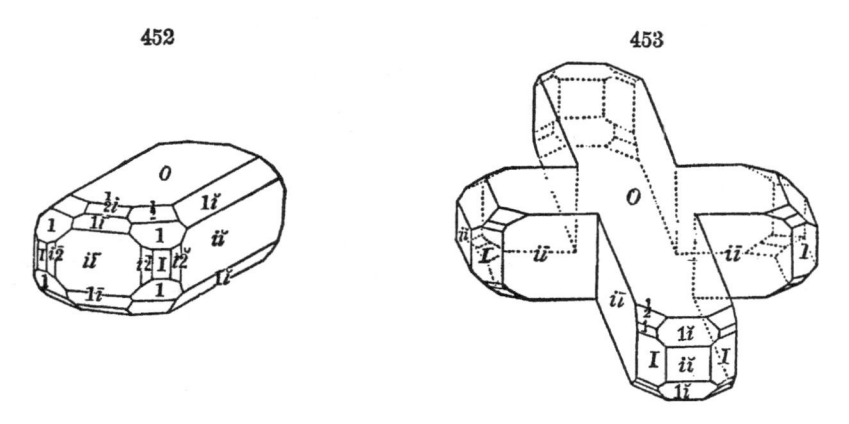

452

453

Comp., Var.—CuPbSbS$_3$ Ramm. (or 3RS+Sb$_2$S$_3$, with 3RS=2PbS+Cu$_2$S)=Sulphur 19·6, antimony 25·0, lead 42·4, copper 13·0=100.

Pyr., etc.—In the closed tube decrepitates, and gives a dark-red sublimate. In the open tube gives sulphurous oxide, and a white sublimate of antimonous oxide. B.B. on charcoal fuses easily, and at first coats the coal white, from antimonous oxide; continued blowing gives a yellow coating of lead oxide; the residue, treated with soda in R.F., gives a globule of copper.

Decomposed by nitric acid, affording a blue solution, and leaving a residue of sulphur, and a white powder containing antimony and lead.

Obs.—Occurs in the Harz; at Kapnik in Transylvania; at Servoz in Piedmont; Bräunsdorf and Gersdorf in Saxony, Olsa in Corinthia, etc.; in Cornwall; in Mexico; at Huasco-Alto in Chili; at Machacamarca in Bolivia; in Peru.

STYLOTYPITE.—An iron-silver-copper bournonite; Copiapo, Chili.

BOULANGERITE.

In plumose masses, exhibiting in the fracture a crystalline structure; also granular and compact.

H.=2·5–3. G.=5.75–6·0. Lustre metallic. Color bluish lead-gray; often covered with yellow spots from oxidation.

Comp.—Pb$_3$Sb$_2$S$_6$ (or 3PbS+Sb$_2$S$_3$)=Sulphur 18·2, antimony 23·1, lead 58·7=100.

Pyr.—Same as for zinkenite.

Obs.—Quite abundant at Molières, department of Gard, in France; also found at Nasafjeld in Lapland; at Nertschinsk; Ober-Lahr in Sayn-Altenkirchen; Wolfsberg in the Harz; near Bottino in Tuscany.

EPIBOULANGERITE.—Probably a decomposition product of boulangerite (Websky); it contains more sulphur and less antimony. Altenberg, Silesia.

WITTICHENITE.—Composition Cu$_3$BiS$_3$ (or 3CuS+Bi$_2$S$_3$)=Sulphur 19·4, bismuth 42.1, copper 38·5=100. Color steel-gray. Wittichen, Baden.

KOBELLITE.—Pb$_2$BiSbS$_6$ (or 3PbS+(Bi,Sb)$_2$S$_3$) Ramm.=Sulphur 16·8, antimony 10·7, bismuth 18·2, lead 54·3=100. Color lead-gray to steel-gray. Hvena, Sweden.

AIKINITE (Nadelerz, Germ.).—CuPbBiS$_3$ (or Cu$_2$S+2PbS+Bi$_2$S$_3$)=Sulphur 167, bismuth 36·2, lead 36·0, copper 11·1=100. In acicular crystals, also massive. Color blackish lead-gray. Beresof, Urals; Gold Hill, North Carolina.

SULPHARSENITES, SULPHANTIMONITES, ETC.   255

(e) GROUP IV. Formula $R_4(As,Sb,Bi)_2S_7 = 4RS + (As,Sb,Bi)_2S_3$.

TETRAHEDRITE.* Gray Copper Ore. Fahlerz; Antimon- and Quecksilberfahlerz, *Germ.*

Isometric; tetrahedral. Twins: twinning-plane octahedral, producing, when the composition is repeated, the form in f. 456. Also massive; granular, coarse, or fine; compact or crypto-crystalline.

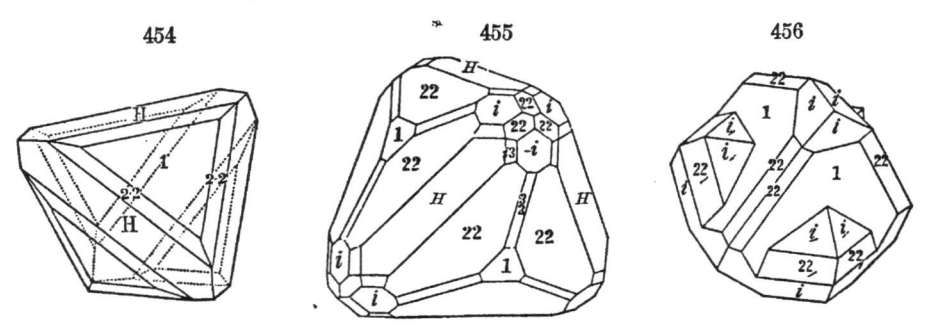

454   455   456

$H. = 3-4 \cdot 5.$ $G. = 4 \cdot 5 - 5 \cdot 56.$ Lustre metallic. Color between light flint-gray and iron-black. Streak generally same as the color; sometimes inclined to brown and cherry-red. Opaque; sometimes subtranslucent in very thin splinters, transmitted color cherry-red. Fracture subconchoidal —uneven. Rather brittle.

Comp., Var.—$Cu_8Sb_2S_7$ (or $4Cu_2S + Sb_2S_3$), with part of the copper (Cu_2) often replaced by iron (Fe), zinc (Zn), silver (Ag_2), or quicksilver (Hg), and rarely cobalt (Co), and part of the antimony by arsenic, and rarely bismuth. Ratio $Ag_2 + Cu_2 : Zn + Fe$ generally $= 2 : 1$. There are thus:
A. An antimonial series; B. An arsenio-antimonial series; C. A bismuthic arsenio-antimonial; besides an *arsenical*, in which arsenic replaces all the antimony, and which is made into a distinct species named *tennantite*.
  Var. 1. *Ordinary.* Containing little or no silver. Color steel-gray to dark-gray.
    2. *Argentiferous; Freibergite.* Light steel-gray, sometimes iron-black.
    3. *Mercuriferous; Schwatzite.* Color gray to iron-black.
The following analyses will serve as examples of these varieties:

	S	Sb	As	Cu	Fe	Zn	Ag	
(1) Müsen	25·46	19·15	4·93	39·88	3·43	3·50	0·60	Ni Co 1·64 = 98·59 Rammelsberg.
(2) Meiseberg	24·80	25·56	—	30·47	3·52	3·39	10·48	Pb 0·78 = 100·00 "
(3) Kotterbach	22·53	19·34	2·94	35·34	0·87	0·69	—	Hg 17·27, Pb 0·21 Bi 0·81 = 100
								v. Rath.

Pyr., etc.—Differ in the different varieties. In the closed tube all fuse and give a dark-red sublimate of antimonous sulphide; when containing mercury, a faint dark-gray sublimate appears at a low red heat; and if much arsenic, a sublimate of arsenous sulphide first forms. In the open tube fuses, gives sulphurous fumes and a white sublimate of antimony; if arsenic is present a crystalline volatile sublimate condenses with the antimony; if the ore contains mercury it condenses in the tube in minute metallic globules. B.B. on charcoal fuses, gives a coating of antimonous oxide and sometimes arsenous acid, zinc oxide, and lead oxide; the arsenic may be detected by the odor when the coating is treated in R.F.; the zinc oxide assumes a green color when heated with cobalt solution. The roasted mineral gives with the fluxes reactions for iron and copper; with soda yields a globule of metallic copper. To determine the presence of a trace of arsenic by the odor, it is best to fuse the mineral on charcoal with soda. The presence of mercury is best ascertained by fusing the pulverized ore in a closed tube with about three times its weight of dry soda, the metal subliming and condensing in minute globules. The silver is determined by cupellation.

Decomposed by nitric acid, with separation of sulphur, and antimonous and arsenous oxides.

Obs.—The Cornish mines, near St. Aust. ; at Andreasberg and Clausthal in the Harz; Kremnitz in Hungary; Freiberg in Saxony ; Przibram in Bohemia ; Kahl in Spessart; Kapnik in Transylvania ; Dillenburg in Nassau ; and other localities. The ore containing mercury occurs in Schmölnitz, Hungary ; at Schwatz in the Tyrol ; and in the valleys of Angina and Costello in Tuscany.

Found in Mexico, at Durango, etc. ; at various mines in Chili ; in Bolivia ; at the Kellogg mines, Arkansas ; at Newburyport, Mass. In California in Mariposa Co. ; in Shasta Co. In Nevada, abundant at the Sheba and De Soto mines, Humboldt Co. ; near Austin in Lander Co. ; in Arizona at the Heintzelman mine, containing 1½ p. c. of silver ; at the Sana Rita mine.

RIONITE (*Brauns*).—A bismuth tetrahedrite from Cremenz. Einfischthal, Switzerland.

MALINOWSKITE.—A tetrahedrite containing 9–13 p. c. lead, and 10–13 p. c. silver. District of Rocuay, Peru. (5th Append. Min. Chili.)

TENNANTITE.* Graukupfererz, *Germ.*

Isometric; holohedral, Phillips. Cleavage: dodecahedral imperfect. Twins as in tetrahedrite. Massive forms unknown.

H.$=3{\cdot}5{-}4$. G.$=4{\cdot}37{-}4{\cdot}53$. Lustre metallic. Color blackish lead-gray to iron-black. Streak dark reddish-gray. Fracture uneven.

Comp.—$Cu_8As_2S_7$ (or $4Cu_2S+As_2S_3$), with Cu_2 replaced in part by Fe, Ag_2, etc., as in tetrahedrite, with which it agrees in crystalline form.

Pyr.—In the closed tube gives a sublimate of arsenous sulphide. In the open tube gives sulphurous fumes, and a sublimate of arsenous oxide. B.B. on charcoal fuses with intumescence and emission of arsenic and sulphur fumes to a dark-gray magnetic globule. The roasted mineral gives reactions for copper and iron with the fluxes; with soda on charcoal gives metallic copper with iron.

Obs.—Found in the Cornish mines. Also at Skutterud in Norway, and in Algeria.

JULIANITE (Websky) is near tennantite. G.$=5{\cdot}12$. Rudelstadt, Silesia.

MENEGHINITE has the composition $Pb_4Sb_2S_7(4PbS+Sb_2S_3)=$ Sulphur 17·3, antimony 16·8, lead 63·9$=100$. Resembles boulangerite. Bottino, Tuscany ; Schwarzenberg, Saxony.

(*f*) GROUP V. Formula $R_5(As,Sb)_2S_8=5RS+(As,Sb)_2S_3$.

STEPHANITE. Sprödglaserz, *Germ.*

Orthorhombic. $I \wedge I = 115° 39'$, $O \wedge 1\text{-}\bar{\imath} = 132° 32\frac{1}{2}'$; $\dot{c} : \bar{b} : \check{a} = 1{\cdot}0897 : 1{\cdot}5844 : 1$. $O \wedge 1 = 127° 51'$, $O \wedge 1\text{-}\check{\imath} = 145° 34$. Cleavage: 2-$\check{\imath}$ and i-$\check{\imath}$ imperfect. Twins: twinning-plane I; forms like those of aragonite frequent. Also massive, compact, and disseminated.

H.$=2{-}2{\cdot}5$. G.$=6{\cdot}269$, Przibram. Lustre metallic. Color and streak iron-black. Fracture uneven.

Comp.—Ag_5SbS_4 (or $5Ag_2S+Sb_2S_3$)=Sulphur 16·2, antimony 15·3, silver 68·5$=100$.

Pyr.—In the closed tube decrepitates, fuses, and after long heating gives a faint sublimate of antimonous sulphide. In the open tube fuses, giving off antimonial fumes and sulphurous oxide. B.B. on charcoal fuses with projection of small particles, coats the coal with antimonous oxide, which after long blowing is colored red from oxidized silver, and a globule of metallic silver is obtained.

Soluble in dilute heated nitric acid, sulphur and oxide of antimony being deposited.

Obs.—At Freiberg and elsewhere in Saxony; at Przibram in Bohemia; in Hungary; at Andreasberg; at Zacatecas in Mexico; and in Peru. In Nevada, an abundant silver ore in the Comstock lode; at Ophir and Mexican mines in fine crystals; in the Reese river and Humboldt and other regions. In Idaho, at the silver mines.

GEOCRONITE.—Composition $Pb_5Sb_2S_8$ (or $5PbS+Sb_2S_3$)=Sulphur 16·7, antimony 15·9, lead 67·4=100 (also contains a little arsenic). Color light lead-gray. Sala, Sweden; Merido, Spain; Val di Castello, Tuscany.

POLYBASITE.

Orthorhombic, DesCl. $I \wedge I$ nearly 120°, $O \wedge 1 = 121° 30'$. Crystals usually short tabular prisms, with the bases triangularly striated parallel to alternate edges. Cleavage: basal imperfect. Also massive and disseminated.

H.=2–3. G.=6·214. Lustre metallic. Color iron-black; in thin crystals cherry-red by transmitted light. Streak iron-black. Opaque except when quite thin. Fracture uneven.

Comp.—Ag_9SbS_6 (or $9Ag_2S+Sb_2S_3$), if containing silver without copper or arsenic, Sulphur 14·8, antimony 9·7, silver 95·5=100. But with Ag_2 replaced in part by Cu_2 (ratio Ag : Cu = 1 : 4 to 1 : 11), and Sb replaced by As (ratio 1 : 1, etc.).

Pyr., etc.—In the open tube fuses, gives sulphurous and antimonial fumes, the latter forming a white sublimate, sometimes mixed with crystalline arsenous oxide. B.B. fuses with spirting to a globule, gives off sulphur (sometimes arsenic), and coats the coal with antimonous oxide; with long-continued blowing some varieties give a faint yellowish-white coating of zinc oxide, and a metallic globule, which with salt of phosphorus reacts for copper, and cupelled with lead gives pure silver.

Decomposed by nitric acid.

Obs.—Occurs in Mexico; at Tres Puntos, Chili; at Freiberg and Przibram. In Nevada, at the Reese mines; in Idaho, at the silver mines of the Owhyhee district.

POLYARGYRITE.—Isometric. Cleavage cubic. Malleable. Comp. $12Ag_2S+Sb_2S_3$. Wolfach, Baden.

ENARGITE.

Orthorhombic. $I \wedge I = 97° 53'$, $O \wedge 1\text{-}\bar{\imath} = 136° 37'$ (Dauber); $\check{a} : \bar{b} : \check{a} = 0.94510 : 1.1480 : 1$. $O \wedge 1\text{-}\check{\imath} = 140° 20'$, $O \wedge 1 = 128° 35'$. Cleavage: I perfect; $i\text{-}\bar{\imath}$, $i\text{-}\check{\imath}$ distinct; O indistinct. Also massive, granular or columnar.

H.=3. G.=4·43–4·45; 4·362, Kenngott. Lustre metallic. Color grayish to iron-black; streak grayish-black, powder having a metallic lustre. Brittle. Fracture uneven.

Comp.—Cu_3AsS_4=Sulphur 32·5, arsenic 19·1, copper 48·4=100, usually containing also a little antimony, and zinc, and sometimes silver.

Pyr.—In the closed tube decrepitates, and gives a sublimate of sulphur; at a higher temperature fuses, and gives a sublimate of arsenous sulphide. In the open tube, heated gently, the powdered mineral gives off sulphurous and arsenous oxides, the latter condensing to a sublimate containing some antimonous oxide. B.B. on charcoal fuses, and gives a faint coating of arsenous oxide, antimonous oxide, and zinc oxide; the roasted mineral with the fluxes gives a globule of metallic copper.

Soluble in nitro-hydrochloric acid.

Obs.—From Morococha, Cordilleras of Peru; Famatina Mts., Argentine Republic; from Chili; mines of Santa Anna, N. Granada; at Cosihuirachi in Mexico; Brewster's gold mine, Chesterfield district, S. Carolina; in Colorado; at Willis's Gulch, near Black Hawk; southern Utah; Morning Star mine, Cal.

FAMATINITE (*Stelzner*).—An antimonial enargite. Massive. Color reddish gray. Famatina Mts., Argentine Republic; Cerro de Pasca, Peru.

LUZONITE.—Similar to enargite in composition, but unlike in form, according to Weisbach. Mancayan Island, Luzon.

CLARITE (*Sandberger*).—Also similar to enargite in composition, but in form monoclinic, and having a perfect cleavage parallel to the clinopinacoid. Schapbach, Black Forest.

EPIGENITE.—Composition S 32·24, As 12·78, Cu 40·68, Fe 14·20=100. Orthorhombic. Color steel-gray. Neuglück mine, Wittichen.

III. COMPOUNDS OF CHLORINE, BROMINE, IODINE.

1. ANHYDROUS CHLORIDES, ETC.

HALITE. COMMON SALT. Kochsalz, Steinsalz, *Germ.*

Isometric. Usually in cubes; rarely in octahedrons; faces of crystals sometimes cavernous, as in f. 458. Cleavage: cubic, perfect. Massive and granular, rarely columnar. H.=2·5. G.=2·1–2·257. Lustre vitreous. Streak white. Color white, also sometimes yellowish, reddish, bluish, purplish; often colorless. Transparent—translucent. Fracture conchoidal. Rather brittle. Soluble; taste purely saline.

Comp.—NaCl=Chlorine 60·7, sodium 39·3=100. Commonly mixed with some calcium sulphate, calcium chloride, and magnesium chloride, and sometimes magnesium sulphate, which render it liable to deliquesce.

Pyr., etc.—In the closed tube fuses, often with decrepitation; when fused on the platinum loop colors the flame deep yellow.

Diff.—Distinguished by its taste, solubility, and perfect cubic cleavage.

Obs.—Common salt occurs in extensive but irregular beds in rocks of various ages, associated with gypsum, polyhalite, calcite, clay, and sandstone; also in solution, and forming salt springs.

The principal mines of Europe are at Wieliczka, in Poland; at Hall, in the Tyrol; Stassfurt, in Prussian Saxony; and along the range through Reichenthal in Bavaria, Hallein in Salzburg, Hallstadt, Ischl, and Ebensee, in upper Austria, and Aussee in Styria; in Transylvania; Wallachia, Galicia, and upper Silesia; Vic and Dieuze in France; Valley of Cardona and elsewhere in Spain, forming hills 300 to 400 feet high; Bex in Switzerland; and Northwich in Cheshire, England. It also occurs near Lake Oroomiah, the Caspian Lake, etc. In Algeria; in Abyssinia; in India in the province of Lahore, and in the valley of Cashmere; in China and Asiatic Russia; in South America, in Peru, and at Zipaquera and Nemocon.

In the United States, salt has been found forming beds with gypsum, in Virginia, Washington Co.; in the Salmon River Mts. of Oregon; in Louisiana. Brine springs are very numerous in the Middle and Western States. These springs are worked at Salina and Syracuse, N. Y.; in the Kanawha Valley, Va.; Muskingum, Ohio; Michigan, at Saginaw and elsewhere; and in Kentucky. Vast lakes of salt water exist in many parts of the world. Lake Timpanogos in the Rocky Mountains, 4,200 feet above the level of the sea, now called the Great Salt Lake, is 2,000 square miles in area. L. Gale found in this water 20·196 per cent. of sodium chloride in 1852; but the greater rainfall of the last few years has diminished the proportion of saline matter. The Dead and Caspian Seas are salt, and the waters of the former contain 20 to 26 parts of solid matter in 100 parts.

HUANTAJAYITE.—Composition 20NaCl+AgCl. Occurs in white cubes in the mine of San Simon, Cerro de Huantajaya, Peru.

SYLVITE.

Isometric. Cleavage cubic. Also compact.
H.=2. G.=1·9–2. White or colorless. Vitreous. Soluble; taste like that of common salt.

Comp.—KCl=Chlorine 47·65, potassium 52·35=100. But often containing impurities.
Pyr., etc.—B.B. in the platinum loop fuses, and gives a violet color to the outer flame. Added to a salt of phosphorus bead, which has been previously saturated with copper oxide, colors the O.F. deep azure-blue. Water completely dissolves it.
Obs.—Occurs at Vesuvius, about the fumaroles of the volcano. Also at Stassfurt; at Leopoldshall (*leopoldite*); at Kalusz, Galicia.

CERARGYRITE. Kerargyrite. Horn Silver. Silberhornerz, *Germ.*

Isometric. Cleavage none. Twins: twinning-plane octahedral. Usually massive and looking like wax; sometimes columnar, or bent columnar; often in crusts.
H.=1–1·5. G.=5·552. Lustre resinous, passing into adamantine. Color pearl-gray, grayish-green, whitish, rarely violet-blue, colorless sometimes when perfectly pure; brown or violet-brown on exposure. Streak shining. Transparent—feebly subtranslucent. Fracture somewhat conchoidal. Sectile.

Comp.—AgCl=Chlorine 24·7, silver 75·3=100.
Pyr., etc.—In the closed tube fuses without decomposition. B.B. on charcoal gives a globule of metallic silver. Added to a bead of salt of phosphorus, previously saturated with copper oxide, and heated in O.F., imparts an intense azure-blue to the flame. A fragment placed on a strip of zinc, and moistened with a drop of water, swells up, turns black, and finally is entirely reduced to metallic silver, which shows the metallic lustre on being pressed with the point of a knife. Insoluble in nitric acid, but soluble in ammonia.
Obs.—Occurs in veins of clay slate, accompanying other ores of silver, and usually only in the higher parts of these veins. It has also been observed with ochreous varieties of brown iron ore; also with several copper ores, with calcite, barite, etc.
The largest masses are brought from Peru, Chili, and Mexico. Also occurs in Nicaragua near Ocotal; in Honduras. It was formerly obtained in the Saxon mining districts of Johanngeorgenstadt and Freiberg, but is now rare. Found in the Altai; at Kongsberg in Norway; in Alsace; rarely in Cornwall, and at Huelgoet in Brittany. In Nevada, about Austin, Lander Co., abundant; at mines of Comstock lode. In Arizona, in the Willow Springs dist., veins of El Dorado cañon, and San Francisco dist. In Idaho, at the Poor Man lode.
Named from κέρας, *horn*, and ἄργυρος, *silver.*
CALOMEL (Quecksilberhornerz, *Germ.*).—Composition HgCl=Chlorine 15·1, mercury 84·9 =100. Color white, grayish, brown. Spain.
SAL AMMONIAC (Salmiak, *Germ.*).—Ammonium chloride, NH₄Cl=Ammonium 33·7, chlorine 66·3=100. Vesuvius, Etna, and many volcanoes.
NANTOKITE (Breithaupt).—Composition CuCl=Chlorine 35·9, copper 64·1=100. Cleavage cubic. Color white. Nantoko, Chili.
EMBOLITE.—Ag(Cl,Br); the ratio of Cl : Br varying from 3 : 1 to 1 : 3. Color grayish-green. At various mines in Chili; also Mexico; Honduras.
BROMYRITE, Bromargyrite (Bromsilber, *Germ.*).—Silver bromide, AgBr=Bromine 42·6, silver 57·4=100. Color when pure bright yellow, slightly greenish. Chili; Mexico.
IODYRITE, Iodargyrite (Iodsilber, *Germ.*).—Silver iodide, AgI=Iodine 54·0, silver 46·0= 100. Color yellow. Mexico; Chili; Spain; Cerro Colorado mine in Arizona.
TOCORNALITE (Domeyko).—Composition AgI+HgI. Amorphous. Color pale yellow. Chañarcillo, Chili.

CHLOROCALCITE (Scacchi).—From Vesuvius, contained 58·76 p. c. CaCl₂; with also KCl, NaCl, MgCl₂. CHLORALUMINITE, CHLORMAGNESITE, and CHLOROTHIONITE are also from Vesuvius.

COTUNNITE.—Lead chloride, $PbCl_2$ = Chlorine 25·5, lead 74·5=100. Soft. White. Vesuvius. PSEUDOCOTUNNITE (Scacchi), Vesuvius.

MOLYSITE.—Composition $FeCl_6$ = Chlorine 65·5, iron 34·5=100. Vesuvius.

2. HYDROUS CHLORIDES.

CARNALLITE.

Massive, granular; flat planes developed by action of water, but no distinct traces of cleavage; lines of striæ sometimes distinguished, which indicate twin-composition.

Lustre shining, greasy. Color milk-white, but often reddish from mixture of oxide of iron. Fracture conchoidal. Soluble. Strongly phosphorescent.

Comp.—$KMgCl_3.6aq = KCl + MgCl_2 + 6aq$ = Magnesium chloride 34·2, potassium chloride 26·9, water 38·9=100.
The brown and red color of the mineral is due partly to iron sesquioxide, which is in hexagonal tables, and partly to organic matters (water-plants, infusoria, sponges, etc.).
Pyr., etc.—B.B. fuses easily. Soluble in water, 100 parts of water at 18·75° C. taking up 64·5 parts.
Obs.—Occurs at Stassfurt, where it forms beds in the upper part of the salt formation, alternating with thinner beds of common salt and kieserite, and also mixed with the common salt. Its beds consist of subordinate beds of different colors, reddish, bluish, brown, deep red, sometimes colorless. Sylvite occurs in the carnallite. Also found at Westeregeln; with salt at Maman in Persia. Its richness in potassium makes it valuable for exploration.
TACHHYDRITE.—Composition $CaMg_2Cl_6 + 12aq = CaCl_2 + 2MgCl_2 + 12aq$ (Ramm.) = Chlorine 40·3, magnesium 9·5, calcium 7·5, water 42·7=100. Color yellowish. Deliquescent. Stassfurt.
KREMERSITE.—Probably $2NH_4Cl + 2KCl + FeCl_6 + 3aq$. Vesuvius.
ERYTHROSIDERITE, also from Vesuvius, is $2KCl + FeCl_6 + 2aq$.

3. OXYCHLORIDES.

ATACAMITE.

Orthorhombic. $I \wedge I = 112° 20'$, $O \wedge 1\text{-}\bar{\imath} = 131° 29'$; $\breve{c} : \bar{b} : \breve{a} = 1.131 : 1.492 : 1$. Usually in modified rectangular prisms, vertically striated; also in rectangular octahedrons. Twins: twinning-plane I; consisting of three individuals. Cleavage: $i\text{-}\bar{\imath}$ perfect, $1\text{-}\bar{\imath}$ imperfect. Occurs also massive lamellar.

H.=3–3·5. G.=3·761 (Klein), 3·898 (Zepharovich). Lustre adamantine—vitreous. Color various shades of bright green, rather darker than emerald, sometimes blackish-green. Streak apple-green. Translucent—subtranslucent.

Comp.—$CuCl_2+3H_2CuO_2=$ Chlorine 16·64, copper 59·45, oxygen 11·25, water 12·66=100. Also other compounds with more water (18 and $22\frac{1}{4}$ p. c.).

Pyr., etc.—In the closed tube gives off much water, and forms a gray sublimate. B.B. or charcoal fuses, coloring the O.F. azure-blue, with a green edge, and giving two coatings, one brownish and the other grayish-white; continued blowing yields a globule of metallic copper; the coatings touched with the R.F. volatilize, coloring the flame azure-blue. In acids easily soluble.

Obs.—Occurs in different parts of Chili; in the district of Tarapaca, Bolivia; at Tocopilla in Bolivia; with malachite in South Australia; Serro do Bembe, near Ambriz, on the west coast of Africa; at the Estrella mine in southern Spain; at St. Just in Cornwall.

TALLINGITE.—Composition $CuCl_2+4H_2CuO_2+4aq$. In thin crusts. Color blue. Botallack mine, Cornwall.

ATELITE.—Composition $CuCl_2+2H_2CuO_2+aq$. Formed from tenorite. Vesuvius.

PERCYLITE.—An oxychloride of lead and copper. Occurs in minute sky-blue cubes. Sonora, Mexico; So. Africa.

MATLOCKITE.—Composition $PbCl_2+PbO=$ Lead chloride 55·5, lead oxide 44·5=100. Cromford, near Matlock, Derbyshire.

MENDIPITE.—Composition $PbCl_2+2PbO=$ Lead chloride 38·4, lead oxide 61·6=100. In columnar masses, often radiated. Color white. Mendip Hills, Somersetshire; Brillon, Westphalia.

SCHWARTZEMBERGITE.—Composition $Pb(I,Cl)_2+2PbO$. Color yellow. Desert of Atacama.

DAUBREITE.—Composition $(Bi_2O_3)_4BiCl_3=Bi_2O_3$ 76·16, $BiCl_3$ 23·84=100. Amorphous. Structure earthy, sometimes fibrous. Color yellowish-gray. H.=2·5. G.=6·4–6·5. From the mine Constancia, Cerro de Tanza, Bolivia (Domeyko).

IV. FLUORINE COMPOUNDS.

1. ANHYDROUS FLUORIDES.

FLUORITE or **FLUOR SPAR.*** Flusspath, *Germ.*

Isometric; forms usually cubic (see f. 39, 40, 41, 52, 55, etc., pp. 16 to 19). Cleavage: octahedral, perfect. Twins: twinning-plane, 1, f. 266, p. 91. Massive. Rarely columnar; usually granular, coarse or fine. Crystals often having the surfaces made up of small cubes, or cavernous with rectangular cavities.

H.=4. G.=3·01–3·25. Lustre vitreous; sometimes splendent; usually glimmering in the massive varieties. Color white, yellow, green, rose, and crimson-red, violet-blue, sky-blue, and brown: wine-yellow, greenish and violet-blue, most common; red, rare. Streak white. Transparent—subtranslucent. Brittle. Fracture of fine massive varieties flat-conchoidal and splintery. Sometimes presenting a bluish fluorescence. Phosphoresces when heated.

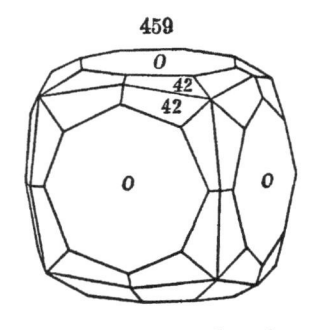

Comp., Var.—Calcium fluoride, CaF_2=Fluorine 48·7, calcium 51·3=100. Berzelius found 0·5 of calcium phosphate in the fluorite of Derbyshire. The presence of chlorine was detected early by Scheele. Kersten found it in fluor from Marienberg and Freiberg. The bright colors, as shown by Kenngott, are lost on heating the mineral; they are attributed mainly to different hydrocarbon compounds by Wyrouboff, the crystallization having taken place from aqueous solution.

Var. *Ordinary*; (*a*) cleavable or crystallized, very various in colors; (*b*) coarse to fine granular; (*c*) earthy, dull, and sometimes very soft. A soft earthy variety from Ratofka, Russia, of a lavender-blue color, is the *ratofkite*. The finely-colored fluorites have been called, according to their colors, *false* ruby, topaz, emerald, amethyst, etc. The colors of the phosphorescent light are various, and are independent of the actual color; and the kind affording a green color is (*d*) the *chlorophane*.

Pyr., etc.—In the closed tube decrepitates and phosphoresces. B.B. in the forceps and on charcoal fuses, coloring the flame red, to an enamel which reacts alkaline to test paper. With soda on platinum foil or charcoal fuses to a clear bead, becoming opaque on cooling; with an excess of soda on charcoal yields a residue of a difficultly fusible enamel, while most of the soda sinks into the coal; with gypsum fuses to a transparent bead, becoming opaque on cooling. Fused in an open tube with fused salt of phosphorus gives the reaction for fluorine. Treated with sulphuric acid gives fumes of hydrofluoric acid which etch glass. Phosphorescence is obtained from the coarsely powdered spar below a red heat. At a high temperature it ceases, but is partially restored by an electric discharge.

Diff.—Recognized by its octahedral cleavage, its etching power when heated in the glass tube, etc.

Obs.—Sometimes in beds, but generally in veins, in gneiss, mica slate, clay slate, and also in limestones, both crystalline and uncrystalline, and sandstones. Often occurs as the gangue of metallic ores. In the North of England, it is the gangue of the lead veins. In Derbyshire it is abundant, and also in Cornwall. Common in the mining district of Saxony; fine near Kongsberg in Norway. In the dolomites of St. Gothard it occurs in pink octahedrons Some American localities are: Trumbull and Plymouth, Conn.; Musculonge Lake, Jefferson Co., N.Y., in gigantic cubes; Rossie, St. Lawrence Co.; near the Franklin furnace, N. J.; Gallatin Co., Ill.; Thunder Bay, Lake Superior; Missouri.

SELLAITE (Strüver).—Magnesium fluoride, MgF_2. Tetragonal. Colorless. Occurs with anhydrite at Gerbulaz in Savoy.

YTTROCERITE.—Composition $2(9CaF_2 + 2YF_2 + CeF_2) + 3aq$ (Ramm.). Color violet-blue, white. Near Fahlun, Sweden; Amity, N. Y.; Paris, Me.; etc.

FLUOCERITE.—Contains (Berzelius) CeO_3 82·64, YO 1·12. Sweden.

FLUELLITE.—Contains (Wollaston) fluorine and aluminum. Cornwall.

CRYPTOHALITE.—Fluosilicate of ammonium. Vesuvius. Also observed at Vesuvius, *hydrofluorite*, HF, and *proidonite*, SiF_4 (Scacchi).

CRYOLITE.*

Triclinic (DesCloizeaux and Websky). Form approaching very closely in appearance and angles to the cube and cubo-octahedron of the isometric system. General habit as in f. 460; $P(O) \wedge T(I) = 90°\ 2'$, $P(O) \wedge M(I') = 90°\ 24'$, $M \wedge T(I \wedge I') = 91°\ 57'$; also $l\ (1-i') \wedge M\ (I') = 124°\ 30'$, $l\ (1-i') \wedge T(I) = 124°\ 14'$ (angles by Websky). Twins common. Cleavage parallel to the three planes P, M, T; in crystals most complete parallel to T, in masses parallel to P. Commonly massive, cleavable.

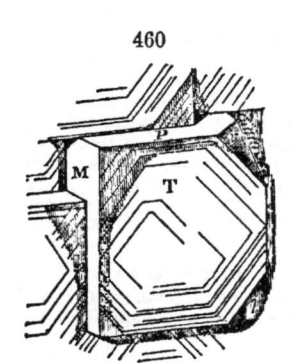

H.=2·5. G.=2·9–3·077. Lustre vitreous; slightly pearly on O. Color snow-white; sometimes reddish or brownish to brick-red and even black. Subtransparent—translucent. Immersion in water increases the transparency. Brittle.

Comp.—Na_6AlF_{12} (or $6NaF + AlF_6$) = Aluminum 13·0, sodium 32·8, fluorine 54·2=100.

Pyr., etc.—Fusible in the flame of a candle. B.B. in the open tube heated so that the flame enters the tube, gives off hydrofluoric acid, etching the glass; the water which condenses at the upper end of the tube reacts for fluorine with Brazil-wood paper. In the forceps fuses very easily, coloring the flame yellow. On the charcoal fuses easily to a clear bead, which on cooling becomes opaque; after long blowing, the assay spreads out, the sodium fluoride is absorbed by the coal, a suffocating odor of fluorine is given off, and a crust of alumina remains, which, when heated with cobalt solution in O.F., gives a blue color. Soluble in sulphuric acid, with evolution of hydrofluoric acid.

Diff.—Distinguished by its extreme fusibility, and its yielding hydrofluoric acid in the open tube.

Obs.—Occurs in a bay in Arksut-fiord, in West Greenland, at Evigtok, where it constitutes a large bed or vein in gneiss. It is used for making soda, and soda and alumina salts; also in Pennsylvania, for the manufacture of a white glass which is a very good imitation of porcelain.

CHIOLITE.—G.=2·84–2·90. Na_3AlF_9 (or $3NaF + AlF_6$). CHODNEFFITE.—G.=3·01. $Na_4Al F_{10}$ (or $4NaF + AlF_6$) Ramm. The two minerals are alike in physical characters, occurring in minute tetragonal pyramids; both from Miask.

2. HYDROUS FLUORIDES.

PACHNOLITE. Thomsenolite.*

Monoclinic, with the lateral axes equal ("clino-quadratic" Nordenskiöld). $\check{c} : b : \check{a} = 1{\cdot}044 : 1 : 1$; $C = 92° 30'$. Prisms slender, a little tapering; I horizontally striated. Cleavage: basal very perfect. Also massive, opal or chalcedony-like.

H. = 2·5–4. G. = 2·929–3·008, of crystals. Lustre vitreous, of a cleavage-face a little pearly, of massive waxy. Color white, or with a reddish tinge. Transparent to translucent.

Comp.—$Na_2Ca_2AlF_{12} + 2aq$, or $2NaF + 2CaF_2 + AlF_6 + 2aq$ = Fluorine 51.28, aluminum 12·28, calcium 17·99, sodium 10·35, water 8·10=100.

Pyr., etc.—Fuses more easily than cryolite to a clear glass. The massive decrepitates remarkably in the flame of a candle. In powder easily decomposed by sulphuric acid.

Obs.—Found incrusting the cryolite of Greenland, and a result of its alteration. The crystals often have an ochre-colored coating, especially the terminal portion; they are sometimes quite large, and have much the appearance of cryolite. The mineral was first described by Knop, and though his description of the crystals does not agree with that given above, there seems to be no doubt that the material was the same, which has since been investigated by Hagemann (*dimetric pachnolite = thomsenolite*), Wöhler (*pyroconite*) and Kœnig, as urged by the latter.

Knop originally described two varieties of the mineral, to which he gave the name pachnolite. The variety, A, appeared in large, cuboidal crystals, with cleavage planes parallel to the faces, intersecting at angles of approximately 90°. These cleavage planes seemed to be continued on into the mass of the cryolite on which the crystals were implanted. The second variety, B, was in small brilliant crystals, of prismatic form, grouped together often in parallel position upon the cryolite (hence the name, from πάχνη, *frost*). The identity of the two varieties chemically was shown by the analyses of Knop and Wöhler. The crystals of variety B, according to Knop, had $I \wedge I = 81° 24'$, etc.

Knop has recently (Jahrb. Min., 1876, 849) suggested the possibility that the crystals of "cryolite," upon which Websky obtained the angles quoted on the preceding page, were really identical with variety A of *pachnolite*. The crystallographic relation of the two species is not yet clearly made out.

ARKSUTITE, HAGEMANNITE, GEARKSUTITE, all from Greenland; and PROSOPITE, from Altenberg.—Fluorine minerals, related to those which precede, but whose exact nature is not yet known.

RALSTONITE (*Brush*).—An hydrous aluminum fluoride, containing also a little magnesium and sodium. Occurs in minute regular octahedrons on the cryolite from Greenland.

V. OXYGEN COMPOUNDS.

1. OXIDES OF METALS OF THE GOLD, IRON, OR TIN GROUPS.

A. ANHYDROUS OXIDES. (a) PROTOXIDES, $\overset{\text{II}}{R}O$ (or $\overset{\text{I}}{R_2}O$).

CUPRITE. Red Copper Ore. Rothkupfererz, *Germ.*

Isometric (see figures on p. 17). Cleavage: octahedral. Sometimes cubes lengthened into capillary forms. Also massive, granular; sometimes earthy.

H.=3·5-4. G.=5·85-6·15. Lustre adamantine or submetallic to earthy. Color red, of various shades, particularly cochineal-red; occasionally crimson-red by transmitted light. Streak several shades of brownish-red, shining. Subtransparent—subtranslucent. Fracture conchoidal, uneven. Brittle.

Comp., Var.—Cu_2O=Oxygen 11·2, copper 88·8=100. Sometimes affords traces of selenium. *Chalcotrichite* is a variety which occurs in capillary or acicular crystallizations, which are cubes elongated in the direction of the octahedral axis. It also occurs earthy; *Tile Ore* (Ziegelerz *Germ.*). Brick-red or reddish-brown and earthy, often mixed with red oxide of iron; sometimes nearly black.

Pyr., etc.—Unaltered in the closed tube. B.B. in the forceps fuses and colors the flame emerald-green; if previously moistened with hydrochloric acid, the color imparted to the flame is momentarily azure-blue from copper chloride. On charcoal first blackens, then fuses, and is reduced to metallic copper. With the fluxes gives reactions for copper oxide. Soluble in concentrated hydrochloric acid.

Obs.—Occurs in Thuringia; on Elba, in cubes; in Cornwall; in Devonshire; in isolated crystals, in lithomarge, at Chessy, near Lyons, which are generally coated with malachite, etc. At the Somerville, and Flemington copper mines, N. J.; at Cornwall, Lebanon Co., Pa.; in the Lake Superior region.

HYDROCUPRITE (*Genth*).—A hydrous cuprite. Occurs in orange-yellow coatings on magnetite. Cornwall, Lebanon Co., Pa.

ZINCITE. Red Zinc Ore. Rothzinkerz, *Germ.*

Hexagonal. $O \wedge 1 = 118° 7'$; $\dot{c} = 1·6208$. In quartzoids with truncated summits, and prismatic faces *I*. Cleavage: basal, eminent; prismatic, sometimes distinct. Usual in foliated grains or coarse particles and masses; also granular.

H.=4-4·5. G.=5·43-5·7. Lustre subadamantine. Streak orange-yellow. Color deep red, also orange-yellow. Translucent—subtranslucent. Fracture subconchoidal. Brittle.

Comp.—ZnO=Oxygen 19·74, zinc 80·26=100; containing manganese as an unessential ingredient. The red color is due probably to the presence of manganese sesquioxide, certainly not to scales of hematite.

Pyr., etc.—Heated in the closed tube blackens, but on cooling resumes the original color B.B. infusible; with the fluxes, on the platinum wire, gives reactions for manganese, and on charcoal in R.F. gives a coating of zinc oxide, yellow while hot, and white on cooling. The coating, moistened with cobalt solution and treated in R.F., assumes a green color. Soluble in acids without effervescence.

Obs.—Occurs with franklinite and also with calcite at Stirling Hill and Mine Hill, Sussex Co., N. J.

CALCOZINCITE.—Impure zincite (mixed with $CaCO_3$, etc.). Stirling Hill, N. J.

TENORITE.* MELACONITE. Schwarzkupfererz (Kupferschwärze), *Germ.*

Orthorhombic (tenorite), crystals from Vesuvius. Earthy; massive; pulverulent (melaconite); also in shining flexible scales; also rarely in cubes with truncated angles (pseudomorphous?).

H.=3. G.=6·25, massive (Whitney). Lustre metallic, and color steel or iron-gray when in thin scales; dull and earthy, with a black or grayish-black color, and ordinarily soiling the fingers when massive or pulverulent.

Comp.—CuO=Oxygen 20·15, copper 79·85=100

Pyr., etc.—B.B. in O.F. infusible; other reactions as for cuprite (p. 244). Soluble in hydrochloric and nitric acids.

Obs.—Found on lava at Vesuvius in minute scales; and also pulverulent (Scacchi, who uses the name melaconise for the mineral). Common in the earthy form (*melaconite*) about copper mines, as a result of the decomposition of chalcopyrite and other copper ores. Ducktown mines in Tennessee, and Keweenaw Point, L. Superior.

PERICLASITE.—Essentially magnesium oxide, MgO, or more exactly $(Mg,Fe)O$, where Mg : Fe=20 : 1, or 30 : 1. Mt. Somma.

BUNSENITE.—NiO. Found at Johanngeorgenstadt. The compound MnO has been found recently in Wermland, in masses of a green color, and with cubic cleavage. See manganosite, p. 431.

MASSICOT (Bleiglätte).—PbO, but generally impure. Badenweiler, Baden. Mexico. Austin's mines, Va.

HYDRARGYRITE.—HgO; with BORDOSITE, $AgCl + HgCl$, at Los Bordos, Chili.

(*b*) SESQUIOXIDES. GENERAL FORMULA RO_3.

CORUNDUM.*

Rhombohedral. $R \wedge R = 86° 4'$, $O \wedge 1(R) = 122° 26'$; (122° 25', Kokscharof); $c = 1·363$. Cleavage: basal, sometimes perfect, but interrupted, commonly imperfect in the blue variety; rhombohedral, often perfect. Large crystals usually rough. Twins: composition-face R. Also massive granular or impalpable; often in layers from composition parallel to R.

H.=9. G.=3·909–4·16. Lustre vitreous; sometimes pearly on the basal planes, and occasionally exhibiting a bright opalescent star of six rays in the direction of the axis. Color blue, red, yellow, brown, gray, and nearly white; streak uncolored. Transparent—translucent. Fracture conchoidal — uneven. Exceedingly tough when compact.

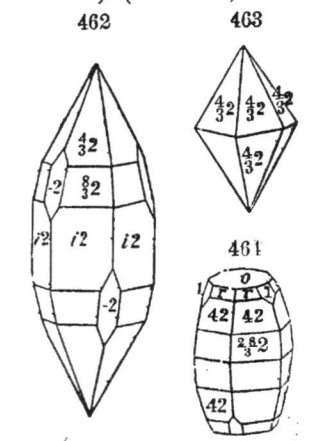

Comp., Var.—Pure alumina AlO_3=Oxygen 46·8, aluminum 53·2=100. There are three subdivisions of the species prominently recognized in the arts, and until early in this century regarded as distinct species; but which actually differ only in purity and state of crystallization or structure.

VAR. 1. SAPPHIRE—Includes the purer kinds of fine colors, transparent to translucent, useful as gems. Stones are named according to their colors; true *Ruby*, or *Oriental Ruby*, red; *O. Topas*, yellow; *O. Emerald*, green; *O. Amethyst*, purple.

2. CORUNDUM.—Includes the kinds of dark or dull colors and not transparent, colors light blue to gray, brown, and black. The original adamantine spar from India has a dark grayish smoky-brown tint, but greenish or bluish by transmitted light, when translucent, and either in distinct crystals often large, or cleavable-massive. It is ground and used as a polishing material, and being purer, is superior in this respect to emery. It was thus employed in ancient times, both in India and Europe.

3. EMERY, Schmirgel, *Germ.*—Includes granular corundum, of black or grayish-black color, and contains magnetite or hematite intimately mixed. Feels and looks much like a black fine-grained iron ore, which it was long considered to be. There are gradations from the evenly fine-grained emery to kinds in which the corundum is in distinct crystals. This last is the case with part of that at Chester, Massachusetts.

Pyr., etc.—B.B. unaltered; slowly dissolved in borax and salt of phosphorus to a clear glass, which is colorless when free from iron; not acted upon by soda. The finely pulverized mineral, after heating with cobalt solution, gives a beautiful blue color. Not acted upon by acids, but converted into a soluble compound by fusion with potassium bisulphate or soda. Friction excites electricity, and in polished specimens the electrical attraction continues for a considerable length of time.

Diff.—Distinguished by its hardness, scratching quartz and topaz; its infusibility and its high specific gravity.

Obs.—This species is associated with crystalline rocks, as granular limestone or dolomite, gneiss, granite, mica slate, chlorite slate. The fine sapphires are usually obtained from the beds of rivers, either in modified hexagonal prisms or in rolled masses, accompanied by grains of magnetic iron ore, and several species of gems. The emery of Asia Minor, according to Dr. Smith, occurs in granular limestone.

Sapphires occur in Ceylon; the East Indies; China. Corundum, at St. Gothard; in Piedmont; Urals; Bohemia. Emery is found in large boulders on some of the Grecian islands; also in Asia Minor, near Ephesus, etc. In N. America, in *Massachusetts*, at Chester, corundum and emery in a large vein; also in Westchester Co., N. Y. In *New York*, at Warwick and Amity. In *Pennsylvania*, in Delaware Co., and Chester Co. In western *N. Carolina*, at many localities in large quantities, and sometimes in crystals of immense size. In *Georgia*, in Cherokee Co. In *California*, in Los Angeles Co.; in the gravel on the Upper Missouri River in Montana.

HEMATITE. Specular Iron. Eisenglanz, Rotheisenerz, *Germ.*

Rhombohedral. $R \wedge R = 86° 10'$, $O \wedge R = 122° 30'$; $\dot{c} = 1.3591$. $O \wedge \frac{4}{3}\text{-}2 = 118° 53'$, $O \wedge 1^3 = 103° 32$, $R \wedge \frac{4}{3}\text{-}2 = 154° 2'$. Cleavage: parallel to R and O; often indistinct. Twins: twinning-plane R; also O

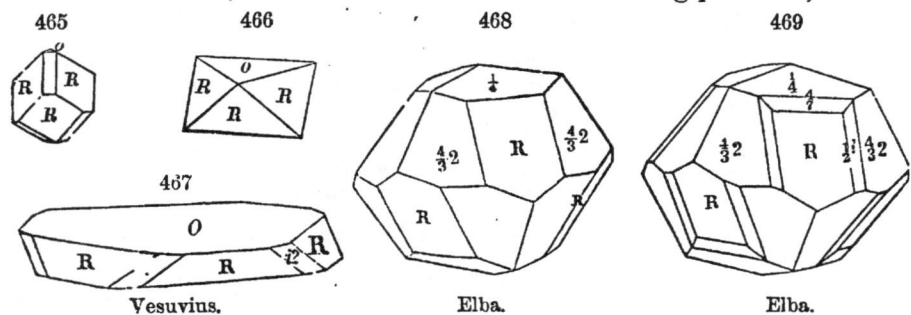

(f. 267, p. 91). Also columnar—granular, botryoidal, and stalactitic shapes; also lamellar, laminæ joined parallel to O, and variously bent, thick or thin; also granular, friable or compact.

H.=5·5–6·5. G.=4·5–5·3 ; of some compact varieties, as low as 4·2. Lustre metallic and occasionally splendent; sometimes earthy. Color dark steel-gray or iron-black; in very thin particles blood-red by transmitted light; when earthy, red. Streak cherry-red or reddish-brown. Opaque, except when in very thin laminæ, which are faintly translucent and blood-red. Fracture subconchoidal, uneven. Sometimes attractable by the magnet, and occasionally even magnetipolar.

Comp., Var.—Iron sesquioxide, FeO_3=Oxygen 30, iron 70=100. Sometimes containing titanium and magnesium.

The varieties depend on texture or state of aggregation, and in some cases the presence of impurities.

Var. 1. *Specular.* Lustre metallic, and crystals often splendent, whence the name *specular iron.* (b) When the structure is foliated or micaceous, the ore is called *micaceous* hematite (Eisenglimmer). 2. *Compact columnar;* or fibrous. The masses often long radiating; lustre submetallic to metallic; color brownish-red to iron-black. Sometimes called *red hematite,* the name hematite among the older mineralogists including the fibrous, stalactitic, and other solid massive varieties of this species, limonite, and turgite. 3. *Red Ochreous.* Red and earthy. Often specimens of the preceding are red ochreous on some parts. *Reddle* and *red chalk* are red ochre, mixed with more or less clay. 4. *Clay Iron-stone; Argillaceous hematite.* Hard, brownish-black to reddish-brown, heavy stone; often in part deep-red ; of submetallic to unmetallic lustre ; and affording, like all the preceding, a red streak. It consists of iron sesquioxide with clay or sand, and sometimes other impurities.

Pyr., etc.—B.B. infusible; on charcoal in R.F. becomes magnetic ; with borax in O.F. gives a bead, which is yellow while hot and colorless on cooling ; if saturated, the bead appears red while hot and yellow on cooling ; in R.F. gives a bottle-green color, and if treated on charcoal with metallic tin, assumes a vitriol-green color. With soda on charcoal in R.F. is reduced to a gray magnetic metallic powder. Soluble in concentrated hydrochloric acid.

Diff.—Distinguished from magnetite by its red streak, also from limonite by the same means, as well as by its not containing water ; from turgite by its greater hardness and by its not decrepitating B.B. It is *hard;* and *infusible.*

Obs.—This ore occurs in rocks of all ages. The specular variety is mostly confined to crystalline or metamorphic rocks, but is also a result of igneous action about some volcanoes, as at Vesuvius. Traversella in Piedmont; the island of Elba, afford fine specimens; also St. Gothard, often in the form of rosettes (*Eisenrose*), and Cavradi in Tavetsch ; and near Limoges, France. At Etna and Vesuvius it is the result of volcanic action. Arendal in Norway, Longban in Sweden, Framont in Lorraine, Dauphiny, also Cleator Moor in Cumberland, are other localities.

In *N. America*, widely distributed, and sometimes in beds of vast thickness in rocks of the Archæan age, as in the Marquette region in northern Michigan ; and in Missouri, at the Pilot Knob and the Iron Mtn.; in Arizona and New Mexico. Some of the localities, interesting for their specimens, are in northern New York, etc.; Woodstock and Aroostook, Me.; at Hawley, Mass.; at Piermont, N. H.

This ore affords a considerable portion of the iron manufactured in different countries. The varieties, especially the specular, require a greater degree of heat to melt than other ores, but the iron obtained is of good quality. Pulverized red hematite is employed in polishing metals, and also as a coloring material. The fine-grained massive variety from England (bloodstone), showing often beautiful conchoidal fracture, is much used for burnishing metals. Red ochre is valuable in making paint.

MARTITE is iron sesquioxide under an isometric form, occurring in octahedrons or dodecahedrons like magnetite, and supposed to be pseudomorphous, mostly after magnetite. H.= 6–7. G.=4·809–4·832, Brazil, Breith.; 5·33, Monroe, N. Y., Hunt. Lustre submetallic. Color iron-black, sometimes with a bronzed tarnish. Streak reddish-brown or purplish-brown. Fracture conchoidal. Not magnetic, or only feebly so. The crystals are sometimes imbedded in the massive sesquioxide. They are distinguished from magnetite by their red streak, and very feeble, if any, action on the magnetic needle.

Found in Vermont at Chittenden; in the Marquette iron region south of L. Superior; Bass lake, Canada West; Digby Neck, Nova Scotia; at Monroe, N. Y.; in Moravia, near Schönberg, in granite.

MENACCANITE.* ILMENITE. Titanic Iron Ore. Titaneisen, *Germ.*

Rhombohedral; tetartohedral to the hexagonal type. $R \wedge R = 85° \, 30'$

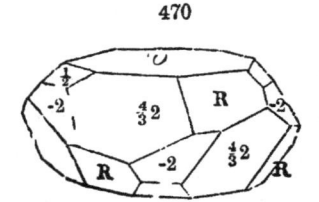

56″ (Koksch.), $\breve{c} = 1.38458$. Angles nearly as in hematite. Often a cleavage parallel with the terminal plane, but probably due to planes of composition. Crystals usually tabular. Twins: twinning-plane O; sometimes producing, when repeated, a form resembling f. 468. Often in thin plates or laminæ; massive; in loose grains as sand. H.=5–6. G.=4·5–5. Lustre submetallic. Color iron-black. Streak submetallic, powder black to brownish-red. Opaque. Fracture conchoidal. Influences slightly the magnetic needle.

Comp., Var.—$(Ti,Fe)_2O_3$ (or hematite, with part of the iron replaced by titanium), the proportion of Ti to Fe varying. Mosander assumes the proportion of FeO : TiO_2 to be always 1 : 1, and that in addition variable amounts of FeO_3 are present in the different varieties. The extensive investigations of Rammelsberg have led him to write the formula like Mosander $(FeO,TiO_2)+nFeO_3$ (notice here that $FeO,TiO_2=RO_3$). This method has the advantage of explaining the presence of the magnesium, occurring sometimes in considerable amount, it replacing the iron (FeO). The first formula given requires the assumption of Mg_2O_3. Friedel and Guérin have recently discussed the same subject (Ann. Ch. Phys., V., viii., 38, 1876).

Sometimes contains manganese. The varieties recognized arise mainly from the proportions of iron to titanium. No satisfactory external distinctions have yet been made out.

The following analyses will illustrate the wide range in composition:

	TiO_2	FeO_3	FeO	MnO	MgO	
1. Ilmen Mts., *Ilmenite*	46·92	10·74	37·86	2·73	1·14=99·39,	Mosander.
2. Snarum	10·02	77·17	8·52	——	1·33, AlO_3 1·46=98·50,	Ramm.
3. Warwick, N. Y.	57·71	——	26·82	0·90	13·71=99·14,	Ramm.

Pyr., etc.—B.B. infusible in O.F. although slightly rounded on the edges in R.F. With borax and salt of phosphorus reacts for iron in O.F., and with the latter flux assumes a more or less intense brownish-red color in R.F.; this treated with tin on charcoal changes to a violet-red color when the amount of titanium is not too small. The pulverized mineral, heated with hydrochloric acid, is slowly dissolved to a yellow solution, which, filtered from the undecomposed mineral and boiled with the addition of tin-foil, assumes a beautiful blue or violet color. Decomposed by fusion with sodium or potassium bisulphate.

Diff.—Resembles hematite, but has a submetallic, nearly black, streak.

Obs.—Some of the principal European localities of this species are: Krageröe, Egersund, Arendal, Norway; Uddewalla, Sweden; Ilmen Mts. (*ilmenite*); Iserwiese, Riesengebirge (*iserine*); Aschaffenburg; Eisenach; St. Cristophe (*crichtonite*).

Occurs in Warwick, Amity, and Monroe, Orange Co., N. Y.; also near Edenville; at Chester and South Royalston, Mass.; at Bay St. Paul in Canada; also with labradorite at Château Richer. Grains are found in the gold sands of California.

PEROFSKITE.*

Isometric, Rose (fr. Ural). Habit cubic, with secondary planes incompletely developed; in cubes, octahedrons, and cubo-octahedrons, from Arkansas. Twins: twinning-plane octahedral, Magnet Cove, Ark.; also like f. 276, p. 93, Achmatovsk. Cleavage: parallel to the cubic faces rather perfect.

H.=5·5. G.=4·02–4·04. Lustre metallic—adamantine. Color pale yellow, honey-yellow, orange-yellow, reddish-brown, grayish-black to iron-black. Streak colorless, grayish. Transparent to opaque. Double refracting.

Comp.—$(Ca+Ti)O_3=\dot{R}O_3=$ Titanic oxide 59·4, lime 40·6=100.

Pyr., etc.—In the forceps and on charcoal infusible. With salt of phosphorus in O.F. dissolves easily, giving a bead greenish while hot, which becomes colorless on cooling; in R.F. the bead changes to grayish-green, and on cooling assumes a violet-blue color. Entirely decomposed by boiling sulphuric acid.

Obs.—Occurs at Achmatovsk, in the Ural; in the valley of Zermatt; at Wildkreuzjoch in the Tyrol. Also at Magnet Cove, Arkansas.

DesCloizeaux has found that the yellow crystals from Zermatt have a complex twinned structure, and are optically biaxial. Kokscharof, in his latest investigations, has shown that the Russian specimens also exhibit phenomena in polarized light analogous to those of biaxial crystals, though irregular. He proves, however, that crystallographically the crystals examined by him were unquestionably isometric, and adds also that almost all the Russian perofskite crystals are penetration-twins. The latter fact explains the commonly observed striations on the cubic planes, as also the incompleteness in the development of the other forms. He refers the optical irregularities to the want of homogeneity in the crystals. DesCloizeaux speaks of inclosed lamellæ of a doubly-refracting substance analogous to the parasite in boracite crystals (p. 176).

HYDROTITANITE.—A decomposition-product of perofskite crystals from Magnet Cove, Arkansas. Form retained but color changed to yellowish-gray (Kœnig).

(c) COMPOUNDS OF PROTOXIDES AND SESQUIOXIDES,* $\overset{..}{R}\overset{...}{R}O_4$ (or $\overset{..}{R}O+\overset{...}{R}O_3$).

Spinel Group. Isometric (Octahedral).

SPINEL.

Isometric. Habit octahedral. Faces of octahedron sometimes convex. Cleavage: octahedral. Twins: twinning-plane 1.

H.=8. G.=3·5–4·1. Lustre vitreous; splendent— nearly dull. Color red of various shades, passing into blue, green, yellow, brown, and black; occasionally almost white. Streak white. Transparent—nearly opaque. Fracture conchoidal.

471

Comp., Var.—The spinels proper have the formula $MgAlO_4(=MgO+AlO_3)$, or in other words contain chiefly magnesium and aluminum, with the former replaced in part by iron (Fe), calcium (Ca), and manganese (Mn); and the latter by iron (Fe). There is hence a gradation into kinds containing little or no magnesium, which stand as distinct species, viz., *Hercynite* and *Gahnite*. $MgAlO_4$=Alumina 72, magnesia 28=100.

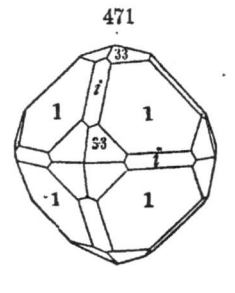

Var. 1. *Ruby*, or *Magnesia Spinel*.—Clear red or reddish; transparent to translucent; sometimes subtranslucent. G.=3·52–3·58. Composition $MgAlO_4$, with little or no Fe, and sometimes chromium as a source of the red color. 2. *Ceylonite*, or *Iron-Magnesia Spinel*. Color dark-green, brown to black, mostly opaque or nearly so. G.=3·5–3·6. Composition $MgAlO_4+FeAlO_4$. Sometimes the Al is replaced in part by Fe. 3. *Picotite*. Contains over 7 p. c. of chromium oxide. Color black. Lustre brilliant. G.=4·08. The original was from a rock occurring about L. Lherz, called *Lherzolite*.

Pyr., etc.—B.B. alone infusible; the red variety turns brown, and even black and opaque, as the temperature increases, and on cooling becomes first green, and then nearly colorless, and at last resumes the red color. Slowly soluble in borax, more readily in salt of phosphorus, with which it gives a reddish bead while hot, becoming faint chrome-green on

---

* The compounds here considered are sometimes regarded as salts of the acids, $H_2\overset{...}{R}O_4$, that is, as *aluminates, ferrates*, etc.

272 DESCRIPTIVE MINERALOGY.

cooling. The black varieties give reactions for iron with the fluxes. Soluble with difficulty in concentrated sulphuric acid. Decomposed by fusion with sodium or potassium bisulphate.

Diff.—Distinguished by its octahedral form, hardness, and infusibility; magnetite is attracted by the magnet, and zircon has a higher specific gravity.

Obs.—Spinel occurs imbedded in granular limestone, and with calcite in serpentine, gneiss, and allied rocks. It also occupies the cavities of masses ejected from some volcanoes, *e.g.*, Mt. Somma.

Fine spinels are found in Ceylon; in Siam, as rolled pebbles in the channels of rivers. Occur at Aker in Sweden; also at Monzoni in the Fassathal.

From Amity, N. Y., to Andover, N. J., a distance of about 30 miles, is a region of granular limestone and serpentine, in which localities of spinel abound; numerous about Warwick, and at Monroe and Cornwall. Franklin, Sterling, Sparta, Hamburgh, and Vernon, N. J., are other localities. At Antwerp, Jefferson Co., N. Y.; at Bolton and elsewhere in Mass.

HERCYNITE.—$FeAlO_4$ (or $FeO+Al_2O_3$). Color black. Massive. Bohemia.

JACOBSITE (*Damour*).—RRO_4, or $(Mn,Mg)(Fe,Mn)O_4$. Color deep black. Occurs in distorted octahedrons (magnetic) in a crystalline limestone at Jacobsberg, Sweden.

GAHNITE. Zinc Spinel.

Isometric. In octahedrons, dodecahedrons, etc., like spinel.

H.$=7\cdot5$–8. G.$=4$–$4\cdot6$. Lustre vitreous, or somewhat greasy. Color dark green, grayish-green, deep leek-green, greenish-black, bluish-black, yellowish- or grayish-brown; streak grayish. Subtranslucent to opaque.

Comp., Var.—$ZnAlO_4$=Alumina 61·3, oxide of zinc 38·7=100; with little or no magnesium. The zinc sometimes replaced in small part by manganese or iron (Mn,Fe), and the aluminum in part by iron (Fe).

Var. 1. *Automolite*, or *Zinc Gahnite;* with sometimes a little iron. G.$=4\cdot1$–$4\cdot6$. Colors as above given. 2. *Dysluite*, or *Zinc-Manganese-Iron Gahnite*. Composition (Zn,Fe,Mn)(Al,Fe)O_4. Color yellowish-brown or grayish-brown. G.$=4$–$4\cdot6$. Form the octahedron, or the same with truncated edges. 3. *Kreittonite*, or *Zinc-Iron Gahnite*. Composition (Zn,Fe,Mg)(Al,Fe)O_4. Occurs in crystals, and granular massive. H.$=7$–8. G.$=4\cdot48$–$4\cdot89$. Color velvet to greenish-black; powder grayish-green. Opaque.

Pyr., etc.—Gives a coating of zinc oxide when treated with a mixture of borax and soda on charcoal. Otherwise like spinel.

Obs.—*Automolite* is found at Fahlun, Sweden; Franklin, N. Jersey; Canton mine, Ga.; *Dysluite* at Sterling, N. J.; *Kreittonite* at Bodenmais in Bavaria.

MAGNETITE. Magnetic Iron Ore. Magneteisenstein, Magneteisenerz, *Germ.*

Isometric. The octahedron and dodecahedron the most common forms.

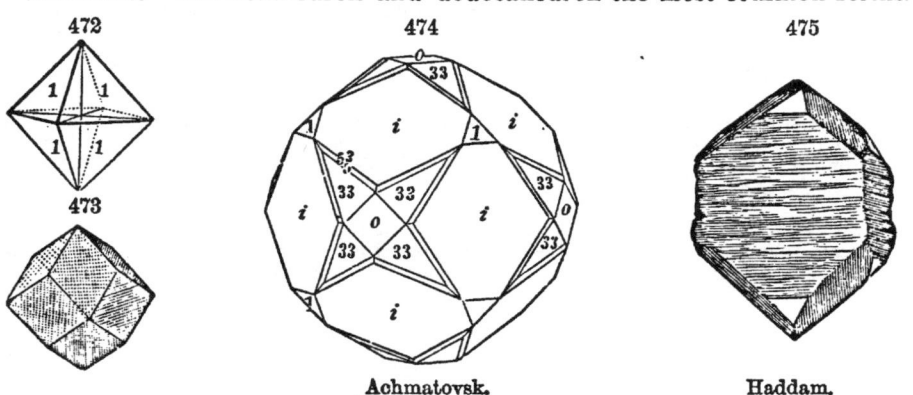

472

473

474 Achmatovsk.

475 Haddam.

Fig. 475 is a distorted dodecahedron. Cleavage: octahedral, perfect to imperfect. Dodecahedral faces commonly striated parallel to the longer diagonal. Twins: twinning-plane, 1; also in dendrites, branching at angles of 60° (f. 277, p. 93). Massive, structure granular—particles of various sizes, sometimes impalpable.

H.=5·5–6·5. G.=4·9–5·2. Lustre metallic—submetallic. Color iron-black; streak black. Opaque; but in mica sometimes transparent or nearly so; and varying from almost colorless to pale smoky-brown and black. Fracture subconchoidal, shining. Brittle. Strongly magnetic, sometimes possessing polarity.

Comp., Var.—$FeFeO_4$ (or Fe_3O_4)=$FeO+FeO_3$=Oxygen 27·6, iron 72·4=100; or iron sesquioxide 68·97, iron protoxide 31·03=100. The iron sometimes replaced in small part by magnesium. Also sometimes titaniferous.

From the normal proportion of Fe to Fe, 1 : 1, there is occasionally a wide variation, and thus a gradual passage to the sesquioxide FeO_3; and this fact may be regarded as evidence that the octahedral FeO_3, martite, is only an altered magnetite.

Pyr., etc.—B.B. very difficultly fusible. In O.F. loses its influence on the magnet. With the fluxes reacts like hematite. Soluble in hydrochloric acid.

Diff.—Distinguished from other members of the spinel group, as also from garnet, by its being attracted by the magnet, as well as by its high specific gravity. Also, when massive, by its black streak from hematite and limonite.

Obs.—Magnetite is mostly confined to crystalline rocks, and is most abundant in metamorphic rocks, though found also in grains in eruptive rocks. In the Archæan rocks the beds are of immense extent, and occur under the same conditions as those of hematite. It is an ingredient in most of the massive variety of corundum called emery. The earthy magnetite is found in bogs like bog-iron ore.

Extensive deposits occur at Arendal, Norway; Dannemora and the Täberg in Smaoland; in Lapland. Fahlun in Sweden, and Corsica, afford octahedral crystals.

In N. America, it constitutes vast beds in the Archæan, in the Adirondack region, in Northern N. York; also in Canada; at Cornwall in Pennsylvania, and at Magnet Cove, Arkansas. Also found in Putnam Co. (Tilly Foster Mine), N. Y., etc. In *Conn.*, at Haddam. In *Penn.*, at Chester Co.; in mica at Pennsbury. In *California*, in Sierra Co.; in Plumas Co., and elsewhere. In *N. Scotia*, Digby Co., Nichol's Mt.

MAGNESIOFERRITE (*magnoferrite*).—$MgFeO_4$. In octahedrons; resembling magnetite. Vesuvius.

FRANKLINITE.

Isometric. Habit octahedral. Cleavage: octahedral, indistinct. Also massive, coarse or fine granular to compact.

H.=5·5–6·5. G.=5·069. Lustre metallic. Color iron-black. Streak dark reddish-brown. Opaque. Fracture conchoidal. Brittle. Acts slightly on the magnet.

Comp.—(Fe,Zn,Mn) (Fe,Mn)O_4, or corresponding to the general formula of the spinel group, though varying much in relative amounts of iron, zinc, and manganese. Analysis, Sterling Hill, N. J., $\frac{1}{4}FeO_3$ 67·42, AlO_3 0·65, FeO 15·65, ZnO 6·78, MnO 9·53=100·12, Seyms. Q. ratio for R : R̶=1 : 1 nearly. In a crystal from Mine Hill, N. J., Seyms found 4·44 p. c. MnO_3.

The evolution of chlorine in the treatment of the mineral is attributed by v. Kobell to the presence of a little MnO_3 (0.80 p. c.) as mixture, which Rammelsberg observes may have come from the oxidation of some of the protoxide of manganese.

Pyr., etc.—B.B. infusible. With borax in O.F. gives a reddish amethystine bead (manganese), and in R.F. this becomes bottle-green (iron). With soda gives a bluish-green manganate, and on charcoal a faint coating of zinc oxide, which is much more marked when a mixture of borax and soda is used. Soluble in hydrochloric acid, with evolution of a small amount of chlorine.

Diff.—Resembles magnetite, but is only slightly attracted by the magnet; it also reacts for zinc on charcoal B.B.

Obs.—Occurs in cubic crystals near Eibach in Nassau; in amorphous masses at Altenberg, near Aix la Chapelle. Abundant at Hamburg, N. J., near the Franklin furnace; also at Stirling Hill, in the same region.

CHROMITE.* Chromic Iron. Chromeisenstein, *Germ.*

Isometric. In octahedrons. Commonly massive; structure fine granular or compact.

H.=5·5. G.=4·321–4·568. Lustre submetallic. Streak brown. Color between iron-black and brownish-black. Opaque. Fracture uneven. Brittle. Sometimes magnetic.

Comp.—$FeCrO_4$, or $(Fe,Mg,Cr)(Al,Fe,Cr)O_4$. $FeCrO_4$=Iron protoxide 32, chromium sesquioxide 68=100. Magnesia is generally present, and in amounts varying from 6–24 p. c.

Pyr., etc.—B. B. in O. F. infusible; in R. F. slightly rounded on the edges, and becomes magnetic. With borax and salt of phosphorus gives beads, which, while hot, show only a reaction for iron, but on cooling become chrome-green; the green color is heightened by fusion on charcoal with metallic tin. Not acted upon by acids, but decomposed by fusion with potassium or sodium bisulphate.

Diff.—Distinguished from magnetite by the reaction for chromic acid with the blowpipe.

Obs.—Occurs in serpentine, forming veins, or in imbedded masses. It assists in giving the variegated color to verde-antique marble. Also occurs in meteorites.

Occurs in Syria; Shetland; in Norway; in the Department du Var in France; in Silesia and Bohemia; in the Urals; in New Caledonia. At Baltimore, Md., in the Bare Hills; at Cooptown. In Pennsylvania, in Chester Co.; at Wood's Mine, near Texas, Lancaster Co., etc. Chester, Mass. In California, in Monterey Co., etc.

This ore affords the chromium oxide, used in painting, etc. The ore employed in England is obtained mostly from Baltimore, Drontheim in Norway, and the Shetland Isles.

CHROMPICOTITE (Petersen).—A magnesian chromite. Color black. New Zealand.

URANINITE* (Pitchblende; Uranpecherz, *Germ.*).—$U_3O_8(UO_2+2UO_3)$. Massive. Black. Saxony, etc.

CHRYSOBERYL.

Orthorhombic. $I \wedge I = 129° 38'$, $O \wedge 1\text{-}\bar{\imath} = 129° 1'$; $\dot{c} : \bar{b} : \check{a} = 1·2285 : 2·1267 : 1$. $i\text{-}\bar{\imath} \wedge 1 = 136° 52'$, $i\text{-}\bar{\imath} \wedge 2\text{-}\check{\imath} = 128° 52'$, $i\text{-}\check{\imath} \wedge 1\text{-}\check{\imath} = 120° 7'$. Plane $i\text{-}\bar{\imath}$ vertically striated; and sometimes also $i\text{-}\check{\imath}$, and other vertical planes. Cleavage: $1\text{-}\check{\imath}$ quite distinct; $i\text{-}\check{\imath}$ imperfect; $i\text{-}\bar{\imath}$ more so. Twins: twinning-plane $3\text{-}\check{\imath}$, as in f. 477 (see p. 97), made up of 6 parts by the crossing of 3 crystals.

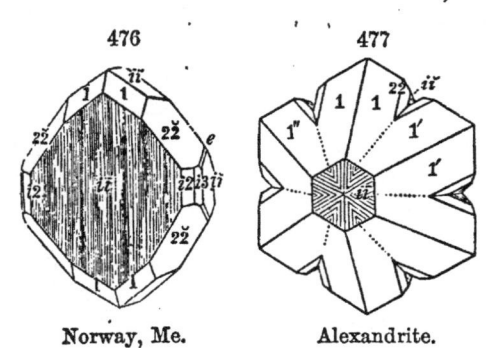

H.=8·5. G.=3·5–3·84. Lustre vitreous. Color asparagus-green, grass-green, emerald-green, greenish-white, and yellowish-green, sometimes raspberry or columbine-red by transmitted light. Streak uncolored. Transparent—translucent. Sometimes a bluish opalescence internally. Fracture conchoidal, uneven.

OXYGEN COMPOUNDS.—ANHYDROUS OXIDES. 275

Var. 1. *Ordinary.*—Color pale green, being colored by iron. G.=3.597, Haddam; 3.734, Brazil; 3.689, Ural, Rose; 3.835, Orenburg, Kokscharof. 2. *Alexandrite.*—Color emerald-green, but columbine-red by transmitted light. G.=3.644, mean of results, Kokscharof. Supposed to be colored by chrome. Crystals often very large, and in twins, like f. 477, either six-sided or six-rayed.

Comp.—$BeAlO_4$=Alumina 80·2, glucina 19·8=100. Iron is also often present, though not in the transparent varieties. Isomorphous with chrysolite.

Pyr., etc.—B.B. alone unaltered; with soda, the surface is merely rendered dull. With borax or salt of phosphorus fuses with great difficulty. With cobalt solution, the powdered mineral gives a bluish color. Not acted upon by acids.

Diff.—Distinguished by its extreme hardness, greater than that of topaz; and its infusibility; also characterized by its tabular crystallization, in contrast with beryl.

Obs.—In Brazil and also Ceylon; at Marchendorf in Moravia; in the Ural; in the Mourne Mts., Ireland; at Haddam, Ct.; at Norway, Me.

When transparent, and of sufficient size, chrysoberyl is cut with facets, and forms a beautiful yellowish-green gem. If opalescent, it is usually cut *en cabochon*.

(*d*) DEUTOXIDES, RO_2.

Rutile Group. Tetragonal.

CASSITERITE. Tin Stone. Zinnstein, Zinnerz, *Germ.*

Tetragonal. $O \wedge 1\text{-}i = 146° 5'$; $\dot{c} = 0.6724$. $1 \wedge 1$, pyr., $= 121° 40'$; $I \wedge 1 = 133° 34'$; $1\text{-}i \wedge 1\text{-}i$, pyr., $= 133° 31'$. Cleavage: I and $i\text{-}i$ hardly distinct. Twins: f. 478, twinning-plane $1\text{-}i$; producing often complex forms through the many modifying planes; sometimes repeated parallel to all the eight planes $1\text{-}i$; also f. 480, a metagenic twin. Often in reniform shapes, structure fibrous divergent; also massive, granular or impalpable.

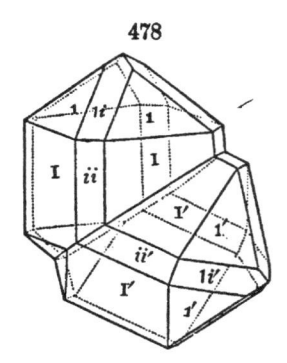

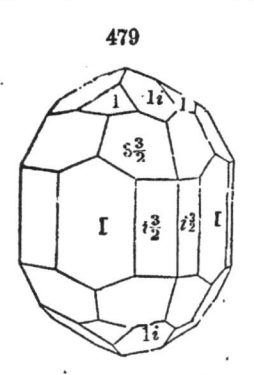

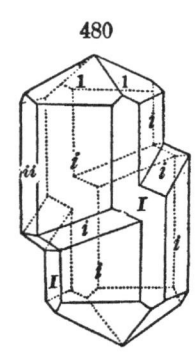

H.=6–7. G.=6·4–7·1. Lustre adamantine, and crystals usually splendent. Color brown or black; sometimes red, gray, white, or yellow. Streak white, grayish, brownish. Nearly transparent—opaque. Fracture subconchoidal, uneven. Brittle.

Var.—1. *Ordinary*, Tin-stone. In crystals and massive. G. of ordinary cryst. 6·96; of colorless, from Tipuani R., Bolivia, 6·832, Forbes. 2. *Wood Tin* (Holz-Zinn, *Germ.*). In botryoidal and reniform shapes, concentric in structure, and radiated fibrous internally

276 DESCRIPTIVE MINERALOGY.

although very compact, with the color brownish, of mixed shades, looking somewhat like dry wood in its colors. G. of one variety 6·514. *Stream tin* is nothing but the ore in the state of sand, as it occurs along the beds of streams or in the gravel of the adjoining region. It has been derived from tin veins or rocks, through the wear and decomposition of the rocks and transportation by water.

Comp.—SnO_2 = Tin 78·6, oxygen 21·4 = 100.

Pyr., etc.—B.B. alone unaltered. On charcoal with soda reduced to metallic tin, and gives a white coating. With the fluxes sometimes gives reactions for iron and manganese, and more rarely for tantalic oxide. Only slightly acted upon by acids.

Diff.—Distinguished by its high specific gravity, its infusibility, and by its yielding metallic tin B.B. from some varieties of garnet, sphalerite, and black tourmaline, to which it has some resemblance. Specific gravity (6·5) higher than that of rutile (4).

Obs.—Tin ore is met with in veins traversing granite, gneiss, mica schist, chlorite or clay schist, and porphyry. Occurs in Cornwall; in Devonshire; in Bohemia and Saxony; at Limoges; also in Galicia; Greenland; Sweden, at Finbo; Finland, at Pitkaranta. In the E. Indies; in Victoria and New South Wales; in large quantities in Queensland. In Bolivia, S. A.; in Mexico.

In the United States, rare: in *Maine*, at Paris; in *N. Hamp.*, at Lyme; in *California*, in San Bernardino Co.; in *Idaho*, near Boonville.

RUTILE.*

Tetragonal. $O \wedge 1\text{-}i = 147°\ 12\frac{1}{2}'$, $\check{c} = 0·6442$. $1 \wedge 1$, pyr., $= 123°\ 7\frac{1}{2}'$, $I \wedge 1 = 132°\ 20'$. Cleavage: I and $i\text{-}i$, distinct; 1, in traces. Vertical planes usually striated. Crystals often acicular. Twins: (1) twinning-plane 1-i (see p. 94). (2) 3-i, making a wedge-shaped crystal consisting of two individuals. (3) 1-i and 3-i in the same crystal (fr. Magnet Cove, Hessenberg). Occasionally compact, massive.

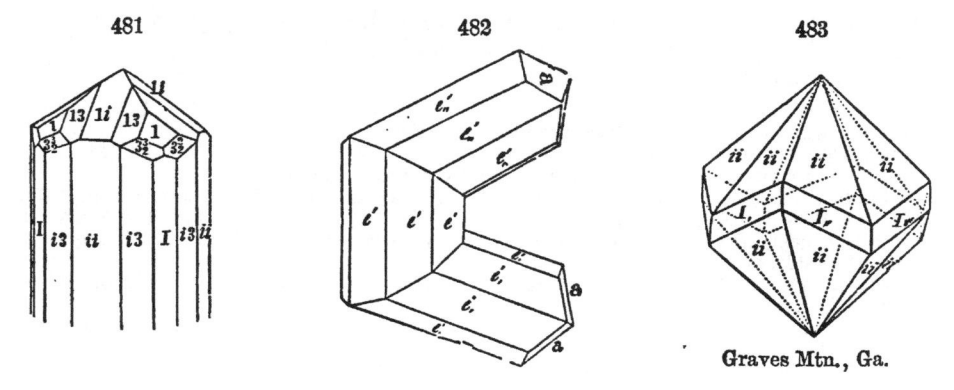

481 482 483

Graves Mtn., Ga.

H. = 6–6·5. G. = 4·18–4·25. Lustre metallic-adamantine. Color reddish-brown, passing into red; sometimes yellowish, bluish, violet, black; rarely grass-green. Streak pale brown. Subtransparent—opaque. Fracture subconchoidal, uneven. Brittle.

Comp., Var.—Titanic oxide, TiO_2 = Oxygen 39, titanium 61 = 100. Sometimes a little iron is present.

Pyr., etc.—B.B. infusible. With salt of phosphorus gives a colorless bead, which in R.F. assumes a violet color on cooling. Most varieties contain iron, and give a brownish-yellow or red bead in R.F., the violet only appearing after treatment of the bead with metallic tin on charcoal. Insoluble in acids; made soluble by fusion with an alkali or alkaline carbonate. The solution containing an excess of acid, with the addition of tin-foil, gives a beautiful violet-color when concentrated.

Diff. Characterized by its peculiar sub-adamantine lustre, and brownish-red color. Differs from tourmaline, vesuvianite, augite in being entirely unaltered when heated alone B.B. Specific gravity about 4, cassiterite 6·5.

Obs.—Rutile occurs in granite, gneiss, mica slate, and syenitic rocks, and sometimes in granular limestone and dolomite. It is generally found in imbedded crystals, often in masses of quartz or feldspar, and frequently in acicular crystals penetrating quartz. Very commonly implanted in regular position upon crystals of hematite, as from Cavradi in the Tavetschthal. Occurs in Norway; Finland; Saualpe, Carinthia; in the Urals; in the Tyrol; at St. Gothard near Freiberg; at Ohlapian in Transylvania.

In *Maine*, at Warren. In *Vermont*, at Waterbury and elsewhere. In *Mass.*, at Barre; Shelburne; Sheffield. In *Conn.*, at Lane's mine, Monroe. In *N. York*, in Orange Co.; Edenville; Warwick. In *Penn.*, Chester Co. In *N. Car.*, at Crowder's Mountain. In *Georgia*, in Habersham Co.; in Lincoln Co., at Graves' Mountain. In *Arkansas*, at Magnet Cove.

Titanium oxide is employed for a yellow color in painting porcelain, and also for giving the requisite tint to artificial teeth.

OCTAHEDRITE.* Anatase.

Tetragonal. $O \wedge 1\text{-}i = 119°\ 22'$; $\check{c} = 1\cdot77771$. Commonly octahedral or tabular. $1 \wedge 1$, pyr., $= 97°\ 51'$. $I \wedge 1 = 158°\ 18'$. Cleavage: 1 and O, perfect.

H.=5·5-6. G.=3·82–3·95; sometimes 4·11-4·16 after heating. Lustre metallic-adamantine. Color various shades of brown, passing into indigo-blue, and black; greenish-yellow by transmitted light. Streak uncolored. Fracture subconchoidal. Brittle.

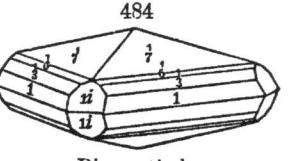

484 Binnenthal.

485

Comp.—Like rutile and brookite, pure titanic oxide.
Pyr., etc.—Same as for rutile.
Obs.—Abundant at Bourg d'Oisans, in Dauphiny; also in the Binnenthal (including here Kenngott's *wiserine*, f. 484, as shown by Klein, Jahrb. Min., 1875, 337); at Pfitsch Joch, Tyrol; near Hof in the Fichtelgebirge; Norway; the Urals; in Devonshire, near Tavistock; at Tremadoc, in North Wales; in Cornwall; in Brazil in quartz. In the U. States, at Smithfield, R. I.

HAUSMANNITE.—$Mn_3O_4 = 2MnO,MnO_2$. Tetragonal, $O \wedge 1\text{-}i = 130°\ 25'$. Color brownish-black. Thuringia; Harz, etc.
BRAUNITE.—$2(2MnO,MnO_2)+MnO_2,SiO_2$. Tetragonal, $O \wedge 1\text{-}i = 135°\ 26'$. Color dark brownish-black. Thuringia; Norway, etc.
MINIUM (Mennige, *Germ.*).—$Pb_3O_4 = PbO_2+2PbO$. Badenweiler; Wythe Co., Va., etc.

BROOKITE.*

Orthorhombic (?). $I \wedge I = 99°\ 50'\ (-100°\ 50')$: $O \wedge 1\text{-}i = 131°\ 42'$; $\check{c} : \bar{b} : \check{a} = 1\cdot1620 : 1\cdot1883 : 1$. Cleavage: I, indistinct; O, still more so.

H.=5·5-6. G.=4·12-4·23, brookite; 4·03-4·085, arkansite. Hair-brown, yellowish, or reddish, with metallic adamantine lustre, and translucent (brookite); also iron-black, opaque, and submetallic (arkansite). Streak uncolored—grayish, yellowish. Brittle.

486 Arkansas. **487** Ellenville, N. Y. **488** Miask, Ural.

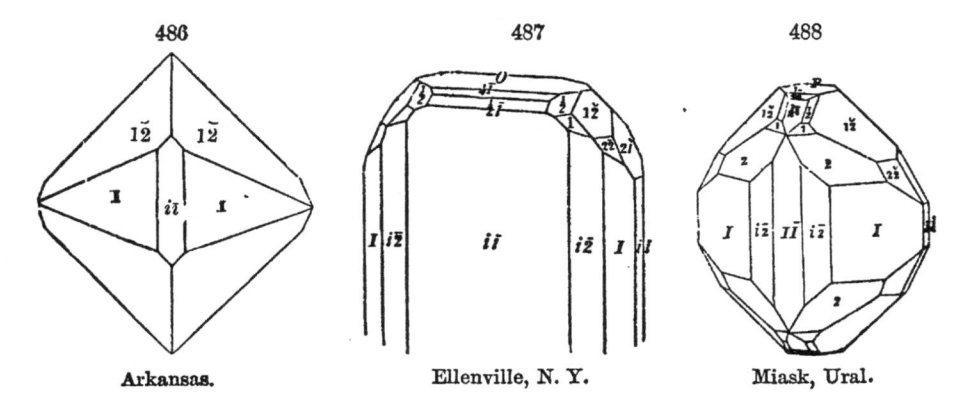

Comp.—Pure titanic oxide, TiO_2, like rutile and octahedrite.
Pyr., etc.—Same as for rutile.
Obs.—Brookite occurs at Bourg d'Oisans in Dauphiny; at St. Gothard; in the Urals, near Miask; in thick black crystals (*arkansite* f. 486) at Magnet Cove, Arkansas, sometimes altered to rutile by *paramorphism;* at Ellenville, Ulster Co., N. Y.; at Paris, Maine.

Schrauf has announced (Atlas Min., Reich. IV.) that he has found brookite to be *monoclinic* (and isomorphous with wolframite). He distinguishes three types having different axial relations. The measurements of v. Rath, however, seem to show that in part it must be *orthorhombic*.

EUMANITE.—From Chesterfield, Mass., may be identical with brookite.

PYROLUSITE.* Polianite.

Orthorhombic. $I \wedge I = 93°\ 40'$, $O \wedge 1\text{-}\bar{\imath} = 142°\ 11'$; $\breve{c} : \breve{b} : \breve{a} = 0.776 : 1.066 : 1$. Cleavage I and $i\text{-}\breve{\imath}$. Also columnar, often divergent; also granular massive, and frequently in reniform coats. Often soils.

489

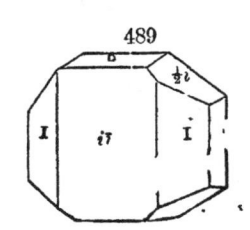

$H. = 2\text{-}2.5$. $G. = 4.82$. Turner. Lustre metallic. Color iron-black, dark steel-gray, sometimes bluish. Streak black or bluish-black, sometimes submetallic. Opaque. Rather brittle.

Comp.—$MnO_2 =$ Manganese 63.2, oxygen $36.8 = 100$.

Pyr., etc.—B.B. alone infusible; on charcoal loses oxygen. A manganese reaction with borax. Affords chlorine with hydrochloric acid.
Diff.—Hardness less than that of psilomelane. Differs from iron ores in its reaction for manganese B.B. Easily distinguished from psilomelane by its inferior hardness, and usually by being crystalline.
Obs.—Occurs extensively at Elgersberg near Ilmenau in Thuringia; at Vorderehrensdorf in Moravia; at Platten in Bohemia, and elsewhere. Occurs in the United States in Vermont, at Brandon, etc.; at Conway, Mass.; at Winchester, N. H.; at Salisbury and Kent, Conn. In California, on Red island, bay of San Francisco. In New Brunswick, near Bathurst. In Nova Scotia, at Walton; Pictou, etc.

Pyrolusite and manganite are the most important of the ores of manganese. Pyrolusite parts with its oxygen at a red heat, and is extensively employed for discharging the brown and green tints of glass. It hence received its name from πῦρ, *fire*, and λύω, *to wash*.

CREDNERITE.—$Cu_3Mn_2O_9$, or $3CuO + 2MnO_2$. Foliated. Color black. Thuringia.

B. HYDROUS OXIDES.

TURGITE.

Compact fibrous and divergent, to massive; often botryoidal and stalactitic like limonite. Also earthy, as red ochre.

H.=5-6. G.=3·56-3·74, from Ural; 4·29-4·49, fr. Hof; 4·681, fr. Horhausen; 4·14, fr. Salisbury. Lustre submetallic and somewhat satin-like in the direction of the fibrous structure; also dull earthy. Color reddish-black, to dark red; bright-red when earthy; botryoidal surface often lustrous, like much limonite. Opaque.

Comp.—$H_2Fe_2O_7$=Iron sesquioxide 94·7, water 5·3=100.
Pyr., etc.—Heated in a closed tube, flies to pieces in a remarkable manner; yields water. Otherwise like hematite.
Diff.—Distinguished from hematite and limonite by its superior hardness, the color of its streak, and B.B. its decrepitation.
Obs.—A very common ore of iron. Occurs at the Turginsk copper mine near Bosgolovsk, in the Ural; near Hof in Bavaria, and Siegen in Prussia; at Horhausen. In the U. S. it occurs at Salisbury, Ct.

DIASPORE.

Orthorhombic. $I \wedge I = 93° \ 42\frac{3}{4}'$, $O \wedge 1\text{-}\bar{\imath} = 147° \ 12\frac{1}{2}'$; $\dot{c} : \bar{b} : \check{a} = 0.64425 : 1.067 : 1$. $\check{\imath}\text{-}\check{\imath} \wedge 1\text{-}\check{\imath} = 121° \ 7\frac{1}{2}'$, $\check{\imath}\text{-}\check{\imath} \wedge 1\text{-}\bar{\imath} = 104° \ 14\frac{1}{2}'$, $\check{\imath}\text{-}\check{\imath} \wedge 1 = 116° \ 54\frac{1}{2}'$. Crystals usually thin, flattened parallel to $\check{\imath}\text{-}\check{\imath}$; sometimes acicular; commonly implanted. Cleavage: $\check{\imath}\text{-}\check{\imath}$ eminent; $\check{\imath}\text{-}\bar{\imath}$ less perfect. Occurs foliated massive and in thin scales; sometimes stalactitic.

490

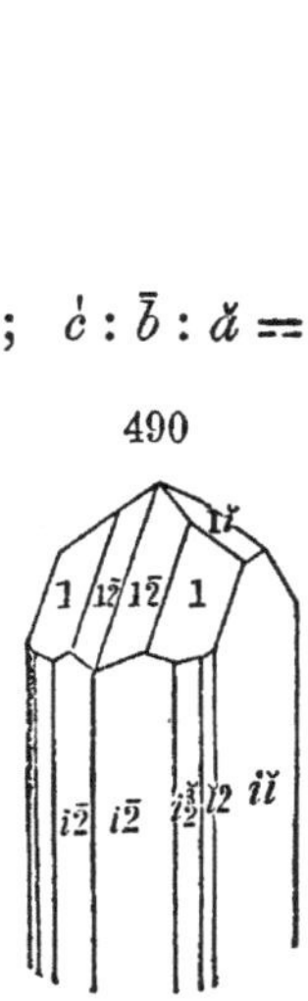

H.=6·5-7. G.=3·3-3·5. Lustre brilliant and pearly on cleavage-face; elsewhere vitreous. Color whitish, grayish-white, greenish-gray, hair-brown, yellowish, to colorless; sometimes violet-blue in one direction, reddish plumb-blue in another, and pale asparagus-green in a third. When thin, translucent—subtranslucent. Very brittle.

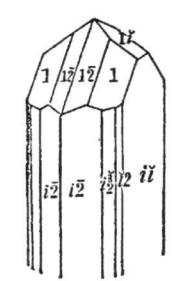

Comp.—H_2AlO_4=Alumina 85·1, water 14·9=100; a little phosphorus pentoxide is often present.
Pyr., etc.—In the closed tube decrepitates strongly, separating into pearly white scales, and at a high temperature yields water. The variety from Schemnitz does not decrepitate. Infusible; with cobalt solution gives a deep blue color. Some varieties react for iron with the fluxes. Not attacked by acids, but after ignition becomes soluble in sulphuric acid.
Diff.—Distinguished (B.B.) by its decrepitation and yielding water; as also by the reaction for alumina with cobalt solution. Resembles some varieties of hornblende, but is harder.
Obs.—Commonly found with corundum or emery. Occurs in the Ural; at Schemnitz; at Broddbo near Fahlun; in Switzerland; in Asia Minor, and the Grecian islands; in Chester Co., Pa.; at the emery mines of Chester, Mass.; N. Carolina.
Diaspore was named by Haüy from διασπείρω, to scatter, alluding to the usual decrepitation before the blowpipe.

GÖTHITE.

Orthorhombic. $I \wedge I = 94° 52'$ (B. & M.); $O \wedge 1\text{-}\bar{\imath} = 146° 33'$; $\breve{c} : \bar{b} : \breve{a} = 0.66 : 1.089 : 1$. In prisms longitudinally striated, and often flattened into scales or tables parallel to the shorter diagonal. Cleavage: brachydiagonal, very perfect. Also fibrous; foliated or in scales; massive; reniform; stalactitic.

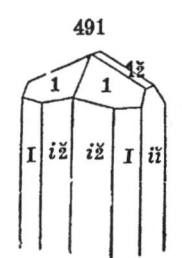

H.=5–5·5. G.=4·0–4·4. Lustre imperfect adamantine. Color yellowish, reddish, and blackish-brown. Often bloodred by transmitted light. Streak brownish-yellow—ochreyellow.

Var.—1. In thin scale-like or tabular crystals, usually attached by one edge. 2. In acicular or capillary (not flexible) crystals, or slender prisms, often radiately grouped: the *Needle-Ironstone* (*Nadeleisenstein*). It passes into (*b*) a variety with a velvety surface: the *Przibramite* (*Sammetblende*) of Przibram is of this kind. Other varieties are columnar or fibrous, scaly-fibrous, or feathery columnar; compact massive, with a flat conchoidal fracture; and sometimes reniform or stalactitic.

Comp.—$H_2FeO_4 = H_6FeO_6 + 2FeO_3$ = Iron sesquioxide 89·9, water 10·1=100.

Pyr., etc.—In the closed tube gives off water and is converted into red iron sesquioxide. With the fluxes like hematite; most varieties give a manganese reaction, and some treated in the forceps in O.F., after moistening in sulphuric acid, impart a bluish-green color to the flame (phosphoric acid). Soluble in hydrochloric acid.

Obs.—Found with the other iron oxides, especially hematite or limonite. Occurs at Eiserfeld; in Nassau; at Zwickau in Saxony; in Cornwall; in Somersetshire, at the Providence iron mines. In the U. States, near Marquette, L. Superior; in Penn., near Easton; in California, at Burns Creek, Mariposa Co.

Named *Göthite* after the poet-philosopher Göthe; and *Pyrrhosiderite* from πυρρός, *fire-red*, and σίδηρος, *iron*.

MANGANITE.

Orthorhombic. $I \wedge I = 99° 40'$, $O \wedge 1\text{-}\bar{\imath} = 147° 9\frac{1}{2}'$; $\breve{c} : \bar{b} : \breve{a} = 0.6455 : 1.185 : 1$. Twins: twinning-plane 1-$\breve{\imath}$ (f. 296, p. 96). Cleavage: $i\text{-}\breve{\imath}$ very perfect, I perfect. Crystals longitudinally striated, and often grouped in bundles. Also columnar; seldom granular; stalactitic.

H.=4. G.=4·2–4·4. Lustre submetallic. Color dark steel-gray—ironblack. Streak reddish-brown, sometimes nearly black. Opaque; minute splinters sometimes brown by transmitted light. Fracture uneven.

Comp.—$H_2MnO_4 = H_6MnO_6 + 2MnO_3$ = Manganese sesquioxide 89·8 (=Mn 62·5, O 27·3), water 10·2=100.

Pyr., etc.—In the closed tube yields water; otherwise like braunite.

Obs.—Occurs in veins traversing porphyry, at Ilefeld in the Harz; in Thuringia; Undenaes in Sweden; Christiansand in Norway; Cornwall, at various places; also in Cumberland, Devonshire, etc. In Nova Scotia, at Cheverie, etc. In New Brunswick, at Shepody mountain, Albert Co., etc.

LIMONITE. Brown Hematite. Brauneisenstein, *Germ.*

Usually in stalactitic and botryoidal or mammillary forms, having a fibrous or subfibrous structure; also concretionary, massive; and occasionally earthy.

H.=5–5·5. G.=3·6–4. Lustre silky, often submetallic; sometimes dull and earthy. Color of surface of fracture various shades of brown, commonly dark, and none bright; sometimes with a nearly black varnish-like exterior; when earthy, brownish-yellow, ochre-yellow. Streak yellowish-brown.

Var.- (1) *Compact.* Submetallic to silky in lustre; often stalactitic, botryoidal, etc. (2) *Ochreous* or earthy, brownish-yellow to ochre-yellow, often impure from the presence of clay, sand, etc. (3) *Bog ore.* The ore from marshy places, generally loose or porous in texture, often petrifying leaves, wood, nuts, etc. (4) *Brown clay-ironstone*, in compact masses, often in concretionary nodules, having a brownish-yellow streak, and thus distinguishable from the clay-ironstone of the species hematite and siderite; it is sometimes (*a*) *pisolitic*, or an aggregation of concretions of the size of small peas (Bohnerz, *Germ.*); or (*b*) *oolitic*.

Comp.—$H_6Fe_2O_9 = H_6FeO_6 + FeO_3 =$ Iron sesquioxide 85·6, water 14·4=100. In the bog ores and ochres, sand, clay, phosphates, manganese oxides, and humic or other acids of organic origin are very common impurities.

Pyr., etc.—Like göthite. Some varieties give a skeleton of silica when fused with salt of phosphorus, and leave a siliceous residue when attacked by acids.

Diff.—Distinguished from hematite by its yellowish streak, inferior hardness, and its reaction for water. Does not decrepitate, B.B., like turgite.

Obs.—Limonite occurs in secondary or more recent deposits, in beds associated at times with barite, siderite, calcite, aragonite, and quartz; and often with ores of manganese; also as a modern marsh deposit. It is in all cases a result of the alteration of other ores, through exposure to moisture, air, and carbonic or organic acids; and is derived largely from the change of pyrite, siderite, magnetite, and various mineral species (such as mica, augite, hornblende, etc.), which contain iron in the protoxide state.

Abundant in the United States. Extensive beds exist at Salisbury and Kent, Conn., also in the neighboring towns of N. Y., and in a similar situation north; at Richmond and Lenox, Mass.; in Vermont, at Bennington, etc.

Limonite is one of the most important ores of iron. The pig iron, from the purer varieties, obtained by smelting with charcoal, is of superior quality. That yielded by bog ore is what is termed *cold short*, owing to the phosphorus present, and cannot therefore be employed in the manufacture of wire, or even of sheet iron, but is valuable for casting. The hard and compact nodular varieties are employed in polishing metallic buttons, etc.

MELANOSIDERITE.—Near limonite, but containing 7·39 p. c. SiO_2, perhaps as an impurity. Cooke regards it as a very basic silicate of iron. G.=3·39. Westchester, Penn.

XANTHOSIDERITE.—$H_4FeO_5 = FeO_3$ 81·6, H_2O 18·4=100; or H_6FeO_6 (Ramm.). In fine needles. Color yellow, brown. Ilmenau; the Harz.

BEAUXITE.—Occurs in concretionary grains. Color whitish to brown. Composition doubtful, perhaps $Al(Fe)O_3+2aq$. Beaux, near Arles, France; near Lake Wochein, Styria (*wocheinite*); French Guiana.

BRUCITE.*

Rhombohedral. $R \wedge R = 82° 22\frac{1}{2}'$, $O \wedge R = 119° 39\frac{1}{2}'$; $c = 1·52078$ (Hessenberg). Crystals often broad tabular. Cleavage: basal, eminent

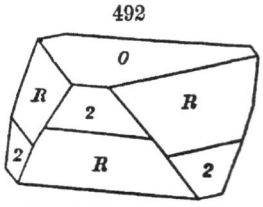

492 — Low's Mine, Texas.

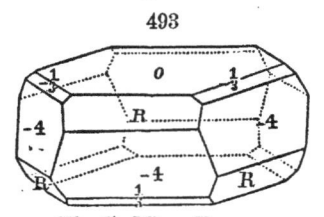

493 — Wood's Mine, Texas.

folia easily separable, nearly as in gypsum. Usually foliated massive. Also fibrous, fibres separable and elastic.

H.=2·5. G.=2·35-2·44. Lustre pearly on a cleavage-face, elsewhere between waxy and vitreous; the fibrous silky. Color white, inclining to gray, blue, or green. Streak white. Translucent—subtranslucent. Sectile. Thin laminæ flexible.

>Comp.—H_2MgO_2=Magnesia 69, water 31=100.
>Var.—1. Foliated. 2. Fibrous; called *nemalite*, containing 4 or 5 p. c. of FeO.
>Pyr., etc.—In the closed tube gives off water, becoming opaque and friable, sometimes turning gray to brown. B.B. infusible. glows with a bright light, and the ignited mineral reacts alkaline to test paper. With cobalt solution gives the violet-red color of magnesia. The pure mineral is soluble in acids without effervescence.
>Diff.—Distinguished by its infusibility. Differs from talc in its solubility in acids.
>Obs.—Brucite accompanies other magnesian minerals in serpentine, and has also been found in limestone. Occurs at Swinaness in Unst, Shetland Isles; in the Urals; at Goujot in France; near Filipstadt in Wermland. It occurs at Hoboken, N. J.; in Richmond Co., N. Y.; at Brewster, N. Y.; at Texas, Pa. The fibrous variety (*nemalite*) occurs at Hoboken, and at Xettes in the Vosges.

GIBBSITE.

Monoclinic (DesCl.). In small hexagonal crystals with replaced lateral edges. Planes vertically striated. Cleavage: basal or O eminent. Occasionally in lamello-radiate spheroidal concretions. Usually stalactitic, or small mammillary and incrusting, with smooth surface, and often a faint fibrous structure within.

H.=2·5-3·5. G.=2·3-2·4. Color white, grayish, greenish, or reddish-white; also reddish-yellow when impure. Lustre of O pearly; of other faces vitreous; of surface of stalactites faint. Translucent; sometimes transparent in crystals. A strong argillaceous odor when breathed on. Tough.

>Var.—1. In crystals: the original *hydrargillite*. 2. Stalactitic; *gibbsite*.
>Comp.—$H_6Al_2O_6$=Alumina 65·5, water 34·5=100.
>Pyr., etc.—In the closed tube becomes white and opaque. and yields water. B.B. infusible, whitens, and does not impart a green color to the flame. With cobalt solution gives a deep-blue color. Soluble in concentrated sulphuric acid.
>Diff.—Resembles chalcedony in appearance, but is softer.
>Obs.—The crystallized gibbsite occurs near Slatoust in the Ural; at Gumuchdagh, Asia Minor; on corundum at Unionville, Pa.; in Brazil. The stalactitic occurs at Richmond, Mass.; at the Clove mine, Duchess Co., N. Y.; in Orange Co., N. Y.
>Rose's hydrargillite (Urals, 1839) is identical with gibbsite (Torrey, 1822), and must receive this name. An uncertain mineral from Richmond afforded Hermann 38 p. c. of phosphoric acid, but a phosphate, if it really occurs there, is *not* gibbsite.
>PYROCHROITE.—H_2MnO_2=Manganese protoxide 79·8, water 20·2=100. Foliated. Color white. Mine of Paisberg. Filipstadt, Sweden.
>HYDROTALCITE from Snarum, Norway, and VÖLKNERITE from the Urals, contain alumina, magnesia, and water with more or less carbon dioxide. Probably mixtures, containing brucite, gibbsite, etc. HOUGHITE from Oxbow and Rossie, N. Y., is a similar mineral derived from the alteration of spinel. NAMAQUALITE (*Church*). A related mineral; from Namaqualand, So. Africa.

PSILOMELANE.*

Massive and botryoidal. Reniform. Stalactitic.
H.=5-6. G.=3·7-4·7. Lustre submetallic. Streak brownish-black, shining. Color iron-black, passing into dark steel-gray. Opaque.

OXYGEN COMPOUNDS.—HYDROUS OXIDES. 283

Comp.—Somewhat doubtful. Contains manganese oxide, with varying amounts of baryta, and potash (lithia), and also water. General formula, according to Rammelsberg, $R_5O_9 = RO + 4MnO_2$, where R is K_2, Ba or Mn. Analyses:

	O	MnO	BaO	K_2O	H_2O		
1. Thüringen	11·43	65·76	16·59	——	5·25	CuO 0·59, CoO 0·79, CaO 0·51=100·72	Olschewsky.
2. Ilmenau	15·82	77·23	0·12	——	5·29	CaO 0·91, CuO 0·40=99·77	Clausbruch.

Pyr., etc.—In the closed tube most varieties yield water, and all lose oxygen on ignition; with the fluxes reacts for manganese. Soluble in hydrochloric acid, with evolution of chlorine.

Obs.—This is a common ore of manganese. It occurs in Devonshire and Cornwall; at Ilefeld in the Harz; also at Johanngeorgenstadt; Schneeberg; Ilmenau; Siegen, etc. It forms mammillary masses at Chittenden, Irasburg, and Brandon, Vt.

WAD.

The manganese ores here included occur in amorphous and reniform masses, either earthy or compact, and sometimes incrusting or as stains. They are mixtures of different oxides, and cannot be considered chemical compounds or distinct mineral species.

H.=0·5–6. G.=3–4·26; often loosely aggregated, and feeling very light to the hands. Color dull black, bluish or brownish-black.

Comp., Var.—Perhaps $H_2Mn_2O_5 = 2MnO_2 + aq$ (Rammelsberg), but in all cases mixed with other ingredients.

Varieties: (A) Manganesian; (B) Cobaltiferous; (C) Cupriferous.

A. BOG MANGANESE.—Consists mainly of manganese dioxide and water, with some iron sesquioxide, and often silica, alumina, baryta.

B. ASBOLITE, or Earthy Cobalt, is wad containing cobalt oxide, which sometimes amounts to 32 p. c. *Lithiophorite*, *heterogenite*, and *rabdionite* belong near here.

C. LAMPADITE, or Cupreous Manganese. A wad containing 4 to 18 p. c. of copper oxide, and often cobalt oxide also. It graduates into black copper (Melaconite). G.=3·1–3·2.

Pyr., etc.— *Wad* reacts like psilomelane. *Earthy cobalt* gives a blue bead with salt of phosphorus, and when heated in R.F. on charcoal with tin, some specimens yield a red opaque bead (copper). *Cupreous manganese* gives similar reactions, and three varieties give a strong manganese reaction with soda, and evolve chlorine when treated with hydrochloric acid.

Obs.—The above ores are results of the decomposition of other ores—partly of oxides, and partly of manganesian carbonates. Wad or bog manganese is abundant in the counties of Columbia and Dutchess, N. Y. There are large deposits of bog manganese at Blue Hill Bay, Dover, and other places in Maine.

Earthy cobalt occurs at Riechelsdorf in Hesse; Saalfeld in Thuringia; at Nertschinsk in Siberia; at Alderly Edge in Cheshire.

CHALCOPHANITE.—Rhombohedral. In druses of minute tabular crystals; also in stalactitic aggregates. H.=2·5. G.=3·907. Lustre metallic. Color bluish-black. Analysis gave MnO_2 59·94, MnO 6·58, ZnO 21·70, FeO_3 0·25, H_2O 11·58=100·05. Composition $2MnO_2 + (Mn,Zn)O + 2aq$. If half the water were basic, the formula might be written $2RMnO_3 + aq$, where $R = Mn, Zn$ and H_2. B.B. becomes of a copper color, hence the name ($\chi\alpha\lambda\kappa\acute{o}s$, *brass, bronze*, and $\varphi\alpha\acute{\iota}\nu\omega$, *to appear*). Stirling Hill, N. J. (*Moore.*)

2. OXIDES of Elements of the Arsenic and Sulphur Groups, Series II

VALENTINITE. Weisspiesglaserz, *Germ.*

Orthorhombic. $I \wedge I = 136° 58'$; $O \wedge 1\text{-}\bar{\imath} = 105° 35'$; $\check{c} : \bar{b} : \check{a} = 3·5868 : 2·5365 : 1$. Often in rectangular plates with the lateral edges bevelled, and in acicular rhombic prisms. Cleavage: I, highly perfect, easily obtained. Also massive; structure lamellar, columnar, granular. H.=2·5–3. G.=5·566, crystals from Bräunsdorf. Lustre adamantine, $i\text{-}i$ often pearly; shining. Color snow-white, occasionally peach-blossom red, and ash-gray to brownish. Streak white. Translucent—subtransparent.

494

Comp.—Sb_2O_3=Oxygen 16·44, antimony 83·56=100.
Obs.—Found at Przibram in Bohemia; at Felsobanya in Hungary; Bräunsdorf in Saxony. Also at South Ham, Canada East.

SENARMONTITE.*—Same composition as the above, but crystallizes in isometric octahedrons. G.=5·2–5·3. Perneck, Hungary; Cornwall; Haraclas in Algeria; S. Ham, Canada.

CLAUDETITE; ARSENOLITE.—Both As_2O_3. The former is orthorhombic, the latter isometric. They thus correspond to the two forms of Sb_2O_3 (see above). *Claudetite* (G.=3·85) occurs in thin plates at the San Domingo mines, Portugal. *Arsenolite* (G.=3·698) occurs usually in capillary crystals, also stalactitic; earthy. Andreasberg; Joachimsthal; Cornwall; Ophir mine, Nevada; California.

BISMITE (Wismuthocker, *Germ*.).—Bi_2O_3. Occurs massive, earthy. Schneeberg; Joachimsthal; Cornwall. KARELINITE.—$3BiO+BiS$. Massive. Color lead-gray. G.=6·60. Savodinsk mine in the Altai.

MOLYBDITE (Molybdänocker, *Germ*.).—Composition MoO_3. In radiated crystallizations, as an incrustation, etc. Occurs with molybdenite. At Westmoreland, New Hampshire; Chester, Penn.; Virginia City, Nevada. ILSEMANNITE, near the above. Bleiberg, Carinthia.

TUNGSTITE.—WO_3. Pulverulent and earthy. Cornwall; Monroe, Ct. MEYMACITE (Carnot).—A hydrated tungstite. Meymac, Corrèze.

KERMESITE (Antimonblende, *Germ*.).—Composition $Sb_2S_2O=2Sb_2S_3+Sb_2O_3$. In capillary crystals. Color cherry-red. Bräunsdorf, Saxony; Allemont; South Ham, Canada East.

CERVANTITE.—$SbO_2=Sb_2O_3+Sb_2O_5$. Color yellow. Results from alteration of stibnite. Spain; Tuscany; Hungary, etc.; South Ham, Canada.

---

3. OXIDES of the Carbon-silicon Group, Series II.

QUARTZ.*

Rhombohedral, and for the most part hemihedral to the rhombohedron (or tetartohedral to the hexagonal prism). $R \wedge R = 94° 15'$, $O \wedge R = 128° 13'$; $\check{c} = 1·0999$. $i \wedge 2\text{-}2 = 142° 2'$, $R \wedge -1$, ov. i, $= 103° 34'$, $R \wedge -1$, adj., $= 133° 44'$, $R \wedge i$, ov. 2-2, $= 113° 8'$. Cleavage: R, -1, and i very indistinct: sometimes effected by plunging a heated crystal in cold water. Crystals sometimes very short, but general habit prismatic; the crystals

OXYGEN COMPOUNDS—SILICA.

much elongated, sometimes fine acicular; usually implanted by one extremity of the prism. Prismatic faces i commonly striated horizontally, and thus distinguishable, in distorted crystals, from the pyramidal. Crystals often grouped by juxtaposition, not proper twins. Frequently in radiated masses with a surface of pyramids, or in druses having a surface of pyramids or short crystals. Twins: twinning-plane, (1), the basal plane O (f. 506); very generally penetration-twins, as illustrated in f. 265, p. 89. (2) The pyramid 1-2, truncating the edge between $+R$ and $-R$, divergence of axes $84° 33'$. Other methods of twinning rare, parallel to i, to R, to $\frac{1}{2}R$, etc. (Jenzsch). Also in pseudo-trillings on calcite, with 2-2 as the approximate twinning-plane (see f. 336, p. 101).

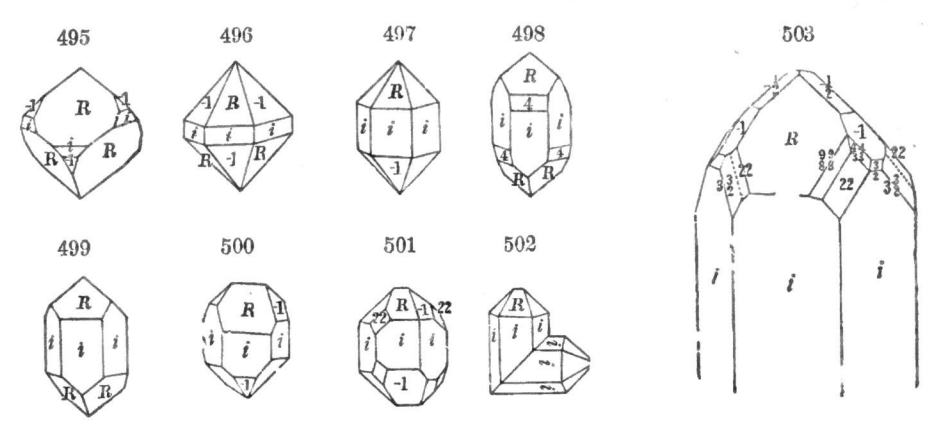

Massive; coarse or fine granular to flint-like or crypto-crystalline. Sometimes mammillary, stalactitic, and in concretionary forms.

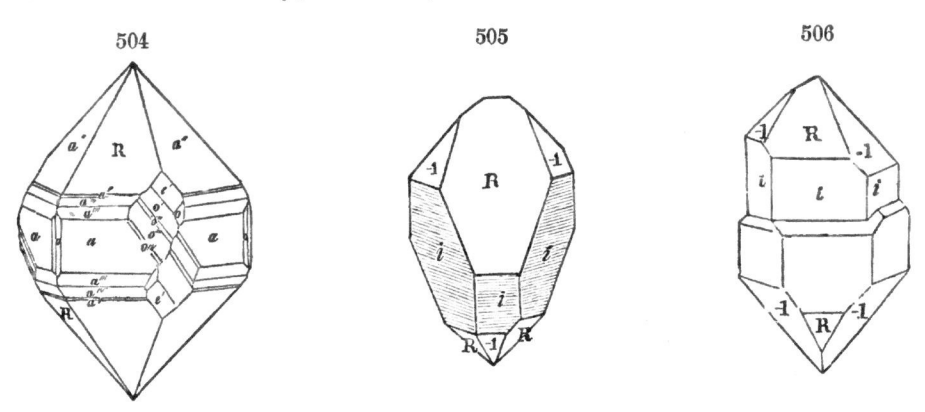

H.=7. G.=2·5–2·8; 2·6413–2·6541 (Beudant). Lustre vitreous, sometimes inclining to resinous; splendent—nearly dull. Colorless when pure; often various shades of yellow, red, brown, green, blue, black. Streak white, of pure varieties; if impure, often the same as the color, but much paler. Transparent—opaque. Fracture perfect conchoidal—subconchoidal. Tough—brittle—friable. Polarization circular, see pp. **142–144**.

Comp.—Pure silica, or SiO_2 = Oxygen 53·33, silicon 46·67 = 100. In massive varieties often mixed with a little opal-silica. Impure varieties contain iron sesquioxide, calcium carbonate, clay, sand, and various minerals.

Var.—1. Crystallized (phenocrystalline), vitreous in lustre. 2. Flint-like, massive, or cryptocrystalline. The first division includes all ordinary vitreous quartz, whether having crystalline faces or not. The varieties under the second are in general acted upon somewhat more by attrition, and by chemical agents, as fluohydric acid, than those of the first. In all kinds made up of layers, as agate, successive layers are unequally eroded.

A. Phenocrystalline or Vitreous Varieties.

1. *Ordinary Crystallized; Rock Crystal.* Colorless quartz, or nearly so, whether in distinct crystals or not.
2. *Asteriated; Star quartz* (Sternquartz, *Germ.*). Containing within the crystal whitish or colored radiations along the diametral planes.
3. *Amethystine; Amethyst.* Clear purple, or bluish-violet. The color is supposed to be due to manganese.
4. *Rose.* Rose-red or pink, but becoming paler on exposure. Common massive, and then usually much cracked. Lustre sometimes a little greasy. Fuchs states that the color is due to titanic oxide. It may come in part from manganese.
5. *Yellow; False Topaz.* Yellow and pellucid, or nearly so; resembling somewhat yellow topaz, but very different in crystallization and in absence of cleavage.
6. *Smoky, Cairngorm Stone.* Smoky-yellow to smoky-brown, and often transparent; but varying to brownish-black, and then nearly opaque in thick crystals. The color is due to organic compounds, according to Forster.
7. *Milky.* Milk-white and nearly opaque. Lustre often greasy, and then called *Greasy* quartz.
8. *Cat's Eye* (Katzenauge, *Germ.*). Exhibiting opalescence, but without prismatic colors, an effect due to fibres of asbestus.
9. *Aventurine.* Spangled with scales of mica or other mineral.
10. *Impure from the presence of distinct minerals* distributed densely through the mass. The more common kinds are those in which the impurities are: (*a*) *ferruginous*, either red or yellow iron oxide; (*b*) *chloritic*, some kind of chlorite; (*c*) *actinolitic;* (*d*) *micaceous;* (*e*) *arenaceous*, or sand. Quartz crystals also occur penetrated by various minerals, as topaz, corundum, chrysoberyl, garnet, different species of the hornblende and pyroxene groups, rutile, hematite, göthite, etc., etc.

Containing liquids in cavities. These liquids are seen to move with the change of position of the crystal, provided an air-bubble be present in the cavity. The liquid is either water (pure, or a mineral solution), carbon dioxide, or some petroleum-like or other compound.

B. Cryptocrystalline Varieties.

1. *Chalcedony.* Having the lustre nearly of wax, and either transparent or translucent. Color white, grayish, pale-brown to dark-brown, black; tendon-color common; sometimes delicate blue. Also of other shades, and then having other names. Often mammillary, botryoidal, stalactitic, and occurring lining or filling cavities in rocks. It is true quartz, with some disseminated opal.
2. *Carnelian.* A clear red chalcedony, pale to deep in shade; also brownish-red to brown, the latter kind reddish-brown by transmitted light.
3. *Chrysoprase.* An apple-green chalcedony, the color due to the presence of nickel oxide.
4. *Prase.* Translucent and dull leek-green; so named from πράσον, *a leek.* Always regarded as a stone of little value. The name is also given to crystalline quartz of the same color.
5. *Plasma.* Rather bright-green to leek-green, and also sometimes nearly emerald-green, and subtranslucent or feebly translucent; sometimes dotted with white. *Heliotrope*, or *Blood-stone*, is the same stone essentially, with small spots of red jasper, looking like drops of blood.
6. *Agate.* A variegated chalcedony. The colors are either banded or in clouds, or due to visible impurities. *a. Banded.* The bands are delicate parallel lines, of white, tendon-like, wax-like, pale and dark-brown, and black colors, and sometimes bluish and other shades. They follow waving or zigzag courses, and are occasionally concentric circular, as in the eye-agate. The bands are the edges of layers of deposition, the agate having been formed by a deposit of silica from solutions intermittently supplied, in irregular cavities in rocks, and

deriving their concentric waving courses from the irregularities of the walls of the cavity. Owing also to the unequal porosity, agates may be varied in color by artificial means. β. *Irregularly* clouded. The colors various, as in banded agate. γ. *Colors due to visible impurities*, including *Moss-agate*, filled with brown moss-like or dendritic forms distributed through the mass; *Dendritic Agate*, containing brown or black dendritic markings. There is also *Agatized wood*: wood petrified with clouded agate.

7. *Onyx.* Like agate in consisting of layers of different colors, but the layers are in even planes, and the banding therefore straight, and hence its use for cameos, the head being cut in one color, and another serving for the background. The colors of the best are perfectly well defined, and either white and black, or white, brown and black alternate.

8. *Sardonyx.* Like onyx in structure, but includes layers of carnelian (sard) along with others of white or whitish, and brown, and sometimes black colors.

9. *Jasper.* Impure opaque colored quartz. (*a*) *Red* iron sesquioxide being the coloring matter. (*b*) *Brownish*, or *ochre-yellow*, colored by *hydrous* iron sesquioxide, and becoming red when so heated as to drive off the water. (*c*) Dark-green and brownish-green. (*d*) Grayish-blue. (*e*) Blackish or brownish-black. (*f*) *Striped* or *riband jasper* (Bandjaspis, *Germ.*), having the colors in broad stripes. (*g*) *Egyptian jasper*, in nodules which are zoned in brown and yellowish colors. *Porcelain jasper* is nothing but baked clay, and differs from true jasper in being B.B. fusible on the edges. *Red porphyry*, or its base, resembles jasper, but is also fusible on the edges, being usually an impure feldspar.

10. *Agate-Jasper.* An agate consisting of jasper with veinings and cloudings of chalcedony.

11. *Siliceous sinter.* Irregularly cellular quartz, formed by deposition from waters containing silica or soluble silicates in solution.

12. *Flint* (Feuerstein, *Germ.*). Somewhat allied to chalcedony, but more opaque, and of dull colors, usually gray, smoky-brown, and brownish-black. The exterior is often whitish, from mixture with lime or chalk, in which it is imbedded. Lustre barely glistening, subvitreous. Breaks with a deeply conchoidal fracture, and a sharp cutting edge. The flint of the chalk formation consists largely of the remains of infusoria (Diatoms), sponges, and other marine productions. The coloring matter of the common kinds is mostly carbonaceous matter.

13. *Hornstone* (Hornstein, *Germ.*). Resembles flint, but more brittle, the fracture more splintery. *Chert* is a term often applied to hornstone, and to any impure flinty rock, including the jaspers.

14. *Basanite, Lydian Stone* or *Touchstone.* A velvet-black siliceous stone or flinty jasper, used on account of its hardness and black color for trying the purity of the precious metals. The color left on the stone after rubbing the metal across it indicates to the experienced eye the amount of alloy. It is not splintery like hornstone.

Pyr., etc.—B.B. unaltered; with borax dissolves slowly to a clear glass; with soda dissolves with effervescence; unacted upon by salt of phosphorus. Insoluble in hydrochloric acid, and only slightly acted upon by solutions of fixed caustic alkalies. When fused and cooled it becomes opal-silica, having $G.=2\cdot2$.

Diff.—Quartz is distinguished by its *hardness*—scratching glass with facility; *infusibility*—not fusing before the blowpipe; *insolubility*—not attacked by water or the acids; *uncleavability*—one variety being tabular, but proper cleavage never being distinctly observed. To these characteristics the action of soda B.B. may be added.

Obs.—Quartz occurs as one of the essential constituents of granite, syenite, gneiss, mica schist, and many related rocks; as the principal constituent of quartz-rock and many sandstones; as an unessential ingredient in some trachyte, porphyry, etc.; as the vein-stone in various rocks, and for a large part of mineral veins; as a foreign mineral in the cavities of trap, basalt, and related rocks, some limestones, etc., making geodes of crystals, or of chalcedony, agate, carnelian, etc.; as imbedded nodules or masses in various limestones, constituting the flint of the chalk formation, the hornstone of other limestones—these nodules sometimes becoming continuous layers; as masses of jasper occasionally in limestone. It is the principal material of the pebbles of gravel beds, and of the sands of the sea-shore and sand beds everywhere. Silica also occurs in solution (but mostly as a soluble alkaline silicate) in heated natural waters, as those of the Geysers of Iceland, New Zealand, and California, and the Yellowstone Park, and very sparingly in many cold mineral waters.

Switzerland, Dauphiny, Piedmont, the Carrara quarries, and numerous other foreign localities, afford fine specimens of rock crystal. Amethysts are brought from India, Ceylon, and Persia, also Transylvania. The amygdaloids of Iceland and the Faroe Islands, afford magnificent specimens of *chalcedony;* also Hüttenberg and Loben in Carinthia, etc. The finest *carnelians* and *agates* are found in Arabia, India, Brazil, Surinam, Oberstein, and Saxony. *Cat's eye*, in Ceylon, the coast of Malabar, and also in the Harz and Bavaria. *Heliotrope*, is Bucharia, Ta tary, Siberia.

In New York, quartz crystals are abundant in Herkimer Co. Fine dodecahedral crystals, at the beds of specular iron in St. Lawrence Co. In Antwerp, Jefferson Co., at Diamond Island and Diamond Point, Lake George, Pelham and Chesterfield, Mass., Paris and Perry, Me., Benton, N. H., Sharon, Vt., Meadow Mount, Md., and Hot Springs, Ark., are other localities of quartz crystal. For other localities, see the catalogue of localities in the latter part of this volume.

Rose quartz, at Albany and Paris, Me., Acworth, N. H., and elsewhere; *smoky quartz*, at Goshen, Mass., Richmond Co., N. Y., Pike's Peak, Colorado, etc.; *amethyst*, at Keweenaw Point and Thunder Bay, etc., Lake Superior; also at Bristol, Rhode Island, near Greensboro, N. C.; Specimen Mountain, Yellowstone Park. Crystallized green quartz, at Providence, Delaware Co., Penn.; at Ellenville, N. Y. Chalcedony and agates about Lake Superior, the Mississippi, and the streams to the west, etc. Red jasper is found in pebbles on the banks of the Hudson at Troy; red and yellow, near Murphy's, Calaveras Co., Cal. Heliotrope occupies veins in slate at Bloomingrove, Orange Co., N. Y.

Several varieties of this species have long been employed in jewelry. The *amethyst* has always been esteemed for its beauty. Cameos are in general made of onyx, which is well fitted for this kind of miniature sculpture. Jasper admits of a brilliant polish, and is often formed into vases, boxes, knife-handles, etc. It is also extensively used in the manufacture of Florentine mosaics. The carnelian is often rich in color, but is too common to be much esteemed; when first obtained from the rock they are usually gray or grayish-red; they receive their fine colors from an exposure of several weeks to the sun's rays, and a subsequent heating in earthen pots. The colors of agate, when indistinct, may be brought out by boiling in oil, and afterward in sulphuric acid; the latter carbonizes the oil absorbed by the porous layers, and thus increases the contrast of the different colors.

TRIDYMITE.*

Hexagonal. $1 \wedge 1 = 124°\ 3'$ (basal); $1 \wedge 1 = 127°\ 35'$ (terminal); $\dot{c} = 1\cdot6304$ (v. Rath). Cleavage O, imperfect. Crystals minute, commonly tabular (f. 507), formed by the prism and basal plane; also frequently in twins and trillings with (1) $\frac{1}{6}$, and (2) $\frac{3}{4}$ as the twinning-planes. Double refraction positive.

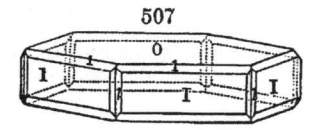

H.$=7$. G.$=2\cdot282$–$2\cdot326$. Lustre vitreous, on the face pearly. Colorless, becoming white on weathering. Fracture conchoidal.

Comp.—Pure silica, or SiO_2, like quartz.

Pyr.—B.B. infusible. Fuses in soda with effervescence, forming a colorless glass. Soluble in a boiling saturated solution of sodium carbonate.

Obs.—First found in cavities in the trachyte from Cerro St. Cristoval, near Pachuca, Mexico. Also in the trachyte of the Siebengebirge, and in related rocks from many localities. Forming on one occasion the mass of white volcanic ashes, from the island Vulcano. Also in microscopic crystals inclosed in opal, and in quartz.

ASMANITE (*Maskelyne*).—A third form of silica, crystallizing in the orthorhombic system, "isomorphous with brookite." H.$=5\cdot5$. G.$=2\cdot245$. Found in very minute crystalline grains, generally rounded, in the meteoric iron of Breitenbach.

OPAL.

Massive, amorphous; sometimes small reniform. stalactitic, or large tuberose. Also earthy.

H.$=5\cdot5$–$6\cdot5$. G.$=1\cdot9$–$2\cdot3$. Lustre vitreous, frequently subvitreous; often inclining to resinous, and sometimes to pearly. Color white, yellow, red, brown, green, gray, generally pale; dark colors arise from foreign admixtures; sometimes a rich play of colors, or different colors by refracted and reflected light. Streak white. Transparent to nearly opaque.

Comp.—Silica, SiO_2, as for quartz, the opal condition being one of lower degrees of hardness and specific gravity. Water is usually present, but it is regarded as unessential. It varies in amount from 2 to 21 p. c.; or, mostly, from 3–9 p. c.

Var.—1. *Precious Opal.* Exhibits a play of delicate colors, or, as Pliny says, presents various refulgent tints in succession, reflecting now one hue and now another. Seldom larger than a hazel-nut. Doubly refracting (biaxial), *Behrens.*
3. *Fire-opal.* Hyacinth-red to honey-yellow colors, with fire-like reflections somewhat irised on turning.
3. *Girasol.* Bluish-white, translucent, with reddish reflections in a bright light.
4. *Common Opal.* In part translucent; (a) milk-white to greenish, yellowish, bluish; (b) *Resin-opal* (Wachsopal, Pechopal, *Germ.*), wax-, honey- to ochre-yellow, with a resinous lustre; (c) dull olive-green and mountain-green; (d) brick-red.
5. *Cacholong.* Opaque, bluish-white, porcelain-white, pale-yellowish or reddish; often adheres to the tongue, and contains a little alumina.
6. *Opal-agate.* Agate-like in structure, but consisting of *opal* of different shades of color.
7. *Jasp-opal.* Opal containing some yellow iron sesquioxide and other impurities, and having the color of yellow jasper, with the lustre of common opal.
8. *Wood-opal* (Holzopal, *Germ.*). Wood petrified by opal.
9. *Hyalite.* Clear as glass and colorless, constituting globular concretions, and also crusts with a globular, reniform, botryoidal, or stalactitic surface; also passing into translucent, and whitish.
10. *Fiorite, Siliceous Sinter.* Includes translucent to opaque, grayish, whitish, or brownish incrustations, porous to firm in texture; sometimes fibrous-like or filamentous, and, when so, pearly in lustre, formed from the decomposition of the siliceous minerals of volcanic rocks about fumaroles, or from the siliceous waters of hot springs. It graduates at times into hyalite. *Geyserite* constitutes concretionary deposits about the Iceland and Yellowstone (*pealite*) geysers, presenting white or grayish, porous, stalactitic, filamentous, cauliflower-like forms; also compact-massive, and scaly-massive; H.=5; rarely transparent, usually opaque; sometimes falling to powder on drying in the air.
11. *Float-stone.* In light concretionary or tuberose masses, white or grayish, sometimes cavernous, rough in fracture. So light, owing to its spongy texture, as to float on water. The concretions sometimes have a flint-like nucleus.
12. *Tripolite.* Formed from the siliceous shells of Diatoms and other microscopic species, as first made known by Ehrenberg, and occurring in deposits, often many miles in area, either uncompacted, or moderately hard. *Infusorial Earth,* or *Earthy Tripolite,* a very fine-grained earth looking often like an earthy chalk, or a clay, but harsh to the feel, and scratching glass when rubbed on it.

Pyr., etc.—Yields water. B.B. infusible, but becomes opaque. Some yellow varieties, containing iron, turn red.

Obs.—Occurs filling cavities and fissures or seams in igneous rocks, porphyry, and some metallic veins. Also imbedded, like flint, in limestone, and sometimes, like other quartz concretions, in argillaceous beds; also formed from the siliceous waters of some hot springs; also resulting from the mere accumulation, or accumulation and partial solution and solidification, of the siliceous shells of infusoria—which consist essentially of opal-silica.

Precious opal occurs in Hungary; in Honduras; and Mexico. *Fire opal* occurs at Zimapan in Mexico; Faröe; near San Antonio, Honduras. *Common opal* is abundant at Telkebanya in Hungary; in Moravia; in Bohemia; Stenzelberg in the Siebengebirge; Faröe, Iceland; the Giant's Causeway, at many localities. In U. S., *hyalite* occurs sparingly in N. York, at the Phillips ore bed, Putnam Co.; in Georgia, in Burke and Scriven Cos.; in Washington Co., good fire opal. At the Geysers on the Fire Hole river, Yellowstone Park, geyserite is abundant.

The precious opal, when large, and exhibiting its peculiar play of colors in perfection, is a gem of high value. It is cut with a convex surface.

MELANOPHLOGITE (*Lasaulx*).—Occurs in minute, colorless, cubes coating sulphur crystals from Girgenti, Sicily. Contains SiO_2 86·3 p. c., SO_3 7·2, H_2O 2·9; chemical nature doubtful. Turns black upon ignition, hence the name.

II. TERNARY OXYGEN COMPOUNDS.

1. SILICATES.—A. ANHYDROUS SILICATES.

a. BISILICATES. GENERAL FORMULA $RSiO_3$.

(a) Amphibole Group. Pyroxene Section.

ENSTATITE. BRONZITE. Protobastite.

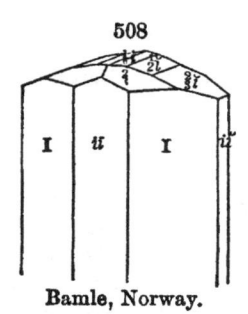

Orthorhombic. $I \wedge I = 88° 16'$ and $91° 44'$ (Breitenbach meteorite, *v. Lang*); $\check{c} : \bar{b} : \check{a} = 0.58853 : 1.03086 : 1$. Cleavage: I, easy; $i\text{-}\check{\imath}$, $i\text{-}\bar{\imath}$, less so. Sometimes a fibrous appearance on the cleavage-surface. Also massive and lamellar.

H.=5·5. G.=3·1–3·3. Lustre a little pearly on cleavage-surfaces to vitreous; often metalloidal in the bronzite variety. Color grayish-white, yellowish-white, greenish-white, to olive-green and brown. Streak uncolored, grayish. Double refraction positive; optic-axial plane brachydiagonal; axes very divergent.

508

Bamle, Norway.

Comp., Var.—$MgSiO_3$=Silica 60, magnesia 40=100; also $(Mg,Fe)SiO_3$.

Var. 1. *With little or no iron; Enstatite.* Color white, yellowish, grayish, or greenish-white; lustre pearly-vitreous; G.=3·10–3·13. *Chladnite*, which makes up 90 p. c. of the Bishopville meteorite, belongs here and is the purest kind; *Victorite (Meunier)*, from the Deesa (Chili) meteoric iron is probably identical.

2. *Ferriferous; Bronzite.* Color grayish-green to olive-green and brown; lustre of cleavage-surface adamantine pearly to submetallic or bronze-like. The ratio of Mg : Fe varies from 11 : 1 to 3 : 1. Analysis of bronzite from Leiperville by Pisani, SiO_2 57·08, AlO_3 0·28, FeO 5·77, MgO 35·59, H_2O 0·90=99·62.

Pyr., etc.—B.B. almost infusible, being only slightly rounded on the thin edges; F.=6. Insoluble in hydrochloric acid.

Diff.—Distinguished by its infusibility from varieties of amphibole, which it resembles.

Obs.—Occurs near Aloysthal in Moravia; in the Vosges; at Kupferberg in Bavaria; at Baste in the Harz (*Protobastite*); in the chrysolite bombs in the Eifel; in immense crystals with apatite, near Bamle, Norway. In Pennsylvania, at Leiperville and Texas; at Brewster, N. Y. Bronzite is quite common in meteorites.

DesCloizeaux first defined the limits of this species, as here laid down.

Named from 'ενστάτης, an *opponent*, because so refractory. The name *bronzite* has priority, but a bronze lustre is not essential, and is far from universal.

HYPERSTHENE.

Orthorhombic. $I \wedge I = 91° 32\frac{1}{2}'$, DesCloizeaux (Mt. Doré); 91° 40' v. Rath (*amblystegite*). Cleavage: $i\text{-}\check{\imath}$ perfect, I and $i\text{-}\bar{\imath}$ distinct but interrupted. Usually foliated massive.

H.=5–6. G.=3·392. Lustre somewhat pearly on a cleavage-surface, and sometimes a little metalloidal; often with a peculiar iridescence due

OXYGEN COMPOUNDS—ANHYDROUS SILICATES.   291

to the presence of minute enclosed tabular crystals (brookite?) in parallel position (Kosmann). Color dark brownish-green, grayish-black, greenish-black, pinchbeck-brown. Streak grayish, brownish-gray. Translucent to nearly opaque. Brittle. Optic-axial plane brachydiagonal; axes very divergent; bisectrix negative.

509

Comp.—(Mg,Fe)SiO$_3$ with Fe : Mg=1 : 5, 1 : 3, etc. It Fe to Mg=1 : 2 the formula requires SiO$_2$ 54·2, FeO 21·7, MgO 24·1=100.
Pyr., etc.—B.B. fuses to a black enamel, and on charcoal yields a magnetic mass. Partially decomposed by hydrochloric acid.
Obs.—Hypersthene occurs at Isle St. Paul, Labrador in Canada; at the Isle of Skye; in Greenland; Norway; Ronsberg in Bohemia; the Tyrol; Elfdalen in Sweden; Laacher See (*amblystegite*); Voigtland; in trachyte of Mt. Doré, Auvergne.

In chemical composition, *enstatite* (and *bronzite*), and *hypersthene* belong together, since they grade insensibly into each other; and in crystalline form they are identical. The essential difference between them, according to DesCloizeaux, lies in the axial dispersion which is *uniformly* $\rho < v$ for enstatite, and $\rho > v$ for hypersthene.

Mt. Doré.

DIACLASITE.—Near bronzite; differs in optical characters. (Mg,Fe,Ca)SiO$_3$. Harzburg; Guadarrama, Spain.

WOLLASTONITE. Tabular Spar. Tafelspath, *Germ*.

Monoclinic. $C = 69°\ 48'$, $I \wedge I = 87°\ 28'$, $O \wedge 2\text{-}i = 137°\ 48'$; $\dot{c} : \bar{b} : \dot{a} = 0.4338 : 0.89789 : 1$. Fig. 510 in the pyroxene or normal position, but with the edge $O/i\text{-}i$ the obtuse edge; f. 511 in the position given the crystals by authors who make $i\text{-}i$ the plane O, and $2\text{-}i$ the plane I. $O \wedge -1\text{-}i = 160°\ 30'$, $O \wedge 1\text{-}i = 154°\ 25'$, $i\text{-}i \wedge -2 = 132°\ 54'$, $i\text{-}i \wedge 2 = 93°\ 52'$. Rarely in distinct tabular crystals. Cleavage: O most distinct; $i\text{-}i$ less so; $1\text{-}i$ and $-1\text{-}i$ in traces. Twins: twinning-plane $i\text{-}i$. Usually cleavable massive, with the surface appearing long fibrous, fibres parallel or reticulated, rather strongly coherent.

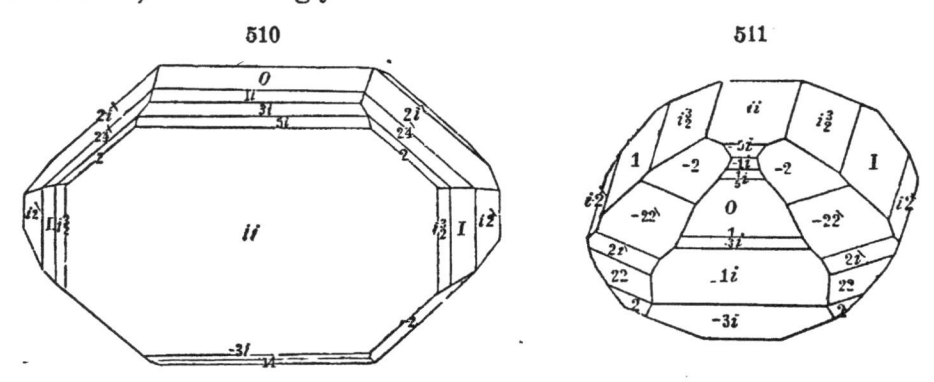

510   511

H. = 4·5–5. G. = 2·78–2·9. Lustre vitreous, inclining to pearly upon the faces of perfect cleavage. Color white, inclining to gray, yellow, red, or brown. Streak white. Subtransparent—translucent. Fracture uneven, sometimes very tough. Optic-axial plane $i\text{-}\bar{\imath}$; divergence 70° 40' for the red rays; bisectrix of the acute angle negative; inclined to a normal to $i\text{-}i$ 57° 48', and to a normal to O 12°, DesCl.

Comp.—$CaSiO_3$=Silica 51·7, lime 48·3=100.

Pyr., etc.—In the matrass no change. B.B. fuses easily on the edges; with some soda, a blebby glass, with more, swells up and is infusible. With hydrochloric acid gelatinizes; most varieties effervesce slightly from the presence of calcite.

Diff.—Differs from asbestus, and tremolite in forming a jelly with acids, as also by its more vitreous fracture; fuses less readily than natrolite and scolecite; when pure does not effervesce with acids like the carbonates.

Obs.—Wollastonite is found in regions of granite and granular limestone; also in basalt and lavas. Occurs in Hungary; in Finland; and in Norway; at Göckum in Sweden; in the Harz; at Auerbach, in granular limestone; at Vesuvius. In the U. S., in *N. York*, at Willsborough; at Lewis; Diana, Lewis Co. In *Penn.*, Bucks Co. At the Cliff Mine, Keweenaw Point, Lake Superior. In *Canada*, at Grenville.

PYROXENE.

Monoclinic. $C = 73° 59'$, $I \wedge I = 87° 5'$, $O \wedge 2\text{-}\check{\imath} = 131° 17'$; $\check{a} : b : \bar{a} = 0.5412 : 0.91346 : 1$. $O \wedge I = 100° 57'$, $O \wedge -1\text{-}i = 155° 51'$, $O \wedge 1\text{-}i = 148° 35'$, $O \wedge -1 = 146° 9'$, $O \wedge 1 = 137° 49'$, $-1 \wedge -1 = 131° 24'$.

Cleavage: I rather perfect, often interrupted; $i\text{-}\check{\imath}$ sometimes nearly per-

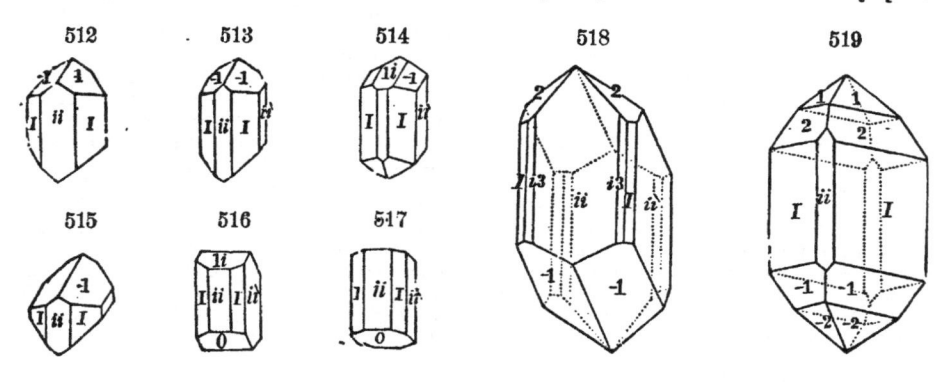

fect; $i\text{-}\check{\imath}$ imperfect; O sometimes easy. Crystals usually thick and stout. Twins: twinning-plane $i\text{-}i$ (f. 521). Often coarse lamellar, in large masses, parallel to O or $i\text{-}i$. Also granular, particles coarse or fine; and fibrous, fibres often fine and long.

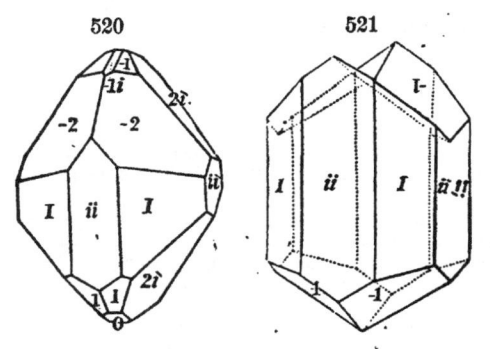

H.=5-6. G.=3·23-3·5. Lustre vitreous, inclining to resinous; some pearly. Color green of various shades, verging on one side to white or grayish-white, and on the other to brown and black. Streak white to gray and grayish-green. Transparent—opaque. Fracture conchoidal—uneven. Brittle. In crystals from Fassa, optic-axial plane $i\text{-}\check{\imath}$; divergence 110° to 113°; bisectrix of the acute angle positive, inclined 51° 6' to a normal to $i\text{-}i$ and 22° 55' to a normal to O, DesCl.

OXYGEN COMPOUNDS —ANHYDROUS SILICATES.

Comp., Var.—A bisilicate, having the general formula $RSiO_3$, where R may be Ca,Mg, Fe,Mn, sometimes also Zn, Ka_2, Na_2. Usually two or more of these bases are present. The first three are most common; but calcium is the only one that is present always and in large percentage. Besides the substitutions of the above bases for one another, these same bases are at times replaced by Al,Fe,Mn, though sparingly, and the silicon occasionally by aluminum.

The varieties proceeding from these isomorphous substitutions are many and diverse; and there are still others depending on the state of crystallization. The foliated and fibrous kinds early received separate names, and for a while were regarded as distinct species. Fibrous or columnar forms are very much less common than in hornblende, and lamellar or foliated kinds more common. The crystals are rarely long and slender, or bladed, like those of that species.

The most prominent division of the species is into (A) the *non-aluminous ;* (B) the *aluminous.* But the former of these groups shades imperceptibly into the latter. These two groups are generally subdivided according to the prevalence of the different protoxide elements. Yet here, also, the gradation from one series to another is in general by almost insensible shades as to composition and chemical characters, as well as all physical qualities.

I. Containing little or no Alumina.

1. *Lime-Magnesia Pyroxene ;* MALACOLITE. Diopside, Alalite, White Coccolite. Color white, yellowish, grayish-white to pale green. In crystals: cleavable and granular massive. Sometimes transparent and colorless. G.$=3\cdot2-3\cdot38$. Formula, $CaMgSi_2O_6=$Silica 55·6, magnesia 18·5, lime 25·9. Sometimes Ca : Mg$=1 : 2$; less than 4 p. c. of iron are present.

2. *Lime-Magnesia-Iron Pyroxene ;* SAHLITE. Color grayish-green to deep green and black; sometimes grayish and yellowish-white. In crystals ; also cleavable and granular massive G.$=3\cdot25-3\cdot4$. Named from Sala in Sweden, one of its localities, where the mineral occurs in masses of a grayish-green color, having a perfect cleavage parallel to the basal plane (O). Formula $(Ca,Mg,Fe)SiO_3$. The ratio of Ca : Mg : Fe varies much, $=3 : 3 : 1, 2 : 2 : 1$, etc. The ratio$=4 : 3 : 1$, corresponds to silica 53·7, magnesia 13·4, lime 24·9, iron protoxide 8·0$=100$.

DIALLAGE. Part of the so-called *diallage*, or thin-foliated pyroxene, belongs here, and the rest under the corresponding division of the aluminous pyroxenes. Color grayish-green to bright grass-green, and deep green; lustre of cleavage surface pearly, sometimes metalloidal or brassy. H.$=4$. G.$=3\cdot2-3\cdot35$. Composition near the preceding; analysis by vom Rath, Neurode, SiO_2 53·60, AlO_3 1·99, FeO 8·95, MnO 0·28, MgO 13·08, CaO 21·06, H_2O 0·86$=99\cdot82$. With this variety belongs part also of what has been called *hypersthene* and *bronzite*—the part that is easily fusible. Common especially in serpentine rocks. Named from διαλλαγή, *difference*, in allusion to the dissimilar cleavages.

3. *Iron-Lime Pyroxene.* HEDENBERGITE. Color black. In crystals, and also lamellar massive ; cleavage easy parallel to i-i. G.$=3\cdot5-3\cdot58$. Formula $CaFeSi_2O_6$ (Mg being absent) $=$Silica 48·39, lime 22·18, iron protoxide 29·43$=100$. *Asteroite* is a similar pyroxene containing also Mn (Igelström), Sweden.

4. *Lime-Iron-Manganese-Zinc Pyroxene ;* JEFFERSONITE. Color greenish-black. Crystals often very large (3-4 in. thick), with the angles generally rounded, and the faces uneven, as if corroded. G.$=3\cdot36$. Analysis, Franklin, N. J., by Pisani, SiO_2 45·95, AlO_3 0·85, FeO 8·91, MnO 10·20, ZnO 10·15, CaO 21·55, MgO 3·61, ign 0·35$=101\cdot57$.

II. Aluminous.

Aluminous Lime-Magnesia Pyroxene ; LEUCAUGITE (*Dana*). Color white or grayish. Analysis, Bathurst, C., by Hunt, SiO_2 51·50, AlO_3 6·15, FeO_3 0·35, MgO 17·69, CaO 23·80, H_2O 1·10$=100\cdot59$. Looks like diopside. H.$=6\cdot5$. G.$=3\cdot19$. Hunt. Named from λευκος, *white.*

Aluminous Lime-Magnesia-Iron Pyroxene ; FASSAITE, AUGITE. Color clear deep-green to greenish-black and black ; in crystals, and also massive ; subtranslucent to opaque. G. $=3\cdot25-3\cdot5$. Contains iron, with calcium and magnesium, also aluminum. Analysis of augite from Montreal by Hunt, SiO_2 49·40, AlO_3 6·70, FeO_3 7·83, MgO 13·06, CaO 21·88, Na_2O 0·74, H_2O 0·50$=100\cdot11$.

a. Fassaite (or *Pyrgom*). Includes the green kinds found in metamorphic rocks. Named from the locality at Fassa in Piedmont, which affords deep-green crystals, sometimes pistachio-green, like the epidote of the locality.

b. Augite. Includes the greenish or brownish-black and black kinds, occurring mostly in eruptive rocks, but also in metamorphic. Named from αυγή, *lustre.*

Pyr., etc.—Varying widely, owing to the wide variations in composition in the different varieties, and often by insensible gradations. Fusibility, from the almost infusible diallage to 3·75 in diopside; 3·5 in sahlite; 3 in jeffersonite and augite; 2·5 in hedenbergite. Varieties rich in iron afford a magnetic globule when fused on charcoal, and in general their fusibility varies with the amount of iron. Jeffersonite gives with soda on charcoal a reaction for zinc and manganese; many others also give with the fluxes reactions for manganese. Most varieties are unacted upon by acids.

Diff.—See Amphibole, p. 297.

Obs.—Pyroxene is a common mineral in crystalline limestone and dolomite, in serpentine, and in volcanic rocks; and occurs also, but less abundantly, in connection with granitic rocks and metamorphic schists. The pyroxene of limestone is mostly the white and light-green or gray varieties; that of most other metamorphic rock, sometimes white or colorless, but usually green of different shades, from pale green to greenish-black, and occasionally black; that of serpentine is sometimes in fine crystals, but often of the foliated green kind called *diallage;* that of eruptive rocks is the black to greenish-black *augite.*

Prominent foreign localities are: *malacolite (diopside),* Traversella, Ala in Piedmont; Sala, Tunaberg, Sweden; Pargas; Achmatovsk; etc. *Sahlite,* Sala; Arendal; Degeröe; Schwarzenberg; etc. *Hedenbergite,* Tunaberg; Arendal. *Augite,* Fassathal; Vesuvius; etc.—in most dolerytic igneous rocks.

In N. America common (see list of localities at the close of the volume). Some localities are: In *Mass.,* at the Bolton quarries. In *Conn.,* at Canaan. In *N. York,* at Warwick, Monroe, Edenville, Diana. In *N. Jersey,* in Franklin. In *Penn.,* near Attleboro'. In *Canada,* at Bytown, at Calumet I., at Grenville.

ACMITE.—Monoclinic. In slender pointed crystals (hence name) in quartz. H.=6. G.= 3·2–3·53. Color brownish to reddish-brown, in the fracture blackish-green. Opaque. Fracture uneven. Brittle. $RSiO_3, R=Na_2, Fe,$ or $Fe(Fe=3R)$; analysis by Rammelsberg, SiO_2 51·66, FeO_3 28·28, FeO 5·23, MnO 0·69, Na_2O 12·46, K_2O 0·43, TiO 1·11, ign 0·39=100·25. Kongsberg, Norway.

ÆGIRITE.—Near pyroxene in form, but contains alkalies. H.=5·5–6. G.=3·45–3·58. Color greenish-black. Subtranslucent to opaque. Analysis Ramm., Brevig, SiO_2 50·25, AlO_3 1·22, FeO_3 22·07, FeO 8·80, MnO 1·40, CaO 5·47, MgO 1·28, Na_2O 9·29, K_2O 0·94=100·72. Also from Magnet Cove, Arkansas.

RHODONITE.

Triclinic, but approximately isomorphous with pyroxene. Cleavage: *I* perfect; *O* less perfect. Usually massive.

522

H.=5·5–6·5. G.=3·4–3·68. Lustre vitreous. Color light brownish-red, flesh-red, sometimes greenish or yellowish, when impure; often black outside from exposure. Streak white. Transparent—opaque. Fracture conchoidal—uneven. Very tough when massive.

Comp., Var.—$MnSiO_3$=Silica 45·9, manganese protoxide 54·1= 100. Usually some Fe and Ca, and occasionally Zn replace part of the Mn. *Ordinary.* (*a*) Crystallized. Either in crystals or foliated. The ore in crystals from Paisberg, Sweden, was named *Paisbergite* under the idea that it was a distinct species. (*b*) Granular massive. *Calciferous;* BUSTAMITE. Contains 9 to 15 p. c. of lime replacing part of the manganese. Often also impure from the presence of calcium carbonate, which suggests that part of the lime replacing the manganese may have come from partial alteration. Grayish-red. *Zinciferous;* FOWLERITE. In crystals and foliated, the latter looking much like cleavable red feldspar; the crystals sometimes half an inch to an inch through. $I \wedge I$=86° 30', Torrey. G.=3·44, Thomson.

Pyr., etc.—B.B. blackens and fuses with slight intumescence at 2·5; with the fluxes gives reactions for manganese; fowlerite gives with soda on charcoal a reaction for zinc. Slightly acted upon by acids. The calciferous varieties often effervesce from mechanical admixture with calcium carbonate. In powder, partly dissolves in hydrochloric acid, and the in soluble part becomes of a white color. Darkens on exposure to the air, and sometimes becomes nearly black.

Obs.—Occurs at Longban, near Philipstadt in Sweden; also in the Harz; in the district of

Katherinenberg in the Ural; in Cornwall, etc. Occurs in Warwick, Mass.; Blue Hill Bay, Maine; near Hinsdale, N. H.; *fowlerite (keatingine)* at Hamburg and Sterling, New Jersey. Named from ρόδον, *a rose*, in allusion to the color.

BABINGTONITE.—Triclinic. $9RSiO_3+FeSi_3O_9$, with $R=Fe(Mn) : Ca(Mg)=2 : 3$ (Ramm.). Analysis, Rammelsberg, SiO_2 51·22, FeO_3 11·00, FeO 10·26, MnO 7·91, MgO 0·77, CaO 19·32, ign=0·44=100·92. Color greenish-black. Arendal; Nassau; Devonshire; Baveno.

SPODUMENE.*

Monoclinic. $C = 69° 40'$ $I \wedge I = 87°$, $O \wedge 2\text{-}i = 130° 30'$. Crystals large. Cleavage: $i\text{-}i$ very perfect; I also perfect; $1\text{-}i$ in traces; in striæ on $i\text{-}i$. Twins: twinning-plane $i\text{-}i$. Also massive, with broad cleavage surface.

H.=6·5–7. G.=3·13–3·19. Lustre pearly. Cross fracture vitreous. Color grayish-green, passing into greenish-white and grayish-white, rarely faint-reddish. Streak uncolored. Translucent—subtranslucent. Fracture uneven.

523

Norwich, Mass.

Comp.—$3RSiO_3+4AlSi_2O_9$; $R=Li_2$ mostly. Silica 64·2, alumina 29·4, lithia 6·4=100. Sometimes Li : Na(K)=20 : 1, Ramm.

Pyr., etc.—B.B. becomes white and opaque, swells up, imparts a purple red color (lithia) to the flame, and fuses at 3·5 to a clear or white glass. The powdered mineral, fused with a mixture of potassium bisulphate and fluor on platinum wire, gives a more intense lithia reaction. Not acted upon by acids.

Diff.—Distinguished by its perfect orthodiagonal, as well as prismatic, cleavage; has a higher specific gravity and more pearly lustre than feldspar or scapolite. Gives a red flame B.B.

Obs.—Occurs on the island of Utö, Sweden; near Sterzing and Lisens in the Tyrol; at Killiney Bay, near Dublin, and at Peterhead in Scotland. At Goshen, Mass.; also at Chesterfield and Norwich, Mass.; at Windham, Maine; at Winchester, N. H.; at Brookfield, Ct.

PETALITE.—$3Li_2Si_2O_5+4AlSi_6O_{15}$=Silica 77·97, alumina 17·79, lithia 3·57, soda 0·67=100. Ramm. Q. ratio Li : Al : Si=1 : 4 : 20, or for bases to silicon=1 : 4. H.=6–6·5. G.=2·5. Colorless; white. Utö, Sweden; Elba (*castorite*); Bolton, Mass.

Amphibole Section.

ANTHOPHYLLITE.

Orthorhombic. $I \wedge I = 125°$ to $125° 25'$. Cleavage: $i\text{-}i$ perfect, I less so, $i\text{-}i$ difficult. Commonly lamellar, or fibrous massive; fibres often very slender.

H.=5·5. G.=3·1–3·2. Lustre somewhat pearly upon a cleavage surface. Color brownish-gray, yellowish-brown, brownish-green, sometimes submetallic. Streak uncolored or grayish. Translucent to subtranslucent. Brittle. Double refraction positive; optical axes in the brachydiagonal section.

Comp.—$(Fe,Mg)SiO_3$, $Fe : Mg = 1 : 3$ = Silica 55·5, magnesia 27·8, iron protoxide 16·7 = 100.

Pyr., etc.—B.B. fuses with great difficulty to a black magnetic enamel; with the fluxes gives reactions for iron; unacted upon by acids.

Obs.—Occurs near Kongsberg in Norway, and near Modum. Also at Hermannschlag, Moravia.

Anthophyllite bears the same relation to the Amphibole Group that enstatite and hypersthene do to the Pyroxene Group.

KUPFFERITE.—Probably $MgSiO_3$, with a little Fe. $I \wedge I = 124°\ 30'$, hence an *enstatite-hornblende*. Color emerald-green (chrome). Tunkinsk Mts., Miask. Analysis of a similar mineral from Perth, Canada, Thomson, SiO_2 57·60, AlO_3 3·20, FeO 2·10, MgO 29·30, CaO 3·55, ign. 3·55 = 99·30.

AMPHIBOLE.* HORNBLENDE.

Monoclinic. $C = 75°\ 2'$, $I \wedge I = 124°\ 30'$, $O \wedge 1\text{-}i = 164°\ 10'$, $\check{c} : \bar{b} : \check{a} = 0·5527 : 1·8825 : 1$. Crystals sometimes stout, often long and bladed. Cleavage: I highly perfect; $i\text{-}i$, $i\text{-}i$ sometimes distinct. Lateral planes often longitudinally striated. Twins: twinning-plane $i\text{-}i$, as in f. 527 (simple form f. 526), and 530. Imperfect crystallizations: fibrous or columnar, coarse or fine, fibres often like flax; sometimes lamellar; also granular massive, coarse or fine, and usually strongly coherent, but sometimes friable.

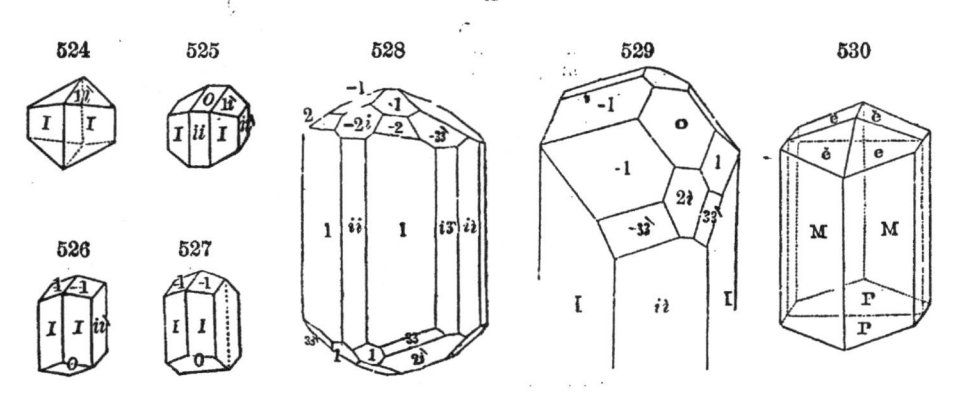

$H. = 5\text{-}6$. $G. = 2·9\text{-}3·4$. Lustre vitreous to pearly on cleavage-faces; fibrous varieties often silky. Color between black and white, through various shades of green, inclining to blackish-green. Streak uncolored, or paler than color. Sometimes nearly transparent; usually subtranslucent—opaque. Fracture subconchoidal, uneven. Bisectrix, in most varieties, inclined about 60° to a normal to O, and 15° to a normal to $i\text{-}i$; and double refraction negative.

Comp., Var.—General formula $RSiO_3$, as for pyroxene. Aluminum is present in most amphibole, and when so it usually replaces silicon. R may correspond to two or more of the basic elements $Mg, Ca, Fe, Mn, Na_2, K_2, H_2$; and R to Al, Fe or Mn. Fe sometimes replaces silicon, like Al. Much amphibole, especially the aluminous, contains some fluorine. The base calcium is absent from some varieties, or nearly so.

The *varieties* of amphibole are as numerous as those of pyroxene, and for the same reasons; and they lead in general to similar subdivisions.

OXYGEN COMPOUNDS—ANHYDROUS SILICATES.

I. Containing little or no Alumina.

Magnesia-Lime Amphibole; TREMOLITE. Grammatite. Colors white to dark-gray. In distinct crystals, either long bladed or short and stout; long and thin columnar, or fibrous; also compact granular massive. $I \wedge I = 124° \ 30'$. H.$=5\cdot0$–$6\cdot5$. G.$=2\cdot9$–$3\cdot1$. Sometimes transparent and colorless. Contains magnesia and lime with little or no iron; formula (Ca, Mg)SiO$_3$, Ca : Mg$=1 : 3=$Silica $57\cdot70$, magnesia $28\cdot85$, lime $13\cdot35=100$. Named *Tremolite* by Pini, from the locality at Tremola in Switzerland.

NEPHRITE.—In part a tough, compact, fine grained tremolite, having a tinge of green or blue, and breaking with a splintery fracture and glistening lustre. H.$=6$–$6\cdot5$. G.$=2\cdot96$–$3\cdot1$. Named from a supposed efficacy in diseases of the kidney, from νεφρός, *kidney*. It occurs usually associated with talcose or magnesian rocks. Nephrite or jade was brought in the form of carved ornaments from Mexico or Peru soon after the discovery of America. A similar stone comes from China and New Zealand.

A nephrite-like mineral, called *bowenite*, from Smithfield, R. I., having the hardness $5\cdot5$ is serpentine in composition. The jade of de Saussure is the *saussurite* (see under ZOISITE) of the younger de Saussure. Another aluminous jade has been called *jadeite* (q. v.) by Damour.

Magnesia-Lime-Iron Amphibole; ACTINOLITE. Strahlstein, *Germ.* Color bright-green and grayish-green. In crystals, either short or long-bladed, as in tremolite; columnar or fibrous; granular massive. G.$=3$–$3\cdot2$. Sometimes transparent. Contains magnesia and lime, with some iron protoxide, but seldom more than 6 p. c.; formula (Ca,Mg.Fe)SiO$_3$. The variety in long bright-green crystals is called *glassy actinolite;* the crystals break easily across the prism. The fibrous and radiated kinds are often called *asbestiform actinolite* and *radiated actinolite.* Actinolite owes its green color to the iron present.

Iron-Magnesia Amphibole; CUMMINGTONITE. Color gray to brown. Usually fibrous or fibro-lamellar, often radiated. G.$=3\cdot1$–$3\cdot32$. Contains much iron, with some magnesia, and little or no lime. Formula (Fe,Mg)SiO$_3$. Named from the locality, Cummington, Mass.

ASBESTUS. Tremolite, actinolite, and other varieties of amphibole, excepting those containing much alumina, pass into fibrous varieties, the fibres of which are sometimes very long, fine, flexible, and easily separable by the fingers, and look like flax. These kinds, like the corresponding of pyroxene, are called *asbestus* (fr. the Greek for *incombustible*). The colors vary from white to green and wood-brown. The name *amianthus* is now applied usually to the finer and more silky kinds. Much that is so called is *chrysotile*, or fibrous serpentine, it containing 12 to 14 p. c. of water. *Mountain leather* is a kind in thin flexible sheets, made of interlaced fibres; and *mountain cork* (Bergkork) the same in thicker pieces; both are so light as to float on water, and they are often hydrous. *Mountain wood* (Bergholz, Holzasbest, *Germ*) is compact fibrous, and gray to brown in color, looking a little like dry wood.

II. Aluminous.

Aluminous Magnesia-Lime Amphibole. (*a*) EDENITE. Color white to gray and pale-green, and also colorless; G.$=3\cdot0$–$3\cdot059$, Ramm. Resembles anthophyllite and tremolite. Named from the locality at Edenville, N. Y. (for analysis, see below.) To this variety belong various pale-colored amphiboles, having less than five p. c. of oxide of iron.

(*b*) SMARAGDITE *Saussure.* A thin-foliated variety, of a light grass-green color, resembling much common green diallage. According to Boulanger it is an aluminous magnesia-lime amphibole, containing less than $3\frac{1}{4}$ p. c. iron protoxide, and is hence related to edenite and the light green Pargas mineral. DesCloizeaux observes that it has the cleavage, and apparently the optical characters, of amphibole. H.$=5$; G.$=3$. It forms, along with whitish or greenish saussurite, a rock.

Aluminous Magnesia-Lime-Iron Amphibole. (*a*) PARGASITE; (*b*) HORNBLENDE. Colors bright, dark, green, and bluish-green to grayish-black and black. $I \wedge I = 124° \ 1'$–$124° \ 25'$; G.$=3\cdot05$–$3\cdot47$. *Pargasite* is usually made to include green and bluish-green kinds, occurring in stout lustrous crystals, or granular; and *hornblende* the greenish-black and black kinds, whether in stout crystals or long bladed, columnar, fibrous, or massive granular. But no line can be drawn between them. Pargasite occurs at Pargas, Finland, in bluish-green and grayish-black crystals.

Composition shown by the following analyses by Rammelsberg; (1) from Edenville; (2) Wolfsburg, Bohemia; (3) Brevig.

	SiO_2	Al_2O_3	Fe_2O_3	FeO	MnO	MgO	CaO	Na_2O	K_2O	H_2O(ign)
(1)	51·67	5·75	2·86	——	——	23·37	12·42	0·75	0·84	0·46=98·12
(2)	41·98	14·31	5·81	7·18	——	14·06	12·55	1·64	1·54	0·26=99·10
(3)	43·28*	6·31	6·62	21·72	1·13	3·62	9·68	3·14	2·65	0·48=98·63

* With 1·01 TiO_2.

Pyr., etc.—The observations under pyroxene apply also to this species, it being impossible to distinguish the varieties by blowpipe characters alone.

Diff.—Distinguished from pyroxene (and tourmaline) by its distinct prismatic cleavage, yielding an angle of 124°. Also in colored varieties by its dichroism, when examined in thin sections. Fibrous and columnar forms are much more common than with pyroxene, lamellar and foliated forms rare. Crystals often long, slender, or bladed. Differs from the fibrous zeolites in not gelatinizing with acids.

Isomorphous and Dimorphous relations to Pyroxene.—The analogy in composition between pyroxene and hornblende has been abundantly illustrated. They have the same general formula; and under this formula there is but one difference of any importance, viz., that lime is a prominent ingredient in *all* the varieties of pyroxene, while it is wanting, or nearly so, in some of those of hornblende. The analogy between the two species in crystallization, or their essential isomorphism, was pointed out by G. Rose in 1831, who showed that the forms of both were referable to one and the same fundamental form. The prism I of hornblende corresponds in angle to i-2 of pyroxene. Calculating from the angle $I \wedge I$ in pyroxene, 87° 5', the angle of i-2 is precisely 124° 30', or the angle $I \wedge I$ in hornblende. But while thus isomorphous in axial relations or form, they are also *dimorphous*. For (1) the cleavage in pyroxene is parallel to the prism of 87° 5', and in hornblende to that of 124¼°. (2) The occurring secondary planes of the latter are in general diverse from those of the former, so that the crystals differ strikingly in habit or system of modifications. Moreover, in pyroxene columnar and fine fibrous forms are uncommon; in hornblende, exceedingly common. (3) The several chemical compounds under pyroxene have *one-tenth* higher specific gravity than the corresponding ones under hornblende.

Vom Rath has described the occurrence of minute crystals of hornblende in parallel position upon crystals of pyroxene (Vesuvius), and in consequence of the relation between the two forms, thus brought out, suggests a change in the commonly accepted fundamental form of the latter. (Jahrb. Min., 1876.) This association of crystals of the two species in parallel position is not uncommon.

Obs.—Amphibole occurs in many crystalline limestones, and metamorphic granitic and schistose rocks, and sparingly in serpentine, and volcanic or igneous rocks. Tremolite, the magnesia-lime variety, is especially common in limestones, particularly magnesian or dolomitic; actinolite, the magnesia-lime-iron variety, in steatitic rocks; and brown, dark-green, and black hornblende, in chlorite schists, mica schist, gneiss, and in various other rocks (syenyte, dioryte, etc.), of which it forms a constituent part. Asbestus is often found in connection with serpentine. Hornblende is often disseminated in black prismatic crystals through trachyte, and also through other igneous rocks, especially the feldspathic kinds.

Aussig and Teplitz in Bohemia, Tunaberg in Sweden, and Pargas in Finland, afford fine specimens of the dark-colored hornblendes. *Actinolite* in the Zillerthal; *tremolite* at St. Gothard, in granular limestone or dolomite; the Tyrol; the Bannat, etc. *Asbestus* is found in Savoy, Salzburg, the Tyrol; in the island of Corsica. Some localities in the U. S. are:— Carlisle, Pelham, etc., *Mass.*, *cummingtonite* at Cummington. In *Conn.*, white crystals of tremolite in dolomite, Canaan. In *N. York*, Willsboro', St. Lawrence Co.; Warwick; with pyroxene at Edenville; near Amity; in Rossie; the variety *pargasite* in large white crystals at Diana, Lewis Co. In *Penn.*, actinolite at Mineral Hill, in Delaware Co.; at Unionville. In *Maryland*, actinolite and asbestus at the Bare Hills; asbestus at Cooptown.

HEXAGONITE.—Described as a new mineral by Goldsmith, but shown by Kœnig to be only a variety of tremolite. From Edwards, St. Lawrence Co., N. Y.

ARFVEDSONITE.—Near hornblende, but contains alkalies. Analysis, Ramm., Greenland. SiO_2 51·22, Al_2O_3 tr., FeO_2 23·75, FeO 7·80, MnO 1·12, CaO 2·08, MgO 0·90, Na_2O 10·58, K_2O 0·68, ign 0·16=98·29. Greenland; Brevig; Arendal.

CROCIDOLITE.—Composition uncertain, near arfvedsonite. Analysis, Stromeyer, SiO_2 51·22, FeO 34·08, MnO 0·10, MgO 2·48, CaO 0·03, Na_2O 7·07, H_2O 4·80=99·78. Fibrous, asbestus-like. Sometimes altered to "*Faserquarz.*" Color lavender-blue or leek-green. Orange river, So. Africa. Vosges Mts.

GASTALDITE.—Monoclinic. Cleavage prismatic, $I \wedge I = 124°\ 25'$ (like amphibole). H.= 6–7. G.=3·044. Color dark-blue to azure-blue. Streak greenish-blue. Q. ratio R : R : Si =1 : 2 : 6; formula $R_3Al_2Si_6O_{27}$, with R=Fe.Mg.Ca Na. Analysis, Strüver, SiO_2 58·55, Al_2O_3 21·40, FeO 9·04, MgO 3·92, CaO 2·03, Na_2O 4·77, K_2O tr=99·71. Occurs in chlorite slate in the valleys of Aosta and Locano.

GLAUCOPHANE.—Monoclinic. Cleavage prismatic, $I \wedge I = 124°\ 51'$. H.=6·5. G.=3·0907

OXYGEN COMPOUNDS—ANHYDROUS SILICATES.

Color blue, bluish-black. Q. ratio for bases to silicon 1 : 2. Analysis from Zermatt, by Bodewig, SiO_2 57·81, AlO_3 12·03, FeO_3 2·17, FeO 5·78. MgO 13·07, CaO 2·20, Na_2O 7·33 =100·45. Also from island of Syra.
WICHTISITE, Finland.—Perhaps identical with glaucophane.

BERYL.*

Hexagonal. $O \wedge 1 = 150° \; 3'$; $\check{c} = 0·499$. Habit prismatic, the prism often vertically striated. Cleavage: basal imperfect; lateral indistinct. Occasionally coarse columnar and large granular.

H. = 7·5–8. G. = 2·63–2·76. Lustre vitreous, sometimes resinous. Color emerald-green, pale green, passing into light-blue, yellow, and white. Streak white. Transparent — subtranslucent. Fracture conchoidal, uneven. Brittle. Double refraction feeble; axis negative.

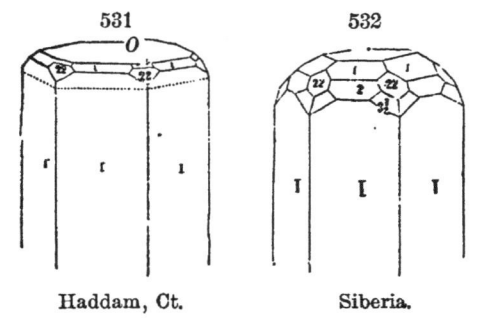

531 Haddam, Ct.   532 Siberia.

Var.—This species is one of the few that occur only in crystals, and that have no essential variations in chemical composition. There are, however, two prominent groups dependent on color, the color varying as chrome or iron is present; but only the merest trace of either exists in any case. The crystals are usually oblong prisms. 1. *Emerald*. Color bright emerald-green, owing to the presence of chromium. Hardness a little less than for beryl, according to the lapidaries. 2. *Beryl*. Colors those of the species, excepting emerald-green, and due mainly to iron. The varieties of beryl depending on color are of importance in the arts, when the crystals are transparent enough to be of value as gems. The transparent bluish-green kinds are called *aquamarine;* also apple-green; greenish-yellow to iron-yellow and honey-yellow. *Davidsonite* is nothing but greenish-yellow beryl from near Aberdeen; and *goshenite* is a colorless or white variety from Goshen, Mass.

Comp.—$Be_3AlSi_6O_{18}$=Silica 66·8, alumina 19·1, glucina 14·1=100.

Pyr., etc.—B.B. alone unchanged or becomes clouded; at a high temperature the edges are rounded, and ultimately a vesicular scoria is formed. Fusibility=5·5 (Kobell). Glass with borax clear and colorless for beryl, a fine green for emerald. Slowly soluble with salt of phosphorus without leaving a siliceous skeleton. A yellowish variety from Broddbo and Finbo yields with soda traces of tin. Unacted upon by acids.

Diff.—Distinguished from apatite by its hardness, not being scratched by a knife, also harder than green tourmaline; from chrysoberyl by its form, and from euclase and topaz by its imperfect cleavage; never massive.

Obs.—Emeralds occur in clay slate, in isolated crystals or in nests (not in veins), near Muso, etc., in N. Gránada; in Siberia. Transparent beryls (*aquamarines*) are found in Siberia, Hindostan, and Brazil. Beautiful crystals also occur at Elba; Ehrenfriedersdorf; Schlackenwald; at St. Michael's Mount in Cornwall; Limoges in France; in Sweden; Fossum in Norway; and elsewhere.

Beryls of gigantic dimensions have been found in the United States, in *N. Hamp.*, at Acworth and Grafton, and in *Mass.*, at Royalston; but they are mostly poor in quality. A crystal from Grafton, according to Prof. Hubbard, measures 45 in. by 24 in its diameter, and a single foot in length by calculation weighs 1,076 lbs., making it, in all nearly 2¼ tons. Other localities are in *Mass.*, at Barre; at Goshen; at Chesterfield. In *Conn.*, at Haddam; Middletown; at Madison. In *Penn.*, at Leiperville and Chester; at Mineral Hill.

EUDIALYTE.—Rhombohedral. Color rose-red. Exact composition uncertain. Analysis, Damour, SiO_2 50·38, ZrO_2 15·60, Ta_2O_5 0·35, FeO 6·37, MnO 1·61, CaO 9·23, Na_2O 13·10, Cl 1·48, H_2O 1·25=99·37. West Greenland. EUCOLITE is similar, but contains also some of the cerium metals. Norway.

POLLUCITE.*—$3R_2AlSi_4O_{12}$+2aq with R = mostly Cs(Na,Li). If Na : Cs=1 : 2, then SiO_2 42·6, AlO 18·2, Cs_2O 33·4, Na_2O 3·7, H_2O 2·1=100. Isometric. Colorless. Island of Elba with castorite.

β. UNISILICATES. GENERAL FORMULA R_2SiO_4.

Chrysolite Group.

CHRYSOLITE.* Olivine. Peridot.

Orthorhombic. $I \wedge I = 94° 2'$; $O \wedge 1\text{-}\bar{i} = 128° 28'$; $\bar{c} : \bar{b} : \bar{a} = 1·2588 :$ $1·0729 : 1$. $O \wedge 1\text{-}i = 130° 26\frac{1}{2}'$. $i\text{-}\bar{2} \wedge i\text{-}\bar{2}$, ov. $i\text{-}\bar{i}, = 130° 2'$. Cleavage: $i\text{-}\bar{i}$ rather distinct. Massive and compact, or granular; usually in imbedded grains.

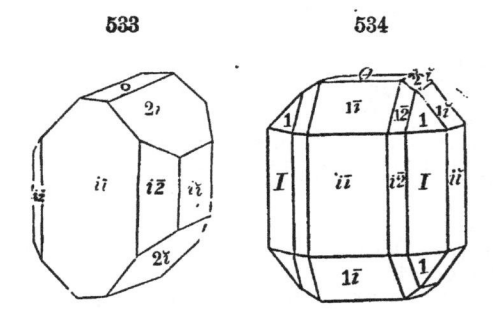

H.=6–7. G.=3·33–3·5. Lustre vitreous. Color green—commonly olive-green, sometimes yellow, brownish, grayish-red, grayish-green. Streak usually uncolored, rarely yellowish. Transparent—translucent. Fracture conchoidal.

Comp., Var.—$(Mg,Fe)_2SiO_4$, with traces at times of Mn, Ca, Ni. The amount of iron varies much. If Mg : Fe=12 : 1, the formula requires Silica 41·39, magnesia 50·90, iron protoxide 7·71=100; Mg : Fe=9 : 1, 6 : 1, etc., and in *hyalosiderite* 2 : 1.

Pyr., etc.—B.B. whitens, but is infusible; with the fluxes gives reactions for iron. Hyalosiderite and other varieties rich in iron fuse to a black magnetic globule. Some varieties give reactions for titanium and manganese. Decomposed by hydrochloric acid with separation of gelatinous silica.

Diff.—Distinguished by its infusibility. Commonly observed in small yellow imbedded grains.

Obs.—A common constituent of some eruptive rocks; and also occurring in or among metamorphic rocks, with talcose schist, hypersthene rocks, and serpentine; or as a rock formation; also a constituent of many meteorites (*e.g.*, the Pallas iron).

Occurs in eruptive rocks at Vesuvius, Sicily, Hecla, Sandwich Islands, and most volcanic islands or regions; in Auvergne; at Unkel, on the Rhine; at the Laacher See; in dolerite or basalt in Canada. Also in labradorite rocks in the White Mountains, N. H. (*hyalosiderite*); in Loudon Co., Va.; in Lancaster Co., Pa., at Wood's Mine.

The following are members of the *Chrysolite Group:*

FORSTERITE.—Mg_2SiO_4. Like chrysolite in physical characters. Vesuvius. BOLTONITE, essentially the same. Bolton, Mass.

MONTICELLITE, from Mt. Somma, and BATRACHITE, from the Tyrol, are $(Ca,Mg)_2SiO_4$, with Ca : Mg=1 : 1. H.=5–5·5. G.=3·03–3·25. Monticellite also occurs in large quantities (v. Rath) on the Pesmeda Alp, Tyrol, altered to serpentine and fassaite.

FAYALITE.—Fe_2SiO_4. G.=4–4·14. Color black. In volcanic rocks at Fayal, Azores; Mourne Mts., Ireland.

HORTONOLITE.—$(Fe,Mg)_2SiO_4$, with Fe : Mg=3 : 2. O'Neil mine, Orange Co., N. Y.

TEPHROITE·—Mn_2SiO_4. G.=4–4·12. Color reddish-brown. Sterling Hill, N. J.; Sweden.

ROEPPERITE.—An iron-manganese-zinc chrysolite. H.=5·5–6. G.=3·95–4·08. Color dark-green to black. Stirling Hill, N. J.

KNEBELITE.—$(Fe,Mn)_2SiO_4$, with Fe : Mn=1 : 1. G.=4·12. Color gray. Dannemora.

LEUCOPHANITE.*—Composition given by the analysis (Ramm.) SiO_2 47·03, AlO_3 1·03, BeO 10·70, CaO 23·37, MgO 0·17, Na_2O 11·26, K_2O 0·30, F 6·57=100·43. Orthorhombic. G.= 2·97. Color greenish-yellow. Occurs in syenite on the island of Lamoë, Norway.

MELIPHANITE (Melinophan).—Composition given by the analysis (Ramm.) SiO_2 43·66, $AlO_3(FeO_3)$ 1·57, BeO 11·74, CaO 26·74, MgO 0·11, Na_2O 8·55, K_2O 1·40, H_2O 0·30, F 5·73 =99·80. G.=3·018. Orthorhombic. Color yellow. Fredriksvärn, Norway.

WÖHLERITE.—Composition given by the analysis (Ramm.) SiO_2 28·43, Cb_2O_5 14·41, ZrO_2 19·63, CaO 26·18, FeO(MnO) 2·50, Na_2O 7·78=98·93. Monoclinic. G.=3·41. Color light-yellow. Near Brevig, Norway.

OXYGEN COMPOUNDS—ANHYDROUS SILICATES. 301

Willemite Group.

WILLEMITE.

Rhombohedral. $R \wedge R = 116° 1'$, $O \wedge R = 142° 17'$; $\check{c} = 0.67378$. Cleavage: i-2 easy in N. Jersey crystals; O easy in those of Moresnet. Also massive and in disseminated grains. Sometimes fibrous.

H.=5·5. G.=3·89–4·18; 4·27, transparent crystals (Cornwall). Lustre vitreo-resinous, rather weak. Color whitish or greenish-yellow, when purest; apple-green, flesh-red, grayish-white, yellowish-brown; often dark-brown when impure. Streak uncolored. Transparent to opaque. Brittle. Fracture conchoidal. Double refraction strong; axis positive.

Var.—The crystals of Moresnet and New Jersey differ in occurring forms. The latter are often quite large, and pass under the name of *troostite;* they are commonly impure from the presence of manganese and iron.

Comp.—Zn_2SiO_4=Silica 27·1, zinc oxide 72·9=100.

Pyr., etc.—B.B. in the forceps glows and fuses with difficulty to a white enamel; the varieties from New Jersey fuse from 3·5 to 4. The powdered mineral on charcoal in R.F. gives a coating yellow while hot and white on cooling, which, moistened with solution of cobalt, and treated in O. F., is colored bright green. With soda the coating is more readily obtained. Decomposed by hydrochloric acid with separation of gelatinous silica.

Obs.—From Vieille-Montagne near Moresnet; also at Stolberg; at Raibel in Carinthia; at Kucsaina in Servia, and in Greenland. In New Jersey, at both Franklin and Stirling in such quantity as to constitute an important ore of zinc. It occurs intimately mixed with zincite and franklinite, and is found massive of a great variety of colors, from pale honey-yellow and light green to dark ash-gray and flesh-red; sometimes in crystals (*troostite*).

DIOPTASE. Emerald-Copper.

Rhombohedral; tetartohedral. $R \wedge R = 126° 24'$; $O \wedge R = 148° 38'$; $\check{c} = 0.5281$. Cleavage: R perfect. Twins: twinning-plane R. Also massive.

H.=5. G.=3·278–3·348. Lustre vitreous. Color emerald-green. Streak green. Transparent—subtranslucent. Fracture conchoidal, uneven. Brittle. Double refraction strong, positive.

Comp.—Q. ratio for Cu : Si : H=1 : 2 : 1; formula H_2CuSiO_4 (Ramm.)=Silica 38·1, copper oxide 50·4, water 11·5=100.

Pyr., etc.—In the closed tube blackens and yields water. B.B. decrepitates, colors the flame emerald-green, but is infusible. With the fluxes gives the reactions for copper. With soda on charcoal a globule of metallic copper. Decomposed by acids with gelatinization.

Obs.—Dioptase occurs disposed in well-defined crystals and amorphous on quartz, occupying seams in a compact limestone west of the hill of Altyn-Tubeh in the Kirghese Steppes; also in the Siberian gold-washings. From Chase Creek, near Clifton, Arizona, in fine crystals, on a "mahogany ore," consisting of limonite and copper oxide.

PHENACITE.—Be_2SiO_4. Rhombohedral. Colorless. Resembles quartz. Takovaja; Miask; Durango, Mexico.

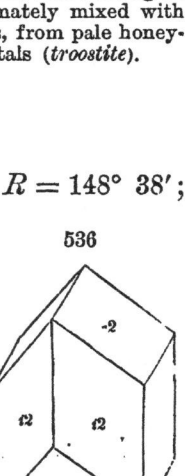

FRIEDELITE.—Rhombohedral. $O \wedge R=147°$; $R \wedge R=123° \; 42'$. Cleavage: O easy. H.=4.75. G.=3.07. Also massive, saccharoidal. Color rose-red. Translucent. Double refraction strong, axis negative. Analysis, SiO_2 36.12, MnO (FeO tr) 53·05, MgO, CaO 2·96, H_2O 7·87=100 This corresponds to the formula $Mn_4Si_3O_{10}+2H_2O$. If the water is basic, as in dioptase, with which it seems to be related in form, the formula is $H_4Mn_4Si_3O_{13}=R_2SiO_4$. This requires SiO_2 36·00, MnO 56·80, H_2O 7·20=100. Occurs with diallogite and alabandite at the manganese mine of Adervielle, Hautes-Pyrénées. (Bertrand, C. R., May, 1876.)

HELVITE.*

Isometric: tetrahedral. Cleavage: octahedral, in traces.

H.=6–6·5. G.=3·1–3·3. Lustre vitreous, inclining to resinous. Color honey-yellow, inclining to yellowish-brown, and siskin-green. Streak uncolored. Subtranslucent. Fracture uneven.

Comp.—Q. ratio for $R : Si = 1 : 2$; for $Mn + Fe : Be = 1 : 1$; formula $3(Be,Mn,Fe)_2SiO_4 + (Mn,Fe)S$ (Ramm.). Analysis by Teich, Lupikko, Finland, SiO_2 30·31, BeO 10·51, MnO 37·87, FeO 10·37, CaO 4·72, ign 0·22, S 5·95=99·95.

Pyr., etc.—Fuses at 3 in R.F. with intumescence to a yellowish-brown opaque bead, becoming darker in R.F. With the fluxes gives the manganese reaction. Decomposed by hydrochloric acid, with evolution of sulphuretted hydrogen, and separation of gelatinous silica.

Obs.—Occurs in gneiss at Schwarzenberg in Saxony; at Breitenbrunn, Saxony; at Hortekulle near Modum, and also at Brevig in Norway, in zircon-syenite.

DANALITE.*

Isometric. In octahedrons, with planes of the dodecahedron; the dodecahedral faces striated parallel to the longer diagonal.

H.=5·5–6. G.=3·427. Lustre vitreo-resinous. Color flesh-red to gray. Streak similar, but lighter. Translucent. Fracture subconchoidal, uneven. Brittle.

Comp.—$3(Be,Fe,Mn,Zn)_2SiO_4+(Fe,Mn,Zn)S$. Analysis: J. P. Cooke, Rockport, SiO_2 31·73, FeO 27·40, MnO 6·28, ZnO 17·51, BeO 13·83, S 5·48=102·23. By subtracting from the analysis oxygen 2·74, equivalent to the sulphur, the sum is 99·49.

Pyr., etc.—B.B. fuses readily on the edges to a black enamel. With soda on charcoal gives a slight coating of zinc oxide. Perfectly decomposed by hydrochloric acid, with evolution of sulphuretted hydrogen and separation of gelatinous silica.

Obs.—Occurs in the Rockport granite, Cape Ann, Mass., small grains being disseminated through this rock; also near Gloucester, Mass.

EULYTITE (Kieselwismuth, *Germ.*).—Isometric, tetrahedral; in minute crystals often aggregated together. H.=4·5–5. G.=6·106. Color grayish-white to brown. *Comp.* A unisilicate of bismuth, $Bi_4Si_3O_{12}$. Schneeberg. *Agricolite.* Composition similar, but form monoclinic. Occurs in globular masses having a radiated structure, and in indistinct groups of crystals. Schneeberg (color hair-brown) and Johanngeorgenstadt (color wine-yellow).

BISMUTOFERRITE.—Cryptocrystalline; generally massive. H.=3·5. G.=4·47. Color olive-green. Analysis (Frenzel) SiO_2 24·05, FeO_3 33·12, Bi_2O_3 42·83=100. Schneeberg. *Hypochlorite* is hornstone mixed with the above mineral and other impurities.

Garnet Group.

GARNET.* Granat, *Germ.*

Isometric; dodecahedron, f. 537, and the trapezohedron 2-2, f. 538, the most common forms; octahedral form very rare. Distorted forms

OXYGEN COMPOUNDS—ANHYDROUS SILICATES.

shown in f. 345-352, pp. 105, 106. Cleavage: dodecahedral, sometimes quite distinct. Twins: twinning-plane octahedral. Also massive; granular, coarse, or fine, and sometimes friable; lamellar, lamellæ thick and bent. Also very compact, crypto-crystalline like saussurite.

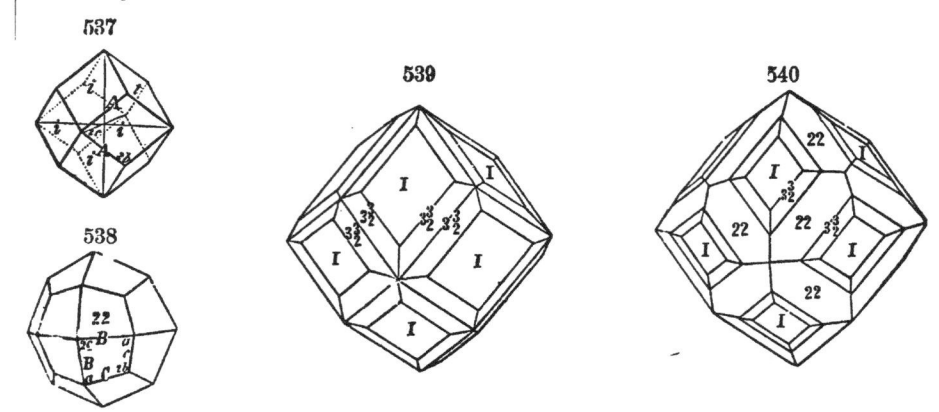

H.=6·5-7·5. G.=3·15-4·3. Lustre vitreous—resinous. Color red, brown, yellow, white, apple-green, black; some red and green colors often bright. Streak white. Transparent—subtranslucent. Fracture subconchoidal, uneven. Brittle, and sometimes friable when granular massive; very tough when compact cryptocrystalline. Sometimes doubly refracting in consequence of lamellar structure, or in some cases from alteration.

Comp., Var.—Garnet is a unisilicate of elements in the sesquioxide and protoxide states, having the general formula $R_2 \ddot{R} Si_3 O_{12}$. There are three prominent groups, based on the nature of the predominating sesquioxide.

I. ALUMINA GARNET, in which *aluminum* ($\dot{A}l$) predominates.
II. IRON GARNET, in which *iron* (Fe) predominates, usually with some aluminum.
III. CHROME GARNET in which *chromium* ($\dot{C}r$) is most prominent.

There are the following varieties or subspecies, based on the predominance of one or another of the protoxides :

A. GROSSULARITE, or *Lime-Alumina garnet*. B. PYROPE, or *Magnesia-Alumina garnet*. C. ALMANDITE, or *Iron-Alumina garnet*. D. SPESSARTITE, or *Manganese-Alumina garnet*. E. ANDRADITE, or *Lime-Iron garnet*, including 1, ordinary; 2, manganesian, or *Rothoffite;* 3, yttriferous, or *Ytter-garnet*. F. BREDBERGITE, or *Lime-Magnesia-Iron garnet*. G. OUVAROVITE, or *Lime-Chrome garnet*. Excepting the last, these subdivisions blend with one another more or less completely.

A. *Lime-Alumina garnet;* GROSSULARITE. Cinnamon stone. A silicate mainly of aluminum and calcium; formula mostly $Ca_3 \ddot{A}l Si_3 O_{12}$=Silica 40·0, alumina 22·8, lime 37·2=100. But some calcium often replaced by iron, and thus graduating toward the Almandite group. Color (*a*) white; (*b*) pale green; (*c*) amber- and honey-yellow; (*d*) wine-yellow, brownish-yellow, cinnamon-brown; rarely (*e*) emerald-green from the presence of chromium. G.=3·4-3·75.

B. *Magnesia-Alumina garnet;* PYROPE. A silicate of aluminum, with various protoxide bases, among which magnesium predominates much in atomic proportions, while in small proportion in other garnets, or absent. Formula $(Mg,Ca,Fe,Mn)_3 \ddot{A}l Si_3 O_{12}$. The original pyrope is the kind containing chromium. In the analysis of the Arendal magnesia-garnet, Mg : Ca : Fe+Mn=3 : 1 : 2; SiO_2 42·45, $\ddot{A}lO_3$ 22·47, FeO 9·29, MnO 6·27, MgO 13·43, CaO 6·53= 100·44 Wacht. G.=3·157. The name *pyrope* is from πυρωπός, *fire-like*.

C. *Iron-Alumina garnet;* ALMANDITE. A silicate mainly of aluminum and iron (Fe); formula $Fe_3 \ddot{A}l Si_3 O_{12}$=Silica 36·1, alumina 20·6, iron protoxide 43·3=100; or Mn may replace some of the Fe, and Fe part of the $\ddot{A}l$. Color fine deep-red and transparent, and then called *precious garnet;* also brownish-red and translucent or subtranslucent, *common garnet;* black, and then referred to var. *melanite*. Part of *common garnet* belongs to the *Andradite* group, or is iron garnet.

D. *Manganese-Alumina garnet;* SPESSARTITE. Color dark hyacinth-red (fr. Spessart), sometimes with a shade of violet, to brownish-red. G.=3·7-4·4. Analysis, Haddam, Ct., SiO_2 36·16, Al_2O_3 19·76, FeO 11·10, MnO 32·18, MgO 0·22, CaO 0·58=100, Ramm.

E. *Lime-Iron garnet;* ANDRADITE. Aplome. Color various, including wine-, topaz-, and greenish-yellow (topazolite), apple-green, brownish-red, brownish-yellow, grayish-green, dark green, brown, grayish-black, black. G.=3.64-4.

Comp.—$Ca_3FeSi_3O_{12}$, this includes: (a) *Topazolite*, having the color and transparency of topaz, and also sometimes green; although resembling essonite, Damour has shown that it belongs here. (b) *Colophonite*, a coarse granular kind, brownish-yellow to dark reddish-brown in color, resinous in lustre, and usually with iridescent hues; named after the resin *colophony*. (c) *Melanite* (named from $μέλας$, *black*), black, either dull or lustrous; but all black garnet is not here included. *Pyreneite* is grayish-black melanite; the original afforded Vauquelin 4 p. c. of water, and was iridescent, indicating incipient alteration. (d) Dark green garnet, not distinguishable from some allochroite, except by chemical means.

F. *Lime-Magnesia Iron garnet;* BREDBERGITE. A variety from Sala, Sweden, is here included. . Formula $(Ca,Mg)_3FeSi_3O_{12}$=Silica 37·2, iron sesquioxide 33·1, magnesia 12·4, lime 17·3=100. It corresponds under Iron garnet nearly to aplome under Alumina garnet.

G. *Lime-Chrome garnet;* OUVAROVITE. A silicate of calcium and chromium. Formula $Ca_3CrSi_3O_{12}$. In the Ural variety, a fourth of the chromium oxide is replaced by aluminum oxide; that is, $\overline{Al}$: $\overline{Cr}$=1 : 3 nearly. Color emerald-green. H.=7·5. G.=3·41-3·52. B.B. infusible; with borax a clear chrome-green glass. Named after the Russian minister, Uvarof.

Pyr., etc.—Most varieties fuse easily to a light-brown or black glass; F.=3 in almandite, spessartite, grossularite, and allochroite; 3·5 in pyrope; but ouvarovite is almost infusible, F.=6. Allochroite and almandite fuse to a magnetic globule. Reactions with the fluxes vary with the bases. Almost all kinds react for iron; strong manganese reaction in spessartite, and less marked in other varieties; a chromium reaction in ouvarovite, and in most pyrope. Some varieties are partially decomposed by acids; all except ouvarovite are decomposed after ignition by hydrochloric acid, and generally with separation of gelatinous silica. Decomposed on fusion with alkaline carbonates.

Diff.—Ordinary garnets are distinguished from zircon by their fusibility B.B., but they fuse *less* readily than vesuvianite; the vitreous lustre, absence of prismatic structure, and usually the form, are characteristic; it has a higher specific gravity than tourmaline.

Obs.—Garnet crystals are very common in mica schist, gneiss, syenitic gneiss, and hornblende and chlorite schist; they occur often, also, in granite, syenite, crystalline limestones, sometimes in serpentine, and occasionally in trap and volcanic tufa and lava.

Some localities are: *Cinnamon-stone (Essonite)*, Ceylon; Mussa-Alp in Piedmont. *Grossularite*, Siberia; Tellemark, Norway; Ural. *Almandite*, Ceylon, Pegu, Brazil, and Greenland. Common garnet in large dodecahedrons, Sweden; Arendal and Kongsberg in Norway, and the Zillerthal. *Melanite* at Vesuvius and in the Hautes-Pyrénées (*Pyreneite*). *Aplome* at Schwarzenberg in Saxony. *Spessartite* at Spessart in Bavaria, Elba, at St. Marcel, Piedmont. *Pyrope* in Bohemia, also at Zöblitz in Saxony. *Ouvarovite* in the Urals.

In N. America in *Maine*, Phippsburg, Rumford, Windham, at Brunswick, etc. In *N. Hamp.*, Warren. In *Mass.*, at Carlisle; massive at Newbury; at Chesterfield. In *Conn.*, trapezohedrons, $\frac{1}{4}$-1 in., in mica slate, at Reading and Monroe; Haddam. In *N. York*, at Roger's Rock; Crown Point, Essex Co.; at Amity. In *N. Jersey*, at Franklin. In *Penn.*, in Chester Co., at Pennsbury; near Knauertown, at Keims' mine; at Chester, brown; in Leiperville, red; near Wilmington. In *California*, in Los Angeles Co., in Mt. Meadows; ouvarovite at New Idria; pyrope, near Santa Fé, New Mexico. In *Canada*, at Marmora, at Grenville; chrome-garnet in Orford, Canada.

The cinnamon-stone from Ceylon (called hyacinth) and the precious garnet are used as gems when large, finely colored, and transparent. The stone is cut quite thin, on account of the depth of color, with a pavilion cut below, and a broad table above bordered with small facets. An octagonal garnet measuring $8\frac{1}{2}$ lines by $6\frac{1}{4}$ has sold for near $700. Pulverized garnet is sometimes employed as a substitute for emery.

Vesuvianite Group.

ZIRCON.*

Tetragonal. $O \wedge 1\text{-}i = 147° 22'$; $c = 0.640373$, Haidinger. $I \wedge 1 = 132° 10'$. Faces of pyramids sometimes convex. Cleavage: I imperfect, 1 less distinct. Also in irregular forms and grains.

OXYGEN COMPOUNDS—ANHYDROUS SILICATES. 305

H.=7·5. G.=4·05–4·75. Lustre adamantine. Colorless, pale yellowish, grayish, yellowish-green, brownish-yellow, reddish-brown. Streak uncolored. Transparent to subtranslucent and opaque. Fracture conchoidal, brilliant. Double refraction strong, positive.

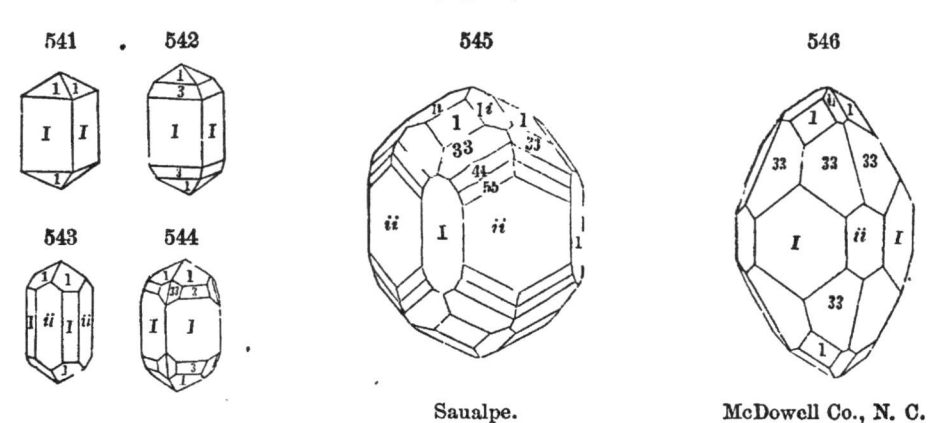

541 . 542   545   546

                         Saualpe.   McDowell Co., N. C.

Var.—The colorless and yellowish or smoky zircons of Ceylon have there been long called *jargons* in jewelry, in allusion to the fact that, while resembling the diamond in lustre, they were comparatively worthless; and thence came the name *zircon*. The brownish, orange, and reddish kinds were called distinctively *hyacinths*—a name applied also in jewelry to some topaz and light-colored garnet.

Comp.—$ZrSiO_4$=Silica 33, zirconia 67=100. Klaproth discovered the earth zirconia in this species in 1789.

Pyr., etc.—Infusible; the colorless varieties are unaltered, the red become colorless, while dark-colored varieties are made white; some varieties glow and increase in density by ignition. Not perceptibly acted upon by salt of phosphorus. In powder is decomposed when fused with soda on the platinum wire, and if the product is dissolved in dilute hydrochloric acid it gives the orange color characteristic of zirconia when tested with turmeric paper. Not acted upon by acids except in fine powder with concentrated sulphuric acid. Decomposed by fusion with alkaline carbonates and bisulphates.

Diff.—Distinguished by its adamantine lustre, hardness, and infusibility; the occurrence of square prismatic forms is also characteristic.

Obs.—Occurs in crystalline rocks, especially granular limestone, chloritic and other schists; gneiss, syenite; also in granite; sometimes in iron-ore beds.

Found in alluvial sands in Ceylon; in the gold regions of the Ural; at Arendal in Norway; at Fredericksvärn, in zircon-syenite; in Transylvania; at Bilin in Bohemia.

In N. America, in *N. York*, at Moriah, Essex Co., and in Orange Co.; in Warwick; near Amity; at Diana in Lewis Co.; also at Rossie. In *N. Jersey*, at Franklin; at Trenton in gneiss. In *N. Car.*, in Buncombe Co.; in the sands of the gold washings of McDowell Co. In *California*, in the auriferous gravel of the north fork of the American river, and elsewhere. In *Canada*, at Grenville, etc.

VESUVIANITE.* IDOCRASE.

Tetragonal. $O \wedge 1\text{-}i = 151°\ 45'$; $\check{c} = 0.537199$ (v. Kokscharof). $O \wedge 1 = 142°\ 46\frac{1}{2}'$ $1 \wedge 1$, ov. $1\text{-}i, = 129°\ 21'$. Cleavage: I not very distinct, O still less so. Columnar structure rare, straight and divergent, or irregular. Sometimes granular massive. Prisms usually terminating in the basal plane O; rarely in a pyramid or zirconoid; sometimes the prism nearly wanting, and the form short pyramidal with truncated summit and edges.

20

$H.=6.5$. $G.=3.349-3.45$. Lustre vitreous; often inclining to resinous. Color brown to green, and the latter frequently bright and clear; occasionally sulphur-yellow, and also pale blue; sometimes green along the axis, and pistachio-green transversely. Streak white. Subtransparent—faintly subtranslucent. Fracture subconchoidal—uneven. Double refraction feeble, axis negative.

547 548 551
549 550

Sandford, Me.

Comp., Var.—Q. ratio for $\dot{R} : \ddot{R} : \ddot{Si} = 4 : 3 : 7$ (according to the latest investigations of Rammelsberg). $\dot{R}=Ca$ (also Mg, Fe, or H_2, K_2, Na_2); $\ddot{R}=\ddot{A}l$ and also Fe. If we neglect the water the empirical formula is $\dot{R}_8\ddot{R}_2\ddot{Si}_7O_{28}$, where the quantivalent ratio of bases to silicon is 1 : 1. The ratio of $\dot{R} : \ddot{R}$ varies much, which, as stated by Rammelsberg, is the explanation of the different varieties. Analyses by Rammelsberg. (1) Monzoni; (2) Wilui, Siberia.

	SiO_2	$\ddot{A}lO_3$	FeO_3	FeO	MgO	CaO	$Na_2O(K_2O)$	H_2O
(1)	37·32	16·08	3·75	2·91	2·11	35·34	0·16	2·08= 99·75
(2)	38·40	13·72	5·54	—	6·88	35·04	0·66	0·82=101·06.

Pyr., etc.—B.B. fuses at 3 with intumescence to a greenish or brownish glass. Magnus states that the density after fusion is 2·93–2·945. With the fluxes gives reactions for iron, and a variety from St. Marcel gives a strong manganese reaction. Cyprine gives a reaction for copper with salt of phosphorus. Partially decomposed by hydrochloric acid, and completely when the mineral has been previously ignited.

Diff.—Resembles some brown varieties of garnet, tourmaline, and epidote, but its tetragonal form and easy fusibility distinguish it.

Obs.—Vesuvianite was first found among the ancient ejections of Vesuvius and the dolomitic blocks of Somma. It has since been met with most abundantly in granular limestone; also in serpentine, chlorite schist, gneiss, and related rocks. It is often associated with lime-garnet and pyroxene. It has been observed imbedded in opal.

Occurs at Vesuvius; at Ala, in Piedmont; at Monzoni in the Fassathal; near Christiansand, Norway; on the Wilui river, near L. Baikal; in the Urals, and elsewhere. In N. America, in *Maine*, at Phippsburg and Rumford, abundant; Sandford (f. 551). In *N. York*, at Amity. In *N. Jersey*, at Newton. In *Canada*, at Calumet Falls; at Grenville. MELILITE from Capo di Bove, and HUMBOLDTILITE from Mt. Somma, are similar in composition. Analysis of the melilite by Damour. SiO_2 38·34, $\ddot{A}lO_3$ 8·61, FeO_3 10·02, CaO 32·05, MgO 6·71, Na_2O 2·12, K_2O 1·51=99·36. Tetragonal. Color honey-yellow.

Epidote Group.

The species of the Epidote Group are characterized by high specific gravity, above 3; hardness above 5; fusibility B.B. below 4; anisometric crystallization, and therefore biaxial polarization; the dominant prismatic angle 112° to 117°; fibrous forms, when they occur, always brittle; colors white, gray, brown, yellowish-green, and deep green to black, and sometimes reddish.

The prismatic angle in zoisite and other orthorhombic species is $I \wedge I$; but in epidote it is the angle over a horizontal edge between the planes O and i-i, the orthodiagonal of epidote corresponding to the vertical axis of zoisite, as explained under the latter species.

OXYGEN COMPOUNDS—ANHYDROUS SILICATES. 307

EPIDOTE. Pistazite.

Monoclinic. $C = 89° 27'$; $i\text{-}2 \wedge i\text{-}2 = 63° 8'$, $O \wedge 1\text{-}i = 122° 23'$; $c : b : a = 0.43436 : 0.30719 : 1$. $O \wedge 1\text{-}i = 154° 3'$, $O \wedge -1\text{-}i = 154° 15'$, $i\text{-}i \wedge -1 = 104° 48'$, $i\text{-}i \wedge 1 = 104° 15'$. Crystals usually lengthened in the direction of the orthodiagonal, or parallel to $i\text{-}i$; sometimes long acicular. Cleavage: $i\text{-}i$ perfect; $1\text{-}i$ less so. Twins : twinning-plane $1\text{-}i$; also $i\text{-}i$. Also fibrous, divergent, or parallel; also granular, particles of various sizes, sometimes fine granular, and forming rock-masses.

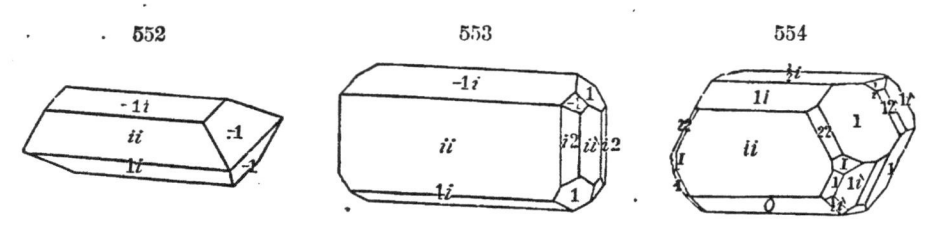

552 553 554

H.=6–7. G.=3·25–3·5. Lustre vitreous, on $i\text{-}i$ inclining to pearly or resinous. Color pistachio-green or yellowish-green to brownish-green, greenish-black, and black; sometimes clear red and yellow; also gray and grayish-white. Pleochroism often distinct, the crystals being usually least yellow in a direction through $1\text{-}i$ (see p. 166). Streak uncolored, grayish. Subtransparent—opaque; generally subtranslucent. Fracture uneven. Brittle.

Var.—Epidote has ordinarily a peculiar yellowish-green (pistachio) color, seldom found in other minerals. But this color passes into dark and light shades—black on one side, and brown on the other. Most of the brown and nearly all the gray epidote belongs to the species *Zoisite;* and the reddish-brown or reddish-black, containing much oxide of manganese, to the species *Piedmontite*, or Manganepidot; while the black is mainly of the species *Allanite*, or Cerium-epidote.

Comp.—Quantivalent ratio for Ca : R : Si=4 : 9 : 12, and H : Ca=1 : 4. The formula is then $H_2Ca_4R_3Si_6O_{26}$. R is Fe or Al, the ratio varying from 1 : 2 to 1 : 6. Analysis, Untersulzbach, Tyrol, by Ludwig : SiO_2 37·83, AlO_3 22·63, FeO_3 15·05, FeO 0·93, CaO 23·27, H_2O 2·05=100·76. As first shown by Ludwig, epidote contains about 2 p. c. water, which is given off only at high temperatures.

Pyr., etc.—In the closed tube gives water at a high temperature. B.B. fuses with intumescence at 3–3·5 to a dark brown or black mass which is generally magnetic. Reacts for iron and sometimes for manganese with the fluxes. Partially decomposed by hydrochloric acid, but when previously ignited, gelatinizes with acid. Decomposed on fusion with alkaline carbonates.

Diff.—Distinguished often by its peculiar yellowish-green color; yields a magnetic globule, B.B. Prismatic forms often longitudinally striated, but they have not the angle, cleavage, or brittleness of tremolite.

Obs.—Epidote is common in many crystalline rocks, as syenite, gneiss, mica schist, hornblendic schist, serpentine, and especially those that contain the ferriferous mineral hornblende. It often accompanies beds of magnetite or hematite in such rocks. It is sometimes found in geodes in trap; and also in sandstone adjoining trap dikes, where it has been formed by metamorphism through the heat of the trap at the time of its ejection. It also occurs at times in nodules in different quartz-rocks or altered sandstones. It is associated often with quartz, pyroxene, feldspar, axinite, chlorite, etc., in the Piedmontese Alps.

Beautiful crystallizations come from Bourg d'Oisans, Ala, and Traversella, in Piedmont, Zermatt and elsewhere in Switzerland; Monzoni in the Fassathal; the Untersulzbachthal and Zillerthal in the Tyrol.

In N. America, occurs in *Mass.*, at Chester; at Athol; at Rome. In *Conn.*, at Haddam,

In *N. York*, at Amity; near Monroe, Orange Co.; at Warwick. In *N. Jersey*, at Franklin. In *Penn.*, at E. Bradford. In *Michigan*, in the Lake Superior region. In *Canada*, at St. Joseph.

PIEDMONTITE (Manganepidot, *Germ.*).—A manganese epidote; formula, $H_2Ca_4\dot{R}_3Si_6O_{26}$, with $\dot{R}$ principally Mn (also Al, Fe). Color reddish-brown. St. Marcel, Aosta valley, Piedmont.

ALLANITE.

Monoclinic, isomorphous with epidote. $C = 89°\ 1'$; $O \wedge 1\text{-}i = 122°\ 50\frac{1}{2}'$, $i\text{-}2 \wedge i\text{-}2 = 63°\ 58'$; $\breve{c} : \bar{b} : \dot{a} = 0·483755 : 0·312187 : 1$. Crystals either short, flat tabular, or long and slender, sometimes acicular. Twins like those of epidote. Cleavage: $i\text{-}i$ in traces. Also massive, and in angular or rounded grains. H.=5·5–6. G.=3·0–4·2. Lustre submetallic, pitchy, or resinous— occasionally vitreous. Color pitch-brown to black, either brownish, greenish, grayish, or yellowish. Streak gray, sometimes slightly greenish or brownish. Subtranslucent—opaque. Fracture uneven or subconchoidal. Brittle. Double refraction either distinct, or wanting.

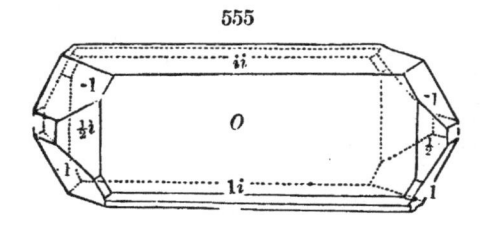

Var.—*Allanite (Cerine).* In tabular crystals or plates. Color black or brownish-black. G.=3·50–3·95; found among specimens from East Greenland, brought to Scotland by C. Giesecké. *Bucklandite* is anhydrous allanite in small black crystals from a mine of magnetite near Arendal, Norway. Referred here by v. Rath on the ground of the angles and physical characters.

Orthite. Including, in its original use, the slender or acicular prismatic crystals, often a foot long, containing some water. But these graduate into massive forms, and some orthites are anhydrous, or as nearly so as much of the allanite. The name is from ὀρθός, *straight*. The tendency to alteration and hydration may be due to the slenderness of the crystals, and the consequent great exposure to the action of moisture and the atmosphere. H.=5–6. G.=2·80–3·75. Lustre vitreous to greasy.

Comp.—Not altogether certain, as analyses vary considerably, some showing the presence of considerable water. According to Rammelsberg the Q. ratio for bases to silicon=1 : 1 (epidote=$1\frac{1}{6}$: 1). Allanite has then the garnet formula, $R_3\ddot{R}Si_3O_{12}$, where R=Ce(La,Di), Fe(Mn), Ca(Mg), and occasionally Y, Na_2, K_2, etc.; $\ddot{R}$=Al or Fe. Analysis, allanite (Ramm.), Fredrikshaab, SiO_2 33·78, Al_2O_3 14·03, Fe_2O_3 6·36, FeO 13·63, CeO 12·63, LaO(DiO) 5·67, CaO 12·12, H_2O 1·78=100.

Pyr., etc.—Some varieties give water in the closed tube. B.B. fuses easily and swells up (F.=2·5) to a dark, blebby, magnetic glass. With the fluxes reacts for iron. Most varieties gelatinize with hydrochloric acid, but if previously ignited are not decomposed by acid.

Obs.—Occurs in albitic and common feldspathic granite, syenite, zircon-syenite, porphyry, white limestone, and often in mines of magnetic iron. *Allanite* occurs in Greenland; at Criffel in Scotland; at Jotun Fjeld in Norway; at Snarum, near Dresden; near Schmiedefeld in the Thüringerwald. *Cerine* occurs at Bastnäs in Sweden. *Orthite* occurs at Finbo and Ytterby in Sweden; also at Krageröe, etc., in Norway; at Miask in the Ural.

In *Mass.*, at the Bolton quarry. In *Conn.*, at Haddam. In *N. York*, Moriah, Essex Co.; at Monroe, Orange Co. In *N. Jersey*, at Franklin. In *Penn.*, at E. Bradford in Chester Co.; at Easton. Amherst Co., Va. In *Canada*, at St. Paul's, C. W.

MUROMONTITE and BODENITE from Marienberg, Saxony; and MICHAELSONITE from Brevig, are minerals related to allanite.

ZOISITE.

Orthorhombic. $I \wedge I = 116°\ 40'$, $O \wedge 1\text{-}\bar{i} = 131°\ 1\frac{1}{2}'$; $\breve{c} : \bar{b} : \dot{a} = 1·1493 : 1·62125 : 1$. Crystals lengthened in the direction of the vertical axis, and vertically deeply striated or furrowed. Cleavage: i-$\bar{i}$ very perfect. Commonly in crystalline masses longitudinally furrowed. Also compact massive.

H.=6–6·5. G.=3·11–3·38. Lustre pearly on i-$\bar{i}$; vitreous on surface of fracture. Color grayish-white, gray, yellowish, brown, greenish-gray, apple-green; also peach-blossom-red to rose-red. Streak uncolored. Transparent to subtranslucent. Double refraction feeble, optic-axial plane i-$\bar{i}$; bisectrix positive, normal to i-$\bar{i}$; DesCl.

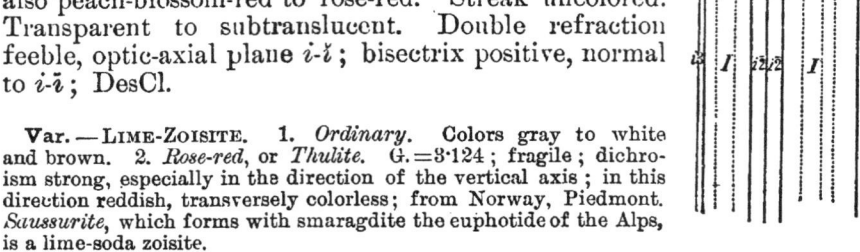

Var.—LIME-ZOISITE. 1. *Ordinary.* Colors gray to white and brown. 2. *Rose-red*, or *Thulite*. G.=3·124; fragile; dichroism strong, especially in the direction of the vertical axis; in this direction reddish, transversely colorless; from Norway, Piedmont. *Saussurite*, which forms with smaragdite the euphotide of the Alps, is a lime-soda zoisite.

Comp.—A lime-epidote, with little or no iron, and thus differing from epidote. Q. ratio as in epidote, H : Ca=1 : 4, and Ca : R̈ : Si=4 : 9 : 12, whence the formula $H_2Ca_4\ddot{R}_3Si_6O_{26}$. Analysis, Ramm., Goshen (G.=3·341) SiO_2 40·06, AlO_3 30·67, FeO_3 2·45, CaO 23·91, MgO 0·49, H_2O 2·25=99·83. The amount of iron sesquioxide varies from 0 to 6·33 p. c.; if much more is present, amounting to a sixth atomically of the protoxide bases, the compound appears to take the monoclinic form of epidote, instead of the orthorhombic of zoisite.

Pyr., etc.—B.B. swells up and fuses at 3–3·5 to a white blebby mass. Not decomposed by acid; when previously ignited gelatinizes with hydrochloric acid.

Obs.—Occurs at Saualpe in Carinthia; Baireuth in the Fichtelgebirge; Sterzing, Tyrol; Lake Geneva; Schwarzwald; Arendal, etc. In the United States, found in *Vermont*, at Willsboro and Montpelier. In *Mass.*, at Goshen, Chesterfield, etc. In *Penn.*, in Chester Co.; at Unionville, white (*Unionite*). In *Tenn.*, at the Ducktown copper mines.

JADEITE is one of the kinds of pale green stones used in China for making ornaments, and passing under the general name of jade or nephrite. Mr. Pumpelly remarks that the *feitsui* is perhaps the most prized of all stones among the Chinese. In composition mainly a silicate of aluminum and sodium. In its high specific gravity like zoisite.

GADOLINITE.—Monoclinic (DesCl.). Color greenish-black. Contains yttrium, cerium, and generally beryllium; though the last is sometimes absent, through alteration (DesCl.). Sweden; Greenland; Norway.

MOSANDRITE.—A silicate containing titanium, cerium, and calcium. Brevig, Norway.

ILVAITE. Lievrite. Yenite.

Orthorhombic. $I \wedge I = 112° 38'$, $O \wedge 1\text{-}\bar{i} = 146° 24'$; $\check{c} : \bar{b} : \check{a} = 0.66608 : 1.5004 : 1$. $O \wedge 1 = 141° 24'$, $O \wedge 2\text{-}\bar{i} = 138° 29'$. Lateral faces usually striated longitudinally. Cleavage: parallel to the longer diagonal, indistinct. Also columnar or compact massive.

H.=5·5–6. G.=3·7–4·2. Lustre submetallic. Color iron-black, or dark grayish-black. Streak black, inclining to green or brown. Opaque. Fracture uneven. Brittle.

Comp.—Q. ratio, for R̈+R : Si : H=9 : 8 : 1, and for bases, including hydrogen, to silicon 5 : 4 (Städeler). Sipöcz by the analysis of entirely unaltered crystals (G.=4·037) from Elba confirms the conclusions of Städeler in regard to the presence of chemically combined water, and adopts the same formula, viz.:—$H_2Ca_2Fe_4FeSi_4O_{18}$. This requires: Silica 29·34, iron sesquioxide 19·56, iron protoxide 35·21, lime 13·69, water 2·20=100; manganese protoxide is also sometimes present in small quantities. Rammelsberg considered the water as due to alteration.

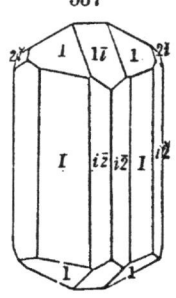

Pyr., etc.—B.B. fuses quietly at 2·5 to a black magnetic bead. With the fluxes reacts for iron. Some varieties give also a reaction for manganese. Gelatinizes with hydrochloric acid.

Obs.—Found in Elba, and at the mine of Temperino in Tuscany. Also at Fossum and at Skeen in Norway; in Siberia; near Andreasberg; near Predazzo, Tyrol; at Schneeberg; at Hebrun in Nassau; at Kangerdluarsuk in Greenland.

Reported as formerly found at Cumberland, R. I.; also at Milk Row quarry, Somerville, Mass.

ARDENNITE (Dewalquite).—Near ilvaite in form. Habit prismatic; vertically striated. Composition given by the analyses, Lasaulx and Bettendorf, SiO_2 29·60, AlO_3 23·50, MnO 25·88, FeO_3 1·68, CaO 1·81, MgO 3·38, V_2O_5 9·20, ign. 4·04=99·09. Color dark rosin-brown. In thin splinters transparent. Other varieties, of a bright sulphur-yellow color (but opaque and dull), contain arsenic (9·33 p. c. As_2O_5) instead of vanadium. Between these two extremes are a series of compounds containing both arsenic and vanadium. Lasaulx regards the arsenic-ardennite as having come from the other through alteration. Locality, Ottrez in the Ardennes, Belgium. ROSCOELITE (p. 367) is another silicate containing vanadium.

AXINITE.

Triclinic. Crystals usually broad, and acute-edged. Making $m = O$, $P = 'I$, $u = I'$, a (brachyd.) : b (macrod.) : $c = 0.49266 : 1 : 0.45112$. Cleavage: i-i (v) quite distinct; in other directions indistinct. Also massive, lamellar, lamellæ often curved; sometimes granular.

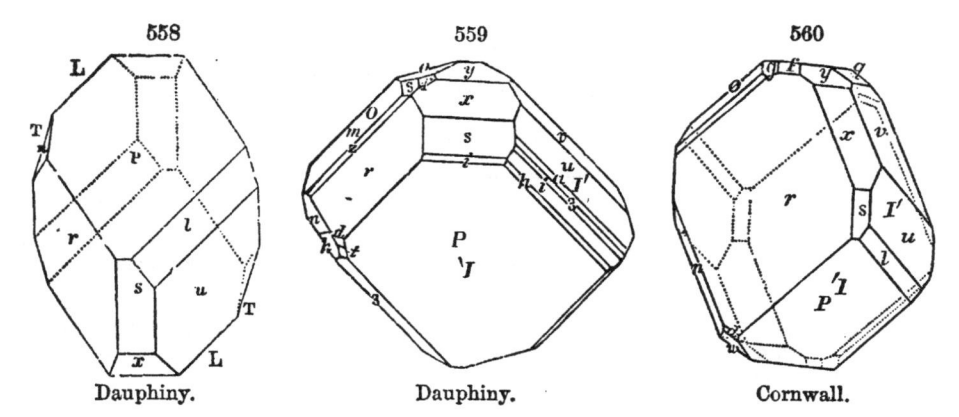

558 559 560

Dauphiny.   Dauphiny.   Cornwall.

H. = 6·5–7. G. = 3·271, Haidinger; a Cornish specimen. Lustre highly glassy. Color clove-brown, plum-blue, and pearl-gray; exhibits trichroism, different colors, as cinnamon-brown, violet-blue, olive-green, being seen in different directions. Streak uncolored. Transparent to subtranslucent. Fracture conchoidal. Brittle. Pyroelectric, with two axes, the analogue (L) and antilogue (T) poles being situated as indicated in f. 558 (G. Rose).

Comp.—Analyses vary. If it contains 2 p. c. water (Ramm.), and if B_2 replaces Al, then it is a unisilicate with the formula $R_7\dot{R}_3Si_8O_{32}$, $R = Fe,Mn,Ca,Mg$, and K_2, while $\dot{R} = B_2,Al$ ($B_2 : Al = 1 : 2$). Analysis (Ramm.), Oisans. Dauphiné, SiO_2 43·46, B_2O_3 5·61, AlO_3 16·33, FeO_3 2·80, FeO 6·78, MnO 2·62, CaO 20·19, MgO 1·73, K_2O 0·11, H_2O 1·45=101·08.

Pyr., etc.—B.B. fuses readily with intumescence, imparts a pale green color to the O.F., and fuses at 2 to a dark green to black glass; with borax in O.F. gives an amethystine bead (manganese), which in R.F. becomes yellow (iron). Fused with a mixture of potassium bisulphate and fluor on the platinum loop colors the flame green (boron). Not decomposed by acids, but when previously ignited, gelatinizes with hydrochloric acid.

Obs.—Axinite occurs near Bourg d'Oisans in Dauphiny; at Santa Maria, Switzerland; at Kongsberg; in Normark in Sweden; in Cornwall; in Devonshire, near Tavistock; at Phipsburg, Maine; at Wales, Maine; at Cold Spring, N. Y.

DANBURITE.*—Triclinic. $CaB_2Si_2O_8$=Silica 48·8, boron trioxide 28·5, lime 22·7 =100. Occurs with feldspar in imbedded masses of yellow color in dolomite, at Danbury, Ct.

IOLITE. Cordierite. Dichroite.

Orthorhombic. In stout prisms often hexagonal. $I \wedge I = 119°\ 10'$ and $60°\ 50'$, $O \wedge 1\text{-}\breve{i} = 150°\ 49'$. Cleavage: $i\text{-}\breve{i}$ distinct; $i\text{-}\bar{i}$ and O indistinct. Crystals often transversely divided or foliated parallel with O. Twins: twinning-plane I. Also massive, compact.

H.=7–7·5. G.=2·56–2·67. Lustre vitreous. Color various shades of blue, light or dark, smoky-blue; pleochroic, being often deep blue along the vertical axis, and brownish-yellow or yellowish-gray perpendicular to it. Streak uncolored. Transparent—translucent. Fracture subconchoidal.

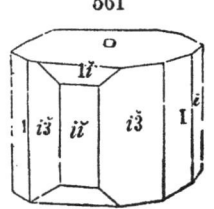

Comp.—Q. ratio for bases and silicon 4 : 5 or 1 : 1¼. The state of oxidation of the iron is still unascertained, and hence there is uncertainty as to the proportion between the protoxides and sesquioxides. The ratio usually deduced for R : Ṙ : Si is 1 : 3 : 5. The formula $R_2\ddot{R}_2Si_5O_{18}$, which corresponds to this ratio, =, if $R=Mg,Fe$ and $Mg : Fe=2 : 1$, Silica 49·4, alumina 33·9, magnesia 8·8, iron protoxide 7·9=100.

Pyr., etc.—B.B. loses transparency and fuses at 5–5·5. Only partially decomposed by acids. Decomposed on fusion with alkaline carbonates.

Obs.—Iolite occurs in granite, gneiss, hornblendic, chlorite and hydro-mica schist, and allied rocks, with quartz, orthoclase or albite, tourmaline, hornblende, andalusite, and sometimes beryl. Also rarely in volcanic rocks. Occurs at Bodenmais, Bavaria; at Ujordlersoak in Greenland; at Krageröe in Norway; Tunaberg in Sweden; Lake Laach. At Haddam, Conn.; at Brimfield, Mass.; also at Richmond, N. H.

Alt.—The alteration of iolite takes place so readily by ordinary exposure, that the mineral is most commonly found in an altered state, or enclosed in the altered iolite. For the distinguishing characters of the different kinds of altered iolite, see PINITE, FAHLUNITE, etc., under HYDROUS SILICATES.

*Mica Group.**

The minerals of the Mica group are alike in having (1) the prismatic angle 120°; (2) eminently perfect basal cleavage, affording readily very thin, tough laminæ; (3) potash almost invariably among the protoxide bases and alumina among the sesquioxide; (4) the crystallization approximately either hexagonal or orthorhombic, and therefore the optic axis, or optic-axial plane, at right angles (or nearly so) to the cleavage surface.

Sodium is sparingly present in some micas, and is characteristic of the hydrous species paragonite (p. 354). Lithium, rubidium, and cæsium occur in lepidolite, and lithium in some biotite. Fluorine is often present, probably replacing oxygen. Titanium is found sparingly in several kinds, and is a prominent ingredient of one species, astrophyllite. It is usually regarded as in the state of titanium dioxide replacing silica; but it is here made basic.

The species of the Mica group graduate into the hydrous micas of the Margarodite group (p. 331); and through these they also approach the foliated species of the Talc and Chlorite groups, especially the latter.

PHLOGOPITE.*

Orthorhombic. $I \wedge I = 120°$, and habit hexagonal. Prisms usually oblong six-sided prisms, more or less tapering, with irregular sides; rarely, when small, with polished lateral planes. Cleavage basal, highly eminent. Not known in compact massive forms.

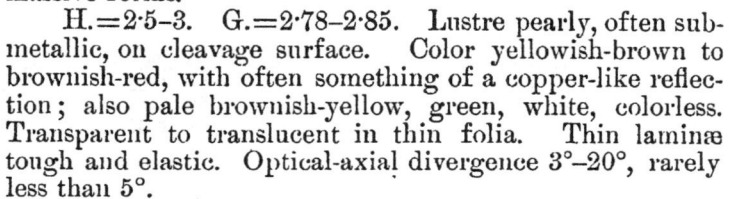

H.=2·5–3. G.=2·78–2·85. Lustre pearly, often submetallic, on cleavage surface. Color yellowish-brown to brownish-red, with often something of a copper-like reflection; also pale brownish-yellow, green, white, colorless. Transparent to translucent in thin folia. Thin laminæ tough and elastic. Optical-axial divergence 3°–20°, rarely less than 5°.

Comp.—The bases include magnesium and little or no iron. Q. ratio R : Si=1 : 1. Formula probably (Ramm.) $K_2Mg_6AlSi_5O_{20}$=Silica 40·73, alumina 13·93, magnesia 32·57, potash 12·77=100.

Pyr., etc.—In the closed tube gives a little water. Some varieties give the reaction for fluorine in the open tube, while most give little or no reaction for iron with the fluxes. B.B. whitens and fuses on the thin edges. Completely decomposed by sulphuric acid, leaving the silica in thin scales.

Obs.—Phlogopite is especially characteristic of serpentine and crystalline limestone or dolomite.

Occurs in limestone in the Vosges. Includes probably the mica found in limestone at Alt-Kemnitz, near Hirschberg; that of Baritti, Brazil, of a golden-yellow color, having the optical angle 5° 30′ and parallel to the shorter diagonal (Grailich); and a brown mica from limestone of Upper Hungary, affording Grailich the angle 4°–5°.

Occurs in New York, at Gouverneur; at Pope's Mills, St. Lawrence Co.; at Edwards; Warwick; Natural Bridge; at Sterling Mine, Morris Co., N. J.; Newton, N. J.; at St. Jerome, Canada; at Burgess, Canada West.

ASPIDOLITE (v. Kobell).—Approaches in composition a soda-phlogopite. Green. Foliated. Zillerthal, Tyrol.

MANGANOPHYLLITE.—Q. ratio for R : R̈ : Si=3 : 1 : 4 (nearly). Foliated like the micas. Color bronze-red. Analysis, Igelström, SiO_2 38·50, AlO_3 11·00, FeO 3·78, MnO 21·40, CaO 3·20, MgO 15·01, $K_2O(Na_2O)$ 5·51, ign. 1·60=100. Paisberg, Sweden.

BIOTITE.*

Hexagonal(?). $R \wedge R = 62° 57'$ (crystals fr. Vesuvius, Hessenberg); $\check{c}$ = 4·911126. Habit often monoclinic. Prisms commonly tabular. Cleavage: basal highly eminent. Often in disseminated scales, sometimes in massive aggregations of cleavable scales.

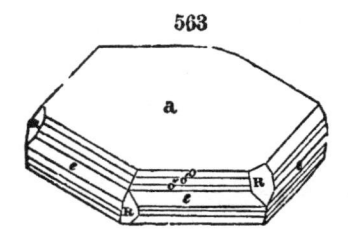

H.=2·5–3. G.=2·7–3·1. Lustre splendent, and more or less pearly on a cleavage surface, and sometimes submetallic when black; lateral surfaces vitreous when smooth and shining. Colors usually green to black, often deep black in thick crystals, and sometimes even in thin laminæ, unless the laminæ are very thin; such thin laminæ green, blood-red, or brown by transmitted light; rarely white.

Streak uncolored. Transparent to opaque. Optically uniaxial. Sometimes biaxial with slight axial divergence, from exceptional irregularities, but the angle not exceeding 5° and seldom 1°.

Comp., Var.—Biotite is a magnesia-iron mica, part of the aluminum (Ᵽl) being replaced by iron (Fe), and Fe and Mg existing among the protoxide bases. Black is the prevailing color, but brown to white also occur. The results of analyses vary much, and for the reason already stated—the non-determination, in most cases, of the degree of oxidation of the iron; and the exact atomic ratio for the species and its limits of variation are therefore not precisely understood. The Q. ratio of bases to silicon is generally 1 : 1, that is the formula in general R_4SiO_4, where $R=K_2(Na_2,Li_2)Fe,Mg(Ca)$, or $Ᵽl,Fe(3R=R)$.
Analyses: 1, Ballyellin; 2, Vesuvius; 3, Portland, Conn.:

	SiO_2	$Ᵽl O_3$	FeO_3	FeO	CaO	MgO	K_2O	Na_2O	Li_2O	ign	
(1)	35·55	17·08	23·70	5·50	——	3·68	9·45	0·35	——	4·30	=99·61, Haughton.
(2)	40·91	17·79	3·00	7·03	0·30	19·04	9·96	——	——	——	=98·03, Chodnew.
(3) $\frac{2}{3}$ 35·61	20·03	0·13	21·85	1·19MnO	5·23	9·69	0·52	0·93	1·87, F 0·76, TiO_2 1·46, Cl tr. =99·27, Hawes.

The above analyses give the ratio of unisilicates, when the water is neglected; in others the ratio of 1 : 1 is obtained only when the water is brought into account.

Pyr., etc.—Same as phlogopite, but with the fluxes it gives strong reactions for iron.

Obs.—A common constituent of many volcanic rocks. Fine specimens obtained at Vesuvius; L. Baikal; Zillerthal; Pargas; Miask; Sala. Also from Greenwood Furnace, N. Y.; Moriah, N. Y.; Easton, Penn.; Topsham, Me., etc.

The biotite of Vesuvius, according to the optical examination of Hintze, is *monoclinic*. (See also Tschermak, Min. Mitth., 1876, 187.)

LEPIDOMELANE.

Hexagonal (?). In small six-sided tables, or an aggregate of minute scales. Cleavage: basal, eminent, as in other micas.

H.=3. G.=3·0. Lustre adamantine, inclining to vitreous, pearly. Color black, with occasionally a leek-green reflection. Streak grayish-green. Opaque, or translucent in very thin laminæ. Somewhat brittle, or but little elastic. Optically uniaxial; or biaxial with a very small axial angle.

Comp.—An iron-potash mica. Q. ratio for bases and silicon 1 : 1; for R : R, mostly 1 : 3, but varying to 1 to more than 3; of doubtful limits, on account of the doubts as to the state of the iron in most of the analyses. Differs from biotite in the smaller proportion of protoxides and little Ᵽl and Mg, but appears to agree with it in optical characters.

Pyr., etc.—B.B. at a red heat becomes brown and fuses to a black magnetic globule. Easily decomposed by hydrochloric acid, depositing silica in scales. Analysis, Cooke, Rockport, Mass.; SiO_2 39·91, $Ᵽl O_3$ 16·73, FeO_3 12·07, FeO 17·48, MnO 0·54, MgO 0·62, K_2O 10·66, $Na_2O(Li_2O)$ 0·59, H_2O 1·50, F 0·45=100.

Obs.—Occurs at Persberg in Wermland, Sweden; at Abborforss in Finland; in Ireland, in Donegal and Leinster Cos.; at Ballyellin, etc. From Cape Ann, Mass. (*Annite*).

ASTROPHYLLITE.—Usually in tabular prisms. Color bronze-yellow. Analysis, Pisani, SiO_2 33·22, TiO_2 7·66, $Ᵽl O_3$ 4·32, FeO_3 4·05, FeO 25·48, MnO 10·70, MgO 1·37, CaO 1·22, Na_2O 2·71, K_2O 6·29, H_2O 2·01=99·03. Brevig, Norway; El Paso County, Colorado.

MUSCOVITE. Kaliglimmer, *Germ.**

Monoclinic (Tschermak). $I \wedge I = 120°$. Cleavage: basal eminent, occasionally also separating in fibres parallel to a diagonal. Twins: often observable by internal markings, or by polarized light; composition parallel

314 DESCRIPTIVE MINERALOGY.

to I consisting of six individuals thus united; sometimes a union of I to
$i\text{-}i$. Folia often aggregated in stellate, plumose, or globular forms; or in
scales, and scaly massive.

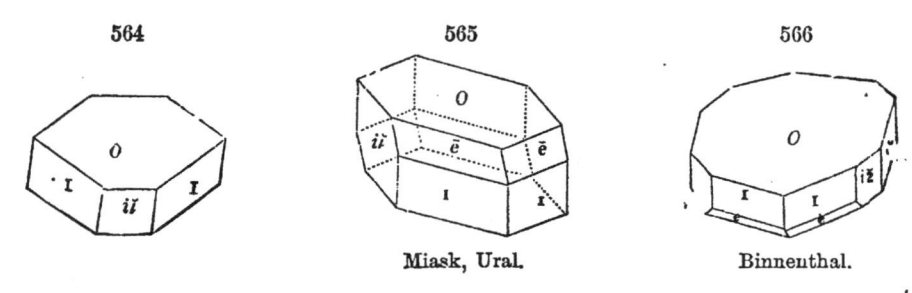

564 565 566

Miask, Ural. Binnenthal.

H.=2–2·5. G.=2·75–3·1. Lustre more or less pearly. Color white, gray, brown, hair-brown, pale green, and violet, yellow, dark olive-green, rarely rose-red; often different for transmitted and reflected light, and different also in vertical and transverse directions. Streak uncolored. Transparent to translucent. Thin laminæ flexible and elastic, very tough. Double refraction strong; optic-axial angle 44°–78°; the axial plane makes an angle of 88° 20′ (Tschermak) with the base.

Comp.—The quantivalent ratio for bases and silicon is generally 4 : 5 (1 . 1¼), rarely 3 . 4, etc. Water is generally present, sometimes as much as 5 p. c.; and the kinds containing from 3 to 5 p. c. water have been referred to the species *margarodite* (p. 353). If the water is regarded as chemically combined, that is, as basic, the Q. ratio for $\overset{\mathrm{I}}{\mathrm{R}}$: R̈ : Si is then
=1 : 3 : 4 (R : Si=1 : 1), also 1 : 6 : 8, 1 : 2 : 4, 1 : 3 : 5, etc. R here is potassium (K) mostly, but also hydrogen (H). R̈=aluminum mostly, also iron. Fluorine is often present, but at most not more than about 1 p. c. Analysis, Smith and Brush, Monroe, Ct., SiO_2 46·50, Al_2O_3 33·91, Fe_2O_3 2·69, MgO 0·90 Na_2O 2·70, K_2O 7·32, H_2O 4·63, F 0·82, Cl 0·31=99·78.

Pyr., etc.—In the closed tube gives water, which with brazil-wood often reacts for fluorine. B.B. whitens and fuses on the thin edges (F.=5·7, v. Kobell) to a gray or yellow glass. With fluxes gives reactions for iron and sometimes manganese, rarely chromium. Not decomposed by acids. Decomposed on fusion with alkaline carbonates.

Obs.—Muscovite is the most common of the micas. It is one of the constituents of granite, gneiss, mica schist, and other related rocks, and is occasionally met with in granular limestone, trachyte, basalt, lava; and occurs also disseminated sparingly in many fragmental rocks. Coarse lamellar aggregations often form the matrix of topaz, tourmaline, and other mineral species in granitic veins.

Siberia affords laminæ of mica sometimes exceeding a yard in diameter; and other remarkable foreign localities are Finbo in Sweden, and Skutterud in Norway. *Fuchsite* or *chromium mica* occurs at Greiner in the Zillerthal, at Passeyr in the Tyrol, and on the Dorfner Alp, as well as at Schwarzenstein.

In *N. Hamp.*, at Acworth, Grafton, etc., in granite, the plates at times a yard across and perfectly transparent. In *Maine*, at Paris; at Buckfield. In *Mass.*, at Chesterfield; at Goshen. In *Conn.*, in Portland; near Middletown. In *N. York*, near Warwick; Edenville; in the town of Edwards. In *Penn.*, at Pennsbury; at Unionville; Delaware Co., at Middletown. In *Maryland*, at Jones's Falls. In western North Carolina, where it is mined.

LEPIDOLITE.* Lithia Mica. Lithionglimmer, *Germ.*

Orthorhombic. $I \wedge I = 120°$. Forms like those of muscovite. Cleavage: basal, highly eminent. Also massive scaly-granular, coarse or fine. H.=2·5–4. G.=2·84–3. Lustre pearly. Color rose-red, violet-gray, or lilac, yellowish, grayish-white, white. Translucent. Optic-axial angle 70°–78°; sometimes 45°–60°.

Comp.—Q. ratio for bases and silicon mostly $1 : 1\frac{1}{2}$; and for $\overset{\text{\tiny I}}{\text{R}} : \text{\r{R}} : \text{Si} = 1 : 3 : 6$, or $1 : 4 : 8$; the formula in the latter case is $\overset{\text{\tiny I}}{\text{R}}_6\text{\r{A}l}_4\text{Si}_{12}\text{O}_{39}$. $\text{\r{R}}$ includes potassium, also lithium, rubidium, and cæsium; and, in the Zinnwald mica, thallium has been detected. Fluorine is present, and the ratio to oxygen mostly 1 : 12. Analysis, Reuter, from Rozena, SiO_2 50·43, AlO_3 28·07, MnO_3 0·88, MgO 1·42, K_2O 10·59, Na_2O 1·46, Li_2O 1·23, F 4·86 = 98·94.

Pyr., etc.—In the closed tube gives water and reaction for fluorine. B.B. fuses with intumescence at 2–2·5 to a white or grayish glass, sometimes magnetic, coloring the flame purplish-red at the moment of fusion (lithia). With the fluxes some varieties give reactions for iron and manganese. Attacked but not completely decomposed by acids. After fusion, gelatinizes with hydrochloric acid.

Obs.—Occurs in granite and gneiss, especially in granitic veins, and is associated sometimes with cassiterite, red, green, or black tourmaline, amblygonite, etc. Found near Utö in Sweden; at Zinnwald in Bohemia; Penig, etc. in Saxony; in the Ural; at Rozena in Moravia; on Elba; at St. Michael's Mount in Cornwall. In the United States, at Paris and Hebron, Me.; near Middletown, Conn.

Named lepidolite from λεπίς, *scale*, after the earlier German name *Schuppenstein*, alluding to the scaly structure of the massive variety of Rozena.

CRYOPHYLLITE (Cooke).—Q. ratio $\text{R} : \text{\r{R}} : \text{Si} = 3 : 4 : 14$, with $\text{R} = \text{Fe,K}_2\text{,Li}_2\text{(Na,Rb,Cs,)}_2$ and $\text{\r{R}} = \text{\r{A}l}$. Orthorhombic. In scales like the micas. Color by transmitted light emerald green. Cape Ann, Mass.

Scapolite Group.

In the species of the Scapolite group, the quantivalent ratio varies from $1 : 1 : 2$, $1 : 2 : 3$, $1 : 3 : 4$, to $1 : 2 : 4$ and $1 : 2 : 6\frac{1}{2}$, but the species are closely alike in the square-prismatic forms of their crystals, in the small number and the kinds of occurring planes, and in their angles. The species are white, or grayish-white, in color, except when impure, and then rarely of dark color; the hardness 5–6·5. G. = 2·5–2·8. The alkali-metal present, when any, is sodium, with only traces of potassium. An increase in the amount of alkali is accompanied by an increase in the silica.

MEIONITE.*

Tetragonal: $O \wedge 1\text{-}i = 156° 18'$; $\check{c} = 0.439$. Sometimes hemihedral in the planes 3-3, the alternate being wanting. Cleavage: $i\text{-}i$ and I rather perfect, but often interrupted.

H. = 5·5–6. G. = 2·6–2·74. Lustre vitreous. Colorless to white. Transparent to translucent; often much cracked within.

Comp.—Q. ratio for $\text{R} : \text{\r{R}} : \text{Si} = 1 : 2 : 3$; formula $\text{R}_5\text{\r{R}}_4\text{Si}_9\text{O}_{36}$. If $\text{R} = \text{Ca} : \text{Na}_2 = 10 : 1$, and $\text{\r{R}} = \text{\r{A}l}$; this is equivalent to Silica 41·6, alumina 31·7, lime 24·1, soda 2·6 = 100. Neminar has found that meionite loses 1 p. c. water at a very high temperature, so that R must be also replaced by H_2; his analysis gives approximately the ratio 1 : 2 : 3.

Pyr., etc.—B.B. fuses with intumescence at 3 to a white blebby glass. Decomposed by acid without gelatinizing (v. Rath).

Obs.—Occurs in small crystals in geodes, usually in limestone blocks, on Monte Somma, near Naples.

WERNERITE.* Scapolite.

Tetragonal: $O \wedge 1\text{-}i = 156° \ 14\frac{1}{2}'$; $\breve{c} = 0.4398$. Often hemihedral in planes 3-3 and i-2 (p. 30). Cleavage: i-i and I rather distinct, but interrupted. Also massive, granular, or with a faint fibrous appearance; sometimes columnar. H.=5-6. G.=2·63-2·8. Lustre vitreous to pearly externally, inclining to resinous; cleavage and cross-fracture surface vitreous. Color white, gray, bluish, greenish, and reddish, usually light. Streak uncolored. Transparent—faintly subtranslucent. Fracture subconchoidal. Brittle.

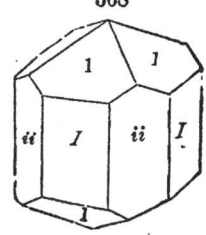

Comp.—Q. ratio for $R : \dot{R} : Si = 1 : 3 : 4$ ($R + \dot{R} : Si = 1 : 1$); formula $\dot{R}\ddot{R}Si_2O_8 = Ca(Na_2)\ddot{A}lSi_2O_8$. Analysis, v. Rath, Pargas, SiO_2 45·46, $\ddot{A}lO_3$ 30·96, CaO 17·22, Na_2O 2·29, K_2O 1·31, H_2O 1·29=98·53. Some varieties vary widely from the above ratio.

Pyr., etc.—B.B. fuses easily with intumescence to a white blebby glass. Imperfectly decomposed by hydrochloric acid.

Diff.—Recognized by its square form; resembles feldspar when massive, but has a characteristic fibrous appearance on the cleavage surface; it is also more fusible, and has a higher specific gravity.

Obs.—Occurs in metamorphic rocks; sometimes in beds of magnetite accompanying limestone. Some localities are: Arendal, Norway; Wermland; Pargas, Finland; L. Baikal, etc. In the following those of the wernerite and ekebergite are not yet distinguished. In *Mass.*, at Bolton; Westfield. In *Conn.*, at Monroe. In *N. York*, in Warwick; in Orange and Essex Co., etc. In *N. Jersey*, at Franklin and Newton. In *Canada*, at G. Calumet Id.; at Hunterstown; Grenville.

The following are other members of the scapolite group:
SARCOLITE.—Q. ratio for $R : \dot{R} : Si = 1 : 1 : 2$. In minute flesh-red crystals at Mt Somma.
PARANTHITE.—Q. ratio=1 : 3 : 4. EKEBERGITE. Q. ratio=1 : 2 : 4½, containing 6-8 p. c. soda. MIZZONITE. Q. ratio=1 : 2 : 5¼, containing 10 p. c. soda. In crystals at Mt. Somma. DIPYRE. Q. ratio=1 : 2 : 6, and for Ca : Na₂=1 : 1. MARIALITE. Q. ratio=1 : 2 : 6, and for Ca : Na₂=1 : 2.

Nephelite Group.

NEPHELITE. Nepheline.

Hexagonal. $O \wedge 1 = 135° \ 55'$; $\breve{c} = 0.839$. Usual forms six-sided and twelve-sided prisms with plane or modified summits. Fig. 569, summit planes of a crystal. Cleavage: I distinct, O imperfect. Also massive, compact; also thin columnar.

H.=5·5-6. G.=2·5-2·65. Lustre vitreous—greasy; a little opalescent in some varieties. Colorless, white, or yellowish; also when massive, dark-green, greenish or bluish-gray, brownish and brick-red. Transparent—opaque. Fracture subconchoidal. Double refraction feeble; axis negative.

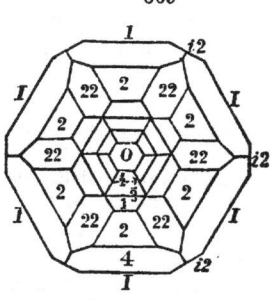

Vesuvius.

Var.—1. *Glassy*, or *Sommite*. Usually in small crystals or grains, with vitreous lustre, first found on Mt. Somma, in the region of Vesuvius. *Davyne* and *cavolinite* belong here.

2. *Elæolite*. In large coarse crystals, or massive, with a greasy lustre.

Comp.—Somewhat uncertain, as all analyses give a little excess of silica beyond what is required for a unisilicate. Assuming that nephelite is a true unisilicate, the Q. ratio for
$\overset{\text{i}}{R} : \overset{..}{R} : Si = 1 : 3 : 4$, and the formula is $(Na,K)_2 AlSi_2O_8$ (Ramm.); some of the Na_2 being replaced by Ca. Analysis, Scheerer, Vesuvius, SiO_2 44·03, AlO_3 33·28, FeO_3 (MnO_3) 0·65, CaO 1·77. Na_2O 15·44, K_2O 4·94, H_2O 0·21 = 100·32. The variety *Elæolite* has the same composition.

Pyr., etc.—B.B. fuses quietly at 3·5 to a colorless glass. Gelatinizes with acids.

Diff.—Distinguished by its gelatinizing with acids from scapolite and feldspar, as also from apatite, from which it differs too in its greater hardness. Massive varieties have a characteristic greasy lustre.

Obs.—Nephelite occurs both in ancient and modern volcanic rocks, and also metamorphic rocks allied to granite and gneiss, the former mostly in glassy crystals or grains (*sommite*), the latter massive or in stout crystals (*elæolite*). Nephelite occurs in crystals in the older lavas of Somma; at Capo di Bove, near Rome; in doleryte of Katzenbuckel, near Heidelberg, etc. Elæolite is found in Norway; in the Ilmen Mts.; Urals; at Litchfield, Me.; in the Ozark Mts., Arkansas.

Named *nepheline* by Haüy (1801), from νεφελή, *a cloud*, in allusion to its becoming cloudy when immersed in strong acid; *elæolite* (by Klaproth), from ἔλαιον, *oil*, in allusion to its greasy lustre.

GIESECKITE is shown by Blum to be a pseudomorph after this species (see p. 330).

CANCRINITE.*—Hexagonal, and in six- and twelve-sided prisms, sometimes with basal edges replaced; also thin columnar and massive. H. = 5–6. G. = 2·42–2·5. Color white, gray, yellow, green, blue, reddish; streak uncolored. Lustre subvitreous, or a little pearly or greasy. Transparent to translucent.

Comp.—Same as for nephelite, with some RCO_3 and water. Analysis, Whitney, Litchfield, Me., SiO_2 37·42, AlO_3 27·70, CaO 3·91, Na_2O 20·98, K_2O 0·67, CO_2 5·95. H_2O 2·82, FeO_3 (MnO_3) 0·86 = 100·31.

Pyr., etc.—In the closed tube gives water. B.B. loses color, and fuses (F. = 2) with intumescence to a white blebby glass, the very easy fusibility distinguishing it readily from nephelite. Effervesces with hydrochloric acid, and forms a jelly on heating, but not before.

Obs.—Found at Miask in the Urals; at Barkevig, Norway; at Ditro in Transylvania (*ditroyte*); at Litchfield, Me.

SODALITE.

Isometric. In dodecahedrons. Cleavage: dodecahedral, more or less distinct. Twins: see f. 272, p. 93. Also massive.

H. = 5·5–6. G. = 2·136–2·401. Lustre vitreous, sometimes inclining to greasy. Color gray, greenish, yellowish, white; sometimes blue, lavender-blue, light red. Subtransparent—translucent. Streak uncolored. Fracture conchoidal—uneven.

Comp.—$3Na_2AlSi_2O_8 + 2NaCl$ = Silica 37·1, alumina 31·71, soda 25·55, chlorine 7·31 = 101·65. Some varieties contain considerably less chlorine.

Pyr., etc.—In the closed tube the blue varieties become white and opaque. B.B. fuses with intumescence, at 3·5–4, to a colorless glass. Decomposed by hydrochloric acid, with separation of gelatinous silica.

Obs.—Occurs in mica slate, granite, syenite, trap, basalt, and volcanic rocks, and is often associated with nephelite (or elæolite) and eudialyte. Found in West Greenland; on Monte Somma; in Sicily; at Miask, in the Ural; near Brevig, Norway. A blue variety occurs at Litchfield, Me., and at Salem, Mass.

MICROSOMMITE.—Occurs in very minute hexagonal crystals in masses of leucitic lava ejected from Mt. Somma. Composition: a unisilicate of potassium, calcium, and aluminum, with small quantities of sodium chloride and calcium sulphate.

HAÜYNITE.

Isometric. In dodecahedrons, octahedrons, etc. Cleavage: dodecahedral distinct. Commonly in rounded grains often looking like crystals with a fused surface.
H.=5·5–6. G.=2·4–2·5. Lustre vitreous, to somewhat greasy. Color bright blue, sky-blue, greenish-blue; asparagus-green. Streak slightly bluish to colorless. Subtransparent to translucent. Fracture flat conchoidal to uneven.

Comp.—$2Na_2(Ca)AlSi_2O_8+CaSO_4$; if in the silicate Na_2 is replaced by Ca, the atomic ratio here being 5 : 1, this gives Silica 34·13, alumina 29·18, lime 10·62, soda 14·69, sulphur trioxide=100. A little potassium is also often present.
Pyr., etc.—In the closed tube retains its color. B.B. in the forceps fuses at 4·5 to a white glass. Fused with soda on charcoal affords a sulphide, which blackens silver. Decomposed by hydrochloric acid with separation of gelatinous silica.
Obs.—Occurs in the Vesuvian lavas, on Somma; in the lavas of the Campagna, Rome; in basalt at Niedermendig and Mayen, L. Laach, etc.
NOSITE (Nosean).—A *soda*-haüynite; $2Na_2AlSi_2O_8+Na_2SO_4$, with also a little calcium. Isometric; often granular massive. Common as a microscopic ingredient of most phonolytes. Lake Laach, etc.
LAPIS-LAZULI (Lasurstein, *Germ.*).—Not a homogeneous mineral according to Fischer and Vogelsang. The latter calls it "a mixture of granular calcite, ekebergite, and an isometric, ultramarine mineral, generally blue or violet." Much used as an ornamental stone.

LEUCITE.*

Tetragonal, according to v. Rath. $\dot{c} = 0.52637$. Usual form as in f. 570, closely resembling a trapezohedron. Twins: twinning-plane 2-i; crystals often very complex, consisting of twinned lamellæ, as indicated by the striations on the planes. Often disseminated in grains; rarely massive granular.
H.=5·5–6. G.=2·44–2·56. Lustre vitreous. Color white, ash-gray or smoke-gray. Streak uncolored. Translucent—opaque. Fracture conchoidal. Brittle. Optically uniaxial; double refraction weak, negative (from Aquacetosa), positive (from Frascati).

Comp.—Formula $K_2AlSi_4O_{12}$=Silica 55·0, alumina 23·5, potash 21·5=100. Q. ratio for K : Al : Si=1 : 3 : 8, for bases to silicon 1 : 2.
Pyr., etc.—B.B. infusible; with cobalt solution gives a blue color (alumina). Decomposed by hydrochloric acid without gelatinization.
Diff.—Distinguished from analcite by its infusibility and greater hardness.
Obs.—Leucite is confined to volcanic rocks, and is common in those of certain parts of Europe; also found in those of the western United States. At Vesuvius and some other parts of Italy it is thickly disseminated through the lava in grains. It is a constituent in the nephelin-doleryte of Merches in the Vogelsberg; abundant in trachyte between Lake Laach and Andernach, on the Rhine.
The question as to whether the crystals of leucite belong to the isometric or the tetragonal system has excited much discussion. Hirschwald (Tsch. Min Mitth., 1875, 227) shows that while implanted crystals are sometimes distinctly *tetragonal*, others, especially those which are imbedded, are as clearly *isometric*, while between the two there exist many transition cases. He claims that the mineral is in fact *isometric*, but having a polysymmetric development, there existing a wide variation from the isometric type. The question cannot be considered as entirely decided.

Feldspar Group.*

The feldspars are characterized by specific gravity below 2·85; hardness 6 to 7, fusibility 3 to 5; oblique or clinohedral crystallization; prismatic angle near 120°; two easy cleavages, one basal, the other brachydiagonal, inclined together either 90°, or very near 90°; cleavage a prominent feature of many massive kinds, and distinct in the grains of granular varieties, giving them angular forms; close isomorphism, and a general resemblance in the systems of occurring crystalline forms; transition from granular varieties to compact, hornstone-like kinds, called felsites, which sometimes occur as rocks; often opalescent, or having a play of colors as seen in a direction a little oblique to i-$\overline{i}$; often aventurine, from the dissemination of microscopic crystals of foreign substances parallel for the most part to the planes O and I.

The bases in the protoxide state are calcium, sodium, potassium, and in one species barium; the sesquioxide base is only aluminum; the quantivalent ratio of $R : \overline{R}$ is constant, 1 : 3; while that of the silicon and bases varies from 1 : 1 to 3 : 1, the amount of silicon increasing with the increase of the alkali metals, and becoming greatest when alkalies are the only protoxides.

The included species are as follows:

		Crystallization.	Approx. Q. ratio $R, \overline{R}, Si$.
ANORTHITE	Lime feldspar	Triclinic	1 : 3 : 4
LABRADORITE	Lime-soda feldspar	"	1 : 3 : 6
HYALOPHANE	Baryta-potash feldspar	Monoclinic	1 : 3 : 8
ANDESITE	Soda-lime feldspar	Triclinic	1 : 3 : 8
OLIGOCLASE	" " "	"	1 : 3 : 9
ALBITE	Soda feldspar	"	1 : 3 : 12
ORTHOCLASE	Potash feldspar	Monoclinic	1 : 3 : 12

To the above list should be added, according to DesCloizeaux, the *triclinic*, potash feldspar, MICROCLINE, which has the composition of orthoclase.

The above ratios are only approximate, for the analyses show a wide variation in the amount of silicon, and an exactly proportionate variation in the amount of alkali; the two elements vary in most cases, as has been long recognized, according to a simple law. There seems hence to be a gradual transition between the successive species; but this is due, in part, to mixtures produced by contemporaneous crystallization (compare *perthite*, p 326, and the description of *microcline*, p. 326).

The unisilicate ratio of 1 : 1 for bases and silicon is found in anorthite only, as shown above. With Ca alone, as in this species, the Q. ratio for $\overline{Al}$ and Si is 3 : 4; with Na₂ alone, 3 : 12; and for kinds containing combinations of the two, exact combinations of these ratios, $mNa_2 : nCa$, giving the ratio $3 : \frac{4m + 12n}{m + n}$.

An explanation of the above fact, and of the variation in ratio shown by analyses, was offered by Hunt, and has since been developed by Tschermak. The existence of two distinct triclinic feldspars is assumed: anorthite $Ca\overline{Al}Si_2O_8$, and albite $Na_2\overline{Al}Si_6O_{16}$, and the other species (sometimes embraced under the general term PLAGIOCLASE) are regarded as due to *isomorphous mixtures* of these two members in different proportions. They have then the general formula $\begin{cases} m(Ca \overline{Al}Si_2O_8) \\ n(Na_2\overline{Al}Si_6O_{16}) \end{cases}$. For labradorite the ratio of $m : n$ is mostly 3 : 2, also 3 : 1, etc.; for andesite the ratio of $m : n$ varies about 1 : 2, and for oligoclase the ratio of $m : n$ is 3 : 10, also 1 : 3, etc. In accordance with the above formula, if Ca : Na=6 : 1, then $\overline{Al}$: Si = 1 : 2·308; for Ca : Na=3 : 1, $\overline{Al}$: Si=1 : 1·257; for Ca : Na=1 : 1, $\overline{Al}$: Si=1 : 3·33; for Ca : Na=1 : 3, $\overline{Al}$: Si=1 : 4·4; for Ca : Na=1 : 6, $\overline{Al}$: Si=1 : 5.

This method of viewing the feldspar species has the advantage of explaining the wide variation in their composition, and is generally accepted among German mineralogists. DesCloizeaux regards his observations upon the optical characters of the feldspars (see p. 298) as showing that they are in fact *distinct* species, and not indeterminate isomorphous mixtures

Optical properties of the triclinic feldspars.—The following table contains the more important optical properties of the feldspar species as determined by DesCloizeaux (C. R., Feb. 8, 1875, and April 17, 1876). Bx=Bisectrix.

	ANORTHITE.	LABRADORITE.	OLIGOCLASE.	ALBITE.	MICROCLINE.
Acute bisectrix.........	always —	always +	generally — sometimes +	always +	always —
Angle made by the +Bx. with a normal to i-i (g)	Position of the Bx. has no simple relation to the planes observed on the crystals.	30° 40'	18° 10'	15°	15° 26'
Same, with normal to $O(p)$..............		56°	68°	78° 35'	
Angle made by the line in which the plane of the optic-axes cuts i-i, with edge i-i/$O(g'/p)$.		27°–28°	Line parallel to the edge $O|i$-i.	20°	5° 6'
Same, with edge i-i I (g' m).............		37°25'–36°25'	" "	96° 28' (front)	
Ordinary dispersion....	$\rho < v(-\text{Bx.})$	$\rho > v(+\text{Bx.})$	$\rho < v(+\text{Bx.})$	$\rho < v(+\text{Bx.})$	$\rho < v(+\text{Bx.})$
Parallel or perpendicular to plane of polarization.	Inclined.	Crossed; also slight inclined.	Crossed; also slight inclined.	Inclined; probably also slight horizontal.	Horizontal (−Bx.) also inclined (+Bx.)
Optic-axial angle (in air) —— for red rays.......	84° 58'	88° 15'	89° 35'	80° 39'	87° 54'
—— for blue rays.....	85° 59' (Somma)	87° 48' (Labrador)	88° 31' (Sunstone, Tvedestrand)	81° 59' (Roc tourné)	Amazonst'ne, Mursinsk.

The axial divergence is quite constant for albite, labradorite, and anorthite, but varies for oligoclase even in different sections taken from the same specimen. Andesine (q. v.) is regarded by DesCloizeaux as an altered oligoclase.

DesCloizeaux gives the following method of *distinguishing between the feldspars* by optical means: It is necessary to obtain a transparent plate parallel to the easiest cleavage (O). Such sections obtained from crystals or lamellar masses of albite, oligoclase, labradorite, and the majority of those of microcline, show hemitropic bands, more or less close together, arranged along the plane parallel to the second cleavage (i-i); for orthoclase and microline in *simple crystals*, two sections placed in opposite positions serve to produce the same effect. These sections are thus brought between the crossed Nicols of a polarization-microscope.

(1) For *orthoclase* the maximum extinction takes place when the two sections are parallel to their plane of contact; the edge O_i/i-i being in the plane of polarization of the microscope.

(2) For *microcline*, the whole structure consists of a multitude of very fine parallel bands; the section may show microcline alone, either hemitropic or not hemitropic, or microcline and orthoclase; the extinction can take place at 30° 54' between the adjoining bands of the same plate of the macle (microcline alone), at 30° 54' between the two plates of the macle (microcline in bands), or at 15° 27' between the adjoining bands (microcline and orthoclase). In the last case the whole of two lamellæ of the macle show at the same time an extinction oblique to the plane of composition, belonging to the microcline, and one parallel to this plane for the orthoclase.

(3) For *albite*, the extinction between two bands takes place at an angle of 6° 32'.

(4) For *oligoclase*, the extinction is simultaneous in the two bands, and when the plane of composition coincides with the plane of polarization of the polariscope, it shows that the structure is homogeneous.

(5) For *labradorite*, the extinction takes place at 10° 24' between the alternate lines of the hemitropic lamellæ.

It follows from this that a plane normal to the plane of the axes cuts the base along a line making with the edge O/i-i the following angles:

        0° in orthoclase,
        15° 27' in microcline,
        3° 16' in albite,
        5° 12' in labradorite.

A variation of one or two degrees from the above mean angles was observed in some specimens. See further on p. 426.

OXYGEN COMPOUNDS—ANHYDROUS SILICATES.

Diff.—The feldspars are distinguished from other species by the characters already stated, prominent among which are: cleavage in two directions, nearly or quite at right angles to each other; also hardness, etc.

The triclinic feldspars can in most cases be distinguished from orthoclase by the fine striation due to repeated twinning. This striation can often be seen by the unaided eye upon the cleavage face (O). And its existence can always be surely tested by the examination of a thin section in polarized light, the alternate bands of color showing the same fact.

The separation of the different triclinic species can be surely made by complete analysis only, or at least by the determination of the amount of alkali present. The degree of fusibility, the color of the flame, and the effect produced by digestion in acids, are often important aids. In the hands of a skilled observer the optical examination may give decisive results.

ANORTHITE. Indianite.

Triclinic. $\breve{c} : \bar{b} : \breve{a} = 0.86663 : 1.57548 : 1$. $I \wedge I' = 120°\ 31'$, $O \wedge i\text{-}\breve{\imath}$, (over $2\text{-}\breve{\imath}$) $= 94°\ 10'$, $O \wedge I' = 114°\ 6\frac{1}{2}'$, $O \wedge I = 110°\ 40'$, $O \wedge 2\text{-}\breve{\imath} = 98°\ 46'$; $a = 93°\ 13\frac{1}{3}'$, $\beta = 115°\ 55\frac{1}{2}'$, $\gamma = 91°\ 11\frac{1}{2}'$ Cleavage: O, $i\text{-}\breve{\imath}$ perfect, the latter least so. Twins similar to those of albite. Also massive. Structure granular, or coarse lamellar.

H.=6–7. G.=2·66–2·78. Lustre of cleavage planes inclining to pearly; of other faces vitreous. Color white, grayish, reddish. Streak uncolored. Transparent — translucent. Fracture conchoidal. Brittle.

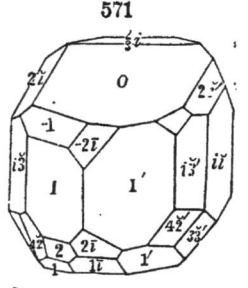

571

Var.—*Anorthite* was described from the glassy crystals of Somma. *Indianite* is a white, grayish, or reddish granular anorthite from India, first described in 1802 by Count Bournon.

Comp.—Q. ratio for R : Ӕl : Si=1 : 3 : 4. Formula $CaӔlSi_2O_8$=Silica 43·1, alumina 36·8, lime 20·1=100. The alkalies are sometimes present in very small amounts.

Pyr., etc.—B.B. fuses at 5 to a colorless glass. Decomposed by hydrochloric acid, with separation of gelatinous silica.

Obs.—Occurs in some granites; occasionally in connection with gabbro and serpentine rocks; in some cases along with corundum; in many volcanic rocks. Found in the old lavas in the ravines of Monte Somma; Pesmeda-Alp, Tyrol; in the Faroe islands; in Iceland; near Bogoslovsk in the Ural, etc.

BYTOWNITE has been shown by Zirkel to be a mixture. Bytown, Canada.

LABRADORITE.

Triclinic. $I \wedge I' = 121°\ 37'$, $O \wedge i\text{-}\breve{\imath} = 93°\ 20'$, $O \wedge I = 110°\ 50'$, $O \wedge I' = 113°\ 34'$; Marignac. Twins: similar to those of albite. Cleavage: O easy; $i\text{-}\breve{\imath}$ less so; I traces. Good crystals rare; generally massive granular, and in grains cleavable; sometimes cryptocrystalline or hornstone-like.

H.=6. G.=2·67–2·76. Lustre of O pearly, passing into vitreous; elsewhere vitreous or subresinous. Color gray, brown, or greenish, sometimes colorless and glassy; rarely porcelain-white; usually a change of colors in cleavable varieties. Streak uncolored. Translucent—subtranslucent.

Comp., Var.—Q. ratio for R : Ӕl : Si=1 : 3 : 6, but varying somewhat (see p. 319). Formula $RӔlSi_3O_{10}$; here R=Ca and Na₂. The atomic ratio for Na : Ca=2 : 3 generally, this corresponds to Silica 52·9, alumina 30·3, lime 12·3, soda 4·5=100.

Var. 1. *Cleavable.* (*a*) Well crystallized to (*b*) massive. Play of colors either wanting, as in some colorless crystals; or pale; or deep; blue and green are the predominant colors; but yellow, fire-red, and pearl-gray also occur. By cutting very thin slices, parallel to i-i, from the original labradorite, they are seen under the microscope to contain, besides striæ, great numbers of minute scales, like the aventurine oligoclase, which are probably göthite or hematite. These scales produce an *aventurine* effect which is quite independent of the play of colors which arises from the interference of the rays of light reflected by innumerable internal lamellæ (*Reusch*). The various forms of minerals (*microplakites, microphyllites*, etc.) enclosed in the labradorite, and their relation to it in position, have been thoroughly investigated by Schrauf (Ber. Ak., Wien, Dec., 1869).

Pyr., etc.—B.B. fuses at 3 to a colorless glass. Decomposed with difficulty by hydrochloric acid, generally leaving a portion of undecomposed mineral.

Obs.—Labradorite is a constituent of some rocks, both metamorphic and igneous; *e.g.*, diabase, doleryte, basalt, etc. The labradoritic metamorphic rocks are most common among the formations of the Archæan or pre-Silurian era. Such are part of those of British America, northern New York, Pennsylvania, Arkansas; those of Greenland, Norway, Finland, Sweden, and probably of the Vosges. Being a feldspar containing comparatively little silica, it occurs mainly in rocks which include little or no quartz (free silica).

Kiew has furnished fine specimens; also Labrador. It is met with in many places in Canada East. Occurs at Essex Co., N. Y.; also in St. Lawrence, Warren, Schoharie, and Green Cos. In Pennsylvania, at Mineral Hill, Chester Co.; in the Witchita Mts., Arkansas, etc.

Labradorite was first brought from the Isle of Paul, on the coast of Labrador, by Mr. Wolfe, a Moravian missionary, about the year 1770, and was called by the early mineralogists Labrador stone (*Labradorstein*), and also chatoyant, opaline, or Labrador feldspar. Labradorite receives a fine polish, and owing to the chatoyant reflections, the specimens are often highly beautiful. It is sometimes used in jewelry.

MASKELYNITE.—Occurs in transparent, isometric, grains in the meteorite of Shergotty. Same composition as labradorite.

ANDESITE. Andesine.

Triclinic. Approximate angles from Esterel crystals (DesCl.): $O \wedge i$-i, left, 87°–88°, $O \wedge I = 111°$–112°, $O \wedge I' = 115°$, $I \wedge i$-$i = 119°$–120°, $I' \wedge i$-$i = 120°$, $O \wedge 2$-$i = 101°$–102°. Twins: resembling those of albite. Seldom in crystals. Cleavage more uneven than in albite. Also granular massive.

H.=5–6. G.=2·61–2·74. Color white, gray, greenish, yellowish, flesh-red. Lustre subvitreous, inclining to pearly.

Comp.—Q. ratio 1 : 3 : 8, but varying to 1 : 3 : 7. General formula $RAlSi_4O_{12}$; $R=Na_2$ and Ca in the ratio 1 : 1 to 3 : 1; if the ratio is 1 : 1, the formula corresponds to Silica 59·8, alumina 25·5, lime 7·0, soda 7·7=100.

Pyr., etc.—Andesite fuses in thin splinters before the blowpipe. Saccharite melts only on thin edges; with borax forms a clear glass. Imperfectly soluble in acids.

Obs.—Occurs in many rocks, especially some trachytes. The original locality was in the Andes, at Marmato; also in the porphyry of l'Esterel, France; in the Vosges Mts.; at Vapnefiord, Iceland, in honey-yellow transparent crystals, etc. In North America, found at Château Richer, Canada, forming with hypersthene and ilmenite a wide-spread rock; color flesh-red.

Andesite is regarded by DesCloizeaux as an altered oligoclase, but many careful analyses point to a feldspar having the composition given above.

HYALOPHANE.

Monoclinic, like orthoclase, and angles nearly the same. $C = 64° 16'$, $I \wedge I = 118° 41'$, $O \wedge 1$-$i = 130° 55\frac{1}{2}'$. Cleavage: O perfect, i-i somewhat less so. In small crystals, single, or in groups of two or three.

$H.=6-6.5$. $G.=2.80$, transparent; 2.905, translucent. Lustre vitreous or like that of adularia. Color white, or colorless; also flesh-red. Transparent to translucent.

Comp.—Q. ratio for $R : \ddot{R} : Si = 1 : 3 : 8$. Formula $(Ba,K_2)\ddot{A}lSi_4O_{12}$. Analysis of hyalophane from the Binnenthal by Stockar-Escher, SiO_2 52·67, AlO_3 21·12, MgO 0·04, CaO 0·46, BaO 15·05, Na_2O 2·14, K_2O 7·82, H_2O 0·58 = 99·88.
Pyr., etc.—B.B. fuses with difficulty to a blebby glass. Unacted upon by acids.
Obs.—Occurs in a granular dolomite near Imfeld, in the Binnenthal, Switzerland; also at Jakobsberg in Sweden.

OLIGOCLASE.

Triclinic. $I \wedge I' = 120°\ 42'$, $O \wedge i\text{-}\breve{\imath}$, ov. $2\text{-}\breve{\imath}' = 93°\ 50'$, $O \wedge I = 110°\ 55'$, $O \wedge I' = 114°\ 40'$. Cleavage: $O, i\text{-}\breve{\imath}$ perfect, the latter least so. Twins: similar to those of albite. Also massive.

$H. = 6-7$. $G. = 2.56-2.72$; mostly 2·65–2·69. Lustre vitreo-pearly or waxy, to vitreous. Color usually whitish, with a faint tinge of grayish-green, grayish-white, reddish-white, greenish, reddish; sometimes aventurine. Transparent, subtranslucent. Fracture conchoidal to uneven.

572

Comp., Var.—Q. ratio for $R : \dot{A}l : Si = 1 : 3 : 9$, though with some variations (see p. 297). Formula $R\ddot{A}lSi_3O_{14}$, with $R=Na_2(K_2)$,Ca   The ratio of 3 : 1 for Na : Ca corresponds in this formula to Silica 61·9, alumina 24·1, lime 5·2, soda 8·8=100.
Var. 1. *Cleavable;* in crystals or massive. 2. *Compact massive; oligoclase-felsite;* includes part, at least, of the so-called compact feldspar or *felsite*, consisting of the feldspar in a compact, either fine granular or flint-like state. 3. *Aventurine oligoclase*, or *sunstone*. Color grayish-white to reddish-gray, usually the latter, with internal yellowish or reddish fire-like reflections proceeding from disseminated crystals of probably either hematite or göthite. 4. *Moonstone* pt. A whitish opalescence.
Pyr., etc.—B.B. fuses at 3·5 to a clear or enamel-like glass. Not materially acted upon by acids.
Obs.—Occurs in porphyry, granite, syenite, serpentine, and also in different eruptive rocks. It is sometimes associated with orthoclase in granite, or other granite-like rocks. Among its localities are Pargas in Finland; Schaitansk, Ural; in protogine of the Mer-de-Glace, in the Alps; in fine crystals at Mt. Somma; as *sunstone* at Tvedestrand, Norway; in Iceland, colorless, at Hafnefjord (*hafnefiordite*). In the United States, at Unionville, Pa.; also at Haddam, Ct.; Mineral Hill, Delaware Co., Pa.; at the emery mine, Chester, Mass.
Named in 1826 by Breithaupt from ὀλίγος, *little*, and κλίω, *to cleave*.

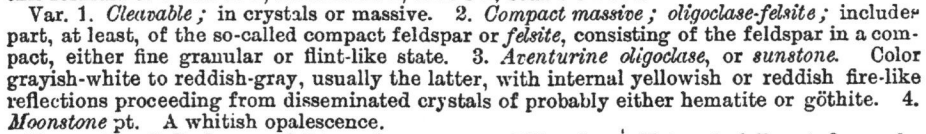

TSCHERMAKITE (v. Kobell).—Supposed to be a *magnesia-feldspar*, but the conclusion was probably based on the analysis of impure material. Later investigations (Hawes, Pisani) make it an oligoclase. Occurs with kjerulfine from Ramle, Norway.

ALBITE.*

Triclinic. $I \wedge I' = 120°\ 47'$, $O \wedge i\text{-}\breve{\imath} = 93°\ 36'$, $O \wedge I' = 114°\ 42'$, $O \wedge I = 110°\ 50'$, $O \wedge 2\text{-}\breve{\imath}' = 136°\ 50'$, $O \wedge 2\text{-}\breve{\imath} = 133°\ 14'$. Cleavage: $O, i\text{-}\breve{\imath}$ perfect, the first most so; $1\text{-}\breve{\imath}$ sometimes distinct. Twins: twinning-plane $i\text{-}\breve{\imath}$, axis of revolution normal to $i\text{-}\breve{\imath}$, this is the most common method, and its repetition gives rise to the fine striations (p. 91) upon the plane O, which are so characteristic of the triclinic feldspars; twinning-plane, $2\text{-}\breve{\imath}$ (f. 578) analogous to the Baveno twins of orthoclase; also twinning-axis, the vertical axis (f. 575); twinning-axis, the macrodiagonal axis* (*b*), the *pericline twins*. Double twins not uncommon. True simple crystals very rare. Also massive, either lamellar or granular; the laminæ sometimes divergent; granular varieties occasionally quite fine to impalpable.

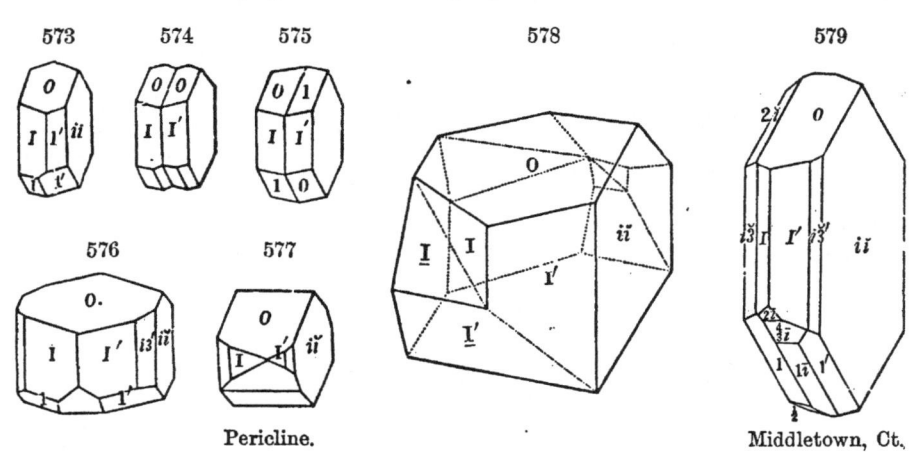

573 574 575 578 579

576 577

Pericline. Middletown, Ct.

H.=6–7. G.=2·59–2·65. Lustre pearly upon a cleavage face; vitreous in other directions. Color white, also occasionally bluish, gray, reddish, greenish, and green; sometimes having a bluish opalescence or play of colors on *O*. Streak uncolored. Transparent—subtranslucent. Fracture uneven. Brittle.

Comp., Var.—Q. ratio Na : Al : Si=1 : 3 : 12. Formula $Na_2AlSi_6O_{16}$=Silica 68·6, alumina 19·6, soda 11·8=100. A small part of the sodium is replaced usually, if not always, by potassium, and also by calcium (here Na_2 by Ca). But these differences are not externally apparent.

Var. 1. *Ordinary*. (*a*) In crystals or cleavable massive. The angles vary somewhat, especially for plane *I'*. (*b*) *Aventurine;* similar to aventurine oligoclase and orthoclase. (*c*) *Moonstone;* similar to moonstone under oligoclase and orthoclase. *Peristerite* is a whitish adularia-like albite, slightly iridescent, having G.=2·626; named from περιστερά, *pigeon*, the colors resembling somewhat those of the neck of a pigeon. (*d*) *Pericline* is in large, opaque, white crystals, short and broad, of the forms in f. 577 (f. 334, p. 101); from the chlorite schists of the Alps. Lamellar; *cleavelandite*, a white kind found at Chesterfield, Mass.

Pyr., etc.—B.B. fuses at 4 to a colorless or white glass, imparting an intense yellow to the flame. Not acted upon by acids.

Obs.—Albite is a constituent of several rocks, as dioryte, etc. It occurs with orthoclase in some granite. It is common also in gneiss, and sometimes in the crystalline schists. Veins of albitic granite are often repositories of the rarer granite minerals and of fine crystallizations of gems, including beryl, tourmaline, allanite, columbite, etc. It occurs also in some trachyte, in phonolyte, in granular limestone in disseminated crystals, as near Modane in Savoy. Some localities for crystals are: Schneeberg in Passeir, in simple crystals; Col du Bonhomme; St. Gothard, and elsewhere in the Alps; Penig, etc., Saxony; Arendal; Greenland; Island of Elba.

In the U. S., in *Maine*, at Paris. In *Mass.*, at Chesterfield; at Goshen. In *Conn.*, at Haddam; at Middletown. In *N. York*, at Granville, Washington Co.; at Moriah, Essex Co. In *Penn.*, at Unionville, Delaware Co.

The name *Albite* is derived from *albus*, white, in allusion to its color, and was given the species by Gahn and Berzelius in 1814.

---

* Vom Rath has recently shown this to be the true method of twinning in this case, and hence that the explanation of Rose (given on p. 101) is incorrect.

ORTHOCLASE.

Monoclinic. $C = 63°\ 53'$, $I \wedge I = 118°\ 48'$, $O \wedge 1\text{-}\check{\imath} = 153°\ 28'$; $\check{c} : b : \check{a} = 0\text{·}844 : 1\text{·}5183 : 1$. $O \wedge 1\text{-}i = 129°\ 41'$, $O \wedge 2\text{-}i = 99°\ 38'$, $O \wedge 2 = 98°\ 4'$. Cleavage: O perfect; $i\text{-}\check{\imath}$ less distinct; $i\text{-}i$ faint; also imperfect in the direction of one of the faces I. Twins: twinning-plane, $i\text{-}i$ (*Carlsbad twins*) f. 582, but the clinopinacoid ($i\text{-}\check{\imath}$) the composition-face (see p. 98); twinning-plane the base (O) f. 583; also the clinodome, 2-$\check{\imath}$ (*Baveno twins*), as in f. 588, in which the prism is made up of two adjoining planes O and two $i\text{-}\check{\imath}$, and is nearly square, because $O \wedge i\text{-}\check{\imath} = 90°$, and $O \wedge 2\text{-}\check{\imath} = 135°\ 3'$; $I \wedge I = 169°\ 28'$; also the same in a twin of 4 crystals, f. 587, each side of the prism then an O (see also p. 99). Often massive, granular; sometimes lamellar. Also compact crypto-crystalline, and sometimes flint-like or jasper-like.

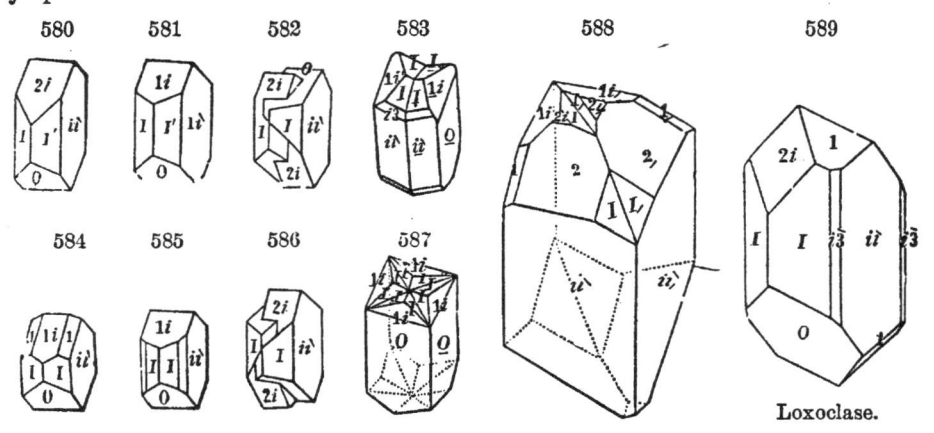

580 581 582 583 588 589

584 585 586 587

Loxoclase.

H.=6–6·5. G.=2·44–2·62, mostly 2·5–2·6. Lustre vitreous; on cleavage-surface sometimes pearly. Color white, gray, flesh-red, common; greenish-white, bright-green. Streak uncolored. Transparent to translucent. Fracture conchoidal to uneven. Optic-axial plane sometimes in the orthodiagonal section and sometimes in the clinodiagonal; acute bisectrix always negative, normal to the orthodiagonal.

Comp., Var.—Q. ratio for K : Al : Si=1 : 3 : 12. Formula $K_2AlSi_6O_{16}$=Silica 64·7, alumina 18·4, potash 16·9=100; with sodium sometimes replacing part of the potassium. The orthoclase of Carlsbad contains rubidium. The varieties depend mainly on structure, variations in angles, the presence of soda, and the presence of impurities.

The amount of sodium detected by analyses varies greatly, the variety *sanidin* (see below) sometimes containing 6 per cent. The variations in angles are large, and they occur sometimes even in specimens of the same locality. The crystallization is normally monoclinic, and the variations are simply irregularities. There are also large optical variations in orthoclase, on which see DesCl. Min., i., 329.

Var. 1. *Ordinary.* In crystals, or cleavable massive. *Adularia* (adular). Transparent, cleavable, usually with pearly opalescent reflections, and sometimes with a play of colors like labradorite, though paler in shade. *Moonstone* belongs in part here, the rest being albite and oligoclase. *Sunstone*, or *aventurine feldspar:* In part orthoclase, rest albite or oligoclase (q. v.). *Amazonstone:* Bright verdigris-green, and cleavable, mostly mixtures of orthoclase and microcline (Dx.). Kœnig concludes that the coloring matter of the Pike's Peak amazonstone is an organic compound of iron, which has been infiltrated into the mass.

Sanidin of Nose, or *glassy feldspar* (including much of the *Ice-spar*, part of which is anorthite). Occurs in transparent glassy crystals, mostly tabular (whence the name from σάνις, a board), in lava, pumice, trachyte, phonolite, etc. Proportion of soda to potash varies from 1 : 20 to 2 : 1. *Rhyacolite* is the same; the name was applied to glassy crystals from Mt. Somma (Eisspath, *Wern.*).

Chesterlite. In white crystals, smooth, but feebly lustrous, implanted on dolomite in Chester Co., Penn., and having wide variations in its angles. It contains but little soda. According to DesCloizeaux the chesterlite consists of a union of parallel bands of orthoclase and a triclinic feldspar of the same composition, which he calls *microcline* (see below).

Loxoclase. In grayish-white or yellowish crystals, a little pearly or greasy in lustre, often large, feebly shining, lengthened usually in the direction of the clinodiagonal. $O \wedge I = 112° 30'$, $O \wedge I' = 112° 50'$, $I \wedge I' = 120° 20'$, $O \wedge i\text{-}\bar{\imath}$ (cleavage angle) $= 90°$, Breith. G. $= 2\cdot6 - 2\cdot62$, Plattner. The analyses find much more soda than potash, the ratio being about 3 : 1, but how far this is due to mixture with albite has not been ascertained. From Hammond, St. Lawrence Co., N. Y. Named from λοξός, *transverse*, and κλάω, *I cleave*, under the idea that the crystals are peculiar in having cleavage parallel to the orthodiagonal section. *Perthite.* A flesh-red aventurine feldspar, consisting of interlaminated albite and orthoclase, as shown by Breithaupt. From Perth, Canada East.

COMPACT ORTHOCLASE or ORTHOCLASE-FELSITE.—This crypto-crystalline variety is common and occurs of various colors, from white and brown to deep red. There are two kinds (*a*) the *jasper-like*, with a subvitreous lustre; and (*b*) the *ceratoid* or *wax-like*, with a waxy lustre. Some red kinds look closely like red jasper, but are easily distinguished by the fusibility. The orthoclase differs from the albite felsite in containing much more potash than soda. The Swedish name *Hälleflinta* means *false flint*.

Pyr., etc.—B.B. fuses at 5; varieties containing much soda are more fusible. Loxoclase fuses at 4. Not acted upon by acids.

Obs.—Orthoclase is an essential constituent of many rocks; here are included granite, gneiss, and mica schist; also syenite, trachyte, phonolyte, etc., etc.

Fine crystals are found at Carlsbad in Bohemia; Katherinenburg, Siberia; Arendal, Norway; Baveno in Piedmont; in Cornwall; in the Urals; the Mourne mountains, Ireland, etc.; in the trachyte of the Drachenfels on the Rhine. In the U. States, orthoclase is found in *N. Hamp.*, at Acworth. In *Conn.*, at Haddam and Middletown. In *N. York*, at Rossie; in the town of Hammond; in Lewis Co.; near Natural Bridge; in Warwick; and at Amity and Edenville. In *Penn.*, in crystals at Leiperville, Delaware Co., etc. In *N. Car.*, at Washington Mine, Davidson Co.; beautiful Amazonstone at Pike's Peak, Col. Massive orthoclase is abundant at many localities.

MICROCLINE.* *A triclinic potash feldspar.*—The name *microcline* was originally given by Breithaupt to a whitish or reddish feldspar from the zircon-syenite of Frederiksvärn and Brevig, Norway, on the ground that it was *triclinic*. It was shown by DesCloizeaux that this feldspar was merely a variety of orthoclase remarkable for its large amount of soda. Recently the latter author has proposed to retain this name for a feldspar found in the midst of granites, pegmatite, and gneiss, which is shown both by the angle between its cleavage planes, and also by its optical properties, to be really *triclinic*.

Form generally like that of orthoclase. Cleavage basal and clinodiagonal, and also easy parallel to both prismatic faces (I and I'); for the optical properties see p. 298. Often associated with orthoclase in regular parallel bands, especially in the amazonstone; albite is also sometimes present, though irregularly. Analysis of a "pure microcline" from Magnet Cove by Pisani. G. $= 2\cdot54$.

SiO_2	AlO_3	FeO_3	K_2O	Na_2O	ign.
64·30	19·70	0·74	15·60	0·48	0·35 = 101·17

The association of orthoclase and microcline was observed in specimens from the Ilmen Mts.; Urals; Arendal; Greenland; Labrador; Leverett, Mass.; Delaware, Chester Co., Penn.; Pike's Peak, Col. The purest microcline was that of a greenish color from Magnet Cove, Ark.; it enclosed crystals of ægirite, and was not mixed with orthoclase.

SUBSILICATES.

Humite or Chondrodite Group, including three sub-species:

I. Humite; II. Chondrodite; III. Clinohumite.

The existence of three types of forms among the crystals of humite (Vesuvius) was early shown by Scacchi; they have since then been further investigated by vom Rath (Pogg. Erg..

Bd. v., 321, 1871; ibid., vi., 385, 1873). The chemical identity of the species humite and chondrodite was shown by Rammelsberg; later Kokscharof proved that the crystals of chondrodite from Pargas, Finland, were identical in form and angles with Scacchi's type II. of humite, and the same has also been shown of the Swedish crystals by vom Rath. In 1875 the author described crystals of chondrodite from Brewster, N. Y., belonging to each of the three types of humite; he showed, moreover, then and later (Feb., 1876), that contrary to what had been previously assumed, the crystals of both type II. and type III. were *monoclinic*, not orthorhombic. DesCloizeaux and Klein have since proved (Jahrb. Min., 1876, No. 6) the monoclinic character of type III. of the Vesuvian humite, and the former that of the Swedish crystals (type II.); he, moreover, proved the orthorhombic character of the crystals of type I., Vesuvius. In accordance with these facts DesCloizeaux has proposed that the three types be regarded as distinct species, with the names given above.

I. **HUMITE.*** Including type I., Scacchi, Vesuvius. Also rare crystals from Brewster, N. Y. The latter large, coarse, and having suffered more or less alteration.

Orthorhombic. Holohedral. $i\text{-}2\,(o^2) \wedge i\text{-}2 = 130°\ 19'$; $O\,(A) \wedge 3\text{-}\bar{i}\,(i^3) = 102°\ 48'$; $O \wedge 1\text{-}\bar{i}\,(i^2) = 124°\ 16'$; $O \wedge 3\text{-}\check{i}\,(e^5) = 103°\ 47'$; $O \wedge 1\text{-}\check{i}\,(e^3) = 126°\ 21'$; $O \wedge 1\text{-}2\,(r^3) = 121°\ 44'$. Twins: twinning-plane $\frac{2}{7}\text{-}\check{i}$, also $\frac{3}{5}\text{-}\check{i}$, in both cases the angle of the horizontal prism is nearly 120°. Optic-axial plane parallel to the base, acute bisectrix positive, normal to $i\text{-}\bar{i}$. Dispersion almost zero. $2Ha = 78°\ 18' - 79°$ for red rays. (DesCl.)

590　　　　　591　　　　　592

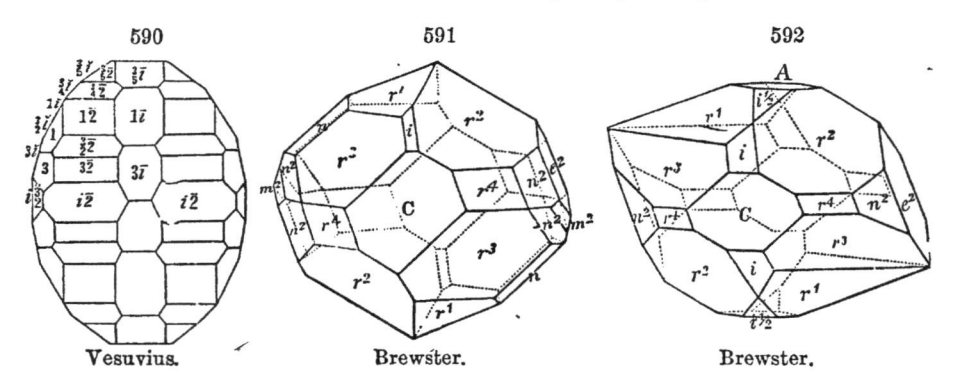

Vesuvius.　　　Brewster.　　　Brewster.

II. **CHONDRODITE.*** Including type II. of Scacchi, Vesuvius; also crystals from Finland, Sweden, and with few exceptions those of Brewster, N. Y.

Monoclinic. $A \wedge i = 122°\ 29'$; $A \wedge e^2 = 109°\ 5'$; $A \wedge e^{2'} = 108°\ 58'$; $A : n^2 = 103°\ 12'$; $A \wedge n^{2'} = 103°\ 9'$; $A \wedge r^1 = 135°\ 20'$; $A \wedge r^2 = 125°\ 50'$; $C \wedge r^3 = 146°\ 24'$; $C \wedge n^2 = 135°\ 40'$; $C \wedge n^{2'} = 135°\ 41'$.

The letters (those employed by Scacchi) correspond to the following symbols:—

$A = O \quad i = 1\text{-}\bar{i} \quad e^2 = -2\text{-}i \quad n^2 = -2 \quad r^1 = -\frac{4}{5}\text{-}2 \quad r^3 = -\frac{4}{3}\text{-}2 \quad m^2 = -6\text{-}\frac{3}{2}.$
$C = i\text{-}\bar{i} \quad i^{\frac{1}{2}} = \frac{1}{2}\text{-}\bar{i} \quad e^{2'} = 2\text{-}i \quad n^{2'} = 2 \quad r^2 = \frac{4}{7}\text{-}2 \quad r^4 = 4\text{-}2 \quad i^1 = \frac{1}{2}\text{-}\bar{i}.$

Twins: twinning plane $\frac{2}{5}\text{-}i\,(\pm?)$ and $\frac{6}{5}\text{-}i\,(\pm?)$, (both having a prismatic angle nearly 120°); also the basal plane O (Brewster, N. Y., f. 593).

Optic-axial plane makes an angle of 26° with the base; acute bisectrix positive, normal to the clinopinacoid (C). $2Ha = 88°\ 48'$ for red rays, Brewster, N. Y. (E. S. D.). $2Ha = 86°\ 14'–87°\ 20'$ (red rays), Sweden, (DesCl.)

The above angles are those given by DesCloizeaux, the author's own measurements on the crystals from Brewster (not yet completed), point to a smaller variation from the rectangular type. DesCloizeaux makes the plane $e^{2'} = i\text{-}i$, and $r^4 = I$, $r^2 = 1$, $r^3 = -1$.

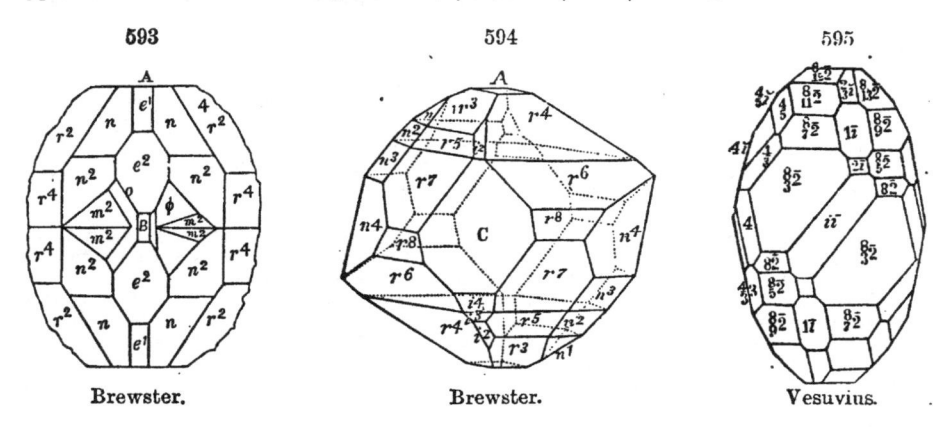

593 594 595

Brewster. Brewster. Vesuvius.

III. CLINOHUMITE. Including type III. of Scacchi, Vesuvius; also rare finely polished red crystals from Brewster, N. Y.

Monoclinic. $A \wedge e^2 = 133°\ 40'$; $A \wedge e^{2'} = 133°\ 40'$; $A \wedge i^2 = 125°\ 13'$; $A \wedge m = 114°\ 55'$; $A \wedge m^2 = 92°\ 58'$; $A \wedge n = 132°\ 14'$; $A \wedge n^2 = 122°\ 57'$; $A \wedge n^4 = 97°\ 23'$; $A \wedge n^{4'} = 97°\ 23'$; $A \wedge r^3 = 131°\ 23$; $A \wedge r^4 = 125°\ 47'$; $C \wedge r^3 = 132°\ 56'$; $C \wedge r^4 = 137°\ 25'$. DesCloizeaux.

These letters (those employed by Scacchi) correspond to the following symbols:—

$A = O$ $i = \tfrac{3}{3}\text{-}i$ $n = \tfrac{4}{7}$ $n^4 = -4$ $r^3 = -\tfrac{8}{11}\text{-}2$ $r^5 = -\tfrac{8}{7}\text{-}2$ $r^7 = -\tfrac{8}{3}\text{-}2$
$C = i\text{-}i$ $i^2 = 1\text{-}i$ $n^2 = -\tfrac{4}{5}$ $n^{4'} = 4$ $r^4 = \tfrac{8}{9}\text{-}2$ $r^6 = \tfrac{8}{5}\text{-}2$ $r^8 = 8\text{-}2$

DesCloizeaux makes the plane $e^{4'} = i\text{-}i$, $r^3 = I$, and $r^4 = -1$, and $r^5 = 1$. Twins: twinning-plane $-\tfrac{4}{3}\text{-}i$; also the basal plane (Brewster). Optic-axial plane makes an angle of $7\tfrac{1}{2}°$ with the base, Brewster (Dana); same angle for Vesuvian crystals equals $12°\ 28'$ (Klein), about $11°$ (DesCl.). Acute bisectrix positive, normal to clinopinacoid. $2Ha = 84°\ 40'–85°\ 15'$, yellow (Kl.). $= 84°\ 38'–85°\ 4'$ white crystals, and $= 86°\ 40'–87°\ 14'$ brown crystals (DesCl.). Sections of crystals often shows a complex twinned structure.

In other physical and in chemical characters these three sub-species are hardly to be distinguished.

H. = 6–6·5. G. = 3·118–3·24. Lustre vitreous—resinous. Color of crystals yellowish-white, citron-yellow, honey-yellow, hyacinth-red, brownish (Vesuvius); also deep garnet-red (Brewster). Color of the mineral occurring massive and in rounded imbedded grains (chondrodite at least in part) as of crystals, also sometimes olive-green, apple-green, gray, black. Streak white, or slightly yellowish, or grayish. Transparent—subtranslucent. Fracture subconchoidal—uneven.

OXYGEN COMPOUNDS—ANHYDROUS SILICATES.   329

Comp.—The chemical investigations of Rammelsberg and vom Rath have served to show a considerable variation in composition in the different varieties, but do not give decidedly different formulas to the three types of Scacchi, that is, the three minerals described above.

In general Q. ratio for Mg : Si=4 : 3 ($1\frac{1}{3}$: 1), and the formula then $Mg_6Si_3O_{14}$; or, as preferred by Rammelsberg, Mg : Si=5 : 4 ($1\frac{1}{4}$: 1), and the formula is then $Mg_5Si_2O_9$. In all cases part of the magnesium is replaced by iron, and part of the oxygen by fluorine (F_2), the amount varying from $2\frac{1}{4}$ to $8\frac{1}{4}$ p. c., but certainly not dependent (v. Rath and Ramm.) upon the three types.

Analyses:—

	SiO_2	FeO	MgO	F		
I. Humite, Vesuvius,	35·63	5·12	54·45	2·43	CaO 0·23 ӔlO_3 0·82	=99·68, v. Rath.
II. Chondrodite, Vesuvius,	33·26	2·30	57·92	5·04	CaO 0·74 ӔlO_3 1·06	=100·32, Ramm.
II. Chondrodite, Brewster,	34·10	7·28	53·72	4·14	——— ӔlO_3 0·48	=99·72, Hawes.
II. Chondrodite, Sweden,	33·96	6·83	53·51	4·24	——— ӔlO_3 0·72	=99·26, v. Rath.
III. Clinohumite, Vesuvius,	36·82	5·48	54·92	2·40	——— ӔlO_3 0·24	=99·86, v. Rath.
Chondrodite (?), N. Jersey,	33·97	3·48	56·97	7·44	——— ———	=101·68, Ramm.

Pyr., etc.—B.B. infusible; some varieties blacken and then burn white. Fused with salt of phosphorus in the open tube gives a reaction for fluorine. With the fluxes a reaction for iron. Gelatinizes with acids. Heated with sulphuric acid gives off silicon fluoride.

Diff.—Distinguishing characters are: infusibility; gelatinizing with acids; fluorine reaction with sulphuric acid.

Obs.—The localities of the crystallized minerals have already been mentioned.

The granular chondrodite (?) occurs mostly in limestone. It is found in Finland and in Sweden; at Taberg in Wermland; at Boden in Saxony; on Loch Ness in Scotland; at Achmatovsk in the Ural, etc. Abundant in the counties of Sussex, N. J., and Orange, N. Y., where it is associated with spinel. In *N. Jersey*, at Bryam; at Sparta; at Vernon, Lockwood, and Franklin. In *N. York*, in Orange Co., in Warwick, Monroe, etc.; near Edenville; at the Tilly Foster Iron Mine, Brewster, Putnam Co. In *Mass.*, at Chelmsford. In *Penn.*, near Chadsford. In *Canada*, in limestone at St. Crosby; St. Jerome; St. Adèle; Grenville, etc., abundant.

TOURMALINE.* Turmalin, *Germ.*

Rhombohedral. $R \wedge R = 103°$, $O \wedge R = 134° \ 3'$; $\dot{c} = 0.89526$. $\frac{1}{4} \wedge \frac{1}{4} =$

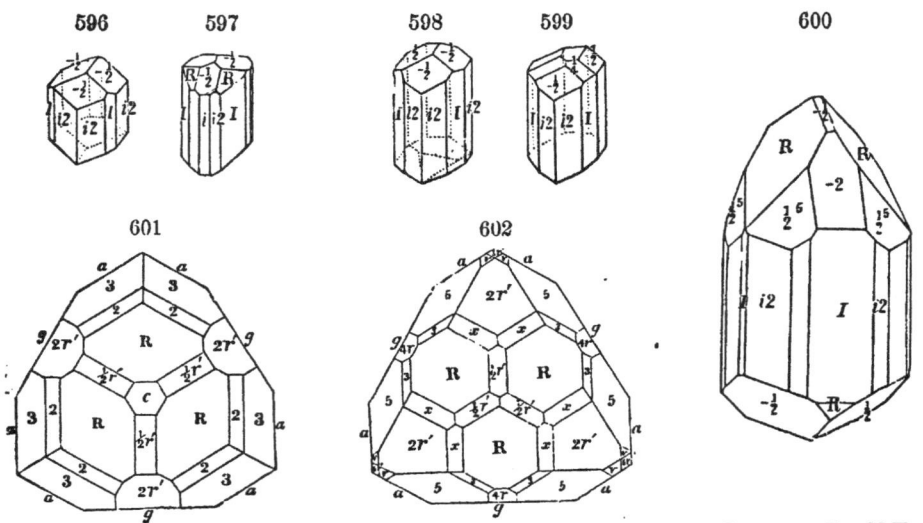

596 597 598 599 600

601 602

Gouverneur, N.Y.   St. Lawrence Co., N.Y.

$154° \ 59'$, $\frac{1}{2} \wedge \frac{1}{2} = 133° \ 8'$, $i\text{-}2 \wedge \frac{1}{2}^5 = 155° \ 14'$, $i\text{-}2 \wedge \frac{1}{2}^3 = 142° \ 26'$. Usually hemihedral, being often unlike at the opposite extremities, or hemimorphic, and the prisms often triangular. Cleavage: R, $-\frac{1}{2}$. and i-2, difficult. Sometimes massive compact; also columnar, coarse or fine, parallel or divergent.

H.=7–7·5. G.=2·94–3·3. Lustre vitreous. Color black, brownish-black, bluish-black, most common; blue, green, red, and sometimes of rich shades; rarely white or colorless; some specimens red internally and green externally; and others red at one extremity, and green, blue, or black at the other. Dichroic (p. 165). Streak uncolored. Transparent—opaque; greater transparency across the prism than in the line of the axis. Fracture subconchoidal—uneven. Brittle. Pyroelectric (p. 169).

Var.—1. *Ordinary*. In crystals. (*a*) *Rubellite;* the red sometimes transparent. (*b*) *Indicolite;* the blue, either pale or bluish-black; named from the indigo-blue color. (*c*) *Brazilian Sapphire* (in jewelry); Berlin-blue and transparent; (*d*) *Brazilian Emerald*, *Chrysolite* (or *Peridot*) *of Brazil;* green and transparent. (*e*) *Peridot of Ceylon;* honey-yellow. (*f*) *Achroite;* colorless tourmaline, from Elba. (*g*) *Aphrizite;* black tourmaline, from Krageröe, Norway. (*h*) *Columnar* and *black;* coarse columnar. Resembles somewhat hornblende, but nas a more resinous fracture, and is without distinct cleavage or anything like a fibrous appearance in the texture.

Comp.—Q. ratio of all varieties for R : Si=3 : 2 (Rammelsberg), consequently the general formula is $\overset{ii}{R}_3(\overset{i}{R}_6,\overset{ii}{R})SiO_5$. R may represent here H, K, Na, Li ; also $\overset{ii}{R}=Mg(Ca),Fe,Mn$, and R=Al,B₂ ; further than this the Si is often in part replaced by F₂. Rammelsberg distinguishes two groups, where the Q. ratio for B : Al : Si=3 : 6 : 8, and (2) with the Q. ratio for B : Al : Si=1 : 3 : 3. In the first group fall most of the yellow, brown, and black varieties, the bivalent elements (Mg,Fe) predominating, the general formula being $\overset{ii}{R}_3(\overset{ii}{R}_6)\overset{i}{R}_2Si_4O_{20}$. The second group includes the colorless, red, and slightly green kinds, the univalent elements appearing most prominent, especially lithium. The general formula is $\overset{i}{R}_6(\overset{ii}{R}_2)\overset{ii}{R}_5Si_9O_{45}$.

Several distinct varieties are made under these groups, which will be sufficiently illustrated by the following analyses, by Rammelsberg. I. Gouverneur, brown·; G.=3·049. II. Haddam, black; G.=3·136. III. Goshen, bluish-black; G.=3·203. IV. Paris, Me., red; G.=3·019. V. Chesterfield, Mass., green; G.=3·069.

	SiO_2	B_2O_3	Al_2O_3	FeO	MnO	MgO	CaO	Na_2O	K_2O	Li_2O	F	H_2O	
I.	38·85	(8·35)	31·32	1·14	—	14·89	1·60	1·28	0·26	—	—	2·31	=100·00
II.	37·50	(9·02)	30·87	8·54	—	8·60	1·33	1·60	0·73	—	—	1·81	=100·00
III.	38·22	10·65	33·35	11·95	1·25	0·63	—	1·75	0·40	0·84	0·82	2·21	=100·82
IV.	38·19	9·97	42·63	—	1·94	0·39	0·45	2·60	0·68	1·17	1·18	2·00	=100·20
V.	38·46	9·73	36·80	6·38	0·78	1·88	—	2·47	0·47	0·72	0·55	2·31	=100·55

Pyr., etc.—I. fuse rather easily to a white blebby glass or slag; II. fuse with a strong heat to a blebby slag or enamel; III. fuse with difficulty, or, in some, only on the edges; IV. fuse on the edges, and often with great difficulty, and some are infusible; V. infusible, but becoming white or paler. With the fluxes many varieties give reactions for iron and manganese. Fused with a mixture of potassium bisulphate and fluorite gives a strong reaction for boracic acid. By heat alone tourmaline loses weight from the evolution of silicon fluoride and perhaps also boron fluoride; and only after previous ignition is the mineral completely decomposed by fluohydric acid. Not decomposed by acids (Ramm.). After fusion perfectly decomposed by sulphuric acid (v. Kobell).

Diff.—Distinguished by its form, occurring commonly in three-sided, or six-sided prisms; absence of cleavage (unlike hornblende). It is less easily fusible than garnet or vesuvianite. B.B. (see above) gives a green flame (boron).

Obs.—Tourmaline is usually found in granite, gneiss, syenite, mica, chloritic or talcose schist, dolomite, granular limestone, and sometimes in sandstone near dykes of igneous rocks. The variety in granular limestone or dolomite is commonly brown.

Prominent localities are Katherinenburg in Siberia; Elba; Windisch Kappell in Carinthia; Rozena; Airolo, Switzerland; St. Gothard. In Great Britain. Bovey Tracey in Devon; Cornwall, at different localities; Aberdeen in Scotland, etc.

In the U. States, in *Maine*, at Paris and Hebron. In *Mass.*, at Chesterfield; at Goshen, blue. In *N. Hamp.*, Grafton; Acworth, etc. In *Conn.*. at Monroe and Haddam, black. In *N. York*,

OXYGEN COMPOUNDS—ANHYDROUS SILICATES. 331

near Gouverneur; near Port Henry, Essex Co., enclosing orthoclase (see p. 109); Pierrepont; near Edenville. In *Penn.*, near Unionville; at Chester; Middletown, and elsewhere. In *Canada*, at G. Calumet Id.; at Fitzroy, C. W.; at Hunterstown, C. E.; at Bathurst and Elmsley, C. W.

GEHLENITE.—Tetragonal. Color grayish-green. Q. ratio for $\dot{R} : \ddot{R} : \ddot{Si} = 3 : 3 : 4$, or $3 : 2$ for bases and silicon. Formula $Ca_3\ddot{R}Si_2O_{10}$, with $\ddot{R}=\ddot{A}l : \ddot{F}e = 5 : 1$; this requires Silica 29·9, alumina 21·5, iron sesquioxide 6·6. lime 4·20=100. Mt. Monzoni, Fassathal, Tyrol.

ANDALUSITE.

Orthorhombic. $I \wedge I = 90°\ 48'$, $O \wedge 1\text{-}\bar{\imath} = 144°\ 32'$; $\check{c} : \bar{b} : \check{a} = 0.71241 : 1.01405 : 1$. Cleavage: I perfect in crystals from Brazil; $i\text{-}\bar{\imath}$ less perfect; $i\text{-}\check{\imath}$ in traces. Massive, imperfectly columnar, sometimes radiated, and granular. H.=7·5; in some opaque kinds 3–6. G.=3·05–3·35, mostly 3·1–3·2. Lustre vitreous; often weak. Color whitish, rose-red, flesh-red, violet, pearl-gray, reddish-brown, olive-green. Streak uncolored. Transparent to opaque, usually subtranslucent. Fracture uneven, subconchoidal.

603

Var.—1. *Ordinary.* H.=7·5 on the basal face, if not elsewhere.
2. *Chiastolite* (macle), Sterling, Mass. Stout crystals having the axis and angles of a different color from the rest, owing to a regular arrangement of impurities through the interior, and hence exhibiting a colored cross, or a tesselated appearance in a transverse section. H.=3–7·5, varying much with the degree of impurity. The following figure shows sections of some crystals (see also p. 110).

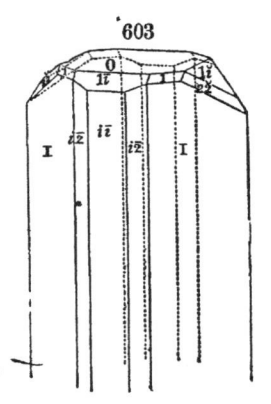

604

Comp.—Q. ratio for $\ddot{R} : \ddot{Si} = 3 : 2$; $\ddot{A}lSiO_5 =$ Silica 36·9, alumina 63·1=100. Sometimes a little FeO_3 is present.
Pyr., etc.—B.B. infusible. With cobalt solution gives a blue color. Not decomposed by acids. Decomposed on fusion with caustic alkalies and alkaline carbonates.
Diff.—Distinguishing characters: infusibility; hardness; and the form, being nearly that of a square prism, unlike staurolite.
Obs.—Most common in argillaceous schist, or other schists imperfectly crystalline; also in gneiss, mica schist, and related rocks. Found in Spain, in Andalusia, and thence the name of the species; in the Tyrol, Lisens valley; in Saxony, at Bräunsdorf, and elsewhere. In Ireland. In Brazil, province of Minas Geraes (transparent). Common in crystalline rocks of New England and Canada; good crystals have been obtained in Delaware Co., Penn., etc. also in California; in Mass., at Sterling (*chiastolite*).

FIBROLITE. Bucholzite. Sillimanite.

Orthorhombic. $I \wedge I = 96°$ to $98°$ in the smoothest crystals; usually larger, the faces I striated, and passing into $i\text{-}2$. Cleavage: $i\text{-}\bar{\imath}$ very perfect, brilliant. Crystals commonly long and slender. Also fibrous or columnar massive, sometimes radiating.

H.=6-7. G.=3·2-3·3. Lustre vitreous, approaching subadamantine. Color hair-brown, grayish-brown, grayish-white, grayish-green, pale olive green. Streak uncolored. Transparent to translucent.

Var.—1. *Sillimanite*. In long, slender crystals, passing into fibrous, with the fibres separable. 2. *Fibrolite*. Fibrous or fine columnar, firm and compact, sometimes radiated; grayish-white to pale brown, and pale olive-green or greenish-gray. *Bucholzite* and *monrolite* are here included; the latter is radiated columnar, and of the greenish color mentioned.
Comp.—$AlSiO_5$, as for andalusite = Silica 36·9, alumina 63·1=100.
Pyr., etc.—Same as given under andalusite.
Diff.—Distinguished from tremolite by its infusibility; also by its brilliant diagonal cleavage, in which and in its specific gravity it differs from cyanite.
Obs.—Occurs in gneiss, mica schist, and related metamorphic rocks. In the Fassathal, Tyrol (*bucholzite*); at Bodenmais in Bavaria, etc. In the United States, at Worcester, *Mass.* Near Norwich, *Conn.*; at Chester, near Saybrook (*sillimanite*). In *N. York*, in Monroe, Orange Co. (*monrolite*). In *Penn.*, at Chester on the Delaware; in Delaware Co., etc. In *Delaware*, at Brandywine Springs. In *N. Carolina*, with corundum.
Fibrolite was much used for stone implements in western Europe in the "Stone age."
WÖRTHITE, a hydrous fibrolite; WESTANITE (Sweden) is related in composition.

CYANITE.* Kyanite. Disthene.

Triclinic. In flattened prisms; O rarely observed. Crystals oblong, usually very long and blade-like. Cleavage: $i\text{-}\bar{i}$ distinct; $i\text{-}\check{i}$ less so; O imperfect. Also coarsely bladed columnar to subfibrous.
H.=5-7·25, the least on the lateral planes. G.=3·45-3·7. Lustre vitreous—pearly. Color blue, white, blue along the centre of the blades or crystals with white margins; also gray, green, black. Streak uncolored. Translucent—transparent.

Var.—The white cyanite is sometimes called *Rhœtizite*.
Comp.—$AlSiO_5$ = Silica 36·9, alumina 63·1=100, like andalusite and fibrolite.
Pyr., etc.—Same as for andalusite.
Diff.—Unlike the amphibole group of minerals in its infusibility; occurrence in thin-bladed prisms characteristic.
Obs.—Occurs principally in gneiss and mica slate. Found at St. Gothard in Switzerland; at Greiner and Pfitsch in the Tyrol; also in Styria; Carinthia; Bohemia. In *Mass.*, at Chesterfield, etc. In *Conn.*, at Litchfield; at Oxford. In *Vermont*, at Thetford. In *Penn.*, in Chester Co.; and Delaware Co. In *N. Carolina*.

TOPAZ.*

Orthorhombic. $I \wedge I = 124°\ 17'$, $O \wedge 1\text{-}i = 138°\ 3'$; $\check{c} : \bar{b} : \check{a} = 0.90243 : 1.8920 : 1$. $O \wedge 1 = 134°\ 25'$, $1 \wedge 1$, macr., $= 141°\ 0'$. Crystals usually hemihedral, the extremities being unlike; habit prismatic. Cleavage: basal, highly perfect. Also firm columnar; also granular, coarse or fine.
H.=8. G.=3·4-3·65. Lustre vitreous. Color straw-yellow, wine-yellow, white, grayish, greenish, bluish, reddish; pale. Streak uncolored Transparent—subtranslucent. Fracture subconchoidal, uneven. Pyro-

OXYGEN COMPOUNDS—ANHYDROUS SILICATES. 333

electric. Optic-axial plane $i\text{-}\breve{\imath}$; divergence very variable, sometimes differing much in different parts of the same crystal; bisectrix positive, normal to O.

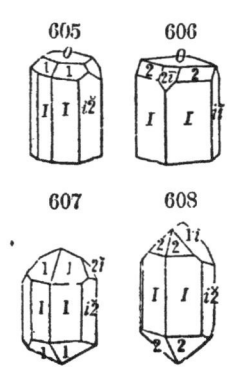

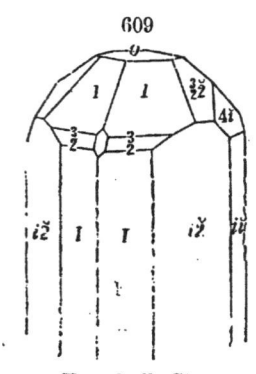

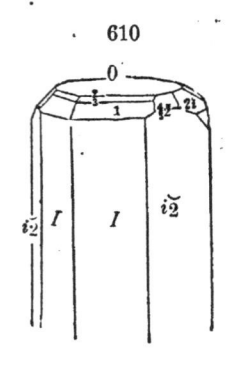

605 606 609 610
607 608
Trumbull, Ct.   Schneckenstein.

Comp.—$AlSiO_5$, with part of the oxygen replaced by fluorine (F_2); ratio of $F_2 : O = 1 : 5 =$ Silicon 15·17, aluminum 29·58, oxygen 34·67, fluorine 20·58=100.

Pyr., etc.—B.B. infusible. Some varieties take a wine-yellow or pink tinge when heated. Fused in the open tube with salt of phosphorus gives the reaction for fluorine. With cobalt solution the pulverized mineral gives a fine blue on heating. Only partially attacked by sulphuric acid.

Diff.—Distinguishing characters:—hardness, greater than that of quartz; infusibility; perfect basal cleavage. B.B. yields fluorine.

Obs.—Topaz occurs in gneiss or granite, with tourmaline, mica, and beryl, occasionally with apatite, fluorite, and tin ore; also in talcose rock, as in Brazil, with euclase, etc., or in mica slate. Fine topazes come from the Urals; Kamschatka; Brazil; in Cairngorm, Aberdeenshire; at the tin mines of Bohemia and Saxony. *Physalite* (a coarse variety), occurs at Fossum, Norway; also in Durango, Mexico; at La Paz, province of Guanaxuato. In the United States, in *Conn.*, at Trumbull. In *N. Car.*, at Crowder's Mountain. In *Utah*, in Thomas's Mts.; from gold washings of Oregon.

EUCLASE.*

Monoclinic. $C = 79°\ 44' = O \wedge i\text{-}i,\ I \wedge I = 115°\ 0',\ O \wedge 1\text{-}\breve{\imath} = 146°\ 45'$; $\dot{c} : \bar{b} : \dot{a} = 1·02943 : 1·5446 : 1 = 1 : 1·50043 : 0·97135$.

Cleavage: $i\text{-}\breve{\imath}$ very perfect and brilliant; O, $i\text{-}i$ much less distinct. Found only in crystals.

H.=7·5. G.=3·098 (Haid.). Lustre vitreous, somewhat pearly on the cleavage-face. Colorless, pale mountain-green, passing into blue and white. Streak uncolored. Transparent; occasionally subtransparent. Fracture conchoidal. Very brittle.

611

Comp.—Q. ratio for H : Be : Al : Si=1 : 2 : 3 : 4, for R : Si=3 : 2 ($H_2=R$, and $3R=Al$), formula, $H_2Be_2AlSi_2O_{10}=$Silica 41·20, alumina 35·22, glucina 17·39, water 6·19=100.

Pyr., etc.—In the closed tube, when strongly ignited, B.B. gives off water (Damour). B.B. in the forceps cracks and whitens, throws out points, and fuses at 5·5 to a white enamel. Not acted on by acids.

Obs.—Occurs in Brazil, at Villa Rica; in southern Ural, near the river Sanarka.

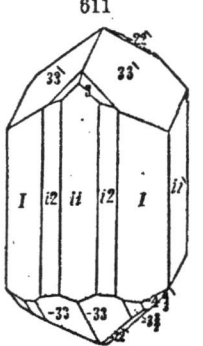

DATOLITE. Humboldtite.

Monoclinic. $C = 89° \, 54' = O$ (below) $\wedge \, i\text{-}i$, $I \wedge I = 115° \, 3'$, $O \wedge 1\text{-}\check{\imath} = 162° \, 27'$; $\dot{c} : \check{b} : \bar{a} = 0.49695 : 1.5712 : 1$. $O \wedge -2\text{-}i = 135° \, 13'$, $O \wedge 1 = 149° \, 33'$, $I \wedge I$ front $= 115° \, 3'$, $2\text{-}\check{\imath} \wedge 2\text{-}\check{\imath}$, ov. $O, = 115° \, 21'$, $i\text{-}2 \wedge i\text{-}2$, ov. $i\text{-}i$. $= 76° \, 18'$, $4\text{-}\check{\imath} \wedge 4\text{-}\check{\imath}$, ov. $O, = 76° \, 88$. Cleavage: O distinct. Also botryoidal and globular, having a columnar structure; also divergent and radiating; also massive, granular to compact.

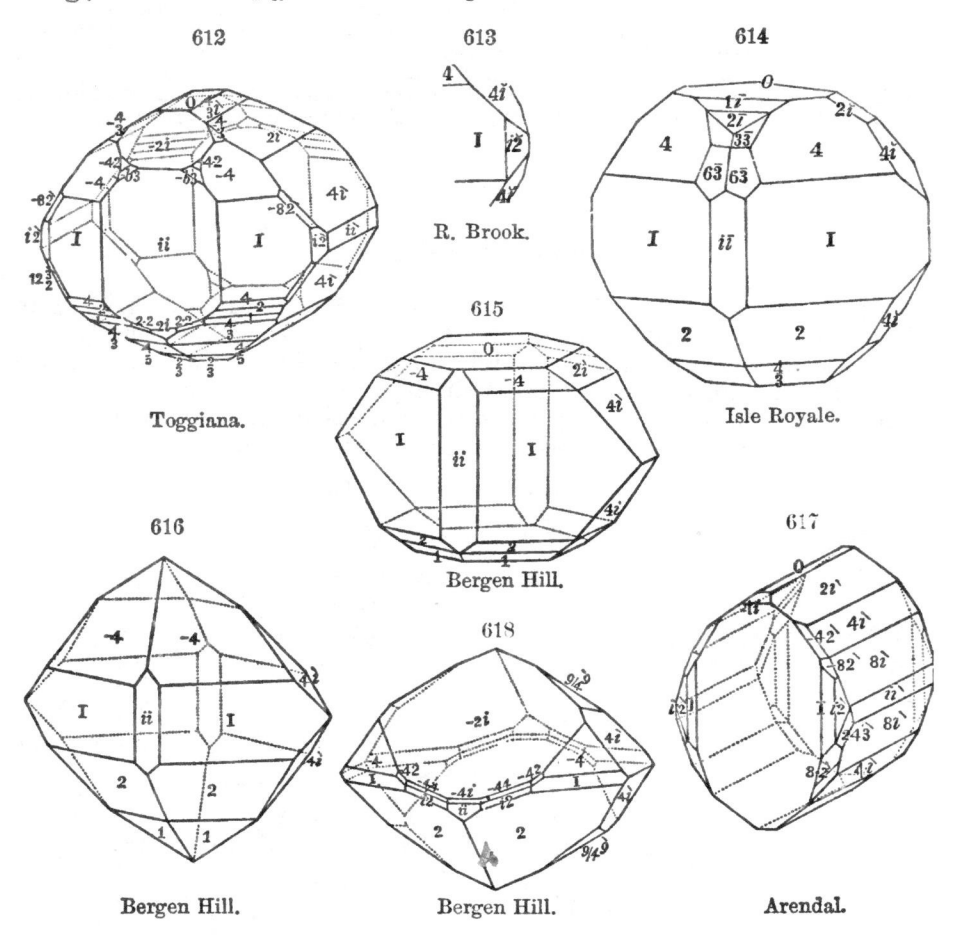

612 — Toggiana.
613 — R. Brook.
614 — Isle Royale.
615 — Bergen Hill.
616 — Bergen Hill.
617 — Arendal.
618 — Bergen Hill.

H.$=5$–5.5. G.$=2.8$–3; 2.989, Arendal, Haidinger. Lustre vitreous, rarely subresinous on a surface of fracture; color white; sometimes grayish, pale-green, yellow, red, or amethystine, rarely dirty olive-green or honey-yellow. Streak white. Translucent; rarely opaque white. Fracture uneven, subconchoidal. Brittle. Plane of optic-axes $i\text{-}\check{\imath}$; angle of divergence very obtuse; bisectrix makes an angle of 4° with a normal to $i\text{-}i$

Var.—1. *Ordinary.* In crystals, glassy in aspect. Usual forms as in figures. **2.** *Compact*

OXYGEN COMPOUNDS—ANHYDROUS SILICATES.   335

massive. White opaque, breaking with the surface of porcelain or Wedgewood ware. From the L. Superior region. 3. *Botryoidal; Botryolite.* Radiated columnar, having a botryoidal surface, and containing more water than the crystals. The original locality of both the crystallized and botryoidal was Arendal, Norway. *Haytorite* is datolite altered to chalcedony, from the Haytor Iron Mine, England.

Comp.—Q. ratio for H : Ca : B : Si=1 : 2 : 3 : 4, like euclase: formula $H_2Ca_2B_2Si_2O_{10}=$ Silica 37·5, boron trioxide 21·9, lime 35·0, water 5·6=100. Botryolite contains 10·64 p.c. water.

Pyr., etc.—In the closed tube gives off much water. B.B. fuses at 2 with intumescence to a clear glass, coloring the flame bright green. Gelatinizes with hydrochloric acid.

Diff.—Distinguishing characters: glassy lustre; usually complex crystallization; B.B. fuses easily with a green flame; gelatinizes with acids.

Obs.—Datolite is found in trappean rocks; also in gneiss, dioryte, and serpentine; in metallic veins; sometimes also in beds of iron ore. Found in Scotland; at Arendal; at Andreasberg; at Baveno near Lago Maggiore; at the Seisser Alp, Tyrol; at Toggiana in Modena, in serpentine. In good specimens at Roaring Brook, near New Haven; also at many other localities in the trap rocks of Connecticut; in N. Jersey, at Bergen Hill; in the Lake Superior region, and on Isle Royale. San Carlos, Inyo Co., Cal., with garnet and vesuvianite.

TITANITE.* SPHENE.

Monoclinic. $C = 60°\ 17' = O \wedge i\text{-}i$; $I \wedge I = 113°\ 31'$, $O \wedge 1\text{-}\check{i} = 159°\ 39'$; $\check{c} : b : \check{a} = 0.56586 : 1.3251 : 1$. Cleavage: I sometimes nearly perfect; $i\text{-}i$ and -1 much less so; rarely (in greenovite) 2 easy, -2 less so; sometimes hemimorphic. Twins: twinning-plane $i\text{-}i$; usually producing thin tables with a reëntering angle along one side; sometimes elongated, as in f. 623. Sometimes massive, compact; rarely lamellar.

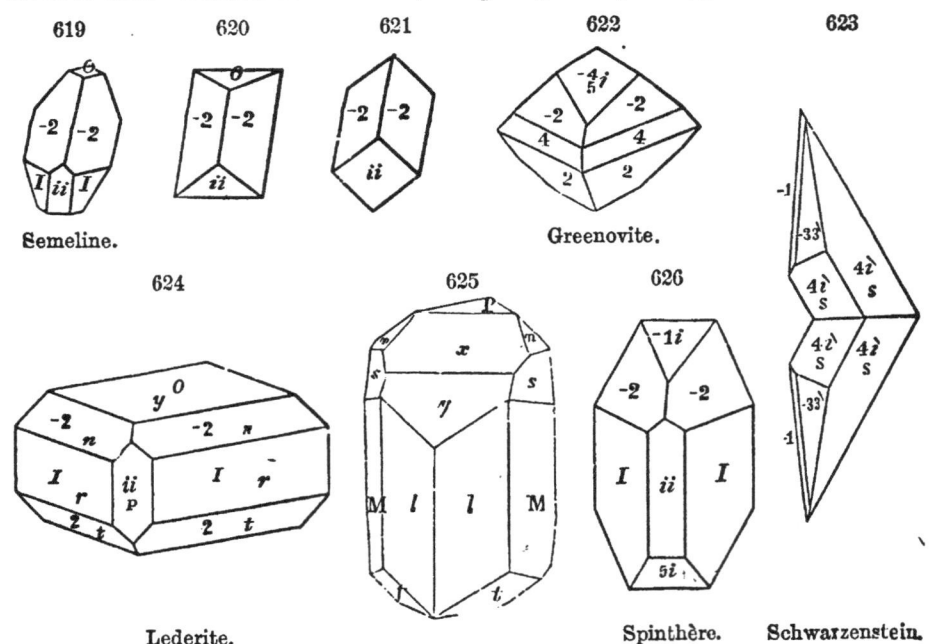

619   620   621   622   623

Semeline.   Greenovite.

624   625   626

Lederite.   Spinthère.   Schwarzenstein.

H.=5-5·5. G.=3·4-3·56. Lustre adamantine—resinous. Color brown, gray, yellow, green, and black. Streak white, slightly reddish in greenovite

Transparent—opaque. Brittle. Optic-axial plane i-$\bar{\imath}$; bisectrix positive, very closely normal to 1-i (x); double refraction strong; axial divergence 53°–56° for the red rays, 46°–45° for the blue; DesCl.

Comp., Var.—Q. ratio for Ca : Ti : Si = 1 : 2 : 2, or making the Ti basic (Ti=2R), R : Si = 3 : 2; formula (equivalent to $RSiO_3$) $CaTiSiO_5$ = Silica 30·61, titanic oxide 40·82, lime 28·57 = 100.

Var.—*Ordinary.* (*a*) *Titanite;* brown to black, the original being thus colored, also opaque or subtranslucent. (*b*) *Sphene* (named from σφήν, *a wedge*); of light shades, as yellow, greenish, etc., and often translucent; the original was yellow. *Manganesian; Greenovite.* Red or rose-colored, owing to the presence of a little manganese. In the crystals there is a great diversity of form, arising from an elongation or not into a prism, and from the occurrence of the elongation in the direction of different diameters of the fundamental form.

Pyr., etc.—B.B. some varieties change color, becoming yellow, and fuse at 3 with intumescence, to a yellow, brown, or black glass. With borax they afford a clear yellowish-green glass. Imperfectly soluble in heated hydrochloric acid; and if the solution be concentrated along with tin, it becomes of a fine violet color. With salt of phosphorus in R.F. gives a violet bead; varieties containing much iron require to be treated with the flux on charcoal with metallic tin. Completely decomposed by sulphuric and fluohydric acids.

Diff.—The resinous lustre is very characteristic; and its commonly occurring wedge-shaped form. B.B. gives a titanium reaction.

Obs.—Titanite occurs in imbedded crystals, in granite, gneiss, mica schist, syenite, chlorite schist, and granular limestone; also in beds of iron ore, and volcanic rocks, and often associated with pyroxene, hornblende, chlorite, scapolite, zircon, etc. Found at St. Gothard, and elsewhere in the Alps; in the protogine of Chamouni (*pictite*, Saus.); at Ala, Piedmont (*ligurite*); at Arendal, in Norway; at Achmatovsk, Urals; at St. Marcel in Piedmont (*greenovite*, Duf.); at Schwarzenstein, Tyrol; in the Untersulzbachthal in Pinzgau; near Tavistock; near Tremadoc, in North Wales.

Occurs in *Canada*, at Grenville, Elmsley, etc. In *Maine*, at Sanford. In *Mass.*, at Bolton; at Pelham. In *N. York*, at Gouverneur; at Diana, in dark-brown crystals (*lederite*); in Orange Co.; near Edenville; near Warwick. In *N. Jersey*, at Franklin. In *Penn.*, Bucks Co., near Attleboro'.

GUARINITE.—Same composition as titanite, but orthorhombic (v. Lang and Guiscardi) in crystallization. Color yellow. Mt. Somma.

KEILHAUITE (Yttrotitanite).—Near sphene in form and composition, but containing alumina and yttria. Arendal, Norway.

TSCHEFFKINITE.—Analogous to keilhauite in composition, containing, besides titanium, also cerium (La,Di). Occurs massive. Ilmen Mts.

STAUROLITE.

Orthorhombic. $I \wedge I = 129° 20'$, $O \wedge 1\text{-}\bar{\imath} = 124° 46'$; $\dot{c} : \bar{b} : \breve{a} = 1·4406 : 2·11233 : 1$. Cleavage: $i\text{-}\breve{\imath}$ distinct, but interrupted; I in traces. Twins

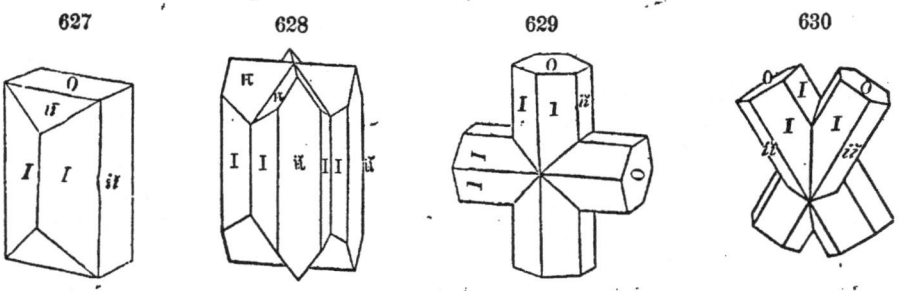

627 628 629 630

cruciform: twinning-plane $i\text{-}\tfrac{\bar{3}}{2}$ (f. 628); $\tfrac{3}{2}\text{-}\breve{\imath}$ (f. 629); and $\tfrac{3}{2}\text{-}\tfrac{\breve{3}}{2}$ (f. 630). Fig.

631 is a drilling according to the last method of twinning, and in f. 632 both methods are combined. See also p. 90 and p. 98. Crystals often with rough surfaces. Massive forms unobserved.

H.=7–7·5. G.=3·4–3·8.. Subvitreous, inclining to resinous. Color dark reddish-brown to brownish-black, and yellowish-brown. Streak uncolored to grayish. Translucent—nearly or quite opaque. Fracture conchoidal.

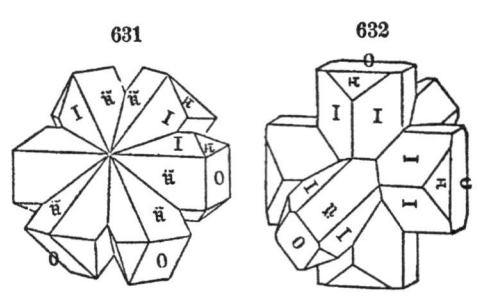

Comp., Var.—Q. ratio, according to Rammelsberg, for $\text{R} : \text{R} : \text{Si} = 2 : 9 : 6$ (where R is Fe and Mg, and also includes H_2, with $H_2 : R = 1 : 3$). Formula $H_2R_3Al_6Si_6O_{34}$ (if Mg : Fe = 1 : 3) = Silica 30·37, alumina 51·92, iron protoxide 13·66, magnesia 2·53, water 1·52 = 100. The iron was first taken as FeO_3, but Mitscherlich showed that it was really FeO. Staurolite often includes impurities, especially free quartz, as first shown by Lechartier, and since then by Fischer, Lasaulx, and Rammelsberg. This is the cause of the variation in the amount of silica appearing in most analyses, there being sometimes as much as 50 p. c.

Pyr., etc.—B.B. infusible, excepting the manganesian variety, which fuses easily to a black magnetic glass. With the fluxes gives reactions for iron, and sometimes for manganese. Imperfectly decomposed by sulphuric acid.

Diff.—Always in crystals; the prisms obtuse, having an angle of 129°.

Obs.—Usually found in mica schist, argillaceous schist, and gneiss; often associated with garnet, cyanite, and tourmaline. Occurs with cyanite in *paragonite* schist, at Mt Campione, Switzerland; at the Greiner mountain, and elsewhere in the Tyrol; in Brittany; in Ireland. Abundant throughout the mica slate of New England. In *Maine*, at Windham, and elsewhere. In *Mass.*, at Chesterfield, etc. In *Penn.* In *Georgia*, at Canton; and in Fannin Co.

SCHORLOMITE.—Q. ratio for $Ca + Fe + Ti : Si = 2 : 1$, nearly. Analysis by Ramm., Arkansas, SiO_2 26·09, TiO_2 21·34, Fe_2O_3 20·11, FeO 1·57, CaO 29·38, MgO 1·36 = 99·85. Color black. Fracture conchoidal. Magnet Cove, Arkansas; Kaiserstuhlgebirge in Breisgau.

HYDROUS SILICATES.

I. GENERAL SECTION. A. BISILICATES.

PECTOLITE.

Monoclinic, isomorphous with wollastonite. Greg. Cleavage: $i\text{-}i$ (orthod.) perfect. Twins: twinning-plane $i\text{-}i$. Usually in close aggregations of acicular crystals. Fibrous massive, radiated to stellate.

H.=5. G.=2·68–2·78. Lustre of the surface of fracture silky or subvitreous. Color whitish or grayish. Subtranslucent to opaque. Tough. For Bergen mineral optic-axial plane parallel to orthodiagonal, and very nearly normal to $i\text{-}i$; acute bisectrix positive, parallel to orthodiagonal, and obtuse bisectrix nearly normal to cleavage-plane or $i\text{-}i$; axial angle in oil, through cleavage-plates, 143°–145°; DesCl.

Var.—Almost always columnar or fibrous, and divergent, the fibres often 2 or 3 inches long, and sometimes, as in Ayrshire, Scotland, a yard. Resembles in aspect fibrous varieties of natrolite, okenite, thomsonite, tremolite, and wollastonite.

Comp.—Q. ratio for H : Na : Ca : Si=1 : 1 : 4 : 12, and for R : Si (where R includes Ca and H_2,Na_2)=1 : 2, like wollastonite; hence formula $HNaCa_2Si_3O_9$=Silica 54·2, lime 33·8, soda 9·3, water 2·7=100. If the H does not belong with the bases, then the formula may be (Ramm.) $Na_2Ca_4Si_6O_{17}$+aq.

Pyr., etc.—In the closed tube yields water. B.B. fuses at 2 to a white enamel. Gelatinizes with hydrochloric acid. Often gives out a light when broken in the dark.

Obs.—Occurs mostly in trap and related rocks, in cavities or seams; occasionally in metamorphic rocks. Found in Scotland, near Edinburgh; in Ayrshire; and at Taliver, etc., I. Skye; at Mt. Baldo and Mt. Monzoni in the Tyrol; in Wermland; at Bergen Hill, N. J.; compact at Isle Royale, L. Superior.

LAUMONTITE. Caporcianite.

Monoclinic. $C = 68°\ 40',\ I \wedge I = 86°\ 16',\ O \wedge 1\text{-}\dot{\imath} = 151°\ 9'$; $\dot{c} : \dot{b} : \dot{a} = 0\text{·}516 : 0\text{·}8727 : 1$. Prism with very oblique terminal plane 2-$\dot{\imath}$, the most common form. Cleavage: $i\text{-}\dot{\imath}$ and I perfect; $i\text{-}\dot{\imath}$ imperfect. Twins: twinning-plane $i\text{-}\dot{\imath}$. Also columnar, radiating or divergent.

H.=3·5-4. G.=2·25-2·36. Lustre vitreous, inclining to pearly upon the faces of cleavage. Color white, passing into yellow or gray, sometimes red. Streak uncolored. Transparent—translucent; becoming opaque and usually pulverulent on exposure. Fracture scarcely observable, uneven. Not very brittle. Double refraction weak; optic-axial plane $i\text{-}\dot{\imath}$; divergence 52° 24' for the red rays; bisectrix negative, making an angle of 20° to 25° with a normal to $i\text{-}\dot{\imath}$; DesCl.

Comp.—Q. ratio for R : R̶ : Si : H=1 : 3 : 8 : 4; and R̶ : Si=1 : 2 (3R=R̶). R=Ca, R̶=Al, and the formula is hence $CaAlSi_4O_{12}$+4aq=Silica 50·0, alumina 21·8, lime 11·9, water 16·3=100.

Pyr., etc.—Loses part of its water over sulphuric acid, but a red heat is needed to drive off all. B.B. swells up and fuses at 2·7-3 to a white enamel. Gelatinizes with hydrochloric acid.

Obs.—Laumontite occurs in the cavities of trap or amygdaloid; also in porphyry and syenite, and occasionally in veins traversing clay slate with calcite. Its principal localities are at the Faröe Islands; Disko in Greenland; in Bohemia, at Eule; St. Gothard in Switzerland; the Fassathal; the Kilpatrick hills, near Glasgow. Nova Scotia affords fine specimens; also Lake Superior, in the copper region, and on I. Royale; also Bergen Hill, N. J.

OKENITE.—Formula $H_2CaSi_2O_6$+aq. having half the water basic=Silica 56·6, lime 26·4, water 17·0=100. Commonly fibrous. Color white, Faröe Is.; Disco, Greenland; Iceland.

GYROLITE.—Occurs in radiated concretions at the Isle of Skye; Nova Scotia. Formula perhaps $H_2Ca_2Si_3O_9$+aq. CENTRALLASSITE. Related to okenite, but contains 1 molecule more water. In trap of Nova Scotia.

CHRYSOCOLLA.* Kieselkupfer, *Germ.*

Cryptocrystalline; often opal-like or enamel-like in texture; earthy. Incrusting, or filling seams. Sometimes botryoidal.

H.=2-4. G.=2-2·238. Lustre vitreous, shining, earthy. Color mountain-green, bluish-green, passing into sky-blue and turquois-blue; brown to black when impure. Streak, when pure, white. Translucent—opaque. Fracture conchoidal. Rather sectile; translucent varieties brittle.

Comp.—Composition varies much through impurities, as with other amorphous substances, resulting from alteration. As the silica has been derived from the decomposition of other silicates, it is natural that an excess should appear in many analyses. True chrysocolla corresponds to the Q ratio for Cu : Si : H, $1 : 2 : 2 = CuSiO_3 + 2aq =$ Silica 34·2, copper oxide 45·3, water 20·5=100. But some analyses afford 1 : 2 : 3, and 1 : 2 : 4. Impure chrysocolla may contain, besides free silica, various other impurities, the color varying from bluish-green to brown and black, the last especially when manganese or copper is present.

Pyr., etc.—In the closed tube blackens and yields water. B.B. decrepitates, colors the flame emerald-green, but is infusible. With the fluxes gives the reactions for copper. With soda and charcoal a globule of metallic copper. Decomposed by acids without gelatinization.

Diff.—Color more bluish-green than that of malachite, and it does not effervesce with acids.

Obs.—Accompanies other copper ores, occurring especially in the upper part of veins. Found in most copper mines in Cornwall; at Libethen in Hungary; at Falkenstein and Schwatz in the Tyrol; in Siberia; the Bannat; Thuringia; Schneeberg, Saxony; Kupferberg, Bavaria; South Australia; Chili, etc. In Somerville and Schuyler's mines, New Jersey; at Morgantown, Pa.; at Cornwall, Lebanon Co.; Nova Scotia, at the Basin of Mines; also in Wisconsin and Michigan.

DEMIDOFFITE; CYANOCHALCITE; RESANITE; near chrysocolla.

CATAPLEIITE.—Analysis (Ramm.), SiO_2 39·78, ZrO_2 40·12, CaO 3·45, Na_2O 7·59, H_2O 9·24 =100·18. Hexagonal. Color yellowish-brown, Lamöe, near Brevig, Norway.

B. UNISILICATES.

CALAMINE. Galmei; Kieselzinkerz, *Germ.*

Orthorhombic; hemimorphic-hemihedral. $I \wedge I = 104°$ 13', $O \wedge 1\text{-}\bar{\imath} =$ 148° 31', Daubar; $\dot{c} : \bar{b} : \breve{a} = 0.6124 : 1·2850 : 1$. Cleavage: I, perfect; O, in traces. Also stalactitic, mammillated, botryoidal, and fibrous forms; also massive and granular.

H.=4·5–5, the latter when crystallized. G.=3·16–3·9. Lustre vitreous, O subpearly, sometimes adamantine. Color white; sometimes with a delicate bluish or greenish shade; also yellowish to brown. Streak white. Transparent—translucent. Fracture uneven. Brittle. Pyroelectric.

Comp.—Q. ratio for R : Si : H=1 : 1 : ½; Zn_2SiO_4+aq=Silica 25·0, zinc oxide 67·5, water 7·5=100.

Pyr., etc.—In the closed tube decrepitates, whitens, and gives off water. B.B. almost infusible (F.=6); moistened with cobalt solution gives a green color when heated. On charcoal with soda gives a coating which is yellow while hot, and white on cooling. Moistened with cobalt solution, and heated in O.F., this coating assumes a bright green color. Gelatinizes with acids even when previously ignited. Decomposed by acetic acid with gelatinization. Soluble in a strong solution of caustic potash.

Diff.—Distinguishing characters: gelatinizing with acids; infusibility; reaction for zinc.

Obs.—Calamine and smithsonite are usually found associated in veins or beds in stratified calcareous rocks accompanying blende, ores of iron, and lead, as at Aix la Chapelle; Bleiberg in Carinthia; Retzbanya; Schemnitz. At Roughten Gill in Cumberland; at Alston Moor; near Matlock in Derbyshire; at Castleton; Leadhills, Scotland.

In the United States occurs with smithsonite in Jefferson county, Missouri. At Stirling Hill, N. J. In Pennsylvania, at the Perkiomen and Phenixville lead mines; at Bethlehem; at Friedensville. Abundant in Virginia, at Austin's mines.

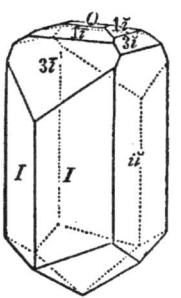

PREHNITE.

Orthorhombic. $I \wedge I = 99° 56'$, $O \wedge 1\text{-}\bar{i} = 146° 11\frac{1}{2}'$; $\check{c} : \bar{b} : \check{a} = 0.66963 : 1.19035 : 1$. Cleavage: basal, distinct. Tabular crystals often united by O, making broken forms, often barrel-shaped. Usually reniform, globular, and stalactitic with a crystalline surface. Structure imperfectly columnar or lamellar, strongly coherent; also compact granular or impalpable.

H.$=6$–6.5. G.$=2.8$–2.953. Lustre vitreous; O weak pearly. Color light green, oil-green, passing into white and gray; often fading on exposure. Subtransparent—translucent; streak uncolored. Fracture uneven. Somewhat brittle.

Comp.—Q. ratio for R : R̈ : Si : H=2 : 3 : 6 : 1, whence, if the water is basic, for bases and silicon, 1 : 1; formula $H_2Ca_2ÄlSi_3O_{12}$ or $Ca_2ÄlSi_3O_{11}+aq=$Silica 43.6, alumina 24.9, lime 27.1, water 4.4=100.

Pyr., etc.—In the closed tube yields water. B.B. fuses at 2 with intumescence to a blebby enamel-like glass. Decomposed by hydrochloric acid without gelatinizing. *Coupholite*, which often contains dust or vegetable matter, blackens and emits a burnt odor.

Diff.—B.B. fuses readily, unlike beryl and chalcedony. Its hardness is greater than that of the zeolites.

Obs.—Occurs in granite, gneiss, syenite, dioryte, and trappean rocks especially the last. At Bourg d'Oisans in Isère; in the Fassathal, Tyrol; Ala in Piedmont; Joachimsthal in Bohemia; near Andreasberg; Arendal, Norway; Ædelfors in Sweden; in Dumbartonshire; in Renfrewshire.

In the United States, in Connecticut; Bergen Hill, N. J.; on north shore of Lake Superior; in large veins in the Lake Superior copper region.

CHLORASTROLITE and ZONOCHLORITE from Lake Superior are mixtures, as shown by Hawes.

VILLARSITE.—Probably an altered chrysolite. Formula $R_2SiO_4+\frac{1}{3}aq$ (or $\frac{1}{4}aq$) R=Mg : Fe =11 : 1. Traversella.

CERITE, Sweden, and TRITOMITE, Norway, contain cerium, lanthanum, and didymium. THORITE and ORANGITE contain thorium. Norway.

PARATHORITE.—In minute orthorhombic crystals, imbedded in danburite at Danbury, Ct. Chemical nature unknown.

PYROSMALITE.—Analysis by Ludwig, SiO_2 34.66, FeO 27.05, MnO 25.60, CaO 0.52, MgO 0.93, H_2O 8.31, Cl 4.88=101.85. In hexagonal tables. Color blackish-green. Nya-Koppaiberg, etc., Sweden.

APOPHYLLITE.*

Tetragonal. $O \wedge 1\text{-}i = 128° 38'$; $\check{c} = 1.2515$. Crystals sometimes nearly cylindrical or barrel-shaped. Twins: twinning-plane the octahedron 1. Cleavage: O highly perfect; I less so. Also massive and lamellar.

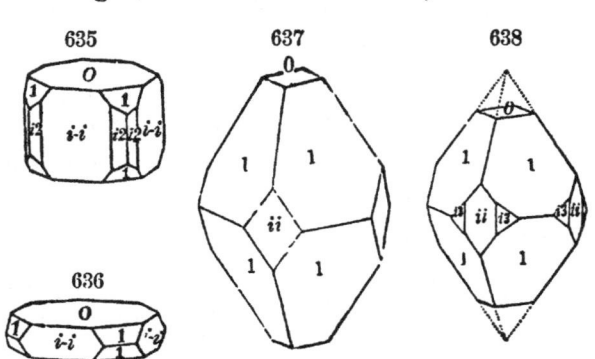

H.$=4.5$–5. G.$=2.3$–2.4. Lustre of O pearly; of the other faces vitreous. Color white, or grayish; occasionally with a greenish, yellowish, or rose-red tint, flesh red. Streak uncolored. Transparent; rarely opaque. Brittle.

OXYGEN COMPOUNDS—HYDROUS SILICATES.

Comp.—Q ratio for R : Si : H usually taken as 1 : 4 : 2, part of the oxygen replaced by fluorine (F_2). According to Rammelsberg the ratio is 9 : 32 : 16; he writes the formula $4(H_2CaSi_2O_6+aq)+KF$. This requires: Silica 52·97, lime 24·72, potash 5·20, water 15·90, fluorine 2·10=100·89. It may be taken as a unisilicate if part of the silica is considered accessory.

Pyr., etc.—In the closed tube exfoliates, whitens, and yields water, which reacts acid. In the open tube, when fused with salt of phosphorus, gives a fluorine reaction. B.B. exfoliates, colors the flame violet (potash), and fuses to a white vesicular enamel. F.=1·5. Decomposed by hydrochloric acid, with separation of slimy silica.

Diff.—Distinguishing characters : its occurrence in square prisms ; its perfect basal cleavage, and pearly lustre on the base.

Obs.—Occurs commonly in amygdaloid and related rocks, with various zeolites; also occasionally in cavities in granite, gneiss, etc. Greenland, Iceland, the Faröe Islands, Andreasberg, the Syhadree Mountains in Bombay, afford fine specimens. In America, found in Nova Scotia; Bergen Hill, N. J.; the Cliff mine, Lake Superior region.

CHALCOMORPHITE (*v. Rath*), from limestone inclosures in the lava of Niedermend'g. Hexagonal. Essentially an hydrous calcium silicate.

EDINGTONITE.—Analysis by Heddle, SiO_2 36·98, AlO_3 22·63, BaO 26·84, CaO tr, Na_2O tr., H_2O 12·46=98·91. Tetragonal. Dumbarton, Scotland.

GISMONDITE.—Analysis, Marignac, SiO_2 35·38, AlO_3 27·23, CaO 13·12, K_2O 2·85, H_2O 21·10 =100·18. Capo di Bove, near Rome; Baumgarten, near Giessen, etc.

CARPHOLITE.—In radiated tufts in the tin mines of Schlackenwald; Wippra in the Harz. Bases mostly in sesquioxide state (Al,Mn,Fe).

SUBSILICATES.

ALLOPHANE.

Amorphous. In incrustations, usually thin, with a mammillary surface, and hyalite-like; sometimes stalactitic. Occasionally almost pulverulent. H.=3. G.=1·85–1·89. Lustre vitreous to subresinous; bright and waxy internally. Color pale sky-blue, sometimes greenish to deep green, brown, yellow, or colorless. Streak uncolored. Translucent. Fracture imperfectly conchoidal and shining, to earthy. Very brittle.

Comp.—Q. ratio for Al : Si : H, mostly=3 : 2 : 6 (or 5) ; $AlSiO_5+6aq$, or $AlSiO_5+5aq=$ Silica 23·75, alumina 40·62, water 35·63=100. *Plumballophane*, from Sardinia, contains a little lead.

The coloring matter of the blue variety is due to traces of chrysocolla, the green to malachite, and that of the yellowish and brown to iron.

Pyr., etc.—Yields much water in the closed tube. B.B. crumbles, but is infusible. Gives a blue color with cobalt solution. Gelatinizes with hydrochloric acid.

Obs.—Allophane is regarded as a result of the decomposition of some aluminous silicate (feldspar, etc.); and it often occurs incrusting fissures or cavities in mines, especially those of copper and limonite, and even in beds of coal. Found at Schneeberg in Saxony; at Gersbach; at the Chessy copper mine, near Lyons; near Woolwich, in Kent, England. In the U. S. it occurs at Richmond, Mass.; at the Friedensville zinc mines, Pa., etc.

COLLYRITE.—A hydrous silicate of aluminum. Clay-like in structure, white. Hove, England; Schemnitz.

URANOPHANE, from Silesia, and URANOTILE , from Wölsendorf, Bavaria, are silicates containing uranium.

II. Zeolite Section.

THOMSONITE. Comptonite.

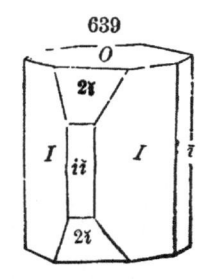

Orthorhombic. $I \wedge I = 90°\ 40'$; $O \wedge 1\text{-}\bar{i} = 144°\ 9'$; $\dot{c} : \bar{b} : \check{a} = 0.7225$:
$1.0117 : 1$. Cleavage: $i\text{-}\bar{i}$ easily obtained; $i\text{-}\check{i}$ less so, O in traces. Twins: cruciform, having the vertical axis in common. Also columnar, structure radiated; in radiated spherical concretions; also amorphous and compact.

H.=5-5·5. G.=2·3-2·4. Vitreous, more or less pearly. Snow-white; impure varieties brown. Streak uncolored. Transparent—translucent. Fracture uneven. Brittle. Pyroelectric. Double refraction weak; optic-axial plane parallel to O; bisectrix positive, normal to $i\text{-}\bar{i}$; divergence $82°-82\frac{1}{2}°$ for red rays, from Dumbarton; DesCl.

Var.—*Ordinary*. (a) In regular crystals, usually more or less rectangular in outline. (b) In slender prisms, often vesicular to radiated. (c) Radiated fibrous. (d) Spherical concretions, consisting of radiated fibres or slender crystals. (e) Massive, granular to impalpable, and white to reddish-brown. *Ozarkite* is massive thomsonite; *rauite* (Norway) is related.

Comp.—Q. ratio for $R(=Ca,Na_2) : \bar{R}(\bar{A}l) : Si : H = 1 : 3 : 4 : 2\frac{1}{2}$, $Ca : Na_2 = 2 : 1$, or $3 : 1$; formula $2(Ca,Na_2)\bar{A}lSi_2O_8+5aq$. Analysis, Rammelsberg, Dumbarton, SiO_2 38·09, $\bar{A}lO_3$ 31·62, CaO 12·60, Na_2O 4·62, H_2O 13·40=100·20.

Pyr., etc.—At a red heat loses 13·3 p. c. of water, and the mineral becomes fused to a white enamel. B.B. fuses with intumescence at 2 to a white enamel. Gelatinizes with hydrochloric acid.

Obs.—Found in cavities in lava and other igneous rocks; and also in some metamorphic rocks, with elæolite. Occurs near Kilpatrick, Scotland; in the lavas of Somma (*comptonite*); in Bohemia; in Sicily; in Faröe; the Tyrol, at Theiss; at Monzoni, Fassathal; at Peter's Point, Nova Scotia; at Magnet Cove, Arkansas (*ozarkite*).

NATROLITE. Mesotype. Nadelzeolith, *Germ*.

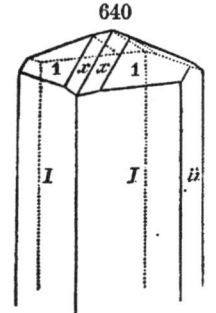

Orthorhombic. $I \wedge I = 91°$, $O \wedge 1\text{-}\bar{i} = 144°\ 23'$; $\dot{c} : \bar{b} : \check{a} = 0.35825$:
$1.0176 : 1$. Crystals usually slender, often acicular; frequently interlacing; divergent, or stellate. Also fibrous, radiating, massive, granular, or compact.

H.=5-5·5. G.=2·17-2·25; 2·249, Bergen Hill, Brush. Lustre vitreous, sometimes inclining to pearly, especially in fibrous varieties. Color white, or colorless; also grayish, yellowish, reddish to red. Streak uncolored. Transparent—translucent. Double refraction weak; optic-axial plane $i\text{-}\bar{i}$; bisectrix positive, parallel to edge I/I; axial divergence $94°-96°$, red rays, for Auvergne crystals; $95°\ 12'$ for brevicite; DesCl.

Comp.—Q. ratio for $R : \bar{R} : Si : H = 1 : 3 : 6 : 2$; and for $R : Si = 2 : 3 (R=Na_2, 3R=\bar{R})$; formula $Na_2\bar{A}lSi_3O_{10}+2aq$=Silica 47·29, alumina 26·96, soda 16·30, water 9·45=100.

Pyr., etc.—In the closed tube loses water, whitens and becomes opaque. B.B. fuses quietly at 2 to a colorless glass. Fusible in the flame of an ordinary stearine or wax candle. Gelatinizes with acids.

OXYGEN COMPOUNDS—HYDROUS SILICATES. 343.

Diff.—Some varieties resemble pectolite, thomsonite, but distinguished B.B.
Obs.—Occurs in cavities in amygdaloidal trap, basalt, and other igneous rocks; and some times in seams in granite, gneiss, and syenite. It is found in Bohemia; in Auvergne; Fassa thal, Tyrol; Kapnik; at Glen Farg in Fifeshire; in Dumbartonshire. In North America, occurs in the trap of Nova Scotia; at Bergen Hill, N. J.; at Copper Falls, Lake Superior.

SCOLECITE. Poonahlite.

Monoclinic. $C = 89°\,6'$, $I \wedge I = 91°\,36'$, $O \wedge 1\text{-}i = 161°\,16\tfrac{1}{2}'$; $\dot{c}:b:a = 0.3485 : 1.0282 : 1$. Crystals long or short prisms, or acicular, rarely well terminated, and always compound. Twins: twinning-plane $i\text{-}i$. Cleavage: I nearly perfect. Also in nodules or massive; fibrous and radiated.
H.=5–5.5. G.=2.16–2.4. Lustre vitreous, or silky when fibrous. Transparent to subtranslucent. Pyroelectric, the free end of the crystals the antilogue pole. Double refraction weak; optic-axial plane normal to $i\text{-}i$; divergence 53° 41', for the red rays; bisectrix negative, parallel to $i\text{-}i$; plane of the axis of the red rays and their bisectrix inclined about 17° 8' to $i\text{-}i$, and 93° 3' to 1-i.

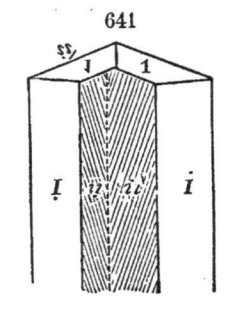

641

Comp.—Q. ratio for $\text{R}:\ddot{\text{R}}:\text{Si}:\text{H}=1:3:6:3$; for $\text{R}(3\ddot{\text{R}}=\ddot{\text{R}}):\text{Si}=2:3$, as in natrolite; $\text{R=Ca, }\ddot{\text{R}}=\ddot{\text{Al}}$; formula $\text{CaAlSi}_3\text{O}_{10}+3\text{aq}=$Silica 45.85, alumina 26.13, lime 14.26, water 13.76=100.
Pyr., etc.—B.B. sometimes curls up like a worm (whence the name from σκώληξ, *a worm*, which gives *scolecite*, and not *scolesite* or *scolezite*); other varieties intumesce but slightly, and all fuse at 2–2.2 to a white blebby enamel. Gelatinizes with acids like natrolite.
Diff.—Characterized by its pyrognostics.
Obs.—Occurs in the Berufiord, Iceland; also at Staffa; in Skye, at Talisker; near Poonah, Hindostan (*Poonahlite*); in Greenland; at Pargas, Finland, etc.
MESOLITE.—$(\text{Ca,Na}_2)\text{AlSi}_3\text{O}_{10}+3\text{aq}$ (5 p. c. Na$_2$O). Near scolecite. Iceland; Nova Scotia.
LEVYNITE.—Rhombohedral. Q. ratio for $\text{R}:\ddot{\text{R}}:\text{Si}:\text{H}=1:3:6:4$. Analysis, Damour, Iceland, SiO$_2$ 45.76, AlO$_3$ 23.56, CaO 10.57, Na$_2$O 1.36, K$_2$O 1.64, H$_2$O 17.33=100.22. Ireland; Faröe; Iceland.

ANALCITE.*

Isometric (?). Usually in trapezohedrons (f. 54, p. 18). Cleavage: cubic, in traces. Also massive granular.
H.=5–5.5. G.=2.22–2.29; 2.278, Thomson. Lustre vitreous. Colorless; white; occasionally grayish, greenish, yellowish, or reddish-white. Streak white. Transparent—nearly opaque. Fracture subconchoidal, uneven. Brittle.

Comp.—Q. ratio for $\text{R}:\ddot{\text{R}}:\text{Si}:\text{H}=1:3:8:2$, R=Na_2, $\ddot{\text{R}}=\ddot{\text{Al}}=3\text{R}$; $\text{R}:\text{Si}=1:2$. Formula $\text{Na}_2\text{AlSi}_4\text{O}_{12}+2\text{aq}=$Silica 54.47, alumina 23.29, soda 14.07, water 8.17=100.
Pyr., etc.—Yields water in the closed tube. B.B. fuses at 2.5 to a colorless glass. Gelatinizes with hydrochloric acid.
Diff.—Distinguishing characters: crystalline form; absence of cleavage; fusion B.B. *without* intumescence to a clear glass (unlike chabazite).
Obs.—Some localities are: the Tyrol; the Kilpatrick Hills in Scotland; the Faröe Islands; Iceland; Aussig, Bohemia; Nova Scotia; Bergen Hill, New Jersey; the Lake Superior region.
Schrauf has found that the analcite of Rrieueck, Bohemia, is properly *tetragonal;* the simplest crystals showing evidence of repeated twinning.

FAUJASITE.—An octahedral zeolite from the Kaiserstuhlgebirge. Analysis, Damour, SiO_2 46·12, AlO_3 16·81, CaO 4·79, Na_2O 5·09, H_2O 27·02=99·83.
EUDNOPHITE. Near analcite. In syenite near Brevig, Norway.
PILINITE.—In slender needles (orthorhombic); white; lustre silky. Analysis SiO_2 55·70, $AlO_3(FeO_3)$ 18·64, CaO 19.51, Li_2O (1·18), H_2O 4·97=100. In granite of Striegau, Silesia (*Lasaulx*).

CHABAZITE.*

Rhombohedral. $R \wedge R = 94° 46'$, $O \wedge R = 129° 15'$; $\check{c} = 1·06$. Twins: twinning-plane O, very common, and usually in compound twins, as in f. 644; also R, rare. Cleavage rhombohedral, rather distinct.

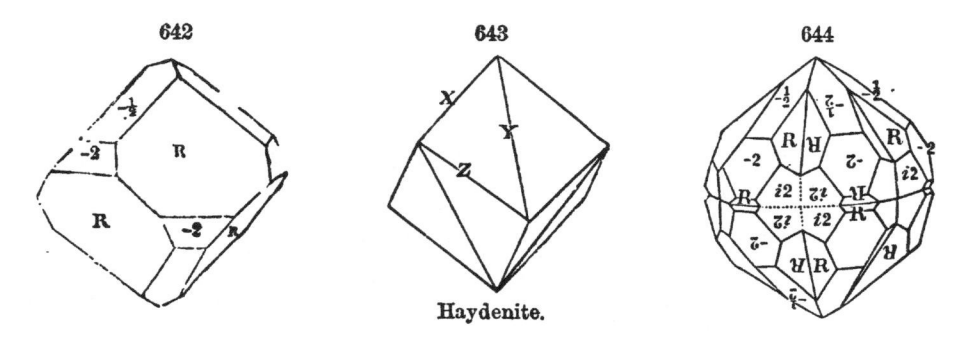

642   643   644

Haydenite.

H.=4–5. G.=2·08–2·19. Lustre vitreous. Color white, flesh-red; streak uncolored. Transparent—translucent. Fracture uneven. Brittle. Double refraction weak; in polarized light, images rather confused; axis in some crystals (Bohemia) negative, in others (from Andreasberg) positive; DesCl.

Var.—1. *Ordinary*. The most common form is the fundamental rhombohedron, in which the angle is so near 90° that the crystals were at first mistaken for cubes. *Acadialite*, from Nova Scotia (*Acadia* of the French of last century), is only a reddish chabazite; sometimes nearly colorless. In some specimens the coloring matter is arranged in a tesselated manner, or in layers, with the angles almost colorless. 2. *Phacolite* is a colorless variety occurring in twins of mostly a hexagonal form, and often much modified so as to be lenticular in shape (whence the name, from φακός, *a bean*); the original was from Leipa in Bohemia; $R \wedge R$ =94° 24', fr. Oberstein, Breith.
Comp.—Making part of the water basic (at 300° C. loses 17–19 p. c.) Rammelsberg writes the formula $(H,K)_2Ca\dot{A}lSi_5O_{15}+6aq$, where the Q. ratio for R : $\ddot{R}$: $Si=2 : 3 : 10$, $R=H_2,Na_2$, Ca; or $(3\ddot{R}=R)$, R : Si=1 : 2. The formula corresponds to Silica 50·50, alumina 17·26, lime 9·43, potash 1·98, water 20·83=100.
Pyr., etc.—B.B. intumesces and fuses to a blebby glass, nearly opaque. Decomposed by hydrochloric acid, with separation of slimy silica.
Diff.—Its rhombohedral form, resembling a cube, is characteristic; is harder, and does not effervesce with acids like calcite; is unlike fluorite in cleavage; fuses B.B. with intumescence to a blebby glass, unlike analcite.
Obs.—Chabazite occurs mostly in trap, basalt, or amygdaloid, and occasionally in gneiss, syenite, mica schist, hornblendic schist. At the Faröe Islands, Greenland, and Iceland; at Aussig in Bohemia; Striegau, Silesia. In Nova Scotia, wine-yellow or flesh-red (the last the *acadialite*), etc.; at Bergen Hill, N. J.; at Jones's Falls, near Baltimore (*haydenite*).
SEEBACHITE (*Bauer*) from Richmond, Victoria, is, according to v. Rath, identical with *phacolite*; and he suggests the same may be true of HERSCHELITE, from Aci Castello, Sicily.

GMELINITE.

Rhombohedral. $R \wedge R = 112° 26'$, $O \wedge R = O \wedge -1 = 140° 3'$; $ð =$ 0·7254. Crystals usually hexagonal in aspect; sometimes habit rhombohedral; i often horizontally striated. Cleavage: i perfect. Observed only in crystals, and never as twins.

H.=4·5. G.=2·04–2·17. Lustre vitreous. Colorless, yellowish-white, greenish-white, reddish-white flesh-red. Transparent to translucent. Brittle.

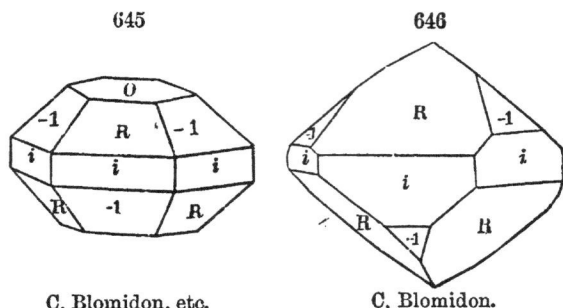

645

C. Blomidon, etc.

646

C. Blomidon.

Comp.—Q. ratio for R : Ṛ : Si : H=1 : 3 : 8 : 6, R=Ca(Na$_2$,K$_2$), Ṛ=Ȧl. Formula (Ca,Na$_2$)ȦlSi$_4$O$_{12}$+6aq. Analysis by Howe, Bergen Hill, SiO$_2$ 48·67, ȦlO$_3$ 18·72, FeO$_3$ 0·10, CaO 2·60, Na$_2$O 9·14, H$_2$O 21·35=100·58 (Am. J. Sci., III., xii., 270, 1876).

Pyr., etc.—In the closed tube crumbles, gives off much water. B.B. fuses easily to a white enamel. Decomposed by hydrochloric acid with gelatinization.

Diff.—Closely resembles some chabazite, but differs decidedly in angle.

Obs.—Occurs at Andreasberg; in Translyvania; in Antrim, Ireland; near Larne; at Talisker in Skye; at Cape Blomidon and other localities in Nova Scotia (*ledererite*); in fine crystals of varied habit at the Bergen Hill tunnel of 1876.

PHILLIPSITE.*

Orthorhombic. $I \wedge I = 91° 12'$; $1 \wedge 1 = 121° 20', 120° 44'$, and $88° 40'$, Marignac. Faces 1 and i-i striated parallel to the edge between them. Simple crystals unknown. Commonly in cruciform crystals, consisting of two crossing crystals, each a twinned prism (f. 647). Crystals either isolated, or grouped in tufts or spheres that are radiated within and bristled with angles at surface.

647

H.=4–4·5.. G.=2·201. Lustre vitreous. Color white, sometimes reddish. Streak uncolored. Translucent—opaque.

Comp.—Q. ratio for R : Ṛ : Si : H=1 : 3 : 8 : 4, R=Ca and K$_2$(Na$_2$); Ca : K$_2$=3 : 1, 2 : 3, etc. Formula RȦlSi$_4$O$_{12}$+4aq. Analysis by Ettling, Nidda, Hessen, SiO$_2$ 48·13, ȦlO$_3$ 21·41, CaO 8·21, K$_2$O 5·20, Na$_2$O 0·70, H$_2$O 16·78= 100·48.

Pyr., etc.—B.B. crumbles and fuses at 3 to a white enamel. Gelatinizes with hydrochloric acid.

Diff.—Resembles harmotome, but distinguished B.B.

Obs.—At the Giant's Causeway, Ireland; at Capo di Bove, near Rome; in Sicily; Annerode, near Giessen; in Silesia; Bohemia; on the west coast of Iceland.

Streng (Jahrb. Min., 1876, 585) shows that the forms are exactly analogous to those of harmotome, and suggests that it may be also monoclinic.

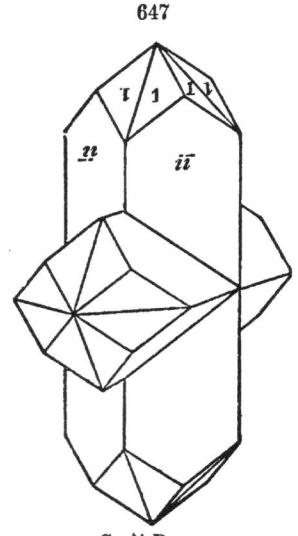

C. di Bove.

HARMOTOME.

Monoclinic (DesCloizeaux).

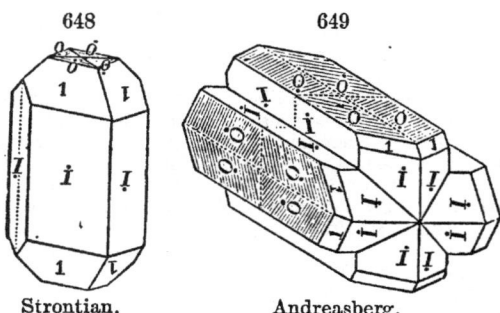

648 — Strontian.
649 — Andreasberg.

Cleavage: I, O, easy. Simple crystals unknown. Occurring in penetration-twins. Unknown massive. H. = 4·5. G. = 2·44–2·45. Lustre vitreous. Color white; passing into gray, yellow, red, or brown. Streak white. Subtransparent—translucent. Fracture uneven, imperfectly conchoidal. Brittle.

Comp.—Q. ratio for $\text{R} : \ddot{\text{R}} : \text{Si} : \text{H} = 1 : 3 : 10 : 5$; here R=Ba mostly, also K_2; $\ddot{\text{R}} = \ddot{\text{Al}}$. Formula $\ddot{\text{R}}\ddot{\text{Al}}\text{Si}_5\text{O}_{14}$ +5aq. If one-fifth of the water is chemically combined (Rammelsberg), then the formula corresponds to $\text{H}_2\ddot{\text{R}}\ddot{\text{Al}}\text{Si}_5\text{O}_{15}$+4aq. Both formulas give Silica 45·91, alumina 15·70, baryta 20·06, potash 3·34, water 14·99=100.

Pyr., etc.—B.B. whitens, then crumbles and fuses at 3·5 without intumescence to a white translucent glass. Some varieties phosphoresce when heated. Decomposed by hydrochloric acid without gelatinizing.

Diff.—Characterized by its crystallization in twins; the presence of barium separates it from other species.

Obs.—Harmotome occurs in amygdaloid. phonolyte, trachyte; also on gneiss, and in some metalliferous veins. At Strontian in Scotland; at Andreasberg; at Rudelstadt in Silesia, Schiffenberg, near Giessen, etc.; Oberstein; in the gneiss of upper New York City.

DesCloizeaux, who has shown the monoclinic character of the species by optical means, has adopted a different position for the crystals ($1 = I$, etc.).

STILBITE.* Desmine.

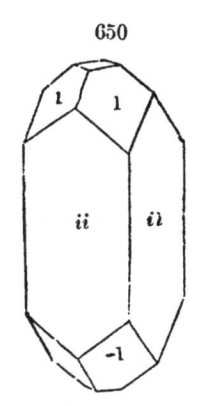

Orthorhombic.

650

$I \wedge I = 94° 16', 1 \wedge 1$, front, $= 119° 16'$, side, $114° 0'$. Cleavage: $i\text{-}\bar{\imath}$ perfect, $i\text{-}\bar{\imath}$ less so. Forms as in f. 650; more common with the prism flattened parallel to $i\text{-}\bar{\imath}$ or the cleavage-face, and pointed at the extremities. Twins: cruciform, twinning-plane. $1\text{-}\bar{\imath}$, rare. Common in sheaf-like aggregations; divergent or radiated; sometimes globular and thin lamellar-columnar.

H.=3·5–4. G.=2·094–2·205. Lustre of $i\text{-}\bar{\imath}$ pearly; of other faces vitreous. Color white; occasionally yellow, brown, or red, to brick-red. Streak uncolored. Transparent—translucent. Fracture uneven. Brittle.

Var.—1. *Ordinary.* Either (a) in crystals, flattened and pearly parallel to the plane of cleavage, or sheaf-like, or divergent groups; or (b) in radiated stars or hemispheres, with the radiating individuals showing a pearly cleavage surface. *Sphærostilbite*, Beud, is in spheres, radiated within with a pearly fracture. rather soft externally.

Comp.—Q. ratio for $\text{R} : \ddot{\text{R}} : \text{Si} : \text{H} = 1 : 3 : 12 : 6$; $\text{R}=\text{Ca}(\text{Na}_2), \ddot{\text{R}}=\ddot{\text{Al}}$. Formula $\ddot{\text{R}}\ddot{\text{Al}}\text{Si}_6\text{O}_{16}$ +6aq. If two parts of water are basic (Ramm.) the ratio becomes $(\text{R}=\text{Ca},\text{H}_2,\text{Na}_2)\ 3 : 3 : 12 : 4$, or $\text{R} : \text{Si}=1 : 2$, and the formula is $\text{H}_4\ddot{\text{R}}\ddot{\text{Al}}\text{Si}_6\text{O}_{18}$+4aq. Analysis, Petersen, Seisser Alp, SiO_2 55·61, $\ddot{\text{Al}}\text{O}_3$ 15·62, CaO 7·33, Na_2O 2·01, K_2O 0·47, H_2O 18·19=99·23.

Pyr., etc.—B.B. exfoliates. swells up, curves into fan-like or vermicular forms, and fuses

OXYGEN COMPOUNDS—HYDROUS SILICATES. 347

to a white enamel. F.=2–2·5. Decomposed by hydrochloric acid, without gelatinizing. The *sphærostilbite* gelatinizes, but Heddle says this is owing to a mixture of *mesolite* with the stilbite.

Diff.—Prominent characters: occurrence in sheaf-like forms, and in the rectangular tabular crystals; lustre on cleavage-face pearly; does not gelatinize with acids.

Obs.—Stilbite occurs mostly in cavities in amygdaloid. It is also found in some metalliferous veins, and in granite and gneiss. The Faröe Islands, Iceland, and the Isle of Skye; in Dumbartonshire, Scotland; at Andreasberg; Arendal in Norway; in the Syhadree Mts., Bombay; near Fahlun, in Sweden. In North America, at Bergen Hill, New Jersey; at the Michipicoten Islands, Lake Superior; Nova Scotia, etc.

The name *stilbite* is from στίλβη, *lustre;* and *desmine* from δέσμη, *a bundle*. The species stilbite, as adopted by Haüy, included Strahlzeolith *Wern.* (radiated zeolite, or the above), and Blätterzeolith *Wern.* (foliated zeolite, or the species heulandite beyond). The former was the typical part of the species, and is the first mentioned in the description; and the latter he added to the species, as he observes, with much hesitation. In 1817, Breithaupt separated the two zeolites, and called the former *desmine* and the latter *euzeolite*, thus throwing aside entirely, contrary to rule and propriety, Haüy's name *stilbite*, which should have been accepted by him in place of desmine, it being the typical part of his species. In 1822, Brooke (apparently unaware of what Breithaupt had done) used *stilbite* for the first, and named the other *heulandite*. In this he has been followed by the French and English mineralogists, while the Germans have unfortunately followed Breithaupt.

EPISTILBITE (*Reissite*).—Composition like heulandite, but form orthorhombic. Iceland; Faröe; Poonah, India, etc.; Bergen Hill, N. J.

FORESITE.—Resembles stilbite in form. Q. ratio for R : R̈ : Si : H = 1 : 6 : 12 : 6. Formula RÄl$_2$Si$_6$O$_{19}$+6aq. (R=Na$_2$: Ca=1 : 3). Occurs in crystalline crusts on tourmaline, in cavities in granite. Island of Elba.

HEULANDITE. Stilbit, *Germ.*

Monoclinic. $C = 88°\,35'$, $I \wedge I = 136°\,4'$, $O \wedge 1\text{-}\breve{\imath} = 156°\,45'$; $\dot{c} : b : \dot{a} = 1\cdot065 : 2\cdot4785 : 1$. Cleavage: clinodiagonal ($\breve{\imath}\text{-}\breve{\imath}$) eminent. Also in globular forms; also granular.

H.=3·5–4. G.=2·2. Lustre of $\breve{\imath}\text{-}\breve{\imath}$ strong pearly; of other faces vitreous. Color various shades of white, passing into red, gray, and brown. Streak white. Transparent—subtranslucent. Fracture subconchoidal, uneven. Brittle. Double refraction weak; optic-axial plane normal to $\breve{\imath}\text{-}\breve{\imath}$; bisectrix positive, parallel to the horizontal diagonal of the base; DesCl.

651

Comp.—Q. ratio for R : R̈ : Si : H = 1 : 3 : 12 : 5; R=Ca(Na$_2$). Formula CaÄlSi$_6$O$_{16}$+5aq, or if 2H$_2$O be basic (Ramm.) then the ratio becomes 1 : 1 : 4 (R̈=Ca and H$_2$), and the formula H$_4$CaÄlSi$_6$O$_{18}$+3aq. Both require Silica 59·06, alumina 16·83, lime 7·88, soda 1·46, water 14·77=100.

Pyr.—B.B. same as with stilbite.

Diff.—Distinguished by its crystalline form. Pearly lustre of $i\text{-}\breve{\imath}$ a prominent character.

Obs.—Heulandite occurs principally in amygdaloidal rocks. Also in gneiss, and occasionally in metalliferous veins. Occurs in Iceland; the Faröe Islands; the Vendayah Mountains, Hindostan. Also in the Kilpatrick Hills, near Glasgow; in the Fassa Valley, Tyrol; Andreasberg; Nova Scotia, etc.; at Bergen Hill, New Jersey; on north shore of Lake Superior; at Jones's Falls, near Baltimore (Levy's *beaumontite*).

For the relation of the synonymes see stilbit, above.

BREWSTERITE.—Q. ratio same as for heulandite, but R is here Ba or Sr (Ca). Formula requires SiO$_2$ 53·5, ÄlO$_3$ 15·3, BaO 7·6, SrO 10·2, H$_2$O 13·4=100. Monoclinic. Strontian in Argyleshire, etc.

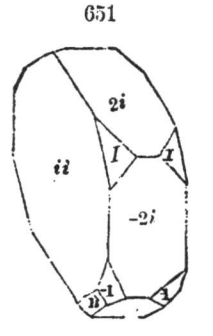

III. MARGAROPHYLLITE SECTION.

BISILICATES.

The Margarophyllites are often foliated like the micas, and the name alludes to the pearly folia. Massive varieties are, however, the most common with a large part of the species, and they often have the compactness of clay or wax. Talc, pyrophyllite, serpentine, are examples of species presenting both extremes of structure; while pinite occurs, as thus far known, only in the compact condition. The true Margarophyllites are below 5 in hardness; greasy to the feel, at least when finely powdered.

TALC.

Orthorhombic. $I \wedge I = 120°$. Occurs rarely in hexagonal prisms and plates. Cleavage: basal, eminent. Foliated massive, sometimes in globular and stellated groups; also granular massive, coarse or fine; also compact or cryptocrystalline.

H.$=1$–$1·5$. G.$=2·565$–$2·8$. Lustre pearly. Color apple-green to white, or silvery-white; also greenish-gray and dark green; sometimes bright green perpendicular to cleavage surface, and brown and less translucent at right angles to this direction; brownish to blackish-green and reddish when impure. Streak usually white; of dark green varieties, lighter than the color. Subtransparent—subtranslucent. Sectile. Thin laminæ flexible, but not elastic. Feel greasy. Optic-axial plane i-i; bisectrix negative, normal to the base; DesCl.

Var.—*Foliated, Talc.* Consists of folia, usually easily separated, having a greasy feel, and presenting ordinarily light green, greenish-white, and white colors. G.$=2·55$–$2·78$. (*a*) *Massive, Steatite* or *Soapstone* (Speckstein, *Germ.*). Coarse granular, gray, grayish-green, and brownish-gray in colors. H.$=1$–$2·5$. (*b*) Fine granular or cryptocrystalline, and soft enough to be used as chalk, as the *French chalk* (*Craie de Briançon*), which is milk-white, with a pearly lustre.

Comp.—Q. ratio for Mg : Si$=2 : 5$, or $3 : 4$, with a varying amount of water in both talc and steatite, from a fraction of a per cent. to 7 p. c. If the water is basic, the ratio becomes for R : Si$=1 : 2$, (R$=$Mg(Fe) and H$_2$), and the formula is $H_2Mg_3Si_4O_{12}$ (Ramm.)$=$Silica 63·49, magnesia 31·75, water 4·76$=100$; the analyses show generally 1 or 2 p. c. of FeO.

Pyr., etc.—In the closed tube B.B., when intensely ignited, most varieties yield water. In the platinum forceps whitens, exfoliates, and fuses with difficulty on the thin edges to a white enamel. Moistened with cobalt solution, assumes on ignition a pale red color. Not decomposed by acids.

Diff.—Recognized by its extreme softness, unctuous feel, and usually foliated structure. Inelastic though flexible. Yields water only on intense ignition.

Obs.—Talc or steatite is a very common mineral, and in the latter form constitutes extensive beds in some regions. It is often associated with serpentine and dolomite, and frequently contains crystals of dolomite, breunerite, asbestus, actinolite, tourmaline, magnetite. Steatite is the material of many pseudomorphs, among which the most common are those after pyroxene, hornblende, mica, scapolite, and spinel. The magnesian minerals are those which commonly afford steatite by alteration; while those, like scapolite and nephelite, which contain soda and no magnesia, most frequently change to pinite-like pseudomorphs. *Rensselaerite* and *pyrallolite* are pseudomorphous varieties.

Apple-green talc occurs near Salzburg; in the Valais; also in Cornwall, near Lizard Point, with serpentine; in Scotland, with serpentine, at Portsoy and elsewhere; etc. In N. America, some localities are: *Vermont*, at Bridgewater; Grafton, etc. In *New Hampshire*, at Pelham, etc. In *R. Island*, at Smithfield. In *N. York*, near Amity. In *Penn.*, at Texas; at Chestnut Hill, on the Schuylkill. In *Maryland*, at Cooptown.

PYROPHYLLITE. Agalmatolite or Pagodite pt.

Orthorhombic. Not observed in distinct crystals. Cleavage: basal eminent. Foliated, radiated lamellar; also granular, to compact or cryptocrystalline; the latter sometimes slaty.

H.=1–2. G.=2·75–2·92. Lustre of folia pearly, like that of talc; of massive kinds dull or glistening. Color white, apple-green, grayish and brownish-green, yellowish to ochre-yellow, grayish-white. Subtransparent to opaque. Laminæ flexible, not elastic. Feel greasy. Optic-axial angle large (about 108°); bisectrix negative, normal to the cleavage-plane.

Var.—(1) Foliated, and often radiated, closely resembling talc in color, feel, lustre, and structure. (2) Compact, massive, white, grayish, and greenish, somewhat resembling compact steatite, or French chalk. This compact variety, as Brush has shown, includes part of what has gone under the name of agalmatolite, from China; it is used for slate-pencils, and is sometimes called *pencil-stone*.

Comp.—Q. ratio for $\text{Al} : \text{Si}=1 : 2$, also in other cases 3 : 8, Formula for the first case= $\text{AlSi}_3\text{O}_9+\text{aq}$ (Ramm.). Analysis, Chesterfield, S. C., by Genth, SiO_2 64·82, AlO_3 28·48, FeO_3 0·96, MgO 0·33, CaO 0·55, H_2O 5·25=100·39.

Pyr., etc.—Yields water. B.B. whitens, and fuses with difficulty on the edges. The radiated varieties exfoliate in fan-like forms, swelling up to many times the original volume of the assay. Heated with cobalt solution gives a deep blue color (alumina). Partially decomposed by sulphuric acid, and completely on fusion with alkaline carbonates.

Obs.—Compact pyrophyllite is the material or base of some schistose rocks. The foliated variety is often the gangue of cyanite. Occurs in the Urals; at Westana, Sweden; near Ottrez in Luxembourg; in Chesterfield Dist., S. C.; in Lincoln Co., Ga.; in Arkansas. The compact pyrophyllite of Deep River, N. C., is extensively used for making slate pencils.

PIHLITE (*cymatolite*), near pyrophyllite.

SEPIOLITE.* Meerschaum, *Germ.* L'Ecume de Mer, *Fr.*

Compact, with a smooth feel, and fine earthy texture, or clay-like. H.=2–2·5. Impressible by the nail. In dry masses floats on water. Color grayish-white, white, or with a faint yellowish or reddish tinge. Opaque.

Comp.—Q. ratio for R : Si : H=1 : 3 : 1, corresponding to $\text{Mg}_2\text{Si}_3\text{O}_8+2\text{aq}$; or, if half the water is basic, 1 : 2 : ½=$\text{H}_2\text{Mg}_2\text{Si}_3\text{O}_9 + \text{aq}$=Silica 60·8, magnesia 27·1, water 12·1=100. The amount of water present is somewhat uncertain.

Pyr., etc.—In the closed tube yields first hygroscopic moisture, and at a higher temperature gives much water and a burnt smell. B.B. some varieties blacken, then burn white, and fuse with difficulty on the thin edges. With cobalt solution a pink color on ignition. Decomposed by hydrochloric acid with gelatinization.

Obs.—Occurs in Asia Minor, in masses in stratified earthy or alluvial deposits at the plains of Eskihi-sher; also found in Greece; at Hrubschitz in Moravia; in Morocco; at Vallecas in Spain, in extensive beds.

The word *meerschaum* is German for *sea-froth*, and alludes to its lightness and color. *Sepiolite*, Glocker, is from σηπια, *cuttle-fish*, the bone of which is light and porous, and also a production of the sea.

APHRODITE.—$4\text{MgSiO}_3+3\text{aq}$. Resembles sepiolite. Longban, Sweden.
SMECTITE.—Fuller's earth pt. A greenish clay from Styria.
MONTMORILLONITE.—A rose-red clay containing more alumina than smectite, from Montmorillon, France.
CELADONITE.—A variety of "green earth" from Mt. Baldo, near Verona.
GLAUCONITE.—Green earth pt. A hydrous silicate of iron and potassium, but always impure. Constitutes the green sand of the chalk and other formations (*e.g.*, in New Jersey).
STILPNOMELANE.—In foliated plates, or as a velvety coating. Essentially a hydrous iron

(Fe) silicate. Color black to yellowish-bronze. Silesia; Weilburg; Nassau; Sterling iron mine; Antwerp, N. Y. (*chalcodite*).

CHLOROPAL.—Compact, earthy. Color greenish-yellow. A hydrated iron silicate. Formula $FeSi_2O_9 + 5aq$. Andreasberg; Steinberg near Göttingen; Nontron (*nontronite*), France, etc.

AERINITE.—Perhaps related to chloropal (*Lasaulx*). Color blue. Spain.

UNISILICATES.

Serpentine Group.

SERPENTINE.*

Orthorhombic (?). In distinct crystals, but only as pseudomorphs. Sometimes foliated, folia rarely separable; also delicately fibrous, the fibres often easily separable, and either flexible or brittle. Usually massive, fine granular to impalpable or cryptocrystalline; also slaty.

H.=2·5–4, rarely 5·5. G.=2·5–2·65; some fibrous varieties 2·2–2·3; retinalite, 2·36–2·55. Lustre subresinous to greasy, pearly, earthy; resinlike, or wax-like; usually feeble. Color leek-green, blackish-green, oil and siskin-green, brownish-red, brownish-yellow; none bright; sometimes nearly white. On exposure, often becoming yellowish-gray. Streak white. slightly shining. Translucent—opaque. Feel smooth, sometimes greasy. Fracture conchoidal or splintery.

Var.—Many unsustained species have been made out of serpentine, differing in structure (massive, slaty, foliated, fibrous), or, as supposed, in chemical composition.

MASSIVE. (1) *Ordinary massive*. (*a*) *Precious* or *Noble Serpentine* (Edler Serpentin, *Germ*.) is of a rich oil-green color, of pale or dark shades, and translucent even when in thick pieces; and (*b*) *Common Serpentine*, when of dark shades of color, and subtranslucent. The former has a hardness of 2·5–3; the latter often of 4 or beyond, owing to impurities. *Bowenite* (Smithfield, R. I.), is a jade-like variety with the hardness 5·5.

FOLIATED. *Marmolite* is thin foliated; the laminæ brittle but easily separable, yet graduating into a variety in which they are not separable. G.=2·41; lustre pearly; colors greenish-white, bluish-white, or pale asparagus-green. From Hoboken, N. J.

FIBROUS. *Chrysotile* is delicately fibrous, the fibres usually flexible and easily separating; lustre silky, or silky metallic; color greenish-white, green, olive-green, yellow, and brownish; G.=2·219. Often constitutes seams in serpentine. It includes most of the silky *amianthus* of serpentine rocks. The original chrysotile was from Reichenstein.

Any serpentine rock cut into slabs and polished is called *serpentine marble*.

Comp.—Q. ratio for Mg : Si : H=3 : 4 : 2, corresponding to $Mg_3Si_2O_7 + 2aq$ = Silica 43·48, magnesia 43·48, water 13·04. But as chrysolite is especially liable to the change to serpentine, and chrysolite is a *unisilicate*, and the change consists in a loss of some Mg, and the addition of water, it is probable that part of the water takes the place of the lost Mg, so that the mineral is essentially a hydrated chrysolite of the formula $H_2Mg_3Si_2O_8 + aq$. The relation in ratio to kaolinite and pinite corresponds with this view of the formula.

Pyr., etc.—In the closed tube yields water. B.B. fuses on the edges with difficulty. F.=6. Gives usually an iron reaction. Decomposed by hydrochloric and sulphuric acids. Chrysotile leaves the silica in fine fibres.

Diff.—Distinguishing characters: compact structure; softness, being easily cut with a knife; low specific gravity; and resinous lustre.

Obs.—Serpentine often constitutes mountain masses. It frequently occurs mixed with more or less of dolomite, magnesite, or calcite, making a rock of clouded green, sometimes veined with white or pale green, called *verd antique*, or *ophiolite*. It results from the alteration of other rocks, frequently chrysolite rocks. Crystals of serpentine (pseudomorphous) occur in the Fassa valley, Tyrol; near Miask; Katharinenberg, and elsewhere; in Norway, at Snarum, etc. Precious serpentines come from Sweden; the Isle of Man; Corsica; Siberia; Saxony, etc. In N. America, in *Vermont*, at New Fane; Roxbury, etc. In *Mass.*, at Newburyport and elsewhere. In *Conn.*, near New Haven and Milford, at the verd-antique quarries. In *N. York*, at Brewster, Putnam Co.; at Antwerp, Jefferson Co.; in Gouverneur, St. Lawrence Co.; in Orange Co.; Richmond Co. In *N. Jersey*, at Hoboken. In *Penn.*. at Texas, Lancaster Co.; also in Chester Co.; in Delaware Co. In *Maryland*, at Bare Hills; at Cooptown, Harford Co.

The following are varieties of serpentine: *retinalite*, Grenville, C. W.; *vorhauserite*, Tyrol; *porcellophite; bowenite*, Smithfield, R. I.; *antigorite*, Piedmont; *williamsite*, Texas, Pa.; *marmolite*, Hoboken; *picrolite; metaxite; refdanskite* (containing Ni); *aquacreptite*.

BASTITE or SCHILLER SPAR.—An impure serpentine, a result of the alteration of a foliated pyroxene. Baste; Todtmoos in the Schwarzwald. ANTILLITE is similar.

DEWEYLITE (*Gymnite*).—$H_4Mg_4Si_3O_{12}+4aq$. Occurs with serpentine at Middlefield and Texas, Penn. HYDROPHITE (*Jenkinsite*), near deweylite, but Mg replaced in part by Fe.

CEROLITE.—$H_2Mg_2Si_2O_7+aq$. Silesia. LIMBACHITE from Limbach, and ZÖBLITZITE from Zöblitz, are varieties of cerolite.

GENTHITE. Nickel-Gymnite.

Amorphous, with a delicately hemispherical or stalactitic surface, incrusting.

H.=3–4; sometimes (as at Michipicoten) so soft as to be polished under the nail, and fall to pieces in water. G.=2·409. Lustre resinous. Color pale apple-green, or yellowish. Streak greenish-white. Opaque to translucent.

Comp.—Q. ratio for R : Si : H=2 : 3 : 3, or the same as for deweylite; formula $H_4(Ni,Mg)_4Si_3O_{12}$, being a nickel-gymnite. Analysis: Genth, Texas, Pa., SiO_2 35·36, NiO 30·64, FeO 0·24, MgO 14·60, CaO 0·26, H_2O 19·09=100·19.

Pyr., etc.—In the closed tube blackens and gives off water. B.B. infusible. With borax in O.F. gives a violet bead, becoming gray in R.F. (Nickel). Decomposed by hydrochloric acid without gelatinizing.

Obs.—From Texas, Lancaster Co., Pa., in thin crusts on chromic iron; from Webster, Jackson Co., N. C.; on Michipicoten Id., Lake Superior.

ALIPITE and PIMELITE, an apple-green silicates containing some nickel. GARNIERITE and NOUMEITE, from New Caledonia are similar, and have been shown by Liversidge to be mixtures.

Kaolinite Group.

KAOLINITE.

Orthorhombic. $I \wedge I = 120°$. In rhombic, rhomboidal, or hexagonal scales or plates; sometimes in fan-shaped aggregations; usually constituting a clay-like mass, either compact, friable, or mealy; base of crystals lined, arising from the edges of superimposed plates. Cleavage: basal, perfect. Twins: the hexagonal plates made up of six sectors.

H.=1–2·5. G.=2·4–2·63. Lustre of plates pearly; of mass, pearly to dull earthy. Color white, grayish-white, yellowish, sometimes brownish, bluish, or reddish. Scales transparent to translucent. Scales flexible, inelastic; usually unctuous and plastic.

Var.—1. *Argilliform*. Soft, clay-like; ordinary kaolinite; under the microscope, if not without, showing that it is made up largely of pearly scales. The constituent of most, if not all, pure kaolin. 2. *Fariniform.* Mealy, hardly coherent, consisting of pearly angular scales. 3. *Indurated; Lithomarge (Steinmark,* Germ.). Firm and compact; $H.=2-2·5$ When pulverized, often shows a scaly texture.

Comp.—Q. ratio for $\dot{R}$: Si : $H=3:4:2$; formula $\ddot{A}lSi_2O_7+2aq$, or making part of the water basic, $H_2\ddot{A}lSi_2O_8+aq=$Silica 46·4, alumina 39·7, water 13·9$=100$.

Pyr., etc.—Yields water. B.B. infusible. Gives a blue color with cobalt solution. Insoluble in acids.

Diff.—Characterized by its unctuous, soapy feel; alumina reaction B.B.

Obs.—Ordinary kaolin is a result of the decomposition of aluminous minerals, especially the feldspars of granitic and gneissoid rocks and porphyries. In some regions where these rocks have decomposed on a large scale, the resulting clay remains in vast beds of *kaolin* usually more or less mixed with free quartz, and sometimes with oxide of iron from some of the other minerals present.

Occurs at Cache-Aprés in Belgium; also in Bohemia; in Saxony. At Yrieix, near Limoges is the best locality of kaolin in Europe, it affords material for the famous Sèvres porcelain manufactory.

In the U. States, kaolin occurs at Newcastle and Wilmington, Del.; at various localities in the limonite region of Vermont (at Branford, etc.); Massachusetts; Pennsylvania; Jacksonville, Ala.; Edgefield, S. C.; near Augusta, Ga.

PHOLERITE, HALLOYSITE, clays allied to kaolinite.

SAPONITE.—A soft magnesian silicate; occurs in cavities in trap.

Pinite Group.

PINITE.

Amorphous; granular to cryptocrystalline; usually the latter. Also in crystals, and sometimes with cleavage, but only because pseudomorphs, the form and cleavage being those of the minerals from which derived. Rarely a submicaceous cleavage, which may belong to the species.

$H.=2·5-3·5$. $G.=2·6-2·85$. Lustre feeble, waxy. Color grayish-white, grayish-green, pea-green, dull green, brownish, reddish. Translucent—opaque. Acts like a gum on polarized light; DesCl.

Comp., Var.—Pinite is essentially a hydrous alkaline silicate. Being a result of alteration, and amorphous, the mineral varies much in composition, and numerous species have been made of the mineral in its various conditions. The varieties of pinite here admitted agree closely in physical characters, and in the amount of potash and water present. Average composition: Silica 46, alumina 30, potash 10, water 6; formula (Ramm.) $H_6K_2\ddot{A}l_2Si_5O_{20}$. The mineral is related chemically, as it is also physically, to *serpentine*; and it is an alkali-alumina serpentine, as pyrophyllite is an alumina talc.

The different kinds are either pseudomorphous crystals after (1) iolite; (2) nephelite; (3) scapolite; (4) some kind of feldspar; (5) spodumene; or (6) other aluminous mineral; or (7) disseminated masses resembling indurated talc, steatite, lithomarge, or kaolinite, also a result of alteration; or (8) the prominent or sole constituent of a metamorphic rock, which is sometimes a *pinite schist* (analogous to, and often much resembling, *talcose schist*, and still more closely related to *pyrophyllite schist*). Some prominent varieties are:

PINITE. Speckstein [fr. the Pini mine at Aue, near Schneeberg]. Occurs in granite, and is supposed to be pseudomorphous after iolite.

GIESECKITE. In 6-sided prisms, probably pseudomorphous after nephelite. $H=3·5$. $G.=2·78-2·85$. Color grayish-green, olive-green, to brownish. Brought by Giesecké from Greenland. Also of similar characters from Diana, N. Y.

AGALMATOLITE. Like ordinary massive pinite in its amorphous compact texture, lustre, and other physical characters, but contains more silica, so as to afford the formula of a bisilicate, or nearly, and it may be a distinct species. *Agalmatolite* was named from αγαλμα, *an image,* and *pagodite* from *pagoda,* the Chinese carving the soft stone into miniature pagodas

Images, etc. Part of the so-called agalmatolite of China is true pinite in composition, another part is compact pyrophyllite (p. 349), and still another steatite (p. 348).

Other minerals belonging in or near the pinite group are: *dyssyntribite* (=gieseckite); *parophite; wilsonite; polyargite; rosite; killinite; giganto'ite; hygrophilite; gümbelite; restormelite*. Also *cataspilite; biharite; palagonite*.

Hydro-mica Group.

FAHLUNITE.

In six- or twelve-sided prisms, but derived from pseudomorphism after iolite. Cleavage: basal sometimes perfect.

H.=3·5-5. G.=2·6-2·8. Lustre of surface of basal cleavage pearly to waxy, glimmering. Color grayish-green, to greenish-brown, olive- or oil-green; sometimes blackish-green to black; streak colorless.

Var.—This species is a result of alteration, and considerable variation in the results of analyses should be expected. The crystalline form is that of the original iolite, while the basal cleavage when distinct is that of the new species fahlunite.

Comp.—Q. ratio for R : Ṙ : Si : H=1 : 3 : 5 : 1; whence the formula $H_4R_2\dot{R}_2Si_5O_{20}$, the water being considered as basic, and as entering to make up the deficiency of bases in the unisilicate. In some kinds, the same with the addition of H_2O. The Q. ratio of iolite, the original of the species, is 1 : 3 : 5. Analysis by Wachtmeister, from Fahlun, SiO_2 44·60, AlO_3 30·10, FeO 3·86, MnO 2·24, MgO 6·75, CaO 1·35, K_2O 1·98, H_2O 9·35, F tr=100·23.

Pyr., etc.—Yields water. B.B. fuses to a white blebby glass. Not acted upon by acids. Pyrargillite is difficultly fusible, but is completely decomposed by hydrochloric acid.

Obs.—*Fahlunite* (and *triclasite*) from Fahlun, Sweden. The following are identical, or nearly so: *Esmarkite* and *praseolite*, Brevig; *raumite*, Raumo, Finland; *chlorophyllite*, Unity, Me.; *pyrargillite*, Helsingfors; *polychroilite*, Krageröe, and *aspasiolite*, Norway; *huronite*, Lake Huron (*Weissite*, Fahlun).

MARGARODITE.

Like muscovite or common mica in crystallization, and in optical and other physical characters, except usually a more pearly lustre, and the color more commonly whitish or silvery.

Comp.—Q. ratio for R : Ṙ : Si : H mostly 1 : 6 : 9 : 2; whence the formula $H_5R_2Al_4Si_9O_{26}$, the water being basic. Sometimes Q. ratio 1 : 9 : 12 : 2; but this division belongs with damourite, if the two are distinguishable. This species appears to be often, if not always, a result of the hydration of muscovite, there being all shades of gradation between it and that species. Muscovite has the Q. ratio for bases and silicon of 4 : 5, or nearly. Analysis, Smith and Brush, Litchfield, Ct., SiO_2 44·60, Al_2O_3 36·23, Fe_2O_3 1·34, MgO 0·37, CaO 0·50, Na_2O 4·10, K_2O 6·20, H_2O 5·26, F tr.=100·60.

For pyrognostics and localities, see muscovite, p. 313.

GILBERTITE.—Essentially identical with margarodite; tin mines, Saxony.

DAMOURITE.

An aggregate of fine scales, mica-like in structure.

H.=2-3. G.=2·792. Lustre pearly. Color yellow or yellowish-white. Optic-axial divergence 10 to 12 degrees; for sterlingite 70°.

Comp.—A hydrous potash-mica, like margarodite, to which it is closely related. Q. ratio for R : Ṙ : Si : H=1 : 9 : 12 : 2, or 1 : 1 for bases to silicon, if the water is basic. Formula $H_4K_2Al_3Si_6O_{24}$. Analysis, Monroe, from Sterling, Mass. (*sterlingite*), SiO_2 43·87, AlO_3 36·45, FeO_3 3·36, K_2O 10·86, H_2O 5·19=99·73.

It is the gangue of cyanite at Pontivy in Brittany; and the same at Horrsjöberg, Wermland. Associated with corundum in North Carolina; with spodumene, at Sterling, Mass.

PARAGONITE. Pregrattite. Cossaite.

Massive, sometimes consisting distinctly of fine scales; the rock slaty or schistose. Cleavage of scales in one direction eminent, mica-like.

H.=2·5–3. G.=2·779, paragonite; 2·895, pregrattite, Œllacher. Lustre strong pearly. Color yellowish, grayish, grayish-white, greenish, light apple-green. Translucent; single scales transparent.

Comp.—A hydrous *sodium* mica. Q. ratio for R : Ṙ : Si : H=1 : 9 : 12 : 2, or 1 : 1 for bases and silicon, if the water be made basic. Formula $H_4Na_2Al_3Si_6O_{24}$(K : Na=1 : 6)= Silica 46·60, alumina 39·96, soda 6·90, potash 1·74, water 4·80=100.

Pyr.—B.B. the paragonite is stated to be infusible. The pregrattite exfoliates somewhat like vermiculite (a property of some clinochlore and other species), and becomes milk-white on the edges.

Obs.—*Paragonite* constitutes the mass of the rock at Monte Campione, in the region of St. Gothard, containing cyanite and staurolite, called paragonitic or talcose schist. The *pregrattite* is from Pregratten in the Pusterthal, Tyrol; cossaite, from mines of Borgofranco, near Ivrea.

IVIGTITE.—Occurs in yellow scales, also granular, with cryolite from Greenland.

EUPHYLLITE.—Associated with tourmaline and corundum at Unionville, Penn. Q. ratio for R : Ṙ : Si : H=1 : 8 : 9 : 2. Average composition, Silica 41·6, alumina 42·3, lime 1·5, potash 3·2, soda 5·9, water 5·5=100.

EPHESITE, LESLEYITE.—Hydro-micas, perhaps identical with damourite. Occur with corundum, and impure from admixture with it.

ŒLLACHERITE.—A hydro-mica, containing 5 p. c. baryta. Pfitschthal, Tyrol.

COOKEITE.—A hydrous lithium mica. From Hebron and Paris, Me., apparently a product of the alteration of rubellite.

HISINGERITE.

Amorphous, compact, without cleavage.

H.=3. G.=3·045. Lustre greasy, inclining to vitreous. Color black to brownish-black. Streak yellowish-brown. Fracture conchoidal.

Comp.—Q. ratio for R+Ṙ : Si : H=2 : 3 : 3; formula $R_6\ddot{R}_2Si_3O_{18}$+4aq (with one-third of the water basic). Ṙ=Fe_2H_2; Ṙ=Fe. Analysis, Cleve, from Solberg, Norway, SiO_2 35·33, FeO_3 32·14, FeO 7·08, MgO 3·60, H_2O 22·04=100·19.

Pyr., etc.—Yields much water. B.B. fuses with difficulty to a black magnetic slag. With the fluxes gives reactions for iron. In hydrochloric acid easily decomposed without gelatinizing.

Obs.—Found at Longban, Tunaberg, Sweden; Riddarhyttan; at Degerö (*degeröite*), near Helsingfors, Finland.

EKMANNITE.—Foliated, also radiated. Color green, resembles chlorite. Analysis, Igelström, SiO_2 34·30, FeO_3 4·97, FeO 35·78, MnO 11·45, MgO 2·99, H_2O 10·51=100. With magnetite at Grythyttan, Sweden.

NEOTOCITE.—Uncertain alteration-products of rhodonite; amorphous. Contains 20–30 p. c. MnO. Paisberg, near Filipstadt, Sweden; Finland, etc.

GILLINGITE ; Sweden. JOLLYTE ; Bodenmais, Bavaria.

Vermiculite Group.*

The VERMICULITES have a micaceous structure. They are all unisilicates, having the general quantivalent ratio $\dot{R}+\ddot{R}:\ddot{S}i:\dot{H}=2:2:1$, the water being solely water of crystallization. The varieties differ in the ratio of the bases present in the protoxide and sesquioxide states.*

JEFFERISITE.

Orthorhombic (?). In broad crystals or crystalline plates. Cleavage: basal eminent, affording easily very thin folia, like mica. Surface of plates often triangularly marked, by the crossing of lines at angles of 60° and 120°.

H.=1·5. G.=2·30. Lustre pearly on cleavage surface. Color dark yellowish-brown and brownish-yellow; light yellow by transmitted light. Transparent only in very thin folia. Flexible, almost brittle. Optically biaxial; DesCl.

Comp.—Q. ratio for $\dot{R}:\ddot{R}:\ddot{S}i:\dot{H}=2:3:5:2\frac{1}{2}$, and $\dot{R}+\ddot{R}:\ddot{S}i:\dot{H}=2:2:1$; whence $\dot{R}_4\ddot{R}_2\ddot{S}i_5O_{20}+5aq$. Analysis: Brush, Westchester, SiO_2 37·10, AlO_3 17·57, FeO_3 10·54, FeO 1·26, MgO 19·65, CaO 0·56, Na_2O tr., K_2O 0·43, H_2O 13·76=100·87.

Pyr., etc.—When heated to 300° C. exfoliates very remarkably (like vermiculite); B.B. in forceps after exfoliation becomes pearly-white and opaque, and ultimately fuses to a dark gray mass. With the fluxes reactions for silica and iron. Decomposed by hydrochloric acid.

Obs.—Occurs in veins in serpentine at Westchester, Pa. Plates often several inches across.

PYROSCLERITE.—Q. ratio for $\dot{R}:\ddot{R}:\ddot{S}i:\dot{H}=4:2:6:3$, and for $\dot{R}+\ddot{R}:\ddot{S}i:\dot{H}=2:2:1$. Silica 38·9, alumina 14·8, magnesia 34·6, water 11·7=100. Color green. Elba. CHONICRITE, also Elba, has the ratio $3:2:5:2$.

VERMICULITE.—Q. ratio for $\dot{R}:\ddot{R}:\ddot{S}i:\dot{H}=4:2:6:3$. Milbury, Mass. CULSAGEEITE. Q. ratio $\dot{R}:\ddot{R}:\ddot{S}i:\dot{H}=2:1:1:1$. Jenk's mine, N. C. HALLITE, same ratio=$2:1:3:2$. East Nottingham, Chester Co., Penn. PELHAMITE, same ratio=$6:4:10:5$. Pelham, Mass. Similar mineral from Lenni, Delaware Co., Pa., above ratio=$6:4:10:5$. In all of the above $\dot{R}$=Mg mostly, and $\ddot{R}$=Al and Fe.

KERRITE.—Q. ratio=$6:3:10:10$; and MACONITE, Q. ratio=$3:6:8:5$, are both from Culsagee mine, Macon Co., N. C. VAALITE, Q. ratio=$6:3:10:4$. South Africa.

DIABANTITE, *Hawes* (diabantachronnyn, *Liebe*).—Fills cavities in amygdaloidal trap. Color dark green. Q. ratio for $\dot{R}:\ddot{R}:\ddot{S}i:\dot{H}=4:2:6:3$, but iron a more prominent ingredient than in pyrosclerite (see above). Analysis: Hawes, Farmington, Ct., $\frac{3}{7}SiO_2$ 33·68, AlO_3 10·84, FeO_3 2·86, FeO 24·33, MnO 0·38, CaO 0·73, MgO 16·52, Na_2O 0·33, H_2O 10·02=99·69.

SUBSILICATES.

Chlorite Group.

PENNINITE. Kämmererite.

Rhombohedral. $R \wedge R = 65° \ 36'$, $O \wedge R = 103° \ 55'$; $\dot{c} = 3·4951$. Cleavage; basal, highly perfect. Crystals often tabular, and in crested groups. Also massive, consisting of an aggregation of scales; also compact cryptocrystalline.

---

* These relations were brought out by Cooke. Proc. Amer. Acad., Boston, 1874, 35; ibid., 1875, 453.

H.=2–2·5; 3, at times, on edges. G.=2·6–2·85. Lustre of cleavage surface pearly; of lateral plates vitreous, and sometimes brilliant. Color green, apple-green, grass-green, grayish-green, olive-green; also reddish, violet, rose-red, pink, grayish-red; occasionally yellowish and silver-white; violet crystals, and sometimes the green, hyacinth-red by transmitted light along the vertical axis. Transparent to subtranslucent. Laminæ flexible, not elastic. Double refraction feeble; axis either negative or positive, and sometimes positive and negative in different laminæ of the same plate or crystal.

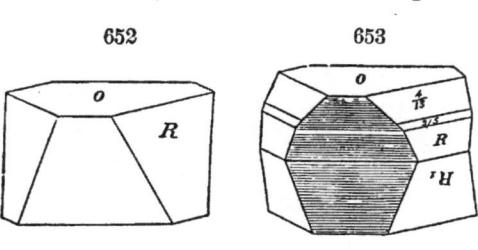

Comp.—Q. ratio for bases and silicon 4 : 3, but varying from 4 : 3 to 5 : 4. Exact deductions from the analyses cannot be made until the state of oxidation of the iron in all cases is ascertained. Analysis: Schweizer, from Zermatt, SiO_2 33·07, AlO_3 9·69, FeO 11·36, MgO 32·34, H_2O 12·58=99·08.

Pyr., etc.—In the closed tube yields water. B.B. exfoliates somewhat and is difficultly fusible. With the fluxes all varieties give reactions for iron, and many varieties react for chromium. Partially decomposed by acids.

Obs.—Occurs with serpentine in the region of Zermatt, Valais, near Mt. Rosa; at Ala, Piedmont; at Schwarzenstein in the Tyrol; at Taberg in Wermland; at Snarum. *Kämmererite* is found near Miask in the Urals; at Haroldswick in Unst, Shetland Isles. Abundant at Texas, Lancaster Co., Pa., along with clinochlore, some crystals being imbedded in clinochlore, or the reverse.

The following names belong here: *tabergite; pseudophite*, compact, massive (*allophite*); *loganite*.

Delessite, euralite, aphrosiderite, chlorophæite are chloritic minerals, occurring under similar conditions, in amygdaloid, etc

RIPIDOLITE. Clinochlore. Klinochlor, *Germ.*

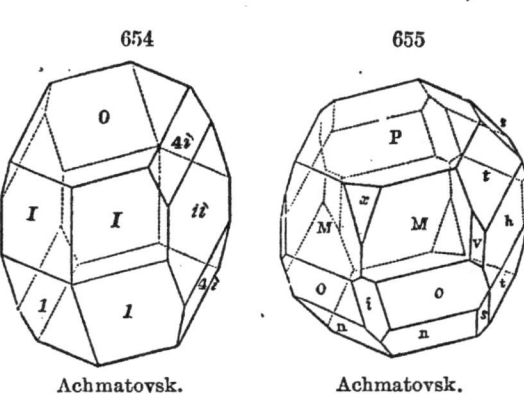

Monoclinic. $C = 62°\ 51' = O \wedge i\text{-}i$, $I \wedge I = 125°\ 37'$, $O \wedge 4\text{-}i = 108°\ 14'$; $\dot{c} : \bar{b} : \dot{a} = 1·47756 : 1·73195 : 1$. Cleavage: O eminent; crystals often tabular, also oblong; frequently rhombohedral in aspect, the plane angles of the base being 60° and 120°. Twins: twinning-plane ³, making stellate groups, as in f. 656, 657, very common. Crystals often grouped in rosettes. Massive coarse scaly granular to fine granular and earthy.

H.=2–2·5. G.=2·65–2·78. Lustre of cleavage-face somewhat pearly. Color deep grass-green to olive-green; also rose-red. Often strongly dichroic. Streak greenish-white to uncolored. Transparent to translucent. Flexible and somewhat elastic.

Comp.—Q. ratio for R : R̈ : Si : H = 5 : 3 : 6 : 4; corresponding to $Mg_5\ddot{A}lSi_3O_{14}+4aq=$ Silica 32·5, alumina 18·6, magnesia 36·0, water 12·9=100. Sometimes part of the Mg is replaced by Fe.

Pyr., etc.—Yields water. B.B. in the platinum forceps whitens and fuses with difficulty on the edges to a grayish-black glass. With borax a clear glass colored by iron, and sometimes chromium. In sulphuric acid wholly decomposed. The variety from Willimantic, Ct., exfoliates in worm-like forms, like vermiculite.

Obs.—Occurs in connection with chloritic and talcose rocks or schist, and serpentine. Found at Achmatovsk; Schwarzenstein; Zillerthal, etc.; red (*kotschubeite*) in the district of Ufaleisk, Southern Ural; at Ala, Piedmont; at Zermatt; at Marienberg, Saxony. In the U. S., at Westchester and Unionville, and Texas, Pa.; Brewster, N. Y.

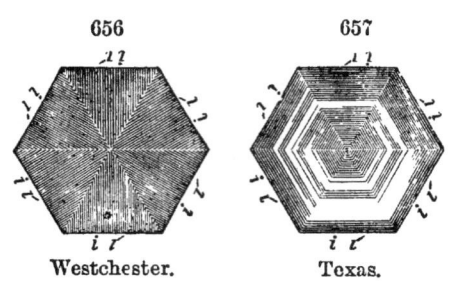

Named *ripidolite* from ῥιπίς, *a fan*, in allusion to a common mode of grouping of the crystals.

LEUCHTENBERGITE.—A prochlorite with the protoxide base almost wholly magnesia. Slatoust, Urals.

PROCHLORITE.

Hexagonal (?). Cleavage: basal, eminent. Crystals often implanted by their sides, and in divergent groups, fan-shaped, or spheroidal. Also in large folia. Massive granular.

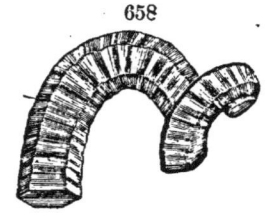

H.=1–2. G.=2·78–2·96. Translucent to opaque; transparent only in very thin folia. Lustre of cleavage surface feebly pearly. Color green, grass-green, olive-green, blackish-green; across the axis by transmitted light sometimes red. Streak uncolored or greenish. Laminæ flexible, not elastic. Double refraction very weak; one optical negative axis (Dauphiny); or two very slightly diverging, apparently normal to plane of cleavage.

Comp.—Q. ratio for R : R̈ : Si : H = 12 : 9 : 14 : 9⅓; for bases and silicon 3 : 2. Average composition=Silica 26·8, alumina 19·7, iron protoxide 27·5, magnesia 15·3, water 10·7=100.

Pyr., etc.—Same as for ripidolite.

Obs.—Like other chlorites in mode of occurrence. Sometimes in implanted crystals, as at St. Gothard, etc.; in the Zillerthal, Tyrol; Traversella in Piedmont; in Styria, Bohemia. Also massive in Cornwall, in tin veins (where it is called *peach*); at Arendal in Norway.

CRONSTEDTITE.—Q. ratio R : R̈ : Si : H = 3 : 3 : 4 : 3. Przibram; Cornwall.

STRIGOVITE.—Q. ratio = 3 : 2 : 4 : 2. In granite of Striegan, Silesia. GROCHAUITE same locality.

MARGARITE. Perlglimmer, *Germ.*

Orthorhombic (?); hemihedral, with a monoclinic aspect. $I \wedge I = 119°$–120°. Lateral planes horizontally striated. Cleavage: basal, eminent. Twins: common, composition-face *I*, and forming, by the crossing of 3 crystals, groups of 6 sectors. Usually in intersecting or aggregated laminæ; sometimes massive, with a scaly structure.

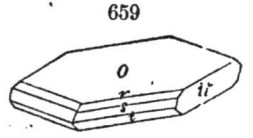

H.=3·5–4·5. G.=2·99, Hermann. Lustre of base pearly, laterally vitreous. Color grayish, reddish-white, yellowish. Translucent, subtranslucent. Laminæ rather brittle.

Optic-axial angle very obtuse; plane of axes parallel to the longer diagonal; dispersion feeble.

Comp.—Q. ratio for $R : \ddot{R} : Si : H = 1 : 6 : 4 : 1$; whence, if the water be basic, for bases and silicon $= 2 : 1$, formula $RRSiO_6$; that is, $H_2Ca\ddot{A}l_2Si_2O_{12}$. Analysis, Smith, Chester, Mass., SiO_2 32·21, $\ddot{A}lO_3$ 48·87, FeO_3 2·50, MgO 0·32, CaO 10·02, $Na_2O(K_2O)$ 1·91, H_2O 4·61, Li_2O 0·32, MnO 0·20 = 100·96.

Pyr., etc.—Yields water in the closed tube. B.B. whitens and fuses on the edges.

Obs.—Margarite occurs in chlorite from the Greiner Mts.; near Sterzing in the Tyrol; at different localities of emery in Asia Minor and the Grecian Archipelago; with corundum in Delaware Co., Pa.; at Unionville, Chester Co., Pa. (*corundellite*); in Madison Co. (*clingmanite*), and elsewhere in North Carolina; at the emery mines of Chester, Mass.

CHLORITOID.

Monoclinic, or triclinic. $I \wedge I'$ about $100°$; O (or cleavage surface) on lateral planes $93°-95°$, DesCl. Cleavage: basal perfect: parallel to a lateral plane imperfect. Usually coarsely foliated massive; folia often curved or bent, and brittle; also in thin scales or small plates disseminated through the containing rock.

$H. = 5·5-6$. $G. = 3·5-3·6$. Color dark gray, greenish-gray, greenish-black, grayish-black, often grass-green in very thin plates; strongly dichroic. Streak uncolored, or grayish, or very slightly greenish. Lustre of surface of cleavage somewhat pearly. Brittle.

Var.—1. The original *chloritoid* (or chloritspath) from Kossoibrod, near Katharinenburg in the Ural. 2. The *Sismondine*, from St. Marcel. 3. *Masonite*, from Natic, R. I., in very broad plates of a dark grayish-green color. The Canada mineral is in small plates, one-fourth in. wide and half this thick, disseminated through a schist (like phyllite), and also in nodules of radiated structure, half an inch through. That of Gumuch-Dagh resembles sismondine, is dark green in thick folia and grass-green in very thin.

Comp.—Q. ratio for $R : \ddot{R} : Si : H = 1 : 3 : 2 : 1$, for most analyses. Analysis by v. Kobell, Bregratten, SiO_2 26·19, $\ddot{A}lO_3$ 38·30, FeO_3 6·00, FeO 21·11, MgO 3·30, H_2O 5·50 = 100·40.

Pyr., etc—In a matrass yields water. B.B. nearly infusible; becomes darker and magnetic. Completely decomposed by sulphuric acid. The masonite fuses with difficulty to a dark green enamel.

Obs.—The Kossoibrod chloritoid is associated with mica and cyanite; the St. Marcel occurs in a dark green chlorite schist, with garnets, magnetite, and pyrite; the Rhode Island, in an argillaceous schist; the Chester, Mass., in talcose schist, with emery, diaspore, etc.

Phyllite (and ottrelite) closely resembles chloritoid, though the analyses hitherto made show a wide discrepancy, perhaps from want of purity in the material analyzed. Occurs in small, oblong, shining scales or plates, in argillaceous schist. Color blackish gray, greenish-gray, black. Phyllite occurs in the schist of Sterling, Goshen, Chesterfield, Plainfield, etc., in Massachusetts, and Newport, R. I. (*newportite*). *Ottrelite* is from a similar rock near Ottrez.

SEYBERTITE.—Orthorhombic. $I \wedge I = 120°$. In tabular crystals, sometimes hexagonal; also foliated massive; sometimes lamellar radiate. Cleavage: basal perfect. Structure thin foliated, or micaceous parallel to the base. $H. = 4-5$. $G. = 3-3·1$. Lustre pearly submetallic. Color reddish-brown, yellowish, copper-red. Folia brittle. Analysis. Brush, Amity, SiO_2 20·24, $\ddot{A}lO_3$ 39·13, FeO_3 3·27, MgO 20·84, CaO 13·69, H_2O 1·04, $Na_2O(K_2O)$ 1·43, ZrO_2 0·75 = 100·39. Amity, N. Y. (*clintonite*); Fassathal (*brandisite*); Slatoust (*xanthophyllite*).

CORUNDOPHILITE.—A chlorite with the Q. ratio $= 1 : 1 : 1 : \frac{3}{5}$. Occurs with corundum at Asheville, N. C.; Chester, Mass.

DUDLEYITE.—Alteration product of margarite. Clay Co., N. C.; Dudleyville, Ala.

WILLCOXITE.—Near margarite. Decomposition product of corundum. Q. ratio for $R : \ddot{R} : Si : H = 3 : 6 : 5 : 1$.

THURINGITE.—Q. ratio $2 : 3 : 3 : 2$. Contains principally iron (Fe and Fe). Hot Springs, Arkansas; Harper's Ferry (*owenite*). *Pattersonite* from Unionville, Pa., near thuringite.

2. TANTALATES, COLUMBATES.

PYROCHLORE.*

Isometric. Commonly in octahedrons. Cleavage: octahedral, sometimes distinct, especially in the smaller crystals.
H.=5–5·5. G.=4·2–4·35. Lustre vitreous or resinous. Color brown, dark reddish- or blackish-brown. Streak light brown, yellowish-brown. Subtranslucent—opaque. Fracture conchoidal.

Comp.—A columbate of calcium, cerium, and other bases in varying amounts. Analysis, by Rammelsberg. Brevig, Cb_2O_5 58·27, TiO_2 5·38, ThO_2 4·96, CeO 5·50, CaO 10·93, FeO(UO_2) 5·53, Na_2O 5·31, F 3·75, H_2O 1·53=101·16.
Obs.—Occurs in syenite at Friederichsvärn and Laurvig, Norway; at Brevig; near Miask in the Urals; Kaiserstuhlgebirge in Breisgau (*koppite*); with samarskite in N. Carolina (G.= 4·794, chemical character unknown).
MICROLITE.*—In minute yellow octahedrons in feldspar. G.=5·5. Near pyrochlore, but probably containing more tantalum pentoxide. Chesterfield, Mass.
PYRRHITE.—In isometric octahedrons. Color orange-yellow. Chemical character unknown. From Mursinsk in the Ural. A mineral supposed to be similar from the Azores contains essentially, according to Hayes, columbium, zirconium, etc.
AZORITE.—In minute tetragonal octahedrons resembling zircon. From the Azores in albite. Chemical character unknown.

TANTALITE.*

Orthorhombic. Observed planes as in the figure. $I \wedge I = 101^c$ 32', $O \wedge 1\text{-}\bar{\imath} = 122°\ 3\frac{1}{2}'$; $\bar{c} : \bar{b} : \check{a} = 1·5967 : 1·2247 : 1$. $O \wedge \frac{3}{2}\text{-}\check{\imath} = 117°\ 2'$, $i\text{-}\bar{\imath} \wedge 1\text{-}2 = 143°\ 6\frac{1}{2}'$, 1-2 $\wedge$ 1-2, adj., = 141° 48', $i\text{-}\bar{\imath} \wedge i\text{-}\frac{2}{3} = 118°\ 33'$. Twins: twinning-plane $i\text{-}\check{\imath}$, common. Also massive.
H.=6–6·5. G.=7–8. Lustre nearly pure metallic, somewhat adamantine. Color iron-black. Streak reddish-brown to black. Opaque. Brittle.

Comp., Var.—A tantalate either (1) of iron, or (2) of iron and manganese, or (3) a stanno-tantalate of these two bases. Formula Fe(Mn)Ta_2O_6. Sn is also often present (as $FeSnO_3$, according to Rammelsberg), and some of the tantalum is often replaced by columbium. Analysis. Ramm., Tammela (G.=7·384), Ta_2O_5 76·34, Cb_2O_5 7·54, SnO_2 0·70, FeO 13·90, MnO 1·42=99·90. Other varieties contain much more Cb_2O_5, the kinds shade into one another.
Pyr., etc.—B.B. unaltered. With borax slowly dissolved, yielding an iron glass, which, at a certain point of saturation, gives, when treated in R.F. and subsequently flamed, a grayish-white bead; if completely saturated becomes of itself cloudy on cooling. With salt of phosphorus dissolves slowly, giving an iron glass, which in R.F., if free from tungsten, is pale yellow on cooling; treated with tin on charcoal it becomes green. If tungsten is present the bead is dark red, and is unchanged in color when treated with tin on charcoal. With soda and nitre gives a greenish-blue manganese reaction. On charcoal, with soda and sufficient borax to dissolve the iron, gives in R.F. metallic tin. Decomposed on fusion with

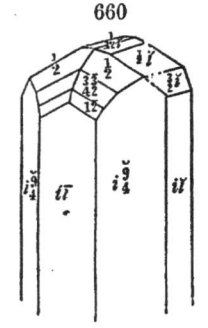

potassium bisulphate in the platinum spoon, and gives on treatment with dilute hydrochloric acid a yellow solution and a heavy white powder. which, on addition of metallic zinc, assumes a smalt-blue color ; on dilution with water the blue color soon disappears (v. Kobell).

Obs.—Tantalite is confined mostly to albite or oligoclase granite, and is usually associated with beryl. Occurs in Finland, at several places ; in Sweden, in Fahlun, at Broddbo and Finbo ; in France, at Chanteloube near Limoges, in pegmatite ; in North Carolina.

Named *Tantalite* by Ekeberg, from the mythic Tantalus, in playful allusion to the difficulties (tantalizing) he encountered in his attempts to make a solution of the Finland mineral in acids.

COLUMBITE.* Niobite. Ferroilmenite.

Orthorhombic. $I \wedge I = 101°\ 26'$, $O \wedge 1\text{-}\bar{\imath} = 134°\ 53\frac{1}{2}'$; $\dot{c} : \bar{b} : \dot{a} = 1·0038 : 1·2225 : 1$. $O \wedge 1\text{-}\check{\imath} = 140°\ 36'$, $O \wedge 1\text{-}\check{\imath} = 138°\ 26'$, $i\text{-}\bar{\imath} \wedge 1\text{-}\check{\imath} = 104°\ 30'$, $1\text{-}\check{\imath} \wedge 1\text{-}\check{\imath}$, adj., $= 151°$, $i\text{-}\check{\imath} \wedge i\text{-}\check{\imath}$, ov. $i\text{-}\check{\imath}, = 135°\ 40'$, $i\text{-}\bar{\imath} \wedge i\text{-}\bar{\imath}$, ov. $i\text{-}\bar{\imath}, = 135°\ 30'$. Twins: twinning-plane 2-$\check{\imath}$. Cleavage : $i\text{-}\bar{\imath}$ and $i\text{-}\check{\imath}$, the former most distinct. Occurs also rarely massive.

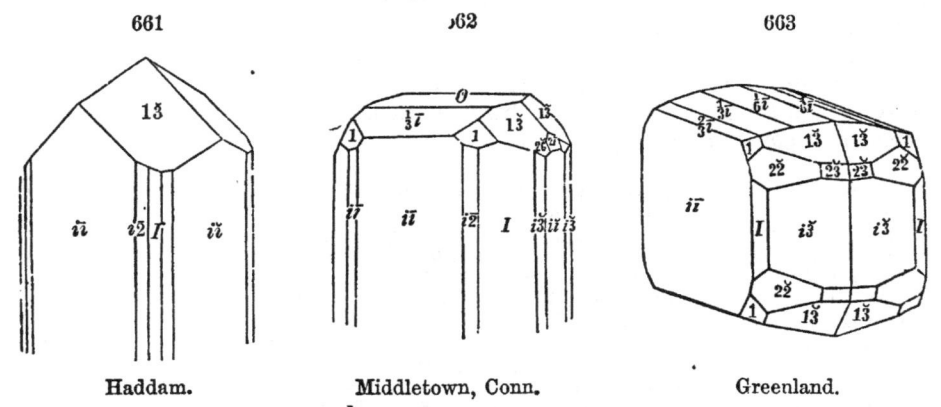

661   662   663

Haddam.   Middletown, Conn.   Greenland.

H.=6. G.=5·4–6·5. Lustre submetallic; a little shining. Color iron-black, brownish-black, grayish-black ; often iridescent. Streak dark red to black. Opaque. Fracture subconchoidal, uneven. Brittle.

Comp., Var.—$FeCb_2(Ta_2)O_6$, with some manganese replacing part of the iron. The ratio of Cb : Ta generally=3 : 1 (Bodenmais, Haddam), sometimes 4 : 1, 8 : 1, 10 : 1, etc.; in the Greenland columbite the Ta_2O_5 is almost entirely absent.

Analyses, Blomstrand, (1) Haddam (G.=6·15), (2) Greenland (G.=5·395).

	Cb_2O_5	Ta_2O_5	WO_3	SnO_2	ZrO_2	FeO	MnO	H_2O
(1)	51·53	28·55	0·76	0·34	0·34	13·54	4·97	0·16=100·19
(2)	77·97	——	0·13	0·73	0·13	17·33	3·51	——= 99·80

Pyr., etc.—Like tantalite. Von Kobell states that when decomposed by fusion with caustic potash, and treated with hydrochloric and sulphuric acids, it gives, on the addition of zinc, a blue color much more lasting than with tantalite ; and the variety *dianite*, when similarly treated, gives, on boiling with tin-foil, and dilution with its volume of water, a sapphire-blue fluid, while, with tantalite and ordinary columbite, the metallic acid remains undissolved. The variety from Haddam, Ct., is partially decomposed when the powdered mineral is evaporated to dryness with concentrated sulphuric acid, its color is changed to white, light gray, or yellow, and when boiled with hydrochloric acid and metallic zinc it gives a beautiful blue. The remarkably pure and unaltered columbite from Arksut-fiord in Greenland is also partially decomposed by sulphuric acid, and the product gives the reaction test with zinc, as above.

Obs.—Occurs at Rabenstein, Bavaria ; at Tirschenreuth, Bavaria ; at Tammela in Finland ; at Chanteloube, near Limoges ; near Miask in the Ilmen Mts.; at Hermanskär, near Björskär, in Finland ; in Greenland, at Evigtok.

OXYGEN COMPOUNDS.—TANTALATES, COLUMBATES.

In the United States, at Haddam, in a granite vein, and near Middletown, Conn.; at Chesterfield, Mass.; Standish, Me.; Acworth, N. H.; also Beverly, Mass.; Northfield, Mass.; Plymouth, N. H.; Greenfield, N. Y.

The Connecticut crystals are usually rather fragile from partial change; while those of Greenland and of Maine are very firm and hard.

HERMANNOLITE (Shepard).—From the columbite locality at Haddam, Ct., and a variety of columbite due to alteration. G.=5·35. Supposed by Hermann to contain "ilmenium" pent oxide (Il_2O_5).

TAPIOLITE.—Tetragonal. $č$=·6464 (rutile $č$=·6442). $FeTa_2(Cb_2)O_6$, with Ta : Cb=4 : 1. Tammela, Finland.

HJELMITE.—A stanno-tantalate of iron, uranium and yttrium. Massive. Color black. Near Fahlun, Sweden.

YTTROTANTALITE. Black Yttrotantalite.

Orthorhombic. $I \wedge I = 123° \ 10'$; $O \wedge 2\text{-}\bar{i} = 103° \ 26'$; $č : \bar{b} : ă = 2·0934$: 1·8482 : 1. Crystals often tabular parallel to $i\text{-}\bar{i}$. Also massive; amorphous.

H.=5–5·5. G.=5·4–5·9. Lustre submetallic to vitreous and greasy. Color black, brown. Streak gray to colorless. Opaque to subtranslucent. Fracture small conchoidal to granular.

664

Ytterby.

Comp.—Mostly $R_3(Ta,Cb)_2O_7$, with two equivalents of water, perhaps from alteration; R=Fe : Ca : Y(Er,Ce)=1 : 2 : 4. Containing also WO_3 and SnO_2. Analysis (Ramm.), Ytterby, Ta_2O_5 46·25, Cb_2O_5 12·32, SnO_2 1·12, WO_3 2·36, UO_2 1·61, YO 10·52, ErO 6·71, FeO 3·80, CeO 2·22, Ca 5·73, H_2O 6·31=98·95.

Pyr., etc.—In the closed tube yields water and turns yellow. On intense ignition becomes white. B.B. infusible. With salt of phosphorus dissolves with at first a separation of a white skeleton of tantalum pentoxide, which with a strong heat is also dissolved; the black variety from Ytterby gives a glass faintly tinted rose-red from the presence of tungsten. With soda and borax on charcoal gives traces of metallic tin (Berzelius). Not decomposed by acids. Decomposed on fusion with potassium bisulphate, and when the product is boiled with hydrychloric acid, metallic zinc gives a pale blue color to the solution which soon fades.

Obs.—Occurs in Sweden at Ytterby; at the Korarfvet mine, etc., near Fahlun.

SAMARSKITE.* Uranotantalite.

Orthorhombic. $I \wedge I = 122° \ 46'$; $1\text{-}\bar{i} \wedge 1\text{-}\bar{i} = 93°$; $č : \bar{b} : ă = 0·949$. 1·833 : 1. Crystals often flattened parallel to $i\text{-}\bar{i}$, also less often to $i\text{-}\bar{i}$. Also in large irregular masses (N. Carolina). In flattened imbedded grains (Urals).

H.=5·5–6. G.=5·614–5·75; 5·45 –5·69, North Carolina. Lustre of surface of fracture shining and submetallic. Color velvet-black. Streak dark reddish-brown. Opaque. Fracture subconchoidal.

665   666

North Carolina.

Comp.—Analyses: 1. Allen (priv. contrib.); 2. Finkener and Stephans:

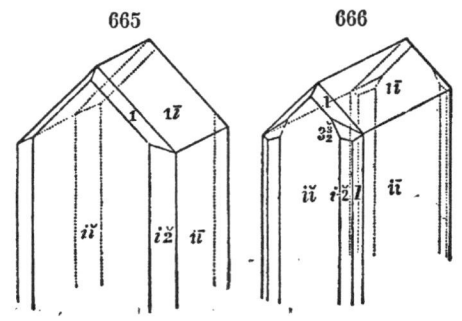

	Cb_2O_5	Ta_2O_5	WO_3	SnO_2	$ThO_2ZrO_2UO_3$	MnO	FeO	CeO*	YO	CaO	H_2O
1. Mitchell Co., N. C.,	37·20	18.60	—	0·08	— —	12·46	0·75	10·90	4·25	14·45	0·55 1·12=
					UO_2						100·36
2. Miask,	47·47	—	1·36	0·05	6·05 4·35 10·95	0·96	11·33†	3·31	12·61	0·73	0·45
										MgO	0·14=99·76

* With LaO, DiO.
† With 0·25 CuO.

Pyr., etc.—In the closed tube decrepitates, glows like gadolinite, cracks open, and turns black, and is of diminished density. B.B. fuses on the edges to a black glass. With borax in O.F. gives a yellowish-green to red bead, in R.F. a yellow to greenish-black, which on flaming becomes opaque and yellowish-brown. With salt of phosphorus in both flames an emerald-green bead. With soda yields a manganese reaction. Decomposed on fusion with potassium bisulphate, yielding a yellow mass which on treatment with dilute hydrochloric acid separates white tantalic acid, and on boiling with metallic zinc gives a fine blue color. Samarskite in powder is also sufficiently decomposed on boiling with concentrated sulphuric acid to give the blue reduction test when the acid fluid is treated with metallic zinc or tin.

Obs.—Occurs in reddish-brown feldspar, near Miask in the Ural; the pieces having the size of hazel-nuts. In masses, sometimes weighing 20 lbs., in the decomposed feldspar of the mica mines of western North Carolina, especially in Mitchell Co. At both localities it is often intimately associated with columbite; at Miask the crystals of the latter species are sometimes implanted in parallel position upon those of the samarskite.

NOHLITE.—Near samarskite, but contains 4·62 p. c. water. Nohl, Sweden.

EUXENITE.

Orthorhombic. Form a rectangular prism with lateral edges replaced, and a pyramid at summit. Cleavage none. Commonly massive.

H.=6·5. G.=4·60–4·99. Lustre brilliant, metallic-vitreous, or somewhat greasy. Color brownish-black; in thin splinters a reddish-brown translucence lighter than the streak. Streak-powder yellowish to reddish-brown. Fracture subconchoidal.

Comp.—According to Rammelsberg $2RTiO_3 + RCb_2O_6 + aq$; here R=Y,Fe,U mostly. Analysis, Ramm., Arendal, Cb_2O_5 35·09, TiO_2 21·16, YO 27·48, ErO 3·40, UO_2 4·78, CeO 3·17, FeO 1·38, H_2O 2·63=99·63.

Obs.—Occurs at Jölster in Norway; near Tvedestrand; at Alve, island of Tromoen, near Arendal; at Möretjär, near Naskilen.

Named by Scheerer from εὔξενος, *a stranger*, in allusion to the rarity of its occurrence.

ÆSCHYNITE.—Orthorhombic. H.=5–6. G.=4·9–5·14. Lustre submetallic to resinous, nearly dull. Color nearly black. Streak gray. Fracture small subconchoidal. Analysis, Ramm., Cb_2O_5 28·81, TiO_2 22·64, SnO_2 0·18, ThO_2 15·75, FeO 3·17, CeO 18·49, LaO(DiO) 5·60, YO 1·12, CaO 2·75, H_2O 1·07=99·58. In feldspar with mica and zircon. Miask in the Urals.

POLYMIGNITE.—Orthorhombic. In slender crystals. H.=6·5. G.=4·77–4·85. Lustre brilliant. Color black. Streak dark brown. Fracture perfect conchoidal. Composition doubtful. Frederiksvärn, Norway. Perhaps identical with æschynite (Frankenheim).

POLYCRASE.—Orthorhombic. H.=5·5. G.=5·09–5·12. Lustre bright. Color black. Streak grayish-brown. Fracture conchoidal. Analysis, Ramm., Cb_2O_5 20·35, Ta_2O_5 4·00, TiO_2 26·59, YO 23·32, FeO 2·72, CeO 2·61, UO_2 7·70 H_2O 4·02=98·84. In crystals in granite at Hitteröe, Norway.

MENGITE.—Occurs in short prisms. H.=5–5·5. G.=5·48. Color iron-black. Contains zirconium, iron, titanium. In granite veins in the Ilmen Mts.

RUTHERFORDITE.—Doubtful; contains titanium, cerium, etc. Rutherford Co., N. C.

FERGUSONITE.* Yellow Yttrotantalite. Tyrite. Bragite.

Tetragonal, hemihedral. $O \wedge 1\text{-}i = 124°\ 20'$; $\check{c} = 1·464$. Cleavage: 1, in distinct traces.

H.=5·5–6. G.=5·838, Allen; 5·800, Turner. Lustre externally dull, on the fracture brilliantly vitreous and submetallic. Color brownish-black; in thin scales pale liver-brown. Streak pale brown. Subtranslucent—opaque. Fracture imperfect conchoidal.

Comp.—According to Rammelsberg, essentially $R_3(Cb,Ta)_2O_8$. Analysis, Ramm., Greenland, Cb_2O_5 44·45, Ta_2O_5 6·30, SnO_2 0·47, WO_3 0·15, YO 24·87. ErO 9·81, CeO 7·63 (5·63 LaO,DiO), UO_2 2·58, FeO 0·74, CaO 0·61, H_2O 1·49=99·10. The amount of water varies from 1·49–7 p. c., and is regarded by Rammelsberg as arising from alteration.

Obs.—*Fergusonite* occurs near Cape Farewell in Greenland, disseminated in quartz. Also found at Ytterby, Sweden; in Silesia. *Bragite* is from Helle, Alve, and elsewhere in Norway. *Tyrite* is associated with euxenite at Hampemyr on the island of Tromoe, and Helle on the mainland; at Næskul, about ten miles east of Arendal.

KOCHELITE.—Near fergusonite. In yellow square-octahedrons and crusts in granite. Kochelwiesen, near Schreiberhau, Silesia.

ADELPHOLITE.—A columbate of iron and manganese, containing 41·8 p. c. of metallic acids, and 9·7 p. c. of water. Tetragonal. H.=3·5–4·5. G.=3·8. Tammela, Finland.

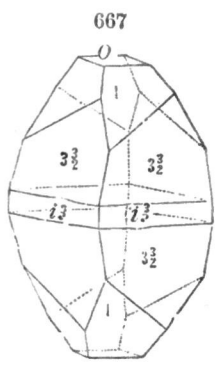

3. PHOSPHATES, ARSENATES, VANADATES, ETC.

Anhydrous Phosphates, Arsenates, etc.

XENOTIME. Ytterspath, *Germ.*

Tetragonal. $O \wedge 1 = 138° 45'$; $\dot{c} = 0.6201$. $1 \wedge 1$, pyram., $= 124° 26'$; basal, $= 82° 30'$. Cleavage: I, perfect.
H.$= 4$–5.   G.$= 4.45$–4.56.   Lustre resinous. Color yellowish-brown, reddish-brown, hair-brown, flesh-red, grayish-white, pale yellow; streak pale brown, yellowish, or reddish. Opaque. Fracture uneven and splintery.

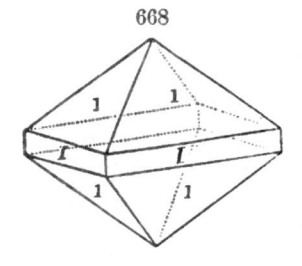

Comp.—$Y_3P_2O_8$=Phosphorus pentoxide (P_2O_5) 37·87, yttria 62·13=100.

Pyr., etc.—B.B. infusible. When moistened with sulphuric acid colors the flame bluish-green. Difficultly soluble in salt of phosphorus. Insoluble in acids.

Obs.—From a granite vein at Hitteröe; at Ytterby, Sweden; St. Gothard; Binnenthal. In the U. S., in the gold washings of Clarksville, Georgia; in McDowell Co., N. C.; in the diamond sands of Bahia, Brazil. The *wiserine* of Kenngott has been shown by Klein to be octahedrite (vide p. 255).

CRYPTOLITE (*Phosphocerite*).—$Ce_3P_2O_8$ (with some Di), like monazite. Occurs in minute grains imbedded in apatite at Arendal; Siberia.

Apatite Group.

APATITE.*

Hexagonal; often hemihedral. $O \wedge 1 = 139° 41' 38''$, Kokscharof; $\dot{c} = 0.734603$. $O \wedge 2$-$2 = 124° 14\frac{1}{2}'$. Cleavage: O, imperfect; I, more so. Also

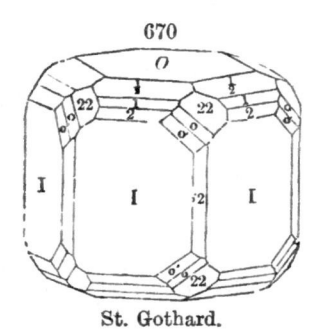

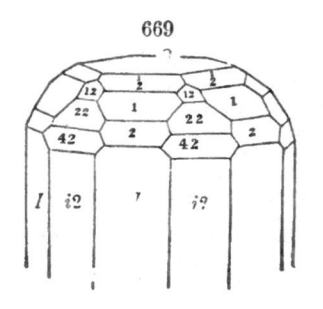

St. Gothard.

globular and reniform, with a fibrous or imperfectly columnar structure, also massive, structure granular.

H.$=5$, sometimes 4·5 when massive. G.$=2·92$–$3·25$. Lustre vitreous, inclining to subresinous. Streak white. Color usually sea-green, bluish-green; often violet-blue; sometimes white; occasionally yellow, gray, red, flesh-red, and brown; none bright. Transparent—opaque. A bluish opalescence sometimes in the direction of the vertical axis, especially in white varieties. Cross fracture conchoidal and uneven. Brittle.

Var.—1. *Ordinary.* Crystallized, or cleavable and granular massive. (*a*) The *asparagus stone* (originally from Murcia, Spain) and *moroxite* (from Arendal) are ordinary apatite. The former was yellowish-green, as the name implies; the latter was in greenish-blue and bluish crystals; and the names have been used for apatite of the same shades from other places. 2. *Fibrous, concretionary, stalactitic.* The name *Phosphorite* was used by Kirwan for all apatite, but in his mind it especially included the fibrous concretionary and partly scaly mineral from Estremadura, Spain, and elsewhere. 3. *Fluor-apatite, Chlor-apatite.* Apatite also varies as to the proportion of fluorine to chlorine, one of these elements sometimes replacing nearly or wholly the other.

Comp.—The formulas of the two varieties are $3Ca_3P_2O_8 + CaCl_2 =$ Phosphorus pentoxide 40·92, lime 53·80, chlorine 6·82$=101·54$; and $3Ca_3P_2O_8 + CaF_2 =$ Phosphorus pentoxide 42·26, lime 55·55, fluorine 3·77$=101·58$. Sometimes both calcium chloride ($CaCl_2$), and calcium fluoride (CaF_2), are present.

Pyr., etc.—B.B. in the forceps fuses with difficulty on the edges (F.$=4·5$–5), coloring the flame reddish-yellow; moistened with sulphuric acid and heated colors the flame pale bluish-green (phosphoric acid); some varieties react for chlorine with salt of phosphorus, when the bead has been previously saturated with copper oxide, while others give fluorine when fused with this salt in an open glass tube. Gives a phosphide with the sodium test.

Dissolves in hydrochloric and nitric acid, yielding with sulphuric acid a copious precipitate of calcium sulphate; the dilute nitric acid solution gives with lead acetate a white precipitate, which B.B. on charcoal fuses, giving a globule with crystalline facets on cooling. Some varieties of apatite phosphoresce on heating.

Diff.—Characterized by its hexagonal form. Distinguished by its softness from beryl; does not effervesce with acids like the carbonates; unlike pyromorphite, yields no lead B.B.

Obs.—Apatite occurs in rocks of various kinds and ages, but is most common in metamorphic crystalline rocks, especially in granular limestone, granitic and many metalliferous veins, particularly those of tin, in gneiss, syenite, hornblendic gneiss, mica schist, beds of iron ore; occasionally in serpentine, and in igneous or volcanic rocks; sometimes in ordinary stratified limestone, beds of sandstone or shale of the Silurian, Carboniferous, Jurassic, Cretaceous, or Tertiary formations; also in microscopic crystals in many igneous rocks, doleryte, etc. It has been observed as the petrifying material of wood.

Among its prominent localities are Ehrenfriedersdorf in Saxony; region of St. Gothard in Switzerland; Mussa-Alp in Piedmont; Untersulzbachthal and elsewhere in the Tyrol; Bohemia; in England, in Cornwall, with tin ores; in Cumberland; in Devonshire; at Wheal Franco (*francolite*), etc. The variety, *moroxite*, occurs at Arendal, Snarum, etc., in Norway. The *asparagus stone* or *Spargelstein* of Jumilla, in Murcia, Spain, is pale yellowish-green in color; and a variety from Zillerthal is wine-yellow. The *phosphorite*, or massive radiated variety, is obtained abundantly near the junction of granite and argillyte, in Estremadura, Spain; at Schlackenwald in Bohemia; at Krageröe, etc.

In *Mass.*, at Norwich; at Bolton, and elsewhere. In *New York*, in St. Lawrence Co., in granular limestone; in Rossie; Sanford mine, Essex Co.; near Edenville, Orange Co. In *New Jersey*, near Suckasunny,; Mt. Pleasant mine, near Mt. Teabo; at Hurdstown, Sussex Co. In *Penn.*, at Leiperville, Delaware Co.; in Chester Co. In *Delaware*, at Dixon's quarry, Wilmington. In *Canada*, in North Elmsley, and passing into South Burgess; similar in Ross; at the foot of Calumet Falls; at St. Roch, on the Achigan.

' Apatite was named by Werner from ἀπατάω, *to deceive*, older mineralogists having referred it to aquamarine, chrysolite, amethyst, fluor, schorl, etc

OSTEOLITE is massive impure altered apatite. The ordinary compact variety looks like lithographic stone of white to gray color. It also occurs earthy. Hanau.

GUANO.—Guano is bone-phosphate of calcium, or osteolite, mixed with the hydrous phosphate, brushite, and generally with some carbonate of calcium, and often a little magnesia, alumina, iron, silica, gypsum, and other impurities. It often contains 9 or 10 p. c. of water. It is often granular or oolitic; also compact through consolidation produced by infiltrating waters, in which case it is frequently lamellar in structure, and also occasionally stalagmitic and stalactitic. Its colors are usually grayish-white, yellowish and dark brown, and sometimes reddish, and the lustre of a surface of fracture earthy to resinous.

PHOSPHATIC NODULES. COPROLITES.—Phosphatic nodules occur in many fossiliferous rocks, which are probably in all cases of organic origin. They sometimes present a spiral or other interior structure, derived from the animal organization that afforded them, and in such cases their coprolitic origin is unquestionable. In other cases there is no structure to aid in deciding whether they are true coprolites or not.

PYROMORPHITE* Grünbleierz, *Germ.*

Hexagonal. Hemihedral. $O \wedge 1 = 139°\ 38'$; $\check{c} = 0.7362$. Cleavage: I and 1 in traces. I commonly striated horizontally. Often globular, reniform, and botryoidal or verruciform, with usually a subcolumnar structure; also fibrous, and granular.

$H. = 3.5-4$. $G. = 6.5-7.1$, mostly when without lime; $5-6.5$, when containing lime. Lustre resinous. Color green, yellow, and brown, of different shades; sometimes wax-yellow and fine orange-yellow; also grayish-white to milk-white. Streak white, sometimes yellowish. Subtransparent—subtranslucent. Fracture subconchoidal, uneven. Brittle.

Comp.—Analogous to apatite, $3Pb_3P_2O_8 + PbCl_2 =$ Phosphorus pentoxide 15·71, lead oxide 82·27, chlorine 2·62 = 100·60. Some varieties contain arsenic replacing part of the phosphorus, and others calcium replacing the lead.

Pyr., etc.—In the closed tube gives a white sublimate of lead chloride. B.B. in the forceps fuses easily (F. = 1·5), coloring the flame bluish-green; on charcoal fuses without reduction to a globule, which on cooling assumes a crystalline polyhedral form, while the coal is coated white from the chloride, and, nearer the assay, yellow from lead oxide. With soda on charcoal yields metallic lead; some varieties contain arsenic, and give the odor of garlic in R.F. on charcoal. With salt of phosphorus, previously saturated with copper oxide, gives an azure-blue color to the flame when treated in O.F. (chlorine). Soluble in nitric acid.

Diff.—Characterized by its high specific gravity, and pyrognostics.

Obs.—Pyromorphite occurs principally in veins, and accompanies other ores of lead. Occurs in Saxony; at Przibram, Mies, and Bleistadt, in Bohemia; near Freiberg; Clausthal in the Harz; at Nassau; Beresof in Siberia; Cornwall, Derbyshire, and Cumberland, in England; Leadhills in Scotland; Wicklow, and elsewhere, Ireland. In the U. S. at Phenixville, Penn.; also in Maine, at Lubec and Lenox; in Davidson Co., N. C.

The figures produced by etching (see p. 118) show that pyromorphite is hemihedral like apatite (Baumhauer).

Named from πῦρ, *fire*; μορφή, *form*, alluding to the crystalline form the globule assumes on cooling.

MIMETITE.* Mimetesite.

Hexagonal. $O \wedge 1 = 139°\ 58'$; $\check{c} = 0.7276$. Cleavage: 1, imperfect. $H. = 3·5$. $G. = 7·0-7·25$, mimetite; $5·4-5·5$, hedyphane. Lustre resinous. Color pale yellow, passing into brown; orange-yellow; white or colorless. Streak white or nearly so. Subtransparent—translucent.

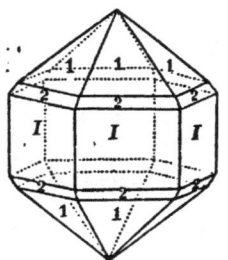

Comp.—Formula $3Pb_3As_2O_8 + PbCl_2 =$ Arsenic pentoxide 23·20, lead oxide 74·96, chlorine 2·39 = 100·55. Generally part of the arsenic is replaced by phosphorus, and often the lead in part by calcium.

Pyr., etc.—In the closed tube like pyromorphite. B.B. fuses at 1, and on charcoal gives in R.F. an arsenical odor, and is easily reduced to metallic lead, coating the coal at first with lead chloride, and later with arsenous oxide and lead oxide. Gives the chlorine reactions as under pyromorphite. Soluble in nitric acid.

Obs.—Occurs at several of the mines in Cornwall; in Cumberland. At St. Prix in France, at Johanngeorgenstadt; at Nertschinsk, Siberia. At the Brookdale mine, Phenixville, Pa.

Mimetite is hemihedral like apatite and pyromorphite, as shown by etching (Baumhauer). Named from μιμητής, *imitator*, it closely resembling pyromorphite.

HEDYPHANE.*—A variety containing much calcium. CAMPYLITE contains much lead phosphate.

VANADINITE.*

Hexagonal. In simple hexagonal prisms, and prisms terminating in planes of the pyramids; $1 \wedge 1$, over terminal edge, $142° 58'$, $O \wedge 1 = 140° 34'$, $I \wedge 1 = 130°$. Usually in implanted globules or incrustations.

H.=2·75–3. G.=6·6623–7.23. Lustre of surface of fracture resinous. Color light brownish-yellow, straw-yellow, reddish-brown. Streak white or yellowish. Subtranslucent—opaque. Fracture uneven, or flat conchoidal. Brittle.

Comp.—Formula $3Pb_3V_2O_8 + PbCl_2 =$ Vanadium pentoxide 19·36, lead oxide 78·70 chlorine 2·50=100·56.

Pyr., etc.—In the closed tube decrepitates and yields a faint white sublimate. B.B. fuses easily, and on charcoal to a black lustrous mass, which in R.F. yields metallic lead and a coating of chloride of lead; after completely oxidizing the lead in O.F the black residue gives with salt of phosphorus an emerald-green bead in R.F., which becomes light yellow in O.F. Gives the chlorine reaction with the copper test. Decomposed by hydrochloric acid.

If nitric acid be dropped on the crystals they become first deep red from the separation of vanadium pentoxide, and then yellow upon its solution.

Obs.—This mineral was first discovered at Zimapan in Mexico, by Del Rio. Since obtained at Wanlockhead in Dumfriesshire; also at Beresof in the Ural; and near Kappel in Carinthia.

DECHENITE.—PbV_2O_6 (or with some Zn)=Vanadium pentoxide 45·1, lead oxide 54·9=100 Massive. Color deep red. Dahn, near Niederschlettenbach, Rhenish Bavaria. Freiberg in Breisgau (*eusynchite*).

DESCLOIZITE.*—$Pb_2V_2O_7$=Vanadium pentoxide 29·1, lead oxide 70·9=100. Orthorhombic. South America. Wheatley Mine, Penn.

PUCHERITE (*Frenzel*).—Orthorhombic, near brookite in form (*Websky*). Occurs in small implanted crystals. Color reddish-brown. In composition a bismuth vanadate, $BiVO_4 =$ Vanadium pentoxide 28·3, bismuth oxide 71·7. Pucher mine, Schneeberg, Saxony.

ROSCOELITE.—Occurs in thin micaceous scales, arranged in stellate or fan-shaped groups. Color dark brownish-green. Soft. G.=2·938 (Genth); 2·902 (Roscoe). Analyses: 1. Roscoe (Proc. Roy. Soc., May 10, 1876); 2. Genth (Am. J. Sci., July, 1876).

	SiO_2	V_2O_5	Al_2O_3	FeO_3	MnO_3	MgO	CaO	K_2O	Na_2O	H_2O
1.	½ 41·25	28·60	14·14	1·13	1·15	2·01	0·61	8·56	0·82	1·08 moisture 2·27=101·62
2.	47·69	22·02 V_6O_{11}	14·10	1·67 FeO	—	2·00	tr.	7·59	0·19 ign. 4·96 0·85 gangue=100·22	

The above analyses, made upon material derived from the same source, differ widely, especially in regard to the state of oxidation of the vanadium. Genth makes it $V_6O_{11} = 2V_2O_3, V_2O_5$. The formula given by Roscoe is $2AlV_2O_6 + K_2Si_9O_{20} + aq$. Found in fissures in the porphyry, and in cavities in quartz at the gold mine at Granite Creek, El Dorado Co., Cal. Named by Dr. Blake, who discovered it. See further on p. 435.

WAGNERITE.

Monoclinic. $C = 71° 53'$, $I \wedge I = 95° 25'$, $O \wedge 1\text{-}\check{\imath} = 144° 25'$, B. & M.; $\check{c} : b : \check{a} = 0.78654 : 1.045 : 1$. Most of the prismatic planes deeply striated. Cleavage : I, and the orthodiagonal, imperfect ; O in traces.
H.=5–5·5. G.=3·068, transparent crystal; 2·985, untransparent, Rammelsberg. Lustre vitreous. Streak white. Color yellow, of different shades; often grayish. Translucent. Fracture uneven and splintery across the prism.

Comp.—$Mg_3P_2O_8 + MgF_2 =$ Phosphorus pentoxide 43·8, magnesia 37·1, fluorine 11·7, magnesium 7·4 = 100.
Pyr., etc.—B.B. in the forceps fuses at 4 to a greenish-gray glass ; moistened with sulphuric acid colors the flame bluish-green. With borax reacts for iron. On fusion with soda effervesces, but is not completely dissolved ; gives a faint manganese reaction. Fused with salt of phosphorus in an open glass tube reacts for fluorine. Soluble in nitric and hydrochloric acids. With sulphuric acid evolves fumes of fluohydric acid.
Obs.—Occurs in the valley of Höllgraben, near Werfen, in Salzburg, Austria.
KJERULFINE (*v. Kobell*).—Stands near wagnerite, but exact nature uncertain. In masses of a pale red color at Bamle, Norway.

MONAZITE.*

Monoclinic. $C = 76° 14'$, $I \wedge I = 93° 10'$, $O \wedge 1\text{-}\check{\imath} = 138° 8'$; $\check{c} : b : \check{a} = 0.94715 : 1.0265 : 1$. Crystals usually flattened parallel to $i\text{-}i$. Cleavage : O very perfect, and brilliant. Twins : twinning plane O.
H. = 5–5·5. G. = 4·9–5·26. Lustre inclining to resinous. Color brownish-hyacinth-red, clove-brown, or yellowish-brown. Subtransparent—subtranslucent. Rather brittle.

672 — Norwich, Ct.
673 — Watertown, Ct.

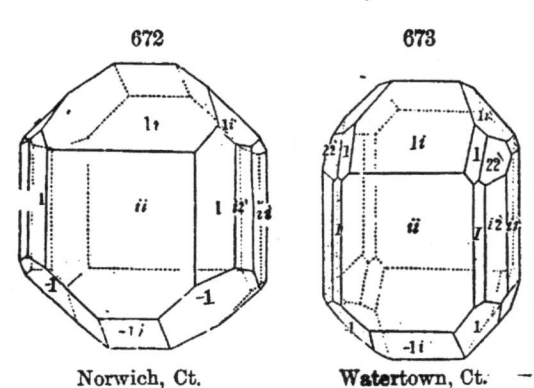

Comp.—According to Rammelsberg, $5R_3P_2O_8 + Th_3P_2O_9$, where $R = Ce, La, Di$. Analysis by Kersten, Slatoust, P_2O_5 28·50, ThO_2 17·95, SnO_2 2·10, CeO 26·00, LaO 23·40, MnO 1·86, CaO 1·68, K_2O and TiO_2 tr. = 101·49.
Pyr., etc.—B.B. infusible, turns gray, and when moistened with sulphuric acid colors the flame bluish-green. With borax gives a bead yellow while hot and colorless on cooling ; a saturated bead becomes enamel-white on flaming. Difficultly soluble in hydrochloric acid.
Diff.—Its brilliant basal cleavage is a prominent character, distinguishing it from titanite.
Obs.—Monazite occurs near Slatoust in the Ilmen Mtn. ; also in the Ural ; near Nöterö in Norway; at Schreiberhau. In the United States, with sillimanite at Norwich ; at Yorktown, Westchester Co., N.Y.; near Crowder's Mountain, N. C.
Named from μονάζω, *to be solitary*, in allusion to its rare occurrence.
TURNERITE.—Identical with monazite, as first suggested by Prof. J. D. Dana. Occurs in minute yellow to brown crystals, rarely twins, at Mt. Sorel, Dauphiny; Santa Brigritta, Tavetsch ; Lercheltiny Alp, Binnenthal; Laacher See (v. Rath.). $\check{c} : b : \check{a} = .921696 : 1 : 0.958444$. $C. = 77° 18'$ (Trechmann).
KORARFVEITE (*Radominski*).—A cerium phosphate containing fluorine ; near monazite Occurs in large crystalline masses of a yellowish color at Korarfvet, near Fahlun, Sweden.

TRIPHYLITE.* Triphyline.

Orthorhombic. $I \wedge I = 98°$, $O \wedge 1\text{-}\bar{i} = 129° 33'$, Tschermak; $\check{c} : \bar{b} : \check{a} =$ 1·211 : 1·1504 : 1. Faces of crystals usually uneven.
Cleavage: O nearly perfect in unaltered crystals.
Massive.
H.=5. G.=3·54–3·6. Subresinous. Color greenish-gray; also bluish; often brownish-black externally. Streak grayish-white. Translucent in thin fragments.

Comp.—$R_3P_2O_8$, where R=Fe, Mn, (Ca) and Li$_2$ (K$_2$, Na$_2$). Analysis by Oesten, from Bodenmais, P$_2$O$_5$ 44·19, FeO 38·21, MnO 5·63, MgO 2·39, CaO 0·76, Li$_2$O 7·69, Na$_2$O 0·74, K$_2$O 0·04, SiO$_2$ 0·40=100·05. The analyses vary much, owing to the impure material employed.

Pyr., etc.—In the closed tube sometimes decrepitates, turns to a dark color, and gives off traces of water. B.B. fuses at 1·5, coloring the flame beautiful lithia-red in streaks, with a pale bluish-green on the exterior of the cone of flame. The coloration of the flame is best seen when the pulverized mineral, moistened with sulphuric acid, is treated on a loop of platinum wire. With borax gives an iron bead; with soda a reaction for manganese. Soluble in hydrochloric acid.

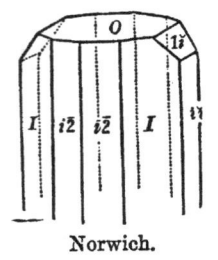

Obs.—Triphylite occurs at Rabenstein near Zwiesel in Bavaria; also at Keityö in Finland; Norwich, Mass.

Named from τρίς, *three-fold*, and φυλή, *family*, in allusion to its containing three phosphates.

TRIPLITE.* Zwieselite.

Orthorhombic. Imperfectly crystalline. Cleavage:—unequal in three directions perpendicular to each other, one much the most distinct.

H.=5–5·5. G.=3·44–3·8. Lustre resinous, inclining to adamantine. Color brown or blackish-brown to almost black. Streak yellowish-gray or brown. Subtranslucent—opaque. Fracture small conchoidal.

Comp.—$R_3P_2O_8+RF_2$; R=Fe, Mn(Ca). Analysis. v. Kobell, Schlackenwald, P$_2$O$_5$ 33·85, FeO$_3$ 3·50, FeO 23·38, MnO 30·00, CaO 2·20, MgO 3·05, F=8·10=104·08.

Pyr., etc.—B.B. fuses easily at 1·5 to a black magnetic globule; moistened with sulphuric acid colors the flame bluish-green. With borax in O.F. gives an amethystine colored glass (manganese); in R.F. a strong reaction for iron. With soda reacts for manganese. With sulphuric acid evolves fluohydric acid. Soluble in hydrochloric acid.

Obs.—Found by Alluaud at Limoges in France, with apatite; at Peilau in Silesia.

Zwieselite, a clove-brown variety, was found near Rabenstein, near Zwiesel in Bavaria, in quartz (G.=3·97, Fuchs).

SARCOPSIDE.—Near triplite. Valley of the Mühlbach, Silesia.

AMBLYGONITE.*

Triclinic. Cleavage: O perfect; $i\text{-}\bar{i}$ nearly perfect, angle between these cleavages 104½°; also I imperfect. Usually massive, cleavable; sometimes columnar.

H.=6. G.=3–3·11. Lustre pearly on face of perfect cleavage (O); vitreous on $i\text{-}\bar{i}$, less perfect cleavage-face; on cross-fracture a little greasy. Color pale mountain or sea-green, white, grayish, brownish-white. Subtransparent—translucent. Fracture uneven. Optical axes very divergent; plane of axes nearly at right angles to $i\text{-}\bar{i}$; bisectrix of the acute angle negative, and parallel to the edge $O/i\text{-}\bar{i}$; DesCl.

Comp.—According to Rammelsberg, $2AlP_2O_8 + 3Li(Na)F$. If Na : Li = 1 : 4, the formula requires : Phosphorus pentoxide 49·24, alumina 35·58, lithia 6·24, soda 3·23, fluorine 9·88 = 104·17.

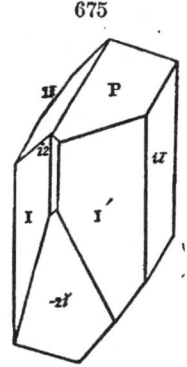

Pyr., etc.—In the closed tube yields water, which at a high heat is acid and corrodes the glass. B.B. fuses easily at 2, with intumescence, and becomes opaque-white on cooling. Colors the flame yellowish-red with traces of green; the Hebron variety gives an intense lithia-red; moistened with sulphuric acid gives a bluish-green to the flame. With cobalt solution assumes a deep blue color (alumina). With borax and salt of phosphorus forms a transparent colorless glass. In fine powder dissolves easily in sulphuric acid, more slowly in hydrochloric.

Diff.—Distinguished by its easy fusibility; reaction for fluorine and lithia; greasy lustre in the mass, etc.

Obs.—Occurs at Chursdorf and Arnsdorf, near Penig in Saxony; also at Arendal, Norway. In the U. States, in Maine, at Hebron (hebronite), imbedded in a coarse granite with lepidolite, albite, quartz, red, green, and black tourmaline; also at Mt. Mica in Paris, 8 m. from Hebron, with tourmaline.

The name is from $ἀμβλύς$, *blunt*, and $γόνν$, *angle*.

Hebronite, Maine.

HEBRONITE.—The mineral from Hebron, Me. (see above), has been shown by DesCloizeaux to differ in optical character ($v > ρ$) from the Penig amblygonite. On this ground, as well as on account of a variation in the composition, it has been proposed (v. Kobell) to make it a new species. The same optical character and composition belong to the mineral from Montebras (called *montebrasite* on the basis of an erroneous analysis). Analysis of hebronite, Pisani, P_2O_5 46·65, AlO; 36·00, Li_2O 9·75, H_2O 4·20, F 5·22 = 101·82.

HERDERITE.—Supposed to be an anhydrous aluminum-calcium phosphate, with fluorine. Color yellowish-white. Ehrenfriedersdorf.

DURANGITE.—Monoclinic. Cleavage prismatic (110° 10'). H. = 5. G. = 3·937–4·07. Color bright orange-red. Analysis, Hawes, Arsenic pentoxide 53·11, alumina 17·19, iron sesquioxide 9·23, manganese sesquioxide 2·08, soda 13·06, lithia 0·65, fluorine 7·67 = 102·99.

Formula $R_2RAs_2O_9$ (with one-ninth of the oxygen replaced by fluorine), or $RAs_2O_8 + 2RF$. Here R = Na : Li = 10 : 1; R = Al : Fe : Mn = 15 : 5 : 1. Other varieties, having a lighter color, have Al : Fe = 5 : 1. Occurs with cassiterite, near Durango, Mexico (Brush).

ANHYDROUS ANTIMONATES.

MONIMOLITE.—Mainly an antimonate of lead. Yellow. G. = 5·94. Paisberg, Sweden.

NADORITE.—$PbSb_2O_4 + PbCl_2$. In yellow translucent crystals. H. = 3. G. = 7·02. Djebel Nador, province of Constantine, Algiers.

ROMEITE.—An antimonate (or antimonite) of calcium. Occurs in groups of minute tetragonal crystals. Color yellow. St. Marcel, Piedmont.

RIVOTITE.—Contains antimonic oxide, carbon dioxide, and copper. Amorphous. Color yellowish-green. Sierra del Cadi.

STIBIOFERRITE.—Amorphous coating on stibnite, from Santa Clara Co., Cal. Mixture (?).

HYDROUS PHOSPHATES, ARSENATES, ETC.

PHARMACOLITE.

Monoclinic. $I \wedge I = 111° 6'$, $i\text{-}\check{\imath} \wedge i\text{-}2 = 109° 26'$, $1 \wedge 1 = 117° 24'$ Cleavage: $i\text{-}\check{\imath}$ eminent. One of the faces 1 often obliterated by the extension of the other. Surfaces $i\text{-}i$ and $i\text{-}2$ usually striated parallel to their mutual intersection. Rarely in crystals; commonly in delicate silky fibres or acicular crystallizations, in stellated groups. Also botryoidal and stalactitic, and sometimes massive.

H.=2–2·5. G.=2·64–2·73. Lustre vitreous; on $i\text{-}i$ inclining to pearly. Color white or grayish; frequently tinged red by arsenate of cobalt. Streak white. Translucent—opaque. Fracture uneven. Thin laminæ flexible.

Comp.—$2HCaAsO_4+5aq$=Arsenic pentoxide 51·1, lime 24·9, water 24·0=100.

Pyr., etc.—In the closed tube yields water and becomes opaque. B.B. in O.F. fuses with intumescence to a white enamel, and colors the flame light blue (arsenic). On charcoal in R.F. gives arsenical fumes, and fuses to a semi-transparent globule, sometimes tinged blue from traces of cobalt. The ignited mineral reacts alkaline to test paper. Insoluble in water, but readily soluble in acids.

Obs.—Found with arsenical ores of cobalt and silver at Wittichen, Baden;_at Andreasberg, and at Riechelsdorf and Bieber; at Joachimsthal.

This species was named, in allusion to its containing arsenic, from φάρμακον, *poison*.

STRUVITE.—An ammonium-magnesium phosphate containing 12 equivalents of water. In guano from Saldanha Bay, Africa.

HAIDINGERITE.—$HCaAsO_4+aq.$=Arsenic pentoxide 58·1, lime 28·3, water 13·6=100. Joachimsthal (?).

BRUSHITE.—$HCaPO_4(R_3P_2O_8)+2aq$=Phosphorus pentoxide 41·3, lime 32·6, water 6·1=100. Monoclinic. G.=2·208. On guano at Aves Island and Sombrero.

METABRUSHITE.—$2HCaPO_4+3aq.$ G.=2·35. Sombrero. ORNITHRITE. Probably altered brushite.

CHURCHITE.—$R_3P_2O_8+4aq$, with R=Ce(Di),Ca. Cornwall.

WAPPLERITE (*Frenzel*).—Triclinic. In minute crystals and in incrustations. Color white. Composition $H_4Ca.Mg)AsO_4+7aq$=(Ca : Mg=4 : 3) arsenic pentoxide 48·7, lime 13·5, magnesia 7·3, water 30·5=100. Found with pharmacolite at Joachimsthal. Schrauf states that *rœsslerite* is a pseudomorph after wapplerite.

HŒRNESITE.—Monoclinic. Color snow-white. Composition $Mg_3As_2O_8+8aq$. From the Banat.

PICROPHARMACOLITE.—Monoclinic. $Ca_3(Mg_3)As_2O_8+6aq$. Riechelsdorf; Freiberg.

VIVIANITE.

Monoclinic. $C=75°\ 34'$, $I\wedge I=108°\ 2'$, $1\wedge 1=120°\ 26'$, $\dot{c}:\bar{b}:\dot{a}=$ ·935792 : 1·33369 : 1; v. Rath. Surface $i\text{-}i$ smooth, others striated. Cleavage: $i\text{-}i$, highly perfect; $i\text{-}i$ and $\frac{1}{2}\text{-}i$ in traces. Often reniform and globular. Structure divergent, fibrous, or earthy; also incrusting.

H.=1·5–2. G.=2·58–2·68. Lustre, $i\text{-}i$ pearly or metallic pearly; other faces vitreous. Color white or colorless, or nearly so, when unaltered; often blue to green, deepening on exposure; usually green when seen perpendicularly to the cleavage-face, and blue transversely; the two colors mingled, producing the ordinary dirty blue color. Streak colorless to bluish-white, soon changing to indigo-blue; color of the dry powder often liver-brown. Transparent—translucent; becoming opaque on exposure. Fracture not observable. Thin laminæ flexible. Sectile.

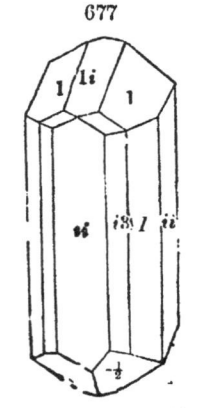

Comp.—$Fe_3P_2O_8+8aq$=Phosphorus pentoxide 28·3, iron protoxide 43·0, water 28·7=100

Pyr., etc.—In the closed tube yields neutral water, whitens and exfoliates. B.B. fuses at 1·5, coloring the flame bluish-green, to a grayish-black magnetic globule. With the fluxes reacts for iron. Soluble in hydrochloric acid.

Diff.—Distinguishing characters: deep-blue color; softness; solubility in acid.

Obs.—Occurs associated with pyrrhotite and pyrite in copper and tin veins; in beds of clay, and sometimes associated with limonite, or bog iron ore; often in cavities of fossils or buried bones. Occurs at Wheal Falmouth, and elsewhere in Cornwall; in Devonshire, near Tavistock; at Bodenmais. The earthy variety, called *blue iron earth* or *native Prussian blue* occurs in Greenland, Carinthia, Cornwall, etc. At Cransac, France.

In N. America, it occurs in *New Jersey*, at Allentown; at Franklin. Also in *Delaware*, near Middletown; near Cape Henlopen. In *Maryland*, in the north part of Somerset and Worcester Cos. In *Virginia*, in Stafford Co. In *Canada*, with limonite at Vandreuil, abundant.

LUDLAMITE (*Field*).—Monoclinic. H.=3·4. G.=3·12. Color clear green, from pale to dark. Transparent, brilliant. Composition $2Fe_3P_2O_8 + H_2FeO_2 + 8aq$ = Phosphorus pentoxide 29·88, iron protoxide 53·06, water 17·06=100. Cornwall.

ERYTHRITE. Cobalt Bloom. Kobaltblüthe, *Germ.*

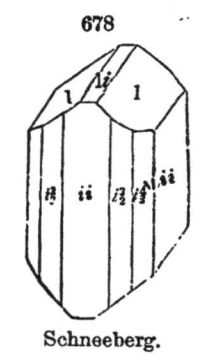

Monoclinic. $C = 70°\ 54'$, $I \wedge I = 111°\ 16'$ $O \wedge 1\text{-}\check{\imath} = 146°\ 19'$; $\check{c} : b : \check{a} = 0.9747 : 1.3818 : 1$. Surfaces $i\text{-}i$ and $1\text{-}i$ vertically striated. Cleavage: $i\text{-}\check{\imath}$ highly perfect, $i\text{-}i$ and $1\text{-}i$ indistinct. Also in globular and reniform shapes, having a drusy surface and a columnar structure; sometimes stellate. Also pulverulent and earthy, incrusting.

H.=1·5–2·5; the lowest on $i\text{-}\check{\imath}$. G.=2·948. Lustre of $i\text{-}\check{\imath}$ pearly; other faces adamantine, inclining to vitreous; also dull and earthy. Color crimson and peach-red, sometimes pearl- or greenish-gray; red tints incline to blue, perpendicular to cleavage-face. Streak a little paler than the color; the dry powder deep lavender-blue. Transparent—subtranslucent. Fracture not observable. Thin laminæ flexible in one direction. Sectile.

Schneeberg.

Comp.—$Co_2As_2O_8 + 8aq$ = Arsenic pentoxide 38·40, cobalt oxide 37·56, water 24·04; Co often partly replaced by Fe, Ca, or Ni.

Pyr., etc.—In the closed tube yields water at a gentle heat and turns bluish; at a higher heat gives off arsenous oxide, which condenses in crystals on the cool glass, and the residue has a dark gray or black color. B.B. in the forceps fuses at 2 to a gray bead, and colors the flame light blue (arsenic). B.B. on charcoal gives an arsenical odor, and fuses to a dark gray arsenide, which with borax gives the deep blue color characteristic of cobalt. Soluble in hydrochloric acid, giving a rose-red solution.

Obs.—Occurs at Schneeberg in Saxony; at Saalfeld in Thuringia; Wolfach and Wittichen in Baden; Modum in Norway; at Allemont in Dauphiny; in Cornwall, at the Botallack mine, etc.

Erythrite, when abundant, is valuable for the manufacture of smalt. Named from ἐρυθρός, red.

ROSELITE.*—Triclinic (Schrauf). Usually in complex twin crystals. H.=3·5. G.=3·585 –3·738. Color rose-red. Composition $R_3As_2O_8 + 2aq$ (or 3aq), with R=Ca, Mg, and Co. Analysis, Winkler, As_2O_5 49·96, CoO 12·45, CaO 23·72, MgO 4·67, H_2O 9·69=100·49. Found at Schneeberg, Saxony; the crystals from the Daniel Mine have a lighter color than those of the Rappold Mine, the latter containing less cobalt and more calcium.

WINKLERITE.—Contains As_2O_5, Cu, Co, Fe, Co, Ni, Ca, H_2O, CO_2, etc. Mixture (?). Pria, Spain.

KÖTTIGITE.—Near erythrite, but contains zinc. Schneeberg.

ANNABERGITE (Nickelblüthe, *Germ.*).—$Ni_3As_2O_8 + 8aq$ = Arsenic pentoxide 38·6, nickel oxide 37·2, water 24·2=100. Soft, earthy. Color apple-green. Allemont; Annaberg; Riechelsdorf.

HUREAULITE.—A hydrous iron-manganese phosphate, occurring in cavities in triphylite at Limoges, France.

CHONDRARSENITE.—Yellow grains in barite; probably a manganese arsenate. Paisberg, Sweden.

OXYGEN COMPOUNDS.—PHOSPHATES, ARSENATES, ETC. 373

LIBETHENITE.

Orthorhombic. $I \wedge I = 92° 20'$, $O \wedge 1\text{-}\bar{\imath} = 143° 50'$; $\check{c} : b$ $\check{a} = 0.7311$
1·0416 : 1. Crystals usually octahedral in aspect.
Cleavage: diagonal, $i\text{-}\bar{\imath}$, $i\text{-}\check{\imath}$, very indistinct. Also globular or reniform, and compact.

H.=4. G.=3·6–3·8. Lustre resinous. Color olive-green, generally dark. Streak olive-green. Translucent to subtranslucent. Fracture subconchoidal—uneven. Brittle.

Comp.—$Cu_4P_2O_9 + aq$, or $Cu_3P_2O_8 + H_2CuO_2$ (Ramm.)=Phosphorus pentoxide 29·7, copper oxide 66·5, water 3·8=100.
Pyr., etc.—In the closed tube yields water and turns black. B.B. fuses at 2 and colors the flame emerald-green. On charcoal with soda gives metallic copper, sometimes also an arsenical odor. Fused with metallic lead on charcoal is reduced to metallic copper, with the formation of lead phosphate, which treated in R.F. gives a crystalline polyhedral bead on cooling. With the fluxes reacts for copper. Soluble in nitric acid.
Obs.—Occurs at Libethen, in Hungary; at Rheinbreitenbach and Ehl on the Rhine; at Nischne Tagilsk in the Ural; in Bolivia; Chili.

OLIVENITE.

Orthorhombic. $I \wedge I = 92° 30'$, $O \wedge 1\text{-}\bar{\imath} = 144° 14'$; $\check{c} : \bar{b} : \check{a} = 0.72 :$
1·0446 : 1. Cleavage: I and 1-$\check{\imath}$ in traces. Sometimes acicular. Also globular and reniform, indistinctly fibrous, fibres straight and divergent, rarely promiscuous; also curved lamellar and granular.

H.=3. G.=4·1–4·4. Lustre adamantine—vitreous; of some fibrous varieties pearly. Color various shades of olive-green, passing into leek-, siskin-, pistachio-, and blackish-green; also liver- and wood-brown; sometimes straw-yellow and grayish-white. Streak olive-green—brown. Subtransparent—opaque. Fracture, when observable, conchoidal—uneven. Brittle.

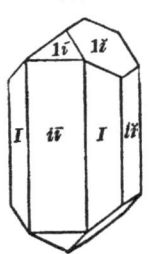

Comp.—$Cu_4As_2O_9 + aq = Cu_3As_2O_8 + H_2CuO_2$ (Ramm.)=Arsenic pentoxide 40·66, copper oxide 56·15, water 3·19=100.
Pyr., etc.—In the closed tube gives water. B.B. fuses at 2, coloring the flame bluish-green, and on cooling the fused mass appears crystalline. B.B. on charcoal fuses with deflagration, gives off arsenical fumes, and yields a metallic arsenide, which, with soda yields a globule of copper. With the fluxes reacts for copper. Soluble in nitric acid.
Obs.—The crystallized varieties occur in many of the Cornwall mines; near Tavistock in Devonshire; also at Alston Moor in Cumberland; at Camsdorf and Saalfeld in Thuringia; the Tyrol; the Banat; Siberia; Chili; and other places.
ADAMITE.—$Zn_3As_2O_8 + H_2ZnO_2$=Arsenic pentoxide 40·2, zinc oxide 56·7, water 3·1=100. Color yellow. Chanarcillo, Chili; Cap Garonne.
TAGILITE —$Cu_4P_2O_9 + 3aq$ ($=Cu_3P_2O_8 + H_2CuO_2 + 2aq$). Color emerald-green. Nischne-Tagilsk. ISOCLASITE. $Ca_4P_2O_9 + 5aq$ ($=Ca_3P_2O_8 + H_2CaO_2 + 4aq$). Colorless to snow-white. Joachimsthal.
EUCHROITE.—$Cu_3As_2O_8 + H_2CuO_2 + 6aq$ (Ramm.)=Arsenic pentoxide 34·1, copper oxide 47·2. water 18·7=100. Color emerald-green. Libethen, Hungary.
CHLOROTILE.—$Cu_3As_2O_8 + 6aq$. In capillary crystals. Also fibrous; massive. Color apple-green. In quartz at Schneeberg and Zinnwald; Thuringia; Chili (*Frenzel*).
VESZELYITE (*Schrauf*).—A hydrous copper phosphate; composition $4Cu_3P_2O_8 + 5aq$. Triclinic. Occurs in crystalline crusts on a garnet-rock at Morawicza in the Banat.

LIROCONITE. Linsenerz, *Germ.*

Monoclinic. $I \wedge I = 74° 21'$, DesCl. $C = 88° 33'$. Cleavage lateral, but obtained with difficulty. Rarely granular.

H.=2–2·5. G.=2·88–2·98. Lustre vitreous, inclining to resinous. Color and streak sky-blue—verdigris-green. Fracture imperfectly conchoidal, uneven. Imperfectly sectile.

Comp.—Formula $Cu_3(Al)As_2(P_2)O_8 + H_6(Cu_3,Al)O_6 + 9aq$, with $Cu_3 : Al = 3 : 2$, and $As : P = 1 : 4$. This requires arsenic pentoxide 23·1, phosphorus pentoxide 3·6, copper oxide 35·9, alumina 10·3, water 27·1=100.

Pyr., etc.—In the closed tube gives much water and turns olive-green. B.B. cracks open, but does not decrepitate; fuses less readily than olivenite to a dark gray slag; on charcoal cracks open, deflagrates, and gives reactions like olivenite. Soluble in nitric acid.

Obs.—With various ores of copper, pyrite, and quartz, at Wheal Gorland, Wheal Muttrell, etc., in Cornwall; also in minute crystals at Herrengrund in Hungary; and in Voigtland.

PSEUDOMALACHITE *Phosphochalcite*. — $Cu_6P_2O_{11} + 3aq = Cu_3P_2O_8 + 3H_2CuO_2 = P_2O_5$ 21·1, CuO 70·9, H_2O 8·0=100. Triclinic (Schrauf). G.=4·34. Color emerald-green. Related sub-species: EHLITE (*Prasine*), $Cu_3P_2O_8 + 2H_2CuO_2 + aq$ (Ramm.); DIHYDRITE, $Cu_3P_2O_8 + 2H_2CuO_2$. Ehl, near Linz, on the Rhine; Libethen, Hungary; Nischne Tagilsk; Cornwall.

ERINITE.—$Cu_3As_2O_8 + 2H_2CuO_2$. In mammillated crystalline groups. Color green. Cornwall.

CORNWALLITE.—$Cu_5As_2O_{10} + 3aq$ (=$Cu_3As_2O_8 + 2H_2CuO_2 + aq$). Amorphous. Color green. Cornwall (*Church*).

PSITTACINITE.—Occurs in thin crypto-crystalline coatings, sometimes having a botryoidal structure; also pulverulent. Color siskin-green to olive-green. Formula $2R_3V_2O_8 + 3H_2CuO_2 + 6aq$, with $R=Pb : Cu = 3 : 1$. This requires: Vanadium pentoxide 19·32, lead oxide 53·15, copper oxide 18·95, water 8·58=100. Found at the gold mines in Silver Star District, Montana (Genth. Am. J. Sci., III., xii., 35, 1876).

MOTTRAMITE.—Occurs as a thin crystalline incrustation, which is sometimes velvety, consisting of minute crystals; more generally compact. H.=3. G.=5·894. Color black by reflected light, in thin particles yellowish, translucent (crystals); purplish-brown, opaque, (compact). Formula $(Pb,Cu)_3V_2O_8 + 2H_2(Pb,Cu)O_2$, which requires vanadium pentoxide 18·74, copper oxide 20·39, lead oxide 57·18, water 3·69=100. Related to dihydrite and erinite. Found in Keuper sandstone at Alderley Edge and Mottram St. Andrew's, in Cheshire, England (Roscoe, Proc. Roy. Soc., xxv., III., 1876).

VOLBORTHITE.—$R_4V_2O_9 + aq$, with $R = Ca : Cu = 2 : 3$ (or 3 : 7), Ramm. From the Urals. Kalk-volborthit (*Germ.*), Friedrichsrode, contains calcium.

CLINOCLASITE. Strahlerz, *Germ.*

Monoclinic. $C = 80° 30'$, $I \wedge I$, front, $= 56°$. Cleavage: basal, highly perfect. Also massive, hemispherical, or reniform; structure radiated fibrous.

681

H.=2·5–3. G.=4·19–4·36. Lustre: O pearly; elsewhere vitreous to resinous. Color internally dark verdigris-green; externally blackish-blue green. Streak bluish-green. Subtranslucent. Not very brittle.

Comp.—$Cu_3As_2O_8 + 3H_2CuO_2$ = Arsenic pentoxide 30·2, copper oxide 62·7, water 7·1=100.

Pyr., etc.—Same as for olivenite.

Obs.—Occurs in Cornwall, with other ores of copper, at several mines. Also found in the Erzgebirge.

TYROLITE (Kupferschaum).—A hydrous arsenate of copper ($Cu_4As_2O_{10} + naq$), containing also calcium carbonate (as an impurity?) Libethen, Hungary; Schneeberg, etc.

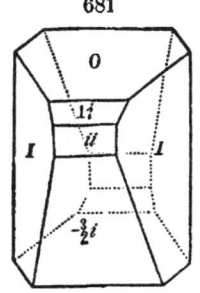

Color pale apple-green.

OXYGEN COMPOUNDS.—PHOSPHATES, ARSENATES, ETC.   375

CHALCOPHYLLITE (Copper mica; Kupferglimmer, *Germ.*).—$Cu_3As_2O_8 + 5H_2CuO_2 + 7H_2O =$ Arsenic pentoxide 21·3, copper oxide 58·7, water 20·0=100. Copper mines of Cornwall, Hungary; Moldawa.

LAZULITE. Blauspath, *Germ.*

Monoclinic. $C = 88° \cdot 15'$, $I \wedge I = 91° 30'$, $O \wedge 1\text{-}\bar{\imath} = 139° 45'$, Prüfer; $\dot{c} : \bar{b} : \dot{a} = 0{\cdot}86904 : 1{\cdot}0260 : 1$. Twins: twinning-plane $i\text{-}i$; also O. Cleavage: lateral, indistinct. Also massive.

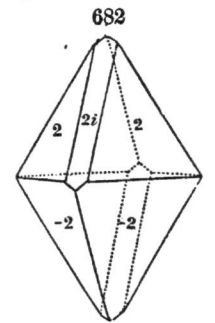

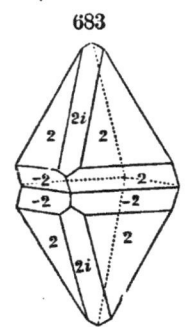

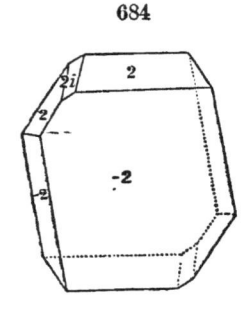

682   683   684

H.=5–6. G.=3·057, Fuchs. Lustre vitreous. Color azure-blue; commonly a fine deep blue viewed along one axis, and a pale greenish-blue along another. Streak white. Subtranslucent—opaque. Fracture uneven. Brittle.

Comp.—$R\ddot{A}lP_2O_9 + aq = \ddot{A}lP_2O_8 + H_2(Mg,Fe)O_2$ (Dana)=Phosphorus pentoxide 46·8, alumina 34·0, magnesia 13·2, water 6·0=100.

Pyr., etc.—In the closed tube whitens and yields water. B.B. with cobalt solution the blue color of the mineral is restored. In the forceps whitens, cracks open, swells up, and without fusion falls to pieces, coloring the flame bluish-green. The green color is made more intense by moistening the assay with sulphuric acid. With the fluxes gives an iron glass; with soda on charcoal an infusible mass. Unacted upon by acids, retaining perfectly its blue color.

Diff.—Characterized by its fine blue color; blue flame B.B.

Obs.—Occurs near Werfen in Salzburg; in Gratz, near Vorau; in Krieglach, in Styria; at Hochthäligrat, at the Gorner glacier, in Switzerland; in Horrsjöberg, Wermland; Westanå, Sweden; also at Tijuco in Minas Geraes, Brazil. Abundant at Crowder's Mt., Lincoln Co., N. C.; and on Graves Mt., Lincoln Co., Ga., 50 m. above Augusta.

SCORODITE.

Orthorhombic. $I \wedge I = 98° 2'$, $O \wedge 1\text{-}\bar{\imath} = 132° 20'$; $\dot{c} : \bar{b} : \breve{a} = 1{\cdot}0977$. 1·1511 : 1, Miller. Cleavage: $i\text{-}\bar{2}$ imperfect, $i\text{-}\bar{\imath}$ and $i\text{-}\check{\imath}$ in traces.

685

H.=3·5–4. G.=3·1–3·3. Lustre vitreous—subadamantine and subresinous. Color pale leek-green or liver-brown. Streak white. Subtransparent—translucent. Fracture uneven.

Comp.—$FeAs_2O_8 + 4aq =$ Arsenic pentoxide 49·8, iron sesquioxide 34·6, water 15·6=100.

Pyr., etc.—In the closed tube yields neutral water and turns yellow. B.B. fuses easily, coloring the flame blue. B.B. on charcoal gives arsenical fumes, and with soda a black magnetic scoria. With the fluxes reacts for iron. Soluble in hydrochloric acid.

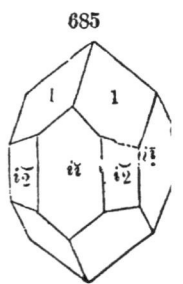

Obs.—Found at Schwarzenberg in Saxony; at Nertschinsk, Siberia; Dernbach in Nassau; in the Cornish mines; at the Minas Geraes, in Brazil; in Popayan; at the gold mines of Victoria in Australia. Occurs in minute crystals and druses, near Edenville, N. Y.; in Cabarras Co., N. C.

WAVELLITE.

Orthorhombic. $I \wedge I = 126°\ 25',\ O \wedge 1\text{-}\bar{i} = 143°\ 23'$; $\check{c} : \bar{b} : \check{a} = 0\cdot 7431 : 1\cdot 4943 : 1$. Cleavage: I rather perfect; also brachydiagonal. Usually in hemispherical or globular concretions, having a radiated structure.

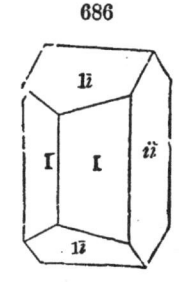

686

H.$=3\cdot 25$–4. G.$=2\cdot 316$–$2\cdot 337$. Lustre vitreous, inclining to pearly and resinous. Color white, passing into yellow, green, gray, brown, and black. Streak white. Translucent.

Comp.—$Al_3P_4O_{19},12aq = 2AlP_2O_8 + H_6AlO_6 + 9aq$ = Phosphorus pentoxide $35\cdot 16$, alumina $38\cdot 10$, water $26\cdot 74 = 100$; 1 to 2 p. c. fluorine is often present, replacing the oxygen.

Pyr., etc.—In the closed tube gives off much water, the last portions of which react acid and color Brazil-wood paper yellow (fluorine), and also etch the tube. B B. in the forceps swells up and splits frequently into fine acicular particles, which are infusible, but color the flame pale green; moistened with sulphuric acid the green becomes more intense. Gives a blue with cobalt solution. Some varieties react for iron and manganese with the fluxes. Heated with sulphuric acid gives off fumes of fluohydric acid, which etch glass. Soluble in hydrochloric acid, and also in caustic potash.

Diff.—Distinguished from the zeolites and from gibbsite by its giving a phosphorus reaction; it dissolves in acid *without* gelatinization.

Obs.—Found near Barnstaple, Devonshire; at Clonmel and Cork, Ireland; in the Shiant Isles of Scotland; at Zbirow in Bohemia; Zajecov in Bohemia; at Frankenberg and Langenstriegis, Saxony; Diensberg, near Giessen, Hesse Darmstadt; in a manganese mine in Weinbach, near Weilburg, in Nassau; at Villa Rica, Minas Geraes, Brazil. In the United States, at the slate quarries of York Co., Pa.; at Washington mine, Davidson Co., N. C.; at White Horse Station, Chester Co., Pa.; Magnet Cove, Ark.

ZEPHAROVICHITE.—Near wavellite. Composition $AlP_2O_8 + 6aq$ (or 5aq, Ramm.). Compact. Color greenish to grayish. Occurs in sandstone at Trenic, Bohemia.

CŒRULEOLACTITE.—Crypto-crystalline. Color milk-white to light blue. Composition (Petersen) $Al_3P_4O_{19} + 10aq$. Katzenellnbogen, Nassau. Also Chester Co., Penn. (Genth, who regards the copper, 4 p. c., as belonging to the mineral.)

PHARMACOSIDERITE. Würfelerz, *Germ.*

Isometric; tetrahedral. Crystals modified cubes and tetrahedrons. Cleavage: cubic, imperfect. O sometimes striated parallel to its edge of intersection with plane 1; planes often curved. Rarely granular.

H.$=2\cdot 5$. G.$=2\cdot 9$–3. Lustre adamantine to greasy, not very distinct Color olive-green, passing into yellowish-brown, bordering sometimes upon hyacinth-red and blackish-brown; also passing into grass-green, emerald-green, and honey-yellow. Streak green—brown, yellow, pale. Subtransparent—subtranslucent. Rather sectile. Pyroelectric.

Comp.—$Fe_4As_6O_{27},15aq = 3FeAs_2O_8 + H_6FeO_6 + 12H_2O$ = Arsenic pentoxide $43\cdot 13$, iron sesquioxide $40\cdot 00$, water $16\cdot 87 = 100$.

Pyr., etc.—Same as for scorodite.

Obs.—Formerly obtained at the mines of Wheal Gorland, Wheal Unity, and Carharrack, in Cornwall; now found at Burdle Gill in Cumberland; in minute tetrahedral crystals at Wheal Jane; also in Australia; at St. Leonard in France and at Schneeberg and Schwarzenberg in Saxony.

Named from φάρμακον, *poison* (in allusion to the arsenic present), and σίδηρος, *iron. Würfelerz*, of the Germans, means *cube-ore.*

RHAGITE (*Weisbach*).—Composition $Bi_{10}As_4O_{25}+9aq=2BiAsO_4+3H_3BiO_3=$Arsenic pentoxide 15·6, bismuth oxide 78·9, water 5·5=100. Spherical crystalline aggregates. Color bright green. Schneeberg, Saxony.

PLUMBOGUMMITE.—Composition uncertain. Contains essentially alumina, lead, water, and phosphorus pentoxide. Huelgoet; Cumberland; Mine la Motte, Mo.

CHILDRENITE.*

Orthorhombic. $I \wedge I = 111° 54'$, $O \wedge 1\text{-}\bar{i} = 136° 26'$; $\check{c} : \bar{b} : \check{a} = 0.9512$: 1·4798 : 1. Plane O sometimes wanting, and the form a double six-sided pyramid, made up of the planes 1, 2-$\bar{i}$, with i-$\bar{i}$ small. Cleavage: i-$\bar{i}$, imperfect.

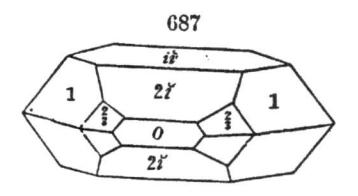

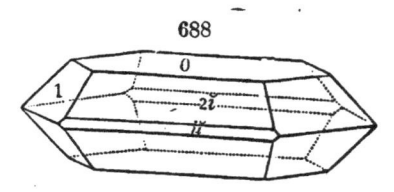

687   688

H.=4·5–5. G.=3·18–3·24. Lustre vitreous, inclining to resinous. Color yellowish-white and pale yellowish-brown, also brownish-black. Streak white, yellowish. Translucent. Fracture uneven.

Comp.—Formula somewhat uncertain. Analysis: Rammelsberg, P_2O_5 28·92, AlO_3 14·44, FeO 30·68, MnO 9·07, MgO 0·14, H_2O 16·98=100·23.

Pyr., etc.—In the closed tube gives off neutral water. B.B. swells up into ramifications, and fuses on the edges to a black mass. coloring the flame pale green. Heated on charcoal turns black and becomes magnetic. With soda gives a reaction for manganese. With borax and salt of phosphorus reacts for iron and manganese. Soluble in hydrochloric acid.

Obs.—Occurs near Tavistock; also at Wheal Crebor, in Devonshire; on slate at Crinnis mine in Cornwall. Hebron, Me. (f. 688.).

TURQUOIS. Callaite. Kallait, Kalait, *Germ.*

Reniform, stalactitic or incrusting. Cleavage none.

H.=6. G.=2·6–2·83. Lustre somewhat waxy, feeble. Color sky-blue, bluish-green to apple-green. Streak white or greenish. Feebly subtranslucent—opaque. Fracture small conchoidal.

Comp.—Hydrous aluminum phosphate, perhaps $Al_2P_2O_{11}+5aq=$Phosphorus pentoxide 32·6, alumina 46·9, water 20·5=100

Pyr., etc.—In the closed tube decrepitates, yields water, and turns brown or black. B.B. in the forceps becomes brown and assumes a glassy appearance, but does not fuse; colors the flame green; moistened with hydrochloric acid the color is at first blue (copper chloride). With the sodium test gives phosphuretted hydrogen. With borax and salt of phosphorus gives beads in O. F. which are yellowish green while hot, and pure green on cooling. With salt of phosphorus and tin on charcoal gives an opaque red bead (copper). Soluble in hydrochloric acid.

Obs.—Occurs in clay slate in a mountainous district in Persia, not far from Nichabour. According to Agaphi, the only naturalist who has visited the locality, turquois occurs only in veins, which traverse the mountain in all directions. An impure variety is found in Silesia, and at Oelsnitz in Saxony. W. P. Blake refers here to a hard yellowish- to bluish-green stone (which he identifies with the *chalchihuitl* of the *Mexicans*) from the mountains Los Cerillas, 20 m. S. E. of Santa Fé. A pale green turquois occurs in the Columbus district, Nevada.

Turquois receives a good polish, and is highly esteemed as a gem. The Persian king is said to retain for his own use all the larger and finely tinted specimens.

PEGANITE.—Composition $Al_2P_2O_{11} + 6aq$ = Phosphorus pentoxide 31·1, alumina 31·1, water 23·7=100. Striegis, Saxony.

DUFRENITE.—Composition $Fe_2P_2O_{11} + 3aq$ ($FeP_2O_{11} + H_6FeO_6$) = Phosphorus pentoxide 27·5, iron sesquioxide 62·0, water 10·5=100. Anglar, Dept. of Haute Vienne; Hirschberg, Westphalia; Allentown, N. J. In deposits of nodules 1 to 6 in. thick, in Rockbridge Co., Va.

ANDREWSITE.—In globular forms, having a radiated structure. H.=4. G.=3·475. Color dark green. Analysis, Flight. P_2O_5 26·09, FeO_3 44·64, AlO_3 0·92, CuO 10·86, FeO 7·11, MnO 0·60, CaO 0·09, SiO_2 0·49, H_2O 8·79=99·59. In a tin lode, West Phenix mine, near Liskeard, Cornwall.

CHALCOSIDERITE.—In bright green crystals (triclinic) on Andrewsite (see above). H.= 4·5. G.=3·108. Analysis, Flight, P_2O_5 29·93, As_2O_5 0·61, FeO_3 42·81, AlO_3 4·45. CuO 8·14, H_2O 15·00, UO_3 tr.=100·94. Also as a coating on dufrenite. Cornwall. Sayn, Westphalia.

HENWOODITE.—In globular forms, with a radiated structure. H.=4-4·5. G.=2·67. Color turquois-blue to bluish-green. B.B. Infusible. Analysis, P_2O_5 48·94, AlO_3 18·24, FeO_3 2·74, CuO 7·10, CaO 0·54, H_2O 17·10, SiO_2 1·37, loss 3·97=100. Occurs on limonite at the West Phenix mine, Cornwall (*Collins*, Min. Mag., 1, p. 11).

CACOXENITE.—Supposed to be an iron wavellite. Composition $Fe_2P_2O_{11} + 12aq$. In radiated tufts. Color yellow. Hrbeck mine, Bohemia.

ARSENIOSIDERITE.—Analysis by Church, As_2O_5 39·86, FeO_3 35·75, CaO 15·53, MgO 0·18, K_2O 0·47, H_2O 7·87=99·66. Formula (Ramm.) $2Ca_3As_2O_8 + FeAs_2O_8 + 3H_6FeO_6$. Romanéche.

ATELESTITE.—Essentially a bismuth arsenate. In minute yellow crystals at Schneeberg.

TORBERNITE. Chalcolite. Kupfer-Uranit, *Germ.*

Tetragonal. $O \wedge 1\text{-}\bar{i} = 134° 8'$; $\dot{c} = 1\cdot03069$. Forms square tables, with often replaced edges; rarely suboctahedral. Cleavage: basal highly perfect, micaceous. Unknown massive or earthy.

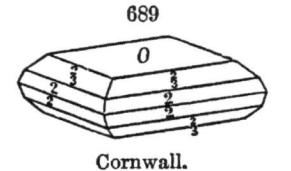

689

Cornwall.

H.=2-2·5. G.=3·4-3·6. Lustre of O pearly, of other faces subadamantine. Color emerald- and grass-green, and sometimes leek-, apple-, and siskin-green. Streak somewhat paler than the color. Transparent—subtranslucent. Fracture not observable. Sectile. Laminæ brittle and not flexible. Optically uniaxial; double refraction negative.

Comp.—Q. ratio for R : U : P : O=1 : 6 : 5 : 8; formula $CuU_2P_2O_{12} + 8aq = 2(UO_2)_3P_2O_8 + Cu_3P_2O_8 + 24aq$. The formula requires: Phosphorus pentoxide 15·1, uranium trioxide 61·2, copper oxide 8·4, water 15·3=100.

Pyr., etc.—In the closed tube yields water. In the forceps fuses at 2·5 to a blackish mass, and colors the flame green. With salt of phosphorus gives a green bead, which with tin on charcoal becomes on cooling opaque red (copper). With soda on charcoal gives a globule of copper. Affords a phosphide with the sodium test. Soluble in nitric acid.

Obs.—Gunnis Lake, Tincroft and Wheal Buller, near Redruth, and elsewhere in Cornwall. Found also at Johanngeorgenstadt, Eibenstock, and Schneeberg, in Saxony; in Bohemia, at Joachimsthal and Zinnwald; in Belgium, at Vielsalm.

Both this species and the autunite have gone under the common name of *uranite;* the former also as *Copper-uranite*, the latter *Lime-uranite*.

AUTUNITE.* Uranit; Kalk-Uranglimmer, Kalk-Uranit, *Germ.*

Orthorhombic; but form very nearly square, and crystals resembling closely those of torbernite. Cleavage: basal eminent, as in torbernite.
H.=2–2·5. G.=3·05–3·19. Lustre of O pearly; elsewhere subadamantine. Color citron- to sulphur-yellow. Streak yellowish. Translucent. Optically biaxial, DesCl.

Comp.—Q. ratio for R : U : P : H=1 : 6 : 5 : 10. Formula $CaU_2P_2O_{12}+10aq$, which may be written $2(UO_2)_3P_2O_8+Ca_3P_2O_8+30aq$. The formula requires: Phosphorus pentoxide 14·9, uranium trioxide (UO_3) 60·4, lime 5·9, water 18·8=100.

Pyr., etc.—Same as for torbernite, but no reaction for copper.

Obs.—Occurs at Johanngeorgenstadt; at Lake Onega, Wolf Island, Russia; near Limoges; near Autun; formerly at South Basset, Wheal Edwards, and near St. Day, England. Occurs sparingly at Middletown, Ct.; also in minute crystals at Chesterfield, Mass.; at Acworth, N. H.

TRÖGERITE.—Composition $U_3As_2O_{14}+12aq=(UO_2)_3As_2O_8+12aq$. This requires: Arsenic pentoxide 17·6, uranium trioxide 65·9, water 16·5=100. Monoclinic. In thin tabular crystals of a lemon-yellow color. Schneeberg, Saxony.

WALPURGITE.—Composition $Bi_{10}U_3As_4O_{34}+12aq=(UO_2)_3As_2O_8+2BiAsO_4+8H_3BiO_3$. This requires: Arsenic pentoxide 11·9, bismuth oxide 60·0, uranium trioxide 22·4, water 5·7=100. Monoclinic. In thin scaly crystals. Color wax-yellow. Schneeberg, Saxony.

URANOSPINITE.—An arsenic autunite. Composition $CaU_2As_2O_{12}+8aq=2(UO_2)_3As_2O_8+Ca_3As_2O_8+24aq$=Arsenic pentoxide 22·9, uranium trioxide 57·2, lime 5·6, water 14·3=100. Color green. Schneeberg, Saxony. URANOSPHÆRITE. Color yellow. Analysis, Winkler: U O_3 50·88, Bi_2O_3 44·34, H_2O 4·75. Schneeberg.

ZEUNERITE.—According to Winkler, an arsenic chalcolite, with which it is isomorphous. Composition $CuU_2As_2O_{12}+8aq=2(UO_2)_3As_2O_8+Cu_3As_2O_8+24aq$=Arsenic pentoxide 22·3, uranium trioxide 56·0, copper oxide 7·7, water 14·0=100. Color bright green. Schneeberg, Zinnwald, Saxony; Cornwall.

PITTICITE.—Iron-sinter. Composition uncertain. contains As_2O_5, FeO_3, SO_3, H_2O. DIADOCHITE is similar, but contains P_2O_5 instead of As_2O_5.

HYDROUS ANTIMONATES.

BINDHEIMITE (Bleinière).—Amorphous, reniform, or spheroidal; also earthy or incrusting. H.=4. G.=4·60–4·76. Color white, gray, brownish, yellowish. Composition uncertain; analysis by Hermann: Sb_2O_5 31·71, PbO 61·83, H_2O 6·46=100. Results from the decomposition of other antimonial ores. From Nertschinsk in Siberia; Horhausen; near Endelliou in Cornwall, with jamesonite, from which it is derived.

NITRATES.

The nitrates are all soluble, and hence are rarely met with in nature. They include:

NITRE, potassium nitrate (KNO_3). Found generally in crusts on the surface of the soil, on walls, rocks, etc. Also found in numerous caves in the Mississippi Valley.

SODA NITRE, sodium nitrate ($NaNO_3$). Tarapaca, Chili.

NITROCALCITE, calcium nitrate (CaN_2O_6). Occurs in silky efflorescences in limestone caverns.

NITROMAGNESITE, magnesium nitrate (MgN_2O_6). From limestone caves. NITROGLAUBERITE, nitro-sulphate of sodium. Desert of Atacama, Chili.

4. BORATES.

SASSOLITE.

Triclinic. $I \wedge I' = 118° 30'$, $O \wedge I = 95° 3'$, $O \wedge I' = 80° 33'$, B. & M. Twins: composition-face O. Cleavage: basal very perfect. Usually in small scales, apparently six-sided tables, and also in stalactitic forms, composed of small scales.

H.$=$1.   G.$=$1·48.   Lustre pearly.   Color white, except when tinged yellow by sulphur; sometimes gray.   Feel smooth and unctuous.   Taste acidulous, and slightly saline and bitter.

Comp.—$H_6B_2O_6=$Boron trioxide (B_2O_3) 56·46, water 43·54$=$100. The native stalactitic salt contains, mechanically mixed, various impurities, as sulphate of magnesium and iron, sulphate of calcium, silica, etc.

Pyr., etc.—In the closed tube gives water. B.B. on platinum wire fuses to a clear glass and tinges the flame yellowish-green. Soluble in water and alcohol.

Obs.—First detected in nature by Höfer in the waters of the Tuscan lagoons of Monte Rotondo and Castelnuovo, and afterward in the solid state at Sasso by Mascagni. The hot vapors of the lagoons consist largely of it. Exists also in other natural waters, as at Wiesbaden; Aachen; Krankenheil near Fölz; Clear Lake in Lake Co., California; and it has been detected in the waters of the ocean. Occurs also abundantly in the crater of Vulcano, one of the Lipari islands, forming a layer on sulphur and about the fumaroles, where it was discovered by Dr. Holland in 1813.

SUSSEXITE (*Brush*).

In fibrous seams or veins.

H.$=$3.   G.$=$3·42.   Lustre silky to pearly.   Color white, with a tinge of pink or yellow.   Translucent.

Comp.—$R_2B_2O_5+$aq, with R$=$Mn : Mg$=$4 : 3$=$Boron trioxide 34·3, manganese protoxide 39·9, magnesia 16·9, water 8·9$=$100.

Pyr., etc.—In the closed tube darkens in color and yields neutral water. If turmeric paper is moistened with this water and then with dilute hydrochloric acid it assumes a red color (boron). Fuses in the flame of a candle, and B.B. in O.F. yields a black crystalline mass coloring the flame intensely yellowish-green. Reacts for manganese with the fluxes. Soluble in hydrochloric acid.

Obs.—Found on Mine Hill, Franklin Furnace, Sussex Co., N. J.; associated with franklinite, zincite, willemite, and other manganese and zinc minerals.

SZAIBELYITE.—A hydrous magnesium borate, $Mg_5B_4O_{11}+$3aq (or $\frac{3}{2}$aq). Occurs in acicular crystals. Color white. Hungary.

LUDWIGITE (*Tschermak*).—Finely fibrous masses. H.$=$5. G.$=$3·907–4·016. Color blackish-green to black. Composition $R_4FeB_2O_{10}$, with R$=$Fe : Mg$=$1 : 5, or 1 : 3. For the latter the formula requires: Boron trioxide 16·6, iron sesquioxide 37·9, iron protoxide 17·1, magnesia 28·4. Occurs in a crystalline limestone with magnetite at Morawicza in the Banat, also altered to limonite.

BORACITE.*

Isometric; tetrahedral. Cleavage: octahedral, in traces. Cubic faces sometimes striated parallel to alternate pairs of edges, as in pyrite.

H.=7, in crystals; 4·5, massive. G.=2·974, Haidinger. Lustre vitreous, inclining to adamantine. Color white, inclining to gray, yellow, and green. Streak white. Subtransparent—translucent. Fracture conchoidal, uneven. Pyroelectric, and polar along the four octahedral axes.

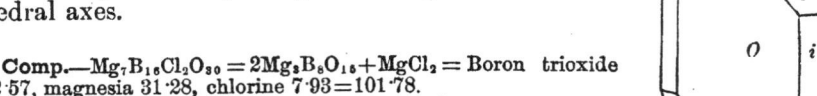

690

Comp.—$Mg_7B_{16}Cl_2O_{30} = 2Mg_3B_8O_{15} + MgCl_2 =$ Boron trioxide 62·57, magnesia 31·28, chlorine 7·93=101·78.

Pyr., etc.—The massive variety gives water in the closed tube. B.B. both varieties fuse at 2 with intumescence to a white crystalline pearl, coloring the flame green; heated after moistening with cobalt solution assumes a deep pink color. Mixed with copper oxide and heated on charcoal colors the flame deep azure-blue (copper chloride). Soluble in hydrochloric acid. Alters very slowly on exposure, owing to the magnesium chloride present, which takes up water.

Obs.—Observed in beds of anhydrite, gypsum, or salt. In crystals at Kalkberg and Schildstein in Lüneberg, Hanover; at Segeberg, near Kiel, in Holstein; at Luneville, La Meurthe, France; massive and crystallized at Stassfurt, Prussia.

BORAX. Tinkal of *India*.

Monoclinic. $C = 73° 25',\ I \wedge I = 87°,\ O \wedge 2\text{-}i = 132° 49';\ \check{c}:b:d =$ 0·4906 : 0·9095 : 1. Cleavage: $i\text{-}i$ perfect; I less so; $i\text{-}i$ in traces.

H.=2–2·5. G.=1·716. Lustre vitreous—resinous; sometimes earthy. Color white; sometimes grayish, bluish, or greenish. Streak white. Translucent—opaque. Fracture conchoidal. Rather brittle. Taste sweetish-alkaline, feeble.

Comp.—$Na_2B_4O_7 + 10aq = 2(NaBO_2 + HBO_2) + 9aq =$ Boron trioxide 36·6, soda 16·2, water 47·2.

Pyr., etc.—B.B. puffs up, and afterwards fuses to a transparent globule, called the glass of borax. Soluble in water, yielding a faintly alkaline solution. Boiling water dissolves double its weight of this salt.

Obs.—Borax was originally brought from a salt lake in Thibet. It is announced by Dr. J. A. Veatch as existing in the waters of the sea along the California coast, and in those of many of the mineral springs of California. Occurs in the mud of Borax Lake, near Clear Lake, Cal. Also found in Peru; at Halberstadt in Transylvania; in Ceylon. It occurs in solution in the mineral springs of Chambly, St. Ours, etc., Canada East. The waters of Borax Lake, California, contain, according to G. E. Moore, 535·08 grains of crystallized borax to the gallon.

ULEXITE. Boronatrocalcite. Natronborocalcite.

In rounded masses, loose in texture, consisting of fine fibres, which are acicular or capillary crystals.

H.=1. G.=1·65, N. Scotia, How. Lustre silky within. Color white. Tasteless.

Comp.—$NaCaB_5O_9 + 5aq =$ Boron trioxide 49·7, lime 15·9, soda 8·8, water 25·6=100.

Pyr., etc.—Yields water. B.B. fuses at 1 with intumescence to a clear blebby glass, color ing the flame deep yellow. Moistened with sulphuric acid the color of the flame is momentarily changed to deep green. Not soluble in cold water, and but little so in hot; the solution alkaline in its reactions.

Obs.—Occurs in the dry plains of Iquique, Southern Peru; in the province of Tarapaca (where it is called *tiza*), in whitish rounded masses, from a hazelnut to a potato in size, which consist of interwoven fibres of the ulexite, with pickeringite, glauberite, halite, gypsum, and other impurities; on the West Africa coast; in Nova Scotia, at Windsor, Brookville, and Newport (H. How), filling narrow cavities, or constituting distinct nodules or mammillated masses imbedded in white gypsum, and associated at Windsor with glauber salt, the lustre internally silky and the color very white; in Nevada, in the salt marsh of the Columbus Mining District, forming layers 2–5 in. thick alternating with layers of salt, and in balls 3–4 in. through in the salt.

BECHILITE. (Borocalcite).—An incrustation at the Tuscany lagoons. Composition CaB_4O_7 + 4aq. Also similar from South America. LARDERELLITE, LAGONITE, rare borates from the Tuscan lagoons.

PRICEITE (*Silliman*).—Compact, chalky. Color milk-white. Composition $Ca_3B_8O_{15} + 6aq$. This requires: Boron trioxide 49·8, lime 29·9, water 20·3=100. Occurs in layers between a bed of slate above and one of steatite below. Near Chetko, Curry Co., Oregon.

HOWLITE, *Silicoborocalcite*.—A hydrous calcium borate (like bechilite), with one-sixth of a silicate analogous to danburite. Near Brookville, and elsewhere in Hants Co., Nova Scotia, in nodules imbedded in anhydrite or gypsum; these nodules sometimes made up of pearly crystalline scales. WINKWORTHITE. In imbedded crystalline nodules from Winkworth, N.S. In composition between selenite and howlite; a mixture (?).

CRYPTOMORPHITE.—Near ulexite in composition. In microscopic rhombic tables. Nova Scotia.

LÜNEBURGITE.—A phospho-borate of magnesium. Flattened masses in gypsiferous marl at Lüneburg.

WARWICKITE.

Monoclinic. $I \wedge I = 91°\ 20'$, DesCl. Usual in rhombic prisms with obtuse edges truncated, and the acute bevelled, summits generally rounded; surfaces of larger crystals not polished. Cleavage: macrodiagonal perfect, affording a surface with vertical striæ and traces of oblique cross cleavage.

H.=3–4. G.=3·19–3·43. Lustre of cleavage surface submetallic-pearly to subvitreous; often nearly dull. Color dark hair-brown to dull black, sometimes a copper-red tinge on cleavage surface. Streak bluish-black. Fracture uneven. Brittle.

Comp.—Essentially a borotitanate of magnesium and iron. Analysis, Smith, B_2O_3 27·80, TiO_2 23·82, FeO_3 7·02, MgO 36·80, SiO_2 1·00, AlO_3 2·21=98·65.

Pyr., etc.—Yields water. B.B. infusible, but becomes lighter in water; moistened with sulphuric acid gives a pale green color to the flame. With salt of phosphorus in O.F. a clear bead, yellow while hot and colorless on cooling; in R.F. on charcoal with tin a violet color (titanium). With soda a slight manganese reaction. Decomposed by sulphuric acid; the product, treated with alcohol and ignited, gives a green flame, and boiled with hydrochloric acid and metallic tin gives on evaporation a violet-colored solution.

Obs.—Occurs in granular limestone 2½ m. S. W. of Edenville, N. Y., with spinel, chondrodite, serpentine, etc. Crystals usually small and slender; sometimes over 2 in. long and ⅜ in. broad.

5. TUNGSTATES, MOLYBDATES, CHROMATES.

WOLFRAMITE.

Monoclinic. $C = 89°\ 22'$, $I \wedge I = 100°\ 37'$, $i\text{-}i \wedge -\tfrac{1}{2}\text{-}i = 118°\ 6'$, $i\text{-}i \wedge +\tfrac{1}{2}\text{-}i = 117°\ 6'$, $1\text{-}\bar{\imath} \wedge 1\text{-}\bar{\imath} = 98°\ 6'$, DesCloizeaux. Cleavage: $i\text{-}\bar{\imath}$ perfect, $i\text{-}i$ imperfect. Twins: planes of twinning $i\text{-}i$ (f. 692), $\tfrac{2}{3}\text{-}i$, and rarely $\tfrac{1}{8}\text{-}\bar{\imath}$. Also irregular lamellar; coarse divergent columnar; massive granular, the particles strongly coherent.

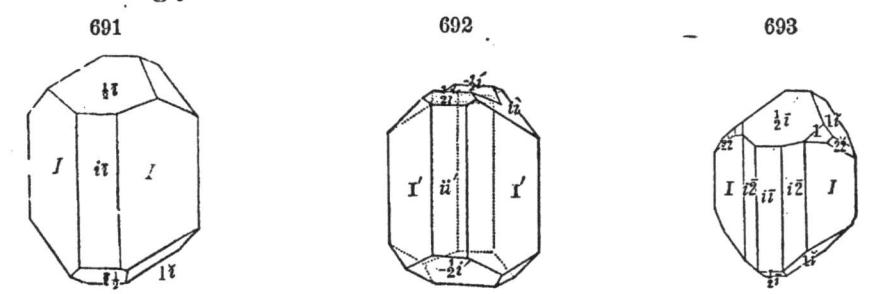

691 692 693

H.=5–5·5. G.=7·1–7·55. Lustre submetallic. Color dark grayish or brownish-black. Streak dark reddish-brown to black. Opaque. Sometimes weak magnetic.

Var.—The most important varieties depend on the proportions of the iron and manganese. Those rich in manganese have G.=7·19–7·54, but generally below 7·25, and the streak is mostly black. Those rich in iron have G.=7·2–7·54, and a dark reddish-brown streak, and they are sometimes feebly attractable by the magnet.

Comp.—$(Fe,Mn)WO_4$, Fe : Mn=2 : 3, mostly; also 4 : 1 and 2 : 1, 3 : 1, 5 : 1, etc. The ratio 2 : 3 corresponds to : Tungsten trioxide 76·47, iron protoxide 9·49, manganese protoxide 14·04=100.

Pyr., etc.—B.B. fuses easily (F.=2·5–3) to a globule, which has a crystalline surface and is magnetic. With salt of phosphorus gives a clear reddish-yellow glass while hot, which is paler on cooling; in R.F. becomes dark red; on charcoal with tin, if not too saturated, the bead assumes on cooling a green color, which continued treatment in R. F. changes to reddish-yellow. With soda and nitre on platinum foil fuses to a bluish-green manganate. Decomposed by aqua regia with separation of tungsten trioxide as a yellow powder, which when treated B.B. reacts as under tungstite (p. 284). Wolfram is sufficiently decomposed by concentrated sulphuric acid, or even hydrochloric acid, to give a colorless solution, which, treated with metallic zinc, becomes intensely blue, but soon bleaches on dilution.

Diff.—Characterized by its high specific gravity and pyrognostics.

Obs.—Wolfram is often associated with tin ores; also in quartz, with native bismuth, scheelite, pyrite, galenite, blende, etc.; and in trachyte, as at Felsöbanya, in Hungary. It occurs at Schlackenwald; Schneeberg; Freiberg; Ehrenfriedersdorf; Zinnwald, and Nertschinsk; at Chanteloup, near Limoges, and at Meymac, Corrèze, in France; near Redruth and elsewhere in Cornwall; in Cumberland. Also in S. America, at Oruro in Bolivia.

In the U. States, occurs at Lane's mine, Monroe, Conn.; at Trumbull, Conn.; on Camdage farm, near Blue Hill Bay, Me.; at the Flowe mine, Mecklenburg Co., N. C.; in Missouri, near Mine la Motte, and in St. Francis Co.; at Mammoth mining district, Nevada.

HÜBNERITE.*—A manganese wolframite, $MnWO_4$ = Tungsten trioxide 76·9, manganese protoxide 23·1 = 100. Mammoth dist., Nevada.

MEGABASITE.—A manganese tungstate, with a little iron. Schlackenwald.

SCHEELITE.

Tetragonal; hemihedral. $O \wedge 1\text{-}i = 123° \ 3'$; $\breve{c} = 1\cdot5369$. Cleavage: 1 most distinct, 1-i interrupted, O traces. Twins: twinning-plane I; also i-i. Crystals usually octahedral in form. Also reniform with columnar structure; and massive granular.

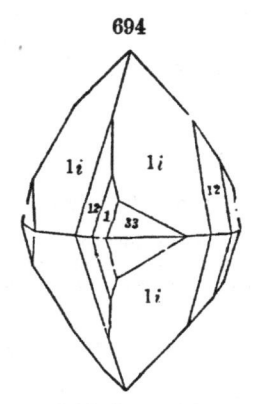

H.=4·5–5. G.=5·9–6·076. Lustre vitreous, inclining to adamantine. Color white, yellowish-white, pale yellow, brownish, greenish, reddish; sometimes almost orange-yellow. Streak white. Transparent —translucent. Fracture uneven. Brittle.

694

Schlackenwald.

Comp.—CaWO$_4$=Tungsten trioxide 80·6, lime 19·4=100. A variety from Coquimbo, Chili, contained 6·2 p. c. vanadium pentoxide; another from Traversella contained didymium.

Pyr., etc.—B.B. in the forceps fuses at 5 to a semi-transparent glass. Soluble with borax to a transparent glass, which afterward becomes opaque and crystalline. With salt of phosphorus forms a glass, colorless in outer flame, in inner green when hot and fine blue cold; varieties containing iron require to be treated on charcoal with tin before the blue color appears. In hydrochloric or nitric acid decomposed, leaving a yellow powder soluble in ammonia.

Diff.—Remarkable among non-metallic minerals for its high specific gravity.

Obs.—Usually associated with crystalline rocks, and commonly found in connection with tin ore, topaz, fluorite, apatite, molybdenite, wolframite, in quartz. Occurs at Schlackenwald and Zinnwald in Bohemia; in the Riesengebirge; at Caldbeck Fell, near Keswick; Neudorf in the Harz; Ehrenfriedersdorf; Pösing in Hungary; Traversella in Piedmont, etc. Llamuco, near Chuapa in Chili. In the U. S., at Lane's mine, Monroe, and Huntington, Conn.; at Chesterfield, Mass.; in the Mammoth mining district, Nevada; at Bangle mine, in Cabarras Co., N. C.; and Flowe mine, Mecklenburg Co.

CUPROSCHEELITE.—A scheelite containing about 6 p. c. copper oxide. Color bright green. La Paz, Lower California. Llamuco, near Santiago, Chili.

CUPROTUNGSTITE.—A copper tungstate, Cu$_2$WO$_3$+aq. Amorphous. Color yellowish-green. With cuproscheelite at the copper mines of Llamuco, Chili.

STOLZITE.—PbWO$_4$=Tungsten trioxide 51, lead oxide 49=100. Tetragonal. Zinnwald; Bleiberg; Coquimbo, Chili.

WULFENITE.* Gelbbleierz, *Germ.*

Tetragonal. Sometimes hemihedral. $O \wedge 1\text{-}i = 122° \ 26'$; $\breve{c} = 1\cdot574$.

695   696   697

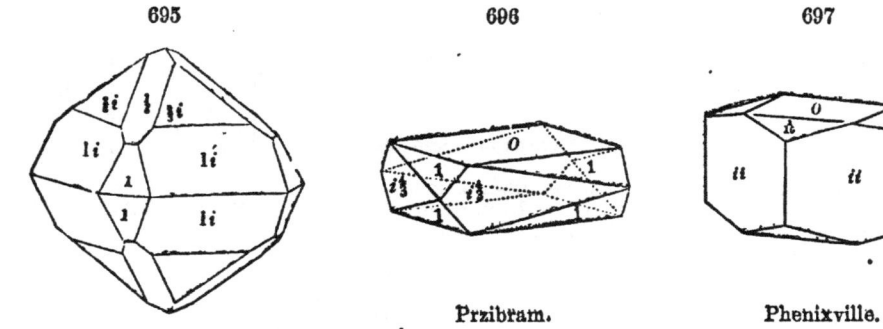

Przibram. Phenixville.

In modified square tables and sometimes very thin octahedrons. Cleavage

1 very smooth; O and $\frac{1}{3}$ much less distinct. Also granularly massive, coarse or fine, firmly cohesive. Often hemihedral in the octagonal prisms, producing thus tables like f. 696, and octahedral forms having the prismatic planes similarly oblique.

H.=2·75–3. G.=6·03–7·01. Lustre resinous or adamantine. Color wax-yellow, passing into orange-yellow; also siskin- and olive-green, yellowish-gray, grayish-white, brown; also orange to bright red. Streak white. Subtransparent—subtranslucent. Fracture subconchoidal. Brittle.

Var.—1. *Ordinary.* Color yellow. 2. *Vanadiferous.* Color orange to bright red, a variety occurring at Phenixville, Pa.

Comp.—$PbMoO_4$ = Molybdenum trioxide 38·5, lead oxide 61·5 = 100. Some varieties contain chromium.

Pyr., etc.—B.B. decrepitates and fuses below 2; with borax in O.F. gives a colorless glass, in R.F. it becomes opaque black or dirty green with black flocks. With salt of phosphorus in O.F. gives a yellowish-green glass, which in R.F. becomes dark green. With soda on charcoal yields metallic lead. Decomposed on evaporation with hydrochloric acid, with the formation of lead chloride and molybdic oxide; on moistening the residue with water and adding metallic zinc, it gives an intense blue color, which does not fade on dilution of the liquid.

Obs.—This species occurs in veins with other ores of lead. Found at Bleiberg, etc., in Carinthia; at Retzbanya; at Przibram; Schneeberg and Johanngeorgenstadt; at Moldava; in the Kirghis Steppes in Russia; at Badenweiler in Baden; in the gold sands of Rio Chico in Antioquia, Columbia, S. A.; Wheatley's mine, near Phenixville, Pa.; at the Comstock lode in Nevada. In fine specimens from the Empire mine, Lucin District, Box Elder County, Utah; at Empire mine, Inyo Co., Cal.; in the Weaver dist., Arizona.

EOSITE (*Schrauf*).—In minute tetragonal octahedrons. Color deep-red. Probably a vanadio-molybdate of lead. Leadhills, Scotland.

ACHREMATITE.—An arsenio-molybdate of lead. Analysis, As_2O_5 18·25, MoO_3 5·01, Cl 2·15, Pb 6·28, PbO 68·31=100·00. Compact; structure indistinctly crystalline. H.=3–4. G.=5·965, 6·178 (powder). Color liver-brown, translucent; in minute grains transparent and color yellow. Brittle. Guanaceré, State of Chihuahua, Mexico. (*Mallet*, J. Ch. Soc., xiii., 1141, New Series.)

CROCOITE. Crocoisite. Rothbleierz, *Germ.*

Monoclinic. $C = 77° 27'$, $I \wedge I = 93° 42'$, $O \wedge 1\text{-}i = 138° 10'$; $\check{c} : \check{b} : \check{a} = 0.95507 : 1.0414 : 1$, Dauber. Cleavage: I tolerably distinct; O and $i\text{-}i$ less so. Surface I streaked longitudinally; the faces mostly smooth and shining. Also imperfectly columnar and granular.

H.=2·5–3. G.=5·9–6·1. Lustre adamantine—vitreous. Color various shades of bright hyacinth-red. Streak orange-yellow. Translucent. Sectile.

Comp.—$PbCrO_4$=Lead oxide 69·0, chromium trioxide 31·0 = 100.

Pyr., etc.—In the closed tube decrepitates, blackens, but recovers its original color on cooling. B.B. fuses at 1·5, and on charcoal is reduced to metallic lead with deflagration, leaving a residue of chromic oxide, and giving a lead coating. With salt of phosphorus gives an emerald-green bead in both flames. Fused with potassium bisulphate in the platinum spoon forms a dark violet mass, which on solidifying becomes reddish, and when cold greenish-white, thus differing from vanadinite, which on similar treatment gives a yellow mass (Plattner).

Obs.—First found at Beresof in Siberia; at Mursinsk and near Nischne Tagilsk in the Ural; in Brazil; at Retzbanya; Moldawa; on Luzon, one of the Philippines.

PHŒNICOCHROITE. Melanochroite.

Orthorhombic (?). Crystals usually tabular, and reticularly interwoven. Cleavage in one direction perfect. Also massive.

H.=3-3·5. G.=5·75. Lustre resinous or adamantine, glimmering. Color between cochineal- and hyacinth-red; becomes lemon-yellow on exposure. Streak brick-red. Subtranslucent—opaque.

Comp.—$Pb_3Cr_2O_9 = 2PbCrO_4 + PbO$ = Chromium trioxide 23·0, lead oxide 77·0=100.
Pyr., etc.—B.B. on charcoal fuses readily to a dark mass, which is crystalline when cold. In R.F. on charcoal gives a coating of lead oxide, with globules of lead and a residue of chromic oxide. Gives the reaction of chrome with fluxes.
Obs.—Occurs in limestone at Beresof in the Ural, with crocoite, vauquelinite, pyromorphite, and galenite.

VAUQUELINITE.

Monoclinic. Crystals usually minute, irregularly aggregated. Also reniform or botryoidal, and granular; amorphous.

H.=2·5-3. G.=5·5-5·78. Lustre adamantine to resinous, often faint. Color green to brown, apple-green, siskin-green, olive-green, ochre-brown, liver-brown; sometimes pearly black. Streak greenish or brownish. Faintly translucent—opaque. Fracture uneven. Rather brittle.

Comp.—$Pb_2CuCr_2O_9 = 2RCrO_4 + RO$. $R=Pb:Cu=2:1$. The formula requires: Chromium trioxide 27·6, lead oxide 61·5, copper oxide 10·9=100.
Pyr., etc.—B.B. on charcoal slightly intumesces and fuses to a gray submetallic globule, yielding at the same time small globules of metal. With borax or salt of phosphorus affords a green transparent glass in the outer flame, which in the inner after cooling is red to black, according to the amount of mineral in the assay; the red color is more distinct with tin. Partly soluble in nitric acid.
Obs.—Occurs with crocoite at Beresof in Siberia, generally in mammillated or amorphous masses, or thin crusts; also at Pont Gibaud in the Puy de Dome; and with the crocoite of Brazil. In the U. States it has been found at the lead mine near Sing Sing, in green and brownish-green mammillary concretions, and also nearly pulverulent; and at the Pequa lead mine in Lancaster Co., Pa., in minute crystals and radiated aggregations on quartz and galenite, of a siskin- to apple-green color, with cerussite.
LAXMANNITE (*phosphochromite*).—Near vauquelinite, but held to be a phospho-chromate. Beresof.

6. SULPHATES.

Anhydrous Sulphates.

Barite Group.

BARITE. Barytes. Heavy Spar. Schwerspath, *Germ.*

Orthorhombic. $I \wedge I = 101° \ 40'$, $O \wedge 1\text{-}\bar{\imath} = 121° \ 50'$; $\bar{c} : \bar{b} : \bar{a} = 1·6107$

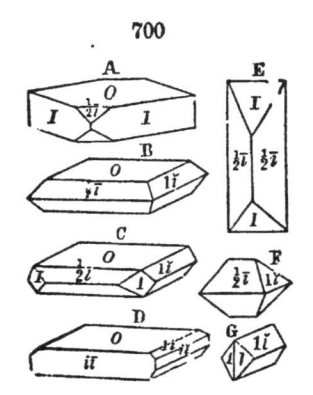

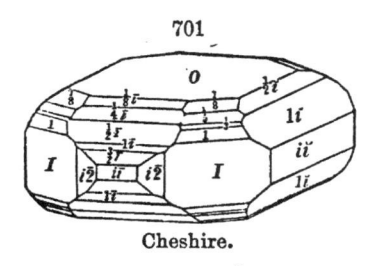

Cheshire.

: 1·2276 : 1. $O \wedge 1 = 115° \ 42'$; $\frac{1}{2}\text{-}\bar{\imath} \wedge \frac{1}{2}\text{-}\bar{\imath}$, top, = 102° 17'; $1\text{-}\check{\imath} \wedge 1\text{-}\check{\imath}$, top, = 74° 36. Crystals usually tabular, as in figures; sometimes prismatic in the direction of the different axes. Cleavage: basal rather perfect; I somewhat less so; $i\text{-}\check{\imath}$ imperfect. Also in globular forms, fibrous or lamellar, crested; coarsely laminated, laminæ convergent and often curved; also granular; colors sometimes banded, as in stalagmite. H.=2·5-3·5. G.=4·3-4·72. Lustre vitreous, inclining to resinous; sometimes pearly. Streak white. Color white; also inclining to yellow, gray, blue, red, or brown, dark brown. Transparent to translucent—opaque. Sometimes fetid, when rubbed. Optic-axial plane brachydiagonal.

Comp.—$BaSO_4$=Sulphur trioxide 34·3, baryta 65·7=100. Strontium and sometimes calcium replace part of the barium; also silica, clay, bituminous or carbonaceous substances are often present as impurities.

Pyr., etc.—B.B. decrepitates and fuses at 3, coloring the flame yellowish-green; the fused mass reacts alkaline with test paper. On charcoal reduced to a sulphide. With soda gives at first a clear pearl, but on continued blowing yields a hepatic mass, which spreads out and soaks into the coal. If a portion of this mass be removed, placed on a clean silver surface, and moistened, it gives a black spot of silver sulphide. Should the barite contain calcium sulphate, this will not be absorbed by the coal when treated in powder with soda. Insoluble in acids.

Diff.—Distinguishing characters: high specific gravity, higher than celestite or aragonite; cleavage; insolubility; green coloration of the blowpipe flame.

Obs.—Occurs commonly in connection with beds or veins of metallic ores, as part of the gangue of the ore. It is met with in secondary limestone, sometimes forming distinct veins, and often in crystals along with calcite and celestite. At Dufton, in Westmoreland. Eng land; in Cornwall, near Liskeard, etc., in Cumberland and Lancashire, in Derbyshire, Staffordshire, etc.; in Scotland, in Argyleshire, at Strontian. Some of the most important European localities are at Felsöbanya and Kremnitz, at Freiberg, Marienberg, Clausthal, Przibram, and at Roya and Roure in Auvergne.

In the U. S., in *Conn.*, at Cheshire. In *N. York*, at Pillar Point; at Scoharie; in St. Lawrence Co.; at Fowler; at Hammond. In *Virginia*, at Eldridge's gold mine in Buckingham Co.; near Lexington, in Rockbridge Co.; Fauquier Co. In *Kentucky*, near Paris; in the W. end of I. Royale, L. Superior, and on Spar Id., N. shore. In *Canada*, at Landsdown. In fine crystals near Fort Wallace, New Mexico.

The white varieties of barite are ground up and employed as a white paint, either alone or mixed with white lead.

CELESTITE.

Orthorhombic. $I \wedge I = 104° \ 2'$ ($103° \ 30'-104° \ 30'$), $O \wedge 1\text{-}\bar{\imath} = 121° \ 19\frac{1}{2}'$; $\bar{c} : \bar{b} : \bar{a} = 1.6432 : 1.2807 : 1$. $O \wedge 1 = 115° \ 38'$, $O \wedge 1\text{-}\bar{\imath} = 127° \ 56'$, $\bar{1} \wedge 1$, mac., $= 112° \ 35'$, $1 \wedge 1$, brach., $= 89° \ 26'$. Cleavage: O perfect; I distinct; $i\text{-}\bar{\imath}$ less distinct. Also fibrous and radiated; sometimes globular; occasionally granular.

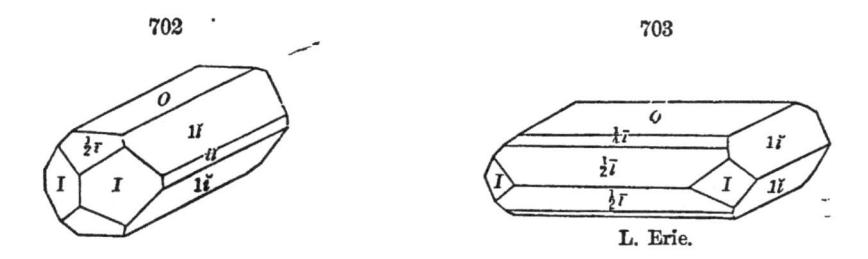

702

703

L. Erie.

H.$=3$-3.5. G.$=3.92$-3.975. Lustre vitreous, sometimes inclining to pearly. Streak white. Color white, often faint bluish, and sometimes reddish. Transparent—subtranslucent. Fracture imperfectly conchoidal—uneven. Very brittle. Trichroism sometimes very distinct.

Comp.—$SrSO_4 =$ Sulphur trioxide 43·6, strontia 56·4$=100$. Wittstein finds that the blue color of the celestite of Jena is due to a trace of a phosphate of iron.

Pyr., etc.—B.B. frequently decrepitates, fuses at 3 to a white pearl, coloring the flame strontia-red; the fused mass reacts alkaline. On charcoal fuses, and in R.F. is converted into a difficultly fusible hepatic mass; this treated with hydrochloric acid and alcohol gives an intensely red flame. With soda on charcoal reacts like barite. Insoluble in acids.

Diff.—Does not effervesce with acids like the carbonates; specific gravity lower than that of barite; colors the blowpipe flame red.

Obs.—Celestite is usually associated with limestone or sandstone. Occurs also in beds of gypsum, rock salt, and clay; and with sulphur in some volcanic regions. Found in Sicily, at Girgenti and elsewhere; at Bex in Switzerland, and Conil in Spain; at Dornburg, near Jena; in the department of the Garonne, France; in the Tyrol; Retzbanya; in rock salt, at Ischl, Austria. Found in the Trenton limestone about Lake Huron, particu'arly on Strontian Island, and at Kingston in Canada; Chaumont Bay, Scoharie, and Lockport, N. Y.; also the Rossie lead mine; at Bell's Mills, Blair Co.. Penn.

Named from *cœlestis, celestial*, in allusion to the faint shade of blue often presented by the mineral.

BARYTOCELESTITE.—Celestite containing barium sulphate 26 p. c. (Grüner), 20·4 p. c. (Turner). $1\text{-}\bar{\imath} \wedge 1\text{-}\bar{\imath} = 74° \ 54\frac{1}{2}'$, $\frac{1}{2}\text{-}\bar{\imath} \wedge \frac{1}{2}\text{-}\bar{\imath} = 100° \ 35'$, on crystals from Imfeld in the Binnenthal (Neminar). Drummond I., Lake Erie; Nörten, Hanover.

ANHYDRITE.

Orthorhombic. $I \wedge I = 100° 30'$, $O \wedge 1\text{-}\bar{i} = 127° 19'$; $\check{c} : \bar{b} : \check{a} = 1·3122 : 1·2024 : 1$. $1\text{-}\check{i} \wedge 1\text{-}\check{i}$, top, $= 85°$. Cleavage: $i\text{-}\bar{i}$ very perfect; $i\text{-}\check{i}$ also perfect; O somewhat less so. Also fibrous, lamellar, granular, and sometimes impalpable. The lamellar and columnar varieties often curved or contorted. H.=3–3·5. G.=2·899–2·985. Lustre: $i\text{-}\check{i}$ and $i\text{-}\bar{i}$ somewhat pearly; O vitreous; in massive varieties, vitreous inclining to pearly. Color white, sometimes a grayish, bluish, or reddish tinge; also brick-red. Streak grayish-white. Fracture uneven; of finely lamellar and fibrous varieties, splintery. Optic-axial plane parallel to $i\text{-}\bar{i}$, or plane of most perfect cleavage; bisectrix normal to O; Grailich.

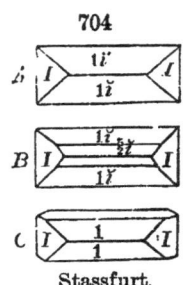

704

Stassfurt.

Var.—(*a*) Crystallized; cleavable in its three rectangular directions. (*b*) fibrous; either parallel, or radiated, or plumose. (*c*) Fine granular. (*d*) Scaly granular. *Vulpinite* is a scaly granular kind from Vulpino in Lombardy; it is cut and polished for ornamental purposes. It does not ordinarily contain more silica than common anhydrite. A kind in contorted concretionary forms is the tripestone (*Gekrösstein*).

Comp.—CaSO$_4$=Sulphur trioxide 58·8, lime 41·2=100.

Pyr., etc.—B.B. fuses at 3, coloring the flame reddish-yellow, and yielding an enamel-like bead which reacts alkaline. On charcoal in R.F. reduced to a sulphide; with soda does not fuse to a clear globule, and is not absorbed by the coal like barite; it is, however, decomposed, and yields a mass which blackens silver; with fluorite fuses to a clear pearl, which is enamel-white on cooling, and by long blowing swells up and becomes infusible. Soluble in hydrochloric acid.

Diff.—Characterized by its cleavage in three rectangular directions; harder than gypsum; does not effervesce with acids like the carbonates.

Obs.—Occurs in rocks of various ages, especially in limestone strata, and often the same that contain ordinary gypsum, and also very commonly in beds of rock salt. Occurs near Hall in Tyrol; at Sulz on the Neckar, in Würtemberg; Bleiberg in Carinthia; Lüneberg, Hanover; Kapnik in Hungary; Ischl; Aussee in Styria; Berchtesgaden; Stassfurt, in fine crystals. In the U. States, at Lockport, N. Y. In Nova Scotia.

ANGLESITE. Bleivitriol, *Germ.*

Orthorhombic. $I \wedge I = 103° 43\frac{1}{2}'$, $O \wedge 1\text{-}\bar{i} = 121° 20\frac{1}{4}'$, Kokscharof; $\check{c} : \bar{b} : \check{a} = 1·64223 : 1·273634 : 1$. $O \wedge 1\text{-}\check{i} = 127° 48'$; $O \wedge 1 = 115° 35\frac{1}{2}'$; $1\text{-}\check{i} \wedge 1\text{-}\check{i}$, top, $= 75° 35\frac{1}{2}'$. Crystals sometimes tabular; often oblong prismatic, and elongated in the direction of either of the axes (as seen in the figures). Cleavage: I, O, but interrupted. The planes I and $i\text{-}\bar{i}$ often vertically striated, and $\frac{1}{2}\text{-}\bar{i}$ horizontally. Also massive, granular, or hardly so. Sometimes stalactitic.

H.=2·75–3. G.=6·12–6·39. Lustre highly adamantine in some specimens, in others inclining to resinous and vitreous. Color white, tinged yellow, gray, green, and sometimes blue. Streak uncolored. Transparent —opaque. Fracture conchoidal. Very brittle.

Comp.—PbSO$_4$=Sulphur trioxide 26·4, lead oxide 73·6=100.

Pyr., etc.—B.B. decrepitates, fuses in the flame of a candle (F.=1·5). On charcoal in O. F. fuses to a clear pearl, which on cooling becomes milk-white; in R.F. is reduced with effervescence to metallic lead. With soda on charcoal in R.F. gives metallic lead, and the soda is absorbed by the coal; when the surface of the coal is removed and placed on bright silver and moistened with water it tarnishes the metal black. Difficultly soluble in nitric acid.

Diff.—Does not effervesce with acid like cerussite (lead carbonate); listinguished by blowpipe tests from other resembling species.

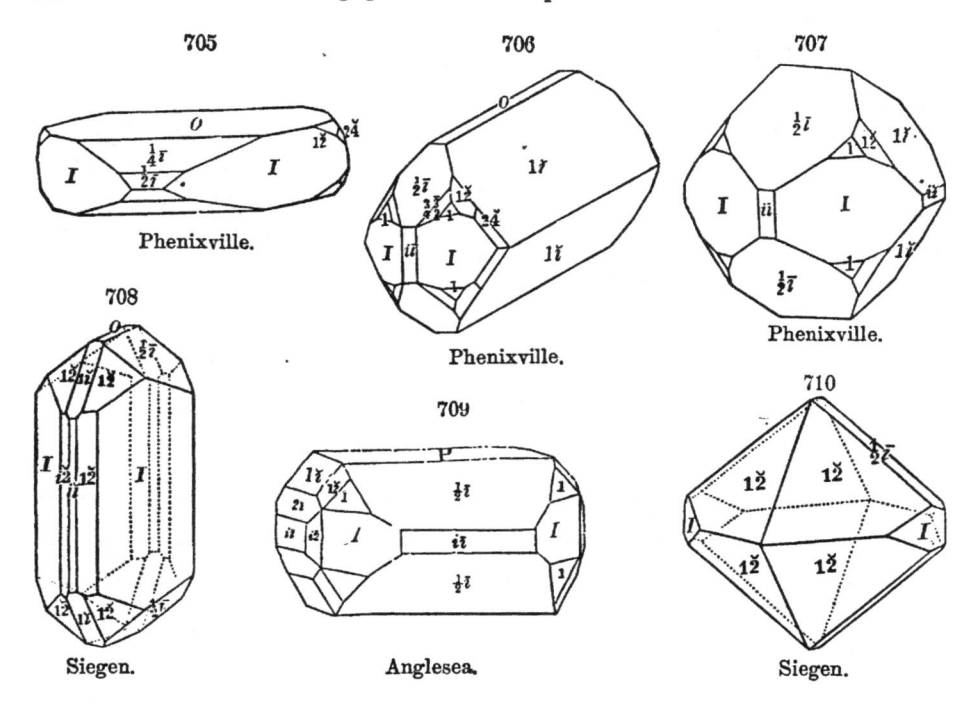

705
Phenixville.

706
Phenixville.

707
Phenixville.

708
Siegen.

709
Anglesea.

710
Siegen.

Obs.—This ore of lead was first observed by Monnet as a result of the decomposition of galenite, and it is often found in its cavities. Occurs in crystals at Leadhills; at Pary's mine in Anglesea; also at Melanoweth in Cornwall; in Derbyshire and in Cumberland: Clausthal, Zillerfeld, and Giepenbach in the Harz; near Siegen in Prussia; Schapbach in the Black Forest; in Sardinia; massive in Siberia. Andalusia, Alston Moor in Cumberland; in Australia. In the U. S., in large crystals at Wheatley's mine, Phenixville, Pa.; in Missouri lead mines; at the lead mines of Southampton, Mass.; at Rossie, N.Y.; at the Walton gold mine, Louisa Co., Va. Compact in Arizona, and Cerro Gordo, Cal.

DREELITE.—Rhombohedral. H.=3·5. G.=3·2–3·4. Color white. Composition given as $CaSO_4 + 3BaSO_4$. Occurs in small crystals at Beaujeau, France; Badenweiler, Baden.

DOLEROPHANITE (*Scacchi*).—Cu_2SO_5. In minute crystals. Monoclinic. Color brown. Vesuvius.

HYDROCYANITE (*Scacchi*).—Anhydrous copper sulphate, $CuSO_4$. Color sky-blue. Very soluble. Vesuvius.

APHTHITALITE, *Arcanite*.—K_2SO_4=Potash 54·1, sulphuric acid 45·9=100. Vesuvius.

THENARDITE.—Sodium sulphate, Na_2SO_4. Spain; Vesuvius.

LEADHILLITE.

Orthorhombic. $I \wedge I = 103° 16'$, $O \wedge 1\text{-}\bar{\imath} = 120°10'$; $\breve{c} : \bar{b} : \breve{a} = 1\cdot7205 : 1\cdot2632 : 1$. Hemihedral in I and some other planes; hence monoclinic in aspect, or rhombohedral when in compound crystals. Cleavage: $i\text{-}\check{\imath}$ very perfect; $i\text{-}\bar{\imath}$ in traces. Twins, f. 712, consisting of three crystals; twinning plane, 1-i (see f. 298, p. 97); also parallel with I.

H.=2·5. G.=6·26-6·44. Lustre of $i\text{-}\bar{\imath}$ pearly, other parts resinous, somewhat adamantine. Color white, passing into yellow, green, or gray. Streak uncolored. Transparent — translucent. Conchoidal fracture scarcely observable. Rather sectile.

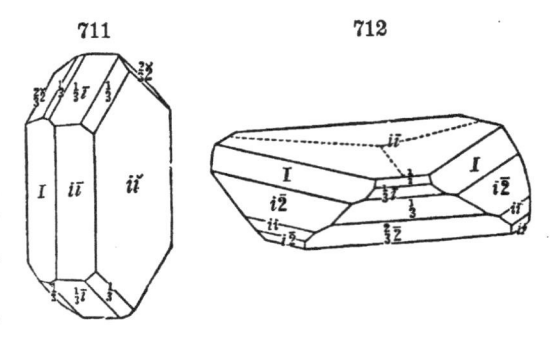

Comp.—Formerly accepted formula, $PbSO_4+3PbCO_3=$ Lead sulphate 27·45, lead carbonate 72·55 = 100. Recent investigations by Laspeyres (J. pr., Ch. II., v., 470; vii., 127; xiii., 370), and Hintze (Pogg. Ann., clii., 156), though not entirely accordant, give different results, both show the presence of some water. Laspeyres writes the formula empirically, $Pb_{18}C_9S_8O_{51} + 5H_2O$, and Hintze, $Pb_7C_4S_2O_{21}+2H_2O$. Analyses: 1. Laspeyres; 2, Hintze:

	SO_3	CO_2	PbO	H_2O	
1.	8·14	8·08	81·91	1·87=100,	Laspeyres.
2.	8·17	9·18	80·80	2·00=100·15,	Hintze.

Pyr., etc.—B.B. intumesces, fuses at 1·5, and turns yellow; but white on cooling. Easily reduced on charcoal. With soda affords the reaction for sulphuric acid. Effervesces briskly in nitric acid, and leaves white lead sulphate undissolved.

Obs.—This ore has been found at Leadhills with other ores of lead; also in crystals at Red Gill, Cumberland, and near Taunton in Somersetshire; at Iglesias, Sardinia (*maxite*).

SUSANNITE.—Composition as for leadhillite, but form rhombohedral. Leadhills; Nertschinsk, Siberia.

CONNELLITE.—Hexagonal. In slender needle-like blue crystals. Contains copper sulphate and copper chloride. Exact composition uncertain. Cornwall.

CALEDONITE.—Monoclinic (*Schrauf*). H.=2·5-3. G.=6·4. Color bluish-green. R_2SO_4 +aq (Flight), with R=Pb : Cu=7 : 3, or $5PbSO_4+3H.CuO_2+2H_2PbO_2$. This requires: Sulphuric trioxide 19·1, lead oxide 65·2, copper oxide 11·4, water 4·3=100. Leadhills, Scotland; Red Gill; Retzbanya; Mine la Motte, Missouri.

LANARKITE.—Monoclinic. H.=2-2·5. G.=6·3-6·4. Color pale yellow, or greenish-white. Transparent. Composition as formerly accepted, $PbSO_4+PbCO_3$. New analyses by Flight, and by Pisani, show the absence of both carbon dioxide and water; composition accordingly $Pb_2SO_5=PbSO_4+PbO$, which requires: Lead sulphate 57·6, lead oxide 42·4=100. Leadhills; Siberia, etc.

GLAUBERITE.

Monoclinic. $C=68°\ 16'$, $I \wedge I=83°\ 20'$, $O \wedge 1\text{-}\bar{\imath}=136°\ 30'$; $\dot{c}:\bar{b}:a = 0·8454 : 0·8267 : 1$. Cleavage: O perfect.

H.=2·5-3. G.=2·64-2·85. Lustre vitreous. Color pale yellow or gray; sometimes brick-red. Streak white. Fracture conchoidal; brittle. Taste slightly saline.

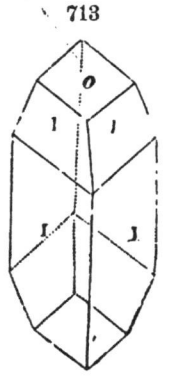

Comp.—$Na_2CaS_2O_8=$ Sulphur trioxide 57·6, lime 20·1, soda 22·3 = 100.

Pyr., etc.—B.B. decrepitates, turns white, and fuses at 1·5 to a white enamel, coloring the flame intensely yellow. On charcoal fuses in O.F. to a clear bead; in R.F. a portion is absorbed by the charcoal, leaving an infusible hepatic residue. With soda on charcoal gives the reaction for sulphur. Soluble in hydrochloric acid. In water it loses its transparency, is partially dissolved, leaving a residue of calcium sulphate, and in a large excess this is completely dissolved. On long exposure absorbs moisture and falls to pieces.

Obs.—In crystals in rock salt at Villa Rubia in New Castile; also at Aussee in Upper Austria; in Bavaria; at the salt mines of Vic in France; and at Borax Lake, California; Province of Tarapaca, Peru.

Hydrous Sulphates.

MIRABILITE. Glauber Salt.

Monoclinic. $C = 72°\ 15'$, $I \wedge I = 86°\ 31'$, $O \wedge 1\text{-}\check{\imath} = 130°\ 19'$; $\check{a} : \bar{b} : \check{a} = 1.1089 : 0.8962 : 1$. Cleavage: $i\text{-}i$ perfect. Usually in efflorescent crusts.

H.$= 1.5-2$. G.$=1.481$. Lustre vitreous. Color white. Transparent—opaque. Taste cool, then feebly saline and bitter.

Comp.—$Na_2SO_4 + 10aq$ = Sulphur trioxide 24·8, soda 19·3, water 55·9=100.
Pyr., etc.—In the closed tube much water; gives an intense yellow to the flame. Very soluble in water; the solution gives with barium salts the reaction for sulphuric acid. Falls to powder on exposure to the air, and becomes anhydrous.
Obs.—Occurs at Ischl and Hallstadt; also in Hungary; Switzerland; Italy; at Guipuzcoa in Spain, etc.; at Kailua on Hawaii; at Windsor, Nova Scotia; also near Sweetwater River, Rocky Mountains.
MASCAGNITE, BOUSSINGAULTITE (cerbolite), LECONTITE, and GUANOVULITE are hydrous sulphates containing ammonium.

GYPSUM.

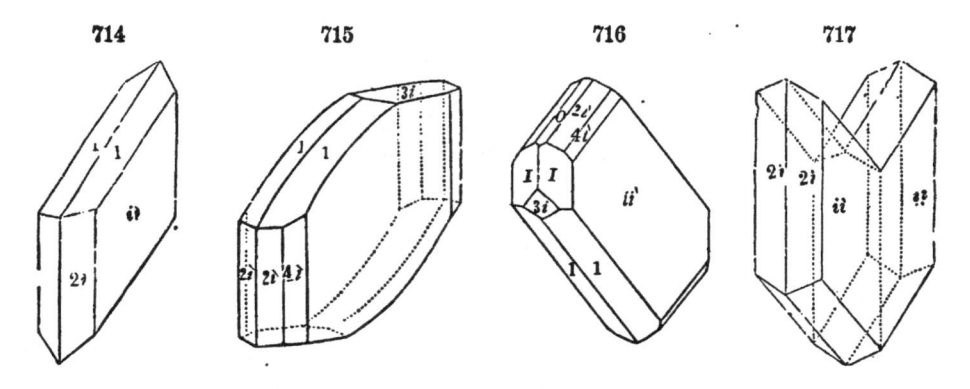

Monoclinic. $C = 66°\ 14'$, if the vertical prism I (see f. 716) correspond to the cleavage prism (second cleavage), and the basal plane O to the direction of the third cleavage. $I \wedge I = 138°\ 28'$, $1\text{-}\check{\imath} \wedge 1\text{-}\check{\imath} = 128°\ 31'$; $\check{a} : \bar{b} : \check{a} = 0.9 : 2.4135 : 1$. $O \wedge 1 = 125°\ 35'$, $O \wedge 2\text{-}\check{\imath} = 145°\ 41'$, $1 \wedge 1 = 143°\ 42'$, $2\text{-}\check{\imath} \wedge 2\text{-}\check{\imath} = 111°\ 42'$.

714 715 716 717

Cleavage: (1) $i\text{-}\check{\imath}$, or clinodiagonal, eminent, affording easily smooth polished folia; (2) I, imperfect, fibrous, and often apparent in internal rifts or linings, making with O (or the edge $2\text{-}\check{\imath}/2\text{-}\check{\imath}$) the angles 66° 14', and 113° 46', corresponding to the obliquity of the fundamental prism; (3) O, or basal, imperfect, but affording a nearly smooth surface. Twins: 1, Twinning-plane O common (f. 717); also $1\text{-}\check{\imath}$, or edge $1/1$. Simple crystals often with warped as well as curved surfaces. Also foliated massive; lamellar stellate; often granular massive; and sometimes nearly impalpable.

H.=1·5–2. G.=2·314–2·328, when pure crystals. Lustre of $i\text{-}i$ pearly and shining, other faces subvitreous. Massive varieties often glistening, sometimes dull earthy. Color usually white; sometimes gray, flesh-red, honey-yellow, ochre-yellow, blue; impure varieties often black, brown, red or reddish-brown. Streak white. Transparent—opaque.

Var.—1. *Crystallized*, or *Selenite ;* either in distinct crystals or in broad folia, the folia sometimes a yard across and transparent throughout. 2. *Fibrous ;* coarse or fine. (*a*) *Satin spar*, when fine-fibrous a variety which has the pearly opalescence of moonstone ; (*b*) *plumose*, when radiately arranged. 3. *Massive ; Alabaster*, a fine-grained variety, either white or delicately shaded ; *scaly-granular ; earthy* or *rock-gypsum*, a dull-colored rock, often impure with clay or calcium carbonate, and sometimes with anhydrite.

Comp.—$CaSO_4 + 2aq$ = Sulphur trioxide 46·5, lime 32·6, water 20·9 = 100.

Pyr., etc.—In the closed tube gives off water and becomes opaque. Fuses at 2·5–3, coloring the flame reddish-yellow. For other reactions, see ANHYDRITE, p. 389. Ignited at a temperature not exceeding 260° C., it again combines with water when moistened, and becomes firmly solid. Soluble in hydrochloric acid, and also in 400 to 500 parts of water.

Diff.—Characterized by its softness ; it does not effervesce nor gelatinize with acids. Some varieties resemble heulandite, stilbite, talc, etc.; and in its fibrous forms it is like some calcite.

Obs.—Gypsum often forms extensive beds in connection with various stratified rocks, especially limestone, and marlytes or clay beds. It occurs occasionally in crystalline rocks. It is also a product of volcanoes; produced by the decomposition of pyrite when lime is present; and often about sulphur springs; also deposited on the evaporation of sea-water and brines, in which it exists in solution.

Fine specimens are found in the salt mines of Bex in Switzerland ; at Hall in the Tyrol; in the sulphur mines of Sicily ; in the gypsum formation near Oçana in Spain ; in the clay of Shotover Hill, near Oxford ; at Montmartre, near Paris. A noted locality of alabaster occurs at Castelino, 35 m. from Leghorn. In the U. S. this species occurs in extensive beds in N. York, Ohio, Illinois, Virginia, Tennessee, and Arkansas; it is usually associated with salt springs. Also in Nova Scotia, Peru, etc. It is characteristic of the so-called triassic, or *red beds*, of the Rocky Mountain region; also of the Cretaceous in the west, particularly of the clays of the Fort Pierre group, in which it occurs in the form of transparent plates.

Handsome selenite and snowy gypsum occur in *N. York*, near Lockport; also near Camillus, Onondaga Co. In *Maryland*, on the St. Mary's, in clay. In *Ohio*, large transparent crystals have been found at Poland and Canfield, Trumbull Co. In *Tenn.*, selenite and alabaster in Davidson Co. In *Kentucky*, in Mammoth Cave, in the form of rosettes, etc. In *N. Scotia*, in Sussex, King's Co., large crystals, often containing much symmetrically disseminated sand (Marsh).

Plaster of Paris (or gypsum which has been heated and ground up) is used for making moulds, taking casts of statues, medals, etc. ; for producing a hard finish on walls; also in the manufacture of artificial marble, as the scagliola tables of Leghorn, and in the glazing of porcelain.

POLYHALITE.

Monoclinic (?). A prism of 115°, with acute edges truncated. Usually in compact fibrous masses.

H.=2·5–3. G.=2·7689. Lustre resinous or slightly pearly. Streak red. Color flesh- or brick-red, sometimes yellowish. Translucent—opaque Taste bitter and astringent, but very weak.

Comp.—$2RSO_4 + aq$, where R=Ca : Mg : K_2 in the ratio 2 : 1 : 1 ; that is, $K_2MgCa_2S_4O_{16}$ $+2aq$ = Calcium sulphate 45·2, magnesium sulphate 19·9, potassium sulphate 28·9, water 6·0=100.

Pyr., etc.—In the closed tube gives water. B.B fuses at 1·5, colors the flame yellow. On charcoal fuses to a reddish globule, which in R.F. becomes white, and on cooling has a saline hepatic taste ; with soda like glauberite. With fluor does not give a clear bead. Partially soluble in water, leaving a residue of calcium sulphate, which dissolves in a large amount of water

Obs.—Occurs at the mines of Ischl, Ebensee, Aussee, Hallstatt, and Hallein in Austria, with common salt, gypsum, and anhydrite; at Berchtesgaden in Bavaria; at Vic in Lorraine.

The name Polyhalite is derived from πολύς, *many*, and ἅλς, *salt*, in allusion to the number of salts in the constitution of the mineral.

SYNGENITE, *v. Zepharovich;* Kaluszite. *Rumpf.*—Near polyhalite. Composition RSO_4 + aq, with R=Ca : K_2=1 : 1, that is, $K_2CaS_2O_8$+aq=Potassium sulphate 53·1, calcium sulphate 41·4, water 5·5=100. Monoclinic. Occurs in small tabular crystals in cavities in halite at Kalusz, East Galicia.

KIESERITE.—$MgSO_4$+aq=Sulphur trioxide 58·0, magnesia 28·0, water 13·0=100. Stassfurt.

PICROMERITE is $K_2MgS_2O_8$+6aq=Sulphur trioxide 39·8, magnesia 9·9, potash 23·4, water 26·9=100. Vesuvius; Stassfurt.

BLOEDITE.—Composition $Na_2MgS_2O_8$+4aq=Sulphur trioxide 47·9, magnesia 12·0, soda 18·6, water 21·5=100. Salt mines of Ischl; also in the Andes. SIMONYITE (*Tschermak*) is identical.

LŒWEITE.—$2Na_2MgS_2O_8$+5aq=Sulphur trioxide 52·1, magnesia 13·0, soda 20·2, water 14·7=100. From Ischl.

EPSOMITE. Epsom Salt. Bittersalz, *Germ.*

Orthorhombic, and generally hemihedral in the octahedral modifications. $I \wedge I = 90°\ 34'$, $O \wedge 1\text{-}\bar{\imath} = 150°\ 2'$; $\check{c} : \bar{b} : \check{a} = 0·5766 : 1·01 : 1$. $1\text{-}\check{\imath} \wedge 1\text{-}\check{\imath}$, basal, $= 59°\ 27'$, $1\text{-}\check{\imath} \wedge 1\text{-}\bar{\imath}$, basal, $= 59°\ 56'$. Cleavage: brachydiagonal, perfect. Also in botryoidal masses and delicately fibrous crusts.

H.=2·25. G.=1·751; 1·685, artificial salt. Lustre vitreous—earthy Streak and color white. Transparent—translucent. Taste bitter and saline.

Comp.—$MgSO_4$+7aq, when pure=Sulphur trioxide 32·5, magnesia 16·3, water 51·2=100.

Pyr., etc.—Liquifies in its water of crystallization. Gives much water in the closed tube at a high temperature; the water is acid. B.B. on charcoal fuses at first, and finally yields an infusible alkaline mass, which, with cobalt solution, gives a pink color on ignition. Very soluble in water, and has a very bitter taste.

Obs.—Common in mineral waters, and as a delicate fibrous or capillary efflorescence on rocks, in the galleries of mines, and elsewhere. In the former state it exists at Epsom, England, and at Sedlitz and Saidschutz in Bohemia. At Idria in Carniola it occurs in silky fibres, and is hence called *hairsalt* by the workmen. Also obtained at the gypsum quarries of Montmartre, near Paris; in Aragon and Catalonia in Spain; in Chili; found at Vesuvius, etc.

The floors of the limestone caves of Kentucky, Tennessee, and Indiana, are in many instances covered with epsomite, in minute crystals, mingled with the earth. In the Mammoth Cave, Ky., it adheres to the roof in loose masses like snowballs.

FAUSERITE.—A hydrous manganese-magnesium sulphate. Hungary.

Copperas Group.

CHALCANTHITE. Blue Vitriol. Kupfervitriol, *Germ.*

Triclinic. $O \wedge I = 109°\ 32'$, $O \wedge I' = 127°\ 40'$, $I \wedge I' = 123°\ 10'$, $O \wedge 1 = 125°\ 38'$, $O \wedge i\text{-}\bar{\imath} = 120°\ 50'$, $O \wedge i\text{-}\check{\imath} = 103°\ 27'$. Cleavage: I imperfect, I' very imperfect. Occurs also amorphous, stalactitic, reniform.

H.=2·5. G.=2·213. Lustre vitreous. Color Berlin-blue to sky-blue, of different shades; sometimes a little greenish. Streak uncolored. Subtransparent—translucent. Taste metallic and nauseous. Somewhat brittle.

Comp.—$CuSO_4$+5aq=Sulphur trioxide 32·1, copper oxide 31·8, water 36·1=100.

Pyr., etc.—In the closed tube yields water, and at a higher temperature sulphuric acid. B.B. with soda on charcoal yields metallic copper. With the fluxes reacts for copper. Soluble in water; a drop of the solution placed on a surface of iron coats it with metallic copper.

Obs.—Blue vitriol is found in waters issuing from mines, and in connection with rocks containing chalcopyrite, by the alteration of which it is formed. Some of its foreign localities are the Rammelsberg mine, near Goslar, in the Harz; Fahlun in Sweden; at Parys mine, Anglesey; at various mines in Co. of Wicklow; Rio Tinto mine, Spain. Found at the Hiwassee copper mine, and other mines, in Polk Co., Tennessee; at the Canton mine, Georgia; at Copiapo, Chili, with stypticite.

When purified it is employed in dyeing operations, and in the printing of cotton and linen, and for various other purposes in the arts. It is manufactured mostly from old sheathing, copper trimmings, and refinery scales.

Other vitriols are:—MELANTERITE, iron vitriol; PISANITE, iron-copper vitriol; GOSLARITE, zinc vitriol; BIEBERITE, cobalt vitriol; MORENOSITE, nickel vitriol; CUPROMAGNESITE, copper-magnesium vitriol (Vesuvius). These are all alike in containing 7 molecules of water of crystallization.

ALUNOGEN (Haarsalz, *Germ.*).—$AlS_3O_{12} + 18aq =$ Sulphur trioxide 36·0, alumina 15·4, water 48·6 = 100. Taste like that of alum. Vesuvius; Königsberg, Hungary.

COQUIMBITE.—$FeS_3O_{12} + 9aq =$ Sulphur trioxide 42·7, iron sesquioxide 28·5, water 28·8 = 100. Coquimbo, Chili.

ETTRINGITE (*Lehmann*).—Analysis, SO_3 16·64, AlO_3 7·76, CaO 27·27, H_2O 45·82. In hexagonal needle-like crystals from the lava at Ettringen, Laacher See.

Alum and Halotrichite Groups.

Here belong: TSCHERMIGITE, ammonium alum. KALINITE, potassium alum, or common alum. MENDOZITE, sodium alum. PICKERINGITE, magnesium alum. APJOHNITE, manganese alum. BOSJEMANNITE, mangano-magnesium alum. HALOTRICHITE, iron alum. Also ROEMERITE, and VOLTAITE.

COPIAPITE.

Hexagonal (?). Loose aggregation of crystalline scales, or granular massive, the scales rhombic or hexagonal tables. Cleavage: basal, perfect. Incrusting.

H. = 1·5. G. = 2·14, Borcher. Lustre pearly. Color sulphur-yellow, citron-yellow. Translucent.

Comp.—$Fe_2S_5O_{21} + 13aq$; $5FeS_3O_{12} + H_6FeO_6 + 36H_2O =$ Sulphur trioxide 41·9, iron sesquioxide 33·5, water 24·5 = 100.

Pyr., etc.—Yields water, and at a higher temperature sulphuric acid. On charcoal becomes magnetic, and with soda affords the reaction for sulphur. With the fluxes reactions for iron. In water insoluble.

Obs.—Common as a result of the decomposition of pyrite at the Rammelsberg mine, near Goslar in the Harz, and elsewhere.

This species is the yellow copperas long called misy, and it might well bear now the name *Misylite.*

RAIMONDITE.—Composition $Fe_2S_3O_{15} + 7aq$. FIBROFERRITE (stypticite).—Composition $FeS_2O_9 + 10aq$.

BOTRYOGEN is red iron vitriol, exact composition uncertain. Fahlun, Sweden. BARTHOLOMITE, West Indies, is related.

IHLEITE.—$Fe\ S_3O_{12} + 12aq$. Occurs as a yellow efflorescence on graphite from Mugrau, Bohemia (*Schrauf*).

ALUMINITE.

Reniform, massive; impalpable.
H. = 1–2. G. = 1·66. Lustre dull, earthy. Color white. Opaque. Fracture earthy. Adheres to the tongue; meagre to the touch.

Comp.—$AlSO_6 + 9aq =$ Sulphur trioxide 23·2, alumina 29·8, water 47·0=100.

Pyr., etc.—In the closed tube gives much water, which, at a high temperature, becomes acid from the evolution of sulphurous and sulphuric oxides. B.B. infusible. With cobalt solution a fine blue color. With soda on charcoal a hepatic mass. Soluble in acids.

Obs.—Occurs in connection with beds of clay in the Tertiary and Post-tertiary formations. Found near Halle; at Newhaven, Sussex; Epernay, in Lunel Vieil, and Auteuil, in France.

WERTHEMANITE.—$AlSO_6 + 3aq$. G.=2·80. Occurs near Chachapoyas, in Peru.

ALUNITE, Alaunstein, *Germ.*—Composition $K_2Al_3S_4O_{22} + 6aq$. Rhombohedral. Also massive, fibrous. Forms seams in trachyte and allied rocks. Tolfa, near Rome; Tuscany; Hungary; Mt. Dore, France, etc.

LÖWIGITE.—Same composition as alunite, but contains 3 parts more of water. Tabrze, Silesia.

LINARITE. Bleilasur, Kupferbleispath, *Germ.*

Monoclinic. $C = 77° 27'$; $I \wedge I$, over i-i, $= 61° 36'$, $O \wedge 1$-$i = 141° 5'$, $\dot{c} : b : \dot{a} = 0·48134 : 0·5819 : 1$, Hessenberg. Twins: twinning-plane i-i common; $O \wedge O' = 154° 54'$. Cleavage: i-i very perfect; O less so.

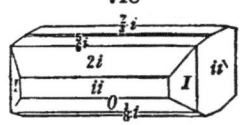

H.=2·5. G.=5·3–5·45. Lustre vitreous or adamantine. Color deep azure-blue. Streak pale blue. Translucent. Fracture conchoidal. Brittle.

Comp.—$PbCuSO_5 + aq = (Pb,Cu)SO_4 + H_2(Pb,Cu)O_2 =$ Sulphur trioxide 20·0, lead oxide 55·7, copper oxide 19·8, water 4·5=100.

Pyr., etc.—In the closed tube yields water and loses its blue color. B.B. on charcoal fuses easily to a pearl, and in R.F. is reduced to a metallic globule which by continued treatment coats the coal with lead oxide, and if fused boron trioxide is added yields a pure globule of copper. With soda gives the reaction for sulphur. Decomposed with nitric acid, leaving a white residue of lead sulphate.

Obs.—Formerly found at Leadhills. Occurs at Roughten Gill, Red Gill, etc., in Cumberland; near Schneeberg, rare; in Dillenburg; at Retzbanya; in Nertschinsk; and near Beresof in the Ural; and supposed formerly to be found at Linares in Spain, whence the name.

BROCHANTITE.

Monoclinic. $C = 89° 27\frac{1}{2}'$. $I \wedge I = 104° 6\frac{1}{2}'$, $O \wedge 1$-$i = 154° 12\frac{1}{2}'$; $\dot{c} : b : \dot{a} = 0·61983 : 1·28242 : 1$. Schrauf distinguishes four types of forms: I. Brochantite from Retzbanya (two varieties), also from Cornwall and Russia, triclinic; II. *Warringtonite* from Cornwall, a third variety from Retzbanya, monoclinic (?); III. Brochantite from Nischne-Tagilsk, monoclinic—triclinic; IV. *Königine* from Russia, and a fourth variety from Retzbanya, monoclinic (or orthorhombic).

Also in groups of acicular crystals and drusy crusts. Cleavage: i-i very perfect; I in traces. Also massive; reniform with a columnar structure.

H.=3·5–4. G.=3·78–3·87, Magnus; 3·9069, G. Rose. Lustre vitreous; a little pearly on the cleavage-face. Color emerald-green, blackish-green. Streak paler green. Transparent—translucent.

Comp.—$Cu_4SO_7 + 3H_2O = CuSO_4 + 3H_2CuO_2 =$ Sulphur trioxide 17·71, copper oxide 70·34, water 11·95=100. This formula belongs to type IV., above; the warringtonite corresponds more nearly to $CuSO_4 + 3H_2CuO_4 + H_2O$, and the existence of other varieties has been also assumed.

Pyr., etc.—Yields water, and at a higher temperature sulphuric acid, in the closed tube, and becomes black. B.B. fuses, and on charcoal affords metallic copper. With soda gives the reaction for sulphuric acid.

Obs.—Occurs at Gumeschevsk and Nischne-Tagilsk in the Ural; the Königine (or *Königite*) was from Gumeschevsk; near Roughten Gill, in Cumberland; in Cornwall (in part *warringtonite*); at Retzbanya; in Nassau; at Krisuvig in Iceland (*krisuvigite*); in Mexico (*brongnartine*); in Chili, at Andacollo; in Australia.

Named after Brochant de Villiers.

LANGITE.—$CuSO_4 + 2H_2CuO_2 + 2aq$. In crystals and concretionary crusts of a blue color. G.$=3.5$. Cornwall.

CYANOTRICHITE, Lettsomite. Kupfersammterz, *Germ.*—In velvety druses. Color blue. A hydrous sulphate of copper and aluminum. Moldava in the Banat. WOODWARDITE, near the above.

KRÖNKITE.—$CuSO_4 + Na_2SO_4 + 2aq =$ Copper sulphate 47.2, sodium sulphate 42.1, water 10.7=100. In irregular crystalline masses of a coarse fibrous structure, prismatic. Color azure-blue. Moist to the touch. Found in the copper mines near Calama, Bolivia. (*Domeyko.*)

PHILLIPITE.—$CuSO_4 + FeS_3O_{12} + n$aq. In irregular fibrous masses, not prismatic. Color blue. In the cordilleras of Condes, Santiago, Chili. (*Domeyko.*)

ENYSITE.—Occurs in stalactitic forms in a cave. H.$=2-2.4$. G.$=1.59$. Color bluish-green. B.B. infusible. Analysis: SO_3 8.12, AlO_3 29.85, CuO 16.91, CaO 1.35, H_2O 39.42, SiO_2 3.40, CO_2 1.05=100. Near St. Agnes, Cornwall. (*Collins*, Min Mag., 1. p. 14.)

URANIUM-SULPHATES.—There are included here *johannite, uranochalcite, medjidite, zippeite, voglianite, uraconite*. These are secondary products found with other uranium minerals at Joachimsthal.

TELLURATES.

MONTANITE.

Incrusting; without distinct crystalline structure. Soft and earthy. Lustre dull to waxy. Color yellowish to white. Opaque.

Comp.—$Bi_2TeO_6 + 2aq =$ Tellurium trioxide 26.1, bismuth oxide 68.6, water 5.3=100.

Pyr., etc.—Yields water in a tube when heated. B.B. gives the reactions of bismuth and tellurium. Soluble in dilute hydrochloric acid.

Obs.—Incrusts tetradymite, at Highland, in Montana; Davidson Co., N. C.

7. CARBONATES.

Anhydrous Carbonates.

Calcite Group.

CALCITE. Calc Spar. Kalkspath, *Germ.*

Rhombohedral. $R \wedge R$, terminal, $= 105° \ 5'$, $O \wedge R = 135° \ 23'$; $\check{c} = 0.8543$. Cleavage: R highly perfect.

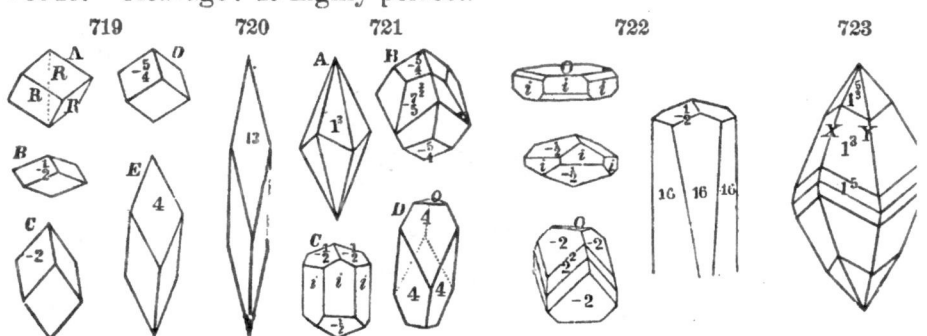

Angles of Rhombohedrons.

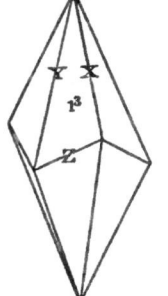

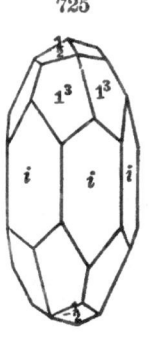

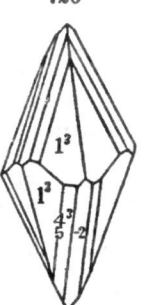

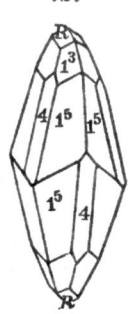

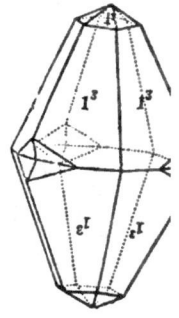

	Term. Edge.	$O \wedge R$		Term. Edge.	$O \wedge R$
$\frac{1}{4}(-\frac{1}{4})$	156° 2′	166° 9′	$-\frac{5}{4}$	95° 28′	129° 2′
$\frac{1}{2}(-\frac{1}{2})$	134° 57′	153° 45′	$2(-2)$	78° 51′	116° 52′
$R(-R)$	105° 5′	135° 23′	$4(-4)$	65° 50′	104° 17′

Angles of Scalenohedrons.

	Edge X (f. 724).	Y.	Z.		Edge X.	Y.	Z.
1^3	138° 5′	159° 24′	64° 54′	$\frac{3}{2}^2$	130° 37′	164° 1′	67° 41′
1^5	128° 15′	146° 10′	90° 20′	$-\frac{4}{5}^3$	107° 38′	145° 15′	124° 39′
1^3	104° 38′	144° 24′	132° 58′	$-\frac{1}{3}^3$	117° 23′	149° 43′	102° 25′
1^5	109° 1′	134° 28′	150° 44′	-2^2	92° 9′	153° 16′	135° 19′

OXYGEN COMPOUNDS.—CARBONATES.

Twins: (1) Twinning-plane basal (or parallel to O). (2) R, the vertical axes of the two forms nearly at right angles. (3) $-2R$. (4) $-\frac{1}{2}R$, the vertical axes of the two forms inclined to one another 127° 34'. (5) Prismatic plane i-2. (6) plane i (see p. 95).

Also fibrous, both coarse and fine; sometimes lamellar; often granular; from coarse to impalpable, and compact to earthy. Also stalactitic, tuberose, nodular, and other imitative forms.

H.=2·5-3·5; some earthy kinds (chalk, etc.) 1. G.=2·508-2·778; pure crystals, 2·7213-2·7234, Beud. Lustre vitreous—subvitreous—earthy. Color white or colorless; also various pale shades of gray, red, green, blue, violet, yellow; also brown and black when impure. Streak white or grayish. Transparent—opaque. Fracture usually conchoidal, but obtained with difficulty when the specimen is crystallized. Double refraction strong.

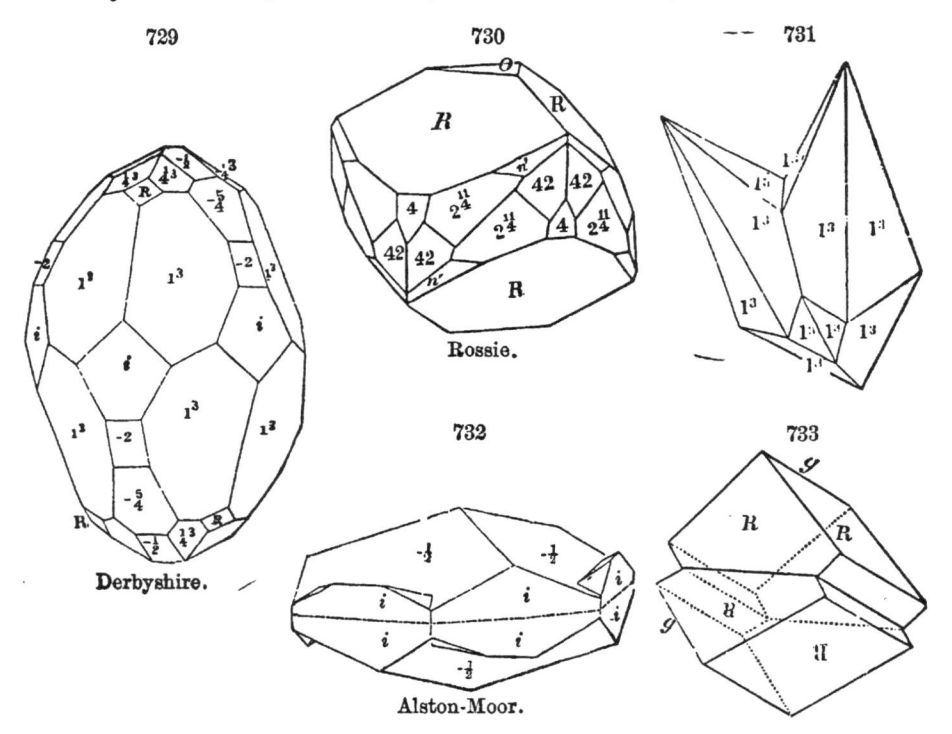

729

730

731

Rossie.

Derbyshire.

732

733

Alston-Moor.

Comp., Var.—Calcite is calcium carbonate, $CaCO_3$=Carbon dioxide 44, lime 56=100. Part of the calcium is sometimes replaced by magnesium, iron, or manganese, more rarely by strontium, barium, zinc, or lead.

The varieties are very numerous, and diverse in appearance. They depend mainly on the following points: (1) differences in crystallization; (2) in structural condition, the extremes being perfect crystals and earthy massive forms; (3) in color, diaphaneity, odor on friction, due to impurities; (4) in modes of origin.

1. *Crystallized.* Crystals and crystallized masses afford easily cleavage rhombohedrons; and when transparent they are called *Iceland Spar*, and also *Doubly-refracting Spar* (Doppelspath, *Germ.*).

The crystals vary in proportions from broad tabular to moderately slender acicular, and take a great diversity of forms. But the extreme kinds so pass into one another through those that are intermediate that no satisfactory classification is possible. Many are stout or short in shape because normally so. But other forms that are long tapering in their full development occur short and stout because abbreviated by an abrupt termination in a broad o, or an obtuse rhombohedron (as $-\frac{1}{2}$ or R), or a low scalenohedron (as $\frac{1}{2}^3$), or a combination of these forms; and thus the crystals having essentially the same combinations of planes vary greatly in shape. The acute scalenohedrons like f. 724, are called *dog-tooth spar*.

Fontainebleau limestone. Crystals of the form in f. 719C, from Fontainebleau and Nemours, France, containing a large amount of sand, some 50 to 63 p. c. Similar sandstone crystals occur at Sievring, near Vienna, and elsewhere. Pseudomorphous scalenohedrons of sandstone, after calcite, are found near Heidelberg.

Satin Spar; fine fibrous, with a silky lustre. Resembles fibrous gypsum, which is also called satin spar, but is much harder and effervesces with acids. *Argentine (Schieferspath)*, a pearly lamellar calcite, the lamellæ more or less undulating; color white, grayish, yellowish, or reddish. *Aphrite*, in its harder and more sparry variety (*Schaumspath*) is a foliated white pearly calcite, near argentine; in its softer kinds (*Schaumerde, Silvery Chalk, Ecume de Terre* H.) it approaches chalk, though lighter, pearly in lustre, silvery-white or yellowish in color, soft and greasy to the touch, and more or less scaly in structure.

2. *Massive Varieties.* *Granular limestone* (*Saccharoidal limestone*, so named because like loaf-sugar in fracture). The texture varies from quite coarse to very fine granular, and the latter passes by imperceptible shades into *compact* limestone. The colors are various, as white, yellow, reddish, green, and usually they are clouded and give a handsome effect when the material is polished. When such limestones are fit for polishing, or for architectural or ornamental use, they are called *marbles*. *Statuary marble* is pure white, fine grained, and firm in texture. *Hard compact limestone*, varies from nearly pure white, through grayish, drab, buff, yellowish, and reddish shades, to bluish-gray, dark brownish-gray, and black, and is sometimes variously veined. The colors dull, excepting ochre-yellow and ochre-red varieties. Many kinds make beautiful marble when polished.

Shell-marble includes kinds cons sting largely of fossil shells. *Ruin-marble* is a kind of compact calcareous marl, showing, when polished, pictures of fortifications, temples, etc., in ruins, due to infiltration of oxide of iron. *Lithographic stone* is a very even grained compact limestone, usually of buff or drab color; as that of Solenhofen. *Breccia marble* is made of fragments of limestone cemented together, and is often very beautiful when the fragments are of different colors, or are imbedded in a base that contrasts well. The colors are very various. *Pudding stone* marble consists of pebbles or rounded stones cemented. It is often called, improperly, breccia marble.

Hydraulic limestone is an impure limestone. The varieties in the United States contain 20 to 40 p. c. of magnesia, and 12 to 30 p. c. of silica and alumina.

Soft compact limestone. *Chalk* is white, grayish-white, or yellowish, and soft enough to leave a trace on a board. The consolidation into a rock of such softness may be owing to the fact that the material is largely the hollow shells of rhizopods. *Calcareous marl* (Mergel-kalk, *Germ.*) is a soft earthy deposit, often hardly at all consolidated, with or without distinct fragments of shells; it generally contains much clay, and graduates into a calcareous clay.

Concretionarg massive. *Oölite* (Rogenstein, *Germ.*) is a granular limestone, but its grains are minute rounded concretions, looking somewhat like the roe of a fish, the name coming from 'ωον, egg. It occurs among all the geological formations, from the Lower Silurian to the most recent, and it is now forming about the coral reefs of Florida. *Pisolite* (Erbsentein *Germ.*) consists of concretions as large often as a small pea, or even larger, the concretions having usually a distinct concentric structure. It is formed in large masses in the vicinity of the Hot Springs at Carlsbad in Bohemia.

Deposited from calcareous springs, streams, or in caverns, etc. (a) *Stalactites* are the calcareous cylinders or cones that hang from the roofs of limestone caverns, and which are formed from the waters that drip through the roof; these waters hold some calcium bicarbonate in solution, and leave calcium carbonate to form the stalactite when evaporation takes place. Stalactites vary from transparent to nearly opaque; from a granular crystalline structure to a radiating fibrous; from a white color and colorless to yellowish-gray and brown. (b) *Stalagmite* is the same material covering the floors of caverns, it being made from the waters that drop from the roofs, or from sources over the bottom or sides; cones of it sometimes rise from the floor to meet the stalactites above.

(c) *Calc-sinter, Travertine, Calc Tufa.* Travertine (*Confetto di Tivoli*) is of essentially the same origin with stalagmite, but is distinctively a deposit from springs or rivers, especially where in large deposits, as along the river Anio, at Tivoli, near Rome, where the deposit is scores of feet in thickness. It has a very cavernous and irregularly banded structure, owing to its mode of formation.

(d) *Agaric mineral; Rock-milk* (*Bergmilch, Montmilch,* Germ.) is a very soft, white material breaking easily in the fingers, deposited sometimes in caverns, or about sources holding lime in solution.

(e) *Rock-meal* (*Bergmehl*, Germ.) is white and light, like cotton, becoming a powder on the slightest pressure. It is an efflorescence, and is common near Paris, especially at the quarries of Nanterre.

Pyr., etc.—In the closed tube sometimes decrepitates, and, if containing metallic oxides, may change its color. B.B. infusible, but becomes caustic, glows, and colors the flame red after ignition the assay reacts alkaline; moistened with hydrochloric acid imparts the characteristic lime color to the flame. In borax dissolves with effervescence, and if saturated, yields on cooling an opaque. milk-white, crystalline bead. Varieties containing metallic oxides color the borax and salt of phosphorus beads accordingly. With soda on platinum foil fuses to a clear mass; on charcoal it at first fuses, but later the soda is absorbed by the coal, leaving an infusible and strongly luminous residue of lime. In the solid mass effervesces when moistened with hydrochloric acid, and fragments dissolve with brisk effervescence even in cold acid.

Diff.—Distinguishing characters: perfect rhombohedral cleavage; softness, can be scratched with a knife; effervescence in cold dilute acid; infusibility. Less hard and of lower specific gravity than aragonite.

Obs.—Andreasberg in the Harz is one of the best European localities of crystallized calcite; there are other localities in the Tyrol, Styria, Carinthia, Hungary, Saxony, Hesse Darmstadt (at Auerbach), Hesse Cassel, Norway, France, and in England in Derbyshire, Cumberland, Cornwall; Scotland; in Iceland.

In the U. States prominent localities are: in *N. York*, in St. Lawrence and Jefferson Cos., especially at the Rossie lead mine; in Antwerp; *dog-tooth spar*, in Niagara Co., near Lockport; near Booneville, Oneida Co. ; at Anthony's Nose, on the Hudson; at Watertown, *Agaric mineral*; at Schoharie, fine *stalactites* in many caverns. In *Conn.*, at the lead mine, Middletown. In *N. Jersey*, at Bergen. In *Virginia*, at the celebrated Wier's cave, *stalactites* of great beauty; also in the large caves of *Kentucky*. At the Lake Superior copper mines, splendid crystals often containing scales of native copper. At Warsaw, *Illinois ;* at Quincy, *Ill.;* at Hazle Green, *Wis*. In Nova Scotia, at Partridge I.

DOLOMITE.

Rhombohedral. $R \wedge R = 106° \; 15'$, $O \wedge R = 136°\; 8\frac{1}{2}'$; $\dot{c} = 0·8322$. $R \wedge R$ varies between $106° \; 10'$ and $106° \; 20'$. Cleavage: R perfect. Faces R often curved, and secondary planes usually with horizontal striæ. Twins: similar to f. 733. Also in imitative shapes; also amorphous, granular, coarse or fine, and grains often slightly coherent.

734

$H. = 3·5-4.$ $G. = 2·8-2·9$, true dolomite. Lustre vitreous, inclining to pearly in some varieties. Color white, reddish, or greenish-white; also rose-red, green, brown, gray, and black. Subtransparent to translucent. Brittle.

Comp., Var.—$(Ca,Mg)CO_3$, the ratio of Ca : Mg in normal or true dolomite is 1 : 1=Calcium carbonate 54·35, magnesium carbonate 45·65. Some kinds included under the name have other proportions; but this may arise from their being mixtures of dolomite with calcite or magnesite. Iron, manganese, and more rarely cobalt or zinc are sometimes present.

The varieties are the following:

Crystallized. *Pearl spar* includes rhombohedral crystallizations with curved faces. *Columnar* or fibrous. *Granular* constitutes many of the kinds of white statuary marble, and white and colored architectural marbles, names of some of which have been mentioned under calcite.

Compact massive, like ordinary limestone. Many of the limestone strata of the globe are here included, and much *hydraulic limestone*, noticed under calcite.

Ferriferous ; Brown spar, in part. Contains iron, and as the proportion increases it graduates into ankerite (q. v.). The color is white to brown, and becomes brownish on exposure through oxidation of the iron. *Manganiferous*. Colorless to flesh-red. $R \wedge R = 106° \; 23'$ 106° 16'. *Cobaltiferous*. Colored reddish; $G. = 2·921$, Gibbs.

The varieties based on variations in the proportions of the carbonates are the following : (*a*) *Normal dolomite*, ratio of Ca to Mg=1 : 1, (*b*) ratio $1\frac{1}{3}$: 1=3 : 2; ratio=2 : 1; ratio 3 : 1; ratio=5 : 1; ratio 1 : 3. The last (*f*) may be dolomitic magnesite; and the others, from (b). dolomitic calcite, or calcite + dolomite. The manner in which dolomite is ofted mi. with calcite, forming its veins and its fossil shells (see below), shows that this is not impr(e) able.

Pyr., etc.—B.B. acts like calcite, but does not give a clear mass when fused with soda (on) platinum foil. Fragments thrown into cold acid are very slowly acted upon, while in powde(r) in warm acid the mineral is readily dissolved with effervescence. The ferriferous dolomite become brown on exposure.

Diff.—Resembles calcite, but generally to be distinguished in that it does not effervesce readily in the mass in cold acid.

Obs.—Massive dolomite constitutes extensive strata, called limestone strata, in various regions. Crystalline and compact varieties are often associated with serpentine and other magnesian rocks, and with ordinary limestones. Some of the prominent localities are at Salzburg; the Tyrol; Schemnitz in Hungary; Kapnik in Transylvania; Freiberg in Saxony; the lead mines at Alston in Derbyshire, etc.

In the U. States, in *Vermont*, at Roxbury. In *Rhode Island*, at Smithfield. In *N. Jersey*, at Hoboken. In *N. York*, at Lockport, Niagara Falls, and Rochester; also at Glenn's Falls, in Richmond Co., and at the Parish ore bed, St. Lawrence Co.; at Brewster, Putnam Co.

Named after Dolomieu, who announced some of the marked characteristics of the rock in 1791—its not effervescing with acids, while burning like limestone, and its solubility after heating in acids.

ANKERITE.

Rhombohedral. $R \wedge R = 106° 7'$, Zepharovich. Also crystalline massive, coarse or fine granular, and compact.

H.=3·5–4. G.=2·95–3·1. Lustre vitreous to pearly. Color white, gray, reddish. Translucent to subtranslucent.

Comp.—$CaCO_3 + FeCO_3 + x(CaMgC_2O_6)$. Here, according to Boricky, x may have the values $\frac{1}{4}, \frac{1}{3}, \frac{1}{2}, \frac{2}{3}, \frac{4}{5}$, 2, 3, 4, 5, 10. The varieties having the five higher values of x he calls *parankerite*, while the others are normal *ankerite*. If $x=1$, the formula is equivalent to $2CaCO_3 + MgCO_3 + FeCO_3$, and requires: Calcium carbonate 50, magnesium carbonate 21, iron carbonate 29=100. Manganese is also sometimes present.

Pyr., etc.—B.B. like dolomite, but darkens in color, and on charcoal becomes black and magnetic; with the fluxes reacts for iron and manganese. Soluble with effervescence in the acids.

Obs.—Occurs with siderite at the Styrian mines; in Bohemia; Siegen; Schneeberg; Nova Scotia, etc.

MAGNESITE.

Rhombohedral. $R \wedge R = 107° 29'$, $O \wedge R = 136° 56'$; $\dot{c} = 0.8095$. Cleavage: rhombohedral, perfect. Also massive; granular, to very compact.

H.=3·5–4·5. G.=3–3·08, cryst.; 2·8, earthy; 3–3·2, when ferriferous. Lustre vitreous; fibrous varieties sometimes silky. Color white, yellowish or grayish-white, brown. Transparent—opaque. Fracture flat conchoidal.

Var.—*Ferriferous, Breunerite;* containing several p. c. of iron protoxide; G.=3–3·2; white, yellowish, brownish, rarely black and bituminous; often becoming brown on exposure, and hence called *Brown Spar*.

Comp.—Magnesium carbonate, $MgCO_3$ = Carbon dioxide 52·4, magnesia 47·6=100; but iron often replacing some magnesium.

Pyr., etc.—B.B. resembles calcite and dolomite, and like the latter is but slightly acted upon by cold acids; in powder is readily dissolved with effervescence in warm hydrochloric acid.

Obs.—Found in talcose schist, serpentine, and other magnesian rocks; as veins in serpentine, or mixed with it so as to form a variety of verd-antique marble (*magnesitic ophiolite* o(r)

Hunt); also in Canada, as a rock, more or less pure, associated with steatite, serpentine, and dolomite.

Occurs at Hrubschütz in Moravia; in Styria, and in the Tyrol; at Frankenstein in Silesia; Snarum, Norway; Baùdissero and Castellamonte in Piedmont. In America, at Bolton, Mass.; at Barehills, near Baltimore, Md.; in Penn., at West Goshen, Chester Co.; near Texas, Lancaster Co.; California.

MESITITE and PISTOMESITE come under the general formula $(Mg, Fe)CO_3$; with the former $Mg : Fe = 2 : 1$; with the latter $= 1 : 1$.

SIDERITE. Spathic Iron. Chalybite. Eisenspath, *Germ.*

Rhombohedral. $R \wedge R = 107°$, $O \wedge R = 136° 37'$; $\dot{c} = 0.81715$. The faces often curved, as below. Cleavage: rhombohedral, perfect. Twins: twinning-plane $-\frac{1}{2}$. Also in botryoidal and globular forms, subfibrous within, occasionally silky fibrous. Often cleavable massive, with cleavage planes undulating. Coarse or fine granular.

H. $= 3.5-4.5$. G. $= 3.7-3.9$. Lustre vitreous, more or less pearly. Streak white. Color ash-gray, yellowish-gray, greenish-gray, also brown and brownish-red, rarely green; and sometimes white. Translucent—subtranslucent. Fracture uneven. Brittle.

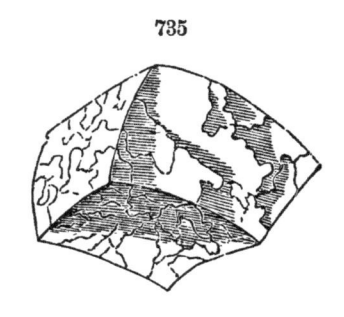

Comp., Var.—Iron carbonate, $FeCO_3 =$ Carbon dioxide 37.9, iron protoxide 62.1. But part of the iron usually replaced by manganese, and often by magnesium or calcium. Some varieties contain 8–10 p. c. MnO.

The principal varieties are the following:

(1) *Ordinary*. (*a*) *Crystallized*. (*b*) *Concretionary = Spherosiderite*; in globular concretions, either solid or concentric scaly, with usually a fibrous structure. (*c*) *Granular* to *compact massive*. (*d*) *Oölitic*, like oölitic limestone in structure. (*e*) *Earthy*, or stony, impure from mixture with clay or sand, constituting a large part of the clay iron-stone of the coal formation and other stratified deposits; H. $= 3$ to 7, the last from the silica present; G. $= 3.0-3.8$, or mostly $3.15-3.65$.

Pyr., etc.—In the closed tube decrepitates, evolves carbon oxide and carbon dioxide, blackens and becomes magnetic. B.B. blackens and fuses at 4.5. With the fluxes reacts for iron, and with soda and nitre on platinum foil generally gives a manganese reaction. Only slowly acted upon by cold acid, but dissolves with brisk effervescence in hot hydrochloric acid.

Diff.—Specific gravity higher than that of calcite and dolomite. B.B. becomes magnetic readily.

Obs.—Siderite occurs in many of the rock strata, in gneiss, mica slate, clay slate, and as clay iron-stone in connection with the Coal formation and many other stratified deposits. It is often associated with metallic ores. At Freiberg it occurs in silver mines. In Cornwall it accompanies tin. It is also found accompanying copper and iron pyrites, galenite, vitreous copper, etc. In New York, according to Beck, it is almost always associated with specular iron. In the region in and about Styria and Carinthia this ore forms extensive tracts in gneiss. At Harzgerode in the Harz, it occurs in fine crystals; also in Cornwall, Alston-Moor, and Devonshire; near Glasgow; also at Mouillar, Magescote, etc., in France, etc.

In the U. States, in *Vermont.* at Plymouth. In *Mass.*, at Sterling. In *Conn.*, at Roxbury. In *N. York*, at the Sterling ore bed in Antwerp, Jefferson Co.; at the Rossie iron mines, St. Lawrence Co. In *N. Carolina*, at Fentress and Harlem mines. The argillaceous carbonate, in nodules and beds (clay iron-stone), is abundant in the coal regions of Penn., Ohio, and many parts of the country.

RHODOCHROSITE.* Dialogite. Manganspath, *Germ.*

Rhombohedral. $R \wedge R = 106° 51'$, $O \wedge R = 136° 31\frac{1}{2}'$; $\dot{c} = 0.8211$. Cleavage: R, perfect. Also globular and botryoidal, having a columnar structure, sometimes indistinct. Also granular massive; occasionally impalpable; incrusting.

H.=3·5–4·5. G.=3·4–3·7. Lustre vitreous, inclining to pearly. Color shades of rose-red, yellowish-gray, fawn-colored, dark red, brown. Streak white. Translucent—subtranslucent. Fracture uneven. Brittle.

Comp.—$MnCO_3$=Carbon dioxide 38·3, manganese protoxide 61·7; but part of the manganese usually replaced by calcium, and often also by magnesium or iron; and sometimes by cobalt.

Pyr., etc.—B.B. changes to gray, brown, and black, and decrepitates strongly, but is infusible. With salt of phosphorus and borax in O.F. gives an amethystine-colored bead in R.F. becomes colorless. With soda on platinum foil a bluish-green manganate. Dissolves with effervescence in warm hydrochloric acid. On exposure to the air changes to brown, and some bright rose-red varieties become paler.

Obs.—Occurs commonly in veins along with ores of silver, lead, and copper, and with other ores of manganese. Found at Schemnitz and Kapnik in Hungary; Nagyag in Transylvania; near Elbingerode in the Harz; at Freiberg in Saxony.

Occurs in New Jersey, at Mine Hill, Franklin Furnace. Abundant at the silver mines of Austin, Nevada; at Placentia Bay, Newfoundland.

Named *rhodochrosite* from ῥόδον, *a rose*, and χρῶσις, *color;* and *dialogite*, from διαλογή, doubt.

SMITHSONITE. Calamine pt. Galmei pt. Zinkspath, *Germ.*

Rhombohedral. $R \wedge R = 107°\ 40'$, $O \wedge R = 137°\ 3'$; $c = 0·8062$. R generally curved and rough. Cleavage: R perfect. Also reniform, botryoidal, or stalactitic, and in crystalline incrustations; also granular, and sometimes impalpable, occasionally earthy and friable.

H.=5. G.=4–4·45. Lustre vitreous, inclining to pearly. Streak white. Color white, often grayish, greenish, brownish-white, sometimes green and brown. Subtransparent—translucent. Fracture uneven—imperfectly conchoidal. Brittle.

Comp., Var.—$ZnCO_3$=Carbon dioxide 35·2, zinc oxide 64·8=100; but part of the zinc often replaced by iron or manganese, and by traces of calcium and magnesium; sometimes by cadmium.

Varieties.—(1) *Ordinary.* (*a*) *Crystallized;* (*b*) *botryoidal* and *stalactitic,* common; (*c*) *granular* to *compact massive;* (*d*) *earthy,* impure, in nodular and cavernous masses, varying from grayish-white to dark gray, brown, brownish-red, brownish-black, and often with drusy surfaces in the cavities; "dry-bone" of American miners.

Pyr., etc.—In the closed tube loses carbon dioxide, and, if pure, is yellow while hot and colorless on cooling. B.B. infusible; moistened with cobalt solution and heated in O.F. gives a green color on cooling. With soda on charcoal gives zinc vapors, and coats the coal yellow while hot, becoming white on cooling; this coating, moistened with cobalt solution, gives a green color after heating in O.F. Cadmiferous varieties, when treated with soda, give at first a deep yellow or brown coating before the zinc coating appears. With the fluxes some varieties react for iron, copper, and manganese. Soluble in hydrochloric acid with effervescence.

Diff.—Distinguished from calamine by its effervescence in acids.

Obs.—Smithsonite is found both in veins and beds, especially in company with galenite and blende; also with copper and iron ores. It usually occurs in calcareous rocks, and is generally associated with calamine, and sometimes with limonite. It is often produced by the action of zinc sulphate upon calcium or magnesium carbonate.

Found at Nertschinsk in Siberia; at Dognatzka in Hungary; Bleiberg and Raibel in Carinthia; Moresnet in Belgium. In England, at Roughten Gill, Alston Moor, near Matlock, in the Mendip Hills, and elsewhere; in Scotland, at Leadhills; in Ireland, at Donegal.

In the U. States, in *N. Jersey*, at Mine Hill, near the Franklin Furnace. In *Penn.*, at Lancaster abundant; at the Perkiomen lead mine; at the Ueberroth mine, near Bethlehem. In *Wisconsin*, at Mineral Point, Shullsburg, etc. In *Minnesota*, at Ewing's diggings, N. W. of Dubuque, etc. In *Missouri* and *Arkansas*, along with the lead ores in Lower Silurian limestone.

Aragonite Group.

ARAGONITE.

Orthorhombic $I \wedge I = 116° \, 10'$, $O \wedge 1\text{-}\bar{\imath} = 130° \, 50'$; $\check{c} : \bar{b} : \check{a} = 1.1571 : 1.6055 : 1$. $O \wedge 1 = 126° \, 15'$, $O \wedge 1\text{-}\breve{\imath} = 137° \, 15'$, $1\text{-}\breve{\imath} \wedge 1\text{-}\breve{\imath}$, top, $= 108° \, 26'$. Crystals usually having O striated parallel to the shorter diagonal; often tapering from the presence of acute domes and pyramids, which have unusual indices. Cleavage: I imperfect; $i\text{-}\breve{\imath}$ distinct; $1\text{-}\breve{\imath}$ imperfect. Twins: twinning-plane I, producing often hexagonal forms, f. 738, compare figures on pp. 96, 97. Twinning often many times repeated in the same crystal, producing successive reversed layers, the alternate of which may be exceedingly thin; often so delicate as to produce by the succession a fine striation of the faces of a prism or of a cleavage plane. Also globular, reniform, and coralloidal shapes; sometimes columnar, composed of straight and divergent fibres; also stalactitic; incrusting.

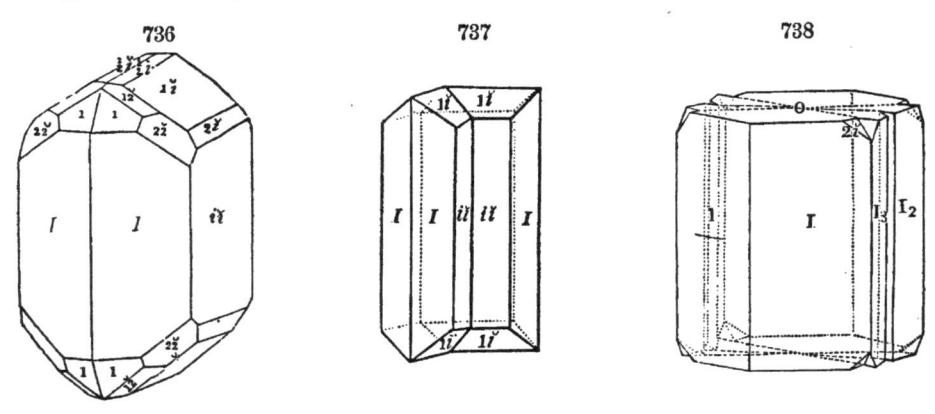

736 737 738

H. = 3.5-4. G. = 2.931, Haidinger. Lustre vitreous, sometimes inclining to resinous on surfaces of fracture. Color white; also gray, yellow, green, and violet; streak uncolored. Transparent—translucent. Fracture subconchoidal. Brittle.

Var.—1. *Ordinary.* (*a*) Crystallized in simple or compound crystals, the latter much the most common; often in radiating groups of acicular crystals. (*b*) Columnar; a fine fibrous variety with silky lustre is called *Satin spar.* (*c*) Massive. Stalactitic or stalagmitic (either compact or fibrous in structure), as with calcite; *Sprudelstein* is stalactitic from Carlsbad. *Coralloidal;* in groupings of delicate interlacing and coalescing stems, of a snow-white color, and looking a little like coral.

Comp.—$CaCO_3$, like calcite, = Carbon dioxide 44, lime 56 = 100.

Pyr., etc.—B.B. whitens and falls to pieces, and sometimes, when containing strontia, imparts a more intensely red color to the flame than lime; otherwise reacts like calcite.

Diff.—See calcite, p. 401.

Obs.—The most common repositories of aragonite are beds of gypsum, beds of iron ore (where it occurs in coralloidal forms, and is denominated *flos-ferri,* "*flower of iron,*" Eisenblüthe, *Germ.*), basalt, and trap rock; occasionally it occurs in lavas. It is often associated with copper and pyrite, galenite, and malachite.

First discovered in Aragon, Spain (whence its name), at Molina and Valencia. Since found at Bilin in Bohemia; at Herrengrund in Hungary, f. 738; at Baumgarten in Silesia;

at Leogang in Salzburg; in Waltsch, Bohemia, and many other places. The *flosferri* variety is found in great perfection in the Styrian mines. In Buckinghamshire, Devonshire, in caverns; at Leadhills in Lanarkshire.

Occurs in serpentine at Hoboken, N. J.; at Edenville, N. Y.; at the Parish ore bed, Rossie, N. Y.; at Haddam, Conn.; at New Garden, in Chester Co., Penn.; at Wood's Mine, Lancaster Co., Penn.; at Warsaw, Ill., lining geodes.

MANGANOCALCITE.—Composition $2MnCO_3+(Ca,Mg)CO_3$, with a little iron replacing part of the manganese. G.$=3·037$. Color flesh-red to reddish-white. Schemnitz, Hungary.

WITHERITE.

Orthorhombic. $I \wedge I = 118° 30'$, $O \wedge 1\text{-}\bar{\imath} = 128° 45'$; $\check{c} : \bar{b} : \check{a} = 1·246 : 1·6808 : 1$. Twins: all the annexed figures, composition parallel to I; reëntering angles sometimes observed. Cleavage: I distinct; also in globular, tuberose, and botryoidal forms; structure either columnar or granular; also amorphous.

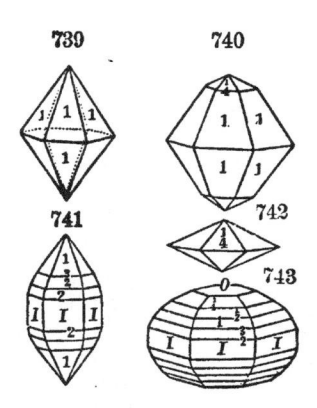

H.$=3-3·75$. G.$=4·29-4·35$. Lustre vitreous, inclining to resinous, on surfaces of fracture. Color white, often yellowish, or grayish. Streak white. Subtransparent—translucent. Fracture uneven. Brittle.

Comp.—$BaCO_3=$ Carbon dioxide 22·3, baryta 77·7$=100$.

Pyr., etc.—B.B. fuses at 2 to a bead, coloring the flame yellowish-green; after fusion reacts alkaline. B.B. on charcoal with soda fuses easily, and is absorbed by the coal. Soluble in dilute hydrochloric acid; this solution, even when very much diluted, gives with sulphuric acid a white precipitate which is insoluble in acids.

Diff.—Distinguishing characters: high specific gravity; effervescence with acids; *green* coloration of the flame B.B.

Obs.—Occurs at Alston-Moor in Cumberland; at Fallowfield, near Hexham in Northumberland; Tarnowitz in Silesia; Leogang in Salzburg; Peggau in Styria; some places in Sicily; the mine of Arqueros, near Coquimbo, Chili; near Lexington, Ky., with barite.

Witherite is extensively mined at Fallowfield, and is used in chemical works in the manufacture of plate-glass, and in France in making beet-sugar.

BROMLITE.—Formula as for barytocalcite, but orthorhombic in form.

STRONTIANITE.

Orthorhombic. $I \wedge I = 117° 19'$, $O \wedge 1\text{-}\bar{\imath} = 130° 5'$; $\check{c} : \bar{b} : \check{a} = 1·1883 : 1·6421 : 1$. $O \wedge 1 = 125° 43'$, $O \wedge 1\text{-}\check{\imath} = 144° 6'$, $1 \wedge 1$, mac., $= 130° 1'$, $1 \wedge 1$, brach., $= 92° 11'$. Cleavage: I nearly perfect, $i\text{-}\check{\imath}$ in traces. Crystals often acicular and in divergent groups. Twins: like those of aragonite. O usually striated parallel to the shorter diagonal. Also in columnar globular forms; fibrous and granular.

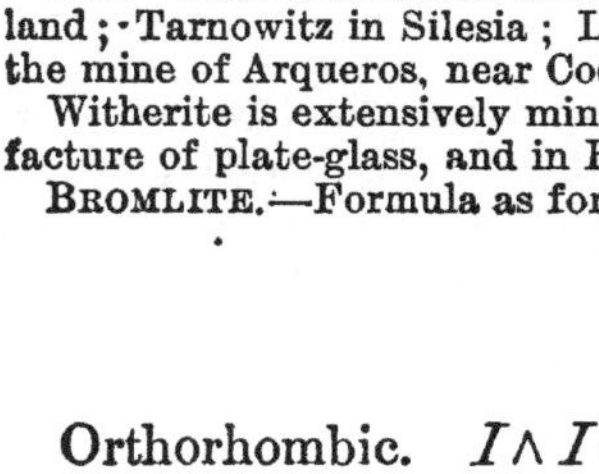

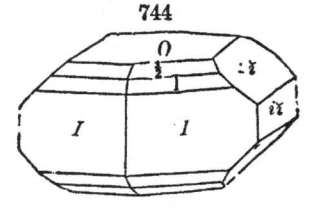

H.$=3·5-4$. G.$=3·605-3·713$. Lustre vitreous; inclining to resinous on uneven faces of fracture. Color pale asparagus-green, apple-green; also white, gray, yellow, and yellowish-brown. Streak white. Transparent—translucent. Fracture uneven. Brittle.

Comp.—$SrCO_3$ = Carbon dioxide 29·7, strontia 70·3; but a small part of the strontium often replaced by calcium.

Pyr., etc.—B.B. swells up, throws out minute sprouts, fuses only on the thin edges, and colors the flame strontia-red; the assay reacts alkaline after ignition. Moistened with hydrochloric acid and treated either B.B. or in the naked lamp gives an intense red color. With soda on charcoal the pure mineral fuses to a clear glass, and is entirely absorbed by the coal; if lime or iron be present they are separated and remain on the surface of the coal. Soluble in hydrochloric acid; the dilute solution when treated with sulphuric acid gives a white precipitate.

Diff.—Differs from related minerals, not carbonates, in effervescing with acids; lower specific gravity than witherite, and colors the flame *red*.

Obs.—Occurs at Strontian in Argyleshire; in Yorkshire, England; Giant's Causeway, Ireland; Clausthal in the Harz; Bräunsdorf, Saxony; Leogang in Salzburg. In the U. States it occurs at Schoharie, N. Y., in granular and columnar masses, and also in crystals. At Muscalonge Lake; at Chaumont Bay and Theresa, in Jefferson Co., N. Y.; Mifflin Co., Penn

CERUSSITE. Weissbleierz, Bleispath, *Germ.*

Orthorhombic. $I \wedge I = 117° 13'$, $O \wedge 1\text{-}\breve{\imath} = 130° 9\frac{1}{2}'$; $\breve{c} : \bar{b} : \breve{a} = 1·1852 : 1·6388 : 1$. $O \wedge 1 = 125° 46'$, $O \wedge 1\text{-}\breve{\imath} = 144° 8'$, $1 \wedge 1$, mac., $= 130°$, $1 \wedge 1$, brach., $= 92° 19'$. Cleavage: I often imperfect; $2\text{-}\breve{\imath}$ hardly less so. Crystals usually thin, broad, and brittle; sometimes stout. Twins: very common; twinning-plane I, producing usually cruciform or stellate forms; also less commonly, twinning-plane $i\text{-}\breve{s}$. Rarely fibrous, often granular massive and compact. Sometimes stalactitic. H. = 3–3·5. G. = 6·465–6·480; some earthy varieties as low as 5·4. Lustre adamantine, inclining to vitreous or resinous; sometimes pearly; sometimes submetallic, if the colors are dark, or from a superficial change. Color white, gray, grayish-black, sometimes tinged blue or green by some of the salts of copper; streak uncolored. Transparent—subtranslucent. Fracture conchoidal. Very brittle.

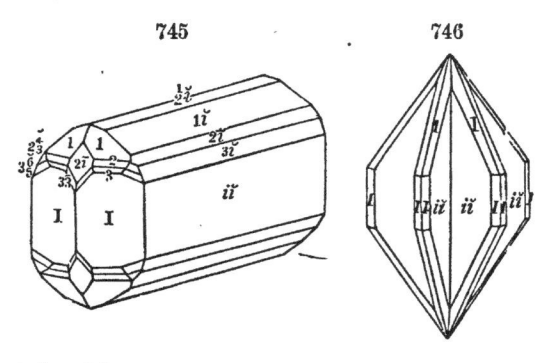

Comp.—$PbCO_3$ = Carbon dioxide 16·5, lead oxide 83·5 = 100.

Pyr., etc.— In the closed tube decrepitates, loses carbon dioxide, turns first yellow, and at a higher temperature dark red, but becomes yellow again on cooling. B.B. on charcoal fuses very easily, and in R.F. yields metallic lead. Soluble in dilute nitric acid with effervescence.

Diff.—Unlike anglesite, it effervesces with nitric acid. Characterized by high specific gravity, and yielding lead B.B.

Obs.—Occurs in connection with other lead minerals, and is formed from galenite, which, as it passes to a sulphate, may be changed to carbonate by means of solutions of calcium bicarbonate. It is found at Johanngeorgenstadt; at Nertschinsk and Beresof in Siberia; at Clausthal in the Harz; at Bleiberg in Carinthia; at Mies and Przibram in Bohemia; at Retzbanya, Hungary; in England, in Cornwall; near Matlock and Wirksworth, Derbyshire; at Leadhills, Scotland; in Wicklow, Ireland.

Found in *Penn.*, at Phenixville; at Perkiomen. In *N. York*, at the Rossie lead mine. In *Virginia*, at Austin's mines, Wythe Co. In *N. Carolina*, at King's mine, Davidson Co., good. In Wisconsin and other lead mines of the northwestern States, rarely in crystals; near the Blue Mounds, Wisc., in stalactites.

BARYTOCALCITE.

Monoclinic. $C = 73° 52'$, $I \wedge I = 106° 54'$, $O \wedge 1\text{-}i = 149°$; $\dot{c} : \bar{b} : \dot{a} = 0.81035 : 1.29583 : 1$. Cleavage: I, perfect; O, less perfect; also massive. H.=4. G.=3·6363–3·66. Lustre vitreous, inclining to resinous. Color white, grayish, greenish, or yellowish. Streak white. Transparent—translucent. Fracture uneven.

Comp.—$(Ba,Ca)CO_3$, where Ba : Ca=1 : 1=Barium carbonate 66·3, calcium carbonate 33·7=100.
Pyr., etc.—B.B. colors the flame yellowish-green, and at a higher temperature fuses on the thin edges and assumes a pale green color; the assay reacts alkaline after ignition. With the fluxes reacts for manganese. With soda on charcoal the lime is separated as an infusible mass, while the remainder is absorbed by the coal. Soluble in dilute hydrochloric acid.
Obs.—Occurs at Alston-Moor in Cumberland, in the Subcarboniferous or mountain limestone.

PARISITE.—A carbonate containing cerium (also La,Di), and calcium with 6 p. c. fluorine. Exact composition uncertain. In hexagonal crystals. Color brownish-yellow. Muso valley, New Granada. KISCHTIMITE, from the gold washing of the Barsovska river, Urals, is similar in composition, but contains no calcium.
BASTNÄSITE (Hamartite).—Composition $2RCO_3+RF_2$, with R=Ce : La=2 : 3. Analysis, Nordenskiöld, CO_2 19·50, LaO 45·77, CeO 28·49, H_2O 1·01, F,O, (5·23)=100. Found in small masses imbedded between allanite crystals. Riddarhyttan, Sweden.

PHOSGENITE. Bleihornerz, *Germ.*

Tetragonal. $O \wedge 1\text{-}i = 132° 37'$; $\dot{c} = 1·0871$. Cleavage: I and $i\text{-}i$ bright; also basal.
H.=2·75–3. G.=6–6·31. Lustre adamantine. Color white, gray, and yellow. Streak white. Transparent—translucent. Rather sectile.

Comp.—$PbCO_3+PbCl_2$=Lead carbonate 49, lead chloride 51=100, or lead oxide 81·9, carbon dioxide 8·1, chlorine 13·0=102·9.
Pyr., etc.—B.B. melts readily to a yellow globule, which on cooling becomes white and crystalline. On charcoal in R.F. gives metallic lead, with a white coating of lead chloride. With a salt of phosphorus bead previously saturated with copper oxide gives the chlorine reaction. Dissolves with effervescence in nitric acid.
Obs.—At Cromford near Matlock in Derbyshire; very rare in Cornwall; in large crystals at Gibbas and Monteponi in Sardinia; near Bobrek in Upper Silesia.

HYDROUS CARBONATES.

TRONA.

Monoclinic. $O \wedge i\text{-}i = 103° 15'$. Cleavage: $i\text{-}i$ perfect. Often fibrous or columnar massive.
H.=2·5–3. G.=2·11. Lustre vitreous, glistening. Color gray or yellowish-white. Translucent. Taste alkaline. Not altered by exposure to a dry atmosphere.

Comp.—$Na_4C_3O_8+3aq$=Carbon dioxide 40·2, soda 37·8, water 22·0.
Pyr., etc.—In the closed tube yields water and carbon dioxide. B.B. imparts an intensely yellow color to the flame. Soluble in water, and effervesces with acids. Reacts alkaline with moistened test paper.
Obs.—The specimen analyzed by Klaproth came from the province of Suckenna, two days' journey from Fezzen,   ica. To this species belongs the urao found at the bottom of a lake

OXYGEN COMPOUNDS.—CARBONATES. 409

In Maracaibo, S. A., a day's journey from Merida. Efflorescences of trona occur near the Sweetwater river, Rocky Mountains, mixed with sodium sulphate and common salt.

NATRON or Soda (sodium carbonate, $Na_2CO_3 + 10aq$). THERMONATRITE, $Na_2CO_3 + aq$. TESCHEMACHERITE, Ammonium carbonate.

GAY-LUSSITE.

Monoclinic. $C = 78° 27'$, $I \wedge I = 68° 50'$ and $111° 10'$, $O \wedge 1\text{-}\check{\imath} = 125° 15'$; $\acute{c} : b : \check{a} = 0.96945 : 0.67137 : 1$. $1\text{-}\check{\imath} \wedge 1\text{-}\check{\imath}$, adj., $= 109° 30'$, $\frac{1}{2} \wedge \frac{1}{2} = 110° 30'$. Crystals often lengthened, and prismatic in the direction of $1\text{-}\check{\imath}$; also in that of $\frac{1}{2}$; also (fr. Nevada) not elongate, but thin in the direction of the orthodiagonal, O being very narrow or wanting; surfaces usually uneven, being formed of minute subordinate planes. Cleavage: I perfect; O less so, but giving a reflected image in a strong light.

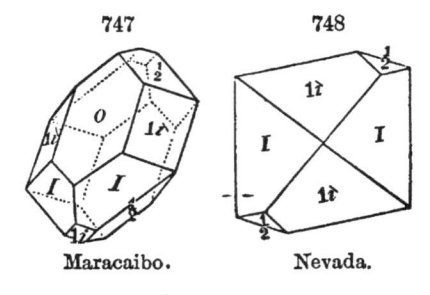

747   748

Maracaibo.   Nevada.

H.=2–3. G.=1·92–1·99. Lustre vitreous. Color white, yellowish-white. Streak uncolored to grayish. Translucent. Fracture conchoidal. Extremely brittle. Not phosphorescent by friction or heat.

Comp.—$Na_2CO_3 + CaCO_3 + 5aq$ = Sodium carbonate 35·9, calcium carbonate 33·8, water 30·3 = 100.

Pyr., etc.—Heated in a matrass the crystals decrepitate and become opaque. B B. fuses easily to a white enamel, and colors the flame intensely yellow. With the fluxes it behaves like calcium carbonate. Dissolves in acids with a brisk effervescence; partly soluble in water, and reddens turmeric.

Obs.—Abundant at Lagunilla, near Merida, in Maracaibo, where its crystals are disseminated at the bottom of a small lake, in a bed of clay, covering *urao;* the natives call it *clavos* or *nails*, in allusion to its crystalline form. Also on a small island in Little Salt Lake, near Ragtown, Nevada, about 1¼ m. S. of the main emigrant road to Humboldt. The lake is in a crater-shaped basin, and its waters are dense and strongly saline.

The distorted crystals from Sangerhausen have been long considered pseudomorphs after gay-lussite, though Des Cloizeaux regards them as pseudomorphs after celestite. Groth regards them as perhaps pseudomorphs after anhydrite. See also thinolite, p. 438.

HYDROMAGNESITE.

Monoclinic. $C = 82°$–$83°$, $I \wedge I = 87° 52'$–$88°$, $O \wedge 2\text{-}\check{\imath} = 137°$; $\acute{c} : b : \check{a} =$ (nearly) $0.455 : 1.0973 : 1$. Crystals small, usually acicular or bladed, and tufted. Also amorphous; as chalky or mealy crusts.

749

H. of crystals 3·5. G.=2·145–2·18, Smith & Brush. Lustre vitreous to silky or subpearly; also earthy. Color and streak white. Brittle.

Comp.—$3MgCO_3 + H_2MgO_2 + 3aq$ = Carbon dioxide 36·3, magnesia 43·9, water 19·8 = 100.

Pyr., etc.—In the closed tube gives off water and carbon dioxide. B.B. infusible, but whitens, and the assay reacts alkaline to turmeric paper. Soluble in acids; the crystalline compact varieties are but slowly acted upon by cold acid, but dissolves with effervescence in hot acid.

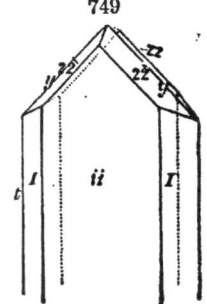

Obs.—Occurs at Hrubschitz, in Moravia, in serpentine; in Negroponte, near Kumi; at Kaiserstuhl, in Baden, impure. In the U. States, near Texas, Lancaster Co., Penn.; at Hoboken, N. J.

HYDRODOLOMITE.—Composition $3(Ca Mg)CO_3 + aq$. From Mt Somma. PENNITE from Texas, Pa., is similar.

PREDAZZITE and PENCATITE are mixtures of calcite and brucite. Tyrol.

DAWSONITE.—In thin-bladed, white, transparent crystals on trachyte. H.=3. G.=2·40. Analysis, Harrington, AlO_3 32·84, MgO tr., CaO 5·95, Na_2O 20·20, K_2O 0·38, H_2O 11·91, CO_2 29·88, SiO_2 0·40=101·56. Regarded as "a hydrous carbonate of aluminum, calcium, and sodium; or perhaps as a hydrate of aluminum with carbonates of calcium and sodium." Montreal, Canada.

HOVITE.—Supposed to be a hydrous carbonate of aluminum and calcium. Soft, white, and friable; earthy in fracture. From Hove, near Brighton, with collyrite.

LANTHANITE.

Orthorhombic. $I \wedge I = 93° \ 30'-94°$, Blake, $92° \ 46'$, v. Lang; $I \wedge 1 = 142° \ 36'$; $\dot{c} : \bar{b} : \check{a} = 0·99898 : 1·0496 : 1$, v. Lang. In thin four-sided plates or minute tables, with bevelled edges. Cleavage micaceous. Also fine granular or earthy.

H.=2·5—3. G.=2·666. Lustre pearly or dull. Color grayish-white, delicate pink, or yellowish.

Comp.—$LaCO_3 + 3aq$=Lanthana 52·6, carbon dioxide 21·3, water 26·1=100. There is some oxide of didymium with the lanthana, according to Smith.

Pyr., etc.—In the closed tube yields water. B.B. infusible; but whitens and becomes opaque, silvery, and brownish; with borax, a glass, slightly bluish, reddish, or amethystine, on cooling; with salt of phosphorus a glass, bluish amethystine while hot, red cold, the bead becoming opaque when but slightly heated, and retaining a pink color. Effervesces in the acids.

Obs.—Found coating cerite at Bastnäs, Sweden; also with the zinc ores of the Saucon valley, Lehigh Co., Pa.; at the Sandford iron-ore bed, Moriah, Essex Co., N. Y.

TENGERITE.—Yttrium carbonate. As a coating on gadolinite from Ytterby.

ZARATITE. Emerald Nickel, *Silliman*. Nickelsmaragd, *Germ.*—Composition Ni_3CO_5+ 6aq, or $NiCO_3 + 2H NiO_1 + 4aq$. This requires: Carbon dioxide 11·8, nickel oxide 59·3, water 28·9=100. Usually as an emerald-green coating; thus on chromite at Texas, Penn., where it was first noticed; Swinnaness, Shetland; Cape Ortegal, Spain.

REMINGTONITE.—A hydrous cobalt carbonate. Finksburg, Md.

HYDROZINCITE. Zinkblüthe, *Germ.*

Massive, earthy or compact. As incrustations, the crusts sometimes concentric and agate-like. At times reniform, pisolitic, stalactitic.

H.=2-2·5. G.=3·58-3·8. Lustre dull. Color pure white, grayish or yellowish. Streak shining. Usually earthy or chalk-like.

Comp.—In part $ZnCO_3 + 2H_2ZnO_1$=Carbon dioxide 13·6, zinc oxide 75·3, water 11·1=100.

Pyr., etc.—In the closed tube yields water; in other respects resembles smithsonite.

Obs.—Occurs at most mines of zinc, and is a result of the alteration of the other ores of this metal. Found in great quantities at the Dolores mine, Udias valley, province of Santander, in Spain; at Bleiberg and Raibel in Carinthia; near Reimsbeck, in Westphalia. In the U. States, at Friedensville, Pa.; at Linden, in Wisconsin; in Marion Co., Arkansas (*marionite*).

AURICHALCITE.—A cupreous hydrozincite. Usually in drusy incrustations. Altai; Matlock, Derbyshire; Spain; Lancaster, Pa.

MALACHITE.

Monoclinic. $C = 88° 32'$, $I \wedge I = 104° 28'$, $i\text{-}i \wedge -1\text{-}i = 118° 15'$, Zepharovich; $\dot{c} : \bar{b} : \dot{a} = 0.51155 : 1.2903 : 1$. Common form f. 750; also same with other terminal planes; also with $i\text{-}i$ wanting; also with $i\text{-}i$, $i\text{-}\bar{i}$ very large, making a rectangular prism; also with the vertical prism very short, as in f. 321. Crystals rarely simple. Twins: twinning-plane $i\text{-}i$, f. 750; often penetration twins, as in f. 321, 322, p. 99. Cleavage: basal, highly perfect; clinodiagonal less distinct. Usually massive or incrusting, with surface tuberose, botryoidal, or stalactitic, and structure divergent; often delicately compact fibrous, and banded in color; frequently granular or earthy.

H.=3·5–4. G.=3·7–4·01. Lustre of crystals adamantine, inclining to vitreous; of fibrous varieties more or less silky; often dull and earthy. Color bright green. Streak paler green. Translucent—subtranslucent—opaque. Fracture subconchoidal, uneven.

Comp.—$Cu_2CO_4 + H_2O = CuCO_3 + H_2CuO_2 =$ Carbon dioxide 19·9, copper oxide 71·9, water 8·2=100.

Pyr., etc.—In the closed tube blackens and yields water. B.B. fuses at 2, coloring the flame emerald-green; on charcoal is reduced to metallic copper; with the fluxes reacts like tenorite. Soluble in acids with effervescence.

Diff.—Differs from other copper ores of a green color in its effervescence with acids.

Obs.—Green malachite accompanies other ores of copper. Perfect crystals are quite rare. Occurs abundantly in the Urals; at Chessy in France; at Schwatz in the Tyrol; in Cornwall and in Cumberland, England; Sandlodge copper mine, Scotland; Limerick, Waterford, and elsewhere, Ireland; at Grimberg, near Siegen in Germany. At the copper mines of Nischne-Tagilsk, belonging to M. Demidoff, a bed of malachite was opened which yielded many tons of malachite. Also in handsome masses at Bembe, on the west coast of Africa; with the copper ores of Cuba; Chili; Australia.

In *N. Jersey*, at New Brunswick. In *Pennsylvania*, near Morgantown, Berks County; at Cornwall, Lebanon Co.; at the Perkiomen and Phenixville lead mines. In *Wisconsin*, at the copper mines of Mineral Point, and elswhere. In *California*, at Hughes's mine in Calaveras Co.

Green malachite admits of a high polish, and when in large masses is cut into tables, snuff-boxes, vases, etc. Named from $\mu\alpha\lambda\alpha\chi\acute{\eta}$, *mallows*, in allusion to the green color.

CUPROCALCITE.—Massive. H.=3. G.=3·90. Color vermilion-red. Analysis, Raymondi, Cu_2O 50·45, CaO 20·16, CO_2 24·00, H_2O 3·20, FeO_3 0·60, AlO_3 0·20, MgO 0·97, SiO_2 0·30=99·86. Occurs with a ferruginous calcite at the copper mines of Canza in Peru.

AZURITE. Kupferlasur, *Germ.*

Monoclinic. $C = 87° 39'$; $I \wedge I = 99° 32'$, $O \wedge 1\text{-}\bar{\imath} = 138° 41'$; $\dot{c} : \bar{b} : \dot{a} = 1.039 : 1.181 : 1$. O usually striated parallel with the clinodiagonal. Cleavage: $2\text{-}\bar{\imath}$ rather perfect; $i\text{-}i$ less distinct; I in traces. Also massive, and presenting imitative shapes, having a columnar composition; also dull and earthy.

H.=3·5–4·25. G.=3·5–3·831. Lustre vitreous, almost adamantine. Color various shades of azure-blue, passing into Berlin-blue. Streak blue, lighter than the color. Transparent—subtranslucent. Fracture conchoidal. Brittle.

Comp.— $Cu_3C_2O_7+H_2O=2CuCO_3+H_2CuO_2=$ Carbon dioxide 25·6, copper **oxide 69·2**, water 5·2=100.

Pyr., etc.—Same as in malachite.

Obs.—Occurs at Chessy, near Lyons, whence its name *Chessy Copper*. Also in Siberia; at Moldava in the Banat; at Wheal Buller, near Redruth in Cornwall · also in Devonshire and Derbyshire.

In *Penn.*, at the Perkiomen lead mine; at Phenixville, in crystals; at Cornwall. In *Wisconsin*, near Mineral Point In *California*, Calaveras Co., at Hughes's mine.

According to Schrauf, who has given a crystallographic monograph of the species, the form is closely related to that of epidote (Ber. Ak. Wien, July 3, 1871).

BISMUTITE. Wismuthspath, *Germ.*

In implanted acicular crystallizations (pseudomorphous); also incrusting or amorphous; pulverulent.

H.=4–4·5. G.=6·86–6·909. Lustre vitreous, when pure; sometimes dull. Color white, mountain-green, and dirty siskin-green; occasionally straw-yellow and yellowish-gray. Streak greenish-gray to colorless. Subtranslucent—opaque. Brittle.

Comp.—$2Bi_6C_3O_{18}+9H_2O$, Ramm. (S. Carolina)=Carbon dioxide 6·38, bismuth oxide 89·75, water 3·87=100.

Pyr., etc.—In the closed tube decrepitates and gives off water. B.B. fuses readily, and on charcoal is reduced to bismuth, and coats the coal with yellow bismuth oxide. Dissolves in nitric acid, with slight effervescence. Dissolves in hydrochloric acid, affording a deep yellow solution.

Obs.—Bismutite occurs at Schneeberg and Johanngeorgenstadt; at Joachimsthal; near Baden; also in the gold district of Chesterfield, S. C.; in Gaston Co., N. C., in yellowish-white concretions.

LIEBIGITE; VOGLITE (Urankalk, *Germ.*).—Carbonates of uranium and calcium, from the decomposition of uraninite. Exact composition doubtful. SCHRÖCKINGERITE is an oxycarbonate of uranium (Schrauf). Orthorhombic. Occurs in six-sided tabular crystals. Joachimsthal.

WHEWELLITE.—An oxalate of calcium. In minute monoclinic crystals on calcite.

HUMBOLDTITE.—A hydrous oxalate of iron, $2FeC_2O_4+3aq$. Compact; earthy. In brown-coal of Koloseruk, near Bilin; also in black shales at Kettle Point; in Bosanquet, Canada.

MELLITE (Honigstein, *Germ.*).—Tetragonal. In octahedrons; also massive, honey-yellow, reddish, or brownish, rarely white. $Al\ C_{12}O_{12}+18aq=$Alumina 14·36, mellitic acid 40·30, water 45·34=100. Artern, Thuringia; Luschitz, Bohemia; Walchow, Moravia; Nertschinsk, etc.

VI. HYDROCARBON COMPOUNDS

The Hydrogen-Carbon Compounds include (1) the SIMPLE HYDROCARBONS; and (2) the OXYGENATED HYDROCARBONS.

1. The SIMPLE HYDRO CARBONS embrace:

(*a*) The Marsh Gas series. General formula C_nH_{2n+2}. Here belong the liquid *naphthas*, the more volatile parts of petroleum; also the butter-like solids *scheererite* and *chrismatite*.

PETROLEUM.—Mineral oil. Kerosene. Bergöl, Steinöl, Erdöl, *Germ.* Petroleum is a thick to thin fluid. Color yellow or brown, or colorless; translucent to transparent. The specific gravity varies from 0·7 to 0·9. Chemically it consists essentially of carbon and hydrogen; containing several members of the naphtha group, as also the oils of the ethylene series, and the paraffins. The proportion of the latter constituents increases with the increase of the density or viscidity of the fluid. It grades insensibly into pittasphalt, and that into solid bitumen.

Occurs in rocks or deposits of nearly all geological ages, from the Lower Silurian to the present epoch. It is associated most abundantly with argillaceous shales and sandstones, but is found also permeating limestones, giving them a bituminous odor, and rendering them sometimes a considerable source of oil. From these oliferous shales and limestones the oil often exudes, and appears floating on the streams or lakes of the region, or rises in oil springs. It also exists collected in subterranean cavities in certain rocks, whence it issues in jets or fountains whenever an outlet is made by boring. These cavities are situated mostly along the course of gentle anticlinals in the rocks of the region; and it is therefore probable, as has been suggested, that they originated for the most part in the displacements of the strata caused by the slight uplift. The oil which fills the cavities has ordinarily been derived from the subjacent rocks; for the strata, in which the cavities exist, are frequently barren sandstones.

Obtained in large quantities from the oil wells of Pennsylvania; also found in eastern Virginia, Kentucky, Ohio, Illinois, Michigan, and New York. In Canada, at several places; in southern California; in Mexico; Trinidad.

Some well-known foreign localities are: Rangoon, Burmah; western shore of the Caspian Sea; in Parma, Italy; Sicily; Galicia; Tegernsee, Bavaria; Hanover.

(*b*) The Olefiant or Ethylene series. General formula C_nH_{2n}. Here belong the pittolium group of liquids, or *pittasphalts* (mineral tar), and the *paraffins*.

PARAFFIN GROUP.—Wax-like in consistence; white and translucent. Sparingly soluble in alcohol, rather easily in ether, and crystallizing more or less perfectly from the solutions. G. about 0·85–0·98. Melting point for the following species, 33°–90°. The different species varying in the value of *n*, vary also in boiling point, and other characters.

Paraffins occur in the Pennsylvania petroleum, a freezing mixture reducing the temperature being sufficient to separate it in crystals. Also in the naphtha of the Caspian, in Rangoon tar, and many other liquid bitumens. It is a result of the destructive distillation of peat, bituminous coal, lignite, coaly or bituminous shales, most viscid bitumens, wood-tar, and many other substances.

The name is from the Latin *parum*, *little*, and *affinis*, alluding to the feeble affinity for other substances, or, in other words, its chemical indifference.

To the Paraffin Group belong:

URPETHITE.—Consistency of soft tallow. Melting point 39° C. Soluble in cold ether. Urpeth Colliery.

HATCHETTITE.—In thin plates or massive. Color yellowish, or greenish-white; blackens on exposure. Melting point 46° C. In the coal-measures of Glamorganshire; Rossitz, Moravia.

OZOCERITE.—Like wax or spermaceti in appearance and consistency. G. = 0·85–0·90. Colorless to white when pure; often leek-green, yellowish, brownish-yellow, brown. Translucent. Greasy to the touch. Fusing point 56° to 63° C. Occurs in beds of coal, or associated bituminous deposits; that of Slanik, Moldavia, beneath a bed of bituminous clay shale: in masses of sometimes 80 to 100 lbs., at the foot of the Carpathians, not far from beds of coal and salt; that of Boryslaw in a bituminous clay associated with calciferous beds in the formation of the Carpathians, in masses. The same compound has been obtained from mineral coal, peat, and petroleum, mineral tar, etc., by destructive distillation. Named from $\delta\zeta\omega$, *smell*, and $\kappa\eta\rho\delta\varsigma$, *wax*, in allusion to the odor.

ELATERITE.—Massive, soft, elastic; often like india-rubber, though sometimes hard and brittle. It is found at Castleton in Derbyshire, in the lead mine of Odin, along with lead ore and calcite, in compact reniform or fungoid masses, and is abundant. Also reported from St Bernard's Well, Edinburgh, etc.

ZIETRISIKITE and PYROPISSITE belong here.

(*c*) The Camphene Series. General Formula C_nH_{2n-4}.

FICHTELITE.—In white monoclinic crystals. Brittle. Solidifies at 36° C. Soluble in ether The mineral occurs in the form of shining scales, flat crystals, and thin layers between the rings of growth and throughout the texture of pine wood (identical in species with the modern *Pinus sylvestris*) from peat beds in the vicinity of Redwitz in the Fichtelgebirge, North Bavaria. In peat near Sobeslau; in a log of Pinus Australis.

HARTITE.—Resembles fichtelite, but melts at 74°–75° C. Found in a kind of pine, like fichtelite, but of a different species, the *Peuce acerosa* Unger, belonging to an earlier geological epoch. From the brown-coal beds of Oberhart, near Gloggnitz, not far from Vienna. Reported also from Rosenthal near Köflach in Styria, and Prävali in Carinthia.

DINITE and IXOLYTE belong here.

(*d*) The Benzole Series, General Formula C_nH_{2n-6}. Including the Benzole liquids and KÖNLITE from Uznach, and Redwitz.

(*e*) The Naphthalin Series. General Formula C_nH_{2n-12}.

NAPHTHALIN.—Occurs in Rangoon tar. IDRIALITE, crystalline in the pure state. Color white. In nature found only impure, being mixed with cinnabar, clay, and some pyrite and gypsum in a brownish-black earthy material, called from its combustibility and the presence of mercury, *inflammable cinnabar* (*Quecksilberbranderz*). Idria, Spain. ARAGOTITE, from New Almaden Mine, Cal., is related to idrialite.

2. The OXYGENATED HYDROCARBONS embrace different groups having ratios of C : H varying from 1 : 2 to 5 : 5½, or less. Some of the more important are:

GEOCERITE. Wax-like. Color white. Melting point near 80° C.; after fusion solidifies as a yellowish wax, hard but not very brittle. Soluble in alcohol of 80 p. c. $C_{28}H_{56}O_2$ = Carbon 79·24, hydrogen 13·21, oxygen 7·55 = 100. From the same *dark-brown* brown coal of Gesterwitz that afforded the geomyricite, and from the same solution.

GEOMYRICITE.—Wax-like. Obtained in a pulverulent form from a solution, the grains consisting of acicular crystals. Color white. Melting point 80°–83° C. After fusion has the aspect of a yellowish brittle wax. Soluble easily in hot absolute alcohol and ether, but slightly in alcohol of 80 p. c. $C_{24}H_{68}O_2$ = Carbon 80·59, hydrogen 13·42, oxygen 5·99 = 100. Burns with a bright flame. Occurs at the Gesterwitz brown coal deposit, in a *dark brown* layer.

SUCCINITE. Amber. Succin, Ambre, *Fr.* Bernstein, *Germ.*

In irregular masses, without cleavage. H.=2–2·5. G.=1·065–1·081. Lustre resinous. Color yellow, sometimes reddish, brownish, and whitish, often clouded. Streak white. Transparent—translucent. Tasteless. Electric on friction. Fuses at 287° C., but without becoming a flowing liquid.

Comp.—Ratio for C : H : O=40 : 64 : 4=Carbon 78·94, hydrogen 10·53, oxygen 10·53= 100. But amber is not a simple resin. According to Berzelius, it consists mainly (85 to 90 p. c.) of a resin which resists all solvents (properly *the species* succinite), along with two other resins soluble in alcohol and ether, an oil, and $2\frac{1}{2}$ to 6 p. c. of succinic acid. Amber is hardly acted on by alcohol. Burns readily with a yellow flame, emitting an agreeable odor, and leaves a black, shining, carbonaceous residue.

Obs.—Occurs abundantly on the Prussian coast of the Baltic; occurring from Dantzig to Memel; also on the coast of Denmark and Sweden; in Galicia, near Lemberg, and at Miszau; in Poland; in Moravia, at Boskowitz, etc. ; in the Urals, Russia ; near Christiania, Norway; in Switzerland, near Bâle; in France, near Paris, in clay. In England, near London, and on the coast of Norfolk, Essex, and Suffolk. In various parts of Asia. Also near Catania, on the Sicilian coast. It has been found in various parts of the Green sand formation of the United States, either loosely imbedded in the soil, or engaged in marl or lignite, as at Gay Head or Martha's Vineyard, near Trenton, and also at Camden in New Jersey, and at Cape Sable, near Magothy river in Maryland. In the royal museum at Berlin there is a mass weighing 18 lbs. Another in the kingdom of Ava, India, is nearly as large as a child's head, and weighs $2\frac{1}{4}$ lbs.

It is now fully ascertained that amber is a vegetable resin altered by fossilization. This is inferred both from its native situation with coal, or fossil wood, and from the occurrence of insects incased in it. Of these insects, some appear evidently to have struggled after being entangled in the then viscous fluid ; and occasionally a leg or a wing is found some distance from the body, which had been detached in the effort to escape.

Amber was early known to the ancients, and called $\eta \lambda \epsilon \kappa \tau \rho o \nu$, *electrum*, whence, on account of its electrical susceptibilities, we have derived the word *electricity.* It was named by some lyncurium, though this name was applied by Theophrastus also to a stone, probably to zircon or tourmaline, both minerals of remarkable electrical properties.

Other related resins are : COPALITE (*retinite* pt.) from Highgate Hill, near London; KRANTZITE, Nienburg; WALCHOWITE, Walchow, Moravia ; AMBRITE, N. Zealand ; BATHVILLITE, occurring in the *torbanite*, or Boghead coal of Bathville, Scotland ; *torbanite* is related to it. SIEGBURGITE, SCHRAUFITE, AMBROSINE, DUXITE.

XYLORETINITE (hartine).—C : H : O=40 : 64 : 4. BOMBICCITE, C : H : O=13 : 7 : 1, in lignite in the valley of the Arno, Tuscany. LEUCOPETRITE. C : H : O=50 : 84 : 3. Gesterwitz, near Weissenfels. EUOSMITE. C : H : O=34 : 29 : 2, from the brown coal at Baiershof in the Fichtelgebirge. ROSTHORNITE. C : H : O=24 : 40 : 1. In coal at Sonnberg, Carinthia. The above species are soluble in ether.

SCLERETINITE.—C : H : O=40 : 64 : 4. Insoluble in ether. Wigan, England.

PYRORETINITE, JAULINGITE, REUSSINITE, GUYAQUILLITE, WHEELERITE (New Mexico), etc. Ratio of C : H=5 : 7 to 5 : $6\frac{1}{2}$.

MIDDLETONITE, STANEKITE, ANTHRACOXENITE. Ratio of C : H=5 : $5\frac{1}{2}$ or less. Insoluble in ether or alcohol.

TASMANITE and DYSODILE are remarkable in containing sulphur, replacing part of the oxygen.

The ACID OXYGENATED HYDROCARBONS include Butyrellite (Bogbutter), Succinellite, Dopplerite, etc., etc.

APPENDIX TO HYDROCARBONS.

ASPHALTUM. Bitumen. Asphalt, Mineral Pitch. Bergpech, E·dpech, *Germ.*

Asphaltum, or mineral pitch, is a mixture of different hydrocarbons, part of which are oxygenated. Its ordinary characters are as follows:
Amorphous. G.=1–1·8; sometimes higher from impurities. Lustre like that of black pitch. Color brownish-black and black. Odor bituminous. Melts ordinarily at 90° to 100° C., and burns with a bright flame. Soluble mostly or wholly in oil of turpentine, and partly or wholly in ether; commonly partly in alcohol.

The more solid kinds graduate into the pittasphalts or mineral tar, and through these there is a gradation to petroleum. The fluid kinds change into the solid by the loss of a vaporizable portion on exposure, and also by a process of oxidation, which consists first in a loss of hydrogen, and finally in the oxygenation of a portion of the mass.

Obs.—Asphaltum belongs to rocks of no particular age. The most abundant deposits are superficial. But these are generally, if not always, connected with rock deposits containing some kind of bituminous material or vegetable remains.

Some of the noted localities of asphaltum are the region of the Dead Sea, or Lake Asphaltites, on Trinidad; at various places in S. America, as at Caxitambo, Peru; at Berengela, Peru, not far from Arica (S.); in California, near the coast of St. Barbara. Also in smaller quantities, sometimes disseminated through shale, and sandstone rocks, and occasionally limestones, or collected in cavities or seams in these rocks; near Matlock, Derbyshire; Poldice mine in Cornwall; Val de Travers, Neuchatel; impregnating dolomite on the island of Brazza in Dalmatia; in the Caucasus; in gneiss and mica schist in Sweden.

The following substances are closely related to asphaltum, and, like it, are mixtures of undetermined carbohydrogens.

GRAHAMITE, *Wurtz.*—Resembles the preceding in its pitch-black, lustrous appearance; H. =2; G.=1·145. Soluble mostly in oil of turpentine; partly in ether, naphtha, or benzole; not at all in alcohol; wholly in chloroform and carbon disulphide. No action with alkalies or hot nitric or hydrochloric acid. Melts only imperfectly, and with a decomposition of the surface; but in this state the interior may be drawn into long threads. Occurs in W. Virginia, about 20 m. in an air line S. of Parkersburg, filling a fissure (shrinkage fissure) in a sandstone of the Carboniferous formation; and supposed to be, like the albertite, an inspissated and oxygenated petroleum.

ALBERTITE, *Robb.*—Differs from ordinary asphaltum in being only partially soluble in oil of turpentine, and in its very imperfect fusion when heated. It has H.=1–2; G.=1·097: lustre brilliant, pitch-like; color jet-black. Softens a little in boiling water; in the flame of a candle shows incipient fusion. According to imperfect determinations, only a trace soluble in alcohol; 4 p. c. in ether; 30 in oil of turpentine. Occurs filling an irregular fissure in rocks of the Subcarboniferous age (or Lower Carboniferous) in Nova Scotia, and is regarded as an inspissated and oxygenated petroleum. This and the above are very valuable in gas-making.

PIAUZITE.—An asphalt-like substance, remarkable for its high melting point, 315° C. It occurs slaty massive; color brownish- or greenish-black; thin splinters colophonite-brown by transmitted light; streak light brown, amber-brown; H.=1·5; G.=1·220; 1·186, Kenngott. It comes from a bed of brown coal at Piauze, near Neustadt in Carniola; on Mt. Chum, near Tüffer in Styria.

WOLLONGONGITE, *Silliman.*—Occurs in cubic blocks without lamination. Fracture broad conchoidal. Color greenish- to brownish-black. Lustre resinous. In the tube does not melt, but decrepitates and gives off oil and gas; yields by dry distillation 82·5 p. c. volatile matter Insoluble in ether or benzole. New South Wales.

MINERAL COAL

The distinguishing characters of Mineral Coal are as follows: Compact massive, without crystalline structure or cleavage; sometimes breaking with a degree of regularity, but from a jointed rather than a cleavage structure. Sometimes laminated; often faintly and delicately banded, successive layers differing slightly in lustre.

H.=0·5-2·5. G.=1-1·80. Lustre dull to brilliant, and either earthy, resinous, or submetallic. Color black, grayish-black, brownish-black, and occasionally iridescent; also sometimes dark brown. Opaque. Fracture conchoidal—uneven. Brittle; rarely somewhat sectile. Without taste, except from impurities present. Insoluble or nearly so in alcohol, ether, naphtha, and benzole. Infusible to subfusible; but often becoming a soft, pliant, or paste-like mass when heated. On distillation most kinds afford more or less of oily and tarry substances, which are mixtures of hydrocarbons and paraffin.

Mineral coal is made up of different kinds of hydrocarbons, with perhaps in some cases free carbon.

Var.—The variations depend partly (1) on the amount of the volatile ingredients afforded on destructive destillation; or (2) on the nature of these volatile compounds, for ingredients of similar composition may differ widely in volatility, etc.; (3) on structure, lustre, and other physical characters.

1. ANTHRACITE. H.=2-2·5. G.=1·32-1·7, Pennsylvania; 1·81, Rhode Island; 1·26-1·36, South Wales. Lustre bright, often submetallic, iron black. and frequently iridescent. Fracture conchoidal. Volatile matter after drying 3 to 6 p. c. Burns with a feeble flame of a pale color. The anthracites of Pennsylvania contain ordinarily 85 to 93 per cent. of carbon; those of South Wales, 88 to 95; of France, 80 to 83; of Saxony, 81; of southern Russia, sometimes 94 per cent. Anthracite graduates into bituminous coal, becoming less hard, and containing more volatile matter; and an intermediate variety is called *free-burning* anthracite.

BITUMINOUS COALS (Steinkohle pt., *Germ.*). Under the head of Bituminous Coals, a number of kinds are included which differ strikingly in the action of heat, and which therefore are of unlike constitution. They have the common characteristic of burning in the fire with a yellow, smoky flame, and giving out on distillation hydrocarbon oils or tar, and hence the name *bituminous*. The *ordinary* bituminous coals contain from 5 to 15 p. c. (rarely 16 or 17) of oxygen (ash excluded); while the so-called *brown coal* or *lignite* contains from 20 to 36 p. c., after the expulsion, at 100° C., of 15 to 36 p. c. of water. The amount of hydrogen in each is from 4 to 7 p. c. Both have usually a bright, pitchy, greasy lustre (whence often called *Pechkohle* in German), a firm compact texture, are rather fragile compared with anthracite, and have G.=1·14-1·40. The *brown* coals have often a brownish-black color, whence the name, and more oxygen, but in these respects and others they shade into ordinary bituminous coals. The ordinary bituminous coal of Pennsylvania has G.=1·26-1·37; of Newcastle, England, 1·27; of Scotland, 1·27-1·32; of France, 1·2-1·33; of Belgium, 1·27-1·3. The most prominent kinds are the following:

2. CAKING COAL. A bituminous coal which softens and becomes pasty or semi-viscid in the fire. This softening takes place at the temperature of incipient decomposition, and is attended with the escape of bubbles of gas. On increasing the heat, the volatile products which result from the ultimate decomposition of the softened mass are driven off, and a coherent, grayish-black, cellular, or fritted mass (*coke*) is left. Amount of coke left (or part not volatile) varies from 50 to 85 p. c. *Byerite* is from Middle Park, Colorado.

3. NON-CAKING COAL. Like the preceding in all external characters, and often in ultimate composition; but burning freely without softening or any appearance of incipient fusion.

4. CANNEL COAL (Parrot Coal). A variety of bituminous coal, and often caking; but differing from the preceding in texture, and to some extent in composition, as shown by its products on distillation. It is compact, with little or no lustre, and without any appearance of a banded structure; and it breaks with a conchoidal fracture and smooth surfaces; color dull black or grayish-black. On distillation it affords, after drying, 40 to 66 ot volatile matter, and the material volatilized includes a large proportion of burning and lubricating oils,

much larger than the above kinds of bituminous coal; whence it is extensively used for the manufacture of such oils. It graduates into oil-producing coaly shales, the more compact of which it much resembles.

5. TORBANITE. A variety of cannel coal of a dark brown color, yellowish streak, without lustre, having a subconchoidal fracture; H.$=2.25$; G.$=1.17$–1.2. Yields over 60 p. c. of volatile matter, and is used for the production of burning and lubricating oils, paraffin, illuminating gas. From Torbane Hill, near Bathgate in Linlithgowshire, Scotland. Also called *Boghead Cannel.*

6. BROWN COAL (Braunkohle *Germ.*, Pechkohle pt. *Germ.*, Lignite). The prominent characteristics of brown coal have already been mentioned. They are non-caking, but afford a large proportion of volatile matter. They are sometimes pitch-black (whence Pechkohle pt. *Germ.*), but often rather dull and brownish-black. G.$=1.15$–1.3; sometimes higher from impurities. It is occasionally somewhat lamellar in structure. Brown coal is often called *lignite.* But this term is sometimes restricted to masses of coal which still retain the form of the original wood. *Jet* is a black variety of brown coal, compact in texture, and taking a good polish, whence its use in jewelry.

7. EARTHY BROWN COAL (*Erdige Braunkohle*) is a brown friable material, sometimes forming layers in beds of brown coal. But it is in general not a true coal, a considerable part of it being soluble in ether and benzole, and often even in alcohol; besides affording largely of oils and paraffin on distillation.

Comp.—Most mineral coal consists mainly, as the best chemists now hold, of *oxygenated hydrocarbons*. Besides oxygenated hydrocarbons, there may also be present *simple hydrocarbons* (that is, containing no oxygen).

Sulphur is present in nearly all coals. It is supposed to be usually combined with iron, and when the coal affords a *red ash* on burning, there is reason for believing this true. But Percy mentions a coal from New Zealand (anal. 18) which gave a peculiarly white ash although containing 2 to 3 p. c. of sulphur, a fact showing that it is present not as a sulphide of iron, but as a constituent of an organic compound. The discovery by Church of a resin containing sulphur (see TASMANITE, p. 415), gives reason for inferring that it may exist in this coal in that state, although its presence as a constituent of other organic compounds is quite possible.

The chemical relations of the different kinds of coals will be understood from the following analyses:

	Carbon.	Hydrogen.	Oxygen.	Nitrogen.	Sulphur.	Ash.
1. Anthracite, S. Wales	92·56	3·33	2·53	——	——	1·58
2. Caking Coal, Northumberland	78·69	6·00	10·07	2·37	1·51	1·36
3. Non-Caking Coal, Zwickau	80·25	4·01	10·98	0·49	2·99	1·57
4. Cannel Coal, Wigan	80·07	5·53	8·10	2·12	1·50	2·70
5. Torbanite, Torbane Hill	64·02	8·90	5·66	0·55	0·50	20·32
6. Brown Coal, Meissen, Sax.	58·90	5·36	21·63	——	6·61	7·50

Coal occurs in beds, interstratified with shales, sandstones, and conglomerates, and sometimes limestones, forming distinct layers, which vary from a fraction of an inch to 30 feet or more in thickness. In the United States, the anthracites occur east of the Alleghany range, in rocks that have undergone great contortions and fracturings, while the bituminous are found farther west, in rocks that have been less disturbed; and this fact and other observations have led some geologists to the view that the anthracites have lost their bitumen by the action of heat. The *origin* of coal is mainly vegetable, though animal life has contributed somewhat to the result. The beds were once beds of vegetation, analogous, in most respects, in mode of formation to the peat beds of modern times, yet in mode of burial often of a very different character. This vegetable origin is proved not only by the occurrence of the leaves, stems, and logs of plants in the coal, but also by the presence throughout its texture, in many cases, of the forms of the original fibres; also by the direct observation that peat is a transition state between unaltered vegetable débris and brown coal, being sometimes found passing completely into true brown coal. *Peat* differs from true coal in want of homogeneity, it visibly containing vegetable fibres only partially altered; and wherever changed to a fine-textured homogeneous material, even though hardly consolidated, it may be true brown coal.

Extensive beds of mineral coal occur in Great Britain, covering 11,859 square miles; in France about 1,719 sq. m.; in Spain about 3,408 sq. m.; in Belgium 518 sq. m.; in Netherlands, Prussia, Bavaria, Austria, northern Italy, Silesia, Spain, Russia on the south near the Azof, and also in the Altai. It is found in Asia, abundantly in China, etc., etc.

In the United States there are four separate coal areas. One of these areas, the Appalachian coal field, commences on the north, in Pennsylvania and southeastern Ohio, and sweep ing south over western Virginia and eastern Kentucky and Tennessee to the west of the Appalachians, or partly involved in their ridges, it continues to Alabama, near Tuscaloosa, where a bed of coal has been opened. It has been estimated to cover 60,000 sq. m. A second coal area (the Illinois) lies adjoining the Mississippi, and covers the larger part of Illinois, though much broken into patches, and a small northwest part of Kentucky. A third covers the central portion of Michigan, not far from 5,000 sq. m. in area. Besides these, there is a smaller coal region (a fourth) in Rhode Island. The total area of workable coal measures in the United States is about 125,000 sq. m. Out of the borders of the United States, on the northeast, commences a fifth coal area, that of Nova Scotia and New Brunswick, which covers, in connection with that of Newfoundland, 18,000 sq. m.

The mines of western Pennsylvania, those of the States west, and those of Cumberland or Frostburg, Maryland, Richmond or Chesterfield, Va., and other mines south, are *bituminous*. Those of eastern Pennsylvania constituting several detached areas—one, the *Schuylkill* coal field—another, the *Wyoming* coal field—those of Rhode Island and Massachusetts, and some patches in Virginia, are *anthracites*. Cannel coal is found near Greensburg, Beaver Co., Pa., in Kenawha Co , Va., at Peytona. etc. ; also in Kentucky, Ohio, Illinois, Missouri, and Indiana ; but part of the so-called cannel is a coaly shale.

Brown coal comes from coal beds more recent than those of the Carboniferous age. But much of this more recent coal is not distinguishable from other bituminous coals. The coal of Richmond, Virginia, is supposed to be of the Liassic or Triassic era; the coal of Brora, in Sutherland, and of Gristhorpe, Yorkshire, is Oolitic in age. Cretaceous coal occurs on Vancouver Island, and Cretaceous and Tertiary coal in many places over the Rocky Mountains, where a "Lignitic formation" is very widely distributed.

PART III.—DESCRIPTIVE MINERALOGY.

SUPPLEMENTARY CHAPTER.*

ABRIACHANITE, Heddle.—A soft blue clay-like substance, filling seams and cavities in granite. Probably near crocidolite (p. 298) in composition. From the Abriachan district near Loch Ness, Scotland.

ADAMITE p. 373.—Occurs in colorless to deep green crystals, and in mammillary groups, at the ancient mines, recently reopened, at Laurium, Greece.

AGLAITE.—Same as cymatolite ; that is, an alteration product of spodumene, consisting of an intimate mixture of albite and muscovite. From Goshen, Mass.

ALASKAITE, König.—Massive. G. = 6·878. Lustre metallic. Color whitish lead-gray. Composition probably $(Ag_2,Cu_2,Pb)S + Bi_2S_3$. Analysis after deducting impurities, S 17·63, Bi 56·97, Sb 0·62, Pb 11·79, Ag 8·74, Cu 3·46, Zn 0·79 = 100. From the Alaska mine, Poughkeepsie Gulch, Colorado. SILBERWISMUTHGLANZ of Rammelsberg, from Morococha, Peru, is pure $Ag_2S + Bi_2S_3$.

ALBITE, p. 323.—Has been made artificially, identical in form and composition with natural crystals, by Hautefeuille.

AMBLYGONITE, p. 369.—Penfield has analyzed specimens from Penig, Montebras, Hebron and Auburn, Me., Branchville, Ct. (including "hebronite" and "montebrasite"). He shows that, while the varieties vary from F 11·26, H_2O 1·75 in one sample to F 1·75, H_2O 6·61, in another, they all conform to the general formula: $Al_2P_2O_8 + 2R(F,OH)$, differing only in the extent to which the hydroxyl replaces the fluorine.

AMPHIBOLE, p. 296.—A variety containing only 0·9 p.c. MgO, has been called *bergamaskite* by Lucchetti Occurs in a hornblende porphyry. Monte Altino, Bergamo, Italy.
Phäactinite (Bertels) is a chloritic alteration product from a rock called isenite. Nassau, Germany.

ANALCITE, p. 343.—On the crystalline system, see p. 189.
Picranalcite, of Bechi. is identical with ordinary analcite, containing only a trace of magnesia, according to Bamberger.

ANIMIKITE, Wurtz.—An impure massive mineral supposed to be a silver antimonide (Sb 11·18, Ag 77·58). Silver Islet, Lake Superior.

ÅNNERÖDITE, Brögger.—A rare columbate, almost identical with samarskite in composition, but in form very near columbite. From a pegmatite vein at Ånneröd, near Moss, Norway.

APATITE, p. 364.—Large deposits of apatite, affording sometimes gigantic crystals, and sometimes mined for commercial purposes, occur in Ottawa County, Quebec, Canada ; also large crystals, with zircon, titanite and amphibole in Renfrew County, Ontario, and elsewhere ; there are similar deposits at Kjörrestad, Bamle, Norway. A variety from San Roque. Argentine Republic, containing 6·7 p.c. MnO, has been called *manganapatite* by Siewert. Penfield found 10·6 p.c. MnO in a bluish-green specimen from Branchville, Ct.
Pseudo-hexagonal, Mallard, see p. 187.

---

* For fuller descriptions of new species, references to original papers, etc., see Appendix III. (1882), System of Mineralogy.

APOPHYLLITE, p. 340.—Pseudo-tetragonal (monoclinic), according to Mallard and Rumpf, but the correctness of their conclusions is doubtful ; see p. 185 et seq.

ARAGONITE, p. 405.—A variety from the Austin mine, Wythe Co., Va., afforded 7·29 p.c. $PbCO_3$.

ARCTOLITE, Blomstrand.—A doubtful silicate, composition near prehnite, prismatic angle near hornblende. Hvitholm, near Spitzbergen.

AREQUIPITE, Raimondi.—A honey-yellow compact substance, supposed to be a silico-antimonate of lead, but probably a mixture. Victoria mine, Province of Arequipa, Peru.

ARFVEDSONITE, p. 298.—Occurs with zircon and astrophyllite in El Paso Co., Colorado.

ARRHENITE, Nordenskiöld.—A silico-tantalate of yttrium, erbium, etc., resembling feldspar in appearance. Probably an uncertain decomposition product. Ytterby, Sweden.

ARSENARGENTITE, Hannay.—An uncertain silver arsenide of doubtful source.

ASMANITE, p. 288.—According to Weisbach and v. Lasaulx, identical with tridymite ; observed in the meteoric iron of Rittersgrün, Saxony.

ASTROPHYLLITE, p. 313.—Referred to the triclinic system by Brögger ; properly a member of the pyroxene group, not one of the true micas.
Occurs with arfvedsonite and zircon in El Paso Co., Colorado.

ATELINE (or atelite), Scacchi.—An alteration product of tenorite at Vesuvius ; near atacamite in composition.

ATOPITE, Nordenskiöld.—In isometric octahedrons. H. = 5·5-6, G. = 5 03. Color yellow to brown. Composition essentially $Ca_2Sb_2O_7$ (near romeite). Imbedded in hedyphane at Långban, Sweden.

AUTUNITE, p. 379.—Monoclinic (or triclinic), according to Brezina.

BALVRAIDITE, Heddle.—A doubtful substance having a saccharoidal structure, and pale purplish-brown color. G. = 2·9. An analysis gave, SiO_2 46·04, Al_2O_3 20·11, Fe_2O_3 2·52, MnO 0·79, MgO 8·30, CaO 13·47, Na_2O 2·72, K_2O 1·36, H_2O 4·71 = 100·02. In limestone at Balvraid, Inverness-shire, Scotland.

BARCENITE, Mallet.—An uncertain alteration product of livingstonite, massive, earthy, color dark gray. G. ≦ 5·343. Huitzuco, Guerrero, Mexico.

BARYLITE, Blomstrand.—In groups of prismatic crystals. Two distinct cleavages (84°). H. = 7. G. = 4·03. White. BB. infusible. A silicate of aluminum and barium (46 p.c. BaO). In limestone at Långban, Sweden.

BEEGERITE, König.—In elongated isometric crystals. Cleavage cubic. G. = 7·273. Color gray. Lustre metallic. Composition, $6PbS + Bi_2S_3$ = S 14·78, Bi 21·36, Pb 63·84 = 100. From the Baltic Lode, Park Co., Colorado.

BERYL, p. 299.—Pseudo-hexagonal, according to Mallard, see p. 186.
A variety in short prismatic to tabular crystals has been called *rosterite* by Grattarola. Locality, Elba.
Found (W. E. Hidden) in fine crystals of large size (to 10 inches in length), and emerald color, in Alexander Co., N. C., also in highly modified crystals of pale green color.

BERZELIITE.—This arsenate from Långban, Sweden, is isometric according to Sjögren ; honey to sulphur yellow, lustre resinous. Lindgren regards the ortho-arsenate of calcium and magnesium, anisotrope, of the same locality, as distinct, and says that earlier descriptions of berzeliite belong to it.

BHRECKITE (or Vreckite), Heddle.—A doubtful soft apple-green substance, coating quartz crystals. A hydrous silicate of alumina, iron, magnesia and lime. From the hill Ben Bhreck, Sutherland, Scotland.

BISMUTOSPHÆRITE, Weisbach.—In spherical forms, with concentric, fine fibrous radiated structure. Regarded as an anhydrous bismuth carbonate. From Neustädtel, Schneeberg, Saxony.

BLOMSTRANDITE, Lindström.—A columbo-titanate of uranium, allied to samarskite. From Nohl, Sweden.

BOLIVITE, Domeyko.—An alteration product of bismuthinite, probably a mechanical mixture of Bi_2O_3 and Bi_2S_3. Mines of Tazna, Province of Choroloque, Bolivia.

BORACITE, p. 381.—On the crystalline system, see p. 189.

BOWLINGITE, Hannay.—A soft, soapy, green substance, containing silica, alumina, iron, magnesia, lime, water; doubtless heterogeneous. Bowling on the Clyde, Scotland.

BRAVAISITE, Mallard.—In fine crystalline fibres, of a grayish color, forming layers in the coal schists at Noyant, Allier Dep't, France. G. = 2·6. Analysis, SiO_2 51·4, Al_2O_3 18·9, Fe_2O_3 4·0, CaO 2·0, MgO 3·3, K_2O 6·5, H_2O 13·3 = 99·4.

BROOKITE, p. 277.—In Mallard's view, brookite, rutile and octahedrite are all monoclinic, having the same primitive form, but differing in the way in which the individuals are grouped, see p. 186.

BRUCITE, p. 281.—*Manganbrucite* (Igelström) is a manganesian variety of brucite (14·16 MnO) from the manganese mines of the Jakobsberg, Wermland, Sweden. In fine granular form with hausmannite in calcite.
Eisenbrucite, Sandberger.—A doubtful substance resulting from the alteration of brucite. Sieberlehn near Freiberg.

CABRERITE.—Occurs in crystals (isomorphous with erythrite) at the zinc mines of Laurium, Greece. An analysis by Damour corresponds to $Ni_3As_2O_8 + 8$ aq.

CALAMINE, p. 329.—According to Groth, the formula should be written $H_2Zn_2SiO_5$.

CALAVERITE, p. 249.—Occurs at the Keystone and Mountain Lion mines, Colorado. Composition (Genth): $(Au,Ag)Te_2$, with Au : Ag = 7 : 1. H. = 2·5. G. = 9·043.

CANCRINITE, p. 317.—An original species (Rauff, Koch), and not an alteration product of nephelite, the carbon dioxide being essential and not due to calcite.

CARYINITE, Lundström.—Massive, monoclinic; two cleavages (130°). H. = 3-3·5. G. = 4·25. Color, brown. Composition, $R_3As_2O_8$, with R = Pb,Mn,Ca,Mg. Occurs with calcite and hausmannite at Långban, Sweden.

CHABAZITE, p. 344.—Triclinic, according to Becke, the crystals being complex twins of several individuals.

CHALCOMENITE, Des Cloizeaux and Damour.—Monoclinic. $I \wedge I = 108° 20'$. $O \wedge i\text{-}i = 89° 9'$. G. = 3·76. Color, bright blue. Composition, $CuSeO_3 + 2$ aq, or a copper selenite. From the Cerro de Cacheuta, Mendoza, Argentine Republic.

CHALCOPYRITE, p. 244.—Found well crystallized, often coated with crystals of tetrahedrite in parallel position, near Central City, Gilpin Co., Colorado.

CHILDRENITE, p. 377.—Formula, as shown by Penfield, $R_2Al_2P_2O_{10} + 4H_2O$, or $Al_2P_2O_8 + 2RH_2O + 2$ aq, with R = Fe principally, also Mn. This requires: P_2O_5 30·80, AlO_3 22·31 FeO 26·37, MnO 4·87, H_2O 15·65.

A mineral closely related to childrenite has been called *eosphorite* by Brush and E S. Dana. Orthorhombic. In prismatic crystals (see fig.), near childrenite. $I \wedge I = 104° 19'$; $p \wedge p (1 \wedge 1) = 133° 32'$ (front), $= 118° 58'$ (side). Here I, and $a (i-\bar{i}) = 2-\bar{i}$ and O of childrenite. Also massive, cleavable to compact. Cleavage parallel $a (i-\bar{i})$ nearly perfect. H. = 5. G. = 3·11–3·145. Lustre vitreous to sub-resinous, also greasy. Color rose pink, yellowish, colorless, when compact various shades of white. Streak white. Transparent to translucent. General formula like childrenite (see above), but with much manganese and little iron (10 : 3). Percentage composition: P_2O_5 30·93, Al_2O_3 22·35, MnO 23·80, FeO 7·24, H_2O 15·68 = 100. B. B. in the forceps cracks opens, sprouts and whitens, colors the flame pale green and fuses at 4 to a black magnetic mass. Reacts for manganese and iron ; is soluble in acids. Occurs with other manganesian phosphates in a vein of pegmatite at Branchville, Conn.

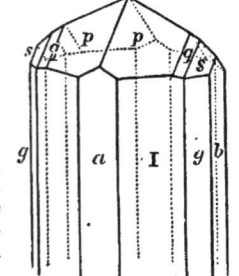

CHLORALLUMINITE, Scacchi.—Hydrous aluminum chloride from Vesuvius.

CHLOROMAGNESITE, Scacchi.—Hydrous magnesium chloride from Vesuvius. *Bischofite* (Ochsenius and Pfeiffer) from Leopoldshall, Prussia, has the composition $MgCl_2 + 6$ aq. Crystalline, massive, foliated or fibrous. Color white. Forms thin layers in halite, with kieserite and carnallite. Readily assumes water on exposure.

CHLOROTHIONITE, Scacchi.—Regarded as a compound salt, $K_2SO_4 + CuCl_2$, forming thin mammillary crusts of a blue color. Vesuvius.

CHONDRODITE, HUMITE, CLINOHUMITE, p. 327.—H. Sjögren has described humite, well crystallized, from the Ladu mine, Wermland, Sweden, and chondrodite from Kaveltorp.

CHROMITE, p. 274.—Not opaque, but in thin sections transmits a yellowish red color, Thoulet. Identified in meteoric irons by J. Lawrence Smith.

CHRYSOCOLLA, p. 338.—*Pilarite*, from Chili, is an aluminous variety, 16·9 p.c. Al_2O_3.

CHRYSOLITE, p. 300.—*Neochrysolite* (Scacchi) is a manganesian variety from Vesuvius. A variety from Zermatt, containing 6 p.c. TiO_2, has been called *titanolivine*.

CLEVEITE, Nordenskiöld.—A mineral closely related to uraninite, but besides uranium (and lead) contains yttrium, erbium, cerium, etc. In isometric crystals. H. = 5·5. G. = 7·49. Color iron black. A decomposition product of a yellow color is called *yttrogummite* (analogous to ordinary gummite). Occurs in feldspar at Garta, near Arendal, Norway.

CLINOCROCITE, Sandberger, Singer.—An imperfectly described sulphate of iron, etc., occurring in saffron-yellow microscopic crystals, derived from the decomposition of pyrite at the Bauersberg, near Bischofsheim vor der Rhön. *Clinophæite*, from the same source, occurs in blackish green microscopic crystals ; formula $5R_2SO_4 + [R_2]H_6O_6 + 5$ aq, with $[R_2] = Fe_2, Al_2$, and $R_2 = Fe, K_2, Na_2$.

CLINTONITE, p. 358.—On the relations of the "clintonite group" of minerals, see Tschermak and Sipöcz, Z. Kryst., iii., 496.

COLORADOITE, Genth.—Massive, granular. H. = 3. G. = 8·627. Lustre metallic. Color iron black. Composition HgTe = tellurium 39, mercury 61 = 100. Occurs with native tellurium, sylvanite, gold, at the Keystone, Mountain Lion, and Smuggler mines in Colorado.

COLUMBITE, p. 360.—Occurs sparingly in small translucent crystals at Branchville, Conn., having the composition $MnCb_2O_6 + MnTa_2O_6$; containing 15·58 p c. MnO, and 0·43 FeO. Also the ordinary variety in groups of very large, though rough, crystals, weighing sometimes 50 pounds, at the same locality. Found with amazonstone at Pike's Peak, Colorado, and in Yancey Co., N. C. Also with monazite, orthite, etc., in Amelia County, Virginia, allied in composition to the above manganesian variety from Branchville.

CORONGUITE, Raimondi.—An earthy, pulverulent substance of a gray to black color. Containing antimony pentoxide, lead, and silver oxides, water, but of doubtful homogeneity. District of Corongo and elsewhere in Peru.

CORUNDOPHILITE, p. 358.—*Amesite* of Shepard, from Chester, Mass., is very near corundophilite.

CORUNDUM, p. 267.—Monoclinic according to Tschermak (orthorhombic, Mallard); often optically biaxial. See p. 18 ; et seq.
Made artificially, with the colors of rubies and sapphires, by Frémy and Feil.

COSALITE, p. 252.—*Bjelkite* of H. Sjögren is identical with cosalite. From the Bjelke mine, Nordmark, Sweden.

COSSYRITE, Foerstner.—Near amphibole in form, but triclinic, and with $I \wedge I' = 114° 5'$. Cleavage prismatic. G. $= 3.75$. Color black. An analysis gave: SiO_2 43.55, Al_2O_3 4.96, Fe_2O_3 7.97, FeO, 32.87, MnO 1.98. CuO 0.39, MgO 0.86, CaO 2.01, Na_2O 5.29, K_2O 0.33 $= 100.21$. In minute crystals weathered out of the ground mass of the liparite lavas of the Island Pantellaria (ancient name Cossyra).

CRAIGTONITE, Heddle.—Doubtful mineral, contains Al_2O_3, Fe_2O_3, MgO, etc. Dendrites in granite at Craigton, Aberdeenshire, Scotland.

CROCOITE, p. 385.—Described by B. Silliman as occurring at the Phenix and other mines in Yavapai Co., Arizona.

CRYOLITE, p. 264.—Observations of Krenner make cryolite monoclinic instead of triclinic. Cryolite and some related fluorides have been found (Cross and Hillebrand) in the Pike's Peak region, El Paso Co., Colorado.

CUPROCALCITE, p. 411.—Mechanical mixture of $CaCO_3$ and Cu_2O, Damour.

CUSPIDINE, Scacchi.—In spear-shaped monoclinic crystals ; color pale rose red. A calcium silicate containing fluorine. Vesuvius.

CYANITE, p. 332.—Recently found in well terminated crystals, Bauer, vom Rath.

CYPRUSITE, Reinsch —A supposed anhydrous iron sulphate, occurring in the western part of the island of Cyprus. Soft. Color yellow. Analysis: SO_3 21.5, Fe_2O_3 (Al_2O_3 tr.) 51.5, insol. silica (shells of Radiolaria) 25, H_2O (hygrosc.) 2 $= 100$.

DANALITE, p. 302.—Occurs at the iron mine of Bartlett, N. H. (Wadsworth).

DANBURITE, p. 311. Occurs (G. J. Brush and E. S. Dana) well crystallized and abundant at Russell, N. Y. Orthorhombic, homœomorphous with topaz and like it in habit. $I \wedge I = 122° 52'$ (topaz $= 124° 17'$), $w \wedge w = 54° 58'$ (topaz $= 55° 20'$), $d \wedge d = 97° 7'$ (topaz $= 96° 6'$). Common forms as in figures, $w = 4\text{-}\bar{i}$, $d = 1\text{-}\bar{i}$, $l = i\text{-}2$, $n = i\text{-}4$, $r = 2\text{-}2$. Color pale wine or honey yellow, colorless. Transparent. Composition $CaB_2Si_2O_8$, as of Danbury mineral.

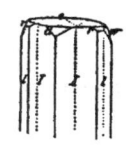

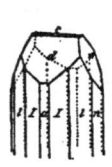

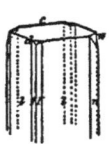

Also from the Skopi, Switzerland, in transparent crystals.

DAVREUXITE, de Koninck.—In aggregates of minute acicular crystals. Color white, with tinge of red. Calculated composition: SiO_2 46·89, Al_2O_3 40·19, MnO 6·93, MgO 1·30, H_2O 4·69 = 100. Occurs in quartz veins in the Ardennes schists at Ottre, Belgium.

DAWSONITE, p. 410.—Occurs (Chaper) in the province of Siena, Pian Castagnaio, Tuscany. Analysis gave Friedel: ($\frac{2}{3}$) CO_2 29·09, Al_2O_3 35·89, Na_2O 19·13, H_2O 12·00, MgO 1·39, CaO 0·42.

DELESSITE, p. 356.—More or less related to the chloritic delessite are: *Subdelessite* from the Thüringer Wald; *Hullite*, Carnmoney Hill, near Belfast, Ireland.

DESCLOIZITE, p. 367.—Occurs in the Sierra de Cordoba, Argentine Republic; perhaps also in Arizona. Composition of South American mineral (Rammelsberg) $R_3V_2O_8 + RH_2O_2$, with R = Pb (56 p.c.), Zn (17 p.c.)
Brackebuschite from Cordoba, Argentine Republic, occurs in small striated crystals. Color black. Composition perhaps $R_3V_2O_8 + H_2O$, with R = Pb : Fe : Mn = 4 : 1 : 1.

DESTINEZITE, *Forir and Jorissen*.—An iron phosphate from Argenteau, Belgium; occurs in yellowish white earthy masses.

DIAMOND, p. 228.—Has been made artificially, in the form of a fine sand, by J. B. Hannay.

DICKINSONITE, G. J. Brush and E. S. Dana.—Monoclinic, pseudo-rhombohedral, $\beta = 61°$ 30'. $c \wedge a = 118° 30'$, $c \wedge p = 118° 52'$, $c \wedge s = 97° 58'$; $c = 0, p = 1, s = 2, x = -3-i$. Commonly foliated to micaceous. Cleavage basal perfect. H. = 3·5–4. G. = 3·338–3·343. Lustre vitreous, on c pearly. Color various shades of green. Composition $4R_3P_2O_8 + 3aq$. with R = Mn,Fe,Ca,Na_2, requiring: P_2O_5 40·05, FeO 12·69, MnO 25·04, CaO 11·85, Na_2O 6·56, H_2O 3·81 = 100. Occurs with eosphorite, triploidite, etc., in pegmatite at Branchville, Conn.

DIETRICHITE, v. Schröckinger.—A zinc-iron-manganese alum, related to mendozite, etc. A recent formation at Felsöbanya, Transylvania.

DOPPLERITE, p. 415.—A black gelatinous hydrocarbon from a stratum of muck below a peat bed at Scranton, Penn., is called by H. C. Lewis *phytocollite;* empirical formula $C_{10}H_{22}O_{16}$.

DOUGLASITE, Ochsenius, Precht.—From Douglasshall, formula, $2KCl,FeCl_2,2H_2O$.

DUMORTIERITE, Damour, Bertrand.—In minute prismatic crystals of a cobalt blue color, imbedded in gneiss. Analysis (Damour): SiO_2 29·85, Al_2O_3 66·02, Fe_2O_3 1·01, MgO 0·45, ign. 2·25 = 99·58; near andalusite. From the gneiss at Chaponost, near Lyons, France.

DUPORTHITE, Collins.—An asbestiform mineral filling fissures in serpentine. Color greenish to brownish gray. Contains silica, alumina, iron, magnesia, and water. Duporth, St. Austell, Cornwall.

DÜRFELDTITE, *Raimondi*.—Massive, indistinctly fibrous. Color light gray. Metallic. Composition $3RS + Sb_2S_3$ (if the results of an analysis after deducting 31 p.c. gangue can be trusted), with R = Pb,Ag_2,Mn, also Fe,Cu_2. From the Irismachay mine, Anquimarca, Peru.

DYSANALYTE, Knop.—The perofskite of the Kaiserstuhl is, according to Knop, a new columbo-titanate of calcium and iron (with also Ce,Na).

EGGONITE, Schrauf.—In minute, grayish-brown crystals (triclinic) near barite in habit. Supposed to be a cadmium silicate. Occurs with calamine and smithsonite at Altenberg.

EKDEMITE, Nordenskiöld.—Massive, coarsely granular, also incrusting. Cleavage basal. H. = 2·5–3. G. = 7·14. Color bright yellow to green. Composition $Pb_3As_2O_8 + 2PbCl_2$ = As_2O_3 10·59, PbO 59·67, Cl 7·58, Pb 22·16 = 100. Found at Långban, Sweden.

ELEONORITE, Nies.—Monoclinic; often in druses and in radiated crusts. Cleavage orthodiagonal. H. = 3-4. Lustre vitreous. Color red brown to dark hyacinth red. Streak yellow. Composition (Streng) $2Fe_2P_2O_8 + Fe_2H_6O_6 + 5$ aq. From the Eleonore mine on the Dünsberg, near Giessen, and the Rothläufchen mine near Waldgirmes. Perhaps identical with the iron phosphate beraunite from Benigna, Bohemia.

ELLONITE, Heddle.—Impure silicate of magnesia, containing SiO_2. In gneiss near Ellon, Aberdeenshire, Scotland.

ELROQUITE, Shepard.—A heterogeneous substance containing silica, alumina, iron oxide, water and (as an impurity) 32 p.c. P_2O_5. Island of Elroque, Caribbean Sea.

ENYSITE, Collins.—A bluish-green stalagmitic substance consisting of aluminum hydrate, basic copper sulphate, calcite, etc. St. Agnes, Cornwall.

EPISTILBITE, p. 347.—Monoclinic, Des Cloizeaux. *Parastilbite* and *reissite* are probably identical.

EPSOMITE, p. 394.—*Reichardtite* (Krause) is a massive variety from Stassfurt and Leopoldshall.

ERILITE, Lewis.—Acicular, wool-like crystals of unknown nature occurring in a cavity in the quartz from Herkimer Co., N. Y.

ERIOCHALCITE, Scacchi.—Copper chloride from Vesuvius.

ERYTHROZINCITE, Damour.—In thin crystalline plates. Color red. Perhaps (Des Cloizeaux) a manganesian variety of wurtzite.

EUCLASE, p. 323.—Found in good crystals in the Tyrol, from the Hohe Tauern, perhaps at Rauris.

EUCRASITE, Paijkull.—A mineral from Brevig, Norway, near thorite.

EUCRYPTITE, G. J. Brush and E. S. Dana.—Hexagonal. In regularly arranged crystals imbedded in albite (like graphic granite, see fig.) both of which have resulted from the alteration of spodumene. G. = 2·667. Composition $Li_2Al_2Si_2O_8 = SiO_2$ 47·51, Al_2O_3 40·61, Li_2O 11·88 = 100. Branchville, Conn.

EULYTITE, p. 302.—Pseudo rhombohedral according to Bertrand.

EUSYNCHITE is (Rammelsberg) $4Pb_3V_2O_8 + 3Zn_3V_2O_8$. Aräoxene is $2(Pb,Zn)_3V_2O_8 + (Pb,Zn)_3As_2O_8$.
Tritochorite (Frenzel) is related, composition $R_3V_2O_8$, with R = Pb (54 p.c.), Cu (7 p.c.), Zn (11 p.c.). Locality uncertain.

FAIRFIELDITE. G. J. Brush and E. S. Dana.—Triclinic. Foliated or lamellar, crystalline; also in radiating masses, curved foliated or fibrous. Cleavage brachydiagonal perfect. Lustre pearly to subadamantine. Color white to pale straw yellow. Transparent. Composition $R_3P_2O_8 + 2aq$, with R = Ca : (Mn + Fe) = 2 : 1. This requires: P_2O_5 39·30, FeO 6·64. MnO 13·10, CaO 30·99, H_2O 9·97 = 100. Occurs with other manganesian phosphates at Branchville, Conn.
Leucomanganite (Sandberger) from Rabenstein, Bavaria, may be identical; not yet described.

FELDSPAR GROUP.—Schuster has shown that in the series of triclinic feldspars there is in optical relations the same gradual transition from the one extreme (albite) to the other (anorthite) as exists in composition. Thus, he finds that the directions of light-extinction, as observed on the basal and clinodiagonal sections, the position of the axes of elasticity, the dispersion of the axes, and the axial angle all show this gradual change in the same direction. These results confirm the accepted view of Tschermak that the intermediate triclinic feldspars are to be regarded as isomorphous mixtures of albite and anorthite in varying proportions; moreover, they explain the apparent difficulties raised by the observations of Des Cloizeaux (p. 319). The angles given on p. 320 are then true only in special cases, since in the varieties varying in composition these values will also vary. The values for angles (given by Schuster) made by the extinction-directions with O and $i-i$ are as follows:

	With O	With $i-i$
Albite	$+4°$ to $+3°$	$+18°$
Varieties between Albite and Oligoclase	$+2°$ to $+1°$	$+12°$
Oligoclase	$+2°$ to $+1°$	$+3°$ to $+2°$
Andesite	$-1°$ to $-2°$	$-4°$ to $-6°$
Labradorite	$-4°$ to $-5°$	$-17°$
Varieties between Labradorite and Anorthite	$-16°$ to $-18°$	$-29°$
Anorthite	$-38°$	$-40°$

FERGUSONITE, p. 362.—New localities: Rockport, Mass. (J. L. Smith); Burke Co., N. C. (Hidden); Mitchell Co., N. C. (Shepard).

FERROTELLURITE, Genth.—In delicate radiating crystalline tufts of a yellow color. Perhaps an iron tellurate. Keystone mine, Magnolia District, Colorado.

FILLOWITE, G. J. Brush and E. S. Dana.—Monoclinic; pseudo-rhombohedral. Generally in granular crystalline masses. H. = 4·5. G. = 3·43. Lustre subresinous to greasy. Color wax yellow, yellowish to reddish brown. Composition $3R_3P_2O_8 + aq$, with $R = $ Mn, Fe, Ca, Na$_2$; requiring: P$_2$O$_5$ 40·19, FeO 6·80, MnO 40·19, CaO 5·28, Na$_2$O 5·84, H$_2$O 1·70 = 100. Occurs with other manganesian phosphates in pegmatite at Branchville, Conn.

FLUORITE, p. 263.—Pseudo-isometric, according to Mallard; see p. 186.

FORESITE, p. 347.—Probably identical with stilbite.

FRANKLANDITE, Reynolds.—Near ulexite. Massive. White. G. = 1·65. Composition Na$_4$Ca$_2$B$_{12}$O$_{22}$, 15H$_2$O. Tarapaca, Peru.

FREYALITE, Esmark, Damour.—A silicate of cerium, thorium, etc. G. = 4·06–4·17. Color brown. From Brevig, Norway.

GADOLINITE, p. 309.—Contains the new earth ytterbium (Marignac), also scandium (Cleve).

GALENOBISMUTITE, H. Sjögren.—Massive, compact. H. = 3–4. G. = 6·88. Lustre metallic. Color tin white. Streak grayish black. Composition PbBi$_2$S$_4$ or PbS + Bi$_2$S$_3$, requiring, S 16·95, Bi 55·62, Pb 27·43 = 100. Occurs with bismutite at the Kogrufva, Nordmark, Sweden.

GANOMALITE, Nordenskiöld.—Massive. H. = 4. G. = 4·98. Lustre greasy. Colorless to white or whitish gray. Transparent. Composition (Pb,Mn)SiO$_3$; analysis (Lindström: SiO$_2$ 34·55, PbO 34·89, MnO 20·01, CaO 4·89, MgO 3·68, alk., ign. 1·88 = 99·58. Occurs with tephroite, native lead, etc., at Långban, Sweden.

GARNET, p. 302.—Pseudo-isometric, according to Mallard and Bertrand, see p. 186. Nearly colorless garnets occur at Hull, Canada; others containing 5 p.c. Cr$_2$O$_3$ at Wakefield, Quebec. Large perfect crystals in mica schist near Fort Wrangell, Alaska.

GARNIERITE, p. 351.—An allied hydrated silicate of magnesium and nickel has been found in Southern Oregon, at Piney Mountain, Cow Creek, Douglas County.

GINILSITE, Fischer.—A doubtful silicate from the Ginilsalp, Graubünden, Switzerland.

GISMONDITE, p. 341.—Triclinic, complex twins, according to Schrauf and v. Lasaulx.

GUANAJUATITE, Fernandez, 1873.—The same mineral as that afterward called frenzeli (p. 223). Composition (Mallet), Bi_2Se_3, with a little Se replaced by S. *Silaonite* is mechanical mixture of this mineral and native bismuth.

GUNNISONITE, Clarke and Perry (Am. Chem. Journ., iv., 140).—A massive substance, a deep purple color, mixed with calcite. An analysis, after deducting 12·75 $CaCO_3$, yielde CaF_2 74·89, CaO 11·44, SiO_2 6·87, Al_2O_3 5·95, Na_2O 0·85 = 100. Probably an impu fluorite; perhaps altered; certainly not a homogeneous mineral.

GUEJARITE, Cumenge.—Orthorhombic; in prismatic crystals, form near that of chalc stibite. H. = 3·5. G. = 5·03. Color steel gray. Composition $Cu_2Sb_4S_7$ or $Cu_2S + 2Sb_2S$ From the copper mines in the district of Guejar, Andalusia.

GUMMITE.—This decomposition product of uraninite occurs in considerable masses the Flat Rock mine, Mitchell Co., N. C.

GYROLITE, p. 328.—*Tobermorite* of Heddle, is near gyrolite and okenite. Massive. Col pinkish white. G. = 2·423. Analysis : SiO_2 46·62, Al_2O_3 3·99, F_2O_3 0·66, FeO 1·08, Ca 33·98, K_2O 0·57, Na_2O 0·89, H_2O 12·11 = 99·81. Filling cavities in rocks near Tobermor Island of Mull.

HALLOYSITE, p. 352.—*Indianaite* of Cox, is a white porcelain clay, useful in the art occurring in considerable beds in Lawrence Co., Indiana.

HANNAYITE, vom Rath.—In triclinic prismatic crystals. G. = 1·893. Compositic $H_4(NH_4)Mg_3P_4O_{16}$ + 8 aq. Occurs in guano of the Skipton Caves, Victoria.

HATCHETTOLITE, J. L. Smith.—Isometric, habit octahedral. H. = 5. G. = 4·77–4·90. Lustr resinous. Color yellowish brown. Translucent. Fracture conchoidal. A columbo-tan talate of uranium and calcium, containing 5 p.c. water; closely related to pyrochlor With samarskite in the mica mines of Mitchell Co., N. C.

HAYESINE.—According to N. H. Darton, this borate occurs sparingly with datolite and ca cite at Bergen Hill, N. J.

HEDYPHANE, p. 367.—A variety from Långban contains (Lindström) 8 p.c. BaO. Mon clinic (Des Cloizeaux), and perhaps isomorphous with caryinite, p. 422; this would sepa rate it from mimetite.

HELDBURGITE, Lüdecke.—In minute tetragonal crystals, resembling guarinite. Col yellow. H. = 6·5. Composition unknown. In feldspar of the phonolyte of the Heldbur near Coburg.

HELVITE, p. 302.—Occurs at the mica mine near Amelia Court House, Amelia Co., Vi ginia. In crystals and crystalline masses, of a sulphur-yellow color, imbedded in orth clase.

HENWOODITE, Collins.—In botryoidal globular masses, crystalline. H. = 4–4·5. G = 2·67. Color turquoise blue. A hydrous phosphate of aluminum and copper (7 p. CuO). West Phenix mine, Cornwall.

HERRENGRUNDITE, Brezina (= Urvölgyite, Szabó).—In spherical groups of six-sided tabu lar crystals (monoclinic). Cleavage basal perfect. H. = 2·5. G. = 3·132. Lustre vitreou pearly on cleavage face. Color emerald to bluish green. A hydrous basic sulphate c copper, allied to langite. From Herrengrund (= Urvölgy) in Hungary.

HESSITE, p. 228.—Pseudo-isometric (triclinic) according to Becke, but the conclusion is not beyond question.

HETÆROLITE (Hetairite), G. E. Moore.—In botryoidal coatings, with radiated structure. H. = 5. G. = 4·933. Stated to be a zinc hausmannite. Occurs with chalcophanite at Sterling Hill, New Jersey.

HEUBACHITE, Sandberger.—In thin soot-like incrustations, also dendritic. Color black. A hydrous oxide of cobalt and nickel. Heubachthal, near Wittichen, Baden.

HEULANDITE, p. 347.—*Oryzite* of Grattarola may be identical with heulandite. In minute white crystals, resembling rice grains ($\delta\rho\upsilon\zeta\alpha$, rice). Elba.

HIBBERTITE, Heddle.—A lemon-yellow powder in kammererite; in composition probably a mixture of magnesium hydrate and calcium carbonate. From the chromite quarry in the island of Unst, Scotland.

HIERATITE, Cossa (Trans. Acad. Linc., III., vi., 14).—A potassium fluo-silicate, $2KF + SiF_4$, obtained in octahedral crystals from an aqueous solution of part of stalactitic concretions found at the fumaroles of the crater of Vulcano. The concretions have a grayish color, a spongy texture, rarely compact, and consist of hieratite, lamellæ of boracic acid, with selensulphur, arsenic sulphide, etc.

HOMILITE, Paijkull.—Near gadolinite and datolite in angles and habit. H. = 4·5-5. G. = 3·34. Lustre resinous to vitreous. Color black or blackish brown. Translucent in thin splinters. Composition $FeCaB_2Si_2O_{10}$, or analogous to datolite. From the Stockö, near Brevig, Norway.

HOPEITE.—Composition probably $Zn_3P_2O_8 + 4$ aq. Orthorhombic. Altenberg.

HÜBNERITE, p. 383.—Found (Jenney) near Deadwood, Black Hills, Dakota. Also in rhodochrosite at Adervielle, in the Hautes Pyrénées.

HUNTILITE, Wurtz.—An impure massive mineral from Silver Islet, Lake Superior, regarded as a basic silver arsenide.

HYALOTEKITE, Nordenskiöld.—Coarsely crystalline, massive. H. = 5-5·5. G. = 3·81. Lustre vitreous to greasy. Color white to pearly gray. Analysis (incomplete): SiO_2 39·62, PbO 25·30, BaO 20·66, CaO 7·00, ign. 0·82, $Al_2O_3K_2O$, etc., tr. From Långban, Sweden.

HYDROCERUSSITE, Nordenskiöld.—A hydrous lead carbonate, occurring in white or colorless crystalline plates on native lead at Långban, Sweden.

HYDROFRANKLINITE, Rœpper.—A hydrous oxide of zinc, manganese and iron, occurring in brilliant regular octahedrons, with perfect octahedral cleavage. Sterling Hill, N. J. Never completely described.

HYDROPHILITE, Adam.—Calcium chloride; see chlorocalcite, p. 260.

HYDRORHODONITE, *Engström.*—A hydrous silicate of manganese ($MnSiO_3 + $ aq). Massive, crystalline. Color red brown. Långban, Sweden.

ILESITE, Wuensch.—In loosely adherent crystalline aggregates. Color white. Taste bitter, astringent. Composition (M. W. Iles) $RSO_4 + 4$ aq, with $R = Mn : Zn : Fe = 5 : 1 : 1$. Occurs in a siliceous gangue in Hall Valley, Park Co., Colorado.

IODOBROMITE, v. Lasaulx.—Isometric, octahedral. G. = 5·713. Color sulphur yellow, sometimes greenish. Composition $2Ag(Cl,Br) + AgI$. From the mine "Schöne Aussicht," Dernbach, Nassau.

IRON, p 226.—The later investigations of the so-called meteoric iron of **Ovifak**, Disco

Bay, Greenland, more especially by Törnebohm and J. Lawrence Smith, leave no doubt that it is in fact terrestrial.

JAMESONITE, p. 251.—Occurs in Sevier Co., Arkansas, with other ores of antimony.

JAROSITE.—Occurs in tabular rhombohedral crystals at the Vulture mine, Arizona (Silliman), and at the Arrow mine, Chaffee Co., Colorado (König). Composition $K_2SO_4 + Fe_2S_3O_{12} + 2Fe_2H_6O_6$.

KENTROLITE, Damour and vom Rath.—In minute orthorhombic crystals, grouped in sheaf-like forms like stilbite. H. = 5. G. = 6·19. Color dark reddish brown. Composition probably $Pb_2Mn_2Si_2O_9$. From Southern Chili.

KRENNERITE, vom Rath (*Bunsenin*, Krenner).—Orthorhombic; in vertically striated prismatic crystals. Color silver white to brass yellow. Lustre metallic, brilliant. A telluride of gold, perhaps related to calaverite. Nagyag, Transylvania.

LAUTITE, Frenzel.—Generally massive. H. = 3–3·5. G. = 4·96. Metallic. Color iron black. Formula given CuAsS, but very probably a mixture. Lauta, Marienberg, Saxony.

LAWRENCITE, Daubrée.—Iron protochloride occurring in the Greenland native iron, etc.

LEADHILLITE, p. 390.—Susannite is very probably identical with leadhillite.

LEIDYITE, König.—In verruciform incrustations, consisting of fine scales. Color various shades of green. A hydrous silicate of aluminum, iron, magnesium, and calcium. Leiperville, Delaware Co., Penn.

LEUCITE, p. 318.—Has been made artificially by Fouqué and Lévy; also an iron leucite has been made by Hautefeuille; optical character as of natural crystals.

LEUCOCHALCITE, Sandberger.—In slender, nearly white crystals. According to an imperfect description, an arsenical tagilite. Wilhelmine mine in the Spessart.

LEUCOPHANITE, p. 300.—Monoclinic (Bertrand, Groth), twins analogous to those of harmotome.

LEUCOTILE, Hare.—In irregularly grouped silky fibres of a green color. Analysis: SiO_2 28·98, Al_2O_3 6·99, Fe_2O_3 8·16, MgO 29·78, CaO 7·37, Na_2O 1·32, K_2O tr., H_2O 17·29 = 99·89. Reichenstein, Silesia.

LIBETHENITE, p. 373.—Pseudo-orthorhombic, monoclinic, according to Schrauf.

LISKEARDITE, Maskelyne.—Massive, incrusting. Color white. Stated to have the composition $Al_6As_2O_{14},16H_2O$. Not fully described. Liskeard, Cornwall.

LIVINGSTONITE, p. 232.—Composition probably $Hg_2S + 4Sb_2S_3$.

LOUISITE, Honeymann.—A transparent, glassy, leek-green mineral. H. = 6·5. G. = 2·41. Analysis (H. Louis): SiO_2 63·74, Al_2O_3 0·57, FeO 1·25, MnO tr., CaO 17·27, MgO 0·38, K_2O 3·38, Na_2O 0·08, H_2O 12·96 = 99·63.

MACFARLANITE, Sibley.—A name given to the complex granular silver ore of Silver Islet, Lake Superior, which has yielded the supposed huntilite.

MAGNOLITE, F. A. Genth.—In radiating tufts of minute acicular crystals. Color white. Lustre silky. Composition perhaps Hg_2TeO_4. A decomposition product of coloradoite, Keystone mine, Magnolia District, Colorado.

MALLARDITE, Carnot.—In colorless cystalline fibrous masses. Composition $MnSO_4 + 7aq$. From the "Lucky Boy" silver mine, Butterfield Cañon, near Salt Lake, Utah.

MANGANOSITE, Blomstrand.—Isometric. Cleavage cubic. H. = 5-6. G. = 5·118. Lustre vitreous. Color emerald green on fresh fracture, becoming black on exposure. Composition MnO. From Långban, and from the Mossgrufva, Nordmark, Sweden.

MARMAIROLITE. Holst.—In fine crystalline needles. H. = 5. G. = 3·07. Color pale yellow. Composition near enstatite, but with 6 p.c. Na_2O and 1·9 p.c. K_2O. Långban, Sweden.

MATRICITE, Holst.—In crystalline masses. H. = 3–4. G. = 2·53. Color gray. Feel greasy. A hydrous silicate of magnesium, near villarsite, but with one molecule H_2O. From the Krangrufva, Wermland, Sweden.

MELANOTEKITE, Lindström.—Massive, cleavable. H. = 6·5. G. = 5·73. Lustre metallic to resinous. Color black to blackish gray. Composition $Pb_2Fe_2Si_2O_9$ (analogous to kentrolite). With magnetite and yellow garnet at Långban, Sweden.

MELANOTHALLITE, Scacchi.—Copper chloride from Vesuvius.

MELANTERITE, p. 395.—*Luckite* of Carnot is a variety containing 1·9 p.c. MnO. "Lucky Boy" silver mine, Butterfield Cañon, near Salt Lake, Utah.

MELIPHANITE, p. 300.—Tetragonal according to Bertrand.

MENACCANITE, p. 269.—*Hydroilmenite* of Blomstrand is a partially altered variety, containing a little water. From Småland, Sweden.

MICA GROUP, pp. 311 to 315.—Tschermak has shown that all the species of the mica group are monoclinic, an axis of elasticity being inclined a few degrees to the plane of cleavage; these conclusions are confirmed by Bauer; and von Kokscharof shows that in angle there is no sensible deviation from the orthorhombic type.
Tschermak divides the species into two groups as follows:

I.	II.
Biotites: Anomite.	Meroxene, Lepidomelane.
Phlogopites:	Phlogopite, Zinnwaldite.
Muscovites: { Lepidolite, Muscovite, Paragonite.	
Margarites: Margarite.	

In group I. are included all the micas in which the optic axial plane is perpendicular to the plane of symmetry; and group II. includes those in which it is parallel to the plane of symmetry. Thus, the former species biotite is divided on this principle into *anomite* (ἄνομος, *contrary to law*) and *meroxene* (Breithaupt's name for the Vesuvian biotite). For example, the mica occurring with diopside in granular calcite at Lake Baikal is anomite, as also that from Greenwood Furnace, N. Y. Meroxene is represented by the Vesuvian magnesian mica. Muscovite includes also some of the "hydro-micas" to all of which belong the formula $(H, K)_2Al_2Si_2O_8$; *phengite* is a name given to some muscovites approaching lepidolite in composition, and thus not conforming to the unisilicate type. For the full discussion of the subject, see the original memoirs of Tschermak and also those of Rammelsberg, etc., referred to in Appendix III.
Haughtonite (Heddle), from Scotch granite, etc., is a variety of biotite, characterized by containing much FeO (to 19 p.c.) and little MgO. *Siderophyllite* (H. C. Lewis) from Colorado contains all FeO (25·5 p.c.) and only a trace of magnesia.

MICROLITE, p. 359.—In small brilliant octahedrons, light grayish yellow to blackish brown (Nordenskiöld), at Utö, Sweden. G. = 5·25. Composition $Ca_2Ta_2O_7$, with also MnO and MgO.

Occurs at the mica mines of Amelia Co., Virginia (Dunnington). In modified octahedrons, also in large (to 4 lbs.) imperfect crystals. G. = 5·656. Composition essentially $Ca_2Ta_2O_7$, with also $\frac{1}{3}$ $CbOF_3$. Also occurs at Branchville, Conn. (Brush and Dana). *Haddamite* of Shepard, from Haddam, Conn., is related, perhaps identical.

MILARITE.—Orthorhombic, pseudo-hexagonal. Composition $HKCa_2Al_2Si_{22}O_{30}$. Originally described from Val Milar, but really (Kuschel) from Val Giuf, Switzerland (giufite).

MIMETITE, p. 366.—According to Bertrand and Jannettaz, crystals of pure lead arsenate are biaxial; as the amount of lead phosphate increases the angle diminishes and pure lead phosphate (pyromorphite) is uniaxial; but this may be due to the grouping of uniaxial crystals in positions not quite parallel. Occurs with vanadinite in Yuma Co., Arizona (Silliman, Blake).

MIXITE, Schrauf.—Incrusting, crypto-crystalline. Color emerald to bluish green. H. = 3-4. G. = 2·66. A hydrous arsenate of copper and bismuth. Joachimsthal.

MOLYBDENITE, p. 233.—Perhaps orthorhombic (Groth).

MOLYBDOMENITE, COBALTOMENITE, Bertrand (Bull. Soc. Min., v. 90).—Minerals belonging to the same group of selenites as chalcomenite. *Molybdomenite* is a lead selenite, occurring in thin white lamellæ, nearly transparent, orthorhombic, two cleavages. *Cobaltomenite* is a cobalt selenite in minute rose-red crystals occurring in the midst of the selenides of lead and cobalt. From Cacheuta, Argentine Republic.

MONAZITE, p. 368.—From Arendal, a normal phosphate (Rammelsberg) of cerium, lanthanum and didymium, containing no thorium nor zirconium. Penfield has proved that the thorium sometimes found is due to admixed thorite. *Turnerite,* according to Pisani, has the same composition.
Occurs in very brilliant highly modified crystals at Milholland's Mill, Alexander Co., N. C.; also at other localities in North Carolina (Hidden). In large masses with microlite at the mica mines of Amelia Co., Va.; also at Portland (near Middletown) Conn.

MONETITE, C. U. Shepard and C. U. Shepard, Jr.—In irregular aggregates of small triclinic crystals. H. = 3·5. G. = 2·75. Lustre vitreous. Color pale yellowish white. Semitransparent. Composition $HCaPO_4$, requiring P_2O_5 52·20, CaO 41·18, H_2O 6·62 = 100. Occurs with gypsum and monite at the guano islands, Moneta and Mona, in the West Indies.
MONITE occurs as a slightly coherent, uncrystalline, snow-white mineral. G. = 2·1. Composition perhaps $Ca_3P_2O_8 + H_2O$.

MORDENITE.—*Steeleite* of How is an altered mordenite from Cape Split, N. S. Mordenite (How) has the composition SiO_2 68·40, Al_2O_3 12·77, CaO 3·46, Na_2O 2·35, H_2O 13·02 = 100.

NAGYAGITE, p. 249.—Perhaps orthorhombic (Schrauf).

NATROLITE, p. 342.—Monoclinic, according to Lüdecke.

NEOCYANITE, Scacchi.—In minute tabular crystals of a blue color. Supposed to be an anhydrous copper silicate. Mt. Vesuvius.

NEPHRITE, p. 297.—The general subject of nephrite and jadeite in their mineralogical and archæological relations has been exhaustively discussed by Fischer in a special work on that subject.

NEWBERYITE, vom Rath.—In rather large tabular orthorhombic crystals. Composition $Mg_2H_2P_2O_8 + 6$ aq. From the guano of the Skipton Caves, Victoria.

NITROBARITE.—Crystals of native barium nitrate have been obtained from Chili; in apparent octahedrons formed of the two tetrahedrons.

NOCERINE, Scacchi.—In white acicular crystals, perhaps rhombohedral; regarded as a double fluoride of calcium and magnesium. From the volcanic bombs of Nocera.

OCTAHEDRITE (Anatase), p. 277.—Belongs to the monoclinic system, according to Mallard's view (see p. 186).
Found in nearly colorless transparent crystals at Brindletown, Burke Co., N. C. (Hidden).

ONOFRITE.—A massive mineral (G. = 7·62), from Marysvale, Utah, has the composition Hg(S,Se), with $S : Se = 6 : 1$. It thus corresponds nearly with Haidinger's onofrite, which has $S : Se = 4 : 1$.

ORPIMENT (p. 231) and realgar (p. 231) occur in Iron Co., Utah (Blake).

ORTHOCLASE, p. 325.—Klockmann (Z. Kryst., vi., 493) has described twins of orthoclase from the Scholzenberg, near Warmbrunn, in Silesia, the twinning planes in different cases were $i-i$, O, $2-i$, $2-\check{i}$, I, $i-\check{3}$.

ORTHITE, p. 308.—Found in imperfect bladed crystals at the mica mines in Amelia Co., Virginia, with monazite, columbite, etc.

OTTRELITE, p. 358.—A variety of ottrelite from Vénasque, in the Pyrenees, has been called *venasquite* (Damour).

OXAMMITE.—Ammonium oxalate (Shepard) from the Guanape Islands. Also called *guanapite* by Raimondi.

OZOCERITE.—A related mineral wax has been found in large quantities in Utah.

PACHNOLITE, p. 265.—See *thomsenolite*, p. 438.

PECKHAMITE, J. L. Smith.—From the Estherville, Emmet Co., Iowa, meteorite. In rounded nodules, with greasy lustre, and light greenish-yellow color. G. = 3·23. Composition equivalent to two molecules of enstatite and one of chrysolite.

PECTOLITE, p. 327.—*Walkerite* (Heddle) is a closely related mineral from the Corstorphine Hill, near Edinburgh, Scotland.

PELAGITE, Church.—A name given to the composite manganese nodules obtained by the "Challenger" from the bottom of the Pacific.

PENWITHITE, Collins.—Described as a hydrated silicate of manganese ($MnSiO_3 + 2$ aq) from Penwith, Cornwall.

PEROFSKITE, p. 270.—Recent observations refer it to the orthorhombic system, the crystals being complex twins. Ben-Saude, however, regards it as isometric and parallel hemihedral, the observed double refraction being due to secondary causes, see p. 190.

PETALITE, p. 295.—Hydrocastorite is an alteration product of castorite from Elba (Grattarola).

PHARMACOSIDERITE, p. 376.—Pseudo-isometric, according to Bertrand, see p. 186.

PHENACITE, p. 301.—Obtained well crystallized from Switzerland, perhaps from Val Giuf. Also (Cross and Hillebrand) from near Pike's Peak, El Paso Co., Colorado.

PHILLIPSITE, p. 345.—Crystalline system monoclinic (Streng), with a higher degree of pseudo-symmetry due to twinning.

PHOSPHURANYLITE, Genth.—As a pulverulent incrustation, of deep lemon-yellow color. Composition probably $(UO_2)_3P_2O_8 + 6$ aq. Occurs with other uranium minerals at the Flat Rock mine, Mitchell Co., N. C.

PICITE, Nies.—An amorphous, dark brown hydrous iron phosphate from the Eleonore mine and the Rothläufchen mine, near Giessen. Of doubtful homogeneity.

PICKERINGITE, p. 395.—*Sonomaite* (Goldsmith), from the Geysers, California, and *picroal lumogene* (Roster), from Elba, are closely related minerals.

PILOLITE, Heddle.—A name suggested for some minerals from Scottish localities of nearly related composition, which have gone by the names "mountain leather" and "mountain cork."

PLAGIOCITRITE, Sandberger, Singer.—A hydrous sulphate of alumina, iron, potassium, sodium, etc., occurring in lemon-yellow microscopic crystals, and formed from the decomposition of pyrite at the Bauersberg, near Bischofsheim vor der Rhön.

PLATINUM, p. 223.—A nugget weighing 104 grams, and consisting of 46 p.c. platinum and 54 p.c. chromite, was found near Plattsburgh, N. Y. (Collier).

PLUMBOMANGANITE, Hannay.—Described as a sulphide of manganese and lead, but doubtless a mixture. Source unknown.

PLUMBOSTANNITE, Raimondi.—An impure massive mineral, described as a sulph-antimonite of tin, lead and iron, but of doubtful homogeneity. From the district of Moho, Peru.

POLYDYMITE, Laspeyres.—Isometric, octahedral. H. = 4·5. G. = 4·808–4·816. Composition Ni_4S_5. From Grünau, Westphalia. Laspeyres regards the saynite of von Kobell grünauite of Nicol, as an impure polydymite.

POLYHALITE, p. 393.—*Krugite* (Precht) is a related mineral from New Stassfurt. Composition, if homogeneous, $K_2SO_4 + MgSO_4 + 4CaSO_4 + 2$ aq.

PRICEITE, p. 382.—*Pandermite* (vom Rath) is a borate from Panderma on the Black Sea, near priceite, if not identical with it.

PSEUDOBROOKITE, Koch.—In thin tabular striated crystals, orthorhombic. H. = 6. G. = 4·98. Lustre adamantine, on crystalline faces. Color dark brown to black. Contains principally the oxides of iron and titanium. From the andesite of the Aranyer Berg, Transylvania, and Riveau Grand, Monte Dore, also with the asparagus stone of Jumilla, Spain (Lewis). Near brookite.

PSEUDONATROLITE, Grattarola.—In minute acicular crystals. Colorless. A hydrous silicate (62·6 p.c. SiO_2) of aluminum and calcium. From San Piero, Elba.

PSILOMELANE, p. 282.—*Calvonigrite* (Laspeyres) from Kälteborn is a variety.

PYRITE, p. 243.—Occurs in highly modified crystals in Gilpin Co., Colorado.

PYROLUSITE, p. 278.—According to Groth, the prismatic angle is 99° 30'.

PYROPHOSPHORITE, C. U. Shepard, Jr.—A massive, earthy, snow-white mineral from the West Indies. Described as a pyrophosphate of calcium and magnesium.

PYRRHOTITE, p. 241.—Perhaps only pseudo-hexagonal, the apparent form due to twinning.

QUARTZ, p. 284.—The smoky quartz of Branchville, Conn., contains very large quantities of liquid CO_2 (Hawes), also N, H_2S, SO_2, H_3N, F (A. W. Wright).

RALSTONITE, p. 265.—Composition (Brandl) $3(Na_2,Mg,Ca)F_2 + 8Al_2F_6 + 6H_2O$.

RANDITE, König.—A canary yellow incrustation on granite at Frankford, near Philadelphia. Contains calcium and uranium, but composition doubtful.

REDDINGITE, G. J. Brush and E. S. Dana.—Orthorhombic; habit octahedral; form near that of scorodite. H. = 3–3·5. G. = 3·10. Lustre vitreous to sub-resinous. Color pale rose pink to yellowish white. Composition $Mn_3P_2O_8 + 3$ aq, with a varying amount of iron (5–8 p.c. FeO). With other manganesian phosphates at Branchville, Conn.

REINITE, K. v. Fritsch, Lüdecke.—A tetragonal iron tungstate ($FeWO_4$) near scheelite in form, and perhaps a pseudomorph. From Kimbosan, Japan.

RESIN.—The following are names recently given to various hydrocarbon compounds: ajkite, bernardinite, celestialite, duxite, gedanite, hofmannite, huminite, ionite, köflachite, muckite, neudorfite, phytocollite, posepnyte.

RHABDOPHANE, Lettsom.—A cerium phosphate, perhaps the same as phosphocerite.

RHODOCHROSITE, p. 403.—A Hungarian variety, containing 39 p.c. $FeCO_3$, has been called *manganosiderite* (Bayer).
Occurs at Branchville, Conn., containing 16·76 p.c. FeO (Penfield).

RHODIZITE.—According to Damour, rhodizite of Rose, from the Ural, is an alkaline boro-aluminate. Pseudo-isometric according to Bertrand.

ROGERSITE, J. L. Smith.—A thin mammillary crust, of a white color, on samarskite. A hydrous columbate of yttrium, etc., exact composition undetermined. Mitchell Co., N. C.

ROSCOELITE, p. 367.—A silicate, according to recent analyses by Genth, having the formula $K(Mg,Fe)(Al_2,V_2)_2Si_{12}O_{32} + 4$ aq; also (Hanks) from Big Red-Ravine, near Sutter's Mill, Cal.

ROSELITE. p. 372.—True composition $R_3As_2O_8 + 2$ aq (Winkler), hence analogous to fairfieldite, p. 426.

RUBISLITE, Heddle.—An uncertain chloritic substance from the granite of Rubislaw, near Aberdeen, Scotland.

RUTILE, p. 276.—Pseudo-tetragonal according to the view of Mallard (see p. 186).
Occurs in splendent crystals in Alexander Co., N. C (Hidden).

SAMARSKITE, p. 361.—The North Carolina mineral has been shown to contain erbium, terbium, phillipium, decipium (Delafontaine, Marignac). A supposed new element, mosandrum, was also announced by Smith. *Vietinghofite* is a ferruginous variety from Lake Baikal, in the Ural.

SARAWAKITE, Frenzel.—Occurs in minute crystals in the native antimony of Borneo; perhaps senarmontite.

SCAPOLITE, p. 317.—The scapolites have been shown by Adams to contain chlorine (up to 2·48 p. c.) when quite unaltered. The analyses of Neminar, Sipöcz, and Becke prove the same.
Ontariolite (Shepard) is a variety occurring in limestone at Galway, Ontario, Canada.

SCHNEEBERGITE, Brezina.—In isometric octahedrons of a honey-yellow color from Schneeberg, Tyrol. Contains lime and antimony, but exact composition unknown.

SCHORLOMITE, p. 337.—The so-called schorlomite of the Kaiserstuhl is, according to Knop, either a titaniferous melanite or pyroxene.

SEMSEYITE, Krenner.—Stated to be related to plagionite ; from Felsöbanya. Not yet described.

SENARMONTITE, p. 284.—Pseudo-isometric according to Mallard (p. 186). Grosse-Bohle, who has investigated the subject, suggests the same for arsenolite.

SEPIOLITE, p. 349.—Chester has analyzed a fibrous variety from Utah.

SERPENTINE, p. 350.—Schrauf (Z. Kryst., vi.. 321) has studied the magnesia silicates from the serpentine región near Budweis, Southern Bohemia. He introduces the following new names : *Kelyphite*, a serpentinous coating of altered crystals of pyrope ; *Enophite*, a chloritic variety of serpentine ; *Lernilite* (wrong orthography for lennilite) in composition near the vermiculite of Lenni (Cooke), hence name ; *Siliciophite*, a heterogeneous substance high in silica ; *Hydrobiotite* (same name used by Lewis) a hydrated biotite ; *Berlauite*, a chloritic substance filling cavities between the granite and serpentine ; *Schuchardtite*, the so-called chrysopraserde from Gläsendorf, Silesia. He also uses the general name parachlorite for substances conforming to $mAl_2Si_3O_{12} + nR_2SiO_4 + p$aq, and protochlorite for those corresponding to $mAl_2SiO_5 + n(R_2SiO_4) + p$aq.

Totaigite (Heddle) is an uncertain serpentinous mineral, derived from the decomposition of malacolite. From Totaig, Rosshire, Scotland.

SERPIERITE, Des Cloizeaux.—In minute tabular crystals; orthorhombic. Color greenish. Stated to be a basic sulphate of copper (Damour). From Laurium, Greece.

SIDERAZOT, Silvestri.—Iron nitride, a coating on lava at Etna.

SIDERONATRITE, Raimondi.—*Sideronatrite*, from Huantajaya, Peru, and *urusite* (Frenzel) from the island Tschleken, Caspian Sea, are hydrous sulphates of iron and sodium, near each other and related to the doubtful bartholomite.

SIPYLITE, Mallet.—Tetragonal, in octahedrons. Form near that of fergusonite. Cleavage octahedral; usually massive, crystalline. $H = 6$. $G. = 4·89$. Color brownish black to brownish orange. Essentially a columbate of erbium, cerium, lanthanum, didymium, uranium, etc. With allanite on the Little Friar Mt., Amherst Co., Va.

SMALTITE, p. 245.—Occurs near Gothic, Gunnison County, Colorado.

SPHÆROCOBALTITE, Weisbach.—In small spherical masses, concentric, radiated. Color within rose-red. $H. = 4$. $G. = 4·02-4·13$. Composition $CoCO_3$. With roselite at Schneeberg, Saxony.

SPODIOSITE, Tiberg.—In flattened prismatic crystals. A calcium phosphate, and perhaps pseudomorphous. From the Krangrufra, Wermland, Sweden.

SPHALERITE, p. 237.—The sphalerite from the Pierrefitte mine, Vallée Argelès, Pyrénées, contains gallium (L. de Boisbaudran), and various American (Cornwall) and Norwegian (Wleugel) varieties afford indium.

SPODUMENE, p. 295.—The true composition is expressed by the formula $Li_2Al_2Si_4O_{12}$, as proved by numerous recent analyses.

Occurs in small prismatic crystals of a deep emerald green to yellowish green color, with beryl (emerald), rutile, monazite, etc., in Alexander Co., N. C. This variety, which has been extensively introduced as a gem, was called *hiddenite* by J. L. Smith, after W. E Hidden.

The alteration products of the spodumene of Chesterfield and Goshen, Mass., have been described by A. A. Julien.

Occurs in immense crystals at Branchville, Conn. (Brush and Dana). The unaltered mineral is of an amethystine purple color and perfectly transparent, but the crystals are mostly altered. This alteration has yielded (1) a substance called β-spodumene, apparently homogeneous, but in fact an intimate mixture of albite and eucryptite (q. v., p. 426); also cymatolite a mixture of albite and muscovite ; also albite alone; muscovite ; microcline, and killinite

STAUROLITE, p. 336.—*Xantholite* (Heddle) from near Milltown, Loch Ness, Scotland, is a closely related mineral.

STERNBERGITE, p. 240.—*Argentopyrite, Argyropyrite* and *Frieseite* are varieties, or at least closely related minerals. They are essentially identical in form. while Streng shows that the composition of the series may be expressed by the general formula $Ag_2S + nFe_nS_{n+1}$.

STIBIANITE, *Goldsmith.*—A doubtful decomposition product of stibnite, near stibiconite. From Victoria.

STIBICONITE.—Extensive deposits of an antimony oxide, near stibiconite, occur at Sonora, Mexico. The ore carries silver chloride.

STIBNITE, p. 232.—Occurs with other antimony minerals in Sevier Co., Arkansas. In groups of large splendent crystals on an island in western Japan.

STILBITE, p. 346.—Monoclinic, and isomorphous with harmotome and phillipsite (v. Lasaulx).

STRENGITE, Nies.—Orthorhombic, and isomorphous with scorodite. Generally in spherical and botryoidal aggregates. H. = 3-4. G. = 2·87. Lustre vitreous. Color various shades of red to colorless. Composition $Fe_2P_2O_8 + 4$ aq. From the Eleonore mine near Geissen, the Rothläufchen mine near Waldgirmes; also in cavities in the dufrenite from Rockbridge Co., Va. (König).

STRONTIANITE, p. 406.—Occurs at Hamm, Westphalia, sometimes in highly modified pseudo-hexagonal crystals, resembling common forms of aragonite (Laspeyres).

STÜTZITE, Schrauf.—A silver telluride, occurring in pseudo-hexagonal crystals of a lead gray color. Named from a single specimen probably from Nagyag.

SZABOITE, Koch.—In minute triclinic crystals, near rhodonite in form. H. = 6-7. G. = 3·505. Lustre vitreous; sometimes tending to metallic and pearly. Color hair brown; in very thin translucent crystals brownish red. A silicate of calcium and iron ($RSiO_3$) related to babingtonite. Occurs with pseudobrookite in the andesite of the Aranyer Berg, Transylvania; Mt. Calvario, Etna; Riveau Grand, Monte Dore.

SZMIKITE, v. Schröckinger.—Amorphous, stalactitic. Color whitish to reddish. Composition $MnSO_4 + H_2O$. Felsöbanya, Transylvania.

TALKTRIPLITE (Igelström).—A phosphate of iron, manganese, magnesium and calcium; probably a triplite remarkable as containing MgO (17·42 p.c.) and CaO (14·91). From Horrsjöberg in Wermland, Sweden.

TANTALITE, p. 359.—Occurs in North Carolina; in Coosa Co., Ala.
Mangantantalite (Nordenskiöld) is a manganesian variety (9 p c. MnO) from Utö, Sweden.

TARAPACAITE, Raimondi.—A supposed potassium chromate, occurring in bright yellow fragments in the midst of the soda nitre from Tarapaca, Peru.

TAZNITE, Domeyko.—Regarded as an arsenio-antimonate of bismuth, but probably a heterogeneous substance.

TELLURITE.—The tellurium oxide (TeO_2) occurs in minute prismatic, yellow to white crystals, imbedded in native tellurium; also incrusting. Keystone, Smuggler and John Jay mines in Colorado.

TELLURIUM, p. 227.—An impure variety from the Mountain Lion mine, Colorado, has been called LIONITE.

TENNANTITE, p. 256.—*Fredricite* (H. Sjögren) is a variety from Falu, Sweden, containing lead (3 p.c.), tin (1·4 p.c.) and silver (2·9 p.c.).

TENORITE, p. 267.—Made triclinic, on optical grounds, by Kalkowsky.

TEQUESQUITE.—A corruption of tequixquitl, a name used in Mexico to designate a mixture of different salts.

TETRAHEDRITE, p. 255.—Occurs near Central City, Gilpin Co., Colorado, in crystals coating chalcopyrite in parallel position. Also at Newburyport, Mass.; in Arizona (16·23 p.c. Pb).
Frigidite (D'Achiardi) is a variety with 12·7 p.c. Fe, etc., from the Valle del Frigido, Apuan Alps.

THAUMASITE, *Nordenskiöld.*—Massive, compact. H. = 3·5. G. = 1·877. Color white. Lustre greasy, dull. Composition deduced $CaSiO_3 + CaCO_3 + CaSO_4 + 14$ aq, but it is very doubtful whether the material analyzed was homogeneous.

THENARDITE, p. 290.—Occurs in large deposits on the Rio Verde, Arizona (Silliman).

THOMSENOLITE, p. 265.—According to Klein and, later, Brandl and Groth, thomsenolite and pachnolite are distinct minerals. *Thomsenolite* is monoclinic, $\beta = 89° 37\frac{1}{2}'$, and c (vert.) : $b : \check{a} = 1·0877 : 1 : 0·9959$, and has the composition $(Na + Ca)F_3 + Al_2F_6 + H_2O$. *Pachnolite* is monoclinic, $\beta = 89° 46'$, c (vert.) : $b : \check{a} = 1·5320 : 1 : 1·626$, and has the composition $(Na + Ca)F_3 + Al_2F_6$. Pachnolite is a cryolite with two sodium atoms replaced by one calcium atom, and thomsenolite is the same, with also one molecule of water.

THOMSONITE, p. 342.—Occurs in amygdules in the diabase of Grand Marais, Lake Superior; also in polished pebbles on the lake shore. The pebbles are sometimes opaque white, like porcelain; sometimes green in color and granular (variety called lintonite); sometimes with fibrous radiated structure, of various colors, and of great beauty. The last are valued as ornaments.

THINOLITE.—Calcium carbonate, forming large tufa-like deposits in Nevada, a shore formation of the former Lake Lahontan. Regarded by King as pseudomorph after gaylussite, but this is doubtful.

THORITE, p. 340.—A variety of thorite is called *uranothorite* by Collier; it contains 9·96 U_2O_3. Massive. G. = 4·126. Color dark red-brown. From the Champlain iron region, N. Y.

TITANITE, p. 335.—Occurs, often in enormous crystals or groups of crystals, at Renfrew, Canada, with zircon (twins), apatite and amphibole.
Alshedite (Blomstrand) is a variety from Småland, Sweden, containing 2·8 p.c. YO.
Titanomorphite is a name given by v. Lasaulx to a part of the white granular aggregates surrounding rutile and menaccanite, and derived from their alteration. It is a calcium titanate, according to Bettendorff's analysis, but Cathrein (Z. Kryst.. vi., 244) shows that it is really a variety of titanite. Leucoxene is a name earlier (1374) given by Gümbel for a similar substance of doubtful chemical nature often observed in rocks; according to Cathrein it is a titanite with or without a mixture of rutile microlites.

TOPAZ, p. 332.—Pseudo-orthorhombic (monoclinic), according to the view of Mallard (see p. 186).
Occurs near Pike's Peak, El Paso Co., Colorado, and at Stoneham, Maine.

TORBANITE, p. 418.—*Wollongongite* (p. 416) is referred to torbanite by Liversidge; it is from Hartley, New South Wales, not Wollongong, so that the name is inappropriate.

TOURMALINE, p. 329.—Pseudo-rhombohedral, according to the view of Mallard (see p. 186).
Occurs in white, nearly colorless crystals, at De Kalb, St. Lawrence Co., N. Y.

TRIDYMITE, p. 288.—Pseudo-hexagonal (triclinic), according to Schuster and also v. Lasaulx. Asmanite is probably identical with it.
Hautefeuille has made it artificially; and it has been observed with zinc spinel as a result of the alteration of zinc muffles.

TRIPHYLITE, p. 369.—The composition (Penfield) is $LiFePO_4 = Li_3PO_4 + Fe_3P_2O_8$, with the iron replaced by manganese in part.
Lithiophilite (Brush and Dana) is a variety almost free from iron (down to 4 p.c.), and corresponding to the formula $LiMnPO_4 = Li_3PO_4 + Mn_3P_2O_8$. Massive, cleavable (*O. I, i-i*). Color salmon,—honey yellow, yellowish brown, light clove brown. Occurs with other manganesian phosphates in pegmatite, at Branchville, Fairfield Co., Conn.

TRIPLOIDITE (G. J. Brush and E. S. Dana).—Monoclinic, near wagnerite in form. Generally in fibrous crystalline aggregates. H. = 4·5–5. G. = 3·697. Lustre vitreous to greasy adamantine. Color yellowish to reddish brown. topaz yellow, hyacinth red. Transparent. Composition $R_3P_2O_8 + R(OH)_2$. with R = Mn : Fe = 3 : 1; hence analogous to triplite, but with (OH) replacing F. With other manganesian phosphates (eosphorite, lithiophilite, etc.) from Branchville, Conn.

TRIPPKEITE, Damour and vom Rath.—In small brilliant crystals, tetragonal. Color bluish green. Stated to be a hydrous arsenite of copper. With olivenite in cuprite from Copiapo, Chili.

TYSONITE, Allen and Comstock.—Hexagonal. Cleavage basal. H. = 4·5–5. G. = 6·13. Lustre vitreous to resinous. Color pale wax yellow. Composition $(Ce,La,Di)_2F_6$. From near Pike's Peak, Colorado. The crystals are mostly altered to *bastnäsite* (also called hamartite), which is a fluo-carbonate, near parisite.

URANINITE, p 274.—Occurs in brilliant black octahedral crystals at Branchville, Conn. G = 9·25. Analysis: UO_3 40·08, UO_2 54·51, PbO 4·27, FeO 0·49, H_2O 0·88 = 100·23. Also from Mitchell Co., N. C.; mostly altered to gummite.

URANOCIRCITE, Weisbach.—Orthorhombic, like autunite. Cleavage basal perfect. G. = 3·53. Color yellow green. Composition $BaU_2P_2O_{12} + 8$ aq. In quartz veins, Saxon Voightland.

URANOTHALLITE, Schrauf (Z. Kryst., vi., 410).—A uranium carbonate from Joachimsthal, originally mentioned by Vogl. Occurs in confused aggregates of orthorhombic crystals. Calculated formula $UC_2O_6 + 2CaCO_3 + 10$ aq.

URANOTILE, p. 341.—Occurs in Mitchell Co., N. C. Genth writes the formula, $Ca_3(UO_2)_6Si_6O_{21} + 18$ aq.

VANADINITE, p. 367.—Occurs in highly modified crystals in the State of Cordoba, Argentine Republic. Also in very beautiful ruby-red crystals at the Hamburg and other mines in Yuma Co., Arizona (Silliman; Blake), and in yellow to nearly white crystals at other localities in Arizona.

VARISCITE.—The so-called peganite from Montgomery Co., Ark., is shown by Chester to be identical with Breithaupt's variscite. Composition $Al_2P_2O_8 + 4$ aq.

VENERITE, Hunt.—An impure chloritic mineral containing copper; mined as copper ore at Jones' mine, near Springfield, Berks Co., Penn.

VERMICULITE, p. 355.—*Protovermiculite* (König) and *philadelphite* (Lewis) are minerals related to the other "vermiculites," the whole group being decomposition products of other micas.

VESBINE, Scacchi.—Forms thin yellow crusts on lava of 1631, Vesuvius; supposed to contain a new element, vesbium.

VESUVIANITE, p. 405.—Pseudo-tetragonal, according to the view of Mallard (see p. 186). A variety from Jordansmühl contains 3 p.c. MnO (manganidocrase).

VESZELYITE, p. 373.—Composition, according to Schrauf, $2(Zn,Cu)_3As_2O_8 + 9(Zn,Cu)H_2O_2 + 9$ aq, with Cu : Zn = 3 : 2, and As : P = 1 : 1.

WAD, p. 283.—*Lepidophæite* (Weisbach) is a related mineral from Kamsdorf, Thuringia. Composition stated to be $CuMn_6O_{12} + 9$ aq.

WAGNERITE, p. 368.—*Kjerulfine* has been shown to be identical with wagnerite in form and composition; often partially altered.

WALPURGITE, p. 379.—Triclinic (pseudo-monoclinic), according to Weisbach.

WATTEVILLITE, Singer.—In minute acicular snow-white crystals. A hydrous sulphate of calcium, sodium, potassium, etc. Formed from the decomposition of pyrite at the Bauersberg, near Bischofsheim vor der Rhön.

WULFENITE, p. 384.—Occurs in fine crystals in the Eureka district, Nevada; also in Yuma Co., Arizona, sometimes in simple octahedral crystals (Silliman).

XANTHOPHYLLITE, p. 358.—Waluewite (v. Kokscharof) is a well crystallized variety from Achmatovsk, Ural.

XENOTIME, p. 364.—Occurs compounded with zircon in Burke Co., N. C. (Hidden).

YOUNGITE, Hannay.—Described as a sulphide of lead, zinc, iron and manganese, but doubtless a mixture.

ZINCALUMINITE, Bertrand and Damour.—In thin hexagonal plates. minute. H. = 2·5-3. G. = 2·26. Composition $2ZnSO_4 + 4ZnH_2O_2 + 3Al_2H_6O_6 + 5$ aq. From the zinc mines of Laurium, Greece.

ZIRCON, p. 304.—Occurs in fine twin crystals ($1-i$, like rutile and cassiterite) with titanite and apatite, in Renfrew Co., Canada (Hidden). Also with astrophyllite and arfvedsonite in El Paso Co., Colorado.
Pseudo-tetragonal, according to the view of Mallard (see p. 186).
Beccarite (Grattarola) is a variety from Ceylon.

APPENDIX A.

SYNOPSIS OF MILLER'S SYSTEM OF CRYSTALLOGRAPHY.

The following pages contain a concise presentation of the System of Crystallography proposed by Prof. W. H. Miller in 1839, and now employed by a large proportion of the workers in Mineralogy. The attempt has been made to present the subject briefly, and yet with sufficient fulness to enable any one having some previous knowledge of Crystallography not only to understand the System, but also to use it himself. For the full development of the subject, especially of its theoretical side, reference must be made to the works of Miller, Grailich, von Lang, Schrauf and Bauerman (see the Introduction), as also to the admirable Lectures of Prof. Maskelyne, printed in the Chemical News for 1873 (vol. xxxi., 3, 13, 24, 63, 101, 111, 121, 153, 200, 232).

GENERAL PRINCIPLES.

The indices of Miller and their relation to those of Naumann.—The position of a plane ABC (f. 751) is determined when the distances OA, OB, OC are known, which it cuts off in the

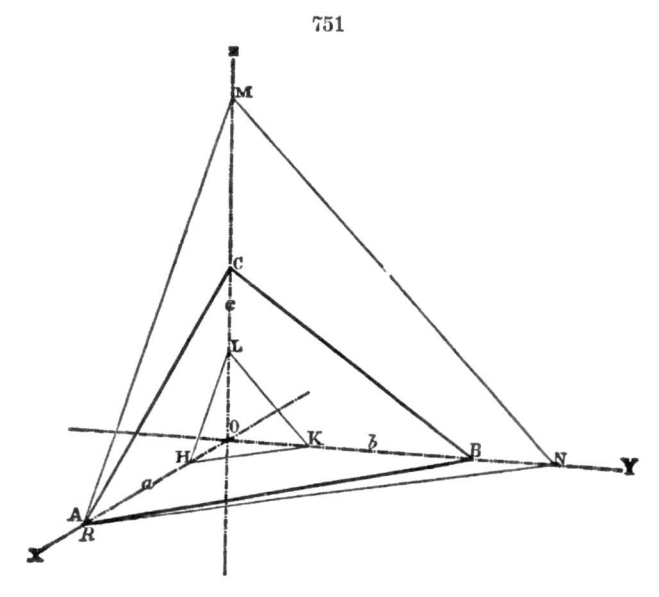

751

assumed axes X, Y, Z from their point of intersection O. The lengths of these axes for a single plane of a crystal being taken as units, thus $OA = a$, $OB = b$, $OC = c$, it is found that the lengths of the corresponding lines OH, OK, OL for any other plane, HKL, of the same crystal always bear some simple relation, expressed in whole numbers, to these assumed units This relation may be expressed as follows:

$$\frac{a}{\mathrm{OH}} = h \qquad \frac{b}{\mathrm{OK}} = k \qquad \frac{c}{\mathrm{OL}} = l,$$

or in the more common form

$$\frac{1}{h} \cdot \frac{a}{\mathrm{OH}} = \frac{1}{k} \cdot \frac{b}{\mathrm{OK}} = \frac{1}{l} \cdot \frac{c}{\mathrm{OL}} = 1 \quad \cdot \quad \cdot \quad \cdot \quad (1)$$

The numbers represented by h, k, l are called the indices of the plane and determine its position, when the *elements* of the crystal—the lengths and mutual inclinations of the axes—are known. When the lines are taken in the opposite direction from O, they are called negative; the corresponding negative character of the indices is indicated by the minus sign placed *over* the index, thus, $\bar{h}$, $\bar{k}$, or $\bar{l}$. When the unit, or fundamental form, is appropriately chosen, the numbers representing h, k, l seldom exceed six.

The above relation may also be written in the form:

$$\frac{\mathrm{OH}}{a} = r \qquad \frac{\mathrm{OK}}{b} = n \qquad \frac{\mathrm{OL}}{c} = m.$$

Here r, n, m, which are obviously the *reciprocals* of the indices h, k, l respectively, are essentially identical with the symbols of Naumann. For example, if $h = 3$, $k = 2$, $l = 2$, then $r = \frac{1}{3}$, $n = \frac{1}{2}$, $m = \frac{1}{2}$, and the symbol (322) of Miller becomes $\frac{1}{3}a : \frac{1}{2}b : \frac{1}{2}c$; but by Naumann's usage this is so transformed that $r = 1$, and $n > 1$ (or sometimes $n = 1$, and $r > 1$), in other words, by multiplying through by 3, in this case, the symbol takes the form $a : \frac{3}{2}b : \frac{3}{2}c$,[*] or, as abbreviated, $\frac{3}{2}\text{-}\frac{3}{2}$ ($\frac{3}{2}\mathrm{P}\frac{3}{2}$). The symbol $a : \frac{3}{2}b : \frac{3}{2}c$ properly belongs to the plane MNR (f. 751), which is parallel to, and hence crystallographically identical (p. 11) with the plane HKL.

Special values of the indices h, k, l. It is obvious that several distinct cases are possible: (1) The three indices h, k, l are all greater than unity, then including the various pyramidal planes. The number of similar planes corresponding to the general form $\left\{hkl\right\}$ depends upon the degree of symmetry of the crystalline system, and upon the special values of h, k, l, e.g., $h = k$, etc. These cases are considered later in their proper place.

(2) One of the three indices may be equal to zero, indicating then that the plane is parallel to the axis corresponding to this index. Thus the symbol $(hk0)$, $= a : nb : \infty c$, or $na : b : \infty c$ (p. 11), belongs to the planes parallel to the vertical axis c, as shown in f. 752. They are called prismatic planes. The symbol $(h0l)$, $= a : \infty b : mc$ (p. 11) belongs to the planes parallel to the axis b, as in f. 753. The symbol $(0kl)$, $= \infty a : b : mc$, belongs to the planes parallel to the axis a, f. 754.

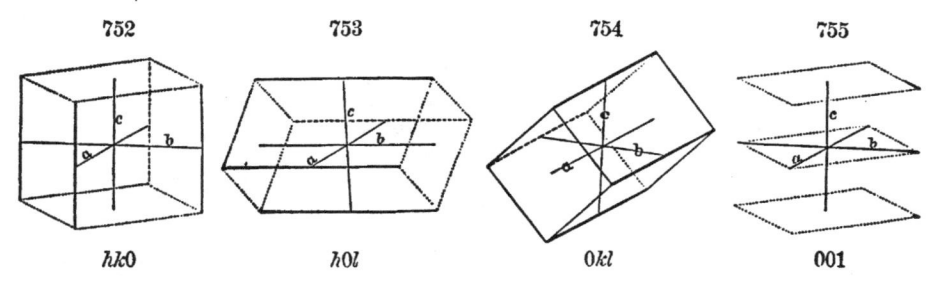

752　　　　　　　753　　　　　　　754　　　　　　　755

$hk0$　　　　　$h0l$　　　　　$0kl$　　　　　001

(3) Two of the indices may be zero, the symbol (hkl) then becomes (001), $= \infty a : \infty b : c$, the basal plane, f. 755; (010), $= \infty a : b : \infty c$; and (100), $= a : \infty b : \infty c$. These are the three diametral or pinacoid planes.

The symbol (010) represents the *clinopinacoid* ($i\text{-}\bar{i}$) of the Monoclinic system, and (following Groth) the *brachypinacoid* ($i\text{-}\bar{i}$) of the Orthorhombic. Similarly $(h0l)$ belongs to the ortho-

---

[*] The symbol is written here in this order to correspond with the ($h\ k\ l$) of Miller; on page 10, and subsequently. the reverse order $\frac{3}{2}c : \frac{3}{2}b : a$ was adopted for the sake of uniformity with Naumann's abbreviated symbols.

domes of the Monoclinic, and the *macrodomes* of the Orthorhombic system; also $(0kl)$ belongs to the clinodomes of the former, and the brachydomes of the latter. See also p. 457.

Spherical Projection.—If the centre of a crystal, that is, the point of intersection of the three axes, be taken as the centre of a sphere, and normals be drawn from it to the successive planes of the crystals, the points, where they meet the surface of the sphere, will be the poles of the respective planes. For example, in f. 756 the common centre of the crystal and sphere is at O, the normal to the plane b meets the surface of the sphere at B, of b' at B', of d and e at D and E respectively, and so on. These poles evidently determine the position of the plane in each case.

It is obvious that the pole of the plane b' $(0\bar{1}0)$ opposite b (010), will be at the opposite extremity of the diameter of the sphere, and so in general, (120) and $(1\bar{2}0)$, etc. It is seen also that all the poles, or normal points, of planes in the same *zone*, that is, planes whose intersection-lines are parallel, are in the same great circle, for instance the planes b (010), d (110), a (100), c $(1\bar{1}0)$, and so on.

It is customary* in the use of the sphere to regard it as projected upon a horizontal plane, usually that normal to the prismatic zone, so that, as in f. 759, the prismatic planes lie in the circumference of the circle, and the other planes within it. The eye being supposed to be situated at the opposite extremity of the diameter of the sphere normal to this plane, the great circles then appear either as arcs of circles, or as straight lines, *i.e.*, diameters.

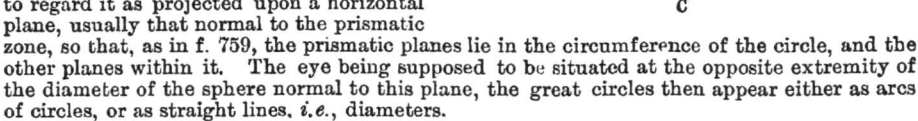

It will be further obvious from f. 756 that the arc BD, between the poles of b and d, measures an angle at the centre (BOD), which is the supplement of the actual interior angle bnd between the two planes. This fact, that the arc of a great circle intercepted between the poles of two planes always gives the supplement of the actual angle between the planes themselves, is most important, and does much to facilitate the ease of calculation. In consequence of this, it is customary with many crystallographers to give for the angle between two planes, not the interfacial angle, but that between their normals.

It is one of the great advantages of this method of projection that it may be employed to show not only the relative positions of the planes, but also those of the optic axes, and the axes of elasticity.

Relation between the indices of a plane and the angle made by it with the axes.—When the assumed axes are at right angles to each other they coincide with the normals to the pinacoid planes (001, 010, 100), and consequently meet the spherical surface at their poles. When the axial angles are not 90°, this is no longer true. In all cases, however, the following relation holds good between the cosines of the angles made by a plane with the axes:

$$\frac{op}{OH} = \cos PX \quad \frac{op}{OK} = \cos PY \quad \frac{op}{OL} = \cos PZ.$$

But from the equation (1) before given, by the introduction of the values of OH, OK, OL, we obtain:

$$\frac{a}{h} \cos PX = \frac{b}{k} \cos PY = \frac{c}{l} \cos PZ. \quad . \quad (2)$$

This equation is fundamental, and many of the relations given beyond are deduced from it. It will be seen that in the case of the orthometric systems the angles PX, PY, PZ are the supplement-angles between any plane (hkl) and the pinacoids (001), (010), (100).

Relations between planes in the same zone.—By the use of the equation (2), it may be shown

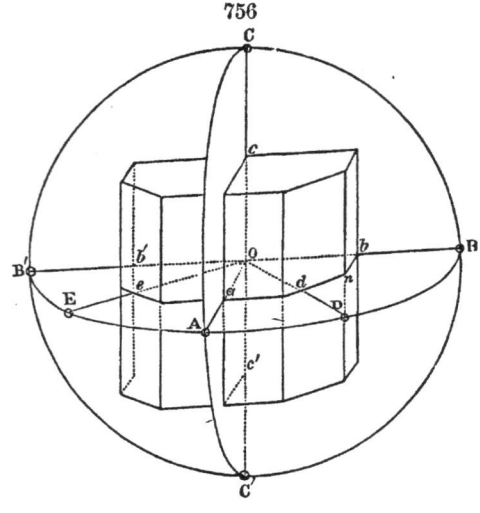

---

* On the construction of the spherical projection, see p. 58.

that if two planes (hkl) and (pqr) lie in the same zone, that the following equation must hold good:

$$ua \cos XQ + vb \cos YQ + wc \cos ZQ = 0.$$

where $\quad u = kr - lq, \quad v = lp - hr, \quad w = hq - kp.$

The letters u, v, w are called the symbol of the zone or great circle PR. Every plane R(xyz) of this zone must satisfy the equation:

$$ux + vy + wz = 0 \quad . \quad . \quad . \quad . \quad . \quad (3)$$

If now (uvw) be the symbol of one zone, and (efg) of another intersecting it, then the point of intersection will be the pole of a plane lying in both zones, whose indices (hkl) must satisfy two equations similar to (3). These indices are equal to:

$$h = gv - fw \qquad k = ew - gu \qquad l = fu - ev.$$

The application of this principle is extremely simple, and its importance cannot be overestimated. Some examples are added here, showing the method of use.

Examples of the methods of calculation by zones.—(1) For the zone of planes between (100) and (001), the zone indices are u = 0, v = −1, w = 0. They are obtained by multiplication in the manner indicated in the following scheme:

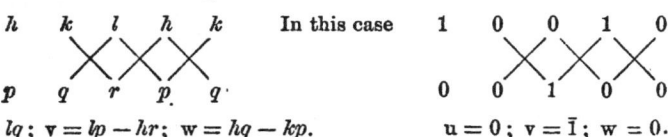

In general $\quad h \quad k \quad l \quad h \quad k \qquad$ In this case $\quad 1 \quad 0 \quad 0 \quad 1 \quad 0$
$\qquad\qquad\quad p \quad q \quad r \quad p \quad q \qquad\qquad\qquad\qquad 0 \quad 0 \quad 1 \quad 0 \quad 0$

$u = kr - lq; \; v = lp - hr; \; w = hq - kp. \qquad u = 0; \; v = \bar{1}; \; w = 0.$

Consequently every plane (hkl) in the zone named must answer the condition: $uh + vk + wl = 0$, that is, in this case $k = 0$. The general symbol is consequently $(h0l)$. Compare f. 759.

(2) For the zone (001), (010), in a similar manner:
$\qquad\qquad\qquad\qquad\qquad\qquad\qquad\qquad 0 \quad 0 \quad 1 \quad 0 \quad 0$
$\qquad\qquad\qquad\qquad\qquad\qquad\qquad\qquad 0 \quad 1 \quad 0 \quad 0 \quad 1$

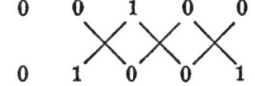

$u = \bar{1}, \; v = 0, \; w = 0,$ and the equation of condition becomes $h = 0$, and the general symbol is $(0kl)$. Compare f. 759.

(3) For the prismatic zone between (100) and (010), the general symbol will be found to be $(hk0)$. Compare f. 759.

758

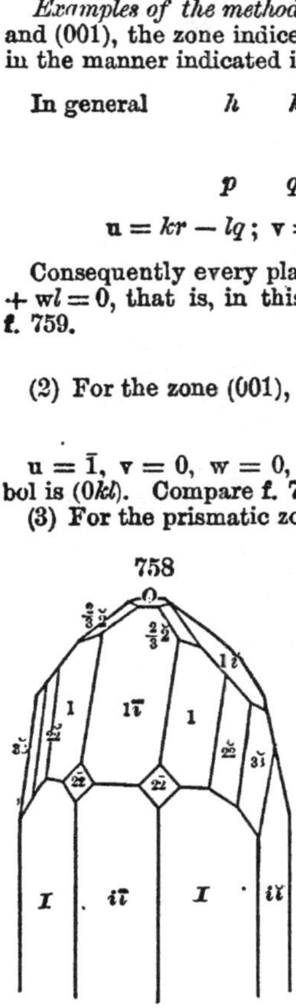

(4) For the pyramidal zone between the basal plane (001) and the unit prism (110), we have the scheme:
$\qquad\qquad\qquad\qquad\qquad\qquad 0 \quad 0 \quad 1 \quad 0 \quad 0$
$\qquad\qquad\qquad\qquad\qquad\qquad 1 \quad 1 \quad 0 \quad 1 \quad 1$

Hence $u = \bar{1}, \; v = 1, \; w = 0$, and the equation of condition becomes $h = k$, and hence the general symbol is hhl for the unit pyramids.

For a plane lying at once in two zones, for instance the plane lettered 2-2̇ in f. 758, lying in the zone $1, 2\text{-}\dot{2}, 1\text{-}\dot{\imath}$, and in the zone $i\text{-}\dot{\imath}, 3\text{-}\dot{3}, 2\text{-}\dot{3}, 1, 1\text{-}\dot{\imath}$. The indices, uvw, for the first zone 1-$\dot{\imath}$ (011), I (110), are, obtained as above, $u = \bar{1}, \; v = 1; \; w = \bar{1}$. Again, for the zone between $i\text{-}\dot{\imath}$ (010), 1-$\bar{\imath}$ (101), the zone indices, efg, are, $e = \bar{1}, \; f = 0, \; g = 1$. The indices (hkl), for the plane (2-2̇) lying in both these zones, and hence answering to two equations of condition, are obtained by multiplication in a scheme exactly like that already given, viz.:

In general $\quad u \quad v \quad w \quad u \quad v \qquad$ In this case $\quad \bar{1} \quad 1 \quad \bar{1} \quad \bar{1} \quad 1$
$\qquad\qquad\quad e \quad f \quad g \quad e \quad f \qquad\qquad\qquad\qquad \bar{1} \quad 0 \quad 1 \quad \bar{1} \quad 0$

$h = gv - fw; \; k = ew - gu; \; l = fu - ev. \qquad h = 1; \; k = 2; \; l = 1.$

The plane has consequently the symbol (211).

MILLER'S SYSTEM OF CRYSTALLOGRAPHY. 445

For the zone of planes, lettered on the figure (f. 758) i-$\bar{\imath}$, 3-$\bar{3}$, 2-$\bar{2}$, etc., the indices, as already shown, are $e = \bar{1}$, $f = 0$, $g = 1$, and consequently the equation of condition reduces to $h = l$, and the general symbol is hkh. This zone is shown on the spherical projection, f. 759, and includes the planes 010 (i-$\bar{\imath}$), 131 (3-$\bar{3}$), 121 (2-$\bar{2}$), 111 (1), 101 (1-$\bar{\imath}$), and so on.

A second example of the above method is afforded by the plane lettered 2-$\bar{2}$ in f. 758. It lies in the zone i-$\bar{\imath}$ (100) to 1-$\bar{\imath}$ (011), whose indices, uvw, obtained as before, are, $u = 0$, $v = \bar{1}$, $w = 1$. It is also in the zone between I(110) and 1-$\bar{\imath}$ (101), whose indices, efg, are, $e = 1$, $f = \bar{1}$, $g = \bar{1}$. Its own symbol (hkl) is deduced as above:

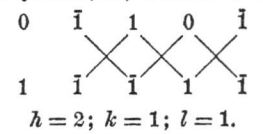

$$\begin{array}{ccccc} 0 & \bar{1} & 1 & 0 & \bar{1} \\ & \times & & \times & \\ 1 & \bar{1} & \bar{1} & 1 & \bar{1} \end{array}$$

$h = 2$; $k = 1$; $l = 1$.

The symbol is consequently (211). The position of this plane is shown on the spherical projection, f. 759, as also that of the zone first mentioned above, whose indices were $u = 0$, $v = \bar{1}$, $w = 1$, and for which the equation (3) consequently reduces to $k = l$; the general symbol is then (hkk), the planes 100 (i-$\bar{\imath}$), 211 (2-$\bar{2}$), 111 (1), 0$\bar{1}$1 (1-$\bar{\imath}$), etc., belong in this zone.

The example employed here serves to show the extensive application of this principle of zones. Supposing that in this crystal, f. 758, I(110), and 1-$\bar{\imath}$ (011) have been assumed as fundamental planes in their respective zones, the symbols of all the others may be obtained in this way, without the necessity of a single measurement; the reflecting goniometer would indicate the presence of the few necessary zones not shown by the parallel intersections.

Methods of Calculation.—In consequence of the wide application of this method of determining the symbols of a plane by the zones in which it lies, actual trigonometrical calculations are not very frequently required. The methods employed are always those of *spherical* trigonometry, and in most cases no formulas are needed, the problems arising requiring nothing but the solution of the triangles, mostly right-angled, seen on the spherical projection. It is to be remembered that an arc of a great circle, between two poles, shown in the projection, is always the supplement of the actual interfacial angle between the planes themselves.

Some of the more commonly used formulas for the solution of spherical triangles, which have been already given on p. 62, are, for the sake of convenience, repeated here.

In right-angled spherical triangles $C = 90°$, $h =$ the hypothenuse.

$$\text{Sin A} = \frac{\sin a}{\sin h} \qquad \sin B = \frac{\sin b}{\sin h}$$

$$\text{Cos A} = \frac{\tan b}{\tan h} \qquad \cos B = \frac{\tan a}{\tan h}$$

$$\text{Tan A} = \frac{\tan a}{\sin b} \qquad \tan B = \frac{\tan b}{\sin a}$$

$$\text{Sin A} = \frac{\cos B}{\cos b} \qquad \sin B = \frac{\cos A}{\cos a}$$

$$\cos h = \cos a \cos b$$
$$\cos h = \cot A \cot B$$

In oblique-angled spherical triangles:

(1) Sin A : sin B = sin a : sin b;
(2) Cos a = cos b cos c + sin b sin c cos A;
(3) Cot b sin c = cos c cos A + sin A cot B;
(4) Cos A = — cos B cos C + sin B sin C cos a.

In calculation it is often more convenient to use, instead of the latter formulas, those especially arranged for logarithms, which will be found in any of the many books devoted to mathematical formulas.

In addition to the mere solution of triangles on the spherical projection, it is also necessary to connect by equations the actually measured angles with the lengths and inclinations of axes of the crystals themselves. These equations are given in connection with the different systems.

The following relation between the planes in the same zone is also of very wide application:

Let P, Q, S, R be the poles of four planes in a zone (f. 760), having the following indices, viz.: $P = (hkl)$, $Q = (pqr)$, $R = (uvw)$, $S = (xyz)$. The folowing relation may be deduced between them, on the supposition that $PQ < PR$.

$$\frac{\cot PS - \cot PR}{\cot PQ - \cot PR} = \frac{(P.Q)}{(Q.R)} \cdot \frac{(S.R)}{(P.S)}. \quad \quad (4)$$

Here,

$$\frac{(P.Q)}{(Q.R)} = \frac{kr - lq}{qw - rv} = \frac{lp - hr}{ru - pw} = \frac{hq - kp}{pv - qu},$$

$$\frac{(S.R)}{(P.S)} = \frac{wy - zv}{kz - ly} = \frac{zu - xw}{lx - hz} = \frac{xv - yu}{hy - kx}. \quad \quad (5)$$

By means of the above equation it is possible to deduce the indices or angle of a fourth plane, when those of the three others are given. In the application of this principle it is essential that the planes should be taken in the proper order, as shown above; to accomplish this it is often necessary to use the indices and corresponding angles, not of (hkl), but its opposite plane $(\bar{h}\bar{k}\bar{l})$, etc.

In the orthometric systems this relation admits of being much simplified.

If one of the above four planes coincides with a pinacoid plane (100), (010), or (001), and another with a plane in a zone with a second pinacoid 90° from the first, then the following relations hold good for two planes $P(hkl)$, and $Q(pqr)$ in this zone:

$$\frac{h}{p} \cdot \frac{\tan PA}{\tan QA} = \frac{k}{q} = \frac{l}{r},$$

$$\frac{h}{p} = \frac{k}{q} \cdot \frac{\tan PB}{\tan QB} = \frac{l}{r},$$

$$\frac{h}{p} = \frac{k}{q} = \frac{l}{r} \cdot \frac{\tan PC}{\tan QC}.$$

As a further simplification of the above equation for the case of a prismatic plane $(hk0)$, or a dome $(h0l)$ or $(0kl)$, between two pinacoid planes 90° from another, we have:

$$\frac{h}{k} = \frac{\tan (100)(110)}{\tan (100)(hk0)}; \quad \frac{h}{l} = \frac{\tan (001)(h0l)}{\tan (001)(101)}; \quad \frac{k}{l} = \frac{\tan (001)(0kl)}{\tan (001)(011)}.$$

These equations are the ones ordinarily employed to determine the symbol of any prismatic plane or dome. It will be seen at once that all the above relations for rectangular zones are essentially identical with those given on p. 59, though here expressed in a clearer and more concise form.

SYSTEMS OF CRYSTALLIZATION.

All crystals are divided into six classes, according to the degree of symmetry which characterizes them. This symmetry, as well as the relations of the different planes of a crystal, is shown in the lengths and position of the axes which are taken for each. With reference to their axial relations crystals are divided into the following six systems:

I. *Isometric System.*—Three equal axes (a, a, a) at right angles to one another.

II. *Tetragonal System.*—Two equal lateral axes (a, a), and a third vertical axis ($\dot{c}$) of un equal length; all at right angles.

MILLER'S SYSTEM OF CRYSTALLOGRAPHY.   447

III. *Hexagonal System.*—Three equal lateral axes (a, a, a) crossing at angles of 60°, and a fourth vertical axis ($\dot{c}$) of unequal length, perpendicular to the plane of the others.
IV. *Orthorhombic System.*—Three unequal axes ($\dot{c}$, $\bar{b}$, $\check{a}$) at right angles to each other.
V. *Monoclinic System*—Three unequal axes ($\dot{c}$, b, $\check{a}$); the angle between $\dot{c}$ and b, and between b and $\check{a}$ = 90°, but the angle between $\dot{c}$ and $\check{a}$ greater and less than 90°.
VI. *Triclinic System.*—Three unequal axes ($\dot{c}$, $\bar{b}$, $\check{a}$); the axial angles all oblique.

I. ISOMETRIC SYSTEM.

The symbol [hkl] embraces all the forms possible under each system in the most general case. Since in the Isometric System all the axes are of equal value, it obviously follows from the symmetry of the system that each one of the indices may be exchanged for each of the others, so that the total number of planes possible will be given by all the arrangements of the indices ±h, ±k, ±l, or as follows:

hkl	hlk	khl	klh	lhk	lkh
$\bar{h}kl$	$\bar{h}lk$	$\bar{k}hl$	$\bar{k}lh$	$\bar{l}hk$	$\bar{l}kh$
$h\bar{k}l$	$h\bar{l}k$	$k\bar{h}l$	$k\bar{l}h$	$l\bar{h}k$	$l\bar{k}h$
$\bar{h}\bar{k}l$	$\bar{h}\bar{l}k$	$\bar{k}\bar{h}l$	$\bar{k}\bar{l}h$	$\bar{l}\bar{h}k$	$\bar{l}\bar{k}h$
$hk\bar{l}$	$hl\bar{k}$	$kh\bar{l}$	$kl\bar{h}$	$lh\bar{k}$	$lk\bar{h}$
$\bar{h}k\bar{l}$	$\bar{h}l\bar{k}$	$\bar{k}h\bar{l}$	$\bar{k}l\bar{h}$	$\bar{l}h\bar{k}$	$\bar{l}k\bar{h}$
$h\bar{k}\bar{l}$	$h\bar{l}\bar{k}$	$k\bar{h}\bar{l}$	$k\bar{l}\bar{h}$	$l\bar{h}\bar{k}$	$l\bar{k}\bar{h}$
$\bar{h}\bar{k}\bar{l}$	$\bar{h}\bar{l}\bar{k}$	$\bar{k}\bar{h}\bar{l}$	$\bar{k}\bar{l}\bar{h}$	$\bar{l}\bar{h}\bar{k}$	$\bar{l}\bar{k}\bar{h}$

A. *Holohedral Forms.*

There are seven cases possible among the holohedral forms of this system, according to the values of h, k, l. These are shown in the list below, to which are added the symbols, after Naumann, given on p. 14, though, as already explained, written in the inverse order. In the most general case [hkl]* the form includes *forty eight* similar planes, and in the most special case [100], there are included *six* similar planes.

MILLER.		NAUMANN.	
1. [hkl] ; $h > k > l$.		$a : na : ma$	[m-n].
2. [hkk] ; $h > k$.		$a : ma : ma$	[m-m].
3. [hhl] ; $h > k$.		$a : a : ma$	[m].
4. [111] ; $h = k = l = 1$.		$a : a : a$	[1].
5. [hk0] ; $l = 0$.		$a : na : \infty a$	[i-n].
6. [110] ; $h = k = 1$; $l = 0$.		$a : a : \infty a$	[i].
7. [100] ; $h = 1$, $k = l = 0$.		$a : \infty a : \infty a$	[H].

The seven distinct forms corresponding to these symbols are as follows, taken in the same order as on pp. 14-20, where the forms are described:
Cube (f. 761).—Symbol [100], including the six planes (100), (010), ($\bar{1}$00), (0$\bar{1}$0), (001), (00$\bar{1}$). See also the spherical projection (f. 766).

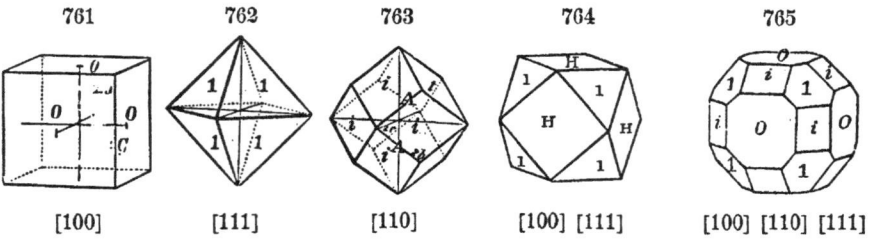

761 762 763 764 765

[100] [111] [110] [100] [111] [100] [110] [111]

Octahedron (f. 762).—Symbol [111], including the eight planes taken in order shown in f. 762, (111), ($\bar{1}$11), ($\bar{1}\bar{1}$1), (1$\bar{1}$1), (11$\bar{1}$), ($\bar{1}$1$\bar{1}$), (1$\bar{1}\bar{1}$), ($\bar{1}\bar{1}\bar{1}$).

---

* In general the indices of any individual plane are written (hkl), whereas the general symbol [hkl] indicates *all* the planes belonging to the form, varying in number in the different systems; thus, in this system, [100] is the general symbol for the six similar planes of the cube.

448   APPENDIX.

Dodecahedron (f. 763).—Symbol [110], including the twelve planes, (110), ($\bar{1}$10), ($1\bar{1}$0), ($\bar{1}\bar{1}$0), (101), (011), ($\bar{1}$01), (0$\bar{1}$1), (10$\bar{1}$), (01$\bar{1}$), ($\bar{1}$0$\bar{1}$), (0$\bar{1}\bar{1}$).
The relations between these three forms are given in full on pp. 15, 16, and need not be repeated. It is to be noticed that the distance between two contiguous poles of [100] and [110] is 45° (see f. 766); between those of [100] and [111] it is 54° 44′, and between (110) and (111) it is 35° 16′. Moreover, the angle between (111) and ($\bar{1}$11) is 70° 32′, and between (111) and ($\bar{1}\bar{1}$1), 109° 28′.

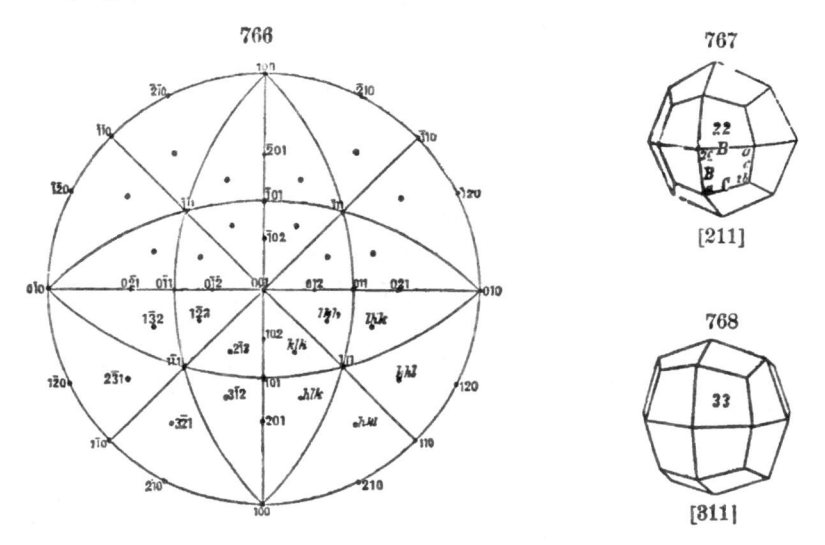

766

767

[211]

768

[311]

Tetragonal trisoctahedron (f. 767, 768).—Symbol [hkk], with $h > k$, comprising twenty-four similar planes.
Trigonal trisoctahedron (f. 769).—Symbol [hhk], with $h > k$, also embracing twenty-four like planes.

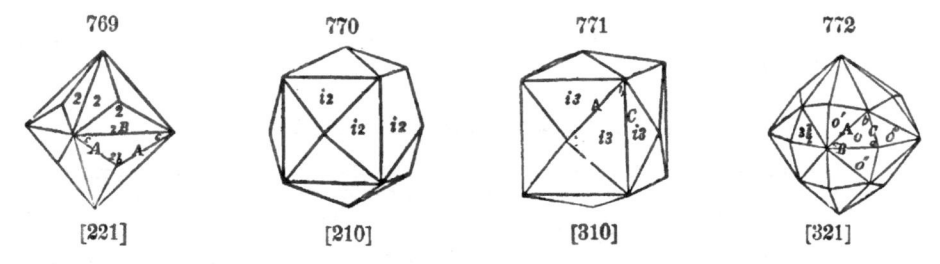

769   770   771   772

[221]   [210]   [310]   [321]

Tetrahexahedron (f. 770, 771).—Symbol [$hk0$] including twenty-four like planes. As seen on the spherical projection (f. 766), the planes of the form [$hk0$] lie in a zone with the dodecahedral planes, between two pinacoid planes.
Hexoctahedron (f. 772), [hkl].—This is the most general form in the system, including the forty-eight planes enumerated on p. 447. Their position ($h = 3, k = 2, l = 1$) is shown on the spherical projection (f. 766).

B. *Hemihedral Forms.*

There are two kinds of hemihedral forms observed, as shown on p. 20: (1) the *hemiholohedral*, where half the quadrants have the whole number of planes; and (2) the *holohemihedral* where all the quadrants have half the full number of planes. The first kind produces *inclined* hemihedrons, indicated by the symbol κ[hkl], and the second kind produces *parallel* hemihedrons, indicated by the symbol π[hkl]. The resulting forms in the several cases are as follows ·

MILLER'S SYSTEM OF CRYSTALLOGRAPHY. 449

INCLINED HEMIHEDRISM.—*Tetrahedron* (±1). Symbol κ[111]. The plus tetrahedron (f. 773) includes the four planes (111), (1̄1̄1), (1̄11̄), (11̄1̄). The minus tetrahedron (f. 774) includes the planes (1̄11), (11̄1), (111̄), (1̄1̄1̄).

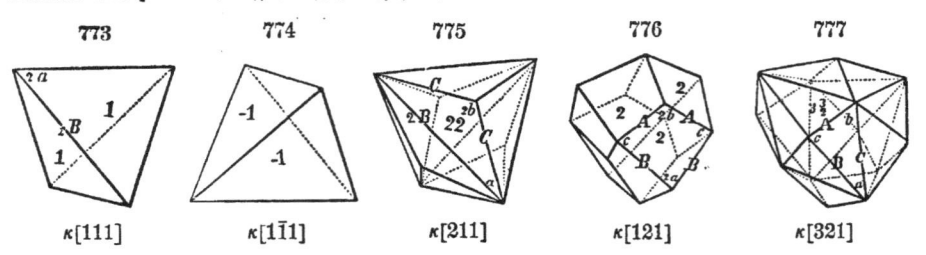

773   774   775   776   777

κ[111]   κ[1̄1̄1]   κ[211]   κ[121]   κ[321]

Hemi-trisoctahedrons.—The symbol κ[*hkk*] denotes the solid shown in f. 775, and κ[*hhk*] the solid shown in f. 776. They are the hemihedral forms of the tetragonal and trigonal trisoctahedrons respectively.

Hemi-hexoctahedron.—The same kind of hemihedrism applied to the hexoctahedron produces the form shown in f. 777, having the general symbol κ[*hkl*].

Inclined hemihedrism as applied to the three other solids of this system produces forms in no way different, in outward appearance, from the holohedral forms.

PARALLEL HEMIHEDRISM produces distinct, independent, forms only in the case of the tetrahexahedron and the hexoctahedron. The symbol of the former is π[*hk*0], and of the latter, π[*hkl*]; they are shown in f. 778–782.

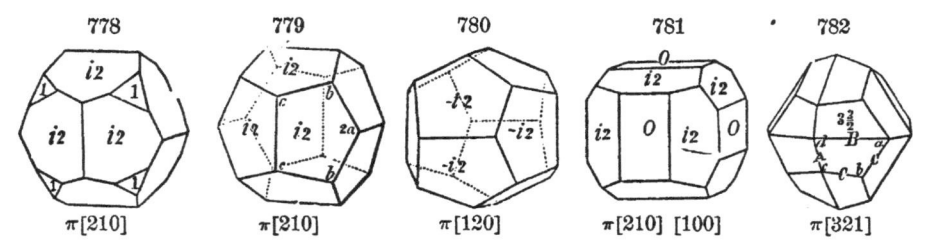

778   779   780   781   782

π[210]   π[210]   π[120]   π[210] [100]   π[321]

Tetartohedral forms of several kinds are possible in this system, but they are of small practical interest.

Mathematical Relations of the Isometric System.

(1) The distance of the pole of any plane P(*hkl*) from the cubic (or pinacoid) planes is given by the following equations. These are derived from equation (2), p. 443. Here PX(=PA) is the distance between (*hkl*) and (100); PY(=PB) is the distance between (*hkl*) and (010); and PZ(=PC) that between (*hkl*) and (001).

The following equations admit of much simplification in special cases, for (*hk*0), (*hhk*), etc.

$$\cos^2 \text{PA} = \frac{h^2}{h^2 + k^2 + l^2}. \quad \cos^2 \text{PB} = \frac{k^2}{h^2 + k^2 + l^2}. \quad \cos^2 \text{PC} = \frac{l^2}{h^2 + k^2 + l^2}.$$

(2) The distance between the poles of any two planes (*hkl*) and (*pqr*) is given by the following equation, which in special cases may also be more or less simplified:

$$\cos \text{PQ} = \frac{hp + kq + lr}{\sqrt{(h^2 + k^2 + l^2)(p^2 + q^2 + r^2)}}.$$

(3) Calculation of the values of *h, k, l*, for the several forms.—(*a*) *Tetragonal trisoctahedron* (f. 767). B and C are the supplement angles of the edges as lettered in the figure.

$$\cos \text{B} = \frac{h^2}{h^2 + 2k^2} \qquad \cos \text{C} = \frac{2hk + k^2}{h^2 + 2k^2}.$$

29

450 APPENDIX.

For the hemihedral form (f. 775), $\cos B = \dfrac{h^2 - 2k^2}{h^2 + 2k^2}$.

(b) *Trigonal trisoctahedron.*—The angles A and C are, as before, the supplements of the interfacial angles of the edges lettered as in f. 769.

$$\cos A = \frac{h^2 + 2hk}{2h^2 + k^2}, \qquad \cos B = \frac{2h^2 - k^2}{2h^2 + k^2}.$$

For the hemihedral form (f. 776), $\cos B = \dfrac{h^2 - 2hk}{2h^2 + k^2}$.

Tetrahexahedron (f. 770),

$$\cos A = \frac{h^2}{h^2 + k^2}; \quad \cos C = \frac{2hk}{h^2 + k^2}.$$

For the hemihedral form (f. 778), $\cos A' = \dfrac{h^2 - k^2}{h^2 + k^2} \cdot \cos C' = \dfrac{hk}{h^2 + k^2}$.

Hexoctahedron (f. 772).

$$\cos A = \frac{h^2 + 2kl}{h^2 + k^2 + l^2}; \quad \cos B = \frac{h^2 + k^2 - l^2}{h^2 + k^2 + l^2}; \quad \cos C = \frac{2hk + l^2}{h^2 + k^2 + l^2}.$$

For the hemihedral form $\kappa[hkl]$ (f. 777), $\cos B' = \dfrac{h^2 - 2kl}{h^2 + k^2 + l^2}$.

For $\pi[hkl]$, $\cos A' = \dfrac{h^2 - k^2 + l^2}{h^2 + k^2 + l^2}; \quad \cos C' = \dfrac{kl + lh + hk}{h^2 + k^2 + l^2}$.

For planes lying in the same zone the methods of calculation given on p. 444 and p. 446 are made use of. In many cases, however, the simplest method of solution of a given problem is by means of the spherical triangles on the projection (f. 766).

II. TETRAGONAL SYSTEM.

In the Tetragonal System, since the vertical axis $\dot{c}$ has a different length from the two equal lateral axes, the index l, referring to it, is never exchangeable for the other indices, h and k. The general form $[hkl]$ consequently embraces all the planes which have as their symbols the different arrangements of $\pm h$, $\pm k$, $\pm l$, in which l always holds the last place. We thus obtain:

hkl	$h\bar{k}l$	$\bar{h}\bar{k}l$	$\bar{h}kl$	khl	$\bar{k}hl$	$\bar{k}\bar{h}l$	$k\bar{h}l$
$hk\bar{l}$	$h\bar{k}\bar{l}$	$\bar{h}\bar{k}\bar{l}$	$\bar{h}k\bar{l}$	$kh\bar{l}$	$\bar{k}h\bar{l}$	$\bar{k}\bar{h}\bar{l}$	$k\bar{h}\bar{l}$

A. *Holohedral Forms.*

According to the values of h, k, and l in this general form ($h = 0$, $k = h$, etc.), different cases may arise. By this means we obtain a list of all the possible distinct holohedral forms in this system. They are analogous to those of the Isometric System.

MILLER.	NAUMANN.	
1. $[hkl]$; $h > k$.	$a : na : mc$	$[m\text{-}n]$.
2. $[hhl]$; $h = k$.	$a : a : mc$	$[m]$.
3. $[h0l]$; h or $k = 0$.	$a : \infty a : mc$	$[m\text{-}i]$.
4. $[hk0]$; $h > k$, $l = 0$.	$a : na : \infty c$	$[i\text{-}n]$.
5. $[110]$; $h = k = 1$, $l = 0$.	$a : a : \infty c$	$[I]$.
6. $[100]$; $k = 0$, $l = 0$.	$a : \infty a : \infty c$	$[i\text{-}i]$.
7. $[001]$; $h = k = 0$.	$\infty a : \infty a : c$	$[O]$.

MILLER'S SYSTEM OF CRYSTALLOGRAPHY.

The forms answering to these general symbols (compare f. 790) are as follows:

Basal planes.—Symbol [001], including the planes (001) and (00$\bar{1}$).

Prisms.—(*a*) *Diametral* prism, or that of the *second series* (f. 783). Symbol [100], including the four planes (100), (010), ($\bar{1}$00), (0$\bar{1}$0).

(*b*) *Unit* prism, or prism of the *first series* (f. 784).—Symbol [110], embracing the four planes (110), (1$\bar{1}$0), ($\bar{1}\bar{1}$0), ($\bar{1}$10). The relation of these two prisms is shown on p. 26.

(*c*) *Octagonal* prism (f. 785).—Symbol [*hk*0], including the eight planes (*hk*0), (*kh*0), ($\bar{k}h$0), ($\bar{h}k$0), ($\bar{h}\bar{k}$0), ($\bar{k}\bar{h}$0), ($k\bar{h}$0), ($h\bar{k}$0).

Octahedrons or *Pyramids.*—There are two series of octahedral planes, corresponding to the two square prisms. (*a*) Octahedrons of the *second*, or *diametral* series. Symbol [*h*0*l*], including eight similar planes. The form [101] is shown in f. 786.

(*b*) Octahedrons of the *first*, or *unit* series.—Symbol [*hkl*], embracing eight similar planes. The form [111] is shown in f. 787.

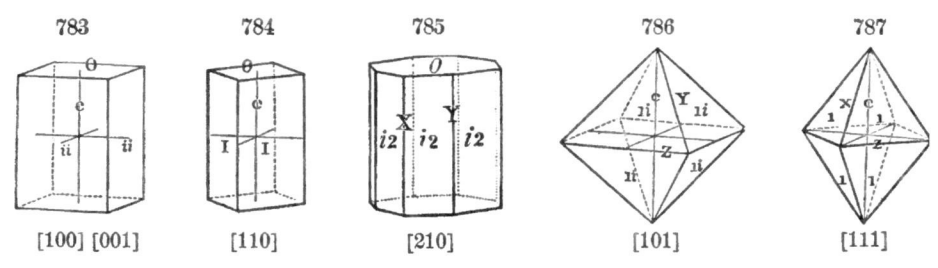

783   784   785   786   787

[100] [001]   [110]   [210]   [101]   [111]

Octagonal Pyramids.—The general symbol [*hkl*] embraces, as already shown, sixteen like planes, which together form the octagonal pyramid shown in f. 788.

788   789   790

[*hkl*]   Meionite.

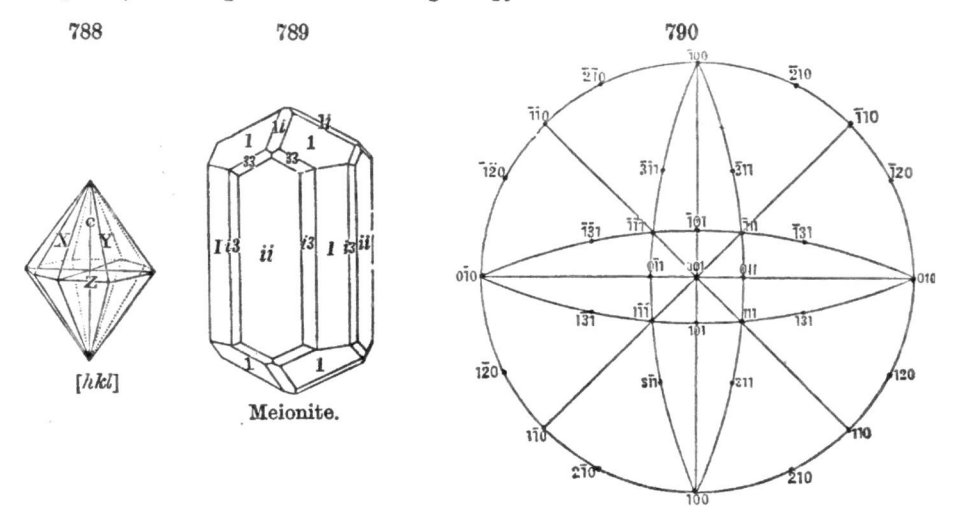

The relations of the various tetragonal forms will be understood by reference to f. 790, showing the projection for the crystal represented in f. 789.

B. *Hemihedral Forms.*

791

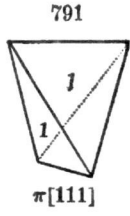

Among the hemihedral forms there are to be distinguished three classes, as shown on p. 28 *et seq.* 1. *Sphenoidal* hemihedrons, corresponding to the *inclined* hemihedrons of the isometric system. They are indicated by the symbol π[*hkl*]. The sphenoid π[111] is shown in f. 791.

2. *Pyramidal* hemihedrons, that is, those which are hemiholohedral, and vertically direct. These are indicated by the symbol κ[*hkl*].

3. *Trapezoidal* hemihedrons, hemiholohedral like those just mentioned, but vertically alternate. They have the symbol κ''[*hkl*].

π[111]

Mathematical Relations of the Tetragonal System.

(1) The distances of the pole of any plane P(hkl) from the pinacoid planes 100 ($=$ PA), 010 $=$ PB), 001 ($=$ PC) are given by the following equations:

$$\cos^2 \text{PA} = \frac{h^2c^2}{h^2c^2 + k^2c^2 + l^2a^2}; \quad \cos^2 \text{PB} = \frac{k^2c^2}{h^2c^2 + k^2c^2 + l^2a^2}; \quad \cos^2 \text{PC} = \frac{l^2a^2}{h^2c^2 + k^2c^2 + l^2a^2}.$$

These may also be expressed in the form:

$$\tan^2 \text{PA} = \frac{k^2c^2 + l^2a^2}{h^2c^2}; \quad \tan^2 \text{PB} = \frac{h^2c^2 + l^2a^2}{k^2c^2}; \quad \tan^2 \text{PC} = \frac{h^2c^2 + k^2c^2}{l^2a^2}.$$

(2) For the distance between the poles of any two planes (hkl), (pqr), we have in general:

$$\cos \text{PQ} = \frac{hpc^2 + kqc^2 + lra^2}{\sqrt{[(h^2+k^2)c^2 + l^2a^2][(p^2+q^2)c^2 + r^2a^2]}}.$$

The above equations take a simpler form for special cases often occurring.

(3) *Planes in the same zone.*—For the general case of planes (hkl) and (pqr) the relation given in equation 4 (p. 446) is made use of. In the special cases, practically of the most importance, where the planes lie in a zone with a pinacoid plane, the simplified formulas are employed.

For the octagonal prism this relation becomes:

$$\tan (100) (hk0) = \cot (010) (hk0) = \frac{k}{h}.$$

Determination of the axis $\dot{c}$.—This follows from equation (1), p. 446, which, for this case, becomes:

$$\frac{1}{h} \cos \text{PA} = \frac{\dot{c}}{l} \cos \text{PC}, \ (a = 1).$$

For an octahedron ($h0l$) in the diametral series, we have:

$$\tan (h0l) (001) = \frac{\dot{c}h}{l}.$$

For the unit octahedron (111), we have:

$$\tan (111) (001) . \cos 45° = \dot{c}.$$

III. Hexagonal System.

The Hexagonal System and its hemihedral, or rhombohedral, division are both included by Miller in his Rhombohedral System (see p. 462). All hexagonal and rhombohedral forms are referred by him to three equal axes, oblique to one another, and normal to the faces of the unit rhombohedron. This method has the great disadvantage of failing to exhibit the hexagonal symmetry existing in the holohedral forms, since in this way the similar planes of a hexagonal pyramid receive two different sets of symbols, having no apparent connection with each other. It, moreover, hides the relation between this system and the tetragonal system, which, optically, are identical, since they possess alike one axis of optical symmetry.

The latter difficulty was avoided by Schrauf, who introduced the Orthohexagonal System. In this the optical axis was made the crystallographical vertical axis, and otherwise two lateral axes, at right angles to each other, were assumed, a and $a \sqrt{3}$. This method, however, does not overcome the other objection named above.

In the method of Weiss and Naumann a vertical axis, coinciding with the optical axis, was adopted, and three lateral axes in a plane at right angles to it, they intersecting at angles of 60°, corresponding to the planes of symmetry in the holohedral forms (see p. 462). In this way only can the symmetry of the hexagonal forms be clearly brought out, and at the same time the relation between the hexagonal and tetragonal systems exhibited. Recently Groth (Tsch. Min. Mitth., 1874, 223, and Phys. Kryst., 1876, p. 252) has shown that the complete symbols of Weiss and Naumann could be translated into a reciprocal, integral form after the manner of Miller. The symbols then obtained, as was also shown, admit of a like convenient use in calculation. Essentially the same method was proposed in 1866 by Bravais, and his suggestion is followed here; the more important equations, expressing the relations between the poles of the planes, their indices, and the axes of the crystal are also added. They are given somewhat in detail, since they are not included in any of the works on Miller's System before referred to.

All hexagonal forms are referred to a vertical axis, c, and three equal lateral axes in a plane at right angles to it, intersecting at angles of 60° and 120° (f. 792). The general symbol for a plane in this system is $(hkli)$, where it is always true that the algebraic sum of h, k, l is zero, that is, $h + k + l = 0$. The indices here are the reciprocals of those of Naumann, except that the index l has the opposite sign, and the order of two of the indices is inverted. According to him the general symbol of any plane is $m\text{-}n$ $(= m\text{P}n)$, or, in full, $\frac{n}{n-1} a : a : na : mc$. Thus the plane $3\text{-}\frac{3}{2}$ $(3\text{P}\frac{3}{2})$ has the full symbol, $3a : a : \frac{3}{2}a : 3c$, or to correspond with the other symbols it must be written, $3a : \frac{3}{2}a : a : 3c$. The reciprocals of the latter indices are $\frac{1}{3} : \frac{2}{3} : 1 : \frac{1}{3}$, or, reduced to integers (and changing the sign of l) $(1\bar{2}31)$, which is the symbol according to the plan here followed. Similarly the plane $(22\bar{4}3)$ gives, on taking the reciprocals, $\frac{1}{2}a : \frac{1}{2}a : \frac{1}{4}a : \frac{1}{3}c$, which is equivalent to $2a : 2a : a : \frac{1}{3}c$, or in Naumann's abbreviated form $\frac{3}{3}\text{-}2$ $(= \frac{1}{3}\text{P}2)$.

It is the great advantage of this method that it makes it possible to change the almost universally adopted symbols of *Weiss* and *Naumann* into a form which allow of all the readiness of calculation and the application to the spherical projection which are the characteristics of Miller's System.

In calculations, both by zone equations and other methods, only two of the indices $h, k,$ or l of the form $(hkli)$ need be employed, with the remaining index i (referring to the vertical axis). This is obviously true, since the three indices named are connected by the equation $h + k + l = 0$. Disregarding, then, in calculation the third index l, as shown beyond, the planes are referred to two equal lateral axes, intersecting at an angle of 120°, and a third vertical axis c.

The symbol $[hkli]$ in its more general form embraces twenty-four planes, as is evident from an inspection of the spherical projection, f. 793. Here h, k, l are of equal value and mutually exchangeable, with the condition, however, that their algebraic sum shall always equal zero. Of the twenty-four planes of the dihexagonal pyramid, the following are those of the upper quadrants mentioned in order from left to right around the circle (f. 793). Those below have the same symbols, except that the index i in each case is minus:

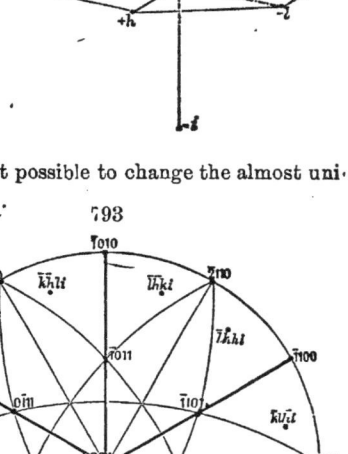

$(hk\bar{l}i)$	$(h\bar{l}ki)$	$(k\bar{l}hi)$	$(\bar{l}khi)$	$(\bar{l}hki)$	$(kh\bar{l}i)$
$(hk\bar{l}i)$	$(h\bar{l}ki)$	$(k\bar{l}hi)$	$(\bar{l}khi)$	$(\bar{l}hki)$	$(kh\bar{l}i)$

In this general form $[hk\bar{l}i]$ the following special cases are possible, each one giving rise to an independent form or group of forms, as seen below:

APPENDIX.

	BRAVAIS-MILLER.		NAUMANN.[*]	
1	$[hkli]$		$\dfrac{n}{n-1} : na : a : mc$	$[m\text{-}n]$
2	$\begin{cases} [hh\,2\bar{h}\,2i] \\ [11\bar{2}2] \end{cases}$;	$\begin{array}{l} k = h \therefore l = 2h \\ h = k = 1 \therefore l = 2, i = 2 \end{array}$	$\begin{cases} 2a : 2a : a : mc \\ 2a : 2a : a : c \end{cases}$	$\begin{array}{l}[m\text{-}2]\\ [1\text{-}2]\end{array}$
3.	$\begin{cases} [0h\bar{h}i] \\ [01\bar{1}1] \end{cases}$;	$\begin{array}{l} k = 0 \therefore l = h \\ h = 1, k = 0 \therefore l = 1 \end{array}$	$\begin{cases} \infty a : a : a : mc \\ \infty a : a : a : c \end{cases}$	$\begin{array}{l}[m]\\ [1]\end{array}$
4.	$[hk\bar{l}0]$;	$i = 0$	$\dfrac{n}{n-1} a : na : a : \infty c$	$[i\text{-}n]$
5.	$[11\bar{2}0]$;	$i = 0, h = k = 1 \therefore l = 2$	$2a : 2a \quad a : \infty c$	$[i\text{-}2]$
6.	$[01\bar{1}0]$;	$i = 0, k = 0, h = 1 \therefore l = 1$	$\infty a : a : a : \infty c$	$[I]$
7	$[0001]$;	$h = k = i = 0.$	$\infty a : \infty a : \infty a : c$	$[O]$

A. *Holohedral Forms.*

The forms to which these symbols belong have been already mentioned on pp. 32-34. They may be briefly recapitulated here. They are taken in the reverse order from that given in the table.

Basal planes.—Symbol (0001) and (000$\bar{1}$).

Prisms.—(a) The *unit* prism (I). General symbol $[01\bar{1}0]$, including (see f. 793, 794) the six planes with the following symbols: $(01\bar{1}0)$, $(1\bar{1}00)$, $(10\bar{1}0)$, $(0\bar{1}10)$, $(\bar{1}100)$, $(10\bar{1}0)$.

(b) The *diagonal* prism (i-2). General symbol $[11\bar{2}0]$, including (f. 793, 795) the following six planes: $(11\bar{2}0)$, $(\bar{1}210)$, $(\bar{2}110)$, $(\bar{1}\bar{1}20)$, $(1\bar{2}10)$, $(2\bar{1}\bar{1}0)$.

(c) The *dihexagonal* prism (i-n). General symbol $[hk\bar{l}0]$, embracing the following twelve planes mentioned in order:

$(hk\bar{l}0)$, $(\bar{h}l\bar{k}0)$, $(\bar{k}lh0)$, $(\bar{l}kh0)$, $(\bar{l}hk0)$, $(\bar{k}h\bar{l}0)$, $(\bar{h}\bar{k}l0)$, $(l\bar{l}k0)$, $(k\bar{l}\bar{h}0)$, $(l\bar{k}\bar{h}0)$, $(l\bar{h}\bar{k}0)$, $(kh\bar{l}0)$.

Hexagonal pyramids, or Quartzoids.—(a) The pyramids of the *first* or *unit series*. General symbol $[0h\bar{h}i]$ embracing twelve similar planes. All the pyramids of this series lie in a zone between the unit prism $[01\bar{1}0]$ and the base $[0001]$. A special case of this is when $h = k = i = 1$. The planes of this form (f. 796) are shown on the projection, f. 793.

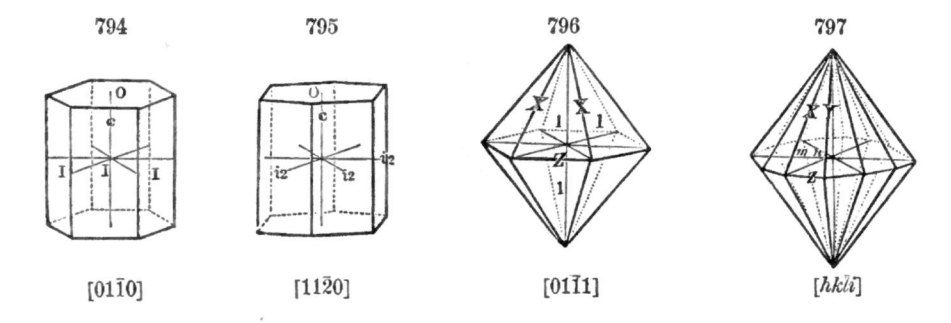

794   795   796   797

$[01\bar{1}0]$ $[11\bar{2}0]$ $[01\bar{1}1]$ $[hkli]$

(b) Pyramids of the *second*, or *diagonal series*. General symbol $[hh\,2\bar{h}\,2i]$, including twelve planes, analogous to those of the pyramid unit series. All the pyramids of this series lie in a zone between the diagonal prism, whose general symbol is $[11\bar{2}0]$, and the basal plane $[0001]$.

Twelve-sided pyramids, or Berylloids (f. 797).—General symbol $[hkli]$, including the twenty-four planes enumerated on p. 453.

---

[*] The order of the terms in the symbols below is made to correspond to that of the indices $h, k, l.$

B. Hemihedral Forms.

The most important of the hemihedral forms in this system are as follows:
1. PYRAMIDAL hemihedrism.—This comes under the head of holohemihedral forms, which are vertically direct (see pp. 34, 35). It is indicated like the corresponding hemihedrism in the tetragonal system $\pi[hkli]$. It is common on apatite.
2. RHOMBOHEDRAL hemihedrism.—These included here are hemiholohedral, and vertically alternate. They are indicated in general by $\kappa[hkli]$. This class is important, since it embraces the RHOMBOHEDRAL DIVISION.

(a) *Rhombohedrons*. Symbol $\kappa[0hh\bar{i}]$; the unit, or fundamental rhombohedron ($+R$, f. 798) has the symbol $\kappa[01\bar{1}1]$, including the six planes: $(01\bar{1}1)$, $(\bar{1}011)$, $(\bar{1}101)$, $(10\bar{1}\bar{1})$, $(1\bar{1}0\bar{1})$, $(0\bar{1}1\bar{1})$. The negative rhombohedron ($-R$, f. 799) includes the planes: $(\bar{1}101)$, $(0\bar{1}11)$, $(10\bar{1}\bar{1})$, $(01\bar{1}\bar{1})$, $(\bar{1}01\bar{1})$, $(1\bar{1}0\bar{1})$.

(b) *Scalenohedrons* (f. 800). Symbol $\kappa[hkli]$.
3. GYROIDAL, or trapezohedral hemihedrism.—The forms here included are holohemihedral, and vertically alternate. They are indicated by $\kappa''[hkli]$. see p. 39.
4. TETRATOHEDRISM.—This may be (1) *rhombohedral*, indicated by $\kappa\pi[hkli]$; or (2) *trapezohedral* (gyroidal), as common on quartz, having the general symbol $\kappa\kappa''[hkli]$.

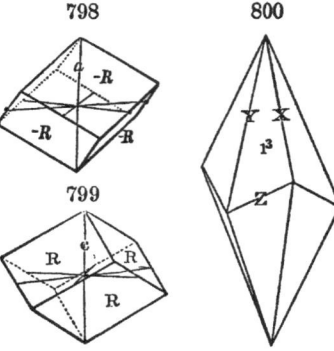

Mathematical Relations of the Hexagonal System.

In the Hexagonal System, as has been explained, the symbol in general has the form $[hkli]$, where the algebraic sum of h, k, and l is zero. This general symbol has four indices, referring respectively to the three equal lateral axes and the vertical axis, as shown in f. 792, thus showing the fundamental *hexagonal* symmetry of the forms. Since, however, the position of a plane is known by its intersection with three axes alone, two of the three indices h, k, l are all that are needed in calculation, the third, l, being a function, as given above, of h and k. The mathematical relations of the planes in this system are brought out by referring them to three axes, viz., two equal lateral axes H, K, ($= a = 1$) oblique (120° and 60°) to one another, and a third axis (c) of unequal length perpendicular to their plane.

This applies also to the calculation by zonal equations. The indices (u, v, w) of the zone in which the planes $(hkli)$, $(pqrt)$ lie, are given by the scheme:

$$\begin{array}{ccccc} h & k & i & h & k \\ & \times & \times & \times & \\ p & q & t & p & q \end{array}$$

$$u = kt - qi \quad v = ip - ht \quad w = hq - kp.$$

(1) The distances (see f. 793) of the pole of any plane $(hkli)$ from the poles of the planes $(10\bar{1}0)$, $(01\bar{1}0)$, $(\bar{1}100)$, and (0001) are given by the following equations:

$$\cos PA = \cos(hkli)(10\bar{1}0) = \frac{\dot{c}(2h+k)}{\sqrt{3i^2 + 4\dot{c}^2(h^2+k^2+hk)}}.$$

$$\cos PB = \cos(hkli)(01\bar{1}0) = \frac{\dot{c}(h+2k)}{\sqrt{3i^2 + 4\dot{c}^2(h^2+k^2+hk)}}.$$

$$\cos PM = \cos(hkli)(\bar{1}100) = \frac{\dot{c}(k-h)}{\sqrt{3i^2 + 4\dot{c}^2(h^2+k^2+hk)}}.$$

$$\cos PC = \cos(hkli)(0001) = \frac{i\sqrt{3}}{\sqrt{3i^2 + 4\dot{c}^2(h^2+k^2+hk)}}.$$

456   APPENDIX.

(2) The distance (PQ) between the poles of any two planes $(hkli)$ and $(pqrt)$ is given by the equation:

$$\cos PQ = \frac{3it + 2\check{c}^2(hq + pk + 2hp + 2kq)}{\sqrt{[3i^2 + 4\check{c}^2(h^2 + k^2 + hk)][3t^2 + 4\check{c}^2(p^2 + q^2 + pq)]}}.$$

(3) For special cases the above formula becomes simplified; it serves to give the value of the normal angles for the several forms in the system. They are as follows:

(a) Hexagonal Pyramid $[0h\bar{h}i]$, f. 796,

$$\cos X \text{ (terminal)} = \frac{3i^2 + 2h^2\check{c}^2}{3i^2 + 4h^2\check{c}^2}; \quad \cos Z \text{ (basal)} = \frac{4h^2\check{c}^2 - 3i^2}{3i^2 + 4h^2\check{c}^2}.$$

For the hexagonal pyramids of the second series $[0h2\bar{h}2i]$ the angles have the same value.

(b) Dihexagonal Pyramid $[hkli]$,

$$\cos X \text{ (see f. 797)} = \frac{3i^2 + 2\check{c}^2(h^2 + k^2 + 4hk)}{3i^2 + 4\check{c}^2(h^2 + k^2 + hk)}.$$

$$\cos Y \text{ (see f. 797)} = \frac{3i^2 + 2\check{c}^2(2k^2 + 2hk - h^2)}{3i^2 + 4\check{c}^2(h^2 + k^2 + hk)}.$$

$$\cos Z \text{ (basal)} = \frac{4\check{c}^2(h^2 + k^2 + hk) - 3i^2}{3i^2 + 4\check{c}^2(h^2 + k^2 + hk)}.$$

(c) Dihexagonal Prism $[hkl0]$,

$$\cos X \text{ (axial)} = \frac{h^2 + k^2 + 4hk}{2(h^2 + k^2 + hk)}.$$

$$\cos Y \text{ (diagonal)} = \frac{2k^2 + 2hk - h^2}{2(h^2 + k^2 + hk)}.$$

(d) Rhombohedron $\kappa[0h\bar{h}i]$,

$$\cos X \text{ (terminal)} = \frac{3i^2 - 2h^2\check{c}^2}{3i^2 + 4\check{c}^2h^2}.$$

(e) Scalenohedron $\kappa[hk\bar{l}i]$,

$$\cos X \text{ (see f. 800)} = \frac{3i^2 + 2\check{c}(2h^2 + 2hk - k^2)}{3i^2 + 4\check{c}^2(h^2 + k^2 + hk)}.$$

$$\cos Y \text{ (see f. 800)} = \frac{3i^2 + 2\check{c}^2(2k^2 + 2hk - h^2)}{3i^2 + 4\check{c}^2(h^2 + k^2 + hk)}.$$

$$\cos Z \text{ (basal)} = \frac{2\check{c}^2(h^2 + k^2 + 4hk) - 3i^2}{3i^2 + 4\check{c}^2(h^2 + k^2 + hk)}.$$

(4) Relations of planes in a zone.—The general equation (3, p. 446) is to be employed. For the pyramidal zones passing through the pole (0001) it takes a simpler form, viz.:

$$\frac{h}{p} = \frac{k}{q} = \frac{i}{t} \cdot \frac{\tan PC}{\tan QC}.$$

If $Q = (01\bar{1}1)$, then:

$$\frac{\tan PC}{\tan QC} = \frac{k}{i}.$$

Determination of the axis $\check{c}$.—The value of $\check{c}$ may be determined from any one of the equations which have been given. The following are simple cases:

$$\tan (hh\, 2\bar{h}\, 2i)\, (0001) = \frac{\check{c}h}{i}.$$

Also $\tan (0h\bar{h}i)\, (0001) \cdot \sin 60° = \frac{\check{c}h}{i}$, or $\tan (01\bar{1}1)\, (0001) \cdot \sin 60° = \check{c}$.

IV. Orthorhombic System.

The Orthorhombic System is characterized by three unequal rectangular axes, $\dot{c}$, $\bar{b}$, $\dot{a}$.[*] The indices h, k, l may be either plus or minus, in the general form $[hkl]$, but they are not exchangeable, since they refer to axes of different lengths. This general symbol then embraces the following planes:

$$(hkl) \qquad (\bar{h}kl) \qquad (\bar{k}\bar{h}l) \qquad (h\bar{k}l)$$
$$(hk\bar{l}) \qquad (\bar{h}k\bar{l}) \qquad (\bar{h}\bar{k}\bar{l}) \qquad (h\bar{k}\bar{l})$$

As different values are given to h, k, l, this general form becomes more or less specialized. The possible forms are as follows:

1. $\begin{cases} [hkl] \; ; \; h > k. \\ [khl] \; ; \; h > k. \\ [hhl] \; ; \; h = k. \end{cases}$ $\quad \dot{a} : n\bar{b} : m\dot{c} \quad [m\text{-}\bar{n}]$
   $\quad n\dot{a} : \bar{b} : m\dot{c} \quad [m\text{-}\check{n}]$
   $\quad \dot{a} : \bar{b} : m\dot{c} \quad [m]$.

2. $[h0l]$; $k = 0$. $\qquad \dot{a} : \infty\bar{b} : m\dot{c} \quad [m\text{-}\bar{i}]$.
3. $[0kl]$; $h = 0$. $\qquad \infty\dot{a} : \bar{b} : m\dot{c} \quad [m\text{-}\check{i}]$.

4. $\begin{cases} [hk0]; \; l = 0, \; h > k. \\ [kh0]; \; l = 0, \; h > k. \\ [110] \; ; \; h = k = 1, \; l = 0. \end{cases}$ $\quad \dot{a} : n\bar{b} : \infty\dot{c} \quad [i\text{-}\bar{n}]$
   $\quad n\dot{a} : \bar{b} : \infty\dot{c} \quad [i\text{-}\check{n}]$.
   $\quad \dot{a} : \bar{b} : \infty\dot{c} \quad [I]$.

5. $[100]$; $k = l = 0$. $\qquad \dot{a} : \infty\bar{b} : \infty\dot{c} \quad [i\text{-}\bar{i}]$.
6. $[010]$; $h = l = 0$. $\qquad \infty\dot{a} : \bar{b} : \infty\dot{c} \quad [i\text{-}\check{i}]$.
7. $[001]$; $h = k = 0$. $\qquad \infty\dot{a} : \infty\bar{b} : \dot{c} \quad [O]$.

These symbols belong to the various distinct forms of this system, as follows:

Pinacoids.—(a) Basal plane. Symbol [001], including the two planes (001) and (00$\bar{1}$). (b) *Macropinacoid.* Symbol [100], including the plane [100], and [$\bar{1}$00] opposite to it. (c) *Brachypinacoid.* Symbol [010], including the planes [010] and [0$\bar{1}$0].

Prisms.—(a) Unit prism (*I*). Symbol 110, including four planes, (110), ($\bar{1}$10), ($\bar{1}\bar{1}$0), (1$\bar{1}$0). (b) Macrodiagonal and brachydiagonal prisms, having respectively the symbols $[hk0]$ and $[kh0]$, if h is greater than k. Thus the symbol $i\text{-}\bar{2}$ corresponds to [210], and $i\text{-}\check{2}$ to [120].

Domes.—(a) Macrodiagonal, or *macrodomes*, having the symbol $[h0l]$; and (b) brachydiagonal, or *brachydomes*, with the symbol $[0kl]$. In each case the symbol embraces four similar planes.

Octahedrons or *Pyramids.*—The symbol $[hhl]$ belongs to the eight planes of the unit pyramids, all lying in the zone between the unit prism [110], and the base [001]. If $h = l$ the form is then [111], and the eight planes are: (111), ($\bar{1}$11), ($\bar{1}\bar{1}$1), (1$\bar{1}$1), (11$\bar{1}$), ($\bar{1}$1$\bar{1}$), ($\bar{1}\bar{1}\bar{1}$), (1$\bar{1}\bar{1}$).

Of the general pyramids two cases are possible, either $[hkl]$ or $[khl]$, when $h > k$, these correspond respectively to the prisms $[hk0]$ and $[kh0]$. They are the macrodiagonal and brachydiagonal pyramids of Naumann; thus $2\text{-}\bar{2}$ ($= \dot{a} : 2\bar{b} : 2\dot{c}$) is [211], according to Miller, and $2\text{-}\check{2}$ ($= 2\dot{a} : \bar{b} : 2\dot{c}$) is [121].

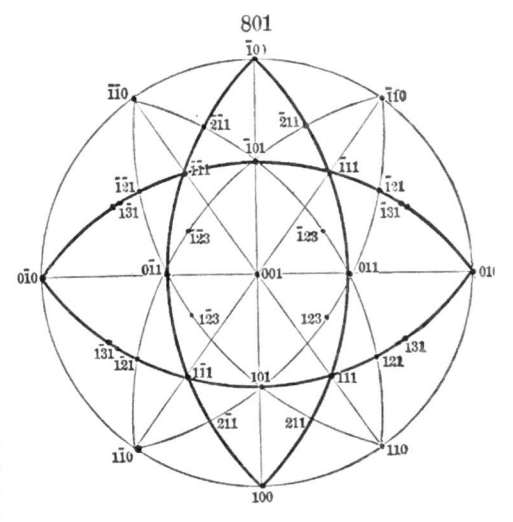

---

[*] The same lettering is employed here as in the early part of this work; it differs from that of Miller in that with him *a* is the *macrodiagonal*, and *b* the *brachydiagonal* axis. Following Groth, and later writers (Bauerman, etc.), the macropinacoid has the symbol (100), and the brachypinacoid the symbol (010); similarly the macrodomes are in general ($h0l$), and the brachydomes (0kl).

For the figures of the above-mentioned forms see pp. 42-44. Their relations will be understood from an examination of f. 801, showing the projection of the crystals in f. 758, p. 444. It will be seen that all the macrodiagonal planes lie between the zonal circles (diameters) (110) (001), and (100) (001), and the brachydiagonal planes between (110)(001) and (010) (001).

Mathematical Relations of the Orthorhombic System.

(1) For the distance between the pole of any plane P (hkl) and the pinacoid planes we have in general:

$$\cos^2 PA = \cos^2(hkl)(100) = \frac{h^2b^2c^2}{h^2b^2c^2 + k^2a^2c^2 + l^2a^2b^2}$$

$$\cos^2 PB = \cos^2(hkl)(010) = \frac{k^2a^2c^2}{h^2b^2c^2 + k^2a^2c^2 + l^2a^2b^2}$$

$$\cos^2 PC = \cos^2(hkl)(001) = \frac{l^2a^2b^2}{h^2b^2c^2 + k^2a^2c^2 + l^2a^2b^2}.$$

(2) For the distance (PQ) between the poles of any two planes (hkl) and (pqr):

$$\cos PQ = \frac{hpb^2c^2 + kqa^2c^2 + lra^2b^2}{\sqrt{[h^2b^2c^2 + k^2a^2c^2 + l^2a^2b^2]\,[p^2b^2c^2 + q^2a^2c^2 + r^2a^2b^2]}}$$

(3) For planes lying in a zone, the general relation (p. 446) is to be employed. For the special cases, practically of most importance, the simplified equations which follow are used.
(4) To determine the lengths of the axes, the general equation may be employed:

$$\frac{\dot{a}}{h} \cos PA = \frac{\bar{b}}{k} \cos PB = \frac{\dot{c}}{l} \cos PC.$$

Here PA, PB, PC are the distances from the pole of any plane (hkl) to the pinacoid planes (100), (010), (001) respectively. The brachydiagonal axis, $\dot{a}$, is made the unit.

If the angle between any dome or prism and the adjoining pinacoid plane is given, the relations follow immediately:

$$\tan PA = \tan(hk0)(100) = \frac{\dot{a}k}{\bar{b}h}$$

$$\tan PB = \tan(0kl)(010) = \frac{\bar{b}l}{\dot{c}k}$$

$$\tan PC = \tan(h0l)(001) = \frac{\dot{c}h}{\dot{a}l}$$

V. Monoclinic System.

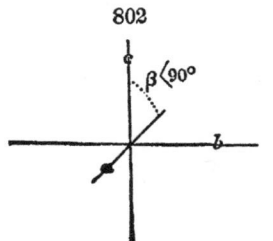

In the Monoclinic System there are three unequal axes, and one of these makes an oblique angle with a second. The axes are lettered as shown in f. 802, $\dot{c}$ is vertical, $\bar{b}$ the orthodiagonal axis, and $\dot{a}$ the clinodiagonal axis oblique to $\dot{c}$, but at right angles to $\bar{b}$. The symbol [hkl] embraces only four similar planes in the most general case, for in consequence of the obliquity of one of the axes, the quadrants above in front correspond alone to those below and behind, and those above behind correspond to those below in front. This is seen clearly in the projection of f. 803. For $\pm h$, $\pm k$, $\pm l$ the symbol [hkl] includes *two* distinct forms, viz.:

      (1)   (hkl)   ($\bar{h}kl$)   ($\bar{h}k\bar{l}$)   ($hk\bar{l}$)
and (2)   ($h\bar{k}l$)   ($\bar{h}\bar{k}l$)   ($\bar{h}\bar{k}\bar{l}$)   ($h\bar{k}\bar{l}$)

The various forms are as follows:

MILLER'S SYSTEM OF CRYSTALLOGRAPHY.   459

Pinacoids.—Base [001]. Orthopinacoid [100]. Clinopinacoid [010]. Each symbol, of course, comprehending two planes only.

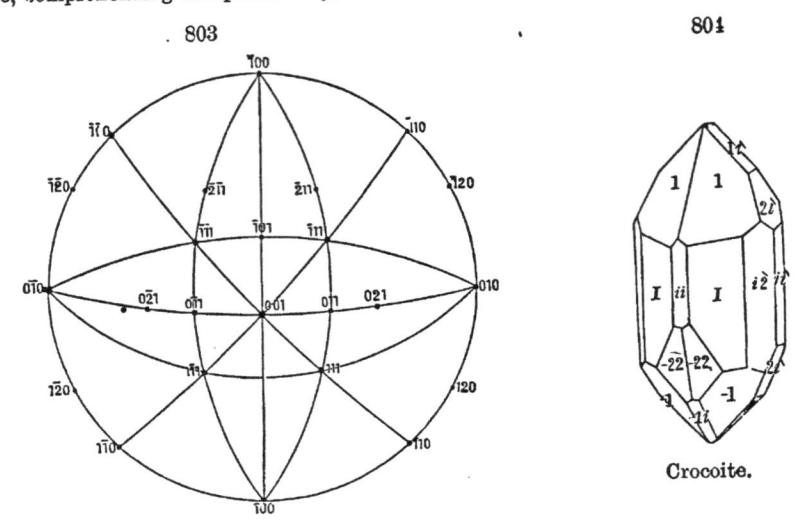

803

804

Crocoite.

Prisms.—(*a*) Unit prism [110], $= d : b : \infty \dot{c}$ (*I*) of Naumann. This symbol embraces four similar prismatic planes. (*b*) Orthodiagonal prisms [*hk*0], where $h > k$, the poles of these prisms fall on the prismatic zonal circle between 100 and 110 (see f. 803). They correspond to the prisms *i-n* ($= d : nb : \infty \dot{c}$) of Naumann. (*c*) Clinodiagonal prisms. Symbol [*kh*0], $h > k$, lying between (110) and (010). They correspond to *i-n̆* ($= nd : b : \infty \dot{c}$) of Naumann.

Domes.—(*a*) Hemi-orthodomes, including two cases, (101) and (10̄1), the *minus* domes of Naumann (opposite the obtuse angle); and also (1̄01) and (10̄1̄)), the plus domes of Naumann (opposite the acute angle β). (*b*) Clinodomes. Symbol [0*kl*], embracing four similar planes (0*kl*) (0*k̄l*), (0*kl̄*), (0*k̄l̄*). The clinodome [011], equivalent to 1-*ĭ* ($= \infty d : b : m\dot{c}$), is one case in this form.

Pyramids.—The pyramids are all hemi-pyramids. (*a*) The symbol [*hhl*] includes the unit pyramids in a zone between [110] and [001]. (*b*) The symbol [*hkl*] includes two sets of hemi-pyramids, whose indices have been given on p. 416, corresponding respectively to −P and +P of Naumann.

If *h* is greater than *k* these are *orthodiagonal* pyramids, corresponding to $\pm(d : nb : \infty \dot{c})$ of Naumann. The symbol [*khl*] on the same supposition includes two sets of planes, like those of p. 458, and differing only in being *clinodiagonal*; equivalent to ($nd : b : \infty \dot{c}$) of Naumann.

The orthodiagonal planes lie between the zone (100), (001) and (110), (001), while the clinodiagonal are between the latter zone and (010) (001), as is seen on f. 803, which gives the projection for f. 804.

Mathematical Relations for the Monoclinic System.

(1) The distances of the pole of any plane (*hkl*) from the pinacoid planes are given by the following equations:

$$\cos PA = \cos (hkl) (100) = \frac{hbc + lab \cos \beta}{\sqrt{h^2b^2c^2 + k^2a^2c^2 \sin^2 \beta + l^2a^2b^2 + 2hlab^2c \cos \beta}};$$

$$\cos PB = \cos (hkl) (010) = \frac{kac \sin \beta}{\sqrt{h^2b^2c^2 + k^2a^2c^2 \sin^2 \beta + l^2a^2b^2 + 2hlab^2c \cos \beta}};$$

$$\cos PC = \cos (hkl) (001) = \frac{lab + hbc \cos \beta}{\sqrt{h^2b^2c^2 + k^2a^2c^2 \sin^2 \beta + l^2a^2b^2 + 2hlab^2c \cos \beta}}.$$

(2) The distance between any two planes may be expressed in general form, but in all practically arising cases the end can be attained by the solution of one or more spherical triangles on the projection.

(3) For the relation between the planes in a zone the general equation before given holds good:

$$\frac{\cot PS - \cot PR}{\cot PQ - \cot PR} = \frac{(PQ).(SR)}{(QR).(PS)}.$$

(4) For all zones passing through the clinopinacoid (010), the value of PR may be taken as 90°, and the above equation consequently simplified:

$$\frac{h}{p} = \frac{k}{q} \cdot \frac{\tan PB}{\tan QB} = \frac{l}{r}$$

This equation is especially valuable for determining the indices of planes in the prismatic and clinodome series.

(5) To determine the axial relations the general equation admits of being transformed so as to read:

$$\frac{h}{l} \cdot \frac{\sin PYA}{\sin PYC} = \frac{p}{r} \cdot \frac{\sin QYA}{\sin QYC} = \frac{a}{c};$$

and

$$\frac{k}{l} \cdot \frac{\sin PYA}{\cot PY} = \frac{q}{r} \cdot \frac{\sin QYA}{\cot QY} = \frac{b}{c}.$$

The angles PYA, PYC are angles which may be calculated directly by spherical triangles from the measured angles. Similarly for QYA, QYC. PY and QY are the angles between the given plane P or Q with the clinopinacoid.

VI. Triclinic System.

In the Triclinic System, since the axes are unequal and all mutually oblique, there can be no plane of symmetry, and there can in no case be more than two planes included in a single form. The three axes are distinguished as a vertical, c, a longer lateral, or macrodiagonal axis, $\bar{b}$, and a shorter lateral, or brachydiagonal axis, $\check{a}$. The position assumed for the axes is shown in f. 259, p. 80.

The general symbol $[hkl]$, which includes eight similar planes in the orthorhombic system, is here resolved into four independent forms, embracing two opposite planes only. They are thus:

(1) $\begin{pmatrix} hkl \\ \bar{h}\bar{k}\bar{l} \end{pmatrix}$ (2) $\begin{pmatrix} h\bar{k}l \\ \bar{h}k\bar{l} \end{pmatrix}$ (3) $\begin{pmatrix} hk\bar{l} \\ \bar{h}\bar{k}l \end{pmatrix}$ (4) $\begin{pmatrix} \bar{h}kl \\ h\bar{k}\bar{l} \end{pmatrix}$

These correspond respectively to $mP'n$ (1), $m'Pn$ (2), mP,n (3), m,Pn (4) of Naumann, or $-m \cdot n'$, $-m \cdot n$, $m \cdot n'$, $m \cdot n'$, as the abbreviated symbols are written in the earlier part of this work.

Contrary to the usage in the orthorhombic system, it is customary to make [100] the macropinacoid ($i\cdot \bar{\imath} = \check{a} : \infty \bar{b} : \infty \check{c}$), and [010] the brachypinacoid ($i\cdot \bar{\imath} = \infty \check{a} : b : \infty c$). Planes having the symbol $[h0l]$ are then macrodomes; and those of the symbol $[0kl]$ are brachydomes. Similarly then pyramids ($h > k$) of the form $[hkl]$ are macrodiagonal planes, and those of the form (hkl) are brachydiagonal planes. The unit prism consists of two independent forms (110), ($\bar{1}\bar{1}0$) ($I' = \infty P,'$), and ($\bar{1}10$), ($1\bar{1}0$) ($I = \infty',P$).

Mathematical Relations of the Triclinic System.

In consequence of the obliquity of the axes in the Triclinic System the mathematical relations are less simple, and the general equations deduced as before become so complicated as to be seldom of much practical value. Most problems which arise may be solved by the zonal relations, or by the solution of the spherical triangles in the projection. Some of the most important relations (given by Schrauf) are as follows:

If the angle between the axes X and Z $= \eta$, between X and Y $= \zeta$, and between Y and Z $= \xi$ (see f. 757); if also α, β, γ are the corresponding angles between the pinacoid planes—then·

$$\cos \xi = \frac{\cos \beta \cos \gamma - \cos \alpha}{\sin \beta \sin \gamma}. \quad \cos \eta = \frac{\cos \gamma \cos \alpha - \cos \beta}{\sin \gamma \sin \alpha}. \quad \cos \zeta = \frac{\cos \beta \cos \alpha - \cos \gamma}{\sin \alpha \sin \beta}.$$

and $\quad \cos^2 PX = \dfrac{h^2 b^2 c^2 A_1}{M_1}. \quad \cos^2 PY = \dfrac{k^2 a^2 c^2 A_1}{M_1}. \quad \cos^2 PZ = \dfrac{l^2 a^2 b^2 A_1}{M_1}$

where $\quad A_1 = [1 + 2 \cos \alpha \cos \beta \cos \gamma - (\cos^2 \alpha + \cos^2 \beta + \cos^2 \gamma)].$

$M_1 = h^2 b^2 c^2 \sin^2 \alpha + k^2 a^2 c^2 \sin^2 \beta + l^2 a^2 b^2 \sin^2 \gamma + 2abc \, (hlb \cos \beta \sin \alpha \sin \gamma + hkc \cos \gamma \sin \alpha \sin \beta + kla \cos \alpha \sin \beta \sin \gamma).$

Also $\quad \cos^2 AX = \dfrac{A_1}{\sin^2 \alpha}; \quad \cos BY = \dfrac{A_1}{\sin^2 \beta}; \quad \cos CZ = \dfrac{A_1}{\sin^2 \gamma}.$

When PX, PY, PZ have been found by calculation, then the following equation gives the relation of the axes:

$$\frac{a}{h} \cos PX = \frac{b}{k} \cos PY = \frac{c}{l} \cos PZ.$$

As seen in f. 805.

$\cos PX = \sin PBC \sin PB = \sin PCB \sin PC;$
$\cos PY = \sin PCA \sin PC = \sin PAC \sin PA;$
$\cos PZ = \sin PAB \sin PA = \sin PBA \sin PB;$

and also from these it follows that—

$\dfrac{b}{k} \sin PAC = \dfrac{c}{l} \sin PAB;$

$\dfrac{c}{l} \sin PBA = \dfrac{a}{h} \sin PBC;$

$\dfrac{a}{h} \sin PCB = \dfrac{b}{k} \sin PCA.$

$\xi = 180° - CAB; \quad \eta = 180° - ABC; \quad \zeta = 180° - ACB.$

RELATIONS OF THE SIX CRYSTALLINE SYSTEMS IN RESPECT TO SYMMETRY.

From a careful study of the spherical projections for the successive systems a very clear idea may be obtained of the degree of symmetry which characterizes each. It is well understood that in the Isometric System there are *nine* planes of symmetry; in the Tetragonal, *five;* in the Hexagonal, *seven;* in the Orthorhombic, *three;* and in the Monoclinic only *one*. These relations are shown on the projections by the symmetrical distribution of the poles about the respective great circles. These zone-circles of symmetry are as follows:

Isometric System (f. 766): 1st, the three diametral zones:

1. (100), (010), ($\bar{1}$00). 2. (100), (001), ($\bar{1}$00). 3. (010), (001), (0$\bar{1}$0).

Also the diagonal zones:

4. (110), (001), ($\bar{1}\bar{1}$0).   6. (100), (011), ($\bar{1}$00).   8. (010), (101), (0$\bar{1}$0).
5. (1$\bar{1}$0), (001), ($\bar{1}$10).   7. (100), (0$\bar{1}$1), ($\bar{1}$00).   9. (010), ($\bar{1}$01), (0$\bar{1}$0).

Tetragonal System (f. 790):

1. (100), (010), ($\bar{1}$00). 2. (100), (001), ($\bar{1}$00). 3. (010), (001), (0$\bar{1}$0).

Also:

4. (110), (001), ($\bar{1}\bar{1}$0).   5. (1$\bar{1}$0), (001), ($\bar{1}$10).

462   APPENDIX.

Hexagonal System (f. 793):

1. $(10\bar{1}0)$, (0001), $(\bar{1}010)$.
4. $(11\bar{2}0)$, (0001), $(\bar{1}\bar{1}20)$.
2. $(01\bar{1}0)$, (0001), $(0\bar{1}10)$.
5. $(\bar{1}2\bar{1}0)$, (0001), $(1\bar{2}10)$.
7. $(10\bar{1}0)$, $(01\bar{1}0)$, $(\bar{1}100)$.
3. $(\bar{1}100)$, (0001), $(1\bar{1}00)$.
6. $(\bar{2}110)$, (0001), $(2\bar{1}\bar{1}0)$.

Orthorhombic System (f. 801):

1. (100), (010), $(\bar{1}00)$.
2. (100), (001), $(\bar{1}00)$.
3. (010), (001), $(0\bar{1}0)$.

Monoclinic System (f. 804):

1. (100), (001), $(\bar{1}00)$.

In the Triclinic System there is no plane of symmetry.

THE RHOMBOHEDRAL DIVISION OF MILLER.

The following projection (f. 806) is added in order to show the relation of the forms in the Hexagonal and Rhombohedral Systems as referred to the three equal oblique axes of Miller. The forms are as follows:

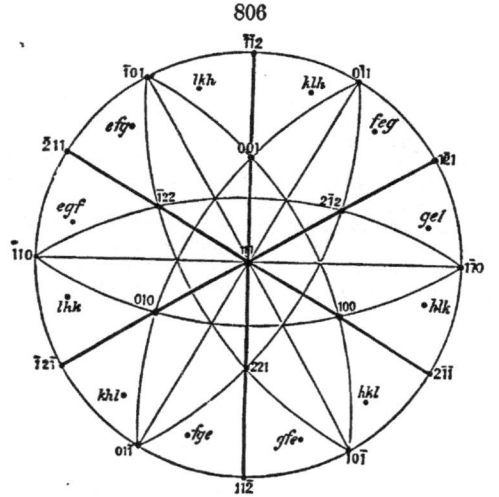

The planes having the indices (100), (010), (001) are those of the (plus) fundamental rhombohedron, while the plane (111) is the base. The planes (221), (121), (122) are those of the minus fundamental rhombohedron; with the planes (100), (010), (001) they form the unit hexagonal pyramid.

The hexagonal unit prism $(I = [01\bar{1}0])$ has the symbols: $(2\bar{1}\bar{1})$, $(1\bar{2}1)$, $(\bar{1}\bar{1}2)$, $(\bar{2}11)$, $(\bar{1}2\bar{1})$, $(11\bar{2})$. The second, or diagonal hexagonal prism $(i\text{-}2 = [11\bar{2}0])$ has the symbols: $(10\bar{1})$, $(1\bar{1}0)$, $(0\bar{1}1)$, $(\bar{1}01)$, $(\bar{1}10)$, $(01\bar{1})$.

The dihexagonal pyramid embraces, like the simple hexagonal pyramid, two forms, $[hkl]$ and $[efg]$; the symbol $[hkl]$ hence belongs to the plus scalenohedron, and $[efg]$ to the minus. In this as in other cases it is true that: $e = -h + 2k + 2l$, $f = 2h - k + 2l$, $g = 2h + 2k - l$.

The dihexagonal prism includes the six planes of the form $[hk0]$, and the remaining six of the form $[ef0]$.

Most of the problems arising under this system can be solved by the zone equations, or by the working out of the spherical triangles on the sphere of projection.

APPENDIX B.

ON THE DRAWING OF FIGURES OF CRYSTALS.

In the projection of crystals, the eye is supposed to be at an infinite distance, so that the rays of light fall from it on the crystal in parallel lines. The plane on which the crystal is projected is termed the *plane of projection*. This plane may be at *right angles* to the vertical axis, may pass *through* the vertical axis, or may intersect it at an *oblique angle*. These different positions give rise, respectively, to the HORIZONTAL, VERTICAL, and OBLIQUE projections. The rays of light may fall *perpendicularly* on the plane of projection, or may be *obliquely* inclined to it; in the former case the projection is termed ORTHOGRAPHIC, in the second CLINOGRAPHIC. In the horizontal position of the plane of projection, the projection is always orthographic. In the other positions, it may be either orthographic or clinographic. It is generally preferable to employ the vertical position and clinographic projection, and this method is elucidated in the following pages.

PROJECTION OF THE AXES.

The projection of the axes of a crystal is the first step preliminary to the projection of the form of the crystal itself. The projection of the axes in the isometric system, which are equal and intersect at right angles, is here first given. The projection of the axes in the other systems, with the exception of the hexagonal, may be obtained by varying the lengths of the projected isometric axes, and also, when oblique, their inclinations, as shown beyond.

Isometric System.—When the eye is directly in front of a face of a cube, neither the sides nor top of the crystal are visible, nor the planes that may be situated on the intermediate edges. On turning the crystal a few degrees from right to left, a side lateral plane is brought in view, and by elevating the eye slightly, the terminal plane becomes apparent. In the following demonstration, the angle of revolution is designated δ, and the angle of the elevation of the eye, ϵ. Fig. 807 represents the normal position of the horizontal axes, supposing the eye to be in the direction of the axis BB; BB is seen as a mere point, while CC appears of its actual length. On revolving the whole through a number of degrees equal to BMB' (δ) the axes have the position exhibited in the dotted lines. The projection of the semiaxis MB is now lengthened to MN, and that of the semiaxis MC is shortened to MH.

If the eye be elevated (at any angle, ϵ), the lines B'N, BM, and C'H will be projected respectively below N, M, and H, and the lengths of these projections (which we may designate b'N, bM, and c'H) will be directly proportional to the lengths of the lines B'N, BM, and C'H.

It is usual to adopt such a revolution and such an elevation of the eye as may be expressed by a simple ratio between the projected axes. The ratio between the two axes, MN : MH, as projected after the revolution, is designated by 1 : r; and the ratio of b'N to MN by 1 : s. Suppose r to equal 3 and s to equal 2, then proceed as follows:

Draw two lines AA', H'H (f. 808), intersecting one another at right angles. Make MH = MH' = b. Divide HH' into 3 (r) parts, and through the points, N, N', thus determined, draw perpendiculars to HH'. On the left hand vertical, set off, below H', a part H'R, equal to $\frac{1}{s}b = \frac{1}{2}$ H'M; and from R draw RM, and extend the same to the vertical N'. B'B is the projection of the front horizontal axis.

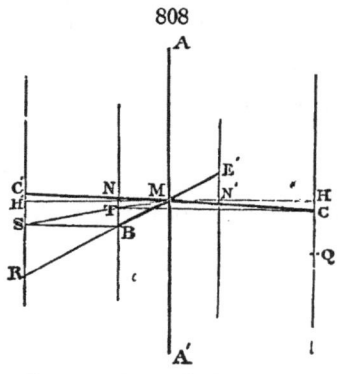

Draw BS parallel with MH' and connect SM. From the point T in which SM intersects BN, draw TC parallel with MH. A line (CC') drawn from C through M, and extended to the left vertical, is the projection of the side horizontal axis.

Lay off on the right vertical, a part HQ equal to $\frac{1}{3}$MH, and make MA = MA' = MQ; AA' is the vertical axis. If, as here, $r = 3$, and $s = 2$, then $\delta = 18°\ 26'$, and $\epsilon = 9°\ 28'$, for cot $\delta = r$, and cot $\epsilon = rs$.

Tetragonal and Orthorhombic Systems.—The axes AA', CC', BB, constructed in the manner described, are equal and at right angles to each other. The projection of the axes of a tetragonal crystal is obtained by simply laying off, with a scale of proportional parts, on MA and MA' taken as units, the value of the vertical axis ($\dot{c}$) for the given species. Thus for zircon, where $\dot{c} = \cdot 64$, we must lay off ·64 of MA above M and the same length below.

For an orthorhombic crystal, where the three axes are unequal, the length of $\dot{c}$ must as before be laid off above and below from M, and that of $\breve{b}$ to the right and left of M, on CC', MC being taken as the unit. It is usual to make the front axis MB = $\breve{a}$ = 1.

Monoclinic System.—The axes $\dot{c}$ and $\breve{a}$ in the monoclinic system are inclined to one another at an oblique angle = β. To project this inclination, and thus adapt the isometric axes to a monoclinic form, lay off (f. 809) on the axis MA, Ma = MA cos β, and on the axis BB' (before or behind M, according as the inclination of $\breve{a}$ on $\dot{c}$, in front, is acute or obtuse) Mb = MB × sin β. From the points b and a, draw lines parallel respectively with the axes AA' and BB', and from their intersection D', draw through M, D'D, making MD = MD'. The line DD' is the clinodiagonal, and the lines AA, C'C, DD' represent the axes in a monoclinic solid in which $a = b = c = 1$. The points a and b and the position of the axis DD' will vary with the angle β. The relative values of the axes may be given them as above explained; that is, if $\breve{a} = 1$, lay off in the direction of MA and MA' a line equal to $\dot{c}$, and in the direction of MC and MC' a line equal to $\breve{b}$, etc.

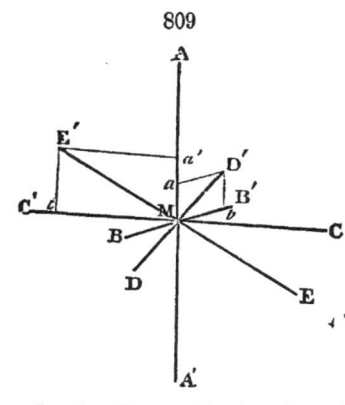

Triclinic System.—The vertical sections through the horizontal axes in the triclinic system are obliquely inclined; also the inclination of the axis a to each axis b and c, is oblique. In the adaptation of the isometric axes to the triclinic forms, it is therefore necessary, in the first place, to give the requisite obliquity to the mutual inclination of the vertical sections, and afterwards to adapt the horizontal axes. The inclination of these sections we may designate A, and as heretofore, the angle between a and b, γ, and a and c, β. BB' is the analogue of the brachydiagonal, and CC' of the macrodiagonal. An oblique inclination may be given the vertical sections, by varying the position of either of these sections. Permitting the brachydiagonal section ABA'B' to remain unaltered, we may vary the other section as follows:

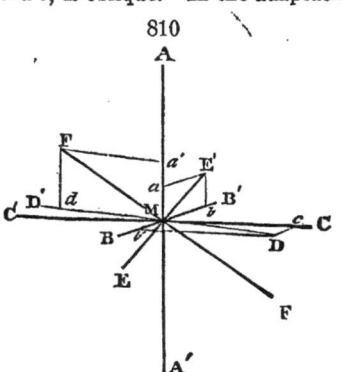

Lay off (f. 810) on MB, Mb' = MB × cos A, and on the axis CC (to the right or left of M, according as the acute angle A is to the right or left), Mc = MC × sin A; completing the parallelogram Mb' Dc, and drawing the diagonal MD, extending the same to D' so as to make MD' = MD, we obtain the line DD', the vertical section passing through this line is the correct macrodiagonal section. The inclination of a to the new macrodiagonal DD' is still a right angle; as also the inclination of a to b, their oblique inclinations may be given them as follows: Lay off on MA (f. 810), $Ma = MA \times \cos \beta$, and on the axis BB' (brachydiagonal), $Mb = MB' \times \sin \beta$. By completing the parallelogram Ma, $E'b$, the point E' is determined. Make $ME = ME$; EE' is the projected brachydiagonal. Again lay off on MA, $Ma' = MA \times \cos a$, and on MD', to the left, $Md = MD' \times \sin a$. Draw lines from a' and d parallel to MD and MA; F', the intersection of these lines, is one extremity of the macrodiagonal; and the line FF', in which $MF = MF'$, is the macrodiagonal. The vertical axis AA' and the horizontal axes EE' (brachydiagonal) and FF' (macrodiagonal) thus obtained, are the axes in a triclinic form, in which $a = b = c = 1$. Different values may be given these axes, according to the method heretofore illustrated.

Hexagonal System.—In this system there are three equal horizontal axes, at right angles to the vertical axis. The normal position of the horizontal axes is represented in f. 811. The eye, placed in the line of the axis YY, observes two of the semiaxes, MZ and MU, projected in the same straight line, while the third, MY, appears a mere point. To give the axes a more eligible position for a representation of the various planes on the solid, we revolve them from right to left through a certain number of degrees δ, and elevate the eye at an angle ϵ. The dotted lines in the figure represent the axes in their new situation, resulting from a revolution through a number of degrees equal to $\delta =$ YMY'. In this position the axis MY is projected upon MP, MU' upon MN, and MZ' on MH. Designating the intermediate axis I, that to the right II, that to the left III, if the revolution is such as to give the projections of I and II the ratio of 1 : 2, the relations of the three projections will be as follows: I : II : III = 1 : 2 : 3.

Let us take $r \cdot (= PM : HM)$ equal to 3, and $s (= b'P : PM)$ equal to 2, these being the most convenient ratios for representing the hexagonal crystalline forms. The following will be the mode of construction:

1. Draw the lines AA, HH (f. 812) at right angles with, and bisecting, each other. Let $HM = b$, or $HH = 2b$. Divide HH into six parts by vertical lines. These lines, including the left- and right-hand verticals, may be numbered from one to six, as in the figure. In the first vertical, below H, lay off $HS = \frac{1}{3}b$, and from S draw a line through M to the fourth vertical. YY' is the projection of the axis I.

2. From Y draw a line to the sixth vertical and parallel with HH. From T, the extremity of this line, draw a line to N in the second vertical. Then from the point U, in which TN intersects the fifth vertical, draw a line through M to the second vertical; UU' is the projection of the axis II.

3. From R, where TN intersects the third vertical, draw RZ to the first vertical parallel with HH. Then from Z draw a line through M to the sixth vertical; this line ZZ' is the projection of the axis III.

4. For the vertical axis, lay off from N on the second vertical (f. 812) a line of any length, and construct upon this line an equilateral triangle; one side (NQ) of this triangle will intersect the first vertical at a distance, HV, from H, corresponding to Z H in f. 811; for in the triangle NHV, the angle HNV is an angle of 30°, and $HN = \frac{1}{2}MH$. MV is therefore the radius of the circle (f. 811). Make therefore $MA = MA' = MV$; AA' is the vertical axis, and YY', UU', ZZ' are the projected horizontal axes.

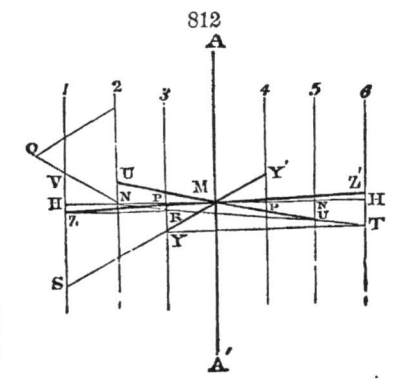

The vertical axis has been constructed equal to the horizontal axes. Its actual length in different hexagonal or rhombohedral forms may be laid off according to the method sufficiently explained.

The projection of the isometric and hexagonal axes, having been once *accurately* made, and that on a conveniently large scale, may be kept on a piece of cardboard, and will then answer all subsequent requirements. Whenever needed for use, these axes may be transferred to a sheet of paper, and then adapted in length, or inclination, or both, to the case in hand.

PROJECTION OF THE FORMS OF CRYSTALS.

Simple forms.—When the axial cross has been constructed for the given species, the unit octahedron is obtained at once by joining the extremities of the axes, AA', BB', CC', as in f. 813. Here as in all cases the lines which fall in front are drawn strongly, while those behind are simply dotted.

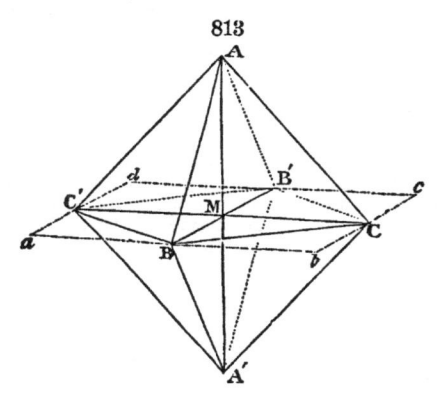

For the *diametral prisms* draw through B, B', C, C', of the projected axes of any species, lines parallel to the axes BB', CC', until they meet; they make the parallelogram, *abcd*, which is a transverse section of the prism, parallel to the base. Through *a, b, c, d* draw lines parallel and equal to the vertical axis, making the parts above and below these points equal to the vertical semiaxis. Then, connect the extremities of these lines by lines parallel to *ab, bc, cd, da*, and the figure will be that of the diametral prism, corresponding to the axes projected.

In the case of the isometric system this diametral prism is the cube, whose faces are represented by the letter H; in the tetragonal system it is the prism $O, i\text{-}i$; in the orthorhombic, the prism $O, i\text{-}i, i\text{-}\bar{\imath}$; in the monoclinic, the prism $O, i\text{-}\bar{\imath}, i\text{-}\bar{\imath}$; in the triclinic, $O, i\text{-}\bar{\imath}, i\text{-}\bar{\imath}$.

The *unit vertical prism* in the tetragonal, orthorhombic, and clinometric systems may be projected by drawing lines parallel to the vertical axis AA' through B, C, B', C', making the parts above and below these points equal to the vertical semiaxis; and then connecting the extremities of these lines by lines parallel to BC, CB', B'C', C'B. The plane BCB'C' is a transverse section of such a prism parallel to its base. It is the prism O, I, in each of the systems excepting the triclinic, and in that O, I, I'; a *square* prism in the tetragonal system; a *right rhombic* in the orthorhombic; an *oblique rhombic* in the monoclinic; an oblique rhomboidal in the triclinic.

Other simple forms under the different systems are constructed in essentially the same way. It is only necessary to lay down upon the axes each plane of the form, in lightly drawn lines, note the points where it intersects the adjoining planes, and draw these in more strongly. When the process is complete the construction lines may be erased. The process will be illustrated by f. 814 and f. 815. In the former case it is required to draw the trigonal trisoctahedron, whose symbol is 2

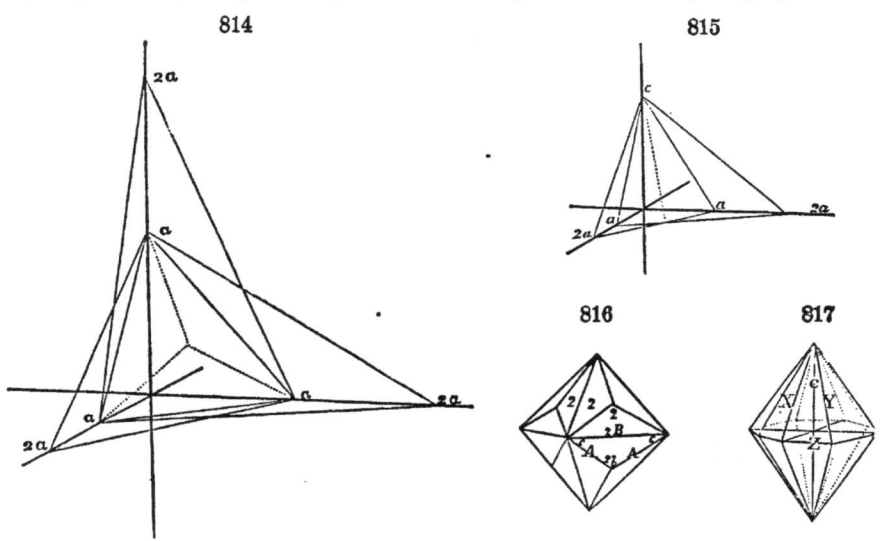

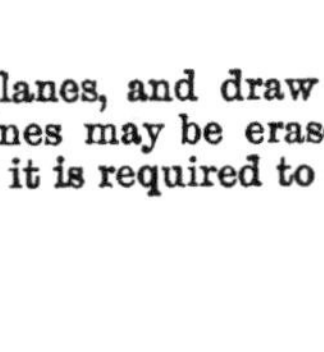

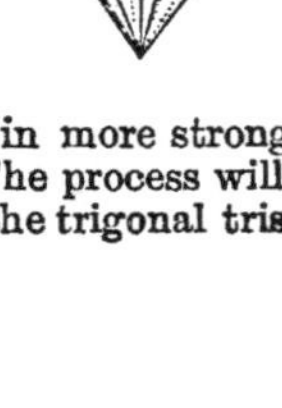

In f. 814 the three planes of the first octant are represented, they are $2:1:1, 1:2:1$, and $1:1:2$. It will be seen here, what is always true, that the two points of intersection required to determine the line of intersection, *lie in the axial planes*. These lines of intersection are represen'ed by the dotted lines in f. 814. If the same process be performed for the other octants, the complete form, as in f. 816, will be obtained.

Similarly in f. 815, the octagonal pyramid 1-2 is constructed; the figure shows the planes of one octant only, $\dot{c}:2a:a$, and $\dot{c}:a:2a$, and the dotted line gives their line of intersection. Carry out the same plane of construction in the other octants, and the form of f. 817 will result.

The construction of the various crystalline forms, by this method, especially those of the isometric system, will be found an interesting and instructive process, and will lead to a clear understanding of the forms themselves and their relations to each other. Another and quicker, though more mechanical method of constructing the isometric forms may also be given.

Projection of Simple Isometric Forms.—This method depends upon the principle that in the different isometric forms the vertices of the solid angles are occupied by one or more of the interaxes (p. 16). If, therefore, these points (the extremities of the interaxes), can be determined in the several crystalline forms, it is only necessary to connect them in order to obtain the projection of the solid itself.

As a preparation for the construction of figures of isometric crystals, it is desirable to have at hand the figure of a cube projected on a large scale, with its axes, and its *trigonal* (octahedral), and *rhombic* (dodecahedral) interaxes.

The values of the interaxes t and r, for a given form, are obtained by adding to their normal length the values of t' and r' respectively given by the following equations; those of the octahedron being taken as a unit:

$$t' = \frac{2mn - (m+n)}{mn + (m+n)} \cdot \quad r' = \frac{n-1}{n+1} \cdot$$

The proportion to be added to the interaxes for some of the common forms is as follows:

	t	r		t	r
2	$\frac{1}{5}$	0	i-2	1	$\frac{1}{3}$
i	$\frac{1}{2}$	0	i-3	$\frac{4}{4}$	$\frac{1}{2}$
3-$\frac{3}{2}$	$\frac{1}{3}$	$\frac{1}{5}$	2-2	$\frac{1}{2}$	$\frac{1}{3}$
4-2	$\frac{4}{7}$	$\frac{1}{3}$	3-3	$\frac{1}{5}$	$\frac{1}{2}$

To construct the form 4-2, the octahedron is first to be projected, and its axes and interaxes drawn. Then add to each half of each trigonal interaxis, five-sevenths of its length; and to each half of each rhombic interaxis, one-third of its length. The extremities of the lines thus extended are situated in the vertices of the solid angles of the hexoctahedron 4-2, and by connecting them, the projection of this form is completed.

In the *inclined hemihedral* isometric forms (p. 20), the rhombic interaxes do not terminate in the vertices of the solid angles, and may therefore be thrown out of view in the projection of these solids. The two halves of each trigonal interaxis terminate in the vertices of dissimilar angles, and are of unequal lengths. One is identical with the corresponding interaxis in the holohedral forms, and is called the holohedral portion of the interaxis; the other is the hemihedral portion. The length of the latter may be determined by adding to the half of the octahedral interaxis that portion of the same indicated in the formula:

$$\frac{2mn - (m-n)}{mn + (m-n)} \cdot$$

If the different halves of the trigonal interaxes be assumed at one time, as the holohedral, and again as the hemihedral portion, the reverse forms $\frac{(m-n)}{2}$ and $-\frac{(m-n)}{2}$ may be projected.

The following table contains the values of the above fraction for several of the inclined hemihedral forms, and also the corresponding values for the holohedral portion of the interaxis:

	Hol. interax.	Hem. interax.		Hol. interax.	Hem. interax.
$\frac{(1)}{2}$ (f. 76, p. 20)	0	2	$\frac{(2)}{1}$ (f. 85)	$\frac{1}{5}$	1
$\frac{(2\text{-}2)}{2}$ (f. 81)	$\frac{1}{3}$	2	$\frac{(3\text{-}\frac{3}{2})}{2}$ (f. 87)	$\frac{1}{3}$	$\frac{4}{5}$
$\frac{(3\text{-}3)}{2}$	$\frac{1}{3}$	2	$\frac{(4\text{-}2)}{2}$	$\frac{4}{7}$	$\frac{3}{5}$

468   APPENDIX.

The *parallel hemihedrons* (for example, the pentagonal dodecahedron, or hemi-tetrahexahedron) contain a solid angle, situated in a line between the extremities of each pair of semiaxes, which is called an *unsymmetrical* solid angle. The vertices of these angles are at unequal distances from the two adjacent axes, and therefore are not in the line of the rhombic interaxes. The co-ordinates of this solid angle for any form, as $\frac{[m\text{-}n]}{2}$, may be found by the formulas $\frac{m(n-1)}{mn-1}$ and $\frac{n(m-1)}{mn-1}$. By means of these formulas, the situation of two points, a and b (f. 818), in each of the axes may be determined: and if lines are drawn through a and b in each semiaxis parallel to the other axes, the intersections $c\,c'$, of these lines will be the vertices of the unsymmetrical solid angles, those marked c of the form $\frac{[m\text{-}n]}{2}$ and those marked c' of the form $-\frac{[m\text{-}n]}{2}$.

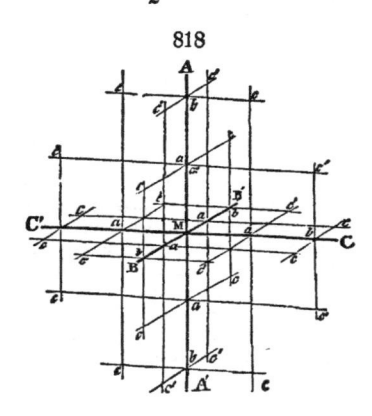

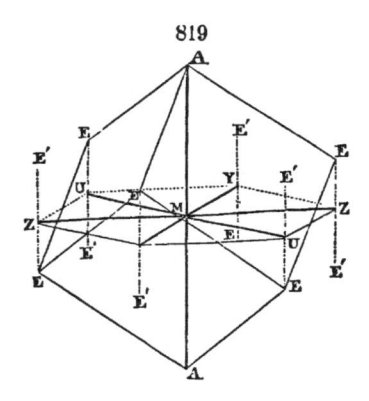

818

819

The trigonal interaxes are of the same length as in the holohedral forms. The values of these interaxes, and of the coördinates of the unsymmetrical solid angle for different parallel hemihedrons, are contained in the following table:

	Trigonal interaxis.	Coörd. of the unsym. S. A.			Trigonal interaxis.	Coörd. of the unsym. S. A.	
$\frac{[3\text{-}\frac{3}{2}]}{2}$ (f. 100, p. 23)	$\frac{1}{2}$	$\frac{3}{7}$	$\frac{4}{7}$	$\frac{[i\text{-}\frac{3}{2}]}{2}$ (sim. f. 92)	$\frac{1}{2}$	$\frac{1}{2}$	1
$\frac{[4\text{-}2]}{2}$	$\frac{1}{2}$	$\frac{3}{7}$	$\frac{4}{7}$	$\frac{[i\text{-}2]}{2}$ (f. 92)	1	$\frac{1}{2}$	1

Projection of a Rhombohedron.—To construct a rhombohedron, lay off verticals through the extremities of the horizontal axes, and make the parts both above and below these extremities equal to the third of the vertical semiaxis (f. 819). The points E, E, E'. E', etc., are thus determined; and if the extremities of the vertical axis be connected with the points E or E', rhombohedrons in different positions, mR, or $-mR$, will be constructed.

Scalenohedron.—The scalenohedron m^n admits of a similar construction with the rhombohedron mR. The only variation required, is to multiply the vertical axis by the number of units in n, after the points E and E' in the rhombohedron mR have been determined; then connect the points E, or the points E', with one another and with the extremities of the vertical axis.

2. *Complex Forms.*—When it is required to figure not only the planes of one form, that is, those embraced in one symbol, but also those of a number modifying one another, a somewhat different process is found desirable. It is possible indeed to construct a complex form in the way mentioned on p. 466, each plane being laid off on the given axes, and its intersection-edges with adjoining planes determined by two points, always in the axial sections, which it has in common with each. In this way, however, the figure will soon become so complex as to be extremely perplexing, and thus lead to error and consequent loss of time.

This difficulty is in part avoided by the use of one projection of the axes on a larger scale, upon which the directions of the intersection-lines are determined, while a second smaller one, placed below and parallel to it on the same sheet of paper, is used for the actual drawing of the crystal. In most cases, however, the crystal may be drawn as conveniently without the use of the second set of axes. The size of the figure may be either that which is to be finally required, or, more advantageously, it may be drawn two or three times larger and then reduced by photography. This method is especially to be recommended when the figures are finally to be engraved on wood, since from the enlarged drawing they may be photographed directly upon the wood of any required size, and thus a very high degree of accuracy attained.

Application of Quenstedt's Projection. — The process of determining the direction of the intersection-edges is much simplified if the principles of Quenstedt's Projection (p. 55) are made use of. In other words, the symbol of every plane is so transformed that for it the length of the vertical axis is *unity*. This extremity of the vertical axis is then *one point of intersection* for all planes whatsoever, and the second point will always lie in the horizontal plane, that of the lateral axes. The change in the symbol requires nothing but that the symbol, expressed in full, should be divided by the coefficient of the vertical axis. The direction of each intersection-edge, when determined, is transferred to the figure in process of construction by means of a small triangle sliding against a ruler some 8 inches in length. It will be found in practice that, especially when this method is employed, it is not necessary to actually draw all the lines representing each plane, but to note simply the required points of intersection. This method and its advantages (see Klein, Einleitung in die Krystallberechnung, II., p. 387) will be made clear by an example.

It is required to project a crystal of andalusite of prismatic habit, showing also the planes $i\text{-}\check{2}$, $i\text{-}\check{\imath}$, $1\text{-}\check{\imath}$, 1, $2\text{-}\check{2}$, $1\text{-}\check{\imath}$, and O.

It is evident that an indefinite number of figures may be made, including the planes mentioned, and yet of very different appearance according to the relative size of each. It is usually desirable, however, to represent the actual appearance of the crystal in nature, only in ideal symmetry, hence it is very important in all cases to have a sketch of the crystal to be represented, showing the relative development of the different planes. If this sketch is made with a little care, so as to show also the parallelism of the intersection-edges in the occurring zones, it will give material aid. The zones, it is to be noted, are a great help in drawing figures of crystals, and they should be carefully studied, since the common direction of the intersection-edge once determined for any two planes in it, will answer for all others.

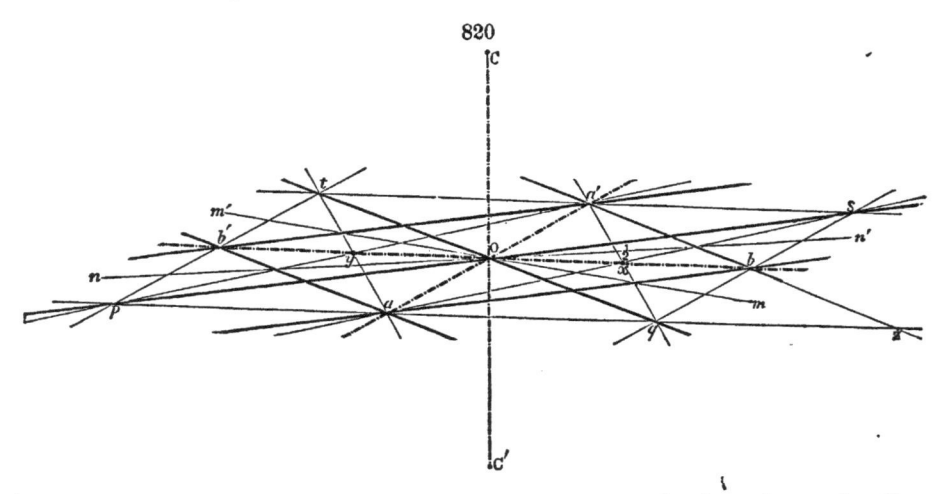

820

The first step is to take the projection of the isometric axes already made once for all on a conveniently large scale, and which, as before suggested, is kept on a card of large size, and ready to be pierced through on to the paper employed. These axes, now of equal length, must be adapted to the species in hand. For andalusite the axial ratio is $\dot{c} : \bar{b} : \breve{a} = 0{\cdot}712 : 1{\cdot}014 : 1$; hence the vertical axis $\dot{c}$ must have a length ·71 of what it now has, and the lateral axis one 1·01; these required lengths are determined in a moment with a scale of equal parts.

The next step is to draw the predominating form, the prism I. Obviously its intersection-edges are parallel to the vertical axis, and its basal edges, intersecting O, are parallel to ps, tq in the projection (f. 820). The planes $i\text{-}\check{\imath}$, and $i\text{-}\check{2}$ are now to be added, whose intersections with each other and with I are parallel to $\dot{c}$. The position of one edge, $I/i\text{-}\check{2}$, having been taken, that of the other on the other side is determined by the point where a line parallel to

470   APPENDIX.

the axis $\bar{b}$ meets the basal edge of the prism. Similarly the position of the same prismatic edges behind are given by the intersection of lines from front to rear parallel to the axis $\breve{a}$.

The prisms drawn, it remains to add the terminal planes, and as they thus modify one another's position, they are drawn together. The required intersection-lines are easily obtained. The macrodome 1-$\bar{i}$ is the plane passing through the point c and intersecting the horizontal plane in the line paq; this line is obviously the direction of its intersection-edge with i-$\bar{i}$ and with O. The prism i-$\check{2}$ appears (f. 820) as the two lines mm', nn'; the line mm' produced beyond m meets paq at z, this will be one common point for the two planes 1-$\bar{i}$ and i-$\check{2}$; the second common point is, as always, the point c, hence the line joining these two points, transferred to the crystal in the way described, gives the required intersection-edge for i-$\check{2}$ and 1-$\bar{i}$. Similarly for i-$\check{2}$ on the right, the two points of intersection are c, and the point where $n'n$ and qap, produced, meet, and this gives the second intersection-edge. The planes 1-$\bar{i}$ and 1 (right) meet at d and c; hence the line cd gives the direction of their intersection-edge, which is also the direction of that of 1-$\bar{i}$ and 1 (left), and of 1 and 2-$\check{2}$, right and left on both sides. Still again, the plane 2-$\check{2}$ has the full symbol $2\frac{1}{2}$: $\bar{b}$: $2\bar{i}$, or $\dot{c}$: $\frac{1}{2}\bar{b}$: $\breve{a}$; and hence intersects the horizontal plane (f. 820) in the lines as (right), at (left), and $a'q$, $a'p$ (behind). Hence the intersection-edge of I, 2-$\check{2}$, 1-$\bar{i}$ has the direction of the line joining the points c and s (right), and similarly to the left and behind. The intersection-edge of 2-$\check{2}$ front, and 2-$\check{2}$ behind, has the direction of the line joining the points c and x (right) and c and y (left).

The method of obtaining the intersection-edges of the planes will be clear from this example. Practical facility in drawing figures by this or any other method is only to be obtained by practice.

821

It will be found that at almost every step there is an opportunity to test the accuracy of the work—thus every point of intersection on the basal plane behind must lie on a line drawn from the corresponding point in front on the basal plane, in the direction of the axis $\breve{a}$; so, too, the point of intersection of 2-$\check{2}$ and I (front), 2-$\check{2}$ and I (behind), on one side, must be in the line of the horizontal axis ($\bar{b}$) with that on the other side, and similarly in other cases.

If it were required, as is generally necessary, to complete the form (f. 821) below, it is unnecessary to obtain any new intersection lines, since every line above has its corresponding line opposite and parallel to it below. Moreover, in an orthorhombic crystal every point above has a corresponding point below on a line parallel to the vertical axis. This, as above, will serve as a control of the accuracy of the work.

There is another method of drawing complex crystalline forms which has many advantages and is sometimes to be preferred to any other; it can be explained in a very few words. After the axes have been obtained the diametral prism is constructed upon them. Upon the solid angles of this each plane of the required form is laid off, the edges being taken instead of the

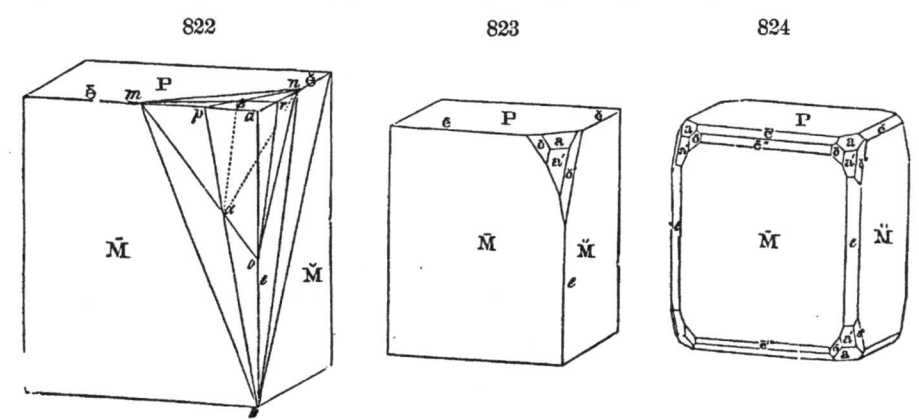

822   823   824

axes. Suppose that f. 822 represents the diametral prism of an orthorhombic crystal. Here obviously the edge $e = 2\dot{c}$, $\bar{e} = 2\bar{b}$, $\check{e} = 2\bar{\imath}$. The plane 1 ($\dot{c}$: $\bar{b}$: $\breve{a}$) may be laid off on it by taking from the angle a equal portions of the edges e, $\bar{e}$, $\check{e}$, for instance, conveniently one

ON THE DRAWING OF FIGURES OF CRYSTALS. 471

half of each, hence the plane appears as mno. Again the plane 2 ($2\dot{c} : \bar{b} : \breve{a}$) is laid off by taking the unit lengths of the edges $\bar{e}$ ($\bar{b}$), and $\breve{e}$ ($\breve{a}$) and twice the unit length of e ($\dot{c}$), the plane is then mnb. Again, the plane 4-$\breve{2}$ ($4\dot{c} : \bar{b} : 2\breve{\imath}$) takes the position npb, since $ap = 2\dot{c}$, $ap = \frac{1}{2}\bar{b}$, and $an = \breve{a}$, the ratio of the edges (axes) being the same as in the symbol. So also the plane 2-$\breve{2}$ ($2\dot{c} : 2\bar{b} : \breve{a}$) has the position rmo, since $ao = \dot{c}$, $am = \bar{b}$, and $ar = \frac{1}{2}\breve{\imath}$, here, too, the ratio of the axes being preserved. By plotting the successive planes of the crystal in this way, each solid angle corresponding to an octant, the direction of the intersection-edges for the given form are at once obtained. For example, the intersection-edge for 1, and the basal plane, as also for 1 and 2, it is the line mn; for 1 and 4-$\breve{2}$ it is the dotted line joining the common points n and a; for 1 and 2-$\breve{2}$ it is the line mo; for 2 and 4-$\breve{2}$, also for 2 and 2-$\breve{2}$, it is the line joining the common points βa.

The direction of the required intersection-edges being obtained in this way, they are used to construct the crystal itself, being transferred to it in the usual way. In f. 823 they have been placed upon the diametral prism, and when this process has been completed for the other angles, and, too, the domes $\bar{e}'$, $\breve{e}'$, are added, the form in f. 824 results.

ON THE DRAWING OF TWIN CRYSTALS.

In order to project a compound or twinned crystal it is generally necessary to obtain first the axes of the second individual, or semi-individual, in the position in which they are brought by the revolution of 180°. This is accomplished in the following manner. In f. 825 a compound crystal of staurolite is represented, in which twinning has taken place (1) on an axis normal to $\frac{3}{2}$-$\breve{\imath}$, and (2) on an axis normal to $\frac{3}{2}$-$\breve{\frac{3}{2}}$. The second, being the more general case, is of the greater importance for the sake of example. In f. 825, cc', bb', aa' represent the rectangular axes of staurolite ($\dot{c} = 1\cdot 441$, $\bar{b} = 2\cdot 112$, $\breve{a} = 1$). The twinning-plane $\frac{3}{2}$-$\breve{\frac{3}{2}}$ ($\frac{3}{2}\dot{c} : -\bar{b} : \frac{3}{2}\breve{a}$)

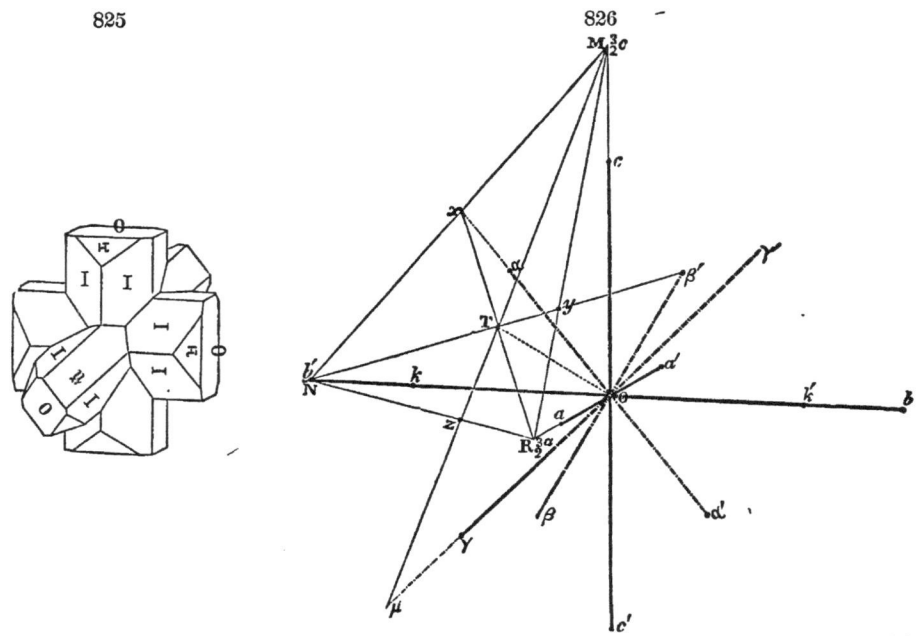

825   826

has the position MNR. It is first necessary to construct a normal from the centre O to this plane. If perpendiculars be drawn from the centre O to the lines MN, NR, MR, they will meet them at the points x, y, z, dividing each line into segments proportional to the squares of the adjacent axes;* or $\mathrm{N}x : \mathrm{M}x = \overline{\mathrm{ON}}^2 : \overline{\mathrm{OM}}^2$. In this way the points x, y, z are fixed, and lines

---

* This is true since the axial angles are right angles. In the Monoclinic System two of the axial intersections are perpendicular, and they are sufficient to allow of the determination of the point T, as above. In the Triclinic System the method needs to be slightly modified.

472   APPENDIX.

drawn from any two of them to the opposite angles R, N, or M will fix the point T. A line joining T and O is normal to the plane (MNR = $\frac{2}{2}$-$\bar{\frac{3}{2}}$). Furthermore, it is obvious that if a revolution of 180° about TO take place, that every point in the plane MNR will remain equally distant from T. Thus, the point M will take the place μ(MT = Tμ), the point b' the place β' (NT = Tβ'), and so on. The lines joining these points μ, β', x, and the common centre O will be the new axes corresponding to MO, NO, RO. In order to obtain the unit axes corresponding to $\dot{c}$, $\bar{b}$, $\dot{a}$ it is merely necessary to draw through c a line parallel to MTμ, meeting μO at γ, then γOγ' is the new vertical axis corresponding to cOc', also βOβ' corresponds to bOb', and aOa' corresponds to aOa'. These three axes then are the axes for the second individual in its twinned position; upon them, in the usual way, the new figure may be constructed and then transferred to its proper position with reference to the normal crystal.

For the second method of twinning, when the axis is normal to $\frac{2}{3}$-$\check{i}$, the construction is more simple. It is obvious the axis is the line Ox, and using this, as before, the new axes are found; κOκ' corresponds to cOc' (sensibly coinciding with bb'), since $O \wedge \frac{2}{3}$-$\check{i}$ = 134° 21', and so on.

In many cases the simplest method is to construct first the normal crystal, then draw through its centre the twinning-plane and the axis of revolution, and determine the angular points of the reversed crystal in the principle alluded to above: that by the revolution every point remains at the same distance from the axis, measured in a plane at right angle to the axis.

827

Calcite.

Thus in f. 827 when the scalenohedron has been drawn, since the twinning-plane is the basal plane, each angular point, by the revolution of 180°, obtains a position equidistant from this plane and directly below it. In this way each angular point is determined, and the compound crystal is completed in a moment.

APPENDIX C.

CATALOGUE OF AMERICAN LOCALITIES OF MINERALS.

The following catalogue * may aid the mineralogical tourist in selecting his routes and arranging the plan of his journeys. Only important localities, which have afforded cabinet specimens, are in general included; and the *names of those minerals which have been obtained in good specimens are distinguished by italics*, the addition of an exclamation mark (!), or of two (!!), indicates the degree of excellence of the specimens. Many of the localities mentioned have been exhausted, others will now yield good specimens only when further explored with blasting, etc. In general, only those of the localities mentioned can be relied upon as likely to reward the visitor liberally where active work is being continually carried on.

MAINE.

ALBANY.—*Beryl! green and black tourmaline, feldspar, rose quartz*, rutile.
AROOSTOOK.—Red hematite.
AUBURN.—*Lepidolite, amblygonite (hebronite), green tourmaline.*
BATH.—Vesuvianite, *garnet*, magnetite, graphite.
BETHEL.—*Cinnamon garnet*, calcite, sphene, beryl, pyroxene, hornblende, epidote, graphite, talc, pyrite, arsenopyrite, magnetite, wad.
BINGHAM.—*Massive pyrite*, galenite, blende, andalusite.
BLUE HILL BAY.—*Arsenical iron, molybdenite! galenite, apatite! fluorite!* black tourmaline (Long Cove), black oxide of manganese (Osgood's farm), rhodonite, bog manganese. wolframite.
BOWDOIN.—*Rose quartz.*
BOWDOINHAM.—*Beryl*, molybdenite.
BRUNSWICK.—*Green mica, garnet! black tourmaline!* molybdenite, epidote, *calcite, muscovite, feldspar*, beryl.
BUCKFIELD.—*Garnet* (estates of Waterman and Lowe), iron ore, *muscovite! tourmaline!* magnetite.
CAMDAGE FARM.—(Near the tide mills), molybdenite, wolframite
CAMDEN.—*Macle*, galenite, epidote, black tourmaline, pyrite, talc, magnetite.
CARMEL (Penobscot Co.).—Stibnite, pyrite, macle.
CORINNA.—*Pyrite*, arsenopyrite.
DEER ISLE.—*Serpentine, verd-antique*, asbestus, diallage, magnetite.
DEXTER.—Galenite, pyrite, blende, chalcopyrite, green talc.
DIXFIELD.—Native copperas, graphite.
EAST WOODSTOCK.—Muscovite.
FARMINGTON.—(Norton's ledge), *pyrite*, graphite, bog ore, garnet, staurolite.
FREEPORT.—*Rose quartz, garnet*, feldspar, scapolite, graphite, *muscovite*.
FRYEBURG.—*Garnet*, beryl.
GEORGETOWN.—(Parker's island), *beryl!* black tourmaline.
GREENWOOD.—Graphite, black manganese, *beryl! arsenopyrite*, cassiterite, *mica, rose quartz, garnet*, corundum, albite, zircon, molybdenite, magnetite, copperas.

---

* The catalogue is essentially the same as that published in the 5th Edition of Dana's System of Mineralogy, 1868. The names of a considerable number of new localities have been added, however, which have been derived from various printed sources, and also from private contributions from Prof. G. J. Brush, Mr. G. W. Hawes, Mr. J. Willcox, and others.
See further on pp. 503 to 508.

HEBRON.—*Cassiterite*, arsenopyrite, idocrase, *lepidolite*, *amblygonite* (*hebronite*), *rubellite !* indicolite, *green tourmaline*, mica, beryl, apatite, albite, childrenite, cookcite.
JEWELL'S ISLAND.—Pyrite.
KATAHDIN IRON WORKS.—Bog-iron ore, pyrite, magnetite. quartz.
LETTER E, Oxford Co.—Staurolite, macle, copperas.
LINNÆUS.—Hematite, limonite, *pyrite*, bog-iron ore.
LITCHFIELD.—*Sodalite, cancrinite, elæolite, zircon,* spodumene, muscovite, pyrrhotite.
LUBEC LEAD MINES.—*Galenite, chalcopyrite, blende.*
MACHIASPORT.—*Jasper,* epidote, laumontite.
MADAWASKA SETTLEMENTS.—*Vivianite.*
MINOT.—*Beryl smoky quartz.*
MONMOUTH.—Actinolite, apatite, *elæolite, zircon,* staurolite, plumose mica, beryl, rutile.
MT. ABRAHAM.—*Andalusite,* staurolite.
NORWAY.—*Chrysoberyl !* molybdenite, *beryl, rose quartz, orthoclase,* cinnamon garnet.
ORR'S ISLAND.—*Steatite,* garnet andalusite.
OXFORD.—*Garnet, beryl,* apatite, wad, zircon, *muscovite, orthoclase.*
PARIS.—*Green ! red ! black,* and *blue tourmaline ! mica ! lepidolite !* feldspar, *albite, quartz crystals ! rose quartz, cassiterite, amblygonite,* zircon, brookite, beryl, smoky quartz, spodumene, *cookcite,* leucopyrite.
PARSONSFIELD.—*Vesuvianite ! yellow garnet, pargasite, adularia, scapolite,* galenite, blende. chalcopyrite.
PERU—*Crystallized pyrite.*
PHIPPSBURG.—*Yellow garnet ! manganesian garnet, vesuvianite, pargasite, axinite, laumontite !* chabazite, an ore of cerium ?
POLAND.—Vesuvianite, smoky quartz, cinnamon garnet.
PORTLAND.—*Prehnite,* actinolite, garnet, epidote, amethyst, calcite.
POWNAL.—*Black tourmaline, feldspar,* scapolite, pyrite. actinolite, apatite, rose quartz.
RAYMOND.—*Magnetite, scapolite, pyroxene, lepidolite, tremolite,* hornblende, epidote, orthoclase, yellow garnet, pyrite, vesuvianite.
ROCKLAND.—Hematite, tremolite, *quartz,* wad, *talc.*
RUMFORD.—*Yellow garnet, vesuvianite, pyroxene,* apatite, scapolite, graphite.
RUTLAND.—Allanite.
SANDY RIVER.—Auriferous sand.
SANFORD, York Co.—*Vesuvianite !* albite, calcite, molybdenite, epidote, black tourmaline, labradorite.
SEARSMONT.—*Andalusite,* tourmaline.
SOUTH BERWICK.—Macle.
STANDISH.—*Columbite !*
STREAKED MOUNTAIN.—*Beryl ! black tourmaline, mica, garnet.*
THOMASTON.—*Calcite, tremolite, hornblende,* sphene, arsenical iron (Owl's head), black manganese (Dodge's mountain), *thomsonite, talc,* blende, pyrite, galenite.
TOPSHAM.—*Quartz,* galenite, blende, tungstite ? beryl, apatite, molybdenite, columbite.
UNION.—Magnetite, bog-iron ore.
WALES.—Axinite in boulder, alum, copperas.
WATERVILLE—*Crystallized pyrite.*
WINDHAM (near the bridge).—*Staurolite, spodumene, garnet,* beryl, amethyst, *cyanite,* tourmaline.
WINSLOW.—Cassiterite.
WINTHROP.—*Staurolite,* pyrite, hornblende, garnet, copperas.
WOODSTOCK.—*Graphite,* hematite, prehnite, epidote, calcite.
YORK.—*Beryl,* vivianite,, oxide of manganese.

NEW HAMPSHIRE.

ACWORTH.—*Beryl ! ! mica ! tourmaline, feldspar, albite, rose quartz, columbite !* cyanite, autunite.
ALSTEAD.—*Mica ! !* albite, *black tourmaline,* molybdenite, andalusite, staurolite.
AMHERST.—*Vesuvianite, yellow garnet,* pargasite, calcite, amethyst, magnetite.
BARTLETT.—Magnetite, hematite, brown iron ore in large veins near Jackson (on "Bald face mountain"), *quartz crystals, smoky quartz.*
BATH.—Galenite, chalcopyrite.
BEDFORD.—Tremolite, epidote, graphite, mica, tourmaline, alum, quartz.
BELLOWS FALLS.—Cyanite, staurolite, wavellite.
BRISTOL.—*Graphite.*

CAMPTON.—*Beryl!*
CANAAN.—Gold in pyrites, garnet.
CHARLESTON.—*Staurolite macle, andalusite macle,* bog-iron ore, prehnite, cyanite.
CORNISH.—Stibnite, tetrahedrite, *rutile in quartz!* (rare), *staurolite.*
CROYDEN.—*Iolite!* chalcopyrite, pyrite, pyrrhotite, blende.
ENFIELD.—Gold, galenite, staurolite, green quartz.
FRANCESTON.—*Soapstone,* arsenopyrite, quartz crystals.
FRANCONIA.—*Hornblende, staurolite! epidote! zoisite, hematite, magnetite, black* and *red manganesian garnets,* arsenopyrite (*danaite*), chalcopyrite, molybdenite, prehnite, green quartz, malachite, azurite.
GILFORD (Gunstock Mt.).—Magnetic iron ore, native "loadstone."
GOSHEN.—*Graphite,* black tourmaline.
GILMANTOWN.—Tremolite, epidote, muscovite, tourmaline, limonite, red and yellow quartz crystals.
GRAFTON.—*Mica!* (extensively quarried at Glass Hill, 2 m. S. of Orange Summit), *albite!* blue, green, and yellow *beryls!* (1 m. S. of O. Summit), *tourmaline, garnets, triphylite,* apatite, fluorite.
GRANTHAM.—*Gray staurolite!*
GROTON.—Arsenopyrite, blue beryl, muscovite crystals.
HANOVER.—*Garnet,* a boulder of quartz containing *rutile! black tourmaline, quartz, cyanite, labradorite,* epidote.
HAVERHILL.—*Garnet!* arsenopyrite, *native arsenic,* galenite, blende, pyrite, chalcopyrite, magnetite, marcasite, steatite.
HILLSBORO' (Campbel.'s mountain).—*Graphite.*
HINSDALE.—*Rhodonite,* black oxide of manganese, molybdenite, indicolite, black tourmaline.
JACKSON.—Drusy quartz, tin ore, *arsenopyrite,* native arsenic, fluorite, apatite, *magnetite, molybdenite,* wolframite, chalcopyrite, arsenate of iron.
JAFFREY (Monadnock Mt.).—*Cyanite,* limonite.
KEENE.—*Graphite,* soapstone, milky quartz, rose quartz.
LANDAFF.—*Molybdenite,* lead and iron ores.
LEBANON.—*Bog-iron ore,* arsenopyrite, galenite, magnetite, pyrite.
LISBON.—*Staurolite,* black and red *garnets, granular magnetite, hornblende, epidote, zoisite,* hematite, arsenopyrite, galenite, gold, ankerite.
LITTLETON.—Ankerite, gold, bornite, chalcopyrite, malachite, menaccanite, chlorite.
LYMAN.—Gold, arsenopyrite, ankerite, dolomite, galenite, pyrite, copper, pyrrhotite.
LYME.—*Cyanite* (N. W. part), *black tourmaline,* rutile, pyrite, chalcopyrite (E. of E. village), *stibnite,* molybdenite, cassiterite.
MADISON.—*Galenite, blende,* chalcopyrite, limonite.
MERRIMACK.—*Rutile!* (in gneiss nodules in granite vein).
MIDDLETOWN.—*Rutile.*
MONADNOCK MOUNTAIN.—Andalusite, hornblende, garnet, graphite, tourmaline, orthoclase.
MOOSILAUKE MT.—*Tourmaline.*
MOULTONBOROUGH (Red Hill).—*Hornbende,* bog ore, pyrite, tourmaline.
NEWINGTON.—Garnet, tourmaline.
NEW LONDON.—Beryl, *molybdenite,* muscovite crystals.
NEWPORT.—Molybdenite.
ORANGE.—*Blue beryls!* Orange Summit, chrysoberyl, *mica* (W. side of mountain), apatite, galenite, limonite.
ORFORD.—*Brown tourmaline* (now obtained with difficulty), *steatite, rutile,* cyanite, brown iron ore, native copper, malachite, galenite, garnet, graphite, molybdenite, pyrrhotite, melaconite, chalcocite, *ripidolite.*
PELHAM.—*Steatite.*
PIERMONT.—*Micaceous iron,* barite, green, white, and brown mica, apatite, titanic iron.
PLYMOUTH.—Columbite, beryl.
RICHMOND.—*Iolite!* rutile, steatite, pyrite, anthophyllite, talc.
RYE.—Chiastolite.
SADDLEBACK MT.—Black tourmaline, garnet, spinel.
SHELBURNE.—*Galenite, black blende, chalcopyrite, pyrite,* pyrolusite.
SPRINGFIELD.—Beryls (very large, eight inches diameter), *manganesian garnets! black tourmaline!* in mica slate, *albite, mica.*
SULLIVAN.—*Tourmaline* (black), in quartz, beryl.
SURREY.—Amethyst, calcite, galenite, limonite, tourmaline.
SWANZEY (near Keene).—*Magnetic iron* (in masses in granite).

TAMWORTH (near White Pond).—Galenite.
UNITY (estate of James Neal).—*Copper and iron pyrites, chlorophyllite, green mica, radiated actinolite*, garnet, *titaniferous iron ore, magnetite,* tourmaline.
WALPOLE (near Bellows Falls).—Macle, staurolite, mica, graphite.
WARE.—Graphite.
WARREN.—*Chalcopyrite, blende, epidote,* quartz, *pyrite,* tremolite, galenite, rutile, talc, molybdenite, *cinnamon stone! pyroxene,* hornblende, *beryl,* cyanite, tourmaline (massive).
WATERVILLE.—Labradorite, chrysolite.
WESTMORELAND (south part).—*Molybdenite! apatite! blue feldspar, bog manganese* (north village), quartz, *fluorite,* chalcopyrite, oxide of molybdenum and uranium.
WHITE MTS. (Notch near the "Crawford House").—Green octahedral fluorite, quartz crystals, black tourmaline, chiastolite, beryl, calcite, amethyst, amazonstone.
WILMOT.—*Beryl.*
WINCHESTER.—Pyrolusite, rhodochrosite, psilomelane, magnetite, granular quartz, spodumene.

VERMONT.

ADDISON.—*Iron sand,* pyrite.
ALBURGH.—Quartz crystals on calcite, pyrite.
ATHENS.—*Steatite, rhomb spar,* actinolite, garnet.
BALTIMORE.—*Serpentine, pyrite!*
BARNET.—Graphite.
BELVIDERE.—Steatite, chlorite.
BENNINGTON.—*Pyrolusite,* brown iron ore, pipe clay, yellow ochre.
BERKSHIRE.—*Epidote,* hematite, magnetite.
BETHEL.—*Actinolite!* talc, chlorite, octahedral iron, *rutile, brown spar in steatite.*
BRANDON.—Braunite, pyrolusite, *psilomelane,* limonite, lignite, white clay, statuary marble; fossil fruits in the lignite, graphite, chalcopyrite.
BRATTLEBOROUGH.—Black tourmaline in quartz, mica, zoisite, rutile, actinolite, scapolite, spodumene, roofing slate.
BRIDGEWATER.—*Talc, dolomite, magnetite,* steatite, chlorite, gold, native copper, blende, galenite, blue spinel, chalcopyrite.
BRISTOL.—*Rutile,* limonite, manganese ores, magnetite.
BROOKFIELD.—Arsenopyrite, *pyrite.*
CABOT.—Garnet, staurolite, hornblende, *albite.*
CASTLETON.—*Roofing slate,* jasper, manganese ores, chlorite.
CAVENDISH.—Garnet, *serpentine, talc, steatite, tourmaline, asbestus, tremolite.*
CHESTER.—*Asbestus,* feldspar, chlorite, *quartz.*
CHITTENDEN.—Psilomelane, pyrolusite, brown iron ore, *hematite* and *magnetite,* galenite, iolite.
COLCHESTER.—Brown iron ore, iron sand, jasper, alum.
CORINTH.—Chalcopyrite (has been mined), pyrrhotite, pyrite, rutile, quartz.
COVENTRY.—Rhodonite.
CRAFTSBURY.—Mica in concentric balls, calcite, rutile.
DERBY.—Mica (*adamsite*).
DUMMERSTON.—Rutile, roofing slate.
FAIR HAVEN.—*Roofing slate,* pyrite.
FLETCHER.—Pyrite, magnetite, acicular tourmaline.
GRAFTON.—The *steatite* quarry referred to Grafton is properly in Athens; *quartz,* actinolite.
GUILFORD.—Scapolite, rutile, roofing slate.
HARTFORD.—Calcite, *pyrite! cyanite* in mica slate, quartz, tourmaline.
IRASBURGH.—Rhodonite, *psilomelane.*
JAY.—*Chromic iron, serpentine,* amianthus, dolomite.
LOWELL.—Picrosmine, amianthus, serpentine, cerolite, talc, chlorite.
MARLBORO'.—*Rhomb spar, steatite,* garnet, *magnetite,* chlorite.
MENDON.—Magnetic iron ore.
MIDDLEBURY.—Zircon.
MIDDLESEX.—Rutile! (exhausted).
MONKTON.—*Pyrolusite,* brown iron ore, pipe clay, feldspar.
MORETOWN.—*Smoky quartz! steatite,* talc, wad, rutile, serpentine.
MORRISTOWN.—Galenite.
MOUNT HOLLY.—*Asbestus,* chlorite.
NEW FANE.—*Glassy* and *asbestiform actinolite, steatite, green quartz* (called chrysoprase

at the locality), chalcedony, drusy quartz, *garnet, chromic and titanic iron, rhomb spar*, serpentine, rutile.
NORWICH.—*Actinolite. feldspar, brown spar* in talc, cyanite, zoisite, chalcopyrite, pyrite.
PITTSFORD.—*Brown iron ore*, manganese ores.
PLYMOUTH.—Siderite, magnetite, hematite, *gold*, galenite.
PLYMPTON.—Massive hornblende.
PUTNEY.—Fluorite, *brown iron ore, rutile*, and *zoisite*, in boulders, staurolite.
READING.—*Glassy actinolite* in talc.
READSBORO'.—*Glassy actinolite, steatite*, hematite.
RIPTON.—*Brown iron ore*, augite in boulders, octahedral pyrite.
ROCHESTER.—Rutile, hematite cryst., *magnetite* in chlorite slate.
ROCKINGHAM (Bellows Falls).—Cyanite, indicolite, feldspar, tourmaline, fluorite, calcite, prehnite, staurolite.
ROXBURY.—*Dolomite, talc*, serpentine, asbestus, quartz.
RUTLAND.—*Magnesite, white marble*, hematite, serpentine, pipe clay.
SALISBURY.—Brown iron ore.
SHARON.—*Quartz crystals*, cyanite.
SHOREHAM.—*Pyrite*, black marble. calcite.
SHREWSBURY.—Magnetite and chalcopyrite.
STARKSBORO'.—Brown iron ore.
STIRLING.—Chalcopyrite, talc, serpentine.
STOCKBRIDGE—Arsenopyrite, magnetite.
STRAFFORD.—Magnetite and *chalcopyrite* (has been worked), native copper, hornblende, copperas.
THETFORD.—Blende, *galenite, cyanite*, chrysolite in basalt, pyrrhotite, *feldspar, roofing slate*, steatite, garnet.
TOWNSHEND.—*Actinolite*, black mica, *talc*, steatite, feldspar.
TROY.—*Magnetite*, talc, serpentine, picrosmine, amianthus, *steatite*, one mile southeast of village of South Troy, on the farm of Mr. Pierce, east side of Missisco, chromite, zaratite.
VERSHIRE.—*Pyrite*, chalcopyrite, tourmaline, arsenopyrite, quartz.
WARDSBORO'.—*Zoisite*, tourmaline, *tremolite*, hematite.
WARREN.—Actinolite, magnetite, wad, serpentine.
WATERBURY.—Arsenopyrite, chalcopyrite, *rutile, quartz*, serpentine.
WATERVILLE.—*Steatite*, actinolite, talc.
WEATHERSFIELD.—*Steatite*, hematite, *pyrite*, tremolite.
WELLS' RIVER.—Graphite.
WESTFIELD.—*Steatite*. chromite, serpentine.
WESTMINSTER.—Zoisite in boulders.
WINDHAM.—*Glassy actinolite, steatite, garnet*, serpentine.
WOODBURY.—Massive pyrite.
WOODSTOCK.—*Quartz crystals*, garnet, zoisite.

MASSACHUSETTS.

ALFORD.—Galenite, pyrite.
ATHOL.—*Allanite*, fibrolite (?), *epidote!* babingtonite?
AUBURN.—*Masonite.*
BARRE.—*Rutile! mica, pyrite, beryl, feldspar, garnet*.
GREAT BARRINGTON.—*Tremolite*.
BEDFORD.—*Garnet*.
BELCHERTON.—Allanite.
BERNARDSTON.—Magnetite.
BEVERLY.—Columbite, *green feldspar*, cassiterite.
BLANFORD.—*Serpentine*, anthophyllite, *actinolite! chromite*, cyanite, rose quartz in boulders.
BOLTON.—*Scapolite! petalite, sphene, pyroxene, nuttalite, diopside, boltonite*, apatite, magnesite, rhomb spar, *allanite, yttrocerite!* cerium ochre? (on the scapolite), spinel.
BOXBOROUGH.—*Scapolite*, spinel, *garnet*, augite, actinolite, apatite.
BRIGHTON.—Asbestus.
BRIMFIELD (road leading to Warren).—*Iolite*, adularia, molybdenite, mica, garnet.
CARLISLE.—*Tourmaline, garnet! scapolite*, actinolite.
CHARLESTOWN.—*Prehnite, laumontite*, stilbite, chabazite, quartz crystals, melanolite.
CHELMSFORD.—*Scapolite* (chelmsfordite), *chondrodite, blue spinel, amianthus!* rose quartz.

478   APPENDIX.

CHESTER.—*Hornblende, scapolite, zoisite, spodumene, indicolite*, apatite, magnetite, chromite, stilbite, heulandite, analcite and chabazite. At the Emery Mine, Chester Factories.—*Corundum, margarite, diaspore*, epidote, corundophilite, chloritoid, tourmaline, *menaccanite!* rutile, biotite, indianite? andesite? *cyanite*, amesite.

CHESTERFIELD.—*Blue, green, and red tourmaline, cleavelandite* (albite), lepidolite, *smoky, quartz, microlite, spodumene, cyanite,* apatite, *rose beryl, garnet, quartz crystals, staurolite,* cassiterite, *columbite,* zoisite, uranite, brookite (eumanite), scheelite, anthophyllite, bornite.

CONWAY.—Pyrolusite, fluorite, zoisite, *rutile!!* native alum, galenite.

CUMMINGTON.—*Rhodonite!* cummingtonite (hornblende), marcasite, *garnet.*

DEDHAM.—Asbestus, galenite.

DEERFIELD.—Chabazite, heulandite, stilbite, amethyst, carnelian, chalcedony, *agate.*

FITCHBURG (Pearl Hill).—*Beryl, staurolite!* garnets, molybdenite.

FOXBOROUGH.—*Pyrite,* anthracite.

FRANKLIN.—Amethyst.

GOSHEN.—*Mica, albite, spodumene! blue and green tourmaline, beryl, zoisite,* smoky quartz, columbite, tin ore, galenite, beryl (goshenite), pihlite (cymatolite).

GREENFIELD (in sandstone quarry, half mile east of village).—Allophane, white and greenish.

HATFIELD.—Barite, yellow quartz crystals, galenite, blende, chalcopyrite.

HAWLEY.—*Micaceous iron,* massive pyrite, magnetite, zoisite.

HEATH.—*Pyrite, zoisite.*

HINSDALE.—Brown iron ore, apatite, zoisite.

HUBBARDSTON.—*Massive pyrite.*

LANCASTER.—*Cyanite, chiastolite!* apatite, staurolite, pinite, andalusite.

LEE.—*Tremolite! sphene!* (east part).

LENOX.—Brown hematite, gibbsite(?)

LEVERETT.—Barite, galenite, blende, chalcopyrite.

LEYDEN.—*Zoisite, rutile.*

LITTLEFIELD.—Spinel, scapolite, apatite.

LYNNFIELD.—Magnesite on serpentine.

MARTHA'S VINEYARD.—Brown iron ore, amber, selenite, radiated pyrite.

MENDON.—*Mica!* chlorite.

MIDDLEFIELD.—*Glassy actinolite, rhomb spar, steatite, serpentine, feldspar,* drusy quartz, apatite, zoisite, nacrite, chalcedony, *talc!* deweylite.

MILBURY.—*Vermiculite.*

MONTAGUE.—Hematite.

NEWBURY.—*Serpentine,* chrysotile, *epidote, massive garnet,* siderite.

NEWBURYPORT.—*Serpentine, nemalite,* uranite.—Argentiferous galenite, tetrahedrite, chalcopyrite, pyrargyrite, etc.

NEW BRAINTREE.—*Black tourmaline.*

NORWICH.—*Apatite! black tourmaline, beryl, spodumene! triphylite* (altered), blende, quartz crystals, cassiterite.

NORTHFIELD.—*Columbite,* fibrolite, cyanite.

PALMER (Three Rivers).—*Feldspar,* prehnite, calc spar.

PELHAM.—*Asbestus,* serpentine, *quartz crystals,* beryl, *molybdenite, green hornstone,* epidote, amethyst, corundum, vermiculite (pelhamite).

PLAINFIELD.—*Cummingtonite, pyrolusite,* rhodonite.

RICHMOND.—*Brown iron ore, gibbsite! allophane.*

ROCKPORT.—*Danalite, cryophyllite, annite, cyrtolite* (altered zircon), *green and white orthoclase.*

ROWE.—Epidote, talc.

SOUTH ROYALSTON.—*Beryl!!* (now obtained with great difficulty), *mica!! feldspar!* allanite. Four miles beyond old loc., on farm of Solomon Heywood, *mica! beryl! feldspar! menaccanite.*

RUSSEL.—Schiller spar (diallage?), *mica,* serpentine, beryl, galenite, chalcopyrite.

SALEM.—In a boulder, cancrinite, sodalite, elæolite.

SAUGUS.—Porphyry, jasper.

SHEFFIELD.—*Asbestus,* pyrite, native alum, pyrolusite, rutile.

SHELBURNE.—Rutile.

SHUTESBURY (east of Locke's Pond).—*Molybdenite.*

SOUTHAMPTON.—*Galenite,* cerussite, anglesite, *wulfenite,* fluorite, barite, pyrite, chalcopyrite, blende, corneous lead, pyromorphite, stolzite, chrysocolla.

STERLING.—*Spodumene, chiastolite,* siderite, arsenopyrite, *blende,* galenite, chalcopyrite, pyrite, sterlingite (damourite).

STONEHAM.—*Nephrite.*

AMERICAN LOCALITIES.

STURBRIDGE.—*Graphite*, garnet, apatite, bog ore.
SWAMPSCOT.—*Orthite*, feldspar.
TAUNTON (one mile south).—Paracolumbite (titanic iron).
TURNER'S FALLS (Conn. River).—Chalcopyrite, prehnite, chlorite, *chlorophæite*, siderite malachite, magnetic iron sand, anthracite.
TYRINGHAM.—Pyroxene, scapolite.
UXBRIDGE.—Galenite.
WARWICK.—*Massive garnet, radiated black tourmaline, magnetite*, beryl, epidote.
WASHINGTON.—*Graphite*.
WESTFIELD.—*Schiller spar* (diallage), *serpentine, steatite*, cyanite, scapolite, actinolite.
WESTFORD.—*Andalusite!*
WEST HAMPTON.—Galenite, *argentine, pseudomorphous quartz*.
WEST SPRINGFIELD.—*Prehnite*, ankerite, satin spar, celestite, bituminous coal.
WEST STOCKBRIDGE.—*Hematite*, fibrous pyrolusite, siderite.
WHATELY.—*Native copper*, galenite.
WILLIAMSBURG.—*Zoisite*, pseudomorphous quartz, apatite, rose and smoky quartz, galenite, pyrolusite, chalcopyrite.
WILLIAMSTOWN.—*Cryst. quartz*.
WINDSOR.—*Zoisite*, actinolite, *rutile!*
WORCESTER.—Arsenopyrite, idocrase, pyroxene, garnet, amianthus, bucholzite, siderite, galenite.
WORTHINGTON.—*Cyanite*.
ZOAR.—Bitter spar, *talc*.

RHODE ISLAND.

BRISTOL.—*Amethyst*.
COVENTRY.—Mica, tourmaline.
CRANSTON.—Actinolite in talc, graphite, cyanite, mica, melanterite, bog iron.
CUMBERLAND.—*Manganese, epidote, actinolite*, garnet, titaniferous iron, magnetite, red hematite, chalcopyrite, bornite, malachite, azurite, calcite, apatite, feldspar, zoisite, mica, quartz crystals, ilvaite.
DIAMOND HILL.—Quartz crystals, hematite.
FOSTER.—*Cyanite*, hematite.
GLOUCESTER.—*Magnetite* in chlorite slate, feldspar.
JOHNSTON.—Talc, brown spar, calcite, garnet, epidote, pyrite, hematite, magnetite, chalcopyrite, malachite, azurite.
LIME ROCK.—Calcite crystals, quartz pyrite.
LINCOLN.—Calcite dolomite.
NATIC.—See WARWICK.
NEWPORT.—*Serpentine*, quartz crystals.
PORTSMOUTH.—*Anthracite*, graphite, asbestus, pyrite, chalcopyrite.
SMITHFIELD.—*Dolomite, calcite, bitter spar, siderite*, nacrite, serpentine (bowenite), tremolite, asbestus, quartz, magnetic iron in chlorite slate, *talc!* octahedrite, feldspar, beryl.
VALLEY FALLS.—Graphite, pyrite, hematite.
WARWICK (Natic village).—*Masonite*, garnet, graphite, bog iron ore.
WESTERLY.—Menaccanite.
WOONSOCKET.—Cyanite.

CONNECTICUT.

BERLIN.—Barite, datolite, blende, quartz crystals.
BOLTON.—Staurolite, chalcopyrite.
BRADLEYVILLE (Litchfield).—Laumontite.
BRISTOL.—*Chalcocite! chalcopyrite*, barite, *bornite*, talc, *allophane*, pyromorphite, *calcite*, malachite, galenite, quartz.
BROOKFIELD.—Galenite, calamine, *blende*, spodumene, pyrrhotite.
CANAAN.—*Tremolite* and white *augite!* in dolomite, canaanite (massive pyroxene).
CHATHAM.—Arsenopyrite, smaltite, chloanthite (chathamite), scorodite, niccolite, *beryl*, erythrite.
CHESHIRE.—*Barite, chalcocite, bornite cryst., malachite*, kaolin, natrolite, prehnite, chabasite, datolite.
CHESTER.—*Sillimanite!* zircon, epidote.

CORNWALL. — *Graphite, pyroxene, actinolite, sphene,* scapolite.
DANBURY.—*Danburite, oligoclase, moonstone,* brown tourmaline, orthoclase, pyroxene, parathorite.
FARMINGTON.—*Prehnite, chabazite,* agate, native copper; in trap, *diabantite.*
GRANBY.—Green malachite.
GREENWICH.—*Black tourmaline.*
HADDAM.—*Chrysoberyl! beryl! epidote! tourmaline! feldspar, garnet! iolite! oligoclase, chlorophyllite! automolite, magnetite, adularia,* apatite, *columbite!* (hermannolite), zircon (calyptolite), *mica,* pyrite, marcasite, *molybdenite,* allanite, bismuth, bismuth ochre, bismutite.
HADLYME.—Chabazite and stilbite in gneiss, with epidote and garnet.
HARTFORD.—*Datolite* (Rocky Hill quarry).
KENT.—*Brown iron ore,* pyrolusite, ochrey iron ore.
LITCHFIELD.—*Cyanite* with corundum, apatite, and andalusite, *menaccanite* (washingtonite), chalcopyrite, diaspore, niccoliferous pyrrhotite, margarodite.
LYME.—Garnet, sunstone.
MERIDEN.—Datolite.
MIDDLEFIELD FALLS.—Datolite, chlorite, etc., in amygdaloid.
MIDDLETOWN.—*Mica, lepidolite* with green and red tourmaline, *albite, feldspar, columbite! prehnite, garnet* (sometimes octahedral), beryl, topaz, uranite, apatite, pitchblende; at lead mine, *galenite, chalcopyrite,* blende, quartz, *calcite,* fluorite, pyrite, sometimes capillary.
MILFORD.—Sahlite, *pyroxene, asbestus,* zoisite, verd-antique, marble, pyrite.
NEW HAVEN.—Serpentine, asbestus, chromic iron, sahlite, stilbite, prehnite, chabazite, gmelinite, apophyllite, topazalite.
NEWTOWN.—*Cyanite, diaspore, rutile,* damourite, cinnabar.
NORWICH.—*Sillimanite, monazite!* zircon, *iolite,* corundum, feldspar.
OXFORD, near Humphreysville.—Cyanite, chalcopyrite.
PLYMOUTH.—Galenite, *heulandite, fluorite, chlorophyllite!* garnet.
READING (near the line of Danbury).—Pyroxene, *garnet.*
ROARING BROOK (Cheshire).—*Datolite!* calcite, prehnite, saponite.
ROXBURY.—*Siderite, blende, pyrite!! galenite,* quartz, chalcopyrite, arsenopyrite, limonite.
SALISBURY.—*Brown iron ore,* ochrey iron, *pyrolusite,* triplite, *turgite.*
SAYBROOK.—*Molybdenite,* stilbite, plumbago.
SEYMOUR.—Native bismuth, arsenopyrite, pyrite.
SIMSBURY.—*Copper glance,* green malachite.
SOUTHBURY.—Rose quartz, laumontite, prehnite, calcite, barite.
SOUTHINGTON.—Barite, datolite, asteriated quartz crystals.
STAFFORD.—Massive pyrites, alum, copperas.
STONINGTON.—Stilbite and *chabazite* on gneiss.
TARIFFVILLE.—*Datolite.*
THATCHERSVILLE (near Bridgeport).—Stilbite on gneiss, babingtonite?
TOLLAND.—Staurolite, massive pyrites.
TRUMBULL and MONROE.—*Chlorophane, topaz, beryl,* diaspore, pyrrhotite, pyrite, niccolite, scheelite, *wolframite* (pseudomorph of scheelite), rutile, native bismuth, tungstic acid, siderite, mispickel, argentiferous galenite, blende, scapolite, *tourmaline, garnet,* albite, augite, graphic tellurium (?), *margarodite.*
WASHINGTON.—*Triplite, menaccanite!* (washingtonite of Shepard), rhodochrosite, natrolite, *andalusite* (New Preston), cyanite.
WATERTOWN, near the Naugatuck.—White sahlite, monazite.
WEST FARMS.—Asbestus.
WILLIMANTIC.—*Topaz, monazite, ripidolite.*
WINCHESTER and WILTON.—Asbestus, garnet.

NEW YORK.

ALBANY CO.—BETHLEHEM.—Calcite, stalactite, stalagmite, calcareous sinter, snowy gypsum.
COEYMAN'S LANDING.—Gypsum, epsom salt, *quartz* crystals at Crystal Hill, three miles south of Albany.
GUILDERLAND.—Petroleum, anthracite, and calcite, on the banks of the Norman's Kill, two miles south of Albany.
WATERVLIET.—*Quartz crystals,* yellow drusy quartz.

ALLEGHANY CO.—CUBA.—Calcareous tufa, petroleum, 3¼ miles from the village.

CATTARAUGUS CO.—FREEDOM.—*Petroleum.*

CAYUGA CO.—AUBURN.—Celestite, calcite, fluor spar, epsomite.
CAYUGA LAKE.—Sulphur.
LUDLOWVILLE.—Epsomite.
UNION SPRINGS.—*Selenite*, gypsum.
SPRINGPORT.—At Thompson's plaster beds. *sulphur! selenite.*
SPRINGVILLE.—Nitrogen springs.

CLINTON CO.—ARNOLD IRON MINE.—*Magnetite*, epidote, molybdenite.
FINCH ORE BED.—*Calcite*, green and purple fluor.

CHATAUQUE CO.—FREDONIA.—*Petroleum, carburetted hydrogen.*
LAONA.—Petroleum.
SHERIDAN.—Alum.

COLUMBIA CO.—AUSTERLITZ.—*Earthy manganese*, wulfenite, chalcocite; Livingston lead mine, vitreous silver?
CHATHAM.—Quartz, pyrite in cubic crystals in slate (Hillsdale).
CANAAN.—Chalcocite, chalcopyrite.
HUDSON.—Epidote, *selenite!*
NEW LEBANON.—Nitrogen springs, graphite, anthracite; at the Ancram lead mine, galenite, barite, *blende, wulfenite* (rare), chalcopyrite, calcareous tufa; near the city of Hudson, epsom salt, brown spar, *wad.*

DUTCHESS CO.—AMENIA.—Dolomite, *limonite, turgite.*
BECKMAN.—*Dolomite.*
DOVER.—Dolomite, tremolite, *garnet* (Foss ore bed), staurolite. *limonite.*
FISHKILL.—Dolomite; near Peekville, talc, asbestus, *graphite, hornblende*, augite, *actinolite*, hydrous anthophyllite, *limonite.*
NORTH EAST.—Chalcocite, chalcopyrite, galenite, blende.
PAWLING.—Dolomite.
RHINEBECK.—Calcite, green feldspar, epidote, tourmaline.
UNION VALE.—At the Clove mine, *gibbsite, limonite.*

ESSEX CO.—ALEXANDRIA.—Kirby's graphite mine, *graphite, pyroxene, scapolite*, sphene.
CROWN POINT.—*Apatite* (eupyrchroite of *Emmons*), *brown tourmaline!* in the apatite, chlorite, quartz crystals, pink and blue calcite, pyrite; a short distance south of J. C. Hammond's house, *garnet, scapolite*, chalcopyrite, *aventurine feldspar*, zircon, magnetic iron (Peru), epidote, mica.
KEENE.—Scapolite.
LEWIS.—*Tabular spar, colophonite*, garnet, *labradorite, hornblende*, actinolite; ten miles south of the village of Keeseville, mispickel.
LONG POND.—Apatite, *garnet, pyroxene,* idocrase, *coccolite!! scapolite*, magnetite, *blue calcite.*
MCINTYRE.—*Labradorite*, garnet, *magnetite.*
MORIAH, at Sandford Ore Bed.—*Magnetite*, apatite, *allanite!* lanthanite, actinolite, and feldspar; at Fisher Ore Bed, *magnetic iron*, feldspar, quartz; at Hall Ore Bed, or "New Ore Bed," *magnetite, zircons;* on Mill brook, *calcite.* pyroxene, hornblende, albite; in the town of Moriah, magnetite, *black mica;* Barton Hill Ore Bed, *albite.*
NEWCOMB.—*Labradorite*, feldspar, magnetite, hypersthene.
PORT HENRY.—*Brown tourmaline, mica, rose quartz, serpentine*, green and *black pyroxene*, hornblende, *cryst. pyrite*, graphite, wollastonite, pyrrhotite, *adularia; phlogopite!* at Cheever Ore Bed, with magnetite and serpentine.
ROGER'S ROCK.—*Graphite, wollastonite, garnet, colophonite, feldspar*, adularia, *pyroxene, sphene*, coccolite.
SCHROON.—*Calcite*, pyroxene, *chondrodite.*
TICONDEROGA.—*Graphite! pyroxene, sahlite, sphene*, black tourmaline, cacoxene? (Mt Defiance).
WESTPORT.—Labradorite, prehnite, magnetite.
WILLSBORO'.—*Wollastonite, colophonite*, garnet, *green coccolite*, hornblende.

ERIE CO.—ELLICOTT'S MILLS.—*Calcareous tufas.*

482 APPENDIX.

FRANKLIN CO.— CHATEAUGAY.—Nitrogen springs, calcareous **tufas**.
MALONE.—*Massive pyrite*, magnetite.

GENESEE CO.—*Acid springs* containing sulphuric acid.

GREENE CO.—CATSKILL.—*Calcite.*
DIAMOND HILL.—Quartz crystals.

HERKIMER CO.—FAIRFIELD.—*Quartz crystals*, fetid barite.
LITTLE FALLS.—*Quartz crystals!* barite, calcite, anthracite, pearl spar, *smoky quartz,* one mile south of Little Falls, calcite. brown spar, feldspar.
MIDDLEVILLE.—*Quartz crystals!* calcite, brown and pearl spar, anthracite.
NEWPORT.—*Quartz crystals.*
SALISBURY.—*Quartz crystals!* blende, galenite, pyrite, chalcopyrite.
STARK.—Fibrous celestite, *gypsum.*

HAMILTON CO.—LONG LAKE.—Blue calcite.

JEFFERSON CO.—ADAMS.—Fluor, calc tufa, barite.
ALEXANDRIA.—On the S.E. bank of Muscolonge Lake, fluorite, *phlogopite*, chalcopyrite, apatite; on High Island, in the St. Lawrence River, feldspar, *tourmaline*, hornblende, *orthoclase,* celestite.
ANTWERP.—Stirling iron mine, hematite, *chalcodite*, siderite, *millerite,* red hematite, crystallized quartz, *yellow aragonite*, niccoliferous pyrite, *quartz crystals*, pyrite; at Oxbow, *calcite!* porous coralloidal heavy spar; near Vrooman's lake, *calcite!* vesuvianite. *phlogopite! pyroxene, sphene,* fluorite, pyrite, chalcopyrite; also *feldspar, bog-iron ore*, scapolite (farm of David Eggleson), *serpentine*, tourmaline (yellow, rare).
BROWNSVILLE.—Celestite in slender crystals, calcite (four miles from Watertown).
NATURAL BRIDGE.—Feldspar, *gieseckite! steatite pseudomorphous* after pyroxene, apatite.
NEW CONNECTICUT.—*Sphene, brown phlogopite.*
OMAR.—*Beryl, feldspar*, hematite.
PHILADELPHIA.—*Garnets* on Indian river, in the village.
PAMELIA.—*Agaric mineral*, calc tufa.
PIERREPONT.—Tourmaline, sphene, scapolite, hornblende.
PILLAR POINT.—*Massive barite* (exhausted).
THERESA.—*Fluorite, calcite,* hematite, hornblende, *quartz crystals,* serpentine (associated with hematite), celestite, strontianite; the Muscolonge Lake locality of fluor is exhausted.
WATERTOWN.—*Tremolite, agaric mineral,* calc tufa, celestite.
WILNA.—One mile north of Natural Bridge, *calcite.*

LEWIS CO.—DIANA (localities mostly near junction of crystalline and sedimentary rocks, and within two miles of Natural Bridge).—*Scapolite!* wollastonite, *green coccolite, feldspar, tremolite, pyroxene! sphene.!!* mica, *quartz crystals,* drusy quartz, cryst. pyrite, pyrrhotite, *blue calcite,* serpentine, *rensselaerite,* zircon, graphite, chlorite, hematite, bog-iron ore, iron sand, *apatite.*
GREIG.—*Magnetite,* pyrite.
LOWVILLE.—*Calcite,* fluorite, pyrite, galenite, blende, calc tufa.
MARTINSBURGH.—Wad, galenite, etc., but mine not now opened, *calcite.*
WATSON, BREMEN.—Bog-iron ore.

MONROE CO.—ROCHESTER.—*Pearl spar,* calcite, snowy gypsum, fluor, celestite, galenite, blende, barite, hornstone.

MONTGOMERY CO.—CANAJOHARIE.—Anthracite.
PALATINE.—*Quartz crystals,* drusy quartz, anthracite, hornstone, agate, garnet.
ROOT.—*Drusy quartz, blende,* barite, stalactite, stalagmite, galenite, pyrite.

NEW YORK CO.—CORLEAR'S HOOK.—Apatite, brown and yellow feldspar, sphene.
KINGSBRIDGE.—*Tremolite, pyroxene, mica, tourmaline,* pyrites. rutile, dolomite.
HARLEM.—Epidote, apophyllite, stilbite, tourmaline, vivianite, lamellar feldspar, mica.
NEW YORK.—*Serpentine, amianthus,* actinolite, *pyroxene,* hydrous anthophyllite, garnet, staurolite, molybdenite, graphite, *chlorite,* jasper, *necronite,* feldspar. In the excavations for the 4th Avenue tunnel, 1875, *harmotome,* stilbite, chabazite, heulandite, etc.

AMERICAN LOCALITIES.

NIAGARA CO.—LEWISTON.—*Epsomite.*
LOCKPORT.—*Celestite, calcite, selenite, anhydrite, fluorite,* dolomite, *blende.*
NIAGARA FALLS.—*Calcite,* flu*o*rite, blende, *dolomite.*

ONEIDA CO.—BOONVILLE.—*Calcite, wollastonite, coccolite.*
CLINTON.—*Blende, lenticular argillaceous iron ore;* in rocks of the Clinton Group, strontianite, celestite, the former covering the latter.

ONONDAGA CO —CAMILLUS.—*Selenite* and *fibrous gypsum.*
COLD SPRING.—Axinite.
MANLIUS.—*Gypsum* and fluor.
SYRACUSE.—*Serpentine,* celestite, selenite, barite.

ORANGE CO.—CORNWALL.—*Zircon, chondrodite, hornblende, spinel, massive feldspar, fibrous epidote,* hudsonite, menaccanite, *serpentine,* coccolite.
DEER PARK.—*Cryst. pyrite,* galenite.
MONROE.—*Mica! sphene! garnet,* colophonite, *epidote, chondrodite, allanite,* bucholzite, brown spar, *spinel,* hornblende, talc, menaccanite, *pyrrhotite,* pyrite, chromite, *graphite,* rastolyte, moronolite.
At WILKS and O'NEIL Mine in Monroe.—Aragonite, *magnetite,* dimagnetite (pseud. ?), jenkinsite, *asbestus,* serpentine, *mica, hortonolite.*
At TWO PONDS in Monroe.—*Pyroxene! chondrodite, hornblende, scapolite! zircon, sphene,* apatite.
At GREENWOOD FURNACE in Monroe.—*Chondrodite, pyroxene! mica, hornblende, spinel, scapolite, biotite!* menaccanite.
At FOREST OF DEAN.—*Pyroxene, spinel,* zircon, scapolite, hornblende.
TOWN OF WARWICK, WARWICK VILLAGE.—*Spinel! zircon, serpentine! brown spar, pyroxene! hornblende! pseudomorphous steatite, feldspar!* (Rock Hill), menaccanite, *clintonite,* tourmaline (R. H.), *rutile, sphene,* molybdenite, arsenopyrite, marcasite, pyrite, yellow iron sinter, quartz, jasper, mica, coccolite.
AMITY.—*Spinel! garnet, scapolite, hornblende, vesuvianite, epidote! clintonite! magnetite, tourmaline,* warwickite, *apatite, chondrodite, talc! pyroxene!* rutile, menaccanite, *zircon, corundum, feldspar,* sphene. calcite, serpentine, schiller spar (?), silvery mica.
EDENVILLE.—*Apatite, chondrodite! hair-brown hornblende!* tremolite, *spinel, tourmaline, warwickite, pyroxene, sphene, mica, feldspar, mispickel,* orpiment, *rutile,* menaccanite, scorodite, chalcopyrite, *leucopyrite* (or löllingite), allanite.
WEST POINT.—*Feldspar, mica,* scapolite, *sphene,* hornblende, allanite.

PUTNAM CO.—BREWSTER, Tilly Foster Iron Mine.—*Chondrodite!* (also humite and clinohumite) crystals very rare, *magnetite, dolomite, serpentine pseudomorphs, brucite,* enstatite, ripidolite, biotite, actinolite, apatite, pyrrhotite, fluorite, albite, epidote, sphene.
CARMEL (Brown's quarry).—Anthophyllite, schiller spar (?), orpiment, arsenopyrite, epidote.
COLD SPRING.—Chabazite, mica, sphene, epidote.
PATTERSON.—*White pyroxene! calcite, asbestus, tremolite,* dolomite, massive pyrite.
PHILLIPSTOWN.—*Tremolite, amianthus, serpentine, sphene,* diopside, green coccolite, hornblende, *scapolite,* stilbite, mica, laumontite, gurhofite, calcite, magnetite, chromite.
PHILLIPS Ore Bed.—Hyalite, *actinolite, massive pyrite.*

RENSSELAER CO.—HOOSIC.—Nitrogen springs.
LANSINGBURGH.—Epsomite. *quartz crystals, pyrite.*
TROY.—*Quartz crystals, pyrite, selenite.*

RICHMOND CO.—ROSSVILLE.—Lignite, *cryst. pyrite.*
QUARANTINE.—*Asbestus, amianthus,* aragonite, *dolomite, gurhofite,* brucite, serpentine talc, magnesite.

ROCKLAND CO.—CALDWELL.—*Calcite.*
GRASSY POINT.—Serpentine, actinolite.
HAVERSTRAW.—*Hornblende,* barite.
LADENTOWN.—Zircon, malachite, cuprite.
PIERMONT.—Datolite, stilbite, apophyllite, stellite, prehnite, thomsonite, calcite, chabazite.
STONY POINT.—Cerolite, lamellar hornblende, asbestus.

ST. LAWRENCE CO.—CANTON.—*Massive pyrite, calcite,* brown tourmaline, *sphene, serpentine,* talc, *rensselaerite,* pyroxene, hematite, chalcopyrite.
DEKALB.—*Hornblende,* barite, *fluorite, tremolite, tourmaline,* blende, graphite, pyroxene, quartz (spongy), serpentine.
EDWARDS.—*Brown and silvery mica!* scapolite, apatite, *quartz crystals.* actinolite, *tremolite!* hematite, serpentine, magnetite.
FINE.—*Black mica,* hornblende.
FOWLER.—*Barite, quartz crystals!* hematite, *blende,* galenite, tremolite, chalcedony, bog ore, satin spar (assoc. with serpentine), pyrite, chalcopyrite, actinolite, *rensselaerite* (near Somerville).
GOUVERNEUR.—*Calcite! serpentine! hornblende! scapolite! orthoclase, tourmaline!* idocrase (one mile south of G.), pyroxene, malacolite, apatite, *rensselaerite,* serpentine, *sphene,* fluorite, barite (farm of Judge Dodge), black *mica,* phlogopite, *tremolite!* asbestus, hematite, graphite, vesuvianite (near Somerville in serpentine), *spinel,* houghite, scapolite, *phlogopite,* dolomite ; three-quarters of a mile west of Somerville, *chondrodite,* spinel ; two miles north of Somerville, *apatite,* pyrite, *brown tourmaline!!*
HAMMOND.—*Apatite! zircon!* (farm of Mr. Hardy), *orthoclase* (loxocase), *pargasite,* barite, pyrite, purple fluorite, dolomite.
HERMON.—*Quartz crystals,* hematite, siderite, pargasite, pyroxene, serpentine, tourmaline, bog-iron ore.
MACOMB.—Blende, mica, *galenite* (on land of James Averil), sphene.
MINERAL POINT, Morristown.—Fluorite, blende, galenite, *phlogopite* (Pope's Mills), barite.
OGDENSBURG.—Labradorite.
PITCAIRN.—Satin spar, associated with serpentine.
POTSDAM.—*Hornblende!*—eight miles from Potsdam, on road to Pierrepont, *feldspar, tourmaline, black mica,* hornblende.
ROSSIE (Iron Mines).—*Barite,* hematite, coralloidal aragonite in mines near Somerville, limonite, *quartz* (sometimes stalactitic at Parish iron mine), *pyrite, pearl spar.*
ROSSIE Lead Mine.—*Calcite! galenite! pyrite, celestite,* chalcopyrite, hematite, cerussite, anglesite, *octahedral fluor, black phlogopite.*
Elsewhere in ROSSIE.—*Calcite,* barite, quartz crystals, chondrodite (near Yellow Lake), *feldspar! pargasite! apatite, pyroxene,* hornblende, sphene, zircon, *mica,* fluorite, serpentine, automolite, pearl spar, graphite.
RUSSEL.—*Pargasite, specular iron, quartz* (dodec.), calcite, serpentine, rensselaerite, magnetite.

SARATOGA CO.—GREENFIELD.—*Chrysoberyl! garnet! tourmaline! mica, feldspar,* apatite, graphite, aragonite (in iron mines).

SCHOHARIE CO.—BALL'S CAVE, and others.—Calcite, stalactites.
CARLISLE.—*Fibrous barite, cryst. and fib. calcite.*
MIDDLEBURY.—Anthracite, calcite.
SHARON.—Calcareous tufa.
SCHOHARIE.—Fibrous celestite, *strontianite! cryst. pyrite!*

SENECA CO.—CANOGA.—*Nitrogen springs.*

SULLIVAN CO.—WURTZBORO'.—*Galenite,* blende, *pyrite, chalcopyrite.*

TOMPKINS CO.—ITHACA.—Calcareous tufa.

ULSTER CO.—ELLENVILLE.—*Galenite,* blende, *chalcopyrite! quartz, brookite.*
MARBLETOWN.—Pyrite.

WARREN CO.—CALDWELL.—*Massive feldspar.*
CHESTER.—*Pyrite,* tourmaline, rutile, chalcopyrite.
DIAMOND ISLE (Lake George).—*Calcite, quartz crystals.*
GLENN'S FALLS.—Rhomb spar.
JOHNSBURG.—*Fluorite! zircon!! graphite,* serpentine, *pyrite.*

WASHINGTON CO.—FORT ANN.—*Graphite,* serpentine.
GRANVILLE.—*Lamellar pyroxene,* massive feldspar, epidote.

WAYNE CO.—WOLCOTT.—Barite.

AMERICAN LOCALITIES. 485

WESTCHESTER CO.—ANTHONY'S NOSE.—*Apatite*, pyrite, *calcite!* in very large tabular crystals, grouped, and sometimes incrusted with drusy quartz.
DAVENPORT'S NECK.—*Serpentine*, garnet, sphene.
EASTCHESTER.—Blende, pyrite, chalcopyrite, dolomite.
HASTINGS.—*Tremolite, white pyroxene.*
NEW ROCHELLE.—*Serpentine*, brucite, quartz, *mica*, tremolite, garnet, magnesite.
PEEKSKILL.—Mica, feldspar, hornblende, stilbite, sphene; three miles south, emery.
RYE.—*Serpentine, chlorite, black tourmaline*, tremolite.
SINGSING.—*Pyroxene, tremolite, pyrite.* beryl, azurite, green malachite, cerussite, pyromorphite, anglesite, vauquelinite, galenite, native silver, chalcopyrite.
WEST FARMS.—Apatite, tremolite, garnet, stilbite, heulandite, chabazite, epidote, sphene.
YONKERS.—*Tremolite*, apatite, calcite, analcite, *pyrite*, tourmaline.
YORKTOWN.—*Sillimanite, monazite*, magnetite.

NEW JERSEY.

ANDOVER IRON MINE (Sussex Co.).—Willemite, brown garnet.
ALLENTOWN (Monmouth Co.).—*Vivianite, dufrenite.*
BELVILLE.—Copper mines.
BERGEN.—*Calcite! datolite! pectolite* (called stellite)! *analcite, apophyllite! gmelinite, prehnite*, sphene, *stilbite, natrolite*, heulandite, laumontite, *chabazite*, pyrite, pseudomorphous steatite, imitative of apophyllite, diabantite.
BRUNSWICK.—Copper mines; *native copper, malachite, mountain leather.*
BRYAM.—Chondrodite, *spinel*, at Roseville, *epidote.*
CANTWELL'S BRIDGE (Newcastle Co.), three miles west.—Vivianite.
DANVILLE (Jemmy Jump Ridge).—*Graphite*, chondrodite, augite, mica.
FLEMINGTON.—*Copper mines.*
FRANKFORT.—*Serpentine.*
FRANKLIN and STERLING.—*Spinel! garnet! rhodonite! willemite! franklinite! zincite! dysluite! hornblende, tremolite, chondrodite, white scapolite, black tourmaline, epidote, pink calcite, mica,* actinolite, augite, sahlite, coccolite, asbestus, *jeffersonite* (augite), calamine, graphite, fluorite, beryl, galenite, serpentine, honey-colored sphene, quartz, chalcedony, amethyst, zircon, molybdenite, vivianite, *tephroite*, rhodochrosite, aragonite, sussexite, chalcophanite, rœpperite, calcozincite, vanuxemite, gahnite. Also *algerite* in gran. limestone.
FRANKLIN and WARWICK MTS.—*Pyrite.*
GREENBROOK.—Copper mines.
GRIGGSTOWN.—Copper mines.
HAMBURGH.—One mile north, *spinel! tourmaline, phlogopite,* hornblende, *limonite*, hematite.
HOBOKEN.—Serpentine (marmolite), *brucite, nemalite* (or fibrous brucite), aragonite, dolomite.
HURDSTOWN.—*Apatite*, pyrrhotite, magnetite.
IMLEYTOWN.—Vivianite.
LOCKWOOD.—*Graphite, chondrodite, talc, augite, quartz, green spinel.*
MONTVILLE (Morris Co.).—Serpentine, *chrysotile.*
MULLICA HILL (Gloucester Co.).—*Vivianite* lining belemnites and other fossils.
NEWTON.—*Spinel*, blue, pink, and white corundum, *mica*, vesuvianite, *hornblende, tourmaline, scapolite*, rutile, pyrite, talc, calcite, barite, *pseudomorphous steatite.*
PATERSON.—*Datolite.*
VERNON.—Serpentine, spinel, hydrotalcite.

PENNSYLVANIA.*

ADAMS CO.—GETTYSBURG.—Epidote, fibrous and massive.

BERKS CO—MORGANTOWN.—At Jones's mines, one mile east of Morgantown, *green malachite*, native copper, *chrysocolla, magnetite*, allophane, pyrite, chalcopyrite, aragonite, apatite, talc; two miles N.E. from Jones's mine, graphite, sphene; at Steele's mine, one mile N.W. from St. Mary's, Chester Co., *magnetite*, micaceous iron, coccolite, brown garnet.
READING.—*Smoky quartz* crystals, zircon, stilbite, iron ore, near Pricetown, zircon, allanite, epidote; at Eckhardt's Furnace, *allanite* with *zircon ;* at Zion's Church, molybdenite;

---

* See also the Report on the Mineralogy of Pennsylvania, by Dr. F A. Genth, 1875.

near Kutztown, in the Crystal Cave, stalactites ; at Fritz Island, *apophyllite*, thomsonite, *chabaite*, calcite, azurite, *malachite*, magnetite, chalcopyrite, stibnite, prochlorite, precious serpentine.

BUCKS CO.—BUCKINGHAM TOWNSHIP.—Crystallized quartz; near New Hope, vesuvianite, epidote, barite.

SOUTHAMPTON.—Near the village of Feasterville, in the quarry of George Van Arsdale *graphite*, pyroxene, sahlite, coccolite, *sphene*, green mica, calcite, *wollastonite*, glassy feldspar sometimes opalescent, phlogopite, *blue quartz*, garnet, zircon, pyrite, moroxite, scapolite

NEW BRITAIN.—Dolomite, galenite, blende, malachite.

CARBON CO.—SUMMIT HILL, in coal mines.—*Kaolinite*.

CHESTER CO.—AVONDALE.—Asbestus, tremolite, garnet, opal.

BIRMINGHAM TOWNSHIP.—Amethyst, *smoky quartz*, serpentine, beryl ; in Ab'm Darlington's lime quarry, calcite.

EAST BRADFORD.—Near Buffington's bridge, on the Brandywine, green, blue, and gray cyanite, the gray cyanite is found loose in the soil, in crystals ; on the farms of Dr. Elwyn Mrs. Foulke, Wm. Gibbons, and Saml. Entrikin, *amethyst*. At Strode's mill, asbestus, *magnesite*, anthophyllite, epidote, aquacrepitite, oligoclase, drusy quartz, *collyrite?* on Osborne's Hill, *wad*, *manganesian garnet* (massive), *sphene*, schorl ; at Caleb Cope's lime quarry *fetid dolomite*, necronite, garnets, blue cyanite, *yellow actinolite in talc ;* near the Black Horse Inn, *indurated talc*, rutile ; on Amor Davis' farm, *orthite!* massive, from a grain to lumps of one pound weight ; near the paper-mill on the Brandywine, zircon, associated with *titaniferous iron* in blue quartz.

WEST BRADFORD.—Near the village of Marshalton, *green cyanite*, rutile, scapolite, pyrite staurolite ; at the Chester County Poor-house limestone quarry, *chesterlite!* in crystals implanted on dolomite, *rutile!* in brilliant acicular crystals, which are finely terminated, calcite in scalenohedrons, zoisite, *damourite?* in radiated groups of crystals on dolomite, *quart crystals ;* on Smith & McMullin's farm, epidote.

CHARLESTOWN.—*Pyromorphite, cerussite, galenite,* quartz.

COVENTRY.—Allanite, near Pughtown.

SOUTH COVENTRY.—In Chrisman's limestone quarry, near Coventry village, augite sphene, graphite, *zircon* in iron ore (about half a mile from the village).

EAST FALLOWFIELD.—Soapstone.

EAST GOSHEN.—Serpentine, *asbestus*, magnetite (loadstone), garnet.

ELK.—Menaccanite with muscovite, chromite ; at Lewisville, *black tourmaline*.

WEST GOSHEN.—On the Barrens, one mile north of West Chester, amianthus, serpentine cellular quartz, jasper, chalcedony, drusy quartz, chlorite, marmolite, indurated talc, *magnesite* in radiated crystals on serpentine, hematite, *asbestus ;* near R. Taylor's mill, chromite in octahedral crystals, *deweylite, radiated magnesite,* aragonite, *staurolite,* garnet, asbestus epidote; *zoisite* on hornblende at West Chester water-works (not accessible at present).

NEW GARDEN.—At Nivin's limestone quarry, *brown tourmaline, necronite,* scapolite, apatite, brown and green mica, rutile, *aragonite, fibrolite, kaolinite,* tremolite.

KENNETT.—Actinolite, brown tourmaline, brown mica, *epidote*, tremolite, scapolite, *aragonite ;* on Wm. Cloud's farm, *sunstone! !* chabazite, sphene. At Pearce's old-mill, zoisite *epidote, sunstone ;* sunstone occurs in good specimens at various places in the range of hornblende rocks running through this township from N.E. to S.W.

LOWER OXFORD.—Garnets, *pyrite* in cubic crystals.

LONDON GROVE.—Rutile, jasper, chalcedony (botryoidal), large and rough quartz crystals epidote ; on Wm. Jackson's farm, *yellow and black tourmaline, tremolite,* rutile, green mica apatite, at Pusey's quarry, rutile, *tremolite*.

EAST MARLBOROUGH.—On the farm of Baily & Brothers, one mile south of Unionville bright *yellow* and nearly white *tourmaline, chesterlite, albite,* pyrite ; near Marlborough meeting-house, epidote, serpentine, acicular black tourmaline in white quartz ; *zircon* in small perfect crystals, loose in the soil at Pusey's saw-mill, two miles S.W. of Unionville.

WEST MARLBOROUGH.—Near Logan's quarry, staurolite, cyanite, yellow tourmaline, rutile garnets ; near Doe Run village, *hematite,* scapolite, *tremolite ;* in R. Baily's limestone quarry two and a half miles S.W. of Unionville, *fibrous tremolite, cyanite,* scapolite ?

NEWLIN.—On the serpentine barrens, one and a half mile N.E. of Unionville, *corundum* massive and crystallized, also in crystals in *albite,* often in loose crystals covered with a thin coating of steatite, spinel (black), talc, picrolite, brucite, *green tourmaline* with flat pyramidal terminations in albite, *unionite* (rare) *euphyllite,* mica in hexagonal crystals, *feldspar beryl!* in hexagonal crystals, one of which weighs 51 lbs., pyrite in cubic crystals, chromic iron, drusy quartz, green quartz, actinolite, *emerylite*, chloritoid, diallage, *oligoclase;* on Johnson Patterson's farm, massive *corundum*, titaniferous iron, *clinochlore, emerylite*, sometimes colored green by chrome, albite, *orthoclase*, halloysite, margarite, garnets, *beryl;* on J. Lesley's farm, *corundum*, crystallized and in massive lumps, one of which weighed 5,200 lbs., *diaspore! ! emerylite! euphyllite crystallized! green tourmaline*, transparent crystals in the *euphyllite*, orthoclase; two miles N. of Unionville, *magnetite* in octahedral crystals; one mile E. of Unionville, *hematite;* in Edwards's old limestone quarry, purple fluorite, rutile.

EAST NOTTINGHAM.—*Sand chrome, asbestus, chromite* in octahedral crystals, hallite, beryl.

WEST NOTTINGHAM.—At Scott's chrome mine, *chromite, foliated talc*, marmolite, serpentine, *chalcedony, rhodochrome;* near Moro Phillip's chrome mine, *asbestus;* at the magnesia quarry, *deweylite*, marmolite, magnesite, leelite, serpentine, sand chrome; near Fremont P.O., corundum.

EAST PIKELAND.—Iron ore.

WEST PIKELAND.—In the iron mines near Chester Springs, *gibbsite, zircon, turgite, hematite* (stalactitical and in geodes), göthite.

PENN.—Garnets, agalmatolite.

PENNSBURY.—On John Craig's farm, brown garnets, *mica;* on J. Dilworth's farm, near Fairville, *muscovite!* in hexagonal prisms from one-quarter to seven inches in diameter; in the village of Fairville, *sunstone;* near Brinton's ford, on the Brandywine, *chondrodite, sphene*, diopside, *augite*, coccolite; at Mendenhall's old limestone quarry, *fetid quartz*, sunstone; at Swain's quarry, crystals of orthoclase.

POCOPSON.—On the farms of John Entrikin and Jos. B. Darlington, *amethyst*.

SADSBURY.—*Rutile!!* splendid geniculated crystals are found loose in the soil for seven miles along the valley, and particularly near the village of Parkesburg, where they sometimes occur weighing one pound, doubly geniculated and of a deep red color; near Sadsbury village, *amethyst*, tourmaline, epidote, *milk quartz*.

SCHUYLKILL.—In the railroad tunnel at PHŒNIXVILLE, *dolomite!* sometimes coated with pyrite, quartz crystals, yellow blende, brookite, *calcite* in hexagonal crystals enclosing *pyrite;* at the WHEATLEY, BROOKDALE, and CHESTER COUNTY LEAD MINES, one and a half mile S. of Phœnixville, *pyromorphite! cerussite! galenite, anglesite!!* quartz crystals, chalcopyrite, barite, *fluorite* (white), stolzite, *wulfenite! calamine, vanadinite, blende! mimetite!* descloizite, göthite, chrysocolla, native copper, malachite, *azurite*, limonite, *calcite*, *sulphur*, pyrite, melaconite, pseudomalachite, gersdorffite, chalcocite? covellite.

THORNBURY.—On Jos. H. Brinton's farm, *muscovite* containing acicular crystals of tourmaline, *rutile*, titaniferous iron.

TREDYFFRIN.—*Pyrite* in cubic crystals loose in the soil.

UWCHLAN.—Massive *blue quartz, graphite*.

WARREN.—*Melanite*, feldspar.

WEST GOSHEN (one mile from West Chester).—Chromite.

WILLISTOWN.—*Magnetite, chromite*, actinolite, asbestus.

WEST-TOWN.—On the serpentine rocks, 3 miles S. of West Chester, *clinochlore! jefferisite!* mica, asbestus, actinolite, magnesite, *talc*, titaniferous iron, magnetite and massive tourmaline.

EAST WHITELAND.—*Pyrite*, in very perfect cubic crystals, is found on nearly every farm in this township, quartz crystals found loose in the soil.

WEST WHITELAND.—At Gen. Trimble's iron mine (south-east), *stalactitic hematite! wavellite!!* in radiated stalactites, gibbsite, cœruleolactite.

WARWICK.—At the Elizabeth mine and Keim's old iron mine adjoining, one mile N. of Knauertown, *aplome garnet!* in brilliant dodecahedrons, *flosferri, pyroxene, micaceous hematite, pyrite* in bright octahedral crystals in calcite, chrysocolla, chalcopyrite massive and in single tetrahedral crystals, magnetite, *fascicular hornblende! bornite*, malachite, *brown garnet*, calcite, *byssolite!* serpentine; near the village of St. Mary's, magnetite in dodecahedral crystals, *melanite, garnet, actinolite* in small radiated nodules; at the Hopewell iron mine, one mile N.W. of St. Mary's, *magnetite* in octahedral crystals.

COLUMBIA CO.—At Webb's mine, yellow blende in calcite; near Bloomburg, cryst. magnetite.

DAUPHIN CO.—NEAR HUMMERSTOWN.—Green garnets, cryst. *smoky quartz*, feldspar.

DELAWARE CO.—ASTON TOWNSHIP.— *Amethyst, corundum*, emerylite, staurolite, *fibrolite*, black tourmaline, *margarite, sunstone, asbestus*, anthophyllite, steatite· near Tyson's mill, garnet, staurolite; at Peter's mill-dam in the creek, *pyrope garnet*.

BIRMINGHAM.—*Fibrolite, kaolin* (abundant), crystals of rutile, *amethyst;* at Bullock's old quarry, zircon, *bucholzite*, nacrite, yellow crystallized quartz, *feldspar*.

BLUE HILL.—Green quartz crystals, spinel.

CHESTER.—*Amethyst, black tourmaline, beryl, crystals of feldspar, garnet,* cryst. pyrite, *molybdenite, molybdite,* chalcopyrite, kaolin, uraninite, *muscovite*, orthoclase, bismutite.

CHICHESTER.—Near Trainer's mill-dam, *beryl,* tourmaline, crystals of *feldspar,* kaolin; on Wm. Eyre's farm, *tourmaline.*

CONCORD.—*Crystals of mica, crystals of feldspar, kaolin* abundant, *drusy quartz* of a blue and green color, meerschaum, stellated *tremolite,* some of the rays 6½ in. diameter, *anthophyllite,* fibrolite, acicular crystals of *rutile,* pyrope in quartz, amethyst, actinolite, *manganesian garnet, beryl;* in Green's creek, *pyrope garnet.*

DARBY.—*Blue* and *gray cyanite,* garnet, staurolite, zoisite, quartz, beryl, chlorite, mica, limonite.

EDGEMONT.—*Amethyst,* oxide of manganese, crystals of *feldspar;* one mile east of Edgemont Hall, *rutile* in quartz.

GREEN'S CREEK.—*Garnet* (so-called pyrope).

HAVERFORD.—Staurolite with garnet.

MARPLE.—*Tourmaline, andalusite,* amethyst, *actinolite, anthophyllite,* talc, *radiated actinolite* in talc, chromite, *drusy quartz,* beryl, cryst. pyrite, *menaccanite in quartz,* chlorite.

MIDDLETOWN.—*Amethyst, beryl,* black mica, *mica* with reticulated magnetite between the plates, *manganesian garnets!* large trapezohedral crystals, some 3 in. in diameter, indurated talc, hexagonal crystals of *rutile, crystals of mica, green quartz! anthophyllite,* radiated tourmaline, staurolite, titanic iron, fibrolite, serpentine; at Lenni, *chlorite,* green and bronze *vermiculite! green feldspar;* at Mineral Hill, fine crystals of *corundum,* one of which weighs 1¾ lb., *actinolite* in great variety, bronzite, *green feldspar, moonstone, sunstone, graphic granite,* magnesite, *octahedral crystals of chromite* in great quantity, *beryl,* chalcedony, asbestus, *fibrous hornblende,* rutile, staurolite, melanosiderite, hallite; at Painter's Farm, near Dismal Run, *zircon* with oligoclase, tremolite, tourmaline; at the Black Horse, near Media, corundum; at Hibbard's Farm and at Fairlamb's Hill, chromite in brilliant octahedrons.

NEWTOWN.—Serpentine, hematite, enstatite, tremolite.

UPPER PROVIDENCE.—*Anthophyllite, tremolite, radiated asbestus, radiated actinolite,* tourmaline, *beryl, green feldspar, amethyst* (one found on Morgan Hunter's farm weighing over 7 lbs.), *andalusite!* (one terminated crystal found on the farm of Jas. Worrall weighs 7½ lbs.); at Blue Hill, very fine crystals of *blue quartz* in chlorite, *amianthus* in serpentine, zircon.

LOWER PROVIDENCE.—*Amethyst, green mica,* garnet, large crystals of *feldspar!* (some over 100 lbs. in weight).

RADNOR.—*Garnet,* marmolite, deweylite, chromite, asbestus, magnesite, talc, blue quartz, picrolite, limonite, magnetite.

SPRINGFIELD.—*Andalusite, tourmaline,* beryl, titanic iron, garnet; on Fell's Laurel Hill, beryl, garnet; near Beattie's mill, staurolite, apatite; near Lewis's paper-mill, tourmaline, *mica.*

THORNBURY.—*Amethyst.*

HUNTINGDON CO.—NEAR FRANKSTOWN.—In the bed of a stream and on the side of a hill, *fibrous celestite* (abundant), *quartz crystals.*

LANCASTER CO.—DRUMORE TOWNSHIP.—Quartz crystals.

FULTON.—At Wood's chrome mine, near the village of Texas, *brucite! !* zaratite (emerald nickel), *pennite! ripidolite! kämmererite! baltimorite, chromic iron,* williamsite, *chrysolite! marmolite, picrolite,* hydromagnesite, *dolomite,* magnesite, *aragonite,* calcite, serpentine, hematite, menaccanite, genthite, chrome-garnet, bronzite, millerite; at Low's mine, *hydromagnesite, brucite* (lancasterite), *picrolite,* magnesite, *williamsite, chromic iron,* ta'c, zaratite, baltimorite, serpentine, hematite; on M. Boice's farm, one mile N.W. of the village, *pyrite* in cubes and various modifications, *anthophyllite;* near Rock Springs, *chalcedony,* carnelian, *moss agate, green tourmaline* in talc, titanic iron, chromite, *octahedral magnetite in chlorite;* at Reynolds's old mine, calcite, *talc,* picrolite, *chromite;* at Carter's chrome mine, brookite.

GAP MINES.—Chalcopyrite, *pyrrhotite* (niccoliferous), *millerite* in botryoidal radiations, *vivianite!* (rare), actinolite, *siderite,* hisingerite, pyrite.

PEQUEA VALLEY.—Eight miles south of Lancaster, argentiferous galenite (said to contain 250 to 300 ounces of silver to the ton?), vauquelinite, rutile at Pequea mine; four miles N.W. of Lancaster, on the Lancaster and Harrisburg Railroad, *calamite,* galenite, blende; *pyrite* in cubic crystals is found in great abundance near the city of Lancaster; at the Lancaster zinc mines, *calamine,* blende, tennantite? *smithsonite* (pseud. of dolomite), *aurichalcite.*

LEBANON CO.—CORNWALL.—*Magnetite, pyrite* (cobaltiferous), chalcopyrite, *native copper, azurite, malachite, chrysocolla, cuprite* (hydrocuprite), *allophane, brochantite,* serpentine, quartz pseudomorphs; *galenite* (with octahedral cleavage), fluorite, covellite, hematite (micaceous), opal, asbestus.

LEHIGH CO —FRIEDENSVILLE.—At the zinc mines, *calamine, smithsonite,* hydrozincite, massive blende, greenockite, quartz, allophane, zinciferous clay, mountain leather, aragonite, sauconite; near Allentown, magnetite, pipe-iron ore; near Bethlehem, on S. Mountain, alianite, with zircon and altered sphene in a single isolated mass of syenite, magnetite, martite, black spinel, tourmaline, chalcocite.

MIFFLIN CO.—Strontianite.

MONROE CO.—In CHERRY VALLEY.—*Calcite,* chalcedony, quartz; in Poconao Valley, near Judge Mervine's, cryst. quartz.

MONTGOMERY CO.—CONSHOHOCKEN.—Fibrous tourmaline, menaccanite, aventurine quartz, phyllite; in the quarry of Geo. Bullock, *calcite* in hexagonal prisms, aragonite.
LOWER PROVIDENCE.—At the Perkiomen lead and copper mines. near the village of Shannonville, azurite, *blende, galenite,* pyromorphite, cerussite, wulfenite, anglesite, barite, calamine, chalcopyrite, malachite, chrysocolla, *brown spar,* cuprite, covellite (rare), melaconite, libethenite, pseudomalachite.
WHITE MARSH.—At D. O. Hitner's iron mine, five and a half miles from Spring Mills, limonite in geodes and stalactites, *göthite,* pyrolusite, wad, lepidocrocite; at Edge Hill Street, North Pennsylvania Railroad, titanic iron, braunite, pyrolusite; one mile S.W. of Hitner's iron mine, *limonite,* velvety, stalactitic, and fibrous, fibres three inches long, turgite, *göthite,* pyrolusite, *velvet manganese,* wad; near Marble Hall, at Hitner's marble quarry, white marble, granular barite, resembling marble; at Spring Mills, limonite, pyrolusite, göthite; at Flat Rock Tunnel, opposite Manayunk, *stilbite, heulandite, chabasite,* ilvaite, beryl, feldspar, mica.
LAFAYETTE, at the Soapstone quarries.—Talc, jefferisite, garnet, albite, serpentine, zoisite, staurolite, chalcopyrite; at Rose's Serpentine quarry, opposite Lafayette, enstatite, serpentine.

NORTHUMBERLAND CO.—Opposite SELIM'S GROVE.—Calamine.

NORTHAMPTON CO.—BUSHKILL TOWNSHIP.—Crystal Spring on Blue Mountain, *quartz crystals.*
Near EASTON.—*Zircon!* (exhausted), nephrite, coccolite, tremolite, pyroxene, sahlite, limonite, magnetite, purple calcite.
WILLIAMS TOWNSHIP.—Pyrolusite in geodes in limonite beds, göthite (lepidocrocite) at Glendon.

PHILADELPHIA CO.—FRANKFORD.—Titanite in gneiss, apophyllite; on the Philadelphia, Trenton and Connecting Railroad, basanite; at the quarries on Frankford Creek, stilbite, molybdenite, hornblende; on the Connecting Railroad, wad, earthy cobalt; at Chestnut Hill, magnetite, green mica, chalcopyrite, fluorite.
FAIRMOUNT WATER WORKS.—In the quarries opposite Fairmount. *autunite! torbernite* crystals of *feldspar,* beryl, pseudomorphs after beryl, tourmaline, albite, wad, menaccanite.
GORGAS' and CREASE'S Lane.—Tourmaline, cyanite, staurolite, hornstone.
Near GERMANTOWN.—*Black tourmaline,* laumontite, *apatite;* York Road, tourmaline, beryl.
HESTONVILLE.—Alunogen, iron alum, orthoclase.
HEFT'S MILL.—Alunogen, tourmaline, cyanite, titanite.
MANAYUNK.—At the soapstone quarries above Manayunk, talc, *steatite,* chlorite, vermiculite, *anthophyllite,* staurolite, dolomite, apatite, asbestus, brown spar, epsomite.
MEAGARGEE'S Paper-mill.—Staurolite, titanic iron, hyalite, *apatite,* green mica, iron garnets in great abundance.
McKINNEY'S Quarry, on Rittenhouse Lane.—Feldspar, *apatite, stilbite,* natrolite, *heulandite,* epidote, hornblende, erubescite, malachite.
SCHUYLKILL FALLS.—Chabazite, titanite, fluorite, epidote, muscovite, tourmaline, prochlorite.

SCHUYLKILL CO.—TAMAQUA, near POTTSVILLE, in coal mines.—*Kaolinite.*

YORK CO.—Bornite, rutile in slender prisms in granular quartz, calcite.

DELAWARE.

NEWCASTLE CO.—BRANDYWINE SPRINGS.—*Bucholzite, fibrolite* abundant, sahlite, pyroxene; Brandywine Hundred, muscovite, enclosing reticulated magnetite.
DIXON'S FELDSPAR QUARRIES, six miles N. W. of Wilmington (these quarries have been worked for the manufacture of porcelain).—*Adularia, albite, oligoclase, beryl, apatite, cinnamon-stone!!* (both granular like that from Ceylon; and crystallized, rare), magnesite, serpentine, asbestus, black *tourmaline!* (rare), *indicolite!* (rare), sphene in pyroxene, cyanite.
DUPONT'S POWDER MILLS.—"Hypersthene."
EASTBURN'S LIMESTONE QUARRIES, near the Pennsylvania line.—*Tremolite, bronzite.*
QUARRYVILLE.—Garnet, spodumene, fibrolite.
Near **NEWARK,** on the railroad.—Sphærosiderite on drusy quartz, jasper (ferruginous opal); cryst. spathic iron in the cavities of cellular quartz.
WAY'S QUARRY, two miles south of Centreville.—*Feldspar* in fine cleavage masses, *apatite, mica, deweylite, granular quartz.*
WILMINGTON.—In Christiana quarries, *metalloidal diallage.*
KENNETT TURNPIKE, near Centreville.—Cyanite and garnet.

HARFORD CO.—Cerolite.

KENT CO.—Near **MIDDLETOWN,** in Wm. Polk's marl pits.—*Vivianite!*
On **CHESAPEAKE AND DELAWARE CANAL.**—Retinasphalt, pyrite, amber.

SUSSEX CO.—Near **CAPE HENLOPEN**—Vivianite.

MARYLAND.

BALTIMORE (Jones's Falls, 1¾ mile from B.).—Chabazite (haydenite), heulandite (beaumontite of Levy), pyrite, lenticular carbonate of iron, *mica, stilbite.*
Sixteen miles from Baltimore, on the Gunpowder.—*Graphite.*
Twenty-three miles from B., on the Gunpowder.—*Talc.*
Twenty-five miles from B., on the Gunpowder.—*Magnetite. sphene,* pycnite.
Thirty miles from B., in Montgomery Co., on farm of S. Eliot.—Gold in quartz.
Eight to twenty miles north of B., in limestone.—*Tremolite, augite, pyrite,* brown and yellow tourmaline.
Fifteen miles north of B.—*Sky-blue chalcedony* in granular limestone.
Eighteen miles north of B., at Scott's mills.—*Magnetite,* cyanite.
BARE HILLS.—*Chromite, asbestus, tremolite, talc,* hornblende. serpentine, chalcedony, meerschaum, baltimorite, *chalcopyrite,* magnetite.
CAPE SABLE, near Magothy R.—Amber, pyrite, alum slate.
CARROLL Co.—Near Sykesville, Liberty Mines, gold, magnetite, *pyrite (octahedrons), chalcopyrite,* linnæite (carrollite); at Patapsco Mines, near Finksburg. bornite, *malachite,* siegenite, *linnæite, remingtonite,* magnetite, *chalcopyrite;* at Mineral Hill mine, *bornite,* chalcopyrite, ore of *nickel* (see above), gold, magnetite.
CECIL Co., north part.—*Chromite* in serpentine.
COOPTOWN, Harford Co.—Olive-colored *tourmaline, diallage, talc* of green, blue, and rose colors, *ligniform asbestus, chromite, serpentine.*
DEER CREEK.—*Magnetite!* in chlorite slate.
FREDERICK Co.—Old Liberty mine, near Liberty Town, black copper, malachite, chalcocite, specular iron; at Dollyhyde mine, *bornite,* chalcopyrite, pyrite, argentiferous galenite in dolomite.
MONTGOMERY Co.—*Oxide of manganese.*
SOMERSET and **WORCESTER COS.,** north part.—*Bog-iron ore, vivianite.*
ST. MARY'S RIVER.—*Gypsum!* in clay.
PYLESVILLE, Harford Co.—Asbestus mine.

VIRGINIA AND DISTRICT OF COLUMBIA.

ALBEMARLE Co., a little west of the Green Mts.—*Steatite, graphite,* galenite.
AMHERST Co., along the west base of Buffalo ridge.—*Copper ores,* allanite. etc.
AUGUSTA Co.—At Weyer's (or Weir's) cave, sixteen miles northeast of Staunton, and eighty-one miles northwest of Richmond, calcite, stalactites.

AMERICAN LOCALITIES 401

BUCKINGHAM CO.—*Gold* at Garnett and Moseley mines, also, pyrite, pyrrhotite, calcite, garnet; at Eldridge mine (now London and Virginia mines) near by, and the Buckingham mines near Maysville, gold, auriferous pyrite, chalcopyrite, tennantite, *barite; cyanite, tourmaline, actinolite.*
CHESTERFIELD CO.—Near this and Richmond Co. bituminous coal, native coke.
CULPEPPER CO., on Rapidan river.—Gold, pyrite.
FRANKLIN CO.—Grayish steatite.
FAUQUIER CO., Barnett's mills.—Asbestus, gold mines, *barite, calcite.*
FLUVANNA CO.—Gold at Stockton's mine; also tetradymite at "Tellurium mine."
PHENIX Copper mines.—*Chalcopyrite*, etc.
GEORGETOWN, D. C.—Rutile.
GOOCHLAND CO.—Gold mines (Moss and Busby's).
HARPER'S FERRY, on both sides of the Potomac.—Thuringite (owenite) with quartz.
JEFFERSON CO., at Shepherdstown. - Fluor.
KENAWHA CO.—At Kenawha, *petroleum*, brine springs, cannel coal.
LOUDON CO.—*Tubular quartz, drase, pyrite, talc, chlorite, soapstone*, asbestus, *chromite, actinolite, quartz crystals; micaceous iron*, bornite, malachite, epidote, near Leesburg (Potomac mine).
LOUISA CO.—Walton gold mine, gold, pyrite, chalcopyrite, argentiferous galenite, siderite, blende, anglesite; boulangerite, blende (at Tinder's mine).
NELSON CO.—Galenite, chalcopyrite, malachite.
ORANGE CO.—Western part, Blue Ridge, specular iron; gold at the Orange Grove and Vaucluse gold mines, worked by the "Freehold" and "Liberty" Mining Companies.
ROCKBRIDGE CO., three miles southwest of Lexington.—Barite.
SHENANDOAH CO., near Woodstock.—Fluorite.
MT. ALTO, Blue Ridge.—Argillaceous iron ore.
SPOTTSYLVANIA CO., two miles northeast of Chancellorville.—*Cyanite;* gold mines at the junction of the Rappahannock and Rapidan; on the Rappahannock (Marshall mine); Whitehall mine, affording also tetradymite.
STAFFORD CO., eight or ten miles from Falmouth—Micaceous iron, gold, tetradymite, silver, galenite, vivianite.
WASHINGTON CO., eighteen miles from Abington.—*Rock salt* with *gypsum.*
WYTHE CO. (Austin's mines).—*Cerussite, minium, plumbic ochre*, blende, *calamine, galenite,* graphite.
On the Potomac, twenty-five miles north of Washington city.—*Native sulphur* in gray compact limestone.

NORTH CAROLINA.

ASHE CO.—Malachite, chalcopyrite.
BUNCOMBE CO., (now called *Madison Co*).—Corundum (from a boulder), *margarite*, corundophilite, *garnet*, chromite, barite, *fluorite*, rutile, iron ores, manganese, *zircon;* at Swannanoa Gap, cyanite.
BURKE CO.—Gold, monazite, zircon, beryl, *corundum, garnet*, sphene, *graphite*, iron ores, tetradymite, montanite.
CABARRUS CO.—Phenix Mine, gold, barite, *chalcopyrite*, auriferous pyrite, quartz, pseudomorph after barite, tetradymite, montanite; Pioneer mines, *gold*, limonite, pyrolusite, *barnhardite, wolfram, scheelite*, cuprotungstite, tungstite, diamond, chrysocolla, chalcocite, molybdenite, *chalcopyrite, pyrite;* White mine, needle ore, chalcopyrite. barite; Long and Muse's mine, argentiferous galenite, pyrite, chalcopyrite, limonite; Boger mine, tetradymite; Fink mine, valuable copper ores; Mt. Makins, tetrahedrite, magnetite, talc, blende, pyrite, proustite, galenite; Bangle mine, scheelite.
CALDWELL CO.—Chromite.
CHATHAM CO.—Mineral coal, pyrite, chloritoid.
CHEROKEE CO.—Iron ores, gold, galenite, corundum, rutile, cyanite, damonite.
CLEVELAND CO.—White Plains, *quartz*, crystals, *smoky quartz*, tourmaline, rutile in quartz.
CLAY CO.—At the Cullakenee Mine and elsewhere, corundum (pink), zoisite, tourmaline, margarite, willcoxite, dudleyite.
DAVIDSON CO.—King's, now Washington mine, native, silver, cerussite, anglesite, scheelite. pyromorphite, galenite, blende, malachite, black copper, *wavellite*, garnet, stilbite; five miles from Washington mine, on Faust's farm, gold, *tetradymite*, oxide of bismuth and tellurium, montanite, chalcopyrite, limonite, spathic iron, epidote; near Squire Ward's, gold in crystals, electrum.
FRANKLIN CO.—At Partiss mine, diamonds.
GASTON CO.—Iron ores, corundum, margarite; near Crowder's Mountain (in what was

formerly Lincoln Co.), *lazulite, cyanite, garnet*, graphite ; also twenty miles northeast, near south end of Clubb's Mtn., lazulite, cyanite, talc, rutile, topaz, *pyrophyllite ;* King's Mountain (or Briggs) Mine, native tellurium, altaite, tedradymite, montanite.

GUILFORD CO.—McCulloch copper and gold mine, twelve miles from Greensboro', *gold, pyrite, chalcopyrite* (worked for copper), *quartz*, siderite. The North Carolina Copper Co. are working the copper ore at the old Fentress mine ; at Deep River, compact *pyrophyllite* (worked for slate-pencils).

HAYWOOD CO.—Corundum, margarite, damourite.

HENDERSON CO.—*Zircon*, sphene (xanthitane).

JACKSON CO.—Alunogen? at Smoky Mt.; at Webster, serpentine, chromite, genthite, *chrysolite*, talc; Hoghalt Mt., pink corundum, margarite, tourmaline.

LINCOLN CO.—Diamond ; at Randleman's, *amethyst*, rose quartz.

MACON CO.—Franklin, Culsagee Mine, *corundum*, spinel, diaspore, tourmaline, damourite, prochlorite, culsageeite, kerrite, maconite.

MCDOWELL CO.—Brookite, monazite, corundum in small crystals red and white, *zircons*, garnet, beryl, sphene, xenotime, rutile, elastic sandstone, iron ores, pyromelane, tetradymite, montanite.

MADISON CO.—20 miles from Asheville, corundum, margarite, chlorite.

MECKLENBURG CO.—Near Charlotte (Rhea and Cathay mines) and elsewhere, *chalcopyrite, gold ;* chalcotrichite at McGinn's mine; barnhardtite near Charlotte ; pyrophyllite in Cotton Stone Mountain, diamond; Flowe mine, scheelite, wolframite ; Todd's Branch, *monazite*.

MITCHELL CO.—*Samarskite*, pyrochlore (?), euxenite, columbite, *muscovite*.

MONTGOMERY CO.—Steele's mine, ripidolite, albite.

MOORE CO.—Carbonton, compact pyrophyllite.

ROWAN CO.—Gold Hill Mines, thirty-eight miles northeast of Charlotte, and fourteen from Salisbury, gold, auriferous pyrite ; ten miles from Salisbury, *feldspar* in crystals, *bismuthinite*.

RANDOLPH CO.—Pyrophyllite.

RUTHERFORD CO.—*Gold, graphite*, bismuthic gold, diamond, euclase, *pseudomorphous quartz?*, chalcedony, corundum in small crystals, *epidote, pyrope*, brookite, zircon, monazite, rutherfordite, samarskite, *quartz crystals*, itacolumyte ; on the road to Cooper's Gap, cyanite.

STOKES AND SURRY COS.—Iron ores, graphite.

UNION CO.—Lemmond gold mine, eighteen miles from Concord (at Stewart's and Moore's mine), gold, quartz, blende, argentiferous galenite (containing 29·4 oz. of gold and 86·5 oz. of silver to the ton, Genth), pyrite, some chalcopyrite.

YANCEY CO.—*Iron ores*, amianthus, *chromite*, garnet (spessartite), samarskite.

SOUTH CAROLINA.

ABBEVILLE.—DIST.—Oakland Grove, *gold* (Dorn mine), galenite, pyromorphite, amethyst, garnet.

ANDERSON DIST.—At Pendleton, *actinolite*, galenite, kaolin, *tourmaline*.

CHARLESTON.—*Selenite*.

CHEOWEE VALLEY.—Galenite, tourmaline, gold.

CHESTERFIELD DIST.—Gold (Brewer's mine), talc, chlorite, pyrophyllite, pyrite, native bismuth, carbonate of bismuth, red and yellow ochre, whetstone, enargite.

DARLINGTON.—Kaolin.

EDGEFIELD DIST.—Psilomelane.

GREENVILLE DIST.—Galenite, pyromorphite, kaolin, chalcedony in buhrstone, beryl, plumbago, epidote, *tourmaline*.

KERSHAW DIST.—*Rutile*.

LANCASTER DIST.—Gold (Hale's mine), talc, chlorite, cyanite, elastic sandstone, pyrite ; gold also at Blackman's mine, Massey's mine, Ezell's mine.

LAURENS DIST.—Corundum, damourite.

NEWBERRY DIST.—Leadhillite.

PICKEN'S DIST.—Gold, manganese ores, kaolin.

RICHLAND DIST.—Chiastolite, novaculite.

SPARTANBURG DIST.—*Magnetite*, chalcedony, *hematite* ; at the Cowpens, limonite, *graphite*, limestone, copperas ; Morgan mine, leadhillite, pyromorphite, cerussite.

SUMTER DIST.—Agate.

UNION DIST.—Fairforest gold mines, pyrite, chalcopyrite.

YORK DIST.—Limestones, whetstones, witherite, barite, tetradymite.

GEORGIA.

BURKE AND SCRIVEN COS.—Hyalite.
CHEROKEE CO.—At Canton Mine, chalcopyrite, galenite, clausthalite, plumbogummite, aitchcockite, *arsenopyrite*, lanthanite, *harrisite*, *cantonite*, pyromorphite, automolite. zinc, staurolite. cyanite ; at Ball-Ground, spodumene.
CLARK CO., near Clarksville.—Gold, *xenotime*, zircon, rutile, cyanite, hematite, garnet, quartz.
DADE CO.—Halloysite, near Rising Fawn.
FANNIN CO.—*Staurolite!* chalcopyrite.
HABERSHAM CO.—*Gold*, pyrite, chalcopyrite, *galenite*, hornblende, garnet, quartz, kaolinite, soapstone, chlorite, *rutile*, iron ores, tourmaline, staurolite, zircon.
HALL CO.—*Gold*, quartz, kaolin, diamond.
HANCOCK CO.—Agate, chalcedony.
HEARD CO.—*Molybdite*, quartz.
LINCOLN CO.—*Lazulite!! rutile!!* hematite, cyanite, menaccanite, *pyrophyllite*, gold, itacolumyte rock.
LOWNS CO.—Corundum.
LUMPKIN CO.—At Field's gold mine, near Dahlonega, *gold, tetradymite*, pyrrhotite, chlorite, menaccanite, allanite, apatite.
RABUN CO.—Gold, *chalcopyrite*.
SPAULDING CO.—Tetradymite.
WASHINGTON CO., near Saundersville.— *Wavellite, fire opal.*

ALABAMA.

BIBB CO., Centreville.—*Iron ores*, marble, *barite*, coal, cobalt.
TUSCALOOSA CO.—*Coal*, galenite, pyrite, vivianite, limonite, calcite, dolomite, cyanite, steatite, quartz crystals, manganese ores.
BENTON CO.—Antimonial lead ore (boulangerite?)
TALLAPOOSA CO., at Dudleyville.—Corundum, spinel, tourmaline.

FLORIDA.

NEAR TAMPA BAY.—Limestone, sulphur springs, chalcedony, carnelian, agate, silicified shells and corals.

KENTUCKY.

ANDERSON CO.—Galenite, barite.
CLINTON CO.—Geodes of quartz.
CRITTENDEN CO.—Galenite, fluorite, calcite.
CUMBERLAND CO.—At mammoth Cave, *gypsum rosettes!* calcite, stalactites, nitre, epsomite.
FAYETTE CO.—Six miles N.E. of Lexington, galenite, barite, witherite, blende.
LIVINGSTONE CO., near the line of Union Co.—Galenite, chalcopyrite, large vein of fluorite.
MERCER CO.—At McAfee, *fluorite*, *pyrite*, calcite, barite. celestite.
OWEN CO.—Galenite, barite.

TENNESSEE.

BROWN'S CREEK.—Galenite, blende, barite, celestite.
CARTER'S CO., foot of Roan Mt.—*Sahlite*, magnetite.
CLAIBORNE CO.—*Calamine*, galenite, smithsonite, chlorite, steatite, magnetite.
COCKE CO., near Brush Creek.—Cacoxene? kraurite, iron sinter, stilpnosiderite, brown hematite.
DAVIDSON CO.—Selenite, with granular and snowy *gypsum*, or alabaster, crystallized and compact *anhydrite*, *fluorite* in crystals? *calcite* in crystals. Near Nashville, blue *celestite*, (crystallized, fibrous, and radiated), with *barite* in limestone. Haysboro', **galenite**, blende, with barite as the gangue of the ore.
DICKSON CO.—Manganite.

JEFFERSON CO.—*Calamine*, galenite, fetid barite.
KNOX CO.—Magnesian limestone, *native iron, variegated marbles!*
MAURY CO.—Wavellite in limestone.
MORGAN CO.—Epsom salt, nitrate of lime.
POLK CO., Ducktown mines, southeast corner of State.—Melaconite, chalcopyrite, pyrite, native copper, bornite, rutile, *zoisite*, galenite, *harrisite*, alisonite, blende, *pyroxene, tremolite, sulphates of copper and iron* in stalactites, allophane, rahtite, chalcocite (ducktownite), chalcotrichite, azurite, malachite, *pyrrhotite*, limonite.
ROAN CO., eastern declivity of Cumberland Mts.—Wavellite in limestone.
SEVIER CO., in caverns.—Epsom salt, soda alum, saltpetre, nitrate of lime, *breccia marble*.
SMITH CO.—Fluorite.
SMOKY MT., on declivity.—Hornblende, garnet, staurolite.
WHITE CO.—*Nitre*.

OHIO.

BAINBRIDGE (Copperas Mt., a few miles east of B.).—Calcite, barite, pyrite, copperas, alum.
CANFIELD.—*Gypsum!*
DUCK CREEK, Monroe Co.—Petroleum.
LAKE ERIE.—Strontian Island, *celestite!* Put-in Bay Island, *celestite! sulphur!* calcite.
LIVERPOOL.—Petroleum.
MARIETTA.—Argillaceous iron ore; iron ore abundant also in Scioto and Lawrence Cos.
OTTAWA CO.—Gypsum.
POLAND.—*Gypsum!*

MICHIGAN.

BREST (Monroe Co.).—*Calcite*, amethystine quartz, apatite, celestite.
GRAND RAPIDS.—*Selenite*, fib. and granular gypsum, *calcite, dolomite, anhydrite*.
*LAKE SUPERIOR MINING REGION.—The four principal regions are Keweenaw Point, Isle Royale, the Ontonagon, and Portage Lake. The mines of Keweenaw Point are along two ranges of elevation, one known as the Greenstone Range, and the other as the Southern or Bohemian Range (Whitney). The copper occurs in the trap or amygdaloid, and in the associated conglomerate. *Native copper! native silver!* chalcopyrite, horn silver, tetrahedrite, manganese ores, epidote, *prehnite, laumontite, datolite*, heulandite, orthoclase, *analcite*, chabazite, compact datolite, chrysocolla, *mesotype* (Copper Falls mine), *leonhardite* (ib.), *analcite* (ib.), *apophyllite* (at Cliff mine), *wollastonite* (ib.), calcite, *quartz* (in crystals at Minnesota mine), compact datolite, orthoclase (Superior mine), *saponite*, melaconite (near Copper Harbor, but exhausted), chrysocolla ; on Chocolate River, galenite and sulphide of copper; chalcopyrite and native copper at Presq' Isle ; at Albion mine, *domeykite ;* at Prince Vein, *barite, calcite, amethyst ;* at Michipicoten Ids., copper nickel, stilbite, analcite ; at Albany and Boston mine, Portage Lake, *prehnite, analcite, orthoclase*, cuprite ; at Sheldon location, *domeykite, whitneyite, algodonite ;* Isle Royale mine, Portage Lake, compact datolite ; Quincy mine, calcite, compact datolite. At the Spurr Mountain Iron mine (magnetite), chlorite pseudomorph after garnet.
MARQUETTE.—Manganite, galenite ; twelve miles west at Jackson Mt., and other mines, *hematite, limonite, göthite!* magnetite, jasper.
MONROE.—Aragonite, apatite.
POINT AUX PEAUX (Monroe Co.).—*Amethystine quartz, apatite*, celestite, *calcite*.
SAGINAW BAY.—At Alabaster, *gypsum*.
STONY POINT (Monroe Co.).—Apatite, amethystine quartz, celestite, calcite.

ILLINOIS.

GALLATIN CO., on a branch of Grand Pierre Creek, sixteen to thirty miles from Shawneetown, down the Ohio, and from half to eight miles from this river.—*Violet fluorite!* in carboniferous limestone, barite, *galenite*, blende, brown iron ore.
HANCOCK CO.—At Warsaw, *quartz geodes!* containing *calcite! chalcedony, dolomite, blende,* brown spar, pyrite, aragonite, gypsum, bitumen.

---

* See also Pumpelly ; on the Paragenesis of copper and its associate minerals on Lake Superior Am. J. Sci., III., x, 17.

AMERICAN LOCALITIES. 495

HARDIN CO.—Near Rosiclare, *calcite*, galenite, blende; five miles back from Elizabeth town, bog-iron; one mile north of the river, between Elizabethtown and Rosiclare, *nitre*.
Jo DAVIESS CO.—At Galena, *galenite*, calcite, *pyrite*, blende; at Marsden's diggings, *galenite! blende, cerussite*, marcasite in stalactitic forms, pyrite.
JOLIET.—*Marble*.
QUINCY.—*Calcite!* pyrite.
SCALES MOUND.—*Barite*, pyrite.

INDIANA.

LIMESTONE CAVERNS; Corydon Caves, etc.—*Epsom salt*.
In most of the southwest counties, *pyrite, iron sulphate*, and *feather alum;* on Sugar Creek, pyrite and *iron sulphate;* in sandstone of Lloyd Co., near the Ohio, *gypsum;* at the top of the blue limestone formation, brown *spar, calcite*.
LAWRENCE CO.—Spice Valle, kaolinite (=indianaite).

MINNESOTA.

NORTH SHORE OF L. SUPERIOR) range of hills running nearly northeast and southwest, extending from Fond du Lac Superieure to the Kamanistiqueia River in Upper Canada).—*Scolecite, apophyllite, prehnite, stilbite, laumontite, heulandite, harmotome*, thomsonite, *fluorite, barite, tourmaline, epidote*, hornblende, calcite, quartz crystals, pyrite, magnetite, steatite, blende, black oxyd of copper, malachite, native copper, chalcopyrite, amethystine quartz, ferruginous quartz, *chalcedony, carnelian, agate*, drusy quartz, hyalite? fibrous quartz, jasper, prase (in the debris of the lake shore), dogtooth, spar, augite, native silver, spodumene? chlorite; between Pigeon Point and Fond du Lac, near Baptism River, saponite (thalite) in amygdaloid.
KETTLE RIVER TRAP RANGE.—Epidote, nail-head calcite, amethystine quartz, calcite, undetermined zeolites, saponite.
STILLWATER.—Blende.
FALLS OF THE ST. CROIX.—Malachite, native copper, epidote, nail-head spar.
RAINY LAKE.—Actinolite, tremolite, fibrous hornblende, garnet, pyrite, magnetite, steatite.

WISCONSIN.

BIG BULL FALLS (near).—Bog iron.
BLUE MOUNDS.—Cerussite.
HAZLE GREEN.—Calcite.
LAC DU FLAMBEAU R.—Garnet, cyanite.
LEFT HAND R. (near small tributary).—Malachite, chalcocite, native copper, red copper ore, earthy malachite, epidote, chlorite? quartz crystals.
LINDEN.—*Galenite, smithsonite, hydrozincite*.
MINERAL POINT and vicinity.—Copper and lead ores, chrysocolla, *azurite!* chalcopyrite, malachite, *galenite*, cerussite, anglesite, blende, *pyrite*, barite, *calcite, marcasite, smithsonite!* (so-called "dry-bone").
MONTREAL RIVER PORTAGE.—Galenite in gneissoid granite.
SANK CO.—Hematite, malachite, chalcopyrite.
SHULLSBURG.—*Galenite!* blende, pyrite; at Emmet's digging, *galenite* and pyrite.

IOWA.

DU BUQUE LEAD MINES, and elsewhere.—*Galenite!* calcite, blende, black oxide of manganese; at Ewing's and Sherard's diggings, *smithsonite*, calamine; at Des Moines, quartz crystals, selenite; Makoqueta R., *brown iron ore;* near Durango, galenite.
CEDAR RIVER, a branch of the Des Moines.—*Selenite* in crystals, in the bituminous shale of the coal measures; also elsewhere on the Des Moines, gypsum abundant; argillaceous iron ore, spathic iron; copperas in crystals on the Des Moines, above the Mouth of Baaj and elsewhere, *pyrite*, blende.
FORT DODGE.—*Celestite*.
MAKOQUETA.—Hematite.
NEW GALENA.—Octahedral galenite, **anglesite**.

MISSOURI.

BIRMINGHAM.—Limonite.
GRANBY.—*Sphalerite, galenite*, calamine, greenockite, as a coating on sphalerite.
JEFFERSON Co., at Valle's diggings.—*Galenite, cerussite*, anglesite, calamine, chalcopyrite malachite, azurite, witherite.
MINE & BURTON.—*Galenite, cerussite, anglesite, barite*, calcite.
DEEP DIGGINGS.—Malachite, *cerussite* in crystals and manganese ore.
MADISON Co.—Wolframite.
MINE LA MOTTE.—*Galenite!* malachite, *earthy cobalt* and *nickel*, bog manganese, sulphide of iron and nickel, *cerussite*, caledonite, plumbogummite, wolframite, *siegenite*, smaltite, aragonite.
ST. LOUIS.—*Millerite*, calcite, dolomite, earthy barite, fluorite.
ST. FRANCIS RIVER.—Wolframite.
PERRY'S DIGGINGS, and elsewhere.—Galenite, etc.
Forty miles west of the Mississippi and ninety south of St. Louis, the iron mountains, specular iron, limonite; 10 m. east of Ironton, wolframite, tungstite.

ARKANSAS.

BATESVILLE.—In bed of White R., some miles above Batesville, gold.
GREEN Co.—Near Gainesville, lignite.
HOT SPRINGS Co.—At Hot Springs. *wavellite*, thuringite; Magnet Cove, *brookite! schorlomite, elæolite*, magnetite, quartz, green coccolite, garnet, apatite, *perofskite* (hydrotitanite), rutile, ripidolite, thomsonite (ozarkite), microcline, ægirite.
INDEPENDENCE Co.—Lafferay Creek, psilomelane.
LAWRENCE Co.—Hoppe, Bath, and Koch mines, *smithsonite*, dolomite, galenite; nitre.
MARION Co.—Wood's mine, smithsonite, hydrozincite (marionite), galenite; Poke bayou, *braunite?*
OUACHITA SPRINGS.—*Quartz?* whetstones.
PULASKI Co.—Kellogg mine, 10 m. north of Little Rock, *tetrahedrite, tennantite*, nacrite galenite, blende, quartz.

CALIFORNIA.

The principal *gold mines* of California are in Tulare, Fresno, Mariposa, Tuolumne, Calaveras, El Dorado, Placer, Nevada, Yuba, Sierra, Butte, Plumas, Shasta, Siskiyou, and Del Norte counties, although gold is found in almost every county of the State. The gold occurs in quartz, associated with sulphides of iron, copper, zinc, and lead; in Calaveras and Tuolomne counties, at the Mellones, Stanislaus, Golden Rule, and Rawhide mines, associated with tellurides of gold and silver; it is also largely obtained from placer diggings, and further it is found in beach washings in Del Norte and Klamath counties.

The *copper mines* are principally at or near Copperopolis, in Calveras county; near Genesee Valley, in Plumas county; near Low Divide, in Del Norte county; on the north fork of Smith's River; at Soledad, in Los Angeles county.

The *mercury mines* are at or near New Almaden and North Almaden, in Santa Clara county; at New Idria and San Carlos, Monterey county; in San Luis Obispo county; at Pioneer mine, and other localities in Lake county; in Santa Barbara county.

ALPINE Co.—Morning Star mine, *enargite*, stephanite, polybasite, barite, quartz, pyrite, tetrahedite.
AMADOR Co.—At Volcano, chalcedony. *hyalite*.
ALAMEDA Co.—Diabolo Range, magnesite.
BUTTE Co.—Cherokee Flat, *diamond*, platinum, iridosmine.
CALAVERAS Co.—Copperopolis, *chalcopyrite*, malachite, *azurite, serpentine, picrolite*, native copper, near Murphy's, jasper, opal; albite, with gold and pyrite; Mellones mine, *calaverite, petzite*.
CONTRA-COSTA Co.—San Antonio, chalcedony.
DEL NORTE Co.—Crescent City, agate, carnelian; Low Divide, chalcopyrite, bornite. malachite; on the coast, iridosmine, platinum.
EL DORADO Co.—Pilot Hill, chalcopyrite, near Georgetown, hessite, from placer diggings; Roger's Claim, Hope Valley, *grossular garnet*, in copper ore; Coloma, *chromite*, Spanish Dry Diggings, *gold;* Granite Creek, roscoelite, gold.

AMERICAN LOCALITIES.

FRESNO Co.—Chowchillas, *andalusite*.
HUMBOLDT Co.—Cryptomorphite.
INGO Co.—Ingo district, *galenite, cerussite,* anglesite, *barite,* atacamite, calcite, *grossular garnet!*
LAKE Co.—Borax Lake, *borax!* sassolite, *glauberite;* Pioneer mine, cinnabar, native mercury, selenide of mercury; near the Geysers, sulphur, hyalite; Redington mine, metacinnabarite.
LOS ANGELES Co.—Near Santa Anna River, *anhydrite;* Williams Pass, chalcedony; Soledad mines, chalcopyrite, *garnet,* gypsum; Mountain Meadows, garnet, in copper ore.
MARIPOSA Co.—Chalcopyrite, itacolumyte; Centreville, cinnabar; Pine Tree Mine, tetrahedrite; Burns Creek, limonite; Geyer Gulch, pyrophyllite; La Victoria mine, *azurite!* near Coulterville, *cinnabar, gold.*
MONO Co.—Partzite.
MONTEREY Co.—Alisal Mine, arsenic; near Paneches, chalcedony; New Idria mine, cinnabar; near New Idria, chromite, zaratite, chrome garnet; near Pacheco's Pass, stibnite.
NEVADA Co.—Grass Valley, *gold!* in quartz veins, with pyrite, chalcopyrite, blende, arsenopyrite, galenite, *quartz,* biotite; near Truckee Pass, gypsum; Excelsior Mine, molybdenite, with molybdenite and gold; Sweet Land, pyrolusite.
PLACER Co.—Miner's Ravine, *epidote!* with *quartz, gold.*
PLUMAS Co.—Genesee Valley, chalcopyrite; Hope mines, *bornite,* sulphur.
SANTA BARBARA Co.—San Amedio Cañon, stibnite, asphaltum, bitumen, maltha, petroleum, cinnabar, iodide of mercury; Santa Clara River, sulphur.
SAN DIEGO Co.—Carisso Creek, gypsum; San Isabel, tourmaline, orthoclase, garnet.
SAN FRANCISCO Co.—Red Island, pyrolusite and manganese ores.
SANTA CLARA Co.—New Almaden, *cinnabar, calcite, aragonite,* serpentine, chrysolite, quartz, aragotite; North Almaden, chromite; Mt. Diabolo Range, magnesite, datolite, with vesuvianite and garnet.
SAN LUIS OBISPO Co.—Asphaltum, cinnabar, native mercury.
SAN BERNARDINO Co.—Colorado River, agate, trona; Temescal, cassiterite; Russ District, galenite, cerussite; Francis mine, cerargyrite.
SHASTA Co.—Near Shasta City, hematite, in large masses.
SISKIYOU Co.—Surprise Valley, selenite, in large slabs.
SONOMA Co.—Actinolite, garnets.
TULARE Co.—Near Visalia, magnesite, asphaltum.
TUOLUMNE Co.—Tourmaline, tremolite; Sonora, *graphite;* York Tent, chromite; Golden Rule mine, *petzite, calaverite,* altaite, hessite, magnesite, tetrahedrite, gold; Whiskey Hill *gold!*
TRINITY Co.—Cassiterite, a single specimen found.

LOWER CALIFORNIA.

LA PAZ.—Cuproscheelite. LORETTO.—Natrolite, siderite, selenite.

UTAH.

BEAVER Co —Bismuthinite, bismite, bismutite.
TINTIC DISTRICT.—At the Shoebridge mine, the Dragon mine, and the Mammoth vein, *enargite* with pyrite.
BOX ELDER Co.—Empire mine, *wulfenite!*
In the Wahsatch and Oquirrh mountains there are extensive mines, especially of ores of lead rich in silver. At the Emma mine occur galenite, cervantite, cerussite, wulfenite, azurite, malachite, calamine, anglesite, linarite, sphalerite, pyrite, argentite, stephanite, etc. At the Lucky Boy mine, Butterfield Cañon., orpiment, realgar.
One hundred and twenty miles south-west of Salt Lake City, *topaz* has been found in colorless crystals.

NEVADA.

CARSON VALLEY.—Chrysolite.
CHURCHILL Co.—Near Ragtown, *gay-lussite,* trona, common salt.
COMSTOCK LODE.—Gold, *native silver, argentite, stephanite, polybasite,* pyrargyrite, proustite, tetrahedrite, cerargyrite, pyrite, chalcopyrite, galenite, blende, pyromorphite, allemontite, arsenolite, quartz, calcite, gypsum, cerussite, cuprite, wulfenite, amethyst, küstelite.

ESMERALDA CO.—Alum, 12 m. north of Silver Creek; at Aurora, fluorite, stibnite; near Mono Lake, native copper and cuprite, obsidian; Columbus district, ulexite; Walker Lake gypsum, hematite; Silver Peak, *salt*, saltpetre, sulphur, silver ores.

HUMBOLDT DISTRICT.—Sheba mine, *native silver, jamesonite*, stibnite, *tetrahedrite*, proustite, blende, cerussite, calcite, bournonite, pyrite, galenite, malachite, xanthocone (?).

MAMMOTH DISTRICT.—*Orthoclase*, turquois, *hübnerite*, scheelite.

REESE RIVER DISTRICT.—Native silver, *proustite, pyrargyrite*, stephanite, blende, polybasite, rhodochrosite, embolite, *tetrahedrite!* cerargyrite, embolite.

SAN ANTONIA.—Belmont mine, stetefeldtite.

SIX MILE CAÑON.—*Selenite.*

ORMSBY CO.—W. of Carson, *epidote.*

STOREY CO.—Alum, natrolite, scolezite.

ARIZONA.

On and near the Colorado, gold, silver, and copper mines; at Bill Williams' Fork, chrysocolla, malachite, atacamite, brochantite; Dayton Lode, gold, fluorite, cerargyrite; Skinner Lode, octahedral fluorite; at various places in the southern part of the territory, silver and copper mines; Heintzelmann mine, *stromeyerite*, chalcocite, tetrahedrite, atacamite. Montgomery mine, Harsayampa Dist., tetradymite. Whitneyite, in Southern Arizona.

OREGON.

Gold is obtained from beach washings on the southern coast; quartz mines and placer mines in the Josephine district; also on the Powder, Burnt, and John Day's rivers, and other places in eastern Oregon; platinum, iridosmine, laurite, on the Rogue River, at Port Oxford, and Cape Blanco. In Curry Co., priceite.

IDAHO.

In the Owyhee, Boise, and Flint districts, *gold*, also extensive silver mines; Poor Man Lode, *cerargyrite! proustite, pyrargyrite! native silver, gold*, pyromorphite, quartz, malachite, polybasite; on Jordan Creek, stream tin; Rising Star mine, *stephanite, argentite*, pyrargyrite.

MONTANA.

Many mines of gold, etc., west of the Missouri R. HIGHLAND DISTRICT.—Tetradymite. SILVER STAR DIST.—Psittacinite.

In the Yellowstone Park, in Montana and Wyoming Territories.—*Geyserite.*—*Amethyst chalcedony*, quartz crystals, quartz on calcite, etc.

COLORADO.*

The principal gold mines of Colorado are in Boulder, Gilpin, Clear Creek, and Jefferson Cos., on a line of country a few miles W. of Denver, extending from Long's Peak to Pike's Peak. A large portion of the gold is associated with veins of pyrite and chalcopyrite; silver and lead mines are at and near Georgetown, Clear Creek Co., and to the westward in Summit Co., on Snake and Swan rivers.

At the GEORGETOWN mines are found:—native silver, pyrargyrite, argentite, tetrahedrite, pyromorphite, galenite, sphalerite, azurite, aragonite, barite, fluorite, mica.

TRAIL CREEK.—Garnet, epidote, hornblende, chlorite; at the Freeland Lode, *tetrahedrite*, tennantite, anglesite, caledonite, cerussite, tenorite, siderite, azurite, minium; at the Champion Lode, tenorite, azurite, chrysocolla, malachite; at the Gold Belt Lode, vivianite; at the Kelly Lode, tenorite; at the Coyote Lode, malachite, cyanotrichite.

Near BLACK HAWK.—At Willis Gulch, enargite, fluorite, pyrite; at the Gilpin County Lode, cerargyrite; on Gregory Hill, feldspar; North Clear Creek, lievrite.—*Galenite!*

---

* See the Catalogue of Minerals of Colorado by J. Alden Smith.

BEAR CREEK.—Fluorite, beryl; near the Malachite Lode, *malachite, cuprite*, vesuvianite, topazolite ; Liberty Lode, chalcocite.
SNAKE RIVER.—Penn District, embolite ; at several lodes, pyrargyrite, native silver, azurite.
RUSSELL DISTRICT.—Delaware Lode, *chalcopyrite,* crystallized *galenite.*—Epidote, pyrite
VIRGINIA CAÑON.—Epidote, fluorite ; at the Crystal Lode, native silver, spinel.
SUGAR LOAF DISTRICT.—Chalcocite, pyrrhotite, garnet (manganesian).
CENTRAL CITY.—Garnet, tenorite ; at Leavitt Lode, molybdenite; on Gunnell Hill, magnetite ; at the Pleasantview mine, cerussite.
GOLDEN CITY.—Aragonite.
BERGEN'S RANCHE.—Garnet, actinolite, calcite.
BOULDER CO., Red Cloud Mine.—Native tellurium, altaite, hessite (petzite), sylvanite, calaverite, schirmerite.
LAKE CITY, at the Hotchkiss Lode.—Petzite, calaverite (?), etc.
PIKE'S PEAK, on Elk Creek.—*Amazon tone!! smoky quartz! aventurine feldspar,* amethyst, *albite,* fluorite, hematite, anhydrite (rare), columbite.

CANADA.

CANADA EAST.

ABERCROMBIE.—Labradorite.
BAY ST. PAUL.—*Mennaccanite!* apatite, allanite, rutile (or brookite ?)
AUBERT.—Gold, iridosmine, platinum.
BOLTON.—*Chromite, magnesite,* serpentine, picrolite, steatite, bitter spar, wad.
BOUCHERVILLE.—*Augite* in trap.
BROME.—*Magnetite,* chalcopyrite, *sphene,* menaccanite, phyllite, sodalite, cancrinite, galenite, chloritoid.
CHAMBLY.—Analcite, chabazite and calcite in trachyte, *menaccanite.*
CHATEAU RICHER.—*Labradorite, hypersthene,* andesite.
DAILLEBOUT.—Blue spinel with clintonite.
GRENVILLE.—Wollastonite, *sphene,* vesuvianite, calcite, pyroxene, steatite (rensselaerite). *garnet* (cinnamon-stone), *zircon, graphite, scapolite.*
HAM.—Chromite in serpentine, diallage, *antimony! senarmontite! kermesite, valentinite,* stibnite.
INVERNESS.—*Variegated copper.*
LAKE ST. FRANCIS.—*Andalusite* in mica slate.
LANDSDOWN.—*Barite.*
LEEDS.—Dolomite, chalcopyrite, gold, *chloritoid.*
MILLE ISLES.—*Labradorite!* menaccanite, hypersthene, andesite, *zircon.*
MONTREAL.—*Calcite, augite,* sphene in trap, chrysolite, natrolite, dawsonite.
MORIN.—*Sphene, apatite, labradorite.*
ORFORD.—White garnet, *chrome garnet, millerite,* serpentine.
OTTAWA.—*Pyroxene.*
POLTON.—Chromite, *steatite,* serpentine, *amianthus.*
ROUGEMONT.—Augite in trap.
SHERBROOK.—At Suffield mine, *albite! native silver,* argentite, chalcopyrite, blende.
ST. ARMAND.—Micaceous iron ore with quartz, epidote.
ST. FRANÇOIS BEAUCE.—Gold, platinum, iridosmine, menaccanite, magnetite, serpentine, chromite, soapstone, barite.
ST. JEROME.—*Sphene, apatite, chondrodite, phlogopite, tourmaline, zircon,* molybdenite, pyrrhotite.
ST. NORBERT.—Amethyst in greenstone.
STUKELEY.—Serpentine, *verd-antique!* schiller spar.
SUTTON.—*Magnetite* in fine crystals, hematite, *rutile,* dolomite, *magnesite,* chromiferous *talc,* bitter spar, steatite.
UPTON.—Chalcopyrite, malachite, calcite.
VAUDREUIL.—Limonite, vivianite.
YAMASKA.—Sphene in trap.

CANADA WEST.

ARNPRIOR.—Calcite.
BALSAM LAKE.—*Molybdenite,* scapolite, quartz, pyroxene, pyrite.
BRANTFORD.—Sulphuric acid spring (4·2 parts of pure sulphuric acid in 1000).
BATHURST.—Barite, *black tourmaline, perthite* (orthoclase), *peristerite* (albite), *bytownite,* pyroxene, wilsonite, scapolite, apatite, titanite.

BROCKVILLE.—Pyrite.
BROME.—Magnetite.
BRUCE MINES.—*Calcite*, dolomite, quartz, chalcopyrite.
BURGESS.—*Pyroxene*, albite, *mica*, *sapphire*, sphene, chalcopyrite, *apatite, black spinel*, spodumene (in a boulder), serpentine, biotite.
BYTOWN.—*Calcite, bytownite*, chondrodite, spinel.
CAPE IPPERWASH, Lake Huron.—Oxalite in shales.
CLARENDON.—*Vesuvianite*.
DALHOUSIE.—Hornblende, dolomite.
DRUMMUND.—Labradorite.
ELIZABETHTOWN.—*Pyrrhotite, pyrite*, calcite, magnetite, talc. phlogopite, siderite, apatite, cacoxenite.
ELMSEY.—Pyroxene, sphene, feldspar, *tourmaline*, apatite, biotite, zircon, red spinel chondrodite.
FITZROY.—Amber, brown *tourmaline*, in quartz.
GŒTINEAU RIVER, Blasdell's Mills.—Calcite, apatite, tourmaline, hornblende, pyroxene.
GRAND CALUMET ISLAND.—*Apatite, phlogopite! pyroxene!* sphene, *vesuvianite!!* serpentine, tremolite, *scapolite*, brown and black *tourmaline!* pyrite, loganite.
HIGH FALLS OF THE MADAWASKA.—*Pyroxene!* hornblende.
HULL.—*Magnetite*, garnet, graphite.
HUNTERSTOWN.—*Scapolite, sphene*, vesuvianite, garnet, *brown tourmaline!*
HUNTINGTON.—*Calcite!*
INNISKILLEN.—Petroleum.
KINGSTON.—*Celestite*.
LAC DES CHATS, Island Portage.—*Brown tourmaline!* pyrite, calcite, quartz.
LANARK.—Raphilite (hornblende), serpentine. asbestus.
LANDSTOWN.—*Barite!* vein 27 in. wide, and fine crystals.
MADOC.—Magnetite.
MAMORA.—Magnetite, chalcolite, garnet, epsomite, specular iron.
MAIMANSE.—*Pitchblende* (coracite).
McNAB.—Hematite, barite.
MICHIPICOTEN ISLAND, Lake Superior.—*Domeykite, niccolite, genthite*.
NEWBOROUGH.—*Chondrodite*, graphite.
PACKENHAM.—Hornblende.
PERTH.—Apatite in large beds, phlogopite.
SOUTH CROSBY.—Chondrodite in limestone, magnetite.
ST. ADELE.—Chondrodite in limestone.
ST. IGNACE ISLAND.—*Calcite*, native copper.
SYDENHAM.—Celestite.
TERRACE COVE, Lake Superior.—Molybdenite.
WALLACE MINE, Lake Huron.—Hematite, nickel ore, nickel vitriol.

NEW BRUNSWICK.[*]

ALBERT Co.—Hopewell, gypsum; Albert mines, coal (albertite); Shepody Mountain, alunite in clay, calcite, iron pyrites, *manganite*, psilomelane, *pyrolusite*.
CARLETON Co.—Woodstock, chalcopyrite, hematite, limonite, wad.
CHARLOTTE Co. — Campobello, at Welchpool, blende, chalcopyrite, bornite, galenite, pyrite; at head of Harbor de Lute, galenite; Deer Island, on west side, calcite, magnetite, quartz crystals; Digdignash River on west side of entrance, *calcite!* (in conglomerate). chalcedony; at Rolling Dam, graphite; Grandmanan, between Northern Head and Dark Harbor, agate, amethyst, *apophyllite, calcite*, hematite, heulandite, jasper, magnetite, natrolite, *stilbite;* at Whale Cove, *calcite!* heulandite, laumontite, stilbite, *semi-opal!* Wagaguadavic River, at entrance, azurite, chalcopyrite in veins, malachite.
GLOUCESTER Co.—Tete-a-Gouche River, eight miles from Bathurst, chalcopyrite (mined), *oxide of manganese!!* formerly mined.
KINGS Co.—Sussex, near Cloat's mills, on road to Belleisle, argentiferous galenite; one mile north of Baxter's Inn, *specular iron* in crystals, limonite; on Capt. McCready's farm, *selenite!!*
RESTIGOUCHE Co.—Belledune Point, *calcite!* serpentine, verd-antique; Dalhousie, agate, carnelian.

---

[*] For a more complete list of localities in New Brunswick, Nova Scotia, and Newfoundland, see catalogue by O. C. Marsh, Am. J. Sci., II. xxxv. 210, 1863

SAINT JOHN CO.—Black River, on coast, calcite, chlorite, chalcopyrite, *hematite!* Brandy Brook, epidote, *hornblende,* quartz crystals; Carleton, near Falls, calcite; Chance Harbor, calcite in quartz veins, chlorite in argillaceous and talcose slate; Little Dipper Harbor, on west side, in greenstone, amethyst, barite, quartz crystals; Moosepath, feldspar, hornblende, muscovite, black tourmaline; Musquash, on east side harbor, copperas, graphite, pyrite; at Shannon's, chrysolite, serpentine; east side of Musquash, *quartz crystals!*; Portland, at the Falls, graphite; at Fort Howe Hill, *calcite,* graphite; Crow's Nest, asbestus, *chryso'ite,* magnetite, *serpentine,* steatite; Lily Lake, white augite* chrysolite, graphite, serpentine steatite, talc; How's Road, two miles out, epidote (in syenite), steatite in limestone, *tremolite;* Drury's Cove, graphite, pyrite, pyrallolite? indurated talc; Quaco, at Lighthouse Point, large bed oxyd of manganese; Sheldon's Point, actinolite, asbestus, calcite, *epidote,* malachite, specular iron; Cape Spenser, asbestus, calcite, chlorite, *specular iron* (in crystals); Westbeach, at east end, on Evans' farm, chlorite, talc, *quartz crystals;* half a mile west, chlorite, chalcopyrite, magnesite (vein), magnetite; Point Wolf and Salmon River, asbestus, chlorite, chrysocolla, chalcopyrite, bornite, pyrite.

VICTORIA CO.—Tabique River, *agate, carne'ian,* jasper; at mouth, south side, galenite; at mouth of Wapskanegan, gypsum, salt spring; three miles above, stalactites (abundant); Quisabis River, blue phosphate of iron, in clay.

WESTMORELAND CO.—Bellevue, pyrite; Dorcester, on Taylor's farm, cannel coal; clay ironstone; on Ayres's farm, asphaltum, petroleum spring; Grandlance, apatite, selenite (in large crystals); Memramcook, coal (albertite); Shediac, four miles up Scadoue River, coal.

YORK CO.—Near Fredericton, stibnite, jamesonite, berthierite; Pokiock River, stibnite, *tin pyrites?* in granite (rare).

NOVA SCOTIA.

ANNAPOLIS CO.—Chute's Cove, *apoyhyllite,* natrolite; Gates' Mountain, analcite, magnetite, *meso'ite! natro'ite,* stilbite; Martial's Cove, *analcite!* chabazite, *heulandite;* Moose River, beds of magnetite; Nictau River, at the Falls, bed of hematite; Paradise River, black tourmaline, *smoky quartz!!;* Port George, farōelite, laumontite, mesolite, stilbite; east of Port George, on coast, apophyllite containing gyrolite; Peter's Point, west side of Stonock's Brook, *apophyllite!* calcite, heulandite, *laumontite!* (abundant), native copper, stilbite; St. Croix Cove, chabazite, heulandite.

COLCHESTER CO.—Five Islands, East River, *barite!* calcite, dolomite (ankerite), hematite, chalcopyrite; Indian Point, malachite, magnetite, red copper, tetrahedrite; Pinnacle Islands, *analcite,* calcite, *chabazite!* natrolite, siliceous sinter; Londonderry, on branch of Great Village River, *barite,* ankerite, hematite, limonite, magnetite; Cook's Brook, ankerite, hematite; Martin's Brook, hematite, limonite; at Folly River, below Falls, ankerite, pyrite; on high land, east of river, ankerite, hematite, limonite; on Archibald's land, ankerite, *barite,* hematite; Salmon River, south branch of, chalcopyrite, hematite; Shubenacadie River, anhydrite, calcite, *barite,* hematite, oxide of manganese; at the Canal, pyrite; Stewiacke River, barite (in limestone).

CUMBERLAND CO.—Cape Chiegnecto, barite; Cape D'Or, *analcite, apophyllite!!* chabazite, farōelite, laumontite, *mesolite,* malachite, *natro'ite, native copper,* obsidian, red copper (rare), vivianite (rare); Horse-shoe Cove, east side of Cape D'Or, analcite, calcite, stilbite; Isle Haute, south side, analcite, *apophyllite!!* calcite, *heulandite!!* natrolite, mesolite, *stilbite!* Joggins, coal, hematite, limonite; malachite and tetrahedrite at Seaman's Brook; Partridge Island, analcite, *apophyllite!* (rare), *amethyst!* agate, apatite (rare), *calcite!!* chabazite (acadialite), chalcedony, cat's-eye (rare), gypsum, hematite, *heulandite!* magnetite, *sti'bite!!;* Swan's Creek, west side, near the Point, calcite, gypsum, *heulandite,* pyrite; east side, at Wasson's Bluff and vicinity, *analcite!! apophyllite!* (rare), *calcite, chabazite!!* (acadialite), gypsum, *heulandite!! natrolite!* siliceous sinter; Two Islands, moss agate, analcite, calcite, chabazite, *heulandite;* McKay's Head, analcite, calcite, heulandite, *siliceous sinter!*

DIGBY CO.—Brier Island, native copper, in trap; Digby Neck, Sandy Cove and vicinity, *agate, amethyst, calcite, chabazite, hematite! laumontite* (abundant), magnetite, *sti'bite, quartz* crystals; Gulliver's Hole, *magnetite, stilbite!;* Mink Cove, amethyst, *chabazite!* quartz crystals; Nichols Mountain, south side, *amethyst, magnetite!;* Williams Brook, near source, *chabazite* (green), heulandite, stilbite, quartz crystal.

GUYSBORO' CO.—Cape Canseau, *andalusite.*

HALIFAX CO.—Gay's river, galenite in limestone; southwest of Halifax, garnet, staurolite, tourmaline: Tangier, *go'd!* in quartz veins in clay slate, associated with auriferous pyrites, galenite, hematite, mispickel, and magnetite; gold has also been found in the same formation, at Country Harbor, Fort Clarence, Isaac's Harbor, Indian Harbor, Laidlow's farm Lawrencetown, Sherbrooke, Salmon River, Wine Cove, and other places.

HANTS CO.—Cheverie, oxide of manganese (in limestone); Petite River, gypsum, oxide of manganese; Windsor, calcite, cryptomorphite (boronatrocalcite), howlite, glauber salt. The last three minerals are found in beds of gypsum.

KINGS CO.—Black Rock, centrallassite, cerinite; cyanolite; a few miles east of Black Rock, prehnite? *stilbite!*; Cape Blomidon, on the coast between the cape and Cape Split, the following minerals occur in many places (some of the best localities are nearly opposite Cape Sharp): *analcite!! agate, amethyst! apophyllite!* calcite, chalcedony, chabazite, *gmelinite* (ledererite), hematite, *heulandite!* laumontite, magnetite, malachite, *mesolite*, native copper (rare), *natrolite!* psilomelane, *stilbite!* thomsonite, faröelite, *quartz;* North Mountains, amethyst, bloodstone (rare), *ferruginous quartz, mesolite* (in soil); Long Point, five miles west of Black Rock, *heulandite, laumontite!! stilbite!!;* Morden, *apophyllite, mordenite;* Scot's Bay, *agate,* amethyst, *chalcedony,* mesolite, natrolite; Woodworth's Cove, a few miles west of Scot's Bay, *agate! chalcedony! jasper.*

LUNENBURG CO.—Chester, Gold River, gold in quartz, pyrite, mispickel; Cape la Have, pyrite; The "Ovens," *gold*, pyrite, arsenopyrite; Petite River, gold in slate.

PICTOU CO.—Pictou, *jet*, oxide of manganese, limonite; at Roder's Hill, six miles west of Pictou, barite; on Carribou River, gray copper and malachite in lignite; at Albion mines, coal, limonite; East River, limonite.

QUEENS CO.—Westfield, gold in quartz, pyrite, arsenopyrite; Five Rivers, near Big Fall, gold in quartz, pyrite, arsenopyrite, limonite.

RICHMOND CO.—West of Plaister Cove, barite and calcite in sandstone; nearer the Cove, calcite, *fluorite* (blue), siderite.

SHELBURNE CO.—Shelburne, near mouth of harbor, garnets (in gneiss); near the town, rose quartz; at Jordan and Sable River, *staurolite* (abundant), schiller spar.

SYDNEY CO.—Hills east of Lochaber Lake, pyrite, chalcopyrite, sideride, hematite; Morristown, epidote in trap, gypsum.

YARMOUTH CO.—Cream Pot, above Cranberry Hill, gold in quartz, pyrite; Cat Rock, Fouchu Point, asbestus, calcite.

NEWFOUNDLAND.

ANTONY'S ISLAND.—*Pyrite.*
CATALINA HARBOR.—On the shore, *pyrite!*
CHALKY HILL.—*Feldspar.*
COPPER ISLAND, one of the Wadham group.—*Chalcopyrite.*
CONCEPTION BAY.—On the shore south of Brigus, bornite and gray copper in trap.
BAY OF ISLANDS.—Southern shore, *pyrite* in slate.
LAWN.—*Galenite, cerargyrite, proustite, argentite.*
PLACENTIA BAY.—At La Manche, two miles eastward of Little Southern Harbor, *galenite!;* on the opposite side of the isthmus from Placentia Bay, barite, in a large vein, occasionally accompanied by chalcopyrite.
SHOAL BAY.—South of St. John's, chalcopyrite.
TRINITY BAY.—Western extremity, barite.
HARBOR GREAT ST. LAWRENCE.—West side, fluoride, galenite.

APPENDIX D.

SUPPLEMENTARY CATALOGUE OF AMERICAN LOCALITIES OF MINERALS.

MAINE.

NORWAY.—Triphylite (lithiophilite), chrysoberyl, cookeite.
PARIS.—Columbite, mica, triphylite.
PARSONFIELD.—Labradorite, crystallized.
PERU.—Triphylite (crystallized), columbite, beryl, spodumene.
STONEHAM.—Triplite, columbite, topaz, curved mica.

NEW HAMPSHIRE.

BARTLETT.—At the iron mine, danalite.

MASSACHUSETTS.

DEERFIELD.—In diabase, datolite, stilbite, chabazite, prehnite, heulandite, natrolite, analcite, calcite, fluorite, albite, epidote, axinite, tourmaline, diabantite, saponite, chlorophæite, kaolin, pyrite, malachite, limonite, wad.
ROCKPORT.—Fergusonite.

CONNECTICUT.

BRANCHVILLE.—In a large vein of pegmatite in gneiss, mica (curved concentric), microcline, albite (also crystallized), quartz (inclosing liquid CO_2), spodumene and various alteration products (eucryptite, cymatolite, killinite, etc.), columbite, apatite (also manganapatite), amblygonite, lithiophilite, eosphorite, triploidite, dickinsonite, reddingite, fairfieldite, fillowite, rhodochrosite, uraninite (crystals), cyrolite, microlite, uranium phosphates, chabazite, stilbite, heulandite and other species.
LITCHFIELD.—Staurolite in mica schist.
NEW HAVEN.—At Mill Rock, contact surface of trap and sandstone, garnet (topazolite); at East Rock, on columnar surfaces of trap, garnet (melanite), magnetite, pyroxene, apatite, calcite.
PORTLAND.—At Pelton's feldspar quarry, monazite.

NEW YORK.

CLINTON CO.—PLATTSBURG, nugget of platinum in drift.
ESSEX CO.—PORT HENRY, black tourmaline enclosing orthoclase; Champlain iron region, uranothorite.
ST. LAWRENCE CO.—DEKALB, white tourmaline.
PICTAIRN.—Titanite.
RUSSELL.—In veins in a granitic rock, danburite with pyroxene, titanite, black mica.

NEW JERSEY.

BERGEN.—Hayesine.
FRANKLIN FURNACE and STERLING.—Chalcophanite, hetærolite, pyrochroite.

PENNSYLVANIA.

BEDFORD CO.—Bridgeport, barite.
BERKS CO.—Jones's mine, aurichalcite, melaconite, byssolite.
BUCKS CO.—Phenixville, ankerite.
Bridgewater Station.—Titanite.
CHESTER CO.—Yellow Springs, allanite.
DELAWARE CO.—Waterville, near Chester, and Upland, chabazite.
Mineral Hill, columbite.
Leiperville, garnet, zoisite, heulandite, leidyite.
FRANKLIN CO.—Lancaster Station, barite.
HUNTINGTON CO.—Broad Top Mountain, barite.
LEHIGH CO.—Shimerville, corundum.
LUZERNE CO.—Scranton, under a peat-bed, phytocollite (dopplerite).
Drifton, pyrophyllite.
MIFFLIN CO.—Strontianite.
MONTGOMERY CO.--Upper Salford mine, azurite.
NORTHAMPTON CO.—Bethlehem, axinite.
PHILADELPHIA CO.—Germantown, fahlunite.
SCHUYLKILL CO., near Mahanoy City, pyrophyllite, alunogen, copiapite, in coal mines.

DELAWARE.

Dixon's Quarry.—Columbite.
Newark.—Quartz crystals, doubly terminated, loose in soil.

VIRGINIA.

AMELIA CO.—From a granite vein (mica mine) in gneiss near Amelia Court House, mica in large sheets, quartz, orthoclase, microlite, monazite, columbite, orthite, helvite with topazolite, beryl, fluorite, amethyst, apatite (rare).
AMHERST CO.—From a feldspar vein in a gneissoid rock on the northwest slope of Little Friar Mt., allanite, sipylite, magnetite, zircon.
ROCKBRIDGE CO.—Underlying limonite, dufrenite in an irregular bed ten inches deep, strengite in cavities in dufrenite.
WYTHE CO.—Austin mine, aragonite (7 p. c. $PbCO_3$).

NORTH CAROLINA.*

Alexander Co.—Near Stony Point, in narrow veins or pockets in a gneissoid rock (in part also loose in overlying soil), spodumene (hiddenite), beryl (emerald), rutile, monazite, allanite, quartz.
At White Plains, quartz crystals, spodumene (hiddenite), beryl, rutile, scorodite, columbite, tourmaline.
At Milholland's mill, rutile, monazite, muscovite, quartz.
Burke Co.—In the auriferous gravels at Brindletown, octahedrite (transparent), brookite, zircon, fergusonite, monazite, xenotime (compounded with zircon), garnet, tourmaline, magnetite and other species.
Mitchell Co.—At the mica mines, muscovite in large quantities, orthoclase, albite, samarskite, columbite, hatchettolite, rogersite, fergusonite, monazite, uraninite, gummite, phosphuranylite, uranotile, allanite, beryl, zoisite, garnet, menaccanite.
Yancey Co.—At the Ray mica mine, muscovite, tantalite (columbite), monazite, beryl, garnet, zircon, rutile, etc.
At Hampton's, chromite, epidote, enstatite, tremolite, chrysolite, serpentine, talc, magnesite, etc.

ALABAMA.

COOSA CO.—Cassiterite, tantalite.

---

* For a complete list of the minerals and mineral localities of North Carolina, see Geology of North Carolina, vol. II., chap. I., Mineralogy by F. A. Genth and W. C. Kerr, with notes by W. E. Hidden; 122 pp., 8vo, Raleigh, 1881.

AMERICAN LOCALITIES. 505

MICHIGAN.

NEGAUNEE.—Manganite, göthite, hematite, barite, kaolinite.
GRAND MARAIS.—Thomsonite (lintonite).

MISSOURI.*

ADAIR CO.—Göthite with calcite in concretionary masses of clay iron-stone.
BARTON CO.—McCarrow's coal bank, pickeringite, as a white efflorescence on sandy shales of coal measures.
BENTON CO —Limonite.
BOLLINGER CO.—Limonite, bog manganese, psilomelane.
CALLAWAY CO.—Hematite, clay iron ore.
CHARITON CO —Selenite.
COLE CO —Barite. At the Eureka mines, galenite, smithsonite.
COOPER CO.—Collins mine, malachite, azurite, chalcopyrite, smithsonite, galenite sphalerite, limonite.
CRAWFORD CO.—Scotia iron banks, hematite, quartz, jasper, amethyst, göthite, malachite.
DADE CO.—Smithsonite.
DENT CO.—Simmon's Mountain, hematite.
FRANKLIN CO.—Cove mines, galenite, cerussite, anglesite, barite.
Mine-à-Burton, galenite, cerussite, anglesite.
Moselle, limonite.
Mount Hope mine, galenite, sphalerite, calamine, smithsonite.
Stanton Copper mines, native copper, chalcotrichite, malachite, azurite, chalcopyrite.
Virginia mines, galenite, anglesite, cerussite, minium.
IRON CO.—PILOT KNOB, hematite, serpentine, magnetite, quartz, manganese ore.
JASPER CO.—Joplin mines, galenite, sphalerite, pyrite, marcasite, cerussite, bitumen.
ORONOGO.—Galenite, sphalerite, cerussite, smithsonite, anglesite.
WEBB CITY.—Galenite, sphalerite.
JEFFERSON CO.—Palmer mines, galenite, cerussite, plumbogummite.
Valle mines, galenite, cerussite, anglesite, calamine, smithsonite, hydrozincite, malachite, azurite.
MADISON CO.—Enistein silver mine, galenite, sphalerite, wolframite, pyrite, quartz, muscovite, actinolite, fluorite.
MINE-LA-MOTTE.—Galenite, linnæite (siegenite), cerussite, anglesite, pyrrhotite, earthy cobalt, bog manganese, plumbogummite, chalcopyrite, annabergite.
In granites, porphyries, etc., quartz, agate, hornblende, asbestos, serpentine, chlorite, epidote, feldspar.
MONITEAU CO —Sampson's coal mine, galenite and sphalerite in cannel coal.
MORGAN CO.—Buffalo mines, galenite.
Humes Hill, barite.
NEWTON CO.—Granby mines, galenite, cerussite, pyromorphite, calamine, greenochite, sphalerite, smithsonite, hydrozincite, buratite, dolomite, calcite.
PHELPS CO —Hematite, siderite, limonite, ankerite.
ST. FRANCOIS CO.—Iron mountain, hematite, apatite, tungstite, wolframite, magnetite, menaccanite.
ST. GENEVIEVE CO.—St. Genevieve copper mines, chalcopyrite, cuprite, malachite, azurite, covellite, chalcocite, bornite, melaconite, chalcanthite.
ST. LOUIS CO.—ST. LOUIS.—In cavities in limestone, millerite, dolomite, calcite, fluorite, anhydite, gypsum, strontianite.
SALINE CO.—Halite in incrustations.
WAYNE CO.—Limonite.

KANSAS.

BROWN CO.—Celestite.

ARKANSAS.

SEVIER Co.—Stibnite, stibiconite, bindheimite, jamesonite.
HOT SPRINGS Co.—Rutile in eightlings, variscite.

---

*See Notes on the Mineralogy of Missouri, by Alexander V. Leonhard, St. Louis, 1882.

COLORADO.

BOULDER Co.—Magnolia district (especially the Keystone, Mountain Lion and Smuggler mines), native tellurium, coloradoite, calaverite, tellurite, magnolite, ferrotellurite, sylvanite.

CHAFFEE Co.—Arrow mine, jarosite with turgite.

CUSTER Co.—Silver cliff, niccolite.

EL PASO COUNTY.—Near Pike's Peak, arfvedsonite, astrophyllite, zircon; siderophyllite, topaz, phenacite, cryolite, thomsenolite (and other fluorides), tysonite, bastnäsite.

GILPIN Co.—Near Central City, pyrite in modified crystals, chalcopyrite often coated by tetrahedrite in parallel position, crystallized gold on pyrite.

GUNNISON Co. Near Gothic, smaltite.

JEFFERSON Co.—Near Golden, in basalt of Table Mountain, chabazite, thomsonite, analcite, apophyllite, calcite, mesolite, laumontite.

LA PLATA Co.—Poughkeepsie Gulch, Alaska mine, alaskaite with tetrahedrite, chalcopyrite, barite.

LAKE Co.—Leadville, cerussite carrying silver, anglesite, pyromorphite, sphalerite, calamine, minium, dechenite (?), rhodochrosite with galenite, chalcopyrite.

Golden Queen mine, scheelite with gold. Ute and Ule silver mine, stephanite, galenite, sphalerite, chalcocite.

PARK Co.—Grant P. O., Baltic lode, beegerite. Hall Valley, ilesite.

CALIFORNIA.

INYO Co.—San Carlos, datolite with grossular garnet and vesuvianite.

LOS ANGELES Co.—Brea Ranch, vivianite in nodules with asphaltum.

OREGON.

DOUGLAS Co.—Cow Creek, Piney Mountain, considerable deposits of a hydrous nickel silicate, allied to garnierite.

GRANT Co.—Canyon City, cinnabar with calcite.

UTAH.

IRON Co.—Coyote District, orpiment and realgar in a thin bed in the horizontal sedimentary formations underlying lava.

PIUTE Co.—Marysvale, onofrite.

SALT LAKE Co.—Butterfield Cañon, mallardite, luckite.

Wahsatch Range, head waters of Spanish Fork, ozocerite in considerable beds.

NEVADA.

ELKO Co.—Emma mine, chrysocolla; Blue Hill mine, azurite, malachite.

LANDER Co.—Austin, polybasite, chalcopyrite, azurite, whitneyite.

LINCOLN Co.—Halite, cerargyrite.

NYE Co.—Anglesite, stetefeldtite, azurite. cerussite, silver ore, cerargyrite.

WHITE PINE Co.—Eberhardt mine, cerargyrite; Paymaster mine, freieslebenite.

NEW MEXICO.*

DOÑA ANA Co.—Lake Valley, cerargyrite in the Sierra mines in large masses, rarely crystallized, associated with embolite, cerussite, galenite, vanadinite in small canary-yellow crystals, native silver, pyrolusite, manganite, fluorite, ankerite, apatite, chert. Victoria mine, 40 miles below Nutt, massive anglesite. Kingston, in Black Range, argentite in large masses.

SOCORRO Co.—Socorro Mt., 3 miles from town of Socorro, large veins of barite carrying cerargyrite, vanadiferous mimetite, vanadinite in barrel-shaped crystals resembling pyromorphite. Magdalena Mountains, 27 miles west of Socorro, cerussite in heavy veins with galenite, sphalerite, etc. Green and blue calamine on the Kelly location. Sophia mine, stromeyerite? Grafton, on a large quartz vein, Ivanhoe mine, gold in black cerussite, chalcocite, bornite, malachite, azurite, chalcopyrite, cerargyrite, amethystine quartz. New Elk Mountain, 100 miles south of Socorro, cerussite carrying silver.

---

* The author is indebted for the following notes, as also for others under Arizona and Montana, to Prof. B. Silliman.

AMERICAN LOCALITIES.

GRANT Co.—Silver City, Bremen's mine, argentite, cerargyrite, argentite pseudomorph of mollusca, barite with cerargyrite, native silver in filagree and dendrites on slate; Santa Rita copper mines, native copper, tenorite. Mogollon and Burro mountains, Coony mining district, Dry Creek; in Mundo mine, melaconite; Silver Twigg mine, bornite, copper; Albatross mine, bornite, malachite; Cooney mine, chalcopyrite, azurite, bornite; Clifton mine, native copper, cuprite, azurite, malachite, wulfenite. Georgetown, Naiad Queen mine, argentite pseudomorph of mollusca, cerargyrite, native silver in dendritic form on slate.

SAN MIGUEL Co.—Cerillos, Mt. Chalchuitl, turquoise in tuff. In the Cerillos district are numerous mineral veins, carrying silver lead and salts of lead, rarely wulfenite and vanadinite, azurite, malachite, sphalerite, etc.

ARIZONA.

In the Silver District, YUMA Co., at the Hamburg, Princess and Red Cloud mines, in connection with quartz veins carrying argentiferous galena, fine ruby-red vanadinite, red wulfenite, massive anglesite. Silent District, Black Rock mine, vanadinite. At the Castle Dome mines, vanadinite, mimetite, wulfenite, cerussite, galenite, fluorite. Also wulfenite at the Melissa mine and Rover mine.

In the Vulture District (also called White Picacho District), YAVAPAI and MARICOPA Cos., numerous veins of gold-bearing quartz, carrying lead. Vulture mine, cryst. gold, jarosite, wulfenite. Hunter's Rest mine, gold in tourmaline rock. Farley's Collateral mine, and the Phenix mine, 20 miles north-east of Vulture, yellow vanadinite with calcite, wulfenite, cerussite, descloizite (?), volborthite (?) crocoite, vauquelinite, phœnicochroite. Montezuma mine, vanadinite, cerussite. Sante Domingo mine, mimetite, argentite. Silver Star mine, native silver, cerussite, argentite, crocoite, vanadinite. Tiger mine, native silver, cerargyrite. Tip Top mine, native silver, sphalerite, argentite, pyrargyrite.

From the Rio Verde, MARICOPA Co., thenardite in large deposits.

MOHAVE Co.—Moss lode, gold in crystalline plates; fluorite a frequent gangue material.

PINAL Co.—Mule Pass, Bisbey, Copper Queen mine, native copper, copper oxide, malachite, azurite, calcite.

From the Silver King mine, Pioneer District, PINAL Co.—Fine crystallized native silver, argentite, sphalerite, pyrite. Stonewall Jackson mine, cryst. silver, argentite.

From the Bon Ton mines, Chase Creek, near Clifton, dioptase with cuprite and limonite.

MONTANA.

BUTTE Co.—Butte City, Alice silver mine, rhodonite, a common gangue of native silver and other silver ores, rhodochrosite. Same in Magna Charter mine. Parrot, Mountain, Bell, and other copper veins yield various copper salts and arsenical copper glance with silver.

"Original Butte mine," wurtzite with pyrite. Clear Grit mine, native silver, argentite, chalcopyrite, sphalerite, calcite, rhodochrosite. Colusa mine, chalcocite.

ALASKA.

Ft. Wrangell at mouth of the Stickeen River, fine garnets in mica schist.

CANADA—PROVINCE OF QUEBEC.

MONTREAL.—Analcite, sodalite, nephelite (in nephelite-syenite).

OTTAWA Co.—Veins carrying apatite and pyroxene in large quantities are common in Buckingham, Burgess, Templeton, and other townships; also calcite, quartz, amphibole, scapolite, garnet, tourmaline, titanite, zircon, orthoclase, phlogopite and other species.

Templeton, vesuvianite, garnet (cinnamonstone), pyroxene.

Hull, colorless garnets, vesuvianite, white pyroxene.

Wakefield, chrome garnet.

CANADA—PROVINCE OF OTTAWA.

FRONTENAC Co.—Scapolite, apatite.

RENFREW Co.—Eganville, large crystals of apatite, titanite, zircon (also twins), amphibole.

NOVA SCOTIA.

CUMBERLAND CO.—Alunogen.
COLCHESTER CO.—New Annan, covellite.
KINGS CO.—Black Rock, in trap with stilbite, ulexite, heulandite.

CANADA—KEEWATIN DISTRICT.

CHURCHILL RIVER.—Lazulite.
KNEE LAKE.—Magnetite Island, magnetite.

CANADA—BRITISH COLUMBIA.

CARIBOO DISTRICT.—Native gold, galenite.
On FRAZER RIVER.—Gold, argentiferous tetrahedrite, cerargyrite, cinnabar. North Thompson River, cyanite.
HOWE SOUND.—Bornite, chalcopyrite, molybdenite, mica.
OMINICA DISTRICT.—Gold, galenite, silver, silver amalgam.
CASSIAR DISTRICT.—Gold.
TEXADA ISLAND.—Magnetite.
QUEEN CHARLOTTE ISLANDS.—Skincuttle Inlet, Harriet Harbor, magnetite, chalcopyrite.

GENERAL INDEX TO MINERAL SPECIES

Abriachanite, 420.
Acadialite, 344.
Acanthite, 239.
Achrematite, 385.
Achroite, 330.
Acmite, 294.
Actinolite, 297.
Adamine, Adamite, 373; 420.
Adelpholite, 363.
Adular, Adularia, 325.
Ægirine, Ægyrite, 294.
Aërinite, 350.
Æschynite, 362.
Agalmatolite, 349, 352.
Agaric mineral, 400.
Agate, 286.
Aglaite, 420.
Agricolite, 302.
Aikinite, 251.
Ajkite, 435.
Akanthit, v. Acanthite.
Akmit, v. Acmite.
Alabandite, 237.
Alabaster, 393.
Alalite, 293.
Alaskaite, 420.
Alaun v. Alum.
Alaunstein, 396.
Albertite, 416.
Albite, 323; 420.
Alexandrite, 275.
Algodonite, 235.
Alipite, 351.
Allanite, 308.
Allemontite, 227.
Allochroite, v. Andradite.
Alloclasite, 248.
Allophane, 341.
Allophite, 356.
Almandin, Almandite, 303.
Alshedite, 438.
Alstonite. v. Bromlite.
Altaite, 237.
Alum, Native, 395.
Alumina = Aluminum oxide.
Aluminum carbonate, 410.
chloride, 260.
fluoride, 264, 265.
fluo-silicate, 332.

Aluminum hydrate, 279, 282.
hydro - sulphate, 395.
mellate, 412.
oxide (Alumina), 267.
phosphate, 375, 376, 377, 378, 439.
silicate, 331, 332, 341, 349, 351.
sulphate, 395, 396.
Aluminite, 395.
Alunite, 396.
Alunogen, 395.
Amalgam, 225.
Amazonstone, 325.
Amber, 415.
Amblygonite, 369; 420.
Amblystegite, 290.
Ambrite, 415.
Ambrosine, 415.
Amesite, 424.
Amethyst, 286.
Amianthus, 297, 350.
Ammonia, v. Ammonium.
Ammonium chloride, 260.
oxalate, 433.
phosphate, 371.
sulphate, 392.
Amphibole, 296; 420.
Analcite, Analcime, 343.
Anatase, 277.
Andalusite, 331.
Andesine, Andesite, 322.
Andradite, 304.
Andrewsite, 378.
Anglesite, 389.
Anhydrite, 389.
Animikite, 420.
Ankerite, 402.
Annabergite, 372.
Ännerödite, 420.
Annite, 313.
Anomite, 431.
Anorthite, 321.
Antholite. v. Anthophyllite.
Anthophyllite, 295.
Anthracite, 417.

Anthracoxenite, 415.
Antigorite, 351.
Antillite, 351.
Antimonblende, 284.
Antimonblüthe, v. Valentinite.
Antimonglanz, 232.
Antimonite, 232.
Antimonsilber, 234.
Antimony, Arsenical, 227.
Gray, 232.
Native, 226.
— Red = Kermesite, 284.
White = Valentinite, 284.
Antimony blende, 284.
bloom, 284.
glance, 232.
ochre, 437.
oxide, 284, 437.
sulphide, 232.
Apatite, 364; 420.
Aphanesite v. Clinoclasite.
Aphrite, 400.
Aphrizite, 330.
Aphrodite, 349.
Aphrosiderite, 356.
Aphthalose, Aphthitalite, 390.
Apjohnite, 395.
Aplome, 304.
Apophyllite, 340; 421.
Aquacreptite, 351.
Aquamarine, 299.
Aræoxene, 426.
Aragonite, 405; 421.
Aragotite, 414.
Arcanite, 390.
Arctolite, 421.
Ardennite, 310.
Arequipite, 421.
Arfvedsonite, 298; 421.
Argentine, 400.
Argentite, 235.
Argentopyrite, 437.
Argyropyrite, 437.
Arite, 243.
Arkansite, 278.
Arksutite, 265.

509

Arquerite, 225.
Arragonite, 405.
Arrhenite, 421.
Arsenargentite, 421.
Arseneisen, v. Leucopyrite.
Arseneisensinter, v. Pitticite.
Arsenic, Antimonial, 227.
　　Native, 226.
　　Red, 284.
　　Yellow, 284.
　　White, 284.
Arsenic oxide, 284.
　　sulphide, 231.
Arsenical Antimony, 227.
Arsenikkies, 247.
Arsenikkupfer, 234.
Arsennickelglanz, 246.
Arseniosiderite, 378.
Arsenite, v. Arsenolite.
Arsenolite, 284.
Arsenopyrite, 247.
Asbestus, 297.
　　Blue, v. Crocidolite.
Asbolan, Asbolite, 283.
Asmanite, 288; 421.
Asparagus-stone, 365.
Aspasiolite, 353.
Asphaltum, 416.
Aspidolite, 312.
Astrakanite, v. Blödite.
Astrophyllite, 313; 421.
Atacamite, 261.
Atelestite, 378.
Ateline, Atelite, 262; 421.
Atopite, 421.
Augite, 293.
Aurichalcite, 410.
Auriferous pyrite, 220.
Auripigmentum, 232.
Automolite, 272.
Autunite, 379; 421.
Aventurine quartz, 286.
　　feldspar, 322, 323, 325.
Axinite, 310.
Azorite, 359.
Azurite, 411.

Babingtonite, 295.
Bagrationite, v. Allanite.
Baikalite, v. Sahlite.
Balvraidite, 421.
Barcenite, 421.
Barnhardtite, 245.
Barite, 387.
Barium carbonate, 406, 408.
　　nitrate, 433.
　　(and uranium) phosphate, 439.
　　silicate, 322, 346, 420.
　　sulphate, 387.
Bartholomite, 395.
Barylite, 421.
Baryt, Barytes, 387.

Baryta = Barium oxide.
Barytocalcite, 408.
Barytocelestite, 388.
Basanite, 287.
Bastite, 351.
Bastnäsite, 408, 438.
Bathvillite, 415.
Batrachite, 300.
Beaumontite, 347.
Beauxite, 281.
Beccarite, 440.
Bechilite, 382.
Beegerite, 421.
Beilstein, v. Nephrite.
Bell metal ore = Stannite, 245.
Belonite, 110.
Benzole, 414.
Beraunite, v. Vivianite.
Bergamaskite, 420.
Bergholz, 297.
Bergkrystall, v. Quartz.
Bergmehl, 401.
Bergmilch, 400.
Bergöl, 413.
Bergpech, 416.
Bergseife, v. Halloysite.
Bergtheer, v. Pittasphalt.
Berlauite, 436.
Bernardinite, 435.
Bernstein, 415.
Beryl, 299; 421.
Beryllium aluminate, 274.
　　silicate, 299, 300, 301, 302, 333.
Berthierite, 251.
Berzelianite, 237.
Berzeliite, 421.
Beyrichite, 241.
Bhreckite, 422.
Bieberite, 395.
Biharite, 353.
Bimsstein, v. Pumice.
Bindheimite, 379.
Binnite, 251; 250.
Biotite, 312.
Bischofite, 423.
Bismite, 284.
Bismuth, Acicular (aikinite), 254.
　　Native, 227.
　　Telluric, 253.
Bismuth arsenate, 377, 379.
　　blende(eulytite), 302.
　　carbonate, 412, 422.
　　chloride, 262.
　　glance, 232.
　　nickel (grünauite), 237.
　　ochre, 284.
　　oxide, 284.
　　selenide, 233.
　　silicate, 302.
　　silver, 420.

Bismuth sulphide, 232.
　　tellurate, 397.
　　telluride, 233.
Bismuthinite, 232.
Bismutite, 412.
Bismutoferrite, 302.
Bismutosphærite, 422.
Bittersalz, 394.
Bitter spar, Bitterspath, v. Dolomite.
Bitumen, 416.
Bituminous coal, 417.
Bjelkite, 424.
Black jack, 237.
Blättererz, Blättertellur, 249.
Blätterzeolith, v. Heulandite.
Blaueisenerz, v. Vivianite.
Blaueisenstein, v. Crocidolite
Blauspath, 375.
Blei, Gediegen, 226.
Bleiglanz, 235.
Bleiglätte, 267.
Bleigumme, v. Plumbogummite.-
Bleilasur, 396.
Bleihornerz, 408.
Bleinière, 379.
Bleinierite, v. Bindheimite.
Bleispath, 407.
Bleivitriol, 389.
Blende, 237.
Blödite, 394.
Blomstrandite, 422.
Bloodstone, 286.
Blue vitriol, 394.
Bodenite, 308.
Bog-butter, 415.
Bog-iron ore, 281.
　　manganese, 283.
Bole, Bolus = Halloysite.
Bolivite, 422.
Boltonite, 300.
Bombiccite, 415.
Boracic acid, 380.
Boracite, 381; 422.
Borax, 381.
Bordosite, 267.
Bornite, 237.
Borocalcite, 382.
Boron trioxide, 380.
Boronatrocalcite, 381.
Bort, 229.
Bosjemanite, 395.
Botallackite, v. Atacamite.
Botryogen, 395.
Botryolite, 325.
Boulangerite, 254.
Bournonite, 253.
Boussingaultite, 392.
Bowenite, 297, 350.
Bowlingite, 422.
Brackebuschite, 425.
Bragite, 362.
Branderz, v. Idrialite.

GENERAL INDEX.

Brandisite, 358.
Brauneisenstein, 280.
Braunite, 277.
Braunkohle, 418.
Braunspath, 401.
Bravaïsite, 422.
Bredbergite, 304.
Breislakite, v. Pyroxene.
Breithauptite, 243.
Breunerite, 402.
Brewsterite, 347.
Brittle silver ore, v. Stephanite.
Brochantite, 396.
Bromargyrite, 260.
Bromlite, 406.
Bromsilber, 260.
Bromyrite, 260.
Brogniardite, 252.
Brongnartine, 397.
Bronzite, 290.
Brookite, 277; 422.
Brown coal, 418.
    iron ore, 280.
    spar, 401, 402.
Brucite, 281; 422.
Brushite, 371.
Bucholzite, 331.
Bucklandite, 308.
Bunsenin, 430.
Bunsenite, 267.
Buntkupfererz, 237.
Bustamite, 294.
Butyrellite, 415.
Byerite, 417.
Bytownite, 321.

Cabrerite, 422.
Cacholong, 289.
Cacoxenite, Cacoxene, 378.
Cadmium sulphide, 242.
Cairngorm stone, 286.
Calaite, v. Callaite.
Calamine, 339, 422; 404.
Calaverite, 249; 422.
Calcareous spar, tufa, 398; 400.
Calcite, 398.
Calcium arsenate, 370, 371.
    antimonate, 370, 421.
    borate, 382.
    boro-silicate, 334.
    carbonate, 398, 405.
    chloride, 260.
    fluoride, 263.
    nitrate, 379.
    oxalate, 412.
    phosphate, 364, 371, 426, 432.
    silicate, 291, 338; 321.
    sulphate, 389, 392; 391.
    sulphide, 235.

Calcium tantalate, 359, 431.
    titanate, 270.
    tungstate, 384.
Calcozincite, 267.
Calc-sinter, 400.
Caledonite, 391.
Callais, Callaite, 377.
Calomel, 260.
Calvonigrite, 434.
Campylite, 367.
Canaanite = White Pyroxene.
Cancrinite, 317; 422.
Cannel Coal, 417.
Capillary pyrites, 241.
Caporcianite, 338.
Carbonado, 229.
Carbon diamantaire, 229.
Carnallite, 261.
Carnelian, 286.
Carpholite, 341.
Caryinite, 422.
Cassiterite, 275.
Castor, Castorite, 295.
Cataplcïte, 339.
Cataspilite, 353.
Cat's eye, 2 6.
Cavolinite, 316.
Celadonite, 349.
Celestialite, 435.
Celestite, Celestine, 388.
Centrallassite, 338.
Cerargyrite, 260.
Cerbolite, 392.
Cerine, 308.
Cerite, 340.
Cerium carbonate, 408.
    fluoride, 439.
    phosphate, 364, 368.
    silicates, 308, 330.
Cerolite, 351.
Cerussite, 407.
Cervantite, 284.
Ceylanite, Ceylonite, 271.
Chabazite, 344; 422.
Chalcanthite, 394.
Chalcedony, 286.
Chalcocite, 239.
Chalcodite, 350.
Chalcolite, 378.
Chalcomenite, 422.
Chalcomorphite, 351.
Chalcophanite, 283.
Chalcophyllite, 375.
Chalcopyrite, 244; 422.
Chalcosiderite, 378.
Chalcosine, 239.
Chalcostibite, 250.
Chalcotrichite, 266.
Chalk, 400.
Chalybite, 403.
Chathamite, 246.
Chert, 287.
Chesterlite, 326. [412.
Chessy Copper, Chessylite,

Chiastolite, 331.
Childrenite, 377; 422.
Chiolite, 264.
Chladnite, 290.
Chloanthite, 245.
Chloralluminite, 260.
Chlor-apatite, 365.
Chlorastrolite, 340.
Chlorite Group, 355.
Chloritoid, 358.
Chloritspath, 358.
Chlormagnesite, 260; 423.
Chlorocalcite, 260.
Chloropal, 350.
Chlorophæite, 356.
Chlorophane, 263.
Chlorophyllite, 353.
Chlorothionite, 260.
Chlorotile, 373.
Chodneffite, 264.
Chondrarsenite, 372.
Chondrodite, 327; 423.
Chonicrite, 355.
Chrismatite, 413.
Chromeisenstein, 274.
Chromglimmer, v. Fuchsite.
Chromic iron, 274.
Chromite, 274; 423.
Chrompicotite, 274.
Chromium oxide, 274.
    sulphide, 242.
Chrysoberyl, 274.
Chrysocolla, 338; 423.
Chrysolite, 300; 423.
Chrysoprase, 286.
Chrysotile, 350.
Churchite, 371.
Cinnabar, 240.
Cinnamon stone, 303.
Clarite, 258.
Claudetite, 284.
Clausthalite, 236.
Clay, 351, et seq.
Cleavelandite, 324.
Cleveite, 423.
Clingmanite, 358.
Clinoclase, Clinoclosite, 374.
Clinochlore, 356.
Clinocrocite, 423.
Clinohumite, 328.
Clinophæite, 423.
Clintonite, 358; 423.
Cloanthite, 245.
Coal, Mineral, 417.
    Boghead, 48.
    Brown, 418.
    Cannel, 417.
Cobalt, Arsenical, 245, 246.
    Black (asbolite), 283.
    Earthy, 283.
    Gray (smaltite), 245.
    Red (erythrite), 372.
    White (cobaltite), 246.

GENERAL INDEX.

Cobalt bloom, 372.
   glance, 246.
   arsenate, 372.
   arsenide, 246; 248.
   carbonate, 436.
   oxide, 283.
   selenite, 432.
   sulphate, 394.
   sulphide, 245.
Cobaltine, Cobaltite, 246.
Cobaltomenite, 432.
Coccolite, 293.
Coke, 417.
Cölestine, v. Celestite.
Cœruleolactite, 376.
Collyrite, 341.
Colophonite, 304.
Coloradoite, 423.
Columbite, 360; 423.
Comptonite, 342.
Connellite, 391.
Cookeite, 354.
Copal, Fossil, 415.
Copaline, Copalite, 415.
Copiapite, 395.
Copper, Antimonial (chalcostibite), 250.
   Arsenical, 234.
   Black (melaconite), 267.
   Blue, 411.
   Emerald (dioptase), 301.
   Gray, 255.
   Indigo, 249.
   Native, 225.
   Purple, 237.
   Red, 266.
   Variegated, 237.
   Vitreous, 239.
Copper arsenate, 373, 374, 375.
   arsenide, 234.
   arsenite (?), 439.
   carbonate, 411.
   chloride, 260.
   chromate, 386.
   glance, 329.
   mica, 375.
   nickel, 242.
   oxide, 266, 267,
   oxychloride, 261, 262.
   phosphate, 373, 374.
   pyrites, 244.
   selenide, 237.
   selenite, 422.
   silicate, 301, 338.
   sulph-antimonite, 250, 254, 255, 257, 428.
   sulph-arsenite, 251, 256, 257, 259.
   sulphate, 390, 394, 396, 397, 428.
   sulphide, 239, 249; 237, 244.

Copper sulpho-bismuthite, 250, 251, 254.
   tungstate, 384.
   vanadate, 374.
   vitriol, v. Chalcanthite.
Copper ore, Red, 266.
   Yellow, 244.
Copperas, 394.
Coprolites, 366.
Coquimbite, 395.
Cordierite, 311.
Cornwallite, 374.
Coronguite, 424.
Corundellite, 358.
Corundophilite, 358; 424.
Corundum, 267; 424.
Corynite, 247.
Cosalite, 252; 424.
Cossaite, 354.
Cossyrite, 424.
Cotunnite, 261.
Covelline, Covellite, 249.
Craigtonite, 424.
Crednerite, 278.
Crichtonite, 270.
Crocidolite, 298.
Crocoite, Crocoisite, 385; 424.
Cronstedtite, 357.
Crookesite, 235.
Cryolite, 264; 424.
Cryophyllite, 315.
Cryptohalite, 264.
Cryptolite, 364.
Cryptomorphite, 382.
Cuban, Cubanite, 245.
Culsageeite, 355.
Cummingtonite, 297.
Cuprocalcite, 411; 424.
Cuprite, 266.
Cupromagnesite, 395.
Cuproscheelite, 384.
Cuprotungstite, 384.
Cuspidine, 424.
Cyanite, 332; 424.
Cyanochalcite, 339.
Cyanotrichite, 397.
Cymatoiite, 349, 436.
Cyprusite, 424.

Damourite, 353.
Danaite, 248.
Danalite, 302; 424.
Danburite, 311; 424.
Datholite, Datolite, 334.
Daubréelite, 242.
Daubreite, 262.
Davidsonite, 299.
Davreuxite, 425.
Davyne, Davina, 316.
Dawsonite, 410; 425.
Dechenite, 367.
Degeroite, 354.
Delessite, 356; 425.

Delvauxite, v. Dufrenite.
Demidoffite, 339.
Derbyshire spar, v. Fluorite
Descloizite, 367; 425.
Desmine, 346.
Destinezite, 425.
Dewalquite, 310.
Deweylite, 351.
Diabantachronnyn, 355.
Diabantite, 355.
Diaclasite, 291.
Diadochite, 379.
Diallage, Green, 293.
Diallogite, Dialogite, 403.
Diamond, 228; 425.
Dianite, v. Columbite.
Diaphorite, 252.
Diaspore, 279.
Dichroite, 311.
Dickinsonite, 425.
Dietrichite, 425.
Dihydrite, 374.
Dimorphite, 232.
Dinite, 414.
Diopside, 293.
Dioptase, 301.
Dipyre, 316.
Discrasite, v. Dyscrasite.
Disterrite = Brandisite.
Disthene, 332.
Ditröyte, 317.
Dog-Tooth Spar, 400.
Dolerophanite, 390.
Dolomite, 401.
Domeykite, 234.
Doppelspath, 399.
Dopplerite, 415; 425.
Douglasite, 425.
Dreelite, 390.
Dry-bone, 404.
Dudleyite, 358.
Dufrenite, 378.
Dufrenoysite, 251.
Dumortierite, 425.
Duporthite, 425.
Durangite, 370.
Dürfeldtite, 425.
Duxite, 415.
Dysanalyte, 425.
Dyscrasite, 234.
Dysluite, 272.
Dysodile, 415.
Dysyntribite, 353.

Earthy Cobalt, 283.
Edenite, 297.
Edingtonite, 341.
Edwardsite, v. Monazite.
Eggonite, 425.
Ehlite, 374.
Eisenblüthe, 405.
Eisenbrucite, 422.
Eisenglanz, 268.
Eisenglimmer, 269.

GENERAL INDEX.

Eisenkies, 243.
Eisenkiesel, v. Quartz.
Eisenrose, 269.
Eisensinter, v. Pitticite.
Eisenspath, 403.
Eisspath, 326.
Ekdemite, 425.
Ekebergite, 336.
Ekmannite, 354.
Elæolite, 316.
Elaterite, 414.
Electrum, 221.
Eleonorite, 426.
Elroquite, 426.
Embolite, 260.
Embrithite, v. Boulangerite.
Emerald, 289.
Emerald nickel, 410.
Emery, 268.
Emplectite, 250.
Enargite, 257.
Enceladite, v. Warwickite.
Enophite, 433.
Enstatite, 230.
Enysite, 397.
Eosite, 385.
Eosphorite, 423.
Ephesite, 354.
Epiboulangerite, 254.
Epidote, 307.
Epigenite, 258.
Epistilbite, 347; 426.
Epsom Salt, Epsomite, 394; 423.
Erbsenstein, 400.
Erdkobalt, 283.
Erdöl, 416.
Erdpech, 416.
Eremite, v. Monazite.
Erilite, 426.
Erinite, 374.
Eriochalcite, 426.
Erubescite, 247.
Erythrite, 372.
Erythrosiderite, 261.
Erythrozincite, 426.
Esmarkite, 353.
Essonite, 304.
Ettringite, 395.
Eucairite, 235.
Euchroite, 373.
Euclase, 333; 426.
Eucolite, 299.
Eucrasite, 426.
Eucryptite, 426.
Eudialyte, Eudyalite, 299.
Eudnophite, 344.
Eugeng'anz, v Polybasite.
Eukairite, v. Eucairite.
Euklas, 333.
Eulytine, Eulytite, 302; 426.
Eumanite, 273.
Euosmite, 415.
Euphyllite, 354.

Eusynchite, 426.
Euxenite, 362.

Fahlerz, 255.
Fahlunite, 353.
Fairfieldite, 426.
Famatinite, 258.
Faserquarz, 298.
Fassaite, 293.
Faujasite, 344.
Fauserite, 394.
Fayalite, 300.
Feather ore, 251.
Federerz, 251.
Feitsui, 309.
Feldspar Group, 319; 426.
Felsite, 323, 326.
Feldspath, v. Feldspar.
Fergusonite, 362; 4.7.
Ferroilmenite, 260.
Ferrotellurite, 427.
Feuerblende, 252.
Feuerstein, 287.
Fibroferrite, 395.
Fibrolite, 331.
Fichtelite, 414.
Fillowite, 427.
Fiorite, 289.
Fireblende, 252.
Flint, 287.
Float-stone, 289.
Flos ferri, 405.
Fluellite, 264.
Fluocerite, 264.
Fluor-apatite, 365.
Fluor, Fluorite, 263; 427.
Fluor Spar, 263.
Flussspath, 263.
Foliated tellurium, v. Nagyagite.
Fontainebleau limestone, 400.
Foresite, 347; 4.7.
Forsterite, 300.
Fowlerite, 294.
Francolite, 365.
Franklandite, 427.
Franklinite, 273.
Fredricite 438.
Freibergite, 255.
Freieslebenite, 252.
Frenzelite, 233.
Freyalite, 427.
Friedelite, 302.
Frieseite, 437.
Frigidite, 438.
Fuchsite, 314.

Gado'in, Gadolinite, 309; 427.
Gahnite, 272.
Galena, Galenite, 235.
Galenobismutite, 427.
Galmei, 339, 404.
Ganomalite, 427.
Garnet, 302; 427.

Garnierite, 351 ; 427.
Gastaldite, 298.
Guanovulite, 392.
Gay-Lussite, 400.
Gearksutite, 265.
Gedanite, 435.
Gehlenite, 331.
Geierite, v. Geyerite.
Gekrösstein, 389.
Gelbbleierz, 384.
Genthite, 351.
Geocerite, 414.
Geocronite, 257.
Geomyricite, 414.
Gersdorffite, 246.
Geyerite, 248.
Geyserite, 289.
Gibbsite, 282.
Gieseckite, 352; 317.
Gigantolite, 353.
Gilbertite, 353.
Gillingite, 354.
Ginilsite, 428.
Girasol, 289.
Gismondine, Gismondite, 341; 428.
Giufite, 432.
Glanzkobalt, v. Cobaltite.
Glaserite, v. Arcanite.
Glaserz, Glanzerz, v. Argentite.
Glauber salt, 392.
Glauberite, 391.
Glaucodot, 248.
Glauconite, 349.
Glaucophane, 298.
Glimmer, v. Mica.
Globulites, 110.
Gmelinite, 345.
Gold, 221.
Gold telluride, 248, 249, 430.
Goldtellur, v. Sylvanite.
Goshenite, 299.
Goslarite, 395.
Göthite, 280.
Grahamite, 416.
Grammatite, 297.
Granat, 302.
Graphic tellurium, 248.
Graphite, 230.
Graukupfererz, v. Tennantite.
Gray antimony, 232.
copper, 255.
Greenockite, 242.
Greenovite, 335.
Grenat, v. Garnet.
Grochamite, 357.
Grossularite, 303.
Grünauite, 237.
Grünbleierz, 366.
Guadalcazarite, 241.
Guanajuatite, 233; 428.
Guanipite, 433.
Guano, 365.

GENERAL INDEX.

Guarinite, 336.
Guejarite, 428.
Gümbelite, 353.
Gummite, 428.
Gunnisonite, 428.
Guyaquillite, 415.
Gymnite, 351.
Gyps, v. Gypsum.
Gypsum, 392.
Gyrolite, 338; 428.

Haarkies, 241; 247.
Haarsalz, 395.
Haddamite, 432.
Hafnefiordite, 523.
Hagemannite, 265.
Haidingerite, 371.
Halite, 259.
Hallite, 355.
Halloysite, 352; 428.
Halotrichite, 395.
Hamartite, 408, 438.
Hannayite, 428.
Harmotome, 346.
Harrisite, 240.
Hartite, 414.
Hatchettite, Hatchettine, 414.
Hatchettolite, 428.
Hauerite, 214.
Haughtonite, 431.
Hausmannite, 277.
Haüyne, Haüynite, 318.
Haydenite, 341.
Hayesine, 428.
Haytorite, 335.
Heavy spar, 387.
Hebronite, 370; 420.
Hedenbergite, 293.
Hedyphane, 367; 428.
Heldburgite, 423.
Heliotrope, 286.
Helvin, Helvite, 302; 428.
Hematite, 263.
  Brown, 280.
Henwoodite, 378.
Hercynite, 272.
Herderite, 370.
Hermannolite, 361.
Herrengrundite, 423.
Herschelite, 344.
Hessite, 238; 429.
Hessonite, v. Essonite.
Hetærolite, Hetairite, 429.
Heteromorphite, v. Jamesonite.
Heubachite, 429.
Heulandite, 347; 429.
Hexagonite, 298.
Hibbertite, 429.
Hiddenite, 436.
Hielmite, 361.
Hieratite, 429.
Highgate resin, 415.
Hisingerite, 354.

Hœrnesite, 371.
Hofmannite, 435.
Holzopal, v. Wood Opal.
Holz Zinn, 275.
Homilite, 429.
Honey-stone, Honigstein, 412.
Hopeite, 429.
Horbachite, 241.
Hornblende, 296.
Horn silver, 260.
Hornstone, 287.
Horse-flesh ore, v. Bornite
Hortonolite, 300.
Houghite, 282.
Hovite, 410.
Howlite, 382.
Huantajayite, 259.
Hübnerite, 383; 429.
Hullite, 425.
Humboldtine, 412.
Humbo'dtilite, 306.
Humboldtite, 334.
Huminite, 4 5.
Humite, 327, 328, 423.
Huntilite, 420.
Hureaulite, 372.
Huronite, 353.
Hyacinth, 304, 305.
Hyalite, 289.
Hyalophane, 322.
Hyalosiderite, 3 .0.
Hyalotekite, 429.
Hydrargillite, 282.
Hydrargyrite, 267.
Hydraulic limestone, 400.
Hydrobiotite, 436.
Hydrocastorite, 433.
Hydrocerussite, 429.
Hydrocuprite, 266.
Hydrocyanite, 390.
Hydrodolomite, 410.
Hydrofluorite, 264.
Hydrofranklinite, 429.
Hydroilmenite, 431.
Hydromagnesite, 409.
Hydro-mica Group, 353.
Hydrophilite, 429.
Hydrophite, 351.
Hydrorhodonite, 429.
Hydrotalcite, 282.
Hydrotitanite, 271.
Hydrozincite, 410.
Hygrophilite, 353.
Hypargyrite, 250.
Hypersthene, 290.
Hypochlorite, 302.

Ice spar, 325.
Iceland spar, 399.
Idocrase, 205.
Idrialine, Idrialite, 314.
Ihleite, 395.
Ilesite, 429.
Ilmenite, 269.

Ilsemannite, 284.
Ilvaite, 309.
Indianaite, 428.
Indianite, 321.
Indicolite, 330.
Iodargyrite, 260.
Iodobromite, 429.
Iodsilber, 260.
Iodyrite, 260.
Iolite, 311.
Ionite, 435.
Iridosmine, 224.
Iron, Arsenical, 247.
  Magnetic, 241, 272.
  Meteoric, 226.
  Native, 226, 429.
  Oligist (hematite), 268.
Iron aluminate, 272.
  arsenate, 375, 376.
  arsenide, 247, 248.
  borate, 380.
  boro-silicate, 429.
  carbonate, 403.
  chloride, 261.
  columbate, 360.
  oxalate, 412.
  oxide, 268, 272, 279, 280.
  phosphate, 369, 371, 372, 378, 426, 437.
  silicate, 300, 354.
  sulphate, 395.
  sulphide, 241, 243, 247.
  sulph-antimonite, 251.
  tantalate, 359.
  tellurate (?) 427.
  tungstate, 383.
Iron pyrites, 243.
  White, 247.
Ironstone, Clay, 269, 281, 403.
Iserine, Iserite, 270.
Isoclasite, 373.
Itacolumyte, 229.
Ivigtite, 354.
Ixolyte, 414.

Jacobsite, 272.
Jade, Common, 297.
Jadeite, 409.
Jamesonite, 251; 430.
Jargon, 305.
Jarosite, 430.
Jasper, 287.
Jaulingite, 415.
Jefferisite, 355.
Jeffersonite, 293.
Jenkinsite, 351.
Jet, 418.
Johannite, 397.
Jollyte, 354.
Jordanite, 251.
Joseite, 233.
Julianite, 256.

N. B.—Many names spelt with an initial K in German, begin with C in English.

Kalait, 377.
Kaliglimmer, 313.
Kalinite, 395.
Kalk-Harmotome, v. Phillipsite.
Kalk-uranit, 379.
Kalkspath, 398.
Kalk-volborthit, 374.
Kallait, 377.
Kaluszite, 394.
Kämmererite, 355.
Kammkies, 247.
Kaolin. Kaolinite, 351.
Karelinite, 284.
Karyinite, 422.
Katzenauge, 286.
Keatingine, 295.
Keilhauite, 333.
Kelyphite, 436.
Kenngottite, 250.
Kentrolite, 430.
Kerargyrite, 260.
Kermes. Kermesite, 284.
Kerolith, v. Cerolite.
Kerrite, 355.
Kiesel, v. Quartz.
Kieselkupfer, 338.
Kieselwismuth, 302.
Kieselzinkerz, 339.
Kieserite, 394.
Killinite, 353, 436.
Kischtimite, 408.
Kjerulfine, 363.
Klaprotholite, 251.
Klinochlor, 356.
Knebelite, 300.
Kobaltblüthe, 372.
Kobaltglanz, 246.
Kobaltkies, v. Linnæite
Kobaltnickelkies, 245.
Kobellite, 254.
Kochelite, 363.
Kochsalz, 259.
Köflachite, 435.
Kohle, v. Coal.
Kokkolit v. Coccolite.
Kongsbergite, 225.
Königine, 396.
Könlite, 414.
Koppite, 359.
Korarfveite, 368.
Köttigite, 372.
Korund, v. Corundum.
Kotschubeite, 357.
Koupholite, 340.
Krantzite, 415.
Kreittonite, 272.
Kremersite, 261.
Krennerite, 430.
Krisuvigite, 397.

Krönkite, 397.
Krugite, 434.
Kupferantimonglanz, 250.
Kupferbleispath, 396.
Kupferglanz, 239.
Kupferglimmer, 375.
Kupferindig, 249.
Kupferkies, 244.
Kupferlasur, 411.
Kupfernickel, 242.
Kupfersammterz, 397.
Kupferschaum, 374.
Kupferschwärze, 267.
Kupfferite, 296.
Kupfer-uranit, 378.
Kupfer-vitriol, 394.
Kupferwismuthglanz, 250.
Kyanite, 332.

Labradorite, 321.
Labrador feldspar, 321.
Lagonite, 382.
Lampadite, 283.
Lanarkite, 391.
Langite, 397.
Lanthanite, 410.
Lapis-lazuli, 418.
Larderellite, 382.
Lasurstein, 418.
Latrobite, v. Anorthite.
Laumonite, Laumontite, 338.
Laurite, 247.
Lautite, 430.
Lawrencite, 430.
Laxmannite, 386.
Lazulite, 375.
Lead, Argentiferous, 223.
  Black (graphite), 230.
  Corneous (phosgenite), 408.
  Native, 226.
Lead antimonate, 370, 379.
  arsenate, 366.
  arsenio-molybdate, 385.
  carbonate, 407.
  chloride, 261.
  chloro-carbonate, 408.
  chromate, 385, 386.
  molybdate 384.
  oxichloride, 262.
  oxide, 267, 277.
  phosphate, 366.
  selenide, 236.
  selenite, 432.
  silicate, 427, 429, 430, 431.
  sulphate, 389, 390, 391.
  sulphato-carbonate, 391.
  sulphide, 235.
  sulpharsenite, 250, 251.
  sulphantimonite, 250, 251, 252, 254.
  sulpho-bismuthite, 252, 421, 427.

Lead telluride, 237, 249.
  tungstate, 384.
  vanadate, 367; 374, 426.
Leadhillite, 390; 430.
Leberkies, v. Marcasite.
Lecontite, 392.
Ledererite, 345.
Lederite, 336.
Lehrbachite, 237.
Leidyite, 430.
Lennilite, 436.
Leopoldite, 260.
Lepidolite, 314.
Lepidomelane, 313.
Lepidophæite, 440.
Lernilite, 436.
Lesleyite, 354.
Lettsomite, 397.
Leucaugite, 293.
Leuchtenbergite, 357.
Leucite, 318; 430.
Leucochalcite, 430.
Leucomanganite, 426.
Leucopetrite, 315.
Leucophanite, 300; 430.
Leucopyrite, 248.
Leucotile, 430.
Leviglianite, 241.
Levyne, Levynite, 343.
Lherzolyte, 271.
Libethenite, 373; 430.
Liebigite, 412.
Lievrite, 309.
Lignite, 418.
Ligurite, 336.
Limbachite, 351.
Lime = Calcium oxide, v. Calcium.
Limestone, 400, 401.
Limonite, 280.
Linarite, 396.
Linnæite, 245.
Linsenerz, 374.
Lintonite, 438.
Lionite, 437.
Liroconite, 374.
Liskeardite, 430.
Lithionglimmer, 314.
Lithiophilite, 368.
Lithographic Stone, 400.
Lithomarge, 352.
Livingstonite, 232; 430.
Loganite, 356.
Löllingite, 248.
Louisite, 430.
Löweite, 394.
Löwigite, 396.
Loxoclase, 326.
Luckite, 431.
Ludlamite, 372.
Ludwigite, 380.
Lüneburgite, 382.
Luzonite, 258.
Lydian stone, 287.

GENERAL INDEX.

Macfarlanite, 430.
Macle, 331.
Maconite, 355.
Magnesia = Magnesium oxide, v. Magnesium.
Magnesioferrite, 273.
Magnesite, 402.
Magnesium aluminate, 271.
    arsenate, 371.
    borate, 380, 381.
    carbonate, 402, 409.
    chloride, 260, 261, 423.
    fluoride, 264.
    fluo - phosphate, 368.
    fluo-silicate, 327.
    hydrate, 281.
    nitrate, 379.
    oxide, 267.
    phosphate, 368, 432.
    silicate, 290, 300, 348, 349, 350.
    sulphate, 394.
Magneteisenstein, 272.
Magnetic iron ore, 272.
Magnetic pyrites, 241.
Magnetite, 272.
Magnetkies, 241.
Magnoferrite, 273.
Magnolite, 430.
Malachite, Blue, 411.
    Green, 411.
Malacolite, 293.
Maldonite, 221.
Malinowskite, 256.
Mallardite, 431.
Manganapatite, 420.
Manganblende, v. Alabandite.
Manganbrucite, 422.
Manganepidot, 308.
Manganese borate, 380.
    carbonate, 403.
    columbate, 423.
    oxide, 277, 278, 280, 282, 283, 431.
    phosphate, 369, 435, 439.
    silicate, 294, 300, 301.
    sulphide, 237, 244.
    sulphate, 431, 437.
    tantalate, 359, 437.
    tungstate, 383.
Manganglanz, 237.
Manganite, 280.
Manganocalcite, 406.
Manganophyllite, 312.
Manganosiderite, 435.
Manganosite, 431.

Manganspath, 403.
Mangantantalite, 437.
Marble, 400.
    Verd-antique, 350.
Marcasite, 247.
Margarite, 357.
Margarites, 110.
Margarodite, 353; 314.
Margarophyllites, 348, et seq.
Marialite, 316.
Marionite. 410.
Marmairolite. 431.
Marmatite, 238.
Marmolite, 350.
Martite, 269.
Mascagnine, Mascagnite, 392.
Maskelynite, 322.
Masonite, 358.
Massicot, 267.
Matlockite, 262.
Matricite, 431.
Maxite, 391.
Medjidite, 397.
Meerschaum, 349.
Megabasite, 383.
Meionite, 315.
Melaconite, 267.
Melanglanz, v. Stephanite.
Melanite, 304.
Melanochroite, 386.
Melanophlogite, 289.
Melanosiderite, 281.
Melanotekite, 431.
Melanothallite, 431.
Melanterite, 395; 431.
Melilite, Mellilite, 306.
Melinophane, 300.
Meliphanite, 300; 431.
Mellite, 412.
Melonite, 249.
Menaccanite, 269, 431.
Mendipite, 262.
Mendozite, 395.
Meneghinite, 256.
Mengite, 362.
Mennige, 277.
Meroxene, 431.
Mercury, Native, 224.
Mercury chloride, 260.
    iodide, 260.
    selenide, 237.
    sulphide, 240, 241.
    telluride, 423.
    tellurate, 430.
    sulph-antimonite, 232.
Mesitine, Mesitite, 403.
Mesolite, 343.
Mesotype, 342.
Metabrushite, 371.
Metacinnabarite, 241.
Metaxite, 351.
Meymacite, 284.
Miargyrite, 249.

Mica Group, 301; 431.
Michaelsonite, 308.
Microcline, 326.
Microlite, 359; 431.
Microphyllites, Microplakites, 322.
Microsommite, 317.
Middletonite, 415.
Mikroklin, v. Microcline.
Milarite, 432.
Millerite, 241.
Mimetene, Mimetite, 366; 432.
Mimetese, Mimetesite, 366.
Mineral coal, 417.
    oil, 413.
    pitch, 416.
    tar, 413.
Minium, 277.
Mirabilite, 392.
Mispickel, 247.
Misy, 395.
Mixite, 432.
Mizzonite, 316.
Molybdänglanz, 233.
Molybdänocker, 284.
Molybdenite, 233; 432.
Molybdenum oxide, 284.
    sulphide, 233.
Molybdite, 284.
Molybdomenite, 432.
Molysite, 261.
Monazite, 368; 432.
Mondstein, v. Moonstone.
Monetite, 432.
Monimolite, 370.
Monite, 432.
Monrolite, 332.
Montanite, 397.
Montebrasite, 370; 420.
Monticellite, 300.
Montmartite, v. Gypsum.
Montmorillonite, 349.
Moonstone, 323, 324, 325.
Mordenite, 432.
Morenosite, 395.
Moroxite, 365.
Mosandrite, 309.
Mottramite, 374.
Mountain cork, 297.
    leather, 297.
Muckite, 435.
Muromontite, 308.
Muscovite, 313.
Müsenite, v. Siegenite.

Nadeleisenstein, 280.
Nadelerz, 254.
Nadelzeolith, 342.
Nadorite, 370.
Nagyagite, 249; 432.
Namaqualite, 282.
Nantokite, 260.
Naphtha, 413.
Naphthaline, 414.

GENERAL INDEX. 517

Natrolite, 342; 432.
Natron, 409.
Natronborocalcite, 381.
Naumannite, 235.
Needle ore, v. Aikinite.
Nemalite, 282.
Neochrysolite, 423.
Neocyanite, 432.
Neotocite, 354.
Nepheline, Nephelite, 316.
Nephrite, 297, 432.
Neudorfite, 435.
Newberyite, 432.
Newjanskite, 224.
Newportite, 358.
Niccolite, 242.
Nickel antimonide, 243, 247.
    arsenate, 372.
    arsenide, 242; 246.
    carbonate, 410.
    oxide, 267.
    silicate, 351, 427.
    sulphate, 395.
    sulphide, 241.
    telluride, 249.
Nickel glance, v. Gersdorffite.
Nickelarsenikglanz, 246.
Nickelarsenikkies, 246.
Nickelblüthe, 372.
Nickel-Gymnite, 351.
Nickelkies, 241.
Nickelsmaragd, 410.
Niobite, 360.
Nitre, 379.
Nitrobarite, 433.
Nitrocalcite, 379.
Nitroglauberite, 379.
Nitromagnesite, 379.
Nocerine, Nocerite, 433.
Nohlite, 362.
Nontronite, 350.
Nosean. Nosite, 318.
Noumeaite, Noumeite, 351.
Nuttalite, v. Wernerite.

Ochre, red, 269.
Octahedrite, 277; 433.
Œllacherite, 354.
Okenite, 338.
Oldhamite, 235.
Oligoclase, 323.
Olivenite, 373.
Olivine, 300.
Onofrite, 433.
Ontariolite, 435.
Onyx, 287.
Oölite, 400.
Opal, 288.
Ophiolite, 350, 402.
Orangite, 340.
Orpiment, 231; 433.
Orthite, 308; 433.
Orthoclase, 325; 433.
Oryzite, 429.

Osmiridium, 224.
Osteolite, 365.
Ottrelite, 358; 433.
Ouvarovite, 304.
Owenite, 358.
Oxammite, 433.
Ozarkite, 342.
Ozocerite, Ozokerit, 414; 433.

Pachnolite, 265; 438.
Pagodite, 349, 352.
Paisbergite, 294.
Palagonite, 353.
Palladium, Native, 224.
Pandermite, 434.
Parachlorite, 436.
Paraffin, 413.
Paragonite, 354.
Parankerite, 402.
Paranthite, 316.
Parasite, v. Boracite.
Parastilbite, 426.
Parathorite, 340.
Pargasite, 297.
Parisite, 408.
Parophite, 353.
Pattersonite, 358.
Pealite, 289.
Pearl-mica, v. Margarite.
Pearl-spar, 401.
Pechkohle, 417.
Pechopal, 289.
Peckhamite, 433.
Pectolite, 337; 433.
Peganite, 378.
Pegmatolite, v. Orthoclase.
Pelagite, 433.
Pelhamite, 355.
Pencatite, 410.
Pennine, Penninite, 355.
Penwithite, 433.
Percylite, 262.
Periclase, Periclasite, 267.
Peridot, 300, 330.
Perikline, Periklin, 324.
Peristérite, 324.
Perlglimmer, 357.
Perthite, 326.
Perofskite, 270; 433.
Perowskit, 270.
Petalite, 295; 433.
Petroleum, 413.
Petzite, 2. 9.
Phacolite, 344.
Phæactinite, 420.
Pharmacolite, 370.
Pharmacosiderite, 376; 433.
Phenacite, Phenakit; 301; 433.
Phengite, 431.
Philadelphite, 439.
Phillipite, 397.
Phillipsite, 345; 433.
Phlogopite, 312.

Phœnicochroite, 386.
Pholerite. 352.
Phosgenite, 408.
Phosphocerite, 364.
Phosphochalcite, 374.
Phosphochromite, 386.
Phosphorite, 365.
Phosphuranylite, 434.
Phyllite, 358.
Physalite, 333.
Phytocollite, 425.
Piauzite, 416.
Picite, 431.
Pickeringite, 395; 434.
Picotite, 271.
Picranalcite, 420.
Picroallumogene, 434.
Picrolite, 351.
Picromerite, 394.
Picropharmacolite, 371.
Pictite, 336.
Piedmontite, 308.
Pihlite, 349.
Pilarite, 423.
Pilinite, 344.
Pilolite, 434.
Pimelite, 351.
Pinite, 352.
Pisanite, 395.
Pisolite, 400.
Pistacite, Pistazit, 307.
Pistomesite, 403.
Pitchblende, 274.
Pittasphalt, 413.
Pitticite, Pittizit, 379.
Plagiocitrite, 434.
Plagioclase, 319.
Plagionite, 251.
Plasma, 286.
Plaster of Paris, 393.
Platinum, Native, 223; 434.
Platiniridium, 224.
Pleonaste, v. Spinel.
Plumbago, 230.
Plumballophane, 341.
Plumbogummite, 377.
Plumbomanganite, 434.
Plumbostannite, 434.
Plumbostib, v. Boulangerite.
Polianite, 278.
Pollucite, Pollux, 299.
Polyargite, 353.
Polyargyrite, 257.
Polybasite, 257.
Polycrase, 362.
Polychroilite, 353.
Polydymite, 434.
Polyhalite, 393; 434.
Polymignite, 362.
Poonahlite, 343.
Porcellophite, 351.
Posepnyte, 435.
Potassium chloride, 260.
    chromate (?), 437.

Potassium nitrate, 379.
    silicate, 313, 325.
    sulphate, 390.
Potash = Potassium oxide, v. Potassium.
Prase, 286.
Prasine, 374.
Praseolite, 353.
Predazzite, 410.
Pregattite, 354.
Prehnite, 340.
Priceite, 382; 434.
Prochlorite, 357.
Proidonite, 264.
Prosopite, 265.
Protobastite, 290.
Protochlorite, 436.
Protovermiculite, 439.
Proustite, 253.
Prussian blue, Native, 372.
Przibramite, 208, 280.
Pseudobrookite, 434.
Pseudocotunnite, 261.
Pseudomalachite, 374.
Pseudonatrolite, 434.
Pseudophite, 356.
Psilomelane, 282; 434.
Psittacinite, 374.
Pucherite, 367.
Purple copper, 237.
Pycnite, v. Topaz.
Pyrallolite, 348.
Pyrargillite, 353.
Pyrargyrite, 252.
Pyreneite, 304.
Pyrgom, 293; 434.
Pyrite, 243.
Pyrites, Arsenical, 247.
    Auriferous, 220.
    Capillary, 241.
    Cockscomb, 247.
    Copper, 244.
    Iron, 243.
    Magnetic, 241.
    Radiated, 247.
    Spear, 247.
    White iron, 247.
Pyrochlore, 359.
Pyrochroite, 282.
Pyroconite, 265.
Pyrolusite, 278; 434.
Pyromorphite, 366.
Pyrope, 303.
Pyrophosphorite, 434.
Pyrophyllite, 349.
Pyropissite, 414.
Pyroretinite, 415.
Pyrosclerite, 355.
Pyrosmalite, 340.
Pyrostilpnite, 252.
Pyroxene, 292.
Pyrrhite, 359.
Pyrrhosiderite, 280.
Pyrrhotite, 241; 434.

Quartz, 284; 434.
Quecksilberbranderz, 414.
Quecksilberhornerz, 260.
Quicksilver, 224.

Rädelerz, 253.
Radiated Pyrites, 247.
Raimondite, 395.
Ralstonite, 265, 435.
Randite, 437.
Ratofkite, 263.
Rauite, 342.
Raumite, 353.
Realgar, 231.
Red copper ore, 266.
    hematite, 269.
    iron ore, 269.
    ochre, 269.
    silver ore, 252, 253.
    zinc ore, 266.
Reddingite, 435.
Refdanskite, 351.
Reichardtite, 426.
Reinite, 4 5.
Reissite, 426.
Remingtonite, 410.
Rensselaerite, 348.
Resanite, 339.
Resin, Mineral, 415, 435.
Restormelite, 353.
Retinalite, 351.
Retinite, 415.
Reussinite, 415.
Rhabdophane, 435.
Rhætizite, 332.
Rhagite, 377.
Rhodizite, 435.
Rhodochrosite, 403; 435.
Rhodonite, 294.
Rhomb-spar, 401.
Rhyacolite, 326.
Rionite, 256.
Ripidolite, 356.
Rittingerite, 252.
Rivotite, 370.
Rock cork, v. Hornblende.
    crystal, 286.
    meal, 401.
    milk, 400.
    salt, 259.
Rœmerite, 395.
Rœpperite, 300.
Rœsslerite, 371.
Rogenstein, 400.
Rogersite, 435.
Romeine, Romeite, 370.
Roscoelite, 367; 435
Rose quartz, 286.?
Roselite, 372; 435.
Rosterite, 420.
Rosthornite, 415.
Rosite, 353.
Rothbleierz, 385.
Rotheisenerz, 268.

Rothgültigerz, 252, 253.
Rothkupfererz, 266.
Rothnickelkies, 242.
Rothoffite, 303.
Rothzinkerz, 266.
Rubellite, 330.
Rubislite, 435.
Ruby, Spinel, Almandine,271.
    Oriental, 268.
Ruby-blende, v. Pyrargyrite.
Ruby silver 252. 253.
Rutherfordite, 362.
Rutile. 276; 435.
Ryacolite, v. Rhyacolite.

Sahlite, 293.
Sal ammoniac, 260.
Salmiak. 260.
Salt, Common, 259.
Samarskite, 361; 435.
Sammetblende, 280.
Sanidin, 325.
Saponite, 352.
Sapphire. 268; 330.
Sarawakite, 435.
Sarcolite, 316.
Sarcopside, 369.
Sard, 287.
Sardonyx, 287.
Sartorite, 250.
Sassolite, Sassolin, 380.
Satin-spar, 393, 400, 405.
Saussurite, 309.
Savite, v. Natrolite.
Scapolite Group, 315; 435.
Schaumspath, 400.
Scheelite, 384.
Scheereite, 413.
Schieferspath, 400.
Schilfglaserz, 252.
Schiller-spar, 351.
Schirmerite, 251.
Schmirgel, 208.
Schneebergite, 437.
Schorlomite, 337; 435.
Schraufite. 415.
Schreibersite, 242.
Schrifterz, Schrift-tellur, 248.
Schröckingerite, 412.
Schuchardtite, 436.
Schuppenstein, 415.
Schwartzembergite, 262.
Schwarzkupfererz, 267.
Schwatzite, 255.
Schwefelkies, 243.
Schwerspath, 387.
Scleretinite, 415.
Scleroclase, 250.
Scolecite, Scolezite, 343.
Scorodite, 375.
Seebachite, 344.
Selenblei, 236.
Selenite, 393.
Selenquecksilber, 237.

Sellaite, 264.
Séméline, 335.
Semseyite, 436.
Senarmontite, 284; 436.
Sepiolite, 349; 436.
Serpentine, 350; 436.
Serpierite, 436.
Seybertite, 358.
Shepardite, 242.
Siderazot, 436.
Siderite, 403.
Sideronatrite, 436.
Siderophyllite, 431.
Siegburgite, 415.
Siegenite, 245.
Silaonite, 233; 428.
Silberamalgam, 225.
Silberglanz, 235.
Silberhornerz, 260.
Silberkupferglanz, 240.
Silberwismuthglanz, 420.
Silex. v. Quartz.
Silicified wood, 286.
Siliceous sinter, 287, 289.
Siliciophite, 436.
Silicoborocalcite, 382.
Sillimanite, 331.
Silver, 223.
   Antimonial. 234.
   Bismuth, 420.
   Horn, 260.
   Native, 223.
   Ruby, 252, 253.
   Vitreous, 235.
Silver antimonide, 234.
   chloride, 260.
   bromide, 260.
   iodide, 260.
   selenide, 235.
   sulph-antimonite, 250, 252, 256, 257.
   sulph-arsenite, 253.
   sulphide, 235, 239.
   sulpho-bismuthite, 420.
   telluride, 238; 248, 437
Silver glance, 235.
Simonyite, 394.
Sinter, Siliceous, 287, 289.
Sipylite, 436.
Sismondine, 358.
Sisserskite, 224.
Skapolith, v. Scapolite.
Skleroklas, v. Sartorite.
Skolezit, v. Scolecite.
Skutterudite, 246.
Smaltine, Smaltite, 245; 436.
Smaragdite, 297.
Smectite, 349.
Smithsonite, 404.
Soapstone, 348.
Soda = Sodium oxide, v. Sodium.
Soda nitre, 381.
Sodalite, 317.

Sodium borate. 381.
   carbonate, 408, 409.
   chloride, 259.
   fluoride, 264.
   nitrate, 379.
   silicate, 323, 342.
   sulphate, 390, 391, 392.
Sommite, 316.
Sonnenstein, v. Sunstone.
Sonomaite, 434.
Spargelstein, 365.
Spathic iron, 403.
Spathiopyrite, 246.
Spear pyrites, 247.
Speckstein, 348, 352.
Specular iron, 268.
Speerkies, 247.
Spessartite, 304.
Speiskobalt, 245.
Sphærocobaltite, 436.
Sphærosiderite, 403.
Sphærostilbite, 346.
Sphalerite, 237; 436.
Sphene, 335.
Spiauterite, 242.
Spinel, 271.
Spinthère, 335.
Spodiosite, 436.
Spodumene, 295; 436.
Sprödglaserz, 256.
Sprudelstein, 405.
Staffelite, v. Phosphorite.
Stalactite, 400.
Stalagmite, 400.
Stanekite, 415.
Stannite, 245.
Staurolite, Staurotide, 336; 437.
Steatite, 348.
Steeleite, 432.
Steinkohle, 417.
Steinmark, 352.
Steinöl, 413.
Steinsalz, 259.
Stephanite, 256.
Sterlingite, 354.
Sternbergite, 240; 437.
Stibianite, 437.
Stibiconite, 437.
Stibioferrite, 370.
Stibnite, 232; 437.
Stilbite, 346, 437; 347.
Stilpnomelane, 349.
Stolzite, 384.
Strahlerz, 374.
Strahlkies, 247.
Strahlstein, 297.
Strahlzeolith, v. Stilbite.
Strengite, 437.
Strigovite, 357.
Stromeyerite, 240.
Strontianite, 406; 437.
Strontium carbonate, 406.

Strontium sulphate, 388.
Struvite, 371.
Stüzite, 437.
Stylotyp, Stylotypite, 254.
Subdelessite, 425.
Succinellite, 415.
Succinite. 415.
Sulphur, Native, 228.
Sunstone, 323, 325.
Susannite, 391.
Sussexite, 380.
Sylvanite, 248.
Sylvine, Sylvite, 260.
Syngenite, 394.
Szaboite, 437.
Szaibelyite, 380.
Szmikite, 437.

Tabergite, 356.
Tabular spar, 291.
Tachhydrite, 261.
Tafelspath, 291.
Tagilite, 373.
Talc, 348.
Talktriplite, 437.
Tallingite, 262.
Tantalite, 359; 437.
Tapalpite, 239.
Tapiolite, 361.
Tarapacaite, 437.
Tasmanite, 415.
Taznite, 437.
Tellur, Gediegen, 227.
Tellurite, 437.
Tellurium, Bismuthic, 233.
   Foliated, 249.
   Graphic, 248.
   Native, 227; 437.
Tellurium oxide, 437.
Tellursilber, 238.
Tellurwismuth, 233.
Tengerite, 410.
Tennantite, 256; 438.
Tenorite, 267; 438.
Tephroite, 300.
Tequesquite, 438.
Tequixquitl, 438.
Tesseralkies, 246.
Tetradymite, 233.
Tetrahedrite, 255; 438.
Thaumasite, 438.
Thenardite, 390; 438.
Thinolite, 438.
Thomsenolite, 265; 438.
Thomsonite, 342; 438.
Thorite, 340; 438.
Thulite, 309.
Thuringite, 358.
Tiemannite, 237.
Tile ore, 266.
Tin, Native, 226.
Tin ore, Tin stone, 275.
   oxide, 275.
   pyrites, v. Stannite.

Tin sulphide, 245.
Tinkal, 381.
Titaneisen, 269.
Titanic iron, 269.
Titanite, 335; 438.
Titanium oxide, 270; 276, 277.
Titanolivine, 423.
Titanomorphite, 438.
Tiza, v. Ulexite.
Tobermorite, 428.
Tocornalite, 260.
Topaz, 332; 438.
    False. 286.
Topazolite, 304.
Torbanite, 415, 418; 438.
Torbernite, Torberite, 378.
Totaigite, 436.
Tourmaline, 329, 438.
Travertine, 400.
Tremolite, 297.
Trichite, 110.
Triclasite, 353.
Tridymite, 288; 439.
Triphylite, Triphyline, 369; 439.
Triplite, 369.
Triploidite, 439.
Tripolite, 289.
Trippkeite, 439.
Tritochorite, 426.
Tritomite, 340.
Trögerite, 379.
Troilite, 242.
Trona, 408.
Troostite, 301.
Tscheffkinite, 336.
Tschermakite, 323.
Tschermigite, 395.
Tufa, Calcareous, 400.
Tungsten oxide, 284.
Tungstite, 284.
Turgite, 279.
Turmalin, 329.
Turnerite, 368, 432.
Turquois, 377.
Tyrite, 362.
Tyrolite, 374.
Tysonite, 439.

Ulexite, 381.
Ullmannite, 247.
Ultramarine, 318.
Unionite, 309.
Uraconise, Uraconite, 397.
Uranglimmer, 378, 379; 439.
Uranin, Uraninite, 272.
Uranite, 378, 379.
Uranium arsenate, 379.
    carbonate, 412, 439.
    oxide, 274.
    phosphate, 378, 379, 434.
    silicate, 341.
    sulphate, 397.

Urankalk, 412.
Uranmica. 378, 379.
Uranochalcite, 397.
Uranocircite, 439.
Uranophane, 341.
Uranospinite, 379.
Uranotantalite, 361.
Uranothallite, 439.
Uranothorite, 438.
Uranotile, 341; 439.
Uranpecherz, 274.
Urao, 409.
Urpethite, 413.
Urusite, 436.
Urvölgyite, 428.
Uwarowit, 304.

Vaalite, 355.
Valentinite, 284.
Vanadinite, 367; 439.
Variscite, 439.
Vauqueline, Vauquelinite, 386.
Venasquite, 433.
Venerite, 439.
Verd-antique, 350.
Vermiculite, 355; 439.
Vesbine, 439.
Vesuvianite, 305, 440.
Veszelyite, 373, 440.
Victorite, 290.
Vietinghofite, 435.
Villarsite, 340.
Vitreous copper, 239.
    silver, 235.
Vitriol, Blue, 394.
Vivianite, 371.
Voglianite, 397.
Voglite, 412.
Völknerite, 282.
Volborthite, 374.
Voltaite, 395.
Vorhauserite, 351.
Vreckite, 422.
Vulpinite, 389.

Wad, 283, 440.
Wagnerite, 368; 440.
Walchowite, 415.
Walkerite, 433.
Walpurgite, 379, 440.
Waluewite, 440.
Wapplerite, 371.
Warringtonite, 396.
Warwickite, 382.
Wattevillite, 440.
Wavellite, 376.
Websterite, v. Aluminite.
Wehrlite, 233.
Weissbleierz, 407.
Weissite, 353.
Weisspiessglaserz, 284.
Wernerite, 316.

Werthemanite, 396.
Westanite, 332.
Wheelerite, 415.
Wheel-ore, 253.
Whewellite, 412.
Whitneyite, 235.
Wichtine, Wichtisite, 299.
Willcoxite, 358.
Willemite, 301.
Williamsite, 351.
Wilsonite, 353.
Winklerite, 372.
Winkworthite, 382.
Wiserine, 277, 364.
Wismuth, Gediegen, 227.
Wismuthglanz, 232.
Wismuthocker, 284.
Wismuthspath, 412.
Witherite, 406.
Wittichenite, 254.
Wocheinite, 281.
Wöhlerite, 300.
Wolfachite, 247.
Wolfram, 383.
Wolframite, 383.
Wollastonite, 291.
Wollongongite, 416; 438.
Wood-opal, 289.
Wood tin, 275.
Woodwardite, 397.
Wörthite, 332.
Wulfenite, 384; 440.
Würfelerz, 376.
Wurtzite, 242, 426.

Xantholite, 437.
Xanthophyllite, 358; 440.
Xanthosiderite, 281.
Xenotime, 364; 440.
Xyloretinite, 415.

Yenite, 309.
Youngite, 440.
Yttergranat, 303.
Ytterspath, 364.
Yttrium phosphate, 364.
Yttrocerite, 264.
Yttrogummite, 423.
Yttrotantalite, 361, 362.
Yttrotitanite, 336.

Zaratite, 410.
Zeolite section, 342.
Zepharovichite, 376.
Zeunerite, 379.
Ziegelerz, 266.
Zietrisikite, 414.
Zinc, Native, 226.
Zinc aluminate 272.
    arsenate, 373.
    blende, 237.
    bloom, v. Hydrozincite,
    carbonate, 404, 410.

Zinc ore, Red, 266.
    oxide, 266, 273.
    silicate, 301, 339.
    sulphate, 395, 440.
    sulphide, 237, 242.
Zincaluminite, 440.
Zincite, 266.
Zinkblüthe, 410.
Zinkenite, 250.
Zinkspath, 404.
Zinnerz, Zinnstein, 275.
Zinnkies, 245.
Zinnober, 240.
Zinnwaldite, *v.* Lepidolite.
Zippeite, 397.
Zircon, 304; 440.
Zoisite, 308.
Zöblitzite, 351.
Zonochlorite, 340.
Zorgite, 237.
Zwieselite, 369.

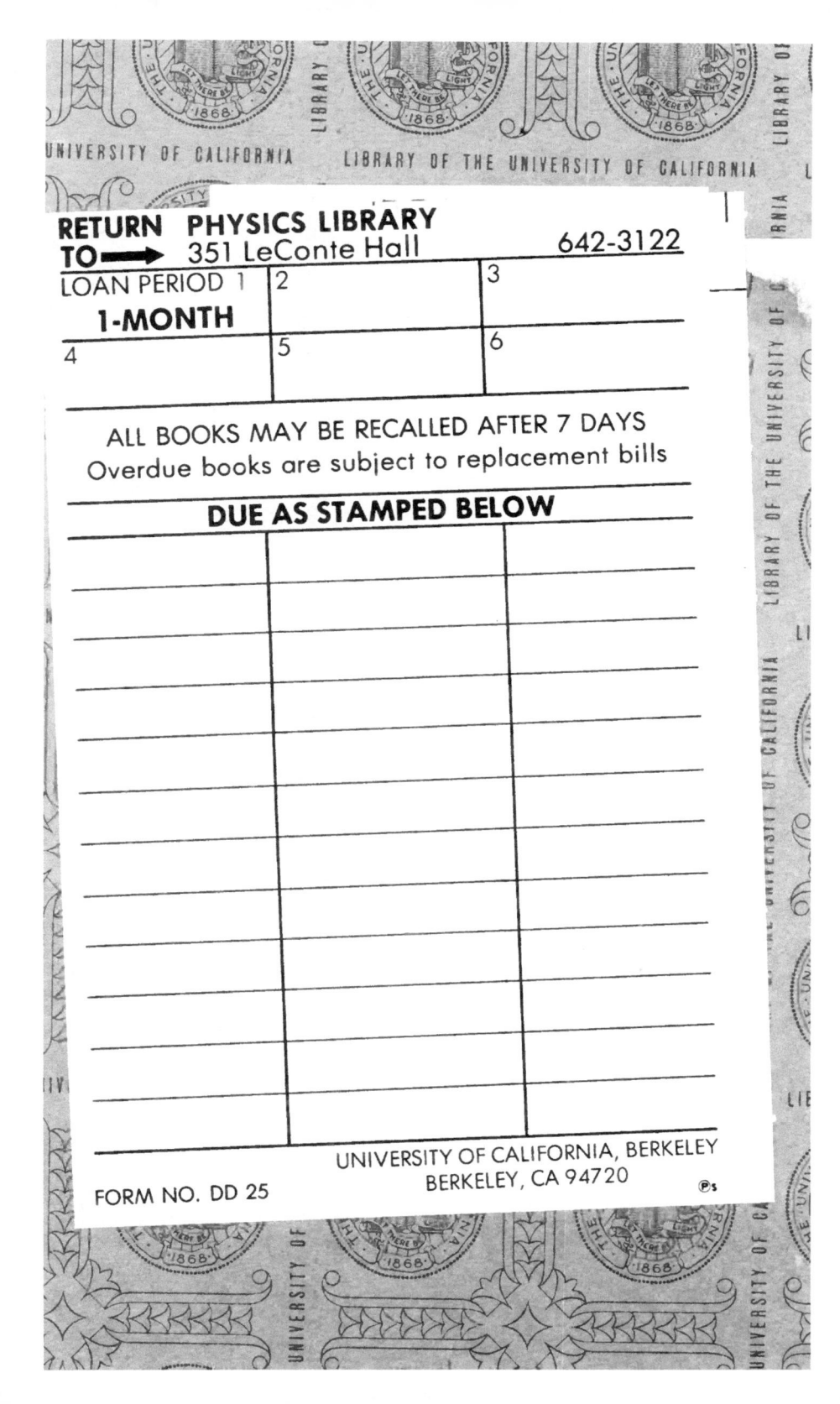

RETURN TO ➡ PHYSICS LIBRARY
351 LeConte Hall   642-3122

LOAN PERIOD 1	2	3
1-MONTH		
4	5	6

ALL BOOKS MAY BE RECALLED AFTER 7 DAYS
Overdue books are subject to replacement bills

DUE AS STAMPED BELOW

FORM NO. DD 25

UNIVERSITY OF CALIFORNIA, BERKELEY
BERKELEY, CA 94720

C032786461

PHYSICS
LIBRARY

ImTheStory.com

Personalized Classic Books in many genre's

Unique gift for kids, partners, friends, colleagues

Customize:
- Character Names
- Upload your own front/back cover images (optional)
- Inscribe a personal message/dedication on the inside page (optional)

Customize many titles Including
- Alice in Wonderland
- Romeo and Juliet
- The Wizard of Oz
- A Christmas Carol
- Dracula
- Dr. Jekyll & Mr. Hyde
- And more...

Emily's Adventures in Wonderland

Ryan & Julia